D1132579

COLLINS
POCKET
GERMAN
DICTIONARY

GERMAN ▶ ENGLISH   ENGLISH ▶ GERMAN

Collins

An Imprint of HarperCollins*Publishers*

fourth edition/vierte Auflage 1999

© HarperCollins Publishers 1996, 1998, 1999
© William Collins Sons & Co. Ltd. 1990

HarperCollins Publishers
P.O. Box, Glasgow G4 0NB, Great Britain
ISBN 0 00 472356-2

The HarperCollins website address is
www.**fire**and**water**.com

Veronika Schnorr • Ute Nicol • Peter Terrell
Bob Grossmith • Helga Holtkamp • Horst Kopleck
Beate Wengel • John Whitlam

editorial staff/Manuskriptbearbeitung
Joyce Littlejohn • Elspeth Anderson
Christine Bahr • John Podbielski

series editor/Gesamtleitung
Lorna Sinclair Knight

Typeset by Morton Word Processing Ltd, Scarborough

*Printed and bound in Great Britain by Caledonian International
Book Manufacturing Ltd, Glasgow, G64*

INTRODUCTION

We are delighted you have decided to buy the Collins Pocket German Dictionary and hope you will enjoy and benefit from using it at home, at school, on holiday or at work.

The innovative use of colour guides you quickly and efficiently to the word you want, and the comprehensive wordlist provides a wealth of modern and idiomatic phrases not normally found in a dictionary this size.

In addition, the supplement provides you with guidance on using the dictionary, along with entertaining ways of improving your dictionary skills.

We hope that you will enjoy using it and that it will significantly enhance your language studies.

ZUM GEBRAUCH IHRES COLLINS TASCHENWÖRTERBUCHS

Das Wörterbuch enthält eine Fülle von Informationen, die mithilfe von unterschiedlichen Schriften und Schriftgrößen, Symbolen, Abkürzungen und Klammern vermittelt werden. Die dabei verwendeten Regeln und Symbole werden in den folgenden Abschnitten erklärt.

Stichwörter

Die Wörter, die Sie im Wörterbuch nachschlagen — „Stichwörter" — sind alphabetisch geordnet. Sie sind **rot** gedruckt, damit man sie schnell erkennt. Die beiden Stichwörter oben links und rechts auf jeder Doppelseite geben das erste bzw. letzte Wort an, das auf den betreffenden Seiten behandelt wird.

Informationen zur Verwendung oder zur Form bestimmter Stichwörter stehen in Klammern hinter der Lautschrift. Sie erscheinen meist in abgekürzter Form und sind kursiv gedruckt (z. B. *(fam)*, *(COMM)*).

Wo es angebracht ist, werden mit dem Stichwort verwandte Wörter im selben Artikel behandelt (z. B. **accept, acceptance**). Sie sind wie das Stichwort fett, aber etwas kleiner gedruckt.

Häufig verwendete Ausdrücke, in denen das Stichwort vorkommt (z. B. **to be cold**), sind in einer anderen Schrift halbfett gedruckt.

Lautschrift

Die Lautschrift für jedes Stichwort (zur Angabe seiner Aussprache) steht in eckigen Klammern direkt hinter dem Stichwort (z. B. **Quark** [kvark]; **knead** [niːd]). Die Symbole der Lautschrift sind auf Seite xii erklärt.

Übersetzungen

Die Übersetzungen des Stichworts sind normal gedruckt. Wenn es mehr als eine Bedeutung oder Verwendung des Stichworts gibt, sind diese durch ein Semikolon voneinander getrennt. Vor den Übersetzungen stehen oft andere, kursiv gedruckte Wörter in Klammern. Sie geben an, in welchem Zusammenhang das Stichwort erscheinen könnte (z. B. **rough** *(voice)* oder *(weather)*), oder sie sind Synonyme (z. B. **rough** *(violent)*).

Schlüsselwörter

Besonders behandelt werden bestimmte deutsche und englische Wörter, die man als „Schlüsselwörter" der jeweiligen Sprache betrachten kann. Diese Wörter kommen beispielsweise sehr häufig vor oder werden unterschiedlich verwendet (z. B. **sein, auch; get, that**). Mithilfe von Rauten und Ziffern können Sie die verschiedenen Wortarten und Verwendungen unterscheiden. Weitere nützliche Hinweise finden Sie kursiv und in Klammern in der jeweiligen Sprache des Benutzers.

Grammatische Informationen

Wortarten stehen in abgekürzter Form kursiv gedruckt hinter der Aussprache des

Stichworts (z. B. *vt, adv, conj*).

Die unregelmäßigen Formen englischer Substantive und Verben stehen in Klammern vor der Wortart (z. B. **man** (*pl* **men**) *n*, **give** (*pt* **gave**, *pp* **given**) *vt*).

Die deutsche Rechtschreibreform
Dieses Wörterbuch folgt durchweg der reformierten deutschen Rechtschreibung. Alle Stichwörter auf der deutsch-englischen Seite, die von der Rechtschreibrefrom betroffen sind, sind mit ▲ gekennzeichnet. Alte Schreibungen, die sich wesentlich von der neuen Schreibung unterscheiden und an einem anderen alphabetischen Ort erscheinen, sind jedoch weiterhin aufgeführt und werden zur neuen Schreibung verwiesen. Diese alten Schreibungen sind mit △ gekennzeichnet.

USING YOUR COLLINS POCKET DICTIONARY

A wealth of information is presented in the dictionary, using various typefaces, sizes of type, symbols, abbreviations and brackets. The conventions and symbols used are explained in the following sections.

Headwords

The words you look up in a dictionary — "headwords" — are listed alphabetically. They are printed in **red type** for rapid identification. The two headwords appearing at the top left and top right of each double page indicate the first and last word dealt with on the pages in question.

Information about the usage or form of certain headwords is given in brackets after the phonetic spelling. This usually appears in abbreviated form and in italics (e.g. (*umg*), (*COMM*)).

Where appropriate, words related to headwords are grouped in the same entry (**Glück, glücken**) in a slightly smaller bold type than the headword.

Common expressions in which the headword appears are shown in a different bold roman type (e.g. **Glück haben**).

Phonetic spellings

The phonetic spelling of each headword (indicating its pronunciation) is given in square brackets immediately after the headword (e.g. **Quark** [kvark]). A list of these symbols is given on page xii.

Meanings

Headword translations are given in ordinary type and, where more than one meaning or usage exists, these are separated by a semi-colon. You will often find other words in italics in brackets before the translations. These offer suggested contexts in which the headword might appear (e.g. **eng** (*Kleidung*) or (*Freundschaft*)) or provide synonyms (e.g. **eng** (*fig: Horizont*)).

"Key" words

Special status is given to certain German and English words which are considered as "key" words in each language. They may, for example, occur very frequently or have several types of usage (e.g. **sein, auch; get, that**). A combination of lozenges and numbers helps you to distinguish different parts of speech and different meanings. Further helpful information is provided in brackets and in italics in the relevant language for the user.

Grammatical information

Parts of speech are given in abbreviated form in italics after the phonetic spellings of headwords (e.g. *vt, adv, konj*).

Genders of German nouns are indicated as follows: *m* for a masculine and *f* for a feminine and *nt* for a neuter noun. The genitive and plural forms of regular nouns are shown on the table on page xi. Nouns which do not follow these rules have the genitive and plural in brackets immediately preceding the gender (e.g. **Spaß**, (**-es**, **⸚e**), *m*).

Adjectives are normally shown in their basic form (e.g. **groß** *adj*), but where they are only used attributively (i.e. before a noun) feminine and neuter endings follow in brackets (**hohe (r, s)** *adj attrib*).

German spelling reform

The German spelling reform has been fully implemented in this dictionary. All headwords on the German-English side which are affected by the spelling changes are marked with ▲, but old spellings which are markedly different from the new ones and have a different alphabetical position are still listed and are cross-referenced to the new spellings. The old spellings are marked with △.

ABKÜRZUNGEN

ABBREVIATIONS

Abkürzung	abk, abbr	abbreviation
Akkusativ	acc	accusative
Adjektiv	adj	adjective
Adverb	adv	adverb
Landwirtschaft	AGR	agriculture
Akkusativ	akk	accusative
Anatomie	ANAT	anatomy
Architektur	ARCHIT	architecture
Astrologie	ASTROL	astrology
Astronomie	ASTRON	astronomy
attributiv	attrib	attributive
Kraftfahrzeuge	AUT	automobiles
Hilfsverb	aux	auxiliary
Luftfahrt	AVIAT	aviation
besonders	bes	especially
Biologie	BIOL	biology
Botanik	BOT	botany
britisch	BRIT	British
Chemie	CHEM	chemistry
Film	CINE	cinema
Handel	COMM	commerce
Komparativ	compar	comparative
Computer	COMPUT	computing
Konjunktion	conj	conjunction
Kochen und Backen	COOK	cooking
zusammengesetztes Wort	cpd	compound
Dativ	dat	dative
bestimmter Artikel	def art	definite article
Diminutiv	dimin	diminutive
kirchlich	ECCL	ecclesiastical
Eisenbahn	EISENB	railways
Elektrizität	ELEK, ELEC	electricity
besonders	esp	especially
und so weiter	etc	et cetera
etwas	etw	something
Euphemismus, Hüllwort	euph	euphemism
Interjektion, Ausruf	excl	exclamation
Femininum	f	feminine
übertragen	fig	figurative
Finanzwesen	FIN	finance
nicht getrennt gebraucht	fus	(phrasal verb) inseparable
Genitiv	gen	genitive
Geografie	GEOG	geography
Geologie	GEOL	geology
Grammatik	GRAM	grammar

Geschichte	HIST	history
unpersönlich	impers	impersonal
unbestimmter Artikel	indef art	indefinite article
umgangssprachlich (! vulgär)	inf(!)	informal (! particularly offensive)
Infinitiv, Grundform	infin	infinitive
nicht getrennt gebraucht	insep	inseparable
unveränderlich	inv	invariable
unregelmäßig	irreg	irregular
jemand	jd	somebody
jemandem	jdm	(to) somebody
jemanden	jdn	somebody
jemandes	jds	somebody's
Rechtswesen	JUR	law
Kochen und Backen	KOCH	cooking
Komparativ	kompar	comparative
Konjunktion	konj	conjunction
Sprachwissenschaft	LING	linguistics
Literatur	LITER	of literature
Maskulinum	m	masculine
Mathematik	MATH	mathematics
Medizin	MED	medicine
Meteorologie	MET	meteorology
Militär	MIL	military
Bergbau	MIN	mining
Musik	MUS	music
Substantiv, Hauptwort	n	noun
nautisch, Seefahrt	NAUT	nautical, naval
Nominativ	nom	nominative
Neutrum	nt	neuter
Zahlwort	num	numeral
Objekt	obj	object
oder	od	or
sich	o.s.	oneself
Parlament	PARL	parliament
abschätzig	pej	pejorative
Fotografie	PHOT	photography
Physik	PHYS	physics
Plural	pl	plural
Politik	POL	politics
Präfix, Vorsilbe	pp	prefix
Präposition	präp, prep	preposition
Typografie	PRINT	printing
Pronomen, Fürwort	pron	pronoun
Psychologie	PSYCH	psychology
1. Vergangenheit, Imperfekt	pt	past tense
Radio	RAD	radio
Eisenbahn	RAIL	railways
Religion	REL	religion

jemand(-en, -em)	**sb**	someone, somebody
Schulwesen	**SCH**	school
Naturwissenschaft	**SCI**	science
Singular, Einzahl	**sg**	singular
etwas	**sth**	something
Konjunktiv	**sub**	subjunctive
Subjekt	**subj**	(grammatical) subject
Superlativ	**superl**	superlative
Technik	**TECH**	technology
Nachrichtentechnik	**TEL**	telecommunications
Theater	**THEAT**	theatre
Fernsehen	**TV**	television
Typografie	**TYP**	printing
umgangssprachlich (! vulgär)	**umg(!)**	informal (! particularly offensive)
Hochschulwesen	**UNIV**	university
unpersönlich	**unpers**	impersonal
unregelmäßig	**unreg**	irregular
(nord)amerikanisch	**US**	(North) America
gewöhnlich	**usu**	usually
Verb	**vb**	verb
intransitives Verb	**vi**	intransitive verb
reflexives Verb	**vr**	reflexive verb
transitives Verb	**vt**	transitive verb
Zoologie	**ZOOL**	zoology
zusammengesetztes Wort	**zW**	compound
zwischen zwei Sprechern	**—**	change of speaker
ungefähre Entsprechung	**≈**	cultural equivalent
eingetragenes Warenzeichen	**®**	registered trademark

Warenzeichen

Wörter, die unseres Wissens eingetragene Warenzeichen darstellen, sind als solche gekennzeichnet. Es ist jedoch zu beachten, dass weder das Vorhandensein noch das Fehlen derartiger Kennzeichnungen die Rechtslage hinsichtlich eingetragener Warenzeichen berührt.

Note on trademarks

Words which we have reason to believe constitute trademarks have been designated as such. However, neither the presence nor the absence of such designation should be regarded as affecting the legal status of any trademark.

REGULAR GERMAN NOUN ENDINGS

nom		*gen*	*pl*
-ant	m	-anten	-anten
-anz	f	-anz	-anzen
-ar	m	-ar(e)s	-are
-chen	nt	-chens	-chen
-e	f	-	-n
-ei	f	-ei	-eien
-elle	f	-elle	-ellen
-ent	m	-enten	-enten
-enz	f	-enz	-enzen
-ette	f	-ette	-etten
-eur	m	-eurs	-eure
-euse	f	-euse	-eusen
-heit	f	-heit	-heiten
-ie	f	-ie	-ien
-ik	f	-ik	-iken
-in	f	-in	-innen
-ine	f	-ine	-inen
-ion	f	-ion	-ionen
-ist	m	-isten	-isten
-ium	nt	-iums	-ien
-ius	m	-ius	-iusse
-ive	f	-ive	-iven
-keit	f	-keit	-keiten
-lein	nt	-leins	-lein
-ling	m	-lings	-linge
-ment	nt	-ments	-mente
-mus	m	-mus	-men
-schaft	f	-schaft	-schaften
-tät	f	-tät	-täten
-tor	m	-tors	-toren
-ung	f	-ung	-ungen
-ur	f	-ur	-uren

PHONETIC SYMBOLS / LAUTSCHRIFT

[ː] *length mark/Längezeichen* ['] *stress mark/Betonung*
[|] *glottal stop/Knacklaut*

all vowel sounds are approximate only
alle Vokallaute sind nur ungefähre Entsprechungen

bet	[b]	**B**all		[e]	M**e**tall
dim	[d]	**d**ann		[eː]	g**e**ben
face	[f]	**F**ass	set	[ɛ]	h**ä**sslich
go	[g]	**G**ast		[ɛ̃ː]	Cous**in**
hit	[h]	**H**err	pity	[ɪ]	B**i**schof
you	[j]	**j**a		[i]	v**i**tal
cat	[k]	**k**alt	green	[iː]	v**ie**l
lick	[l]	**L**ast	rot	[ɔ]	P**o**st
must	[m]	**M**ast	board	[ɔː]	
nut	[n]	**N**uss		[o]	M**o**ral
bang	[ŋ]	la**ng**		[oː]	**o**ben
pepper	[p]	**P**akt		[õ]	Champig**non**
red	[r]	**R**egen		[ø]	**ö**konomisch
sit	[s]	**R**asse		[œ]	g**ö**nnen
shame	[ʃ]	**Sch**al	full	[u]	k**u**lant
tell	[t]	**T**al	root	[uː]	H**u**t
chat	[tʃ]	**tsch**üs	come	[ʌ]	
vine	[v]	**w**as		[ʊ]	P**u**lt
wine	[w]			[y]	ph**y**sisch
lo**ch**	[x]	Ba**ch**		[yː]	f**ü**r
	[ç]	i**ch**		[ʏ]	M**ü**ll
zero	[z]	**H**ase	above	[ə]	bitt**e**
leisure	[ʒ]	**G**enie	girl	[əː]	
join	[dʒ]				
thin	[θ]		lie	[aɪ]	w**ei**t
this	[ð]		now	[au]	
	[a]	H**a**st		[aʊ]	H**au**t
hat	[æ]		day	[eɪ]	
	[aː]	B**a**hn	fair	[ɛə]	
farm	[ɑː]		beer	[ɪə]	
	[ã]	**En**semble	toy	[ɔɪ]	
fiancé	[ãː]			[ɔʏ]	H**eu**
			pure	[uə]	

[ʳ] r can be pronounced before a vowel; Bindungs-R

ZAHLEN   # NUMBERS

ein(s)	1	one
zwei	2	two
drei	3	three
vier	4	four
fünf	5	five
sechs	6	six
sieben	7	seven
acht	8	eight
neun	9	nine
zehn	10	ten
elf	11	eleven
zwölf	12	twelve
dreizehn	13	thirteen
vierzehn	14	fourteen
fünfzehn	15	fifteen
sechzehn	16	sixteen
siebzehn	17	seventeen
achtzehn	18	eighteen
neunzehn	19	nineteen
zwanzig	20	twenty
einundzwanzig	21	twenty-one
zweiundzwanzig	22	twenty-two
dreißig	30	thirty
vierzig	40	forty
fünfzig	50	fifty
sechzig	60	sixty
siebzig	70	seventy
achtzig	80	eighty
neunzig	90	ninety
hundert	100	a hundred
hunderteins	101	a hundred and one
zweihundert	200	two hundred
zweihunderteins	201	two hundred and one
dreihundert	300	three hundred
dreihunderteins	301	three hundred and one
tausend	1000	a thousand
tausend(und)eins	1001	a thousand and one
fünftausend	5000	five thousand
eine Million	1000000	a million

erste(r, s)	1.	first	1st
zweite(r, s)	2.	second	2nd
dritte(r, s)	3.	third	3rd
vierte(r, s)	4.	fourth	4th
fünfte(r, s)	5.	fifth	5th
sechste(r, s)	6.	sixth	6th

siebte(r, s)	7.	seventh	7th
achte(r, s)	8.	eighth	8th
neunte(r, s)	9.	ninth	9th
zehnte(r, s)	10.	tenth	10th
elfte(r, s)	11.	eleventh	11th
zwölfte(r, s)	12.	twelfth	12th
dreizehnte(r, s)	13.	thirteenth	13th
vierzehnte(r, s)	14.	fourteenth	14th
fünfzehnte(r, s)	15.	fifteenth	15th
sechzehnte(r, s)	16.	sixteenth	16th
siebzehnte(r, s)	17.	seventeenth	17th
achtzehnte(r, s)	18.	eighteenth	18th
neunzehnte(r, s)	19.	nineteenth	19th
zwanzigste(r, s)	20.	twentieth	20th
einundzwanzigste(r, s)	21.	twenty-first	21st
dreißigste(r, s)	30.	thirtieth	30th
hundertste(r, s)	100.	hundredth	100th
hunderterste(r, s)	101.	hundred-and-first	101st
tausendste(r, s)	1000.	thousandth	1000th

Brüche usw.

Fractions etc.

ein Halb	$\frac{1}{2}$	a half	
ein Drittel	$\frac{1}{3}$	a third	
ein Viertel	$\frac{1}{4}$	a quarter	
ein Fünftel	$\frac{1}{5}$	a fifth	
null Komma fünf	0,5	(nought) point five	0.5
drei Komma vier	3,4	three point four	3.4
sechs Komma acht neun	6,89	six point eight nine	6.89
zehn Prozent	10%	ten per cent	
hundert Prozent	100%	a hundred per cent	

Beispiele

Examples

er wohnt in Nummer 10	he lives at number 10
es steht in Kapitel 7	it's in chapter 7
auf Seite 7	on page 7
er wohnt im 7. Stock	he lives on the 7th floor
er wurde 7.	he came in 7th
Maßstab eins zu zwanzigtausend	scale one to twenty thousand

UHRZEIT

THE TIME

wie viel Uhr ist es?, wie spät ist es?

what time is it?

es ist ...

it's ...

Mitternacht, zwölf Uhr nachts	midnight, twelve p.m.
ein Uhr (morgens *or* früh)	one o'clock (in the morning), one (a.m.)
fünf nach eins, ein Uhr fünf	five past one
zehn nach eins, ein Uhr zehn	ten past one
Viertel nach eins, ein Uhr fünfzehn	a quarter past one, one fifteen
fünf vor halb zwei, ein Uhr fünfundzwanzig	twenty-five past one, one twenty-five
halb zwei, ein Uhr dreißig	half past one, one thirty
fünf nach halb zwei, ein Uhr fünfunddreißig	twenty-five to two, one thirty-five
zwanzig vor zwei, ein Uhr vierzig	twenty to two, one forty
Viertel vor zwei, ein Uhr fünfundvierzig	a quarter to two, one forty-five
zehn vor zwei, ein Uhr fünfzig	ten to two, one fifty
zwölf Uhr (mittags), Mittag	twelve o'clock, midday, noon
halb eins (mittags *or* nachmittags), zwölf Uhr dreißig	half past twelve, twelve thirty (p.m.)
zwei Uhr (nachmittags)	two o'clock (in the afternoon), two (p.m.)
halb acht (abends)	half past seven (in the evening), seven thirty (p.m.)

um wie viel Uhr?

at what time?

um Mitternacht	at midnight
um sieben Uhr	at seven o'clock
in zwanzig Minuten	in twenty minutes
vor fünfzehn Minuten	fifteen minutes ago

WÖRTERBUCH
DEUTSCH-ENGLISCH

GERMAN-ENGLISH
DICTIONARY

DEUTSCH – ENGLISCH
GERMAN – ENGLISH

A, a

Aal [aːl] (-(e)s, -e) *m* eel
Aas [aːs] (-es, -e *od* **Äser**) *nt* carrion

SCHLÜSSELWORT

ab [ap] *präp* +*dat* from; **Kinder ab 12 Jahren** children from the age of 12; **ab morgen** from tomorrow; **ab sofort** as of now
♦ *adv* 1 off; **links ab** to the left; **der Knopf ist ab** the button has come off; **ab nach Hause!** off you go home
2 (*zeitlich*): **von da ab** from then on; **von heute ab** from today, as of today
3 (*auf Fahrplänen*): **München ab 12.20** leaving Munich 12.20
4: **ab und zu** *od* **an** now and then *od* again

Abänderung [ˈapˌɛndəruŋ] *f* alteration
Abbau [ˈapbau] (-(e)s) *m* (+*gen*) dismantling; (*Verminderung*) reduction (in); (*Verfall*) decline (in); (*MIN*) mining; quarrying; (*CHEM*) decomposition; **a~en** *vt* to dismantle; (*MIN*) to mine; to quarry; (*verringern*) to reduce; (*CHEM*) to break down
abbeißen [ˈapbaisən] (*unreg*) *vt* to bite off
abbekommen [ˈapbəkɔmən] (*unreg*) *vt* (*Deckel, Schraube, Band*) to loosen; **etwas ~** (*beschädigt werden*) to get damaged; (: *Person*) to get injured
abbestellen [ˈapbəʃtɛlən] *vt* to cancel
abbezahlen [ˈapbətsaːlən] *vt* to pay off
abbiegen [ˈapbiːgən] (*unreg*) *vi* to turn off; (*Straße*) to bend ♦ *vt* to bend; (*verhindern*) to ward off
abbilden [ˈapbɪldən] *vt* to portray; **Abbildung** *f* illustration
abblenden [ˈapblɛndən] *vt, vi* (*AUT*) to dip (*BRIT*), to dim (*US*)
Abblendlicht [ˈapblɛntlɪçt] *nt* dipped (*BRIT*) *od* dimmed (*US*) headlights *pl*

abbrechen [ˈapbrɛçən] (*unreg*) *vt, vi* to break off; (*Gebäude*) to pull down; (*Zelt*) to take down; (*aufhören*) to stop; (*COMPUT*) to abort
abbrennen [ˈapbrɛnən] (*unreg*) *vt* to burn off; (*Feuerwerk*) to let off ♦ *vi* (*aux sein*) to burn down
abbringen [ˈapbrɪŋən] (*unreg*) *vt*: **jdn von etw ~** to dissuade sb from sth; **jdn vom Weg ~** to divert sb
abbröckeln [ˈapbrœkəln] *vt, vi* to crumble off *od* away
Abbruch [ˈapbrʊx] *m* (*von Verhandlungen etc*) breaking off; (*von Haus*) demolition; **jdm/ etw ~ tun** to harm sb/sth; **a~reif** *adj* only fit for demolition
abbrühen [ˈapbryːən] *vt* to scald; **abgebrüht** (*umg*) hard-boiled
abbuchen [ˈapbuːxən] *vt* to debit
abdanken [ˈapdaŋkən] *vi* to resign; (*König*) to abdicate; **Abdankung** *f* resignation; abdication
abdecken [ˈapdɛkən] *vt* (*Loch*) to cover; (*Tisch*) to clear; (*Plane*) to uncover
abdichten [ˈapdɪçtən] *vt* to seal; (*NAUT*) to caulk
abdrehen [ˈapdreːən] *vt* (*Gas*) to turn off; (*Licht*) to switch off; (*Film*) to shoot ♦ *vi* (*Schiff*) to change course
Abdruck [ˈapdrʊk] *m* (*Nachdrucken*) reprinting; (*Gedrucktes*) reprint; (*Gipsabdruck, Wachsabdruck*) impression; (*Fingerabdruck*) print; **a~en** *vt* to print, to publish
abdrücken [ˈapdrʏkən] *vt* (*Waffe*) to fire; (*Person*) to hug, to squeeze
Abend [ˈaːbənt] (-s, -e) *m* evening; **guten ~** good evening; **zu ~ essen** to have dinner *od* supper; **heute ~** this evening; **~brot** *nt* supper; **~essen** *nt* supper; **~garderobe** *f*

Spelling Reform: ▲ *new spelling* △ *old spelling (to be phased out)*

evening dress; **~kasse** *f* box office; **~kleid**
nt evening dress; **~kurs** *m* evening classes
pl; **~land** *nt* (*Europa*) West; **a~lich** *adj*
evening; **~mahl** *nt* Holy Communion; **~rot**
nt sunset; **a~s** *adv* in the evening

Abenteuer ['a:bəntɔʏər] **(-s, -)** *nt* adventure;
a~lich *adj* adventurous; **~urlaub** *m*
adventure holiday

Abenteurer (-s, -) *m* adventurer; **~in** *f*
adventuress

aber ['a:bər] *konj* but; (*jedoch*) however
♦ *adv*: **das ist ~ schön** that's really nice;
nun ist ~ Schluss! now that's enough!;
vielen Dank – ~ bitte! thanks a lot – you're
welcome; **A~glaube** *m* superstition;
~gläubisch *adj* superstitious

aberkennen ['ap|ɛrkɛnən] (*unreg*) *vt* (*JUR*):
jdm etw ~ to deprive sb of sth, to take sth
(away) from sb

abermals ['a:bəma:ls] *adv* once again

Abertausend, abertausend
['a:bətauzənt] *indef pron* **tausend** *od*
Tausend und ~ thousands upon thousands

Abf. *abk* (= *Abfahrt*) dep.

abfahren ['apfa:rən] (*unreg*) *vi* to leave, to
depart ♦ *vt* to take *od* cart away; (*Strecke*)
to drive; (*Reifen*) to wear; (*Fahrkarte*) to use

Abfahrt ['apfa:rt] *f* departure; (*SKI*) descent;
(*Piste*) run; **~szeit** *f* departure time

Abfall ['apfal] *m* waste; (*von Speisen etc*)
rubbish (*BRIT*), garbage (*US*); (*Neigung*)
slope; (*Verschlechterung*) decline; **~eimer** *m*
rubbish bin (*BRIT*), garbage can (*US*); **a~en**
(*unreg*) *vi* (*auch fig*) to fall *od* drop off; (*sich
neigen*) to fall *od* drop away

abfällig ['apfɛlɪç] *adj* disparaging,
deprecatory

abfangen ['apfaŋən] (*unreg*) *vt* to intercept;
(*Person*) to catch; (*unter Kontrolle bringen*) to
check

abfärben ['apfɛrbən] *vi* to lose its colour;
(*Wäsche*) to run; (*fig*) to rub off

abfassen ['apfasən] *vt* to write, to draft

abfertigen ['apfɛrtɪgən] *vt* to prepare for
dispatch, to process; (*an der Grenze*) to
clear; (*Kundschaft*) to attend to

Abfertigungsschalter *m* (*Flughafen*)

check-in desk

abfeuern ['apfɔʏərn] *vt* to fire

abfinden ['apfɪndən] (*unreg*) *vt* to pay off
♦ *vr* to come to terms; **sich mit jdm ~/
nicht ~** to put up with/not get on with sb

Abfindung *f* (*von Gläubigern*) payment;
(*Geld*) sum in settlement

abflauen ['apflauən] *vi* (*Wind, Erregung*) to
die away, to subside; (*Nachfrage, Geschäft*)
to fall *od* drop off

abfliegen ['apfli:gən] (*unreg*) *vi* (*Flugzeug*) to
take off; (*Passagier auch*) to fly ♦ *vt* (*Gebiet*)
to fly over

abfließen ['apfli:sən] (*unreg*) *vi* to drain
away

Abflug ['apflu:k] *m* departure; (*Start*) take-
off; **~halle** *f* departure lounge; **~zeit** *f*
departure time

Abfluss ▲ ['apflʊs] *m* draining away;
(*Öffnung*) outlet; **~rohr** *nt* drain pipe; (*von
sanitären Anlagen auch*) waste pipe

abfragen ['apfra:gən] *vt* (*bes SCH*) to test
orally (on)

Abfuhr ['apfu:r] **(-, -en)** *f* removal; (*fig*)
snub, rebuff

abführen ['apfy:rən] *vt* to lead away;
(*Gelder, Steuern*) to pay ♦ *vi* (*MED*) to have a
laxative effect

Abführmittel ['apfy:rmɪtəl] *nt* laxative,
purgative

abfüllen ['apfʏlən] *vt* to draw off; (*in
Flaschen*) to bottle

Abgabe ['apga:bə] *f* handing in; (*von Ball*)
pass; (*Steuer*) tax; (*eines Amtes*) giving up;
(*einer Erklärung*) giving

Abgang ['apgaŋ] *m* (*von Schule*) leaving;
(*THEAT*) exit; (*Abfahrt*) departure; (*der Post,
von Waren*) dispatch

Abgas ['apga:s] *nt* waste gas; (*AUT*) exhaust

abgeben ['apge:bən] (*unreg*) *vt* (*Gegenstand*)
to hand *od* give in; (*Ball*) to pass; (*Wärme*)
to give off; (*Amt*) to hand over; (*Schuss*) to
fire; (*Erklärung, Urteil*) to give; (*darstellen,
sein*) to make ♦ *vr*: **sich mit jdm/etw ~** to
associate with sb/bother with sth; **jdm etw
~** (*überlassen*) to let sb have sth

abgebrüht ['apgəbry:t] (*umg*) *adj* (*skrupellos*)

Rechtschreibreform: ▲ *neue Schreibung* △ *alte Schreibung (auslaufend)*

hard-boiled

abgehen ['apge:ən] (*unreg*) *vi* to go away, to leave; (*THEAT*) to exit; (*Knopf etc*) to come off; (*Straße*) to branch off ♦ *vt* (*Strecke*) to go *od* walk along; **etw geht jdm ab** (*fehlt*) sb lacks sth

abgelegen ['apgəle:gən] *adj* remote

abgemacht ['apgəmaxt] *adj* fixed; **~!** done!

abgeneigt ['apgənaikt] *adj* disinclined

abgenutzt ['apgənʊtst] *adj* worn

Abgeordnete(r) ['apgəʔɔrdnətə(r)] *f(m)* member of parliament; elected representative

abgeschlossen ['apgəʃlɔsən] *adj attrib* (*Wohnung*) self-contained

abgeschmackt ['apgəʃmakt] *adj* tasteless

abgesehen ['apgəze:ən] *adj*: **es auf jdn/ etw ~ haben** to be after sb/sth; **~ von ...** apart from ...

abgespannt ['apgəʃpant] *adj* tired out

abgestanden ['apgəʃtandən] *adj* stale; (*Bier auch*) flat

abgestorben ['apgəʃtɔrbən] *adj* numb; (*BIOL, MED*) dead

abgetragen ['apgətra:gən] *adj* shabby, worn out

abgewinnen ['apgəvɪnən] (*unreg*) *vt*: **einer Sache etw/Geschmack ~** to get sth/ pleasure from sth

abgewöhnen ['apgəvø:nən] *vt*: **jdm/sich etw ~** to cure sb of sth/give sth up

abgrenzen ['apgrɛntsən] *vt* (*auch fig*) to mark off; to fence off

Abgrund ['apgrʊnt] *m* (*auch fig*) abyss

abhacken ['apʰakən] *vt* to chop off

abhaken ['apʰa:kən] *vt* (*auf Papier*) to tick off

abhalten ['apʰaltən] (*unreg*) *vt* (*Versammlung*) to hold; **jdn von etw ~** (*fern halten*) to keep sb away from sth; (*hindern*) to keep sb from sth

abhanden [ap'handən] *adj*: **~ kommen** to get lost

Abhandlung ['apʰandlʊŋ] *f* treatise, discourse

Abhang ['apʰaŋ] *m* slope

abhängen ['apʰɛŋən] *vt* (*Bild*) to take down; (*Anhänger*) to uncouple; (*Verfolger*) to shake off ♦ *vi* (*unreg*: *Fleisch*) to hang; **von jdm/ etw ~** to depend on sb/sth

abhängig ['apʰɛŋɪç] *adj*: **~ (von)** dependent (on); **A~keit** *f*: **A~keit (von)** dependence (on)

abhärten ['apʰɛrtən] *vt, vr* to toughen (o.s.) up; **sich gegen etw ~** to inure o.s. to sth

abhauen ['apʰaʊən] (*unreg*) *vt* to cut off; (*Baum*) to cut down ♦ *vi* (*umg*) to clear off *od* out

abheben ['apʰe:bən] (*unreg*) *vt* to lift (up); (*Karten*) to cut; (*Geld*) to withdraw, to take out ♦ *vi* (*Flugzeug*) to take off; (*Rakete*) to lift off ♦ *vr* to stand out

abheften ['apʰɛftən] *vt* (*Rechnungen etc*) to file away

abhetzen ['apʰɛtsən] *vr* to wear *od* tire o.s. out

Abhilfe ['apʰɪlfə] *f* remedy; **~ schaffen** to put things right

abholen ['apʰo:lən] *vt* (*Gegenstand*) to fetch, to collect; (*Person*) to call for; (*am Bahnhof etc*) to pick up, to meet

abholzen ['apʰɔltsən] *vt* (*Wald*) to clear

abhorchen ['apʰɔrçən] *vt* (*MED*) to listen to a patient's chest

abhören ['apʰø:rən] *vt* (*Vokabeln*) to test; (*Telefongespräch*) to tap; (*Tonband etc*) to listen to

Abhörgerät *nt* bug

Abitur [abi'tu:r] (**-s, -e**) *nt* German school-leaving examination; **~i'ent(in)** *m(f)* candidate for school-leaving certificate

---

Abitur

*The **Abitur** is the German school-leaving examination taken in four subjects by pupils at a **Gymnasium** at the age of 18 or 19. It is necessary for entry to university.*

Abk. *abk* (= *Abkürzung*) abbr.

abkapseln ['apkapsəln] *vr* to shut *od* cut o.s. off

abkaufen ['apkaʊfən] *vt*: **jdm etw ~** (*auch fig*) to buy sth from sb

---

abkehren ['apke:rən] *vt* (*Blick*) to avert, to turn away ♦ *vr* to turn away

abklingen ['apklıŋən] (*unreg*) *vi* to die away; (*Radio*) to fade out

abknöpfen ['apknœpfən] *vt* to unbutton; **jdm etw ~** (*umg*) to get sth off sb

abkochen ['apkɔxən] *vt* to boil

abkommen ['apkɔmən] (*unreg*) *vi* to get away; **von der Straße/von einem Plan ~** to leave the road/give up a plan; **A~ (-s, -)** *nt* agreement

abkömmlich ['apkœmlıç] *adj* available, free

abkratzen ['apkratsən] *vt* to scrape off ♦ *vi* (*umg*) to kick the bucket

abkühlen ['apky:lən] *vt* to cool down ♦ *vr* (*Mensch*) to cool down *od* off; (*Wetter*) to get cool; (*Zuneigung*) to cool

abkürzen ['apkyrtsən] *vt* to shorten; (*Wort auch*) to abbreviate; **den Weg ~** to take a short cut

Abkürzung *f* (*Wort*) abbreviation; (*Weg*) short cut

abladen ['apla:dən] (*unreg*) *vt* to unload

Ablage ['apla:gə] *f* (*für Akten*) tray; (*für Kleider*) cloakroom

ablassen ['aplasən] (*unreg*) *vt* (*Wasser, Dampf*) to let off; (*vom Preis*) to knock off ♦ *vi*: **von etw ~** to give sth up, to abandon sth

Ablauf ['aplaʊf] *m* (*Abfluss*) drain; (*von Ereignissen*) course; (*einer Frist, Zeit*) expiry (*BRIT*), expiration (*US*); **a~en** (*unreg*) *vi* (*abfließen*) to drain away; (*Ereignisse*) to happen; (*Frist, Zeit, Pass*) to expire ♦ *vt* (*Sohlen*) to wear down *od* out)

ablegen ['aple:gən] *vt* to put *od* lay down; (*Kleider*) to take off; (*Gewohnheit*) to get rid of; (*Prüfung*) to take, to sit; (*Zeugnis*) to give

Ableger (-s, -) *m* layer; (*fig*) branch, offshoot

ablehnen ['aple:nən] *vt* to reject; (*Einladung*) to decline, to refuse ♦ *vi* to decline, to refuse

ablehnend *adj* (*Haltung, Antwort*) negative; (*Geste*) disapproving; **ein ~er Bescheid** a rejection

Ablehnung *f* rejection; refusal

ableiten ['aplaɪtən] *vt* (*Wasser*) to divert; (*deduzieren*) to deduce; (*Wort*) to derive; **Ableitung** *f* diversion; deduction; derivation; (*Wort*) derivative

ablenken ['aplɛŋkən] *vt* to turn away, to deflect; (*zerstreuen*) to distract ♦ *vi* to change the subject; **Ablenkung** *f* distraction

ablesen ['aple:zən] (*unreg*) *vt* to read out; (*Messgeräte*) to read

ablichten ['aplıçtən] *vt* to photocopy

abliefern ['apli:fərn] *vt* to deliver; **etw bei jdm ~** to hand sth over to sb

Ablieferung *f* delivery

ablösen ['aplø:zən] *vt* (*abtrennen*) to take off, to remove; (*in Amt*) to take over from; (*Wache*) to relieve

Ablösung *f* removal; relieving

abmachen ['apmaxən] *vt* to take off; (*vereinbaren*) to agree; **Abmachung** *f* agreement

abmagern ['apma:gərn] *vi* to get thinner

Abmagerungskur *f* diet; **eine ~ machen** to go on a diet

abmarschieren ['apmarʃi:rən] *vi* to march off

abmelden ['apmɛldən] *vt* (*Zeitungen*) to cancel; (*Auto*) to take off the road ♦ *vr* to give notice of one's departure; (*im Hotel*) to check out; **jdn bei der Polizei ~** to register sb's departure with the police

abmessen ['apmɛsən] (*unreg*) *vt* to measure; **Abmessung** *f* measurement

abmontieren ['apmɔnti:rən] *vt* to take off

abmühen ['apmy:ən] *vr* to wear o.s. out

Abnahme ['apna:mə] *f* (+*gen*) removal; (*COMM*) buying; (*Verringerung*) decrease (in)

abnehmen ['apne:mən] (*unreg*) *vt* to take off, to remove; (*Führerschein*) to take away; (*Prüfung*) to hold; (*Maschen*) to decrease ♦ *vi* to decrease; (*schlanker werden*) to lose weight; **(jdm) etw ~** (*Geld*) to get sth (out of sb); (*kaufen, umg: glauben*) to buy sth (from sb); **jdm Arbeit ~** to take work off sb's shoulders

Abnehmer (-s, -) *m* purchaser, customer

Abneigung ['apnaɪguŋ] *f* aversion, dislike

abnorm [ap'nɔrm] *adj* abnormal

abnutzen ['apnʊtsən] *vt* to wear out; **Abnutzung** *f* wear (and tear)

Abo ['abo] (*umg*) *nt abk* = **Abonnement**

Abonnement [abɔn(ə)'mã:] (**-s, -s**) *nt* subscription; **Abonnent(in)** [abɔ'nɛnt(ɪn)] *m(f)* subscriber; **abonnieren** *vt* to subscribe to

Abordnung ['apˌɔrdnʊŋ] *f* delegation

abpacken ['appakən] *vt* to pack

abpassen ['appasən] *vt* (*Person, Gelegenheit*) to wait for

Abpfiff ['appfɪf] *m* final whistle

abplagen ['appla:gən] *vr* to wear o.s. out

abprallen ['appralən] *vi* to bounce off; to ricochet

abraten ['apra:tən] (*unreg*) *vi*: **jdm von etw ~** to advise *or* warn sb against sth

abräumen ['apˌrɔymən] *vt* to clear up *od* away

abreagieren ['apreagi:rən] *vt*: **seinen Zorn (an jdm/etw) ~** to work one's anger off (on sb/sth) ♦ *vr* to calm down

abrechnen ['aprɛçnən] *vt* to deduct, to take off ♦ *vi* to settle up; (*fig*) to get even **Abrechnung** *f* settlement; (*Rechnung*) bill

Abrede ['apre:də] *f*: **etw in ~ stellen** to deny *od* dispute sth

Abreise ['apraızə] *f* departure; **a~n** *vi* to leave, to set off

abreißen ['apraısən] (*unreg*) *vt* (*Haus*) to tear down; (*Blatt*) to tear off

abrichten ['aprɪçtən] *vt* to train

abriegeln ['apri:gəln] *vt* (*Straße, Gebiet*) to seal off

Abruf ['apru:f] *m*: **auf ~** on call; **a~en** (*unreg*) *vt* (*Mensch*) to call away; (*COMM: Ware*) to request delivery of

abrunden ['aprʊndən] *vt* to round off

abrupt [a'brʊpt] *adj* abrupt

abrüsten ['aprʏstən] *vi* to disarm; **Abrüstung** *f* disarmament

abrutschen ['aprʊtʃən] *vi* to slip; (*AVIAT*) to sideslip

Abs. *abk* (= *Absender*) sender, from

Absage ['apza:gə] *f* refusal; **a~n** *vt* to cancel, to call off; (*Einladung*) to turn down

♦ *vi* to cry off; (*ablehnen*) to decline

absahnen ['apza:nən] *vt* to skim ♦ *vi* (*fig*) to rake in

Absatz ['apzats] *m* (*COMM*) sales *pl*; (*Bodensatz*) deposit; (*neuer Abschnitt*) paragraph; (*Treppenabsatz*) landing; (*Schuhabsatz*) heel; **~gebiet** *nt* (*COMM*) market

abschaffen ['apʃafən] *vt* to abolish, to do away with; **Abschaffung** *f* abolition

abschalten ['apʃaltən] *vt, vi* (*auch umg*) to switch off

abschätzen ['apʃɛtsən] *vt* to estimate; (*Lage*) to assess; (*Person*) to size up

abschätzig ['apʃɛtsɪç] *adj* disparaging, derogatory

Abschaum ['apʃaum] (**-(e)s**) *m* scum

Abscheu ['apʃɔy] (**-(e)s**) *m* loathing, repugnance; **~ erregend** repulsive, loathsome; **a~lich** [ap'ʃɔylɪç] *adj* abominable

abschicken ['apʃɪkən] *vt* to send off

abschieben ['apʃi:bən] (*unreg*) *vt* to push away; (*Person*) to pack off; (: *POL*) to deport

Abschied ['apʃi:t] (**-(e)s, -e**) *m* parting; (*von Armee*) discharge; (**von jdm**) **~ nehmen** to say goodbye (to sb), to take one's leave (of sb); **seinen ~ nehmen** (*MIL*) to apply for discharge; **~sbrief** *m* farewell letter; **~sfeier** *f* farewell party

abschießen ['apʃi:sən] (*unreg*) *vt* (*Flugzeug*) to shoot down; (*Geschoss*) to fire

abschirmen ['apʃɪrmən] *vt* to screen

abschlagen ['apʃla:gən] (*unreg*) *vt* (*abhacken, COMM*) to knock off; (*ablehnen*) to refuse; (*MIL*) to repel

abschlägig ['apʃlɛ:gɪç] *adj* negative

Abschlagszahlung *f* interim payment

Abschlepp- ['apʃlɛp] *zW*: **~dienst** *m* (*AUT*) breakdown service (*BRIT*), towing company (*US*); **a~en** *vt* (to take in) tow; **~seil** *nt* towrope

abschließen ['apʃli:sən] (*unreg*) *vt* (*Tür*) to lock; (*beenden*) to conclude, to finish; (*Vertrag, Handel*) to conclude ♦ *vr* (*sich isolieren*) to cut o.s. off; **~d** *adj* concluding

Abschluss ▲ ['apʃlʊs] *m* (*Beendigung*) close,

conclusion; (COMM: *Bilanz*) balancing; (*von Vertrag, Handel*) conclusion; **zum ~** in conclusion; **~feier** f (SCH) end of term party; **~prüfung** f final exam

abschneiden ['apʃnaɪdən] (*unreg*) vt to cut off ♦ vi to do, to come off

Abschnitt ['apʃnɪt] m section; (MIL) sector; (*Kontrollabschnitt*) counterfoil; (MATH) segment; (*Zeitabschnitt*) period

abschrauben ['apʃraubən] vt to unscrew

abschrecken ['apʃrɛkən] vt to deter, to put off; (*mit kaltem Wasser*) to plunge in cold water; **~d** adj deterrent; **~des Beispiel** warning

abschreiben ['apʃraibən] (*unreg*) vt to copy; (*verloren geben*) to write off; (COMM) to deduct

Abschrift ['apʃrɪft] f copy

Abschuss ▲ ['apʃʊs] m (*eines Geschützes*) firing; (*Herunterschießen*) shooting down; (*Tötung*) shooting

abschüssig ['apʃʏsɪç] adj steep

abschwächen ['apʃvɛçən] vt to lessen; (*Behauptung, Kritik*) to tone down ♦ vr to lessen

abschweifen ['apʃvaifən] vi to digress

abschwellen ['apʃvɛlən] (*unreg*) vi (*Geschwulst*) to go down; (*Lärm*) to die down

abschwören ['apʃvøːrən] vi (+dat) to renounce

absehbar ['apzeːbaːr] adj foreseeable; **in ~er Zeit** in the foreseeable future; **das Ende ist ~** the end is in sight

absehen ['apzeːən] (*unreg*) vt (*Ende, Folgen*) to foresee ♦ vi: **von etw ~** to refrain from sth; (*nicht berücksichtigen*) to leave sth out of consideration

abseilen ['apzailən] vr (*Bergsteiger*) to abseil (down)

abseits ['apzaits] adv out of the way ♦ präp +gen away from; **A~** nt (SPORT) offside

absenden ['apzɛndən] (*unreg*) vt to send off, to dispatch

Absender (-s, -) m sender

absetzen ['apzɛtsən] vt (*niederstellen, aussteigen lassen*) to put down; (*abnehmen*) to take off; (COMM: *verkaufen*) to sell; (FIN: *abziehen*) to deduct; (*entlassen*) to dismiss; (*König*) to depose; (*streichen*) to drop; (*hervorheben*) to pick out ♦ vr (*sich entfernen*) to clear off; (*sich ablagern*) to be deposited

Absetzung f (FIN: *Abzug*) deduction; (*Entlassung*) dismissal; (*von König*) deposing

absichern ['apzɪçərn] vt to make safe; (*schützen*) to safeguard ♦ vr to protect o.s.

Absicht ['apzɪçt] f intention; **mit ~** on purpose; **a~lich** adj intentional, deliberate

absinken ['apzɪŋkən] (*unreg*) vi to sink; (*Temperatur, Geschwindigkeit*) to decrease

absitzen ['apzɪtsən] (*unreg*) vi to dismount ♦ vt (*Strafe*) to serve

absolut [apzo'luːt] adj absolute; **A~ismus** m absolutism

absolvieren [apzɔl'viːrən] vt (SCH) to complete

absonder- ['apzɔndər] zW: **~lich** adj odd, strange; **~n** vt to separate; (*ausscheiden*) to give off, to secrete ♦ vr to cut o.s. off; **A~ung** f separation; (MED) secretion

abspalten ['apʃpaltən] vt to split off

abspannen ['apʃpanən] vt (*Pferde*) to unhitch; (*Wagen*) to uncouple

abspeisen ['apʃpaizən] vt (fig) to fob off

abspenstig ['apʃpɛnstɪç] adj: **(jdm) ~ machen** to lure away (from sb)

absperren ['apʃpɛrən] vt to block od close off; (*Tür*) to lock; **Absperrung** f (*Vorgang*) blocking od closing off; (*Sperre*) barricade

abspielen ['apʃpiːlən] vt (*Platte, Tonband*) to play; (SPORT: *Ball*) to pass ♦ vr to happen

Absprache ['apʃpraːxə] f arrangement

absprechen ['apʃprɛçən] (*unreg*) vt (*vereinbaren*) to arrange; **jdm etw ~** to deny sb sth

abspringen ['apʃprɪŋən] (*unreg*) vi to jump down/off; (*Farbe, Lack*) to flake off; (AVIAT) to bale out; (*sich distanzieren*) to back out

Absprung ['apʃprʊŋ] m jump

abspülen ['apʃpyːlən] vt to rinse; (*Geschirr*) to wash up

abstammen ['apʃtamən] vi to be descended; (*Wort*) to be derived; **Abstammung** f descent; derivation

Abstand ['apʃtant] *m* distance; (*zeitlich*) interval; **davon ~ nehmen, etw zu tun to** refrain from doing sth; **mit ~ der Beste** by far the best

abstatten ['apʃtatən] *vt* (*Dank*) to give; (*Besuch*) to pay

abstauben ['apʃtaʊbən] *vt, vi* to dust; (*umg: stehlen*) to pinch; (: *schnorren*) to scrounge

Abstecher ['apʃtɛçər] (**-s, -**) *m* detour

abstehen ['apʃteːən] (*unreg*) *vi* (*Ohren, Haare*) to stick out; (*entfernt sein*) to stand away

absteigen ['apʃtaɪgən] (*unreg*) *vi* (*vom Rad etc*) to get off, to dismount; **(in die zweite Liga) ~** to be relegated (to the second division)

abstellen ['apʃtɛlən] *vt* (*niederstellen*) to put down; (*entfernt stellen*) to pull out; (*hinstellen: Auto*) to park; (*ausschalten*) to turn *od* switch off; (*Missstand, Unsitte*) to stop

Abstellraum *m* storage room

abstempeln ['apʃtɛmpəln] *vt* to stamp

absterben ['apʃtɛrbən] (*unreg*) *vi* to die; (*Körperteil*) to go numb

Abstieg ['apʃtiːk] (**-(e)s, -e**) *m* descent; (*SPORT*) relegation; (*fig*) decline

abstimmen ['apʃtɪmən] *vi* to vote ♦ *vt:* **~ (auf** +*akk*) (*Instrument*) to tune (to); (*Interessen*) to match (with); (*Termine, Ziele*) to fit in (with) ♦ *vr* to agree

Abstimmung *f* vote

Abstinenz [apsti'nɛnts] *f* abstinence; teetotalism; **~ler(in) (-s, -)** *m(f)* teetotaller

abstoßen ['apʃtoːsən] (*unreg*) *vt* to push off *od* away; (*verkaufen*) to unload; (*anekeln*) to repel, to repulse; **~d** *adj* repulsive

abstrakt [ap'ʃtrakt] *adj* abstract ♦ *adv* abstractly, in the abstract

abstreiten ['apʃtraɪtən] (*unreg*) *vt* to deny

Abstrich ['apʃtrɪç] *m* (*Abzug*) cut; (*MED*) smear; **~e machen** to lower one's sights

abstufen ['apʃtuːfən] *vt* (*Hang*) to terrace; (*Farben*) to shade; (*Gehälter*) to grade

Absturz ['apʃtʊrts] *m* fall; (*AVIAT*) crash

abstürzen ['apʃtʏrtsən] *vi* to fall; (*AVIAT*) to crash

absuchen ['apzuːxən] *vt* to scour, to search

absurd [ap'zʊrt] *adj* absurd

Abszess ▲ [aps'tsɛs] (**-es, -e**) *m* abscess

Abt [apt] (**-(e)s, ⁺e**) *m* abbot

Abt. *abk* (= *Abteilung*) dept.

abtasten ['aptastən] *vt* to feel, to probe

abtauen ['aptaʊən] *vt, vi* to thaw

Abtei [ap'taɪ] (**-, -en**) *f* abbey

Abteil [ap'taɪl] (**-(e)s, -e**) *nt* compartment; **'a~n** *vt* to divide up; (*abtrennen*) to divide off; **~ung** *f* (*in Firma, Kaufhaus*) department; (*in Krankenhaus*) section; (*MIL*) unit

abtippen ['aptɪpən] *vt* (*Text*) to type up

abtransportieren ['aptranspɔrtiːrən] *vt* to take away, to remove

abtreiben ['aptraɪbən] (*unreg*) *vt* (*Boot, Flugzeug*) to drive off course; (*Kind*) to abort ♦ *vi* to be driven off course; to abort

Abtreibung *f* abortion

abtrennen ['aptrɛnən] *vt* (*lostrennen*) to detach; (*entfernen*) to take off; (*abteilen*) to separate off

abtreten ['aptreːtən] (*unreg*) *vt* to wear out; (*überlassen*) to hand over, to cede ♦ *vi* to go off; (*zurücktreten*) to step down

Abtritt ['aptrɪt] *m* resignation

abtrocknen ['aptrɔknən] *vt, vi* to dry

abtun ['aptuːn] (*unreg*) *vt* (*fig*) to dismiss

abwägen ['apvɛːgən] (*unreg*) *vt* to weigh up

abwälzen ['apvɛltsən] *vt* (*Schuld, Verantwortung*): **~ (auf** +*akk*) to shift (onto)

abwandeln ['apvandəln] *vt* to adapt

abwandern ['apvandərn] *vi* to move away; (*FIN*) to be transferred

abwarten ['apvartən] *vt* to wait for ♦ *vi* to wait

abwärts ['apvɛrts] *adv* down

Abwasch ['apvaʃ] (**-(e)s**) *m* washing-up; **a~en** (*unreg*) *vt* (*Schmutz*) to wash off; (*Geschirr*) to wash (up)

Abwasser ['apvasər] (**-s, -wässer**) *nt* sewage

abwechseln ['apvɛksəln] *vi, vr* to alternate; (*Personen*) to take turns; **~d** *adj* alternate; **Abwechslung** *f* change; **abwechslungsreich** *adj* varied

abwegig ['apveːgɪç] *adj* wrong

Spelling Reform: ▲ *new spelling* △ *old spelling (to be phased out)*

Abwehr ['apveːr] (-) *f* defence; (*Schutz*) protection; (~*dienst*) counterintelligence (service); **a~en** *vt* to ward off; (*Ball*) to stop

abweichen ['apvaiçən] (*unreg*) *vi* to deviate; (*Meinung*) to differ

abweisen ['apvaizən] (*unreg*) *vt* to turn away; (*Antrag*) to turn down; **~d** *adj* (*Haltung*) cold

abwenden ['apvɛndən] (*unreg*) *vt* to avert
♦ *vr* to turn away

abwerfen ['apvɛrfən] (*unreg*) *vt* to throw off; (*Profit*) to yield; (*aus Flugzeug*) to drop; (*Spielkarte*) to discard

abwerten ['apvɛrtən] *vt* (*FIN*) to devalue

abwertend *adj* (*Worte, Sinn*) pejorative

Abwertung *f* (*von Währung*) devaluation

abwesend ['apveːzənt] *adj* absent

Abwesenheit ['apveːzənhait] *f* absence

abwickeln ['apvikəln] *vt* to unwind; (*Geschäft*) to wind up

abwimmeln ['apviməln] (*umg*) *vt* (*Menschen*) to get shot of

abwischen ['apviʃən] *vt* to wipe off *od* away; (*putzen*) to wipe

Abwurf ['apvurf] *m* throwing off; (*von Bomben etc*) dropping; (*von Reiter, SPORT*) throw

abwürgen ['apvyrgən] (*umg*) *vt* to scotch; (*Motor*) to stall

abzahlen ['aptsaːlən] *vt* to pay off

abzählen ['aptsɛːlən] *vt, vi* to count (up)

Abzahlung *f* repayment; **auf ~ kaufen** to buy on hire purchase

abzapfen ['aptsapfən] *vt* to draw off; **jdm Blut ~** to take blood from sb

abzäunen ['aptsɔynən] *vt* to fence off

Abzeichen ['aptsaiçən] *nt* badge; (*Orden*) decoration

abzeichnen ['aptsaiçnən] *vt* to draw, to copy; (*Dokument*) to initial ♦ *vr* to stand out; (*fig: bevorstehen*) to loom

abziehen ['aptsiːən] (*unreg*) *vt* to take off; (*Tier*) to skin; (*Bett*) to strip; (*Truppen*) to withdraw; (*subtrahieren*) to take away, to subtract; (*kopieren*) to run off ♦ *vi* to go away; (*Truppen*) to withdraw

abzielen ['aptsiːlən] *vi*: **~ auf** +*akk* to be aimed at

Abzug ['aptsuːk] *m* departure; (*von Truppen*) withdrawal; (*Kopie*) copy; (*Subtraktion*) subtraction; (*Betrag*) deduction; (*Rauchabzug*) flue; (*von Waffen*) trigger

abzüglich ['aptsyːkliç] *präp* +*gen* less

abzweigen ['aptsvaigən] *vi* to branch off
♦ *vt* to set aside

Abzweigung *f* junction

ach [ax] *excl* oh; **~ ja!** (oh) yes; **~ so!** I see; **mit A~ und Krach** by the skin of one's teeth

Achse ['aksə] *f* axis; (*AUT*) axle

Achsel ['aksəl] (-, -n) *f* shoulder; **~höhle** *f* armpit

acht [axt] *num* eight; **~ Tage** a week; **A~**[1] (-, -en) *f* eight; (*beim Eislaufen etc*) figure eight

Acht[2] (-, -en) *f*: **~ geben** (**auf** +*akk*) to pay attention (to); **sich in ~ nehmen** (**vor** +*dat*) to be careful (of), to watch out (for); **etw außer ~ lassen** to disregard sth; **a~bar** *adj* worthy

acht- *zW*: **~e(r, s)** *adj* eighth; **A~el** *num* eighth; **~en** *vt* to respect ♦ *vi*: **~en** (**auf** +*akk*) to pay attention (to); **~en, daß ...** to be careful that ...

ächten ['ɛçtən] *vt* to outlaw, to ban

Achterbahn ['axtər-] *f* roller coaster

acht- *zW*: **~fach** *adj* eightfold; **~geben** △ (*unreg*) *vi siehe* **Acht**[2]; **~hundert** *num* eight hundred; **~los** *adj* careless; **~mal** *adv* eight times; **~sam** *adj* attentive

Achtung ['axtʊŋ] *f* attention; (*Ehrfurcht*) respect ♦ *excl* look out!; (*MIL*) attention!; **alle ~!** good for you/him *etc*

achtzehn *num* eighteen

achtzig *num* eighty

ächzen ['ɛçtsən] *vi* to groan

Acker ['akər] (-s, ¨) *m* field; **a~n** *vt, vi* to plough; (*umg*) to slog away

ADAC [aːdeːʔaˈtseː] *abk* (= *Allgemeiner Deutscher Automobil-Club*) ≃ AA, RAC

Adapter [aˈdaptər] (-s, -) *m* adapter

addieren [aˈdiːrən] *vt* to add (up); **Addition** [aditsiˈoːn] *f* addition

Adel ['aːdəl] (-s) *m* nobility; **a~ig** *adj* noble;

a~n vt to raise to the peerage

Ader ['a:dər] **(-, -n)** f vein

Adjektiv ['atjekti:f] **(-s, -e)** nt adjective

Adler ['a:dlər] **(-s, -)** m eagle

adlig adj noble

Adopt- zW: **a~ieren** [adɔp'ti:rən] vt to adopt; **~ion** [adɔptsi'o:n] f adoption; **~iveltern** pl adoptive parents; **~ivkind** nt adopted child

Adressbuch ▲ nt directory; (privat) address book

Adress- zW: **~e** [a'dresə] f address; **a~ieren** [adre'si:rən] vt: **a~ieren (an** +akk) to address (to)

Adria ['a:dria] **(-)** f Adriatic

Advent [at'vɛnt] **(-(e)s, -e)** m Advent; **~skalender** m Advent calendar; **~skranz** m Advent wreath

Adverb [at'vɛrp] nt adverb

Aerobic [ae'ro:bik] nt aerobics sg

Affäre [a'fɛ:rə] f affair

Affe ['afə] **(-n, -n)** m monkey

Affekt [a'fɛkt] **(-(e)s, -e)** m: **im ~ handeln** to act in the heat of the moment; **a~iert** [afɛk'ti:rt] adj affected

Affen- zW: **a~artig** adj like a monkey; **mit a~artiger Geschwindigkeit** like a flash; **~hitze** (umg) f incredible heat

affig ['afɪç] adj affected

Afrika ['a:frika] **(-s)** nt Africa; **~ner(in)** ['ka:nər(ɪn)] **(-s, -)** m(f) African; **a~nisch** adj African

AG [a:'ge:] abk (= Aktiengesellschaft) ≈ plc (BRIT), ≈ Inc. (US)

Agent [a'gɛnt] m agent; **~ur** f agency

Aggregat [agre'ga:t] **(-(e)s, -e)** nt aggregate; (TECH) unit

Aggress- zW: **~ion** [agresi'o:n] f aggression; **a~iv** [agrɛ'si:f] adj aggressive; **~ivität** [agresivi'tɛ:t] f aggressiveness

Agrarpolitik [a'gra:r-] f agricultural policy

Ägypten [ɛ'gyptən] **(-s)** nt Egypt; **ägyptisch** adj Egyptian

aha [a'ha:] excl aha

ähneln ['ɛ:nəln] vi +dat to be like, to resemble ♦ vr to be alike od similar

ahnen ['a:nən] vt to suspect; (Tod, Gefahr) to

have a presentiment of

ähnlich ['ɛ:nlɪç] adj (+dat) similar (to); **Ä~keit** f similarity

Ahnung ['a:nʊŋ] f idea, suspicion; presentiment; **a~slos** adj unsuspecting

Ahorn ['a:hɔrn] **(-s, -e)** m maple

Ähre ['ɛ:rə] f ear

Aids [e:dz] nt AIDS sg

Airbag ['ɛ:əbɛk] **(-s, -s)** m airbag

Akademie [akade'mi:] f academy; **Aka'demiker(in) (-s, -)** m(f) university graduate; **akademisch** adj academic

akklimatisieren [aklimati'zi:rən] vr to become acclimatized

Akkord [a'kɔrt] **(-(e)s, -e)** m (MUS) chord; **Im ~ arbeiten** to do piecework

Akkordeon [a'kɔrdeɔn] **(-s, -s)** nt accordion

Akku ['aku] **(-s, -s)** m rechargeable battery

Akkusativ ['akuzati:f] **(-s, -e)** m accusative

Akne ['akne] f acne

Akrobat(in) [akro'ba:t(ɪn)] **(-en, -en)** m(f) acrobat

Akt [akt] **(-(e)s, -e)** m act; (KUNST) nude

Akte ['aktə] f file

Akten- zW: **~koffer** m attaché case; **a~kundig** adj on the files; **~schrank** m filing cabinet; **~tasche** f briefcase

Aktie ['aktsiə] f share

Aktien- zW: **~gesellschaft** f public limited company; **~index (-(es), -e** od **-indices)** m share index; **~kurs** m share price

Aktion [aktsi'o:n] f campaign; (Polizeiaktion, Suchaktion) action

Aktionär [aktsio'nɛ:r] **(-s, -e)** m shareholder

aktiv [ak'ti:f] adj active; (MIL) regular; **~ieren** [-'vi:rən] vt to activate; **A~ität** f activity

Aktualität [aktuali'tɛ:t] f topicality; (einer Mode) up-to-dateness

aktuell [aktu'ɛl] adj topical; up-to-date

Akupunktur [akupʊŋk'tu:ər] f acupuncture

Akustik [a'kʊstɪk] f acoustics pl

akut [a'ku:t] adj acute

Akzent [ak'tsɛnt] m accent; (Betonung) stress

akzeptabel [aktsɛp'ta:bl] adj acceptable

akzeptieren [aktsɛp'ti:rən] vt to accept

Alarm [a'larm] **(-(e)s, -e)** m alarm; **a~bereit** adj standing by; **~bereitschaft** f stand-by;

a~**ieren** [-'miːrən] *vt* to alarm
Albanien [al'baːniən] **(-s)** *nt* Albania
albanisch *adj* Albanian
albern ['albərn] *adj* silly
Albtraum ▲ ['alptraʊm] *m* nightmare
Album ['albʊm] **(-s, Alben)** *nt* album
Alge ['algə] *f* algae
Algebra ['algebra] **(-)** *f* algebra
Algerier(in) [al'geːriːɐ] **(-s, -)** *m(f)* Algerian
algerisch *adj* Algerian
alias ['aːlias] *adv* alias
Alibi ['aːlibi] **(-s, -s)** *nt* alibi
Alimente [ali'mentə] *pl* alimony *sg*
Alkohol ['alkohɔl] **(-s, -e)** *m* alcohol; a~**frei**
  adj non-alcoholic; ~**iker(in)**
  [alko'hoːlikər(ɪn)] **(-s, -)** *m(f)* alcoholic;
  a~**isch** *adj* alcoholic; ~**verbot** *nt* ban on
  alcohol
All [al] **(-s)** *nt* universe
all'abendlich *adj* every evening
'**allbekannt** *adj* universally known

alle(r, s) ['alə(r,s)] *adj* **1** (*sämtliche*) all; **wir
alle** all of us; **alle Kinder waren da** all the
children were there; **alle Kinder mögen ...**
all children like ...; **alle beide** both of us/
them; **sie kamen alle** they all came; **alles
Gute** all the best; **alles in allem** all in all
2 (*mit Zeit- oder Maßangaben*) every; **alle
vier Jahre** every four years; **alle fünf
Meter** every five metres
♦ *pron* everything; **alles was er sagt**
everything he says, all that he says
♦ *adv* (*zu Ende, aufgebraucht*) finished; **die
Milch ist alle** the milk's all gone, there's
no milk left; **etw alle machen** to finish sth
up

Allee [a'leː] *f* avenue
allein [a'laɪn] *adv* alone; (*ohne Hilfe*) on one's
own, by oneself ♦ *konj* but, only; **nicht ~**
(*nicht nur*) not only; ~ **stehend** single;
A~**erziehende(r)** *f(m)* single parent;
A~**gang** *m*: **im A~gang** on one's own
allemal ['alə'maːl] *adv* (*jedes Mal*) always;
(*ohne weiteres*) with no bother; *siehe* **Mal**

allenfalls ['alən'fals] *adv* at all events;
(*höchstens*) at most
aller- ['alər] *zW*: ~**beste(r, s)** *adj* very best;
~**dings** *adv* (*zwar*) admittedly; (*gewiss*)
certainly
Allergie [aler'giː] *f* allergy; al'**lergisch** *adj*
allergic
aller- *zW*: ~**hand** (*umg*) *adj inv* all sorts of;
das ist doch ~hand! that's a bit much;
~**hand!** (*lobend*) good show!; A~'**heiligen**
nt All Saints' Day; ~**höchstens** *adv* at the
very most; ~**lei** *adj inv* all sorts of;
~**letzte(r, s)** *adj* very last; A~**seelen** **(-s)**
nt All Souls' Day; ~**seits** *adv* on all sides;
prost ~seits! cheers everyone!

i **Allerheiligen** (*All Saints' Day*) is
celebrated on November 1st and is a
public holiday in some parts of Germany
and in Austria. **Allerseelen** (*All Souls'
Day*) is celebrated on November 2nd in the
Roman Catholic Church. It is customary to
visit cemeteries and place lighted candles on
the graves of relatives and friends.

Allerwelts- *in zW* (*Durchschnitts-*) common;
(*nichts sagend*) commonplace
alles *pron* everything; ~ **in allem** all in all; ~
Gute! all the best!
Alleskleber **(-s, -)** *m* multi-purpose glue
allgemein ['algəmaɪn] *adj* general; **im A~en**
in general; ~ **gültig** generally accepted;
A~**wissen** *nt* general knowledge
Alliierte(r) [ali'iːrtə(r)] *m* ally
all- *zW*: ~**jährlich** *adj* annual; ~**mächtig**
adj almighty; ~**mählich** *adj* gradual;
A~**tag** *m* everyday life; ~**täglich** *adj, adv*
daily; (*gewöhnlich*) commonplace; ~**tags**
adv on weekdays; ~'**wissend** *adj*
omniscient; ~**zu** *adv* all too; ~ **oft** all too
often; ~ **viel** too much
Allzweck- ['altsvɛk-] *in zW* multi-purpose
Alm [alm] **(-, -en)** *f* alpine pasture
Almosen ['almoːzən] **(-s, -)** *nt* alms *pl*
Alpen ['alpən] *pl* Alps; ~**vorland** *nt* foothills
pl of the Alps

Alphabet [alfa'be:t] **(-(e)s, -e)** *nt* alphabet;
a~isch *adj* alphabetical

Alptraum ['alptraʊm] = **Albtraum**

SCHLÜSSELWORT

als [als] *konj* 1 *(zeitlich)* when; *(gleichzeitig)*
as; **damals, als ...** (in the days) when ...;
gerade, als ... just as ...
2 *(in der Eigenschaft)* than; **als Antwort** as
an answer; **als Kind** as a child
3 *(bei Vergleichen)* than; **ich kam später als
er** I came later than he (did) *od* later than
him; **lieber ... als ...** rather ... than ...;
nichts als Ärger nothing but trouble
4: **als ob / wenn** as if

also ['alzo:] *konj* so; *(folglich)* therefore; **~ gut
od schön!** okay then; **~, so was!** well
really!; **na ~!** there you are then!

Alsterwasser ['alstər-] *nt* shandy *(BRIT)*,
beer and lemonade

Alt [alt] **(-s, -e)** *m (MUS)* alto

alt *adj* old; **alles beim A~en lassen** to leave
everything as it was

Altar [al'ta:r] **(-(e)s, -äre)** *m* altar

Alt- *zW:* **~bau** *m* old building; **a~bekannt**
adj long-known; **~bier** *nt* top-fermented
German dark beer; **~'eisen** *nt* scrap iron

Alten(wohn)heim *nt* old people's home

Alter ['altər] **(-s, -)** *nt* age; *(hohes)* old age;
im ~ von at the age of; **a~n** *vi* to grow
old, to age

Alternativ- [alterna'ti:f] *in zW* alternative;
~e *f* alternative

Alters- *zW:* **~grenze** *f* age limit; **~heim** *nt*
old people's home; **~rente** *f* old age
pension; **a~schwach** *adj (Mensch)* frail;
~versorgung *f* old age pension

Altertum ['altərtuːm] *nt* antiquity

alt- *zW:* **A~glas** *nt* glass for recycling;
A~glascontainer *m* bottle bank; **~klug**
adj precocious; **~modisch** *adj* old-
fashioned; **A~papier** *nt* waste paper;
A~stadt *f* old town

Alufolie ['a:lufo:liə] *f* aluminium foil

Aluminium [alu'mi:niʊm] **(-s)** *nt* aluminium,
aluminum *(US)*

Alzheimerkrankheit ['altshaɪmər'kraŋkhaɪt]
f Alzheimer's (disease)

am [am] = **an dem**; **~ Schlafen**; *(umg)*
sleeping; **~ 15. März** on March 15th; **~
besten / schönsten** best/most beautiful

Amateur [ama'tø:r] *m* amateur

Amboss ▲ ['ambɔs] **(-es, -e)** *m* anvil

ambulant [ambu'lant] *adj* outpatient;
Ambulanz *f* outpatients *sg*

Ameise ['a:maɪzə] *f* ant

Ameisenhaufen *m* ant hill

Amerika [a'me:rika] **(-s)** *nt* America;
~ner(in) [-'ka:nər(ɪn)] **(-s, -)** *m(f)* American;
a~nisch [-'ka:nɪʃ] *adj* American

Amnestie [amnɛs'tiː] *f* amnesty

Ampel ['ampəl] **(-, -n)** *f* traffic lights *pl*

amputieren [ampu'ti:rən] *vt* to amputate

Amsel ['amzəl] **(-, -n)** *f* blackbird

Amt [amt] **(-(e)s, -er)** *nt* office; *(Pflicht)* duty;
(TEL) exchange; **a~ieren** [am'ti:rən] *vi* to
hold office; **a~lich** *adj* official

Amts- *zW:* **~richter** *m* district judge;
~stunden *pl* office hours; **~zeichen** *nt*
dialling tone; **~zeit** *f* period of office

amüsant [amy'zant] *adj* amusing

amüsieren [amy'zi:rən] *vt* to amuse ♦ *vr* to
enjoy o.s.

Amüsierviertel *nt* nightclub district

SCHLÜSSELWORT

an [an] *präp +dat* 1 *(räumlich: wo?)* at; *(auf,
bei)* on; *(nahe bei)* near; **an diesem Ort** at
this place; **an der Wand** on the wall; **zu
nahe an etw** too near to sth; **unten am
Fluss** down by the river; **Köln liegt am
Rhein** Cologne is on the Rhine
2 *(zeitlich: wann?)* on; **an diesem Tag** on
this day; **an Ostern** at Easter
3: **arm an Fett** low in fat; **an etw sterben**
to die of sth; **an (und für) sich** actually
♦ *präp +akk* 1 *(räumlich: wohin?)* to; **er ging
ans Fenster** he went (over) to the
window; **etw an die Wand hängen /
schreiben** to hang/write sth on the wall
2 *(zeitlich: woran?)*: **an etw denken** to think
of sth
3 *(gerichtet an)* to; **ein Gruß / eine Frage**

Spelling Reform: ▲ *new spelling* △ *old spelling (to be phased out)*

an dich greetings/a question to you
♦ *adv* **1** (*ungefähr*) about; **an die hundert** about a hundred
2 (*auf Fahrplänen*): **Frankfurt an 18.30** arriving Frankfurt 18.30
3 (*ab*): **von dort/heute an** from there/today onwards
4 (*angeschaltet, angezogen*) on; **das Licht ist an** the light is on; **ohne etwas an** with nothing on; *siehe auch* **am**

analog [ana'lo:k] *adj* analogous; **A~ie** [-'gi:] *f* analogy
Analphabet(in) [an|alfa'be:t(ɪn)] (**-en, -en**) *m(f)* illiterate (person)
Analyse [ana'ly:zə] *f* analysis
analysieren [analy'zi:rən] *vt* to analyse
Ananas ['ananas] (**-, -** *od* **-se**) *f* pineapple
Anarchie [anar'çi:] *f* anarchy
Anatomie [anato'mi:] *f* anatomy
anbahnen ['anba:nən] *vt, vr* to open up
Anbau ['anbau] *m* (*AGR*) cultivation; (*Gebäude*) extension; **a~en** *vt* (*AGR*) to cultivate; (*Gebäudeteil*) to build on
anbehalten ['anbəhaltən] (*unreg*) *vt* to keep on
anbei [an'bai] *adv* enclosed
anbeißen ['anbaisən] (*unreg*) *vt* to bite into ♦ *vi* to bite; (*fig*) to swallow the bait; **zum A~** (*umg*) good enough to eat
anbelangen ['anbəlaŋən] *vt* to concern; **was mich anbelangt** as far as I am concerned
anbeten ['anbe:tən] *vt* to worship
Anbetracht ['anbətraxt] *m*: **in ~** +*gen* in view of
anbieten ['anbi:tən] (*unreg*) *vt* to offer ♦ *vr* to volunteer
anbinden ['anbindən] (*unreg*) *vt* to tie up; **kurz angebunden** (*fig*) curt
Anblick ['anblɪk] *m* sight; **a~en** *vt* to look at
anbraten ['anbra:tən] *vt* to brown
anbrechen ['anbrɛçən] (*unreg*) *vt* to start; (*Vorräte*) to break into ♦ *vi* to start; (*Tag*) to break; (*Nacht*) to fall
anbrennen ['anbrɛnən] (*unreg*) *vi* to catch fire; (*KOCH*) to burn

anbringen ['anbrɪŋən] (*unreg*) *vt* to bring; (*Ware*) to sell; (*festmachen*) to fasten
Anbruch ['anbrʊx] *m* beginning; **~ des Tages/der Nacht** dawn/nightfall
anbrüllen ['anbrylən] *vt* to roar at
Andacht ['andaxt] (**-, -en**) *f* devotion; (*Gottesdienst*) prayers *pl*; **andächtig** *adj* ['andɛçtɪç] devout
andauern ['andauərn] *vi* to last, to go on; **~d** *adj* continual
Anden ['andən] *pl* Andes
Andenken ['andɛŋkən] (**-s, -**) *nt* memory; souvenir
andere(r, s) ['andərə(r, z)] *adj* other; (*verschieden*) different; **ein ~s Mal** another time; **kein ~r** nobody else; **von etw ~m sprechen** to talk about something else; **~rseits** *adv* on the other hand
andermal *adv*: **ein ~** some other time
ändern ['ɛndərn] *vt* to alter, to change ♦ *vr* to change
andernfalls ['andərnfals] *adv* otherwise
anders ['andərs] *adv*: **~ (als)** differently (from); **wer ~?** who else?; **jd/irgendwo ~** sb/somewhere else; **~ aussehen/klingen** to look/sound different; **~artig** *adj* different; **~herum** *adv* the other way round; **~wo** *adv* somewhere else; **~woher** *adv* from somewhere else
anderthalb ['andərt'halp] *adj* one and a half
Änderung ['ɛndərʊŋ] *f* alteration, change
Änderungsschneiderei *f* tailor (*who does alterations*)
anderweitig ['andər'vaitɪç] *adj* other ♦ *adv* otherwise; (*anderswo*) elsewhere
andeuten ['andɔytən] *vt* to indicate; (*Wink geben*) to hint at; **Andeutung** *f* indication; hint
Andrang ['andraŋ] *m* crush
andrehen ['andre:ən] *vt* to turn *od* switch on; **jdm etw ~** (*umg*) to unload sth onto sb
androhen ['andro:ən] *vt*: **jdm etw ~** to threaten sb with sth
aneignen ['an|aignən] *vt*: **sich** *dat* **etw ~** to acquire sth; (*widerrechtlich*) to appropriate sth

Rechtschreibreform: ▲ *neue Schreibung* △ *alte Schreibung (auslaufend)*

aneinander [anǀaɪˈnandər] *adv* at/on/to *etc* one another *od* each other; **~ geraten** to clash

Anekdote [anɛkˈdoːtə] *f* anecdote

anekeln [ˈanǀeːkəln] *vt* to disgust

anerkannt [ˈanǀɛrkant] *adj* recognized, acknowledged

anerkennen [ˈanǀɛrkɛnən] (*unreg*) *vt* to recognize, to acknowledge; (*würdigen*) to appreciate; **~d** *adj* appreciative

Anerkennung *f* recognition, acknowledgement; appreciation

anfachen [ˈanfaxən] *vt* to fan into flame; (*fig*) to klndle

anfahren [ˈanfaːrən] (*unreg*) *vt* to deliver; (*fahren gegen*) to hit; (*Hafen*) to put into; (*fig*) to bawl out ♦ *vi* to drive up; (*losfahren*) to drive off

Anfahrt [ˈanfaːrt] *f* (*~sweg, ~szeit*) journey

Anfall [ˈanfal] *m* (*MED*) attack; **a~en** (*unreg*) *vt* to attack; (*fig*) to overcome ♦ *vi* (*Arbeit*) to come up; (*Produkt*) to be obtained

anfällig [ˈanfɛlɪç] *adj* delicate; **~ für etw** prone to sth

Anfang [ˈanfaŋ] (**-(e)s, -fänge**) *m* beginning, start; **von ~ an** right from the beginning; **zu ~** at the beginning; **~ Mai** at the beginning of May; **a~en** (*unreg*) *vt, vi* to begin, to start; (*machen*) to do

Anfänger(in) [ˈanfɛŋər(ɪn)] (**-s, -**) *m(f)* beginner

anfänglich [ˈanfɛŋlɪç] *adj* initial

anfangs *adv* at first; **A~buchstabe** *m* initial *od* first letter; **A~gehalt** *nt* starting salary

anfassen [ˈanfasən] *vt* to handle; (*berühren*) to touch ♦ *vi* to lend a hand ♦ *vr* to feel

anfechten [ˈanfɛçtən] (*unreg*) *vt* to dispute

anfertigen [ˈanfɛrtɪgən] *vt* to make

anfeuern [ˈanfɔʏərn] *vt* (*fig*) to spur on

anflehen [ˈanfleːən] *vt* to implore

anfliegen [ˈanfliːgən] (*unreg*) *vt* to fly to

Anflug [ˈanfluːk] *m* (*AVIAT*) approach; (*Spur*) trace

anfordern [ˈanfɔrdərn] *vt* to demand; (*COMM*) to requisition

Anforderung *f* (*+gen*) demand (for)

Anfrage [ˈanfraːgə] *f* inquiry; **a~n** *vi* to inquire

anfreunden [ˈanfrɔʏndən] *vr* to make friends

anfügen [ˈanfyːgən] *vt* to add; (*beifügen*) to enclose

anfühlen [ˈanfyːlən] *vt, vr* to feel

anführen [ˈanfyːrən] *vt* to lead; (*zitieren*) to quote; (*umg: betrügen*) to lead up the garden path

Anführer *m* leader

Anführungszeichen *pl* quotation marks, inverted commas

Angabe [ˈangaːbə] *f* statement; (*TECH*) specification; (*umg: Prahlerei*) boasting; (*SPORT*) service

angeben [ˈangeːbən] (*unreg*) *vt* to give; (*anzeigen*) to inform on; (*bestimmen*) to set ♦ *vi* (*umg*) to boast; (*SPORT*) to serve

Angeber (-s, -) (*umg*) *m* show-off; **Angebe'rei** (*umg*) *f* showing off

angeblich [ˈangeːplɪç] *adj* alleged

angeboren [ˈangəboːrən] *adj* inborn, innate

Angebot [ˈangəboːt] *nt* offer; **~ (an** +*dat*) (*COMM*) supply (of)

angebracht [ˈangəbraxt] *adj* appropriate, in order

angegriffen [ˈangəɡrɪfən] *adj* exhausted

angeheitert [ˈangəhaɪtərt] *adj* tipsy

angehen [ˈangeːən] (*unreg*) *vt* to concern; (*angreifen*) to attack; (*bitten*): **jdn ~ (um)** to approach sb (for) ♦ *vi* (*Feuer*) to light; (*umg: beginnen*) to begin; **~d** *adj* prospective

angehören [ˈangəhøːrən] *vi* (+ *dat*) to belong to; (*Partei*) to be a member of

Angehörige(r) *f(m)* relative

Angeklagte(r) [ˈangəklaːktə(r)] *f(m)* accused

Angel [ˈaŋəl] (**-, -n**) *f* fishing rod; (*Türangel*) hinge

Angelegenheit [ˈangəleːgənhaɪt] *f* affair, matter

Angel- *zW*: **~haken** *m* fish hook; **a~n** *vt* to catch ♦ *vi* to fish; **~n (-s)** *nt* angling, fishing; **~rute** *f* fishing rod; **~schein** *m* fishing permit

angemessen [ˈangəmɛsən] *adj* appropriate, suitable

angenehm [ˈangəneːm] *adj* pleasant; **~!** (*bei Vorstellung*) pleased to meet you

angeregt [angəreːkt] *adj* animated, lively

angesehen [ˈangəzeːən] *adj* respected

angesichts [ˈangəzɪçts] *präp +gen* in view of, considering

angespannt [ˈangəʃpant] *adj* (*Aufmerksamkeit*) close; (*Arbeit*) hard

Angestellte(r) [ˈangəʃtɛltə(r)] *f(m)* employee

angestrengt [ˈangəʃtrɛŋt] *adv* as hard as one can

angetan [ˈangətaːn] *adj*: **von jdm/etw ~ sein** to be impressed by sb/sth; **es jdm ~ haben** to appeal to sb

angetrunken [ˈangətrʊŋkən] *adj* tipsy

angewiesen [ˈangəviːzən] *adj*: **auf jdn/etw ~ sein** to be dependent on sb/sth

angewöhnen [ˈangəvøːnən] *vt*: **jdm/sich etw ~** to get sb/become accustomed to sth

Angewohnheit [ˈangəvoːnhaɪt] *f* habit

angleichen [ˈanglaɪçən] (*unreg*) *vt, vr* to adjust

Angler [ˈaŋlər] **(-s, -)** *m* angler

angreifen [ˈangraɪfən] (*unreg*) *vt* to attack; (*beschädigen*) to damage

Angreifer (-s, -) *m* attacker

Angriff [ˈangrɪf] *m* attack; **etw in ~ nehmen** to make a start on sth

Angst (-, ⁺e) *f* fear; **jdm ist a~** sb is afraid *od* scared; **~ haben** (**vor** +*dat*) to be afraid *od* scared (of); **~ haben um jdn/etw** to be worried about sb/sth; **jdm ~ machen** to scare sb; **~hase** (*umg*) *m* chicken, scaredy-cat

ängst- [ˈɛŋst] *zW*: **~igen** *vt* to frighten ♦ *vr*: **sich ~igen** (**vor** +*dat od* **um**) to worry (o.s.) (about); **~lich** *adj* nervous; (*besorgt*) worried; **Ä~lichkeit** *f* nervousness

anhaben [ˈanhaːbən] (*unreg*) *vt* to have on; **er kann mir nichts ~** he can't hurt me

anhalt- [ˈanhalt] *zW*: **~en** (*unreg*) *vt* to stop ♦ *vi* to stop; (*andauern*) to persist; **(jdm) etw ~en** to hold sth up (against sb); **jdn zur Arbeit/Höflichkeit ~en** to make sb work/be polite; **~end** *adj* persistent;

A~er(in) (-s, -) *m(f)* hitch-hiker; **per A~er fahren** to hitch-hike; **A~spunkt** *m* clue

anhand [anˈhant] *präp +gen* with

Anhang [ˈanhaŋ] *m* appendix; (*Leute*) family; supporters *pl*

anhäng- [ˈanhɛŋ] *zW*: **~en** (*unreg*) *vt* to hang up; (*Wagen*) to couple up; (*Zusatz*) to add (on); **A~er (-s, -)** *m* supporter; (*AUT*) trailer; (*am Koffer*) tag; (*Schmuck*) pendant; **A~erschaft** *f* supporters *pl*; **~lich** *adj* devoted; **A~lichkeit** *f* devotion; **A~sel (-s, -)** *nt* appendage

Anhäufung [ˈanhɔyfʊŋ] *f* accumulation

anheben [ˈanheːbən] (*unreg*) *vt* to lift up; (*Preise*) to raise

anheizen [ˈanhaɪtsən] *vt* (*Stimmung*) to lift; (*Moral*) to boost

Anhieb [ˈanhiːb] *m*: **auf ~** at the very first go; (*kurz entschlossen*) on the spur of the moment

Anhöhe [ˈanhøːə] *f* hill

anhören [ˈanhøːrən] *vt* to listen to; (*anmerken*) to hear ♦ *vr* to sound

animieren [aniˈmiːrən] *vt* to encourage, to urge on

Anis [aˈniːs] **(-es, -e)** *m* aniseed

Ank. *abk* (= *Ankunft*) arr.

Ankauf [ˈankaʊf] *m* (*von Wertpapieren, Devisen, Waren*) purchase; **a~en** *vt* to purchase, to buy

Anker [ˈaŋkər] **(-s, -)** *m* anchor; **vor ~ gehen** to drop anchor

Anklage [ˈanklaːgə] *f* accusation; (*JUR*) charge; **~bank** *f* dock; **a~n** *vt* to accuse; **jdn (eines Verbrechens) a~n** (*JUR*) to charge sb (with a crime)

Ankläger [ˈanklɛːgər] *m* accuser

Anklang [ˈanklaŋ] *m*: **bei jdm ~ finden** to meet with sb's approval

Ankleidekabine *f* changing cubicle

ankleiden [ˈanklaɪdən] *vt, vr* to dress

anklopfen [ˈanklɔpfən] *vi* to knock

anknüpfen [ˈanknʏpfən] *vt* to fasten *od* tie on; (*fig*) to start ♦ *vi* (*anschließen*): **~ an** +*akk* to refer to

ankommen [ˈankɔmən] (*unreg*) *vi* to arrive; (*näher kommen*) to approach; (*Anklang* *finden*): **bei jdm (gut)** ~ to go down well with sb; **es kommt darauf an** it depends; (*wichtig sein*) that (is what) matters; **es darauf ~ lassen** to let things take their course; **gegen jdn/etw ~** to cope with sb/sth; **bei jdm schlecht ~** to go down badly with sb

ankreuzen ['ankrɔʏtsən] *vt* to mark with a cross; (*hervorheben*) to highlight

ankündigen ['ankʏndɪgən] *vt* to announce; **Ankündigung** *f* announcement

Ankunft ['ankʊnft] (-, **-künfte**) *f* arrival; **~szeit** *f* time of arrival

ankurbeln ['ankʊrbəln] *vt* (*fig*) to boost

Anlage ['anlaːgə] *f* disposition; (*Begabung*) talent; (*Park*) gardens *pl*; (*Beilage*) enclosure; (*TECH*) plant; (*FIN*) investment; (*Entwurf*) layout

Anlass ▲ ['anlas] (**-es, -lässe**) *m*: ~ **(zu)** cause (for); (*Ereignis*) occasion; **aus ~** +*gen* on the occasion of; ~ **zu etw geben** to give rise to sth; **etw zum ~ nehmen** to take the opportunity of sth

anlassen (*unreg*) *vt* to leave on; (*Motor*) to start ♦ *vr* (*umg*) to start off

Anlasser (-s, -) *m* (*AUT*) starter

anlässlich ▲ ['anlɛslɪç] *präp* +*gen* on the occasion of

Anlauf ['anlaʊf] *m* run-up; **a~en** (*unreg*) *vi* to begin; (*neuer Film*) to show; (*SPORT*) to run up; (*Fenster*) to mist up; (*Metall*) to tarnish ♦ *vt* to call at; **rot a~en** to blush; **angelaufen kommen** to come running up

anlegen ['anleːgən] *vt* to put; (*anziehen*) to put on; (*gestalten*) to lay out; (*Geld*) to invest ♦ *vi* to dock; **etw an etw** *akk* ~ to put sth against *od* on sth; **ein Gewehr ~ (auf** +*akk*) to aim a weapon (at); **es auf etw** *akk* ~ to be out for sth/to do sth; **sich mit jdm ~** (*umg*) to quarrel with sb

Anlegestelle *f* landing place

anlehnen ['anleːnən] *vt* to lean; (*Tür*) to leave ajar; **(sich) an etw** *akk* ~ to lean on/against sth

Anleihe ['anlaɪə] *f* (*FIN*) loan

anleiten ['anlaɪtən] *vt* to instruct; **Anleitung** *f* instructions *pl*

anliegen ['anliːgən] (*unreg*) *vi* (*Kleidung*) to cling; **A~** (-s, -) *nt* matter; (*Wunsch*) wish; **~d** *adj* adjacent; (*beigefügt*) enclosed

Anlieger (-s, -) *m* resident; „~ **frei"** "residents only"

anmachen ['anmaxən] *vt* to attach; (*Elektrisches*) to put on; (*Zigarette*) to light; (*Salat*) to dress

anmaßen ['anmaːsən] *vt*: **sich** *dat* **etw ~** (*Recht*) to lay claim to sth; **~d** *adj* arrogant

Anmaßung *f* presumption

anmelden ['anmeldən] *vt* to announce ♦ *vr* (*sich ankündigen*) to make an appointment; (*polizeilich, für Kurs etc*) to register

Anmeldung *f* announcement; appointment; registration

anmerken ['anmɛrkən] *vt* to observe; (*anstreichen*) to mark; **sich** *dat* **nichts ~ lassen** to not give anything away

Anmerkung *f* note

anmieten ['anmiːtən] *vt* to rent; (*auch Auto*) to hire

Anmut ['anmuːt] (-) *f* grace; **a~en** *vt* to give a feeling; **a~ig** *adj* charming

annähen ['annɛːən] *vt* to sew on

annähern ['annɛːərn] *vr* to get closer; **~d** *adj* approximate

Annäherung *f* approach

Annäherungsversuch *m* advances *pl*

Annahme ['annaːmə] *f* acceptance; (*Vermutung*) assumption

annehm- ['annɛːm] *zW*: **~bar** *adj* acceptable; **~en** (*unreg*) *vt* to accept; (*Namen*) to take; (*Kind*) to adopt; (*vermuten*) to suppose, to assume ♦ *vr* (+*gen*) to take care (of); **A~lichkeit** *f* comfort

Annonce [a'nõːsə] *f* advertisement

annoncieren [anõ'siːrən] *vt, vi* to advertise

annullieren [anʊ'liːrən] *vt* to annul

anonym [ano'nyːm] *adj* anonymous

Anorak ['anorak] (-s, -s) *m* anorak

anordnen ['anɔrdnən] *vt* to arrange; (*befehlen*) to order

Anordnung *f* arrangement; order

anorganisch ['anɔrgaːnɪʃ] *adj* inorganic

anpacken ['anpakən] *vt* to grasp; (*fig*) to tackle; **mit ~** to lend a hand

Spelling Reform: ▲ *new spelling* △ *old spelling (to be phased out)*

anpassen ['anpasən] *vt*: **(jdm)** ~ to fit (on sb); (*fig*) to adapt ♦ *vr* to adapt

anpassungsfähig *adj* adaptable

Anpfiff ['anpfɪf] *m* (*SPORT*) (starting) whistle; kick-off; (*umg*) rocket

anprallen ['anpralən] *vi*: ~ **(gegen** *od* **an** +*akk*) to collide (with)

anprangern ['anpraŋərn] *vt* to denounce

anpreisen ['anpraɪzən] (*unreg*) *vt* to extol

Anprobe ['anproːbə] *f* trying on

anprobieren ['anprobiːrən] *vt* to try on

anrechnen ['anrɛçnən] *vt* to charge; (*fig*) to count; **jdm etw hoch** ~ to think highly of sb for sth

Anrecht ['anrɛçt] *nt*: ~ **(auf** +*akk*) right (to)

Anrede ['anreːdə] *f* form of address; **a~n** *vt* to address; (*belästigen*) to accost

anregen ['anreːgən] *vt* to stimulate; **angeregte Unterhaltung** lively discussion; **~d** *adj* stimulating

Anregung *f* stimulation; (*Vorschlag*) suggestion

anreichern ['anraɪçərn] *vt* to enrich

Anreise ['anraɪzə] *f* journey; **a~n** *vi* to arrive

Anreiz ['anraɪts] *m* incentive

Anrichte ['anrɪçtə] *f* sideboard; **a~n** *vt* to serve up; **Unheil a~n** to make mischief

anrüchig ['anryçɪç] *adj* dubious

anrücken ['anrʏkən] *vi* to approach; (*MIL*) to advance

Anruf ['anruːf] *m* call; **~beantworter** [-bə-'|antvɔrtər] **(-s, -)** *m* answering machine; **a~en** (*unreg*) *vt* to call out to; (*bitten*) to call on; (*TEL*) to ring up, to phone, to call

ans [ans] = **an das**

Ansage ['anzaːgə] *f* announcement; **a~n** *vt* to announce ♦ *vr* to say one will come; **~r(in) (-s, -)** *m(f)* announcer

ansammeln ['anzaməln] *vt* (*Reichtümer*) to amass ♦ *vr* (*Menschen*) to gather, to assemble; (*Wasser*) to collect; **Ansammlung** *f* collection; (*Leute*) crowd

ansässig ['anzɛsɪç] *adj* resident

Ansatz ['anzats] *m* start; (*Haaransatz*) hairline; (*Halsansatz*) base; (*Verlängerungsstück*) extension; (*Veranschlagung*) estimate; **~punkt** *m* starting point

anschaffen ['anʃafən] *vt* to buy, to purchase; **Anschaffung** *f* purchase

anschalten ['anʃaltən] *vt* to switch on

anschau- ['anʃaʊ] *zW*: **~en** *vt* to look at; **~lich** *adj* illustrative; **A~ung** *f* (*Meinung*) view; **aus eigener A~ung** from one's own experience

Anschein ['anʃaɪn] *m* appearance; **allem ~ nach** to all appearances; **den ~ haben** to seem, to appear; **a~end** *adj* apparent

anschieben ['anʃiːbən] *vt* to push

Anschlag ['anʃlaːk] *m* notice; (*Attentat*) attack; (*COMM*) estimate; (*auf Klavier*) touch; (*Schreibmaschine*) character; **a~en** ['anʃlaːgən] (*unreg*) *vt* to put up; (*beschädigen*) to chip; (*Akkord*) to strike; (*Kosten*) to estimate ♦ *vi* to hit; (*wirken*) to have an effect; (*Glocke*) to ring; **an etw** *akk* **a~en** to hit against sth

anschließen ['anʃliːsən] (*unreg*) *vt* to connect up; (*Sender*) to link up ♦ *vi*: **an etw** *akk* ~ to adjoin sth; (*zeitlich*) to follow sth ♦ *vr*: **sich jdm/etw** ~ to join sb/sth; (*beipflichten*) to agree with sb/sth; **sich an etw** *akk* ~ to adjoin sth; **~d** *adj* adjacent; (*zeitlich*) subsequent ♦ *adv* afterwards

Anschluss ▲ ['anʃlʊs] *m* (*ELEK, EISENB*) connection; (*von Wasser etc*) supply; **im ~ an** +*akk* following; **~ finden** to make friends; **~flug** *m* connecting flight

anschmiegsam ['anʃmiːkzaːm] *adj* affectionate

anschnallen ['anʃnalən] *vt* to buckle on ♦ *vr* to fasten one's seat belt

anschneiden ['anʃnaɪdən] (*unreg*) *vt* to cut into; (*Thema*) to introduce

anschreiben ['anʃraɪbən] (*unreg*) *vt* to write (up); (*COMM*) to charge up; (*benachrichtigen*) to write to

anschreien ['anʃraɪən] (*unreg*) *vt* to shout at

Anschrift ['anʃrɪft] *f* address

Anschuldigung ['anʃʊldɪɡʊŋ] *f* accusation

anschwellen ['anʃvɛlən] (*unreg*) *vi* to swell (up)

anschwindeln ['anʃvɪndəln] *vt* to lie to

ansehen ['anzeːən] (*unreg*) *vt* to look at;

jdm etw ~ to see sth (from sb's face); **jdn/etw als etw ~** to look on sb/sth as sth; **~ für** to consider; **A~ (-s)** nt respect; (Ruf) reputation

ansehnlich ['anzeːnlɪç] adj fine-looking; (beträchtlich) considerable

ansetzen ['anzɛtsən] vt (festlegen) to fix; (entwickeln) to develop; (Fett) to put on; (Blätter) to grow; (zubereiten) to prepare ♦ vi (anfangen) to start, to begin; (Entwicklung) to set in; (dick werden) to put on weight ♦ vr (Rost etc) to start to develop; **~ an** +akk (anfügen) to fix on to; (anlegen, an Mund etc) to put to

Ansicht ['anzɪçt] f (Anblick) sight; (Meinung) view, opinion; **zur ~** on approval; **meiner ~ nach** in my opinion; **~skarte** f picture postcard; **~ssache** f matter of opinion

ansonsten [an'zɔnstən] adv otherwise

anspannen ['anʃpanən] vt to harness; (Muskel) to strain; **Anspannung** f strain

anspielen ['anʃpiːlən] vi (SPORT) to start play; **auf etw akk ~** to refer od allude to sth

Anspielung f: **~ (auf +akk)** reference (to), allusion (to)

Anspitzer ['anʃpɪtsər] (-s, -) m pencil sharpener

Ansporn ['anʃpɔrn] (-(e)s) m incentive

Ansprache ['anʃpraːxə] f address

ansprechen ['anʃprɛçən] (unreg) vt to speak to; (bitten, gefallen) to appeal to ♦ vi: **(auf etw akk) ~** to react (to sth); **jdn auf etw akk (hin) ~** to ask sb about sth; **~d** adj attractive

anspringen ['anʃprɪŋən] (unreg) vi (AUT) to start ♦ vt to jump at

Anspruch ['anʃprʊx] m (Recht): **~ (auf +akk)** claim (to); **hohe Ansprüche stellen/haben** to demand/expect a lot; **jdn/etw in ~ nehmen** to occupy sb/take up sth; **a~slos** adj undemanding; **a~svoll** adj demanding

anstacheln ['anʃtaxəln] vt to spur on

Anstalt ['anʃtalt] (-, -en) f institution; **~en machen, etw zu tun** to prepare to do sth

Anstand ['anʃtant] m decency

anständig ['anʃtɛndɪç] adj decent; (umg) proper; (groß) considerable

anstandslos adv without any ado

anstarren ['anʃtarən] vt to stare at

anstatt [an'ʃtat] präp +gen instead of ♦ konj: **~ etw zu tun** instead of doing sth

Ansteck- ['anʃtɛk] zW: **a~en** vt to pin on; (MED) to infect; (Pfeife) to light; (Haus) to set fire to ♦ vr: **ich habe mich bei ihm angesteckt** I caught it from him ♦ vi (fig) to be infectious; **a~end** adj infectious; **~ung** f infection

anstehen ['anʃteːən] (unreg) vi to queue (up) (BRIT), to line up (US)

ansteigen ['anʃtaɪgən] vt (Straße) to climb; (Gelände, Temperatur, Preise) to rise

anstelle, an Stelle [an'ʃtɛlə] präp +gen in place of; **~n** ['an-] vt (einschalten) to turn on; (Arbeit geben) to employ; (machen) to do ♦ vr to queue (up) (BRIT), to line up (US); (umg) to act

Anstellung f employment; (Posten) post, position

Anstieg ['anʃtiːk] **(-(e)s, -e)** m (+gen) climb; (fig: von Preisen etc) increase (in)

anstiften ['anʃtɪftən] vt (Unglück) to cause; **jdn zu etw ~** to put sb up to sth

anstimmen ['anʃtɪmən] vt (Lied) to strike up with; (Geschrei) to set up

Anstoß ['anʃtoːs] m impetus; (Ärgernis) offence; (SPORT) kick-off; **der erste ~** the initiative; **~ nehmen an** +dat to take offence at; **a~en** (unreg) vt to push; (mit Fuß) to kick ♦ vi to knock, to bump; (mit der Zunge) to lisp; (mit Gläsern): **a~en (auf +akk)** to drink (to), to drink a toast (to)

anstößig ['anʃtøːsɪç] adj offensive, indecent

anstreichen ['anʃtraɪçən] (unreg) vt to paint

anstrengen ['anʃtrɛŋən] vt to strain; (JUR) to bring ♦ vr to make an effort; **~d** adj tiring

Anstrengung f effort

Anstrich ['anʃtrɪç] m coat of paint

Ansturm ['anʃtʊrm] m rush; (MIL) attack

Antarktis [ant|'arktɪs] (-) f Antarctic

antasten ['antastən] vt to touch; (Recht) to infringe upon; (Ehre) to question

Anteil ['antaɪl] **(-s, -e)** m share; (Mitgefühl)

Spelling Reform: ▲ new spelling △ old spelling (to be phased out)

sympathy; **~ nehmen (an** +*dat*) to share (in); (*sich interessieren*) to take an interest (in); **~nahme** (-) *f* sympathy

Antenne [an'tɛnə] *f* aerial

Anti- ['anti] *in zW* anti; **~alko'holiker** *m* teetotaller; **a~autori'tär** *adj* anti-authoritarian; **~babypille** *f* contraceptive pill; **~biotikum** [antibi'o:tikʊm] **(-s, -ka)** *nt* antibiotic

antik [an'ti:k] *adj* antique; **A~e** *f* (*Zeitalter*) ancient world

Antiquariat [antikvari'a:t] **(-(e)s, -e)** *nt* secondhand bookshop

Antiquitäten [antikvi'tɛ:tən] *pl* antiques; **~händler** *m* antique dealer

Antrag ['antra:k] **(-(e)s, -träge)** *m* proposal; (*PARL*) motion; (*Gesuch*) application; **~steller(in)** **(-s, -)** *m(f)* claimant; (*für Kredit*) applicant

antreffen ['antrɛfən] (*unreg*) *vt* to meet

antreiben ['antraɪbən] (*unreg*) *vt* to drive on; (*Motor*) to drive

antreten ['antre:tən] (*unreg*) *vt* (*Amt*) to take up; (*Erbschaft*) to come into; (*Beweis*) to offer; (*Reise*) to start, to begin ♦ *vi* (*MIL*) to fall in; (*SPORT*) to line up; **gegen jdn ~** to play/fight (against) sb

Antrieb ['antri:p] *m* (*auch fig*) drive; **aus eigenem ~** of one's own accord

antrinken ['antrɪŋkən] (*unreg*) *vt* (*Flasche, Glas*) to start to drink from; **sich** *dat* **Mut/ einen Rausch ~** to give o.s. Dutch courage/get drunk; **angetrunken sein** to be tipsy

Antritt ['antrɪt] *m* beginning, commencement; (*eines Amts*) taking up

antun ['antu:n] (*unreg*) *vt*: **jdm etw ~** to do sth to sb; **sich** *dat* **Zwang ~** to force o.s.; **sich** *dat* **etwas ~** to (try to) take one's own life

Antwort ['antvɔrt] **(-, -en)** *f* answer, reply; **a~en** *vi* to answer, to reply

anvertrauen ['anfɛrtrauən] *vt*: **jdm etw ~** to entrust sb with sth; **sich jdm ~** to confide in sb

anwachsen ['anvaksən] (*unreg*) *vi* to grow; (*Pflanze*) to take root

Anwalt ['anvalt] **(-(e)s, -wälte)** *m* solicitor; lawyer; (*fig*) champion

Anwältin ['anvɛltɪn] *f siehe* **Anwalt**

Anwärter ['anvɛrtər] *m* candidate

anweisen ['anvaɪzən] (*unreg*) *vt* to instruct; (*zuteilen*) to assign

Anweisung *f* instruction; (*COMM*) remittance; (*Postanweisung, Zahlungsanweisung*) money order

anwend- ['anvɛnd] *zW*: **~bar** ['anvɛnt-] *adj* practicable, applicable; **~en** (*unreg*) *vt* to use, to employ; (*Gesetz, Regel*) to apply; **A~ung** *f* use; application

anwesend ['anve:zənt] *adj* present; **die A~en** those present

Anwesenheit *f* presence

anwidern ['anvi:dərn] *vt* to disgust

Anwohner(in) ['anvo:nər(ɪn)] **(-s, -)** *m(f)* neighbour

Anzahl ['antsa:l] *f*: **~ (an** +*dat*) number (of); **a~en** *vt* to pay on account; **~ung** *f* deposit, payment on account

Anzeichen ['antsaɪçən] *nt* sign, indication

Anzeige ['antsaɪɡə] *f* (*Zeitungsanzeige*) announcement; (*Werbung*) advertisement; (*bei Polizei*) report; **~ erstatten gegen jdn** to report sb (to the police); **a~n** *vt* (*zu erkennen geben*) to show; (*bekannt geben*) to announce; (*bei Polizei*) to report

anziehen ['antsi:ən] (*unreg*) *vt* to attract; (*Kleidung*) to put on; (*Mensch*) to dress; (*Seil*) to pull tight; (*Schraube*) to tighten; (*Knie*) to draw up ♦ *vr* to get dressed; **~d** *adj* attractive

Anziehung *f* (*Reiz*) attraction; **~skraft** *f* power of attraction; (*PHYS*) force of gravitation

Anzug ['antsu:k] *m* suit; (*Herankommen*): **im ~ sein** to be approaching

anzüglich ['antsy:klɪç] *adj* personal; (*anstößig*) offensive; **A~keit** *f* offensiveness; (*Bemerkung*) personal remark

anzünden ['antsyndən] *vt* to light

anzweifeln ['antsvaɪfəln] *vt* to doubt

apathisch [a'pa:tɪʃ] *adj* apathetic

Apfel ['apfəl] **(-s, ⁻)** *m* apple; **~saft** *m* apple juice; **~sine** [-'zi:nə] *f* orange; **~wein** *m* cider

Apostel [a'pɔstəl] **(-s, -)** m apostle

Apotheke [apo'te:kə] f chemist's (shop), drugstore (US); **a~npflichtig** [-pflɪçtɪç] adj available only at a chemist's shop (BRIT) or pharmacy; **~r(in) (-s, -)** m(f) chemist, druggist (US)

Apotheke

i The **Apotheke** is a pharmacy selling medicines available only on prescription and toiletries. The pharmacist is qualified to give advice on medicines and treatments.

Apparat [apa'ra:t] **(-(e)s, -e)** m piece of apparatus; camera; telephone; (RADIO, TV) set; **am ~!** speaking!; **~ur** [-'tu:r] f apparatus

Appartement [apart(ə)'mã:] **(-s, -s)** nt flat

appellieren [ape'li:rən] vi: **~ (an** +akk) to appeal (to)

Appetit [ape'ti:t] **(-(e)s, -e)** m appetite; **guten ~!** enjoy your meal; **a~lich** adj appetizing; **~losigkeit** f lack of appetite

Applaus [ap'laʊs] **(-es, -e)** m applause

Aprikose [apri'ko:zə] f apricot

April [a'prɪl] **(-(s), -e)** m April

Aquarell [akva'rɛl] **(-s, -e)** nt watercolour

Äquator [ɛ'kva:tɔr] **(-s, -)** m equator

Arab- ['arab] zW: **~er(in) (-s, -)** m(f) Arab; **~ien** [a'ra:biən] **(-s)** nt Arabia; **a~isch** [a'ra:bɪʃ] adj Arabian

Arbeit ['arbaɪt] **(-, -en)** f work no art; (Stelle) job; (Erzeugnis) piece of work; (wissenschaftliche) dissertation; (Klassenarbeit) test; **das war eine ~** that was a hard job; **a~en** vi to work ♦ vt to work, to make; **~er(in) (-s, -)** m(f) worker; (ungelernt) labourer; **~erschaft** f workers pl, labour force; **~geber (-s, -)** m employer; **~nehmer (-s, -)** m employee

Arbeits- in zW labour; **a~am** adj industrious; **~amt** nt employment exchange; **~erlaubnis** f work permit; **a~fähig** adj fit for work, able-bodied; **~gang** m operation; **~kräfte** pl (Mitarbeiter) workforce; **a~los** adj unemployed, out-of-work; **~lose(r)** f(m) unemployed person; **~losigkeit** f unemployment; **~markt** m job market; **~platz** m job; place of work; **a~scheu** adj workshy; **~tag** m work(ing) day; **a~unfähig** adj unfit for work; **~zeit** f working hours pl; **~zimmer** nt study

Archäologe [arçɛo'lo:gə] **(-n, -n)** m archaeologist

Architekt(in) [arçi'tɛkt(ɪn)] **(-en, -en)** m(f) architect; **~ur** [-'tu:r] f architecture

Archiv [ar'çi:f] **(-s, -e)** nt archive

arg [ark] adj bad, awful ♦ adv awfully, very

Argentinien [argen'ti:niən] **(-s)** nt Argentina, the Argentine

argentinisch adj Argentinian

Ärger ['ɛrgər] **(-s)** m (Wut) anger; (Unannehmlichkeit) trouble; **ä~lich** adj (zornig) angry; (lästig) annoying, aggravating; **ä~n** vt to annoy ♦ vr to get annoyed

arg- zW: **~listig** adj cunning, insidious; **~los** adj guileless, innocent

Argument [argu'mɛnt] nt argument

argwöhnisch adj suspicious

Arie ['a:riə] f aria

Aristokrat [arɪsto'kra:t] **(-en, -en)** m aristocrat; **~ie** [-'ti:] f aristocracy

Arktis ['arktɪs] **(-)** f Arctic

Arm [arm] **(-(e)s, -e)** m arm; (Flussarm) branch

arm adj poor

Armatur [arma'tu:r] f (ELEK) armature; **~enbrett** nt instrument panel; (AUT) dashboard

Armband nt bracelet; **~uhr** f (wrist) watch

Arme(r) f(m) poor man (woman); **die ~n** the poor

Armee [ar'me:] f army

Ärmel ['ɛrməl] **(-s, -)** m sleeve; **etw aus dem ~ schütteln** (fig) to produce sth just like that; **~kanal** m English Channel

ärmlich ['ɛrmlɪç] adj poor

armselig adj wretched, miserable

Armut ['armu:t] **(-)** f poverty

Aroma [a'ro:ma] **(-s, Aromen)** nt aroma; **~therapie** f aromatherapy; **a~tisch**

[aro'maːtɪʃ] *adj* aromatic

arrangieren [arãˈʒiːrən] *vt* to arrange ♦ *vr* to come to an arrangement

Arrest [aˈrɛst] **(-(e)s, -e)** *m* detention

arrogant [aroˈgant] *adj* arrogant

Arsch [arʃ] **(-es, ⁻e)** *(umg!)* *m* arse *(BRIT!)*, ass *(US!)*

Art [aːrt] **(-, -en)** *f* (Weise) way; (Sorte) kind, sort; (BIOL) species; **eine ~ (von) Frucht** a kind of fruit; **Häuser aller ~** houses of all kinds; **es ist nicht seine ~, das zu tun** it's not like him to do that; **ich mache das auf meine ~** I do that my (own) way

Arterie [arˈteːriə] *f* artery; **~nverkalkung** *f* arteriosclerosis

artig [ˈaːrtɪç] *adj* good, well-behaved

Artikel [arˈtiːkəl] **(-s, -)** *m* article

Artillerie [artɪləˈriː] *f* artillery

Artischocke [artiˈʃɔkə] *f* artichoke

Artist(in) [arˈtɪst(ɪn)] **(-en, -en)** *m(f)* (circus/variety) artiste *od* performer

Arznei [aːrtsˈnai] *f* medicine; **~mittel** *nt* medicine, medicament

Arzt [aːrtst] **(-es, ⁻e)** *m* doctor; **~helferin** *f* (doctor's) receptionist

Ärztin [ˈɛːrtstɪn] *f* doctor

ärztlich [ˈɛːrtstlɪç] *adj* medical

As △ [as] **(-ses, -se)** *nt* = **Ass**

Asche [ˈaʃə] *f* **(-, -n)** ash, cinder

Aschen- *zW:* **~bahn** *f* cinder track; **~becher** *m* ashtray

Aschermittwoch *m* Ash Wednesday

Äser [ˈɛːzər] *pl von* **Aas**

Asiat(in) [aziˈaːt(ɪn)] **(-en, -en)** *m(f)* Asian; **asiatisch** [-ˈaːtɪʃ] *adj* Asian

Asien [ˈaːziən] **(-s)** *nt* Asia

asozial [ˈazotsiaːl] *adj* antisocial; (Familien) asocial

Aspekt [asˈpɛkt] **(-(e)s, -e)** *m* aspect

Asphalt [asˈfalt] **(-(e)s, -e)** *m* asphalt; **a~ieren** *vt* to asphalt

Ass ▲ [as] **(-es, -e)** *nt* ace

aß *etc* [aːs] *vb siehe* **essen**

Assistent(in) [asɪsˈtɛnt(ɪn)] *m(f)* assistant

Assoziation [asotsiatsiˈoːn] *f* association

Ast [ast] **(-(e)s, ⁻e)** *m* bough, branch

ästhetisch [ɛsˈteːtɪʃ] *adj* aesthetic

Asthma [ˈastma] **(-s)** *nt* asthma; **~tiker(in)** **(-s, -)** *m(f)* asthmatic

Astro- [astro] *zW:* **~loge (-n, -n)** *m* astrologer; **~lo'gie** *f* astrology; **~'naut (-en, -en)** *m* astronaut; **~'nom (-en, -en)** *m* astronomer; **~no'mie** *f* astronomy

Asyl [aˈzyːl] **(-s, -e)** *nt* asylum; (Heim) home; (Obdachlosenasyl) shelter; **~ant(in)** [azyˈlant(ɪn)] **(-en, -en)** *m(f)* asylum-seeker

Atelier [atəliˈeː] **(-s, -s)** *nt* studio

Atem [ˈaːtəm] **(-s)** *m* breath; **den ~ anhalten** to hold one's breath; **außer ~** out of breath; **a~beraubend** *adj* breathtaking; **a~los** *adj* breathless; **~not** *f* difficulty in breathing; **~pause** *f* breather; **~zug** *m* breath

Atheismus [ateˈɪsmʊs] *m* atheism

Atheist *m* atheist; **a~isch** *adj* atheistic

Athen [aˈteːn] **(-s)** *nt* Athens

Äthiopien [etiˈoːpiən] **(-s)** *nt* Ethiopia

Athlet [atˈleːt] **(-en, -en)** *m* athlete

Atlantik [atˈlantɪk] **(-s)** *m* Atlantic (Ocean)

Atlas [ˈatlas] **(- od -ses, -se od Atlanten)** *m* atlas

atmen [ˈaːtmən] *vt, vi* to breathe

Atmosphäre [atmoˈsfɛːrə] *f* atmosphere; **atmosphärisch** *adj* atmospheric

Atmung [ˈaːtmʊŋ] *f* respiration

Atom [aˈtoːm] **(-s, -e)** *nt* atom; **a~ar** *adj* atomic; **~bombe** *f* atom bomb; **~energie** *f* atomic *od* nuclear energy; **~kern** *m* atomic nucleus; **~kraftwerk** *nt* nuclear power station; **~krieg** *m* nuclear *od* atomic war; **~müll** *m* atomic waste; **~strom** *m* (electricity generated by) nuclear power; **~versuch** *m* atomic test; **~waffen** *pl* atomic weapons; **a~waffenfrei** *adj* nuclear-free; **~zeitalter** *nt* atomic age

Attentat [atenˈtaːt] **(-(e)s, -e)** *nt:* **~ (auf +akk)** (attempted) assassination (of)

Attentäter [atenˈtɛːtər] *m* (would-be) assassin

Attest [aˈtɛst] **(-(e)s, -e)** *nt* certificate

Attraktion [atraktsiˈoːn] *f* (Tourismus, Zirkus) attraction

attraktiv [atrakˈtiːf] *adj* attractive

Attrappe [aˈtrapə] *f* dummy

Attribut [atri'bu:t] (-(e)s, -e) *nt* (*GRAM*) attribute

ätzen ['ɛtsən] *vi* to be caustic; **~d** *adj* (*Säure*) corrosive; (*fig: Spott*) cutting

au [aʊ] *excl* ouch!; **~ ja!** oh yes!

Aubergine [obɛr'ʒi:nə] *f* aubergine, eggplant

SCHLÜSSELWORT

---

auch [aʊx] *adv* **1** (*ebenfalls*) also, too, as well; **das ist auch schön** that's nice too *od* as well; **er kommt - ich auch** he's coming - so am I, me too; **auch nicht** not ... either; **ich auch nicht** nor I, me neither; **oder auch** or; **auch das noch!** not that as well! **2** (*selbst, sogar*) even; **auch wenn das Wetter schlecht ist** even if the weather is bad; **ohne auch nur zu fragen** without even asking
3 (*wirklich*) really; **du siehst müde aus - bin ich auch** you look tired - (so) I am; **so sieht es auch aus** it looks like it too
4 (*auch immer*): **wer auch** whoever; **was auch** whatever; **wie dem auch sei** be that as it may; **wie sehr er sich auch bemühte** however much he tried

---

SCHLÜSSELWORT

---

auf [aʊf] *präp +dat* (*wo?*) on; **auf dem Tisch** on the table; **auf der Reise** on the way; **auf der Post/dem Fest** at the post office/party; **auf der Straße** on the road; **auf dem Land/der ganzen Welt** in the country/the whole world
♦ *präp +akk* **1** (*wohin?*) on(to); **auf den Tisch** on(to) the table; **auf die Post gehen** go to the post office; **auf das Land** into the country; **etw auf einen Zettel schreiben** to write sth on a piece of paper
2: **auf Deutsch** in German; **auf Lebenszeit** for my/his lifetime; **bis auf ihn** except for him; **auf einmal** at once; **auf seinen Vorschlag (hin)** at his suggestion
♦ *adv* **1** (*offen*) open; **auf sein** (*umg*) (*Tür, Geschäft*) to be open; **das Fenster ist auf** the window is open

2 (*hinauf*) up; **auf und ab** up and down; **auf und davon** up and away; **auf!** (*los!*) come on!
3 (*aufgestanden*) up; **auf sein** to be up; **ist er schon auf?** is he up yet?
♦ *konj*: **auf dass** (so) that

aufatmen ['aʊfʔa:tmən] *vi* to heave a sigh of relief

aufbahren ['aʊfba:rən] *vt* to lay out

Aufbau ['aʊfbaʊ] *m* (*Bauen*) building, construction; (*Struktur*) structure; (*aufgebautes Teil*) superstructure; **a~en** *vt* to erect, to build (up); (*Existenz*) to make; (*gestalten*) to construct; **a~en (auf** +*dat*) (*gründen*) to found *od* base (on)

aufbauschen ['aʊfbaʊʃən] *vt* to puff out; (*fig*) to exaggerate

aufbekommen ['aʊfbəkɔmən] (*unreg*) *vt* (*öffnen*) to get open; (*Hausaufgaben*) to be given

aufbessern ['aʊfbɛsərn] *vt* (*Gehalt*) to increase

aufbewahren ['aʊfbəva:rən] *vt* to keep; (*Gepäck*) to put in the left-luggage office (*BRIT*) *od* baggage check (*US*)

Aufbewahrung *f* (safe)keeping; (*Gepäckaufbewahrung*) left-luggage office (*BRIT*), baggage check (*US*)

aufbieten ['aʊfbi:tən] (*unreg*) *vt* (*Kraft*) to summon (up); (*Armee, Polizei*) to mobilize

aufblasen ['aʊfbla:zən] (*unreg*) *vt* to blow up, to inflate ♦ *vr* (*umg*) to become bigheaded

aufbleiben ['aʊfblaɪbən] (*unreg*) *vi* (*Laden*) to remain open; (*Person*) to stay up

aufblenden ['aʊfblɛndən] *vt* (*Scheinwerfer*) to switch on full beam ♦ *vi* (*Fahrer*) to have the lights on full beam; (*AUT: Scheinwerfer*) to be on full beam

aufblicken ['aʊfblɪkən] *vi* to look up; **~ zu** to look up at; (*fig*) to look up to

aufblühen ['aʊfbly:ən] *vi* to blossom, to flourish

aufbrauchen ['aʊfbraʊxən] *vt* to use up

aufbrausen ['aʊfbraʊzən] *vi* (*fig*) to flare up; **~d** *adj* hot-tempered

---

Spelling Reform: ▲ *new spelling* △ *old spelling (to be phased out)*

aufbrechen ['aʊfbrɛçən] (*unreg*) *vt* to break *od* prise (*BRIT*) open ♦ *vi* to burst open; (*gehen*) to start, to set off

aufbringen ['aʊfbrɪŋən] (*unreg*) *vt* (*öffnen*) to open; (*in Mode*) to bring into fashion; (*beschaffen*) to procure; (*FIN*) to raise; (*ärgern*) to irritate; **Verständnis für etw ~** to be able to understand sth

Aufbruch ['aʊfbrʊx] *m* departure

aufbrühen ['aʊfbry:ən] *vt* (*Tee*) to make

aufbürden ['aʊfbʏrdən] *vt*: **jdm etw ~** to burden sb with sth

aufdecken ['aʊfdɛkən] *vt* to uncover

aufdrängen ['aʊfdrɛŋən] *vt*: **jdm etw ~** to force sth on sb ♦ *vr* (*Mensch*): **sich jdm ~** to intrude on sb

aufdrehen ['aʊfdre:ən] *vt* (*Wasserhahn etc*) to turn on; (*Ventil*) to open up

aufdringlich ['aʊfdrɪŋlɪç] *adj* pushy

aufeinander [aʊfaɪˈnandər] *adv* on top of each other; (*schießen*) at each other; (*vertrauen*) each other; **~ folgen** to follow one another; **~ folgend** consecutive; **~ prallen** to hit one another

Aufenthalt ['aʊfɛnthalt] *m* stay; (*Verzögerung*) delay; (*EISENB: Halten*) stop; (*Ort*) haunt

Aufenthaltserlaubnis *f* residence permit

auferlegen ['aʊfɛrleːgən] *vt*: **(jdm) ~** to impose (upon sb)

Auferstehung ['aʊfɛrʃteːʊŋ] *f* resurrection

aufessen ['aʊfɛsən] (*unreg*) *vt* to eat up

auffahr- ['aʊffaːr] *zW*: **~en** (*unreg*) *vi* (*herankommen*) to draw up; (*hochfahren*) to jump up; (*wütend werden*) to flare up; (*in den Himmel*) to ascend ♦ *vt* (*Kanonen, Geschütz*) to bring up; **~en auf** +*akk* (*Auto*) to run *od* crash into; **~end** *adj* hot-tempered; **A~t** *f* (*Hausauffahrt*) drive; (*Autobahnauffahrt*) slip road (*BRIT*), (*freeway*) entrance (*US*); **A~unfall** *m* pile-up

auffallen ['aʊffalən] (*unreg*) *vi* to be noticeable; **A~t** *f* (*Hausauffahrt*) drive; **jdm ~** to strike sb

auffällig ['aʊffɛlɪç] *adj* conspicuous, striking

auffangen ['aʊffaŋən] (*unreg*) *vt* to catch; (*Funkspruch*) to intercept; (*Preise*) to peg

auffassen ['aʊffasən] *vt* to understand, to comprehend; (*auslegen*) to see, to view

Auffassung *f* (*Meinung*) opinion; (*Auslegung*) view, concept; (*auch*: **~sgabe**) grasp

auffindbar ['aʊffɪntbaːr] *adj* to be found

auffordern ['aʊffɔrdərn] *vt* (*befehlen*) to call upon, to order; (*bitten*) to ask

Aufforderung *f* (*Befehl*) order; (*Einladung*) invitation

auffrischen ['aʊffrɪʃən] *vt* to freshen up; (*Kenntnisse*) to brush up; (*Erinnerungen*) to reawaken ♦ *vi* (*Wind*) to freshen

aufführen ['aʊffyːrən] *vt* (*THEAT*) to perform; (*in einem Verzeichnis*) to list, to specify ♦ *vr* (*sich benehmen*) to behave

Aufführung *f* (*THEAT*) performance; (*Liste*) specification

Aufgabe ['aʊfgaːbə] *f* task; (*SCH*) exercise; (*Hausaufgabe*) homework; (*Verzicht*) giving up; (*von Gepäck*) registration; (*von Post*) posting; (*von Inserat*) insertion

Aufgang ['aʊfgaŋ] *m* ascent; (*Sonnenaufgang*) rise; (*Treppe*) staircase

aufgeben ['aʊfgeːbən] (*unreg*) *vt* (*verzichten*) to give up; (*Paket*) to send, to post; (*Gepäck*) to register; (*Bestellung*) to give; (*Inserat*) to insert; (*Rätsel, Problem*) to set ♦ *vi* to give up

Aufgebot ['aʊfgəboːt] *nt* supply; (*Eheaufgebot*) banns *pl*

aufgedunsen ['aʊfgədʊnzən] *adj* swollen, puffed up

aufgehen ['aʊfgeːən] (*unreg*) *vi* (*Sonne, Teig*) to rise; (*sich öffnen*) to open; (*klar werden*) to become clear; (*MATH*) to come out exactly; **~ (in** +*dat*) (*sich widmen*) to be absorbed (in); **in Rauch/Flammen ~** to go up in smoke/flames

aufgelegt ['aʊfgəleːkt] *adj*: **gut/schlecht ~ sein** to be in a good/bad mood; **zu etw ~ sein** to be in the mood for sth

aufgeregt ['aʊfgəreːkt] *adj* excited

aufgeschlossen ['aʊfgəʃlɔsən] *adj* open, open-minded

aufgeweckt ['aʊfgəvɛkt] *adj* bright, intelligent

aufgießen ['aʊfgiːsən] (*unreg*) *vt* (*Wasser*) to

pour over; (*Tee*) to infuse

aufgreifen ['aʊfɡraɪfən] (*unreg*) *vt* (*Thema*) to take up; (*Verdächtige*) to pick up, to seize

aufgrund, auf Grund [aʊf'ɡrʊnt] *präp* +*gen* on the basis of; (*wegen*) because of

aufhaben ['aʊfhaːbən] (*unreg*) *vt* to have on; (*Arbeit*) to have to do

aufhalsen ['aʊfhalzən] (*umg*) *vt*: **jdm etw ~** to saddle *od* lumber sb with sth

aufhalten ['aʊfhaltən] (*unreg*) *vt* (*Person*) to detain; (*Entwicklung*) to check; (*Tür, Hand*) to hold open; (*Augen*) to keep open ♦ *vr* (*wohnen*) to live; (*bleiben*) to stay; **sich mit etw ~** to waste time over sth

aufhängen ['aʊfhɛŋən] (*unreg*) *vt* (*Wäsche*) to hang up; (*Menschen*) to hang ♦ *vr* to hang o.s.

Aufhänger (**-s, -**) *m* (*am Mantel*) loop; (*fig*) peg

aufheben ['aʊfheːbən] (*unreg*) *vt* (*hochheben*) to raise, to lift; (*Sitzung*) to wind up; (*Urteil*) to annul; (*Gesetz*) to repeal, to abolish; (*aufbewahren*) to keep ♦ *vr* to cancel itself out; **bei jdm gut aufgehoben sein** to be well looked after at sb's; **viel A~(s) machen (von)** to make a fuss (about)

aufheitern ['aʊfhaɪtərn] *vt, vr* (*Himmel, Miene*) to brighten; (*Mensch*) to cheer up

aufhellen ['aʊfhɛlən] *vt, vr* to clear up; (*Farbe, Haare*) to lighten

aufhetzen ['aʊfhɛtsən] *vt* to stir up

aufholen ['aʊfhoːlən] *vt* to make up ♦ *vi* to catch up

aufhorchen ['aʊfhɔrçən] *vi* to prick up one's ears

aufhören ['aʊfhøːrən] *vi* to stop; **~, etw zu tun** to stop doing sth

aufklappen ['aʊfklapən] *vt* to open

aufklären ['aʊfklɛːrən] *vt* (*Geheimnis etc*) to clear up; (*Person*) to enlighten; (*sexuell*) to tell the facts of life to; (*MIL*) to reconnoitre ♦ *vr* to clear up

Aufklärung *f* (*von Geheimnis*) clearing up; (*Unterrichtung, Zeitalter*) enlightenment; (*sexuell*) sex education; (*MIL, AVIAT*) reconnaissance

aufkleben ['aʊfkleːbən] *vt* to stick on;

Aufkleber (**-s, -**) *m* sticker

aufknöpfen ['aʊfknœpfən] *vt* to unbutton

aufkommen ['aʊfkɔmən] (*unreg*) *vi* (*Wind*) to come up; (*Zweifel, Gefühl*) to arise; (*Mode*) to start; **für jdn/etw ~** to be liable *od* responsible for sb/sth

aufladen ['aʊflaːdən] (*unreg*) *vt* to load

Auflage ['aʊflaːɡə] *f* edition; (*Zeitung*) circulation; (*Bedingung*) condition

auflassen ['aʊflasən] (*unreg*) *vt* (*offen*) to leave open; (*aufgesetzt*) to leave on

auflauern ['aʊflaʊərn] *vi*: **jdm ~** to lie in wait for sb

Auflauf ['aʊflaʊf] *m* (*KOCH*) pudding; (*Menschenauflauf*) crowd

aufleben ['aʊfleːbən] *vi* (*Mensch, Gespräch*) to liven up; (*Interesse*) to revive

auflegen ['aʊfleːɡən] *vt* to put on; (*Telefon*) to hang up; (*TYP*) to print

auflehnen ['aʊfleːnən] *vt* to lean on ♦ *vr* to rebel

Auflehnung *f* rebellion

auflesen ['aʊfleːzən] (*unreg*) *vt* to pick up

aufleuchten ['aʊflɔʏçtən] *vi* to light up

auflisten ['aʊflɪstən] *vt* to list

auflockern ['aʊflɔkərn] *vt* to loosen; (*fig: Eintönigkeit etc*) to liven up

auflösen ['aʊfløːzən] *vt* to dissolve; (*Haare etc*) to loosen; (*Missverständnis*) to sort out ♦ *vr* to dissolve; to come undone; to be resolved; (**in Tränen**) **aufgelöst sein** to be in tears

Auflösung *f* dissolving; (*fig*) solution

aufmachen ['aʊfmaxən] *vt* to open; (*Kleidung*) to undo; (*zurechtmachen*) to do up ♦ *vr* to set out

Aufmachung *f* (*Kleidung*) outfit, get-up; (*Gestaltung*) format

aufmerksam ['aʊfmɛrkzaːm] *adj* attentive; **jdn auf etw** *akk* **~ machen** to point sth out to sb; **A~keit** *f* attention, attentiveness

aufmuntern ['aʊfmʊntərn] *vt* (*ermutigen*) to encourage; (*erheitern*) to cheer up

Aufnahme ['aʊfnaːmə] *f* reception; (*Beginn*) beginning; (*in Verein etc*) admission; (*in Liste etc*) inclusion; (*Notieren*) taking down; (*PHOT*) shot; (*auf Tonband etc*) recording;

Spelling Reform: ▲ *new spelling* △ *old spelling (to be phased out)*

a~fähig *adj* receptive; **~prüfung** *f* entrance test

aufnehmen ['aʊfneːmən] (*unreg*) *vt* to receive; (*hochheben*) to pick up; (*beginnen*) to take up; (*in Verein etc*) to admit; (*in Liste etc*) to include; (*fassen*) to hold; (*notieren*) to take down; (*fotografieren*) to photograph; (*auf Tonband, Platte*) to record; (*FIN: leihen*) to take out; **es mit jdm ~ können** to be able to compete with sb

aufopfern ['aʊfʔɔpfərn] *vt, vr* to sacrifice; **~d** *adj* selfless

aufpassen ['aʊfpasən] *vi* (*aufmerksam sein*) to pay attention; **auf jdn/etw ~** to look after *od* watch sb/sth; **aufgepasst!** look out!

Aufprall ['aʊfpral] (**-s, -e**) *m* impact; **a~en** *vi* to hit, to strike

Aufpreis ['aʊfpraɪs] *m* extra charge

aufpumpen ['aʊfpʊmpən] *vt* to pump up

aufräumen ['aʊfrɔʏmən] *vt, vi* (*Dinge*) to clear away; (*Zimmer*) to tidy up

aufrecht ['aʊfrɛçt] *adj* (*auch fig*) upright; **~erhalten** (*unreg*) *vt* to maintain

aufreg- ['aʊfreːg] *zW*: **~en** *vt* to excite ♦ *vr* to get excited; **~end** *adj* exciting; **A~ung** *f* excitement

aufreibend ['aʊfraɪbənt] *adj* strenuous

aufreißen ['aʊfraɪsən] (*unreg*) *vt* (*Umschlag*) to tear open; (*Augen*) to open wide; (*Tür*) to throw open; (*Straße*) to take up

aufreizen ['aʊfraɪtsən] *vt* to incite, to stir up; **~d** *adj* exciting, stimulating

aufrichten ['aʊfrɪçtən] *vt* to put up, to erect; (*moralisch*) to console ♦ *vr* to rise; (*moralisch*): **sich ~ (an** +*dat*) to take heart (from)

aufrichtig ['aʊfrɪçtɪç] *adj* sincere, honest; **A~keit** *f* sincerity

aufrücken ['aʊfrʏkən] *vi* to move up; (*beruflich*) to be promoted

Aufruf ['aʊfruːf] *m* summons; (*zur Hilfe*) call; (*des Namens*) calling out; **a~en** (*unreg*) *vt* (*Namen*) to call out; (*auffordern*): **jdn a~en (zu)** to call upon sb (for)

Aufruhr ['aʊfruːr] (**-(e)s, -e**) *m* uprising, revolt

aufrührerisch ['aʊfryːrərɪʃ] *adj* rebellious

aufrunden ['aʊfrʊndən] *vt* (*Summe*) to round up

Aufrüstung ['aʊfrʏstʊŋ] *f* rearmament

aufrütteln ['aʊfrʏtəln] *vt* (*auch fig*) to shake up

aufs [aʊfs] = **auf das**

aufsagen ['aʊfzaːgən] *vt* (*Gedicht*) to recite

aufsässig ['aʊfzɛsɪç] *adj* rebellious

Aufsatz ['aʊfzats] *m* (*Geschriebenes*) essay; (*auf Schrank etc*) top

aufsaugen ['aʊfzaʊgən] (*unreg*) *vt* to soak up

aufschauen ['aʊfʃaʊən] *vi* to look up

aufscheuchen ['aʊfʃɔʏçən] *vt* to scare *od* frighten away

aufschieben ['aʊfʃiːbən] (*unreg*) *vt* to push open; (*verzögern*) to put off, to postpone

Aufschlag ['aʊfʃlaːk] *m* (*Ärmelaufschlag*) cuff; (*Jackenaufschlag*) lapel; (*Hosenaufschlag*) turn-up; (*Aufprall*) impact; (*Preisaufschlag*) surcharge; (*Tennis*) service; **a~en** [-gən] (*unreg*) *vt* (*öffnen*) to open; (*verwunden*) to cut; (*hochschlagen*) to turn up; (*aufbauen: Zelt, Lager*) to pitch, to erect; (*Wohnsitz*) to take up ♦ *vi* (*aufprallen*) to hit; (*teurer werden*) to go up; (*Tennis*) to serve

aufschließen ['aʊfʃliːsən] (*unreg*) *vt* to open up, to unlock ♦ *vi* (*aufrücken*) to close up

aufschlussreich ▲ *adj* informative, illuminating

aufschnappen ['aʊfʃnapən] *vt* (*umg*) to pick up ♦ *vi* to fly open

aufschneiden ['aʊfʃnaɪdən] (*unreg*) *vt* (*Brot*) to cut up; (*MED*) to lance ♦ *vi* to brag

Aufschneider (**-s, -**) *m* boaster, braggart

Aufschnitt ['aʊfʃnɪt] *m* (slices of) cold meat

aufschrauben ['aʊfʃraʊbən] *vt* (*festschrauben*) to screw on; (*lösen*) to unscrew

aufschrecken ['aʊfʃrɛkən] *vt* to startle ♦ *vi* (*unreg*) to start up

aufschreiben ['aʊfʃraɪbən] (*unreg*) *vt* to write down

aufschreien ['aʊfʃraɪən] (*unreg*) *vi* to cry out

Aufschrift ['aʊfʃrɪft] *f* (*Inschrift*) inscription; (*auf Etikett*) label

Rechtschreibreform: ▲ *neue Schreibung* △ *alte Schreibung (auslaufend)*

Aufschub ['aʊfʃuːp] **(-(e)s, -schübe)** *m* delay, postponement

Aufschwung ['aʊfʃvʊŋ] *m* (*Elan*) boost; (*wirtschaftlich*) upturn, boom; (*SPORT*) circle

aufsehen ['aʊfzeːən] (*unreg*) *vi* to look up; **~ zu** to look up at; (*fig*) to look up to; **A~ (-s)** *nt* sensation, stir; **~ erregend** sensational

Aufseher(in) **(-s, -)** *m(f)* guard; (*im Betrieb*) supervisor; (*Museumsaufseher*) attendant; (*Parkaufseher*) keeper

auf sein ▲ *siehe* **auf**

aufsetzen ['aʊfzetsən] *vt* to put on; (*Dokument*) to draw up ♦ *vr* to sit up(right) ♦ *vi* (*Flugzeug*) to touch down

Aufsicht ['aʊfzɪçt] *f* supervision; **die ~ haben** to be in charge

Aufsichtsrat *m* (supervisory) board

aufsitzen ['aʊfzɪtsən] (*unreg*) *vi* (*aufrecht hinsitzen*) to sit up; (*aufs Pferd, Motorrad*) to mount, to get on; (*Schiff*) to run aground; **jdm ~** (*umg*) to be taken in by sb

aufsparen ['aʊfʃpaːrən] *vt* to save (up)

aufsperren ['aʊfʃpɛrən] *vt* to unlock; (*Mund*) to open wide

aufspielen ['aʊfʃpiːlən] *vr* to show off

aufspießen ['aʊfʃpiːsən] *vt* to spear

aufspringen ['aʊfʃprɪŋən] (*unreg*) *vi* (*hochspringen*) to jump up; (*sich öffnen*) to spring open; (*Hände, Lippen*) to become chapped; **auf etw** *akk* **~** to jump onto sth

aufspüren ['aʊfʃpyːrən] *vt* to track down, to trace

aufstacheln ['aʊfʃtaxəln] *vt* to incite

Aufstand ['aʊfʃtant] *m* insurrection, rebellion; **aufständisch** ['aʊfʃtɛndɪʃ] *adj* rebellious, mutinous

aufstehen ['aʊfʃteːən] (*unreg*) *vi* to get up; (*Tür*) to be open

aufsteigen ['aʊfʃtaɪɡən] (*unreg*) *vi* (*hochsteigen*) to climb; (*Rauch*) to rise; **auf etw** *akk* **~** to get onto sth

aufstellen ['aʊfʃtɛlən] *vt* (*aufrecht stellen*) to put up; (*aufreihen*) to line up; (*nominieren*) to nominate; (*formulieren: Programm etc*) to draw up; (*leisten: Rekord*) to set up

Aufstellung *f* (*SPORT*) line-up; (*Liste*) list

Aufstieg ['aʊfʃtiːk] **(-(e)s, -e)** *m* (*auf Berg*) ascent; (*Fortschritt*) rise; (*beruflich, SPORT*) promotion

aufstocken ['aʊfʃtɔkən] *vt* (*Kapital*) to increase

aufstoßen ['aʊfʃtoːsən] (*unreg*) *vt* to push open ♦ *vi* to belch

aufstützen ['aʊfʃtʏtsən] *vt* (*Körperteil*) to prop, to lean; (*Person*) to prop up ♦ *vr*: **sich auf etw** *akk* **~** to lean on sth

aufsuchen ['aʊfzuːxən] *vt* (*besuchen*) to visit; (*konsultieren*) to consult

Auftakt ['aʊftakt] *m* (*MUS*) upbeat; (*fig*) prelude

auftanken ['aʊftaŋkən] *vi* to get petrol (*BRIT*) *od* gas (*US*) ♦ *vt* to refuel

auftauchen ['aʊftaʊxən] *vi* to appear; (*aus Wasser etc*) to emerge; (*U-Boot*) to surface; (*Zweifel*) to arise

auftauen ['aʊftaʊən] *vt* to thaw ♦ *vi* to thaw; (*fig*) to relax

aufteilen ['aʊftaɪlən] *vt* to divide up; (*Raum*) to partition; **Aufteilung** *f* division; partition

Auftrag ['aʊftraːk] **(-(e)s, -träge)** *m* order; (*Anweisung*) commission; (*Aufgabe*) mission; **im ~ von** on behalf of; **a~en** [-ɡən] (*unreg*) *vt* (*Essen*) to serve; (*Farbe*) to put on; (*Kleidung*) to wear out; **jdm etw a~en** to tell sb sth; **dick a~en** (*fig*) to exaggerate; **~geber (-s, -)** *m* (*COMM*) purchaser, customer

auftreiben ['aʊftraɪbən] (*unreg*) *vt* (*umg: beschaffen*) to raise

auftreten ['aʊftreːtən] (*unreg*) *vt* to kick open ♦ *vi* to appear; (*mit Füßen*) to tread; (*sich verhalten*) to behave; **A~ (-s)** *nt* (*Vorkommen*) appearance; (*Benehmen*) behaviour

Auftrieb ['aʊftriːp] *m* (*PHYS*) buoyancy, lift; (*fig*) impetus

Auftritt ['aʊftrɪt] *m* (*des Schauspielers*) entrance; (*Szene: auch fig*) scene

aufwachen ['aʊfvaxən] *vi* to wake up

aufwachsen ['aʊfvaksən] (*unreg*) *vi* to grow up

Aufwand ['aʊfvant] **(-(e)s)** *m* expenditure; (*Kosten auch*) expense; (*Luxus*) show

Spelling Reform: ▲ *new spelling* △ *old spelling (to be phased out)*

aufwändig ▲ ['aʊfvɛndɪç] *adj* costly
aufwärmen ['aʊfvɛrmən] *vt* to warm up; *(alte Geschichten)* to rake up
aufwärts ['aʊfvɛrts] *adv* upwards; **A~entwicklung** *f* upward trend
Aufwasch ['aʊfvaʃ] *m* washing-up
aufwecken ['aʊfvɛkən] *vt* to wake up, to waken up
aufweisen ['aʊfvaɪzən] *(unreg) vt* to show
aufwenden ['aʊfvɛndən] *(unreg) vt* to expend; *(Geld)* to spend; *(Sorgfalt)* to devote
aufwendig *adj siehe* **aufwändig**
aufwerfen ['aʊfvɛrfən] *(unreg) vt (Fenster etc)* to throw open; *(Probleme)* to throw up, to raise
aufwerten ['aʊfvɛrtən] *vt (FIN)* to revalue; *(fig)* to raise in value
aufwickeln ['aʊfvɪkəln] *vt (aufrollen)* to roll up; *(umg: Haar)* to put in curlers
aufwiegen ['aʊfviːgən] *(unreg) vt* to make up for
Aufwind ['aʊfvɪnt] *m* up-current
aufwirbeln ['aʊfvɪrbəln] *vt* to whirl up; **Staub ~** *(fig)* to create a stir
aufwischen ['aʊfvɪʃən] *vt* to wipe up
aufzählen ['aʊftsɛːlən] *vt* to list
aufzeichnen ['aʊftsaɪçnən] *vt* to sketch; *(schriftlich)* to jot down; *(auf Band)* to record
Aufzeichnung *f (schriftlich)* note; *(Tonbandaufzeichnung)* recording; *(Filmaufzeichnung)* record
aufzeigen ['aʊftsaɪgən] *vt* to show, to demonstrate
aufziehen ['aʊftsiːən] *(unreg) vt (hochziehen)* to raise, to draw up; *(öffnen)* to pull open; *(Uhr)* to wind; *(umg: necken)* to tease; *(großziehen: Kinder)* to raise, to bring up; *(Tiere)* to rear
Aufzug ['aʊftsuːk] *m (Fahrstuhl)* lift, elevator; *(Aufmarsch)* procession, parade; *(Kleidung)* get-up; *(THEAT)* act
aufzwingen ['aʊftsvɪŋən] *(unreg) vt:* **jdm etw ~** to force sth upon sb
Augapfel ['aʊkapfəl] *m* eyeball; *(fig)* apple of one's eye
Auge ['aʊgə] **(-s, -n)** *nt* eye; *(Fettauge)*

globule of fat; **unter vier ~n** in private
Augen- *zW:* **~blick** *m* moment; **im ~blick** at the moment; **a~blicklich** *adj (sofort)* instantaneous; *(gegenwärtig)* present; **~braue** *f* eyebrow; **~optiker(in)** *m(f)* optician; **~weide** *f* sight for sore eyes; **~zeuge** *m* eye witness
August [aʊ'gʊst] **(-(e)s** *od* **-, -e)** *m* August
Auktion [aʊktsi'oːn] *f* auction
Aula ['aʊla] **(-, Aulen** *od* **-s)** *f* assembly hall

SCHLÜSSELWORT

aus [aʊs] *präp +dat* **1** *(räumlich)* out of; *(von ... her)* from; **er ist aus Berlin** he's from Berlin; **aus dem Fenster** out of the window
2 *(gemacht/hergestellt aus)* made of; **ein Herz aus Stein** a heart of stone
3 *(auf Ursache deutend)* out of; **aus Mitleid** out of sympathy; **aus Erfahrung** from experience; **aus Spaß** for fun
4: aus ihr wird nie etwas she'll never get anywhere
♦ *adv* **1** *(zu Ende)* finished, over; **aus sein** to be over; **aus und vorbei** over and done with
2 *(ausgeschaltet, ausgezogen)* out; *(Aufschrift an Geräten)* off; **aus sein** *(nicht brennen)* to be out; *(abgeschaltet sein: Radio, Herd)* to be off; **Licht aus!** lights out!
3 *(nicht zu Hause):* **aus sein** to be out
4 *(in Verbindung mit von):* **von Rom aus** from Rome; **vom Fenster aus** out of the window; **von sich aus** *(selbstständig)* of one's own accord; **von ihm aus** as far as he's concerned

ausarbeiten ['aʊsarbaɪtən] *vt* to work out
ausarten ['aʊsartən] *vi* to degenerate
ausatmen ['aʊsaːtmən] *vi* to breathe out
ausbaden ['aʊsbaːdən] *(umg) vt:* **etw ~ müssen** to carry the can for sth
Ausbau ['aʊsbaʊ] *m* extension, expansion; removal; **a~en** *vt* to extend, to expand; *(herausnehmen)* to take out, to remove; **a~fähig** *adj (fig)* worth developing
ausbessern ['aʊsbɛsərn] *vt* to mend, to

repair

ausbeulen ['aʊsbɔylən] *vt* to beat out

Ausbeute ['aʊsbɔytə] *f* yield; (*Fische*) catch; **a~n** *vt* to exploit; (*MIN*) to work

ausbild- ['aʊsbɪld] *zW:* **~en** *vt* to educate; (*Lehrling, Soldat*) to instruct, to train; (*Fähigkeiten*) to develop; (*Geschmack*) to cultivate; **A~er (-s, -)** *m* instructor; **A~ung** *f* education; training, instruction; development; cultivation

ausbleiben ['aʊsblaɪbən] (*unreg*) *vi* (*Personen*) to stay away, not to come; (*Ereignisse*) to fail to happen, not to happen

Ausblick ['aʊsblɪk] *m* (*auch fig*) prospect, outlook, view

ausbrechen ['aʊsbrɛçən] (*unreg*) *vi* to break out ♦ *vt* to break off; **in Tränen/Gelächter ~** to burst into tears/out laughing

ausbreiten ['aʊsbraɪtən] *vt* to spread (out); (*Arme*) to stretch out ♦ *vr* to spread; **sich über ein Thema ~** to expand *od* enlarge on a topic

ausbrennen ['aʊsbrɛnən] (*unreg*) *vt* to scorch; (*Wunde*) to cauterize ♦ *vi* to burn out

Ausbruch ['aʊsbrʊx] *m* outbreak; (*von Vulkan*) eruption; (*Gefühlsausbruch*) outburst; (*von Gefangenen*) escape

ausbrüten ['aʊsbryːtən] *vt* (*auch fig*) to hatch

Ausdauer ['aʊsdaʊər] *f* perseverance, stamina; **a~nd** *adj* persevering

ausdehnen ['aʊsdeːnən] *vt, vr* (*räumlich*) to expand; (*zeitlich, auch Gummi*) to stretch; (*Nebel, fig: Macht*) to extend

ausdenken ['aʊsdɛŋkən] (*unreg*) *vt:* **sich** *dat* **etw ~** to think sth up

Ausdruck ['aʊsdrʊk] *m* expression, phrase; (*Kundgabe, Gesichtsausdruck*) expression; (*COMPUT*) print-out, hard copy; **a~en** *vt* (*COMPUT*) to print out

ausdrücken ['aʊsdrʏkən] *vt* (*auch vr:* formulieren, zeigen) to express; (*Zigarette*) to put out; (*Zitrone*) to squeeze

ausdrücklich *adj* express, explicit

ausdrucks- *zW:* **~los** *adj* expressionless, blank; **~voll** *adj* expressive; **A~weise** *f*

mode of expression

auseinander [aʊsʔaɪˈnandər] *adv* (*getrennt*) apart; **~ schreiben** to write as separate words; **~ bringen** to separate; **~ fallen** to fall apart; **~ gehen** (*Menschen*) to separate; (*Meinungen*) to differ; (*Gegenstand*) to fall apart; **~ halten** to tell apart; **~ nehmen** to take to pieces, to dismantle; **~ setzen** (*erklären*) to set forth, to explain; **sich ~ setzen** (*sich verständigen*) to come to terms, to settle; (*sich befassen*) to concern o.s.; **A~setzung** *f* argument

ausfahren ['aʊsfaːrən] (*unreg*) *vt* (*spazieren fahren: im Auto*) to take for a drive; (: *im Kinderwagen*) to take for a walk; (*liefern*) to deliver

Ausfahrt *f* (*des Zuges etc*) leaving, departure; (*Autobahnausfahrt*) exit; (*Garagenausfahrt etc*) exit, way out; (*Spazierfahrt*) drive, excursion

Ausfall ['aʊsfal] *m* loss; (*Nichtstattfinden*) cancellation; (*MIL*) sortie; (*radioaktiv*) fall-out; **a~en** (*unreg*) *vi* (*Zähne, Haare*) to fall *od* come out; (*nicht stattfinden*) to be cancelled; (*wegbleiben*) to be omitted; (*Person*) to drop out, (*Lohn*) to be stopped; (*nicht funktionieren*) to break down; (*Resultat haben*) to turn out; **~straße** *f* arterial road

ausfertigen ['aʊsfɛrtɪgən] *vt* (*förmlich: Urkunde, Pass*) to draw up; (*Rechnung*) to make out

Ausfertigung ['aʊsfɛrtɪgʊn] *f* drawing up; making out; (*Exemplar*) copy

ausfindig ['aʊsfɪndɪç] *adj:* **~ machen** to discover

ausfließen ['aʊsfliːsən] (*unreg*) *vt* (*her~*): **~ (aus)** to flow out (of); (*auslaufen: Öl etc*): **~ (aus)** to leak (out of)

Ausflucht ['aʊsflʊxt] (**-, -flüchte**) *f* excuse

Ausflug ['aʊsfluːk] *m* excursion, outing; **Ausflügler** ['aʊsflyːklər] (**-s, -**) *m* tripper

Ausflugslokal *nt* tourist café

Ausfluss ▲ ['aʊsflʊs] *m* outlet; (*MED*) discharge

ausfragen ['aʊsfraːgən] *vt* to interrogate, to question

ausfressen ['aʊsfrɛsən] (*unreg*) *vt* to eat up;

Spelling Reform: ▲ new spelling △ old spelling (to be phased out)

(*aushöhlen*) to corrode; (*umg: anstellen*) to be up to

Ausfuhr ['aʊsfuːr] (-, **-en**) *f* export, exportation ♦ *in zW* export

ausführ- ['aʊsfyːr] *zW:* **~en** *vt* (*verwirklichen*) to carry out; (*Person*) to take out; (*Hund*) to take for a walk; (*COMM*) to export; (*erklären*) to give details of; **~lich** *adj* detailed ♦ *adv* in detail; **A~lichkeit** *f* detail; **A~ung** *f* execution, performance; (*Durchführung*) completion; (*Herstellungsart*) version; (*Erklärung*) explanation

ausfüllen ['aʊsfʏlən] *vt* to fill up; (*Fragebogen etc*) to fill in; (*Beruf*) to be fulfilling for

Ausgabe ['aʊsgaːbə] *f* (*Geld*) expenditure, outlay; (*Aushändigung*) giving out; (*Gepäckausgabe*) left-luggage office; (*Buch*) edition; (*Nummer*) issue; (*COMPUT*) output

Ausgang ['aʊsgaŋ] *m* way out, exit; (*Ende*) end; (*~spunkt*) starting point; (*Ergebnis*) result; (*Ausgehtag*) free time, time off; **kein ~** no exit

Ausgangs- *zW:* **~punkt** *m* starting point; **~sperre** *f* curfew

ausgeben ['aʊsgeːbən] (*unreg*) *vt* (*Geld*) to spend; (*austeilen*) to issue, to distribute ♦ *vr:* **sich für etw/jdn ~** to pass o.s. off as sth/sb

ausgebucht ['aʊsgəbuːxt] *adj* (*Vorstellung, Flug, Maschine*) fully booked

ausgedient ['aʊsgədiːnt] *adj* (*Soldat*) discharged; (*verbraucht*) no longer in use; **~ haben** to have done good service

ausgefallen ['aʊsgəfalən] *adj* (*ungewöhnlich*) exceptional

ausgeglichen ['aʊsgəglɪçən] *adj* (well-) balanced; **A~heit** *f* balance; (*von Mensch*) even-temperedness

ausgehen ['aʊsgeːən] (*unreg*) *vi* to go out; (*zu Ende gehen*) to come to an end; (*Benzin*) to run out; (*Haare, Zähne*) to fall *od* come out; (*Feuer, Ofen, Licht*) to go out; (*Strom*) to go off; (*Resultat haben*) to turn out; **mir ging das Benzin aus** I ran out of petrol (*BRIT*) *od* gas (*US*); **von etw ~** (*wegführen*) to lead away from sth; (*herrühren*) to come

from sth; (*zugrunde legen*) to proceed from sth; **wir können davon ~, dass ...** we can take as our starting point that ...; **leer ~** to get nothing

ausgelassen ['aʊsgəlasən] *adj* boisterous, high-spirited

ausgelastet ['aʊsgəlastət] *adj* fully occupied

ausgelernt ['aʊsgəlɛrnt] *adj* trained, qualified

ausgemacht ['aʊsgəmaxt] *adj* settled; (*umg: Dummkopf etc*) out-and-out, downright; **es war eine ~e Sache, dass ...** it was a foregone conclusion that ...

ausgenommen ['aʊsgənɔmən] *präp +gen* except ♦ *konj* except; **Anwesende sind ~** present company excepted

ausgeprägt ['aʊsgəprɛːkt] *adj* distinct

ausgerechnet ['aʊsgərɛçnət] *adv* just, precisely; **~ du/heute** you of all people/ today of all days

ausgeschlossen ['aʊsgəʃlɔsən] *adj* (*unmöglich*) impossible, out of the question

ausgeschnitten ['aʊsgəʃnɪtən] *adj* (*Kleid*) low-necked

ausgesprochen ['aʊsgəʃprɔxən] *adj* (*Faulheit, Lüge etc*) out-and-out; (*unverkennbar*) marked ♦ *adv* decidedly

ausgezeichnet ['aʊsgətsaɪçnət] *adj* excellent

ausgiebig ['aʊsgiːbɪç] *adj* (*Gebrauch*) thorough, good; (*Essen*) generous, lavish; **~ schlafen** to have a good sleep

ausgießen ['aʊsgiːsən] *vt* to pour out; (*Behälter*) to empty

Ausgleich ['aʊsglaɪç] (**-(e)s, -e**) *m* balance; (*Vermittlung*) reconciliation; (*SPORT*) equalization; **zum ~ einer Sache** *gen* in order to offset sth; **a~en** (*unreg*) *vt* to balance (out); to reconcile; (*Höhe*) to even up ♦ *vi* (*SPORT*) to equalize

ausgraben ['aʊsgraːbən] (*unreg*) *vt* to dig up; (*Leichen*) to exhume; (*fig*) to unearth

Ausgrabung *f* excavation; (*Ausgraben auch*) digging up

Ausguss ▲ ['aʊsgʊs] *m* (*Spüle*) sink; (*Abfluss*) outlet; (*Tülle*) spout

aushalten ['aʊshaltən] (*unreg*) *vt* to bear, to

stand; (*Geliebte*) to keep ♦ *vi* to hold out;
das ist nicht zum A~ that is unbearable
aushandeln ['aushandǝln] *vt* to negotiate
aushändigen ['aushɛndɪgǝn] *vt*: **jdm etw ~**
to hand sth over to sb
Aushang ['aushaŋ] *m* notice
aushängen ['aushɛŋǝn] (*unreg*) *vt* (*Meldung*)
to put up; (*Fenster*) to take off its hinges
♦ *vi* to be displayed
ausharren ['ausharǝn] *vi* to hold out
ausheben ['aushe:bǝn] (*unreg*) *vt* (*Erde*) to
lift out; (*Grube*) to hollow out; (*Tür*) to take
off its hinges; (*Diebesnest*) to clear out; (*MIL*)
to enlist
aushecken ['aushɛkǝn] (*umg*) *vt* to cook up
aushelfen ['aushɛlfǝn] (*unreg*) *vi*: **jdm ~** to
help sb out
Aushilfe ['aushɪlfǝ] *f* help, assistance;
(*Person*) (temporary) worker
Aushilfs- *zW*: **~kraft** *f* temporary worker;
a~weise *adv* temporarily, as a stopgap
ausholen ['ausho:lǝn] *vi* to swing one's arm
back; (*zur Ohrfeige*) to raise one's hand;
(*beim Gehen*) to take long strides
aushorchen ['aushɔrçǝn] *vt* to sound out,
to pump
auskennen ['auskɛnǝn] (*unreg*) *vr* to know a
lot; (*an einem Ort*) to know one's way
about; (*in Fragen etc*) to be knowledgeable
Ausklang ['ausklaŋ] *m* end
auskleiden ['ausklaɪdǝn] *vr* to undress ♦ *vt*
(*Wand*) to line
ausklingen ['ausklɪŋǝn] (*unreg*) *vi* (*Ton, Lied*)
to die away; (*Fest*) to peter out
ausklopfen ['ausklɔpfǝn] *vt* (*Teppich*) to
beat; (*Pfeife*) to knock out
auskochen ['auskɔxǝn] *vt* to boil; (*MED*) to
sterilize; **ausgekocht** (*fig*) out-and-out
Auskommen (**-s**) *nt*: **sein A~ haben** to
have a regular income; **a~** (*unreg*) *vi*: **mit
jdm a~** to get on with sb; **mit etw a~** to
get by with sth
auskosten ['auskɔstǝn] *vt* to enjoy to the
full
auskundschaften ['auskʊntʃaftǝn] *vt* to
spy out; (*Gebiet*) to reconnoitre
Auskunft ['auskʊnft] (**-, -künfte**) *f*

information; (*nähere*) details *pl*, particulars
pl; (*Stelle*) information office; (*TEL*) directory
inquiries *sg*
auslachen ['auslaxǝn] *vt* to laugh at, to
mock
ausladen ['ausla:dǝn] (*unreg*) *vt* to unload;
(*umg: Gäste*) to cancel an invitation to
Auslage ['ausla:gǝ] *f* shop window (display);
~n *pl* (*Ausgabe*) outlay *sg*
Ausland ['auslant] *nt* foreign countries *pl*;
im ~ abroad; **ins ~** abroad
Ausländer(in) ['auslɛndǝr(ɪn)] (**-s, -**) *m(f)*
foreigner
ausländisch *adj* foreign
Auslands- *zW*: **~gespräch** *nt*
international call; **~reise** *f* trip abroad;
~schutzbrief *m* international travel cover
auslassen ['auslasǝn] (*unreg*) *vt* to leave
out; (*Wort etc auch*) to omit; (*Fett*) to melt;
(*Kleidungsstück*) to let out ♦ *vr*: **sich über
etw** *akk* **~** to speak one's mind about sth;
seine Wut *etc* **an jdm ~** to vent one's rage
etc on sb
Auslassung *f* omission
Auslauf ['auslauf] *m* (*für Tiere*) run; (*Ausfluss*)
outflow, outlet; **a~en** (*unreg*) *vi* to run out;
(*Behälter*) to leak; (*NAUT*) to put out (to
sea); (*langsam aufhören*) to run down
Ausläufer ['auslɔyfǝr] *m* (*von Gebirge*) spur;
(*Pflanze*) runner; (*MET: von Hoch*) ridge;
(: *von Tief*) trough
ausleeren ['ausle:rǝn] *vt* to empty
auslegen ['ausle:gǝn] *vt* (*Waren*) to lay out;
(*Köder*) to put down; (*Geld*) to lend;
(*bedecken*) to cover; (*Text etc*) to interpret
Auslegung *f* interpretation
ausleiern ['auslaɪǝrn] *vi* (*Gummi*) to wear
out
Ausleihe ['auslaɪǝ] *f* issuing; (*Stelle*) issue
desk; **a~n** (*unreg*) *vt* (*verleihen*) to lend; **sich**
dat **etw a~n** to borrow sth
Auslese ['ausle:zǝ] *f* selection; (*Elite*) elite;
(*Wein*) choice wine; **a~n** (*unreg*) *vt* to
select; (*umg: zu Ende lesen*) to finish
ausliefern ['ausli:fǝrn] *vt* to deliver (up), to
hand over; (*COMM*) to deliver; **jdm/etw
ausgeliefert sein** to be at the mercy of

sb/sth

auslöschen ['aʊslœʃən] *vt* to extinguish; (*fig*) to wipe out, to obliterate

auslosen ['aʊsloːzən] *vt* to draw lots for

auslösen ['aʊsløːzən] *vt* (*Explosion, Schuss*) to set off; (*hervorrufen*) to cause, to produce; (*Gefangene*) to ransom; (*Pfand*) to redeem

ausmachen ['aʊsmaxən] *vt* (*Licht, Radio*) to turn off; (*Feuer*) to put out; (*entdecken*) to make out; (*vereinbaren*) to agree; (*beilegen*) to settle; (*Anteil darstellen, betragen*) to represent; (*bedeuten*) to matter; **macht es Ihnen etwas aus, wenn ...?** would you mind if ...?

ausmalen ['aʊsmaːlən] *vt* to paint; (*fig*) to describe; **sich** *dat* **etw ~** to imagine sth

Ausmaß ['aʊsmaːs] *nt* dimension; (*fig auch*) scale

ausmessen ['aʊsmɛsən] (*unreg*) *vt* to measure

Ausnahme ['aʊsnaːmə] *f* exception; **~fall** *m* exceptional case; **~zustand** *m* state of emergency

ausnahms- *zW*: **~los** *adv* without exception; **~weise** *adv* by way of exception, for once

ausnehmen ['aʊsneːmən] (*unreg*) *vt* to take out, to remove; (*Tier*) to gut; (*Nest*) to rob; (*umg: Geld abnehmen*) to clean out; (*ausschließen*) to make an exception of ♦ *vr* to look, to appear; **~d** *adj* exceptional

ausnützen ['aʊsnʏtsən] *vt* (*Zeit, Gelegenheit*) to use, to turn to good account; (*Einfluss*) to use; (*Mensch, Gutmütigkeit*) to exploit

auspacken ['aʊspakən] *vt* to unpack

auspfeifen ['aʊspfaɪfən] (*unreg*) *vt* to hiss/boo at

ausplaudern ['aʊsplaʊdərn] *vt* (*Geheimnis*) to blab

ausprobieren ['aʊsprobiːrən] *vt* to try (out)

Auspuff ['aʊspʊf] (**-(e)s, -e**) *m* (*TECH*) exhaust; **~rohr** *nt* exhaust (pipe)

ausradieren ['aʊsradiːrən] *vt* to erase, to rub out; (*fig*) to annihilate

ausrangieren ['aʊsrãʒiːrən] (*umg*) *vt* to chuck out

ausrauben ['aʊsraʊbən] *vt* to rob

ausräumen ['aʊsrɔymən] *vt* (*Dinge*) to clear away; (*Schrank, Zimmer*) to empty; (*Bedenken*) to dispel

ausrechnen ['aʊsrɛçnən] *vt* to calculate, to reckon

Ausrede ['aʊsreːdə] *f* excuse; **a~n** *vi* to have one's say ♦ *vt*: **jdm etw a~n** to talk sb out of sth

ausreichen ['aʊsraɪçən] *vi* to suffice, to be enough; **~d** *adj* sufficient, adequate; (*SCH*) adequate

Ausreise ['aʊsraɪzə] *f* departure; **bei der ~** when leaving the country; **~erlaubnis** *f* exit visa; **a~n** *vi* to leave the country

ausreißen ['aʊsraɪsən] (*unreg*) *vt* to tear *od* pull out ♦ *vi* (*Riss bekommen*) to tear; (*umg*) to make off, to scram

ausrenken ['aʊsrɛŋkən] *vt* to dislocate

ausrichten ['aʊsrɪçtən] *vt* (*Botschaft*) to deliver; (*Gruß*) to pass on; (*Hochzeit etc*) to arrange; (*in gerade Linie bringen*) to get in a straight line; (*angleichen*) to bring into line; (*TYP*) to justify; **ich werde es ihm ~** I'll tell him; **etwas/nichts bei jdm ~** to get somewhere/nowhere with sb

ausrotten ['aʊsrɔtən] *vt* to stamp out, to exterminate

Ausruf ['aʊsruːf] *m* (*Schrei*) cry, exclamation; (*Bekanntmachung*) proclamation; **a~en** (*unreg*) *vt* to cry out, to exclaim; to call out; **~ezeichen** *nt* exclamation mark

ausruhen ['aʊsruːən] *vt, vr* to rest

ausrüsten ['aʊsrʏstən] *vt* to equip, to fit out

Ausrüstung *f* equipment

ausrutschen ['aʊsrʊtʃən] *vi* to slip

Aussage ['aʊszaːgə] *f* (*JUR*) statement; **a~n** *vt* to say, to state ♦ *vi* (*JUR*) to give evidence

ausschalten ['aʊsʃaltən] *vt* to switch off; (*fig*) to eliminate

Ausschank ['aʊsʃaŋk] (**-(e)s, -schänke**) *m* dispensing, giving out; (*COMM*) selling; (*Theke*) bar

Ausschau ['aʊsʃaʊ] *f*: **~ halten (nach)** to look out (for), to watch (for); **a~en** *vi*: **a~en (nach)** to look out (for), to be on the look-out (for)

ausscheiden ['aʊsʃaɪdən] (*unreg*) *vt* to take

out; (*MED*) to secrete ♦ *vi*: **~ (aus)** to leave; (*SPORT*) to be eliminated (from) *od* knocked out (of)

Ausscheidung *f* separation; secretion; elimination; (*aus Amt*) retirement

ausschenken ['aʊsʃɛŋkən] *vt* (*Alkohol, Kaffee*) to pour out; (*COMM*) to sell

ausschildern ['aʊsʃɪldərn] *vt* to signpost

ausschimpfen ['aʊsʃɪmpfən] *vt* to scold, to tell off

ausschlafen ['aʊsʃlaːfən] (*unreg*) *vi, vr* to have a good sleep ♦ *vt* to sleep off; **ich bin nicht ausgeschlafen** I didn't have *od* get enough sleep

Ausschlag ['aʊsʃlaːk] *m* (*MED*) rash; (*Pendelausschlag*) swing; (*Nadelausschlag*) deflection; **den ~ geben** (*fig*) to tip the balance; **a~en** [-ɡən] (*unreg*) *vt* to knock out; (*auskleiden*) to deck out; (*verweigern*) to decline ♦ *vi* (*Pferd*) to kick out; (*BOT*) to sprout; **a~gebend** *adj* decisive

ausschließen ['aʊsʃliːsən] (*unreg*) *vt* to shut *od* lock out; (*fig*) to exclude

ausschließlich *adj* exclusive ♦ *adv* exclusively ♦ *präp +gen* exclusive of, excluding

Ausschluss ▲ ['aʊsʃlʊs] *m* exclusion

ausschmücken ['aʊsʃmykən] *vt* to decorate; (*fig*) to embellish

ausschneiden ['aʊsʃnaɪdən] (*unreg*) *vt* to cut out; (*Büsche*) to trim

Ausschnitt ['aʊsʃnɪt] *m* (*Teil*) section; (*von Kleid*) neckline; (*Zeitungsausschnitt*) cutting; (*aus Film etc*) excerpt

ausschreiben ['aʊsʃraɪbən] (*unreg*) *vt* (*ganz schreiben*) to write out (in full); (*ausstellen*) to write (out); (*Stelle, Wettbewerb etc*) to announce, to advertise

Ausschreitung ['aʊsʃraɪtʊŋ] *f* (*usu pl*) riot

Ausschuss ▲ ['aʊsʃʊs] *m* committee, board; (*Abfall*) waste, scraps *pl*; (*COMM: auch:* **~ware**) reject

ausschütten ['aʊsʃytən] *vt* to pour out; (*Eimer*) to empty; (*Geld*) to pay ♦ *vr* to shake (with laughter)

ausschweifend ['aʊsʃvaɪfənt] *adj* (*Leben*) dissipated, debauched; (*Fantasie*)

extravagant

aussehen ['aʊszeːən] (*unreg*) *vi* to look; **es sieht nach Regen aus** it looks like rain; **es sieht schlecht aus** things look bad; **A~ (-s)** *nt* appearance

aus sein ▲ *siehe* **aus**

außen ['aʊsən] *adv* outside; (*nach ~*) outwards; **~ ist es rot** it's red (on the) outside

Außen- *zW*: **~dienst** *m*: **im ~dienst sein** to work outside the office; **~handel** *m* foreign trade; **~minister** *m* foreign minister; **~ministerium** *nt* foreign office; **~politik** *f* foreign policy; **a~politisch** *adj* (*Entwicklung, Lage*) foreign; **~seite** *f* outside; **~seiter (-s, -)** *m* outsider; **~stände** *pl* outstanding debts; **~stehende(r)** *f(m)* outsider; **~welt** *f* outside world

außer ['aʊsər] *präp +dat* (*räumlich*) out of; (*abgesehen von*) except ♦ *konj* (*ausgenommen*) except; **~ Gefahr** out of danger; **~ Zweifel** beyond any doubt; **~ Betrieb** out of order; **~ Dienst** retired; **~ Landes** abroad; **~ sich** *dat* **sein** to be beside o.s.; **~ sich** *akk* **geraten** to go wild; **~ wenn** unless; **~ dass** except; **~dem** *konj* besides, in addition

äußere(r, s) ['ɔʏsərə(r,s)] *adj* outer, external

außergewöhnlich *adj* unusual

außerhalb *präp +gen* outside ♦ *adv* outside

äußerlich *adj* external

äußern *vt* to utter, to express; (*zeigen*) to show ♦ *vr* to give one's opinion; (*Krankheit etc*) to show itself

außerordentlich *adj* extraordinary

außerplanmäßig *adj* unscheduled

äußerst ['ɔʏsərst] *adv* extremely, most; **~e(r, s)** *adj* utmost; (*räumlich*) farthest; (*Termin*) last possible; (*Preis*) highest

Äußerung *f* remark, comment

aussetzen ['aʊszɛtsən] *vt* (*Kind, Tier*) to abandon; (*Boote*) to lower; (*Belohnung*) to offer; (*Urteil, Verfahren*) to postpone ♦ *vi* (*aufhören*) to stop; (*Pause machen*) to have a break; **jdm/etw ausgesetzt sein** to be exposed to sb/sth; **an jdm/etw etwas ~ to**

find fault with sb/sth

Aussicht ['aʊszɪçt] *f* view; (*in Zukunft*) prospect; **etw in ~ haben** to have sth in view

Aussichts- *zW*: **a~los** *adj* hopeless; **~punkt** *m* viewpoint; **a~reich** *adj* promising; **~turm** *m* observation tower

aussöhnen ['aʊszøːnən] *vt* to reconcile ♦ *vr* to reconcile o.s., to become reconciled

aussondern ['aʊszɔndərn] *vt* to separate, to select

aussortieren ['aʊszɔrtiːrən] *vt* to sort out

ausspannen ['aʊsʃpanən] *vt* to spread *od* stretch out; (*Pferd*) to unharness; (*umg: Mädchen*): **(jdm) jdn ~** to steal sb (from sb) ♦ *vi* to relax

aussperren ['aʊsʃpɛrən] *vt* to lock out

ausspielen ['aʊsʃpiːlən] *vt* (*Karte*) to lead; (*Geldprämie*) to offer as a prize ♦ *vi* (*KARTEN*) to lead; **jdn gegen jdn ~** to play sb off against sb; **ausgespielt haben** to be finished

Aussprache ['aʊsʃpraːxə] *f* pronunciation; (*Unterredung*) (frank) discussion

aussprechen ['aʊsʃprɛçən] (*unreg*) *vt* to pronounce; (*äußern*) to say, to express ♦ *vr* (*sich äußern*): **sich ~ (über** +*akk*) to speak (about); (*sich anvertrauen*) to unburden o.s. (about *od* on); (*diskutieren*) to discuss ♦ *vi* (*zu Ende sprechen*) to finish speaking

Ausspruch ['aʊsʃprʊx] *m* saying, remark

ausspülen ['aʊsʃpyːlən] *vt* to wash out; (*Mund*) to rinse

Ausstand ['aʊsʃtant] *m* strike; **in den ~ treten** to go on strike

ausstatten ['aʊsʃtatən] *vt* (*Zimmer etc*) to furnish; (*Person*) to equip, to kit out

Ausstattung *f* (*Ausstatten*) provision; (*Kleidung*) outfit; (*Aufmachung*) make-up; (*Einrichtung*) furnishing

ausstechen ['aʊsʃtɛçən] (*unreg*) *vt* (*Augen, Rasen, Graben*) to dig out; (*Kekse*) to cut out; (*übertreffen*) to outshine

ausstehen ['aʊsʃteːən] (*unreg*) *vt* to stand, to endure ♦ *vi* (*noch nicht da sein*) to be outstanding

aussteigen ['aʊsʃtaɪɡən] (*unreg*) *vi* to get out, to alight

ausstellen ['aʊsʃtɛlən] *vt* to exhibit, to display; (*umg: ausschalten*) to switch off; (*Rechnung etc*) to make out; (*Pass, Zeugnis*) to issue

Ausstellung *f* exhibition; (*FIN*) drawing up; (*einer Rechnung*) making out; (*eines Passes etc*) issuing

aussterben ['aʊsʃtɛrbən] (*unreg*) *vi* to die out

Aussteuer ['aʊsʃtɔyər] *f* dowry

Ausstieg ['aʊsʃtiːk] (**-(e)s, -e**) *m* exit

ausstopfen ['aʊsʃtɔpfən] *vt* to stuff

ausstoßen ['aʊsʃtoːsən] (*unreg*) *vt* (*Luft, Rauch*) to give off, to emit; (*aus Verein etc*) to expel, to exclude; (*Auge*) to poke out

ausstrahlen ['aʊsʃtraːlən] *vt, vi* to radiate; (*RADIO*) to broadcast

Ausstrahlung *f* radiation; (*fig*) charisma

ausstrecken ['aʊsʃtrɛkən] *vt, vr* to stretch out

ausstreichen ['aʊsʃtraɪçən] (*unreg*) *vt* to cross out; (*glätten*) to smooth (out)

ausströmen ['aʊsʃtrøːmən] *vi* (*Gas*) to pour out, to escape ♦ *vt* to give off; (*fig*) to radiate

aussuchen ['aʊszuːxən] *vt* to select, to pick out

Austausch ['aʊstaʊʃ] *m* exchange; **a~bar** *adj* exchangeable; **a~en** *vt* to exchange, to swap

austeilen ['aʊstaɪlən] *vt* to distribute, to give out

Auster ['aʊstər] (**-, -n**) *f* oyster

austoben ['aʊstoːbən] *vr* (*Kind*) to run wild; (*Erwachsene*) to sow one's wild oats

austragen ['aʊstraːɡən] (*unreg*) *vt* (*Post*) to deliver; (*Streit etc*) to decide; (*Wettkämpfe*) to hold

Australien [aʊsˈtraːliən] (**-s**) *nt* Australia; **Australier(in)** (**-s, -**) *m(f)* Australian; **australisch** *adj* Australian

austreiben ['aʊstraɪbən] (*unreg*) *vt* to drive out, to expel; (*Geister*) to exorcize

austreten ['aʊstreːtən] (*unreg*) *vi* (*zur Toilette*) to be excused ♦ *vt* (*Feuer*) to tread out, to trample; (*Schuhe*) to wear out; (*Treppe*) to

wear down; **aus etw ~** to leave sth
austrinken ['austrɪŋkən] (*unreg*) *vt* (*Glas*) to
drain; (*Getränk*) to drink up ♦ *vi* to finish
one's drink, to drink up
Austritt ['austrɪt] *m* emission; (*aus Verein,
Partei etc*) retirement, withdrawal
austrocknen ['austrɔknən] *vt, vi* to dry up
ausüben ['aus|y:bən] *vt* (*Beruf*) to practise,
to carry out; (*Funktion*) to perform; (*Einfluss*)
to exert; **einen Reiz auf jdn ~** to hold an
attraction for sb; **eine Wirkung auf jdn ~**
to have an effect on sb
Ausverkauf ['ausfɛrkauf] *m* sale; **a~en** *vt* to
sell out; (*Geschäft*) to sell up; **a~t** *adj*
(*Karten, Artikel*) sold out; (*THEAT: Haus*) full
Auswahl ['ausva:l] *f*: **eine ~ (an** +*dat*) a
selection (of), a choice (of)
auswählen ['ausvɛ:lən] *vt* to select, to
choose
Auswander- ['ausvandər] *zW*: **~er** *m*
emigrant; **a~n** *vi* to emigrate; **~ung** *f*
emigration
auswärtig ['ausvɛrtɪç] *adj* (*nicht am/vom Ort*)
out-of-town; (*ausländisch*) foreign
auswärts ['ausvɛrts] *adv* outside; (*nach
außen*) outwards; **~ essen** to eat out;
A~spiel ['ausvɛrtsʃsi:l] *nt* away game
auswechseln ['ausvɛksəln] *vt* to change, to
substitute
Ausweg ['ausve:k] *m* way out; **a~los** *adj*
hopeless
ausweichen ['ausvaiçən] (*unreg*) *vi*: **jdm/
etw ~** to move aside *od* make way for sb/
sth; (*fig*) to side-step sb/sth; **~d** *adj* evasive
ausweinen ['ausvainən] *vr* to have a (good)
cry
Ausweis ['ausvais] (**-es, -e**) *m* identity card;
passport; (*Mitgliedsausweis, Bibliotheksausweis
etc*) card; **a~en** [-zən] (*unreg*) *vt* to expel, to
banish ♦ *vr* to prove one's identity;
~kontrolle *f* identity check; **~papiere** *pl*
identity papers; **~ung** *f* expulsion
ausweiten ['ausvaitən] *vt* to stretch
auswendig ['ausvɛndɪç] *adv* by heart
auswerten ['ausvɛrtən] *vt* to evaluate;
Auswertung *f* evaluation, analysis;
(*Nutzung*) utilization

auswirken ['ausvɪrkən] *vr* to have an effect;
Auswirkung *f* effect
auswischen ['ausvɪʃən] *vt* to wipe out; **jdm
eins ~** (*umg*) to put one over on sb
Auswuchs ['ausvu:ks] *m* (out)growth; (*fig*)
product
auszahlen ['austsa:lən] *vt* (*Lohn, Summe*) to
pay out; (*Arbeiter*) to pay off; (*Miterbe*) to
buy out ♦ *vr* (*sich lohnen*) to pay
auszählen ['austsɛ:lən] *vt* (*Stimmen*) to
count
auszeichnen ['austsaiçnən] *vt* to honour;
(*MIL*) to decorate; (*COMM*) to price ♦ *vr* to
distinguish o.s.
Auszeichnung *f* distinction; (*COMM*)
pricing; (*Ehrung*) awarding of decoration;
(*Ehre*) honour; (*Orden*) decoration; **mit ~**
with distinction
ausziehen ['austsi:ən] (*unreg*) *vt* (*Kleidung*)
to take off; (*Haare, Zähne, Tisch etc*) to pull
out; (*nachmalen*) to trace ♦ *vr* to undress
♦ *vi* (*aufbrechen*) to leave; (*aus Wohnung*) to
move out
Auszubildende(r) ['austsubɪldəndə(r)] *f(m)*
trainee
Auszug ['austsu:k] *m* (*aus Wohnung*)
removal; (*aus Buch etc*) extract; (*Konto~*)
statement; (*Ausmarsch*) departure
Auto ['auto] (**-s, -s**) *nt* (motor)car; **~ fahren**
to drive; **~atlas** *m* road atlas; **~bahn** *f*
motorway; **~bahndreieck** *nt* motorway
junction; **~bahngebühr** *f* toll;
~bahnkreuz *nt* motorway intersection;
~bus *m* bus; **~fähre** *f* car ferry;
~fahrer(in) *m(f)* motorist, driver; **~fahrt** *f*
drive; **a~gen** [-'ge:n] *adj* autogenous;
~'gramm *nt* autograph

Autobahn

i *An* **Autobahn** *is a motorway. In former
West Germany there is a widespread
motorway network but in the former* **DDR**
*the motorways are somewhat less extensive.
There is no overall speed limit but a limit of
130 km/hour is recommended and there are
lower mandatory limits on certain stretches
of road. As yet there are no tolls payable on*

German Autobahnen. However, a yearly toll is payable in Switzerland and tolls have been introduced in Austria.

Auto- *zW:* **~'mat (-en, -en)** *m* machine; **~matik** [auto'ma:tɪk] *f* (*AUT*) automatic; **a~'matisch** *adj* automatic; **a~nom** [-'no:m] *adj* autonomous

Autor(in) ['autɔr(ɪn)] **(-s, -en)** *m(f)* author

Auto- *zW:* **~radio** *nt* car radio; **~reifen** *m* car tyre; **~reisezug** *m* motorail train; **~rennen** *nt* motor racing

autoritär [autori'tɛ:r] *adj* authoritarian

Autorität *f* authority

Auto- *zW:* **~telefon** *nt* car phone; **~unfall** *m* car *od* motor accident; **~vermietung** *f* car hire (*BRIT*) *od* rental (*US*); **~waschanlage** *f* car wash

Axt [akst] **(-, ⁺e)** *f* axe

B, b

Baby ['be:bi] **(-s, -s)** *nt* baby; **~nahrung** *f* baby food; **~sitter (-s, -)** *m* baby-sitter

Bach [bax] **(-(e)s, ⁺e)** *m* stream, brook

Backbord ['bakbɔrt] **(-(e)s, -e)** *nl* (*NAUT*) port

Backe ['bakə] *f* cheek

backen ['bakən] (*unreg*) *vt, vi* to bake

Backenzahn *m* molar

Bäcker ['bɛkər(ɪn)] **(-s, -)** *m* baker; **~ei** *f* bakery; (*~eiladen*) baker's (shop)

Back- *zW:* **~form** *f* baking tin; **~obst** *nt* dried fruit; **~ofen** *m* oven; **~pflaume** *f* prune; **~pulver** *nt* baking powder; **~stein** *m* brick

Bad [ba:t] **(-(e)s, ⁺er)** *nt* bath; (*Schwimmen*) bathe; (*Ort*) spa

Bade- ['ba:də] *zW:* **~anstalt** *f* (swimming) baths *pl*; **~anzug** *m* bathing suit; **~hose** *f* bathing *od* swimming trunks *pl*; **~kappe** *f* bathing cap; **~mantel** *m* bath(ing) robe; **~meister** *m* baths attendant; **b~n** *vi* to bathe, to have a bath ♦ *vt* to bath; **~ort** *m* spa; **~tuch** *nt* bath towel; **~wanne** *f* bath (tub); **~zimmer** *nt* bathroom

Bagatelle [baga'tɛlə] *f* trifle

Bagger ['bagər] **(-s, -)** *m* excavator; (*NAUT*) dredger; **b~n** *vt, vi* to excavate; to dredge

Bahn [ba:n] **(-, -en)** *f* railway, railroad (*US*); (*Weg*) road, way; (*Spur*) lane; (*Rennbahn*) track; (*ASTRON*) orbit; (*Stoffbahn*) length; **b~brechend** *adj* pioneering; **~Card** ['ba:nka:rd] **(-, -s)** ® *f* ≈ railcard; **~damm** *m* railway embankment; **b~en** *vt:* **sich/ jdm einen Weg b~en** to clear a way/a way for sb; **~fahrt** *f* railway journey; **~fracht** *f* rail freight; **~hof (-, -s)** *m* station; **auf dem ~hof** at the station; **~hofshalle** *f* station concourse; **~linie** *f* (railway) line; **~steig** *m* platform; **~übergang** *m* level crossing, grade crossing (*US*)

Bahre ['ba:rə] *f* stretcher

Bakterien [bak'te:riən] *pl* bacteria *pl*

Balance [ba'lã:sə] *f* balance, equilibrium

balan'cieren [balt] *vt, vi* to balance

bald [balt] *adv* (*zeitlich*) soon; (*beinahe*) almost; **~ig** ['baldɪç] *adj* early, speedy

Baldrian ['baldria:n] **(-s, -e)** *m* valerian

Balkan ['balka:n] **(-s)** *m:* **der ~** the Balkans *pl*

Balken ['balkən] **(-s, -)** *m* beam; (*Tragbalken*) girder; (*Stützbalken*) prop

Balkon [bal'kõ:] **(-s, -s** *od* **-e)** *m* balcony; (*THEAT*) (dress) circle

Ball [bal] **(-(e)s, ⁺e)** *m* ball; (*Tanz*) dance, ball

Ballast ['balast] **(-(e)s, -e)** *m* ballast; (*fig*) weight, burden

Ballen ['balən] **(-s, -)** *m* bale; (*ANAT*) ball; **b~** *vt* (*formen*) to make into a ball; (*Faust*) to clench ♦ *vr* (*Wolken etc*) to build up; (*Menschen*) to gather

Ballett [ba'lɛt] **(-(e)s, -e)** *nt* ballet

Ballkleid *nt* evening dress

Ballon [ba'lõ:] **(-s, -s** *od* **-e)** *m* balloon

Ballspiel *nt* ball game

Ballungsgebiet ['baluŋsgəbi:t] *nt* conurbation

Baltikum ['baltikʊm] **(-s)** *nt:* **das ~** the Baltic States

Banane [ba'na:nə] *f* banana

Band¹ [bant] **(-(e)s, ⁺e)** *m* (*Buchband*) volume

Rechtschreibreform: ▲ *neue Schreibung* △ *alte Schreibung (auslaufend)*

Band² (-(e)s, ⸚er) nt (Stoffband) ribbon, tape; (Fließband) production line; (Tonband) tape; (ANAT) ligament; **etw auf ~ aufnehmen** to tape sth; **am laufenden ~** (umg) non-stop

Band³ (-(e)s, -e) nt (Freundschaftsband etc) bond

Band⁴ [bɛnt] (-, -s) f band, group

band etc vb siehe **binden**

Bandage [ban'daːʒə] f bandage

banda'gieren vt to bandage

Bande ['bandə] f band; (Straßenbande) gang

bändigen ['bɛndɪgən] vt (Tier) to tame; (Trieb, Leidenschaft) to control, to restrain

Bandit [ban'diːt] (-en, -en) m bandit

Band- zW: **~nudel** f (KOCH: gew pl) ribbon noodles pl; **~scheibe** f (ANAT) disc; **~wurm** m tapeworm

bange ['baŋə] adj scared; (besorgt) anxious; **jdm wird es ~** sb is becoming scared; **jdm B~ machen** to scare sb; **~n** vi: **um jdn/ etw ~n** to be anxious od worried about sb/sth

Bank¹ [baŋk] (-, ⸚e) f (Sitz~) bench; (Sand~ etc) (sand)bank, (sand)bar

Bank² [baŋk] (-, -en) f (Geldbank) bank; **~anweisung** f banker's order; **~einzug** m direct debit

Bankett [baŋ'kɛt] (-(e)s, -e) nt (Essen) banquet; (Straßenrand) verge (BRIT), shoulder (US)

Bankier [baŋki'eː] (-s, -s) m banker

Bank- zW: **~konto** m bank account; **~leitzahl** f bank sort code number; **~note** f banknote; **~raub** m bank robbery

Bankrott [baŋ'krɔt] (-(e)s, -e) m bankruptcy; **~ machen** to go bankrupt; **b~** adj bankrupt

Bankverbindung f banking arrangements pl; **geben Sie bitte Ihre ~ an** please give your account details

Bann [ban] (-(e)s, -e) m (HIST) ban; (Kirchenbann) excommunication; (fig: Zauber) spell; **b~en** vt (Geister) to exorcize; (Gefahr) to avert; (bezaubern) to enchant; (HIST) to banish

Banner (-s, -) nt banner, flag

Bar (-, -s) f bar

bar [baːr] adj (+gen) (unbedeckt) bare; (frei von) lacking (in); (offenkundig) utter, sheer; **~e(s) Geld** cash; **etw (in) ~ bezahlen** to pay sth (in) cash; **etw für ~e Münze nehmen** (fig) to take sth at its face value

Bär [bɛːr] (-en, -en) m bear

Baracke [ba'rakə] f hut

barbarisch [bar'baːrɪʃ] adj barbaric, barbarous

Bar- zW: **b~fuß** adj barefoot; **~geld** nt cash, ready money; **b~geldlos** adj non-cash

Barkauf m cash purchase

Barkeeper ['baːrkiːpər] (-s, -) m barman, bartender

barmherzig [barm'hɛrtsɪç] adj merciful, compassionate

Baron [ba'roːn] (-s, -e) m baron; **~in** f baroness

Barren ['barən] (-s, -) m parallel bars pl; (Goldbarren) ingot

Barriere [bari'ɛːrə] f barrier

Barrikade [bari'kaːdə] f barricade

Barsch [barʃ] (-(e)s, -e) m perch

barsch [barʃ] adj brusque, gruff

Bar- zW: **~schaft** f ready money; **~scheck** m open od uncrossed cheque (BRIT), open check (US)

Bart [baːrt] (-(e)s, ⸚e) m beard; (Schlüsselbart) bit; **bärtig** ['bɛːrtɪç] adj bearded

Barzahlung f cash payment

Base ['baːzə] f (CHEM) base; (Kusine) cousin

Basel ['baːzəl] nt Basle

Basen pl von **Base**; **Basis**

basieren [ba'ziːrən] vt to base ♦ vi to be based

Basis ['baːzɪs] (-, **Basen**) f basis

Bass ▲ [bas] (-es, ⸚e) m bass

Bassin [ba'sɛ̃ː] (-s, -s) nt pool

basteln ['bastəln] vt to make ♦ vi to do handicrafts

bat etc [baːt] vb siehe **bitten**

Bataillon [batal'joːn] (-s, -e) nt battalion

Batik ['baːtɪk] f (Verfahren) batik

Batterie [batə'riː] f battery

Bau [bau] (-(e)s) m (~en) building,

construction; (*Aufbau*) structure; (*Körperbau*) frame; (*~stelle*) building site; (*pl ~e: Tierbau*) hole, burrow; (*: MIN*) working(s); (*pl ~ten: Gebäude*) building; **sich im ~ befinden** to be under construction; **~arbeiten** *pl* building *od* construction work *sg*; **~arbeiter** *m* building worker

Bauch [baʊx] **(-(e)s, Bäuche)** *m* belly; (*ANAT auch*) stomach, abdomen; **~fell** *nt* peritoneum; **b~ig** *adj* bulbous; **~nabel** *m* navel; **~redner** *m* ventriloquist; **~schmerzen** *pl* stomachache; **~weh** *nt* stomachache

Baudenkmal *nt* historical monument

bauen ['baʊən] *vt, vi* to build; (*TECH*) to construct; **auf jdn/etw ~** to depend *od* count upon sb/sth

Bauer[1] ['baʊər] **(-n** *od* **-s, -n)** *m* farmer; (*Schach*) pawn

Bauer[2] ['baʊər] **(-s, -)** *nt od m* (bird)cage

Bäuerin ['bɔʏərɪn] *f* farmer; (*Frau des Bauers*) farmer's wife

bäuerlich *adj* rustic

Bauern- *zW:* **~haus** *nt* farmhouse; **~hof** *m* farm(yard)

Bau- *zW:* **b~fällig** *adj* dilapidated; **~gelände** *f* building site; **~genehmigung** *f* building permit; **~gerüst** *nt* scaffolding; **~herr** *m* purchaser; **~kasten** *m* box of bricks; **~land** *nt* building land; **b~lich** *adj* structural

Baum [baʊm] **(-(e)s, Bäume)** *m* tree

baumeln ['baʊməln] *vi* to dangle

bäumen ['bɔʏmən] *vr* to rear (up)

Baum- *zW:* **~schule** *f* nursery; **~stamm** *m* tree trunk; **~stumpf** *m* tree stump; **~wolle** *f* cotton

Bau- *zW:* **~plan** *m* architect's plan; **~platz** *m* building site

bauspar- *zW:* **~en** *vi* to save with a building society; **B~kasse** *f* building society; **B~vertrag** *m* building society savings agreement

Bau- *zW:* **~stein** *m* building stone, freestone; **~stelle** *f* building site; **~teil** *nt* prefabricated part (of building); **~ten** *pl von* **Bau;** **~unternehmer** *m* building

contractor; **~weise** *f* (method of) construction; **~werk** *nt* building; **~zaun** *m* hoarding

Bayern ['baɪərn] *nt* Bavaria

bayrisch ['baɪrɪʃ] *adj* Bavarian

Bazillus [ba'tsɪlʊs] **(-, Bazillen)** *m* bacillus

beabsichtigen [bə'apzɪçtɪgən] *vt* to intend

beacht- [bə'axt] *zW:* **~en** *vt* to take note of; (*Vorschrift*) to obey; (*Vorfahrt*) to observe; **~lich** *adj* considerable; **B~ung** *f* notice, attention, observation

Beamte(r) [bə'amtə(r)] **(-n, -n)** *m* official; (*Staatsbeamte*) civil servant; (*Bankbeamte etc*) employee

Beamtin *f siehe* **Beamte(r)**

beängstigend [bə'ɛŋstɪgənt] *adj* alarming

beanspruchen [bə'anʃprʊxən] *vt* to claim; (*Zeit, Platz*) to take up, to occupy; **jdn ~** to take up sb's time

beanstanden [bə'anʃtandən] *vt* to complain about, to object to

beantragen [bə'antra:gən] *vt* to apply for, to ask for

beantworten [bə'antvɔrtən] *vt* to answer; **Beantwortung** *f* (*+gen*) reply (to)

bearbeiten [bə'arbaɪtən] *vt* to work; (*Material*) to process; (*Thema*) to deal with; (*Land*) to cultivate; (*CHEM*) to treat; (*Buch*) to revise; (*umg: beeinflussen wollen*) to work on

Bearbeitung *f* processing; cultivation; treatment; revision

Bearbeitungsgebühr *f* handling charge

Beatmung [bə'a:tmʊŋ] *f* respiration

beaufsichtigen [bə'aʊfzɪçtɪgən] *vt* to supervise; **Beaufsichtigung** *f* supervision

beauftragen [bə'aʊftra:gən] *vt* to instruct; **jdn mit etw ~** to entrust sb with sth

Beauftragte(r) *f(m)* representative

bebauen [bə'baʊən] *vt* to build on; (*AGR*) to cultivate

beben ['be:bən] *vi* to tremble, to shake; **B~ (-s, -)** *nt* earthquake

Becher ['bɛçər] **(-s, -)** *m* mug; (*ohne Henkel*) tumbler

Becken ['bɛkən] **(-s, -)** *nt* basin; (*MUS*) cymbal; (*ANAT*) pelvis

bedacht [bə'daxt] *adj* thoughtful, careful;
auf etw *akk* ~ **sein** to be concerned about
sth

bedächtig [bə'dεçtıç] *adj* (*umsichtig*)
thoughtful, reflective; (*langsam*) slow,
deliberate

bedanken [bə'daŋkən] *vr*: **sich (bei jdm)** ~
to say thank you (to sb)

Bedarf [bə'darf] **(-(e)s)** *m* need,
requirement; (*COMM*) demand; **je nach** ~
according to demand; **bei** ~ if necessary; ~
an etw *dat* **haben** to be in need of sth

Bedarfs- *zW*: **~fall** *m* case of need;
~haltestelle *f* request stop

bedauerlich [bə'dauərlıç] *adj* regrettable

bedauern [bə'dauərn] *vt* to be sorry for;
(*bemitleiden*) to pity; **B~ (-s)** *nt* regret;
~swert *adj* (*Zustände*) regrettable; (*Mensch*)
pitiable, unfortunate

bedecken [bə'dεkən] *vt* to cover

bedeckt *adj* covered; (*Himmel*) overcast

bedenken [bə'dεŋkən] (*unreg*) *vt* to think
over, to consider

Bedenken (-s, -) *nt* (*Überlegen*)
consideration; (*Zweifel*) doubt; (*Skrupel*)
scruple

bedenklich *adj* doubtful; (*bedrohlich*)
dangerous, risky

Bedenkzeit *f* time to think

bedeuten [bə'dɔʏtən] *vt* to mean; to signify;
(*wichtig sein*) to be of importance; **~d** *adj*
important; (*beträchtlich*) considerable

bedeutsam *adj* (*wichtig*) significant

Bedeutung *f* meaning; significance;
(*Wichtigkeit*) importance; **b~slos** *adj*
insignificant, unimportant; **b~svoll** *adj*
momentous, significant

bedienen [bə'di:nən] *vt* to serve; (*Maschine*)
to work, to operate ♦ *vr* (*beim Essen*) to
help o.s.; **sich jds/einer Sache** ~ to make
use of sb/sth

Bedienung *f* service; (*Kellnerin*) waitress;
(*Verkäuferin*) shop assistant; (*Zuschlag*)
service (charge)

Bedienungsanleitung *f* operating
instructions *pl*

bedingen [bə'dıŋən] *vt* (*verursachen*) to

cause

bedingt *adj* (*Richtigkeit, Tauglichkeit*) limited;
(*Zusage, Annahme*) conditional

Bedingung *f* condition; (*Voraussetzung*)
stipulation; **b~slos** *adj* unconditional

bedrängen [bə'drεŋən] *vt* to pester, to
harass

bedrohen [bə'dro:ən] *vt* to threaten;
Bedrohung *f* threat, menace

bedrücken [bə'drʏkən] *vt* to oppress, to
trouble

bedürf- [bə'dʏrf] *zW*: **~en** (*unreg*) *vi* +*gen* to
need, to require; **~nis (-ses, -se)** *nt*
need; **~tig** *adj* in need, poor, needy

beeilen [bə'|aılən] *vr* to hurry

beeindrucken [bə'|aındrʊkən] *vt* to
impress, to make an impression on

beeinflussen [bə'|aınflʊsən] *vt* to influence

beeinträchtigen [bə'|aıntrεçtıgən] *vt* to
affect adversely; (*Freiheit*) to infringe upon

beend(ig)en [bə'|εnd(ıg)ən] *vt* to end, to
finish, to terminate

beengen [bə'|εŋən] *vt* to cramp; (*fig*) to
hamper, to oppress

beerben [bə'|εrbən] *vt*: **jdn** ~ to inherit from
sb

beerdigen [bə'|e:rdıgən] *vt* to bury;
Beerdigung *f* funeral, burial

Beere ['be:rə] *f* berry; (*Traubenbeere*) grape

Beet [he:t] **(-(e)s, -e)** *nt* bed

befähigen [bə'fε:ıgən] *vt* to enable

befähigt *adj* (*begabt*) talented; ~ **(für)**
(*fähig*) capable (of)

Befähigung *f* capability; (*Begabung*) talent,
aptitude

befahrbar [bə'fa:rba:r] *adj* passable; (*NAUT*)
navigable

befahren [bə'fa:rən] (*unreg*) *vt* to use, to
drive over; (*NAUT*) to navigate ♦ *adj* used

befallen [bə'falən] (*unreg*) *vt* to come over

befangen [bə'faŋən] *adj* (*schüchtern*) shy,
self-conscious; (*voreingenommen*) biased

befassen [bə'fasən] *vr* to concern o.s.

Befehl [bə'fe:l] **(-(e)s, -e)** *m* command,
order; **b~en** (*unreg*) *vt* to order ♦ *vi* to give
orders; **jdm etw b~en** to order sb to do
sth; **~sverweigerung** *f* insubordination

Spelling Reform: ▲ *new spelling* △ *old spelling (to be phased out)*

befestigen [bə'fɛstɪgən] *vt* to fasten; (*stärken*) to strengthen; (*MIL*) to fortify; **~ an** +*dat* to fasten to

Befestigung *f* fastening; strengthening; (*MIL*) fortification

befeuchten [bə'fɔyçtən] *vt* to damp(en), to moisten

befinden [bə'fɪndən] (*unreg*) *vr* to be; (*sich fühlen*) to feel ♦ *vt*: **jdn/etw für** *od* **als etw ~** to deem sb/sth to be sth ♦ *vi*: **~ (über** +*akk*) to decide (on), to adjudicate (on); **B~ (-s)** *nt* health, condition; (*Meinung*) view, opinion

befolgen [bə'fɔlgən] *vt* to comply with, to follow

befördern [bə'fœrdərn] *vt* (*senden*) to transport, to send; (*beruflich*) to promote; **Beförderung** *f* transport; promotion

befragen [bə'fra:gən] *vt* to question

befreien [bə'fraɪən] *vt* to set free; (*erlassen*) to exempt; **Befreiung** *f* liberation, release; (*Erlassen*) exemption

befreunden [bə'frɔyndən] *vr* to make friends; (*mit Idee etc*) to acquaint o.s.

befreundet *adj* friendly

befriedigen [bə'fri:dɪgən] *vt* to satisfy; **~d** *adj* satisfactory

Befriedigung *f* satisfaction, gratification

befristet [bə'frɪstət] *adj* limited

befruchten [bə'frʊxtən] *vt* to fertilize; (*fig*) to stimulate

Befruchtung *f*: **künstliche ~** artificial insemination

Befugnis [bə'fu:knɪs] **(-, -se)** *f* authorization, powers *pl*

befugt *adj* authorized, entitled

Befund [bə'fʊnt] **(-(e)s, -e)** *m* findings *pl*; (*MED*) diagnosis

befürchten [bə'fyrçtən] *vt* to fear; **Befürchtung** *f* fear, apprehension

befürworten [bə'fy:rvɔrtən] *vt* to support, to speak in favour of; **Befürworter (-s, -)** *m* supporter, advocate

begabt [bə'ga:pt] *adj* gifted

Begabung [bə'ga:bʊŋ] *f* talent, gift

begann *etc* [bə'gan] *vb siehe* **beginnen**

begeben [bə'ge:bən] (*unreg*) *vr* (*gehen*) to betake o.s.; (*geschehen*) to occur; **sich ~ nach** *od* **zu** to proceed to(wards); **B~heit** *f* occurrence

begegnen [bə'ge:gnən] *vi*: **jdm ~** to meet sb; (*behandeln*) to treat sb; **einer Sache** *dat* **~** to meet with sth

Begegnung *f* meeting

begehen [bə'ge:ən] (*unreg*) *vt* (*Straftat*) to commit; (*abschreiten*) to cover; (*Straße etc*) to use, to negotiate; (*Feier*) to celebrate

begehren [bə'ge:rən] *vt* to desire

begehrt *adj* in demand; (*Junggeselle*) eligible

begeistern [bə'gaɪstərn] *vt* to fill with enthusiasm, to inspire ♦ *vr*: **sich für etw ~** to get enthusiastic about sth

begeistert *adj* enthusiastic

Begierde [bə'gi:rdə] *f* desire, passion

begierig [bə'gi:rɪç] *adj* eager, keen

begießen [bə'gi:sən] (*unreg*) *vt* to water; (*mit Alkohol*) to drink to

Beginn [bə'gɪn] **(-(e)s)** *m* beginning; **zu ~** at the beginning; **b~en** (*unreg*) *vt*, *vi* to start, to begin

beglaubigen [bə'glaʊbɪgən] *vt* to countersign; **Beglaubigung** *f* countersignature

begleichen [bə'glaɪçən] (*unreg*) *vt* to settle, to pay

Begleit- [bə'glaɪt] *zW*: **b~en** *vt* to accompany; (*MIL*) to escort; **~er (-s, -)** *m* companion; (*Freund*) escort; (*MUS*) accompanist; **~schreiben** *nt* covering letter; **~umstände** *pl* concomitant circumstances; **~ung** *f* company; (*MIL*) escort; (*MUS*) accompaniment

beglücken [bə'glʏkən] *vt* to make happy, to delight

beglückwünschen [bə'glʏkvʏnʃən] *vt*: **~ (zu)** to congratulate (on)

begnadigen [bə'gna:dɪgən] *vt* to pardon; **Begnadigung** *f* pardon, amnesty

begnügen [bə'gny:gən] *vr* to be satisfied, to content o.s.

begonnen *etc* [bə'gɔnən] *vb siehe* **beginnen**

begraben [bə'gra:bən] (*unreg*) *vt* to bury; **Begräbnis (-ses, -se)** [bə'grɛ:pnɪs] *nt* burial, funeral

Rechtschreibreform: ▲ *neue Schreibung* △ *alte Schreibung (auslaufend)*

begreifen [bə'graɪfən] (unreg) vt to understand, to comprehend

begreiflich [bə'graɪflɪç] adj understandable

begrenzen [bə'grɛntsən] vt (beschränken) to limit

Begrenztheit [bə'grɛntsthaɪt] f limitation, restriction; (fig) narrowness

Begriff [bə'grɪf] (-(e)s, -e) m concept, idea; **im ~ sein, etw zu tun** to be about to do sth; **schwer von ~** (umg) slow, dense

begriffsstutzig adj slow, dense

begründ- [bə'grʏnd] zW: **~en** vt (Gründe geben) to justify; **~et** adj well-founded, justified; **B~ung** f justification, reason

begrüßen [bə'gry:sən] vt to greet, to welcome; **Begrüßung** f greeting, welcome

begünstigen [bə'gʏnstɪgən] vt (Person) to favour; (Sache) to further, to promote

begutachten [bə'gu:tʲaxtən] vt to assess

begütert [bə'gy:tərt] adj wealthy, well-to-do

behaart [bə'ha:rt] adj hairy

behagen [bə'ha:gən] vi: **das behagt ihm nicht** he does not like it

behaglich [bə'ha:klɪç] adj comfortable, cosy; **B~keit** f comfort, cosiness

behalten [bə'haltən] (unreg) vt to keep, to retain; (im Gedächtnis) to remember

Behälter [bə'hɛltər] (-s, -) m container, receptacle

behandeln [bə'handəln] vt to treat; (Thema) to deal with; (Maschine) to handle

Behandlung f treatment; (von Maschine) handling

beharren [bə'harən] vi: **auf etw** dat **~** to stick od keep to sth

beharrlich [bə'harlɪç] adj (ausdauernd) steadfast, unwavering; (hartnäckig) tenacious, dogged; **B~keit** f steadfastness; tenacity

behaupten [bə'haʊptən] vt to claim, to assert, to maintain; (sein Recht) to defend ♦ vr to assert o.s.

Behauptung f claim, assertion

beheben [bə'he:bən] (unreg) vt to remove

behelfen [bə'hɛlfən] (unreg) vr: **sich mit etw ~** to make do with sth

behelfsmäßig adj improvised, makeshift; (vorübergehend) temporary

behelligen [bə'hɛlɪgən] vt to trouble, to bother

beherbergen [bə'hɛrbɛrgən] vt to put up, to house

beherrsch- [bə'hɛrʃ] zW: **~en** vt (Volk) to rule, to govern; (Situation) to control; (Sprache, Gefühle) to master ♦ vr to control o.s.; **~t** adj controlled; **B~ung** f rule; control; mastery

beherzigen [bə'hɛrtsɪgən] vt to take to heart

beherzt adj courageous, brave

behilflich [bə'hɪlflɪç] adj helpful; **jdm ~ sein (bei)** to help sb (with)

behindern [bə'hɪndərn] vt to hinder, to impede

Behinderte(r) f(m) disabled person

Behinderung f hindrance; (Körperbehinderung) handicap

Behörde [bə'hø:rdə] f (auch pl) authorities pl

behördlich [bə'hø:rtlɪç] adj official

behüten [bə'hy:tən] vt to guard; **jdn vor etw** dat **~** to preserve sb from sth

behutsam [bə'hu:tza:m] adj cautious, careful; **B~keit** f caution, carefulness

---
SCHLÜSSELWORT
---

bei [baɪ] präp +dat **1** (nahe bei) near; (zum Aufenthalt) at, with; (unter, zwischen) among; **bei München** near Munich; **bei uns** at our place; **beim Friseur** at the hairdresser's; **bei seinen Eltern wohnen** to live with one's parents; **bei einer Firma arbeiten** to work for a firm; **etw bei sich haben** to have sth on one; **jdn bei sich haben** to have sb with one; **bei Goethe** in Goethe; **beim Militär** in the army

2 (zeitlich) at, on; (während) during; (Zustand, Umstand) in; **bei Nacht** at night; **bei Nebel** in fog; **bei Regen** if it rains; **bei solcher Hitze** in such heat; **bei meiner Ankunft** on my arrival; **bei der Arbeit** when I'm etc working; **beim Fahren** while driving

beibehalten ['baɪbəhaltən] (unreg) vt to keep, to retain

Spelling Reform: ▲ new spelling △ old spelling (to be phased out)

beibringen ['baɪbrɪŋən] (*unreg*) *vt* (*Beweis, Zeugen*) to bring forward; (*Gründe*) to adduce; **jdm etw ~** (*lehren*) to teach sb sth; (*zu verstehen geben*) to make sb understand sth; (*zufügen*) to inflict sth on sb

Beichte ['baɪçtə] *f* confession; **b~n** *vt* to confess ♦ *vi* to go to confession

beide(s) ['baɪdə(s)] *pron, adj* both; **meine ~n Brüder** my two brothers, both my brothers; **die ersten ~n** the first two; **wir ~** we two; **einer von ~n** one of the two; **alles ~s** both (of them)

beider- ['baɪdər] *zW*: **~lei** *adj inv* of both; **~seitig** *adj* mutual, reciprocal; **~seits** *adv* mutually ♦ *präp +gen* on both sides of

beieinander [baɪaɪ'nandər] *adv* together

Beifahrer ['baɪfaːrər] *m* passenger

Beifall ['baɪfal] (**-(e)s**) *m* applause; (*Zustimmung*) approval

beifügen ['baɪfyːgən] *vt* to enclose

beige ['beːʒ] *adj* beige, fawn

beigeben ['baɪgeːbən] (*unreg*) *vt* (*zufügen*) to add; (*mitgeben*) to give ♦ *vi* (*nachgeben*) to give in

Beihilfe ['baɪhɪlfə] *f* aid, assistance; (*Studienbeihilfe*) grant; (*JUR*) aiding and abetting

beikommen ['baɪkɔmən] (*unreg*) *vi +dat* to get at; (*einem Problem*) to deal with

Beil [baɪl] (**-(e)s, -e**) *nt* axe, hatchet

Beilage ['baɪlaːgə] *f* (*Buchbeilage etc*) supplement; (*KOCH*) vegetables and potatoes *pl*

beiläufig ['baɪlɔyfɪç] *adj* casual, incidental ♦ *adv* casually, by the way

beilegen ['baɪleːgən] *vt* (*hinzufügen*) to enclose, to add; (*beimessen*) to attribute, to ascribe; (*Streit*) to settle

Beileid ['baɪlaɪt] *nt* condolence, sympathy; **herzliches ~** deepest sympathy

beiliegend ['baɪliːgənt] *adj* (*COMM*) enclosed

beim [baɪm] = **bei dem**

beimessen ['baɪmɛsən] (*unreg*) *vt* (*+dat*) to attribute (to), to ascribe (to)

Bein [baɪn] (**-(e)s, -e**) *nt* leg

beinah(e) ['baɪnaː(ə)] *adv* almost, nearly

Beinbruch *m* fracture of the leg

beinhalten [bə'ʔɪnhaltən] *vt* to contain

Beipackzettel ['baɪpaktsetəl] *m* instruction leaflet

beipflichten ['baɪpflɪçtən] *vi*: **jdm/etw ~** to agree with sb/sth

beisammen [baɪ'zamən] *adv* together; **B~sein** (**-s**) *nt* get-together

Beischlaf ['baɪʃlaːf] *m* sexual intercourse

Beisein ['baɪzaɪn] (**-s**) *nt* presence

beiseite [baɪ'zaɪtə] *adv* to one side, aside; (*stehen*) on one side, aside; **etw ~ legen** (*sparen*) to put sth by

beisetzen ['baɪzɛtsən] *vt* to bury; **Beisetzung** *f* funeral

Beisitzer ['baɪzɪtsər] (**-s, -**) *m* (*bei Prüfung*) assessor

Beispiel ['baɪʃpiːl] (**-(e)s, -e**) *nt* example; **sich +dat an jdm ein ~ nehmen** to take sb as an example; **zum ~** for example; **b~haft** *adj* exemplary; **b~los** *adj* unprecedented; **b~sweise** *adv* for instance *od* example

beißen ['baɪsən] (*unreg*) *vt, vi* to bite; (*stechen: Rauch, Säure*) to burn ♦ *vr* (*Farben*) to clash; **~d** *adj* biting, caustic; (*fig auch*) sarcastic

Beistand ['baɪʃtant] (**-(e)s, ⁻e**) *m* support, help; (*JUR*) adviser

beistehen ['baɪʃteːən] (*unreg*) *vi*: **jdm ~** to stand by sb

beisteuern ['baɪʃtɔyərn] *vt* to contribute

Beitrag ['baɪtraːk] (**-(e)s, ⁻e**) *m* contribution; (*Zahlung*) fee, subscription; (*Versicherungsbeitrag*) premium; **b~en** ['baɪtraːgən] (*unreg*) *vt, vi*: **b~en (zu)** to contribute (to); (*mithelfen*) to help (with)

beitreten ['baɪtreːtən] (*unreg*) *vi +dat* to join

Beitritt ['baɪtrɪt] *m* joining, membership

Beiwagen ['baɪvaːgən] *m* (*Motorradbeiwagen*) sidecar

beizeiten [baɪ'tsaɪtən] *adv* in time

bejahen [bə'jaːən] *vt* (*Frage*) to say yes to, to answer in the affirmative; (*gutheißen*) to agree with

bekämpfen [bə'kɛmpfən] *vt* (*Gegner*) to fight; (*Seuche*) to combat ♦ *vr* to fight;

Bekämpfung f fight, struggle

bekannt [bə'kant] adj (well-)known; (nicht fremd) familiar; **~ geben** to announce publicly; **mit jdm ~ sein** to know sb; **~ machen** to announce; **jdn mit jdm ~ machen** to introduce sb to sb; **das ist mir ~** I know that; **es/sie kommt mir ~ vor** it/she seems familiar; **B~e(r)** f(m) acquaintance; friend; **B~enkreis** m circle of friends; **~lich** adv as is well known, as you know; **B~machung** f publication; announcement; **B~schaft** f acquaintance

bekehren [bə'ke:rən] vt to convert ♦ vr to be od become converted

bekennen [bə'kɛnən] (unreg) vt to confess; (Glauben) to profess; **Farbe ~** (umg) to show where one stands

Bekenntnis [bə'kɛntnɪs] (-ses, -se) nt admission, confession; (Religion) confession, denomination

beklagen [bə'kla:gən] vt to deplore, to lament ♦ vr to complain

bekleiden [bə'klaɪdən] vt to clothe; (Amt) to occupy, to fill

Bekleidung f clothing

beklemmen [bə'klɛmən] vt to oppress

beklommen [bə'klɔmən] adj anxious, uneasy

bekommen [bə'kɔmən] (unreg) vt to get, to receive; (Kind) to have; (Zug) to catch, to get ♦ vi: **jdn ~** to agree with sb

bekömmlich [bə'kœmlɪç] adj easily digestible

bekräftigen [bə'krɛftɪgən] vt to confirm, to corroborate

bekreuzigen [bə'krɔʏtsɪgən] vr to cross o.s.

bekunden [bə'kundən] vt (sagen) to state; (zeigen) to show

belächeln [bə'lɛçəln] vt to laugh at

beladen [bə'la:dən] (unreg) vt to load

Belag [bə'la:k] (-(e)s, ⁻e) m covering, coating; (Brotbelag) spread; (Zahnbelag) tartar; (auf Zunge) fur; (Bremsbelag) lining

belagern [bə'la:gərn] vt to besiege; **Belagerung** f siege

Belang [bə'laŋ] (-(e)s) m importance; **~e** pl (Interessen) interests, concerns; **b~los** adj trivial, unimportant

belassen [bə'lasən] (unreg) vt (in Zustand, Glauben) to leave; (in Stellung) to retain

belasten [bə'lastən] vt to burden; (fig: bedrücken) to trouble, to worry; (COMM: Konto) to debit; (JUR) to incriminate ♦ vr to weigh o.s. down; (JUR) to incriminate o.s.; **~d** adj (JUR) incriminating

belästigen [bə'lɛstɪgən] vt to annoy, to pester; **Belästigung** f annoyance, pestering

Belastung [bə'lastuŋ] f load; (fig: Sorge etc) weight; (COMM) charge, debit(ing); (JUR) incriminatory evidence

belaufen [bə'laufən] (unreg) vr: **sich ~ auf** +AKK to amount to

beleben [bə'le:bən] vt (anregen) to liven up; (Konjunktur, jds Hoffnungen) to stimulate ♦ vr (Augen) to light up; (Stadt) to come to life

belebt [bə'le:pt] adj (Straße) busy

Beleg [bə'le:k] (-(e)s, -e) m (COMM) receipt; (Beweis) documentary evidence, proof; (Beispiel) example; **b~en** vt to cover; (Kuchen, Brot) to spread; (Platz) to reserve, to book; (Kurs, Vorlesung) to register for; (beweisen) to verify, to prove; (MIL: mit Bomben) to bomb; **~schaft** f personnel, staff; **b~t** adj: **b~tes Brot** open sandwich

belehren [bə'le:rən] vt to instruct, to teach; **Belehrung** f instruction

beleibt [bə'laɪpt] adj stout, corpulent

beleidigen [bə'laɪdɪgən] vt to insult, to offend; **Beleidigung** f insult; (JUR) slander, libel

beleuchten [bə'lɔʏçtən] vt to light, to illuminate; (fig) to throw light on

Beleuchtung f lighting, illumination

Belgien ['bɛlgiən] nt Belgium; **Belgier(in)** m(f) Belgian; **belgisch** adj Belgian

belichten [bə'lɪçtən] vt to expose

Belichtung f exposure; **~smesser** m exposure meter

Belieben [bə'li:bən] nt: **(ganz) nach ~** (just) as you wish

beliebig [bə'li:bɪç] adj any you like ♦ adv as you like; **ein ~es Thema** any subject you like od want; **~ viel/viele** as much/many as you like

beliebt [bə'li:pt] *adj* popular; **sich bei jdm ~ machen** to make o.s. popular with sb; **B~heit** *f* popularity

beliefern [bə'li:fərn] *vt* to supply

bellen ['bɛlən] *vi* to bark

belohnen [bə'lo:nən] *vt* to reward; **Belohnung** *f* reward

Belüftung [bə'lʏftʊŋ] *f* ventilation

belügen [bə'ly:gən] (*unreg*) *vt* to lie to, to deceive

belustigen [bə'lʊstɪgən] *vt* to amuse; **Belustigung** *f* amusement

bemalen [bə'ma:lən] *vt* to paint

bemängeln [bə'mɛŋəln] *vt* to criticize

bemerk- [bə'mɛrk] *zW:* **~bar** *adj* perceptible, noticeable; **sich ~bar machen** (*Person*) to make od get o.s. noticed; (*Unruhe*) to become noticeable; **~en** *vt* (*wahrnehmen*) to notice, to observe; (*sagen*) to say, to mention; **~enswert** *adj* remarkable, noteworthy; **B~ung** *f* remark; (*schriftlich auch*) note

bemitleiden [bə'mɪtlaɪdən] *vt* to pity

bemühen [bə'my:ən] *vr* to take trouble od pains; **Bemühung** *f* trouble, pains *pl*, effort

benachbart [bə'naxba:rt] *adj* neighbouring

benachrichtigen [bə'na:xrɪçtɪgən] *vt* to inform; **Benachrichtigung** *f* notification, information

benachteiligen [bə'na:xtaɪlɪgən] *vt* to put at a disadvantage; to victimize

benehmen [bə'ne:mən] (*unreg*) *vr* to behave; **B~** (**-s**) *nt* behaviour

beneiden [bə'naɪdən] *vt* to envy; **~swert** *adj* enviable

benennen [bə'nɛnən] (*unreg*) *vt* to name

Bengel ['bɛŋəl] (**-s, -**) *m* (little) rascal od rogue

benommen [bə'nɔmən] *adj* dazed

benoten [bə'no:tən] *vt* to mark

benötigen [bə'nø:tɪgən] *vt* to need

benutzen [bə'nʊtsən] *vt* to use

Benutzer (**-s, -**) *m* user

Benutzung *f* utilization, use

Benzin [bɛnt'si:n] (**-s, -e**) *nt* (*AUT*) petrol

(*BRIT*), gas(oline) (*US*); **~kanister** *m* petrol (*BRIT*) od gas (*US*) can; **~tank** *m* petrol tank (*BRIT*), gas tank (*US*); **~uhr** *f* petrol (*BRIT*) od gas (*US*) gauge

beobachten [bə'|o:baxtən] *vt* to observe; **Beobachter** (**-s, -**) *m* observer; (*eines Unfalls*) witness; (*PRESSE, TV*) correspondent; **Beobachtung** *f* observation

bepacken [bə'pakən] *vt* to load, to pack

bequem [bə'kve:m] *adj* comfortable; (*Ausrede*) convenient; (*Person*) lazy, indolent; **~en** *vr*: **sich ~en(, etw zu tun)** to condescend (to do sth); **B~lichkeit** [-'lɪçkaɪt] *f* convenience, comfort; (*Faulheit*) laziness, indolence

beraten [bə'ra:tən] (*unreg*) *vt* to advise; (*besprechen*) to discuss, to debate ♦ *vr* to consult; **gut/schlecht ~ sein** to be well/ill advised; **sich ~ lassen** to get advice

Berater (**-s, -**) *m* adviser

Beratung *f* advice; (*Besprechung*) consultation; **~sstelle** *f* advice centre

berauben [bə'raubən] *vt* to rob

berechenbar [bə'rɛçənba:r] *adj* calculable

berechnen [bə'rɛçnən] *vt* to calculate; (*COMM: anrechnen*) to charge; **~d** *adj* (*Mensch*) calculating, scheming

Berechnung *f* calculation; (*COMM*) charge

berechtigen [bə'rɛçtɪgən] *vt* to entitle; to authorize; (*fig*) to justify

berechtigt [bə'rɛçtɪçt] *adj* justifiable, justified

Berechtigung *f* authorization; (*fig*) justification

bereden [bə're:dən] *vt* (*besprechen*) to discuss; (*überreden*) to persuade ♦ *vr* to discuss

Bereich [bə'raɪç] (**-(e)s, -e**) *m* (*Bezirk*) area; (*PHYS*) range; (*Ressort, Gebiet*) sphere

bereichern [bə'raɪçərn] *vt* to enrich ♦ *vr* to get rich

bereinigen [bə'raɪnɪgən] *vt* to settle

bereisen [bə'raɪzən] *vt* (*Land*) to travel through

bereit [bə'raɪt] *adj* ready, prepared; **zu etw ~ sein** to be ready for sth; **sich ~ erklären** to declare o.s. willing; **~en** *vt* to prepare, to make ready; (*Kummer, Freude*) to cause;

~**halten** (*unreg*) *vt* to keep in readiness;
~**legen** *vt* to lay out; ~**machen** *vt, vr* to
prepare, to get ready; ~**s** *adv* already;
B~schaft *f* readiness; (*Polizei*) alert;
B~schaftsdienst *m* emergency service;
~**stehen** (*unreg*) *vi* (*Person*) to be prepared;
(*Ding*) to be ready; ~**stellen** *vt* (*Kisten,
Pakete etc*) to put ready; (*Geld etc*) to make
available; (*Truppen, Maschinen*) to put at the
ready; ~**willig** *adj* willing, ready;
B~willigkeit *f* willingness, readiness

bereuen [bə'rɔʏən] *vt* to regret

Berg [bɛrk] **(-(e)s, -e)** *m* mountain; hill;
b~ab *adv* downhill; ~**arbeiter** *m* miner;
b~auf *adv* uphill; ~**bahn** *f* mountain
railway; ~**bau** *m* mining

bergen ['bɛrgən] (*unreg*) *vt* (*retten*) to rescue;
(*Ladung*) to salvage; (*enthalten*) to contain

Berg- *zW*: ~**führer** *m* mountain guide;
~**gipfel** *m* peak, summit; **b~ig** ['bɛrgɪç] *adj*
mountainous; hilly; ~**kette** *f* mountain
range; ~**mann** (*pl* ~**leute**) *m* miner;
~**rettungsdienst** *m* mountain rescue
team; ~**rutsch** *m* landslide; ~**steigen** *nt*
mountaineering; ~**steiger(in)** (**-s, -**) *m(f)*
mountaineer, climber; ~**tour** *f* mountain
climb

Bergung ['bɛrgʊŋ] *f* (*von Menschen*) rescue;
(*von Material*) recovery; (*NAUT*) salvage

Berg- *zW*: ~**wacht** *f* mountain rescue
service; ~**wanderung** *f* hike in the
mountains; ~**werk** *nt* mine

Bericht [bə'rɪçt] **(-(e)s, -e)** *m* report,
account; **b~en** *vt, vi* to report; ~**erstatter**
(**-s, -**) *m* reporter; (newspaper)
correspondent

berichtigen [bə'rɪçtɪgən] *vt* to correct;
Berichtigung *f* correction

Bernstein ['bɛrnʃtaɪn] *m* amber

bersten ['bɛrstən] (*unreg*) *vi* to burst, to split

berüchtigt [bə'rʏçtɪçt] *adj* notorious,
infamous

berücksichtigen [bə'rʏkzɪçtɪgən] *vt* to
consider, to bear in mind;
Berücksichtigung *f* consideration

Beruf [bə'ru:f] **(-(e)s, -e)** *m* occupation,
profession; (*Gewerbe*) trade; **b~en** (*unreg*)

vt: **b~en zu** to appoint to ♦ *vr*: **sich auf
jdn/etw b~en** to refer *od* appeal to sb/sth
♦ *adj* competent, qualified; **b~lich** *adj*
professional

Berufs- *zW*: ~**ausbildung** *f* job training;
~**berater** *m* careers adviser; ~**beratung** *f*
vocational guidance; ~**geheimnis** *nt*
professional secret; ~**leben** *nt* professional
life; ~**schule** *f* vocational *od* trade school;
~**sportler** [-ʃpɔrtlər] *m* professional
(sportsman); **b~tätig** *adj* employed;
b~unfähig *adj* unfit for work; ~**verkehr** *m*
rush-hour traffic

Berufung *f* vocation, calling; (*Ernennung*)
appointment; (*JUR*) appeal; ~ **einlegen** to
appeal

beruhen [bə'ru:ən] *vi*: **auf etw** *dat* ~ to be
based on sth; **etw auf sich** ~ **lassen** to
leave sth at that

beruhigen [bə'ru:ɪgən] *vt* to calm, to pacify,
to soothe ♦ *vr* (*Mensch*) to calm (o.s.)
down; (*Situation*) to calm down

Beruhigung *f* soothing; (*der Nerven*)
calming; **zu jds** ~ (in order) to reassure sb;
~**smittel** *nt* sedative

berühmt [bə'ry:mt] *adj* famous; **B~heit** *f*
(*Ruf*) fame; (*Mensch*) celebrity

berühren [bə'ry:rən] *vt* to touch;
(*gefühlsmäßig bewegen*) to affect; (*flüchtig
erwähnen*) to mention, to touch on ♦ *vr* to
meet, to touch

Berührung *f* contact

besagen [bə'za:gən] *vt* to mean

besänftigen [bə'zɛnftɪgən] *vt* to soothe, to
calm

Besatz [bə'zats] **(-es, ⁺e)** *m* trimming,
edging

Besatzung *f* garrison; (*NAUT, AVIAT*) crew

Besatzungsmacht *f* occupying power

beschädigen [bə'ʃɛːdɪgən] *vt* to damage;
Beschädigung *f* damage; (*Stelle*)
damaged spot

beschaffen [bə'ʃafən] *vt* to get, to acquire
♦ *adj*: **das ist so ~, dass** that is such that;
B~heit *f* (*von Mensch*) constitution, nature

Beschaffung *f* acquisition

beschäftigen [bə'ʃɛftɪgən] *vt* to occupy;

(*beruflich*) to employ ♦ *vr* to occupy *od* concern o.s.

beschäftigt *adj* busy, occupied

Beschäftigung *f* (*Beruf*) employment; (*Tätigkeit*) occupation; (*Befassen*) concern

beschämen [bə'ʃɛ:mən] *vt* to put to shame; ~**d** *adj* shameful; (*Hilfsbereitschaft*) shaming

beschämt *adj* ashamed

Bescheid [bə'ʃaıt] (**-(e)s, -e**) *m* information; (*Weisung*) directions *pl*; ~ **wissen** (**über** +*akk*) to be well-informed (about); **ich weiß** ~ I know; **jdm** ~ **geben** *od* **sagen** to let sb know

bescheiden [bə'ʃaıdən] (*unreg*) *vr* to content o.s. ♦ *adj* modest; **B~heit** *f* modesty

bescheinen [bə'ʃaınən] (*unreg*) *vt* to shine on

bescheinigen [bə'ʃaınıgən] *vt* to certify; (*bestätigen*) to acknowledge

Bescheinigung *f* certificate; (*Quittung*) receipt

beschenken [bə'ʃɛŋkən] *vt*: **jdn mit etw** ~ to give sb sth as a present

bescheren [bə'ʃe:rən] *vt*: **jdm etw** ~ to give sb sth as a Christmas present; **jdn** ~ to give Christmas presents to sb

Bescherung *f* giving of Christmas presents; (*umg*) mess

beschildern [bə'ʃıldərn] *vt* to put signs/a sign on

beschimpfen [bə'ʃımpfən] *vt* to abuse; **Beschimpfung** *f* abuse; insult

Beschlag [bə'ʃla:k] (**-(e)s, ⁼e**) *m* (*Metallband*) fitting; (*auf Fenster*) condensation; (*auf Metall*) tarnish; finish; (*Hufeisen*) horseshoe; **jdn/etw in** ~ **nehmen** *od* **mit** ~ **belegen** to monopolize sb/sth; **b~en** [bə'ʃla:gən] (*unreg*) *vt* to cover; (*Pferd*) to shoe ♦ *vi*, *vr* (*Fenster etc*) to mist over; **b~en sein** (**in** *od* **auf** +*dat*) to be well versed (in); **b~nahmen** *vt* to seize, to confiscate; to requisition; ~**nahmung** *f* confiscation, sequestration

beschleunigen [bə'ʃlɔynıgən] *vt* to accelerate, to speed up ♦ *vi* (*AUT*) to accelerate; **Beschleunigung** *f* acceleration

beschließen [bə'ʃli:sən] (*unreg*) *vt* to decide on; (*beenden*) to end, to close

Beschluss ▲ [bə'ʃlʊs] (**-es, ⁼e**) *m* decision, conclusion; (*Ende*) conclusion, end

beschmutzen [bə'ʃmʊtsən] *vt* to dirty, to soil

beschönigen [bə'ʃø:nıgən] *vt* to gloss over

beschränken [bə'ʃrɛŋkən] *vt*, *vr* (**sich**) ~ (**auf** +*akk*) to limit *od* restrict (o.s.) (to)

beschränk- *zW*: ~**t** *adj* confined, restricted; (*Mensch*) limited, narrow-minded; **B~ung** *f* limitation

beschreiben [bə'ʃraıbən] (*unreg*) *vt* to describe; (*Papier*) to write on

Beschreibung *f* description

beschriften [bə'ʃrıftən] *vt* to mark, to label; **Beschriftung** *f* lettering

beschuldigen [bə'ʃʊldıgən] *vt* to accuse; **Beschuldigung** *f* accusation

Beschuss ▲ [bə'ʃʊs] *m*: **jdn/etw unter** ~ **nehmen** (*MIL*) to open fire on sb/sth

beschützen [bə'ʃʏtsən] *vt*: ~ (**vor** +*dat*) to protect (from); **Beschützer** (**-s, -**) *m* protector

Beschwerde [bə'ʃve:rdə] *f* complaint; (*Mühe*) hardship; ~**n** *pl* (*Leiden*) trouble

beschweren [bə'ʃve:rən] *vt* to weight down; (*fig*) to burden ♦ *vr* to complain

beschwerlich *adj* tiring, exhausting

beschwichtigen [bə'ʃvıçtıgən] *vt* to soothe, to pacify

beschwindeln [bə'ʃvındəln] *vt* (*betrügen*) to cheat; (*belügen*) to fib to

beschwingt [bə'ʃvıŋt] *adj* in high spirits

beschwipst [bə'ʃvıpst] (*umg*) *adj* tipsy

beschwören [bə'ʃvø:rən] (*unreg*) *vt* (*Aussage*) to swear to; (*anflehen*) to implore; (*Geister*) to conjure up

beseitigen [bə'zaıtıgən] *vt* to remove; **Beseitigung** *f* removal

Besen ['be:zən] (**-s, -**) *m* broom; ~**stiel** *m* broomstick

besessen [bə'zɛsən] *adj* possessed

besetz- [bə'zɛts] *zW*: ~**en** *vt* (*Haus, Land*) to occupy; (*Platz*) to take, to fill; (*Posten*) to fill; (*Rolle*) to cast; (*mit Edelsteinen*) to set; ~**t** *adj* full; (*TEL*) engaged, busy; (*Platz*) taken;

(*WC*) engaged; **B~tzeichen** *nt* engaged tone; **B~ung** *f* occupation; filling; (*von Rolle*) casting; (*die Schauspieler*) cast

besichtigen [bəˈzɪçtɪgən] *vt* to visit, to have a look at; **Besichtigung** *f* visit

besiegen [bəˈziːgən] *vt* to defeat, to overcome

besinn- [bəˈzɪn] *zW:* **~en** (*unreg*) *vr* (*nachdenken*) to think, to reflect; (*erinnern*) to remember; **sich anders ~en** to change one's mind; **B~ung** *f* consciousness; **zur B~ung kommen** to recover consciousness; (*fig*) to come to one's senses; **~ungslos** *adj* unconscious

Besitz [bəˈzɪts] **(-es)** *m* possession; (*Eigentum*) property; **b~en** (*unreg*) *vt* to possess, to own; (*Eigenschaft*) to have; **~er(in)** **(-s, -)** *m(f)* owner, proprietor; **~ergreifung** *f* occupation, seizure

besoffen [bəˈzɔfən] (*umg*) *adj* drunk, stoned

besohlen [bəˈzoːlən] *vt* to sole

Besoldung [bəˈzɔldʊŋ] *f* salary, pay

besondere(r, s) [bəˈzɔndərə(r, s)] *adj* special; (*eigen*) particular; (*gesondert*) separate; (*eigentümlich*) peculiar

Besonderheit [bəˈzɔndərhaɪt] *f* peculiarity

besonders [bəˈzɔndərs] *adv* especially, particularly; (*getrennt*) separately

besonnen [bəˈzɔnən] *adj* sensible, level-headed

besorg- [bəˈzɔrg] *zW:* **~en** *vt* (*beschaffen*) to acquire; (*kaufen auch*) to purchase; (*erledigen: Geschäfte*) to deal with; (*sich kümmern um*) to take care of; **B~nis (-, -se)** *f* anxiety, concern; **~t** [bəˈzɔrçt] *adj* anxious, worried; **B~ung** *f* acquisition; (*Kauf*) purchase

bespielen [bəˈʃpiːlən] *vt* to record

bespitzeln [bəˈʃpɪtsəln] *vt* to spy on

besprechen [bəˈʃprɛçən] (*unreg*) *vt* to discuss; (*Tonband etc*) to record, to speak onto; (*Buch*) to review ♦ *vr* to discuss, to consult; **Besprechung** *f* meeting, discussion; (*von Buch*) review

besser [ˈbɛsər] *adj* better; **es geht ihm ~** he is feeling better; **~n** *vt* to make better, to improve ♦ *vr* to improve; (*Menschen*) to

reform; **B~ung** *f* improvement; **gute B~ung!** get well soon!; **B~wisser (-s, -)** *m* know-all

Bestand [bəˈʃtant] **(-(e)s, ⸚e)** *m* (*Fortbestehen*) duration, stability; (*Kassenbestand*) amount, balance; (*Vorrat*) stock; **~ haben, von ~ sein** to last long, to endure

beständig [bəˈʃtɛndɪç] *adj* (*ausdauernd: auch fig*) constant; (*Wetter*) settled; (*Stoffe*) resistant; (*Klagen etc*) continual

Bestandsaufnahme [bəˈʃtantsaʊfnaːmə] *f* stocktaking

Bestandteil *m* part, component; (*Zutat*) ingredient

bestärken [bəˈʃtɛrkən] *vt:* **jdn in etw** *dat* **~** to strengthen *od* confirm sb in sth

bestätigen [bəˈʃtɛːtɪgən] *vt* to confirm; (*anerkennen, COMM*) to acknowledge; **Bestätigung** *f* confirmation; acknowledgement

bestatten [bəˈʃtatən] *vt* to bury

Bestattung *f* funeral

Bestattungsinstitut *nt* funeral director's

bestaunen [bəˈʃtaʊnən] *vt* to marvel at, gaze at in wonder

beste(r, s) [ˈbɛstə(r, s)] *adj* best; **so ist es am ~n** it's best that way; **am ~n gehst du gleich** you'd better go at once; **jdn zum B~n haben** to pull sb's leg; **einen Witz** *etc* **zum B~n geben** to tell a joke *etc*; **aufs B~** *od* **~** in the best possible way; **zu jds B~n** for the benefit of sb

bestechen [bəˈʃtɛçən] (*unreg*) *vt* to bribe; **bestechlich** *adj* corruptible; **Bestechung** *f* bribery, corruption

Besteck [bəˈʃtɛk] **(-(e)s, -e)** *nt* knife, fork and spoon, cutlery; (*MED*) set of instruments

bestehen [bəˈʃteːən] (*unreg*) *vi* to be; to exist; (*andauern*) to last ♦ *vt* (*Kampf, Probe, Prüfung*) to pass; **~ auf** +*dat* to insist on; **~ aus** to consist of

bestehlen [bəˈʃteːlən] (*unreg*) *vt:* **jdn (um etw) ~** to rob sb (of sth)

besteigen [bəˈʃtaɪgən] (*unreg*) *vt* to climb, to ascend; (*Pferd*) to mount; (*Thron*) to ascend

Bestell- [bə'ʃtɛl] *zW:* **~buch** *nt* order book; **b~en** *vt* to order; (*kommen lassen*) to arrange to see; (*nominieren*) to name; (*Acker*) to cultivate; (*Grüße, Auftrag*) to pass on; **~formular** *nt* order form; **~nummer** *f* order code; **~ung** *f* (*COMM*) order; (*~en*) ordering

bestenfalls ['bɛstən'fals] *adv* at best

bestens ['bɛstəns] *adv* very well

besteuern [bə'ʃtɔʏɐrn] *vt* (*jdn, Waren*) to tax

Bestie ['bɛstiə] *f* (*auch fig*) beast

bestimm- [bə'ʃtɪm] *zW:* **~en** *vt* (*Regeln*) to lay down; (*Tag, Ort*) to fix; (*beherrschen*) to characterize; (*vorsehen*) to mean; (*ernennen*) to appoint; (*definieren*) to define; (*veranlassen*) to induce; **~t** *adj* (*entschlossen*) firm; (*gewiss*) certain, definite; (*Artikel*) definite ♦ *adv* (*gewiss*) definitely, for sure; **suchen Sie etwas B~tes?** are you looking for something in particular?; **B~theit** *f* firmness; certainty; **B~ung** *f* (*Verordnung*) regulation; (*Festsetzen*) determining; (*Verwendungszweck*) purpose; (*Schicksal*) fate; (*Definition*) definition; **B~ungsland** *nt* (country of) destination; **B~ungsort** *m* (place of) destination

Bestleistung *f* best performance

bestmöglich *adj* best possible

bestrafen [bə'ʃtraːfən] *vt* to punish; **Bestrafung** *f* punishment

bestrahlen [bə'ʃtraːlən] *vt* to shine on; (*MED*) to treat with X-rays

Bestrahlung *f* (*MED*) X-ray treatment, radiotherapy

Bestreben [bə'ʃtreːbən] (**-s**) *nt* endeavour, effort

bestreiten [bə'ʃtraɪtən] (*unreg*) *vt* (*abstreiten*) to dispute; (*finanzieren*) to pay for, to finance

bestreuen [bə'ʃtrɔʏən] *vt* to sprinkle, to dust; (*Straße*) to grit

bestürmen [bə'ʃtʏrmən] *vt* (*mit Fragen, Bitten etc*) to overwhelm, to swamp

bestürzend [bə'ʃtʏrtsənd] *adj* (*Nachrichten*) disturbing

bestürzt [bə'ʃtʏrtst] *adj* dismayed

Bestürzung *f* consternation

Besuch [bə'zuːx] (**-(e)s, -e**) *m* visit; (*Person*) visitor; **einen ~ machen bei jdm** to pay sb a visit *od* call; **~ haben** to have visitors; **bei jdm auf** *od* **zu ~ sein** to be visiting sb; **b~en** *vt* to visit; (*SCH etc*) to attend; **gut b~t** well-attended; **~er(in)** (**-s, -**) *m(f)* visitor, guest; **~szeit** *f* visiting hours *pl*

betätigen [bə'tɛːtɪgən] *vt* (*bedienen*) to work, to operate ♦ *vr* to involve o.s.; **sich als etw ~** to work as sth

Betätigung *f* activity; (*beruflich*) occupation; (*TECH*) operation

betäuben [bə'tɔʏbən] *vt* to stun; (*fig: Gewissen*) to still; (*MED*) to anaesthetize

Betäubung *f* (*Narkose*): **örtliche ~** local anaesthetic

Betäubungsmittel *nt* anaesthetic

Bete ['beːtə] *f*: **Rote ~** beetroot (*BRIT*), beet (*US*)

beteilig- [bə'taɪlɪg] *zW:* **~en** *vr*: **sich ~en (an** +*dat*) to take part (in), to participate (in), to share (in); (*an Geschäft: finanziell*) to have a share (in) ♦ *vt*: **jdn ~en (an** +*dat*) to give sb a share *od* interest (in); **B~te(r)** *f(m)* (*Mitwirkender*) partner; (*finanziell*) shareholder; **B~ung** *f* participation; (*Anteil*) share, interest; (*Besucherzahl*) attendance

beten ['beːtən] *vt, vi* to pray

beteuern [bə'tɔʏɐrn] *vt* to assert; (*Unschuld*) to protest

Beton [be'tõ:] (**-s, -s**) *m* concrete

betonen [bə'toːnən] *vt* to stress

betonieren [beto'niːrən] *vt* to concrete

Betonung *f* stress, emphasis

betr. *abk* (= *betrifft*) re

Betracht [bə'traxt] *m*: **in ~ kommen** to be considered *od* relevant; **etw in ~ ziehen** to take sth into consideration; **außer ~ bleiben** not to be considered; **b~en** *vt* to look at; (*fig*) to look at, to consider; **~er(in)** (**-s, -**) *m(f)* observer

beträchtlich [bə'trɛçtlɪç] *adj* considerable

Betrachtung *f* (*Ansehen*) examination; (*Erwägung*) consideration

Betrag [bə'traːk] (**-(e)s, ⁺e**) *m* amount; **b~en** (*unreg*) *vt* to amount to ♦ *vr* to behave; **~en** (**-s**) *nt* behaviour

Betreff *m*: ~ **Ihr Schreiben vom ...** re your letter of ...

betreffen [bə'trɛfən] (*unreg*) *vt* to concern, to affect; **was mich betrifft** as for me; ~**d** *adj* relevant, in question

betreffs [bə'trɛfs] *präp +gen* concerning, regarding; (*COMM*) re

betreiben [bə'traɪbən] (*unreg*) *vt* (*ausüben*) to practise; (*Politik*) to follow; (*Studien*) to pursue; (*vorantreiben*) to push ahead; (*TECH: antreiben*) to drive

betreten [bə'tre:tən] (*unreg*) *vt* to enter; (*Bühne etc*) to step onto ♦ *adj* embarrassed; **B~ verboten** keep off/out

Betreuer(in) [bə'trɔʏər(ɪn)] (**-s, -**) *m(f)* (*einer Person*) caretaker; (*eines Gebäudes, Arbeitsgebiets*) caretaker; (*SPORT*) coach

Betreuung *f* care

Betrieb [bə'tri:p] (**-(e)s, -e**) *m* (*Firma*) firm, concern; (*Anlage*) plant; (*Tätigkeit*) operation; (*Treiben*) traffic; **außer ~ sein** to be out of order; **in ~ sein** to be in operation

Betriebs- *zW*: ~**ausflug** *m* works outing; **b~bereit** *adj* operational; **b~fähig** *adj* in working order; ~**ferien** *pl* company holidays (*BRIT*), company vacation *sg* (*US*); ~**klima** *nt* (working) atmosphere; ~**kosten** *pl* running costs; ~**rat** *m* workers' council; **b~sicher** *adj* safe (to operate); ~**störung** *f* breakdown; ~**system** *nt* (*COMPUT*) operating system; ~**unfall** *m* industrial accident; ~**wirtschaft** *f* economics

betrinken [bə'trɪŋkən] (*unreg*) *vr* to get drunk

betroffen [bə'trɔfən] *adj* (*bestürzt*) full of consternation; **von etw ~ werden** *od* **sein** to be affected by sth

betrüben [bə'try:bən] *vt* to grieve

betrübt [bə'try:pt] *adj* sorrowful, grieved

Betrug [bə'tru:k] (**-(e)s**) *m* deception; (*JUR*) fraud

betrügen [bə'try:gən] (*unreg*) *vt* to cheat; (*JUR*) to defraud; (*Ehepartner*) to be unfaithful to ♦ *vr* to deceive o.s.

Betrüger (**-s, -**) *m* cheat, deceiver; **b~isch** *adj* deceitful; (*JUR*) fraudulent

betrunken [bə'trʊŋkən] *adj* drunk

Bett [bɛt] (**-(e)s, -en**) *nt* bed; **ins** *od* **zu ~ gehen** to go to bed; ~**bezug** *m* duvet cover; ~**decke** *f* blanket; (*Daunenbett*) quilt; (*Überwurf*) bedspread

Bettel- ['bɛtəl] *zW*: **b~arm** *adj* very poor, destitute; ~**ei** [bɛtə'laɪ] *f* begging; **b~n** *vi* to beg

bettlägerig ['bɛtlɛːgərɪç] *adj* bedridden

Bettlaken *nt* sheet

Bettler(in) ['bɛtlər(ɪn)] (**-s, -**) *m(f)* beggar

Bett- *zW*: ~**tuch** ▲ *nt* sheet; ~**vorleger** *m* bedside rug; ~**wäsche** *f* bed linen; ~**zeug** *nt* bed linen *pl*

beugen ['bɔʏgən] *vt* to bend; (*GRAM*) to inflect ♦ *vr* (*sich fügen*) to bow

Beule ['bɔʏlə] *f* bump, swelling

beunruhigen [bə'ʊnru:ɪgən] *vt* to disturb, to alarm ♦ *vr* to become worried

Beunruhigung *f* worry, alarm

beurlauben [bə'u:rlaʊbən] *vt* to give leave *od* a holiday to (*BRIT*), to grant vacation time to (*US*)

beurteilen [bə'ʊrtaɪlən] *vt* to judge; (*Buch etc*) to review

Beurteilung *f* judgement; review; (*Note*) mark

Beute ['bɔʏtə] (**-**) *f* booty, loot

Beutel (**-s, -**) *m* bag; (*Geldbeutel*) purse; (*Tabakbeutel*) pouch

Bevölkerung [bə'tœlkərʊŋ] *f* population

bevollmächtigen [bə'fɔlmɛçtɪgən] *vt* to authorize

Bevollmächtigte(r) *f(m)* authorized agent

bevor [bə'fo:r] *konj* before; ~**munden** *vt insep* to treat like a child; ~**stehen** (*unreg*) *vi*: **(jdm) ~stehen** to be in store (for sb); ~**stehend** *adj* imminent, approaching; ~**zugen** *vt insep* to prefer

bewachen [bə'vaxən] *vt* to watch, to guard

Bewachung *f* (*Bewachen*) guarding; (*Leute*) guard, watch

bewaffnen [bə'vafnən] *vt* to arm

Bewaffnung *f* (*Vorgang*) arming; (*Ausrüstung*) armament, arms *pl*

bewahren [bə'va:rən] *vt* to keep; **jdn vor jdm/etw ~** to save sb from sb/sth

Spelling Reform: ▲ *new spelling* △ *old spelling (to be phased out)*

bewähren [bə'vɛːrən] *vr* to prove o.s.;
(*Maschine*) to prove its worth
bewahrheiten [bə'vaːrhaɪtən] *vr* to come
true
bewährt *adj* reliable
Bewährung *f* (*JUR*) probation
bewältigen [bə'vɛltɪgən] *vt* to overcome;
(*Arbeit*) to finish; (*Portion*) to manage
bewandert [bə'vandərt] *adj* expert,
knowledgeable
bewässern [bə'vɛsərn] *vt* to irrigate
Bewässerung *f* irrigation
bewegen [bə'veːgən] *vt, vr* to move; **jdn zu
etw ~** to induce sb to do sth; **~d** *adj*
touching, moving
Beweg- [bə'veːk] *zW:* **~grund** *m* motive;
b~lich *adj* movable, mobile; (*flink*) quick;
b~t *adj* (*Leben*) eventful; (*Meer*) rough;
(*ergriffen*) touched
Bewegung *f* movement, motion; (*innere*)
emotion; (*körperlich*) exercise; **~sfreiheit** *f*
freedom of movement; (*fig*) freedom of
action; **b~ungslos** *adj* motionless
Beweis [bə'vaɪs] (**-es, -e**) *m* proof; (*Zeichen*)
sign; **b~en** [-zən] (*unreg*) *vt* to prove;
(*zeigen*) to show; **~mittel** *nt* evidence
Bewerb- [bə'vɛrb] *zW:* **b~en** (*unreg*) *vr* to
apply (for); **~er(in)** (**-s, -**) *m(f)* applicant;
~ung *f* application
bewerkstelligen [bə'vɛrkʃtɛlɪgən] *vt* to
manage, to accomplish
bewerten [bə'veːrtən] *vt* to assess
bewilligen [bə'vɪlɪgən] *vt* to grant, to allow
Bewilligung *f* granting
bewirken [bə'vɪrkən] *vt* to cause, to bring
about
bewirten [bə'vɪrtən] *vt* to feed, to entertain
(to a meal)
bewirtschaften [bə'vɪrtʃaftən] *vt* to
manage
Bewirtung *f* hospitality
bewog *etc* [bə'voːk] *vb siehe* **bewegen**
bewohn- [bə'voːn] *zW:* **~bar** *adj* habitable;
~en *vt* to inhabit, to live in; **B~er(in)** (**-s,
-**) *m(f)* inhabitant; (*von Haus*) resident
bewölkt [bə'vœlkt] *adj* cloudy, overcast
Bewölkung *f* clouds *pl*

Bewunder- [bə'vʊndər] *zW:* **~er (-s, -)** *m*
admirer; **b~n** *vt* to admire; **b~nswert** *adj*
admirable, wonderful; **~ung** *f* admiration
bewusst ▲ [bə'vʊst] *adj* conscious;
(*absichtlich*) deliberate; **sich** *dat* **einer
Sache** *gen* **~ sein** to be aware of sth; **~los**
adj unconscious; **B~losigkeit** *f*
unconsciousness; **B~sein** *nt* consciousness;
bei B~sein conscious
bezahlen [bə'tsaːlən] *vt* to pay for
Bezahlung *f* payment
bezaubern [bə'tsaʊbərn] *vt* to enchant, to
charm
bezeichnen [bə'tsaɪçnən] *vt* (*kennzeichnen*)
to mark; (*nennen*) to call; (*beschreiben*) to
describe; (*zeigen*) to show, to indicate; **~d**
adj: **~d (für)** characteristic (of), typical (of)
Bezeichnung *f* (*Zeichen*) mark, sign;
(*Beschreibung*) description
bezeugen [bə'tsɔʏgən] *vt* to testify to
Bezichtigung [bə'tsɪçtɪguŋ] *f* accusation
beziehen [bə'tsiːən] (*unreg*) *vt* (*mit Überzug*)
to cover; (*Bett*) to make; (*Haus, Position*) to
move into; (*Standpunkt*) to take up;
(*erhalten*) to receive; (*Zeitung*) to subscribe
to, to take ♦ *vr* (*Himmel*) to cloud over; **etw
auf jdn/etw ~** to relate sth to sb/sth; **sich
~ auf** +*akk* to refer to
Beziehung *f* (*Verbindung*) connection;
(*Zusammenhang*) relation; (*Verhältnis*)
relationship; (*Hinsicht*) respect; **~en haben**
(*vorteilhaft*) to have connections *od*
contacts; **b~sweise** *adv* or; (*genauer gesagt
auch*) that is, or rather
Bezirk [bə'tsɪrk] (**-(e)s, -e**) *m* district
Bezug [bə'tsuːk] (**-(e)s, ⁻e**) *m* (*Hülle*)
covering; (*COMM*) ordering; (*Gehalt*)
income, salary; (*Beziehung*): **~ (zu)**
relation(ship) (to); **in ~ auf** +*akk* with
reference to; **~ nehmen auf** +*akk* to refer
to
bezüglich [bə'tsyːklɪç] *präp* +*gen* concerning,
referring to ♦ *adj* (*GRAM*) relative; **auf etw**
akk **~** relating to sth
bezwecken [bə'tsvɛkən] *vt* to aim at
bezweifeln [bə'tsvaɪfəln] *vt* to doubt, to
query

Rechtschreibreform: ▲ neue Schreibung △ alte Schreibung (auslaufend)

BH *m abk von* **Büstenhalter**

Bhf. *abk* (= *Bahnhof*) station

Bibel ['biːbəl] (-, -n) *f* Bible

Biber ['biːbər] (-s, -) *m* beaver

Biblio- [biːblio] *zW:* **~grafie** ▲ [-graˈfiː] *f* bibliography; **~thek** [-ˈteːk] (-, -en) *f* library; **~thekar(in)** [-teˈkaːr(ɪn)] (-s, -e) *m(f)* librarian

biblisch ['biːblɪʃ] *adj* biblical

bieder ['biːdər] *adj* upright, worthy; (*Kleid etc*) plain

bieg- ['biːg] *zW:* **~en** (*unreg*) *vt, vr* to bend ♦ *vi* to turn; **~sam** ['biːk-] *adj* flexible; **B~ung** *f* bend, curve

Biene ['biːnə] *f* bee

Bienenhonig *m* honey

Bienenwachs *nt* beeswax

Bier [biːr] (-(e)s, -e) *nt* beer; **~deckel** *m* beer mat; **~garten** *m* beer garden; **~krug** *m* beer mug; **~zelt** *nt* beer tent

Biest [biːst] (-s, -er) (*umg: pej*) *nt* (*Tier*) beast, creature; (*Mensch*) beast

bieten ['biːtən] (*unreg*) *vt* to offer; (*bei Versteigerung*) to bid ♦ *vr* (*Gelegenheit*): **sich jdm ~** to present itself to sb; **sich** *dat* **etw ~ lassen** to put up with sth

Bikini [biˈkiːni] (-s, -s) *m* bikini

Bilanz [biˈlants] *f* balance; (*fig*) outcome; **~ ziehen (aus)** to take stock (of)

Bild [bɪlt] (-(e)s, -er) *nt* (*auch fig*) picture; *photo*; (*Spiegelbild*) reflection; **~bericht** *m* photographic report

bilden ['bɪldən] *vt* to form; (*erziehen*) to educate; (*ausmachen*) to constitute ♦ *vr* to arise; (*erziehen*) to educate o.s.

Bilderbuch *nt* picture book

Bilderrahmen *m* picture frame

Bild- *zW:* **~fläche** *f* screen; (*fig*) scene; **~hauer** (-s, -) *m* sculptor; **b~hübsch** *adj* lovely, pretty as a picture; **b~lich** *adj* figurative; pictorial; **~schirm** *m* television screen; (*COMPUT*) monitor; **~schirmschoner** *m* (*COMPUT*) screen saver; **b~schön** *adj* lovely

Bildung [bɪlduŋ] *f* formation; (*Wissen, Benehmen*) education

Billard ['bɪljart] (-s, -e) *nt* billiards *sg*;

~kugel *f* billiard ball

billig ['bɪlɪç] *adj* cheap; (*gerecht*) fair, reasonable; **~en** ['bɪlɪgən] *vt* to approve of

Binde ['bɪndə] *f* bandage; (*Armbinde*) band; (*MED*) sanitary towel; **~gewebe** *nt* connective tissue; **~glied** *nt* connecting link; **~hautentzündung** *f* conjunctivitis; **b~n** (*unreg*) *vt* to bind, to tie; **~strich** *m* hyphen

Bindfaden ['bɪnt-] *m* string

Bindung *f* bond, tie; (*Skibindung*) binding

binnen ['bɪnən] *präp* (+*dat od gen*) within; **B~hafen** *m* river port; **B~handel** *m* internal trade

Bio- [bio-] *in zW* bio-; **~chemie** *f* biochemistry; **~grafie** ▲ [-graˈfiː] *f* biography; **~laden** *m* wholefood shop; **~loge** [-ˈloːgə] (-n, -n) *m* biologist; **~logie** [-loˈgiː] *f* biology; **b~logisch** [-ˈloːgɪʃ] *adj* biological; **~top** *m od nt* biotope

> **Bioladen**
>
> *A* **Bioladen** *is a shop specializing in environmentally-friendly products such as phosphate-free washing powders, recycled paper and organically-grown vegetables.*

Birke ['bɪrkə] *f* birch

Birne ['bɪrnə] *f* pear; (*ELEK*) (light) bulb

> *SCHLÜSSELWORT*

bis [bɪs] *präp +akk, adv* **1** (*zeitlich*) till, until; (*bis spätestens*) by; **Sie haben bis Dienstag Zeit** you have until *od* till Tuesday; **bis Dienstag muss es fertig sein** it must be ready by Tuesday; **bis auf weiteres** until further notice; **bis in die Nacht** into the night; **bis bald/gleich** see you later/soon **2** (*räumlich*) (up) to; **ich fahre bis Köln** I'm going *od* I'm going as far as Cologne; **bis an unser Grundstück** (right *od* up) to our plot; **bis hierher** this far **3** (*bei Zahlen*) up to; **bis zu** up to **4**: **bis auf etw** *akk* (*außer*) except sth; (*einschließlich*) including sth ♦ *konj* **1** (*mit Zahlen*) to; **10 bis 20** 10 to 20 **2** (*zeitlich*) till, until; **bis es dunkel wird** till *od* until it gets dark; **von ... bis ...** from ... to ...

Bischof ['bɪʃɔf] (**-s, ⁼e**) *m* bishop; **bischöflich** ['bɪʃøːflɪç] *adj* episcopal

bisher [bɪs'heːr] *adv* till now, hitherto; **~ig** *adj* till now

Biskuit [bɪs'kviːt] (**-(e)s, -s** *od* **-e**) *m od nt* (fatless) sponge

Biss ▲ [bɪs] (**-es, -e**) *m* bite

biss ▲ *etc vb siehe* **beißen**

bisschen ▲ ['bɪsçən] *adj, adv* bit

Bissen ['bɪsən] (**-s, -**) *m* bite, morsel

bissig ['bɪsɪç] *adj* (*Hund*) snappy; (*Bemerkung*) cutting, biting

bist [bɪst] *vb siehe* **sein**

bisweilen [bɪs'vaɪlən] *adv* at times, occasionally

Bitte ['bɪtə] *f* request; **b~** *excl* please; (*wie b~?*) (I beg your) pardon?; ♦ *interj* (*als Antwort auf Dank*) you're welcome; **darf ich? - aber b~!** may I? - please do; **b~ schön!** it was a pleasure; **b~n** (*unreg*) *vt, vi*: **b~n (um)** to ask (for); **b~nd** *adj* pleading, imploring

bitter ['bɪtər] *adj* bitter; **~böse** *adj* very angry; **B~keit** *f* bitterness; **~lich** *adj* bitter

Blähungen ['blɛːʊŋən] *pl* (*MED*) wind *sg*

blamabel [bla'maːbəl] *adj* disgraceful

Blamage [bla'maːʒə] *f* disgrace

blamieren [bla'miːrən] *vr* to make a fool of o.s., to disgrace o.s. ♦ *vt* to let down, to disgrace

blank [blaŋk] *adj* bright; (*unbedeckt*) bare; (*sauber*) clean, polished; (*umg: ohne Geld*) broke; (*offensichtlich*) blatant

blanko ['blaŋko] *adv* blank; **B~scheck** *m* blank cheque

Blase ['blaːzə] *f* bubble; (*MED*) blister; (*ANAT*) bladder; **~balg** (**-(e)s, -bälge**) *m* bellows *pl*; **b~n** (*unreg*) *vt, vi* to blow; **~nentzündung** *f* cystitis

Blas- ['blaːs] *zW*: **~instrument** *nt* wind instrument; **~kapelle** *f* brass band

blass ▲ [blas] *adj* pale

Blässe ['blɛsə] (**-**) *f* paleness, pallor

Blatt [blat] (**-(e)s, ⁼er**) *nt* leaf; (*von Papier*)

sheet; (*Zeitung*) newspaper; (*KARTEN*) hand

blättern ['blɛtərn] *vi*: **in etw** *dat* **~** to leaf through sth

Blätterteig *m* flaky *od* puff pastry

blau [blaʊ] *adj* blue; (*umg*) drunk, stoned; (*KOCH*) boiled; (*Auge*) black; **~er Fleck** bruise; **Fahrt ins B~e** mystery tour; **~äugig** *adj* blue-eyed

Blech [blɛç] (**-(e)s, -e**) *nt* tin, sheet metal; (*Backblech*) baking tray; **~büchse** *f* tin, can; **~dose** *f* tin, can; **b~en** (*umg*) *vt, vi* to fork out; **~schaden** *m* (*AUT*) damage to bodywork

Blei [blaɪ] (**-(e)s, -e**) *nt* lead

Bleibe ['blaɪbə] *f* roof over one's head; **b~n** (*unreg*) *vi* to stay, to remain; **~ lassen** to leave alone; **b~nd** *adj* (*Erinnerung*) lasting; (*Schaden*) permanent

bleich [blaɪç] *adj* faded, pale; **~en** *vt* to bleach

Blei- *zW*: **b~ern** *adj* leaden; **b~frei** *adj* (*Benzin*) lead-free; **~stift** *m* pencil

Blende ['blɛndə] *f* (*PHOT*) aperture; **b~n** *vt* to blind, to dazzle; (*fig*) to hoodwink; **b~nd** (*umg*) *adj* grand; **b~nd aussehen** to look smashing

Blick [blɪk] (**-(e)s, -e**) *m* (*kurz*) glance, glimpse; (*Anschauen*) look; (*Aussicht*) view; **b~en** *vi* to look; **sich b~en lassen** to put in an appearance; **~fang** *m* eye-catcher

blieb *etc* [bliːp] *vb siehe* **bleiben**

blind [blɪnt] *adj* blind; (*Glas etc*) dull; **~er Passagier** stowaway; **B~darm** *m* appendix; **B~darmentzündung** *f* appendicitis; **B~enschrift** ['blɪndən-] *f* Braille; **B~heit** *f* blindness; **~lings** *adv* blindly

blink- ['blɪŋk] *zW*: **~en** *vi* to twinkle, to sparkle; (*Licht*) to flash, to signal; (*AUT*) to indicate ♦ *vt* to flash, to signal; **B~er** (**-s, -**) *m* (*AUT*) indicator; **B~licht** *nt* (*AUT*) indicator; (*an Bahnübergängen usw*) flashing light

blinzeln ['blɪntsəln] *vi* to blink, to wink

Blitz [blɪts] (**-es, -e**) *m* (flash of) lightning; **~ableiter** *m* lightning conductor; **b~en** *vi* (*aufleuchten*) to flash, to sparkle; **es b~t**

(*MET*) there's a flash of lightning; **~licht** *nt* flashlight; **b~schnell** *adj* lightning ♦ *adv* (as) quick as a flash

Block [blɔk] (**-(e)s, ~e**) *m* block; (*von Papier*) pad; **~ade** [blɔˈkaːdə] *f* blockade; **~flöte** *f* recorder; **b~frei** *adj* (*POL*) unaligned; **~haus** *nt* log cabin; **b~ieren** [blɔˈkiːrən] *vt* to block ♦ *vi* (*Räder*) to jam; **~schrift** *f* block letters *pl*

blöd [bløːt] *adj* silly, stupid; **~eln** [ˈbløːdəln] (*umg*) *vi* to act the goat (*fam*), to fool around; **B~sinn** *m* nonsense; **b~sinnig** *adj* silly, idiotic

blond [blɔnt] *adj* blond, fair-haired

--- SCHLÜSSELWORT ---

bloß [bloːs] *adj* **1** (*unbedeckt*) bare; (*nackt*) naked; **mit der bloßen Hand** with one's bare hand; **mit bloßem Auge** with the naked eye

2 (*alleinig, nur*) mere; **der bloße Gedanke** the very thought; **bloßer Neid** sheer envy ♦ *adv* only, merely; **lass das bloß!** just don't do that!; **wie ist das bloß passiert?** how on earth did that happen?

Blöße [ˈbløːsə] *f* bareness; nakedness; (*fig*) weakness

bloßstellen *vt* to show up

blühen [ˈblyːən] *vi* to bloom (*lit*), to be in bloom; (*fig*) to flourish; **~d** *adj* (*Pflanze*) blooming; (*Aussehen*) blooming, radiant; (*Handel*) thriving, booming

Blume [ˈbluːmə] *f* flower; (*von Wein*) bouquet

Blumen- *zW*: **~kohl** *m* cauliflower; **~topf** *m* flowerpot; **~zwiebel** *f* bulb

Bluse [ˈbluːzə] *f* blouse

Blut [bluːt] (**-(e)s**) *nt* blood; **b~arm** *adj* anaemic; (*fig*) penniless; **b~befleckt** *adj* bloodstained; **~bild** *nt* blood count; **~druck** *m* blood pressure

Blüte [ˈblyːtə] *f* blossom; (*fig*) prime

Blut- *zW*: **b~en** *vi* to bleed; **~er** *m* (*MED*) haemophiliac; **~erguss** ▲ *m* haemorrhage; (*auf Haut*) bruise

Blütezeit *f* flowering period; (*fig*) prime

Blut- *zW*: **~gruppe** *f* blood group; **b~ig** *adj* bloody; **b~jung** *adj* very young; **~probe** *f* blood test; **~spender** *m* blood donor; **~transfusion** *f* (*MED*) blood transfusion; **~ung** *f* bleeding, haemorrhage; **~vergiftung** *f* blood poisoning; **~wurst** *f* black pudding

Bö [bøː] (**-, -en**) *f* squall

Bock [bɔk] (**-(e)s, ~e**) *m* buck, ram; (*Gestell*) trestle, support; (*SPORT*) buck; **~wurst** *f* *type of pork sausage*

Boden [ˈboːdən] (**-s, ~**) *m* ground; (*Fußboden*) floor; (*Meeresboden, Fassboden*) bottom; (*Speicher*) attic; **b~los** *adj* bottomless; (*umg*) incredible; **~nebel** *m* ground mist; **~personal** *nt* (*AVIAT*) ground staff; **~schätze** *pl* mineral resources; **~see** *m*: **der ~see** Lake Constance; **~turnen** *nt* floor exercises *pl*

Böe [ˈbøːə] *f* squall

Bogen [ˈboːgən] (**-s, -**) *m* (*Biegung*) curve; (*ARCHIT*) arch; (*Waffe, MUS*) bow; (*Papier*) sheet

Bohne [ˈboːnə] *f* bean

bohnern *vt* to wax, to polish

Bohnerwachs *nt* floor polish

Bohr- *zW*: **b~en** *vt* to bore; **~er** (**-s, -**) *m* drill; **~insel** *f* oil rig; **~maschine** *f* drill; **~turm** *m* derrick

Boiler [ˈbɔylər] (**-s, -**) *m* (hot-water) tank

Boje [ˈbɔːjə] *f* buoy

Bolzen [ˈbɔltsən] (**-s, -**) *m* bolt

bombardieren [bɔmbarˈdiːrən] *vt* to bombard; (*aus der Luft*) to bomb

Bombe [ˈbɔmbə] *f* bomb

Bombenangriff *m* bombing raid

Bombenerfolg (*umg*) *m* smash hit

Bon [bɔŋ] (**-s, -s**) *m* voucher, chit

Bonbon [bõˈbõː] (**-s, -s**) *m* od *nt* sweet

Boot [boːt] (**-(e)s, -e**) *nt* boat

Bord [bɔrt] (**-(e)s, -e**) *m* (*AVIAT, NAUT*) board ♦ *nt* (*Brett*) shelf; **an ~** on board

Bordell [bɔrˈdɛl] (**-s, -e**) *nt* brothel

Bordstein *m* kerb(stone)

borgen [ˈbɔrgən] *vt* to borrow; **jdm etw ~** to lend sb sth

borniert [bɔrˈniːrt] *adj* narrow-minded

Börse ['bœːrzə] *f* stock exchange; (*Geldbörse*) purse; **~nmakler** *m* stockbroker

Borte ['bɔrtə] *f* edging; (*Band*) trimming

bös [bøːs] *adj* = **böse**

bösartig ['bøːz-] *adj* malicious

Böschung ['bœʃʊŋ] *f* slope; (*Uferböschung etc*) embankment

böse ['bøːzə] *adj* bad, evil; (*zornig*) angry

boshaft ['boːshaft] *adj* malicious, spiteful

Bosheit *f* malice, spite

Bosnien ['bɔsniən] **(-s)** *nt* Bosnia; **~ und Herzegowina** [-hɛrtsəˈɡoːvina] *nt* Bosnia (and) Herzegovina

böswillig ['bøːsvɪlɪç] *adj* malicious

bot *etc* [boːt] *vb siehe* **bieten**

Botanik [boˈtaːnɪk] *f* botany; **botanisch** *adj* botanical

Bot- ['boːt] *zW:* **~e (-n, -n)** *m* messenger; **~schaft** *f* message, news; (*POL*) embassy; **~schafter (-s, -)** *m* ambassador

Bottich ['bɔtɪç] **(-(e)s, -e)** *m* vat, tub

Bouillon [buˈljõː] **(-, -s)** *f* consommé

Bowle ['boːlə] *f* punch

Box- ['bɔks] *zW:* **b~en** *vi* to box; **~er (-s, -)** *m* boxer; **~kampf** *m* boxing match

boykottieren [bɔykɔˈtiːrən] *vt* to boycott

brach *etc* [braːx] *vb siehe* **brechen**

brachte *etc* ['braxtə] *vb siehe* **bringen**

Branche ['brãːʃə] *f* line of business

Branchenverzeichnis *nt* Yellow Pages® *pl*

Brand [brant] **(-(e)s, ⸚e)** *m* fire; (*MED*) gangrene; **b~en** ['brandən] *vi* to surge; (*Meer*) to break; **b~marken** *vt* to brand; (*fig*) to stigmatize; **~salbe** *f* ointment for burns; **~stifter** [-ʃtɪftər] *m* arsonist, fire raiser; **~stiftung** *f* arson; **~ung** *f* surf

Branntwein ['brantvaɪn] *m* brandy

Brasilien [braˈziːliən] *nt* Brazil

Brat- ['braːt] *zW:* **~apfel** *m* baked apple; **b~en** (*unreg*) *vt* to roast; to fry; **~en (-s, -)** *m* roast, joint; **~hähnchen** *nt* roast chicken; **~huhn** *nt* roast chicken; **~kartoffeln** *pl* fried *od* roast potatoes; **~pfanne** *f* frying pan

Bratsche ['braːtʃə] *f* viola

Bratspieß *m* spit

Bratwurst *f* grilled/fried sausage

Brauch [braʊx] **(-(e)s, Bräuche)** *m* custom; **b~bar** *adj* usable, serviceable; (*Person*) capable; **b~en** *vt* (*bedürfen*) to need; (*müssen*) to have to; (*umg: verwenden*) to use

Braue ['braʊə] *f* brow

brauen ['braʊən] *vt* to brew

Braueˈrei *f* brewery

braun [braʊn] *adj* brown; (*von Sonne auch*) tanned; **~ gebrannt** tanned

Bräune ['brɔynə] **(-)** *f* brownness; (*Sonnenbräune*) tan; **b~n** *vt* to make brown; (*Sonne*) to tan

Brause ['braʊzə] *f* shower bath; (*von Gießkanne*) rose; (*Getränk*) lemonade; **b~n** *vi* to roar; (*auch vr: duschen*) to take a shower

Braut [braʊt] **(-, Bräute)** *f* bride; (*Verlobte*) fiancée

Bräutigam ['brɔytigam] **(-s, -e)** *m* bridegroom; fiancé

Brautpaar *nt* bride and (bride)groom, bridal pair

brav [braːf] *adj* (*artig*) good; (*ehrenhaft*) worthy, honest

bravo ['braːvo] *excl* well done

BRD ['beːˈʔɛrˈdeː] **(-)** *f abk* = **Bundesrepublik Deutschland**

<table><tr><td>BRD</td></tr></table>

ⓘ   *The* **BRD** *(Bundesrepublik Deutschland) is the official name for the Federal Republic of Germany. It comprises 16* **Länder** *(see* **Land***). It was formerly the name given to West Germany as opposed to East Germany (the* **DDR***). The two Germanies were reunited on 3rd October 1990.*

Brech- ['brɛç] *zW:* **~eisen** *nt* crowbar; **b~en** (*unreg*) *vt, vi* to break; (*Licht*) to refract; (*fig: Mensch*) to crush; (*speien*) to vomit; **~reiz** *m* nausea, retching

Brei [braɪ] **(-(e)s, -e)** *m* (*Masse*) pulp; (*KOCH*) gruel; (*Haferbrei*) porridge

breit [braɪt] *adj* wide, broad; **sich ~ machen** to spread o.s. out; **B~e** *f* width; (*bes bei*

Maßangaben) breadth; *(GEOG)* latitude; **~en**
vt: **etw über etw** *akk* **~en** to spread sth
over sth; **B~engrad** *m* degree of latitude;
~treten *(unreg) (umg) vt* to go on about
Brems- ['brɛms] *zW:* **~belag** *m* brake
lining; **~e** [-zə] *f* brake; *(ZOOL)* horsefly;
b~en [-zən] *vi* to brake ♦ *vt (Auto)* to brake;
(fig) to slow down; **~flüssigkeit** *f* brake
fluid; **~licht** *nt* brake light; **~pedal** *nt*
brake pedal; **~spur** *f* skid mark(s *pl*); **~weg**
m braking distance
Brenn- ['brɛn] *zW:* **b~bar** *adj* inflammable;
b~en *(unreg) vi* to burn, to be on fire;
(Licht, Kerze etc) to burn ♦ *vt (Holz etc)* to
burn; *(Ziegel, Ton)* to fire; *(Kaffee)* to roast;
darauf b~en, etw zu tun to be dying to
do sth; **~nessel** ▲ *f* stinging nettle;
~punkt *m (PHYS)* focal point; *(Mittelpunkt)*
focus; **~stoff** *m* fuel
brenzlig ['brɛntslɪç] *adj (fig)* precarious
Bretagne [brə'tanjə] *f:* **die ~** Brittany
Brett [brɛt] **(-(e)s, -er)** *nt* board, plank;
(Bord) shelf; *(Spielbrett)* board; **~er** *pl (SKI)*
skis; *(THEAT)* boards; **schwarzes ~** notice
board; **~erzaun** *m* wooden fence; **~spiel**
nt board game
Brezel ['bre:tsəl] **(-, -n)** *f* pretzel
brichst *etc* [brɪçst] *vb siehe* **brechen**
Brief [bri:f] **(-(e)s, -e)** *m* letter; **~freund** *m*
penfriend; **~kasten** *m* letterbox; **b~lich**
adj, adv by letter; **~marke** *f* (postage
stamp; **~papier** *nt* notepaper; **~tasche** *f*
wallet; **~träger** *m* postman; **~umschlag**
m envelope; **~waage** *f* letter scales;
~wechsel *m* correspondence
brief *etc* [bri:t] *vb siehe* **braten**
Brikett [bri'kɛt] **(-s, -s)** *nt* briquette
brillant [brɪl'jant] *adj (fig)* brilliant; **B~ (-en,
-en)** *m* brilliant, diamond
Brille ['brɪlə] *f* spectacles *pl*; *(Schutzbrille)*
goggles *pl*; *(Toilettenbrille)* (toilet) seat;
~ngestell *nt* (spectacle) frames
bringen ['brɪŋən] *(unreg) vt* to bring;
(mitnehmen, begleiten) to take; *(einbringen:
Profit)* to bring in; *(veröffentlichen)* to
publish; *(THEAT, CINE)* to show; *(RADIO, TV)* to
broadcast; *(in einen Zustand versetzen)* to

get; *(umg: tun können)* to manage; **jdn
dazu ~, etw zu tun** to make sb do sth; **jdn
nach Hause ~** to take sb home; **jdn um
etw ~** to make sb lose sth; **jdn auf eine
Idee ~** to give sb an idea
Brise ['bri:zə] *f* breeze
Brit- ['bri:t] *zW:* **~e** *m* Briton; **~in** *f* Briton;
b~isch *adj* British
bröckelig ['brœkəlɪç] *adj* crumbly
Brocken ['brɔkən] **(-s, -)** *m* piece, bit;
(Felsbrocken) lump of rock
brodeln ['bro:dəln] *vi* to bubble
Brokkoli ['brɔkoli] *pl (BOT)* broccoli
Brombeere ['brɔmbe:rə] *f* blackberry,
bramble *(BRIT)*
Bronchien ['brɔnçiən] *pl* bronchia(l tubes)
pl
Bronchitis [brɔn'çi:tɪs] **(-)** *f* bronchitis
Bronze ['brõ:sə] *f* bronze
Brosche ['brɔʃə] *f* brooch
Broschüre [brɔ'ʃy:rə] *f* pamphlet
Brot [bro:t] **(-(e)s, -e)** *nt* bread; *(Laib)* loaf
Brötchen ['brø:tçən] *nt* roll
Bruch [brʊx] **(-(e)s, ⁺e)** *m* breakage;
(zerbrochene Stelle) break; *(fig)* split, breach;
(MED: Eingeweidebruch) rupture, hernia;
(Beinbruch etc) fracture; *(MATH)* fraction
brüchig ['brʊçɪç] *adj* brittle, fragile; *(Haus)*
dilapidated
Bruch- *zW:* **~landung** *f* crash landing;
~strich *m (MATH)* line; **~stück** *nt*
fragment; **~teil** *m* fraction; **~zahl** [brʊxtsa:l]
f (MATH) fraction
Brücke ['brʊkə] *f* bridge; *(Teppich)* rug
Bruder ['bru:dər] **(-s, ⁺)** *m* brother;
brüderlich *adj* brotherly
Brühe ['bry:ə] *f* broth, stock; *(pej)* muck
brüllen ['brʊlən] *vi* to bellow, to roar
brummen ['brʊmən] *vi (Bär, Mensch etc)* to
growl; *(Insekt)* to buzz; *(Motoren)* to roar;
(murren) to grumble
brünett [brʏ'nɛt] *adj* brunette, dark-haired
Brunnen ['brʊnən] **(-s, -)** *m* fountain; *(tief)*
well; *(natürlich)* spring
Brust [brʊst] **(-, ⁺e)** *f* breast; *(Männerbrust)*
chest
brüsten ['brʏstən] *vr* to boast

Brust- *zW:* **~kasten** *m* chest; **~schwimmen** *nt* breast-stroke

Brüstung ['brʏstʊŋ] *f* parapet

Brut [bruːt] **(-, -en)** *f* brood; *(Brüten)* hatching

brutal [bru'taːl] *adj* brutal

Brutali'tät *f* brutality

brüten ['bryːtən] *vi* (*auch fig*) to brood

Brutkasten *m* incubator

brutto ['brʊto] *adv* gross; **B~einkommen** *nt* gross salary; **B~gehalt** *nt* gross salary; **B~gewicht** *nt* gross weight; **B~lohn** *m* gross wages *pl*; **B~sozialprodukt** *nt* gross national product

BSE *f abk* (= *Bovine Spongiforme Enzephalopathie*) BSE

Bube ['buːbə] **(-n, -n)** *m* (*Schurke*) rogue; (*KARTEN*) jack

Buch [buːx] **(-(e)s, ⁻er)** *nt* book; (*COMM*) account book; **~binder** *m* bookbinder; **~drucker** *m* printer

Buche *f* beech tree

buchen *vt* to book; (*Betrag*) to enter

Bücher- ['byːçər] *zW:* **~brett** *nt* book-shelf; **~ei** [-'raɪ] *f* library; **~regal** *nt* book-shelves *pl*, bookcase; **~schrank** *m* book-case

Buch- *zW:* **~führung** *f* book-keeping, accounting; **~halter(in)** **(-s, -)** *m(f)* book-keeper; **~handel** *m* book trade; **~händler(in)** *m(f)* bookseller; **~handlung** *f* bookshop

Büchse ['bʏksə] *f* tin, can; (*Holzbüchse*) box; (*Gewehr*) rifle; **~nfleisch** *nt* tinned meat; **~nmilch** *f* (*KOCH*) evaporated milk, tinned milk; **~nöffner** *m* tin *od* can opener

Buchstabe **(-ns, -n)** *m* letter (of the alphabet)

buchstabieren [buːxʃta'biːrən] *vt* to spell

buchstäblich ['buːxʃtɛːplɪç] *adj* literal

Bucht ['bʊxt] **(-, -en)** *f* bay

Buchung ['buːxʊŋ] *f* booking; (*COMM*) entry

Buckel ['bʊkəl] **(-s, -)** *m* hump

bücken ['bʏkən] *vr* to bend

Bude ['buːdə] *f* booth, stall; (*umg*) digs *pl* (*BRIT*)

Büfett [bʏ'fet] **(-s, -s)** *nt* (*Anrichte*) sideboard; (*Geschirrschrank*) dresser; **kaltes ~** cold buffet

Büffel ['bʏfəl] **(-s, -)** *m* buffalo

Bug [buːk] **(-(e)s, -e)** *m* (*NAUT*) bow; (*AVIAT*) nose

Bügel ['byːgəl] **(-s, -)** *m* (*Kleider~*) hanger; (*Steig~*) stirrup; (*Brillen~*) arm; **~brett** *nt* ironing board; **~eisen** *nt* iron; **~falte** *f* crease; **b~frei** *adj* crease-resistant, noniron; **b~n** *vt, vi* to iron

Bühne ['byːnə] *f* stage; **~nbild** *nt* set, scenery

Buhruf ['buːruːf] *m* boo

buk *etc* [buːk] *vb siehe* **backen**

Bulgarien [bʊl'gaːriən] *nt* Bulgaria

Bull- ['bʊl] *zW:* **~auge** *nt* (*NAUT*) porthole; **~dogge** *f* bulldog; **~dozer** ['bʊldoːzər] **(-s, -)** *m* bulldozer; **~e** **(-n, -n)** *m* bull

Bumerang ['buːməraŋ] **(-s, -e)** *m* boomerang

Bummel ['bʊməl] **(-s, -)** *m* stroll; (*Schaufensterbummel*) window-shopping; **~ant** [-'lant] *m* slowcoach; **~ei** [-'laɪ] *f* wandering; dawdling; skiving; **b~n** *vi* to wander, to stroll; (*trödeln*) to dawdle; (*faulenzen*) to skive, to loaf around; **~streik** ['bʊməlʃtraɪk] *m* go-slow

Bund¹ [bʊnt] **(-(e)s, ⁻e)** *m* (*Freundschaftsbund etc*) bond; (*Organisation*) union; (*POL*) confederacy; (*Hosenbund, Rockband*) waistband

Bund² **(-(e)s, -e)** *nt* bunch; (*Strohbund*) bundle

Bündel ['bʏndəl] **(-s, -)** *nt* bundle, bale; **b~n** *vt* to bundle

Bundes- ['bʊndəs] *in zW* Federal; **~bürger** *m* German citizen; **~hauptstadt** *f* Federal capital; **~kanzler** *m* Federal Chancellor; **~land** *nt* Land; **~liga** *f* football league; **~präsident** *m* Federal President; **~rat** *m* upper house of German Parliament; **~regierung** *f* Federal government; **~republik** *f* Federal Republic (of Germany); **~staat** *m* Federal state; **~straße** *f* Federal road; **~tag** *m* German Parliament; **~wehr** *f* German Armed Forces *pl*; **b~weit** *adj* nationwide

Rechtschreibreform: ▲ *neue Schreibung* △ *alte Schreibung (auslaufend)*

| **Bundespräsident** |

i *The* **Bundespräsident** *is the head of state of the Federal Republic of Germany. He is elected every 5 years - no-one can be elected more than twice - by the members of the* **Bundesversammlung**, *a body formed especially for this purpose. His role is to represent Germany at home and abroad. In Switzerland the* **Bundespräsident** *is the head of the government, known as the Bundesrat. The* **Bundesrat** *is the Upper House of the German Parliament whose 68 members are nominated by the parliaments of the* **Länder**. *Its most important function is to approve federal laws concerned with the jurisdiction of the* **Länder***; it can raise objections to other laws, but can be outvoted by the* **Bundestag**. *In Austria the* **Länder** *are also represented in the* **Bundesrat**.

| **Bundestag** |

i *The* **Bundestag** *is the Lower House of the German Parliament and is elected by the people by proportional representation. There are 672 MPs, half of them elected directly from the first vote (***Erststimme***), and half from the regional list of parliamentary candidates resulting from the second vote (***Zweitstimme***). The* **Bundestag** *exercises parliamentary control over the government.*

Bündnis ['byntnɪs] (-ses, -se) *nt* alliance
bunt [bʊnt] *adj* coloured; (*gemischt*) mixed; **jdm wird es zu ~** it's getting too much for sb; **B~stift** *m* coloured pencil, crayon
Burg [bʊrk] (-, -en) *f* castle, fort
Bürge ['byrgə] (-n, -n) *m* guarantor; **b~n vi: b~n für** to vouch for
Bürger(in) ['byrgər(ɪn)] (-s, -) *m(f)* citizen; member of the middle class; **~krieg** *m* civil war; **b~lich** *adj* (*Rechte*) civil; (*Klasse*) middle-class; (*pej*) bourgeois; **~meister** *m*

mayor; **~recht** *nt* civil rights *pl*; **~schaft** *f* (*Vertretung*) City Parliament; **~steig** *m* pavement
Bürgschaft *f* surety; **~ leisten** to give security
Büro [by'roː] (-s, -s) *nt* office; **~angestellte(r)** *f(m)* office worker; **~klammer** *f* paper clip; **~kra'tie** *f* bureaucracy; **b~'kratisch** *adj* bureaucratic; **~schluss** ▲ *m* office closing time
Bursche ['bʊrʃə] (-n, -n) *m* lad, fellow; (*Diener*) servant
Bürste ['byrstə] *f* brush; **b~n** *vt* to brush
Bus [bʊs] (-ses, -se) *m* bus; **~bahnhof** *m* bus/coach (*BRIT*) station
Busch [bʊʃ] (-(e)s, ⁺e) *m* bush, shrub
Büschel ['byʃəl] (-s, -) *nt* tuft
buschig *adj* bushy
Busen ['buːzən] (-s, -) *m* bosom; (*Meerbusen*) inlet, bay
Bushaltestelle *f* bus stop
Buße ['buːsə] *f* atonement, penance; (*Geld*) fine
büßen ['byːsən] *vi* to do penance, to atone ♦ *vt* to do penance for, to atone for
Bußgeld ['buːsɡɛlt] *nt* fine; **~bescheid** *m* notice of payment due (*for traffic offence etc*)
Büste ['bystə] *f* bust; **~nhalter** *m* bra
Butter ['bʊtər] (-) *f* butter; **~blume** *f* buttercup; **~brot** *nt* (piece of) bread and butter; (*umg*) sandwich; **~brotpapier** *nt* greaseproof paper; **~dose** *f* butter dish; **~milch** *f* buttermilk; **b~weich** ['bʊtərvaɪç] *adj* soft as butter; (*fig, umg*) soft
b. w. *abk* (= *bitte wenden*) p.t.o.
bzgl. *abk* (= *bezüglich*) re
bzw. *abk* = **beziehungsweise**

C, c

ca. [ka] *abk* (= *circa*) approx.
Café [ka'feː] (-s, -s) *nt* café
Cafeteria [kafete'riːa] (-, -s) *f* cafeteria
Camcorder (-s, -) *m* camcorder
Camp- ['kɛmp] *zW*: **c~en** *vi* to camp; **~er**

(-s, -) *m* camper; **~ing** (-s) *nt* camping; **~ingführer** *m* camping guide (book); **~ingkocher** *m* camping stove; **~ingplatz** *m* camp(ing) site

CD-Spieler *m* CD (player)

Cello ['tʃɛlo] (-s, -s *od* **Celli**) *nt* cello

Celsius ['tsɛlziʊs] (-) *nt* centigrade

Champagner [ʃam'panjər] (-s, -) *m* champagne

Champignon ['ʃampɪnjõ] (-s, -s) *m* button mushroom

Chance ['ʃã:s(ə)] *f* chance, opportunity

Chaos ['ka:ɔs] (-, -) *nt* chaos; **chaotisch** [ka'o:tɪʃ] *adj* chaotic

Charakter [ka'raktər, *pl* karak'te:rə] (-s, -e) *m* character; **c~fest** *adj* of firm character, strong; **c~i'sieren** *vt* to characterize; **c~istisch** [karakte'rɪstɪʃ] *adj*: **c~istisch (für)** characteristic (of), typical (of); **c~los** *adj* unprincipled; **~losigkeit** *f* lack of principle; **~schwäche** *f* weakness of character; **~stärke** *f* strength of character; **~zug** *m* characteristic, trait

charmant [ʃar'mant] *adj* charming

Charme [ʃarm] (-s) *m* charm

Charterflug ['tʃartərfluːk] *m* charter flight

Chauffeur [ʃɔ'føːr] *m* chauffeur

Chauvinist [ʃovi'nɪst] *m* chauvinist, jingoist

Chef [ʃɛf] (-s, -s) *m* head; (*umg*) boss; **~arzt** *m* senior consultant; **~in** (*umg*) *f* boss

Chemie [çe'mi:] (-) *f* chemistry; **~faser** *f* man-made fibre

Chemikalie [çemi'ka:liə] *f* chemical

Chemiker ['çe:mikər] (-s, -) *m* (industrial) chemist

chemisch ['çe:mɪʃ] *adj* chemical; **~e Reinigung** dry cleaning

Chicorée ['ʃikore:] (-s) *m od* f chicory

Chiffre ['ʃɪfrə] *f* (*Geheimzeichen*) cipher; (*in Zeitung*) box number

Chile ['tʃi:le] *nt* Chile

Chin- ['çi:n] *zW*: **~a** *nt* China; **~akohl** *m* Chinese leaves; **~ese** [-'ne:zə] *m* Chinese; **~esin** *f* Chinese; **c~esisch** *adj* Chinese

Chip [tʃɪp] (-s, -s) *m* (*Kartoffelchips*) crisp (*BRIT*), chip (*US*); (*COMPUT*) chip; **~karte** *f* smart card

Chirurg [çi'rʊrg] (-en, -en) *m* surgeon; **~ie** [-'gi:] *f* surgery; **c~isch** *adj* surgical

Chlor [klo:r] (-s) *nt* chlorine; **~o'form** (-s) *nt* chloroform

cholerisch [ko'le:rɪʃ] *adj* choleric

Chor [ko:r] (-(e)s, ⁺e) *m* choir; (*Musikstück, THEAT*) chorus; **~al** [ko'ra:l] (-s, -äle) *m* chorale

Choreograf ▲ [koreo'gra:f] (-en, -en) *m* choreographer

Christ [krɪst] (-en, -en) *m* Christian; **~baum** *m* Christmas tree; **~entum** *nt* Christianity; **~in** *f* Christian; **~kind** *nt* ≈ Father Christmas; (*Jesus*) baby Jesus; **c~lich** *adj* Christian; **~us** (-) *m* Christ

Chrom [kro:m] (-s) *nt* (*CHEM*) chromium; chrome

Chron- ['kro:n] *zW*: **~ik** *f* chronicle; **c~isch** *adj* chronic; **c~ologisch** [-o'lo:gɪʃ] *adj* chronological

circa ['tsɪrka] *adv* about, approximately

Clown [klaʊn] (-s, -s) *m* clown

Cocktail ['kɔkteːl] (-s, -s) *m* cocktail

Cola ['ko:la] (-, -s) *f* Coke ®

Computer [kɔm'pju:tər] (-s, -) *m* computer; **~spiel** *nt* computer game

Cord [kɔrt] (-s) *m* cord, corduroy

Couch [kaʊtʃ] (-, -es *od* -en) *f* couch

Coupon [ku'põ] (-s, -s) *m* = **Kupon**

Cousin [ku'zɛ̃:] (-s, -s) *m* cousin; **~e** [ku'zi:nə] *f* cousin

Creme [krɛːm] (-, -s) *f* cream; (*Schuhcreme*) polish; (*Zahncreme*) paste; (*KOCH*) mousse; **c~farben** *adj* cream(-coloured)

cremig ['kre:mɪç] *adj* creamy

Curry ['kari] (-s) *m od* nt curry powder; **~pulver** *nt* curry powder; **~wurst** *f* curried sausage

D, d

da [da:] *adv* **1** (*örtlich*) there; (*hier*) here; **da draußen** out there; **da sein** to be there; **da**

bin ich here I am; **da, wo** where; **ist noch Milch da?** is there any milk left?
2 (*zeitlich*) then; (*folglich*) so
3: da haben wir Glück gehabt we were lucky there; **da kann man nichts machen** nothing can be done about it
♦ *konj* (*weil*) as, since

dabehalten (*unreg*) *vt* to keep

dabei [da'baɪ] *adv* (*räumlich*) close to it; (*noch dazu*) besides; (*zusammen mit*) with them; (*zeitlich*) during this; (*obwohl doch*) but, however; **was ist schon ~?** what of it?; **es ist doch nichts ~, wenn ...** it doesn't matter if ...; **bleiben wir ~** let's leave it at that; **es bleibt ~** that's settled; **das Dumme / Schwierige ~** the stupid/difficult part of it; **er war gerade ~ zu gehen** he was just leaving; **~ sein** (*anwesend*) to be present; (*beteiligt*) to be involved; **~stehen** (*unreg*) *vi* to stand around

Dach [dax] **(-(e)s, ⁓er)** *nt* roof; **~boden** *m* attic, loft; **~decker (-s, -)** *m* slater, tiler; **~fenster** *nt* skylight; **~gepäckträger** *m* roof rack; **~luke** *f* skylight; **~pappe** *f* roofing felt; **~rinne** *f* gutter

Dachs [daks] **(-es, -e)** *m* badger

dachte *etc* ['daxtə] *vb siehe* **denken**

Dackel ['dakəl] **(-s, -)** *m* dachshund

dadurch [da'dʊrç] *adv* (*räumlich*) through it; (*durch diesen Umstand*) thereby, in that way; (*deshalb*) because of that, for that reason
♦ *konj*: **~, dass** because

dafür [da'fy:r] *adv* for it; (*anstatt*) instead; **er kann nichts ~** he can't help it; **er ist bekannt ~** he is well-known for that; **was bekomme ich ~?** what will I get for it?

dagegen [da'ge:gən] *adv* against it; (*im Vergleich damit*) in comparison with it; (*bei Tausch*) for it/them ♦ *konj* however; **ich habe nichts ~** I don't mind; **ich war ~** I was against it; **~ kann man nichts tun** one can't do anything about it; **~halten** (*unreg*) *vt* (*vergleichen*) to compare with it; (*entgegnen*) to object to it; **~sprechen** (*unreg*) *vi*: **es spricht nichts ~** there's no reason why not

daheim [da'haɪm] *adv* at home; **D~ (-s)** *nt* home

daher [da'he:r] *adv* (*räumlich*) from there; (*Ursache*) from that ♦ *konj* (*deshalb*) that's why

dahin [da'hɪn] *adv* (*räumlich*) there; (*zeitlich*) then; (*vergangen*) gone; **~ gehend** on this matter; **~gegen** *konj* on the other hand; **~gestellt** *adv*: **~gestellt bleiben** to remain to be seen; **~gestellt sein lassen** to leave open *od* undecided

dahinten [da'hɪntən] *adv* over there

dahinter [da'hɪntər] *adv* behind it; **~ kommen** to get to the bottom of it

dalli ['dali] (*umg*) *adv* chop chop

damalig ['da:ma:lɪç] *adj* of that time, then

damals ['da:ma:ls] *adv* at that time, then

Dame ['da:mə] *f* lady; (*SCHACH, KARTEN*) queen; (*Spiel*) draughts *sg*; **~nbinde** *f* sanitary towel *od* napkin (*US*); **d~nhaft** *adj* ladylike; **~ntoilette** *f* ladies' toilet *od* restroom (*US*); **~nwahl** *f* ladies' excuse-me

damit [da'mɪt] *adv* with it; (*begründend*) by that ♦ *konj* in order that, so that; **was meint er ~?** what does he mean by that?; **genug ~!** that's enough!

dämlich ['de:mlɪç] (*umg*) *adj* silly, stupid

Damm [dam] **(-(e)s, ⁓e)** *m* dyke; (*Staudamm*) dam; (*Hafendamm*) mole; (*Bahndamm, Straßendamm*) embankment

dämmen ['dɛmən] *vt* (*Wasser*) to dam up; (*Schmerzen*) to keep back

dämmer- *zW*: **~ig** *adj* dim, faint; **~n** *vi* (*Tag*) to dawn; (*Abend*) to fall; **D~ung** *f* twilight; (*Morgendämmerung*) dawn; (*Abenddämmerung*) dusk

Dampf [dampf] **(-(e)s, ⁓e)** *m* steam; (*Dunst*) vapour; **d~en** *vi* to steam

dämpfen ['dɛmpfən] *vt* (*KOCH*) to steam; (*bügeln*) to iron with a damp cloth; (*fig*) to dampen, to subdue

Dampf- *zW*: **~schiff** *nt* steamship; **~walze** *f* steamroller

danach [da'na:x] *adv* after that; (*zeitlich*) after that, afterwards; (*gemäß*) accordingly; according to which; according to that; **er sieht ~ aus** he looks it

Däne ['dɛːnə] (-n, -n) *m* Dane
daneben [da'neːbən] *adv* beside it; (*im Vergleich*) in comparison; **~benehmen** (*unreg*) *vr* to misbehave; **~gehen** (*unreg*) *vi* to miss; (*Plan*) to fail
Dänemark ['dɛːnəmark] *nt* Denmark; **Dänin** *f* Dane; **dänisch** *adj* Danish
Dank [daŋk] (-(e)s) *m* thanks *pl*; **vielen** *od* **schönen ~** many thanks; **jdm ~ sagen** to thank sb; **d~** *präp* (+*dat od gen*) thanks to; **d~bar** *adj* grateful; (*Aufgabe*) rewarding; **~barkeit** *f* gratitude; **d~e** *excl* thank you, thanks; **d~en** *vi* +*dat* to thank; **d~enswert** *adj* (*Arbeit*) worthwhile; rewarding; (*Bemühung*) kind; **d~sagen** *vi* to express one's thanks
dann [dan] *adv* then; **~ und wann** now and then
daran [da'ran] *adv* on it; (*stoßen*) against it; **es liegt ~, dass ...** the cause of it is that ...; **gut/schlecht ~ sein** to be well-/badly off; **das Beste/Dümmste ~** the best/stupidest thing about it; **ich war nahe ~ zu ...** I was on the point of ...; **er ist ~ gestorben** he died from it *od* of it; **~gehen** (*unreg*) *vi* to start; **~setzen** *vt* to stake
darauf [da'rauf] *adv* (*räumlich*) on it; (*zielgerichtet*) towards it; (*danach*) afterwards; **es kommt ganz ~ an, ob ...** it depends whether ...; **die Tage ~** the days following *od* thereafter; **am Tag ~** the next day; **~ folgend** (*Tag, Jahr*) next, following; **~ legen** to lay *od* put on top
daraus [da'raus] *adv* from it; **was ist ~ geworden?** what became of it?; **~ geht hervor, dass ...** this means that ...
Darbietung ['daːrbiːtʊŋ] *f* performance
darf *etc* [darf] *vb siehe* **dürfen**
darin [da'rɪn] *adv* in (there), in it
darlegen ['daːrleːgən] *vt* to explain, to expound, to set forth; **Darlegung** *f* explanation
Darleh(e)n (-s, -) *nt* loan
Darm [darm] (-(e)s, ⁼e) *m* intestine; (*Wurstdarm*) skin; **~grippe** *f* (*MED*) gastric influenza *od* flu

darstell- ['daːrʃtɛl] *zW:* **~en** *vt* (*abbilden, bedeuten*) to represent; (*THEAT*) to act; (*beschreiben*) to describe ♦ *vr* to appear to be; **D~er(in)** (-s, -) *m(f)* actor (actress); **D~ung** *f* portrayal, depiction
darüber [da'ryːbər] *adv* (*räumlich*) over it, above it; (*fahren*) over it; (*mehr*) more; (*währenddessen*) meanwhile; (*sprechen, streiten*) about it; **~ geht nichts** there's nothing like it
darum [da'rʊm] *adv* (*räumlich*) round it ♦ *konj* that's why; **er bittet ~** he is pleading for it; **es geht ~, dass ...** the thing is that ...; **er würde viel ~ geben, wenn ...** he would give a lot to ...; **ich tue es ~, weil ...** I am doing it because ...
darunter [da'rʊntər] *adv* (*räumlich*) under it; (*dazwischen*) among them; (*weniger*) less; **ein Stockwerk ~** one floor below (it); **was verstehen Sie ~?** what do you understand by that?
das [das] *def art* the ♦ *pron* that
Dasein ['daːzain] (-s) *nt* (*Leben*) life; (*Anwesenheit*) presence; (*Bestehen*) existence
da sein ▲ *siehe* **da**
dass ▲ [das] *konj* that
dasselbe [das'zɛlbə] *art, pron* the same
dastehen ['daːʃteːən] (*unreg*) *vi* to stand there
Datei [da'tai] *f* file
Daten- ['daːtən] *zW:* **~bank** *f* data base; **~schutz** *m* data protection; **~verarbeitung** *f* data processing
datieren [da'tiːrən] *vt* to date
Dativ ['daːtiːf] (-s, -e) *m* dative (case)
Dattel ['datəl] (-, -n) *f* date
Datum ['daːtʊm] (-s, Daten) *nt* date; **Daten** *pl* (*Angaben*) data *pl*
Dauer ['dauər] (-, -n) *f* duration; (*gewisse Zeitspanne*) length; (*Bestand, Fortbestehen*) permanence; **es war nur von kurzer ~** it didn't last long; **auf die ~** in the long run; (*auf längere Zeit*) indefinitely; **~auftrag** *m* standing order; **d~haft** *adj* lasting, durable; **~karte** *f* season ticket; **~lauf** *m* jog(ging); **d~n** *vi* to last; **es hat sehr lang gedauert, bis er ...** it took him a long time to ...;

d~nd *adj* constant; **~parkplatz** *m* long-stay car park; **~welle** *f* perm, permanent wave; **~wurst** *f* German salami; **~zustand** *m* permanent condition

Daumen ['daʊmən] **(-s, -)** *m* thumb

Daune ['daʊnə] *f* down; **~ndecke** *f* down duvet, down quilt

davon [da'fɔn] *adv* of it; (*räumlich*) away; (*weg von*) from it; (*Grund*) because of it; **das kommt ~!** that's what you get; **~ abgesehen** apart from that; **~ sprechen/wissen** to talk/know of *od* about it; **was habe ich ~?** what's the point?; **~kommen** (*unreg*) *vi* to escape; **~laufen** (*unreg*) *vi* to run away

davor [da'foːr] *adv* (*räumlich*) in front of it; (*zeitlich*) before (that); **~ warnen** to warn about it

dazu [da'tsuː] *adv* (*legen, stellen*) by it; (*essen, singen*) with it; **und ~ noch** and in addition; **ein Beispiel/seine Gedanken ~** one example for/his thoughts on this; **wie komme ich denn ~?** why should I?; **~ fähig sein** to be capable of it; **sich ~ äußern** to say something on it; **~gehören** *vi* to belong to it; **~kommen** (*unreg*) *vi* (*Ereignisse*) to happen too; (*an einen Ort*) to come along

dazwischen [da'tsvɪʃən] *adv* in between; (*räumlich auch*) between (them); (*zusammen mit*) among them; **~kommen** (*unreg*) *vi* (*hineingeraten*) to get caught in it; **es ist etwas ~gekommen** something cropped up; **~reden** *vi* (*unterbrechen*) to interrupt; (*sich einmischen*) to interfere; **~treten** (*unreg*) *vi* to intervene

Debatte [de'batə] *f* debate

Deck [dɛk] **(-(e)s, -s** *od* **-e)** *nt* deck; **an ~ gehen** to go on deck

Decke *f* cover; (*Bettdecke*) blanket; (*Tischdecke*) tablecloth; (*Zimmerdecke*) ceiling; **unter einer ~ stecken** to be hand in glove; **~l (-s, -)** *m* lid; **d~n** *vt* to cover ♦ *vr* to coincide

Deckung *f* (*Schützen*) covering; (*Schutz*) cover; (*SPORT*) defence; (*Übereinstimmen*) agreement

Defekt [de'fɛkt] **(-(e)s, -e)** *m* fault, defect; **d~** *adj* faulty

defensiv [defɛn'siːf] *adj* defensive

definieren [defi'niːrən] *vt* to define; **Definition** [definitsi'oːn] *f* definition

Defizit ['deːfitsɪt] **(-s, -e)** *nt* deficit

deftig ['dɛftɪç] *adj* (*Essen*) large; (*Witz*) coarse

Degen ['deːgən] **(-s, -)** *m* sword

degenerieren [degene'riːrən] *vi* to degenerate

dehnbar ['deːnbaːr] *adj* elastic; (*fig: Begriff*) loose

dehnen *vt, vr* to stretch

Deich [daɪç] **(-(e)s, -e)** *m* dyke, dike

deichseln (*umg*) *vt* (*fig*) to wangle

dein(e) [daɪn(ə)] *adj* your; **~e(r, s)** *pron* yours; **~er** (*gen von* **du**) *pron* of you; **~erseits** *adv* on your part; **~esgleichen** *pron* people like you; **~etwegen** *adv* (*für dich*) for your sake; (*wegen dir*) on your account; **~etwillen** *adv*: **um ~etwillen = deinetwegen**; **~ige** *pron*: **der/die/das ~ige** *od* **D~ige** yours

Deklination [deklinatsi'oːn] *f* declension

deklinieren [dekli'niːrən] *vt* to decline

Dekolleté, Dekolletee ▲ [dekɔl'teː] **(-s, -s)** *nt* low neckline

Deko- [deko] *zW*: **~rateur** [-ra'tøːr] *m* window dresser; **~ration** [-ratsi'oːn] *f* decoration; (*in Laden*) window dressing; **d~rativ** [-ra'tiːf] *adj* decorative; **d~rieren** [-'riːrən] *vt* to decorate; (*Schaufenster*) to dress

Spelling Reform: ▲ *new spelling* △ *old spelling (to be phased out)*

Delegation [delegatsi'o:n] *f* delegation

delegieren [dele'gi:rən] *vt*: ~ **an** +*akk* (*Aufgaben*) to delegate to

Delfin ▲ [dɛl'fi:n] (**-s, -e**) *m* dolphin

delikat [deli'ka:t] *adj* (*zart, heikel*) delicate; (*köstlich*) delicious

Delikatesse [delika'tesə] *f* delicacy; **~n** *pl* (*Feinkost*) delicatessen food; **~ngeschäft** *nt* delicatessen

Delikt [de'lɪkt] (**-(e)s, -e**) *nt* (*JUR*) offence

Delle ['dɛlə] (*umg*) *f* dent

Delphin △ [dɛl'fi:n] (**-s, -e**) *m* = **Delfin**

dem [de(:)m] *art dat von* **der**

Demagoge [dema'go:gə] (**-n, -n**) *m* demagogue

dementieren [demɛn'ti:rən] *vt* to deny

dem- *zW*: **~gemäß** *adv* accordingly; **~nach** *adv* accordingly; **~nächst** *adv* shortly

Demokrat [demo'kra:t] (**-en, -en**) *m* democrat; **~ie** [-'ti:] *f* democracy; **d~isch** *adj* democratic; **d~isieren** [-i'zi:rən] *vt* to democratize

demolieren [demo'li:rən] *vt* to demolish

Demon- [demɔn] *zW*: **~strant(in)** [-'strant(ɪn)] *m(f)* demonstrator; **~stration** [-stratsi'o:n] *f* demonstration; **d~strativ** [-stra'ti:f] *adj* demonstrative; (*Protest*) pointed; **d~strieren** [-'stri:rən] *vt, vi* to demonstrate

Demoskopie [demosko'pi:] *f* public opinion research

Demut ['de:mu:t] (**-**) *f* humility

demütig ['de:my:tɪç] *adj* humble; **~en** ['de:my:tɪgən] *vt* to humiliate; **D~ung** *f* humiliation

demzufolge ['de:mtsu'fɔlgə] *adv* accordingly

den [de(:)n] *art akk von* **der**

denen ['de:nən] *pron dat pl von* **der**; **die**; **das**

Denk- [dɛŋk] *zW*: **d~bar** *adj* conceivable; **~en** (**-s**) *nt* thinking; **d~en** (*unreg*) *vt, vi* to think; **d~faul** *adj* lazy; **~fehler** *m* logical error; **~mal** (**-s, ⁀er**) *nt* monument; **~malschutz** *m* protection of historical monuments; **unter ~malschutz stehen** to be classified as a historical monument; **d~würdig** *adj* memorable; **~zettel** *m*: **jdm**

einen ~zettel verpassen to teach sb a lesson

denn [dɛn] *konj* for ♦ *adv* then; (*nach Komparativ*) than; **warum ~?** why?

dennoch ['dɛnnɔx] *konj* nevertheless

Denunziant [denuntsi'ant(ɪn)] *m* informer

Deodorant [de|odo'rant] (**-s, -s** *od* **-e**) *nt* deodorant

Deponie [depo'ni:] *f* dump

deponieren [depo'ni:rən] *vt* (*COMM*) to deposit

Depot [de'po:] (**-s, -s**) *nt* warehouse; (*Busdepot, EISENB*) depot; (*Bankdepot*) strongroom, safe (*US*)

Depression [deprɛsi'o:n] *f* depression; **depres'siv** *adj* depressive

deprimieren [depri'mi:rən] *vt* to depress

der [de(:)r] (*f* **die**, *nt* **das**, *gen* **des, der, des**, *dat* **dem, der, dem**, *akk* **den, die, das**, *pl* **die**) *def art* the; **der Rhein** the Rhine; **der Klaus** (*umg*) Klaus; **die Frau** (*im Allgemeinen*) women; **der Tod / das Leben** death/life; **der Fuß des Berges** the foot of the hill; **gib es der Frau** give it to the woman; **er hat sich die Hand verletzt** he has hurt his hand

♦ *relativ pron* (*bei Menschen*) who, that; (*bei Tieren, Sachen*) which, that; **der Mann, den ich gesehen habe** the man who *od* whom *od* that I saw

♦ *demonstrativ pron* he/she/it; (*jener, dieser*) that; (*pl*) those; **der / die war es** it was him/her; **der mit der Brille** the one with glasses; **ich will den (da)** I want that one

derart ['de:r|a:rt] *adv* so; (*solcher Art*) such; **~ig** *adj* such, this sort of

derb [dɛrp] *adj* sturdy; (*Kost*) solid; (*grob*) coarse

der- *zW*: **'~'gleichen** *pron* such; **'~jenige** *pron* he; she; it; the one (who); that (which); **'~'maßen** *adv* to such an extent, so; **~'selbe** *art, pron* the same; **'~'weil(en)** *adv* in the meantime; **'~'zeitig** *adj* present, current; (*damalig*) then

des [dɛs] *art gen von* **der**

desertieren [dɛzɛr'tiːrən] *vi* to desert

desgleichen ['dɛs'glaɪçən] *adv* likewise, also

deshalb ['dɛs'halp] *adv* therefore, that's why

Desinfektion [dɛzɪnfɛktsi'oːn] *f* disinfection; **~smittel** *nt* disinfectant

desinfizieren [dɛzɪnfi'tsiːrən] *vt* to disinfect

dessen ['dɛsən] *pron gen von* **der**; **das**; **~ ungeachtet** nevertheless, regardless

Dessert [dɛ'sɛːr] **(-s, -s)** *nt* dessert

destillieren [dɛstɪ'liːrən] *vt* to distil

desto ['dɛsto] *adv* all the, so much the; **~ besser** all the better

deswegen ['dɛs'veːgən] *konj* therefore, hence

Detail [de'taɪ] **(-s, -s)** *nt* detail

Detektiv [detɛk'tiːf] **(-s, -e)** *m* detective

deut- ['dɔʏt] *zW:* **~en** *vt* to interpret, to explain ♦ *vi:* **~en (auf** +*akk*) to point (to *od* at); **~lich** *adj* clear; (*Unterschied*) distinct; **D~lichkeit** *f* clarity; distinctness

Deutsch [dɔʏtʃ] *nt* German

deutsch *adj* German; **auf D~** in German; **D~e Demokratische Republik** (*HIST*) German Democratic Republic, East Germany; **~es Beefsteak** ≈ hamburger; **D~e(r)** *mf* German; **ich bin D~er** I am German; **D~land** *nt* Germany

Devise [de'viːzə] *f* motto, device; **~n** *pl* (*FIN*) foreign currency, foreign exchange

Dezember [de'tsɛmbər] **(-s, -)** *m* December

dezent [de'tsɛnt] *adj* discreet

dezimal [detsi'maːl] *adj* decimal; **D~system** *nt* decimal system

d. h. *abk* (= *das heißt*) i.e.

Dia ['diːa] **(-s, -s)** *nt* (*PHOT*) slide, transparency

Diabetes [dia'beːtes] **(-, -)** *m* (*MED*) diabetes

Diagnose [dia'gnoːzə] *f* diagnosis

diagonal [diago'naːl] *adj* diagonal

Dialekt [dia'lɛkt] **(-(e)s, -e)** *m* dialect; **d~isch** *adj* dialectal; (*Logik*) dialectical

Dialog [dia'loːk] **(-(e)s, -e)** *m* dialogue

Diamant [dia'mant] *m* diamond

Diaprojektor ['diːaprojɛktɔr] *m* slide projector

Diät [di'ɛːt] **(-, -en)** *f* diet

dich [dɪç] (*akk von du*) *pron* you; yourself

dicht [dɪçt] *adj* dense; (*Nebel*) thick; (*Gewebe*) close; (*undurchlässig*) (water)tight; (*fig*) concise ♦ *adv:* **~ an/bei** close to; **~ bevölkert** densely *od* heavily populated; **D~e** *f* density; thickness; closeness; (water)tightness; (*fig*) conciseness

dichten *vt* (*dicht machen*) to make watertight, to seal; (*NAUT*) to caulk; (*LITER*) to compose, to write ♦ *vi* to compose, to write

Dichter(in) **(-s, -)** *m(f)* poet; (*Autor*) writer; **d~isch** *adj* poetical

dichthalten (*unreg*) (*umg*) *vi* to keep one's mouth shut

Dichtung *f* (*TECH*) washer; (*AUT*) gasket; (*Gedichte*) poetry; (*Prosa*) (piece of) writing

dick [dɪk] *adj* thick; (*fett*) fat; **durch ~ und dünn** through thick and thin; **D~darm** *m* (*ANAT*) colon; **D~e** *f* thickness; fatness; **~flüssig** *adj* viscous; **D~icht** **(-s, -e)** *nt* thicket; **D~kopf** *m* mule; **D~milch** *f* soured milk

die [diː] *def art siehe* **der**

Dieb(in) [diːp, 'diːbɪn] **(-(e)s, -e)** *m(f)* thief; **d~isch** *adj* thieving; (*umg*) immense; **~stahl** **(-(e)s, ⁻e)** *m* theft; **~stahlversicherung** *f* insurance against theft

Diele ['diːlə] *f* (*Brett*) board; (*Flur*) hall, lobby

dienen ['diːnən] *vi:* **(jdm) ~** to serve (sb)

Diener **(-s, -)** *m* servant; **~in** *f* (maid)servant; **~schaft** *f* servants *pl*

Dienst [diːnst] **(-(e)s, -e)** *m* service; **außer ~** retired; **~ haben** to be on duty; **~ habend** (*Arzt*) on duty

Dienstag ['diːnstaːk] *m* Tuesday; **d~s** *adv* on Tuesdays

Dienst- *zW:* **~bote** *m* servant; **~geheimnis** *nt* official secret; **~gespräch** *nt* business call; **~leistung** *f* service; **d~lich** *adj* official; **~mädchen** *nt* (house)maid; **~reise** *f* business trip; **~stelle** *f* office; **~vorschrift** *f* official regulations *pl*; **~weg** *m* official channels *pl*; **~zeit** *f* working hours *pl*; (*MIL*) period of service

dies [diːs] *pron (demonstrativ: sg)* this; (: *pl*) these; **~bezüglich** *adj (Frage)* on this matter; **~e(r, s)** ['diːzə(r, s)] *pron* this (one)

Diesel ['diːzəl] *m (Kraftstoff)* diesel

dieselbe [diːˈzɛlbə] *pron, art* the same

Dieselmotor *m* diesel engine

diesig ['diːzɪç] *adj* drizzly

dies- *zW:* **~jährig** *adj* this year's; **~mal** *adv* this time; **~seits** *präp +gen* on this side; **D~seits** (-) *nt* this life

Dietrich ['diːtrɪç] (**-s, -e**) *m* picklock

diffamieren [dɪfaˈmiːrən] (*pej*) *vt* to defame

Differenz [dɪfəˈrɛnts] (**-, -en**) *f (Unterschied)* difference; **~en** *pl (Meinungsverschiedenheit)* difference (of opinion); **d~ieren** *vt* to make distinctions in; **d~iert** *adj (Mensch etc)* complex

differenzial ▲ [dɪfərɛntsiaˈl] *adj* differential; **D~rechnung** *f* differential calculus

digital [digiˈtaːl] *adj* digital; **D~fernsehen** *f* digital TV

Dikt- [dɪkt] *zW:* **~afon, ~aphon** [-aˈfoːn] *nt* dictaphone; **~at** [-ˈtaːt] (**-(e)s, -e**) *nt* dictation; **~ator** [-ˈtaːtɔr] *m* dictator; **d~atorisch** [-aˈtoːrɪʃ] *adj* dictatorial; **~atur** [-aˈtuːr] *f* dictatorship; **d~ieren** [-ˈtiːrən] *vt* to dictate

Dilemma [diˈlɛma] (**-s, -s** *od* **-ta**) *nt* dilemma

Dilettant [dileˈtant] *m* dilettante, amateur; **d~isch** *adj* amateurish, dilettante

Dimension [dimɛnziˈoːn] *f* dimension

DIN *f abk (= Deutsche Industrie-Norm)* German Industrial Standard

Ding [dɪŋ] (**-(e)s, -e**) *nt* thing, object; **d~lich** *adj* real, concrete; **~s(bums)** ['dɪŋks(bʊms)] (-) (*umg*) *nt* thingummybob

Diplom [diˈploːm] (**-(e)s, -e**) *nt* diploma, certificate; **~at** [-ˈmaːt] (**-en, -en**) *m* diplomat; **~atie** [-aˈtiː] *f* diplomacy; **d~atisch** [-ˈmaːtɪʃ] *adj* diplomatic; **~ingenieur** *m* qualified engineer

dir [diːr] (*dat von* **du**) *pron* (to) you

direkt [diˈrɛkt] *adj* direct; **D~flug** *m* direct flight; **D~or** *m* director; (*SCH*) principal, headmaster; **D~übertragung** *f* live broadcast

Dirigent [diriˈgɛnt(ɪn)] *m* conductor

dirigieren [diriˈgiːrən] *vt* to direct; (*MUS*) to conduct

Diskette [dɪsˈkɛtə] *f* diskette, floppy disk

Diskont [dɪsˈkɔnt] (**-s, -e**) *m* discount; **~satz** *m* rate of discount

Diskothek [dɪskoˈteːk] (**-, -en**) *f* disco(theque)

diskret [dɪsˈkreːt] *adj* discreet; **D~ion** *f* discretion

diskriminieren [dɪskrimiˈniːrən] *vt* to discriminate against

Diskussion [dɪskʊsiˈoːn] *f* discussion; debate; **zur ~ stehen** to be under discussion

diskutieren [dɪskuˈtiːrən] *vt, vi* to discuss; to debate

Distanz [dɪsˈtants] *f* distance; **distanˈzieren** *vr*: **sich von jdm/etw d~ieren** to distance o.s. from sb/sth

Distel ['dɪstəl] (**-, -n**) *f* thistle

Disziplin [dɪstsiˈpliːn] *f* discipline

Dividende [diviˈdɛndə] *f* dividend

dividieren [diviˈdiːrən] *vt*: **(durch etw) ~** to divide (by sth)

DM [deːˈʔɛm] *abk (= Deutsche Mark)* German Mark

D-Mark ['deːmark] *f* D Mark, German Mark

SCHLÜSSELWORT

---

doch [dɔx] *adv* **1** *(dennoch)* after all; *(sowieso)* anyway; **er kam doch noch** he came after all; **du weißt es ja doch besser** you know better than I do anyway; **und doch ...** and yet ...

2 *(als bejahende Antwort)* yes I do/it does *etc*; **das ist nicht wahr - doch!** that's not true - yes it is!

3 *(auffordernd)*: **komm doch** do come; **lass ihn doch** just leave him; **nicht doch!** oh no!

4: **sie ist doch noch so jung** but she's still so young; **Sie wissen doch, wie das ist** you know how it is (, don't you?); **wenn doch** if only

♦ *konj (aber)* but; *(trotzdem)* all the same;

---

und doch hat er es getan but still he did it

Docht [dɔxt] (-(e)s, -e) *m* wick
Dock [dɔk] (-s, -s *od* -e) *nt* dock
Dogge ['dɔgə] *f* bulldog
Dogma ['dɔgma] (-s, -men) *nt* dogma; **d~tisch** *adj* dogmatic
Doktor ['dɔktɔr, *pl* -'to:rən] (-s, -en) *m* doctor
Dokument [dokumɛnt] *nt* document
Dokumentar- [dokumɛn'ta:r] *zW*: **~bericht** *m* documentary; **~film** *m* documentary (film); **d~isch** *adj* documentary
Dolch [dɔlç] (-(e)s, -e) *m* dagger
dolmetschen ['dɔlmɛtʃən] *vt, vi* to interpret; **Dolmetscher(in)** (-s, -) *m(f)* interpreter
Dom [do:m] (-(e)s, -e) *m* cathedral
dominieren [domi'ni:rən] *vt* to dominate ♦ *vi* to predominate
Donau ['do:nau] *f* Danube
Donner ['dɔnər] (-s, -) *m* thunder; **d~n** *vi unpers* to thunder
Donnerstag ['dɔnərsta:k] *m* Thursday
doof [do:f] (*umg*) *adj* daft, stupid
Doppel ['dɔpəl] (-s, -) *nt* duplicate; (*SPORT*) doubles; **~bett** *nt* double bed; **d~deutig** *adj* ambiguous; **~fenster** *nt* double glazing; **~gänger** (-s, -) *m* double; **~punkt** *m* colon; **~stecker** *m* two-way adaptor; **d~t** *adj* double; **in d~ter Ausführung** in duplicate; **~verdiener** *m* person with two incomes; (*pl: Paar*) two-income family; **~zentner** *m* 100 kilograms; **~zimmer** *nt* double room
Dorf [dɔrf] (-(e)s, -er) *nt* village; **~bewohner** *m* villager
Dorn [dɔrn] (-(e)s, -en) *m* (*BOT*) thorn; **d~ig** *adj* thorny
Dörrobst ['dœro:pst] *nt* dried fruit
Dorsch [dɔrʃ] (-(e)s, -e) *m* cod
dort [dɔrt] *adv* there; **~ drüben** over there; **~her** *adv* from there; **~hin** *adv* (to) there; **~ig** *adj* of that place; in that town
Dose ['do:zə] *f* box; (*Blechdose*) tin, can
Dosen *pl von* **Dose**; **Dosis**

Dosenöffner *m* tin *od* can opener
Dosis ['do:zɪs] (-, Dosen) *f* dose
Dotter ['dɔtər] (-s, -) *m* (egg) yolk
Drache ['draxə] (-n, -n) *m* (*Tier*) dragon
Drachen (-s, -) *m* kite; **~fliegen** (-s) *nt* hang-gliding
Draht [dra:t] (-(e)s, -e) *m* wire; **auf ~ sein** to be on the ball; **d~ig** *adj* (*Mann*) wiry; **~seil** *nt* cable; **~seilbahn** *f* cable railway, funicular
Drama ['dra:ma] (-s, Dramen) *nt* drama, play; **~tiker** [-'ma:tikər] (-s, -) *m* dramatist; **d~tisch** [-'ma:tɪʃ] *adj* dramatic
dran [dran] (*umg*) *adv*: **jetzt bin ich ~!** it's my turn now; *siehe* **daran**
Drang [draŋ] (-(e)s, -e) *m* (*Trieb*): **~ (nach)** impulse (for), urge (for), desire (for); (*Druck*) pressure
drängeln ['drɛŋəln] *vt, vi* to push, to jostle
drängen ['drɛŋən] *vt* (*schieben*) to push, to press; (*antreiben*) to urge ♦ *vi* (*eilig sein*) to be urgent; (*Zeit*) to press; **auf etw** *akk* **~ to** press for sth
drastisch ['drastɪʃ] *adj* drastic
drauf [drauf] (*umg*) *adv* = **darauf**; **D~gänger** (-s, -) *m* daredevil
draußen ['drausən] *adv* outside
Dreck [drɛk] (-(e)s) *m* mud, dirt; **d~ig** *adj* dirty, filthy
Dreh- ['dre:] *zW*: **~arbeiten** *pl* (*CINE*) shooting *sg*; **~bank** *f* lathe; **~buch** *nt* (*CINE*) script; **d~en** *vt* to turn, to rotate; (*Zigaretten*) to roll; (*Film*) to shoot ♦ *vi* to turn, to rotate ♦ *vr* to turn; (*handeln von*): **es d~t sich um ...** it's about ...; **~orgel** *f* barrel organ; **~tür** *f* revolving door; **~ung** *f* (*Rotation*) rotation; (*Umdrehung, Wendung*) turn; **~zahl** *f* rate of revolutions; **~zahlmesser** *m* rev(olution) counter
drei [drai] *num* three; **~ viertel** three quarters; **D~eck** *nt* triangle; **~eckig** *adj* triangular; **~einhalb** *num* three and a half; **~erlei** *adj inv* of three kinds; **~fach** *adj* triple, treble ♦ *adv* three times; **~hundert** *num* three hundred; **D~'königsfest** *nt* Epiphany; **~mal** *adv* three times; **~malig** *adj* three times

dreinreden ['draɪnreːdən] *vi:* **jdm ~** *(dazwischenreden)* to interrupt sb; *(sich einmischen)* to interfere with sb

Dreirad *nt* tricycle

dreißig ['draɪsɪç] *num* thirty

dreist [draɪst] *adj* bold, audacious

drei- *zW:* **~viertel** △ *num siehe* **drei**; **D~viertelstunde** *f* three-quarters of an hour; **~zehn** *num* thirteen

dreschen ['drɛʃən] *(unreg) vt (Getreide)* to thresh; *(umg: verprügeln)* to beat up

dressieren [drɛ'siːrən] *vt* to train

drillen ['drɪlən] *vt (bohren)* to drill, to bore; *(MIL)* to drill; *(fig)* to train

Drilling *m* triplet

drin [drɪn] *(umg) adv* = **darin**

dringen ['drɪŋən] *(unreg) vi (Wasser, Licht, Kälte):* **~ (durch/in** +*akk)* to penetrate (through/into); **auf etw** *akk* **~** to insist on sth

dringend ['drɪŋənt] *adj* urgent

Dringlichkeit *f* urgency

drinnen ['drɪnən] *adv* inside, indoors

dritte(r, s) ['drɪtə(r, s)] *adj* third; **D~ Welt** Third World; **D~s Reich** Third Reich; **D~l** **(-s, -)** *nt* third; **~ns** *adv* thirdly

DRK [deːʔɛr'kaː] *nt abk* (= *Deutsches Rotes Kreuz)* German Red Cross

droben ['droːbən] *adv* above, up there

Droge ['droːgə] *f* drug

drogen *zW:* **~abhängig** *adj* addicted to drugs; **D~händler** *m* drug pedlar, pusher

Drogerie [droːgə'riː] *f* chemist's shop

Drogerie

The **Drogerie** *as opposed to the* **Apotheke** *sells medicines not requiring a prescription. It tends to be cheaper and also sells cosmetics, perfume and toiletries.*

Drogist [dro'gɪst] *m* pharmacist, chemist

drohen ['droːən] *vi:* **(jdm) ~** to threaten (sb)

dröhnen ['drøːnən] *vi (Motor)* to roar; *(Stimme, Musik)* to ring, to resound

Drohung ['droːʊŋ] *f* threat

drollig ['drɔlɪç] *adj* droll

Drossel ['drɔsəl] **(-, -n)** *f* thrush

drüben ['dryːbən] *adv* over there, on the other side

drüber ['dryːbər] *(umg) adv* = **darüber**

Druck [drʊk] **(-(e)s, -e)** *m (PHYS: Zwang)* pressure; *(TYP: Vorgang)* printing; *(: Produkt)* print; *(fig: Belastung)* burden, weight; **~buchstabe** *m* block letter

drücken ['drʏkən] *vt (Knopf, Hand)* to press; *(zu eng sein)* to pinch; *(fig: Preise)* to keep down; *(: belasten)* to oppress, to weigh down ♦ *vi* to press; to pinch ♦ *vr:* **sich vor etw** *dat* **~** to get out of (doing) sth; **~d** *adj* oppressive

Drucker **(-s, -)** *m* printer

Drücker **(-s, -)** *m* button; *(Türdrücker)* handle; *(Gewehrdrücker)* trigger

Druck- *zW:* **~erei** *f* printing works, press; **~erschwärze** *f* printer's ink; **~fehler** *m* misprint; **~knopf** *m* press stud, snap fastener; **~sache** *f* printed matter; **~schrift** *f* block *od* printed letters *pl*

drum [drʊm] *(umg) adv* = **darum**

drunten ['drʊntən] *adv* below, down there

Drüse ['dryːzə] *f* gland

Dschungel ['dʒʊŋəl] **(-s, -)** *m* jungle

du [duː] *(nom) pron* you; **~ sagen** = **duzen**

Dübel ['dyːbəl] **(-s, -)** *m* Rawlplug ®

ducken ['dʊkən] *vt (Kopf, Person)* to duck; *(fig)* to take down a peg or two ♦ *vr* to duck

Duckmäuser ['dʊkmɔʏzər] **(-s, -)** *m* yes man

Dudelsack ['duːdəlzak] *m* bagpipes *pl*

Duell [du'ɛl] **(-s, -e)** *nt* duel

Duft [dʊft] **(-(e)s, ▪e)** *m* scent, odour; **d~en** *vi* to smell, to be fragrant; **d~ig** *adj (Stoff, Kleid)* delicate, diaphanous

dulden ['dʊldən] *vt* to suffer; *(zulassen)* to tolerate ♦ *vi* to suffer

dumm [dʊm] *adj* stupid; *(ärgerlich)* annoying; **der D~e sein** to be the loser; **~erweise** *adv* stupidly; **D~heit** *f* stupidity; *(Tat)* blunder, stupid mistake; **D~kopf** *m* blockhead

dumpf [dʊmpf] *adj (Ton)* hollow, dull; *(Luft)*

musty; *(Erinnerung, Schmerz)* vague

Düne ['dy:nə] *f* dune

düngen ['dyŋən] *vt* to manure

Dünger (-s, -) *m* dung, manure; *(künstlich)* fertilizer

dunkel ['dʊŋkəl] *adj* dark; *(Stimme)* deep; *(Ahnung)* vague; *(rätselhaft)* obscure; *(verdächtig)* dubious, shady; **im D~n tappen** *(fig)* to grope in the dark

Dunkel- *zW*: **~heit** *f* darkness; *(fig)* obscurity; **~kammer** *f (PHOT)* darkroom; **d~n** *vi unpers* to grow dark; **~ziffer** *f estimated number of unreported cases*

dünn [dyn] *adj* thin; **~flüssig** *adj* watery, thin

Dunst [dʊnst] **(-es, ~e)** *m* vapour; *(Wetter)* haze

dünsten ['dynstən] *vt* to steam

dunstig ['dʊnstɪç] *adj* vaporous; *(Wetter)* hazy, misty

Duplikat [dupli'ka:t] **(-(e)s, -e)** *nt* duplicate

Dur [du:r] **(-, -)** *nt (MUS)* major

SCHLÜSSELWORT

durch [dʊrç] *präp +akk* **1** *(hindurch)* through; **durch den Urwald** through the jungle; **durch die ganze Welt reisen** to travel all over the world

2 *(mittels)* through, by (means of); *(aufgrund)* due to, owing to; **Tod durch Herzschlag/den Strang** death from a heart attack/by hanging; **durch die Post** by post; **durch seine Bemühungen** through his efforts

♦ *adv* **1** *(hindurch)* through; **die ganze Nacht durch** all through the night; **den Sommer durch** during the summer; **8 Uhr durch** past 8 o'clock; **durch und durch** completely

2 *(durchgebraten etc)*: **(gut) durch** well-done

---

durch- *zW*: **~arbeiten** *vt, vi* to work through ♦ *vr* to work one's way through; **~'aus** *adv* completely; *(unbedingt)* definitely; **~aus nicht** absolutely not

Durchblick ['dʊrçblɪk] *m* view; *(fig)* comprehension; **d~en** *vi* to look through;

(umg: verstehen): **(bei etw) d~en** to understand (sth); **etw d~en lassen** *(fig)* to hint at sth

durchbrechen ['dʊrçbrɛçən] *(unreg) vt, vi* to break

durch'brechen ['dʊrçbrɛçən] *(unreg) vt insep (Schranken)* to break through; *(Schallmauer)* to break; *(Gewohnheit)* to break free from

durchbrennen ['dʊrçbrɛnən] *(unreg) vi (Draht, Sicherung)* to burn through; *(umg)* to run away

durchbringen *(unreg) vt (Kranken)* to pull through; *(umg: Familie)* to support; *(durchsetzen: Antrag, Kandidat)* to get through; *(vergeuden: Geld)* to get through, to squander

Durchbruch ['dʊrçbrʊx] *m (Öffnung)* opening; *(MIL)* breach; *(von Gefühlen etc)* eruption; *(der Zähne)* cutting; *(fig)* breakthrough; **zum ~ kommen** to break through

durch- *zW*: **~dacht** [-'daxt] *adj* well thought-out; **~'denken** *(unreg) vt* to think out; **~drehen** *vt (Fleisch)* to mince ♦ *vi (umg)* to crack up

durcheinander [dʊrçaɪ'nandər] *adv* in a mess, in confusion; *(umg: verwirrt)* confused; **~ bringen** to mess up; *(verwirren)* to confuse; **~ reden** to talk at the same time; **D~ (-s)** *nt (Verwirrung)* confusion; *(Unordnung)* mess

durch- *zW*: **~fahren** *(unreg) vi (~ Tunnel usw)* to drive through; *(ohne Unterbrechung)* to drive straight through; *(ohne anzuhalten)*: **der Zug fährt bis Hamburg ~** the train runs direct to Hamburg; *(ohne Umsteigen)*: **können wir ~fahren?** can we go direct?, can we go non-stop?; **D~fahrt** *f* transit; *(Verkehr)* thoroughfare; **D~fall** *m (MED)* diarrhoea; **~fallen** *(unreg) vi* to fall through; *(in Prüfung)* to fail; **~finden** *(unreg) vr* to find one's way through; **~fragen** *vr* to find one's way by asking

durchführ- ['dʊrçfy:r] *zW*: **~bar** *adj* feasible, practicable; **~en** *vt* to carry out; **D~ung** *f* execution, performance

---

Spelling Reform: ▲ *new spelling* △ *old spelling (to be phased out)*

Durchgang ['dʊrçgaŋ] *m* passage(way); (*bei Produktion, Versuch*) run; (*SPORT*) round; (*bei Wahl*) ballot; „~ **verboten**" "no thoroughfare"

Durchgangsverkehr *m* through traffic

durchgefroren ['dʊrçgəfroːrən] *adj* (*Mensch*) frozen stiff

durchgehen ['dʊrçgeːən] (*unreg*) *vt* (*behandeln*) to go over ♦ *vi* to go through; (*ausreißen: Pferd*) to break loose; (*Mensch*) to run away; **mein Temperament ging mit mir durch** my temper got the better of me; **jdm etw ~ lassen** to let sb get away with sth; **~d** *adj* (*Zug*) through; (*Öffnungszeiten*) continuous

durch- *zW*: **~greifen** (*unreg*) *vi* to take strong action; **~halten** (*unreg*) *vi* to last out ♦ *vt* to keep up; **~kommen** (*unreg*) *vi* to get through; (*überleben*) to pull through; **~'kreuzen** *vt insep* to thwart, to frustrate; **~lassen** (*unreg*) *vt* (*Person*) to let through; (*Wasser*) to let in; **~lesen** (*unreg*) *vt* to read through; **~leuchten** *vt insep* to X-ray; **~machen** *vt* to go through; **die Nacht ~machen** to make a night of it

Durchmesser (-s, -) *m* diameter

durch- *zW*: **~'nässen** *vt insep* to soak (through); **~nehmen** (*unreg*) *vt* to go over; **~nummerieren** ▲ *vt* to number consecutively; **~queren** [dʊrç'kveːrən] *vt insep* to cross; **D~reise** *f* transit; **auf der D~reise** passing through; (*Güter*) in transit; **~ringen** (*unreg*) *vr* to reach a decision after a long struggle

durchs [dʊrçs] = **durch das**

Durchsage ['dʊrçzaːgə] *f* intercom *od* radio announcement

durchschauen ['dʊrçʃaʊən] *vi* to look *od* see through; (*Person, Lüge*) to see through

durchscheinen ['dʊrçʃaɪnən] (*unreg*) *vi* to shine through; **~d** *adj* translucent

Durchschlag ['dʊrçʃlaːk] *m* (*Doppel*) carbon copy; (*Sieb*) strainer; **d~en** [-gən] (*unreg*) *vt* (*entzweischlagen*) to split (in two); (*sieben*) to sieve ♦ *vi* (*zum Vorschein kommen*) to emerge, to come out ♦ *vr* to get by

durchschlagend *adj* resounding

durchschneiden ['dʊrçʃnaɪdən] (*unreg*) *vt* to cut through

Durchschnitt ['dʊrçʃnɪt] *m* (*Mittelwert*) average; **über/unter dem ~** above/below average; **im ~** on average; **d~lich** *adj* average ♦ *adv* on average

Durchschnittswert *m* average

durch- *zW*: **D~schrift** *f* copy; **~sehen** (*unreg*) *vt* to look through; **~setzen** *vt* to enforce ♦ *vr* (*Erfolg haben*) to succeed; (*sich behaupten*) to get one's way; **seinen Kopf ~setzen** to get one's way; **~'setzen** *vt insep* to mix

Durchsicht ['dʊrçzɪçt] *f* looking through, checking; **d~ig** *adj* transparent

durch- *zW*: **~'sprechen** (*unreg*) *vt* to talk over; **~'stehen** (*unreg*) *vt* to live through; **~stellen** *vt* (*an Telefon*) to put through; **~stöbern** (*auch untr*) *vt* (*Kisten*) to rummage through, to rifle through; (*Haus, Wohnung*) to ransack; **~'streichen** (*unreg*) *vt* to cross out; **~'suchen** *vt insep* to search; **D~'suchung** *f* search; **~'wachsen** *adj* (*Speck*) streaky; (*fig: mittelmäßig*) so-so; **D~wahl** *f* (*TEL*) direct dialling; **~weg** *adv* throughout, completely; **~ziehen** (*unreg*) *vt* (*Faden*) to draw through ♦ *vi* to pass through; **D~zug** *m* (*Luft*) draught; (*von Truppen, Vögeln*) passage

---
SCHLÜSSELWORT
---

dürfen ['dʏrfən] (*unreg*) *vi* **1** (*Erlaubnis haben*) to be allowed to; **ich darf das** I'm allowed to (do that); **darf ich?** may I?; **darf ich ins Kino?** can *od* may I go to the cinema?; **es darf geraucht werden** you may smoke

2 (*in Verneinungen*): **er darf das nicht** he's not allowed to (do that); **das darf nicht geschehen** that must not happen; **da darf sie sich nicht wundern** that shouldn't surprise her

3 (*in Höflichkeitsformeln*): **darf ich Sie bitten, das zu tun?** may *od* could I ask you to do that?; **was darf es sein?** what can I do for you?

Rechtschreibreform: ▲ *neue Schreibung* △ *alte Schreibung (auslaufend)*

4 (*können*): **das dürfen Sie mir glauben** you can believe me
5 (*Möglichkeit*): **das dürfte genug sein** that should be enough; **es dürfte Ihnen bekannt sein, dass ...** as you will probably know ...

dürftig ['dʏrftɪç] *adj* (*ärmlich*) needy, poor; (*unzulänglich*) inadequate

dürr [dʏr] *adj* dried-up; (*Land*) arid; (*mager*) skinny, gaunt; **D~e** *f* aridity; (*Zeit*) drought; (*Magerkeit*) skinniness

Durst [dʊrst] **(-(e)s)** *m* thirst; **~ haben** to be thirsty; **d~ig** *adj* thirsty

Dusche ['dʊʃə] *f* shower; **d~en** *vi, vr* to have a shower

Düse ['dy:zə] *f* nozzle; (*Flugzeugdüse*) jet

Düsen- *zW*: **~antrieb** *m* jet propulsion; **~flugzeug** *nt* jet (plane); **~jäger** *m* jet fighter

Dussel ['dʊsəl] **(-s, -)** (*umg*) *m* twit

düster ['dy:stər] *adj* dark; (*Gedanken, Zukunft*) gloomy

Dutzend ['dʊtsənt] **(-s, -e)** *nt* dozen; **~(e)** *od* **d~(e) Mal(e)** a dozen times

duzen ['du:tsən] *vt*: (**jdn**) **~** to use the familiar form of address "du" (to *od* with sb)

> duzen

ⓘ There are two different forms of address in Germany: du and Sie. Duzen means addressing someone as 'du' - used with children, family and close friends - and siezen means addressing someone as 'Sie' - used for all grown-ups and older teenagers. Students almost always use 'du' to each other.

Dynamik [dy'na:mɪk] *f* (*PHYS*) dynamics *sg*; (*fig: Schwung*) momentum; (*von Mensch*) dynamism; **dynamisch** *adj* (*auch fig*) dynamic

Dynamit [dyna'mi:t] **(-s)** *nt* dynamite

Dynamo [dy'na:mo] **(-s, -s)** *m* dynamo

DZ *nt abk* = **Doppelzimmer**

D-Zug ['de:tsu:k] *m* through train

E, e

Ebbe ['ɛbə] *f* low tide

eben ['e:bən] *adj* level, flat; (*glatt*) smooth
♦ *adv* just; (*bestätigend*) exactly; **~ deswegen** just because of that; **~bürtig** *adj*: **jdm ~bürtig sein** to be sb's equal; **E~e** *f* plain; (*fig*) level; **~falls** *adv* likewise; **~so** *adv* just as

Eber ['e:bər] **(-s, -)** *m* boar

ebnen ['e:bnən] *vt* to level

Echo ['ɛço] **(-s, -s)** *nt* echo

echt [ɛçt] *adj* genuine; (*typisch*) typical; **E~heit** *f* genuineness

Eck- ['ɛk] *zW*: **~ball** *m* corner (kick); **~e** *f* corner; (*MATH*) angle; **e~ig** *adj* angular; **~zahn** *m* eye tooth

ECU [e'ky:] **(-, -s)** *m* (*FIN*) ECU

edel ['e:dəl] *adj* noble; **E~metall** *nt* rare metal; **E~stahl** *m* high-grade steel; **E~stein** *m* precious stone

EDV [e:de:'fau] **(-)** *f abk* (= *elektronische Datenverarbeitung*) electronic data processing

Efeu ['e:fɔy] **(-s)** *m* ivy

Effekt [ɛ'fɛkt] **(-s, -e)** *m* effect

Effekten [ɛ'fɛktən] *pl* stocks

effektiv [ɛfɛk'ti:f] *adj* effective, actual

EG ['e:'ge:] *f abk* (= *Europäische Gemeinschaft*) EC

egal [e'ga:l] *adj* all the same

Ego- [e'go] *zW*: **~ismus** [-'ɪsmʊs] *m* selfishness, egoism; **~ist** [-'ɪst] *m* egoist; **e~istisch** *adj* selfish, egoistic

Ehe ['e:ə] *f* marriage

ehe *konj* before

Ehe- *zW*: **~beratung** *f* marriage guidance (counselling); **~bruch** *m* adultery; **~frau** *f* married woman; wife; **~leute** *pl* married people; **e~lich** *adj* matrimonial; (*Kind*) legitimate

ehemalig *adj* former

ehemals *adv* formerly

Ehe- *zW*: **~mann** *m* married man; husband; **~paar** *nt* married couple

Spelling Reform: ▲ *new spelling* △ *old spelling (to be phased out)*

eher ['e:ər] *adv* (*früher*) sooner; (*lieber*) rather, sooner; (*mehr*) more

Ehe- *zW*: **~ring** *m* wedding ring; **~schließung** *f* marriage ceremony

eheste(r, s) ['e:əstə(r, s)] *adj* (*früheste*) first, earliest; **am ~n** (*liebsten*) soonest; (*meist*) most; (*wahrscheinlichst*) most probably

Ehr- ['e:r] *zW*: **e~bar** *adj* honourable, respectable; **~e** *f* honour; **e~en** *vt* to honour

Ehren- ['e:rən] *zW*: **e~amtlich** *adj* honorary; **~gast** *m* guest of honour; **e~haft** *adj* honourable; **~platz** *m* place of honour *od* (*US*) honor; **~runde** *f* lap of honour; **~sache** *f* point of honour; **e~voll** *adj* honourable; **~wort** *nt* word of honour

Ehr- *zW*: **~furcht** *f* awe, deep respect; **e~fürchtig** *adj* reverent; **~gefühl** *nt* sense of honour; **~geiz** *m* ambition; **e~geizig** *adj* ambitious; **e~lich** *adj* honest; **~lichkeit** *f* honesty; **e~los** *adj* dishonourable; **~ung** *f* honour(ing); **e~würdig** *adj* venerable

Ei [aɪ] **(-(e)s, -er)** *nt* egg

Eich- *zW*: **~e** [aɪçə] *f* oak (tree); **~l** (-, -n) *f* acorn; **~hörnchen** *nt* squirrel

Eichmaß *nt* standard

Eid [aɪt] **(-(e)s, -e)** *m* oath

Eidechse ['aɪdɛksə] *f* lizard

eidesstattlich *adj*: **~e Erklärung** affidavit

Eidgenosse *m* Swiss

Eier- *zW*: **~becher** *m* eggcup; **~kuchen** *m* omelette; pancake; **~likör** *m* advocaat; **~schale** *f* eggshell; **~stock** *m* ovary; **~uhr** *f* egg timer

Eifer ['aɪfər] **(-s)** *m* zeal, enthusiasm; **~sucht** *f* jealousy; **e~süchtig** *adj*: **e~süchtig (auf +***akk***)** jealous (of)

eifrig ['aɪfrɪç] *adj* zealous, enthusiastic

Eigelb ['aɪgɛlp] **(-(e)s, -)** *nt* egg yolk

eigen ['aɪgən] *adj* own; (*~artig*) peculiar; **mit der/dem ihm ~en ...** with that ... peculiar to him; **sich** *dat* **etw zu E~ machen** to make sth one's own; **E~art** *f* peculiarity; characteristic; **~artig** *adj* peculiar; **E~bedarf** *m*: **zum E~bedarf** for (one's own) personal use/domestic requirements; **der Vermieter machte E~bedarf geltend** the landlord showed he needed the house/flat for himself; **~händig** *adj* with one's own hand; **E~heim** *nt* owner-occupied house; **E~heit** *f* peculiarity; **~mächtig** *adj* high-handed; **E~name** *m* proper name; **~s** *adv* expressly, on purpose; **E~schaft** *f* quality, property, attribute; **E~sinn** *m* obstinacy; **~sinnig** *adj* obstinate; **~tlich** *adj* actual, real ♦ *adv* actually, really; **E~tor** *nt* own goal; **E~tum** *nt* property; **E~tümer(in)** **(-s, -)** *m(f)* owner, proprietor; **~tümlich** *adj* peculiar; **E~tümlichkeit** *f* peculiarity; **E~tumswohnung** *f* freehold flat

eignen ['aɪgnən] *vr* to be suited; **Eignung** *f* suitability

Eil- [aɪl] *zW*: **~bote** *m* courier; **~brief** *m* express letter; **~e** *f* haste; **es hat keine ~e** there's no hurry; **e~en** *vi* (*Mensch*) to hurry; (*dringend sein*) to be urgent; **e~ends** *adv* hastily; **~gut** *nt* express goods *pl*, fast freight (*US*); **e~ig** *adj* hasty, hurried; (*dringlich*) urgent; **es e~ig haben** to be in a hurry; **~zug** *m* semi-fast train, limited stop train

Eimer ['aɪmər] **(-s, -)** *m* bucket, pail

ein [aɪn] *adv*: **nicht ~ noch aus wissen** not to know what to do

ein(e) ['aɪn(ə)] *num* one ♦ *indef art* a, an

einander [aɪˈnandər] *pron* one another, each other

einarbeiten ['aɪn|arbaɪtən] *vt* to train ♦ *vr*: **sich in etw** *akk* **~** to familiarize o.s. with sth

einatmen ['aɪn|a:tmən] *vt*, *vi* to inhale, to breathe in

Einbahnstraße ['aɪnba:nʃtrasə] *f* one-way street

Einband ['aɪnbant] *m* binding, cover

einbauen ['aɪnbauən] *vt* to build in; (*Motor*) to install, to fit

Einbaumöbel *pl* built-in furniture *sg*

einbegriffen ['aɪnbəgrɪfən] *adj* included

einberufen ['aɪnbəru:fən] (*unreg*) *vt* to convene; (*MIL*) to call up

Einbettzimmer *nt* single room

einbeziehen ['aɪnbətsi:ən] (*unreg*) *vt* to

include
einbiegen ['aɪnbiːɡən] (*unreg*) *vi* to turn
einbilden ['aɪnbɪldən] *vt*: **sich** *dat* **etw ~** to
imagine sth
Einbildung *f* imagination; (*Dünkel*) conceit;
~skraft *f* imagination
Einblick ['aɪnblɪk] *m* insight
einbrechen ['aɪnbrɛçən] (*unreg*) *vi* (*in Haus*)
to break in; (*Nacht*) to fall; (*Winter*) to set
in; (*durchbrechen*) to break; **~ in** +*akk* (*MIL*)
to invade
Einbrecher (**-s, -**) *m* burglar
einbringen ['aɪnbrɪŋən] (*unreg*) *vt* to bring
in; (*Geld, Vorteil*) to yield; (*mitbringen*) to
contribute
Einbruch ['aɪnbrʊx] *m* (*Hauseinbruch*) break-
in, burglary; (*Eindringen*) invasion; (*des
Winters*) onset; (*Durchbrechen*) break; (*MET*)
approach; (*MIL*) penetration; (**bei/vor**) **~
der Nacht** at/before nightfall; **e~sicher**
adj burglar-proof
einbürgern ['aɪnbʏrɡərn] *vt* to naturalize
♦ *vr* to become adopted
einbüßen ['aɪnbyːsən] *vt* to lose, to forfeit
einchecken ['aɪntʃɛkən] *vt, vi* to check in
eincremen ['aɪnkreːmən] *vt* to put cream
on
eindecken ['aɪndɛkən] *vr*: **sich (mit etw) ~**
to lay in stocks (of sth); to stock up (with
sth)
eindeutig ['aɪndɔʏtɪç] *adj* unequivocal
eindringen ['aɪndrɪŋən] (*unreg*) *vi*: **~ (in**
+*akk*) to force one's way in(to); (*in Haus*) to
break in(to); (*in Land*) to invade; (*Gas,
Wasser*) to penetrate; (**auf jdn**) **~** (*mit Bitten*)
to pester (sb)
eindringlich *adj* forcible, urgent
Eindringling *m* intruder
Eindruck ['aɪndrʊk] *m* impression
eindrücken ['aɪndrʏkən] *vt* to press in
eindrucksvoll *adj* impressive
eine(r, s) *pron* one; (*jemand*) someone
eineiig ['aɪnʔaɪɪç] *adj* (*Zwillinge*) identical
eineinhalb ['aɪnʔaɪnʰhalp] *num* one and a
half
einengen ['aɪnʔɛŋən] *vt* to confine, to
restrict

einer- ['aɪnər] *zW*: **'E~lei (-s)** *nt* sameness;
'~'lei *adj* (*gleichartig*) the same kind of; **es
ist mir ~lei** it is all the same to me; **~seits**
adv on the one hand
einfach ['aɪnfax] *adj* simple; (*nicht mehrfach*)
single ♦ *adv* simply; **E~heit** *f* simplicity
einfädeln ['aɪnfɛːdəln] *vt* (*Nadel, Faden*) to
thread; (*fig*) to contrive
einfahren ['aɪnfaːrən] (*unreg*) *vt* to bring in;
(*Barriere*) to knock down; (*Auto*) to run in
♦ *vi* to drive in; (*Zug*) to pull in; (*MIN*) to go
down
Einfahrt *f* (*Vorgang*) driving in; pulling in;
(*MIN*) descent; (*Ort*) entrance
Einfall ['aɪnfal] *m* (*Idee*) idea, notion;
(*Lichteinfall*) incidence; (*MIL*) raid; **e~en**
(*unreg*) *vi* (*Licht*) to fall; (*MIL*) to raid;
(*einstürzen*) to fall in, to collapse;
(*einstimmen*): (**in etw** *akk*) **e~en** to join in
(with sth); **etw fällt jdm ein** sth occurs to
sb; **das fällt mir gar nicht ein** I wouldn't
dream of it; **sich** *dat* **etw e~en lassen** to
have a good idea
einfältig ['aɪnfɛltɪç] *adj* simple(-minded)
Einfamilienhaus [aɪnfa'miːliənhaʊs] *nt*
detached house
einfarbig ['aɪnfarbɪç] *adj* all one colour;
(*Stoff etc*) self-coloured
einfetten ['aɪnfɛtən] *vt* to grease
einfließen ['aɪnfliːsən] (*unreg*) *vi* to flow in
einflößen ['aɪnfløːsən] *vt*: **jdm etw ~** to give
sb sth; (*fig*) to instil sth in sb
Einfluss ▲ ['aɪnflʊs] *m* influence; **~bereich**
m sphere of influence
einförmig ['aɪnfœrmɪç] *adj* uniform; **E~keit**
f uniformity
einfrieren ['aɪnfriːrən] (*unreg*) *vi* to freeze
(up) ♦ *vt* to freeze
einfügen ['aɪnfyːɡən] *vt* to fit in; (*zusätzlich*)
to add
Einfuhr ['aɪnfuːr] (**-**) *f* import;
~beschränkung *f* import restrictions *pl*;
~bestimmungen *pl* import regulations
einführen ['aɪnfyːrən] *vt* to bring in;
(*Mensch, Sitten*) to introduce; (*Ware*) to
import
Einführung *f* introduction

Spelling Reform: ▲ *new spelling* △ *old spelling (to be phased out)*

Eingabe [ˈaɪngaːbə] *f* petition; (*COMPUT*) input

Eingang [ˈaɪngaŋ] *m* entrance; (*COMM: Ankunft*) arrival; (*Erhalt*) receipt

eingeben [ˈaɪngeːbən] (*unreg*) *vt* (*Arznei*) to give; (*Daten etc*) to enter

eingebildet [ˈaɪngəbɪldət] *adj* imaginary; (*eitel*) conceited

Eingeborene(r) [ˈaɪngəboːrənə(r)] *f(m)* native

Eingebung *f* inspiration

eingefleischt [ˈaɪngəflaɪʃt] *adj* (*Gewohnheit, Vorurteile*) deep-rooted

eingehen [ˈaɪngeːən] (*unreg*) *vi* (*Aufnahme finden*) to come in; (*Sendung, Geld*) to be received; (*Tier, Pflanze*) to die; (*Firma*) to fold; (*schrumpfen*) to shrink ♦ *vt* to enter into; (*Wette*) to make; **auf etw** *akk* **~** to go into sth; **auf jdn ~** to respond to sb; **jdm ~** (*verständlich sein*) to be comprehensible to sb; **~d** *adj* exhaustive, thorough

Eingemachte(s) [ˈaɪngəmaːxtə(s)] *nt* preserves *pl*

eingenommen [ˈaɪngənɔmən] *adj*: **~ (von)** fond (of), partial (to); **~ (gegen)** prejudiced (against)

eingeschrieben [ˈaɪngəʃriːbən] *adj* registered

eingespielt [ˈaɪngəʃpiːlt] *adj*: **aufeinander ~ sein** to be in tune with each other

Eingeständnis [ˈaɪngəʃtɛntnɪs] (*-ses, -se*) *nt* admission, confession

eingestehen [ˈaɪngəʃteːən] (*unreg*) *vt* to confess

eingestellt [ˈaɪngəʃtɛlt] *adj*: **auf etw ~ sein** to be prepared for sth

eingetragen [ˈaɪngətraːgən] *adj* (*COMM*) registered

Eingeweide [ˈaɪngəvaɪdə] (*-s, -*) *nt* innards *pl*, intestines *pl*

Eingeweihte(r) [ˈaɪngəvaɪtə(r)] *f(m)* initiate

eingewöhnen [ˈaɪngəvøːnən] *vr*: **sich ~ in** +*akk* to settle (down) in

eingleisig [ˈaɪnglaɪzɪç] *adj* single-track

eingreifen [ˈaɪngraɪfən] (*unreg*) *vi* to intervene, to interfere; (*Zahnrad*) to mesh

Eingriff [ˈaɪngrɪf] *m* intervention,

interference; (*Operation*) operation

einhaken [ˈaɪnhaːkən] *vt* to hook in ♦ *vr*: **sich bei jdm ~** to link arms with sb ♦ *vi* (*sich einmischen*) to intervene

Einhalt [ˈaɪnhalt] *m*: **~ gebieten** +*dat* to put a stop to; **e~en** (*unreg*) *vt* (*Regel*) to keep ♦ *vi* to stop

einhändigen [ˈaɪnhɛndɪgən] *vt* to hand in

einhängen [ˈaɪnhɛŋən] *vt* to hang; (*Telefon*) to hang up ♦ *vi* (*TEL*) to hang up; **sich bei jdm ~** to link arms with sb

einheimisch [ˈaɪnhaɪmɪʃ] *adj* native; **E~e(r)** *f(m)* local

Einheit [ˈaɪnhaɪt] *f* unity; (*Maß, MIL*) unit; **e~lich** *adj* uniform; **~spreis** *m* standard price

einholen [ˈaɪnhoːlən] *vt* (*Tau*) to haul in; (*Fahne, Segel*) to lower; (*Vorsprung aufholen*) to catch up with; (*Verspätung*) to make up; (*Rat, Erlaubnis*) to ask ♦ *vi* (*einkaufen*) to shop

einhüllen [ˈaɪnhylən] *vt* to wrap up

einhundert [ˈaɪnhʊndərt] *num* one hundred, a hundred

einig [ˈaɪnɪç] *adj* (*vereint*) united; **~ gehen** to agree; **sich** *dat* **~ sein** to be in agreement; **~ werden** to agree

einige(r, s) [ˈaɪnɪgə(r, s)] *adj, pron* some ♦ *pl* some; (*mehrere*) several; **~ Mal** a few times

einigen *vt* to unite ♦ *vr*: **sich ~ (auf** +*akk*) to agree (on)

einigermaßen *adv* somewhat; (*leidlich*) reasonably

einig- *zW*: **E~keit** *f* unity; (*Übereinstimmung*) agreement; **E~ung** *f* agreement; (*Vereinigung*) unification

einkalkulieren [ˈaɪnkalkuliːrən] *vt* to take into account, to allow for

Einkauf [ˈaɪnkaʊf] *m* purchase; **e~en** *vt* to buy ♦ *vi* to shop; **e~en gehen** to go shopping

Einkaufs- *zW*: **~bummel** *m* shopping spree; **~korb** *m* shopping basket; **~wagen** *m* shopping trolley; **~zentrum** *nt* shopping centre

einklammern [ˈaɪnklamərn] *vt* to put in brackets, to bracket

Rechtschreibreform: ▲ *neue Schreibung* △ *alte Schreibung (auslaufend)*

Einklang ['aɪnklaŋ] *m* harmony

einklemmen ['aɪnklɛmən] *vt* to jam

einkochen ['aɪnkɔxən] *vt* to boil down; (*Obst*) to preserve, to bottle

Einkommen ['aɪnkɔmən] (**-s, -**) *nt* income; **~(s)steuer** *f* income tax

Einkünfte ['aɪnkynftə] *pl* income *sg*, revenue *sg*

einladen ['aɪnla:dən] (*unreg*) *vt* (*Person*) to invite; (*Gegenstände*) to load; **jdn ins Kino ~** to take sb to the cinema

Einladung *f* invitation

Einlage ['aɪnla:gə] *f* (*Programmeinlage*) interlude; (*Spareinlage*) deposit; (*Schuheinlage*) insole; (*Fußstütze*) support; (*Zahneinlage*) temporary filling; (*KOCH*) noodles *pl*, vegetables *pl etc* in soup

einlagern ['aɪnla:gərn] *vt* to store

Einlass ▲ ['aɪnlas] (**-es, ˷e**) *m* (*Zutritt*) admission

einlassen ['aɪnlasən] (*unreg*) *vt* to let in; (*einsetzen*) to set in ♦ *vr*: **sich mit jdm/auf etw** *akk* **~** to get involved with sb/sth

Einlauf ['aɪnlaʊf] *m* arrival; (*von Pferden*) finish; (*MED*) enema; **e~en** (*unreg*) *vi* to arrive, to come in; (*in Hafen*) to enter; (*SPORT*) to finish; (*Wasser*) to run in; (*Stoff*) to shrink ♦ *vt* (*Schuhe*) to break in ♦ *vr* (*SPORT*) to warm up; (*Motor, Maschine*) to run in; **jdm das Haus e~en** to invade sb's house

einleben ['aɪnle:bən] *vr* to settle down

einlegen ['aɪnle:gən] *vt* (*einfügen: Blatt, Sohle*) to insert; (*KOCH*) to pickle; (*Pause*) to have; (*Protest*) to make; (*Veto*) to use; (*Berufung*) to lodge; (*AUT: Gang*) to engage

einleiten ['aɪnlaɪtən] *vt* to introduce, to start; (*Geburt*) to induce; **Einleitung** *f* introduction; induction

einleuchten ['aɪnlɔyçtən] *vi*: (**jdm**) **~** to be clear *od* evident (to sb); **~d** *adj* clear

einliefern ['aɪnli:fərn] *vt*: **~ (in** +*akk*) to take (into)

Einlieferungsschein *m* certificate of posting

Einliegerwohnung ['aɪnli:gərvo:nʊŋ] *f* self-contained flat; (*für Eltern, Großeltern*) granny flat

einlösen ['aɪnløːzən] *vt* (*Scheck*) to cash; (*Schuldschein, Pfand*) to redeem; (*Versprechen*) to keep

einmachen ['aɪnmaxən] *vt* to preserve

einmal ['aɪnma:l] *adv* once; (*erstens*) first; (*zukünftig*) sometime; **nehmen wir ~ an** just let's suppose; **noch ~** once more; **nicht ~ not** even; **auf ~** all at once; **es war ~** once upon a time there was/were; **E~'eins** *nt* multiplication tables *pl*; **~ig** *adj* unique; (*nur einmal erforderlich*) single; (*prima*) fantastic

Einmarsch ['aɪnmarʃ] *m* entry; (*MIL*) invasion; **e~ieren** *vi* to march in

einmischen ['aɪnmɪʃən] *vr*: **sich ~ (in** +*akk*) to interfere (with)

einmütig ['aɪnmy:tɪç] *adj* unanimous

Einnahme ['aɪnna:mə] *f* (*von Medizin*) taking; (*MIL*) capture, taking; **~n** *pl* (*Geld*) takings, revenue *sg*; **~quelle** *f* source of income

einnehmen ['aɪnne:mən] (*unreg*) *vt* to take; (*Stellung, Raum*) to take up; **~ für/gegen** to persuade in favour of/against; **~d** *adj* charming

einordnen ['aɪnɔrdnən] *vt* to arrange, to fit in ♦ *vr* to adapt; (*AUT*) to get into lane

einpacken ['aɪnpakən] *vt* to pack (up)

einparken ['aɪnparkən] *vt* to park

einpendeln ['aɪnpɛndəln] *vr* to even out

einpflanzen ['aɪnpflantsən] *vt* to plant; (*MED*) to implant

einplanen ['aɪnpla:nən] *vt* to plan for

einprägen ['aɪnprɛ:gən] *vt* to impress, to imprint; (*beibringen*): (**jdm**) **~** to impress (on sb); **sich** *dat* **etw ~** to memorize sth

einrahmen ['aɪnra:mən] *vt* to frame

einräumen ['aɪnrɔymən] *vt* (*ordnend*) to put away; (*überlassen: Platz*) to give up; (*zugestehen*) to admit, to concede

einreden ['aɪnre:dən] *vt*: **jdm/sich etw ~** to talk sb/o.s. into believing sth

einreiben ['aɪnraɪbən] (*unreg*) *vt* to rub in

einreichen ['aɪnraɪçən] *vt* to hand in; (*Antrag*) to submit

Einreise ['aɪnraɪzə] *f* entry;

Spelling Reform: ▲ *new spelling* △ *old spelling (to be phased out)*

~bestimmungen *pl* entry regulations;
~erlaubnis *f* entry permit;
~genehmigung *f* entry permit; **e~n** *vi*:
(in ein Land) e~n to enter (a country)

einrichten ['aɪnrɪçtən] *vt* (*Haus*) to furnish;
(*schaffen*) to establish, to set up; (*arrangieren*) to arrange; (*möglich machen*) to manage ♦ *vr* (*in Haus*) to furnish one's house; **sich ~ (auf** +*akk*) (*sich vorbereiten*) to prepare o.s. (for); (*sich anpassen*) to adapt (to)

Einrichtung *f* (*Wohnungseinrichtung*) furnishings *pl*; (*öffentliche Anstalt*) organization; (*Dienste*) service

einrosten ['aɪnrɔstən] *vi* to get rusty

einrücken ['aɪnrʏkən] *vi* (*MIL*: *in Land*) to move in

Eins [aɪns] (**-, -en**) *f* one; **e~** *num* one; **es ist mir alles e~** it's all one to me

einsam ['aɪnzaːm] *adj* lonely, solitary;
E~keit *f* loneliness, solitude

einsammeln ['aɪnzaməln] *vt* to collect

Einsatz ['aɪnzats] *m* (*Teil*) inset; (*an Kleid*) insertion; (*Verwendung*) use, employment; (*Spieleinsatz*) stake; (*Risiko*) risk; (*MIL*) operation; (*MUS*) entry; **im ~** in action;
e~bereit *adj* ready for action

einschalten ['aɪnʃaltən] *vt* (*einfügen*) to insert; (*Pause*) to make; (*ELEK*) to switch on;
(*Anwalt*) to bring in ♦ *vr* (*dazwischentreten*) to intervene

einschärfen ['aɪnʃɛrfən] *vt*: **jdm etw ~** to impress sth (up)on sb

einschätzen ['aɪnʃɛtsən] *vt* to estimate, to assess ♦ *vr* to rate o.s.

einschenken ['aɪnʃɛŋkən] *vt* to pour out

einschicken ['aɪnʃɪkən] *vt* to send in

einschl. *abk* (= *einschließlich*) incl.

einschlafen ['aɪnʃlaːfən] (*unreg*) *vi* to fall asleep, to go to sleep

einschläfernd ['aɪnʃlɛːfɛrnt] *adj* (*MED*) soporific; (*langweilig*) boring; (*Stimme*) lulling

Einschlag ['aɪnʃlaːk] *m* impact; (*fig*: *Beimischung*) touch, hint; **e~en** [-gən] (*unreg*) *vt* to knock in; (*Fenster*) to smash, to break; (*Zähne, Schädel*) to smash in; (*AUT*: *Räder*) to turn; (*kürzer machen*) to take up; (*Ware*) to pack, to wrap up; (*Weg, Richtung*) to take ♦ *vi* to hit; (*sich einigen*) to agree;
(*Anklang finden*) to work, to succeed; **in etw** *akk*/**auf jdn e~en** to hit sth/sb

einschlägig ['aɪnʃlɛːgɪç] *adj* relevant

einschließen ['aɪnʃliːsən] (*unreg*) *vt* (*Kind*) to lock in; (*Häftling*) to lock up; (*Gegenstand*) to lock away; (*Bergleute*) to cut off;
(*umgeben*) to surround; (*MIL*) to encircle;
(*fig*) to include, to comprise ♦ *vr* to lock o.s. in

einschließlich *adv* inclusive ♦ *präp* +*gen* inclusive of, including

einschmeicheln ['aɪnʃmaɪçəln] *vr*: **sich ~ (bei)** to ingratiate o.s. (with)

einschnappen ['aɪnʃnapən] *vi* (*Tür*) to click to; (*fig*) to be touchy; **eingeschnappt sein** to be in a huff

einschneidend ['aɪnʃnaɪdənt] *adj* drastic

Einschnitt ['aɪnʃnɪt] *m* cutting; (*MED*) incision; (*Ereignis*) decisive point

einschränken ['aɪnʃrɛŋkən] *vt* to limit, to restrict; (*Kosten*) to cut down, to reduce ♦ *vr* to cut down (on expenditure);
Einschränkung *f* restriction, limitation; reduction; (*von Behauptung*) qualification

Einschreib- ['aɪnʃraɪb] *zW*: **~(e)brief** *m* recorded delivery letter; **e~en** (*unreg*) *vt* to write in; (*Post*) to send recorded delivery ♦ *vr* to register; (*UNIV*) to enrol; **~en** *nt* recorded delivery letter

einschreiten ['aɪnʃraɪtən] (*unreg*) *vi* to step in, to intervene; **~ gegen** to take action against

einschüchtern ['aɪnʃʏçtərn] *vt* to intimidate

einschulen ['aɪnʃuːlən] *vt*: **eingeschult werden** (*Kind*) to start school

einsehen ['aɪnzeːən] (*unreg*) *vt* (*hineinsehen in*) to realize; (*Akten*) to have a look at;
(*verstehen*) to see; **E~ (-s)** *nt* understanding; **ein E~ haben** to show understanding

einseitig ['aɪnzaɪtɪç] *adj* one-sided

Einsend- ['aɪnzɛnt] *zW*: **e~en** (*unreg*) *vt* to send in; **~er (-s, -)** *m* sender, contributor;
~ung *f* sending in

Rechtschreibreform: ▲ *neue Schreibung* △ *alte Schreibung (auslaufend)*

einsetzen ['aınzɛtsən] vt to put (in); (in Amt) to appoint, to install; (Geld) to stake; (verwenden) to use; (MIL) to employ ♦ vi (beginnen) to set in; (MUS) to enter, to come in ♦ vr to work hard; **sich für jdn/ etw ~** to support sb/sth

Einsicht ['aınzıçt] f insight; (in Akten) look, inspection; **zu der ~ kommen, dass ...** to come to the conclusion that ...; **e~ig** adj (Mensch) judicious; **e~slos** adj unreasonable; **e~svoll** adj understanding

einsilbig ['aınzılbıç] adj (auch fig) monosyllabic; (Mensch) uncommunicative

einspannen ['aınʃpanən] vt (Papier) to insert; (Pferde) to harness; (umg: Person) to rope in

Einsparung ['aınʃpa:roŋ] f economy, saving

einsperren ['aınʃpɛrən] vt to lock up

einspielen ['aınʃpi:lən] vr (SPORT) to warm up ♦ vt (Film: Geld) to bring in; (Instrument) to play in; **sich aufeinander ~** to become attuned to each other; **gut eingespielt** running smoothly

einsprachig ['aınʃpra:xıç] adj monolingual

einspringen ['aınʃprıŋən] (unreg) vi (aushelfen) to help out, to step into the breach

Einspruch ['aınʃprox] m protest, objection; **~srecht** nt veto

einspurig ['aınʃpu:rıç] adj (EISENB) single-track; (AUT) single-lane

einst [aınst] adv once; (zukünftig) one day, some day

einstecken ['aınʃtɛkən] vt to stick in, to insert; (Brief) to post; (ELEK: Stecker) to plug in; (Geld) to pocket; (mitnehmen) to take; (überlegen sein) to put in the shade; (hinnehmen) to swallow

einstehen ['aınʃte:ən] (unreg) vi: **für jdn/ etw ~** to guarantee sb/sth; (verantworten): **für etw ~** to answer for sth

einsteigen ['aınʃtaıgən] (unreg) vi to get in od on; (in Schiff) to go on board; (sich beteiligen) to come in; (hineinklettern) to climb in

einstellen ['aınʃtɛlən] vt (aufhören) to stop; (Geräte) to adjust; (Kamera etc) to focus;

(Sender, Radio) to tune in; (unterstellen) to put; (in Firma) to employ, to take on ♦ vi (Firma) to take on staff/workers ♦ vr (anfangen) to set in; (kommen) to arrive; **sich auf jdn ~** to adapt to sb; **sich auf etw** akk ~ to prepare o.s. for sth

Einstellung f (Aufhören) suspension; adjustment; focusing; (von Arbeiter etc) appointment; (Haltung) attitude

Einstieg ['aınʃti:k] (-(e)s, -e) m entry; (fig) approach

einstig ['aınstıç] adj former

einstimmig ['aınʃtımıç] adj unanimous; (MUS) for one voice

einstmals adv once, formerly

einstöckig ['aınʃtœkıç] adj two-storeyed

Einsturz ['aınʃtorts] m collapse

einstürzen ['aınʃtʏrtsən] vi to fall in, to collapse

einst- zW: **~weilen** adv meanwhile; (vorläufig) temporarily, for the time being; **~weilig** adj temporary

eintägig ['aınte:gıç] adj one-day

eintauschen ['aıntauʃən] vt: **~ (gegen** od **für)** to exchange (for)

eintausend ['aın'tauzənt] num one thousand

einteilen ['aıntaılən] vt (in Teile) to divide (up); (Menschen) to assign

einteilig adj one-piece

eintönig ['aıntø:nıç] adj monotonous

Eintopf ['aıntɔpf] m stew

Eintracht ['aıntraxt] (-) f concord, harmony; **einträchtig** ['aıntrɛçtıç] adj harmonious

Eintrag ['aıntra:k] (-(e)s, **²e**) m entry; **amtlicher ~** entry in the register; **e~en** [-gən] (unreg) vt (in Buch) to enter; (Profit) to yield ♦ vr to put one's name down

einträglich ['aıntrɛ:klıç] adj profitable

eintreffen ['aıntrɛfən] (unreg) vi to happen; (ankommen) to arrive

eintreten ['aıntre:tən] (unreg) vi to occur; (sich einsetzen) to intercede ♦ vt (Tür) to kick open; **~ in** +akk to enter; (in Klub, Partei) to join

Eintritt ['aıntrıt] m (Betreten) entrance; (Anfang) commencement; (in Klub etc)

Spelling Reform: ▲ new spelling △ old spelling (to be phased out)

joining

Eintritts- *zW:* **~geld** *nt* admission charge; **~karte** *f* (admission) ticket; **~preis** *m* admission charge

einüben ['aɪnˌyːbən] *vt* to practise

Einvernehmen ['aɪnferneːmən] **(-s, -)** *nt* agreement, harmony

einverstanden ['aɪnferʃtandən] *excl* agreed, okay ♦ *adj:* **~ sein** to agree, to be agreed

Einverständnis ['aɪnferʃtɛntnɪs] *nt* understanding; (*gleiche Meinung*) agreement

Einwand ['aɪnvant] **(-(e)s, ⁺e)** *m* objection

Einwand- *zW:* **~erer** ['aɪnvandərər] *m* immigrant; **e~ern** *vi* to immigrate; **~erung** *f* immigration

einwandfrei *adj* perfect ♦ *adv* absolutely

Einweg- ['aɪnveːg-] *zW:* **~flasche** *f* no-deposit bottle; **~spritze** *f* disposable syringe

einweichen ['aɪnvaɪçən] *vt* to soak

einweihen ['aɪnvaɪən] *vt* (*Kirche*) to consecrate; (*Brücke*) to open; (*Gebäude*) to inaugurate; **~ (in** +*akk*) (*Person*) to initiate (in); **Einweihung** *f* consecration; opening; inauguration; initiation

einweisen ['aɪnvaɪzən] (*unreg*) *vt* (*in Amt*) to install; (*in Arbeit*) to introduce; (*in Anstalt*) to send

einwenden ['aɪnvɛndən] (*unreg*) *vt:* **etwas ~ gegen** to object to, to oppose

einwerfen ['aɪnverfən] (*unreg*) *vt* to throw in; (*Brief*) to post; (*Geld*) to put in, to insert; (*Fenster*) to smash; (*äußern*) to interpose

einwickeln ['aɪnvɪkəln] *vt* to wrap up; (*fig: umg*) to outsmart

einwilligen ['aɪnvɪlɪgən] *vi:* **~ (in** +*akk*) to consent (to), to agree (to); **Einwilligung** *f* consent

einwirken ['aɪnvɪrkən] *vi:* **auf jdn/etw ~** to influence sb/sth

Einwohner ['aɪnvoːnər] **(-s, -)** *m* inhabitant; **~'meldeamt** *nt* registration office; **~schaft** *f* population, inhabitants *pl*

Einwurf ['aɪnvʊrf] *m* (*Öffnung*) slot; (*von Münze*) insertion; (*von Brief*) posting; (*Einwand*) objection; (*SPORT*) throw-in

Einzahl ['aɪntsaːl] *f* singular; **e~en** *vt* to pay

in; **~ung** *f* paying in; **~ungsschein** *m* paying-in slip, deposit slip

einzäunen ['aɪntsɔynən] *vt* to fence in

Einzel ['aɪntsəl] **(-s, -)** *nt* (*TENNIS*) singles; **~fahrschein** *m* one-way ticket; **~fall** *m* single instance, individual case; **~handel** *m* retail trade; **~handelspreis** *m* retail price; **~heit** *f* particular, detail; **~kind** *nt* only child; **e~n** *adj* single; (*vereinzelt*) the odd ♦ *adv* singly; **e~n angeben** to specify; **der/die E~ne** the individual; **das E~ne** the particular; **ins E~ne gehen** to go into detail(s); **~teil** *nt* component (part); **~zimmer** *nt* single room; **~zimmerzuschlag** *m* single room supplement

einziehen ['aɪntsiːən] (*unreg*) *vt* to draw in, to take in; (*Kopf*) to duck; (*Fühler, Antenne, Fahrgestell*) to retract; (*Steuern, Erkundigungen*) to collect; (*MIL*) to draft, to call up; (*aus dem Verkehr ziehen*) to withdraw; (*konfiszieren*) to confiscate ♦ *vi* to move in; (*Friede, Ruhe*) to come; (*Flüssigkeit*) to penetrate

einzig ['aɪntsɪç] *adj* only; (*ohnegleichen*) unique; **das E~e** the only thing; **der/die E~e** the only one; **~artig** *adj* unique

Einzug ['aɪntsuːk] *m* entry, moving in

Eis [aɪs] **(-es, -)** *nt* ice; (*Speiseeis*) ice cream; **~bahn** *f* ice *od* skating rink; **~bär** *m* polar bear; **~becher** *m* sundae; **~bein** *nt* pig's trotters *pl*; **~berg** *m* iceberg; **~café** *nt* ice-cream parlour (*BRIT*) *od* parlor (*US*); **~decke** *f* sheet of ice; **~diele** *f* ice-cream parlour

Eisen ['aɪzən] **(-s, -)** *nt* iron

Eisenbahn *f* railway, railroad (*US*); **~er (-s, -)** *m* railwayman, railway employee, railroader (*US*); **~schaffner** *m* railway guard; **~wagen** *m* railway carriage

Eisenerz *nt* iron ore

eisern ['aɪzərn] *adj* iron; (*Gesundheit*) robust; (*Energie*) unrelenting; (*Reserve*) emergency

Eis- *zW:* **e~frei** *adj* clear of ice; **~hockey** *nt* ice hockey; **e~ig** ['aɪzɪç] *adj* icy; **e~kalt** *adj* icy cold; **~kunstlauf** *m* figure skating; **~laufen** *nt* ice skating; **~pickel** *m* ice axe; **~schrank** *m* fridge, icebox (*US*); **~würfel**

m ice cube; **~zapfen** *m* icicle; **~zeit** *f* ice age

eitel ['aɪtəl] *adj* vain; **E~keit** *f* vanity

Eiter ['aɪtər] (**-s**) *m* pus; **e~ig** *adj* suppurating; **e~n** *vi* to suppurate

Eiweiß (**-es, -e**) *nt* white of an egg; (CHEM) protein

Ekel¹ ['eːkəl] (**-s, -**) *nt* (*umg*: *Mensch*) nauseating person

Ekel² ['eːkəl] (**-s**) *m* nausea, disgust; **~ erregend** nauseating, disgusting; **e~haft** *adj* nauseating, disgusting; **e~ig** *adj* nauseating, disgusting; **e~n** *vt* to disgust ♦ *vr*: **sich e~n (vor** +*dat*) to loathe, to be disgusted (at); **es e~t jdn** *od* **jdm** sb is disgusted, **eklig** *adj* nauseating, disgusting

Ekstase [ɛk'staːzə] *f* ecstasy

Ekzem [ɛk'tseːm] (**-s, -e**) *nt* (MED) eczema

Elan [e'lãː] (**-s**) *m* elan

elastisch [e'lastɪʃ] *adj* elastic

Elastizität [elastitsi'tɛːt] *f* elasticity

Elch [ɛlç] (**-(e)s, -e**) *m* elk

Elefant [ele'fant] *m* elephant

elegant [ele'gant] *adj* elegant

Eleganz [ele'gants] *f* elegance

Elek- [e'lɛk] *zW*: **~triker** [-trɪkər] (**-s, -**) *m* electrician; **e~trisch** [-trɪʃ] *adj* electric; **e~trisieren** [-tri'ziːrən] *vt* (*auch fig*) to electrify; (*Mensch*) to give an electric shock to ♦ *vr* to get an electric shock; **~trizität** [tritsi'tɛːt] *f* electricity; **~trizitätswerk** *nt* power station; (*Gesellschaft*) electric power company

Elektro- [e'lɛktro] *zW*: **~de** [-'troːdə] *f* electrode; **~gerät** *nt* electrical appliance; **~herd** *m* electric cooker; **~n** (**-s, -en**) *nt* electron; **~nenrechner** [elɛk'troːnən-] *m* computer; **~nik** *f* electronics *sg*; **e~nisch** *adj* electronic; **~rasierer** *m* electric razor; **~technik** *f* electrical engineering

Element [ele'mɛnt] (**-s, -e**) *nt* element; (*ELEK*) cell, battery; **e~ar** [-'taːr] *adj* elementary; (*naturhaft*) elemental

Elend ['eːlɛnt] (**-(e)s**) *nt* misery; **e~** *adj* miserable; **~sviertel** *nt* slum

elf [ɛlf] *num* eleven; **E~** (**-, -en**) *f* (SPORT) eleven

Elfe *f* elf

Elfenbein *nt* ivory

Elfmeter *m* (SPORT) penalty (kick)

Elite [e'liːtə] *f* elite

Ell- *zW*: **~bogen** *m* elbow; **~e** ['ɛlə] *f* ell; (*Maß*) yard; **~enbogen** *m* elbow; **~(en)bogenfreiheit** *f* (*fig*) elbow room

Elsass ▲ ['ɛlzas] (**-**) *nt*: **das ~** Alsace

Elster ['ɛlstər] (**-, -n**) *f* magpie

Eltern ['ɛltərn] *pl* parents; **~beirat** *m* (SCH) ≈ PTA (BRIT), parents' council; **~haus** *nt* home; **e~los** *adj* parentless

E-Mail ['iːmeːl] (**-, -s**) *f* E-mail

Emaille [e'maljə] (**-s, -s**) *nt* enamel

emaillieren [ema'jiːrən] *vt* to enamel

Emanzipation [emantsipatsi'oːn] *f* emancipation

emanzi'pieren *vt* to emancipate

Embryo ['ɛmbryo] (**-s, -s** *od* **Embryonen**) *m* embryo

Emi- *zW*: **~'grant(in)** *m(f)* emigrant; **~gration** *f* emigration; **e~grieren** *vi* to emigrate

Emissionen [emisi'oːnən] *fpl* emissions

Empfang [ɛm'pfaŋ] (**-(e)s, ⸚e**) *m* reception; (*Erhalten*) receipt; **in ~ nehmen** to receive; **e~en** (*unreg*) *vt* to receive ♦ *vi* (*schwanger werden*) to conceive

Empfäng- [ɛm'pfɛŋ] *zW*: **~er** (**-s, -**) *m* receiver; (COMM) addressee, consignee; **~erabschnitt** *m* receipt slip; **e~lich** *adj* receptive, susceptible; **~nis** (**-, -se**) *f* conception; **~nisverhütung** *f* contraception

Empfangs- *zW*: **~bestätigung** *f* acknowledgement; **~dame** *f* receptionist; **~schein** *m* receipt; **~zimmer** *nt* reception room

empfehlen [ɛm'pfeːlən] (*unreg*) *vt* to recommend ♦ *vr* to take one's leave; **~swert** *adj* recommendable

Empfehlung *f* recommendation

empfiehlst *etc* [ɛm'pfiːlst] *vb siehe* **empfehlen**

empfind- [ɛm'pfɪnt] *zW*: **~en** [-dən] (*unreg*) *vt* to feel; **~lich** *adj* sensitive; (*Stelle*) sore; (*reizbar*) touchy; **~sam** *adj* sentimental;

E~ung [-dʊŋ] f feeling, sentiment
empfohlen etc [ɛm'pfoːlən] vb siehe
  empfehlen
empor [ɛm'poːr] adv up, upwards
empören [ɛm'pøːrən] vt to make indignant;
to shock ♦ vr to become indignant; **~d** adj
outrageous
Emporkömmling [ɛm'poːrkœmlɪŋ] m
upstart, parvenu
Empörung f indignation
emsig ['ɛmzɪç] adj diligent, busy
End- ['ɛnd] in zW final; **~e (-s, -n)** nt end;
am ~e at the end; (schließlich) in the end;
am ~e sein to be at the end of one's
tether; **~e Dezember** at the end of
December; **zu ~e sein** to be finished;
e~en vi to end; **e~gültig** ['ɛnt-] adj final,
definite
Endivie [ɛn'diːviə] f endive
End- zW: **e~lich** adj final; (MATH) finite
♦ adv finally; **e~lich!** at last!; **komm e~lich!**
come on!; **e~los** adj endless, infinite;
~spiel nt final match(s); **~spurt** m (SPORT) final
spurt; **~station** f terminus; **~ung** f ending
Energie [enɛr'giː] f energy; **~bedarf** m
energy requirement; **e~los** adj lacking in
energy, weak; **~verbrauch** m energy
consumption; **~versorgung** f supply of
energy; **~wirtschaft** f energy industry
energisch [e'nɛrgɪʃ] adj energetic
eng [ɛŋ] adj narrow; (Kleidung) tight; (fig:
Horizont) narrow, limited; (Freundschaft,
Verhältnis) close; **~ an etw** dat close to sth
Engagement [ãgaʒə'mãː] (-s, -s) nt
engagement; (Verpflichtung) commitment
engagieren [ãga'ʒiːrən] vt to engage ♦ vr to
commit o.s.
Enge ['ɛŋə] f (auch fig) narrowness;
(Landenge) defile; (Meerenge) straits pl; **jdn
in die ~ treiben** to drive sb into a corner
Engel ['ɛŋəl] (-s, -) m angel; **e~haft** adj
angelic
England ['ɛŋlant] nt England;
Engländer(in) m(f) Englishman(-woman);
englisch adj English
Engpass ▲ m defile, pass; (fig, Verkehr)
bottleneck

en gros [ãˈgro] adv wholesale
engstirnig ['ɛnʃtɪrnɪç] adj narrow-minded
Enkel ['ɛŋkəl] (-s, -) m grandson; **~in** f
granddaughter; **~kind** nt grandchild
enorm [e'nɔrm] adj enormous
Ensemble [ãˈsãbəl] (-s, -s) nt company,
ensemble
entbehr- [ɛnt'beːr-] zW: **~en** vt to do
without, to dispense with; **~lich** adj
superfluous; **E~ung** f deprivation
entbinden [ɛnt'bɪndən] (unreg) vt (+gen) to
release (from); (MED) to deliver ♦ vi (MED)
to give birth; **Entbindung** f release; (MED)
confinement; **Entbindungsheim** nt
maternity hospital
entdeck- [ɛnt'dɛk] zW: **~en** vt to discover;
E~er (-s, -) m discoverer; **E~ung** f
discovery
Ente ['ɛntə] f duck; (fig) canard, false report
enteignen [ɛnt'aignən] vt to expropriate;
(Besitzer) to dispossess
enterben [ɛnt'ɛrbən] vt to disinherit
entfallen [ɛnt'falən] (unreg) vi to drop, to
fall; (wegfallen) to be dropped; **jdm ~**
(vergessen) to slip sb's memory; **auf jdn ~**
to be allotted to sb
entfalten [ɛnt'faltən] vt to unfold; (Talente)
to develop ♦ vr to open; (Mensch) to
develop one's potential; **Entfaltung** f
unfolding; (von Talenten) development
entfern- [ɛnt'fɛrn] zW: **~en** vt to remove;
(hinauswerfen) to expel ♦ vr to go away, to
withdraw; **~t** adj distant; **weit davon ~t
sein, etw zu tun** to be far from doing sth;
E~ung f distance; (Wegschaffen) removal
entfremden [ɛnt'frɛmdən] vt to estrange, to
alienate; **Entfremdung** f alienation,
estrangement
entfrosten [ɛnt'frɔstən] vt to defrost
Entfroster (-s, -) m (AUT) defroster
entführ- [ɛnt'fyːr] zW: **~en** vt to carry off,
to abduct; to kidnap; **E~er** m kidnapper;
E~ung f abduction; kidnapping
entgegen [ɛnt'geːgən] präp +dat contrary to,
against ♦ adv towards; **~bringen** (unreg) vt
to bring; **jdm etw ~bringen** (fig) to show
sb sth; **~gehen** (unreg) vi +dat to go to

meet, to go towards; **~gesetzt** *adj* opposite; (*widersprechend*) opposed; **~halten** (*unreg*) *vt* (*fig*) to object; **E~kommen** *nt* obligingness; **~kommen** (*unreg*) *vi +dat* to approach; to meet; (*fig*) to accommodate; **~kommend** *adj* obliging; **~nehmen** (*unreg*) *vt* to receive, to accept; **~sehen** (*unreg*) *vi +dat* to await; **~setzen** (*unreg*) *vi* to oppose; **~treten** (*unreg*) *vi +dat* to step up to; (*fig*) to oppose, to counter; **~wirken** *vi +dat* to counteract

entgegnen [ɛnt'geːgnən] *vt* to reply, to retort

entgehen [ɛnt'geːən] (*unreg*) *vi* (*fig*): **jdm ~** to escape sb's notice; **sich** *dat* **etw ~ lassen** to miss sth

Entgelt [ɛnt'gɛlt] **(-(e)s, -e)** *nt* compensation, remuneration

entgleisen [ɛnt'glaɪzən] *vi* (*EISENB*) to be derailed; (*fig: Person*) to misbehave; **~ lassen** to derail

entgräten [ɛnt'grɛːtən] *vt* to fillet, to bone

Enthaarungscreme [ɛnt'haːrʊŋs-] *f* hair-removing cream

enthalten [ɛnt'haltən] (*unreg*) *vt* to contain ♦ *vr*: **sich (von etw) ~** to abstain (from sth), to refrain (from sth)

enthaltsam [ɛnt'haltzaːm] *adj* abstinent, abstemious

enthemmen [ɛnt'hɛmən] *vt*: **jdn ~** to free sb from his inhibitions

enthüllen [ɛnt'hylən] *vt* to reveal, to unveil

Enthusiasmus [ɛntuzi'asmʊs] *m* enthusiasm

entkommen [ɛnt'kɔmən] (*unreg*) *vi*: **~ (aus** *od* **+dat)** to get away (from), to escape (from)

entkräften [ɛnt'krɛftən] *vt* to weaken, to exhaust; (*Argument*) to refute

entladen [ɛnt'laːdən] (*unreg*) *vt* to unload; (*ELEK*) to discharge ♦ *vr* (*ELEK: Gewehr*) to discharge; (*Ärger etc*) to vent itself

entlang [ɛnt'laŋ] *adv* along; **~ dem Fluss, den Fluss ~** along the river; **~gehen** (*unreg*) *vi* to walk along

entlarven [ɛnt'larfən] *vt* to unmask, to expose

entlassen [ɛnt'lasən] (*unreg*) *vt* to discharge; (*Arbeiter*) to dismiss; **Entlassung** *f* discharge; dismissal

entlasten [ɛnt'lastən] *vt* to relieve; (*Achse*) to relieve the load on; (*Angeklagten*) to exonerate; (*Konto*) to clear

Entlastung *f* relief; (*COMM*) crediting

Entlastungszug *m* relief train

entlegen [ɛnt'leːgən] *adj* remote

entlocken [ɛnt'lɔkən] *vt*: **(jdm etw) ~** to elicit (sth from sb)

entmutigen [ɛnt'muːtɪgən] *vt* to discourage

entnehmen [ɛnt'neːmən] (*unreg*) *vt* (*+dat*) to take out (of), to take (from); (*folgern*) to infer (from)

entreißen [ɛnt'raɪsən] (*unreg*) *vt*: **jdm etw ~** to snatch sth (away) from sb

entrichten [ɛnt'rɪçtən] *vt* to pay

entrosten [ɛnt'rɔstən] *vt* to remove rust from

entrümpeln [ɛnt'rʏmpəln] *vt* to clear out

entrüst- [ɛnt'rʏst] *zW*: **~en** *vt* to incense, to outrage ♦ *vr* to be filled with indignation; **~et** *adj* indignant, outraged; **E~ung** *f* indignation

entschädigen [ɛnt'ʃɛːdɪgən] *vt* to compensate; **Entschädigung** *f* compensation

entschärfen [ɛnt'ʃɛrfən] *vt* to defuse; (*Kritik*) to tone down

Entscheid [ɛnt'ʃaɪt] **(-(e)s, -e)** *m* decision; **e~en** [-dən] (*unreg*) *vt*, *vi*, *vr* to decide; **e~end** *adj* decisive; (*Stimme*) casting; **~ung** *f* decision

entschieden [ɛnt'ʃiːdən] *adj* decided; (*entschlossen*) resolute; **E~heit** *f* firmness, determination

entschließen [ɛnt'ʃliːsən] (*unreg*) *vr* to decide

entschlossen [ɛnt'ʃlɔsən] *adj* determined, resolute; **E~heit** *f* determination

Entschluss ▲ [ɛnt'ʃlʊs] *m* decision; **e~freudig** *adj* decisive; **~kraft** *f* determination, decisiveness

entschuldigen [ɛnt'ʃʊldɪgən] *vt* to excuse ♦ *vr* to apologize

Entschuldigung *f* apology; (*Grund*)

excuse; **jdn um ~ bitten** to apologize to sb; **~!** excuse me; (*Verzeihung*) sorry

entsetz- [ɛntˈzɛts] *zW*: **~en** *vt* to horrify; (*MIL*) to relieve ♦ *vr* to be horrified *od* appalled; **E~en (-s)** *nt* horror, dismay; **~lich** *adj* dreadful, appalling; **~t** *adj* horrified

Entsorgung [ɛntˈzɔrɡʊŋ] *f* (*von Kraftwerken, Chemikalien*) (waste) disposal

entspannen [ɛntˈʃpanən] *vt*, *vr* (*Körper*) to relax; (*POL*: *Lage*) to ease

Entspannung *f* relaxation, rest; (*POL*) détente; **~spolitik** *f* policy of détente

entsprechen [ɛntˈʃprɛçən] (*unreg*) *vi* +*dat* to correspond to; (*Anforderungen, Wünschen*) to meet, to comply with; **~d** *adj* appropriate ♦ *adv* accordingly

entspringen [ɛntˈʃprɪŋən] (*unreg*) *vi* (+*dat*) to spring (from)

entstehen [ɛntˈʃteːən] (*unreg*) *vi*: **~ (aus** *od* **durch)** to arise (from), to result (from)

Entstehung *f* genesis, origin

entstellen [ɛntˈʃtɛlən] *vt* to disfigure; (*Wahrheit*) to distort

entstören [ɛntˈʃtøːrən] *vt* (*RADIO*) to eliminate interference from

enttäuschen [ɛntˈtɔʏʃən] *vt* to disappoint; **Enttäuschung** *f* disappointment

entwaffnen [ɛntˈvafnən] *vt* (*lit, fig*) to disarm

entwässern [ɛntˈvɛsərn] *vt* to drain; **Entwässerung** *f* drainage

entweder [ɛntˈveːdər] *konj* either

entwenden [ɛntˈvɛndən] (*unreg*) *vt* to purloin, to steal

entwerfen [ɛntˈvɛrfən] (*unreg*) *vt* (*Zeichnung*) to sketch; (*Modell*) to design; (*Vortrag, Gesetz etc*) to draft

entwerten [ɛntˈveːrtən] *vt* to devalue; (*stempeln*) to cancel

Entwerter (-s, -) *m* ticket punching machine

entwickeln [ɛntˈvɪkəln] *vt*, *vr* (*auch PHOT*) to develop; (*Mut, Energie*) to show (o.s.), to display (o.s.)

Entwicklung [ɛntˈvɪklʊŋ] *f* development; (*PHOT*) developing

Entwicklungs- *zW*: **~hilfe** *f* aid for developing countries; **~land** *nt* developing country

entwöhnen [ɛntˈvøːnən] *vt* to wean; (*Süchtige*): **(einer Sache** *dat od* **von etw) ~** to cure (of sth)

Entwöhnung *f* weaning; cure, curing

entwürdigend [ɛntˈvyrdɪɡənt] *adj* degrading

Entwurf [ɛntˈvʊrf] *m* outline, design; (*Vertragsentwurf, Konzept*) draft

entziehen [ɛntˈtsiːən] (*unreg*) *vt* (+*dat*) to withdraw (from), to take away (from); (*Flüssigkeit*) to draw (from), to extract (from) ♦ *vr* (+*dat*) to escape (from); (*jds Kenntnis*) to be outside *od* beyond; (*der Pflicht*) to shirk

Entziehung *f* withdrawal; **~sanstalt** *f* drug addiction/alcoholism treatment centre; **~skur** *f* treatment for drug addiction/alcoholism

entziffern [ɛntˈtsɪfərn] *vt* to decipher; to decode

entzücken [ɛntˈtsʏkən] *vt* to delight; **E~ (-s)** *nt* delight; **~d** *adj* delightful, charming

entzünden [ɛntˈtsʏndən] *vt* to light, to set light to; (*fig, MED*) to inflame; (*Streit*) to spark off ♦ *vr* (*auch fig*) to catch fire; (*Streit*) to start; (*MED*) to become inflamed

Entzündung *f* (*MED*) inflammation

entzwei [ɛntˈtsvaɪ] *adv* broken; in two; **~brechen** (*unreg*) *vt*, *vi* to break in two; **~en** *vt* to set at odds ♦ *vr* to fall out; **~gehen** (*unreg*) *vi* to break (in two)

Enzian [ˈɛntsiaːn] **(-s, -e)** *m* gentian

Epidemie [epideˈmiː] *f* epidemic

Epilepsie [epileˈpsiː] *f* epilepsy

Episode [epiˈzoːdə] *f* episode

Epoche [eˈpɔxə] *f* epoch; **~ machend** epoch-making

Epos [ˈeːpɔs] **(-, Epen)** *nt* epic (poem)

er [eːr] (*nom*) *pron* he; it

erarbeiten [ɛrˈarbaɪtən] *vt* to work for, to acquire; (*Theorie*) to work out

erbarmen [ɛrˈbarmən] *vr* (+*gen*) to have pity *od* mercy (on); **E~ (-s)** *nt* pity

erbärmlich [ɛrˈbɛrmlɪç] *adj* wretched,

Rechtschreibreform: ▲ *neue Schreibung* △ *alte Schreibung (auslaufend)*

pitiful; **E~keit** *f* wretchedness

erbarmungslos [ɛr'barmʊŋsloːs] *adj* pitiless, merciless

erbau- [ɛr'bau] *zW:* **~en** *vt* to build, to erect; (*fig*) to edify; **E~er (-s, -)** *m* builder; **~lich** *adj* edifying

Erbe1 ['ɛrbə] **(-n, -n)** *m* heir

Erbe2 ['ɛrbə] *nt* inheritance; (*fig*) heritage

erben *vt* to inherit

erbeuten [ɛr'bɔytən] *vt* to carry off; (*MIL*) to capture

Erb- [ɛrb] *zW:* **~faktor** *m* gene; **~folge** *f* (line of) succession; **~in** *f* heiress

erbittern [ɛr'bɪtərn] *vt* to embitter; (*erzürnen*) to incense

erbittert [ɛr'bɪtərt] *adj* (*Kampf*) fierce, bitter

erblassen [ɛr'blasən] *vi* to (turn) pale

erblich ['ɛrplɪç] *adj* hereditary

erblinden [ɛr'blɪndən] *vi* to go blind

erbrechen [ɛr'brɛçən] (*unreg*) *vt, vr* to vomit

Erbschaft *f* inheritance, legacy

Erbse ['ɛrpsə] *f* pea

Erbstück *nt* heirloom

Erd- ['ɛːrd] *zW:* **~achse** *f* earth's axis; **~atmosphäre** *f* earth's atmosphere; **~beben** *nt* earthquake; **~beere** *f* strawberry; **~boden** *m* ground; **~e** *f* earth; **zu ebener ~e** at ground level; **e~en** *vt* (*ELEK*) to earth

erdenklich [ɛr'dɛŋklɪç] *adj* conceivable

Erd- *zW:* **~gas** *nt* natural gas; **~geschoss** ▲ *nt* ground floor; **~kunde** *f* geography; **~nuss** ▲ *f* peanut; **~öl** *nt* (mineral) oil

erdrosseln [ɛr'drɔsəln] *vt* to strangle, to throttle

erdrücken [ɛr'drykən] *vt* to crush

Erd- *zW:* **~rutsch** *m* landslide; **~teil** *m* continent

erdulden [ɛr'dʊldən] *vt* to endure, to suffer

ereignen [ɛr'|aignən] *vr* to happen

Ereignis [ɛr'|aignɪs] **(-ses, -se)** *nt* event; **e~los** *adj* uneventful; **e~reich** *adj* eventful

ererbt [ɛr'|ɛrpt] *adj* (*Haus*) inherited; (*Krankheit*) hereditary

erfahren [ɛr'faːrən] (*unreg*) *vt* to learn, to find out; (*erleben*) to experience ♦ *adj* experienced

Erfahrung *f* experience; **e~sgemäß** *adv* according to experience

erfassen [ɛr'fasən] *vt* to seize; (*fig: einbeziehen*) to include, to register; (*verstehen*) to grasp

erfind- [ɛr'fɪnd] *zW:* **~en** (*unreg*) *vt* to invent; **E~er (-s, -)** *m* inventor; **~erisch** *adj* inventive; **E~ung** *f* invention

Erfolg [ɛr'fɔlk] **(-(e)s, -e)** *m* success; (*Folge*) result; **~ versprechend** promising; **e~en** [-gən] *vi* to follow; (*sich ergeben*) to result; (*stattfinden*) to take place; (*Zahlung*) to be effected; **e~los** *adj* unsuccessful; **~losigkeit** *f* lack of success; **e~reich** *adj* successful

erforderlich *adj* requisite, necessary

erfordern [ɛr'fɔrdərn] *vt* to require, to demand

erforschen [ɛr'fɔrʃən] *vt* (*Land*) to explore; (*Problem*) to investigate; (*Gewissen*) to search; **Erforschung** *f* exploration; investigation; searching

erfreuen [ɛr'frɔyən] *vr:* **sich ~ an** +*dat* to enjoy ♦ *vt* to delight; **sich einer Sache** *gen* **~** to enjoy sth

erfreulich [ɛr'frɔylɪç] *adj* pleasing, gratifying; **~erweise** *adv* happily, luckily

erfrieren [ɛr'friːrən] (*unreg*) *vi* to freeze (to death); (*Glieder*) to get frostbitten; (*Pflanzen*) to be killed by frost

erfrischen [ɛr'frɪʃən] *vt* to refresh; **Erfrischung** *f* refreshment

Erfrischungs- *zW:* **~getränk** *nt* (liquid) refreshment; **~raum** *m* snack bar, cafeteria

erfüllen [ɛr'fylən] *vt* (*Raum etc*) to fill; (*fig: Bitte etc*) to fulfil ♦ *vr* to come true

ergänzen [ɛr'gɛntsən] *vt* to supplement, to complete ♦ *vr* to complement one another; **Ergänzung** *f* completion; (*Zusatz*) supplement

ergeben [ɛr'geːbən] (*unreg*) *vt* to yield, to produce ♦ *vr* to surrender; (*folgen*) to result ♦ *adj* devoted, humble

Ergebnis [ɛr'geːpnɪs] **(-ses, -se)** *nt* result; **e~los** *adj* without result, fruitless

ergehen [ɛr'geːən] (*unreg*) *vi* to be issued, to go out ♦ *vi unpers:* **es ergeht ihm gut/**

Spelling Reform: ▲ *new spelling* △ *old spelling (to be phased out)*

schlecht he's faring *od* getting on well/ badly ♦ *vr:* **sich in etw** *dat* ~ to indulge in sth; **etw über sich ~ lassen** to put up with sth

ergiebig [ɛrˈgiːbɪç] *adj* productive

Ergonomie [ɛrgonoˈmiː] *f* ergonomics *sg*

Ergonomik [ɛrgoˈnoːmɪk] *f* = **Ergonomie**

ergreifen [ɛrˈgraɪfən] *(unreg) vt (auch fig)* to seize; *(Beruf)* to take up; *(Maßnahmen)* to resort to; *(rühren)* to move; **~d** *adj* moving, touching

ergriffen [ɛrˈgrɪfən] *adj* deeply moved

Erguss ▲ [ɛrˈgʊs] *m* discharge; *(fig)* outpouring, effusion

erhaben [ɛrˈhaːbən] *adj* raised, embossed; *(fig)* exalted, lofty; **über etw** *akk* ~ **sein** to be above sth

erhalten [ɛrˈhaltən] *(unreg) vt* to receive; *(bewahren)* to preserve, to maintain; **gut** ~ in good condition

erhältlich [ɛrˈhɛltlɪç] *adj* obtainable, available

Erhaltung *f* maintenance, preservation

erhärten [ɛrˈhɛrtən] *vt* to harden; *(These)* to substantiate, to corroborate

erheben [ɛrˈheːbən] *(unreg) vt* to raise; *(Protest, Forderungen)* to make; *(Fakten)* to ascertain, to establish ♦ *vr* to rise (up)

erheblich [ɛrˈheːplɪç] *adj* considerable

erheitern [ɛrˈhaɪtərn] *vt* to amuse, to cheer (up)

Erheiterung *f* exhilaration; **zur allgemeinen** ~ to everybody's amusement

erhitzen [ɛrˈhɪtsən] *vt* to heat ♦ *vr* to heat up; *(fig)* to become heated

erhoffen [ɛrˈhɔfən] *vt* to hope for

erhöhen [ɛrˈhøːən] *vt* to raise; *(verstärken)* to increase

erhol- [ɛrˈhoːl] *zW:* **~en** *vr* to recover; *(entspannen)* to have a rest; **~sam** *adj* restful; **E~ung** *f* recovery; relaxation, rest; **~ungsbedürftig** *adj* in need of a rest, run-down; **E~ungsgebiet** *nt* ≈ holiday area; **E~ungsheim** *nt* convalescent home

erhören [ɛrˈhøːrən] *vt (Gebet etc)* to hear; *(Bitte etc)* to yield to

erinnern [ɛrˈ|ɪnərn] *vt:* ~ **(an** +*akk)* to remind (of) ♦ *vr:* **sich (an** *akk* **etw)** ~ to remember (sth)

Erinnerung *f* memory; *(Andenken)* reminder

erkältet [ɛrˈkɛltət] *adj* with a cold; ~ **sein** to have a cold

Erkältung *f* cold

erkennbar *adj* recognizable

erkennen [ɛrˈkɛnən] *(unreg) vt* to recognize; *(sehen, verstehen)* to see

erkennt- *zW:* **~lich** *adj:* **sich ~lich zeigen** to show one's appreciation; **E~lichkeit** *f* gratitude; *(Geschenk)* token of one's gratitude; **E~nis (-, -se)** *f* knowledge; *(das Erkennen)* recognition; *(Einsicht)* insight; **zur E~nis kommen** to realize

Erkennung *f* recognition

Erkennungszeichen *nt* identification

Erker [ˈɛrkər] **(-s, -)** *m* bay

erklär- [ɛrˈklɛːr] *zW:* **~bar** *adj* explicable; **~en** *vt* to explain; **~lich** *adj* explicable; *(verständlich)* understandable; **E~ung** *f* explanation; *(Aussage)* declaration

erkranken [ɛrˈkraŋkən] *vi* to fall ill; **Erkrankung** *f* illness

erkund- [ɛrˈkʊnd] *zW:* **~en** *vt* to find out, to ascertain; *(bes MIL)* to reconnoitre, to scout; **~igen** *vr:* **sich ~igen (nach)** to inquire (about); **E~igung** *f* inquiry; **E~ung** *f* reconnaissance, scouting

erlahmen [ɛrˈlaːmən] *vi* to tire; *(nachlassen)* to flag, to wane

erlangen [ɛrˈlaŋən] *vt* to attain, to achieve

Erlass ▲ [ɛrˈlas] **(-es, ⁼e)** *m* decree; *(Aufhebung)* remission

erlassen *(unreg) vt (Verfügung)* to issue; *(Gesetz)* to enact; *(Strafe)* to remit; **jdm etw** ~ to release sb from sth

erlauben [ɛrˈlaʊbən] *vt:* **(jdm etw)** ~ to allow *od* permit (sb (to do) sth) ♦ *vr* to permit o.s., to venture

Erlaubnis [ɛrˈlaʊpnɪs] **(-, -se)** *f* permission; *(Schriftstück)* permit

erläutern [ɛrˈlɔytərn] *vt* to explain; **Erläuterung** *f* explanation

erleben [ɛrˈleːbən] *vt* to experience; *(Zeit)* to live through; *(miterleben)* to witness; *(noch* *miterleben)* to live to see

Erlebnis [ɛr'le:pnɪs] **(-ses, -se)** *nt* experience

erledigen [ɛr'le:dɪgən] *vt* to take care of, to deal with; *(Antrag etc)* to process; *(umg: erschöpfen)* to wear out; *(: ruinieren)* to finish; *(: umbringen)* to do in

erleichtern [ɛr'laıçtərn] *vt* to make easier; *(fig: Last)* to lighten; *(lindern, beruhigen)* to relieve; **Erleichterung** *f* facilitation; lightening; relief

erleiden [ɛr'laıdən] *(unreg) vt* to suffer, to endure

erlernen [ɛr'lɛrnən] *vt* to learn, to acquire

erlesen [ɛr'le:zən] *adj* select, choice

erleuchten [ɛr'lɔʏçtən] *vt* to illuminate; *(fig)* to inspire

Erleuchtung *f (Einfall)* inspiration

Erlös [ɛr'løːs] **(-es, -e)** *m* proceeds *pl*

erlösen [ɛr'løːzən] *vt* to redeem, to save; **Erlösung** *f* release; *(REL)* redemption

ermächtigen [ɛr'mɛçtɪgən] *vt* to authorize, to empower; **Ermächtigung** *f* authorization; authority

ermahnen [ɛr'ma:nən] *vt* to exhort, to admonish; **Ermahnung** *f* admonition, exhortation

ermäßigen [ɛr'mɛsɪgən] *vt* to reduce; **Ermäßigung** *f* reduction

ermessen [ɛr'mɛsən] *(unreg) vt* to estimate, to gauge; **E~ (-s)** *nt* estimation; discretion; **in jds E~ liegen** to lie within sb's discretion

ermitteln [ɛr'mɪtəln] *vt* to determine; *(Täter)* to trace ♦ *vi:* **gegen jdn ~** to investigate sb

Ermittlung [ɛr'mɪtlʊŋ] *f* determination; *(Polizeiermittlung)* investigation

ermöglichen [ɛr'møː:klɪçən] *vt (+dat)* to make possible (for)

ermorden [ɛr'mɔrdən] *vt* to murder

ermüden [ɛr'my:dən] *vt, vi* to tire; *(TECH)* to fatigue; **~d** *adj* tiring; *(fig)* wearisome

Ermüdung *f* fatigue

ermutigen [ɛr'mu:tɪgən] *vt* to encourage

ernähr- [ɛr'nɛ:r] *zW:* **~en** *vt* to feed, to nourish; *(Familie)* to support ♦ *vr* to support o.s., to earn a living; **sich ~en von** to live

on; **E~er (-s, -)** *m* breadwinner; **E~ung** *f* nourishment; nutrition; *(Unterhalt)* maintenance

ernennen [ɛr'nɛnən] *(unreg) vt* to appoint; **Ernennung** *f* appointment

erneu- [ɛr'nɔʏ] *zW:* **~ern** *vt* to renew; to restore; to renovate; **E~erung** *f* renewal; restoration; renovation; **~t** *adj* renewed, fresh ♦ *adv* once more

ernst [ɛrnst] *adj* serious; **~ gemeint** meant in earnest, serious; **E~ (-es)** *m* seriousness; **das ist mein E~** I'm quite serious; **im E~** in earnest; **E~ machen mit etw** to put sth into practice; **E~fall** *m* emergency; **~haft** *adj* serious; **E~haftigkeit** *f* seriousness; **~lich** *adj* serious

Ernte ['ɛrntə] *f* harvest; **e~n** *vt* to harvest; *(Lob etc)* to earn

ernüchtern [ɛr'nʏçtərn] *vt* to sober up; *(fig)* to bring down to earth

Erober- [ɛr'|oːbər] *zW:* **~er (-s, -)** *m* conqueror; **e~n** *vt* to conquer; **~ung** *f* conquest

eröffnen [ɛr'|œfnən] *vt* to open ♦ *vr* to present itself; **jdm etw ~** to disclose sth to sb

Eröffnung *f* opening

erörtern [ɛr'|œrtərn] *vt* to discuss

Erotik [e'ro:tɪk] *f* eroticism; **erotisch** *adj* erotic

erpress- [ɛr'prɛs] *zW:* **~en** *vt (Geld etc)* to extort; *(Mensch)* to blackmail; **E~er (-s, -)** *m* blackmailer; **E~ung** *f* extortion; blackmail

erprobt [ɛr'pro:pt] *adj (Gerät, Medikamente)* proven, tested

erraten [ɛr'ra:tən] *(unreg) vt* to guess

erreg- [ɛr're:g] *zW:* **~en** *vt* to excite; *(ärgern)* to infuriate; *(hervorrufen)* to arouse, to provoke ♦ *vr* to get excited *od* worked up; **E~er (-s, -)** *m* causative agent; **E~ung** *f* excitement

erreichbar *adj* accessible, within reach

erreichen [ɛr'raıçən] *vt* to reach; *(Zweck)* to achieve; *(Zug)* to catch

errichten [ɛr'rɪçtən] *vt* to erect, to put up; *(gründen)* to establish, to set up

erringen [ɛr'rɪŋən] (*unreg*) *vt* to gain, to win

erröten [ɛr'røːtən] *vi* to blush, to flush

Errungenschaft [ɛr'rʊŋənʃaft] *f* achievement; (*umg*: *Anschaffung*) acquisition

Ersatz [ɛr'zats] (**-es**) *m* substitute; replacement; (*Schadenersatz*) compensation; (*MIL*) reinforcements *pl*; **~dienst** *m* (*MIL*) alternative service; **~reifen** *m* (*AUT*) spare tyre; **~teil** *nt* spare (part)

erschaffen [ɛr'ʃafən] (*unreg*) *vt* to create

erscheinen [ɛr'ʃaɪnən] (*unreg*) *vi* to appear; **Erscheinung** *f* appearance; (*Geist*) apparition; (*Gegebenheit*) phenomenon; (*Gestalt*) figure

erschießen [ɛr'ʃiːsən] (*unreg*) *vt* to shoot (dead)

erschlagen [ɛr'ʃlaːgən] (*unreg*) *vt* to strike dead

erschöpf- [ɛr'ʃœpf] *zW*: **~en** *vt* to exhaust; **~end** *adj* exhaustive, thorough; **E~ung** *f* exhaustion

erschrecken [ɛr'ʃrɛkən] *vt* to startle, to frighten ♦ *vi* to be frightened *od* startled; **~d** *adj* alarming, frightening

erschrocken [ɛr'ʃrɔkən] *adj* frightened, startled

erschüttern [ɛr'ʃʏtərn] *vt* to shake; (*fig*) to move deeply; **Erschütterung** *f* shaking; shock

erschweren [ɛr'ʃveːrən] *vt* to complicate

erschwinglich [ɛr'ʃvɪŋlɪç] *adj* within one's means

ersetzen [ɛr'zɛtsən] *vt* to replace; **jdm Unkosten** *etc* **~** to pay sb's expenses *etc*

ersichtlich [ɛr'zɪçtlɪç] *adj* evident, obvious

ersparen [ɛr'ʃpaːrən] *vt* (*Ärger etc*) to spare; (*Geld*) to save

Ersparnis (**-**, **-se**) *f* saving

SCHLÜSSELWORT
---

erst [eːrst] *adv* **1** first; **mach erst mal die Arbeit fertig** finish your work first; **wenn du das erst mal hinter dir hast** once you've got that behind you

2 (*nicht früher als, nur*) only; (*nicht bis*) not till; **erst gestern** only yesterday; **erst morgen** not until tomorrow; **erst als** only when, not until; **wir fahren erst später**

we're not going until later; **er ist (gerade) erst angekommen** he's only just arrived

3: **wäre er doch erst zurück!** if only he were back!

---

erstatten [ɛr'ʃtatən] *vt* (*Kosten*) to (re)pay; **Anzeige** *etc* **gegen jdn ~** to report sb; **Bericht ~** to make a report

Erstattung *f* (*von Kosten*) refund

Erstaufführung ['eːrst|aʊffyːrʊŋ] *f* first performance

erstaunen [ɛr'ʃtaʊnən] *vt* to astonish ♦ *vi* to be astonished; **E~** (**-s**) *nt* astonishment

erstaunlich *adj* astonishing

erst- ['eːrst] *zW*: **E~ausgabe** *f* first edition; **~beste(r, s)** *adj* first that comes along; **~e(r, s)** *adj* first

erstechen [ɛr'ʃtɛçən] (*unreg*) *vt* to stab (to death)

erstehen [ɛr'ʃteːən] (*unreg*) *vt* to buy ♦ *vi* to (a)rise

erstens ['eːrstəns] *adv* firstly, in the first place

ersticken [ɛr'ʃtɪkən] *vt* (*auch fig*) to stifle; (*Mensch*) to suffocate; (*Flammen*) to smother ♦ *vi* (*Mensch*) to suffocate; (*Feuer*) to be smothered; **in Arbeit ~** to be snowed under with work

erst- *zW*: **~klassig** *adj* first-class; **~malig** *adj* first; **~mals** *adv* for the first time

erstrebenswert [ɛr'ʃtreːbənsveːrt] *adj* desirable, worthwhile

erstrecken [ɛr'ʃtrɛkən] *vr* to extend, to stretch

ersuchen [ɛr'zuːxən] *vt* to request

ertappen [ɛr'tapən] *vt* to catch, to detect

erteilen [ɛr'taɪlən] *vt* to give

Ertrag [ɛr'traːk] (**-(e)s**, **ᵂe**) *m* yield; (*Gewinn*) proceeds *pl*

ertragen [ɛr'traːgən] (*unreg*) *vt* to bear, to stand

erträglich [ɛr'trɛːklɪç] *adj* tolerable, bearable

ertrinken [ɛr'trɪŋkən] (*unreg*) *vi* to drown; **E~** (**-s**) *nt* drowning

erübrigen [ɛr'|yːbrɪgən] *vt* to spare ♦ *vr* to be unnecessary

erwachen [ɛr'vaxən] *vi* to awake

erwachsen [ɛr'vaksən] *adj* grown-up; **E~e(r)** *f(m)* adult; **E~enbildung** *f* adult education

erwägen [ɛr'vɛ:gən] *(unreg) vt* to consider; **Erwägung** *f* consideration

erwähn- [ɛr'vɛ:n] *zW:* **~en** *vt* to mention; **~enswert** *adj* worth mentioning; **E~ung** *f* mention

erwärmen [ɛr'vɛrmən] *vt* to warm, to heat ♦ *vr* to get warm, to warm up; **sich ~ für** to warm to

Erwarten *nt:* **über meinen/unseren** *usw* **~** beyond my/our *etc* expectations; **wider ~** contrary to expectations

erwarten [ɛr'vartən] *vt* to expect; *(warten auf)* to wait for; **etw kaum ~ können** to be hardly able to wait for sth

Erwartung *f* expectation

erwartungsgemäß *adv* as expected

erwartungsvoll *adj* expectant

erwecken [ɛr'vɛkən] *vt* to rouse, to awake; **den Anschein ~** to give the impression

Erweis [ɛr'vais] **(-es, -e)** *m* proof; **e~en** *(unreg) vt* to prove ♦ *vr:* **sich e~en (als)** to prove (to be); **jdm einen Gefallen/Dienst e~en** to do sb a favour/service

Erwerb [ɛr'vɛrp] **(-(e)s, -e)** *m* acquisition; *(Beruf)* trade; **e~en** [-bən] *(unreg) vt* to acquire

erwerbs- *zW:* **~los** *adj* unemployed; **E~quelle** *f* source of income; **~tätig** *adj* (gainfully) employed

erwidern [ɛr'vi:dərn] *vt* to reply; *(vergelten)* to return

erwischen [ɛr'vɪʃən] *(umg) vt* to catch, to get

erwünscht [ɛr'vʏnʃt] *adj* desired

erwürgen [ɛr'vʏrgən] *vt* to strangle

Erz [ɛːrts] **(-es, -e)** *nt* ore

erzähl- [ɛr'tsɛːl] *zW:* **~en** *vt* to tell ♦ *vi:* **sie kann gut ~en** she's a good story-teller; **E~er (-s, -)** *m* narrator; **E~ung** *f* story, tale

Erzbischof *m* archbishop

erzeug- [ɛr'tsɔyg] *zW:* **~en** *vt* to produce; *(Strom)* to generate; **E~nis (-ses, -se)** *nt* product, produce; **E~ung** *f* production; generation

erziehen [ɛr'tsi:ən] *(unreg) vt* to bring up; *(bilden)* to educate, to train; **Erzieher(in) (-s, -)** *m(f)* *(Berufsbezeichnung)* teacher; **Erziehung** *f* bringing up; *(Bildung)* education; **Erziehungsbeihilfe** *f* educational grant; **Erziehungsberechtigte(r)** *f(m)* parent; guardian

erzielen [ɛr'tsi:lən] *vt* to achieve, to obtain; *(Tor)* to score

erzwingen [ɛr'tsvɪŋən] *(unreg) vt* to force, to obtain by force

es [ɛs] *(nom, akk) pron* it

Esel ['eːzəl] **(-s, -)** *m* donkey, ass

Eskalation [ɛskalatsi'oːn] *f* escalation

ess- ▲ ['ɛs] *zW:* **~bar** ['ɛsbaːr] *adj* eatable, edible; **E~besteck** *nt* knife, fork and spoon; **E~ecke** *f* dining area

essen ['ɛsən] *(unreg) vt, vi* to eat; **E~ (-s, -)** *nt* meal; food

Essig ['ɛsɪç] **(-s, -e)** *m* vinegar

Ess- ▲ *zW:* **~kastanie** *f* sweet chestnut; **~löffel** *m* tablespoon; **~tisch** *m* dining table; **~waren** *pl* foodstuffs, provisions; **~zimmer** *nt* dining room

etablieren [eta'bli:rən] *vr* to become established; to set up in business

Etage [e'taːʒə] *f* floor, storey; **~nbetten** *pl* bunk beds; **~nwohnung** *f* flat

Etappe [e'tapə] *f* stage

Etat [e'taː] **(-s, -s)** *m* budget

etc *abk* (= *et cetera*) etc

Ethik ['eːtɪk] *f* ethics *sg*; **ethisch** *adj* ethical

Etikett [eti'kɛt] **(-(e)s, -e)** *nt* label; tag; **~e** *f* etiquette, manners *pl*

etliche ['ɛtlɪçə] *pron pl* some, quite a few; **~s** *pron* a thing or two

Etui [ɛt'viː] **(-s, -s)** *nt* case

etwa ['ɛtva] *adv (ungefähr)* about; *(vielleicht)* perhaps; *(beispielsweise)* for instance; **nicht ~** by no means; **~ig** ['ɛtvaɪç] *adj* possible

etwas *pron* something; anything; *(ein wenig)* a little ♦ *adv* a little

euch [ɔyç] *pron (akk von ihr)* you; yourselves; *(dat von ihr)* (to) you

euer ['ɔyər] *pron (gen von ihr)* of you ♦ *adj* your

Eule ['ɔʏlə] f owl

eure ['ɔʏrə] adj f siehe **euer**

eure(r, s) ['ɔʏrɐ(r, s)] pron yours; **~rseits** adv on your part; **~s** adj nt siehe **euer**; **~sgleichen** pron people like you; **~twegen** adv (für euch) for your sakes; (wegen euch) on your account; **~twillen** adv: **um ~twillen = euretwegen**

eurige ['ɔʏrɪɡə] pron: **der/die/das ~** od **E~** yours

Euro- ['ɔʏro:] (-, -s) m (FIN) euro

Euro- zW: **~pa** [ɔʏ'ro:pa] nt Europe; **~päer(in)** [ɔʏro'pɛːɐr(ɪn)] m(f) European; **e~päisch** adj European; **~pameister** [ɔʏ'ro:pa-] m European champion; **~paparlament** nt European Parliament; **~scheck** m (FIN) eurocheque

Euter ['ɔʏtɐr] (-s, -) nt udder

ev. abk = **evangelisch**

evakuieren [evaku'iːrən] vt to evacuate

evangelisch [evaŋˈɡeːlɪʃ] adj Protestant

Evangelium [evaŋˈɡeːliom] nt gospel

eventuell [eventu'ɛl] adj possible ♦ adv possibly, perhaps

evtl. abk = **eventuell**

EWG [eːveːˈɡeː] (-) f abk (= Europäische Wirtschaftsgemeinschaft) EEC, Common Market

ewig ['eːvɪç] adj eternal; **E~keit** f eternity

EWU [eːveːˈʔuː] f abk (= Europäische Währungsunion) EMU

exakt [ɛˈksakt] adj exact

Examen [ɛˈksaːmən] (-s, - od **Examina**) nt examination

Exemplar [ɛksɛmˈplaːr] (-s, -e) nt specimen; (Buchexemplar) copy; **e~isch** adj exemplary

Exil [ɛˈksiːl] (-s, -e) nt exile

Existenz [ɛksɪsˈtɛnts] f existence; (Unterhalt) livelihood, living; (pej: Mensch) character; **~minimum** (-s) nt subsistence level

existieren [ɛksɪsˈtiːrən] vi to exist

exklusiv [ɛkskluˈziːf] adj exclusive; **~e** adv exclusive of, not including ♦ präp +gen exclusive of, not including

exotisch [ɛˈksoːtɪʃ] adj exotic

Expedition [ɛkspeditsiˈoːn] f expedition

Experiment [ɛksperiˈmɛnt] nt experiment;

e~ell [-ˈtɛl] adj experimental; **e~ieren** [-ˈtiːrən] vi to experiment

Experte [ɛksˈpɛrtə] (-n, -n) m expert, specialist

Expertin f expert, specialist

explo- [ɛksplo] zW: **~dieren** [-ˈdiːrən] vi to explode; **E~sion** [-ziˈoːn] f explosion; **~siv** [-ˈziːf] adj explosive

Export [ɛksˈpɔrt] (-(e)s, -e) m export; **~eur** [-ˈtøːr] m exporter; **~handel** m export trade; **e~ieren** [-ˈtiːrən] vt to export; **~land** nt exporting country

Express- ▲ [ɛksˈprɛs] zW: **~gut** nt express goods pl, express freight; **~zug** m express (train)

extra ['ɛkstra] adj inv (umg: gesondert) separate; (besondere) extra ♦ adv (gesondert) separately; (speziell) specially; (absichtlich) on purpose; (vor Adjektiven, zusätzlich) extra; **E~** (-s, -s) nt extra; **E~ausgabe** f special edition; **E~blatt** nt special edition

Extrakt [ɛksˈtrakt] (-(e)s, -e) m extract

extravagant [ɛkstravaˈɡant] adj extravagant

extrem [ɛksˈtreːm] adj extreme; **~istisch** [-ˈmɪstɪʃ] adj (POL) extremist; **E~itäten** [-miˈtɛːtən] pl extremities

exzentrisch [ɛksˈtsɛntrɪʃ] adj eccentric

EZ nt abk = **Einzelzimmer**

F, f

Fa. abk (= Firma) firm; (in Briefen) Messrs

Fabel ['faːbəl] (-, -n) f fable; **f~haft** adj fabulous, marvellous

Fabrik [faˈbriːk] f factory; **~ant** [-ˈkant] m (Hersteller) manufacturer; (Besitzer) industrialist; **~arbeiter** m factory worker; **~at** [-ˈkaːt] (-(e)s, -e) nt manufacture, product; **~gelände** nt factory site

Fach [fax] (-(e)s, er) nt compartment; (Sachgebiet) subject; **ein Mann vom ~** an expert; **~arbeiter** m skilled worker; **~arzt** m (medical) specialist; **~ausdruck** m technical term

Fächer ['fɛçɐr] (-s, -) m fan

Fach- zW: **~geschäft** nt specialist shop;

~hochschule f technical college; **~kraft** f skilled worker, trained employee; **f~kundig** adj expert, specialist; **f~lich** adj professional; expert; **~mann** (pl **-leute**) m specialist; **f~männisch** adj professional; **~schule** f technical college; **f~simpeln** vi to talk shop; **~werk** nt timber frame

Fackel ['fakəl] (-, -n) f torch

fad(e) [fa:t, 'fa:də] adj insipid; (langweilig) dull

Faden ['fa:dən] (-s, ⁈) m thread; **f~scheinig** adj (auch fig) threadbare

fähig ['fɛːɪç] adj: **~ (zu** od +gen) capable (of); able (to); **F~keit** f ability

fahnden ['fa:ndən] vi: **~ nach** to search for; **Fahndung** f search

Fahndungsliste f list of wanted criminals, wanted list

Fahne ['fa:nə] f flag, standard; **eine ~ haben** (umg) to smell of drink; **~nflucht** f desertion

Fahr- zW: **~ausweis** m ticket; **~bahn** f carriageway (BRIT), roadway

Fähre ['fɛːrə] f ferry

fahren ['fa:rən] (unreg) vt to drive; (Rad) to ride; (befördern) to drive, to take; (Rennen) to drive in ♦ vi (sich bewegen) to go; (Schiff) to sail; (abfahren) to leave; **mit dem Auto / Zug ~** to go od travel by car/train; **mit der Hand ~ über** +akk to pass one's hand over

Fahr- zW: **~er(in)** (-s, -) m(f) driver; **~erflucht** f hit-and-run; **~gast** m passenger; **~geld** nt fare; **~karte** f ticket; **~kartenausgabe** f ticket office; **~kartenautomat** m ticket machine; **~kartenschalter** m ticket office; **f~lässig** adj negligent; **f~lässige Tötung** manslaughter; **~lehrer** m driving instructor; **~plan** m timetable; **f~planmäßig** adj scheduled; **~preis** m fare; **~prüfung** f driving test; **~rad** nt bicycle; **~radweg** m cycle lane; **~schein** m ticket; **~scheinentwerter** m (automatic) ticket stamping machine

Fährschiff ['fɛːrʃɪf] nt ferry(boat)

Fahr- zW: **~schule** f driving school; **~spur** f lane; **~stuhl** m lift (BRIT), elevator (US)

Fahrt [fa:rt] (-, -en) f journey; (kurz) trip;

(AUT) drive; (Geschwindigkeit) speed; **gute ~!** have a good journey

Fährte ['fɛːrtə] f track, trail

Fahrt- zW: **~kosten** pl travelling expenses; **~richtung** f course, direction

Fahrzeit f time for the journey

Fahrzeug nt vehicle; **~brief** m log book; **~papiere** pl vehicle documents

fair [fɛːr] adj fair

Fakt [fakt] (-(e)s, -en) m fact

Faktor ['faktɔr] m factor

Fakultät [fakʊl'tɛːt] f faculty

Falke ['falkə] (-n, -n) m falcon

Fall [fal] (-(e)s, ⁈e) m (Sturz) fall; (Sachverhalt, JUR, GRAM) case; **auf jeden ~, auf alle Fälle** in any case, (bestimmt) definitely; **auf keinen ~!** no way!

Falle f trap

fallen (unreg) vi to fall; **etw ~ lassen** to drop sth; (Bemerkung) to make sth; (Plan) to abandon sth, to drop sth

fällen ['fɛlən] vt (Baum) to fell; (Urteil) to pass

fällig ['fɛlɪç] adj due

falls [fals] adv in case, if

Fallschirm m parachute; **~springer** m parachutist

falsch [falʃ] adj false; (unrichtig) wrong

fälschen ['fɛlʃən] vt to forge

fälsch- zW: **~lich** adj false; **~licherweise** adv mistakenly; **F~ung** f forgery

Falte ['faltə] f (Knick) fold, crease; (Hautfalte) wrinkle; (Rockfalte) pleat; **f~n** vt to fold; (Stirn) to wrinkle

faltig ['faltɪç] adj (Hände, Haut) wrinkled; (zerknittert: Rock) creased

familiär [famili'ɛːr] adj familiar

Familie [fa'mi:liə] f family

Familien- zW: **~betrieb** m family business; **~kreis** m family circle; **~mitglied** nt member of the family; **~name** m surname; **~stand** m marital status

Fanatiker [fa'na:tikər] (-s, -) m fanatic; **fanatisch** adj fanatical

fand etc [fant] vb siehe **finden**

Fang [faŋ] (-(e)s, ⁈e) m catch; (Jagen) hunting; (Kralle) talon, claw; **f~en** (unreg) vt to catch ♦ vr to get caught; (Flugzeug) to level out; (*Mensch: nicht fallen*) to steady o.s.; (*fig*) to compose o.s.; (*in Leistung*) to get back on form

Fantasie ▲ [fanta'zi:] *f* imagination; **f~los** *adj* unimaginative; **f~ren** *vi* to fantasize; **f~voll** *adj* imagainative

fantastisch ▲ [fan'tastɪʃ] *adj* fantastic

Farb- ['farb] *zW:* **~abzug** *m* colour print; **~aufnahme** *f* colour photograph; **~band** *m* typewriter ribbon; **~e** *f* colour; (*zum Malen etc*) paint; (*Stoffarbe*) dye; **f~echt** *adj* colourfast

färben ['fɛrbən] *vt* to colour; (*Stoff, Haar*) to dye

farben- ['farbən] *zW:* **~blind** *adj* colour-blind; **~freudig** *adj* colourful; **~froh** *adj* colourful, gay

Farb- *zW:* **~fernsehen** *nt* colour television; **~film** *m* colour film; **~foto** *nt* colour photograph; **f~ig** *adj* coloured; **~ige(r)** *f(m)* coloured (person); **~kasten** *m* paintbox; **f~lich** *adj* colour; **f~los** *adj* colourless; **~stift** *m* coloured pencil; **~stoff** *m* dye; **~ton** *m* hue, tone

Färbung ['fɛrbʊŋ] *f* colouring; (*Tendenz*) bias

Farn [farn] (**-(e)s, -e**) *m* fern; bracken

Fasan [fa'za:n] (**-(e)s, -e(n)**) *m* pheasant

Fasching ['faʃɪŋ] (**-s, -e** *od* **-s**) *m* carnival

Faschismus [fa'ʃɪsmʊs] *m* fascism

Faschist *m* fascist

Faser ['fa:zər] (**-, -n**) *f* fibre; **f~n** *vi* to fray

Fass ▲ [fas] (**-es, er**) *nt* vat, barrel; (*für Öl*) drum; **Bier vom ~** draught beer

Fassade [fa'sa:də] *f* façade

fassen ['fasən] *vt* (*ergreifen*) to grasp, to take; (*inhaltlich*) to hold; (*Entschluss etc*) to take; (*verstehen*) to understand; (*Ring etc*) to set; (*formulieren*) to formulate, to phrase ♦ *vr* to calm down; **nicht zu ~** unbelievable

Fassung ['fasʊŋ] *f* (*Umrahmung*) mounting; (*Lampenfassung*) socket; (*Wortlaut*) version; (*Beherrschung*) composure; **jdn aus der ~ bringen** to upset sb; **f~slos** *adj* speechless

fast [fast] *adv* almost, nearly

fasten ['fastən] *vi* to fast; **F~zeit** *f* Lent

Fastnacht *f* Shrove Tuesday; carnival

faszinieren [fastsi'ni:rən] *vt* to fascinate

fatal [fa'ta:l] *adj* fatal; (*peinlich*) embarrassing

faul [faʊl] *adj* rotten; (*Person*) lazy; (*Ausreden*) lame; **daran ist etwas ~** there's something fishy about it; **~en** *vi* to rot; (*verwesen*) to idle; **F~enzer** (**-s, -**) *m* idler, loafer; **F~heit** *f* laziness; **~ig** *adj* putrid

Faust ['faʊst] (**-, Fäuste**) *f* fist; **auf eigene ~** off one's own bat; **~handschuh** *m* mitten

Favorit [favo'ri:t] (**-en, -en**) *m* favourite

Fax [faks] (**-, -(e)**) *nt* fax

faxen ['faksən] *vt* to fax; **jdm etw ~** to fax sth to sb

FCKW *m abk* (= *Fluorchlorkohlenwasserstoff*) CFC

Februar ['fe:brua:r] (**-(s), -e**) *m* February

fechten ['fɛçtən] (*unreg*) *vi* to fence

Feder ['fe:dər] (**-, -n**) *f* feather; (*Schreibfeder*) pen nib; (*TECH*) spring; **~ball** *m* shuttlecock; **~bett** *nt* continental quilt; **~halter** *m* penholder, pen; **f~leicht** *adj* light as a feather; **f~n** *vi* (*nachgeben*) to be springy; (*sich bewegen*) to bounce ♦ *vt* to spring; **~ung** *f* (*AUT*) suspension

Fee [fe:] *f* fairy

fegen ['fe:gən] *vt* to sweep

fehl [fe:l] *adj:* **~ am Platz** *od* **Ort** out of place; **F~betrag** *m* deficit; **~en** *vi* to be wanting *od* missing; (*abwesend sein*) to be absent; **etw ~t jdm** sb lacks sth; **du ~st mir** I miss you; **was ~t ihm?** what's wrong with him?; **F~er** (**-s, -**) *m* mistake, error; (*Mangel, Schwäche*) fault; **~erfrei** *adj* faultless; without any mistakes; **~erhaft** *adj* incorrect; faulty; **~erlos** *adj* flawless, perfect; **F~geburt** *f* miscarriage; **~gehen** (*unreg*) *vi* to go astray; **F~griff** *m* blunder; **F~konstruktion** *f* badly designed thing; **~schlagen** (*unreg*) *vi* to fail; **F~start** *m* (*SPORT*) false start; **F~zündung** *f* (*AUT*) misfire, backfire

Feier ['faɪər] (**-, -n**) *f* celebration; **~abend** *m* time to stop work; **~abend machen** to stop, to knock off; **jetzt ist ~abend!** that's enough!; **f~lich** *adj* solemn; **~lichkeit** *f* solemnity; **~lichkeiten** *pl* (*Veranstaltungen*) festivities; **f~n** *vt, vi* to celebrate; **~tag** *m* holiday

feig(e) [faɪk, 'faɪgə] *adj* cowardly

Feige ['faɪgə] *f* fig

Feigheit *f* cowardice

Feigling *m* coward

Feile ['faɪlə] *f* file

feilschen ['faɪlʃən] *vi* to haggle

fein [faɪn] *adj* fine; (*vornehm*) refined; (*Gehör etc*) keen; **~!** great!

Feind [faɪnt] **(-(e)s, -e)** *m* enemy; **f~lich** *adj* hostile; **~schaft** *f* enmity; **f~selig** *adj* hostile

Fein- *zW:* **f~fühlig** *adj* sensitive; **~gefühl** *nt* delicacy, tact; **~heit** *f* fineness; refinement; keenness; **~kostgeschäft** *nt* delicatessen (shop); **~schmecker (-s, -)** *m* gourmet; **~wäsche** *f* delicate clothing (*when washing*); **~waschmittel** *nt* mild detergent

Feld [fɛlt] **(-(e)s, -er)** *nt* field; (*SCHACH*) square; (*SPORT*) pitch; **~herr** *m* commander; (*SPORT*); **~stecher (-s, -)** *m* binoculars *pl*; **~weg** *m* path; **~zug** *m* (*fig*) campaign

Felge ['fɛlgə] *f* (wheel) rim

Fell [fɛl] **(-(e)s, -e)** *nt* fur; coat; (*von Schaf*) fleece; (*von toten Tieren*) skin

Fels [fɛls] **(-en, -en)** *m* rock; (*Klippe*) cliff

Felsen ['fɛlzən] **(-s, -)** *m* = **Fels**; **f~fest** *adj* firm

feminin [femi'niːn] *adj* feminine

Fenster ['fɛnstər] **(-s, -)** *nt* window; **~bank** *f* windowsill; **~laden** *m* shutter; **~leder** *nt* chamois (leather); **~scheibe** *f* windowpane

Ferien ['feːrɪən] *pl* holidays, vacation *sg* (*US*); **~ haben** to be on holiday; **~bungalow** [-bʊŋgalo] **(-s, -s)** *m* holiday bungalow; **~haus** *nt* holiday home; **~kurs** *m* holiday course; **~lager** *nt* holiday camp; **~reise** *f* holiday; **~wohnung** *f* holiday apartment

Ferkel ['fɛrkəl] **(-s, -)** *nt* piglet

fern [fɛrn] *adj, adv* far-off, distant; **~ von hier** a long way (away) from here; **der F~e Osten** the Far East; **~ halten** to keep away; **F~bedienung** *f* remote control; **F~e** *f* distance; **~er** *adj* further ♦ *adv* further; (*weiterhin*) in future; **F~gespräch** *nt* trunk call; **F~glas** *nt* binoculars *pl*; **F~licht** *nt* (*AUT*) full beam; **F~rohr** *nt* telescope; **F~ruf** *m* (*förmlich*) telephone number; **F~schreiben** *nt* telex; **F~sehapparat** *m* television set; **F~sehen (-s)** *nt* television; **im F~sehen** on television; **~sehen** (*unreg*) *vi* to watch television; **F~seher** *m* television; **F~sehturm** *m* television tower; **F~sprecher** *m* telephone; **F~steuerung** *f* remote control; **F~straße** *f* ≈ 'A' road (*BRIT*), highway (*US*); **F~verkehr** *m* long-distance traffic

Ferse ['fɛrzə] *f* heel

fertig ['fɛrtɪç] *adj* (*bereit*) ready; (*beendet*) finished; (*gebrauchsfertig*) ready-made; **~ bringen** (*fähig sein*) to be capable of; **~ machen** (*beenden*) to finish; (*umg: Person*) to finish; (*: körperlich*) to exhaust; (*: moralisch*) to get down; **sich ~ machen** to get ready; **~ stellen** to complete; **F~gericht** *nt* precooked meal; **F~haus** *nt* kit house, prefab; **F~keit** *f* skill

Fessel ['fɛsəl] **(-, -n)** *f* fetter; **f~n** *vt* to bind; (*mit ~n*) to fetter; (*fig*) to spellbind; **f~nd** *adj* fascinating, captivating

Fest **(-(e)s, -e)** *nt* party; festival; **frohes ~!** Happy Christmas!

fest [fɛst] *adj* firm; (*Nahrung*) solid; (*Gehalt*) regular; **~e Kosten** fixed cost ♦ *adv* (*schlafen*) soundly; **~ angestellt** permanently employed; **~binden** (*unreg*) *vt* to tie, to fasten; **~bleiben** (*unreg*) *vi* to stand firm; **F~essen** *nt* banquet; **~halten** (*unreg*) *vt* to seize, to hold fast; (*Ereignis*) to record ♦ *vr:* **sich ~halten (an** *+dat*) to hold on (to); **~igen** *vt* to strengthen; **F~igkeit** *f* strength; **F~ival** ['fɛstɪval] **(-s, -s)** *nt* festival; **F~land** *nt* mainland; **~legen** *vt* to fix ♦ *vr* to commit o.s.; **~lich** *adj* festive; **~liegen** (*unreg*) *vi* (*~stehen: Termin*) to be confirmed, be fixed; **~machen** *vt* to fasten; (*Termin etc*) to fix; **F~nahme** *f* arrest; **~nehmen** (*unreg*) *vt* to arrest; **F~preis** *m* (*COMM*) fixed price; **F~rede** *f* address; **~setzen** *vt* to fix, to settle; **F~spiele** *pl* (*Veranstaltung*) festival *sg*; **~stehen** (*unreg*) *vi* to be certain; **~stellen** *vt* to establish; (*sagen*) to remark; **F~tag** *m*

feast day, holiday; **F~ung** *f* fortress;
F~wochen *pl* festival *sg*
Fett [fɛt] **(-(e)s, -e)** *nt* fat, grease
fett *adj* fat; (*Essen etc*) greasy; (*TYP*) bold;
~arm *adj* low fat; **~en** *vt* to grease;
F~fleck *m* grease stain; **~ig** *adj* greasy,
fatty
Fetzen ['fɛtsən] **(-s, -)** *m* scrap
feucht [fɔʏçt] *adj* damp; (*Luft*) humid;
F~igkeit *f* dampness; humidity;
F~igkeitscreme *f* moisturizing cream
Feuer ['fɔʏər] **(-s, -)** *nt* fire; (*zum Rauchen*) a
light; (*fig: Schwung*) spirit; **~alarm** *m* fire
alarm; **f~fest** *adj* fireproof; **~gefahr** *f*
danger of fire; **f~gefährlich** *adj*
inflammable; **~leiter** *f* fire escape ladder;
~löscher **(-s, -)** *m* fire extinguisher;
~melder **(-s, -)** *m* fire alarm; **f~n** *vt, vi*
(*auch fig*) to fire; **~stein** *m* flint; **~treppe** *f*
fire escape; **~wehr** **(-, -en)** *f* fire brigade;
~wehrauto *nt* fire engine; **~wehrmann**
m fireman; **~werk** *nt* fireworks *pl*; **~zeug**
nt (cigarette) lighter
Fichte ['fɪçtə] *f* spruce, pine
Fieber ['fiːbər] **(-s, -)** *nt* fever, temperature;
f~haft *adj* feverish; **~thermometer** *nt*
thermometer; **fiebrig** *adj* (*Erkältung*)
feverish
fiel *etc* [fiːl] *vb siehe* **fallen**
fies [fiːs] (*umg*) *adj* nasty
Figur [fi'guːr] **(-, -en)** *f* figure; (*Schachfigur*)
chessman, chess piece
Filet [fi'leː] **(-s, -s)** *nt* (*KOCH*) fillet
Filiale [fili'aːlə] *f* (*COMM*) branch
Film [fɪlm] **(-(e)s, -e)** *m* film; **~aufnahme** *f*
shooting; **f~en** *vt, vi* to film; **~kamera** *f*
cine camera
Filter ['fɪltər] **(-s, -)** *m* filter; **f~n** *vt* to filter;
~papier *nt* filter paper; **~zigarette** *f*
tipped cigarette
Filz [fɪlts] **(-es, -e)** *m* felt; **f~en** *vt* (*umg*) to
frisk ♦ *vi* (*Wolle*) to mat; **~stift** *m* felt-tip
pen
Finale [fi'naːlə] **(-s, -(s))** *nt* finale; (*SPORT*)
final(s)
Finanz [fi'nants] *f* finance; **~amt** *nt* Inland
Revenue office; **~beamte(r)** *m* revenue

officer; **f~iell** [-tsi'ɛl] *adj* financial; **f~ieren**
[-'tsiːrən] *vt* to finance; **f~kräftig** *adj*
financially strong; **~minister** *m* Chancellor
of the Exchequer (*BRIT*), Minister of Finance
Find- ['fɪnd] *zW:* **f~en** (*unreg*) *vt* to find;
(*meinen*) to think ♦ *vr* to be (found); (*sich
fassen*) to compose o.s.; **ich f~e nichts
dabei, wenn ...** I don't see what's wrong if
...; **das wird sich f~en** things will work
out; **~er** **(-s, -)** *m* finder; **~erlohn** *m*
reward (*for sb who finds sth*); **f~ig** *adj*
resourceful
fing *etc* [fɪŋ] *vb siehe* **fangen**
Finger ['fɪŋər] **(-s, -)** *m* finger; **~abdruck** *m*
fingerprint; **~nagel** *m* fingernail; **~spitze** *f*
fingertip
fingiert *adj* made-up, fictitious
Fink [fɪŋk] **(-en, -en)** *m* finch
Finn- [fɪn] *zW:* **~e** **(-n, -n)** *m* Finn; **~in** *f*
Finn; **f~isch** *adj* Finnish; **~land** *nt* Finland
finster ['fɪnstər] *adj* dark, gloomy;
(*verdächtig*) dubious; (*verdrossen*) grim;
(*Gedanke*) dark; **F~nis** **(-)** *f* darkness, gloom
Firma ['fɪrma] **(-, -men)** *f* firm
Firmen- ['fɪrmən] *zW:* **~inhaber** *m* owner
of firm; **~schild** *nt* (shop) sign; **~wagen**
m company car; **~zeichen** *nt* trademark
Fisch [fɪʃ] **(-(e)s, -e)** *m* fish; **~e** *pl* (*ASTROL*)
Pisces *sg*; **f~en** *vt, vi* to fish; **~er** **(-s, -)** *m*
fisherman; **~e'rei** *f* fishing, fishery; **~fang**
m fishing; **~geschäft** *nt* fishmonger's
(shop); **~gräte** *f* fishbone; **~stäbchen**
[-stɛːpçən] *nt* fish finger (*BRIT*), fish stick (*US*)
fit [fɪt] *adj* fit; '**F~ness** ▲ **(-, -)** *f* (physical)
fitness
fix [fɪks] *adj* fixed; (*Person*) alert, smart; **~ und
fertig** finished; (*erschöpft*) done in;
F~er(in) *m(f)* (*umg*) junkie; **F~erstube** *f*
(*umg*) junkies centre; **~ieren** [fɪ'ksiːrən] *vt*
to fix; (*anstarren*) to stare at
flach [flax] *adj* flat; (*Gefäß*) shallow
Fläche ['flɛçə] *f* area; (*Oberfläche*) surface
Flachland *nt* lowland
flackern ['flakərn] *vi* to flare, to flicker
Flagge ['flagə] *f* flag; **f~n** *vi* to fly a flag
flämisch ['flɛːmɪʃ] *adj* (*LING*) Flemish
Flamme ['flamə] *f* flame

Flandern ['flandərn] *nt* Flanders

Flanke ['flaŋkə] *f* flank; (*SPORT: Seite*) wing

Flasche ['flaʃə] *f* bottle; (*umg: Versager*) wash-out

Flaschen- *zW:* **~bier** *nt* bottled beer; **~öffner** *m* bottle opener; **~zug** *m* pulley

flatterhaft *adj* flighty, fickle

flattern ['flatərn] *vi* to flutter

flau [flau] *adj* weak, listless; (*Nachfrage*) slack; **jdm ist ~** sb feels queasy

Flaum [flaum] **(-(e)s)** *m* (*Feder*) down; (*Haare*) fluff

flauschig ['flauʃɪç] *adj* fluffy

Flaute ['flautə] *f* calm; (*COMM*) recession

Flechte ['flɛçtə] *f* plait; (*MED*) dry scab; (*BOT*) lichen; **f~n** (*unreg*) *vt* to plait; (*Kranz*) to twine

Fleck [flɛk] **(-(e)s, -e)** *m* spot; (*Schmutzfleck*) stain; (*Stofffleck*) patch; (*Makel*) blemish; **nicht vom ~ kommen** (*auch fig*) not to get any further; **vom ~ weg** straight away

Flecken **(-s, -)** *m* = **Fleck**; **f~los** *adj* spotless; **~mittel** *nt* stain remover; **~wasser** *nt* stain remover

fleckig *adj* spotted; stained

Fledermaus ['fle:dərmaus] *f* bat

Flegel ['fle:gəl] **(-s, -)** *m* (*Mensch*) lout; **f~haft** *adj* loutish, unmannerly; **~jahre** *pl* adolescence *sg*

flehen ['fle:ən] *vi* to implore; **~tlich** *adj* imploring

Fleisch ['flaiʃ] **(-(e)s)** *nt* flesh; (*Essen*) meat; **~brühe** *f* beef tea, meat stock; **~er** **(-s, -)** *m* butcher; **~e'rei** *f* butcher's (shop); **f~ig** *adj* fleshy; **f~los** *adj* meatless, vegetarian

Fleiß ['flais] **(-es)** *m* diligence, industry; **f~ig** *adj* diligent, industrious

fletschen ['flɛtʃən] *vt* (*Zähne*) to show

flexibel [flɛ'ksi:bəl] *adj* flexible

Flicken ['flɪkən] **(-s, -)** *m* patch; **f~** *vt* to mend

Flieder ['fli:dər] **(-s, -)** *m* lilac

Fliege ['fli:gə] *f* fly; (*Kleidung*) bow tie; **f~n** (*unreg*) *vt, vi* to fly; **auf jdn/etw f~n** (*umg*) to be mad about sb/sth; **~npilz** *m* toadstool; **~r** **(-s, -)** *m* flier, airman

fliehen ['fli:ən] (*unreg*) *vi* to flee

Fliese ['fli:zə] *f* tile

Fließ- ['fli:s] *zW:* **~band** *nt* production *od* assembly line; **f~en** (*unreg*) *vi* to flow; **f~end** *adj* flowing; (*Rede, Deutsch*) fluent; (*Übergänge*) smooth

flimmern ['flɪmərn] *vi* to glimmer

flink [flɪŋk] *adj* nimble, lively

Flinte ['flɪntə] *f* rifle; shotgun

Flitterwochen *pl* honeymoon *sg*

flitzen ['flɪtsən] *vi* to flit

Flocke ['flɔkə] *f* flake

flog *etc* [flo:k] *vb siehe* **fliegen**

Floh [flo:] **(-(e)s, ¨e)** *m* flea; **~markt** *m* flea market

florieren [flo'ri:rən] *vi* to flourish

Floskel ['flɔskəl] **(-, -n)** *f* set phrase

Floß [flɔs] **(-es, ¨e)** *nt* raft, float

floss ▲ *etc vb siehe* **fließen**

Flosse ['flɔsə] *f* fin

Flöte ['flø:tə] *f* flute; (*Blockflöte*) recorder

flott [flɔt] *adj* lively; (*elegant*) smart; (*NAUT*) afloat; **F~e** *f* fleet, navy

Fluch [flu:x] **(-(e)s, ¨e)** *m* curse; **f~en** *vi* to curse, to swear

Flucht [fluxt] **(-, -en)** *f* flight; (*Fensterflucht*) row; (*Zimmerflucht*) suite; **f~artig** *adj* hasty

flücht- ['flʏçt] *zW:* **~en** *vi, vr* to flee, to escape; (*vergänglich*) transitory; (*oberflächlich*) superficial; (*eilig*) fleeting; **F~igkeltsfehler** *m* careless slip; **F~ling** *m* fugitive, refugee

Flug [flu:k] **(-(e)s, ¨e)** *m* flight; **~blatt** *nt* pamphlet

Flügel ['fly:gəl] **(-s, -)** *m* wing; (*MUS*) grand piano

Fluggast *m* airline passenger

Flug- *zW:* **~gesellschaft** *f* airline (company); **~hafen** *m* airport; **~lärm** *m* aircraft noise; **~linie** *f* airline; **~plan** *m* flight schedule; **~platz** *m* airport; (*klein*) airfield; **~reise** *f* flight; **~schein** *m* (*Ticket*) plane ticket; (*Pilotenschein*) pilot's licence; **~steig** [-staik] **(-(e)s, -e)** *m* gate; **~verbindung** *f* air connection; **~verkehr** *m* air traffic; **~zeug** *nt* (aero)plane, airplane (*US*); **~zeugentführung** *f* hijacking of a plane; **~zeughalle** *f* hangar; **~zeugträger**

m aircraft carrier

Flunder ['flʊndər] (-, -n) *f* flounder

flunkern ['flʊŋkərn] *vi* to fib, to tell stories

Fluor ['fluːɔr] (-s) *nt* fluorine

Flur [fluːr] (-(e)s, -e) *m* hall; (*Treppenflur*) staircase

Fluss ▲ [flʊs] (-es, ⸚e) *m* river; (*Fließen*) flow

flüssig ['flʏsɪç] *adj* liquid; **~ machen** (*Geld*) to make available; **F~keit** *f* liquid; (*Zustand*) liquidity

flüstern ['flʏstərn] *vt, vi* to whisper

Flut [fluːt] (-, -en) *f* (*auch fig*) flood; (*Gezeiten*) high tide; **f~en** *vi* to flood; **~licht** *nt* floodlight

Fohlen ['foːlən] (-s, -) *nt* foal

Föhn¹ [føːn] (-(e)s, -e) *m* (*warmer Fallwind*) föhn

Föhn² ▲ (-(e)s, -e) *m* (*Haartrockner*) hair-dryer; **f~en** ▲ *vt* to (blow) dry; **~frisur** ▲ *f* blow-dry hairstyle

Folge ['fɔlɡə] *f* series, sequence; (*Fortsetzung*) instalment; (*Auswirkung*) result; **in rascher ~** in quick succession; **etw zur ~ haben** to result in sth; **~n haben** to have consequences; **einer Sache** *dat* **~ leisten** to comply with sth; **f~n** *vi* to follow; (*gehorchen*) to obey; **jdm f~n können** (*fig*) to follow *od* understand sb; **f~nd** *adj* following; **f~ndermaßen** *adv* as follows, in the following way; **f~rn** *vt*: **f~rn (aus)** to conclude (from); **~rung** *f* conclusion

folglich ['fɔlklɪç] *adv* consequently

folgsam ['fɔlkzaːm] *adj* obedient

Folie ['foːliə] *f* foil

Folklore ['fɔlkloːər] *f* folklore

Folter ['fɔltər] (-, -n) *f* torture; (*Gerät*) rack; **f~n** *vt* to torture

Fön [føːn] (-(e)s, -e) ® *m* hair dryer

Fondue [fõdyː] (-s, -s *od* -, -s) *nt od f* (*KOCH*) fondue

fönen △ *vt siehe* **föhnen**

Fönfrisur △ *f siehe* **Föhnfrisur**

Fontäne [fɔn'tɛːnə] *f* fountain

Förder- ['fœrdər] *zW*: **~band** *nt* conveyor belt; **~korb** *m* pit cage; **f~lich** *adj* beneficial

fordern ['fɔrdərn] *vt* to demand

fördern ['fœrdərn] *vt* to promote; (*unterstützen*) to help; (*Kohle*) to extract

Forderung ['fɔrdərʊŋ] *f* demand

Förderung ['fœrdərʊŋ] *f* promotion; help; extraction

Forelle [fo'rɛlə] *f* trout

Form [fɔrm] (-, -en) *f* shape; (*Gestaltung*) form; (*Gussform*) mould; (*Backform*) baking tin; **in ~ sein** to be in good form *od* shape; **in ~ von** in the shape of

Formali'tät *f* formality

Format [fɔr'maːt] (-(e)s, -e) *nt* format; (*fig*) distinction

formbar *adj* malleable

Formblatt *nt* form

Formel (-, -n) *f* formula

formell [fɔr'mɛl] *adj* formal

formen *vt* to form, to shape

Formfehler *m* faux pas, gaffe; (*JUR*) irregularity

formieren [fɔr'miːrən] *vt* to form ♦ *vr* to form up

förmlich ['fœrmlɪç] *adj* formal; (*umg*) real; **F~keit** *f* formality

formlos *adj* shapeless; (*Benehmen etc*) informal

Formular [fɔrmu'laːr] (-s, -e) *nt* form

formulieren [fɔrmu'liːrən] *vt* to formulate

forsch [fɔrʃ] *adj* energetic, vigorous

forsch- *zW*: **~en** *vi*: **~en (nach)** to search (for); (*wissenschaftlich*) to (do) research; **~end** *adj* searching; **F~er** (-s, -) *m* research scientist; (*Naturforscher*) explorer; **F~ung** *f* research

Forst [fɔrst] (-(e)s, -e) *m* forest

Förster ['fœrstər] (-s, -) *m* forester; (*für Wild*) gamekeeper

fort [fɔrt] *adv* away; (*verschwunden*) gone; (*vorwärts*) on; **und so ~** and so on; **in einem ~** on and on; **~bestehen** (*unreg*) *vi* to survive; **~bewegen** *vt, vr* to move away; **~bilden** *vr* to continue one's education; **~bleiben** (*unreg*) *vi* to stay away; **F~dauer** *f* continuance; **~fahren** (*unreg*) *vi* to depart; (*~setzen*) to go on, to continue; **~führen** *vt* to continue, to carry on; **~gehen** (*unreg*) *vi* to go away;

~geschritten adj advanced; **~pflanzen** vr to reproduce; **F~pflanzung** f reproduction

fort- zW: **~schaffen** vt to remove; **~schreiten** (unreg) vi to advance

Fortschritt ['fɔrtʃrɪt] m advance; **~e machen** to make progress; **f~lich** adj progressive

fort- zW: **~setzen** vt to continue; **F~setzung** f continuation; (folgender Teil) instalment; **F~setzung folgt** to be continued; **~während** adj incessant, continual

Foto ['foːto] (-s, -s) nt photo(graph); **~apparat** m camera; **~'graf** m photographer; **~gra'fie** f photography; (Bild) photograph; **f~gra'fieren** vt to photograph ♦ vi to take photographs; **~kopie** f photocopy

Fr. abk (= Frau) Mrs, Ms

Fracht [fraxt] (-, -en) f freight; (NAUT) cargo; (Preis) carriage; **~ zahlt Empfänger** (COMM) carriage forward; **~er** (-s, -) m freighter, cargo boat; **~gut** nt freight

Frack [frak] (-(e)s, ⁺e) m tails pl

Frage ['fraːgə] (-, -n) f question; **jdm eine ~ stellen** to ask sb a question, to put a question to sb; siehe **infrage**; **~bogen** m questionnaire; **f~n** vt, vi to ask; **~zeichen** nt question mark

fraglich adj questionable, doubtful

fraglos adv unquestionably

Fragment [fra'gmɛnt] nt fragment

fragwürdig ['fraːkvyrdɪç] adj questionable, dubious

Fraktion [fraktsi'oːn] f parliamentary party

frankieren [fraŋ'kiːrən] vt to stamp, to frank

franko ['fraŋko] adv post-paid; carriage paid

Frankreich ['fraŋkraɪç] (-s) nt France

Franzose [fran'tsoːzə] m Frenchman; **Französin** [fran'tsøːzɪn] f Frenchwoman; **französisch** adj French

fraß etc [fras] vb siehe **fressen**

Fratze ['fratsə] f grimace

Frau [frau] (-, -en) f woman; (Ehefrau) wife; (Anrede) Mrs, Ms; **~ Doktor** Doctor

Frauen- zW: **~arzt** m gynaecologist; **~bewegung** f feminist movement; **~haus**

nt women's refuge; **~zimmer** nt female, broad (US)

Fräulein ['frɔʏlaɪn] nt young lady; (Anrede) Miss, Ms

fraulich ['fraulɪç] adj womanly

frech [frɛç] adj cheeky, impudent; **F~heit** f cheek, impudence

frei [fraɪ] adj free; (Stelle, Sitzplatz) free, vacant; (Mitarbeiter) freelance; (unbekleidet) bare; **von etw ~ sein** to be free of sth; **im F~en** in the open air; **~ sprechen** to talk without notes; **~ Haus** (COMM) carriage paid; **~er Wettbewerb** (COMM) fair/open competition; **F~bad** nt open-air swimming pool; **~bekommen** (unreg) vt: **einen Tag ~bekommen** to get a day off; **~beruflich** adj self-employed; **~gebig** adj generous; **~halten** (unreg) vt to keep free; **~händig** adv (fahren) with no hands; **F~heit** f freedom; **~heitlich** adj liberal; **F~heitsstrafe** f prison sentence; **F~karte** f free ticket; **~lassen** (unreg) vt to (set) free; **~legen** vt to expose; **~lich** adv certainly, admittedly; **ja ~lich** yes of course; **F~lichtbühne** f open-air theatre; **F~lichtmuseum** nt open-air museum; **~machen** vt (Post) to stamp ♦ vr to arrange to be free; (entkleiden) to undress; **Tage ~machen** to take days off; **~nehmen** ▲ (unreg) vt: **sich** dat **einen Tag ~nehmen** to take a day off; **~sprechen** (unreg) vt: **~sprechen (von)** to acquit (of); **F~spruch** m acquittal; **~stehen** (unreg) vi: **es steht dir ~, das zu tun** you're free to do that; (leer stehen: Wohnung, Haus) to lie/stand empty; **~stellen** vt: **jdm etw ~stellen** to leave sth (up) to sb; **F~stoß** m free kick

Freitag m Friday; **~s** adv on Fridays

frei- zW: **~willig** adj voluntary; **F~zeit** f spare od free time; **F~zeitpark** m amusement park; **F~zeitzentrum** nt leisure centre; **~zügig** adj liberal, broad-minded; (mit Geld) generous

fremd [frɛmt] adj (unvertraut) strange; (ausländisch) foreign; (nicht eigen) someone else's; **etw ist jdm ~** sth is foreign to sb; **~artig** adj strange; **F~enführer** ['frɛmdən-]

Spelling Reform: ▲ *new spelling* △ *old spelling (to be phased out)*

m (tourist) guide; **F~enverkehr** *m* tourism; **F~enverkehrsamt** *nt* tourist board; **F~enzimmer** *nt* guest room; **F~körper** *m* foreign body; **~ländisch** *adj* foreign; **F~sprache** *f* foreign language; **F~wort** *nt* foreign word

Frequenz [freˈkvɛnts] *f* (*RADIO*) frequency

fressen [ˈfrɛsən] (*unreg*) *vt, vi* to eat

Freude [ˈfrɔydə] *f* joy, delight

freudig *adj* joyful, happy

freuen [ˈfrɔyən] *vt unpers* to make happy *od* pleased ♦ *vr* to be glad *od* happy; **freut mich!** pleased to meet you; **sich auf etw** *akk* **~** to look forward to sth; **sich über etw** *akk* **~** to be pleased about sth

Freund [frɔynt] *(-(e)s, -e)* *m* friend; boyfriend; **~in** [-dɪn] *f* friend; girlfriend; **f~lich** *adj* kind, friendly; **f~licherweise** *adv* kindly; **~lichkeit** *f* friendliness, kindness; **~schaft** *f* friendship; **f~schaftlich** *adj* friendly

Frieden [ˈfriːdən] *(-s, -)* *m* peace; **im ~** in peacetime

Friedens- *zW*: **~schluss** ▲ *m* peace agreement; **~vertrag** *m* peace treaty; **~zeit** *f* peacetime

fried- [ˈfriːt] *zW*: **~fertig** *adj* peaceable; **F~hof** *m* cemetery; **~lich** *adj* peaceful

frieren [ˈfriːrən] (*unreg*) *vt, vi* to freeze; **ich friere, es friert mich** I'm freezing, I'm cold

Frikadelle [frɪkaˈdɛlə] *f* rissole

Frikassee [frɪkaˈseː] *(-s, -s)* *nt* (*KOCH*) fricassee

frisch [frɪʃ] *adj* fresh; (*lebhaft*) lively; **~ gestrichen!** wet paint!; **sich ~ machen** to freshen (o.s.) up; **F~e** *f* freshness; liveliness; **F~haltefolie** *f* cling film

Friseur [friˈzøːr] *m* hairdresser

Friseuse [friˈzøːzə] *f* hairdresser

frisieren [friˈziːrən] *vt* to do (one's) hair; (*fig: Abrechnung*) to fiddle, to doctor ♦ *vr* to do one's hair

Frisiersalon *m* hairdressing salon

frisst ▲ [frɪst] *vb siehe* **fressen**

Frist [frɪst] *(-, -en)* *f* period; (*Termin*) deadline; **f~gerecht** *adj* within the stipulated time *od* period; **f~los** *adj*

(*Entlassung*) instant

Frisur [friˈzuːr] *f* hairdo, hairstyle

frivol [friˈvoːl] *adj* frivolous

froh [froː] *adj* happy, cheerful; **ich bin ~, dass ...** I'm glad that ...

fröhlich [ˈfrøːlɪç] *adj* merry, happy; **F~keit** *f* merriness, gaiety

fromm [frɔm] *adj* pious, good; (*Wunsch*) idle; **Frömmigkeit** [ˈfrœmɪçkaɪt] *f* piety

Fronleichnam [froːnˈlaɪçnaːm] *(-(e)s)* *m* Corpus Christi

Front [frɔnt] *(-, -en)* *f* front; **f~al** [frɔnˈtaːl] *adj* frontal

fror *etc* [froːr] *vb siehe* **frieren**

Frosch [frɔʃ] *(-(e)s, ⁻e)* *m* frog; (*Feuerwerk*) squib; **~mann** *m* frogman; **~schenkel** *m* frog's leg

Frost [frɔst] *(-(e)s, ⁻e)* *m* frost; **~beule** *f* chilblain

frösteln [ˈfrœstəln] *vi* to shiver

frostig *adj* frosty

Frostschutzmittel *nt* antifreeze

Frottier(hand)tuch [frɔˈtiːr(hant)tuːx] *nt* towel

Frucht [frʊxt] *(-, ⁻e)* *f* (*auch fig*) fruit; (*Getreide*) corn; **f~bar** *adj* fruitful, fertile; **~barkeit** *f* fertility; **f~ig** *adj* (*Geschmack*) fruity; **f~los** *adj* fruitless; **~saft** *m* fruit juice

früh [fryː] *adj, adv* early; **heute ~** this morning; **F~aufsteher** *(-s, -)* *m* early riser; **F~e** *f* early morning; **~er** *adj* earlier; (*ehemalig*) former ♦ *adv* formerly; **~er war das anders** that used to be different; **~estens** *adv* at the earliest; **F~jahr** *nt*, **F~ling** *m* spring; **~reif** *adj* precocious; **F~stück** *nt* breakfast; **~stücken** *vi* to (have) breakfast; **F~stücksbüfett** *nt* breakfast buffet; **~zeitig** *adj* early; (*pej*) untimely

frustrieren [frʊsˈtriːrən] *vt* to frustrate

Fuchs [fʊks] *(-es, ⁻e)* *m* fox; **f~en** (*umg*) *vt* to rile, to annoy; **f~teufelswild** *adj* hopping mad

Fuge [ˈfuːɡə] *f* joint; (*MUS*) fugue

fügen [ˈfyːɡən] *vt* to place, to join ♦ *vr*: **sich ~ (in** +*dat*) to be obedient (to); (*anpassen*) to adapt oneself (to) ♦ *vr unpers* to happen

fühl- zW: **~bar** adj perceptible, noticeable; **~en** vt, vi, vr to feel; **F~er (-s, -)** m feeler

fuhr etc [fuːr] vb siehe **fahren**

führen ['fyːrən] vt to lead; (Geschäft) to run; (Name) to bear; (Buch) to keep ♦ vi to lead ♦ vr to behave

Führer ['fyːrər] **(-s, -)** m leader; (Fremdenführer) guide; **~schein** m driving licence

Führung ['fyːruŋ] f leadership; (eines Unternehmens) management; (MIL) command; (Benehmen) conduct; (Museumsführung) conducted tour; **~szeugnis** nt certificate of good conduct

Fülle ['fylə] f wealth, abundance; **f~n** vt to fill; (KOCH) to stuff ♦ vi to fill (up)

Füll- zW: **~er (-s, -)** m fountain pen; **~federhalter** m fountain pen; **~ung** f filling; (Holzfüllung) panel

fummeln ['fuməln] (umg) vi to fumble

Fund [fɔnt] **(-(e)s, -e)** m find

Fundament [fɔndaˈmɛnt] nt foundation; **fundamenˈtal** adj fundamental

Fund- zW: **~büro** nt lost property office, lost and found (US); **~grube** f (fig) treasure trove

fundiert [fʊnˈdiːrt] adj sound

fünf [fynf] num five; **~hundert** num five hundred; **~te(r, s)** adj fifth; **F~tel (-s, -)** nt fifth; **~zehn** num fifteen; **~zig** num fifty

Funk [fʊŋk] **(-s)** m radio, wireless; **~e (-no, -n)** m (auch fig) spark; **f~eln** vi to sparkle; **~en (-s, -)** m (auch fig) spark; **f~en** vi (durch Funk) to signal, to radio; (umg: richtig funktionieren) to work ♦ vt (Funken sprühen) to shower with sparks; **~er (-s, -)** m radio operator; **~gerät** nt radio set; **~rufempfänger** m pager, paging device; **~streife** f police radio patrol; **~telefon** nt cellphone

Funktion [fʊŋktsiˈoːn] f function; **f~ieren** [-ˈniːrən] vi to work, to function

für [fyːr] präp +akk for; **was ~** what kind od sort of; **das F~ und Wider** the pros and cons pl; **Schritt ~ Schritt** step by step

Furche ['fʊrçə] f furrow

Furcht [fʊrçt] **(-)** f fear; **f~bar** adj terrible, frightful

fürchten ['fyrçtən] vt to be afraid of, to fear ♦ vr: **sich ~ (vor** +dat) to be afraid (of)

fürchterlich adj awful

furchtlos adj fearless

füreinander [fyːraɪˈnandər] adv for each other

Furnier [fʊrˈniːr] **(-s, -e)** nt veneer

fürs [fyːrs] = **für das**

Fürsorge ['fyːrzɔrgə] f care; (Sozialfürsorge) welfare; **f~r(in) (-s, -)** m(f) welfare worker; **~unterstützung** f social security, welfare benefit (US); **fürsorglich** adj attentive, caring

Fürsprache f recommendation; (um Gnade) intercession

Fürsprecher m advocate

Fürst [fyrst] **(-en, -en)** m prince; **~entum** nt principality; **~in** f princess; **f~lich** adj princely

Fuß [fuːs] **(-es, ⁿe)** m foot; (von Glas, Säule etc) base; (von Möbel) leg; **zu ~** on foot; **~ball** m football; **~ballplatz** m football pitch; **~ballspiel** nt football match; **~ballspieler** m footballer; **~boden** m floor; **~bremse** f (AUT) footbrake; **~ende** nt foot; **~gänger(in) (-s, -)** m(f) pedestrian; **~gängerzone** f pedestrian precinct; **~nagel** m toenail; **~note** f footnote; **~spur** f footprint; **~tritt** m kick; (Spur) footstep; **~weg** m footpath

Futter ['fʊtər] **(-s, -)** nt fodder, feed; (Stoff) lining; **~al** [-ˈraːl] **(-s, -e)** nt case

füttern ['fʏtərn] vt to feed; (Kleidung) to line

Futur [fuˈtuːr] **(-s, -e)** nt future

G, g

g abk = **Gramm**

gab etc [gaːp] vb siehe **geben**

Gabe ['gaːbə] f gift

Gabel ['gaːbəl] **(-, -n)** f fork; **~ung** f fork

gackern ['gakərn] vi to cackle

gaffen ['gafən] vi to gape

Gage ['gaːʒə] f fee; salary

gähnen ['gɛːnən] vi to yawn

Galerie [galə'ri:] f gallery

Galgen ['galgən] **(-s, -)** m gallows sg; **~frist** f respite; **~humor** m macabre humour

Galle ['galə] f gall; (*Organ*) gall bladder; **~nstein** m gallstone

gammeln ['gaməln] (*umg*) vi to bum around; **Gammler(in) (-s, -)** (*pej*) m(f) layabout, loafer (*inf*)

Gämse ▲ ['gɛmzə] f chamois

Gang [gaŋ] m **(-(e)s, ⁺e)** m walk; (*Botengang*) errand; (*~art*) gait; (*Abschnitt eines Vorgangs*) operation; (*Essensgang, Ablauf*) course; (*Flur etc*) corridor; (*Durchgang*) passage; (*TECH*) gear; **in ~ bringen** to start up; (*fig*) to get off the ground; **in ~ sein** to be in operation; (*fig*) to be under way

gang adj: **~ und gäbe** usual, normal

gängig ['gɛŋɪç] adj common, current; (*Ware*) in demand, selling well

Gangschaltung f gears pl

Ganove [ga'no:və] **(-n, -n)** (*umg*) m crook

Gans [gans] **(-, ⁺e)** f goose

Gänse- ['gɛnzə] zW: **~blümchen** nt daisy; **~füßchen** (*umg*) pl (*Anführungszeichen*) inverted commas; **~haut** f goose pimples pl; **~marsch** m: **im ~marsch** in single file; **~rich (-s, -e)** m gander

ganz [gants] adj whole; (*vollständig*) complete ♦ adv quite; (*völlig*) completely; **~ Europa** all Europe; **sein ~es Geld** all his money; **~ und gar nicht** not at all; **es sieht ~ so aus** it really looks like it; **aufs G~e gehen** to go for the lot

gänzlich ['gɛntslɪç] adj complete, entire ♦ adv completely, entirely

Ganztagsschule f all-day school

gar [ga:r] adj cooked, done ♦ adv quite; **~ nicht/nichts/keiner** not/nothing/nobody at all; **~ nicht schlecht** not bad at all

Garage [ga'ra:ʒə] f garage

Garantie [garan'ti:] f guarantee; **g~ren** vt to guarantee; **er kommt g~rt** he's guaranteed to come

Garbe ['garbə] f sheaf

Garde ['gardə] f guard

Garderobe [gardə'ro:bə] f wardrobe; (*Abgabe*) cloakroom; **~nfrau** f cloakroom

attendant

Gardine [gar'di:nə] f curtain

garen ['ga:rən] vt, vi to cook

gären ['gɛ:rən] (*unreg*) vi to ferment

Garn [garn] **(-(e)s, -e)** nt thread; yarn (*auch fig*)

Garnele [gar'ne:lə] f shrimp, prawn

garnieren [gar'ni:rən] vt to decorate; (*Speisen, fig*) to garnish

Garnison [garni'zo:n] **(-, -en)** f garrison

Garnitur [garni'tu:r] f (*Satz*) set; (*Unterwäsche*) set of (matching) underwear; **erste ~** (*fig*) top rank; **zweite ~** (*fig*) second rate

garstig ['garstɪç] adj nasty, horrid

Garten ['gartən] **(-s, ⁺)** m garden; **~arbeit** f gardening; **~gerät** nt gardening tool; **~lokal** nt beer garden; **~tür** f garden gate

Gärtner(in) ['gɛrtnər(ɪn)] **(-s, -)** m(f) gardener; **~ei** [-'raɪ] f nursery; (*Gemüsegärtnerei*) market garden (*BRIT*), truck farm (*US*)

Gärung ['gɛ:rʊŋ] f fermentation

Gas [ga:s] **(-es, -e)** nt gas; **~ geben** (*AUT*) to accelerate, to step on the gas; **~hahn** m gas tap; **~herd** m gas cooker; **~kocher** m gas cooker; **~leitung** f gas pipe; **~pedal** nt accelerator, gas pedal

Gasse ['gasə] f lane, alley

Gast [gast] **(-es, ⁺e)** m guest; (*in Lokal*) patron; **bei jdm zu ~ sein** to be sb's guest; **~arbeiter(in)** m(f) foreign worker

Gäste- ['gɛstə] zW: **~buch** nt visitors' book, guest book; **~zimmer** nt guest od spare room

Gast- zW: **g~freundlich** adj hospitable; **~geber (-s, -)** m host; **~geberin** f hostess; **~haus** nt hotel, inn; **~hof** m hotel, inn; **g~ieren** [-'ti:rən] vi (*THEAT*) to (appear as a) guest; **g~lich** adj hospitable; **~rolle** f guest role; **~spiel** nt (*THEAT*) guest performance; **~stätte** f restaurant; pub; **~wirt** m innkeeper; **~wirtschaft** f hotel, inn

Gaswerk nt gasworks sg

Gaszähler m gas meter

Gatte ['gatə] **(-n, -n)** m husband, spouse

Gattin f wife, spouse

Rechtschreibreform: ▲ *neue Schreibung* △ *alte Schreibung (auslaufend)*

Gattung ['gatʊŋ] *f* genus; kind

Gaudi ['gaʊdi] (*umg: SÜDD, ÖSTERR*) *nt od f* fun

Gaul [gaʊl] **(-(e)s, Gäule)** *m* horse; nag

Gaumen ['gaʊmən] **(-s, -)** *m* palate

Gauner ['gaʊnər] **(-s, -)** *m* rogue; **~ei** [-'raɪ] *f* swindle

geb. *abk* = **geboren**

Gebäck [gə'bɛk] **(-(e)s, -e)** *nt* pastry

gebacken [gə'bakən] *adj* baked; (*gebraten*) fried

Gebälk [gə'bɛlk] **(-(e)s)** *nt* timberwork

Gebärde [gə'bɛːrdə] *f* gesture; **g~n** *vr* to behave

gebären [gə'bɛːrən] (*unreg*) *vt* to give birth to, to bear

Gebärmutter *f* uterus, womb

Gebäude [gə'bɔʏdə] **(-s, -)** *nt* building; **~komplex** *m* (building) complex

geben ['geːbən] (*unreg*) *vt, vi* to give; (*Karten*) to deal ♦ *vb unpers*: **es gibt** there is/are; there will be ♦ *vr* (*sich verhalten*) to behave, to act; (*aufhören*) to abate; **jdm etw ~** to give sb sth *od* sth to sb; **was gibts?** what's up?; **was gibt es im Kino?** what's on at the cinema?; **sich geschlagen ~** to admit defeat; **das wird sich schon ~** that'll soon sort itself out

Gebet [gə'beːt] **(-(e)s, -e)** *nt* prayer

gebeten [gə'beːtən] *vb siehe* **bitten**

Gebiet [gə'biːt] **(-(e)s, -e)** *nt* area; (*Hoheitsgebiet*) territory; (*fig*) field; **g~en** (*unreg*) *vt* to command; to demand; **g~erisch** *adj* imperious

Gebilde [gə'bɪldə] **(-s, -)** *nt* object

gebildet *adj* cultured, educated

Gebirge [gə'bɪrgə] **(-s, -)** *nt* mountain chain

Gebiss [gə'bɪs] **(-es, -e)** *nt* teeth *pl*; (*künstlich*) dentures *pl*

gebissen *vb siehe* **beißen**

geblieben [gə'bliːbən] *vb siehe* **bleiben**

geblümt [gə'blyːmt] *adj* (*Kleid, Stoff, Tapete*) floral

geboren [gə'boːrən] *adj* born; (*Frau*) née

geborgen [gə'bɔrgən] *adj* secure, safe

Gebot [gə'boːt] **(-(e)s, -e)** *nt* command; (*REL*) commandment; (*bei Auktion*) bid

geboten [gə'boːtən] *vb siehe* **bieten**

Gebr. *abk* (= *Gebrüder*) Bros.

gebracht [gə'braxt] *vb siehe* **bringen**

gebraten [gə'braːtən] *adj* fried

Gebrauch [gə'braʊx] **(-(e)s, Gebräuche)** *m* use; (*Sitte*) custom; **g~en** *vt* to use

gebräuchlich [gə'brɔʏçlɪç] *adj* usual, customary

Gebrauchs- *zW*: **~anweisung** *f* directions *pl* for use; **g~fertig** *adj* ready for use; **~gegenstand** *m* commodity

gebraucht [gə'braʊxt] *adj* used; **G~wagen** *m* secondhand *od* used car

gebrechlich [gə'brɛçlɪç] *adj* frail

Gebrüder [gə'bryːdər] *pl* brothers

Gebrüll [gə'brʏl] **(-(e)s)** *nt* roaring

Gebühr [gə'byːr] **(-, -en)** *f* charge, fee; **nach ~** fittingly; **über ~** unduly; **g~en** *vi*: **jdm g~en** to be sb's due *od* due to sb ♦ *vr* to be fitting; **g~end** *adj* fitting, appropriate ♦ *adv* fittingly, appropriately

Gebühren- *zW*: **~einheit** *f* (*TEL*) unit; **~erlass** ▲ *m* remission of fees; **~ermäßigung** *f* reduction of fees; **g~frei** *adj* free of charge; **~ordnung** *f* scale of charges, tariff; **g~pflichtig** *adj* subject to a charge

gebunden [gə'bʊndən] *vb siehe* **binden**

Geburt [gə'buːrt] **(-, -en)** *f* birth

Geburtenkontrolle *f* birth control

Geburtenregelung *f* birth control

gebürtig [gə'bʏrtɪç] *adj* born in, native of; **~e Schweizerin** native of Switzerland

Geburts- *zW*: **~anzeige** *f* birth notice; **~datum** *nt* date of birth; **~jahr** *nt* year of birth; **~ort** *m* birthplace; **~tag** *m* birthday; **~urkunde** *f* birth certificate

Gebüsch [gə'bʏʃ] **(-(e)s, -e)** *nt* bushes *pl*

gedacht [gə'daxt] *vb siehe* **denken**

Gedächtnis [gə'dɛçtnɪs] **(-ses, -se)** *nt* memory; **~feier** *f* commemoration

Gedanke [gə'daŋkə] **(-ns, -n)** *m* thought; **sich über etw** *akk* **~n machen** to think about sth

Gedanken- *zW*: **~austausch** *m* exchange of ideas; **g~los** *adj* thoughtless; **~strich** *m* dash; **~übertragung** *f* thought transference, telepathy

Gedeck [gə'dɛk] **(-(e)s, -e)** *nt* cover(ing); (*Speisenfolge*) menu; **ein ~ auflegen** to lay a place

gedeihen [gə'daɪən] (*unreg*) *vi* to thrive, to prosper

Gedenken *nt*: **zum ~ an jdn** in memory of sb

gedenken [gə'dɛŋkən] (*unreg*) *vi +gen* (*beabsichtigen*) to intend; (*sich erinnern*) to remember

Gedenk- *zW*: **~feier** *f* commemoration; **~minute** *f* minute's silence; **~stätte** *f* memorial; **~tag** *m* remembrance day

Gedicht [gə'dɪçt] **(-(e)s, -e)** *nt* poem

gediegen [gə'diːgən] *adj* (good) quality; (*Mensch*) reliable, honest

Gedränge [gə'drɛŋə] **(-s)** *nt* crush, crowd

gedrängt *adj* compressed; **~ voll** packed

gedrückt [gə'drʏkt] *adj* (*deprimiert*) low, depressed

gedrungen [gə'drʊŋən] *adj* thickset, stocky

Geduld [gə'dʊlt] *f* patience; **g~en** [gə'dʊldən] *vr* to be patient; **g~ig** *adj* patient, forbearing; **~sprobe** *f* trial of (one's) patience

gedurft [gə'dʊrft] *vb siehe* **dürfen**

geehrt [gə'|eːrt] *adj*: **Sehr ~e Frau X!** Dear Mrs X

geeignet [gə'|aɪgnət] *adj* suitable

Gefahr [gə'faːr] **(-, -en)** *f* danger; **~ laufen, etw zu tun** to run the risk of doing sth; **auf eigene ~** at one's own risk

gefährden [gə'fɛːrdən] *vt* to endanger

Gefahren- *zW*: **~quelle** *f* source of danger; **~zulage** *f* danger money

gefährlich [gə'fɛːrlɪç] *adj* dangerous

Gefährte [gə'fɛːrtə] **(-n, -n)** *m* companion; (*Lebenspartner*) partner

Gefährtin [gə'fɛːrtɪn] *f* (female) companion; (*Lebenspartner*) (female) partner

Gefälle [gə'fɛlə] **(-s, -)** *nt* gradient, incline

Gefallen¹ [gə'falən] **(-s, -)** *m* favour

Gefallen² [gə'falən] **(-s)** *nt* pleasure; **an etw** *dat* **~ finden** to derive pleasure from sth

gefallen *pp von* **fallen** ♦ *vi*: **jdm ~** to please

sb; **er/es gefällt mir** I like him/it; **das gefällt mir an ihm** that's one thing I like about him; **sich** *dat* **etw ~ lassen** to put up with sth

gefällig [gə'fɛlɪç] *adj* (*hilfsbereit*) obliging; (*erfreulich*) pleasant; **G~keit** *f* favour; helpfulness; **etw aus G~keit tun** to do sth out of the goodness of one's heart

gefangen [gə'faŋən] *adj* captured; (*fig*) captivated; **~ halten** to keep prisoner; **~ nehmen** to take prisoner; **G~e(r)** *f(m)* prisoner, captive; **G~nahme** *f* capture; **G~schaft** *f* captivity

Gefängnis [gə'fɛŋnɪs] **(-ses, -se)** *nt* prison; **~strafe** *f* prison sentence; **~wärter** *m* prison warder; **~zelle** *f* prison cell

Gefäß [gə'fɛːs] **(-es, -e)** *nt* vessel; (*auch ANAT*) container

gefasst ▲ [gə'fast] *adj* composed, calm; **auf etw** *akk* **~ sein** to be prepared *od* ready for sth

Gefecht [gə'fɛçt] **(-(e)s, -e)** *nt* fight; (*MIL*) engagement

Gefieder [gə'fiːdər] **(-s, -)** *nt* plumage, feathers *pl*

gefleckt [gə'flɛkt] *adj* spotted, mottled

geflogen [gə'floːgən] *vb siehe* **fliegen**

geflossen [gə'flɔsən] *vb siehe* **fließen**

Geflügel [gə'flyːgəl] **(-s)** *nt* poultry

Gefolgschaft [gə'fɔlkʃaft] *f* following

gefragt [gə'fraːkt] *adj* in demand

gefräßig [gə'frɛːsɪç] *adj* voracious

Gefreite(r) [gə'fraɪtə(r)] *m* lance corporal; (*NAUT*) able seaman; (*AVIAT*) aircraftman

Gefrierbeutel *m* freezer bag

gefrieren [gə'friːrən] (*unreg*) *vi* to freeze

Gefrier- *zW*: **~fach** *nt* icebox; **~fleisch** *nt* frozen meat; **g~getrocknet** [-gətrɔknət] *adj* freeze-dried; **~punkt** *m* freezing point; **~schutzmittel** *nt* antifreeze; **~truhe** *f* deep-freeze

gefroren [gə'froːrən] *vb siehe* **frieren**

Gefühl [gə'fyːl] **(-(e)s, -e)** *nt* feeling; **etw im ~ haben** to have a feel for sth; **g~los** *adj* unfeeling

gefühls- *zW*: **~betont** *adj* emotional; **G~duselei** [-duːzə'laɪ] *f* over-sentimentality;

~mäßig adj instinctive
gefüllt [gə'fʏlt] adj (KOCH) stuffed
gefunden [gə'fʊndən] vb siehe **finden**
gegangen [gə'gaŋən] vb siehe **gehen**
gegeben [gə'ge:bən] vb siehe **geben** ♦ adj
given; **zu ~er Zeit** in good time
gegebenenfalls [gə'ge:bənənfals] adv if
need be

SCHLÜSSELWORT
---

gegen ['ge:gən] präp +akk 1 against; **nichts
gegen jdn haben** to have nothing against
sb; **X gegen Y** (SPORT, JUR) X versus Y; **ein
Mittel gegen Schnupfen** something for
colds
2 (in Richtung auf) towards; **gegen Osten**
to(wards) the east; **gegen Abend** towards
evening; **gegen einen Baum fahren** to
drive into a tree
3 (ungefähr) round about; **gegen 3 Uhr**
around 3 o'clock
4 (gegenüber) towards; (ungefähr) around;
gerecht gegen alle fair to all
5 (im Austausch für) for; **gegen bar** for cash;
gegen Quittung against a receipt
6 (verglichen mit) compared with

Gegenangriff m counter-attack
Gegenbeweis m counter-evidence
Gegend ['ge:gənt] (-, -en) f area, district
Gegen- zW: **~einander** adv against one
another; **~fahrbahn** f oncoming
carriageway; **~frage** f counter-question;
~gewicht nt counterbalance; **~gift** nt
antidote; **~leistung** f service in return;
~maßnahme f countermeasure; **~mittel**
nt antidote, cure; **~satz** m contrast; **~sätze
überbrücken** to overcome differences;
g~sätzlich adj contrary, opposite;
(widersprüchlich) contradictory; **g~seitig** adj
mutual, reciprocal; **sich g~seitig helfen** to
help each other; **~spieler** m opponent;
~sprechanlage f (two-way) intercom;
~stand m object; **~stimme** f vote against;
~stoß m counterblow; **~stück** nt
counterpart; **~teil** nt opposite; **im ~teil** on
the contrary; **g~teilig** adj opposite,

contrary
gegenüber [ge:gən'|y:bər] präp +dat
opposite; (zu) to(wards); (angesichts) in the
face of ♦ adv opposite; **G~ (-s, -)** nt person
opposite; **~liegen** (unreg) vr to face each
other; **~stehen** (unreg) vr to be opposed
(to each other); **~stellen** vt to confront;
(fig) to contrast; **G~stellung** f
confrontation; (fig) contrast; **~treten**
(unreg) vi +dat to face
Gegen- zW: **~verkehr** m oncoming traffic;
~vorschlag m counterproposal; **~wart** f
present; **g~wärtig** adj present ♦ adv at
present; **das ist mir nicht mehr g~wärtig**
that has slipped my mind; **~wert** m
equivalent; **~wind** m headwind;
g~zeichnen vt, vi to countersign
gegessen [gə'gesən] vb siehe **essen**
Gegner ['ge:gnər] (-s, -) m opponent;
g~isch adj opposing
gegr. abk (= gegründet) est.
gegrillt [gə'grɪlt] adj grilled
Gehackte(s) [gə'hakta(s)] nt mince(d meat)
Gehalt¹ [gə'halt] (-(e)s, -e) m content
Gehalt² [gə'halt] (-(e)s, ⸚er) nt salary
Gehalts- zW: **~empfänger** m salary
earner; **~erhöhung** f salary increase;
~zulage f salary increment
gehaltvoll [gə'haltfɔl] adj (nahrhaft)
nutritious
gehässig [gə'hɛsɪç] adj spiteful, nasty
Gehäuse [gə'hɔʏzə] (-s, -) nt case; casing;
(von Apfel etc) core
Gehege [gə'he:gə] (-s, -) nt reserve; (im Zoo)
enclosure
geheim [gə'haɪm] adj secret; **~ halten** to
keep secret; **G~dienst** m secret service,
intelligence service; **G~nis (-ses, -se)** nt
secret; mystery; **~nisvoll** adj mysterious;
G~polizei f secret police
gehemmt [gə'hɛmt] adj inhibited, self-
conscious
gehen ['ge:ən] (unreg) vt, vi to go; (zu Fuß ~)
to walk ♦ vb unpers: **wie geht es (dir)?**
how are you od things?; **~ nach** (Fenster) to
face; **mir/ihm geht es gut** I'm/he's (doing)
fine; **geht das?** is that possible?; **gehts**

noch? can you manage?; **es geht** not too bad, O.K.; **das geht nicht** that's not on; **es geht um etw** it has to do with sth, it's about sth; **sich ~ lassen** (*unbeherrscht sein*) to lose control (of o.s.); **jdn ~ lassen** to let/leave sb alone; **lass mich ~!** leave me alone!

geheuer [gə'hɔyər] *adj*: **nicht ~** eerie; (*fragwürdig*) dubious

Gehilfe [gə'hɪlfə] (**-n, -n**) *m* assistant; **Gehilfin** *f* assistant

Gehirn [gə'hɪrn] (**-(e)s, -e**) *nt* brain; **~erschütterung** *f* concussion; **~hautentzündung** *f* meningitis

gehoben [gə'hoːbən] *pp von* **heben** ♦ *adj* (*Position*) elevated; high

geholfen [gə'hɔlfən] *vb siehe* **helfen**

Gehör [gə'høːr] (**-(e)s**) *nt* hearing; **musikalisches ~** ear; **~ finden** to gain a hearing; **jdm ~ schenken** to give sb a hearing

gehorchen [gə'hɔrçən] *vi +dat* to obey

gehören [gə'høːrən] *vi* to belong ♦ *vr unpers* to be right *od* proper

gehörig *adj* proper; **~ zu** *od +dat* belonging to; part of

gehörlos *adj* deaf

gehorsam [gə'hoːrzaːm] *adj* obedient; **G~** (**-s**) *m* obedience

Geh- ['geː-] *zW*: **~steig** *m* pavement, sidewalk (*US*); **~weg** *m* pavement, sidewalk (*US*)

Geier ['gaɪər] (**-s, -**) *m* vulture

Geige ['gaɪɡə] *f* violin; **~r** (**-s, -**) *m* violinist

geil [gaɪl] *adj* randy (*BRIT*), horny (*US*)

Geisel ['gaɪzəl] (**-, -n**) *f* hostage

Geist [gaɪst] (**-(e)s, -er**) *m* spirit; (*Gespenst*) ghost; (*Verstand*) mind

geisterhaft *adj* ghostly

Geistes- *zW*: **g~abwesend** *adj* absent-minded; **~blitz** *m* brainwave; **~gegenwart** *f* presence of mind; **g~krank** *adj* mentally ill; **~kranke(r)** *f(m)* mentally ill person; **~krankheit** *f* mental illness; **~wissenschaften** *pl* the arts; **~zustand** *m* state of mind

geist- *zW*: **~ig** *adj* intellectual; mental;

(*Getränke*) alcoholic; **~ig behindert** mentally handicapped; **~lich** *adj* spiritual, religious; clerical; **G~liche(r)** *m* clergyman; **G~lichkeit** *f* clergy; **~los** *adj* uninspired, dull; **~reich** *adj* clever; witty; **~voll** *adj* intellectual; (*weise*) wise

Geiz [gaɪts] (**-es**) *m* miserliness, meanness; **g~en** *vi* to be miserly; **~hals** *m* miser; **g~ig** *adj* miserly, mean; **~kragen** *m* miser

gekannt [gə'kant] *vb siehe* **kennen**

gekonnt [gə'kɔnt] *adj* skilful ♦ *vb siehe* **können**

gekünstelt [ge'kʏnstəlt] *adj* artificial, affected

Gel [geːl] (**-s, -e**) *nt* gel

Gelächter [gə'lɛçtər] (**-s, -**) *nt* laughter

geladen [ge'laːdən] *adj* loaded; (*ELEK*) live; (*fig*) furious

gelähmt [gə'lɛːmt] *adj* paralysed

Gelände [gə'lɛndə] (**-s, -**) *nt* land, terrain; (*von Fabrik, Sportgelände*) grounds *pl*; (*Bau~*) site; **~lauf** *m* cross-country race

Geländer [gə'lɛndər] (**-s, -**) *nt* railing; (*Treppengeländer*) banister(s)

gelangen [gə'laŋən] *vi*: **~ (an** *+akk od* **zu)** to reach; (*erwerben*) to attain; **in jds Besitz** *akk* **~** to come into sb's possession

gelangweilt [gə'laŋvaɪlt] *adj* bored

gelassen [gə'lasən] *adj* calm, composed; **G~heit** *f* calmness, composure

Gelatine [ʒela'tiːnə] *f* gelatine

geläufig [gə'lɔyfɪç] *adj* (*üblich*) common; **das ist mir nicht ~** I'm not familiar with that

gelaunt [gə'laʊnt] *adj*: **schlecht/gut ~** in a bad/good mood; **wie ist er ~?** what sort of mood is he in?

gelb [gɛlp] *adj* yellow; (*Ampellicht*) amber; **~lich** *adj* yellowish; **G~sucht** *f* jaundice

Geld [gɛlt] (**-(e)s, -er**) *nt* money; **etw zu ~ machen** to sell sth off; **~anlage** *f* investment; **~automat** *m* cash dispenser; **~beutel** *m* purse; **~börse** *f* purse; **~geber** (**-s, -**) *m* financial backer; **g~gierig** *adj* avaricious; **~schein** *m* banknote; **~schrank** *m* safe, strongbox; **~strafe** *f* fine; **~stück** *nt* coin; **~wechsel**

m exchange (of money)

Gelee [ʒeˈleː] **(-s, -s)** *nt od m* jelly

gelegen [gəˈleːgən] *adj* situated; (*passend*) convenient, opportune ♦ *vb siehe* **liegen**; **etw kommt jdm ~** sth is convenient for sb

Gelegenheit [gəˈleːgənhaɪt] *f* opportunity; (*Anlaß*) occasion; **bei jeder ~** at every opportunity; **~sarbeit** *f* casual work; **~skauf** *m* bargain

gelegentlich [gəˈleːgəntlɪç] *adj* occasional ♦ *adv* occasionally; (*bei Gelegenheit*) some time (or other) ♦ *präp +gen* on the occasion of

gelehrt [gəˈleːrt] *adj* learned; **G~e(r)** *f(m)* scholar; **G~heit** *f* scholarliness

Geleise [gəˈlaɪzə] **(-s, -)** *nt* = **Gleis**

Geleit [gəˈlaɪt] **(-(e)s, -e)** *nt* escort; **g~en** *vt* to escort

Gelenk [gəˈlɛŋk] **(-(e)s, -e)** *nt* joint; **g~ig** *adj* supple

gelernt [gəˈlɛrnt] *adj* skilled

Geliebte(r) [gəˈliːptə(r)] *f(m)* sweetheart, beloved

geliehen [gəˈliːən] *vb siehe* **leihen**

gelind(e) [gəˈlɪnd(ə)] *adj* mild, light; (*fig: Wut*) fierce; **~ gesagt** to put it mildly

gelingen [gəˈlɪŋən] (*unreg*) *vi* to succeed; **es ist mir gelungen, etw zu tun** I succeeded in doing sth

geloben [gəˈloːbən] *vt, vi* to vow, to swear

gelten [ˈgɛltən] (*unreg*) *vt* (*wert sein*) to be worth ♦ *vi* (*gültig sein*) to be valid; (*erlaubt sein*) to be allowed ♦ *vb unpers*: **es gilt, etw zu tun** it is necessary to do sth; **jdm viel/ wenig ~** to mean a lot/not to mean much to sb; **was gilt die Wette?** what do you bet?; **etw ~ lassen** to accept sth; **als** *od* **für etw ~** to be considered to be sth; **jdm** *od* **für jdn ~** (*betreffen*) to apply to *od* for sb; **~d** *adj* prevailing; **etw ~d machen** to assert sth; **sich ~d machen** to make itself/ o.s. felt

Geltung [ˈgɛltʊŋ] *f*: **~ haben** to have validity; **sich/etw** *dat* **~ verschaffen** to establish one's position/the position of sth; **etw zur ~ bringen** to show sth to its best advantage; **zur ~ kommen** to be seen/ heard *etc* to its best advantage

Geltungsbedürfnis *nt* desire for admiration

Gelübde [gəˈlʏpdə] **(-s, -)** *nt* vow

gelungen [gəˈlʊŋən] *adj* successful

gemächlich [gəˈmɛːçlɪç] *adj* leisurely

Gemahl [gəˈmaːl] **(-(e)s, -e)** *m* husband; **~in** *f* wife

Gemälde [gəˈmɛːldə] **(-s, -)** *nt* picture, painting

gemäß [gəˈmɛːs] *präp +dat* in accordance with ♦ *adj (+dat)* appropriate (to)

gemäßigt *adj* moderate; (*Klima*) temperate

gemein [gəˈmaɪn] *adj* common; (*niederträchtig*) mean; **etw ~ haben (mit)** to have sth in common (with)

Gemeinde [gəˈmaɪndə] *f* district, community; (*Pfarrgemeinde*) parish; (*Kirchengemeinde*) congregation; **~steuer** *f* local rates *pl*; **~verwaltung** *f* local administration; **~wahl** *f* local election

Gemein- *zW*: **g~gefährlich** *adj* dangerous to the public; **~heit** *f* commonness; mean thing to do/to say; **g~nützig** *adj* charitable; **g~nütziger Verein** non-profit-making organization; **g~sam** *adj* joint, common (*AUCH MATH*) ♦ *adv* together, jointly; **g~same Sache mit jdm machen** to be in cahoots with sb; **etw g~sam haben** to have sth in common; **~samkeit** *f* community, having in common; **~schaft** *f* community; **in ~schaft mit** jointly *od* together with; **g~schaftlich** *adj* = **gemeinsam**; **~schaftsarbeit** *f* teamwork; team effort; **~sinn** *m* public spirit

Gemenge [gəˈmɛŋə] **(-s, -)** *nt* mixture; (*Handgemenge*) scuffle

gemessen [gəˈmɛsən] *adj* measured

Gemetzel [gəˈmɛtsəl] **(-s, -)** *nt* slaughter, carnage, butchery

Gemisch [gəˈmɪʃ] **(-es, -e)** *nt* mixture; **g~t** *adj* mixed

gemocht [gəˈmɔxt] *vb siehe* **mögen**

Gemse △ [ˈgɛmzə] *f siehe* **Gämse**

Gemurmel [gəˈmʊrməl] **(-s)** *nt* murmur(ing)

Gemüse [gəˈmyːzə] **(-s, -)** *nt* vegetables *pl*; **~garten** *m* vegetable garden; **~händler** *m* greengrocer

gemusst ▲ [gə'mʊst] *vb siehe* **müssen**

gemustert [gə'mʊstərt] *adj* patterned

Gemüt [gə'my:t] **(-(e)s, -er)** *nt* disposition, nature; person; **sich** *dat* **etw zu ~e führen** (*umg*) to indulge in sth; **die ~er erregen** to arouse strong feelings; **g~lich** *adj* comfortable, cosy; (*Person*) good-natured; **~lichkeit** *f* comfortableness, cosiness; amiability

Gemüts- *zW*: **~mensch** *m* sentimental person; **~ruhe** *f* composure; **~zustand** *m* state of mind

Gen [ge:n] **(-s, -e)** *nt* gene

genannt [gə'nant] *vb siehe* **nennen**

genau [gə'nau] *adj* exact, precise ♦ *adv* exactly, precisely; **etw ~ nehmen** to take sth seriously; **~ genommen** strictly speaking; **G~igkeit** *f* exactness, accuracy; **~so** *adv* just the same; **~so gut** just as good

genehm [gə'ne:m] *adj* agreeable, acceptable; **~igen** *vt* to approve, to authorize; **sich** *dat* **etw ~igen** to indulge in sth; **G~igung** *f* approval, authorization; (*Schriftstück*) permit

General [gene'ra:l] **(-s, -e** *od* **-e)** *m* general; **~direktor** *m* director general; **~konsulat** *nt* consulate general; **~probe** *f* dress rehearsal; **~streik** *m* general strike; **g~überholen** *vt* to overhaul thoroughly; **~versammlung** *f* general meeting

Generation [generatsi'o:n] *f* generation

Generator [gene'ra:tɔr] *m* generator, dynamo

generell [genə'rɛl] *adj* general

genesen [gə'ne:zən] (*unreg*) *vi* to convalesce, to recover; **Genesung** *f* recovery, convalescence

genetisch [ge'ne:tɪʃ] *adj* genetic

Genf ['gɛnf] *nt* Geneva; **der ~er See** Lake Geneva

genial [geni'a:l] *adj* brilliant

Genick [gə'nɪk] **(-(e)s, -e)** *nt* (back of the) neck

Genie [ʒe'ni:] **(-s, -s)** *nt* genius

genieren [ʒe'ni:rən] *vt* to bother ♦ *vr* to feel

awkward *od* self-conscious

genieß- *zW*: **~bar** *adj* edible; drinkable; **~en** [gə'ni:sən] (*unreg*) *vt* to enjoy; to eat; to drink; **G~er** **(-s, -)** *m* epicure; pleasure lover; **~erisch** *adj* appreciative ♦ *adv* with relish

genmanipuliert ['ge:nmanipuli:rt] *adj* genetically modified

genommen [gə'nɔmən] *vb siehe* **nehmen**

Genosse [gə'nɔsə] **(-n, -n)** *m* (*bes POL*) comrade, companion; **~nschaft** *f* cooperative (association)

Genossin *f* (*bes POL*) comrade, companion

Gentechnik ['ge:ntɛçnɪk] *f* genetic engineering

genug [gə'nu:k] *adv* enough

Genüge [gə'ny:gə] *f*: **jdm/etw ~ tun** *od* **leisten** to satisfy sb/sth; **g~n** *vi* (+*dat*) to be enough (for); **g~nd** *adj* sufficient

genügsam [gə'ny:kza:m] *adj* modest, easily satisfied; **G~keit** *f* moderation

Genugtuung [gə'nu:ktu:ʊŋ] *f* satisfaction

Genuss ▲ [gə'nʊs] **(-es, -e)** *m* pleasure; (*Zusichnehmen*) consumption; **in den ~ von etw kommen** to receive the benefit of sth

genüsslich ▲ [gə'nʏslɪç] *adv* with relish

Genussmittel ▲ *pl* (semi-)luxury items

geöffnet [gə'œfnət] *adj* open

Geograf ▲ [geo'gra:f] **(-en, -en)** *m* geographer; **Geogra'fie** ▲ *f* geography; **g~isch** *adj* geographical

Geologe [geo'lo:gə] **(-n, -n)** *m* geologist; **Geolo'gie** *f* geology

Geometrie [geome'tri:] *f* geometry

Gepäck [gə'pɛk] **(-(e)s)** *nt* luggage, baggage; **~abfertigung** *f* luggage office; **~annahme** *f* luggage office; **~aufbewahrung** *f* left-luggage office (*BRIT*), baggage check (*US*); **~aufgabe** *f* luggage office; **~ausgabe** *f* luggage office; (*AVIAT*) luggage reclaim; **~netz** *nt* luggage rack; **~träger** *m* porter; (*Fahrrad*) carrier; **~versicherung** *f* luggage insurance; **~wagen** *m* luggage van (*BRIT*), baggage car (*US*)

gepflegt [gə'pfle:kt] *adj* well-groomed; (*Park etc*) well looked after

---

Rechtschreibreform: ▲ *neue Schreibung* △ *alte Schreibung (auslaufend)*

Gerade [gə'ra:də] f straight line; **g~'aus** adv straight ahead; **g~he'raus** adv straight out, bluntly; **g~stehen** (unreg) vi: **für jdn/etw g~stehen** to be answerable for sb('s actions)/sth; **g~wegs** adv direct, straight; **g~zu** adv (beinahe) virtually, almost

---
SCHLÜSSELWORT
---

gerade [gə'ra:də] adj straight; (aufrecht) upright; **eine gerade Zahl** an even number

♦ adv **1** (genau) just, exactly; (speziell) especially; **gerade deshalb** that's just od exactly why; **das ist es ja gerade!** that's just it!; **gerade du** why me especially; **warum gerade ich?** why me (of all people)?; **jetzt gerade nicht!** not now!; **gerade neben** right next to

2 (eben, soeben) just; **er wollte gerade aufstehen** he was just about to get up; **gerade erst** only just; **gerade noch** (only) just

---

gerannt [gə'rant] vb siehe **rennen**
Gerät [gə'rɛːt] (-(e)s, -e) nt device; (Werkzeug) tool; (SPORT) apparatus; (Zubehör) equipment no pl
geraten [gə'ra:tən] (unreg) vi (gedeihen) to thrive; (gelingen): **(jdm) ~** to turn out well (for sb); **gut/schlecht ~** to turn out well/badly; **an jdn ~** to come across sb; **in etw akk ~** to get into sth; **nach jdm ~** to take after sb
Geratewohl [gəra:tə'vo:l] nt: **aufs ~** on the off chance; (bei Wahl) at random
geräuchert [gə'rɔʏçɐt] adj smoked
geräumig [gə'rɔʏmɪç] adj roomy
Geräusch [gə'rɔʏʃ] (-(e)s, -e) nt sound, noise; **g~los** adj silent
gerben ['gɛrbən] vt to tan
gerecht [gə'rɛçt] adj just, fair; **jdm/etw ~ werden** to do justice to sb/sth; **G~igkeit** f justice, fairness
Gerede [gə're:də] (-s) nt talk, gossip
geregelt [gə're:gəlt] adj (Arbeit) steady, regular; (Mahlzeiten) regular, set

gereizt [gə'raɪtst] adj irritable; **G~heit** f irritation
Gericht [gə'rɪçt] (-(e)s, -e) nt court; (Essen) dish; **mit jdm ins ~ gehen** (fig) to judge sb harshly; **das Jüngste ~** the Last Judgement; **g~lich** adj judicial, legal ♦ adv judicially, legally
Gerichts- zW: **~barkeit** f jurisdiction; **~hof** m court (of law); **~kosten** pl (legal) costs; **~medizin** f forensic medicine; **~saal** m courtroom; **~verfahren** nt legal proceedings pl; **~verhandlung** f trial; **~vollzieher** m bailiff
gerieben [gə'ri:bən] adj grated; (umg: schlau) smart, wily ♦ vb siehe **reiben**
gering [gə'rɪŋ] adj slight, small; (niedrig) low; (Zeit) short; **~fügig** adj slight, trivial; **~schätzig** adj disparaging
geringste(r, s) adj slightest, least; **~nfalls** adv at the very least
gerinnen [gə'rɪnən] (unreg) vi to congeal; (Blut) to clot; (Milch) to curdle
Gerippe [gə'rɪpə] (-s, -) nt skeleton
gerissen [gə'rɪsən] adj wily, smart
geritten [gə'rɪtən] vb siehe **reiten**
gern(e) ['gɛrn(ə)] adv willingly, gladly; **~ haben, ~ mögen** to like; **etwas ~ tun** to like doing something; **ich möchte ~ ...** I'd like ...; **ja, ~** yes, please; yes, I'd like to; **~ geschehen** it's a pleasure
gerochen [gə'rɔxən] vb siehe **riechen**
Geröll [gə'rœl] (-(e)s, -e) nt scree
Gerste ['gɛrstə] f barley; **~nkorn** nt (im Auge) stye
Geruch [gə'rʊx] (-(e)s, "e) m smell, odour; **g~los** adj odourless
Gerücht [gə'rʏçt] (-(e)s, -e) nt rumour
geruhsam [gə'ru:za:m] adj (Leben) peaceful; (Nacht, Zeit) peaceful, restful; (langsam: Arbeitsweise, Spaziergang) leisurely
Gerümpel [gə'rʏmpəl] (-s) nt junk
Gerüst [gə'rʏst] (-(e)s, -e) nt (Baugerüst) scaffold(ing); frame
gesalzen [gə'zaltsən] pp von **salzen** ♦ adj (umg: Preis, Rechnung) steep
gesamt [gə'zamt] adj whole, entire; (Kosten) total; (Werke) complete; **im G~en** all in all;

~**deutsch** *adj* all-German; **G~eindruck** *m* general impression; **G~heit** *f* totality, whole; **G~schule** *f* ≈ comprehensive school

Gesamtschule

🛈 The **Gesamtschule** *is a comprehensive school for pupils of different abilities. Traditionally pupils go to either a* **Gymnasium, Realschule** *or* **Hauptschule,** *depending on ability. The* **Gesamtschule** *seeks to avoid the elitism of many* **Gymnasien.** *However, these schools are still very controversial, with many parents still preferring the traditional education system.*

gesandt [gə'zant] *vb siehe* **senden**

Gesandte(r) [gə'zantə(r)] *m* envoy

Gesandtschaft [gə'zantʃaft] *f* legation

Gesang [gə'zaŋ] (**-(e)s, ⸚e**) *m* song; (*Singen*) singing; ~**buch** *nt* (*REL*) hymn book

Gesäß [gə'zɛːs] (**-es, -e**) *nt* seat, bottom

Geschäft [gə'ʃɛft] (**-(e)s, -e**) *nt* business; (*Laden*) shop; (~*sabschluß*) deal; **g~ig** *adj* active, busy; (*pej*) officious; **g~lich** *adj* commercial ♦ *adv* on business

Geschäfts- *zW*: ~**bedingungen** *pl* terms *pl* of business; ~**bericht** *m* financial report; ~**frau** *f* businesswoman; ~**führer** *m* manager; (*Klub*) secretary; ~**geheimnis** *nt* trade secret; ~**jahr** *nt* financial year; ~**lage** *f* business conditions *pl*; ~**mann** *m* businessman; **g~mäßig** *adj* businesslike; ~**partner** *m* business partner; ~**reise** *f* business trip; ~**schluss** ▲ *m* closing time; ~**stelle** *f* office, place of business; **g~tüchtig** *adj* business-minded; ~**viertel** *nt* business quarter; shopping centre; ~**wagen** *m* company car; ~**zeit** *f* business hours *pl*

geschehen [gə'ʃeːən] (*unreg*) *vi* to happen; **es war um ihn** ~ that was the end of him

gescheit [gə'ʃaɪt] *adj* clever

Geschenk [gə'ʃɛŋk] (**-(e)s, -e**) *nt* present, gift

Geschichte [gə'ʃɪçtə] *f* story; (*Sache*) affair;

(*Historie*) history

geschichtlich *adj* historical

Geschick [gə'ʃɪk] (**-(e)s, -e**) *nt* aptitude; (*Schicksal*) fate; ~**lichkeit** *f* skill, dexterity; **g~t** *adj* skilful

geschieden [gə'ʃiːdən] *adj* divorced

geschienen [gə'ʃiːnən] *vb siehe* **scheinen**

Geschirr [gə'ʃɪr] (**-(e)s, -e**) *nt* crockery; pots and pans *pl*; (*Pferdegeschirr*) harness; ~**spülmaschine** *f* dishwasher; ~**spülmittel** *nt* washing-up liquid; ~**tuch** *nt* dish cloth

Geschlecht [gə'ʃlɛçt] (**-(e)s, -er**) *nt* sex; (*GRAM*) gender; (*Gattung*) race; family; **g~lich** *adj* sexual

Geschlechts- *zW*: ~**krankheit** *f* venereal disease; ~**teil** *nt* genitals *pl*; ~**verkehr** *m* sexual intercourse

geschlossen [gə'ʃlɔsən] *adj* shut ♦ *vb siehe* **schließen**

Geschmack [gə'ʃmak] (**-(e)s, ⸚e**) *m* taste; **nach jds** ~ to sb's taste; ~ **finden an etw** *dat* to (come to) like sth; **g~los** *adj* tasteless; (*fig*) in bad taste; ~**ssinn** *m* sense of taste; **g~voll** *adj* tasteful

geschmeidig [gə'ʃmaɪdɪç] *adj* supple; (*formbar*) malleable

Geschnetzelte(s) [gə'ʃnɛtsəltə(s)] *nt* (*KOCH*) strips of meat stewed to produce a thick sauce

geschnitten [gə'ʃnɪtən] *vb siehe* **schneiden**

Geschöpf [gə'ʃœpf] (**-(e)s, -e**) *nt* creature

Geschoss ▲ [gə'ʃɔs] (**-es, -e**) *nt* (*MIL*) projectile, missile; (*Stockwerk*) floor

geschossen [gə'ʃɔsən] *vb siehe* **schießen**

geschraubt [gə'ʃraʊpt] *adj* stilted, artificial

Geschrei [gə'ʃraɪ] (**-s**) *nt* cries *pl*, shouting; (*fig: Aufheben*) noise, fuss

geschrieben [gə'ʃriːbən] *vb siehe* **schreiben**

Geschütz [gə'ʃʏts] (**-es, -e**) *nt* gun, cannon; **ein schweres** ~ **auffahren** (*fig*) to bring out the big guns

geschützt *adj* protected

Geschw. *abk siehe* **Geschwister**

Geschwätz [gə'ʃvɛts] (**-es**) *nt* chatter, gossip; **g~ig** *adj* talkative

geschweige [gə'ʃvaɪgə] *adv*: ~ (**denn**) let

alone, not to mention

geschwind [gəˈʃvɪnt] *adj* quick, swift;
G~igkeit [-dɪçkaɪt] *f* speed, velocity;
G~igkeitsbeschränkung *f* speed limit;
G~igkeitsüberschreitung *f* exceeding
the speed limit

Geschwister [gəˈʃvɪstər] *pl* brothers and
sisters

geschwommen [gəˈʃvɔmən] *vb siehe*
schwimmen

Geschworene(r) [gеˈʃvоːrənə(r)] *f(m)* juror;
~n *pl* jury

Geschwulst [gəˈʃvʊlst] (-, ¨e) *f* swelling;
growth, tumour

geschwungen [gəˈʃvʊŋən] *pp von*
schwingen ♦ *adj* curved, arched

Geschwür [gəˈʃvyːr] (-(e)s, -e) *nt* ulcer

Gesell- [gəˈzɛl] *zW:* **~e** (-n, -n) *m* fellow;
(*Handwerkgeselle*) journeyman; **g~ig** *adj*
sociable; **~igkeit** *f* sociability; **~schaft** *f*
society; (*Begleitung*, COMM) company;
(*Abendgesellschaft etc*) party; **g~schaftlich**
adj social; **~schaftsordnung** *f* social
structure; **~schaftsschicht** *f* social
stratum

gesessen [gəˈzɛsən] *vb siehe* **sitzen**

Gesetz [gəˈzɛts] (-es, -e) *nt* law; **~buch** *nt*
statute book; **~entwurf** *m* (draft) bill;
~gebung *f* legislation; **g~lich** *adj* legal,
lawful; **g~licher Feiertag** statutory holiday;
g~los *adj* lawless; **g~mäßig** *adj* lawful;
g~t *adj* (*Mensch*) sedate; **g~widrig** *adj*
illegal, unlawful

Gesicht [gəˈzɪçt] (-(e)s, -er) *nt* face; **das
zweite ~** second sight; **das ist mir nie zu
~ gekommen** I've never laid eyes on that

Gesichts- *zW:* **~ausdruck** *m* (facial)
expression; **~creme** *f* face cream; **~farbe**
f complexion; **~punkt** *m* point of view;
~wasser *nt* face lotion; **~züge** *pl* features

Gesindel [gəˈzɪndəl] (-s) *nt* rabble

gesinnt [gəˈzɪnt] *adj* disposed, minded

Gesinnung [gəˈzɪnʊŋ] *f* disposition; (*Ansicht*)
views *pl*

gesittet [gəˈzɪtət] *adj* well-mannered

Gespann [gəˈʃpan] (-(e)s, -e) *nt* team;
(*umg*) couple

gespannt *adj* tense, strained; (*begierig*)
eager; **ich bin ~, ob** I wonder if *od*
whether; **auf etw/jdn ~ sein** to look
forward to sth/meeting sb

Gespenst [gəˈʃpɛnst] (-(e)s, -er) *nt* ghost,
spectre

gesperrt [gəˈʃpɛrt] *adj* closed off

Gespött [gəˈʃpœt] (-(e)s) *nt* mockery; **zum ~
werden** to become a laughing stock

Gespräch [gəˈʃprɛːç] (-(e)s, -e) *nt*
conversation; discussion(s); (*Anruf*) call;
g~ig *adj* talkative

gesprochen [gəˈʃprɔxən] *vb siehe* **sprechen**

gesprungen [gəˈʃprʊŋən] *vb siehe* **springen**

Gespür [gəˈʃpyːr] (-s) *nt* feeling

Gestalt [gəˈʃtalt] (-, -en) *f* form, shape;
(*Person*) figure; **in ~ von** in the form of; **~
annehmen** to take shape; **g~en** *vt* (*formen*)
to shape, to form; (*organisieren*) to arrange,
to organize ♦ *vr:* **sich g~en (zu)** to turn out
(to be); **~ung** *f* formation; organization

gestanden [gəˈʃtandən] *vb siehe* **stehen**

Geständnis [gəˈʃtɛntnɪs] (-ses, -se) *nt*
confession

Gestank [gəˈʃtaŋk] (-(e)s) *m* stench

gestatten [gəˈʃtatən] *vt* to permit, to allow;
~ Sie? may I?; **sich** *dat* **~, etw zu tun** to
take the liberty of doing sth

Geste [ˈɡɛstə] *f* gesture

gestehen [gəˈʃteːən] (*unreg*) *vt* to confess

Gestein [gəˈʃtaɪn] (-(e)s, -e) *nt* rock

Gestell [gəˈʃtɛl] (-(e)s, -e) *nt* frame; (*Regal*)
rack, stand

gestern [ˈɡɛstərn] *adv* yesterday; **~ Abend /
Morgen** yesterday evening/morning

Gestirn [gəˈʃtɪrn] (-(e)s, -e) *nt* star;
(*Sternbild*) constellation

gestohlen [gəˈʃtoːlən] *vb siehe* **stehlen**

gestorben [gəˈʃtɔrbən] *vb siehe* **sterben**

gestört [gəˈʃtøːrt] *adj* disturbed

gestreift [gəˈʃtraɪft] *adj* striped

gestrichen [gəˈʃtrɪçən] *adj* cancelled

gestrig [ˈɡɛstrɪç] *adj* yesterday's

Gestrüpp [gəˈʃtrʏp] (-(e)s, -e) *nt*
undergrowth

Gestüt [gəˈʃtyːt] (-(e)s, -e) *nt* stud farm

Gesuch [gəˈzuːx] (-(e)s, -e) *nt* petition;

(*Antrag*) application; **g~t** *adj* (*COMM*) in demand; wanted; (*fig*) contrived

gesund [gə'zʊnt] *adj* healthy; **wieder ~ werden** to get better; **G~heit** *f* health(iness); **G~heit!** bless you!; **~heitlich** *adj* health *attrib*, physical ♦ *adv*: **wie geht es Ihnen ~heitlich?** how's your health?; **~heitsschädlich** *adj* unhealthy; **G~heitswesen** *nt* health service; **G~heitszustand** *m* state of health

gesungen [gə'zʊŋən] *vb siehe* **singen**

getan [gə'taːn] *vb siehe* **tun**

Getöse [gə'tøːzə] (*-s*) *nt* din, racket

Getränk [gə'trɛŋk] (*-(e)s, -e*) *nt* drink; **~ekarte** *f* wine list

getrauen [gə'traʊən] *vr* to dare, to venture

Getreide [gə'traɪdə] (*-s, -*) *nt* cereals *pl*, grain; **~speicher** *m* granary

getrennt [gə'trɛnt] *adj* separate

Getriebe [gə'triːbə] (*-s, -*) *nt* (*Leute*) bustle; (*AUT*) gearbox

getrieben *vb siehe* **treiben**

getroffen [gə'trɔfən] *vb siehe* **treffen**

getrost [gə'troːst] *adv* without any bother

getrunken [gə'trʊŋkən] *vb siehe* **trinken**

Getue [gə'tuːə] (*-s*) *nt* fuss

geübt [gə'yːpt] *adj* experienced

Gewächs [gə'vɛks] (*-es, -e*) *nt* growth; (*Pflanze*) plant

gewachsen [gə'vaksən] *adj*: **jdm/etw ~ sein** to be sb's equal/equal to sth

Gewächshaus *nt* greenhouse

gewagt [gə'vaːkt] *adj* daring, risky

gewählt [gə'vɛːlt] *adj* (*Sprache*) refined, elegant

Gewähr [gə'vɛːr] (*-*) *f* guarantee; **keine ~ übernehmen für** to accept no responsibility for; **g~en** *vt* to grant; (*geben*) to provide; **g~leisten** *vt* to guarantee

Gewahrsam [gə'vaːrzaːm] (*-s, -e*) *m* safekeeping; (*Polizeigewahrsam*) custody

Gewalt [gə'valt] (*-, -en*) *f* power; (*große Kraft*) force; (*~taten*) violence; **mit aller ~** with all one's might; **~anwendung** *f* use of force; **g~ig** *adj* tremendous, huge; **~marsch** *m* forced march; **g~sam** *adj* forcible; **g~tätig** *adj* violent

Gewand [gə'vant] (*-(e)s, ⁺er*) *nt* gown, robe

gewandt [gə'vant] *adj* deft, skilful; (*erfahren*) experienced; **G~heit** *f* dexterity, skill

gewann *etc* [gə'van] *vb siehe* **gewinnen**

Gewässer [gə'vɛsər] (*-s, -*) *nt* waters *pl*

Gewebe [gə'veːbə] (*-s, -*) *nt* (*Stoff*) fabric; (*BIOL*) tissue

Gewehr [gə'veːr] (*-(e)s, -e*) *nt* gun; rifle; **~lauf** *m* rifle barrel

Geweih [gə'vaɪ] (*-(e)s, -e*) *nt* antlers *pl*

Gewerb- [gə'vɛrb] *zW*: **~e** (*-s, -*) *nt* trade, occupation; **Handel und ~e** trade and industry; **~eschule** *f* technical school; **~ezweig** *m* line of trade

Gewerkschaft [gə'vɛrkʃaft] *f* trade union; **~ler** (*-s, -*) *m* trade unionist; **~sbund** *m* trade unions federation

gewesen [gə'veːzən] *pp von* **sein**

Gewicht [gə'vɪçt] (*-(e)s, -e*) *nt* weight; (*fig*) importance

gewieft [gə'viːft] *adj* shrewd, cunning

gewillt [gə'vɪlt] *adj* willing, prepared

Gewimmel [gə'vɪməl] (*-s*) *nt* swarm

Gewinde [gə'vɪndə] (*-s, -*) *nt* (*Kranz*) wreath; (*von Schraube*) thread

Gewinn [gə'vɪn] (*-(e)s, -e*) *m* profit; (*bei Spiel*) winnings *pl*; **~ bringend** profitable; **etw mit ~ verkaufen** to sell sth at a profit; **~- und Verlustrechnung** (*COMM*) profit and loss account; **~beteiligung** *f* profit-sharing; **g~en** (*unreg*) *vt* to win; (*erwerben*) to gain; (*Kohle, Öl*) to extract ♦ *vi* to win; (*profitieren*) to gain; **an etw** *dat* **g~en** to gain (in) sth; **g~end** *adj* (*Lächeln, Aussehen*) winning, charming; **~er(in)** (*-s, -*) *m(f)* winner; **~spanne** *f* profit margin; **~ung** *f* winning; gaining; (*von Kohle etc*) extraction

Gewirr [gə'vɪr] (*-(e)s, -e*) *nt* tangle; (*von Straßen*) maze

gewiss ▲ [gə'vɪs] *adj* certain ♦ *adv* certainly

Gewissen [gə'vɪsən] (*-s, -*) *nt* conscience; **g~haft** *adj* conscientious; **g~los** *adj* unscrupulous

Gewissens- *zW*: **~bisse** *pl* pangs of conscience, qualms; **~frage** *f* matter of conscience; **~konflikt** *m* moral conflict

gewissermaßen [gəvɪsər'maːsən] *adv* more

or less, in a way

Gewissheit ▲ [gə'vɪshaɪt] f certainty

Gewitter [gə'vɪtər] **(-s, -)** nt thunderstorm; **g~n** vi unpers: **es g~t** there's a thunderstorm

gewitzt [gə'vɪtst] adj shrewd, cunning

gewogen [gə'vo:gən] adj (+dat) well-disposed (towards)

gewöhnen [gə'vø:nən] vt: **jdn an etw** akk **~** to accustom sb to sth; (erziehen zu) to teach sb sth ♦ vr: **sich an etw** akk **~** to get used od accustomed to sth

Gewohnheit [gə'vo:nhaɪt] f habit; (Brauch) custom; **aus ~** from habit; **zur ~ werden** to become a habit

Gewohnheits- zW: **~mensch** m creature of habit; **~recht** nt common law

gewöhnlich [gə'vø:nlɪç] adj usual; ordinary; (pej) common; **wie ~** as usual

gewohnt [gə'vo:nt] adj usual; **etw ~ sein** to be used to sth

Gewöhnung f: **~ (an** +akk) getting accustomed (to)

Gewölbe [gə'vœlbə] **(-s, -)** nt vault

gewollt [gə'vɔlt] adj affected, artificial

gewonnen [gə'vɔnən] vb siehe **gewinnen**

geworden [gə'vɔrdən] vb siehe **werden**

geworfen [gə'vɔrfən] vb siehe **werfen**

Gewühl [gə'vy:l] **(-(e)s)** nt throng

Gewürz [gə'vʏrts] **(-es, -e)** nt spice, seasoning; **g~t** adj spiced

gewusst ▲ [gə'vʊst] vb siehe **wissen**

Gezeiten [gə'tsaɪtən] pl tides

gezielt [gə'tsi:lt] adj with a particular aim in mind, purposeful; (Kritik) pointed

gezogen [gə'tso:gən] vb siehe **ziehen**

Gezwitscher [gə'tsvɪtʃər] **(-s)** nt twitter(ing), chirping

gezwungen [gə'tsvʊŋən] adj forced; **~ermaßen** adv of necessity

ggf. abk von **gegebenenfalls**

gibst etc [gi:pst] vb siehe **geben**

Gicht [gɪçt] **(-)** f gout

Giebel ['gi:bəl] **(-s, -)** m gable; **~dach** nt gable(d) roof; **~fenster** nt gable window

Gier [gi:r] **(-)** f greed; **g~ig** adj greedy

gießen ['gi:sən] (unreg) vt to pour; (Blumen)

to water; (Metall) to cast; (Wachs) to mould

Gießkanne f watering can

Gift [gɪft] **(-(e)s, -e)** nt poison; **g~ig** adj poisonous; (fig: boshaft) venomous; **~müll** m toxic waste; **~stoff** m toxic substance; **~zahn** m fang

ging etc [gɪŋ] vb siehe **gehen**

Gipfel ['gɪpfəl] **(-s, -)** m summit, peak; (fig: Höhepunkt) height; **g~n** vi to culminate; **~treffen** nt summit (meeting)

Gips [gɪps] **(-es, -e)** m plaster; (MED) plaster (of Paris); **~abdruck** m plaster cast; **g~en** vt to plaster; **~verband** m plaster (cast)

Giraffe [gi'rafə] f giraffe

Girlande [gɪr'landə] f garland

Giro ['ʒi:ro] **(-s, -s)** nt giro; **~konto** nt current account

Gitarre [gi'tarə] f guitar

Gitter ['gɪtər] **(-s, -)** nt grating, bars pl; (für Pflanzen) trellis; (Zaun) railing(s); **~bett** nt cot; **~fenster** nt barred window; **~zaun** m railing(s)

Glanz [glants] **(-es)** m shine, lustre; (fig) splendour

glänzen ['glɛntsən] vi to shine (also fig), to gleam ♦ vt to polish; **~d** adj shining; (fig) brilliant

Glanz- zW: **~leistung** f brilliant achievement; **g~los** adj dull; **~zeit** f heyday

Glas [gla:s] **(-es, ⁺er)** nt glass; **~er** **(-s, -)** m glazier; **~faser** f fibreglass; **g~ieren** [gla'zi:rən] vt to glaze; **g~ig** adj glassy; **~scheibe** f pane; **~ur** [gla'zu:r] f glaze; (KOCH) icing

glatt [glat] adj smooth; (rutschig) slippery; (Absage) flat; (Lüge) downright; **Glätte** f smoothness; slipperiness

Glatteis nt (black) ice; **jdn aufs ~ führen** (fig) to take sb for a ride

glätten vt to smooth out

Glatze ['glatsə] f bald head; **eine ~ bekommen** to go bald

Glaube ['glaubə] **(-ns, -n)** m: **~ (an** +akk) faith (in); belief (in); **g~n** vt, vi to believe; to think; **jdm g~n** to believe sb; **an etw** akk **g~n** to believe in sth; **daran g~n müssen**

(umg) to be for it
glaubhaft ['glaubhaft] *adj* credible
gläubig ['glɔybɪç] *adj* (REL) devout; *(vertrauensvoll)* trustful; **G~e(r)** *f(m)* believer; **die G~en** the faithful; **G~er (-s, -)** *m* creditor
glaubwürdig ['glaubvʏrdɪç] *adj* credible; *(Mensch)* trustworthy; **G~keit** *f* credibility; trustworthiness
gleich [glaiç] *adj* equal; *(identisch)* (the) same, identical ♦ *adv* equally; *(sofort)* straight away; *(bald)* in a minute; **es ist mir ~** it's all the same to me; **~ bleibend** constant; **~ gesinnt** like-minded; **2 mal 2 ~ 4** 2 times 2 is *od* equals 4; **~ groß** the same size; **~ nach/an** right after/at; **~altrig** *adj* of the same age; **~artig** *adj* similar; **~bedeutend** *adj* synonymous; **G~berechtigung** *f* equal rights *pl*; **~en** *(unreg)* *vi*: **jdm/etw ~en** to be like sb/sth; **viel ~en** to be alike; **~falls** *adv* likewise; **danke ~falls!** the same to you; **G~förmigkeit** *f* uniformity; **G~gewicht** *nt* equilibrium, balance; **~gültig** *adj* indifferent; *(unbedeutend)* unimportant; **G~gültigkeit** *f* indifference; **G~heit** *f* equality; **~kommen** *(unreg)* *vi +dat* to be equal to; **~mäßig** *adj* even, equal; **~sam** *adv* as it were; **G~schritt** *m*: **im G~schritt gehen** to walk in step; **~stellen** *vt* *(rechtlich etc)* to treat as (an) equal; **G~strom** *m* (ELEK) direct current; **~tun** *(unreg)* *vi*: **es jdm ~tun** to match sb; **G~ung** *f* equation; **~viel** *adv* no matter; **~wertig** *adj* *(Geld)* of the same value; *(Gegner)* evenly matched; **~zeitig** *adj* simultaneous
Gleis [glais] **(-es, -e)** *nt* track, rails *pl*; *(Bahnsteig)* platform
gleiten ['glaitən] *(unreg)* *vi* to glide; *(rutschen)* to slide
Gleitzeit *f* flex(i)time
Gletscher ['glɛtʃər] **(-s, -)** *m* glacier; **~spalte** *f* crevasse
Glied [gliːt] **(-(e)s, -er)** *nt* member; *(Arm, Bein)* limb; *(von Kette)* link; *(MIL)* rank(s); **g~ern** [-dərn] *vt* to organize, to structure; **~erung** *f* structure, organization

glimmen ['glɪmən] *(unreg)* *vi* to glow, to gleam
glimpflich ['glɪmpflɪç] *adj* mild, lenient; **~ davonkommen** to get off lightly
glitschig ['glɪtʃɪç] *adj* (Fisch, Weg) slippery
glitzern ['glɪtsərn] *vi* to glitter; to twinkle
global [glo'baːl] *adj* global
Globus ['gloːbʊs] **(- od -ses, Globen od -se)** *m* globe
Glocke ['glɔkə] *f* bell; **etw an die große ~ hängen** *(fig)* to shout sth from the rooftops
Glocken- zW: **~blume** *f* bellflower; **~geläut** *nt* peal of bells; **~spiel** *nt* chime(s); (MUS) glockenspiel; **~turm** *m* bell tower
Glosse ['glɔsə] *f* comment
glotzen ['glɔtsən] *(umg)* *vi* to stare
Glück [glʏk] **(-(e)s)** *nt* luck, fortune; *(Freude)* happiness; **~ haben** to be lucky; **viel ~!** good luck!; **zum ~** fortunately; **g~en** *vi* to succeed; **es g~te ihm, es zu bekommen** he succeeded in getting it
gluckern ['glʊkərn] *vi* to glug
glück- zW: **~lich** *adj* fortunate; *(froh)* happy; **~licherweise** *adv* fortunately; **~'selig** *adj* blissful
Glücks- zW: **~fall** *m* stroke of luck; **~kind** *nt* lucky person; **~sache** *f* matter of luck; **~spiel** *nt* game of chance
Glückwunsch *m* congratulations *pl*, best wishes *pl*
Glüh- ['glyː] zW: **~birne** *f* light bulb; **g~en** *vi* to glow; **~wein** *m* mulled wine; **~würmchen** *nt* glow-worm
Glut [gluːt] **(-, -en)** *f* (Röte) glow; *(Feuersglut)* fire; *(Hitze)* heat; *(fig)* ardour
GmbH [geːʔɛmbeː'haː] *f abk* (= *Gesellschaft mit beschränkter Haftung*) limited company, Ltd
Gnade ['gnaːdə] *f* (Gunst) favour; *(Erbarmen)* mercy; *(Milde)* clemency
Gnaden- zW: **~frist** *f* reprieve, respite; **g~los** *adj* merciless; **~stoß** *m* coup de grâce
gnädig ['gnɛːdɪç] *adj* gracious; *(voll Erbarmen)* merciful
Gold [gɔlt] **(-(e)s)** *nt* gold; **g~en** *adj* golden; **~fisch** *m* goldfish; **~grube** *f* goldmine;

Rechtschreibreform: ▲ *neue Schreibung* △ *alte Schreibung (auslaufend)*

g~ig ['gɔldɪç] (*umg*) *adj* (*fig: allerliebst*) sweet, adorable; **~regen** *m* laburnum; **~schmied** *m* goldsmith

Golf¹ [gɔlf] (**-(e)s, -e**) *m* gulf

Golf² [gɔlf] (**-s**) *nt* golf; **~platz** *m* golf course; **~schläger** *m* golf club

Golfstrom *m* Gulf Stream

Gondel ['gɔndəl] (**-, -n**) *f* gondola; (*Seilbahn*) cable car

gönnen ['gœnən] *vt*: **jdm etw ~** not to begrudge sb sth; **sich** *dat* **etw ~** to allow o.s. sth

Gönner (**-s, -**) *m* patron; **g~haft** *adj* patronizing

Gosse ['gɔsə] *f* gutter

Gott [gɔt] (**-es, ¨er**) *m* god; **mein ~!** for heaven's sake!; **um ~es Willen!** for heaven's sake!; **grüß ~!** hello; **~ sei Dank!** thank God!; **~heit** *f* deity

Göttin ['gœtɪn] *f* goddess

göttlich *adj* divine

gottlos *adj* godless

Götze ['gœtsə] (**-n, -n**) *m* idol

Grab [gra:p] (**-(e)s, ¨er**) *nt* grave; **g~en** ['gra:bən] (*unreg*) *vt* to dig; **~en** (**-s, ¨**) *m* ditch; (*MIL*) trench; **~stein** *m* gravestone

Grad [gra:t] (**-(e)s, -e**) *m* degree

Graf [gra:f] (**-en, -en**) *m* count, earl

Grafiker(in) ▲ ['gra:fɪkər(ɪn)] (**-s, -**) *m(f)* graphic designer

grafisch ▲ ['gra:fɪʃ] *adj* graphic

Gram [gra:m] (**-(e)s**) *m* grief, sorrow

grämen ['grɛːmən] *vr* to grieve

Gramm [gram] (**-s, -e**) *nt* gram(me)

Grammatik [gra'matɪk] *f* grammar

Granat [gra'na:t] (**-(e)s, -e**) *m* (*Stein*) garnet

Granate *f* (*MIL*) shell; (*Handgranate*) grenade

Granit [gra'ni:t] (**-(e)s, -e**) *m* granite

Gras [gra:s] (**-es, ¨er**) *nt* grass; **g~en** ['gra:zən] *vi* to graze; **~halm** *m* blade of grass

grassieren [gra'si:rən] *vi* to be rampant, to rage

grässlich ▲ ['grɛslɪç] *adj* horrible

Grat [gra:t] (**-(e)s, -e**) *m* ridge

Gräte ['grɛːtə] *f* fishbone

gratis ['gra:tɪs] *adj, adv* free (of charge);

G~probe *f* free sample

Gratulation [gratulatsi'o:n] *f* congratulation(s)

gratulieren [gratu'li:rən] *vi*: **jdm ~ (zu etw)** to congratulate sb (on sth); **(ich) gratuliere!** congratulations!

grau [grau] *adj* grey

Gräuel ▲ ['grɔyəl] (**-s, -**) *m* horror, revulsion; **etw ist jdm ein ~** sb loathes sth

Grauen (**-s**) *nt* horror; **g~** *vi unpers*: **es graut jdm vor etw** sb dreads sth, sb is afraid of sth ♦ *vr*: **sich g~ vor** to dread, to have a horror of; **g~haft** *adj* horrible

grauhaarig *adj* grey-haired

gräulich ▲ ['grɔylɪç] *adj* horrible

grausam ['grauzaːm] *adj* cruel; **G~keit** *f* cruelty

Grausen ['grauzən] (**-s**) *nt* horror; **g~** *vb* – **grauen**

gravieren [gra'vi:rən] *vt* to engrave; **~d** *adj* grave

graziös [gratsi'øːs] *adj* graceful

greifbar *adj* tangible, concrete; **in ~er Nähe** within reach

greifen ['graifən] (*unreg*) *vt* to seize; to grip; **nach etw ~** to reach for sth; **um sich ~** (*fig*) to spread; **zu etw ~** (*fig*) to turn to sth

Greis [grais] (**-es, -e**) *m* old man; **g~enhaft** *adj* senile; **~in** *f* old woman

grell [grɛl] *adj* harsh

Grenz- ['grɛnts] *zW*: **~beamte(r)** *m* frontier official; **~e** *f* boundary; (*Staatsgrenze*) frontier; (*Schranke*) limit; **g~en** *vi*: **g~en (an** *+akk*) to border (on); **g~enlos** *adj* boundless; **~fall** *m* borderline case; **~kontrolle** *f* border control; **~übergang** *m* frontier crossing

Greuel △ ['grɔyəl] (**-s, -**) *m siehe* **Gräuel**

greulich △ *adj siehe* **gräulich**

Griech- ['gri:ç] *zW*: **~e** (**-n, -n**) *m* Greek; **~enland** *nt* Greece; **~in** *f* Greek; **g~isch** *adj* Greek

griesgrämig ['gri:sgrɛːmɪç] *adj* grumpy

Grieß [gri:s] (**-es, -e**) *m* (*KOCH*) semolina

Griff [grɪf] (**-(e)s, -e**) *m* grip; (*Vorrichtung*) handle; **g~bereit** *adj* handy

Grill [grɪl] *m* grill; **~e** *f* cricket; **g~en** *vt* to grill; **~fest** nt barbecue party

Grimasse [gri'masə] f grimace

grimmig ['grɪmɪç] adj furious; (heftig) fierce, severe

grinsen ['grɪnzən] vi to grin

Grippe ['grɪpə] f influenza, flu

grob [gro:p] adj coarse, gross; (Fehler, Verstoß) gross; **G~heit** f coarseness; coarse expression

grölen ['grø:lən] (pej) vt to bawl, to bellow

Groll [grɔl] **(-(e)s)** m resentment; **g~en** vi (Donner) to rumble; **g~en (mit** od +dat) to bear ill will (towards)

groß [gro:s] adj big, large; (hoch) tall; (fig) great ♦ adv greatly; **im G~en und Ganzen** on the whole; **bei jdm ~ geschrieben werden** to be high on sb's list of priorities; **~artig** adj great, splendid; **G~aufnahme** f (CINE) close-up; **G~britannien** nt Great Britain

Größe ['grø:sə] f size; (Höhe) height; (fig) greatness

Groß- zW: **~einkauf** m bulk purchase; **~eltern** pl grandparents; **g~enteils** adv mostly; **~format** nt large size; **~handel** m wholesale trade; **~händler** m wholesaler; **~macht** f great power; **~mutter** f grandmother; **~rechner** m mainframe (computer); **g~schreiben** (unreg) vt (Wort) to write in block capitals; siehe **groß**; **g~spurig** adj pompous; **~stadt** f city, large town

größte(r, s) [grø:stə(r, s)] adj superl von **groß**; **größtenteils** adv for the most part

Groß- zW: **g~tun** (unreg) vi to boast; **~vater** m grandfather; **g~ziehen** (unreg) vt to raise; **g~zügig** adj generous; (Planung) on a large scale

grotesk [gro'tɛsk] adj grotesque

Grotte ['grɔtə] f grotto

Grübchen ['gry:pçən] nt dimple

Grube ['gru:bə] f pit; mine

grübeln ['gry:bəln] vi to brood

Gruft [gruft] **(-, ⁻e)** f tomb, vault

grün [gry:n] adj green; **der ~e Punkt** green spot symbol on recyclable packaging

The grüner Punkt is a green spot which appears on packaging that should be kept separate from normal household refuse to be recycled through the recycling company, DSD (Duales System Deutschland). The recycling is financed by licences bought by the packaging manufacturer from DSD. These costs are often passed on to the consumer.

Grünanlage f park

Grund [grʊnt] **(-(e)s, ⁻e)** m ground; (von See, Gefäß) bottom; (fig) reason; **im ~e genommen** basically; siehe **aufgrund**; **~ausbildung** f basic training; **~besitz** m land(ed property), real estate; **~buch** nt land register

gründen [grʏndən] vt to found ♦ vr: **sich ~ (auf** +dat) to be based (on); **~ auf** +akk to base on; **Gründer (-s, -)** m founder

Grund- zW: **~gebühr** f basic charge; **~gesetz** nt constitution; **~lage** f foundation; **g~legend** adj fundamental

gründlich adj thorough

Grund- zW: **g~los** adj groundless; **~regel** f basic rule; **~riss ▲** m plan; (fig) outline; **~satz** m principle; **g~sätzlich** adj fundamental; (Frage) of principle ♦ adv fundamentally; (prinzipiell) on principle; **~schule** f elementary school; **~stein** m foundation stone; **~stück** nt estate; plot

Grundwasser nt ground water

The Grundschule is a primary school which children attend for 4 years from the age of 6 to 10. There are no formal examinations in the Grundschule but parents receive a report on their child's progress twice a year. Many children attend a Kindergarten from 3-6 years before going to the Grundschule, though no formal instruction takes place in the Kindergarten.

Grünstreifen *m* central reservation

grunzen ['grʊntsən] *vi* to grunt

Gruppe ['grʊpə] *f* group; **~nermäßigung** *f* group reduction; **g~nweise** *adv* in groups

gruppieren [grʊ'piːrən] *vt, vr* to group

gruselig *adj* creepy

gruseln ['gruːzəln] *vi unpers*: **es gruselt jdm vor etw** sth gives sb the creeps ♦ *vr* to have the creeps

Gruß [gruːs] **(-es, ¨e)** *m* greeting; (*MIL*) salute; **viele Grüße** best wishes; **mit freundlichen Grüßen** yours sincerely; **Grüße an** *+akk* regards to

grüßen ['gryːsən] *vt* to greet, (*MIL*) to salute; **jdn von jdm ~** to give sb sb's regards; **jdn ~ lassen** to send sb one's regards

gucken ['gʊkən] *vi* to look

gültig ['gʏltɪç] *adj* valid; **G~keit** *f* validity

Gummi ['gʊmi] **(-s, -s)** *nt od m* rubber; (*~harze*) gum; **~band** *nt* rubber *od* elastic band; (*Hosenband*) elastic; **~bärchen** *nt* ≈ jelly baby (*BRIT*); **~baum** *m* rubber plant; **g~eren** [gʊ'miːrən] *vt* to gum; **~stiefel** *m* rubber boot

günstig ['gʏnstɪç] *adj* convenient; (*Gelegenheit*) favourable; **das habe ich ~ bekommen** it was a bargain

Gurgel ['gʊrgəl] **(-, -n)** *f* throat; **g~n** *vi* to gurgle; (*im Mund*) to gargle

Gurke ['gʊrkə] *f* cucumber; **saure ~** pickled cucumber, gherkin

Gurt [gʊrt] **(-(e)s, -e)** *m* belt

Gürtel ['gʏrtəl] **(-s, -)** *m* belt; (*GEOG*) zone; **~reifen** *m* radial tyre

GUS *f abk* (= *Gemeinschaft unabhängiger Staaten*) CIS

Guss ▲ [gʊs] **(-es, ¨e)** *m* casting; (*Regenguß*) downpour; (*KOCH*) glazing; **~eisen** *nt* cast iron

---
SCHLÜSSELWORT
---

gut *adj* good; **alles Gute** all the best; **also gut** all right then
♦ *adv* well; **gut gehen** to work, to come off; **es geht jdm gut** sb's doing fine; **gut gemeint** well meant; **gut schmecken** to taste good; **jdm gut tun** to do sb good; **gut, aber ...** OK, but ...; **(na) gut, ich komme** all right, I'll come; **gut drei Stunden** a good three hours; **das kann gut sein** that may well be; **lass es gut sein** that'll do

---

Gut [guːt] **(-(e)s, ¨er)** *nt* (*Besitz*) possession; **Güter** *pl* (*Waren*) goods; **~achten (-s, -)** *nt* (expert) opinion; **~achter (-s, -)** *m* expert; **g~artig** *adj* good-natured; (*MED*) benign; **g~bürgerlich** *adj* (*Küche*) (good) plain; **~dünken** *nt*: **nach ~dünken** at one's discretion

Güte ['gyːtə] *f* goodness, kindness; (*Qualität*) quality

Güter- *zW*: **~abfertigung** *f* (*EISENB*) goods office; **~bahnhof** *m* goods station; **~wagen** *m* goods waggon (*BRIT*), freight car (*US*); **~zug** *m* goods train (*BRIT*), freight train (*US*)

Gütezeichen *nt* quality mark; ≈ kite mark

gut- *zW*: **~gehen** △ (*unreg*) *vi unpers siehe* **gut**; **~gemeint** △ *adj siehe* **gut**; **~gläubig** *adj* trusting; **G~haben (-s)** *nt* credit; **~heißen** (*unreg*) *vt* to approve (of)

gütig ['gyːtɪç] *adj* kind

Gut- *zW*: **g~mütig** *adj* good-natured; **~schein** *m* voucher; **g~schreiben** (*unreg*) *vt* to credit; **~schrift** *f* (*Betrag*) credit; **g~tun** △ (*unreg*) *vi siehe* **gut**; **g~willig** *adj* willing

Gymnasium [gym'naːziʊm] *nt* grammar school (*BRIT*), high school (*US*)

Gymnasium

ℹ The **Gymnasium** *is a selective secondary school. After nine years of study pupils sit the* **Abitur** *so they can go on to higher education. Pupils who successfully complete six years at a* **Gymnasium** *automatically gain the* **mittlere Reife**.

Gymnastik [gym'nastɪk] *f* exercises *pl*, keep fit

H, h

Haag [haːk] *m*: **Den ~** the Hague

Haar [haːr] (**-(e)s, -e**) *nt* hair; **um ein ~** nearly; **an den ~en herbeigezogen** (*umg: Vergleich*) very far-fetched; **~bürste** *f* hairbrush; **h~en** *vi, vr* to lose hair; **~esbreite** *f*: **um ~esbreite** by a hair's-breadth; **~festiger** (**-s, -**) *m* (hair) setting lotion; **h~genau** *adv* precisely; **h~ig** *adj* hairy; (*fig*) nasty; **~klammer** *f* hairgrip; **~nadel** *f* hairpin; **h~scharf** *adv* (*beobachten*) very sharply; (*daneben*) by a hair's breadth; **~schnitt** *m* haircut; **~spange** *f* hair slide; **h~sträubend** *adj* hair-raising; **~teil** *nt* hairpiece; **~waschmittel** *nt* shampoo

Habe [ˈhaːbə] (**-**) *f* property

haben [ˈhaːbən] (*unreg*) *vt, vb aux* to have; **Hunger/Angst ~** to be hungry/afraid; **woher hast du das?** where did you get that from?; **was hast du denn?** what's the matter (with you)?; **du hast zu schweigen** you're to be quiet; **ich hätte gern** I would like; **H~** (**-s, -**) *nt* credit

Habgier *f* avarice; **h~ig** *adj* avaricious

Habicht [ˈhaːbɪçt] (**-s, -e**) *m* hawk

Habseligkeiten [ˈhaːpzeːlɪçkaɪtən] *pl* belongings

Hachse [ˈhaksə] *f* (*KOCH*) knuckle

Hacke [ˈhakə] *f* hoe; (*Ferse*) heel; **h~n** *vt* to hack, to chop; (*Erde*) to hoe

Hackfleisch *nt* mince, minced meat

Hafen [ˈhaːfən] (**-s, ⁴**) *m* harbour, port; **~arbeiter** *m* docker; **~rundfahrt** *f* boat trip round the harbour; **~stadt** *f* port

Hafer [ˈhaːfər] (**-s, -**) *m* oats *pl*; **~flocken** *pl* rolled oats; **~schleim** *m* gruel

Haft [haft] (**-**) *f* custody; **h~bar** *adj* liable, responsible; **~befehl** *m* warrant (for arrest); **h~en** *vi* to stick, to cling; **h~en für** to be liable *od* responsible for; **h~en bleiben (an** +*dat*) to stick (to); **Häftling** *m* prisoner; **~pflicht** *f* liability; **~pflichtversicherung** *f* (*AUT*) third party

insurance; **~schalen** *pl* contact lenses; **~ung** *f* liability; **~ungsbeschränkung** *f* limitation of liability

Hagebutte [ˈhaːgəbʊtə] *f* rose hip

Hagel [ˈhaːgəl] (**-s**) *m* hail; **h~n** *vi unpers* to hail

hager [ˈhaːgər] *adj* gaunt

Hahn [haːn] (**-(e)s, ⁴e**) *m* cock; (*Wasserhahn*) tap, faucet (*US*)

Hähnchen [ˈhɛːnçən] *nt* cockerel; (*KOCH*) chicken

Hai(fisch) [ˈhaɪ(fɪʃ)] (**-(e)s, -e**) *m* shark

häkeln [ˈhɛːkəln] *vt* to crochet

Haken [ˈhaːkən] (**-s, -**) *m* hook; (*fig*) catch; **~kreuz** *nt* swastika; **~nase** *f* hooked nose

halb [halp] *adj* half; **~ eins** half past twelve; **~ offen** half-open; **ein ~es Dutzend** half a dozen; **H~dunkel** *nt* semi-darkness

halber [ˈhalbər] *präp* +*gen* (*wegen*) on account of; (*für*) for the sake of

Halb- *zW*: **~heit** *f* half-measure; **h~ieren** *vt* to halve; **~insel** *f* peninsula; **~jahr** *nt* six months; (*auch: COMM*) half-year; **h~jährlich** *adj* half-yearly; **~kreis** *m* semicircle; **~leiter** *m* semiconductor; **~mond** *m* half-moon; (*fig*) crescent; **~pension** *f* half-board; **~schuh** *m* shoe; **h~tags** *adv*: **h~tags arbeiten** to work part-time, to work mornings/afternoons; **h~wegs** *adv* halfway; **h~wegs besser** more or less better; **~zeit** *f* (*SPORT*) half; (*Pause*) half-time

Halde [ˈhaldə] *f* (*Kohlen*) heap

half [half] *vb siehe* **helfen**

Hälfte [ˈhɛlftə] *f* half

Halfter [ˈhalftər] (**-s, -**) *m od nt* (*für Tiere*) halter

Halle [ˈhalə] *f* hall; (*AVIAT*) hangar; **h~n** *vi* to echo, to resound; **~nbad** *nt* indoor swimming pool

hallo [haˈloː] *excl* hello

Halluzination [halutsinatsiˈoːn] *f* hallucination

Halm [halm] (**-(e)s, -e**) *m* blade; stalk

Halogenlampe [haloˈgeːnlampə] *f* halogen lamp

Hals [hals] (**-es, ˝e**) *m* neck; (*Kehle*) throat; ~ **über Kopf** in a rush; ~**band** *nt* (*von Hund*) collar; ~**kette** *f* necklace; ~-**Nasen-Ohren-Arzt** *m* ear, nose and throat specialist; ~**schmerzen** *pl* sore throat *sg*; ~**tuch** *nt* scarf

Halt [halt] (**-(e)s, -e**) *m* stop; (*fester ~*) hold; (*innerer ~*) stability; ~ *od* **h~!** stop!, halt!; ~ **machen** to stop; **h~bar** *adj* durable; (*Lebensmittel*) non-perishable; (*MIL, fig*) tenable; ~**barkeit** *f* durability; (non-)perishability

halten [ʹhaltən] (*unreg*) *vt* to keep; (*festhalten*) to hold ♦ *vi* to hold; (*frisch bleiben*) to keep; (*stoppen*) to stop ♦ *vr* (*frisch bleiben*) to keep; (*sich behaupten*) to hold out; ~ **für** to regard as; ~ **von** to think of; **an sich** ~ to restrain o.s.; **sich rechts/links** ~ to keep to the right/left

Halte- *zW*: ~**stelle** *f* stop; ~**verbot** *nt*: **hier ist** ~**verbot** there's no waiting here

Halt- *zW*: **h~los** *adj* unstable; **h~machen** △ *vi siehe* **Halt**; ~**ung** *f* posture; (*fig*) attitude; (*Selbstbeherrschung*) composure

Halunke [haʹlʊŋkə] (**-n, -n**) *m* rascal

hämisch [ʹhɛːmɪʃ] *adj* malicious

Hammel [ʹhaməl] (**-s, ˝ od -**) *m* wether; ~**fleisch** *nt* mutton

Hammer [ʹhamər] (**-s, ˝**) *m* hammer

hämmern [ʹhɛmərn] *vt, vi* to hammer

Hämorr(ho)iden [hɛmɔroʹiːdən, hɛmɔʹriːdn] *pl* haemorrhoids

Hamster [ʹhamstər] (**-s, -**) *m* hamster; ~**ei** [-ʹraɪ] *f* hoarding; **h~n** *vi* to hoard

Hand [hant] (**-, ˝e**) *f* hand; ~**arbeit** *f* manual work; (*Nadelarbeit*) needlework; ~**ball** *m* (*SPORT*) handball; ~**bremse** *f* handbrake; ~**buch** *nt* handbook, manual

Händedruck [ʹhɛndədrʊk] *m* handshake

Handel [ʹhandəl] (**-s**) *m* trade; (*Geschäft*) transaction

Handeln [ʹhandəln] (**-s**) *nt* action

handeln *vi* to trade; (*agieren*) to act ♦ *vr unpers*: **sich** ~ **um** to be a question of, to be about; ~ **von** to be about

Handels- *zW*: ~**bilanz** *f* balance of trade;

~**kammer** *f* chamber of commerce; ~**reisende(r)** *m* commercial traveller; ~**schule** *f* business school; **h~üblich** *adj* customary; (*Preis*) going *attrib*; ~**vertreter** *m* sales representative

Hand- *zW*: ~**feger** (**-s, -**) *m* hand brush; **h~fest** *adj* hefty; **h~gearbeitet** *adj* handmade; ~**gelenk** *nt* wrist; ~**gemenge** *nt* scuffle; ~**gepäck** *nt* hand luggage; **h~geschrieben** *adj* handwritten; **h~greiflich** *adj* palpable; **h~greiflich werden** to become violent; ~**griff** *m* flick of the wrist; **h~haben** *vt insep* to handle

Händler [ʹhɛndlər] (**-s, -**) *m* trader, dealer

handlich [ʹhantlɪç] *adj* handy

Handlung [ʹhandlʊŋ] *f* act(ion); (*in Buch*) plot; (*Geschäft*) shop

Hand- *zW*: ~**schelle** *f* handcuff; ~**schrift** *f* handwriting; (*Text*) manuscript; ~**schuh** *m* glove; ~**stand** *m* (*SPORT*) handstand; ~**tasche** *f* handbag; ~**tuch** *nt* towel; ~**umdrehen** *nt* **im** ~**umdrehen** in the twinkling of an eye; ~**werk** *nt* trade, craft; ~**werker** (**-s, -**) *m* craftsman, artisan; ~**werkzeug** *nt* tools *pl*

Handy [ʹhɛndɪ] (**-s, -s**) *nt* mobile (telephone)

Hanf [hanf] (**-(e)s**) *m* hemp

Hang [haŋ] (**-(e)s, ˝e**) *m* inclination; (*Abhang*) slope

Hänge- [ʹhɛŋə] *in zW* hanging; ~**brücke** *f* suspension bridge; ~**matte** *f* hammock

hängen [ʹhɛŋən] (*unreg*) *vi* to hang ♦ *vt*: **etw (an etw** *akk*) ~ to hang sth (on sth); ~ **an** +*dat* (*fig*) to be attached to; **sich** ~ **an** +*akk* to hang on to, to cling to; ~ **bleiben** to be caught; (*fig*) to remain, to stick; ~ **bleiben an** +*dat* to catch *od* get caught on; ~ **lassen** (*vergessen*) to leave; **den Kopf** ~ **lassen** to get downhearted

Hannover [haʹnoːfər] (**-s**) *nt* Hanover

hänseln [ʹhɛnzəln] *vt* to tease

Hansestadt [ʹhanzəʃtat] *f* Hanse town

hantieren [hanʹtiːrən] *vi* to work, to be busy; **mit etw** ~ to handle sth

hapern [ʹhaːpərn] *vi unpers*: **es hapert an etw** *dat* there is a lack of sth

Happen ['hapən] **(-s, -)** *m* mouthful
Harfe ['harfə] *f* harp
Harke ['harkə] *f* rake; **h~n** *vt, vi* to rake
harmlos ['harmlo:s] *adj* harmless; **H~igkeit** *f* harmlessness
Harmonie [harmo'ni:] *f* harmony; **h~ren** *vi* to harmonize
harmonisch [har'mo:nɪʃ] *adj* harmonious
Harn ['harn] **(-(e)s, -e)** *m* urine; **~blase** *f* bladder
Harpune [har'pu:nə] *f* harpoon
harren ['harən] *vi:* **~ (auf** +*akk*) to wait (for)
hart [hart] *adj* hard; (*fig*) harsh; **~ gekocht** hard-boiled
Härte ['hertə] *f* hardness; (*fig*) harshness
hart- *zW:* **~herzig** *adj* hard-hearted; **~näckig** *adj* stubborn
Harz [ha:rts] **(-es, -e)** *nt* resin
Haschee [ha'ʃe:] **(-s, -s)** *nt* hash
Haschisch ['haʃɪʃ] **(-)** *nt* hashish
Hase ['ha:zə] **(-n, -n)** *m* hare
Haselnuss ▲ ['ha:zəlnʊs] *f* hazelnut
Hasenscharte *f* harelip
Hass ▲ [has] **(-es)** *m* hate, hatred
hassen ['hasən] *vt* to hate
hässlich ▲ ['heslɪç] *adj* ugly; (*gemein*) nasty; **H~keit** *f* ugliness; nastiness
Hast [hast] *f* haste
hast *vb siehe* **haben**
hasten *vi* to rush
hastig *adj* hasty
hat [hat] *vb siehe* **haben**
hatte *etc* ['hatə] *vb siehe* **haben**
Haube ['haʊbə] *f* hood; (*Mütze*) cap; (*AUT*) bonnet, hood (*US*)
Hauch [haʊx] **(-(e)s, -e)** *m* breath; (*Lufthauch*) breeze; (*fig*) trace; **h~dünn** *adj* extremely thin
Haue ['haʊə] *f* hoe, pick; (*umg*) hiding; **h~n** (*unreg*) *vt* to hew, to cut; (*umg*) to thrash
Haufen ['haʊfən] **(-s, -)** *m* heap; (*Leute*) crowd; **ein ~ (x)** (*umg*) loads *od* a lot (of x); **auf einem ~** in one heap
häufen ['hɔyfən] *vt* to pile up ♦ *vr* to accumulate
haufenweise *adv* in heaps; in droves; **etw ~ haben** to have piles of sth

häufig ['hɔyfɪç] *adj* frequent ♦ *adv* frequently; **H~keit** *f* frequency
Haupt [haʊpt] **(-(e)s, Häupter)** *nt* head; (*Oberhaupt*) chief ♦ *in zW* main; **~bahnhof** *m* central station; **h~beruflich** *adv* as one's main occupation; **~darsteller(in)** *m(f)* leading actor (actress); **~fach** *nt* (*SCH, UNIV*) main subject, major (*US*); **~gericht** *nt* (*KOCH*) main course
Häuptling ['hɔyptlɪŋ] *m* chief(tain)
Haupt- *zW:* **~mann** (*pl* **-leute**) *m* (*MIL*) captain; **~person** *f* central figure; **~quartier** *nt* headquarters *pl*; **~rolle** *f* leading part; **~sache** *f* main thing; **h~sächlich** *adj* chief ♦ *adv* chiefly; **~saison** *f* high season, peak season; **~schule** *f* ≈ secondary school; **~stadt** *f* capital; **~straße** *f* main street; **~verkehrszeit** *f* rush-hour, peak traffic hours *pl*

Hauptschule

i The **Hauptschule** *is a non-selective school which pupils may attend after the* **Grundschule.** *They complete five years of study and most go on to do some vocational training.*

Haus [haʊs] **(-es, Häuser)** *nt* house; **~ halten** (*sparen*) to economize; **nach ~e** home; **zu ~e** at home; **~apotheke** *f* medicine cabinet; **~arbeit** *f* housework; (*SCH*) homework; **~arzt** *m* family doctor; **~aufgabe** *f* (*SCH*) homework; **~besitzer(in)** *m(f)* house owner; **~besuch** *m* (*von Arzt*) house call; **~durchsuchung** *f* police raid; **h~eigen** *adj* belonging to a/ the hotel/firm
Häuser- ['hɔyzər] *zW:* **~block** *m* block (of houses); **~makler** *m* estate agent (*BRIT*), real estate agent (*US*)
Haus- *zW:* **~flur** *m* hallway; **~frau** *f* housewife; **h~gemacht** *adj* home-made; **~halt** *m* household; (*POL*) budget; **h~halten** (*unreg*) *vi* △ *siehe* **Haus**; **~hälterin** *f* housekeeper; **~haltsgeld** *nt* housekeeping (money); **~haltsgerät** *nt*

domestic appliance; **~herr** m host; (*Vermieter*) landlord; **h~hoch** adv: **h~hoch verlieren** to lose by a mile

hausieren [hau'ziːrən] vi to peddle

Hausierer (**-s, -**) m pedlar (*BRIT*), peddler (*US*)

häuslich ['hɔyslɪç] adj domestic

Haus- zW: **~meister** m caretaker, janitor; **~nummer** f street number; **~ordnung** f house rules pl; **~putz** m house cleaning; **~schlüssel** m front door key; **~schuh** m slipper; **~tier** nt pet; **~tür** f front door; **~wirt** m landlord; **~wirtschaft** f domestic science; **~zelt** nt frame tent

Haut [haut] (**-, Häute**) f skin, (*Tierhaut*) hide, **~creme** f skin cream; **h~eng** adj skin tight; **~farbe** f complexion; **~krebs** m skin cancer

Haxe ['haksə] f = **Hachse**

Hbf. abk = **Hauptbahnhof**

Hebamme ['heːp|amə] f midwife

Hebel ['heːbəl] (**-s, -**) m lever

heben ['heːbən] (*unreg*) vt to raise, to lift

Hecht [hɛçt] (**-(e)s, -e**) m pike

Heck [hɛk] (**-(e)s, -e**) nt stern; (*von Auto*) rear

Hecke ['hɛkə] f hedge

Heckenschütze m sniper

Heckscheibe f rear window

Heer [heːr] (**-(e)s, -e**) nt army

Hefe ['heːfə] f yeast

Heft [hɛft] (**-(e)s, -e**) nt exercise book; (*Zeitschrift*) number; (*von Messer*) haft; **h~en** vt: **h~en (an** +akk) to fasten (to); (*nähen*) to tack ((on) to); **etw an etw** akk **h~en** to fasten sth to sth; **~er** (**-s, -**) m folder

heftig adj fierce, violent; **H~keit** f fierceness, violence

Heft- zW: **~klammer** f paper clip; **~pflaster** nt sticking plaster; **~zwecke** f drawing pin

hegen ['heːgən] vt (*Wild, Bäume*) to care for, to tend; (*fig, geh: empfinden: Wunsch*) to cherish; (: *Misstrauen*) to feel

Hehl [heːl] m od nt: **kein(en) ~ aus etw machen** to make no secret of sth; **~er** (**-s,**

-) m receiver (of stolen goods), fence

Heide[1] ['haidə] (**-n, -n**) m heathen, pagan

Heide[2] ['haidə] f heath, moor; **~kraut** nt heather

Heidelbeere f bilberry

Heidentum nt paganism

Heidin f heathen, pagan

heikel ['haikəl] adj awkward, thorny

Heil [hail] (**-(e)s**) nt well-being; (*Seelenheil*) salvation; **h~** adj in one piece, intact; **~and** (**-(e)s, -e**) m saviour; **h~bar** adj curable; **h~en** vt to cure ♦ vi to heal; **h~froh** adj very relieved

heilig ['hailɪç] adj holy; **~ sprechen** to canonize, **H~abend** m Christmas Eve; **H~e(r)** f(m) saint; **~en** vt to sanctify, to hallow; **H~enschein** m halo; **H~keit** f holiness; **H~tum** nt shrine; (*Gegenstand*) relic

Heil- zW: **h~los** adj unholy; (*fig*) hopeless; **~mittel** nt remedy; **~praktiker(in)** m(f) non-medical practitioner; **h~sam** adj (*fig*) salutary; **~sarmee** f Salvation Army; **~ung** f cure

Heim [haim] (**-(e)s, -e**) nt home; **h~** adv home

Heimat ['haimaːt] (**-, -en**) f home (town/ country etc); **~land** nt homeland; **h~lich** adj native, home attrib; (*Gefühle*) nostalgic; **h~los** adj homeless; **~ort** m home town/ area

Heim- zW: **~computer** m home computer; **h~fahren** (*unreg*) vi to drive home; **~fahrt** f journey home; **h~gehen** (*unreg*) vi to go home; (*sterben*) to pass away; **h~isch** adj (*gebürtig*) native; **sich h~isch fühlen** to feel at home; **~kehr** (**-, -en**) f homecoming; **h~kehren** vi to return home; **h~lich** adj secret; **~lichkeit** f secrecy; **~reise** f journey home; **~spiel** nt (*SPORT*) home game; **h~suchen** vt to afflict; (*Geist*) to haunt; **~trainer** m exercise bike; **h~tückisch** adj malicious; **~weg** m way home; **~weh** nt homesickness; **~werker** (**-s, -**) m handyman; **h~zahlen** vt: **jdm etw h~zahlen** to pay sb back for sth

Heirat ['hairaːt] (**-, -en**) f marriage; **h~en** vt

to marry ♦ *vi* to marry, to get married ♦ *vr* to get married; **~santrag** *m* proposal

heiser ['haɪzər] *adj* hoarse; **H~keit** *f* hoarseness

heiß [haɪs] *adj* hot; **~e(s) Eisen** (*umg*) hot potato; **~blütig** *adj* hot-blooded

heißen ['haɪsən] (*unreg*) *vi* to be called; (*bedeuten*) to mean ♦ *vt* to command; (*nennen*) to name ♦ *vi unpers*: **es heißt** it says; it is said; **das heißt** that is (to say)

Heiß- *zW*: **~hunger** *m* ravenous hunger; **h~laufen** (*unreg*) *vi, vt* to overheat

heiter ['haɪtər] *adj* cheerful; (*Wetter*) bright; **H~keit** *f* cheerfulness; (*Belustigung*) amusement

Heiz- ['haɪts] *zW*: **h~bar** *adj* heated; (*Raum*) with heating; **h~en** *vt* to heat; **~körper** *m* radiator; **~öl** *nt* fuel oil; **~sonne** *f* electric fire; **~ung** *f* heating

hektisch ['hɛktɪʃ] *adj* hectic

Held [hɛlt] (**-en, -en**) *m* hero; **h~enhaft** *adj* heroic; **~in** *f* heroine

helfen ['hɛlfən] (*unreg*) *vi* to help; (*nützen*) to be of use ♦ *vb unpers*: **es hilft nichts, du musst ...** it's no use, you'll have to ...; **jdm (bei etw) ~** to help sb (with sth); **sich** *dat* **zu ~ wissen** to be resourceful

Helfer (**-s, -**) *m* helper, assistant; **~shelfer** *m* accomplice

hell [hɛl] *adj* clear, bright; (*Farbe, Bier*) light; **~blau** *adj* light blue; **~blond** *adj* ash blond; **H~e** (**-**) *f* clearness, brightness; **~hörig** *adj* (*Wand*) paper-thin; **~hörig werden** (*fig*) to prick up one's ears; **H~seher** *m* clairvoyant; **~wach** *adj* wide-awake

Helm ['hɛlm] (**-(e)s, -e**) *m* (*auf Kopf*) helmet

Hemd [hɛmt] (**-(e)s, -en**) *nt* shirt; (*Unterhemd*) vest; **~bluse** *f* blouse

hemmen ['hɛmən] *vt* to check, to hold up; **gehemmt sein** to be inhibited; **Hemmung** *f* check; (*PSYCH*) inhibition; **hemmungslos** *adj* unrestrained, without restraint

Hengst [hɛŋst] (**-es, -e**) *m* stallion

Henkel ['hɛŋkəl] (**-s, -**) *m* handle

Henker (**-s, -**) *m* hangman

Henne ['hɛnə] *f* hen

SCHLÜSSELWORT

her [he:r] *adv* **1** (*Richtung*): **komm her zu mir** come here (to me); **von England her** from England; **von weit her** from a long way away; **her damit!** hand it over!; **wo hat er das her?** where did he get that from?

2 (*Blickpunkt*): **von der Form her** as far as the form is concerned

3 (*zeitlich*): **das ist 5 Jahre her** that was 5 years ago; **wo bist du her?** where do you come from?; **ich kenne ihn von früher her** I know him from before

herab [hɛ'rap] *adv* down(ward(s)); **~hängen** (*unreg*) *vi* to hang down; **~lassen** (*unreg*) *vt* to let down ♦ *vr* to condescend; **~lassend** *adj* condescending; **~setzen** *vt* to lower, to reduce; (*fig*) to belittle, to disparage

heran [hɛ'ran] *adv*: **näher ~!** come up closer!; **~ zu mir!** come up to me!; **~bringen** (*unreg*) *vt*: **~bringen (an +***akk*) to bring up (to); **~fahren** (*unreg*) *vi*: **~fahren (an +***akk*) to drive up (to); **~kommen** (*unreg*) *vi*: **(an jdn/etw) ~kommen** to approach (sb/sth), to come near (to sb/sth); **~machen** *vr*: **sich an jdn ~machen** to make up to sb; **~treten** (*unreg*) *vi*: **mit etw an jdn ~treten** to approach sb with sth; **~wachsen** (*unreg*) *vi* to grow up; **~ziehen** (*unreg*) *vt* to pull nearer; (*aufziehen*) to raise; (*ausbilden*) to train; **jdn zu etw ~ziehen** to call upon sb to help in sth

herauf [hɛ'raʊf] *adv* up(ward(s)), up here; **~beschwören** (*unreg*) *vt* to conjure up, to evoke; **~bringen** (*unreg*) *vt* to bring up; **~setzen** *vt* (*Preise, Miete*) to raise, put up

heraus [hɛ'raʊs] *adv* out; **~bekommen** (*unreg*) *vt* to get out; (*fig*) to find *od* figure out; **~bringen** (*unreg*) *vt* (*Geheimnis*) to elicit; **~finden** (*unreg*) *vt* to find out; **~fordern** *vt* to challenge; **H~forderung** *f* challenge; provocation; **~geben** (*unreg*) *vt* to hand over, to surrender; (*zurückgeben*) to give back; (*Buch*) to edit; (*veröffentlichen*) to publish; **H~geber** (-s, -) *m* editor; (*Verleger*) publisher; **~gehen** (*unreg*) *vi:* **aus sich ~gehen** to come out of one's shell; **~halten** (*unreg*) *vr:* **sich aus etw ~halten** to keep out of sth; **~hängen**[1] *vt* to hang out; **~hängen**[2] (*unreg*) *vi* to hang out; **~holen** *vt:* **~holen (aus)** to get out (of); **~kommen** (*unreg*) *vi* to come out; **dabei kommt nichts ~** nothing will come of it; **~nehmen** (*unreg*) *vt* to remove (from), take out (of); **sich dat etw ~nehmen** to take liberties; **~reißen** (*unreg*) *vt* to tear out; to pull out; **~rücken** *vt* (*Geld*) to fork out, to hand over; **mit etw ~rücken** (*fig*) to come out with sth; **~stellen** *vr:* **sich ~stellen (als)** to turn out (to be); **~suchen** *vt:* **sich** *dat* **jdn/etw ~suchen** to pick sb/sth out; **~ziehen** (*unreg*) *vt* to pull out, to extract

herb [hɛrp] *adj* (slightly) bitter, acid; (*Wein*) dry; (*fig: schmerzlich*) bitter

herbei [hɛrˈbaɪ] *adv* (over) here; **~führen** *vt* to bring about; **~schaffen** *vt* to procure

herbemühen [ˈheːrbəmyːən] *vr* to take the trouble to come

Herberge [ˈhɛrbɛrgə] *f* shelter; hostel, inn

Herbergsmutter *f* warden

Herbergsvater *m* warden

herbitten (*unreg*) *vt* to ask to come (here)

Herbst [hɛrpst] (-(e)s, -e) *m* autumn, fall (*US*); **h~lich** *adj* autumnal

Herd [heːrt] (-(e)s, -e) *m* cooker; (*fig, MED*) focus, centre

Herde [ˈheːrdə] *f* herd; (*Schafherde*) flock

herein [hɛˈraɪn] *adv* in (here); here; **~!** come in!; **~bitten** (*unreg*) *vt* to ask in; **~brechen** (*unreg*) *vi* to set in; **~bringen** (*unreg*) *vt* to bring in; **~fallen** (*unreg*) *vi* to be caught, to be taken in; **~fallen auf** +*akk* to fall for; **~kommen** (*unreg*) *vi* to come in; **~lassen** (*unreg*) *vt* to admit; **~legen** *vt:* **jdn ~legen** to take sb in; **~platzen** (*umg*) *vi* to burst in

Her- *zW:* **~fahrt** *f* journey here; **h~fallen** (*unreg*) *vi:* **h~fallen über** +*akk* to fall upon; **~gang** *m* course of events; **h~geben**

(*unreg*) *vt* to give, to hand (over); **sich zu etw h~geben** to lend one's name to sth; **h~gehen** (*unreg*) *vi:* **hinter jdm h~gehen** to follow sb; **es geht hoch h~** there are a lot of goings-on; **h~halten** (*unreg*) *vt* to hold out; **h~halten müssen** (*umg*) to have to suffer; **h~hören** *vi* to listen

Hering [ˈheːrɪŋ] (-s, -e) *m* herring

her- [hɛr] *zW:* **~kommen** (*unreg*) *vi* to come; **komm mal ~!** come here!; **~kömmlich** *adj* traditional; **H~kunft** (-, -künfte) *f* origin; **H~kunftsland** *nt* country of origin; **H~kunftsort** *m* place of origin; **~laufen** (*unreg*) *vi:* **~laufen hinter** +*dat* to run after

hermetisch [hɛrˈmeːtɪʃ] *adj* hermetic ♦ *adv* hermetically

her'nach *adv* afterwards

Heroin [heroˈiːn] (-s) *nt* heroin

Herr [hɛr] (-(e)n, -en) *m* master; (*Mann*) gentleman; (*REL*) Lord; (*vor Namen*) Mr.; **mein ~!** sir!; **meine ~en!** gentlemen!

Herren- *zW:* **~haus** *nt* mansion; **~konfektion** *f* menswear; **h~los** *adj* ownerless; **~toilette** *f* men's toilet *od* restroom (*US*)

herrichten [ˈheːrrɪçtən] *vt* to prepare

Herr- *zW:* **~in** *f* mistress; **h~isch** *adj* domineering; **h~lich** *adj* marvellous, splendid; **~lichkeit** *f* splendour, magnificence; **~schaft** *f* power, rule; (~ *und* ~*in*) master and mistress; **meine ~schaften!** ladies and gentlemen!

herrschen [ˈhɛrʃən] *vi* to rule; (*bestehen*) to prevail, to be

Herrscher(in) (-s, -) *m(f)* ruler

her- *zW:* **~rühren** *vi* to arise, to originate; **~sagen** *vt* to recite; **~stellen** *vt* to make, to manufacture; **H~steller** (-s, -) *m* manufacturer; **H~stellung** *f* manufacture

herüber [hɛˈryːbər] *adv* over (here), across

herum [hɛˈrʊm] *adv* about, (a)round; **um etw ~** around sth; **~führen** *vt* to show around; **~gehen** (*unreg*) *vi* to walk about; **um etw ~gehen** to walk *od* go round sth; **~kommen** (*unreg*) *vi* (*um Kurve etc*) to come round, to turn (round); **~kriegen**

(umg) vt to bring *od* talk around; **~lungern** *(umg)* vi to hang about *od* around; **~sprechen** *(unreg)* vr to get around, to be spread; **~treiben** vi, vr to drift about; **~ziehen** vi, vr to wander about

herunter [hɛˈrʊntər] adv downward(s), down (there); **~gekommen** adj run-down; **~kommen** *(unreg)* vi to come down; *(fig)* to come down in the world; **~machen** vt to take down; *(schimpfen)* to have a go at

hervor [hɛrˈfoːr] adv out, forth; **~bringen** *(unreg)* vt to produce; *(Wort)* to utter; **~gehen** *(unreg)* vi to emerge, to result; **~heben** *(unreg)* vt to stress; *(als Kontrast)* to set off; **~ragend** adj *(fig)* excellent; **~rufen** *(unreg)* vt to cause, to give rise to; **~treten** *(unreg)* vi to come out (from behind/ between/below); *(Adern)* to be prominent

Herz [hɛrts] **(-ens, -en)** nt heart; *(KARTEN)* hearts pl; **~anfall** m heart attack; **~fehler** m heart defect; **h~haft** adj hearty

herziehen [ˈhɛːrtsiːən] *(unreg)* vi: **über jdn/ etw ~** *(umg: auch fig)* to pull sb/sth to pieces *(inf)*

Herz- zW: **~infarkt** m heart attack; **~klopfen** nt palpitation; **h~lich** adj cordial; **h~lichen Glückwunsch** congratulations pl; **h~liche Grüße** best wishes; **h~los** adj heartless

Herzog [ˈhɛrtsoːk] **(-(e)s, ⁀e)** m duke; **~tum** nt duchy

Herz- zW: **~schlag** m heartbeat; *(MED)* heart attack; **~stillstand** m cardiac arrest; **h~zerreißend** adj heartrending

Hessen [ˈhɛsən] **(-s)** nt Hesse

hessisch adj Hessian

Hetze [ˈhɛtsə] f *(Eile)* rush; **h~n** vt to hunt; *(verfolgen)* to chase ♦ vi *(eilen)* to rush; **jdn/etw auf jdn/etw h~n** to set sb/sth on sb/sth; **h~n gegen** to stir up feeling against; **h~n zu** to agitate for

Heu [hɔy] **(-(e)s)** nt hay; **Geld wie ~** stacks of money

Heuch- [ˈhɔyç] zW: **~elei** [-ǝˈlaɪ] f hypocrisy; **h~eln** vt to pretend, to feign ♦ vi to be hypocritical; **~ler(in)** **(-s, -)** m(f) hypocrite; **h~lerisch** adj hypocritical

heulen [ˈhɔylən] vi to howl; to cry

Heurige(r) [ˈhɔyrɪgə(r)] m new wine

Heu- zW: **~schnupfen** m hay fever; **'~schrecke** f grasshopper; locust

heute [ˈhɔytə] adv today; **~ Abend/früh** this evening/morning

heutig [ˈhɔytɪç] adj today's

heutzutage [ˈhɔyttsutaːgə] adv nowadays

Hexe [ˈhɛksə] f witch; **h~n** vi to practise witchcraft; **ich kann doch nicht h~n** I can't work miracles; **~nschuss** ▲ m lumbago; **~'rei** f witchcraft

Hieb [hiːp] **(-(e)s, -e)** m blow; *(Wunde)* cut, gash; *(Stichelei)* cutting remark; **~e bekommen** to get a thrashing

hielt etc [hiːlt] vb siehe **halten**

hier [hiːr] adv here; **~ behalten** to keep here; **~ bleiben** to stay here; **~ lassen** to leave here; **~auf** adv thereupon; *(danach)* after that; **~bei** adv herewith, enclosed; **~durch** adv by this means; *(örtlich)* through here; **~her** adv this way, here; **~hin** adv here; **~mit** adv hereby; **~nach** adv hereafter; **~von** adv about this, hereof; **~zulande, ~ zu Lande** adv in this country

hiesig [ˈhiːzɪç] adj of this place, local

hieß etc [hiːs] vb siehe **heißen**

Hilfe [ˈhɪlfə] f help; aid; **erste ~** first aid; **~!** help!

Hilf- zW: **h~los** adj helpless; **~losigkeit** f helplessness; **h~reich** adj helpful

Hilfs- zW: **~arbeiter** m labourer; **h~bedürftig** adj needy; **h~bereit** adj ready to help; **~kraft** f assistant, helper

hilfst [hɪlfst] vb siehe **helfen**

Himbeere [ˈhɪmbeːrə] f raspberry

Himmel [ˈhɪməl] **(-s, -)** m sky; *(REL, auch fig)* heaven; **~bett** nt four-poster bed; **h~blau** adj sky-blue; **~fahrt** f Ascension; **~srichtung** f direction

himmlisch [ˈhɪmlɪʃ] adj heavenly

SCHLÜSSELWORT
---

hin [hɪn] adv **1** *(Richtung)*: **hin und zurück** there and back; **hin und her** to and fro; **bis zur Mauer hin** up to the wall; **wo ist**

---

er hin? where has he gone?; **Geld hin, Geld her** money or no money

2 (*auf ... hin*): **auf meine Bitte hin** at my request; **auf seinen Rat hin** on the basis of his advice

3: mein Glück ist hin my happiness has gone

hinab [hɪ'nap] *adv* down; **~gehen** (*unreg*) *vi* to go down; **~sehen** (*unreg*) *vi* to look down

hinauf [hɪ'nauf] *adv* up; **~arbeiten** *vr* to work one's way up; **~steigen** (*unreg*) *vi* to climb

hinaus [hɪ'naus] *adv* out; **~gehen** (*unreg*) *vi* to go out; **~gehen über** +*akk* to exceed; **~laufen** (*unreg*) *vi* to run out; **~laufen auf** +*akk* to come to, to amount to; **~schieben** (*unreg*) *vt* to put off, to postpone; **~werfen** (*unreg*) *vt* (*Gegenstand, Person*) to throw out; **~wollen** *vi* to want to go out; **~wollen auf** +*akk* to drive at, to get at

Hinblick ['hɪnblɪk] *m*: **in** *od* **im ~ auf** +*akk* in view of

hinder- ['hɪndər] *zW*: **~lich** *adj*: **~lich sein** to be a hindrance *od* nuisance; **~n** *vt* to hinder, to hamper; **jdn an etw** *dat* **~n** to prevent sb from doing sth; **H~nis** (**-ses, -se**) *nt* obstacle; **H~nisrennen** *nt* steeplechase

hindeuten ['hɪndɔytən] *vi*: **~ auf** +*akk* to point to

hindurch [hɪn'dʊrç] *adv* through; across; (*zeitlich*) through(out)

hinein [hɪ'naɪn] *adv* in; **~fallen** (*unreg*) *vi* to fall in; **~fallen in** +*akk* to fall into; **~gehen** (*unreg*) *vi* to go in; **~gehen in** +*akk* to go into, to enter; **~geraten** (*unreg*) *vi*: **~geraten in** +*akk* to get into; **~passen** *vi* to fit in; **~passen in** +*akk* to fit into; (*fig*) to fit in with; **~steigern** *vr* to get worked up; **~versetzen** *vr*: **sich ~versetzen in** +*akk* to put o.s. in the position of; **~ziehen** (*unreg*) *vt* to pull in ♦ *vi* to go in

hin- ['hɪn] *zW*: **~fahren** (*unreg*) *vi* to go; to drive ♦ *vt* to take; to drive; **H~fahrt** *f*

journey there; **~fallen** (*unreg*) *vi* to fall (down); **~fällig** *adj* frail; (*fig: ungültig*) invalid; **H~flug** *m* outward flight; **H~gabe** *f* devotion; **~geben** (*unreg*) *vr* +*dat* to give o.s. up to, to devote o.s. to; **~gehen** (*unreg*) *vi* to go; (*Zeit*) to pass; **~halten** (*unreg*) *vt* to hold out; (*warten lassen*) to put off, to stall

hinken ['hɪŋkən] *vi* to limp; (*Vergleich*) to be unconvincing

hinkommen (*unreg*) *vi* (*an Ort*) to arrive

hin- ['hɪn] *zW*: **~legen** *vt* to put down ♦ *vr* to lie down; **~nehmen** (*unreg*) *vt* (*fig*) to put up with, to take; **H~reise** *f* journey out; **~reißen** (*unreg*) *vt* to carry away, to enrapture; **sich ~reißen lassen, etw zu tun** to get carried away and do sth; **~richten** *vt* to execute; **H~richtung** *f* execution; **~setzen** *vt* to put down ♦ *vr* to sit down; **~sichtlich** *präp* +*gen* with regard to; **~stellen** *vt* to put (down) ♦ *vr* to place o.s.

hinten ['hɪntən] *adv* at the back; behind; **~herum** *adv* round the back; (*fig*) secretly

hinter ['hɪntər] *präp* (+*dat od akk*) behind; (*: nach*) after; **~ jdm her sein** to be after sb; **H~achse** *f* rear axle; **H~bliebene(r)** *f(m)* surviving relative; **~e(r, s)** *adj* rear, back; **~einander** *adv* one after the other; **H~gedanke** *m* ulterior motive; **~gehen** (*unreg*) *vt* to deceive; **H~grund** *m* background; **H~halt** *m* ambush; **~hältig** *adj* underhand, sneaky; **~her** *adv* afterwards, after; **H~hof** *m* backyard; **H~kopf** *m* back of one's head; **~'lassen** (*unreg*) *vt* to leave; **~'legen** *vt* to deposit; **H~list** *f* cunning, trickery; (*Handlung*) trick, dodge; **~listig** *adj* cunning, crafty; **H~mann** *m* person behind; **H~rad** *nt* back wheel; **H~radantrieb** *m* (*AUT*) rear wheel drive; **~rücks** *adv* from behind; **H~tür** *f* back door; (*fig: Ausweg*) loophole; **~'ziehen** (*unreg*) *vt* (*Steuern*) to evade

hinüber [hɪ'ny:bər] *adv* across, over; **~gehen** (*unreg*) *vi* to go over *od* across

hinunter [hɪ'nʊntər] *adv* down; **~bringen** (*unreg*) *vt* to take down; **~schlucken** *vt* (*auch fig*) to swallow; **~steigen** (*unreg*) *vi* to descend

Hinweg ['hɪnveːk] *m* journey out

hinweghelfen [hɪn'vɛk-] (*unreg*) *vi*: **jdm über etw** *akk* **~** to help sb to get over sth

hinwegsetzen [hɪn'vɛk-] *vr*: **sich ~ über** +*akk* to disregard

hin- ['hɪn] *zW*: **H~weis** (**-es, -e**) *m* (*Andeutung*) hint; (*Anweisung*) instruction; (*Verweis*) reference; **~weisen** (*unreg*) *vi*: **~weisen auf** +*akk* (*anzeigen*) to point to; (*sagen*) to point out, to refer to; **~werfen** (*unreg*) *vt* to throw down; **~ziehen** (*unreg*) *vr* (*fig*) to drag on

hinzu [hɪn'tsuː] *adv* in addition; **~fügen** *vt* to add; **~kommen** (*unreg*) *vi* (*Mensch*) to arrive, to turn up; (*Umstand*) to ensue

Hirn [hɪrn] (**-(e)s, -e**) *nt* brain(s); **~gespinst** (**-(e)s, -e**) *nt* fantasy

Hirsch [hɪrʃ] (**-(e)s, -e**) *m* stag

Hirt ['hɪrt] (**-en, -en**) *m* herdsman; (*Schafhirt, fig*) shepherd

hissen ['hɪsən] *vt* to hoist

Historiker [hɪs'toːrikər] (**-s, -**) *m* historian

historisch [hɪs'toːrɪʃ] *adj* historical

Hitze ['hɪtsə] (**-**) *f* heat; **h~beständig** *adj* heat-resistant; **h~frei** *adj*: **h~frei haben** *to have time off school because of excessively hot weather*; **~welle** *f* heat wave

hitzig ['hɪtsɪç] *adj* hot-tempered; (*Debatte*) heated

Hitzkopf *m* hothead

Hitzschlag *m* heatstroke

hl. *abk von* **heilig**

H-Milch ['haːmɪlç] *f* long-life milk

Hobby ['hɔbi] (**-s, -s**) *nt* hobby

Hobel ['hoːbəl] (**-s, -**) *m* plane; **~bank** *f* carpenter's bench; **h~n** *vt, vi* to plane; **~späne** *pl* wood shavings

Hoch (**-s, -s**) *nt* (*Ruf*) cheer; (*MET*) anticyclone

hoch [hoːx] (*attrib* **hohe(r, s)**) *adj* high; ♦ *adv*: **~ achten** to respect; **~ begabt** extremely gifted; **~ dotiert** highly paid; **H~achtung** *f* respect, esteem; **~achtungsvoll** *adv* yours faithfully; **H~amt** *nt* high mass; **~arbeiten** *vr* to

work one's way up; **H~betrieb** *m* intense activity; (*COMM*) peak time; **H~burg** *f* stronghold; **H~deutsch** *nt* High German; **H~druck** *m* high pressure; **H~ebene** *f* plateau; **H~form** *f* top form; **H~gebirge** *nt* high mountains *pl*; **H~glanz** *m* (*PHOT*) high gloss print; **etw auf H~glanz bringen** to make sth sparkle like new; **~halten** (*unreg*) *vt* to hold up; (*fig*) to uphold, to cherish; **H~haus** *nt* multi-storey building; **~heben** (*unreg*) *vt* to lift (up); **H~konjunktur** *f* boom; **H~land** *nt* highlands *pl*; **~leben** *vi*: **jdn ~leben lassen** to give sb three cheers; **H~mut** *m* pride; **~mütig** *adj* proud, haughty; **~näsig** *adj* stuck-up, snooty; **H~ofen** *m* blast furnace; **~prozentig** *adj* (*Alkohol*) strong; **H~rechnung** *f* projection; **H~saison** *f* high season; **H~schule** *f* college; university; **H~sommer** *m* middle of summer; **H~spannung** *f* high tension; **H~sprung** *m* high jump

höchst [høːçst] *adv* highly, extremely

Hochstapler ['hoːxʃtaːplər] (**-s, -**) *m* swindler

höchste(r, s) *adj* highest; (*äußerste*) extreme

Höchst- *zW*: **h~ens** *adv* at the most; **~geschwindigkeit** *f* maximum speed; **h~persönlich** *adv* in person; **~preis** *m* maximum price; **h~wahrscheinlich** *adv* most probably

Hoch- *zW*: **~verrat** *m* high treason; **~wasser** *nt* high water; (*Überschwemmung*) floods *pl*

Hochzeit ['hɔxtsaɪt] (**-, -en**) *f* wedding; **~sreise** *f* honeymoon

hocken ['hɔkən] *vi, vr* to squat, to crouch

Hocker (**-s, -**) *m* stool

Höcker ['hœkər] (**-s, -**) *m* hump

Hoden ['hoːdən] (**-s, -**) *m* testicle

Hof [hoːf] (**-(e)s, ⁺e**) *m* (*Hinterhof*) yard; (*Bauernhof*) farm; (*Königshof*) court

hoff- ['hɔf] *zW*: **~en** *vi*: **~en (auf** +*akk*) to hope (for); **~entlich** *adv* I hope, hopefully; **H~nung** *f* hope

Hoffnungs- *zW*: **h~los** *adj* hopeless;

~losigkeit f hopelessness; **h~voll** adj hopeful

höflich ['hø:flɪç] adj polite, courteous; **H~keit** f courtesy, politeness

hohe(r, s) ['ho:ə(r, s)] adj attrib siehe **hoch**

Höhe ['hø:ə] f height; (Anhöhe) hill

Hoheit ['ho:haɪt] f (POL) sovereignty; (Titel) Highness

Hoheits- zW: **~gebiet** nt sovereign territory; **~gewässer** nt territorial waters pl

Höhen- ['hø:ən] zW: **~luft** f mountain air; **~messer (-s, -)** m altimeter; **~sonne** f sun lamp; **~unterschied** m difference in altitude

Höhepunkt m climax

höher adj, adv higher

hohl [ho:l] adj hollow

Höhle ['hø:lə] f cave, hole; (Mundhöhle) cavity; (fig, ZOOL) den

Hohlmaß nt measure of volume

Hohn [ho:n] **(-(e)s)** m scorn

höhnisch adj scornful, taunting

holen ['ho:lən] vt to get, to fetch; (Atem) to take; **jdn/etw ~ lassen** to send for sb/sth

Holland ['hɔlant] nt Holland; **Holländer** ['hɔlɛndər] m Dutchman; **holländisch** adj Dutch

Hölle ['hœlə] f hell

höllisch ['hœlɪʃ] adj hellish, infernal

holperig ['hɔlpərɪç] adj rough, bumpy

Holunder [ho'lʊndər] **(-s, -)** m elder

Holz [hɔlts] **(-es, ⁻er)** nt wood

hölzern ['hœltsərn] adj (auch fig) wooden

Holz- zW: **~fäller (-s, -)** m lumberjack, woodcutter; **h~ig** adj woody; **~kohle** f charcoal; **~schuh** m clog; **~weg** m (fig) wrong track; **~wolle** f fine wood shavings pl

Homöopathie [homøopa'ti:] f homeopathy

homosexuell [homozɛksu'ɛl] adj homosexual

Honig ['ho:nɪç] **(-s, -e)** m honey; **~melone** f (BOT, KOCH) honeydew melon; **~wabe** f honeycomb

Honorar [hono'ra:r] **(-s, -e)** nt fee

Hopfen ['hɔpfən] **(-s, -)** m hops pl

hopsen ['hɔpsən] vi to hop

Hörapparat m hearing aid

hörbar adj audible

horchen ['hɔrçən] vi to listen; (pej) to eavesdrop

Horde ['hɔrdə] f horde

hör- ['hø:r] zW: **~en** vt, vi to hear; **Musik/Radio ~en** to listen to music/the radio; **H~er (-s, -)** m hearer; (RADIO) listener; (UNIV) student; (Telefonhörer) receiver; **H~funk (-s)** m radio; **~geschädigt** [-gəʃɛ:dɪçt] adj hearing-impaired

Horizont [hori'tsɔnt] **(-(e)s, -e)** m horizon; **h~al** [-'ta:l] adj horizontal

Hormon [hɔr'mo:n] **(-s, -e)** nt hormone

Hörmuschel f (TEL) earpiece

Horn [hɔrn] **(-(e)s, ⁻er)** nt horn; **~haut** f horny skin

Hornisse [hɔr'nɪsə] f hornet

Horoskop [horo'sko:p] **(-s, -e)** nt horoscope

Hörspiel nt radio play

Hort [hɔrt] **(-(e)s, -e)** m (SCH) day centre for schoolchildren whose parents are at work

horten ['hɔrtən] vt to hoard

Hose ['ho:zə] f trousers pl, pants pl (US)

Hosen- zW: **~anzug** m trouser suit; **~rock** m culottes pl; **~tasche** f (trouser) pocket; **~träger** m braces pl (BRIT), suspenders pl (US)

Hostie ['hɔstiə] f (REL) host

Hotel [ho'tɛl] **(-s, -s)** nt hotel; **~ier (-s, -s)** [hotɛl'eː] m hotelkeeper, hotelier; **~verzeichnis** nt hotel register

Hubraum ['hu:p-] m (AUT) cubic capacity

hübsch [hypʃ] adj pretty, nice

Hubschrauber ['hu:pʃraʊbər] **(-s, -)** m helicopter

Huf ['hu:f] **(-(e)s, -e)** m hoof; **~eisen** nt horseshoe

Hüft- ['hyft] zW: **~e** f hip; **~gürtel** m girdle; **~halter (-s, -)** m girdle

Hügel ['hy:gəl] **(-s, -)** m hill; **h~ig** adj hilly

Huhn [hu:n] **(-(e)s, ⁻er)** nt hen; (KOCH) chicken

Hühner- ['hy:nər] zW: **~auge** nt corn; **~brühe** f chicken broth

Hülle ['hylə] f cover(ing); wrapping; **in ~**

und Fülle galore; **h~n** vt: **h~n (in** +akk) to cover (with); to wrap (in)

Hülse ['hʏlzə] f husk, shell; **~nfrucht** f pulse

human [hu'ma:n] adj humane; **~i'tär** adj humanitarian; **H~i'tät** f humanity

Hummel ['hʊməl] (-, -n) f bumblebee

Hummer ['hʊmər] (-s, -) m lobster

Humor [hu'mo:r] (-s, -e) m humour; **~ haben** to have a sense of humour; **~ist** [-'rɪst] m humorist; **h~voll** adj humorous

humpeln ['hʊmpəln] vi to hobble

Humpen ['hʊmpən] (-s, -) m tankard

Hund [hʊnt] (-(e)s, -e) m dog

Hunde- [hʊndə] zW: **~hütte** f (dog) kennel; **h~müde** (umg) adj dog-tired

hundert ['hʊndərt] num hundred; **H~'jahrfeier** f centenary; **~prozentig** adj, adv one hundred per cent

Hundesteuer f dog licence fee

Hündin ['hʏndɪn] f bitch

Hunger ['hʊŋər] (-s) m hunger; **~ haben** to be hungry; **h~n** vi to starve; **~snot** f famine

hungrig ['hʊŋrɪç] adj hungry

Hupe ['hu:pə] f horn; **h~n** vi to hoot, to sound one's horn

hüpfen ['hʏpfən] vi to hop; to jump

Hürde ['hʏrdə] f hurdle; (für Schafe) pen; **~nlauf** m hurdling

Hure ['hu:rə] f whore

hurtig ['hʊrtɪç] adj brisk, quick ♦ adv briskly, quickly

huschen ['hʊʃən] vi to flit; to scurry

Husten ['hu:stən] (-s) m cough; **h~** vi to cough; **~anfall** m coughing fit; **~bonbon** m od nt cough drop; **~saft** m cough mixture

Hut[1] [hu:t] (-(e)s, ⁺e) m hat

Hut[2] [hu:t] (-) f care; **auf der ~ sein** to be on one's guard

hüten ['hy:tən] vt to guard ♦ vr to watch out; **sich ~, zu** to take care not to; **sich ~ (vor)** to beware (of), to be on one's guard (against)

Hütte ['hʏtə] f hut; cottage; (Eisenhütte) forge

Hütten- zW: **~käse** m (KOCH) cottage

cheese; **~schuh** m slipper sock

Hydrant [hy'drant] m hydrant

hydraulisch [hy'draʊlɪʃ] adj hydraulic

Hygiene [hygi'e:nə] (-) f hygiene

hygienisch [hygi'e:nɪʃ] adj hygienic

Hymne ['hʏmnə] f hymn; anthem

Hypno- [hʏp'no:] zW: **~se** f hypnosis; **h~tisch** adj hypnotic; **~tiseur** [-ti'zø:r] m hypnotist; **h~ti'sieren** vt to hypnotize

Hypothek [hypo'te:k] (-, -en) f mortgage

Hypothese [hypo'te:zə] f hypothesis

Hysterie [hʏste'ri:] f hysteria

hysterisch [hʏs'te:rɪʃ] adj hysterical

I, i

ICE [i:tse:'|e:] m abk = Intercity-Expresszug

Ich (-(s), -(s)) nt self; (PSYCH) ego

ich [ɪç] pron I; **~ bins!** it's me!

Ideal [ide'a:l] (-s, -e) nt ideal; **ideal** adj ideal; **idealistisch** [-'lɪstɪʃ] adj idealistic

Idee [i'de:, pl i'de:ən] f idea

identifizieren [idɛntifi'tsi:rən] vt to identify

identisch [i'dɛntɪʃ] adj identical

Identität [idɛnti'tɛ:t] f identity

Ideo- [ideo] zW: **~loge** [-'lo:gə] (-n, -n) m ideologist; **~logie** [-lo'gi:] f ideology; **ideologisch** [-'lo:gɪʃ] adj ideological

Idiot [idi'o:t] (-en, -en) m idiot; **idiotisch** adj idiotic

idyllisch [i'dʏlɪʃ] adj idyllic

Igel ['i:gəl] (-s, -) m hedgehog

ignorieren [ɪgno'ri:rən] vt to ignore

ihm [i:m] (dat von er, es) pron (to) him; (to) it

ihn [i:n] (akk von er, es) pron him; it; **~en** (dat von sie pl) pron (to) them; **Ihnen** (dat von Sie pl) pron (to) you

---

SCHLÜSSELWORT

ihr [i:r] pron 1 (nom pl) you; **ihr seid es** it's you

2 (dat von sie) to her; **gib es ihr** give it to her; **er steht neben ihr** he is standing beside her

♦ possessiv pron 1 (sg) her; (: bei Tieren,

Dingen) its; **ihr Mann** her husband
2 (*pl*) their; **die Bäume und ihre Blätter**
the trees and their leaves

ihr(e) [iːr] *adj* (*sg*) her, its; (*pl*) their; **Ihr(e)**
adj your

ihre(r, s) *pron* (*sg*) hers, its; (*pl*) theirs;
Ihre(r, s) *pron* yours; ~**r** (*gen von* **sie** *sg/pl*)
pron of her/them; **Ihrer** (*gen von* **Sie**) *pron*
of you; ~**rseits** *adv* for her/their part;
~**sgleichen** *pron* people like her/them;
(*von Dingen*) others like it; ~**twegen** *adv*
(*für sie*) for her/its/their sake; (*wegen ihr*) on
her/its/their account; ~**twillen** *adv*: **um**
~**twillen** = **ihretwegen**

Ihrige ['iːrɪgə] *pron*: **der/die/das** ~ *od* **l**~
hers; its; theirs

illegal ['ɪlegaːl] *adj* illegal

Illusion [ɪluzi'oːn] *f* illusion

illusorisch [ɪlu'zoːrɪʃ] *adj* illusory

illustrieren [ɪlʊs'triːrən] *vt* to illustrate

Illustrierte *f* magazine

im [ɪm] = **in dem**

Imbiss ▲ ['ɪmbɪs] (**-es, -e**) *m* snack;
~**stube** *f* snack bar

imitieren [imi'tiːrən] *vt* to imitate

Imker ['ɪmkər] (**-s, -**) *m* beekeeper

immatrikulieren [ɪmatriku'liːrən] *vi, vr* to
register

immer ['ɪmər] *adv* always; ~ **wieder** again
and again; ~ **noch** still; ~ **noch nicht** still
not; ~ **für** forever; ~ **wenn ich ...** every
time I ...; ~ **schöner/trauriger** more and
more beautiful/sadder and sadder; **was/
wer (auch)** ~ whatever/whoever; ~**hin** *adv*
all the same; ~**zu** *adv* all the time

Immobilien [ɪmo'biːliən] *pl* real estate *sg*;
~**makler** *m* estate agent (*BRIT*), realtor
(*US*)

immun [ɪ'muːn] *adj* immune; **Immunität**
[-i'tɛːt] *f* immunity; **Immunsystem** *nt*
immune system

Imperfekt ['ɪmpɛrfɛkt] (**-s, -e**) *nt* imperfect
(tense)

Impf- ['ɪmpf] *zW*: **impfen** *vt* to vaccinate;
~**stoff** *m* vaccine, serum; ~**ung** *f*
vaccination

imponieren [ɪmpo'niːrən] *vi* +*dat* to impress

Import [ɪm'pɔrt] (**-(e)s, -e**) *m* import; ~**eur**
m importer; **importieren** *vt* to import

imposant [ɪmpo'zant] *adj* imposing

impotent ['ɪmpotɛnt] *adj* impotent

imprägnieren [ɪmprɛ'gniːrən] *vt* to
(water)proof

improvisieren [ɪmproviˈziːrən] *vt, vi* to
improvise

Impuls [ɪm'pʊls] (**-es, -e**) *m* impulse;
impulsiv [-'ziːf] *adj* impulsive

imstande, im Stande [ɪm'ʃtandə] *adj*: ~
sein to be in a position; (*fähig*) to be able

SCHLÜSSELWORT

in [ɪn] *präp* +*akk* **1** (*räumlich: wohin?*) in, into;
in die Stadt into town; **in die Schule
gehen** to go to school
2 (*zeitlich*): **bis ins 20. Jahrhundert** into *od*
up to the 20th century
♦ *präp* +*dat* **1** (*räumlich: wo*) in; **in der Stadt**
in town; **in der Schule sein** to be at
school
2 (*zeitlich: wann*): **in diesem Jahr** this year;
(*in jenem Jahr*) in that year; **heute in zwei
Wochen** two weeks today

Inanspruchnahme [ɪn'anʃpruxnaːmə] *f*
(+*gen*) demands *pl* (on)

Inbegriff ['ɪnbəgrɪf] *m* embodiment,
personification; **inbegriffen** *adv* included

indem [ɪn'deːm] *konj* while; ~ **man etw
macht** (*dadurch*) by doing sth

Inder(in) ['ɪndər(ɪn)] *m(f)* Indian

indes(sen) [ɪn'dɛs(ən)] *adv* however;
(*inzwischen*) meanwhile ♦ *konj* while

Indianer(in) [ɪndi'aːnər(ɪn)] (**-s, -**) *m(f)*
American Indian, native American;
indianisch *adj* Red Indian

Indien ['ɪndiən] *nt* India

indirekt ['ɪndirɛkt] *adj* indirect

indisch ['ɪndɪʃ] *adj* Indian

indiskret ['ɪndɪskreːt] *adj* indiscreet

indiskutabel ['ɪndɪskutaːbəl] *adj* out of the
question

individuell [ɪndividu'ɛl] *adj* individual

Individuum [ɪndi'viːduʊm] (**-s, -en**) *nt*
individual

Spelling Reform: ▲ *new spelling* △ *old spelling (to be phased out)*

Indiz [ɪn'diːts] **(-es, -ien)** *nt* (*JUR*) clue; ~ **(für)** sign (of)

industrialisieren [ɪndʊstriali'tsiːrən] *vt* to industrialize

Industrie [ɪndʊs'triː] *f* industry ♦ *in zW* industrial; ~**gebiet** *nt* industrial area; ~-**und Handelskammer** *f* chamber of commerce; ~**zweig** *m* branch of industry

ineinander [ɪn|aɪ'nandər] *adv* in(to) one another *od* each other

Infarkt [ɪn'farkt] **(-(e)s, -e)** *m* coronary (thrombosis)

Infektion [ɪnfɛktsi'oːn] *f* infection; ~**skrankheit** *f* infectious disease

Infinitiv ['ɪnfinitiːf] **(-s, -e)** *m* infinitive

infizieren [ɪnfi'tsiːrən] *vt* to infect ♦ *vr*: **sich (bei jdm)** ~ to be infected (by sb)

Inflation [ɪnflatsi'oːn] *f* inflation

inflationär [ɪnflatsio'nɛːr] *adj* inflationary

infolge [ɪn'fɔlgə] *präp +gen* as a result of, owing to; ~**dessen** [-'dɛsən] *adv* consequently

Informatik [ɪnfɔr'matɪk] *f* information studies *pl*

Information [ɪnfɔrmatsi'oːn] *f* information *no pl*

informieren [ɪnfɔr'miːrən] *vt* to inform ♦ *vr*: **sich** ~ **(über** +*akk*) to find out (about)

infrage, in Frage *adv*: ~ **stellen** to question sth; **nicht** ~ **kommen** to be out of the question

Ingenieur [ɪnʒeni'øːr] *m* engineer; ~**schule** *f* school of engineering

Ingwer ['ɪnvər] **(-s)** *m* ginger

Inh. *abk* (= *Inhaber*) prop.; (= *Inhalt*) contents

Inhaber(in) ['ɪnhaːbər(ɪn)] **(-s, -)** *m(f)* owner; (*Hausinhaber*) occupier; (*Lizenzinhaber*) licensee, holder; (*FIN*) bearer

inhaftieren [ɪnhaf'tiːrən] *vt* to take into custody

inhalieren [ɪnha'liːrən] *vt, vi* to inhale

Inhalt ['ɪnhalt] **(-(e)s, -e)** *m* contents *pl*; (*eines Buchs etc*) content; (*MATH*) area; volume; **inhaltlich** *adj* as regards content

Inhalts- *zW*: ~**angabe** *f* summary; ~**verzeichnis** *nt* table of contents

inhuman ['ɪnhumaːn] *adj* inhuman

Initiative [initsia'tiːvə] *f* initiative

inklusive [ɪnklu'ziːvə] *präp +gen* inclusive of ♦ *adv* inclusive

In-Kraft-Treten [ɪn'krafttreːtən] **(-s)** *nt* coming into force

Inland ['ɪnlant] **(-(e)s)** *nt* (*GEOG*) inland; (*POL, COMM*) home (country); ~**flug** *m* domestic flight

inmitten [ɪn'mɪtən] *präp +gen* in the middle of; ~ **von** amongst

innehaben ['ɪnəhaːbən] (*unreg*) *vt* to hold

innen ['ɪnən] *adv* inside; **Innenarchitekt** *m* interior designer; **Inneneinrichtung** *f* (interior) furnishings *pl*; **Innenhof** *m* inner courtyard; **Innenminister** *m* minister of the interior, Home Secretary (*BRIT*); **Innenpolitik** *f* domestic policy; ~**politisch** *adj* (*Entwicklung, Lage*) internal, domestic; **Innenstadt** *f* town/city centre

inner- ['ɪnər] *zW*: ~**e(r, s)** *adj* inner; (*im Körper, inländisch*) internal; **Innere(s)** *nt* inside; (*Mitte*) centre; (*fig*) heart; **Innereien** [-'raɪən] *pl* innards; ~**halb** *adv* within; (*räumlich*) inside ♦ *präp +gen* within; inside; ~**lich** *adj* internal; (*geistig*) inward; ~**ste(r, s)** *adj* innermost; **Innerste(s)** *nt* heart

innig ['ɪnɪç] *adj* (*Freundschaft*) close

inoffiziell ['ɪn|ɔfitsiel] *adj* unofficial

ins [ɪns] = **in das**

Insasse ['ɪnzasə] **(-n, -n)** *m* (*Anstalt*) inmate; (*AUT*) passenger

Insassenversicherung *f* passenger insurance

insbesondere [ɪnsbə'zɔndərə] *adv* (e)specially

Inschrift ['ɪnʃrɪft] *f* inscription

Insekt [ɪn'zɛkt] **(-(e)s, -en)** *nt* insect

Insektenschutzmittel *nt* insect repellent

Insel ['ɪnzəl] **(-, -n)** *f* island

Inser- *zW*: ~**at** [ɪnzə'raːt] **(-(e)s, -e)** *nt* advertisement; ~**ent** [ɪnzə'rɛnt] *m* advertiser; **inserieren** [ɪnzə'riːrən] *vt, vi* to advertise

insgeheim [ɪnsgə'haɪm] *adv* secretly

insgesamt [ɪnsgə'zamt] *adv* altogether, all in all

Rechtschreibreform: ▲ *neue Schreibung* △ *alte Schreibung (auslaufend)*

insofern [ɪnzo'fɛrn] *adv* in this respect ♦ *konj* if; *(deshalb)* (and) so; **~ als** in so far as

insoweit [ɪnzo'vaɪt] = **insofern**

Installateur [ɪnstala'tøːr] *m* electrician; plumber

Instandhaltung [ɪn'ʃtanthaltʊŋ] *f* maintenance

inständig [ɪn'ʃtɛndɪç] *adj* urgent

Instandsetzung [ɪn'ʃtant-] *f* overhaul; *(eines Gebäudes)* restoration

Instanz [ɪn'stants] *f* authority; *(JUR)* court

Instinkt [ɪn'stɪŋkt] *(-(e)s, -e)* *m* instinct; **instinktiv** [-'tiːf] *adj* instinctive

Institut [ɪnsti'tuːt] *(-(e)s, -e)* *nt* institute

Instrument [ɪnstru'mɛnt] *nt* instrument

Intell- [ɪntɛl] *zW:* **Intellektuell** [-ɛktu'ɛl] *adj* intellectual; **intelligent** [-i'gɛnt] *adj* intelligent; **~igenz** [-i'gɛnts] *f* intelligence; *(Leute)* intelligentsia *pl*

Intendant [ɪntɛn'dant] *m* director

intensiv [ɪntɛn'ziːf] *adj* intensive; **Intensivstation** *f* intensive care unit

Intercity- [ɪntər'sɪti] *zW:* **~-Expresszug** ▲ *m* high-speed train; **~-Zug** *m* intercity (train); **~-Zuschlag** *m* intercity supplement

Interess- *zW:* **interessant** [ɪntɛrɛ'sant] *adj* interesting; **interessanterweise** *adv* interestingly enough; **~e** [ɪntɛ'rɛsə] *(-s, -n)* *nt* interest; **~e haben an** +*dat* to be interested in; **~ent** [ɪntɛrɛ'sɛnt] *m* interested party; **interessieren** [ɪntɛrɛ'siːrən] *vt* to interest ♦ *vr:* **sich interessieren für** to be interested in

intern [ɪn'tɛrn] *adj (Angelegenheiten, Regelung)* internal; *(Besprechung)* private

Internat [ɪntɛr'naːt] *(-(e)s, -e)* *nt* boarding school

inter- [ɪntɛr] *zW:* **~national** [-natsio'naːl] *adj* international; **I~net** ['ɪntərnɛt] *(-s)* *nt*: **das I~net** the Internet; **I~net-Café** *nt* Internet café; **~pretieren** [-pre'tiːrən] *vt* to interpret; **Intervall** [-'val] *(-s, -e)* *nt* interval; **Interview** [-'vjuː] *(-s, -s)* *nt* interview; **~viewen** [-'vjuːən] *vt* to interview

intim [ɪn'tiːm] *adj* intimate; **Intimität** *f* intimacy

intolerant ['ɪntolɛrant] *adj* intolerant

Intrige [ɪn'triːgə] *f* intrigue, plot

Invasion [ɪnvazi'oːn] *f* invasion

Inventar [ɪnvɛn'taːr] *(-s, -e)* *nt* inventory

Inventur [ɪnvɛn'tuːr] *f* stocktaking; **~ machen** to stocktake

investieren [ɪnvɛs'tiːrən] *vt* to invest

inwie- [ɪnvi'] *zW:* **~fern** *adv* how far, to what extent; **~weit** *adv* how far, to what extent

inzwischen [ɪn'tsvɪʃən] *adv* meanwhile

Irak [i'raːk] *(-s)* *m*: **der ~** Iraq; **irakisch** *adj* Iraqi

Iran [i'raːn] *(-s)* *m*: **der ~** Iran; **iranisch** *adj* Iranian

irdisch ['ɪrdɪʃ] *adj* earthly

Ire ['iːrə] *(-n, -n)* *m* Irishman

irgend ['ɪrgɛnt] *adv* at all; **wann/was/wer ~** whenever/whatever/whoever; **~etwas** *pron* something/anything; **~jemand** *pron* somebody/anybody; **~ein(e, s)** *adj* some, any; **~einmal** *adv* sometime or other; *(fragend)* ever; **~wann** *adv* sometime; **~wie** *adv* somehow; **~wo** *adv* somewhere; anywhere; **~wohin** *adv* somewhere; anywhere

Irin ['iːrɪn] *f* Irishwoman

Irland ['ɪrlant] *(-s)* *nt* Ireland

Ironie [iro'niː] *f* irony; **ironisch** [i'roːnɪʃ] *adj* ironic(al)

irre ['ɪrə] *adj* crazy, mad; **Irre(r)** *f(m)* lunatic; **~führen** *vt* to mislead; **~machen** *vt* to confuse; **~n** *vi* to be mistaken; *(umherirren)* to wander, to stray ♦ *vr* to be mistaken; **Irrenanstalt** *f* lunatic asylum

Irr- *zW:* **~garten** *m* maze; **i~ig** ['ɪrɪç] *adj* incorrect, wrong; **i~itieren** [ɪri'tiːrən] *vt* *(verwirren)* to confuse; *(ärgern)* to irritate; *(stören)* to annoy; **irrsinnig** *adj* mad, crazy; *(umg)* terrific; **~tum** *(-s, -tümer)* *m* mistake, error; **irrtümlich** *adj* mistaken

Island ['iːslant] *(-s)* *nt* Iceland

Isolation [izolatsi'oːn] *f* isolation; *(ELEK)* insulation

Isolier- [izo'liːr] *zW:* **~band** *nt* insulating tape; **isolieren** *vt* to isolate; *(ELEK)* to insulate; **~station** *f* *(MED)* isolation ward;

~**ung** *f* isolation; (*ELEK*) insulation
Israel ['ɪsraeːl] (**-s**) *nt* Israel; ~**i** (**-s, -s**) [-'eːli]
m Israeli; **israelisch** *adj* Israeli
isst ▲ [ɪst] *vb siehe* **essen**
ist [ɪst] *vb siehe* **sein**
Italien [i'taːliən] (**-s**) *nt* Italy; ~**er(in)** (**-s**)
m(f) Italian; **italienisch** *adj* Italian
i. V. *abk* = **in Vertretung**

J, j

ja [jaː] *adv* **1** yes; **haben Sie das gesehen? -
ja** did you see it? - yes(, I did); **ich glaube
ja** (yes) I think so
2 (*fragend*) really?; **ich habe gekündigt -
ja?** I've quit - have you?; **du kommst, ja?**
you're coming, aren't you?
3: **sei ja vorsichtig** do be careful; **Sie
wissen ja, dass ...** as you know, ...; **tu
das ja nicht!** don't do that!; **ich habe es
ja gewusst** I just knew it; **ja, also ...** well
you see ...

Jacht [jaxt] (**-, -en**) *f* yacht
Jacke ['jakə] *f* jacket; (*Wolljacke*) cardigan
Jackett [ʒa'ket] (**-s, -s** *od* **-e**) *nt* jacket
Jagd [jaːkt] (**-, -en**) *f* hunt; (*Jagen*) hunting;
~**beute** *f* kill; ~**flugzeug** *nt* fighter;
~**hund** *m* hunting dog
jagen ['jaːgən] *vi* to hunt; (*eilen*) to race ♦ *vt*
to hunt; (*wegjagen*) to drive (off); (*verfolgen*)
to chase
Jäger ['jeːgər] (**-s, -**) *m* hunter; ~**schnitzel**
nt (*KOCH*) *pork in a spicy sauce with
mushrooms*
jäh [jeː] *adj* sudden, abrupt; (*steil*) steep,
precipitous
Jahr [jaːr] (**-(e)s, -e**) *nt* year; **j~elang** *adv* for
years
Jahres- *zW*: ~**abonnement** *nt* annual
subscription; ~**abschluss** ▲ *m* end of the
year; (*COMM*) annual statement of account;
~**beitrag** *m* annual subscription; ~**karte** *f*

yearly season ticket; ~**tag** *m* anniversary;
~**wechsel** *m* turn of the year; ~**zahl** *f*
date; year; ~**zeit** *f* season
Jahr- *zW*: ~**gang** *m* age group; (*von Wein*)
vintage; ~'**hundert** (**-s, -e**) *nt* century;
jährlich ['jeːrlɪç] *adj, adv* yearly; ~**markt** *m*
fair; ~**tausend** *nt* millennium; ~'**zehnt** *nt*
decade
Jähzorn ['jeːtsɔrn] *m* sudden anger; hot
temper; **j~ig** *adj* hot-tempered
Jalousie [ʒalu'ziː] *f* venetian blind
Jammer ['jamər] (**-s**) *m* misery; **es ist ein ~,
dass ...** it is a crying shame that ...
jämmerlich ['jemərlɪç] *adj* wretched,
pathetic
jammern *vi* to wail ♦ *vt unpers*: **es jammert
jdn** it makes sb feel sorry
Januar ['januaːr] (**-(s), -e**) *m* January
Japan ['jaːpan] (**-s**) *nt* Japan; ~**er(in)**
[-'paːnər(ɪn)] (**-s**) *m(f)* Japanese; **j~isch** *adj*
Japanese
jäten ['jeːtən] *vt*: **Unkraut ~** to weed
jauchzen ['jaʊxtsən] *vi* to rejoice
jaulen ['jaʊlən] *vi* to howl
jawohl [ja'voːl] *adv* yes (of course)
Jawort ['jaːvɔrt] *nt* consent
Jazz [dʒæz] (**-**) *m* Jazz

je [jeː] *adv* **1** (*jemals*) ever; **hast du so was je
gesehen?** did you ever see anything like
it?
2 (*jeweils*) every, each; **sie zahlten je 3
Mark** they paid 3 marks each
♦ *konj* **1**: **je nach** depending on; **je
nachdem** it depends; **je nachdem, ob ...**
depending on whether ...
2: **je eher, desto** *od* **umso besser** the
sooner the better

Jeans [dʒiːnz] *pl* jeans
jede(r, s) ['jeːdə(r, s)] *adj* every, each ♦ *pron*
everybody; (~ *Einzelne*) each; ~**s Mal** every
time, each time; **ohne ~ x** without any x
jedenfalls *adv* in any case
jedermann *pron* everyone
jederzeit *adv* at any time

jedoch [je'dɔx] *adv* however

jeher ['je:he:r] *adv*: **von/seit ~** always

jemals ['je:ma:ls] *adv* ever

jemand ['je:mant] *pron* somebody; anybody

jene(r, s) ['je:nə(r, s)] *adj* that ♦ *pron* that one

jenseits ['je:nzaits] *adv* on the other side ♦ *präp* +*gen* on the other side of, beyond

Jenseits *nt*: **das ~** the hereafter, the beyond

jetzig ['jɛtsɪç] *adj* present

jetzt [jɛtst] *adv* now

jeweilig *adj* respective

jeweils *adv*: **~ zwei zusammen** two at a time; **zu ~ 5 DM** at 5 marks each; **~ das Erste** the first each time

Jh. *abk* = **Jahrhundert**

Job [dʒɔp] **(-s, -s)** *m* (*umg*) job; **j~ben** ['dʒɔbən] *vi* (*umg*) to work

Jockei ['dʒɔke] **(-s, -s)** *m* jockey

Jod [jo:t] **(-e)s)** *nt* iodine

jodeln ['jo:dəln] *vi* to yodel

joggen ['dʒɔgən] *vi* to jog

Jog(h)urt ['jo:gʊrt] **(-s, -s)** *m od nt* yogurt

Johannisbeere [jo'hanisbe:rə] *f* redcurrant; **schwarze ~** blackcurrant

johlen ['jo:lən] *vi* to yell

jonglieren [ʒõ'gliːrən] *vi* to juggle

Journal- [ʒʊrnal] *zW*: **~ismus** ['lismʊs] *m* journalism; **~ist(in)** [-'lɪst(ɪn)] *m(f)* journalist; **journa'listisch** *adj* journalistic

Jubel ['juːbəl] **(-s)** *m* rejoicing; **j~n** *vi* to rejoice

Jubiläum [jubi'lɛːʊm] **(-s, Jubiläen)** *nt* anniversary; jubilee

jucken ['jʊkən] *vi* to itch ♦ *vt*: **es juckt mich am Arm** my arm is itching

Juckreiz ['jʊkraits] *m* itch

Jude ['juːdə] **(-n, -n)** *m* Jew

Juden- *zW*: **~tum** (-) *nt* Judaism; Jewry; **~verfolgung** *f* persecution of the Jews

Jüdin ['jyːdɪn] *f* Jewess

jüdisch ['jyːdɪʃ] *adj* Jewish

Jugend ['juːgənt] (-) *f* youth; **j~frei** *adj* (*CINE*) U (*BRIT*), G (*US*), suitable for children; **~herberge** *f* youth hostel; **~herbergsausweis** *m* youth hostelling

card; **j~lich** *adj* youthful; **~liche(r)** *f(m)* teenager, young person

Jugoslaw- [jugɔ'slaːv] *zW*: **~ien (-s)** *nt* Yugoslavia; **j~isch** *adj* Yugoslavian

Juli ['juːli] **(-(s), -s)** *m* July

jun. *abk* (= *junior*) jr.

jung [jʊŋ] *adj* young; **J~e (-n, -n)** *m* boy, lad ♦ *nt* young animal; **J~en** *pl* (*von Tier*) young *pl*

Jünger ['jʏŋər] **(-s, -)** *m* disciple

jünger *adj* younger

Jung- *zW*: **~frau** *f* virgin; (*ASTROL*) Virgo; **~geselle** *m* bachelor; **~gesellin** *f* unmarried woman

jüngst [jʏŋst] *adv* lately, recently; **~e(r, s)** *adj* youngest, (*neueste*) latest

Juni ['juːni] **(-(s), -s)** *m* June

Junior ['juːniɔr] **(-s, -en)** *m* junior

Jurist [ju'rɪst] *m* jurist, lawyer; **j~isch** *adj* legal

Justiz [jʊs'tiːts] (-) *f* justice; **~beamte(r)** *m* judicial officer; **~irrtum** *m* miscarriage of justice; **~minister** *m* ≃ Lord (High) Chancellor (*BRIT*), ≃ Attorney General (*US*)

Juwel [ju'veːl] **(-s, -en)** *nt od m* jewel

Juwelier [juve'liːr] **(-s, -e)** *m* jeweller; **~geschäft** *nt* jeweller's (shop)

Jux [jʊks] **(-es, -e)** *m* joke, lark

K, k

Kabarett [kaba'rɛt] **(-s, -e od -s)** *nt* cabaret; **~ist** [-'tɪst] *m* cabaret artiste

Kabel ['kaːbəl] **(-s, -)** *nt* (*ELEK*) wire; (*stark*) cable; **~fernsehen** *nt* cable television

Kabeljau ['kaːbəljau] **(-s, -e od -s)** *m* cod

Kabine [ka'biːnə] *f* cabin; (*Zelle*) cubicle

Kabinenbahn *f* cable railway

Kabinett [kabi'nɛt] **(-s, -e)** *nt* (*POL*) cabinet

Kachel ['kaxəl] **(-, -n)** *f* tile; **k~n** *vt* to tile; **~ofen** *m* tiled stove

Käfer ['kɛːfər] **(-s, -)** *m* beetle

Kaffee ['kafe] **(-s, -s)** *m* coffee; **~haus** *nt* café; **~kanne** *f* coffeepot; **~löffel** *m* coffee spoon

Käfig ['kɛːfɪç] **(-s, -e)** *m* cage

kahl [kaːl] *adj* bald; ~ **geschoren** shaven, shorn; ~**köpfig** *adj* bald-headed

Kahn [kaːn] (-(e)s, ⸚e) *m* boat, barge

Kai [kaɪ] (-s, -e *od* -s) *m* quay

Kaiser ['kaɪzər] (-s, -) *m* emperor; ~**in** *f* empress; **k~lich** *adj* imperial; ~**reich** *nt* empire; ~**schnitt** *m* (MED) Caesarian (section)

Kakao [ka'kaːo] (-s, -s) *m* cocoa

Kaktee [kak'teː(ə)] (-, -n) *f* cactus

Kaktus ['kaktʊs] (-, -teen) *m* cactus

Kalb [kalp] (-(e)s, ⸚er) *nt* calf; **k~en** ['kalbən] *vi* to calve; ~**fleisch** *nt* veal; ~**sleder** *nt* calf(skin)

Kalender [ka'lɛndər] (-s, -) *m* calendar; (*Taschenkalender*) diary

Kaliber [ka'liːbər] (-s, -) *nt* (*auch fig*) calibre

Kalk [kalk] (-(e)s, -e) *m* lime; (BIOL) calcium; ~**stein** *m* limestone

kalkulieren [kalku'liːrən] *vt* to calculate

Kalorie [kalo'riː] *f* calorie

kalt [kalt] *adj* cold; **mir ist (es) ~** I am cold; ~ **bleiben** (*fig*) to remain unmoved; ~ **stellen** to chill; ~**blütig** *adj* cold-blooded; (*ruhig*) cool

Kälte ['kɛltə] (-) *f* cold; coldness; ~**grad** *m* degree of frost *od* below zero; ~**welle** *f* cold spell

kalt- *zW*: ~**herzig** *adj* cold-hearted; ~**schnäuzig** *adj* cold, unfeeling; ~**stellen** *vt* (*fig*) to leave out in the cold

kam *etc* [kaːm] *vb siehe* **kommen**

Kamel [ka'meːl] (-(e)s, -e) *nt* camel

Kamera ['kamera] (-, -s) *f* camera

Kamerad [kamə'raːt] (-en, -en) *m* comrade, friend; ~**schaft** *f* comradeship; **k~schaftlich** *adj* comradely

Kameramann (-(e)s, -männer) *m* cameraman

Kamille [ka'mɪlə] *f* camomile; ~**ntee** *m* camomile tea

Kamin [ka'miːn] (-s, -e) *m* (*außen*) chimney; (*innen*) fireside, fireplace; ~**kehrer** (-s, -) *m* chimney sweep

Kamm [kam] (-(e)s, ⸚e) *m* comb; (*Bergkamm*) ridge; (*Hahnenkamm*) crest

kämmen ['kɛmən] *vt* to comb ♦ *vr* to comb

Kammer ['kamər] (-, -n) *f* chamber; small bedroom

Kammerdiener *m* valet

Kampagne [kam'panjə] *f* campaign

Kampf [kampf] (-(e)s, ⸚e) *m* fight, battle; (*Wettbewerb*) contest; (*fig: Anstrengung*) struggle; **k~bereit** *adj* ready for action

kämpfen ['kɛmpfən] *vi* to fight

Kämpfer (-s, -) *m* fighter, combatant

Kampf- *zW*: ~**handlung** *f* action; **k~los** *adj* without a fight; ~**richter** *m* (SPORT) referee; (TENNIS) umpire; ~**stoff** *m*: **chemischer/biologischer ~stoff** chemical/biological weapon

Kanada ['kanada] (-s) *nt* Canada; **Kanadier(in)** (-s, -) [ka'naːdiər(ɪn)] *m(f)* Canadian; **ka'nadisch** *adj* Canadian

Kanal [ka'naːl] (-s, Kanäle) *m* (*Fluss*) canal; (*Rinne, Ärmelkanal*) channel; (*für Abfluss*) drain; ~**inseln** *pl* Channel Islands; ~**isation** [-izatsi'oːn] *f* sewage system; ~**tunnel** *m*: **der ~tunnel** the Channel Tunnel

Kanarienvogel [ka'naːriənfoːgəl] *m* (ZOOL) canary

kanarisch [ka'naːrɪʃ] *adj*: **K~e Inseln** Canary Islands, Canaries

Kandi- [kandi] *zW*: ~**dat** [-'daːt] (-en, -en) *m* candidate; ~**datur** [-da'tuːr] *f* candidature, candidacy; **k~dieren** [-'diːrən] *vi* to stand, to run

Kandis(zucker) ['kandɪs(tsʊkər)] (-) *m* candy

Känguru ▲ ['kɛŋguru] (-s, -s) *nt* kangaroo

Kaninchen [ka'niːnçən] *nt* rabbit

Kanister [ka'nɪstər] (-s, -) *m* can, canister

Kännchen ['kɛnçən] *nt* pot

Kanne ['kanə] *f* (*Krug*) jug; (*Kaffeekanne*) pot; (*Milchkanne*) churn; (*Gießkanne*) can

kannst *etc* [kanst] *vb siehe* **können**

Kanone [ka'noːnə] *f* gun; (HIST) cannon; (*fig: Mensch*) ace

Kantate [kan'taːtə] *f* cantata

Kante ['kantə] *f* edge

Kantine [kan'tiːnə] *f* canteen

Kanton [kan'toːn] (-s, -e) *m* canton

Kanton

i **Kanton** *is the term for a state or region of Switzerland. Under the Swiss constitution the* **Kantone** *enjoy considerable autonomy. The Swiss* **Kantone** *are Aargau, Appenzell, Basel, Bern, Fribourg, Geneva, Glarus, Graubünden, Luzern, Neuchâtel, St. Gallen, Schaffhausen, Schwyz, Solothurn, Ticino, Thurgau, Unterwalden, Uri, Valais, Vaud, Zug and Zürich.*

Kanu ['ka:nu] (**-s, -s**) *nt* canoe
Kanzel ['kantsəl] (**-, -n**) *f* pulpit
Kanzler ['kantslər] (**-s, -**) *m* chancellor
Kap [kap] (**-s, -s**) *nt* cape (GEOG)
Kapazität [kapatsi'tɛːt] *f* capacity; (*Fachmann*) authority
Kapelle [ka'pɛlə] *f* (*Gebäude*) chapel; (MUS) band
kapieren [ka'piːrən] (*umg*) *vt, vi* to get, to understand
Kapital [kapi'taːl] (**-s, -e** *od* **-ien**) *nt* capital; **~anlage** *f* investment; **~ismus** [-'lɪsmʊs] *m* capitalism; **~ist** [-'lɪst] *m* capitalist; **k~istisch** *adj* capitalist
Kapitän [kapi'tɛːn] (**-s, -e**) *m* captain
Kapitel [ka'pɪtəl] (**-s, -**) *nt* chapter
Kapitulation [kapitulatsi'oːn] *f* capitulation
kapitulieren [kapitu'liːrən] *vi* to capitulate
Kappe ['kapə] *f* cap; (*Kapuze*) hood
kappen *vt* to cut
Kapsel ['kapsəl] (**-, -n**) *f* capsule
kaputt [ka'pʊt] (*umg*) *adj* kaput, broken; (*Person*) exhausted, finished; **am Auto ist etwas ~** there's something wrong with the car; **~gehen** (*unreg*) *vi* to break; (*Schuhe*) to fall apart; (*Firma*) to go bust; (*Stoff*) to wear out; (*sterben*) to cop it (*umg*); **~machen** *vt* to break; (*Mensch*) to exhaust, to wear out
Kapuze [ka'puːtsə] *f* hood
Karamell ▲ [kara'mɛl] (**-s**) *m* caramel; **~bonbon** *m od nt* toffee
Karate [ka'raːtə] (**-s**) *nt* karate
Karawane [kara'vaːnə] *f* caravan

Kardinal [kardi'naːl] (**-s, Kardinäle**) *m* cardinal; **~zahl** *f* cardinal number
Karfreitag [kaːr'fraita:k] *m* Good Friday
karg [kark] *adj* (*Landschaft, Boden*) barren; (*Lohn*) meagre
kärglich ['kɛrklɪç] *adj* poor, scanty
Karibik [ka'riːbɪk] (**-**) *f*: **die ~** the Caribbean
karibisch [ka'riːbɪʃ] *adj*: **K~e Inseln** Caribbean Islands
kariert [ka'riːrt] *adj* (*Stoff*) checked; (*Papier*) squared
Karies ['kaːriɛs] (**-**) *f* caries
Karikatur [karika'tuːr] *f* caricature; **~ist** [-'rɪst] *m* cartoonist
Karneval ['karnəval] (**-s, -e** *od* **-s**) *m* carnival

Karneval

i **Karneval** *is the time immediately before Lent when people gather to eat, drink and generally have fun before the fasting begins.* **Rosenmontag***, the day before Shrove Tuesday, is the most important day of* **Karneval** *on the Rhine. Most firms take a day's holiday on that day to enjoy the celebrations. In South Germany and Austria* **Karneval** *is called* **Fasching***.*

Karo ['kaːro] (**-s, -s**) *nt* square; (KARTEN) diamonds
Karosserie [karɔsə'riː] *f* (AUT) body(work)
Karotte [ka'rɔtə] *f* carrot
Karpfen ['karpfən] (**-s, -**) *m* carp
Karre ['karə] *f* cart, barrow
Karren (**-s, -**) *m* cart, barrow
Karriere [kari'eːrə] *f* career; **~ machen** to get on, to get to the top; **~macher** (**-s, -**) *m* careerist
Karte ['kartə] *f* card; (*Landkarte*) map; (*Speisekarte*) menu; (*Eintrittskarte, Fahrkarte*) ticket; **alles auf eine ~ setzen** to put all one's eggs in one basket
Kartei [kar'tai] *f* card index; **~karte** *f* index card
Kartell [kar'tɛl] (**-s, -e**) *nt* cartel
Karten- *zW*: **~spiel** *nt* card game; pack of cards; **~telefon** *nt* cardphone;

~vorverkauf *m* advance booking office

Kartoffel [kar'tɔfəl] **(-, -n)** *f* potato; **~brei** *m* mashed potatoes *pl*; **~mus** *nt* mashed potatoes *pl*; **~püree** *nt* mashed potatoes *pl*; **~salat** *m* potato salad

Karton [kar'tõː] **(-s, -s)** *m* cardboard; (*Schachtel*) cardboard box; **k~iert** [karto'niːrt] *adj* hardback

Karussell [karʊ'sel] **(-s, -s)** *nt* roundabout (*BRIT*), merry-go-round

Karwoche ['kaːrvɔxə] *f* Holy Week

Käse ['kɛːzə] **(-s, -)** *m* cheese; **~glocke** *f* cheese (plate) cover; **~kuchen** *m* cheesecake

Kaserne [ka'zɛrnə] *f* barracks *pl*; **~nhof** *m* parade ground

Kasino [ka'ziːno] **(-s, -s)** *nt* club; (*MIL*) officers' mess; (*Spielkasino*) casino

Kaskoversicherung ['kasko-] *f* (*Teilkasko*) ≈ third party, fire and theft insurance; (*Vollkasko*) ≈ fully comprehensive insurance

Kasse ['kasə] *f* (*Geldkasten*) cashbox; (*in Geschäft*) till, cash register; cash desk, checkout; (*Kinokasse, Theaterkasse etc*) box office; ticket office; (*Krankenkasse*) health insurance; (*Sparkasse*) savings bank; **~ machen** to count the money; **getrennte ~ führen** to pay separately; **an der ~** (*in Geschäft*) at the desk; **gut bei ~ sein** to be in the money

Kassen- *zW*: **~arzt** *m* panel doctor (*BRIT*); **~bestand** *m* cash balance; **~patient** *m* panel patient (*BRIT*); **~prüfung** *f* audit; **~sturz** *m*: **~sturz machen** to check one's money; **~zettel** *m* receipt

Kassette [ka'setə] *f* small box; (*Tonband, PHOT*) cassette; (*Bücherkassette*) case

Kassettenrekorder **(-s, -)** *m* cassette recorder

kassieren [ka'siːrən] *vt* to take ♦ *vi*: **darf ich ~?** would you like to pay now?

Kassierer [ka'siːrər] **(-s, -)** *m* cashier; (*von Klub*) treasurer

Kastanie [kas'taːniə] *f* chestnut; (*Baum*) chestnut tree

Kasten ['kastən] **(-s, ")** *m* (*auch SPORT*) box; case; (*Truhe*) chest

kastrieren [kas'triːrən] *vt* to castrate

Katalog [kata'loːk] **(-(e)s, -e)** *m* catalogue

Katalysator [kataly'zaːtɔr] *m* catalyst; (*AUT*) catalytic converter

katastrophal [katastro'faːl] *adj* catastrophic

Katastrophe [kata'stroːfə] *f* catastrophe, disaster

Kat-Auto ['kat|aʊto] *nt* car fitted with a catalytic converter

Kategorie [katego'riː] *f* category

kategorisch [kate'goːrɪʃ] *adj* categorical

Kater ['kaːtər] **(-s, -)** *m* tomcat; (*umg*) hangover

kath. *abk* (= *katholisch*) Cath.

Kathedrale [kate'draːlə] *f* cathedral

Katholik [kato'liːk] **(-en, -en)** *m* Catholic

katholisch [ka'toːlɪʃ] *adj* Catholic

Kätzchen ['kɛtsçən] *nt* kitten

Katze ['katsə] *f* cat; **für die Katz** (*umg*) in vain, for nothing

Katzen- *zW*: **~auge** *nt* cat's eye; (*Fahrrad*) rear light; **~sprung** (*umg*) *m* stone's throw; short journey

Kauderwelsch ['kaʊdərvelʃ] **(-(s))** *nt* jargon; (*umg*) double Dutch

kauen ['kaʊən] *vt, vi* to chew

kauern ['kaʊərn] *vi* to crouch down; (*furchtsam*) to cower

Kauf [kaʊf] **(-(e)s, Käufe)** *m* purchase, buy; (*~en*) buying; **ein guter ~** a bargain; **etw in ~ nehmen** to put up with sth; **k~en** *vt* to buy

Käufer(in) ['kɔyfər(ɪn)] **(-s, -)** *m(f)* buyer

Kauf- *zW*: **~frau** *f* businesswoman; **~haus** *nt* department store; **~kraft** *f* purchasing power

käuflich ['kɔyflɪç] *adj* purchasable, for sale; (*pej*) venal ♦ *adv*: **~ erwerben** to purchase

Kauf- *zW*: **k~lustig** *adj* interested in buying; **~mann** (*pl* **-leute**) *m* businessman; shopkeeper; **k~männisch** *adj* commercial; **k~männischer Angestellter** office worker; **~preis** *m* purchase price; **~vertrag** *m* bill of sale

Kaugummi ['kaʊgʊmi] *m* chewing gum

Kaulquappe ['kaʊlkvapə] *f* tadpole

kaum [kaʊm] *adv* hardly, scarcely

Kaution [kaʊtsiˈoːn] f deposit; (JUR) bail

Kauz [kaʊts] (**-es, Käuze**) m owl; (fig) queer fellow

Kavalier [kavaˈliːr] (**-s, -e**) m gentleman, cavalier; **~sdelikt** nt peccadillo

Kaviar [ˈkaːviar] m caviar

keck [kɛk] adj daring, bold

Kegel [ˈkeːgəl] (**-s, -**) m skittle; (MATH) cone; **~bahn** f skittle alley; bowling alley; **k~n** vi to play skittles

Kehle [ˈkeːlə] f throat

Kehlkopf m larynx

Kehre [ˈkeːrə] f turn(ing), bend; **k~n** vt, vi (wenden) to turn; (mit Besen) to sweep; **sich an etw** dat **nicht k~n** not to heed sth

Kehricht [ˈkeːrɪçt] (**-s**) m sweepings pl

Kehrseite f reverse, other side; wrong side; bad side

kehrtmachen vi to turn about, to about-turn

keifen [ˈkaɪfən] vi to scold, to nag

Keil [kaɪl] (**-(e)s, -e**) m wedge; (MIL) arrowhead; **~riemen** m (AUT) fan belt

Keim [kaɪm] (**-(e)s, -e**) m bud; (MED, fig) germ; **k~en** vi to germinate; **k~frei** adj sterile; **~zelle** f (fig) nucleus

kein [kaɪn] adj no, not ... any; **~e(r, s)** pron no one, nobody; none; **~erlei** adj attrib no ... whatsoever

keinesfalls adv on no account

keineswegs adv by no means

keinmal adv not once

Keks [keːks] (**-es, -e**) m od nt biscuit

Kelch [kɛlç] (**-(e)s, -e**) m cup, goblet, chalice

Kelle [ˈkɛlə] f (Suppenkelle) ladle; (Maurerkelle) trowel

Keller [ˈkɛlər] (**-s, -**) m cellar

Kellner(in) [ˈkɛlnər(ɪn)] (**-s, -**) m(f) waiter (-tress)

keltern [ˈkɛltərn] vt to press

kennen [ˈkɛnən] (unreg) vt to know; **~ lernen** to get to know; **sich ~ lernen** to get to know each other; (zum ersten Mal) to meet

Kenner (**-s, -**) m connoisseur

kenntlich adj distinguishable, discernible;

etw **~ machen** to mark sth

Kenntnis (**-, -se**) f knowledge no pl; **etw zur ~ nehmen** to note sth; **von etw ~ nehmen** to take notice of sth; **jdn in ~ setzen** to inform sb

Kenn- zW: **~zeichen** nt mark, characteristic; **k~zeichnen** vt insep to characterize; **~ziffer** f reference number

kentern [ˈkɛntərn] vi to capsize

Keramik [keˈraːmɪk] (**-, -en**) f ceramics pl, pottery

Kerbe [ˈkɛrbə] f notch, groove

Kerker [ˈkɛrkər] (**-s, -**) m prison

Kerl [kɛrl] (**-s, -e**) m chap, bloke (BRIT), guy

Kern [kɛrn] (**-(e)s, -e**) m (Obstkern) pip, stone; (Nusskern) kernel; (Atomkern) nucleus; (fig) heart, core; **~energie** f nuclear energy; **~forschung** f nuclear research; **~frage** f central issue; **k~gesund** adj thoroughly healthy, fit as a fiddle; **k~ig** adj (kraftvoll) robust; (Ausspruch) pithy; **~kraftwerk** nt nuclear power station; **k~los** adj seedless, without pips; **~physik** f nuclear physics sg; **~spaltung** f nuclear fission; **~waffen** pl nuclear weapons

Kerze [ˈkɛrtsə] f candle; (Zündkerze) plug; **k~ngerade** adj straight as a die; **~nständer** m candle holder

kess ▲ [kɛs] adj saucy

Kessel [ˈkɛsəl] (**-s, -**) m kettle; (von Lokomotive etc) boiler; (GEOG) depression; (MIL) encirclement

Kette [ˈkɛtə] f chain; **k~n** vt to chain; **~nrauchen** (**-s**) nt chain smoking; **~nreaktion** f chain reaction

Ketzer [ˈkɛtsər] (**-s, -**) m heretic

keuchen [ˈkɔʏçən] vi to pant, to gasp

Keuchhusten m whooping cough

Keule [ˈkɔʏlə] f club; (KOCH) leg

keusch [kɔʏʃ] adj chaste; **K~heit** f chastity

kfm. abk = **kaufmännisch**

Kfz [kaːɛfˈtset] nt abk = **Kraftfahrzeug**

KG [kaːˈgeː] (**-, -s**) f abk (= Kommanditgesellschaft) limited partnership

kg abk = **Kilogramm**

kichern [ˈkɪçərn] vi to giggle

kidnappen ['kɪtnɛpən] *vt* to kidnap

Kiefer[1] ['kiːfər] (-s, -) *m* jaw

Kiefer[2] ['kiːfər] (-, -n) *f* pine; **~nzapfen** *m* pine cone

Kiel [kiːl] (-(e)s, -e) *m* (*Federkiel*) quill; (*NAUT*) keel

Kieme ['kiːmə] *f* gill

Kies [kiːs] (-es, -e) *m* gravel

Kilo ['kiːlo] *nt* kilo; **~gramm** [kilo'gram] *nt* kilogram; **~meter** [kilo'meːtər] *m* kilometre; **~meterzähler** *m* milometer

Kind [kɪnt] (-(e)s, -er) *nt* child; **von ~ auf** from childhood

Kinder- ['kɪndər] *zW*: **~betreuung** *f* crèche; **~ei** [-'raɪ] *f* childishness; **~garten** *m* nursery school, playgroup; **~gärtnerin** *f* nursery school teacher; **~geld** *nt* child benefit (*BRIT*); **~heim** *nt* children's home; **~krippe** *f* crèche; **~lähmung** *f* poliomyelitis; **k~leicht** *adj* childishly easy; **k~los** *adj* childless; **~mädchen** *nt* nursemaid; **k~reich** *adj* with a lot of children; **~sendung** *f* (*RADIO, TV*) children's programme; **~sicherung** *f* (*AUT*) childproof safety catch; **~spiel** *nt* (*fig*) child's play; **~tagesstätte** *f* day nursery; **~wagen** *m* pram, baby carriage (*US*); **~zimmer** *nt* (*für ~*) children's room; (*für Säugling*) nursery

---

Kindergarten

*A **Kindergarten** is a nursery school for children aged between 3 and 6 years. The children sing and play but do not receive any formal instruction. Most Kindergärten are financed by the town or the church with parents paying a monthly contribution towards the cost.*

Kind- *zW*: **~heit** *f* childhood; **k~isch** *adj* childish; **k~lich** *adj* childlike

Kinn [kɪn] (-(e)s, -e) *nt* chin; **~haken** *m* (*BOXEN*) uppercut

Kino ['kiːno] (-s, -s) *nt* cinema; **~besucher** *m* cinema-goer; **~programm** *nt* film programme

Kiosk [ki'ɔsk] (-(e)s, -e) *m* kiosk

Kippe ['kɪpə] *f* cigarette end; (*umg*) fag; **auf der ~ stehen** (*fig*) to be touch and go

kippen *vi* to topple over, to overturn ♦ *vt* to tilt

Kirch- ['kɪrç] *zW*: **~e** *f* church; **~enlied** *nt* hymn; **~ensteuer** *f* church tax; **~gänger** (-s, -) *m* churchgoer; **~hof** *m* churchyard; **k~lich** *adj* ecclesiastical

Kirmes ['kɪrmɛs] (-, -sen) *f* fair

Kirsche ['kɪrʃə] *f* cherry

Kissen ['kɪsən] (-s, -) *nt* cushion; (*Kopfkissen*) pillow; **~bezug** *m* pillowslip

Kiste ['kɪstə] *f* box; chest

Kitsch [kɪtʃ] (-(e)s, -e) *m* kitsch; **k~ig** *adj* kitschy

Kitt [kɪt] (-(e)s, -e) *m* putty

Kittel (-s, -) *m* overall, smock

kitten *vt* to putty; (*fig: Ehe etc*) to cement

kitzelig ['kɪtsəliç] *adj* (*auch fig*) ticklish

kitzeln *vi* to tickle

Kiwi ['kiːvi] (-, -s) *f* (*BOT, KOCH*) kiwi fruit

KKW [kaːkaːˈveː] *nt abk* = **Kernkraftwerk**

Klage ['klaːgə] *f* complaint; (*JUR*) action; **k~n** *vi* (*wehklagen*) to lament, to wail; (*sich beschweren*) to complain; (*JUR*) to take legal action

Kläger(in) ['klɛːgər(ɪn)] (-s, -) *m(f)* plaintiff

kläglich ['klɛːkliç] *adj* wretched

klamm [klam] *adj* (*Finger*) numb; (*feucht*) damp

Klammer ['klamər] (-, -n) *f* clamp; (*in Text*) bracket; (*Büroklammer*) clip; (*Wäscheklammer*) peg; (*Zahnklammer*) brace; **k~n** *vr*: **sich k~n an** +*akk* to cling to

Klang [klaŋ] (-(e)s, ⁺e) *m* sound; **k~voll** *adj* sonorous

Klappe ['klapə] *f* valve; (*Ofenklappe*) damper; (*umg: Mund*) trap; **k~n** *vi* (*Geräusch*) to click; (*Sitz etc*) to tip ♦ *vt* to tip ♦ *vb unpers* to work

Klapper ['klapər] (-, -n) *f* rattle; **k~ig** *adj* run-down, worn-out; **k~n** *vi* to clatter, to rattle; **~schlange** *f* rattlesnake; **~storch** *m* stork

Klapp- *zW*: **~messer** *nt* jackknife; **~rad** *nt* collapsible bicycle; **~stuhl** *m* folding chair; **~tisch** *m* folding table

---

Klaps [klaps] (**-es, -e**) *m* slap

klar [klaːr] *adj* clear; (*NAUT*) ready for sea; (*MIL*) ready for action; **sich** *dat* **(über etw** *akk***) ~ werden** to get (sth) clear in one's mind; **sich** *dat* **im K~en sein über** +*akk* to be clear about; **ins K~e kommen** to get clear; **(na) ~!** of course!; **~ sehen** to see clearly

Kläranlage *f* purification plant

klären ['klɛːrən] *vt* (*Flüssigkeit*) to purify; (*Probleme*) to clarify ♦ *vr* to clear (itself) up

Klarheit *f* clarity

Klarinette [klari'nɛtə] *f* clarinet

klar- *zW*: **~legen** *vt* to clear up, to explain; **~machen** *vt* (*Schiff*) to get ready for sea; **jdm etw ~machen** to make sth clear to sb; **~sehen** △ (*unreg*) *vi siehe* **klar**; **K~sichtfolie** *f* transparent film; **~stellen** *vt* to clarify

Klärung ['klɛːrʊŋ] *f* (*von Flüssigkeit*) purification; (*von Problemen*) clarification

klarwerden △ (*unreg*) *vi siehe* **klar**

Klasse ['klasə] *f* class; (*SCH*) class, form

klasse (*umg*) *adj* smashing

Klassen- *zW*: **~arbeit** *f* test; **~gesellschaft** *f* class society; **~lehrer** *m* form master; **k~los** *adj* classless; **~sprecher(in)** *m(f)* form prefect; **~zimmer** *nt* classroom

klassifizieren [klasifi'tsiːrən] *vt* to classify

Klassik ['klasɪk] *f* (*Zeit*) classical period; (*Stil*) classicism; **~er** (**-s, -**) *m* classic

klassisch *adj* (*auch fig*) classical

Klatsch [klatʃ] (**-(e)s, -e**) *m* smack, crack; (*Gerede*) gossip; **~base** *f* gossip, scandalmonger; **~e** (*umg*) *f* crib; **k~en** *vi* (*Geräusch*) to clash; (*reden*) to gossip; (*applaudieren*) to applaud, to clap ♦ *vt*: **jdm Beifall k~en** to applaud sb; **~mohn** *m* (corn) poppy; **k~nass** ▲ *adj* soaking wet

Klaue ['klaʊə] *f* claw; (*umg: Schrift*) scrawl; **k~n** (*umg*) *vt* to pinch

Klausel ['klaʊzəl] (**-, -n**) *f* clause

Klausur [klaʊ'zuːr] *f* seclusion; **~arbeit** *f* examination paper

Klavier [kla'viːr] (**-s, -e**) *nt* piano

Kleb- ['kleːb] *zW*: **k~en** ['kleːbən] *vt, vi*: **k~en (an** +*akk*) to stick (to); **k~rig** *adj* sticky; **~stoff** *m* glue; **~streifen** *m* adhesive tape

kleckern ['klɛkərn] *vi* to make a mess ♦ *vt* to spill

Klecks [klɛks] (**-es, -e**) *m* blot, stain

Klee [kleː] (**-s**) *m* clover; **~blatt** *nt* cloverleaf; (*fig*) trio

Kleid [klaɪt] (**-(e)s, -er**) *nt* garment; (*Frauenkleid*) dress; **~er** *pl* (**~ung**) clothes; **k~en** ['klaɪdən] *vt* to clothe, to dress; to suit ♦ *vr* to dress

Kleider- [klaɪdər] *zW*: **~bügel** *m* coat hanger; **~bürste** *f* clothes brush; **~schrank** *m* wardrobe

Kleid- *zW*: **k~sam** *adj* flattering; **~ung** *f* clothing; **~ungsstück** *nt* garment

klein [klaɪn] *adj* little, small; **~ hacken** to chop, to mince; **~ schneiden** to chop up; **K~e(r, s)** *mf* little one; **K~format** *nt* small size; **im K~format** small-scale; **K~geld** *nt* small change; **K~igkeit** *f* trifle; **K~kind** *nt* infant; **K~kram** *m* details *pl*; **~laut** *adj* dejected, quiet; **~lich** *adj* petty, paltry; **K~od** ['klaɪnoːt] (**-s, -odien**) *nt* gem, jewel; treasure; **K~stadt** *f* small town; **~städtisch** *adj* provincial; **~stmöglich** *adj* smallest possible

Kleister ['klaɪstər] (**-s, -**) *m* paste

Klemme ['klɛmə] *f* clip; (*MED*) clamp; (*fig*) jam; **k~n** *vt* (*festhalten*) to jam; (*quetschen*) to pinch, to nip ♦ *vr* to catch o.s.; (*sich hineinzwängen*) to squeeze o.s. ♦ *vi* (*Tür*) to stick, to jam; **sich hinter jdn/etw k~n** to get on to sb/down to sth

Klempner ['klɛmpnər] (**-s, -**) *m* plumber

Klerus ['kleːrʊs] (**-**) *m* clergy

Klette ['klɛtə] *f* burr

Kletter- ['klɛtər] *zW*: **~er** (**-s, -**) *m* climber; **k~n** *vi* to climb; **~pflanze** *f* creeper

Klient(in) [kli'ɛnt(ɪn)] *m(f)* client

Klima ['kliːma] (**-s, -s** *od* **-te**) *nt* climate; **~anlage** *f* air conditioning; **~wechsel** *m* change of air

klimpern ['klɪmpərn] (*umg*) *vi* (*mit Münzen, Schlüsseln*) to jingle; (*auf Klavier*) to plonk (away)

Klinge ['klɪŋə] f blade; sword

Klingel ['klɪŋəl] (-, -n) f bell; **~beutel** m collection bag; **k~n** vi to ring

klingen ['klɪŋən] (*unreg*) vi to sound; (*Gläser*) to clink

Klinik ['kliːnɪk] f hospital, clinic

Klinke ['klɪŋkə] f handle

Klippe ['klɪpə] f cliff; (*im Meer*) reef; (*fig*) hurdle

klipp und klar ['klɪp|ʊntklaːr] adj clear and concise

klirren ['klɪrən] vi to clank, to jangle; (*Gläser*) to clink; **~de Kälte** biting cold

Klischee [klɪ'ʃeː] (-s, -s) nt (*Druckplatte*) plate, block; (*fig*) cliché; **~vorstellung** f stereotyped idea

Klo [kloː] (-s, -s) (*umg*) nt loo (*BRIT*), john (*US*)

Kloake [klo'aːkə] f sewer

klobig ['kloːbɪç] adj clumsy

Klopapier (*umg*) nt loo paper (*BRIT*)

klopfen ['klɔpfən] vi to knock; (*Herz*) to thump ♦ vt to beat; **es klopft** somebody's knocking; **jdm auf die Schulter ~** to tap sb on the shoulder

Klopfer (-s, -) m (*Teppichklopfer*) beater; (*Türklopfer*) knocker

Klops [klɔps] (-es, -e) m meatball

Klosett [klo'zɛt] (-s, -e od -s) nt lavatory, toilet; **~papier** nt toilet paper

Kloß [kloːs] (-es, ⁓e) m (*im Hals*) lump; (*KOCH*) dumpling

Kloster ['kloːstər] (-s, ⁓) nt (*Männerkloster*) monastery; (*Frauenkloster*) convent; **klösterlich** ['kløːstərlɪç] adj monastic; convent cpd

Klotz [klɔts] (-es, ⁓e) m log; (*Hackklotz*) block; **ein ~ am Bein** (*fig*) a drag, a millstone round (sb's) neck

Klub [klʊp] (-s, -s) m club; **~sessel** m easy chair

Kluft [klʊft] (-, ⁓e) f cleft, gap; (*GEOG*) gorge, chasm

klug [kluːk] adj clever, intelligent; **K~heit** f cleverness, intelligence

Klumpen ['klʊmpən] (-s, -) m (*Erdklumpen*) clod; (*Blutklumpen*) clot; (*Goldklumpen*)

nugget; (*KOCH*) lump

km *abk* = **Kilometer**

knabbern ['knabərn] vt, vi to nibble

Knabe ['knaːbə] (-n, -n) m boy

Knäckebrot ['knɛkəbroːt] nt crispbread

knacken ['knakən] vt, vi (*auch fig*) to crack

Knacks [knaks] (-es, -e) m crack; (*fig*) defect

Knall [knal] (-(e)s, -e) m bang; (*Peitschenknall*) crack; **~ und Fall** (*umg*) unexpectedly; **~bonbon** nt cracker; **k~en** vi to bang; to crack; **k~rot** adj bright red

knapp [knap] adj tight; (*Geld*) scarce; (*Sprache*) concise; **eine ~e Stunde** just under an hour; **~ unter/neben** just under/ by; **K~heit** f tightness; scarcity; conciseness

knarren ['knarən] vi to creak

Knast [knast] (-(e)s) (*umg*) m (*Haftstrafe*) porridge, time (*inf*); (*Gefängnis*) slammer (*inf*), clink (*inf*)

knattern ['knatərn] vi to rattle; (*Maschinengewehr*) to chatter

Knäuel ['knɔɪəl] (-s, -) m od nt (*Wollknäuel*) ball; (*Menschenknäuel*) knot

Knauf [knaʊf] (-(e)s, Knäufe) m knob; (*Schwertknauf*) pommel

Knebel ['kneːbəl] (-s, -) m gag

kneifen ['knaɪfən] (*unreg*) vt to pinch ♦ vi to pinch; (*sich drücken*) to back out; **vor etw ~** to dodge sth

Kneipe ['knaɪpə] (*umg*) f pub

kneten ['kneːtən] vt to knead; (*Wachs*) to mould

Knick [knɪk] (-(e)s, -e) m (*Sprung*) crack; (*Kurve*) bend; (*Falte*) fold; **k~en** vt, vi (*springen*) to crack; (*brechen*) to break; (*Papier*) to fold; **geknickt sein** to be downcast

Knicks [knɪks] (-es, -e) m curtsey

Knie [kniː] (-s, -) nt knee; **~beuge** f knee bend; **~bundhose** m knee breeches; **~gelenk** nt knee joint; **~kehle** f back of the knee; **k~n** vi to kneel; **~scheibe** f kneecap; **~strumpf** m knee-length sock

Kniff [knɪf] (-(e)s, -e) m (*fig*) trick, knack; **k~elig** adj tricky

---

Rechtschreibreform: ▲ *neue Schreibung* △ *alte Schreibung (auslaufend)*

knipsen ['knɪpsən] *vt* (*Fahrkarte*) to punch; (*PHOT*) to take a snap of, to snap ♦ *vi* to take a snap *od* snaps

Knirps [knɪrps] (**-es, -e**) *m* little chap; (®: *Schirm*) telescopic umbrella

knirschen ['knɪrʃən] *vi* to crunch; **mit den Zähnen ~** to grind one's teeth

knistern ['knɪstərn] *vi* to crackle

Knitter- ['knɪtər] *zW:* **~falte** *f* crease; **k~frei** *adj* non-crease; **k~n** *vi* to crease

Knoblauch ['knoːblaʊx] (**-(e)s**) *m* garlic; **~zehe** *f* (*KOCH*) clove of garlic

Knöchel ['knœçəl] (**-s, -**) *m* knuckle; (*Fußknöchel*) ankle

Knochen ['knɔxən] (**-s, -**) *m* bone; **~bruch** *m* fracture; **~gerüst** *nt* skeleton; **~mark** *nt* bone marrow

knöchern ['knœçərn] *adj* bone

knochig ['knɔxɪç] *adj* bony

Knödel ['knøːdəl] (**-s, -**) *m* dumpling

Knolle ['knɔlə] *f* tuber

Knopf [knɔpf] (**-(e)s, ⸚e**) *m* button; (*Kragenknopf*) stud

knöpfen ['knœpfən] *vt* to button

Knopfloch *nt* buttonhole

Knorpel ['knɔrpəl] (**-s, -**) *m* cartilage, gristle; **k~ig** *adj* gristly

Knospe ['knɔspə] *f* bud

Knoten ['knoːtən] (**-s, -**) *m* knot; (*BOT*) node; (*MED*) lump; **k~** *vt* to knot; **~punkt** *m* junction

Knüller ['knʏlər] (**-s, -**) (*umg*) *m* hit; (*Reportage*) scoop

knüpfen ['knʏpfən] *vt* to tie; (*Teppich*) to knot; (*Freundschaft*) to form

Knüppel ['knʏpəl] (**-s, -**) *m* cudgel; (*Polizeiknüppel*) baton, truncheon; (*AVIAT*) (joy)stick

knurren ['knʊrən] *vi* (*Hund*) to snarl, to growl; (*Magen*) to rumble; (*Mensch*) to mutter

knusperig ['knʊspərɪç] *adj* crisp; (*Keks*) crunchy

k. o. [kaːˈoː] *adj* knocked out; (*fig*) done in

Koalition [koalitsiˈoːn] *f* coalition

Kobold ['koːbɔlt] (**-(e)s, -e**) *m* goblin, imp

Koch [kɔx] (**-(e)s, ⸚e**) *m* cook; **~buch** *nt* cook(ery) book; **k~en** *vt, vi* to cook; (*Wasser*) to boil; **~er** (**-s, -**) *m* stove, cooker; **~gelegenheit** *f* cooking facilities *pl*

Köchin ['kœçɪn] *f* cook

Koch- *zW:* **~löffel** *m* kitchen spoon; **~nische** *f* kitchenette; **~platte** *f* hotplate; **~salz** *nt* cooking salt; **~topf** *m* saucepan, pot

Köder ['køːdər] (**-s, -**) *m* bait, lure

ködern *vt* (*Tier*) to trap with bait; (*Person*) to entice, to tempt

Koexistenz [koɛksɪsˈtɛnts] *f* coexistence

Koffein [kɔfeˈiːn] (**-s**) *nt* caffeine; **k~frei** *adj* decaffeinated

Koffer ['kɔfər] (**-s, -**) *m* suitcase; (*Schrankkoffer*) trunk; **~kuli** *m* (luggage) trolley; **~radio** *nt* portable radio; **~raum** *m* (*AUT*) boot (*BRIT*), trunk (*US*)

Kognak ['kɔnjak] (**-s, -s**) *m* brandy, cognac

Kohl [koːl] (**-(e)s, -e**) *m* cabbage

Kohle ['koːlə] *f* coal; (*Holzkohle*) charcoal; (*CHEM*) carbon; **~hydrat** (**-(e)s, -e**) *nt* carbohydrate

Kohlen- *zW:* **~dioxid** (**-(e)s, -e**) *nt* carbon dioxide; **~händler** *m* coal merchant, coalman; **~säure** *f* carbon dioxide; **~stoff** *m* carbon

Kohlepapier *nt* carbon paper

Koje ['koːjə] *f* cabin; (*Bett*) bunk

Kokain [kokaˈiːn] (**-s**) *nt* cocaine

kokett [koˈkɛt] *adj* coquettish, flirtatious

Kokosnuss ▲ ['koːkɔsnʊs] *f* coconut

Koks [koːks] (**-es, -e**) *m* coke

Kolben ['kɔlbən] (**-s, -**) *m* (*Gewehrkolben*) rifle butt; (*Keule*) club; (*CHEM*) flask; (*TECH*) piston; (*Maiskolben*) cob

Kolik ['koːlɪk] *f* colic, the gripes *pl*

Kollaps [kɔˈlaps] (**-es, -e**) *m* collapse

Kolleg [kɔˈleːk] (**-s, -s** *od* **-ien**) *nt* lecture course; **~e** [kɔˈleːgə] (**-n, -n**) *m* colleague; **~in** *f* colleague; **~ium** *nt* working party; (*SCH*) staff

Kollekte [kɔˈlɛktə] *f* (*REL*) collection

kollektiv [kɔlɛkˈtiːf] *adj* collective

Köln [kœln] (**-s**) *nt* Cologne

Kolonie [koloˈniː] *f* colony

kolonisieren [koloni'ziːrən] *vt* to colonize

Kolonne [ko'lɔnə] *f* column; (*von Fahrzeugen*) convoy

Koloss ▲ [ko'lɔs] (**-es, -e**) *m* colossus; **kolo'ssal** *adj* colossal

Kölsch [kœlʃ] (**-, -**) *nt* (*Bier*) ≈ (strong) lager

Kombi- ['kɔmbi] *zW*: **~nation** [-natsi'oːn] *f* combination; (*Vermutung*) conjecture; (*Hemdhose*) combinations *pl*; **k~nieren** [-'niːrən] *vt* to combine ♦ *vi* to deduce, to work out; (*vermuten*) to guess; **~wagen** *m* station wagon; **~zange** *f* (pair of) pliers *pl*

Komet [ko'meːt] (**-en, -en**) *m* comet

Komfort [kɔm'foːr] (**-s**) *m* luxury

Komik ['koːmɪk] *f* humour, comedy; **~er** (**-s, -**) *m* comedian

komisch ['koːmɪʃ] *adj* funny

Komitee [komi'teː] (**-s, -s**) *nt* committee

Komma ['kɔma] (**-s, -s** *od* **-ta**) *nt* comma; **2 ~ 3** 2 point 3

Kommand- [ko'mand] *zW*: **~ant** [-'dant] *m* commander, commanding officer; **k~ieren** [-'diːrən] *vt, vi* to command; **~o** (**-s, -s**) *nt* command, order; (*Truppe*) detachment, squad; **auf ~o** to order

kommen ['kɔmən] (*unreg*) *vi* to come; (*näher kommen*) to approach; (*passieren*) to happen; (*gelangen, geraten*) to get; (*Blumen, Zähne, Tränen etc*) to appear; (*in die Schule, das Zuchthaus etc*) to go; **~ lassen** to send for; **das kommt in den Schrank** that goes in the cupboard; **zu sich ~** to come round *od* to; **zu etw ~** to acquire sth; **um etw ~** to lose sth; **nichts auf jdn/etw ~ lassen** to have nothing said against sb/sth; **jdm frech ~** to get cheeky with sb; **auf jeden vierten kommt ein Platz** there's one place for every fourth person; **wer kommt zuerst?** who's first?; **unter ein Auto ~** to be run over by a car; **wie hoch kommt das?** what does that cost?; **komm gut nach Hause!** safe journey (home); **~den Sonntag** next Sunday; **K~** (**-s**) *nt* coming

Kommentar [kɔmɛn'taːr] *m* commentary; **kein ~** no comment; **k~los** *adj* without comment

Kommentator [kɔmɛn'taːtɔr] *m* (*TV*) commentator

kommentieren [kɔmɛn'tiːrən] *vt* to comment on

kommerziell [kɔmɛrtsi'ɛl] *adj* commercial

Kommilitone [kɔmili'toːnə] (**-n, -n**) *m* fellow student

Kommissar [kɔmɪ'saːr] *m* police inspector

Kommission [kɔmɪsi'oːn] *f* (*COMM*) commission; (*Ausschuss*) committee

Kommode [kɔ'moːdə] *f* (chest of) drawers

kommunal [kɔmu'naːl] *adj* local; (*von Stadt auch*) municipal

Kommune [kɔ'muːnə] *f* commune

Kommunikation [kɔmunikatsi'oːn] *f* communication

Kommunion [kɔmuni'oːn] *f* communion

Kommuniqué, Kommunikee ▲ [kɔmyni'keː] (**-s, -s**) *nt* communiqué

Kommunismus [kɔmu'nɪsmʊs] *m* communism

Kommunist(in) [kɔmu'nɪst(ɪn)] *m(f)* communist; **k~isch** *adj* communist

kommunizieren [kɔmuni'tsiːrən] *vi* to communicate

Komödie [ko'møːdiə] *f* comedy

Kompagnon [kɔmpan'jõː] (**-s, -s**) *m* (*COMM*) partner

kompakt [kɔm'pakt] *adj* compact

Kompanie [kɔmpa'niː] *f* company

Kompass ▲ ['kɔmpas] (**-es, -e**) *m* compass

kompatibel [kɔmpa'tiːbəl] *adj* compatible

kompetent [kɔmpe'tɛnt] *adj* competent

Kompetenz *f* competence, authority

komplett [kɔm'plɛt] *adj* complete

Komplex [kɔm'plɛks] (**-es, -e**) *m* (*Gebäudekomplex*) complex

Komplikation [kɔmplikatsi'oːn] *f* complication

Kompliment [kɔmpli'mɛnt] *nt* compliment

Komplize [kɔm'pliːtsə] (**-n, -n**) *m* accomplice

kompliziert [kɔmpli'tsiːrt] *adj* complicated

komponieren [kɔmpo'niːrən] *vt* to compose

Komponist [kɔmpo'nɪst(ɪn)] *m* composer

Komposition [kɔmpozitsi'oːn] *f* composition

Kompost [kɔm'pɔst] (**-(e)s, -e**) *m* compost

Kompott [kɔm'pɔt] **(-(e)s, -e)** *nt* stewed fruit

Kompromiss ▲ [kɔmpro'mɪs] **(-es, -e)** *m* compromise; **k~bereit** *adj* willing to compromise

Kondens- [kɔn'dɛns] *zW:* **~ation** [kɔndenzatsi'o:n] *f* condensation; **k~ieren** [kɔndɛn'zi:rən] *vt* to condense; **~milch** *f* condensed milk

Kondition [kɔnditsi'o:n] *f* (COMM, FIN) condition; (*Durchhaltevermögen*) stamina; (*körperliche Verfassung*) physical condition, state of health

Konditionstraining [kɔnditsi'o:nstrɛːnɪŋ] *nt* fitness training

Konditor [kɔn'di:tɔr] *m* pastry cook; **~ei** [-'raɪ] *f* café; cake shop

Kondom [kɔn'do:m] **(-s, -e)** *nt* condom

Konferenz [kɔnfe'rɛnts] *f* conference, meeting

Konfession [kɔnfɛsi'o:n] *f* (religious) denomination; **k~ell** [-'nɛl] *adj* denominational; **k~slos** *adj* non-denominational

Konfirmand [kɔnfɪr'mant] *m* candidate for confirmation

Konfirmation [kɔnfɪrmatsi'o:n] *f* (REL) confirmation

konfirmieren [kɔnfɪr'mi:rən] *vt* to confirm

konfiszieren [kɔnfis'tsi:rən] *vt* to confiscate

Konfitüre [kɔnfi'ty:rə] *f* jam

Konflikt [kɔn'flɪkt] **(-(e)s, -e)** *m* conflict

konfrontieren [kɔnfrɔn'ti:rən] *vt* to confront

konfus [kɔn'fu:s] *adj* confused

Kongress ▲ [kɔn'grɛs] **(-es, -e)** *m* congress; **~zentrum** *nt* conference centre

Kongruenz [kɔngru'ɛnts] *f* agreement, congruence

König ['kø:nɪç] **(-(e)s, -e)** *m* king; **~in** ['kø:nɪgɪn] *f* queen; **k~lich** *adj* royal; **~reich** *nt* kingdom

Konjugation [kɔnjugatsi'o:n] *f* conjugation

konjugieren [kɔnju'gi:rən] *vt* to conjugate

Konjunktion [kɔnjʊŋktsi'o:n] *f* conjunction

Konjunktiv ['kɔnjʊŋkti:f] **(-s, -e)** *m* subjunctive

Konjunktur [kɔnjʊŋk'tu:r] *f* economic situation; (*Hochkonjunktur*) boom

konkret [kɔn'kre:t] *adj* concrete

Konkurrent(in) [kɔnkʊ'rɛnt(ɪn)] *m(f)* competitor

Konkurrenz [kɔnkʊ'rɛnts] *f* competition; **k~fähig** *adj* competitive; **~kampf** *m* competition; rivalry, competitive situation

konkurrieren [kɔnkʊ'ri:rən] *vi* to compete

Konkurs [kɔn'kʊrs] **(-es, -e)** *m* bankruptcy

Können **(-s)** *nt* ability

SCHLÜSSELWORT

können ['kœnən] (*pt* **konnte**, *pp* **gekonnt** *od* (*als Hilfsverb*) **können**) *vt, vi* **1** to be able to; **ich kann es machen** I can do it, I am able to do it, **ich kann es nicht machen** I can't do it, I'm not able to do it; **ich kann nicht ...** I can't ..., I cannot ...; **ich kann nicht mehr** I can't go on

2 (*wissen, beherrschen*) to know; **können Sie Deutsch?** can you speak German?; **er kann gut Englisch** he speaks English well; **sie kann keine Mathematik** she can't do mathematics

3 (*dürfen*) to be allowed to; **kann ich gehen?** can I go?; **könnte ich ...?** could I ...?; **kann ich mit?** (*umg*) can I come with you?

4 (*möglich sein*): **Sie könnten Recht haben** you may be right; **das kann sein** that's possible; **kann sein** maybe

Könner *m* expert

konnte *etc* ['kɔntə] *vb siehe* **können**

konsequent [kɔnze'kvɛnt] *adj* consistent

Konsequenz [kɔnze'kvɛnts] *f* consistency; (*Folgerung*) conclusion

Konserv- [kɔn'zɛrv] *zW:* **k~ativ** [-a'ti:f] *adj* conservative; **~ative** [-a'ti:və] *f(m)* (POL) conservative; **~e** *f* tinned food; **~enbüchse** *f* tin, can; **k~ieren** [-'vi:rən] *vt* to preserve; **~ierung** *f* preservation; **~ierungsstoff** *m* preservatives

Konsonant [kɔnzo'nant] *m* consonant

konstant [kɔn'stant] *adj* constant

konstru- *zW:* **~ieren** [kɔnstru'i:rən] *vt* to construct; **K~kteur** [kɔnstrʊk'tø:r] *m* designer; **K~ktion** [kənstrʊktsi'oːn] *f* construction; **~ktiv** [kɔnstrʊk'tiːf] *adj* constructive

Konsul ['kɔnzʊl] **(-s, -n)** *m* consul; **~at** [-'laːt] *nt* consulate

konsultieren [kɔnzʊl'tiːrən] *vt* to consult

Konsum [kɔn'zuːm] **(-s)** *m* consumption; **~artikel** *m* consumer article; **~ent** [-'mɛnt] *m* consumer; **k~ieren** [-'miːrən] *vt* to consume

Kontakt [kɔn'takt] **(-(e)s, -e)** *m* contact; **k~arm** *adj* unsociable; **k~freudig** *adj* sociable; **~linsen** *pl* contact lenses

kontern ['kɔntərn] *vt, vi* to counter

Kontinent [kɔnti'nɛnt] *m* continent

Kontingent [kɔntɪŋ'gɛnt] **(-(e)s, -e)** *nt* quota; (*Truppenkontingent*) contingent

kontinuierlich [kɔntinu'iːrlɪç] *adj* continuous

Konto ['kɔnto] **(-s, Konten)** *nt* account; **~auszug** *m* statement (of account); **~inhaber(in)** *m(f)* account holder; **~stand** *m* balance

Kontra ['kɔntra] **(-s, -s)** *nt* (*KARTEN*) double; **jdm ~ geben** (*fig*) to contradict sb; **~bass** ▲ *m* double bass; **~hent** *m* (*COMM*) contracting party; **~punkt** *m* counterpoint

Kontrast [kɔn'trast] **(-(e)s, -e)** *m* contrast

Kontroll- [kɔn'trɔl] *zW:* **~e** *f* control, supervision; (*Passkontrolle*) passport control; **~eur** [-'løːr] *m* inspector; **k~ieren** [-'liːrən] *vt* to control, to supervise; (*nachprüfen*) to check

Konvention [kɔnvɛntsi'oːn] *f* convention; **k~ell** [-'nɛl] *adj* conventional

Konversation [kɔnvɛrzatsi'oːn] *f* conversation; **~slexikon** *nt* encyclop(a)edia

Konvoi ['kɔnvɔy] **(-s, -s)** *m* convoy

Konzentration [kɔntsɛntratsi'oːn] *f* concentration

Konzentrationslager *nt* concentration camp

konzentrieren [kɔntsɛn'triːrən] *vt, vr* to concentrate

konzentriert *adj* concentrated ♦ *adv* (*zuhören, arbeiten*) intently

Konzern [kɔn'tsɛrn] **(-s, -e)** *m* combine

Konzert [kɔn'tsɛrt] **(-(e)s, -e)** *nt* concert; (*Stück*) concerto; **~saal** *m* concert hall

Konzession [kɔntsesi'oːn] *f* licence; (*Zugeständnis*) concession

Konzil [kɔn'tsiːl] **(-s, -e** *od* **-ien)** *nt* council

kooperativ [koʔopera'tiːf] *adj* cooperative

koordinieren [koʔɔrdi'niːrən] *vt* to coordinate

Kopf [kɔpf] **(-(e)s, ⁺e)** *m* head; **~haut** *f* scalp; **~hörer** *m* headphones *pl*; **~kissen** *nt* pillow; **k~los** *adj* panic-stricken; **k~rechnen** *vi* to do mental arithmetic; **~salat** *m* lettuce; **~schmerzen** *pl* headache *sg*; **~sprung** *m* header, dive; **~stand** *m* headstand; **~stütze** *f* (*im Auto etc*) headrest, head restraint; **~tuch** *nt* headscarf; **~weh** *nt* headache; **~zerbrechen** *nt*: **jdm ~zerbrechen machen** to be a headache for sb

Kopie [ko'piː] *f* copy; **k~ren** *vt* to copy

Kopiergerät *nt* photocopier

Koppel¹ ['kɔpəl] **(-, -n)** *f* (*Weide*) enclosure

Koppel² ['kɔpəl] **(-s, -)** *nt* (*Gürtel*) belt

koppeln *vt* to couple

Koppelung *f* coupling

Koralle [ko'ralə] *f* coral

Korb [kɔrp] **(-(e)s, ⁺e)** *m* basket; **jdm einen ~ geben** (*fig*) to turn sb down; **~ball** *m* basketball; **~stuhl** *m* wicker chair

Kord [kɔrt] **(-(e)s, -e)** *m* cord, corduroy

Kordel ['kɔrdəl] **(-, -n)** *f* cord, string

Kork [kɔrk] **(-(e)s, -e)** *m* cork; **~en (-s, -)** *m* stopper, cork; **~enzieher (-s, -)** *m* corkscrew

Korn [kɔrn] **(-(e)s, ⁺er)** *nt* corn, grain; (*Gewehr*) sight

Körper ['kœrpər] **(-s, -)** *m* body; **~bau** *m* build; **k~behindert** *adj* disabled; **~geruch** *m* body odour; **~gewicht** *nt* weight; **~größe** *f* height; **k~lich** *adj* physical; **~pflege** *f* personal hygiene; **~schaft** *f* corporation; **~schaftssteuer** *f* corporation tax; **~teil** *m* part of the body; **~verletzung** *f* bodily *od* physical injury

korpulent [kɔrpu'lɛnt] *adj* corpulent

korrekt [kɔ'rɛkt] *adj* correct; **K~ur** [-'tuːr] *f*

(eines Textes) proofreading; *(Text)* proof; *(SCH)* marking, correction

Korrespond- [kɔrɛspɔnd] *zW:* **~ent(in)** [-'dɛnt(ɪn)] *m(f)* correspondent; **~enz** [-'dɛnts] *f* correspondence; **k~ieren** [-'diːrən] *vi* to correspond

Korridor ['kɔridoːr] **(-s, -e)** *m* corridor

korrigieren [kɔri'giːrən] *vt* to correct

Korruption [kɔrʊptsi'oːn] *f* corruption

Kose- ['koːzə] *zW:* **~form** *f* pet form; **~name** *m* pet name; **~wort** *nt* term of endearment

Kosmetik [kɔs'meːtɪk] *f* cosmetics *pl;* **~erin** *f* beautician

kosmetisch *adj* cosmetic; *(Chirurgie)* plastic

kosmisch ['kɔsmɪʃ] *adj* cosmic

Kosmo- [kɔsmo] *zW:* **~naut** [-'naʊt] **(-en, -en)** *m* cosmonaut; **k~politisch** *adj* cosmopolitan; **~s (-)** *m* cosmos

Kost [kɔst] **(-)** *f (Nahrung)* food; *(Verpflegung)* board; **k~bar** *adj* precious; *(teuer)* costly, expensive; **~barkeit** *f* preciousness, costliness, expensiveness; *(Wertstück)* valuable

Kosten *pl* cost(s); *(Ausgaben)* expenses; **auf ~ von** at the expense of; **k~** *vt* to cost; *(versuchen)* to taste ♦ *vi* to taste; **was kostet ...?** what does ... cost?, how much is ...?; **~anschlag** *m* estimate; **k~los** *adj* free (of charge)

köstlich ['kœstlɪç] *adj* precious; *(Einfall)* delightful; *(Essen)* delicious; **sich ~ amüsieren** to have a marvellous time

Kostprobe *f* taste; *(fig)* sample

kostspielig *adj* expensive

Kostüm [kɔs'tyːm] **(-s, -e)** *nt* costume; *(Damenkostüm)* suit; **~fest** *nt* fancy-dress party; **k~ieren** [kɔsty'miːrən] *vt, vr* to dress up; **~verleih** *m* costume agency

Kot [koːt] **(-(e)s)** *m* excrement

Kotelett [kotə'let] **(-(e)s, -e** *od* **-s)** *nt* cutlet, chop; **~en** *pl (Bart)* sideboards

Köter ['køːtər] **(-s, -)** *m* cur

Kotflügel *m (AUT)* wing

kotzen ['kɔtsən] *(umg!)* *vi* to puke *(umg)*, to throw up *(umg)*

Krabbe ['krabə] *f* shrimp; **k~ln** *vi* to crawl

Krach [krax] **(-(e)s, -s** *od* **-e)** *m* crash; *(andauernd)* noise; *(umg: Streit)* quarrel, argument; **k~en** *vi* to crash; *(beim Brechen)* to crack ♦ *vr (umg)* to argue, to quarrel

krächzen ['krɛçtsən] *vi* to croak

Kraft [kraft] **(-, ⁻e)** *f* strength; power; force; *(Arbeitskraft)* worker; **in ~ treten** to come into force; **k~** *präp* +*gen* by virtue of; **~fahrer** *m* (motor) driver; **~fahrzeug** *nt* motor vehicle; **~fahrzeugbrief** *m* logbook; **~fahrzeugsteuer** *f* ≈ road tax; **~fahrzeugversicherung** *f* car insurance

kräftig ['krɛftɪç] *adj* strong; **~en** *vt* to strengthen

Kraft- *zW:* **k~los** *adj* weak; powerless; *(JUR)* invalid; **~probe** *f* trial of strength; **~stoff** *m* fuel; **k~voll** *adj* vigorous; **~werk** *nt* power station

Kragen ['kraːgən] **(-s, -)** *m* collar; **~weite** *f* collar size

Krähe ['krɛːə] *f* crow; **k~n** *vi* to crow

Kralle ['kralə] *f* claw; *(Vogelkralle)* talon; **k~n** *vt* to clutch; *(krampfhaft)* to claw

Kram [kraːm] **(-(e)s)** *m* stuff, rubbish; **k~en** *vi* to rummage; **~laden** *m (pej)* small shop

Krampf [krampf] **(-(e)s, ⁻e)** *m* cramp; *(zuckend)* spasm; **~ader** *f* varicose vein; **k~haft** *adj* convulsive; *(fig: Versuche)* desperate

Kran [kraːn] **(-(e)s, ⁻e)** *m* crane; *(Wasserkran)* tap, faucet *(US)*

krank [kraŋk] *adj* ill, sick; **K~e(r)** *f(m)* sick person, invalid; patient; **~en** *vi:* **an etw** *dat* **~en** *(fig)* to suffer from sth

kränken ['krɛŋkən] *vt* to hurt

Kranken- *zW:* **~geld** *nt* sick pay; **~gymnastik** *f* physiotherapy; **~haus** *nt* hospital; **~kasse** *f* health insurance; **~pfleger** *m* nursing orderly; **~schein** *m* health insurance card; **~schwester** *f* nurse; **~versicherung** *f* health insurance; **~wagen** *m* ambulance

Krank- *zW:* **k~haft** *adj* diseased; *(Angst etc)* morbid; **~heit** *f* illness; disease; **~heitserreger** *m* disease-causing agent

kränklich ['krɛŋklɪç] *adj* sickly

Kränkung *f* insult, offence

Kranz [krants] (**-es, ⁼e**) *m* wreath, garland

krass ▲ [kras] *adj* crass

Krater ['kraːtər] (**-s, -**) *m* crater

Kratz- ['krats] *zW:* **~bürste** *f* (*fig*) crosspatch; **k~en** *vt, vi* to scratch; **~er** (**-s, -**) *m* scratch; (*Werkzeug*) scraper

Kraul [kraʊl] (**-s**) *nt* crawl; **~ schwimmen** to do the crawl; **k~en** *vi* (*schwimmen*) to do the crawl ♦ *vt* (*streicheln*) to fondle

kraus [kraʊs] *adj* crinkly; (*Haar*) frizzy; (*Stirn*) wrinkled

Kraut [kraʊt] (**-(e)s, Kräuter**) *nt* plant; (*Gewürz*) herb; (*Gemüse*) cabbage

Krawall [kra'val] (**-s, -e**) *m* row, uproar

Krawatte [kra'vatə] *f* tie

kreativ [krea'tiːf] *adj* creative

Krebs [kreːps] (**-es, -e**) *m* crab; (*MED, ASTROL*) cancer; **k~krank** *adj* suffering from cancer

Kredit [kre'diːt] (**-(e)s, -e**) *m* credit; **~institut** *nt* bank; **~karte** *f* credit card

Kreide ['kraɪdə] *f* chalk; **k~bleich** *adj* as white as a sheet

Kreis [kraɪs] (**-es, -e**) *m* circle; (*Stadtkreis etc*) district; **im ~ gehen** (*auch fig*) to go round in circles

kreischen ['kraɪʃən] *vi* to shriek, to screech

Kreis- *zW:* **~el** ['kraɪzəl] (**-s, -**) *m* top; (*~verkehr*) roundabout (*BRIT*), traffic circle (*US*); **k~en** ['kraɪzən] *vi* to spin; **~lauf** *m* (*MED*) circulation; (*fig: der Natur etc*) cycle; **~säge** *f* circular saw; **~stadt** *f* county town; **~verkehr** *m* roundabout traffic

Krematorium [krema'toːriʊm] *nt* crematorium

Kreml ['kreːml] (**-s**) *m* Kremlin

krepieren [kre'piːrən] (*umg*) *vi* (*sterben*) to die, to kick the bucket

Krepp [krɛp] (**-s, -s** *od* **-e**) *m* crepe; **~papier** ▲ *nt* crepe paper

Kresse ['krɛsə] *f* cress

Kreta ['kreːta] (**-s**) *nt* Crete

Kreuz [krɔʏts] (**-es, -e**) *nt* cross; (*ANAT*) small of the back; (*KARTEN*) clubs; **k~en** *vt, vr* to cross ♦ *vi* (*NAUT*) to cruise; **~er** (**-s, -**) *m* (*Schiff*) cruiser; **~fahrt** *f* cruise; **~feuer** *nt* (*fig*): **ins ~feuer geraten** to be under fire from all sides; **~gang** *m* cloisters *pl*;

k~igen *vt* to crucify; **~igung** *f* crucifixion; **~ung** *f* (*Verkehrskreuzung*) crossing, junction; (*Züchten*) cross; **~verhör** *nt* cross-examination; **~weg** *m* crossroads; (*REL*) Way of the Cross; **~worträtsel** *nt* crossword puzzle; **~zug** *m* crusade

Kriech- ['kriːç] *zW:* **k~en** (*unreg*) *vi* to crawl, to creep; (*pej*) to grovel, to crawl; **~er** (**-s, -**) *m* crawler; **~spur** *f* crawler lane; **~tier** *nt* reptile

Krieg [kriːk] (**-(e)s, -e**) *m* war

kriegen ['kriːgən] (*umg*) *vt* to get

Kriegs- *zW:* **~erklärung** *f* declaration of war; **~fuß** *m:* **mit jdm/etw auf ~fuß stehen** to be at loggerheads with sb/to have difficulties with sth; **~gefangene(r)** *m* prisoner of war; **~gefangenschaft** *f* captivity; **~gericht** *nt* court-martial; **~schiff** *nt* warship; **~verbrecher** *m* war criminal; **~versehrte(r)** *m* person disabled in the war; **~zustand** *m* state of war

Krim [krɪm] (**-**) *f* Crimea

Krimi ['kriːmi] (**-s, -s**) (*umg*) *m* thriller

Kriminal- [krimi'naːl] *zW:* **~beamte(r)** *m* detective; **~i'tät** *f* criminality; **~'polizei** *f* ≈ Criminal Investigation Department (*BRIT*), Federal Bureau of Investigation (*US*); **~ro'man** *m* detective story

kriminell [krimi'nɛl] *adj* criminal; **K~e(r)** *m* criminal

Krippe ['krɪpə] *f* crib; (*Kinderkrippe*) crèche

Krise ['kriːzə] *f* crisis; **k~ln** *vi:* **es k~lt** there's a crisis

Kristall [krɪs'tal] (**-s, -e**) *m* crystal ♦ *nt* (*Glas*) crystal

Kriterium [kri'teːriʊm] *nt* criterion

Kritik [kri'tiːk] *f* criticism; (*Zeitungskritik*) review, write-up; **~er** ['kriːtikər] (**-s, -**) *m* critic; **k~los** *adj* uncritical

kritisch ['kriːtɪʃ] *adj* critical

kritisieren [kriti'ziːrən] *vt, vi* to criticize

kritzeln ['krɪtsəln] *vt, vi* to scribble, to scrawl

Kroatien [kro'aːtsiən] *nt* Croatia

Krokodil [kroko'diːl] (**-s, -e**) *nt* crocodile

Krokus ['kroːkʊs] (**-, -** *od* **-se**) *m* crocus

Krone ['kroːnə] *f* crown; (*Baumkrone*) top

krönen ['krøːnən] *vt* to crown

Kron- zW: **~korken** m bottle top;
~leuchter m chandelier; **~prinz** m crown
prince
Krönung ['krø:nʊŋ] f coronation
Kropf [krɔpf] (-(e)s, ⁻e) m (MED) goitre; (von
Vogel) crop
Kröte ['krø:tə] f toad
Krücke ['krʏkə] f crutch
Krug [kru:k] (-(e)s, ⁻e) m jug; (Bierkrug) mug
Krümel ['kry:məl] (-s, -) m crumb; **k~n** vt, vi
to crumble
krumm [krʊm] adj (auch fig) crooked;
(kurvig) curved; **jdm etw ~ nehmen** to take
sth amiss; **~beinig** adj bandy-legged;
~lachen (umg) vr to laugh o.s. silly
Krümmung ['krʏmʊŋ] f bend, curve
Krüppel ['krʏpəl] (-s, -) m cripple
Kruste ['krʊstə] f crust
Kruzifix [krutsi'fɪks] (-es, -e) nt crucifix
Kübel ['ky:bəl] (-s, -) m tub; (Eimer) pail
Kubikmeter [ku'bi:kme:tər] m cubic metre
Küche ['kʏçə] f kitchen; (Kochen) cooking,
cuisine
Kuchen ['ku:xən] (-s, -) m cake; **~form** f
baking tin; **~gabel** f pastry fork
Küchen- zW: **~herd** m cooker, stove;
~schabe f cockroach; **~schrank** m
kitchen cabinet
Kuckuck ['kʊkʊk] (-s, -e) m cuckoo; **~suhr**
f cuckoo clock
Kugel ['ku:gəl] (-, -n) f ball; (MATH) sphere;
(MIL) bullet; (Erdkugel) globe; (SPORT) shot;
k~förmig adj spherical; **~lager** nt ball
bearing; **k~rund** adj (Gegenstand) round;
(umg: Person) tubby; **~schreiber** m ballpoint (pen), Biro ®; **k~sicher** adj
bulletproof; **~stoßen** (-s) nt shot put
Kuh [ku:] (-, ⁻e) f cow
kühl [ky:l] adj (auch fig) cool; **K~anlage** f
refrigeration plant; **K~e** (-) f coolness; **~en**
vt to cool; **K~er** (-s, -) m (AUT) radiator;
K~erhaube f (AUT) bonnet (BRIT), hood
(US); **K~raum** m cold storage chamber;
K~schrank m refrigerator; **K~truhe** f
freezer; **K~ung** f cooling; **K~wasser** nt
radiator water
kühn [ky:n] adj bold, daring; **K~heit** f
boldness
Kuhstall m byre, cattle shed
Küken ['ky:kən] (-s, -) nt chicken
kulant [ku'lant] adj obliging
Kuli ['ku:li] (-s, -s) m coolie; (umg:
Kugelschreiber) Biro ®
Kulisse [ku'lɪsə] f scenery
kullern ['kʊlərn] vi to roll
Kult [kʊlt] (-(e)s, -e) m worship, cult; **mit
etw einen ~ treiben** to make a cult out of
sth
kultivieren [kʊlti'vi:rən] vt to cultivate
kultiviert adj cultivated, refined
Kultur [kʊl'tu:r] f culture; civilization; (des
Bodens) cultivation; **~banause** (umg) m
philistine, low-brow; **~beutel** m toilet bag;
k~ell [-u'rɛl] adj cultural; **~ministerium** nt
ministry of education and the arts
Kümmel ['kʏməl] (-s, -) m caraway seed;
(Branntwein) kümmel
Kummer ['kʊmər] (-s) m grief, sorrow
kümmerlich ['kʏmərlɪç] adj miserable,
wretched
kümmern ['kʏmərn] vt to concern ♦ vr: **sich
um jdn ~** to look after sb; **das kümmert
mich nicht** that doesn't worry me; **sich
um etw ~** to see to sth
Kumpel ['kʊmpəl] (-s, -) (umg) m mate
kündbar ['kʏntba:r] adj redeemable,
recallable; (Vertrag) terminable
Kunde¹ ['kʊndə] (-n, -n) m customer
Kunde² [-] f (Botschaft) news
Kunden- zW: **~dienst** m after-sales service;
~konto nt charge account; **~nummer** f
customer number
Kund- zW: **k~geben** (unreg) vt to
announce; **~gebung** f announcement;
(Versammlung) rally
Künd- ['kʏnd] zW: **k~igen** vi to give in
one's notice ♦ vt to cancel; **jdm k~igen** to
give sb his notice; **die Stellung/Wohnung
k~igen** to give notice that one is leaving
one's job/house; **jdm die Stellung/
Wohnung k~igen** to give sb notice to
leave his/her job/house; **~igung** f notice;
~igungsfrist f period of notice;
~igungsschutz m protection against

wrongful dismissal

Kundin f customer

Kundschaft f customers pl, clientele

künftig ['kʏnftɪç] adj future ♦ adv in future

Kunst [kʊnst] (-, ¨e) f art; (Können) skill; **das ist doch keine ~** it's easy; **~dünger** m artificial manure; **~faser** f synthetic fibre; **~fertigkeit** f skilfulness; **~gegenstand** m art object; **~gerecht** adj skilful; **~geschichte** f history of art; **~gewerbe** nt arts and crafts pl; **~griff** m trick, knack; **~händler** m art dealer

Künstler(in) ['kʏnstlər(ɪn)] (-s, -) m(f) artist; **k~isch** adj artistic; **~name** m pseudonym

künstlich ['kʏnstlɪç] adj artificial

Kunst- zW: **~sammler** (-s, -) m art collector; **~seide** f artificial silk; **~stoff** m synthetic material; **~stück** nt trick; **~turnen** nt gymnastics sg; **k~voll** adj artistic; **~werk** nt work of art

kunterbunt ['kʊntərbʊnt] adj higgledy-piggledy

Kupee ▲ [ku'pe:] (-s, -s) nt coupé

Kupfer ['kʊpfər] (-s) nt copper; **k~n** adj copper

Kupon [ku'põ:, ku'pɔŋ] (-s, -s) m coupon; (Stoff~) length of cloth

Kuppe ['kʊpə] f (Bergkuppe) top; (Fingerkuppe) tip

Kuppel (-, -n) f dome; **k~n** vi (JUR) to procure; (AUT) to declutch ♦ vt to join

Kupplung f coupling; (AUT) clutch

Kur [ku:r] (-, -en) f cure, treatment

Kür [ky:r] (-, -en) f (SPORT) free exercises pl

Kurbel ['kʊrbəl] (-, -n) f crank, winder; (AUT) starting handle; **~welle** f crankshaft

Kürbis ['kʏrbɪs] (-ses, -se) m pumpkin; (exotisch) gourd

Kurgast m visitor (to a health resort)

kurieren [ku'ri:rən] vt to cure

kurios [kuri'o:s] adj curious, odd; **K~i'tät** f curiosity

Kurort m health resort

Kurs [kʊrs] (-es, -e) m course; (FIN) rate; **~buch** nt timetable; **k~ieren** [kʊr'zi:rən] vi to circulate; **k~iv** [kʊr'zi:f] adv in italics; **~us** ['kʊrzʊs] (-, Kurse) m course; **~wagen**

m (EISENB) through carriage

Kurtaxe [-taksə] (-, -n) f visitors' tax (at health resort or spa)

Kurve ['kʊrvə] f curve; (Straßenkurve) curve, bend; (einer Straße) bend; **kurvig** adj (Straße) bendy

kurz [kʊrts] adj short; **~ gesagt** in short; **~ halten** to keep short; **zu ~ kommen** to come off badly; **den Kürzeren ziehen** to get the worst of it; **K~arbeit** f short-time work; **~ärm(e)lig** adj short-sleeved

Kürze ['kʏrtsə] f shortness, brevity; **k~n** vt to cut short; (in der Länge) to shorten; (Gehalt) to reduce

kurz- zW: **~erhand** adv on the spot; **~fristig** adj short-term; **K~geschichte** f short story; **~halten** △ (unreg) vt siehe **kurz**; **~lebig** adj short-lived

kürzlich ['kʏrtslɪç] adv lately, recently

Kurz- zW: **~schluss** ▲ m (ELEK) short circuit; **k~sichtig** adj short-sighted

Kürzung f (eines Textes) abridgement; (eines Theaterstück, des Gehalts) cut

Kurzwelle f short wave

kuscheln ['kʊʃəln] vr to snuggle up

Kusine [ku'zi:nə] f cousin

Kuss ▲ [kʊs] (-es, ¨e) m kiss

küssen ['kʏsən] vt, vr to kiss

Küste ['kʏstə] f coast, shore

Küstenwache f coastguard

Küster ['kʏstər] (-s, -) m sexton, verger

Kutsche ['kʊtʃə] f coach, carriage; **~r** (-s, -) m coachman

Kutte ['kʊtə] f habit

Kuvert [ku'vɛrt] (-s, -e od -s) nt envelope; cover

KZ nt abk von **Konzentrationslager**

L, l

l. abk = **Liter**

labil [la'bi:l] adj (MED: Konstitution) delicate

Labor [la'bo:r] (-s, -e od -s) nt lab; **~ant(in)** m(f) lab(oratory) assistant

Labyrinth [laby'rɪnt] (-s, -e) nt labyrinth

Lache ['laxə] f (Flüssigkeit) puddle; (von Blut, Benzin etc) pool

lächeln ['lɛçəln] *vi* to smile; **L~ (-s)** *nt* smile

lachen ['laxən] *vi* to laugh

lächerlich ['lɛçərliç] *adj* ridiculous

Lachgas *nt* laughing gas

lachhaft *adj* laughable

Lachs [laks] **(-es, -e)** *m* salmon

Lack [lak] **(-(e)s, -e)** *m* lacquer, varnish; *(von Auto)* paint; **l~ieren** [la'ki:rən] *vt* to varnish; *(Auto)* to spray; **~ierer** [la'ki:rər] **(-s, -)** *m* varnisher

Laden ['la:dən] **(-s, ⁵)** *m* shop; *(Fensterladen)* shutter

laden ['la:dən] *(unreg) vt (Lasten)* to load; *(JUR)* to summon; *(einladen)* to invite

Laden- *zW:* **~dieb** *m* shoplifter; **~diebstahl** *m* shoplifting; **~schluss** ▲ *m* closing time; **~tisch** *m* counter

Laderaum *m* freight space; *(AVIAT, NAUT)* hold

Ladung ['la:dʊŋ] *f (Last)* cargo, load; *(Beladen)* loading; *(JUR)* summons; *(Einladung)* invitation; *(Sprengladung)* charge

Lage ['la:gə] *f* position, situation; *(Schicht)* layer; **in der ~ sein** to be in a position

Lageplan *m* ground plan

Lager ['la:gər] **(-s, -)** *nt* camp; *(COMM)* warehouse; *(Schlaflager)* bed; *(von Tier)* lair; *(TECH)* bearing; **~bestand** *m* stocks *pl*; **~feuer** *nt* campfire; **~haus** *nt* warehouse, store

lagern ['la:gərn] *vi (Dinge)* to be stored; *(Menschen)* to camp ♦ *vt* to store; *(betten)* to lay down; *(Maschine)* to bed

Lagune [la'gu:nə] *f* lagoon

lahm [la:m] *adj* lame; **~ legen** to paralyse; **~en** *vi* to be lame

Lähmung *f* paralysis

Laib [laıp] **(-s, -e)** *m* loaf

Laie ['laıə] **(-n, -n)** *m* layman; **l~nhaft** *adj* amateurish

Laken ['la:kən] **(-s, -)** *nt* sheet

Lakritze [la'krıtsə] *f* liquorice

lallen ['lalən] *vt, vi* to slur; *(Baby)* to babble

Lamelle [la'mɛlə] *f* lamella; *(ELEK)* lamina; *(TECH)* plate

Lametta [la'mɛta] **(-s)** *nt* tinsel

Lamm [lam] **(-(e)s, ⁵er)** *nt* lamb

Lampe ['lampə] *f* lamp

Lampen- *zW:* **~fieber** *nt* stage fright; **~schirm** *m* lampshade

Lampion [lampi'õ:] **(-s, -s)** *m* Chinese lantern

Land [lant] **(-(e)s, ⁵er)** *nt* land; *(Nation, nicht Stadt)* country; *(Bundesland)* state; **auf dem ~(e)** in the country; *siehe* **hierzulande**; **~besitz** *m* landed property; **~ebahn** *f* runway; **l~en** ['landən] *vt, vi* to land

---

Land

i A **Land** *(plural* **Länder)** *is a member state of the* **BRD** *and of Austria. There are 16* **Länder** *in Germany, namely Baden-Württemberg, Bayern, Berlin, Brandenburg, Bremen, Hamburg, Hessen, Mecklenburg-Vorpommern, Niedersachsen, Nordrhein-Westfalen, Rheinland-Pfalz, Saarland, Sachsen, Sachsen-Anhalt, Schleswig-Holstein and Thüringen. Each* **Land** *has its own parliament and constitution. The 9* **Länder** *of Austria are Vorarlberg, Tirol, Salzburg, Oberösterreich, Niederösterreich, Kärnten, Steiermark, Burgenland and Wien.*

Landes- ['landəs] *zW:* **~farben** *pl* national colours; **~innere(s)** *nt* inland region; **~sprache** *f* national language; **l~üblich** *adj* customary; **~verrat** *m* high treason; **~währung** *f* national currency; **l~weit** *adj* nationwide

Land- *zW:* **~haus** *nt* country house; **~karte** *f* map; **~kreis** *m* administrative region; **l~läufig** *adj* customary

ländlich ['lɛntlıç] *adj* rural

Land- *zW:* **~schaft** *f* countryside; *(KUNST)* landscape; **~schaftsschutzgebiet** *nt* nature reserve; **~sitz** *m* country seat; **~straße** *f* country road; **~streicher (-s, -)** *m* tramp; **~strich** *m* region

Landung ['landʊŋ] *f* landing; **~sbrücke** *f* jetty, pier

Land- *zW:* **~weg** *m:* **etw auf dem ~weg befördern** to transport sth by land; **~wirt**

---

m farmer; **~wirtschaft** *f* agriculture;
~zunge *f* spit
lang [laŋ] *adj* long; (*Mensch*) tall; **~atmig** *adj*
long-winded; **~e** *adv* for a long time;
(*dauern, brauchen*) a long time
Länge ['lɛŋə] *f* length; (*GEOG*) longitude
langen ['laŋən] *vi* (*ausreichen*) to do, to
suffice; (*fassen*) **~ (nach)** to reach (for)
♦ *vt*: **jdm etw ~** to hand *od* pass sb sth; **es
langt mir** I've had enough
Längengrad *m* longitude
Längenmaß *nt* linear measure
lang- *zW*: **~sam** *adj* slow; **L~samkeit** *f*
slowness; **L~schläfer(in)** *m(f)* late riser
längst [lɛŋst] *adv*: **das ist ~ fertig** that was
finished a long time ago, that has been
finished for a long time; **~e(r, s)** *adj*
longest
lang- *zW*: **~weilen** *vt* to bore ♦ *vr* to be
bored; **~weilig** *adj* boring, tedious;
L~welle *f* long wave; **~wierig** *adj* lengthy,
long-drawn-out
Lanze ['lantsə] *f* lance
Lappalie [la'paːliə] *f* trifle
Lappen ['lapən] (**-s, -**) *m* cloth, rag; (*ANAT*)
lobe
läppisch ['lɛpɪʃ] *adj* foolish
Lapsus ['lapsʊs] (**-, -**) *m* slip
Laptop ['lɛptɔp] (**-s, -s**) *m* laptop
(computer)
Lärche ['lɛrçə] *f* larch
Lärm [lɛrm] (**-(e)s**) *m* noise; **l~en** *vi* to be
noisy, to make a noise
Larve ['larfə] *f* (*BIOL*) larva
lasch [laʃ] *adj* slack
Laser ['leːzər] (**-s, -**) *m* laser

SCHLÜSSELWORT

lassen ['lasən] (*pt* **ließ**, *pp* **gelassen** *od* (*als
Hilfsverb*) **lassen**) *vt* **1** (*unterlassen*) to stop;

(*momentan*) to leave; **lass das (sein)!** don't
(do it)!; (*hör auf*) stop it!; **lass mich!** leave
me alone; **lassen wir das!** let's leave it; **er
kann das Trinken nicht lassen** he can't
stop drinking
2 (*zurücklassen*) to leave; **etw lassen, wie
es ist** to leave sth (just) as it is
3 (*überlassen*): **jdn ins Haus lassen** to let
sb into the house
♦ *vi*: **lass mal, ich mache das schon** leave
it, I'll do it
♦ *Hilfsverb* **1** (*veranlassen*): **etw machen
lassen** to have*od* get sth done; **sich** *dat*
etw schicken lassen to have sth sent (to
one)
2 (*zulassen*): **jdn etw wissen lassen** to let
sb know sth; **das Licht brennen lassen** to
leave the light on; **jdn warten lassen** to
keep sb waiting; **das lässt sich machen**
that can be done
3: **lass uns gehen** let's go

lässig ['lɛsɪç] *adj* casual; **L~keit** *f* casualness
Last [last] (**-, -en**) *f* load, burden; (*NAUT,
AVIAT*) cargo; (*meist pl: Gebühr*) charge; **jdm
zur ~ fallen** (to be a burden to sb; **~auto**
nt lorry, truck; **l~en** *vi*: **l~en auf** +*dat* to
weigh on; **~enaufzug** *m* goods lift *od*
elevator (*US*)
Laster ['lastər] (**-s, -**) *nt* vice
lästern ['lɛstərn] *vt, vi* (*Gott*) to blaspheme;
(*schlecht sprechen*) to mock
Lästerung *f* jibe; (*Gotteslästerung*)
blasphemy
lästig ['lɛstɪç] *adj* troublesome, tiresome
Last- *zW*: **~kahn** *m* barge; **~kraftwagen**
m heavy goods vehicle; **~schrift** *f* debit;
~wagen *m* lorry, truck; **~zug** *m* articulated
lorry
Latein [la'tain] (**-s**) *nt* Latin; **~amerika** *nt*
Latin America
latent [la'tɛnt] *adj* latent
Laterne [la'tɛrnə] *f* lantern; (*Straßenlaterne*)
lamp, light; **~npfahl** *m* lamppost
latschen ['laːtʃən] (*umg*) *vi* (*gehen*) to
wander, to go; (*lässig*) to slouch
Latte ['latə] *f* lath; (*SPORT*) goalpost; (*quer*)

Rechtschreibreform: ▲ *neue Schreibung* △ *alte Schreibung (auslaufend)*

crossbar

Latzhose ['latshoːzə] f dungarees pl

lau [laʊ] adj (Nacht) balmy; (Wasser) lukewarm

Laub [laʊp] (-(e)s) nt foliage; ~**baum** m deciduous tree; ~**frosch** m tree frog; ~**säge** f fretsaw

Lauch [laʊx] (-(e)s, -e) m leek

Lauer ['laʊər] f: **auf der ~ sein** od **liegen** to lie in wait; **l~n** vi to lie in wait; (Gefahr) to lurk

Lauf [laʊf] (-(e)s, Läufe) m run; (Wettlauf) race; (Entwicklung, ASTRON) course; (Gewehrlauf) barrel; **einer Sache** dat **ihren ~ lassen** to let sth take its course; ~**bahn** f career

laufen ['laʊfən] (unreg) vt, vi to run; (umg: gehen) to walk; ~**d** adj running; (Monat, Ausgaben) current; **auf dem ~den sein/halten** to be/keep up to date; **am ~den Band** (fig) continuously

Läufer ['lɔʏfər] (-s, -) m (Teppich, SPORT) runner; (Fußball) half-back; (Schach) bishop

Lauf- zW: ~**masche** f run, ladder (BRIT); ~**pass** ▲ m: **jdm den ~pass geben** (umg) to send sb packing (inf); ~**stall** m playpen; ~**steg** m catwalk; ~**werk** nt (COMPUT) disk drive

Lauge ['laʊgə] f soapy water; (CHEM) alkaline solution

Laune ['laʊnə] f mood, humour; (Einfall) caprice; (schlechte) temper; **l~nhaft** adj capricious, changeable

launisch adj moody; bad-tempered

Laus [laʊs] (-, Läuse) f louse

lauschen ['laʊʃən] vi to eavesdrop, to listen in

lauschig ['laʊʃɪç] adj snug

lausig ['laʊzɪç] (umg: pej) adj measly; (Kälte) perishing

laut [laʊt] adj loud ♦ adv loudly; (lesen) aloud ♦ präp (+gen od dat) according to; **L~** (-(e)s, -e) m sound

Laute ['laʊtə] f lute

lauten ['laʊtən] vi to say; (Urteil) to be

läuten ['lɔʏtən] vt, vi to ring, to sound

lauter ['laʊtər] adj (Wasser) clear, pure; (Wahrheit, Charakter) honest ♦ adj inv (Freude, Dummheit etc) sheer ♦ adv nothing but, only

laut- zW: ~**hals** adv at the top of one's voice; ~**los** adj noiseless, silent; **L~schrift** f phonetics pl; **L~sprecher** m loudspeaker; ~**stark** adj vociferous; **L~stärke** f (RADIO) volume

lauwarm ['laʊvarm] adj (auch fig) lukewarm

Lavendel [la'vɛndəl] (-s, -) m lavender

Lawine [la'viːnə] f avalanche; ~**ngefahr** f danger of avalanches

lax [laks] adj lax

Lazarett [latsa'rɛt] (-(e)s, -e) nt (MIL) hospital, infirmary

leasen ['liːzən] vt to lease

Leben (-s, -) nt life

leben ['leːbən] vt, vi to live; ~**d** adj living; ~**dig** [le'bɛndɪç] adj living, alive; (lebhaft) lively; **L~digkeit** f liveliness

Lebens- zW: ~**art** f way of life; ~**erwartung** f life expectancy; **l~fähig** adj able to live; ~**freude** f zest for life; ~**gefahr** f: **in ~gefahr** dangerously ill; **l~gefährlich** adj dangerous; (Verletzung) critical; ~**haltungskosten** pl cost of living sg; ~**jahr** nt year of life; **l~länglich** adj (Strafe) for life; ~**lauf** m curriculum vitae; ~**mittel** pl food sg; ~**mittelgeschäft** nt grocer's (shop); ~**mittelvergiftung** f (MED) food poisoning; **l~müde** adj tired of life; ~**retter** m lifesaver; ~**standard** m standard of living; ~**unterhalt** m livelihood; ~**versicherung** f life insurance; ~**wandel** m way of life; ~**weise** f lifestyle, way of life; **l~wichtig** adj vital, essential; ~**zeichen** nt sign of life

Leber ['leːbər] (-, -n) f liver; ~**fleck** m mole; ~**tran** m cod-liver oil; ~**wurst** f liver sausage

Lebewesen nt creature

leb- ['leːp] zW: ~**haft** adj lively, vivacious; **L~kuchen** m gingerbread; ~**los** adj lifeless

Leck [lɛk] (-(e)s, -e) nt leak; **l~** adj leaky, leaking; **l~en** vi (Loch haben) to leak; (schlecken) to lick ♦ vt to lick

Spelling Reform: ▲ new spelling △ old spelling (to be phased out)

lecker ['lɛkər] *adj* delicious, tasty; **L~bissen** *m* dainty morsel

Leder ['le:dər] **(-s, -)** *nt* leather; **~hose** *f* lederhosen; **l~n** *adj* leather; **~waren** *pl* leather goods

ledig ['le:dɪç] *adj* single; **einer Sache** *gen* **~ sein** to be free of sth; **~lich** *adv* merely, solely

leer [le:r] *adj* empty; vacant; **~ machen** to empty; **~ stehend** empty; **L~e (-)** *f* emptiness; **~en** *vt, vr* to empty; **L~gewicht** *nt* weight when empty; **L~gut** *nt* empties *pl*; **L~lauf** *m* neutral; **L~ung** *f* emptying; *(Post)* collection

legal [le'ga:l] *adj* legal, lawful; **~i'sieren** *vt* to legalize

legen ['le:gən] *vt* to lay, to put, to place; *(Ei)* to lay ♦ *vr* to lie down; *(fig)* to subside

Legende [le'gɛndə] *f* legend

leger [le'ʒe:r] *adj* casual

Legierung [le'gi:rʊŋ] *f* alloy

Legislative [legɪsla'ti:və] *f* legislature

legitim [legi'ti:m] *adj* legitimate

legitimieren [legiti'mi:rən] *vt* to legitimate ♦ *vr* to prove one's identity

Lehm [le:m] **(-(e)s, -e)** *m* loam; **l~ig** *adj* loamy

Lehne ['le:nə] *f* arm; back; **l~n** *vt, vr* to lean

Lehnstuhl *m* armchair

Lehr- *zW:* **~amt** *nt* teaching profession; **~buch** *nt* textbook

Lehre ['le:rə] *f* teaching, doctrine; *(beruflich)* apprenticeship; *(moralisch)* lesson; *(TECH)* gauge; **l~n** *vt* to teach

Lehrer(in) **(-s, -)** *m(f)* teacher; **~zimmer** *nt* staff room

Lehr- *zW:* **~gang** *m* course; **~jahre** *pl* apprenticeship *sg;* **~kraft** *f (förmlich)* teacher; **~ling** *m* apprentice; **~plan** *m* syllabus; **l~reich** *adj* instructive; **~stelle** *f* apprenticeship; **~zeit** *f* apprenticeship

Leib [laɪp] **(-(e)s, -er)** *m* body; **halt ihn mir vom ~!** keep him away from me!; **l~haftig** *adj* personified; *(Teufel)* incarnate; **l~lich** *adj* bodily; *(Vater etc)* own; **~schmerzen** *pl* stomach pains; **~wache** *f* bodyguard

Leiche ['laɪçə] *f* corpse; **~nhalle** *f* mortuary;

~nwagen *m* hearse

Leichnam ['laɪçna:m] **(-(e)s, -e)** *m* corpse

leicht [laɪçt] *adj* light; *(einfach)* easy; **jdm ~ fallen** to be easy for sb; **es sich** *dat* **~ machen** to make things easy for o.s.; **L~athletik** *f* athletics *sg;* **~fertig** *adj* frivolous; **~gläubig** *adj* gullible, credulous; **~hin** *adv* lightly; **L~igkeit** *f* easiness; **mit L~igkeit** with ease; **L~sinn** *m* carelessness; **~sinnig** *adj* careless

Leid [laɪt] **(-(e)s)** *nt* grief, sorrow; **es tut mir/ihm ~** I am/he is sorry; **er/das tut mir ~** I am sorry for him/it; **l~** *adj:* **etw l~ haben** *od* **sein** to be tired of sth; **l~en** *(unreg)* *vt* to suffer; *(erlauben)* to permit ♦ *vi* to suffer; **jdn/etw nicht l~en können** not to be able to stand sb/sth; **~en** ['laɪdən] **(-s, -)** *nt* suffering; *(Krankheit)* complaint; **~enschaft** *f* passion; **l~enschaftlich** *adj* passionate

leider ['laɪdər] *adv* unfortunately; **ja, ~** yes, I'm afraid so; **~ nicht** I'm afraid not

leidig ['laɪdɪç] *adj* worrying, troublesome

leidlich ['laɪtlɪç] *adj* tolerable ♦ *adv* tolerably

Leid- *zW:* **~tragende(r)** *f(m)* bereaved; *(Benachteiligter)* one who suffers; **~wesen** *nt:* **zu jds ~wesen** to sb's disappointment

Leier ['laɪər] **(-, -n)** *f* lyre; *(fig)* old story; **~kasten** *m* barrel organ

Leihbibliothek *f* lending library

Leihbücherei *f* lending library

leihen ['laɪən] *(unreg)* *vt* to lend; **sich** *dat* **etw ~** to borrow sth

Leih- *zW:* **~gebühr** *f* hire charge; **~haus** *nt* pawnshop; **~wagen** *m* hired car

Leim [laɪm] **(-(e)s, -e)** *m* glue; **l~en** *vt* to glue

Leine ['laɪnə] *f* line, cord; *(Hundeleine)* leash, lead

Leinen *nt* linen; **l~** *adj* linen

Leinwand *f (KUNST)* canvas; *(CINE)* screen

leise ['laɪzə] *adj* quiet; *(sanft)* soft, gentle

Leiste ['laɪstə] *f* ledge; *(Zierleiste)* strip; *(ANAT)* groin

leisten ['laɪstən] *vt (Arbeit)* to do; *(Gesellschaft)* to keep; *(Ersatz)* to supply; *(vollbringen)* to achieve; **sich** *dat* **etw ~**

können to be able to afford sth
Leistung f performance; (*gute*) achievement; **~sdruck** m pressure; **l~sfähig** adj efficient
Leitartikel m leading article
Leitbild nt model
leiten ['laɪtən] vt to lead; (*Firma*) to manage; (*in eine Richtung*) to direct; (*ELEK*) to conduct
Leiter¹ ['laɪtər] (**-s, -**) m leader, head; (*ELEK*) conductor
Leiter² ['laɪtər] (**-, -n**) f ladder
Leitfaden m guide
Leitplanke f crash barrier
Leitung f (*Führung*) direction; (*CINE, THEAT etc*) production; (*von Firma*) management; directors pl; (*Wasserleitung*) pipe; (*Kabel*) cable; **eine lange ~ haben** to be slow on the uptake
Leitungs- zW: **~draht** m wire; **~rohr** nt pipe; **~wasser** nt tap water
Lektion [lɛktsiˈoːn] f lesson
Lektüre [lɛkˈtyːrə] f (*Lesen*) reading; (*Lesestoff*) reading matter
Lende ['lɛndə] f loin; **~nstück** nt fillet
lenk- ['lɛŋk] zW: **~bar** adj (*Fahrzeug*) steerable; (*Kind*) manageable; **~en** vt to steer; (*Kind*) to guide; (*Blick, Aufmerksamkeit*): **~en (auf +akk)** to direct (at); **L~rad** nt steering wheel; **L~radschloss** ▲ nt steering (wheel) lock; **L~stange** f handlebars pl; **L~ung** f steering
Lepra ['leːpra] (**-**) f leprosy
Lerche ['lɛrçə] f lark
lernbegierig adj eager to learn
lernen ['lɛrnən] vt to learn
lesbar ['leːsbaːr] adj legible
Lesbierin ['lɛsbiərɪn] f lesbian
lesbisch ['lɛsbɪʃ] adj lesbian
Lese ['leːzə] f (*Wein*) harvest
Lesebrille f reading glasses
Lesebuch nt reading book, reader
lesen (*unreg*) vt, vi to read; (*ernten*) to gather, to pick
Leser(in) (**-s, -**) m(f) reader; **~brief** m reader's letter; **l~lich** adj legible
Lesezeichen nt bookmark

Lesung ['leːzʊŋ] f (*PARL*) reading
letzte(r, s) ['lɛtstə(r, s)] adj last; (*neueste*) latest; **zum ~n Mal** for the last time; **~ns** adv lately; **~re(r, s)** adj latter
Leuchte ['lɔʏçtə] f lamp, light; **l~n** vi to shine, to gleam; **~r (-s, -)** m candlestick
Leucht- zW: **~farbe** f fluorescent colour; **~rakete** f flare; **~reklame** f neon sign; **~röhre** f strip light; **~turm** m lighthouse
leugnen ['lɔʏɡnən] vt to deny
Leukämie [lɔʏkɛˈmiː] f leukaemia
Leukoplast [lɔʏkoˈplast] (®; **-(e)s, -e**) nt Elastoplast ®
Leumund ['lɔʏmʊnt] (**-(e)s, -e**) m reputation
Leumundszeugnis nt character reference
Leute ['lɔʏtə] pl people pl
Leutnant ['lɔʏtnant] (**-s, -s** od **-e**) m lieutenant
leutselig ['lɔʏtzeːlɪç] adj amiable
Lexikon ['lɛksikɔn] (**-s, Lexiken** od **Lexika**) nt encyclop(a)edia
Libelle [liˈbɛlə] f dragonfly; (*TECH*) spirit level
liberal [libeˈraːl] adj liberal; **L~e(r)** f(m) liberal
Licht [lɪçt] (**-(e)s, -er**) nt light; **~bild** nt photograph; (*Dia*) slide; **~blick** m cheering prospect; **l~empfindlich** adj sensitive to light; **l~en** vt to clear; (*Anker*) to weigh ♦ vr to clear up; (*Haar*) to thin; **l~erloh** adv: **l~erloh brennen** to be ablaze; **~hupe** f flashing of headlights; **~jahr** nt light year; **~maschine** f dynamo; **~schalter** m light switch; **~schutzfaktor** m protection factor
Lichtung f clearing, glade
Lid [liːt] (**-(e)s, -er**) nt eyelid; **~schatten** m eyeshadow
lieb [liːp] adj dear; **das ist ~ von dir** that's kind of you; **~ gewinnen** to get fond of; **~ haben** to be fond of; **~äugeln** ['liːbɔʏɡəln] vi insep: **mit etw ~äugeln** to have one's eye on sth; **mit dem Gedanken ~äugeln, etw zu tun** to toy with the idea of doing sth
Liebe ['liːbə] f love; **l~bedürftig** adj: **l~bedürftig sein** to need love; **l~n** vt to love; to like

liebens- *zW:* **~wert** *adj* loveable; **~würdig** *adj* kind; **~würdigerweise** *adv* kindly; **L~würdigkeit** *f* kindness

lieber ['liːbər] *adv* rather, preferably; **ich gehe ~ nicht** I'd rather not go; *siehe auch* **gern; lieb**

Liebes- *zW:* **~brief** *m* love letter; **~kummer** *m:* **~kummer haben** to be lovesick; **~paar** *nt* courting couple, lovers *pl*

liebevoll *adj* loving

lieb- [liːp] *zW:* **~gewinnen** △ (*unreg*) *vt siehe* **lieb;** **~haben** △ (*unreg*) *vt siehe* **lieb;** **L~haber** (**-s, -**) *m* lover; **L~habe'rei** *f* hobby; **~kosen** ['liːpkoːzən] *vt insep* to caress; **~lich** *adj* lovely, charming; **L~ling** *m* darling; **L~lings-** *in zW* favourite; **~los** *adj* unloving; **L~schaft** *f* love affair

Lied [liːt] **(-(e)s, -er)** *nt* song; (*REL*) hymn; **~erbuch** ['liːdər-] *nt* songbook; hymn book

liederlich ['liːdərlɪç] *adj* slovenly; (*Lebenswandel*) loose, immoral; **L~keit** *f* slovenliness; immorality

lief *etc* [liːf] *vb siehe* **laufen**

Lieferant [liːfəˈrant] *m* supplier

Lieferbedingungen *pl* terms of delivery

liefern ['liːfərn] *vt* to deliver; (*versorgen mit*) to supply; (*Beweis*) to produce

Liefer- *zW:* **~schein** *m* delivery note; **~termin** *m* delivery date; **~ung** *f* delivery; supply; **~wagen** *m* van; **~zeit** *f* delivery period

Liege ['liːgə] *f* bed

liegen ['liːgən] (*unreg*) *vi* to lie; (*sich befinden*) to be; **mir liegt nichts/viel daran** it doesn't matter to me/it matters a lot to me; **es liegt bei Ihnen, ob ...** it's up to you whether ...; **Sprachen ~ mir nicht** languages are not my line; **woran liegt es?** what's the cause?; **~ bleiben** (*im Bett*) to stay in bed; (*nicht aufstehen*) to stay lying down; (*vergessen werden*) to be left (behind); **~ lassen** (*vergessen*) to leave behind

Liege- *zW:* **~sitz** *m* (*AUT*) reclining seat; **~stuhl** *m* deck chair; **~wagen** *m* (*EISENB*) couchette

Lift [lɪft] **(-(e)s, -e** *od* **-s)** *m* lift

Likör [liˈkøːr] **(-s, -e)** *m* liqueur

lila ['liːla] *adj inv* purple, lilac; **L~ (-s, -s)** *nt* (*Farbe*) purple, lilac

Lilie ['liːliə] *f* lily

Limonade [limoˈnaːdə] *f* lemonade

Limone [liˈmoːnə] *f* lime

Linde ['lɪndə] *f* lime tree, linden

lindern ['lɪndərn] *vt* to alleviate, to soothe; **Linderung** *f* alleviation

Lineal [lineˈaːl] **(-s, -e)** *nt* ruler

Linie ['liːniə] *f* line

Linien- *zW:* **~blatt** *nt* ruled sheet; **~flug** *m* scheduled flight; **~richter** *m* linesman

linieren [liˈniːrən] *vt* to line

Linke ['lɪŋkə] *f* left side; left hand; (*POL*) left

linkisch *adj* awkward, gauche

links [lɪŋks] *adv* left; **to** *od* **on the left;** **~ von mir** on *od* to my left; **L~händer(in)** **(-s, -)** *m(f)* left-handed person; **L~kurve** *f* left-hand bend; **L~verkehr** *m* driving on the left

Linoleum [liˈnoːleʊm] **(-s)** *nt* lino(leum)

Linse ['lɪnzə] *f* lentil; (*optisch*) lens *sg*

Lippe ['lɪpə] *f* lip; **~nstift** *m* lipstick

lispeln ['lɪspəln] *vi* to lisp

Lissabon ['lɪsabɔn] *nt* Lisbon

List [lɪst] **(-, -en)** *f* cunning; trick, ruse

Liste ['lɪstə] *f* list

listig ['lɪstɪç] *adj* cunning, sly

Liter ['liːtər] **(-s, -)** *nt od m* litre

literarisch [liteˈraːrɪʃ] *adj* literary

Literatur [literaˈtuːr] *f* literature

Litfaßsäule ['lɪtfasɔʏlə] *f* advertising pillar

Liturgie [lɪturˈgiː] *f* liturgy

liturgisch [liˈturɡɪʃ] *adj* liturgical

Litze ['lɪtsə] *f* braid; (*ELEK*) flex

Lizenz [liˈtsɛnts] *f* licence

Lkw [ɛlkaːˈveː] **(-(s), -(s))** *m abk =* **Lastkraftwagen**

Lob [loːp] **(-(e)s)** *nt* praise

Lobby ['lɔbi] *f* lobby

loben ['loːbən] *vt* to praise; **~swert** *adj* praiseworthy

löblich ['løːplɪç] *adj* praiseworthy, laudable

Loch [lɔx] **(-(e)s, ¨er)** *nt* hole; **l~en** *vt* to punch holes in; **~er (-s, -)** *m* punch

löcherig ['lœçərɪç] *adj* full of holes

Lochkarte *f* punch card

Lochstreifen *m* punch tape

Locke ['lɔkə] *f* lock, curl; **l~n** *vt* to entice; (*Haare*) to curl; **~nwickler (-s, -)** *m* curler

locker ['lɔkər] *adj* loose; **~lassen** (*unreg*) *vi*: **nicht ~lassen** not to let up; **~n** *vt* to loosen

lockig ['lɔkɪç] *adj* curly

lodern ['lo:dərn] *vi* to blaze

Löffel ['lœfəl] **(-s, -)** *m* spoon

löffeln *vt* to spoon

Loge ['lo:ʒə] *f* (*THEAT*) box; (*Freimaurer*) (masonic) lodge; (*Pförtnerloge*) office

Logik ['lo:gɪk] *f* logic

logisch ['lo:gɪʃ] *adj* logical

Logopäde [logo'pɛ:də] **(-n, -n)** *m* speech therapist

Lohn [lo:n] **(-(e)s, ⁼e)** *m* reward; (*Arbeitslohn*) pay, wages *pl*; **~büro** *nt* wages office; **~empfänger** *m* wage earner

lohnen ['lo:nən] *vr unpers* to be worth it ♦ *vt*: (**jdm etw) ~** to reward (sb for sth); **~d** *adj* worthwhile

Lohn- *zW*: **~erhöhung** *f* pay rise; **~steuer** *f* income tax; **~steuerkarte** *f* (income) tax card; **~streifen** *m* pay slip; **~tüte** *f* pay packet

Lokal [lo'ka:l] **(-(e)s, -e)** *nt* pub(lic house)

lokal *adj* local; **~isieren** *vt* to localize

Lokomotive [lokomo'ti:və] *f* locomotive

Lokomotivführer *m* engine driver

Lorbeer ['lɔrbe:r] **(-s, -en)** *m* (*auch fig*) laurel; **~blatt** *nt* (*KOCH*) bay leaf

Los [lo:s] **(-es, -e)** *nt* (*Schicksal*) lot, fate; (*Lotterielos*) lottery ticket

los [lo:s] *adj* (*locker*) loose; **~!** go on!; **etw ~ sein** to be rid of sth; **was ist ~?** what's the matter?; **dort ist nichts/viel ~** there's nothing/a lot going on there; **~binden** (*unreg*) *vt* to untie

Löschblatt ['lœʃblat] *nt* sheet of blotting paper

löschen ['lœʃən] *vt* (*Feuer, Licht*) to put out, to extinguish; (*Durst*) to quench; (*COMM*) to cancel; (*COMPUT*) to delete; (*Tonband*) to erase; (*Fracht*) to unload ♦ *vi* (*Feuerwehr*) to

put out a fire; (*Tinte*) to blot

Lösch- *zW*: **~fahrzeug** *nt* fire engine; fire boat; **~gerät** *nt* fire extinguisher; **~papier** *nt* blotting paper

lose ['lo:zə] *adj* loose

Lösegeld *nt* ransom

losen ['lo:zən] *vi* to draw lots

lösen ['lø:zən] *vt* to loosen; (*Rätsel etc*) to solve; (*Verlobung*) to call off; (*CHEM*) to dissolve; (*Partnerschaft*) to break up; (*Fahrkarte*) to buy ♦ *vr* (*aufgehen*) to come loose; (*Zucker etc*) to dissolve; (*Problem, Schwierigkeit*) to (re)solve itself

los- *zW*: **~fahren** (*unreg*) *vi* to leave; **~gehen** *vi* to set out; (*anfangen*) to start; (*Bombe*) to go off; **auf jdn ~gehen** to go for sb; **~kaufen** *vt* (*Gefangene, Geißeln*) to pay ransom for; **~kommen** (*unreg*) *vi*: **von etw ~kommen** to get away from sth; **~lassen** (*unreg*) *vt* (*Seil*) to let go of; (*Schimpfe*) to let loose; **~laufen** (*unreg*) *vi* to run off

löslich ['lø:slɪç] *adj* soluble; **L~keit** *f* solubility

los- *zW*: **~lösen** *vt*: **(sich) ~lösen** to free (o.s.); **~machen** *vt* to loosen; (*Boot*) to unmoor *vr* to get away; **~schrauben** *vt* to unscrew

Losung ['lo:zʊŋ] *f* watchword, slogan

Lösung ['lø:zʊŋ] *f* (*Lockermachen*) loosening; (*eines Rätsels, CHEM*) solution; **~smittel** *nt* solvent

los- *zW*: **~werden** (*unreg*) *vt* to get rid of; **~ziehen** (*unreg*) (*umg*) *vi* (*sich aufmachen*) to set off

Lot [lo:t] **(-(e)s, -e)** *nt* plumbline; **im ~** vertical; (*fig*) on an even keel

löten ['lø:tən] *vt* to solder

Lothringen ['lo:trɪŋən] **(-s)** *nt* Lorraine

Lotse ['lo:tsə] **(-n, -n)** *m* pilot; (*AVIAT*) air traffic controller; **l~n** *vt* to pilot; (*umg*) to lure

Lotterie [lɔtə'ri:] *f* lottery

Lotto ['lɔto] **(-s, -s)** *nt* national lottery; **~zahlen** *pl* winning lottery numbers

Löwe ['lø:və] **(-n, -n)** *m* lion; (*ASTROL*) Leo; **~nanteil** *m* lion's share; **~nzahn** *m*

Spelling Reform: ▲ *new spelling* △ *old spelling (to be phased out)*

dandelion

loyal [loaˈjaːl] *adj* loyal; **L~ität** *f* loyalty

Luchs [lʊks] **(-es, -e)** *m* lynx

Lücke [ˈlykə] *f* gap

Lücken- *zW:* **~büßer (-s, -)** *m* stopgap;
l~haft *adj* full of gaps; *(Versorgung, Vorräte etc)* inadequate; **l~los** *adj* complete

Luft [lʊft] **(-, -ͤe)** *f* air; *(Atem)* breath; **in der ~ liegen** to be in the air; **jdn wie ~ behandeln** to ignore sb; **~angriff** *m* air raid; **~ballon** *m* balloon; **~blase** *f* air bubble; **l~dicht** *adj* airtight; **~druck** *m* atmospheric pressure

lüften [ˈlʏftən] *vt* to air; *(Hut)* to lift, to raise
♦ *vi* to let some air in

Luft- *zW:* **~fahrt** *f* aviation; **~fracht** *f* air freight; **l~gekühlt** *adj* air-cooled;
~gewehr *nt* air rifle, airgun; **l~ig** *adj* *(Ort)* breezy; *(Raum)* airy; *(Kleider)* summery;
~kissenfahrzeug *nt* hovercraft; **~kurort** *m* health resort; **l~leer** *adj:* **l~leerer Raum** vacuum; **~linie** *f*: **in der ~linie** as the crow flies; **~loch** *nt* air hole; *(AVIAT)* air pocket;
~matratze *f* Lilo ® *(BRIT)*, air mattress;
~pirat *m* hijacker; **~post** *f* airmail;
~pumpe *f* air pump; **~röhre** *f* *(ANAT)* windpipe; **~schlange** *f* streamer;
~schutzkeller *m* air-raid shelter;
~verkehr *m* air traffic; **~verschmutzung** *f* air pollution; **~waffe** *f* air force; **~zug** *m* draught

Lüge [ˈlyːgə] *f* lie; **jdn/etw ~n strafen** to give the lie to sb/sth; **l~n** *(unreg)* *vi* to lie

Lügner(in) **(-s, -)** *m(f)* liar

Luke [ˈluːkə] *f* dormer window; hatch

Lump [lʊmp] **(-en, -en)** *m* scamp, rascal

Lumpen [ˈlʊmpən] **(-s, -)** *m* rag

lumpen [ˈlʊmpən] *vi:* **sich nicht ~ lassen** not to be mean

lumpig [ˈlʊmpɪç] *adj* shabby

Lupe [ˈluːpə] *f* magnifying glass; **unter die ~ nehmen** *(fig)* to scrutinize

Lust [lʊst] **(-, -ͤe)** *f* joy, delight; *(Neigung)* desire; **~ haben zu** *od* **auf etw** *akk* / **etw zu tun** to feel like sth/doing sth

lüstern [ˈlʏstərn] *adj* lustful, lecherous

lustig [ˈlʊstɪç] *adj* *(komisch)* amusing, funny;

(fröhlich) cheerful

Lust- *zW:* **l~los** *adj* unenthusiastic; **~mord** *m* sex(ual) murder; **~spiel** *nt* comedy

lutschen [ˈlʊtʃən] *vt, vi* to suck; **am Daumen ~** to suck one's thumb

Lutscher **(-s, -)** *m* lollipop

luxuriös [lʊksuriˈøːs] *adj* luxurious

Luxus [ˈlʊksʊs] **(-)** *m* luxury; **~artikel** *pl* luxury goods; **~hotel** *nt* luxury hotel

Luzern [luˈtsɛrn] **(-s)** *nt* Lucerne

Lymphe [ˈlʏmfə] *f* lymph

lynchen [ˈlʏnçən] *vt* to lynch

Lyrik [ˈlyːrɪk] *f* lyric poetry; **~er (-s, -)** *m* lyric poet

lyrisch [ˈlyːrɪʃ] *adj* lyrical

M, m

m *abk* = **Meter**

Machart *f* make

machbar *adj* feasible

SCHLÜSSELWORT

machen [ˈmaxən] *vt* **1** to do; *(herstellen, zubereiten)* to make; **was machst du da?** what are you doing (there)?; **das ist nicht zu machen** that can't be done; **das Radio leiser machen** to turn the radio down; **aus Holz gemacht** made of wood

2 *(verursachen, bewirken)* to make; **jdm Angst machen** to make sb afraid; **das macht die Kälte** it's the cold that does that

3 *(ausmachen)* to matter; **das macht nichts** that doesn't matter; **die Kälte macht mir nichts** I don't mind the cold

4 *(kosten, ergeben)* to be; **3 und 5 macht 8** 3 and 5 is *od* are 8; **was** *od* **wie viel macht das?** how much does that make?

5: was macht die Arbeit? how's the work going?; **was macht dein Bruder?** how is your brother doing?; **das Auto machen lassen** to have the car done; **machs gut!** take care!; *(viel Glück)* good luck!

♦ *vi:* **mach schnell!** hurry up!; **Schluss machen** to finish (off); **mach schon!** come on!; **das macht müde** it makes you tired; **in etw** *dat* **machen** to be *od* deal in sth ♦ *vr* to come along (nicely); **sich an etw** *akk* **machen** to set about sth; **sich verständlich machen** to make o.s. understood; **sich** *dat* **viel aus jdm/etw machen** to like sb/sth

Macht [maxt] (-, ⸚e) *f* power; ~**haber** (-s, -) *m* ruler

mächtig ['mɛçtɪç] *adj* powerful, mighty; (*umg: ungeheuer*) enormous

Macht- *zW:* **m~los** *adj* powerless; ~**probe** *f* trial of strength; ~**wort** *nt:* **ein ~wort sprechen** to exercise one's authority

Mädchen ['mɛ:tçən] *nt* girl, **m~haft** *adj* girlish; ~**name** *m* maiden name

Made ['ma:də] *f* maggot

madig ['ma:dɪç] *adj* maggoty; **jdm etw ~ machen** to spoil sth for sb

mag *etc* [ma:k] *vb siehe* **mögen**

Magazin [maga'tsi:n] (-s, -e) *nt* magazine

Magen ['ma:gən] (-s, - *od* ⸚) *m* stomach; ~**geschwür** *nt* (*MED*) stomach ulcer; ~**schmerzen** *pl* stomachache *sg*

mager ['ma:gər] *adj* lean; (*dünn*) thin; **M~keit** *f* leanness; thinness

Magie [ma'gi:] *f* magic

magisch ['ma:gɪʃ] *adj* magical

Magnet [ma'gne:t] (-s *od* -en, -en) *m* magnet; **m~isch** *adj* magnetic; ~**nadel** *f* magnetic needle

mähen ['mɛ:ən] *vt, vi* to mow

Mahl [ma:l] (-(e)s, -e) *nt* meal; **m~en** (*unreg*) *vt* to grind; ~**zeit** *f* meal ♦ *excl* enjoy your meal

Mahnbrief *m* reminder

Mähne ['mɛ:nə] *f* mane

mahn- ['ma:n] *zW:* ~**en** *vt* to remind; (*warnen*) to warn; (*wegen Schuld*) to demand payment from; **M~mal** *nt* memorial; **M~ung** *f* reminder; admonition, warning

Mai [mai] (-(e)s, -e) *m* May; ~**glöckchen** *nt* lily of the valley

Mailand ['mailant] *nt* Milan

mailändisch *adj* Milanese

Mais [mais] (-es, -e) *m* maize, corn (*US*); ~**kolben** *m* corncob; ~**mehl** *nt* (*KOCH*) corn meal

Majestät [majes'tɛ:t] *f* majesty; **m~isch** *adj* majestic

Majonäse ▲ [majo'nɛ:zə] *f* mayonnaise

Major [ma'jo:r] (-s, -e) *m* (*MIL*) major; (*AVIAT*) squadron leader

Majoran [majo'ra:n] (-s, -e) *m* marjoram

makaber [ma'ka:bər] *adj* macabre

Makel ['ma:kəl] (-s, -) *m* blemish; (*moralisch*) stain; **m~los** *adj* immaculate, spotless

mäkeln ['mɛ:kəln] *vi* to find fault

Makler(in) ['ma:klər(ın)] (-s, -) *m(f)* broker

Makrele [ma'kre:lə] *f* mackerel

Mal [ma:l] (-(e)s, -e) *nt* mark, sign; (*Zeitpunkt*) time; **ein für alle ~** once and for all; **m~** *adv* times; (*umg*) *siehe* **einmal** ♦ *suffix:* -**m~** -times

malen *vt, vi* to paint

Maler (-s, -) *m* painter; **Male'rei** *f* painting; **m~isch** *adj* picturesque

Malkasten *m* paintbox

Mallorca [ma'jɔrka, ma'lɔrka] (-s) *nt* Majorca

malnehmen (*unreg*) *vt, vi* to multiply

Malz [malts] (-es) *nt* malt; ~**bier** *nt* (*KOCH*) malt beer; ~**bonbon** *nt* cough drop; ~**kaffee** *m* malt coffee

Mama ['mama:] (-, -s) (*umg*) *f* mum(my) (*BRIT*), mom(my) (*US*)

Mami ['mami] (-, -s) = **Mama**

Mammut ['mamʊt] (-s, -e *od* -s) *nt* mammoth

man [man] *pron* one, you; ~ **sagt, ...** they *od* people say ...; **wie schreibt ~ das?** how do you write it?, how is it written?

manch [manç] (*unver*) *pron* many a

manche(r, s) ['mançə(r, s)] *adj* many a; (*pl: einige*) a number of ♦ *pron* some

mancherlei [mançər'lai] *adj inv* various ♦ *pron inv* a variety of things

manchmal *adv* sometimes

Mandant(in) [man'dant(ın)] *m(f)* (*JUR*) client

Mandarine [manda'ri:nə] *f* mandarin, tangerine

Mandat [man'da:t] (-(e)s, -e) nt mandate

Mandel ['mandəl] (-, -n) f almond; (*ANAT*) tonsil; ~**entzündung** f (*MED*) tonsillitis

Manege [ma'ne:ʒə] f ring, arena

Mangel ['maŋəl] (-s, ˵) m lack; (*Knappheit*) shortage; (*Fehler*) defect, fault; ~ **an** +*dat* shortage of; ~**erscheinung** f deficiency symptom; **m~haft** *adj* poor; (*fehlerhaft*) defective, faulty; **m~n** *vi unpers*: **es m~t jdm an etw** *dat* sb lacks sth ♦ *vt* (*Wäsche*) to mangle

mangels *präp* +*gen* for lack of

Manie [ma'ni:] f mania

Manier [ma'ni:r] (-) f manner; style; (*pej*) mannerism; ~**en** *pl* (*Umgangsformen*) manners; **m~lich** *adj* well-mannered

Manifest [mani'fest] (-es, -e) nt manifesto

Maniküre [mani'ky:rə] f manicure

manipulieren [manipu'li:rən] *vt* to manipulate

Manko ['maŋko] (-s, -s) nt deficiency; (*COMM*) deficit

Mann [man] (-(e)s, ˵er) m man; (*Ehemann*) husband; (*NAUT*) hand; **seinen ~ stehen** to hold one's own

Männchen ['mɛnçən] nt little man; (*Tier*) male

Mannequin [manə'kɛ̃:] (-s, -s) nt fashion model

männlich ['mɛnlɪç] *adj* (*BIOL*) male; (*fig, GRAM*) masculine

Mannschaft f (*SPORT, fig*) team; (*AVIAT, NAUT*) crew; (*MIL*) other ranks *pl*

Manöver [ma'nø:vər] (-s, -) nt manoeuvre

manövrieren [manø'vri:rən] *vt, vi* to manoeuvre

Mansarde [man'zardə] f attic

Manschette [man'ʃetə] f cuff; (*TECH*) collar; sleeve; ~**nknopf** m cufflink

Mantel ['mantəl] (-s, ˵) m coat; (*TECH*) casing, jacket

Manuskript [manu'skrɪpt] (-(e)s, -e) nt manuscript

Mappe ['mapə] f briefcase; (*Aktenmappe*) folder

Märchen ['mɛːrçən] nt fairy tale; **m~haft** *adj* fabulous; ~**prinz** m Prince Charming

Margarine [marga'ri:nə] f margarine

Margerite [margə'ri:tə] f (*BOT*) marguerite

Marienkäfer [ma'ri:ənke:fər] m ladybird

Marine [ma'ri:nə] f navy; **m~blau** *adj* navy blue

marinieren [mari'ni:rən] *vt* to marinate

Marionette [mario'netə] f puppet

Mark[1] [mark] (-, -) f (*Münze*) mark

Mark[2] [mark] (-(e)s) nt (*Knochenmark*) marrow; **jdm durch ~ und Bein gehen** to go right through sb

markant [mar'kant] *adj* striking

Marke ['markə] f mark; (*Warensorte*) brand; (*Fabrikat*) make; (*Rabattmarke, Briefmarke*) stamp; (*Essenmarke*) ticket; (*aus Metall etc*) token, disc

Markenartikel m proprietary article

markieren [mar'ki:rən] *vt* to mark; (*umg*) to act ♦ *vi* (*umg*) to act it

Markierung f marking

Markise [mar'ki:zə] f awning

Markstück nt one-mark piece

Markt [markt] (-(e)s, ˵e) m market; ~**forschung** f market research; ~**lücke** f (*COMM*) opening, gap in the market; ~**platz** m market place; **m~üblich** *adj* (*Preise, Mieten*) standard, usual; ~**wert** m (*COMM*) market value; ~**wirtschaft** f market economy

Marmelade [marmə'la:də] f jam

Marmor ['marmor] (-s, -e) m marble; **m~ieren** [-'ri:rən] *vt* to marble

Marokko [ma'rɔko] (-s) nt Morocco

Marone [ma'ro:nə] (-, -n *od* **Maroni**) f chestnut

Marotte [ma'rɔtə] f fad, quirk

Marsch[1] [marʃ] (-, -en) f marsh

Marsch[2] [marʃ] (-(e)s, ˵e) m march ♦ *excl* march!; ~**befehl** m marching orders *pl*; **m~bereit** *adj* ready to move; **m~ieren** [mar'ʃi:rən] *vi* to march

Märtyrer(in) ['mɛrtyrər(ɪn)] (-s, -) m(f) martyr

März [mɛrts] (-(es), -e) m March

Marzipan [martsi'pa:n] (-s, -e) nt marzipan

Masche ['maʃə] f mesh; (*Strickmasche*) stitch; **das ist die neueste ~** that's the

latest thing; **~ndraht** *m* wire mesh;
m~nfest *adj* run-resistant

Maschine [ma'ʃiːnə] *f* machine; (*Motor*)
engine; (*Schreibmaschine*) typewriter; **~
schreiben** to type; **m~ll** [maʃiˈnɛl] *adj*
machine(-); mechanical

Maschinen- *zW:* **~bauer** *m* mechanical
engineer; **~gewehr** *nt* machine gun;
~pistole *f* submachine gun; **~schaden** *m*
mechanical fault; **~schlosser** *m* fitter;
~schrift *f* typescript

Maschinist [maʃiˈnɪst] *m* engineer

Maser ['maːzər] (**-**, **-n**) *f* (*von Holz*) grain; **~n**
pl (*MED*) measles *sg*

Maske ['maskə] *f* mask; **~nball** *m* fancy-
dress ball

maskieren [mas'kiːrən] *vt* to mask;
(*verkleiden*) to dress up ♦ *vr* to disguise o.s.;
to dress up

Maskottchen [mas'kɔtçən] *nt* (lucky)
mascot

Maß¹ [maːs] (**-es**, **-e**) *nt* measure;
(*Mäßigung*) moderation; (*Grad*) degree,
extent; **~ halten** to exercise moderation

Maß² [maːs] (**-**, **-(e)**) *f* litre of beer

Massage [ma'saːʒə] *f* massage

Maßanzug *m* made-to-measure suit

Maßarbeit *f* (*fig*) neat piece of work

Masse ['masə] *f* mass

Maßeinheit *f* unit of measurement

Massen- *zW:* **~artikel** *m* mass-produced
article; **~grab** *nt* mass grave; **m~haft** *adj*
loads of; **~medien** *pl* mass media *pl*;
~veranstaltung *f* mass meeting;
m~weise *adv* on a large scale

Masseur [ma'søːr] *m* masseur; **~in** *f*
masseuse

maßgebend *adj* authoritative

maßhalten △ (*unreg*) *vi siehe* **Maß¹**

massieren [ma'siːrən] *vt* to massage; (*MIL*)
to mass

massig ['masɪç] *adj* massive; (*umg*) massive
amount of

mäßig ['mɛːsɪç] *adj* moderate; **~en**
['mɛːsɪɡən] *vt* to restrain, to moderate;
M~keit *f* moderation

Massiv (**-s**, **-e**) *nt* massif

massiv [ma'siːf] *adj* solid; (*fig*) heavy, rough

Maß- *zW:* **~krug** *m* tankard; **m~los** *adj*
extreme; **~nahme** *f* measure, step; **~stab**
m rule, measure; (*fig*) standard; (*GEOG*)
scale; **m~voll** *adj* moderate

Mast [mast] (**-(e)s**, **-e(n)**) *m* mast; (*ELEK*)
pylon

mästen ['mɛstən] *vt* to fatten

Material [materi'aːl] (**-s**, **-ien**) *nt* material(s);
~fehler *m* material defect; **~ismus** [-
'lɪsmʊs] *m* materialism; **m~istisch** [-'lɪstɪʃ]
adj materialistic

Materie [ma'teːriə] *f* matter, substance

materiell [materi'ɛl] *adj* material

Mathematik [matema'tiːk] *f* mathematics
sg; **~er(in)** [mate'maːtikər(ɪn)] (**-s**, **-**) *m(f)*
mathematician

mathematisch [mate'maːtɪʃ] *adj*
mathematical

Matjeshering ['matjəsheːrɪŋ] *m* (*KOCH*)
young herring

Matratze [ma'tratsə] *f* mattress

Matrixdrucker ['maːtrɪks-] *m* dot-matrix
printer

Matrose [ma'troːzə] (**-n**, **-n**) *m* sailor

Matsch [matʃ] (**-(e)s**) *m* mud;
(*Schneematsch*) slush; **m~ig** *adj* muddy;
slushy

matt [mat] *adj* weak; (*glanzlos*) dull; (*PHOT*)
matt; (*SCHACH*) mate

Matte ['matə] *f* mat

Mattscheibe *f* (*TV*) screen

Mauer ['mauər] (**-**, **-n**) *f* wall; **m~n** *vi* to
build; to lay bricks ♦ *vt* to build

Maul [maul] (**-(e)s**, **Mäuler**) *nt* mouth;
m~en (*umg*) *vi* to grumble; **~esel** *m* mule;
~korb *m* muzzle; **~sperre** *f* lockjaw;
~tasche *f* (*KOCH*) *pasta envelopes stuffed
and used in soup*; **~tier** *nt* mule; **~wurf** *m*
mole

Maurer ['maurər] (**-s**, **-**) *m* bricklayer

Maus [maus] (**-**, **Mäuse**) *f* (*auch COMPUT*)
mouse

Mause- ['mauzə] *zW:* **~falle** *f* mousetrap;
m~n *vi* to catch mice ♦ *vt* (*umg*) to pinch;
m~tot *adj* stone dead

Maut- ['maut] *zW:* **~gebühr** *f* toll (charge);

Spelling Reform: ▲ *new spelling* △ *old spelling (to be phased out)*

~straße f toll road

maximal [maksi'ma:l] adj maximum ♦ adv at most

Mayonnaise [majo'nɛːzə] f mayonnaise

Mechan- [me'çaːn] zW: **~ik** f mechanics sg; (Getriebe) mechanics pl; **~iker (-s, -)** m mechanic, engineer; **m~isch** adj mechanical; **~ismus** m mechanism

meckern ['mɛkərn] vi to bleat; (umg) to moan

Medaille [me'daljə] f medal

Medaillon [medal'jõː] **(-s, -s)** nt (Schmuck) locket

Medikament [medika'mɛnt] nt medicine

Meditation [meditatsi'oːn] f meditation

meditieren [medi'tiːrən] vi to meditate

Medizin [medi'tsiːn] **(-, -en)** f medicine; **m~isch** adj medical

Meer [meːr] **(-(e)s, -e)** nt sea; **~enge** f straits pl; **~esfrüchte** pl seafood sg; **~esspiegel** m sea level; **~rettich** m horseradish; **~schweinchen** nt guinea-pig

Mehl [meːl] **(-(e)s, -e)** nt flour; **m~ig** adj floury; **~schwitze** f (KOCH) roux; **~speise** f (KOCH) flummery

mehr [meːr] adj, adv more; **~deutig** adj ambiguous; **~ere** adj several; **~eres** pron several things; **~fach** adj multiple; (wiederholt) repeated; **M~fahrtenkarte** f multi-journey ticket; **M~heit** f majority; **~malig** adj repeated; **~mals** adv repeatedly; **~stimmig** adj for several voices; **~stimmig singen** to harmonize; **M~wertsteuer** f value added tax; **M~zahl** f majority; (GRAM) plural

Mehrzweck- in zW multipurpose

meiden ['maɪdən] (unreg) vt to avoid

Meile ['maɪlə] f mile; **~nstein** m milestone; **m~nweit** adj for miles

mein(e) [maɪn] adj my; **~e(r, s)** pron mine

Meineid ['maɪnʔaɪt] m perjury

meinen ['maɪnən] vi to think ♦ vt to think; (sagen) to say; (sagen wollen) to mean; **das will ich ~** I should think so

mein- zW: **~erseits** adv for my part; **~etwegen** adv (für mich) for my sake; (wegen mir) on my account; (von mir aus) as

far as I'm concerned; I don't care od mind; **~etwillen** adv: **um ~etwillen** for my sake, on my account

Meinung ['maɪnʊŋ] f opinion; **ganz meine ~** I quite agree; **jdm die ~ sagen** to give sb a piece of one's mind

Meinungs- zW: **~austausch** m exchange of views; **~umfrage** f opinion poll; **~verschiedenheit** f difference of opinion

Meise ['maɪzə] f tit(mouse)

Meißel ['maɪsəl] **(-s, -)** m chisel

meist [maɪst] adj most ♦ adv mostly; **am ~en** the most; **~ens** adv generally, usually

Meister ['maɪstər] **(-s, -)** m master; (SPORT) champion; **m~haft** adj masterly; **m~n** vt (Schwierigkeiten etc) to overcome, conquer; **~schaft** f mastery; (SPORT) championship; **~stück** nt masterpiece; **~werk** nt masterpiece

Melancholie [melaŋko'liː] f melancholy; **melancholisch** [melaŋ'koːlɪʃ] adj melancholy

Melde- ['mɛldə] zW: **~frist** f registration period; **m~n** vt to report ♦ vr to report; (SCH) to put one's hand up; (freiwillig) to volunteer; (auf etw, am Telefon) to answer; **sich m~n bei** to report to; to register with; **sich zu Wort m~n** to ask to speak; **~pflicht** f obligation to register with the police; **~schluss** ▲ m closing date; **~stelle** f registration office

Meldung ['mɛldʊŋ] f announcement; (Bericht) report

meliert [me'liːrt] adj (Haar) greying; (Wolle) flecked

melken ['mɛlkən] (unreg) vt to milk

Melodie [melo'diː] f melody, tune

melodisch [me'loːdɪʃ] adj melodious, tuneful

Melone [me'loːnə] f melon; (Hut) bowler (hat)

Membran [mɛm'braːn] **(-, -en)** f (TECH) diaphragm

Memoiren [memo'aːrən] pl memoirs

Menge ['mɛŋə] f quantity; (Menschenmenge) crowd; (große Anzahl) lot (of); **m~n** vt to mix ♦ vr: **sich m~n in** +akk to meddle

with; ~**nlehre** f (*MATH*) set theory;
~**nrabatt** m bulk discount

Mensch [mɛnʃ] (**-en, -en**) m human being,
man; person ♦ *excl* hey!; **kein ~** nobody

Menschen- *zW:* ~**affe** m (*ZOOL*) ape;
m~freundlich adj philanthropical;
~**kenner** m judge of human nature;
m~leer adj deserted; **m~möglich** adj
humanly possible; ~**rechte** pl human
rights; **m~unwürdig** adj beneath human
dignity; ~**verstand** m: **gesunder**
~**verstand** common sense

Mensch- *zW:* ~**heit** f humanity, mankind;
m~lich adj human; (*human*) humane;
~**lichkeit** f humanity

Menstruation [mɛnstruatsi'oːn] f
menstruation

Mentalität [mɛntaliˈtɛːt] f mentality

Menü [meˈnyː] (**-s, -s**) nt (*auch COMPUT*)
menu

Merk- [ˈmɛrk] *zW:* ~**blatt** nt instruction
sheet *od* leaflet; **m~en** vt to notice; **sich**
dat **etw m~en** to remember sth; **m~lich**
adj noticeable; ~**mal** nt sign, characteristic;
m~würdig adj odd

messbar ▲ [ˈmɛsbaːr] adj measurable

Messbecher ▲ m measuring jug

Messe [ˈmɛsə] f fair; (*ECCL*) mass; ~**gelände**
nt exhibition centre; ~**halle** f pavilion at a
fair

messen (*unreg*) vt to measure ♦ vr to
compete

Messer (**-s, -**) nt knife; ~**spitze** f knife
point; (*in Rezept*) pinch

Messestand m stall at a fair

Messgerät ▲ nt measuring device, gauge

Messing [ˈmɛsɪŋ] (**-s**) nt brass

Metall [meˈtal] (**-s, -e**) nt metal; **m~isch** adj
metallic

Meter [ˈmeːtər] (**-s, -**) nt od m metre; ~**maß**
nt tape measure

Methode [meˈtoːdə] f method;
methodisch adj methodical

Metropole [metroˈpoːlə] f metropolis

Metzger [ˈmɛtsgər] (**-s, -**) m butcher; ~**ei**
[-ˈraɪ] f butcher's (shop)

Meute [ˈmɔʏtə] f pack; ~'**rei** f mutiny;

m~rn vi to mutiny

miauen [miˈaʊən] vi to miaow

mich [mɪç] (*akk von* **ich**) pron me; myself

Miene [ˈmiːnə] f look, expression

mies [miːs] (*umg*) adj lousy

Miet- [ˈmiːt] *zW:* ~**auto** nt hired car; ~**e** f
rent; **zur ~e wohnen** to live in rented
accommodation; **m~en** vt to rent; (*Auto*)
to hire; ~**er(in)** (**-s, -**) m(f) tenant; ~**shaus**
nt tenement, block of (rented) flats;
~**vertrag** m lease

Migräne [miˈɡrɛːnə] f migraine

Mikro- [ˈmikro] *zW:* ~**fon, ~phon**
[-ˈfoːn] (**-s, -e**) nt microphone; ~**skop**
[-ˈskoːp] (**-s, -e**) nt microscope;
m~skopisch adj microscopic;
~**wellenherd** m microwave (oven)

Milch [mɪlç] (**-**) f milk; ~**glas** nt frosted
glass; **m~ig** adj milky; ~**kaffee** m white
coffee; ~**mann** (pl **-männer**) m milkman;
~**mixgetränk** nt (*KOCH*) milkshake;
~**pulver** nt powdered milk; ~**straße** f
Milky Way; ~**zahn** m milk tooth

mild [mɪlt] adj mild; (*Richter*) lenient;
(*freundlich*) kind, charitable; **M~e** f
mildness; leniency; ~**ern** vt to mitigate, to
soften; (*Schmerz*) to alleviate; ~**ernde**
Umstände extenuating circumstances

Milieu [miliˈøː] (**-s, -s**) nt background,
environment; **m~geschädigt** adj
maladjusted

Mili- [mili] *zW:* **m~tant** [-ˈtant] adj militant;
~**tär** [-ˈtɛːr] (**-s**) nt military, army;
~'**tärgericht** nt military court; **m~'tärisch**
adj military

Milli- [ˈmili] *zW:* ~**ardär** [-arˈdɛːr] m
multimillionaire; ~**arde** [-ˈardə] f milliard;
billion (*BES US*); ~**meter** m millimetre;
~**meterpapier** nt graph paper

Million [miliˈoːn] (**-, -en**) f million; ~**är**
[-oˈnɛːr] m millionaire

Milz [mɪlts] (**-, -en**) f spleen

Mimik [ˈmiːmɪk] f mime

Mimose [miˈmoːzə] f mimosa; (*fig*) sensitive
person

minder [ˈmɪndər] adj inferior ♦ adv less;
M~heit f minority; ~**jährig** adj minor;

M~jährige(r) *f(m)* minor; **~n** *vt, vr* to decrease, to diminish; **M~ung** *f* decrease; **~wertig** *adj* inferior;
M~wertigkeitskomplex *m* inferiority complex

Mindest- ['mɪndəst] *zW:* **~alter** *nt* minimum age; **~betrag** *m* minimum amount; **m~e(r, s)** *adj* least; **zum ~en** *od* **m~en** at least; **m~ens** *adv* at least; **~haltbarkeitsdatum** *nt* best-before date; **~lohn** *m* minimum wage; **~maß** *nt* minimum

Mine ['mi:nə] *f* mine; *(Bleistiftmine)* lead; *(Kugelschreibermine)* refill

Mineral [mine'ra:l] *(-s, -e od -ien)* *nt* mineral; **m~isch** *adj* mineral; **~wasser** *nt* mineral water

Miniatur [minia'tu:r] *f* miniature

Mini- *zW:* **~golf** ['mɪnɪgɔlf] *nt* miniature golf, crazy golf; **m~mal** [mini'ma:l] *adj* minimal; **~mum** ['minimʊm] *nt* minimum; **~rock** *nt* miniskirt

Minister [mi'nɪstər] *(-s, -)* *m* minister; **m~iell** *adj* ministerial; **~ium** *nt* ministry; **~präsident** *m* prime minister

Minus ['mi:nʊs] *(-, -)* *nt* deficit

minus *adv* minus; **M~zeichen** *nt* minus sign

Minute [mi'nu:tə] *f* minute

Minze ['mɪntsə] *f* mint

mir [mi:r] *(dat von ich) pron* (to) me; **~ nichts, dir nichts** just like that

Misch- ['mɪʃ] *zW:* **~brot** *nt* bread made *from more than one kind of flour*; **~ehe** *f* mixed marriage; **m~en** *vt* to mix; **~ling** *m* half-caste; **~ung** *f* mixture

miserabel [mizə'ra:bəl] *(umg) adj (Essen, Film)* dreadful

Miss- ▲ ['mɪs] *zW:* **~behagen** *nt* discomfort, uneasiness; **~bildung** *f* deformity; **m~'billigen** *vt insep* to disapprove of; **~brauch** *m* abuse; *(falscher Gebrauch)* misuse; **m~'brauchen** *vt insep* to abuse; **jdn zu** *od* **für etw m~brauchen** to use sb for *od* to do sth; **~erfolg** *m* failure; **~fallen** *(-s)* *nt* displeasure; **m~'fallen** *(unreg) vi insep:* **jdm m~fallen** to displease sb; **~geschick** *nt* misfortune; **m~glücken** [mɪs'glʏkən] *vi insep* to fail; **jdm m~glückt etw** sb does not succeed with sth; **~griff** *m* mistake; **~gunst** *f* envy; **m~günstig** *adj* envious; **m~'handeln** *vt insep* to ill-treat; **~'handlung** *f* ill-treatment

Mission [mɪsi'o:n] *f* mission; **~ar(in)** *m(f)* missionary

Miss- ▲ *zW:* **~klang** *m* discord; **~kredit** *m* discredit; **m~lingen** [mɪs'lɪŋən] *(unreg) vi insep* to fail; **~mut** *m* sullenness; **m~mutig** *adj* sullen; **m~'raten** *(unreg) vi insep* to turn out badly ♦ *adj* ill-bred; **~stand** *m* bad state of affairs; abuse; **m~'trauen** *vi insep* to mistrust; **~trauen** *(-s)* *nt* distrust, suspicion; **~trauensantrag** *m (POL)* motion of no confidence; **m~trauisch** *adj* distrustful, suspicious; **~verhältnis** *nt* disproportion; **~verständnis** *nt* misunderstanding; **m~verstehen** *(unreg) vt insep* to misunderstand; **~wirtschaft** *f* mismanagement

Mist [mɪst] *(-(e)s)* *m* dung; dirt; *(umg)* rubbish

Mistel *(-, -n)* *f* mistletoe

Misthaufen *m* dungheap

mit [mɪt] *präp +dat* with; *(~tels)* by ♦ *adv* along, too; **~ der Bahn** by train; **~ 10 Jahren** at the age of 10; **wollen Sie ~?** do you want to come along?

Mitarbeit ['mɪtʔarbaɪt] *f* cooperation; **m~en** *vi* to cooperate, to collaborate; **~er(in)** *m(f)* collaborator; co-worker ♦ *pl (Personal)* staff

Mit- *zW:* **~bestimmung** *f* participation in decision-making; **m~bringen** *(unreg) vt* to bring along

miteinander [mɪtʔaɪ'nandər] *adv* together, with one another

miterleben *vt* to see, to witness

Mitesser ['mɪtʔɛsər] *(-s, -)* *m* blackhead

mitfahr- *zW:* **~en** *vi* to accompany; *(auf Reise auch)* to travel with; **M~gelegenheit** *f* lift; **M~zentrale** *f* agency for arranging lifts

mitfühlend *adj* sympathetic, compassionate

Mit- *zW*: **m~geben** (*unreg*) *vt* to give; **~gefühl** *nt* sympathy; **m~gehen** (*unreg*) *vi* to go/come along; **m~genommen** *adj* done in, in a bad way; **~gift** *f* dowry

Mitglied ['mɪtɡliːt] *nt* member; **~sbeitrag** *m* membership fee; **~schaft** *f* membership

Mit- *zW*: **m~halten** (*unreg*) *vi* to keep up; **m~helfen** (*unreg*) *vi* to help; **~hilfe** *f* help, assistance; **m~hören** *vt* to listen in to; **m~kommen** (*unreg*) *vi* to come along; (*verstehen*) to keep up, to follow; **~läufer** *m* hanger-on; (*POL*) fellow traveller

Mitleid *nt* sympathy; (*Erbarmen*) compassion; **m~ig** *adj* sympathetic; **m~slos** *adj* pitiless, merciless

Mit- *zW*: **m~machen** *vt* to join in, to take part in; **~mensch** *m* fellow man; **m~nehmen** (*unreg*) *vt* to take along/away; (*anstrengen*) to wear out, to exhaust; **zum ~nehmen** to take away; **m~reden** *vi*: **bei etw m~reden** to have a say in sth; **m~reißen** (*unreg*) *vt* to carry away/along; (*fig*) to thrill, captivate

mitsamt [mɪt'zamt] *präp +dat* together with

Mitschuld *f* complicity; **m~ig** *adj*: **m~ig (an +dat)** implicated (in); (*an Unfall*) partly responsible (for)

Mit- *zW*: **~schüler(in)** *m(f)* schoolmate; **m~spielen** *vi* to join in, to take part; **~spieler(in)** *m(f)* partner

Mittag ['mɪtaːk] *m* midday, lunchtime; **(zu) ~ essen** to have lunch; **heute/morgen ~** today/tomorrow at lunchtime *od* noon; **~essen** *nt* lunch, dinner

mittags *adv* at lunchtime *od* noon; **M~pause** *f* lunch break; **M~schlaf** *m* early afternoon nap, siesta

Mittäter(in) ['mɪttɛːtər(ɪn)] *m(f)* accomplice

Mitte ['mɪtə] *f* middle; (*POL*) centre; **aus unserer ~** from our midst

mitteilen ['mɪttaɪlən] *vt*: **jdm etw ~** to inform sb of sth, to communicate sth to sb

Mitteilung *f* communication

Mittel ['mɪtəl] (**-s -**) *nt* means; method; (*MATH*) average; (*MED*) medicine; **ein ~ zum Zweck** a means to an end; **~alter** *nt*

Middle Ages *pl*; **m~alterlich** *adj* mediaeval; **~ding** *nt* cross; **~europa** *nt* Central Europe; **~gebirge** *nt* low mountain range; **m~mäßig** *adj* mediocre, middling; **~mäßigkeit** *f* mediocrity; **~meer** *nt* Mediterranean; **~ohrentzündung** *f* inflammation of the middle ear; **~punkt** *m* centre; **~stand** *m* middle class; **~streifen** *m* central reservation; **~stürmer** *m* centre-forward; **~weg** *m* middle course; **~welle** *f* (*RADIO*) medium wave

mitten ['mɪtən] *adv* in the middle; **~ auf der Straße/in der Nacht** in the middle of the street/night

Mitternacht ['mɪtərnaxt] *f* midnight

mittlere(r, s) ['mɪtlərə(r, s)] *adj* middle; (*durchschnittlich*) medium, average; **~ Reife** ≈ O-levels

---

┌─────────────────────────────┐
│ **mittlere Reife** │
└─────────────────────────────┘

ⓘ The **mittlere Reife** is the standard certificate gained at a **Realschule** or **Gymnasium** on successful completion of 6 years' education there. If a pupil at a **Realschule** attains good results in several subjects he is allowed to enter the 11th class of a **Gymnasium** to study for the **Abitur**.

---

mittlerweile ['mɪtlər'vaɪlə] *adv* meanwhile

Mittwoch ['mɪtvɔx] (**-(e)s, -e**) *m* Wednesday; **m~s** *adv* on Wednesdays

mitunter [mɪt'ʔʊntər] *adv* occasionally, sometimes

Mit- *zW*: **m~verantwortlich** *adj* jointly responsible; **m~wirken** *vi*: **m~wirken (bei)** to contribute (to); (*THEAT*) to take part (in); **~wirkung** *f* contribution; participation

Mobbing ['mɔbɪŋ] (**-s**) *nt* workplace bullying

Möbel ['møːbəl] *pl* furniture *sg*; **~wagen** *m* furniture *od* removal van

mobil [mo'biːl] *adj* mobile; (*MIL*) mobilized; **M~iar** [mobili'aːr] (**-s, -e**) *nt* furnishings *pl*; **M~machung** *f* mobilization; **M~telefon** *nt* mobile phone

möblieren [mø'bliːrən] *vt* to furnish;

Spelling Reform: ▲ *new spelling* △ *old spelling (to be phased out)*

möbliert wohnen to live in furnished accommodation

möchte *etc* ['mœçtə] *vb siehe* **mögen**

Mode ['mo:də] *f* fashion

Modell [mo'dɛl] **(-s, -e)** *nt* model; **m~ieren** [-'li:rən] *vt* to model

Modenschau *f* fashion show

moderig ['mo:dərıç] *adj* (*Keller*) musty; (*Luft*) stale

modern [mo'dɛrn] *adj* modern; (*modisch*) fashionable; **~i'sieren** *vt* to modernize

Mode- *zW:* **~schau** *f* fashion show; **~schmuck** *m* fashion jewellery; **~schöpfer(in)** *m(f)* fashion designer; **~wort** *nt* fashionable word, buzz word

modisch ['mo:dıʃ] *adj* fashionable

Mofa ['mo:fa] **(-s, -s)** *nt* small moped

mogeln ['mo:gəln] (*umg*) *vi* to cheat

⌐ *SCHLÜSSELWORT* ┐

mögen ['mø:gən] [*pt* **mochte**, *pp* **gemocht** *od* (*als Hilfsverb*) **mögen**] *vt, vi* to like; **magst du/mögen Sie ihn?** do you like him?; **ich möchte ...** I would like ..., I'd like ...; **er möchte in die Stadt** he'd like to go into town; **ich möchte nicht, dass du ...** I wouldn't like you to ...; **ich mag nicht mehr** I've had enough

♦ *Hilfsverb* to like to; (*wollen*) to want; **möchtest du etwas essen?** would you like something to eat?; **sie mag nicht bleiben** she doesn't want to stay; **das mag wohl sein** that may well be; **was mag das heißen?** what might that mean?; **Sie möchten zu Hause anrufen** could you please call home?

└─────────────────────┘

möglich ['mø:klıç] *adj* possible; **~erweise** *adv* possibly; **M~keit** *f* possibility; **nach M~keit** if possible; **~st** *adv* as ... as possible

Mohn [mo:n] **(-(e)s, -e)** *m* (*~blume*) poppy; (*~samen*) poppy seed

Möhre ['mø:rə] *f* carrot

Mohrrübe ['mo:rry:bə] *f* carrot

mokieren [mo'ki:rən] *vr:* **sich ~ über** *+akk* to make fun of

Mole ['mo:lə] *f* (harbour) mole

Molekül [mole'ky:l] **(-s, -e)** *nt* molecule

Molkerei [mɔlkə'raı] *f* dairy

Moll [mɔl] **(-, -)** *nt* (*MUS*) minor (key)

mollig *adj* cosy; (*dicklich*) plump

Moment [mo'mɛnt] **(-(e)s, -e)** *m* moment ♦ *nt* factor; **im ~** at the moment; **~ (mal)!** just a moment; **m~an** [-'ta:n] *adj* momentary ♦ *adv* at the moment

Monarch [mo'narç] **(-en, -en)** *m* monarch; **~ie** [monar'çi:] *f* monarchy

Monat ['mo:nat] **(-(e)s, -e)** *m* month; **m~elang** *adv* for months; **m~lich** *adj* monthly

Monats- *zW:* **~gehalt** *nt:* **das dreizehnte ~gehalt** Christmas bonus (*of one month's salary*); **~karte** *f* monthly ticket

Mönch [mœnç] **(-(e)s, -e)** *m* monk

Mond [mo:nt] **(-(e)s, -e)** *m* moon; **~finsternis** *f* eclipse of the moon; **m~hell** *adj* moonlit; **~landung** *f* moon landing; **~schein** *m* moonlight

Mono- [mono] *in zW* mono; **~log** [-'lo:k] **(-s, -e)** *m* monologue; **~pol** [-'po:l] **(-s, -e)** *nt* monopoly; **m~polisieren** [-poli'zi:rən] *vt* to monopolize; **m~ton** [-'to:n] *adj* monotonous; **~tonie** [-to'ni:] *f* monotony

Montag ['mo:nta:k] **(-(e)s, -e)** *m* Monday

Montage [mɔn'ta:ʒə] *f* (*PHOT etc*) montage; (*TECH*) assembly; (*Einbauen*) fitting

Monteur [mɔn'tø:r] *m* fitter

montieren [mɔn'ti:rən] *vt* to assemble

Monument [monu'mɛnt] *nt* monument; **m~al** [-'ta:l] *adj* monumental

Moor [mo:r] **(-(e)s, -e)** *nt* moor

Moos [mo:s] **(-es, -e)** *nt* moss

Moped ['mo:pɛt] **(-s, -s)** *nt* moped

Moral [mo'ra:l] **(-, -en)** *f* morality; (*einer Geschichte*) moral; **m~isch** *adj* moral

Morast [mo'rast] **(-(e)s, -e)** *m* morass, mire; **m~ig** *adj* boggy

Mord [mɔrt] **(-(e)s, -e)** *m* murder; **~anschlag** *m* murder attempt

Mörder(in) ['mœrdər(ın)] **(-s, -)** *m(f)* murderer (murderess)

mörderisch *adj* (*fig: schrecklich*) terrible, dreadful ♦ *adv* (*umg: entsetzlich*) terribly, dreadfully

Rechtschreibreform: ▲ *neue Schreibung* △ *alte Schreibung (auslaufend)*

Mord- *zW:* **~kommission** *f* murder squad; **~sglück** (*umg*) *nt* amazing luck; **m~smäßig** (*umg*) *adj* terrific, enormous; **~verdacht** *m* suspicion of murder; **~waffe** *f* murder weapon

morgen ['mɔrgən] *adv* tomorrow; **~ früh** tomorrow morning; **M~** (**-s, -**) *m* morning; **M~mantel** *m* dressing gown; **M~rock** *m* dressing gown; **M~röte** *f* dawn; **~s** *adv* in the morning

morgig ['mɔrgɪç] *adj* tomorrow's; **der ~e Tag** tomorrow

Morphium ['mɔrfiʊm] *nt* morphine

morsch [mɔrʃ] *adj* rotten

Morsealphabet ['mɔrzə|alfabe:t] *nt* Morse code

morsen *vi* to send a message by Morse code

Mörtel ['mœrtəl] (**-s, -**) *m* mortar

Mosaik [moza'i:k] (**-s, -en** *od* **-e**) *nt* mosaic

Moschee [mɔ'ʃe:] (**-, -n**) *f* mosque

Moskito [mɔs'ki:to] (**-s, -s**) *m* mosquito

Most [mɔst] (**-(e)s, -e**) *m* (unfermented) fruit juice; (*Apfelwein*) cider

Motel [mo'tel] (**-s, -s**) *nt* motel

Motiv [mo'ti:f] (**-s, -e**) *nt* motive; (*MUS*) theme; **~ation** [-vatsi'o:n] *f* motivation; **m~ieren** [moti'vi:rən] *vt* to motivate

Motor ['mo:tɔr, *pl* mo'to:rən] (**-s, -en**) *m* engine; (*bes ELEK*) motor; **~boot** *nt* motorboat; **~haube** *f* (*von Auto*) bonnet (*BRIT*), hood (*US*); **m~isieren** *vt* to motorize; **~öl** *nt* engine oil; **~rad** *nt* motorcycle; **~roller** *m* (motor) scooter; **~schaden** *m* engine trouble *od* failure

Motte ['mɔtə] *f* moth; **~nkugel** *f* mothball(s)

Motto ['mɔto] (**-s, -s**) *nt* motto

Möwe ['mø:və] *f* seagull

Mücke ['mʏkə] *f* midge, gnat; **~nstich** *m* midge *od* gnat bite

müde ['my:də] *adj* tired

Müdigkeit ['my:dɪçkaɪt] *f* tiredness

Muffel (**-s, -**) (*umg*) *m* killjoy, sourpuss

muffig *adj* (*Luft*) musty

Mühe ['my:ə] *f* trouble, pains *pl*; **mit Müh und Not** with great difficulty; **sich** *dat* **~**

geben to go to a lot of trouble; **m~los** *adj* without trouble, easy; **m~voll** *adj* laborious, arduous

Mühle ['my:lə] *f* mill; (*Kaffeemühle*) grinder

Müh- *zW:* **~sal** (**-, -e**) *f* tribulation; **m~sam** *adj* arduous, troublesome; **m~selig** *adj* arduous, laborious

Mulde ['mʊldə] *f* hollow, depression

Mull [mʊl] (**-(e)s, -e**) *m* thin muslin

Müll [mʏl] (**-(e)s**) *m* refuse; **~abfuhr** *f* rubbish disposal; (*Leute*) dustmen *pl*; **~ableplatz** *m* rubbish dump; **~binde** *f* gauze bandage; **~eimer** *m* dustbin, garbage can (*US*); **~haufen** *m* rubbish heap; **~schlucker** (**-s, -**) *m* garbage disposal unit; **~tonne** *f* dustbin; **~verbrennungsanlage** *f* incinerator

mulmig ['mʊlmɪç] *adj* rotten; (*umg*) dodgy; **jdm ist ~** sb feels funny

multiplizieren [mʊltipli'tsi:rən] *vt* to multiply

Mumie ['mu:miə] *f* mummy

Mumm [mʊm] (**-s**) (*umg*) *m* gumption, nerve

Mumps [mʊmps] (**-**) *m od f* (*MED*) mumps

München ['mʏnçən] (**-s**) *nt* Munich

Mund [mʊnt] (**-(e)s, ⁻er**) *m* mouth; **~art** *f* dialect

münden ['mʏndən] *vi:* **~ in** +*akk* to flow into

Mund- *zW:* **m~faul** *adj* taciturn; **~geruch** *m* bad breath; **~harmonika** *f* mouth organ

mündig ['mʏndɪç] *adj* of age; **M~keit** *f* majority

mündlich ['mʏntlɪç] *adj* oral

Mundstück *nt* mouthpiece; (*Zigarettenmundstück*) tip

Mündung ['mʏndʊŋ] *f* (*von Fluss*) mouth; (*Gewehr*) muzzle

Mund- *zW:* **~wasser** *nt* mouthwash; **~werk** *nt:* **ein großes ~werk haben** to have a big mouth; **~winkel** *m* corner of the mouth

Munition [munitsi'o:n] *f* ammunition; **~slager** *nt* ammunition dump

munkeln ['mʊŋkəln] *vi* to whisper, to

mutter

Münster ['mʏnstər] *(-s, -)* nt minster

munter ['mʊntər] *adj* lively

Münze ['mʏntsə] *f* coin; **m~n** *vt* to coin, to mint; **auf jdn gemünzt sein** to be aimed at sb

Münzfernsprecher ['mʏntsfɛrnʃpreçər] *m* callbox (*BRIT*), pay phone

mürb(e) ['mʏrb(ə)] *adj* (*Gestein*) crumbly; (*Holz*) rotten; (*Gebäck*) crisp; **jdn ~ machen** to wear sb down; **M~eteig** ['mʏrbətaɪç] *m* shortcrust pastry

murmeln ['mʊrməln] *vt, vi* to murmur, to mutter

murren ['mʊrən] *vi* to grumble, to grouse

mürrisch ['mʏrɪʃ] *adj* sullen

Mus [muːs] *(-es, -e)* nt purée

Muschel ['mʊʃəl] *(-, -n)* f mussel; (*~schale*) shell; (*Telefonmuschel*) receiver

Muse ['muːzə] *f* muse

Museum [mu'zeːʊm] *(-s, Museen)* nt museum

Musik [mu'ziːk] *f* music; (*Kapelle*) band; **m~alisch** [-kaːlɪʃ] *adj* musical; **~ant(in)** [-'kant(ɪn)] *(-en, -en)* m(f) musician; **~box** *f* jukebox; **~er** *(-s, -)* m musician; **~hochschule** *f* college of music; **~instrument** nt musical instrument

musisch ['muːzɪʃ] *adj* (*Mensch*) artistic

musizieren [muzi'tsiːrən] *vi* to make music

Muskat [mʊs'kaːt] *(-(e)s, -e)* m nutmeg

Muskel ['mʊskəl] *(-s, -n)* m muscle; **~kater** *m*: **~kater haben** to be stiff

Muskulatur [mʊskula'tuːr] *f* muscular system

muskulös [mʊsku'løːs] *adj* muscular

Müsli ['myːsli] *(-s, -)* nt (*KOCH*) muesli

Muss ▲ [mʊs] *(-)* nt necessity, must

Muße ['muːsə] *(-)* f leisure

SCHLÜSSELWORT

---

müssen ['mʏsən] *(pt* **musste,** *pp* **gemusst** *od (als Hilfsverb)* **müssen)** *vi* 1 (*Zwang*) must (*nur im Präsens*), to have to; **ich muss es tun** I must do it, I have to do it; **ich musste es tun** I had to do it; **er muss es**

nicht tun he doesn't have to do it; **muss ich?** must I?, do I have to?; **wann müsst ihr zur Schule?** when do you have to go to school?; **er hat gehen müssen** he (has) had to go; **muss das sein?** is that really necessary?; **ich muss mal** (*umg*) I need the toilet

2 (*sollen*): **das musst du nicht tun!** you oughtn't to *od* shouldn't do that; **Sie hätten ihn fragen müssen** you should have asked him

3: **es muss geregnet haben** it must have rained; **es muss nicht wahr sein** it needn't be true

---

müßig ['myːsɪç] *adj* idle

Muster ['mʊstər] *(-s, -)* nt model; (*Dessin*) pattern; (*Probe*) sample; **m~gültig** *adj* exemplary; **m~n** *vt* (*Tapete*) to pattern; (*fig, MIL*) to examine; (*Truppen*) to inspect; **~ung** *f* (*von Stoff*) pattern; (*MIL*) inspection

Mut [muːt] *m* courage; **nur ~!** cheer up!; **jdm ~ machen** to encourage sb; **m~ig** *adj* courageous; **m~los** *adj* discouraged, despondent

mutmaßlich ['muːtmaːslɪç] *adj* presumed ♦ *adv* probably

Mutprobe *f* test *od* trial of courage

Mutter¹ ['mʊtər] *(-, ̈)* f mother

Mutter² ['mʊtər] *(-, -n)* f (*Schraubenmutter*) nut

mütterlich ['mʏtərlɪç] *adj* motherly; **~erseits** *adv* on the mother's side

Mutter- *zW*: **~liebe** *f* motherly love; **~mal** nt birthmark; **~milch** *f* mother's milk; **~schaft** *f* motherhood, maternity; **~schutz** *m* maternity regulations; **'~'seelena|llein** *adj* all alone; **~sprache** *f* native language; **~tag** *m* Mother's Day

Mutti ['mʊti] *(-, -s)* f mum(my) (*BRIT*), mom(my) (*US*)

mutwillig ['muːtvɪlɪç] *adj* malicious, deliberate

Mütze ['mʏtsə] *f* cap

MwSt *abk* (= *Mehrwertsteuer*) VAT

mysteriös [mʏsteri'øːs] *adj* mysterious

Mythos ['myːtɔs] *(-, Mythen)* m myth

Rechtschreibreform: ▲ *neue Schreibung* △ *alte Schreibung (auslaufend)*

N, n

na [na] *excl* well; ~ **gut** okay then
Nabel ['na:bəl] (**-s, -**) *m* navel; ~**schnur** *f* umbilical cord

---
SCHLÜSSELWORT
---

nach [na:x] *präp +dat* **1** (*örtlich*) to; **nach Berlin** to Berlin; **nach links/rechts** (to the) left/right; **nach oben/hinten** up/back
2 (*zeitlich*) after; **einer nach dem anderen** one after the other; **nach Ihnen!** after you!; **zehn (Minuten) nach drei** ten (minutes) past three
3 (*gemäß*) according to; **nach dem Gesetz** according to the law; **dem Namen nach** judging by his/her name; **nach allem, was ich weiß** as far as I know
♦ *adv*: **ihm nach!** after him!; **nach und nach** gradually, little by little; **nach wie vor** still

nachahmen ['na:x|a:mən] *vt* to imitate
Nachbar(in) ['na:xba:r(ɪn)] (**-s, -n**) *m(f)* neighbour; ~**haus** *nt*: **im** ~**haus** next door; **n~lich** *adj* neighbourly; ~**schaft** *f* neighbourhood; ~**staat** *m* neighbouring state
nach- *zW*: ~**bestellen** *vt*: **50 Stück** ~**bestellen** to order another 50; **N~bestellung** *f* (*COMM*) repeat order; **N~bildung** *f* imitation, copy; ~**blicken** *vi* to gaze after; ~**datieren** *vt* to postdate
nachdem [na:x'de:m] *konj* after; (*weil*) since; **je** ~ (**ob**) it depends (whether)
nachdenken (*unreg*) *vi*: ~ **über** *+akk* to think about; **N~** (**-s**) *nt* reflection, meditation
nachdenklich *adj* thoughtful, pensive
Nachdruck ['na:xdrʊk] *m* emphasis; (*TYP*) reprint, reproduction
nachdrücklich ['na:xdrʏklɪç] *adj* emphatic
nacheinander [na:x|aɪ'nandər] *adv* one after the other
nachempfinden ['na:x|empfɪndən] (*unreg*)

vt: **jdm etw** ~ to feel sth with sb
Nacherzählung ['na:x|ɛrtsɛ:lʊŋ] *f* reproduction (of a story)
Nachfahr ['na:xfa:r] (**-s, -en**) *m* descendant
Nachfolge ['na:xfɔlgə] *f* succession; **n~n** *vi* +*dat* to follow; ~**r(in)** (**-s, -**) *m(f)* successor
nachforschen *vt, vi* to investigate
Nachforschung *f* investigation
Nachfrage ['na:xfra:gə] *f* inquiry; (*COMM*) demand; **n~n** *vi* to inquire
nach- *zW*: ~**füllen** *vt* to refill; ~**geben** (*unreg*) *vi* to give way, to yield; **N~gebühr** *f* (*POST*) excess postage
nachgehen ['na:xge:ən] (*unreg*) *vi* (+*dat*) to follow; (*erforschen*) to inquire (into); (*Uhr*) to be slow
Nachgeschmack ['na:xgəʃmak] *m* aftertaste
nachgiebig ['na:xgi:bɪç] *adj* soft, accommodating; **N~keit** *f* softness
nachhaltig ['na:xhaltɪç] *adj* lasting; (*Widerstand*) persistent
nachhause *adv* (*österreichisch, schweizerisch*) home
nachhelfen ['na:xhɛlfən] (*unreg*) *vi* +*dat* to assist, to help
nachher [na:x'he:r] *adv* afterwards
Nachhilfeunterricht ['na:xhɪlfə|ʊntərrɪçt] *m* extra tuition
nachholen ['na:xho:lən] *vt* to catch up with; (*Versäumtes*) to make up for
Nachkomme ['na:xkɔmə] (**-, -n**) *m* descendant
nachkommen (*unreg*) *vi* to follow; (*einer Verpflichtung*) to fulfil; **N~schaft** *f* descendants *pl*
Nachkriegszeit *f* postwar period
Nach- *zW*: ~**lass** ▲ (**-es, -lässe**) *m* (*COMM*) discount, rebate; (*Erbe*) estate; **n~lassen** (*unreg*) *vt* (*Strafe*) to remit; (*Summe*) to take off; (*Schulden*) to cancel
♦ *vi* to decrease, to ease off; (*Sturm*) to die down, to ease off; (*schlechter werden*) to deteriorate; **er hat n~gelassen** he has got worse; **n~lässig** *adj* negligent, careless
nachlaufen ['na:xlaʊfən] (*unreg*) *vi* +*dat* to run after, to chase

Spelling Reform: ▲ *new spelling* △ *old spelling (to be phased out)*

nachlösen ['na:xlø:zən] *vi (Zuschlag)* to pay on the train, pay at the other end; *(zur Weiterfahrt)* to pay the supplement

nachmachen ['na:xmaxən] *vt* to imitate, to copy; *(fälschen)* to counterfeit

Nachmittag ['na:xmɪta:k] *m* afternoon; **am ~** in the afternoon; **n~s** *adv* in the afternoon

Nach- *zW:* **~nahme** *f* cash on delivery; **per ~nahme** C.O.D.; **~name** *m* surname; **~porto** *nt* excess postage

nachprüfen ['na:xpry:fən] *vt* to check, to verify

nachrechnen ['na:xrɛçnən] *vt* to check

nachreichen ['na:xraɪçən] *vt (Unterlagen)* to hand in later

Nachricht ['na:xrɪçt] **(-, -en)** *f* (piece of) news; *(Mitteilung)* message; **~en** *pl (Neuigkeiten)* news

Nachrichten- *zW:* **~agentur** *f* news agency; **~dienst** *m (MIL)* intelligence service; **~sprecher(in)** *m(f)* newsreader; **~technik** *f* telecommunications *sg*

Nachruf ['na:xru:f] *m* obituary

nachsagen ['na:xza:gən] *vt* to repeat; **jdm etw ~** to say sth of sb

Nachsaison ['na:xzɛzõː] *f* off-season

nachschicken ['na:xʃɪkən] *vt* to forward

nachschlagen ['na:xʃla:gən] *(unreg) vt* to look up

Nachschlagewerk *nt* reference book

Nachschlüssel *m* duplicate key

Nachschub ['na:xʃu:p] *m* supplies *pl*; *(Truppen)* reinforcements *pl*

nachsehen ['na:xze:ən] *(unreg) vt (prüfen)* to check ♦ *vi (erforschen)* to look and see; **jdm etw ~** to forgive sb sth; **das N~ haben** to come off worst

Nachsendeantrag *m* application to have one's mail forwarded

nachsenden ['na:xzɛndən] *(unreg) vt* to send on, to forward

nachsichtig *adj* indulgent, lenient

nachsitzen ['na:xzɪtsən] *(unreg) vi:* **~ (müssen)** *(SCH)* to be kept in

Nachspeise ['na:xʃpaɪzə] *f* dessert, sweet, pudding

Nachspiel ['na:xʃpi:l] *nt* epilogue; *(fig)* sequel

nachsprechen ['na:xʃprɛçən] *(unreg) vt:* **(jdm) ~** to repeat (after sb)

nächst [nɛːçst] *präp +dat (räumlich)* next to; *(außer)* apart from; **~beste(r, s)** *adj* first that comes along; *(zweitbeste)* next best; **N~e(r)** *f(m)* neighbour; **~e(r, s)** *adj* next; *(~gelegen)* nearest

nachstellen ['na:xʃtɛlən] *vt (TECH: neu einstellen)* to adjust

nächst *zW:* **N~enliebe** *f* love for one's fellow men; **~ens** *adv* shortly, soon; **~liegend** *adj* nearest; *(fig)* obvious; **~möglich** *adj* next possible

Nacht [naxt] **(-, ⁻e)** *f* night; **~dienst** *m* night shift

Nachteil ['na:xtaɪl] *m* disadvantage; **n~ig** *adj* disadvantageous

Nachthemd *nt (Herrennachthemd)* nightshirt; *(Damennachthemd)* nightdress

Nachtigall ['naxtɪgal] **(-, -en)** *f* nightingale

Nachtisch ['na:xtɪʃ] *m* = **Nachspeise**

Nachtklub *m* night club

Nachtleben *nt* nightlife

nächtlich ['nɛçtlɪç] *adj* nightly

Nachtlokal *nt* night club

Nacht- *zW:* **~trag (-(e)s, -träge)** *m* supplement; **n~tragen** *(unreg) vt* to carry; *(zufügen)* to add; **jdm etw n~tragen** to hold sth against sb; **n~träglich** *adj* later, subsequent; additional ♦ *adv* subsequently; additionally; **n~trauern** *vi:* **jdm/etw n~trauern** to mourn the loss of sb/sth

Nacht- *zW:* **n~s** *adv* at *od* by night; **~schicht** *f* nightshift; **~schwester** *f* night nurse; **~tarif** *m* off-peak tariff; **~tisch** *m* bedside table; **~wächter** *m* night watchman

Nach- *zW:* **~untersuchung** *f* checkup; **n~wachsen** *(unreg) vi* to grow again; **~wahl** *f (POL)* ≃ by-election

Nachweis ['na:xvaɪs] **(-es, -e)** *m* proof; **n~bar** *adj* provable, demonstrable; **n~en** *(unreg) vt* to prove; **jdm etw n~en** to point sth out to sb; **n~lich** *adj* evident,

Rechtschreibreform: ▲ *neue Schreibung* △ *alte Schreibung (auslaufend)*

demonstrable

nach- zW: **~wirken** vi to have after-effects; **N~wirkung** f aftereffect; **N~wort** nt epilogue; **N~wuchs** m offspring; (beruflich etc) new recruits pl; **~zahlen** vt, vi to pay extra; **N~zahlung** f additional payment; (zurückdatiert) back pay; **~ziehen** (unreg) vt (hinter sich herziehen: Bein) to drag; **N~zügler** (-s, -) m straggler

Nacken ['nakən] (-s, -) m nape of the neck

nackt [nakt] adj naked; (Tatsachen) plain, bare; **N~badestrand** m nudist beach; **N~heit** f nakedness

Nadel ['na:dəl] (-, -n) f needle; (Stecknadel) pin; **~öhr** nt eye of a needle; **~wald** m coniferous forest

Nagel ['na:gəl] (-s, ⁼) m nail; **~bürste** f nailbrush; **~feile** f nailfile; **~lack** m nail varnish od polish (BRIT); **n~n** vt, vi to nail; **n~neu** adj brand-new; **~schere** f nail scissors pl

nagen ['na:gən] vt, vi to gnaw

Nagetier ['na:gəti:r] nt rodent

nah(e) ['na:(ə)] adj (räumlich) near(by); (Verwandte) near; (Freunde) close; (zeitlich) near, close ♦ adv near(by); near, close; (verwandt) closely ♦ präp (+dat) near (to), close to; **der Nahe Osten** the Near East; **~gehen** (+dat) to grieve; **~ kommen** (+dat) to get close (to); **jdm etw ~ legen** to suggest sth to sb; **~ liegen** to be obvious; **~ liegend** obvious; **~ stehen** (+dat) to be close (to); **einer Sache ~ stehen** to sympathize with sth; **~ stehend** close; **jdm (zu) ~ treten** to offend sb

Nahaufnahme f close-up

Nähe ['nɛ:ə] (-) f nearness, proximity; (Umgebung) vicinity; **in der ~** close by; at hand; **aus der ~** from close to

nah(e)bei adv nearby

nahen vi, vr to approach, to draw near

nähen ['nɛ:ən] vt, vi to sew

näher adj, adv nearer; (Erklärung, Erkundigung) more detailed; **(sich) ~ kommen** to get closer; **N~e(s)** nt details pl, particulars pl

Naherholungsgebiet nt recreational area

(close to a town)

nähern vr to approach

nahezu adv nearly

Nähgarn nt thread

Nahkampf m hand-to-hand fighting

Nähkasten m sewing basket, workbox

nahm etc [na:m] vb siehe **nehmen**

Nähmaschine f sewing machine

Nähnadel f needle

nähren ['nɛ:rən] vt to feed ♦ vr (Person) to feed o.s.; (Tier) to feed

nahrhaft ['na:rhaft] adj nourishing, nutritious

Nahrung ['na:ruŋ] f food; (fig auch) sustenance

Nahrungs- zW: **~mittel** nt foodstuffs pl; **~mittelindustrie** f food industry; **~suche** f search for food

Nährwert m nutritional value

Naht [na:t] (-, ⁼e) f seam; (MED) suture; (TECH) join; **n~los** adj seamless; **n~los ineinander übergehen** to follow without a gap

Nah- zW: **~verkehr** m local traffic; **~verkehrszug** m local train; **~ziel** nt immediate objective

Name ['na:mə] (-ns, -n) m name; **im ~n von** on behalf of; **n~ns** adv by the name of; **~nstag** m name day, saint's day; **n~ntlich** adj by name ♦ adv particularly, especially

---
Namenstag
---

i In Catholic areas of Germany the **Namenstag** is often a more important celebration than a birthday. This is the day dedicated to the saint after whom a person is called, and on that day the person receives presents and invites relatives and friends round to celebrate.

---

namhaft ['na:mhaft] adj (berühmt) famed, renowned; (beträchtlich) considerable; **~ machen** to name

nämlich ['nɛ:mlɪç] adv that is to say, namely; (denn) since

nannte etc ['nantə] vb siehe **nennen**

Napf [napf] (-(e)s, ⁼e) m bowl, dish

Narbe ['narbə] f scar; **narbig** adj scarred

Narkose [nar'koːzə] f anaesthetic

Narr [nar] **(-en, -en)** m fool; **n~en** vt to fool; **Närrin** ['nɛrɪn] f fool; **närrisch** adj foolish, crazy

Narzisse [nar'tsɪsə] f narcissus; daffodil

naschen ['naʃən] vt, vi to nibble; (heimlich kosten) to pinch a bit

naschhaft adj sweet-toothed

Nase ['naːzə] f nose

Nasen- zW: **~bluten (-s)** nt nosebleed; **~loch** nt nostril; **~tropfen** pl nose drops

naseweis adj pert, cheeky; (neugierig) nosey

Nashorn ['naːshɔrn] nt rhinoceros

nass ▲ [nas] adj wet

Nässe ['nɛsə] **(-)** f wetness; **n~n** vt to wet

nasskalt ▲ adj wet and cold

Nassrasur ▲ f wet shave

Nation [natsi'oːn] f nation

national [natsio'naːl] adj national; **N~feiertag** m national holiday; **N~hymne** f national anthem; **~isieren** [-i'ziːrən] vt to nationalize; **N~ismus** [-'lɪsmʊs] m nationalism; **~istisch** [-'lɪstɪʃ] adj nationalistic; **N~i'tät** f nationality; **N~mannschaft** f national team; **N~sozialismus** m national socialism

Natron ['naːtrɔn] **(-s)** nt soda

Natter ['natər] **(-, -n)** f adder

Natur [na'tuːr] f nature; (körperlich) constitution; **~ell (-es, -e)** nt disposition; **~erscheinung** f natural phenomenon od event; **n~farben** adj natural coloured; **n~gemäß** adj natural; **~gesetz** nt law of nature; **n~getreu** adj true to life; **~katastrophe** f natural disaster

natürlich [na'tyːrlɪç] adj natural ♦ adv naturally; **ja, ~!** yes, of course; **N~keit** f naturalness

Natur- zW: **~park** m ≃ national park; **~produkt** nt natural product; **n~rein** adj natural, pure; **~schutz** m nature conservation; **unter ~schutz stehen** to be legally protected; **~schutzgebiet** nt nature reserve; **~wissenschaft** f natural science; **~wissenschaftler(in)** m(f)

scientist

nautisch ['naʊtɪʃ] adj nautical

Nazi ['naːtsi] **(-s, -s)** m Nazi

NB abk (= nota bene) nb

n. Chr. abk (= nach Christus) A.D.

Nebel ['neːbəl] **(-s, -)** m fog, mist; **n~ig** adj foggy, misty; **~scheinwerfer** m fog lamp

neben ['neːbən] präp (+akk od dat) next to; (+dat: außer) apart from, besides; **~an** [neːbən'an] adv next door; **N~anschluss** ▲ m (TEL) extension; **N~ausgang** m side exit; **~bei** [neːbən'baɪ] adv at the same time; (außerdem) additionally; (beiläufig) incidentally; **N~beruf** m second job; **N~beschäftigung** f second job; **N~buhler(in) (-s, -)** m(f) rival; **~einander** [neːbən|aɪ'nandər] adv side by side; **~einander legen** to put next to each other; **N~eingang** m side entrance; **N~fach** nt subsidiary subject; **N~fluss** ▲ m tributary; **N~gebäude** nt annexe; **N~geräusch** nt (RADIO) atmospherics pl, interference; **~her** [neːbən'heːr] adv (zusätzlich) besides; (gleichzeitig) at the same time; (daneben) alongside; **N~kosten** pl extra charges, extras; **N~produkt** nt by-product; **N~sache** f trifle, side issue; **~sächlich** adj minor, peripheral; **N~saison** f low season; **N~straße** f side street; **N~verdienst** m secondary income; **N~wirkung** f side effect; **N~zimmer** nt adjoining room

neblig ['neːblɪç] adj foggy, misty

Necessaire [nesɛ'sɛːr] **(-s, -s)** nt (Nähnecessaire) needlework box; (Nagelnecessaire) manicure case

necken ['nekən] vt to tease

Neckerei [nekə'raɪ] f teasing

Neffe ['nɛfə] **(-n, -n)** m nephew

negativ ['neːgatiːf] adj negative; **N~ (-s, -e)** nt (PHOT) negative

Neger ['neːgər] **(-s, -)** m negro; **~in** f negress

nehmen ['neːmən] (unreg) vt to take; **jdn zu sich ~** to take sb in; **sich ernst ~** to take o.s. seriously; **nimm dir doch bitte** please help yourself

Neid [naɪt] **(-(e)s)** *m* envy; **~er (-s, -)** *m* envier; **n~isch** ['naɪdɪʃ] *adj* envious, jealous

neigen ['naɪɡən] *vt* to incline, to lean; (*Kopf*) to bow ♦ *vi*: **zu etw ~** to tend to sth

Neigung *f* (*des Geländes*) slope; (*Tendenz*) tendency, inclination; (*Vorliebe*) liking; (*Zuneigung*) affection

nein [naɪn] *adv* no

Nektarine [nɛktaˈriːnə] *f* (*Frucht*) nectarine

Nelke ['nɛlkə] *f* carnation, pink; (*Gewürz*) clove

Nenn- ['nɛn] *zW*: **n~en** (*unreg*) *vt* to name; (*mit Namen*) to call; **wie n~t man ...?** what do you call ...?; **n~enswert** *adj* worth mentioning; **~er (-s, -)** *m* denominator; **~wert** *m* nominal value; (*COMM*) par

Neon ['neːɔn] **(-s)** *nt* neon; **~licht** *nt* neon light; **~röhre** *f* neon tube

Nerv [nɛrf] **(-s, -en)** *m* nerve; **jdm auf die ~en gehen** to get on sb's nerves; **n~enaufreibend** *adj* nerve-racking; **~enbündel** *nt* bundle of nerves; **~enheilanstalt** *f* mental home; **n~enkrank** *adj* mentally ill; **~ensäge** (*umg*) *f* pain (in the neck) (*umg*); **~ensystem** *nt* nervous system; **~enzusammenbruch** *m* nervous breakdown; **n~lich** *adj* (*Belastung*) affecting the nerves; **n~ös** [nɛrˈvøːs] *adj* nervous; **~osiˈtät** *f* nervousness; **n~tötend** *adj* nerve-racking; (*Arbeit*) soul destroying

Nerz [nɛrts] **(-es, -e)** *m* mink

Nessel ['nɛsəl] **(-, -n)** *f* nettle

Nessessär ▲ [nɛseˈsɛːr] **(-s, -s)** *nt* = Necessaire

Nest [nɛst] **(-(e)s, -er)** *nt* nest; (*umg: Ort*) dump

nett [nɛt] *adj* nice; (*freundlich*) nice, kind; **~erweise** *adv* kindly

netto ['nɛtoː] *adv* net

Netz [nɛts] **(-es, -e)** *nt* net; (*Gepäcknetz*) rack; (*Einkaufsnetz*) string bag; (*Spinnennetz*) web; (*System*) network; **jdm ins ~ gehen** (*fig*) to fall into sb's trap; **~anschluss** ▲ *m* mains connection

Netzhaut *f* retina

neu [nɔʏ] *adj* new; (*Sprache, Geschichte*)

modern; **seit ~estem** (since) recently; **die ~esten Nachrichten** the latest news; **~ schreiben** to rewrite, to write again; **N~anschaffung** *f* new purchase *od* acquisition; **~artig** *adj* new kind of; **N~bau** *m* new building; **N~e(r)** *f(m)* the new man/woman; **~erdings** *adv* (*kürzlich*) (since) recently; (*von ~em*) again; **N~erscheinung** *f* (*Buch*) new publication; (*Schallplatte*) new release; **N~erung** *f* innovation, new departure; **N~gier** *f* curiosity; **~gierig** *adj* curious; **N~heit** *f* newness, novelty; **N~igkeit** *f* news *sg*; **N~jahr** *nt* New Year; **~lich** *adv* recently, the other day; **N~ling** *m* novice; **N~mond** *m* new moon

neun [nɔʏn] *num* nine; **~zehn** *num* nineteen; **~zig** *num* ninety

neureich *adj* nouveau riche; **N~e(r)** *f(m)* nouveau riche

neurotisch *adj* neurotic

Neuseeland [nɔʏˈzeːlant] *nt* New Zealand; **Neuseeländer(in)** [nɔʏˈzeːlɛndər(ɪn)] *m(f)* New Zealander

neutral [nɔʏˈtraːl] *adj* neutral; **~iˈsieren** *vt* to neutralize

Neutrum ['nɔʏtrʊm] **(-s, -a** *od* **-en)** *nt* neuter

Neu- *zW*: **~wert** *m* purchase price; **n~wertig** *adj* (as) new, not used; **~zeit** *f* modern age; **n~zeitlich** *adj* modern, recent

---

SCHLÜSSELWORT

nicht [nɪçt] *adv* **1** (*Verneinung*) not; **er ist es nicht** it's not him, it isn't him; **er raucht nicht** (*gerade*) he isn't smoking; (*gewöhnlich*) he doesn't smoke; **ich kann das nicht - ich auch nicht** I can't do it - neither *od* nor can I; **es regnet nicht mehr** it's not raining any more; **nicht rostend** stainless

2 (*Bitte, Verbot*): **nicht!** don't!, no!; **nicht berühren!** do not touch!; **nicht doch!** don't!

3 (*rhetorisch*): **du bist müde, nicht (wahr)?** you're tired, aren't you?; **das ist schön,**

nicht (wahr)? it's nice, isn't it?
4: was du nicht sagst! the things you say!

Nichtangriffspakt [nɪçt'|angrɪfspakt] *m* non-aggression pact

Nichte ['nɪçtə] *f* niece

nichtig ['nɪçtɪç] *adj (ungültig)* null, void; *(wertlos)* futile

Nichtraucher(in) *m(f)* non-smoker

nichts [nɪçts] *pron* nothing; **für ~ und wieder ~** for nothing at all; **~ sagend** meaningless; **N~ (-)** *nt* nothingness; *(pej: Person)* nonentity

Nichtschwimmer *m* non-swimmer

nichts- *zW:* **~desto'weniger** *adv* nevertheless; **N~nutz (-es, -e)** *m* good-for-nothing; **~nutzig** *adj* worthless, useless; **N~tun (-s)** *nt* idleness

Nichtzutreffende(s) *nt:* **~s od nicht Zutreffendes (bitte) streichen!** (please) delete where appropriate

Nickel ['nɪkəl] **(-s)** *nt* nickel

nicken ['nɪkən] *vi* to nod

Nickerchen ['nɪkərçən] *nt* nap

nie [niː] *adv* never; **~ wieder** *od* **mehr** never again; **~ und nimmer** never ever

nieder ['niːdər] *adj* low; *(gering)* inferior
♦ *adv* down; **N~gang** *m* decline; **~gedrückt** *adj (deprimiert)* dejected, depressed; **~gehen** *(unreg) vi* to descend; *(AVIAT)* to come down; *(Regen)* to fall; *(Boxer)* to go down; **~geschlagen** *adj* depressed, dejected; **N~lage** *f* defeat; **N~lande** *pl* Netherlands; **N~länder(in)** *m(f)* Dutchman(-woman); **~ländisch** *adj* Dutch; **~lassen** *(unreg) vr (sich setzen)* to sit down; *(an Ort)* to settle (down); *(Arzt, Rechtsanwalt)* to set up a practice; **N~lassung** *f* settlement; *(COMM)* branch; **~legen** *vt* to lay down; *(Arbeit)* to stop; *(Amt)* to resign; **N~sachsen** *nt* Lower Saxony; **N~schlag** *m (MET)* precipitation; rainfall; **~schlagen** *(unreg) vt (Gegner)* to beat down; *(Gegenstand)* to knock down; *(Augen)* to lower; *(Aufstand)* to put down ♦ *vr (CHEM)* to precipitate; **~trächtig** *adj* base, mean; **N~trächtigkeit** *f* meanness,

baseness; outrage; **N~ung** *f (GEOG)* depression; *(Mündungsgebiet)* flats *pl*

niedlich ['niːtlɪç] *adj* sweet, cute

niedrig ['niːdrɪç] *adj* low; *(Stand)* lowly, humble; *(Gesinnung)* mean

niemals ['niːmaːls] *adv* never

niemand ['niːmant] *pron* nobody, no-one

Niemandsland ['niːmantslant] *nt* no-man's-land

Niere ['niːrə] *f* kidney

nieseln ['niːzəln] *vi* to drizzle

niesen ['niːzən] *vi* to sneeze

Niete ['niːtə] *f (TECH)* rivet; *(Los)* blank; *(Reinfall)* flop; *(Mensch)* failure; **n~n** *vt* to rivet

---

St. Nikolaus

i On December 6th, **St. Nikolaus** visits German children to reward those who have been good by filling shoes they have left out with sweets and small presents.

Nikotin [niko'tiːn] **(-s)** *nt* nicotine

Nilpferd [niːl-] *nt* hippopotamus

Nimmersatt ['nɪmərzat] **(-(e)s, -e)** *m* glutton

nimmst *etc* [nɪmst] *vb siehe* **nehmen**

nippen ['nɪpən] *vt, vi* to sip

nirgend- ['nɪrgənt] *zW:* **~s** *adv* nowhere; **~wo** *adv* nowhere; **~wohin** *adv* nowhere

Nische ['niːʃə] *f* niche

nisten ['nɪstən] *vi* to nest

Niveau [ni'voː] **(-s, -s)** *nt* level

Nixe ['nɪksə] *f* water nymph

nobel ['noːbəl] *adj (großzügig)* generous; *(elegant)* posh *(inf)*

SCHLÜSSELWORT

noch [nɔx] *adv* 1 *(weiterhin)* still; **noch nicht** not yet; **noch nie** never (yet); **noch immer** *od* **immer noch** still; **bleiben Sie doch noch** stay a bit longer
2 *(in Zukunft)* still, yet; **das kann noch passieren** that might still happen; **er wird noch kommen** he'll come (yet)
3 *(nicht später als)*: **noch vor einer Woche** only a week ago; **noch am selben Tag** the

---

very same day; **noch im 19. Jahrhundert** as late as the 19th century; **noch heute** today

4 (*zusätzlich*): **wer war noch da?** who else was there?; **noch einmal** once more, again; **noch dreimal** three more times; **noch einer** another one

5 (*bei Vergleichen*): **noch größer** even bigger; **das ist noch besser** that's better still; **und wenn es noch so schwer ist** however hard it is

6: **Geld noch und noch** heaps (and heaps) of money; **sie hat noch und noch versucht, ...** she tried again and again to ...

♦ *konj*: **weder A noch B** neither A nor B

noch- *zW*: **~mal** ['nɔxmaːl] *adv* again, once more; **~malig** ['nɔxmaːlıç] *adj* repeated; **~mals** *adv* again, once more

Nominativ ['noːminatiːf] (**-s, -e**) *m* nominative

nominell [nomi'nɛl] *adj* nominal

Nonne ['nɔnə] *f* nun

Nord(en) ['nɔrd(ən)] (**-s**) *m* north

Nord'irland *nt* Northern Ireland

nordisch *adj* northern

nördlich ['nœrtlıç] *adj* northerly, northern ♦ *präp +gen* (to the) north of; **~ von** (to the) north of

Nord- *zW*: **~pol** *m* North Pole; **~rhein-Westfalen** *nt* North Rhine-Westphalia; **~see** *f* North Sea; **n~wärts** *adv* northwards

nörgeln ['nœrgəln] *vi* to grumble; **Nörgler** (**-s, -**) *m* grumbler

Norm [nɔrm] (**-, -en**) *f* norm; (*Größenvorschrift*) standard; **n~al** [nɔr'maːl] *adj* normal; **~al(benzin)** *nt* ≈ 2-star petrol (*BRIT*), regular petrol (*US*); **n~alerweise** *adv* normally; **n~ali'sieren** *vt* to normalize ♦ *vr* to return to normal

normen *vt* to standardize

Norwegen ['nɔrveːgən] *nt* Norway; **norwegisch** *adj* Norwegian

Nostalgie [nɔstal'giː] *f* nostalgia

Not [noːt] (**-, ⁻e**) *f* need; (*Mangel*) want;

(*Mühe*) trouble; (*Zwang*) necessity; **~leidend** needy; **zur ~** if necessary; (*gerade noch*) just about

Notar [no'taːr] (**-s, -e**) *m* notary; **n~i'ell** *adj* notarial

Not- *zW*: **~arzt** *m* emergency doctor; **~ausgang** *m* emergency exit; **~behelf** (**-s, -e**) *m* makeshift; **~bremse** *f* emergency brake; **~dienst** *m* (*Bereitschaftsdienst*) emergency service; **n~dürftig** *adj* scanty; (*behelfsmäßig*) makeshift

Note ['noːtə] *f* note; (*SCH*) mark (*BRIT*), grade (*US*)

Noten- *zW*: **~blatt** *nt* sheet of music; **~schlüssel** *m* clef; **~ständer** *m* music stand

Not- *zW*: **~fall** *m* (case of) emergency; **n~falls** *adv* if need be; **n~gedrungen** *adj* necessary, unavoidable; **etw n~gedrungen machen** to be forced to do sth

notieren [no'tiːrən] *vt* to note; (*COMM*) to quote

Notierung *f* (*COMM*) quotation

nötig ['nøːtıç] *adj* necessary; **etw ~ haben** to need sth; **~en** [-gən] *vt* to compel, to force; **~enfalls** *adv* if necessary

Notiz [no'tiːts] (**-, -en**) *f* note; (*Zeitungsnotiz*) item; **~ nehmen** to take notice; **~block** *m* notepad; **~buch** *nt* notebook

Not- *zW*: **~lage** *f* crisis, emergency; **n~landen** *vi* to make a forced *od* emergency landing; **n~leidend** △ *adj* siehe **Not**; **~lösung** *f* temporary solution; **~lüge** *f* white lie

notorisch [no'toːrıʃ] *adj* notorious

Not- *zW*: **~ruf** *m* emergency call; **~rufsäule** *f* emergency telephone; **~stand** *m* state of emergency; **~unterkunft** *f* emergency accommodation; **~verband** *m* emergency dressing; **~wehr** (**-**) *f* self-defence; **n~wendig** *adj* necessary; **~wendigkeit** *f* necessity

Novelle [no'vɛlə] *f* short novel; (*JUR*) amendment

November [no'vɛmbər] (**-s, -**) *m* November

Nu [nuː] *m*: **im ~** in an instant

Nuance [ny'ã:sə] f nuance
nüchtern ['nγçtərn] adj sober; (*Magen*) empty; (*Urteil*) prudent; **N~heit** f sobriety
Nudel ['nu:dəl] (**-, -n**) f noodle; **~n** pl (*Teigwaren*) pasta sg; (*in Suppe*) noodles
Null [nʊl] (**-, -en**) f nought, zero; (*pej: Mensch*) washout; **n~** num zero; (*Fehler*) no; **n~ Uhr** midnight; **n~ und nichtig** null and void; **~punkt** m zero; **auf dem ~punkt** at zero
numerisch [nu'me:rɪʃ] adj numerical
Nummer ['nʊmər] (**-, -n**) f number; (*Größe*) size; **n~ieren** ▲ vt to number; **~nschild** nt (*AUT*) number od license (*US*) plate
nun [nu:n] adv now ♦ excl well; **das ist ~ mal so** that's the way it is
nur [nu:r] adv just, only; **wo bleibt er ~?** (just) where is he?
Nürnberg ['nγrnbεrk] (**-s**) nt Nuremberg
Nuss ▲ [nʊs] (**-, ⁻e**) f nut; **~baum** m walnut tree; **~knacker** (**-s, -**) m nutcracker
nutz [nʊts] adj: **zu nichts ~ sein** to be no use for anything; **~bringend** adj (*Verwendung*) profitable
nütze ['nγtsə] adj = nutz
Nutzen (**-s**) m usefulness; (*Gewinn*) profit; **von ~** useful; **n~** vi to be of use ♦ vt: **etw zu etw n~** to use sth for sth; **was nutzt es?** what's the use?, what use is it?
nützen vi, vt = nutzen
nützlich ['nγtslɪç] adj useful; **N~keit** f usefulness
Nutz- zW: **n~los** adj useless; **~losigkeit** f uselessness; **~nießer** (**-s, -**) m beneficiary
Nylon ['naɪlɔn] (**-(s)**) nt nylon

O, o

Oase [o'a:zə] f oasis
ob [ɔp] konj if, whether; **~ das wohl wahr ist?** can that be true?; **und ~!** you bet!
obdachlos adj homeless
Obdachlose(r) f(m) homeless person; **~nasyl** nt shelter for the homeless
Obduktion [ɔpdʊktsi'o:n] f post-mortem
obduzieren [ɔpdu'tsi:rən] vt to do a post-

mortem on
O-Beine ['o:baɪnə] pl bow od bandy legs
oben ['o:bən] adv above; (*in Haus*) upstairs; **~ erwähnt, ~ genannt** above-mentioned; **nach ~** up; **von ~ nach unten** down; **~ ohne** topless; **jdn von ~ bis unten ansehen** to look sb up and down; **~an** adv at the top; **~auf** adv up above, on the top ♦ adj (*munter*) in form; **~drein** adv into the bargain
Ober ['o:bər] (**-s, -**) m waiter; **die ~en** pl (*umg*) the bosses; (*ECCL*) the superiors; **~arm** m upper arm; **~arzt** m senior physician; **~aufsicht** f supervision; **~bayern** nt Upper Bavaria; **~befehl** m supreme command; **~befehlshaber** m commander-in-chief; **~bekleidung** f outer clothing; **~'bürgermeister** m lord mayor; **~deck** nt upper od top deck; **o~e(r, s)** adj upper; **~fläche** f surface; **o~flächlich** adj superficial; **~geschoss** ▲ nt upper storey; **o~halb** adv above ♦ präp +gen above; **~haupt** nt head, chief; **~haus** nt (*POL*) upper house, House of Lords (*BRIT*); **~hemd** nt shirt; **~herrschaft** f supremacy, sovereignty; **~in** f matron; (*ECCL*) Mother Superior; **~kellner** m head waiter; **~kiefer** m upper jaw; **~körper** m upper part of body; **~leitung** f direction; (*ELEK*) overhead cable; **~licht** nt skylight; **~lippe** f upper lip; **~schenkel** m thigh; **~schicht** f upper classes pl; **~schule** f grammar school (*BRIT*), high school (*US*); **~schwester** f (*MED*) matron
Oberst ['o:bərst] (**-en** od **-s, -en** od **-e**) m colonel; **o~e(r, s)** adj very top, top-most
Ober- zW: **~stufe** f upper school; **~teil** nt upper part; **~weite** f bust/chest measurement
obgleich [ɔp'glaɪç] konj although
Obhut ['ɔphu:t] (**-**) f care, protection; **in jds ~ sein** to be in sb's care
obig ['o:bɪç] adj above
Objekt [ɔp'jεkt] (**-(e)s, -e**) nt object; **~iv** [-'ti:f] (**-s, -e**) nt lens; **o~iv** adj objective; **~ivi'tät** f objectivity
Oblate [o'bla:tə] f (*Gebäck*) wafer; (*ECCL*) host

obligatorisch [obliga'to:rɪʃ] adj compulsory, obligatory

Obrigkeit ['o:brɪçkaɪt] f (Behörden) authorities pl, administration; (Regierung) government

obschon [ɔp'ʃo:n] konj although

Observatorium [ɔpzɛrva'to:riʊm] nt observatory

obskur [ɔps'ku:r] adj obscure; (verdächtig) dubious

Obst [o:pst] (-(e)s) nt fruit; ~baum m fruit tree; ~garten m orchard; ~händler m fruiterer, fruit merchant; ~kuchen m fruit tart

obszön [ɔps'tsø:n] adj obscene; O~i'tät f obscenity

obwohl [ɔp'vo:l] konj although

Ochse ['ɔksə] (-n, -n) m ox; o~n (umg) vt, vi to cram, to swot (BRIT)

Ochsenschwanzsuppe f oxtail soup

Ochsenzunge f oxtongue

öd(e) ['ø:d(ə)] adj (Land) waste, barren; (fig) dull; Ö~ f desert, waste(land); (fig) tedium

oder ['o:dər] konj or; das stimmt, ~? that's right, isn't it?

Ofen ['o:fən] (-s, ⸚) m oven; (Heizofen) fire, heater; (Kohlenofen) stove; (Hochofen) furnace; (Herd) cooker, stove; ~rohr nt stovepipe

offen ['ɔfən] adj open; (aufrichtig) frank; (Stelle) vacant; ~ bleiben (Fenster) to stay open; (Frage, Entscheidung) to remain open; ~ halten to keep open; ~ lassen to leave open; ~ stehen to be open; (Rechnung) to be unpaid; es steht Ihnen ~, es zu tun you are at liberty to do it; ~ gesagt to be honest; ~bar adj obvious; ~baren [ɔfən'ba:rən] vt to reveal, to manifest; O~'barung f (REL) revelation; O~heit f candour, frankness; ~herzig adj candid, frank; (Kleid) revealing; ~kundig adj well-known; (klar) evident; ~sichtlich adj evident, obvious

offensiv [ɔfɛn'zi:f] adj offensive; O~e [-'zi:və] f offensive

öffentlich ['œfəntlɪç] adj public; Ö~keit f (Leute) public; (einer Versammlung etc) public nature; in aller Ö~keit in public; an die Ö~keit dringen to reach the public ear

offiziell [ɔfitsi'ɛl] adj official

Offizier [ɔfi'tsi:r] (-s, -e) m officer; ~skasino nt officers' mess

öffnen ['œfnən] vt, vr to open; jdm die Tür ~ to open the door for sb

Öffner ['œfnər] (-s, -) m opener

Öffnung ['œfnʊŋ] f opening; ~szeiten pl opening times

oft [ɔft] adv often

öfter ['œftər] adv more often od frequently; ~s adv often, frequently

oh [o:] excl oh; ~ je! oh dear

OHG abk (= Offene Handelsgesellschaft) general partnership

ohne ['o:nə] präp +akk without ♦ konj without; das ist nicht ~ (umg) it's not bad; ~ weiteres without a second thought; (sofort) immediately; ~ zu fragen without asking; ~ dass er es wusste without him knowing it; ~dies [o:nə'di:s] adv anyway; ~gleichen [o:nə'glaɪçən] adj unsurpassed, without equal; ~hin [o:nə'hɪn] adv anyway, in any case

Ohnmacht ['o:nmaxt] f faint; (fig) impotence; in ~ fallen to faint

ohnmächtig ['o:nmɛçtɪç] adj in a faint, unconscious; (fig) weak, impotent; sie ist ~ she has fainted

Ohr [o:r] (-(e)s, -en) nt ear

Öhr [ø:r] (-(e)s, -e) nt eye

Ohren- zW: ~arzt m ear specialist; o~betäubend adj deafening; ~schmalz nt earwax; ~schmerzen pl earache sg

Ohr- zW: ~feige f slap on the face; box on the ears; o~feigen vt: jdn o~feigen to slap sb's face; to box sb's ears; ~läppchen nt ear lobe; ~ring m earring; ~wurm m earwig; (MUS) catchy tune

Öko- [øko] zW: ~laden m wholefood shop; ö~logisch [-'lo:gɪʃ] adj ecological; ö~nomisch [-'no:mɪʃ] adj economical

Oktober [ɔk'to:bər] (-s, -) m October; ~fest nt Munich beer festival

---

Oktoberfest

i The annual beer festival, the **Oktoberfest**, takes place in Munich at the end of September in a huge area where beer tents and various amusements are set up. People sit at long wooden tables, drink beer from enormous beer mugs, eat pretzels and listen to brass bands. It is a great attraction for tourists and locals alike.

ökumenisch [øku'me:nɪʃ] *adj* ecumenical

Öl [ø:l] (-(e)s, -e) *nt* oil; ~**baum** *m* olive tree; **ö~en** *vt* to oil; (*TECH*) to lubricate; ~**farbe** *f* oil paint; ~**feld** *nt* oilfield; ~**film** *m* film of oil; ~**heizung** *f* oil-fired central heating; **ö~ig** *adj* oily; ~**industrie** *f* oil industry

oliv [o'li:f] *adj* olive-green; **O~e** *f* olive

Öl- *zW:* ~**messstab** ▲ *m* dipstick; ~**sardine** *f* sardine; ~**stand** *m* oil level; ~**standanzeiger** *m* (*AUT*) oil gauge; ~**tanker** *m* oil tanker; ~**ung** *f* lubrication; oiling; (*ECCL*) anointment; **die Letzte ~ung** Extreme Unction; ~**wechsel** *m* oil change

Olymp- [o'lymp] *zW:* ~**iade** [olympi'a:də] *f* Olympic Games *pl*; ~**iasieger(in)** [-iazi:gər(ɪn)] *m(f)* Olympic champion; ~**iateilnehmer(in)** *m(f)* Olympic competitor; **o~isch** *adj* Olympic

Ölzeug *nt* oilskins *pl*

Oma ['o:ma] (-, -s) (*umg*) *f* granny

Omelett [ɔm(ə)'lɛt] (-(e)s, -s) *nt* omelet(te)

ominös [omi'nø:s] *adj* (*unheilvoll*) ominous

Onanie [ona'ni:] *f* masturbation; **o~ren** *vi* to masturbate

Onkel ['ɔŋkəl] (-s, -) *m* uncle

Opa ['o:pa] (-s, -s) (*umg*) *m* grandpa

Oper ['o:pər] (-, -n) *f* opera; opera house

Operation [operatsi'o:n] *f* operation; ~**ssaal** *m* operating theatre

Operette [ope'rɛtə] *f* operetta

operieren [ope'ri:rən] *vt* to operate on ♦ *vi* to operate

Opern- *zW:* ~**glas** *nt* opera glasses *pl*; ~**haus** *nt* opera house

Opfer ['ɔpfər] (-s, -) *nt* sacrifice; (*Mensch*) victim; **o~n** *vt* to sacrifice; ~**ung** *f* sacrifice

opponieren [ɔpo'ni:rən] *vi:* **gegen jdn/etw ~** to oppose sb/sth

Opportunist [ɔpɔrtu'nɪst] *m* opportunist

Opposition [ɔpozitsi'o:n] *f* opposition; **o~ell** *adj* opposing

Optik ['ɔptɪk] *f* optics *sg*; ~**er** (-s, -) *m* optician

optimal [ɔpti'ma:l] *adj* optimal, optimum

Optimismus [ɔpti'mɪsmʊs] *m* optimism

Optimist [ɔpti'mɪst] *m* optimist; **o~isch** *adj* optimistic

optisch ['ɔptɪʃ] *adj* optical

Orakel [o'ra:kəl] (-s, -) *nt* oracle

oral [o'ra:l] *adj* (*MED*) oral

Orange [o'rãːʒə] *f* orange; **o~** *adj* orange; ~**ade** [orã'ʒa:də] *f* orangeade; ~**at** [orã'ʒa:t] (-s, -e) *nt* candied peel

Orchester [ɔr'kɛstər] (-s, -) *nt* orchestra

Orchidee [ɔrçi'de:ə] *f* orchid

Orden ['ɔrdən] (-s, -) *m* (*ECCL*) order; (*MIL*) decoration; ~**sschwester** *f* nun

ordentlich ['ɔrdəntlɪç] *adj* (*anständig*) decent, respectable; (*geordnet*) tidy, neat; (*umg: annehmbar*) not bad; (: *tüchtig*) real, proper ♦ *adv* properly; ~**er Professor** (full) professor; **O~keit** *f* respectability; tidiness, neatness

ordinär [ɔrdi'nɛ:r] *adj* common, vulgar

ordnen ['ɔrdnən] *vt* to order, to put in order

Ordner (-s, -) *m* steward; (*COMM*) file

Ordnung *f* order; (*Ordnen*) ordering; (*Geordnetsein*) tidiness; ~ **machen** to tidy up; **in ~!** okay!

Ordnungs- *zW:* **o~gemäß** *adj* proper, according to the rules; **o~liebend** *adj* orderly, methodical; ~**strafe** *f* fine; **o~widrig** *adj* contrary to the rules, irregular; ~**widrigkeit** [-vɪdrɪçkaɪt] *f* infringement (*of law or rule*); ~**zahl** *f* ordinal number

Organ [ɔr'ga:n] (-s, -e) *nt* organ; (*Stimme*) voice; ~**isation** [-izatsi'o:n] *f* organization; ~**isator** [i'za:tɔr] *m* organizer; **o~isch** *adj* organic; **o~isieren** [-i'zi:rən] *vt* to organize, to arrange; (*umg: beschaffen*) to acquire ♦ *vr* to organize; ~**ismus** [-'nɪsmʊs] *m*

---

organism; **~ist** [-'nɪst] m organist;
~spende f organ donation;
~spenderausweis m donor card

Orgasmus [ɔr'ɡasmʊs] m orgasm

Orgel ['ɔrɡəl] (-, -n) f organ

Orgie ['ɔrɡiə] f orgy

Orient ['oːriɛnt] (-s) m Orient, east;
o~alisch [-'taːlɪʃ] adj oriental

orientier- zW: **~en** [-'tiːrən] vt (örtlich) to
locate; (fig) to inform ♦ vr to find one's way
od bearings; to inform o.s.; **O~ung** [-'tiːrʊŋ]
f orientation; (fig) information;
O~ungssinn m sense of direction;
O~ungsstufe f period during which pupils
are selected for different schools

Orientierungsstufe

i The **Orientierungsstufe** *is the name
given to the first two years spent in a*
Realschule *or* **Gymnasium**, *during which
a child is assessed as to his or her
suitability for that type of school. At the
end of two years it may be decided to
transfer the child to a school more suited to
his or her ability.*

---

original [ɔriɡiˈnaːl] adj original; **O~** (-s, -e)
nt original; **O~fassung** f original version;
O~i'tät f originality

originell [ɔriɡiˈnɛl] adj original

Orkan [ɔrˈkaːn] (-(e)s, -e) m hurricane;
o~artig adj (Wind) gale-force; (Beifall)
thunderous

Ornament [ɔrnaˈmɛnt] nt decoration,
ornament; **o~al** [-ˈtaːl] adj decorative,
ornamental

Ort [ɔrt] (-(e)s, -e od ⁼er) m place; **an ~ und
Stelle** on the spot; **o~en** vt to locate

ortho- [ɔrto-] zW: **~dox** [-ˈdɔks] adj orthodox;
O~grafie ▲ [-ɡraˈfiː] f spelling,
orthography; **~'grafisch** ▲ adj
orthographic; **O~päde** [-ˈpɛːdə] m
orthopaedist; **O~pädie** [-pɛˈdiː] f
orthopaedics sg; **~'pädisch** adj
orthopaedic

örtlich ['œrtlɪç] adj local; **Ö~keit** f locality

ortsansässig adj local

Ortschaft f village, small town

Orts- zW: **o~fremd** adj non-local;
~gespräch nt local (phone)call; **~name**
m place name; **~netz** nt (TEL) local
telephone exchange area; **~tarif** m (TEL)
tariff for local calls; **~zeit** f local time

Ortung f locating

Öse ['øːzə] f loop, eye

Ostasien [ɔsˈtaːziən] nt Eastern Asia

Osten ['ɔstən] (-s) m east

Oster- ['oːstər] zW: **~ei** nt Easter egg; **~fest**
nt Easter; **~glocke** f daffodil; **~hase** m
Easter bunny; **~montag** m Easter Monday;
~n (-s, -) nt Easter

Österreich ['øːstəraɪç] (-s) nt Austria;
~er(in) (-s, -) m(f) Austrian; **ö~isch** adj
Austrian

Ostküste f east coast

östlich ['œstlɪç] adj eastern, easterly

Ostsee f: **die ~** the Baltic (Sea)

Ouvertüre [uverˈtyːrə] f overture

oval [oˈvaːl] adj oval

Ovation [ovatsiˈoːn] f ovation

Oxid, Oxyd [ɔˈksyːt] (-(e)s, -e) nt oxide;
o~ieren vt, vi to oxidize; **~ierung** f
oxidization

Ozean ['oːtseaːn] (-s, -e) m ocean;
~dampfer m (ocean-going) liner

Ozon [oˈtsoːn] (-s) nt ozone; **~loch** nt ozone
hole; **~schicht** f ozone layer

P, p

Paar [paːr] (-(e)s, -e) nt pair; (Ehepaar)
couple; **ein p~** a few; **ein p~ Mal** a few
times; **p~en** vt, vr to couple; (Tiere) to
mate; **~lauf** m pair skating; **~ung** f
combination; mating; **p~weise** adv in
pairs; in couples

Pacht [paxt] (-, -en) f lease; **p~en** vt to
lease

Pächter ['pɛçtər] (-s, -) m leaseholder,
tenant

Pack¹ [pak] (-(e)s, -e od ⁼e) m bundle,
pack

Pack² [pak] (-(e)s) nt (pej) mob, rabble

Päckchen ['pɛkçən] *nt* small package; (*Zigaretten*) packet; (*Postpäckchen*) small parcel

Pack- *zW:* **p~en** *vt* to pack; (*fassen*) to grasp, to seize; (*umg: schaffen*) to manage; (*fig: fesseln*) to grip; **~en** (**-s, -**) *m* bundle; (*fig: Menge*) heaps of; **~esel** *m* (*auch fig*) packhorse; **~papier** *nt* brown paper, wrapping paper; **~ung** *f* packet; (*Pralinenpackung*) box; (*MED*) compress; **~ungsbeilage** *f* enclosed instructions *pl* for use

Pädagog- [pɛda'goːg] *zW:* **~e** (**-n, -n**) *m* teacher; **~ik** *f* education; **p~isch** *adj* educational, pedagogical

Paddel ['padəl] (**-s, -**) *nt* paddle; **~boot** *nt* canoe; **p~n** *vi* to paddle

Page ['paːʒə] (**-n, -n**) *m* page

Paket [pa'keːt] (**-(e)s, -e**) *nt* packet; (*Postpaket*) parcel; **~karte** *f* dispatch note; **~post** *f* parcel post; **~schalter** *m* parcels counter

Pakt [pakt] (**-(e)s, -e**) *m* pact

Palast [pa'last] (**-es, Paläste**) *m* palace

Palästina [palɛ'stiːna] (**-s**) *nt* Palestine

Palme ['palmə] *f* palm (tree)

Pampelmuse ['pampəlmuːzə] *f* grapefruit

panieren [pa'niːrən] *vt* (*KOCH*) to bread

Paniermehl [pa'niːrmeːl] *nt* breadcrumbs *pl*

Panik ['paːnɪk] *f* panic

panisch ['paːnɪʃ] *adj* panic-stricken

Panne [panə] *f* (*AUT etc*) breakdown; (*Missgeschick*) slip; **~nhilfe** *f* breakdown service

panschen ['panʃən] *vi* to splash about ♦ *vt* to water down

Pantoffel [pan'tɔfəl] (**-s, -n**) *m* slipper

Pantomime [panto'miːmə] *f* mime

Panzer ['pantsər] (**-s, -**) *m* armour; (*Platte*) armour plate; (*Fahrzeug*) tank; **~glas** *nt* bulletproof glass; **p~n** *vt* to armour ♦ *vr* (*fig*) to arm o.s.

Papa [pa'paː] (**-s, -s**) (*umg*) *m* dad, daddy

Papagei [papa'gaɪ] (**-s, -en**) *m* parrot

Papier [pa'piːr] (**-s, -e**) *nt* paper; (*Wertpapier*) security; **~fabrik** *f* paper mill; **~geld** *nt* paper money; **~korb** *m* wastepaper basket;

~taschentuch *nt* tissue

Papp- ['pap] *zW:* **~deckel** *m* cardboard; **~e** *f* cardboard; **~el** (**-, -n**) *f* poplar; **p~en** (*umg*) *vt, vi* to stick; **p~ig** *adj* sticky

Paprika ['paprika] (**-s, -s**) *m* (*Gewürz*) paprika; (*~schote*) pepper

Papst [paːpst] (**-(e)s, ▾e**) *m* pope

päpstlich ['pɛːpstlɪç] *adj* papal

Parabel [pa'raːbəl] (**-, -n**) *f* parable; (*MATH*) parabola

Parabolantenne [para'boːlantɛnə] *f* satellite dish

Parade [pa'raːdə] *f* (*MIL*) parade, review; (*SPORT*) parry

Paradies [para'diːs] (**-es, -e**) *nt* paradise; **p~isch** *adj* heavenly

Paradox [para'dɔks] (**-es, -e**) *nt* paradox; **p~** *adj* paradoxical

Paragraf ▲ [para'graːf] (**-en, -en**) *m* paragraph; (*JUR*) section

parallel [para'leːl] *adj* parallel; **P~e** *f* parallel

Parasit [para'ziːt] (**-en, -en**) *m* (*auch fig*) parasite

parat [pa'raːt] *adj* ready

Pärchen ['pɛːrçən] *nt* couple

Parfüm [par'fyːm] (**-s, -s** *od* **-e**) *nt* perfume; **~erie** [-ə'riː] *f* perfumery; **p~frei** *adj* non-perfumed; **p~ieren** *vt* to scent, to perfume

parieren [pa'riːrən] *vt* to parry ♦ *vi* (*umg*) to obey

Paris [pa'riːs] (**-**) *nt* Paris; **~er** *adj* Parisian ♦ *m* Parisian; **~erin** *f* Parisian

Park [park] (**-s, -s**) *m* park; **~anlage** *f* park; (*um Gebäude*) grounds *pl*; **p~en** *vt, vi* to park; **~ett** (**-(e)s, -e**) *nt* parquet (floor); (*THEAT*) stalls *pl*; **~gebühr** *f* parking fee; **~haus** *nt* multi-storey car park; **~lücke** *f* parking space; **~platz** *m* parking place; car park, parking lot (*US*); **~scheibe** *f* parking disc; **~schein** *m* car park ticket; **~uhr** *f* parking meter; **~verbot** *nt* parking ban

Parlament [parla'mɛnt] *nt* parliament; **~arier** [-'taːriər] (**-s, -**) *m* parliamentarian; **p~arisch** [-'taːrɪʃ] *adj* parliamentary

Parlaments- *zW:* **~beschluss** ▲ *m* vote of parliament; **~mitglied** *nt* member of parliament; **~sitzung** *f* sitting (of parliament)

Parodie [paro'di:] *f* parody; **p~ren** *vt* to parody

Parole [pa'ro:lə] *f* password; (*Wahlspruch*) motto

Partei [par'tai] *f* party; ~ **ergreifen für jdn** to take sb's side; **p~isch** *adj* partial, bias(s)ed; **p~los** *adj* neutral, impartial; **~mitglied** *nt* party member; **~programm** *nt* (party) manifesto; **~tag** *m* party conference

Parterre [par'tɛr] (**-s, -s**) *nt* ground floor; (*THEAT*) stalls *pl*

Partie [par'ti:] *f* part; (*Spiel*) game; (*Ausflug*) outing; (*Mann, Frau*) catch; (*COMM*) lot; **mit von der ~ sein** to join in

Partizip [parti'tsi:p] (**-s, -ien**) *nt* participle

Partner(in) ['partnər(ɪn)] (**-s, -**) *m(f)* partner; **~schaft** *f* partnership; (*von Städten*) twinning; **p~schaftlich** *adj* as partners; **~stadt** *f* twin town

Party ['pa:rti] (**-, -s**) *f* party

Pass ▲ [pas] (**-es, ⁺e**) *m* pass; (*Ausweis*) passport

passabel [pa'sa:bəl] *adj* passable, reasonable

Passage [pa'sa:ʒə] *f* passage

Passagier [pasa'ʒi:r] (**-s, -e**) *m* passenger; **~flugzeug** *nt* airliner

Passamt ▲ *nt* passport office

Passant [pa'sant] *m* passer-by

Passbild ▲ *nt* passport photograph

passen ['pasən] *vi* to fit; (*Farbe*) to go; (*auf Frage, KARTEN, SPORT*) to pass; **das passt mir nicht** that doesn't suit me; **~ zu** (*Farbe, Kleider*) to go with; **er passt nicht zu dir** he's not right for you; **~d** *adj* suitable; (*zusammenpassend*) matching; (*angebracht*) fitting; (*Zeit*) convenient

passier- [pa'si:r] *zW:* **~bar** *adj* passable; **~en** *vt* to pass; (*durch Sieb*) to strain ♦ *vi* to happen; **P~schein** *m* pass, permit

Passion [pasi'o:n] *f* passion; **p~iert** [-'ni:rt] *adj* enthusiastic, passionate; **~sspiel** *nt* Passion Play

passiv ['pasi:f] *adj* passive; **P~** (**-s, -e**) *nt* passive; **P~a** *pl* (*COMM*) liabilities; **P~i'tät** *f*

passiveness; **P~rauchen** *nt* passive smoking

Pass- ▲ *zW:* **~kontrolle** *f* passport control; **~stelle** *f* passport office; **~straße** *f* (mountain) pass

Paste ['pastə] *f* paste

Pastete [pas'te:tə] *f* pie

pasteurisieren [pastøri'zi:rən] *vt* to pasteurize

Pastor ['pastɔr] *m* vicar; pastor, minister

Pate ['pa:tə] (**-n, -n**) *m* godfather; **~nkind** *nt* godchild

Patent [pa'tɛnt] (**-(e)s, -e**) *nt* patent; (*MIL*) commission; **p~** *adj* clever; **~amt** *nt* patent office

Patentante *f* godmother

patentieren [patɛn'ti:rən] *vt* to patent

Patentinhaber *m* patentee

pathetisch [pa'te:tɪʃ] *adj* emotional; bombastic

Pathologe [pato'lo:gə] (**-n, -n**) *m* pathologist

pathologisch *adj* pathological

Pathos ['pa:tɔs] (**-**) *nt* emotiveness, emotionalism

Patient(in) [patsi'ɛnt(ɪn)] *m(f)* patient

Patin ['pa:tɪn] *f* godmother

Patriot [patri'o:t] (**-en, -en**) *m* patriot; **p~isch** *adj* patriotic; **~ismus** [-'tɪsmʊs] *m* patriotism

Patrone [pa'tro:nə] *f* cartridge

Patrouille [pa'trʊljə] *f* patrol

patrouillieren [patrʊl'ji:rən] *vi* to patrol

patsch [patʃ] *excl* splash; **P~e** (*umg*) *f* (*Bedrängnis*) mess, jam; **~en** *vi* to smack, to slap; (*im Wasser*) to splash; **~nass** ▲ *adj* soaking wet

patzig ['patsɪç] (*umg*) *adj* cheeky, saucy

Pauke ['pauka] *f* kettledrum; **auf die ~ hauen** to live it up

pauken *vt* (*intensiv lernen*) to swot up (*inf*) ♦ *vi* to swot (*inf*), cram (*inf*)

pausbäckig ['pausbɛkɪç] *adj* chubby-cheeked

pauschal [pau'ʃa:l] *adj* (*Kosten*) inclusive; (*Urteil*) sweeping; **P~e** *f* flat rate; **P~gebühr** *f* flat rate; **P~preis** *m* all-in

Spelling Reform: ▲ new spelling △ old spelling (to be phased out)

price; **P~reise** f package tour; **P~summe**
f lump sum

Pause ['pauzə] f break; (*THEAT*) interval;
(*Innehalten*) pause; (*Kopie*) tracing

pausen vt to trace; **~los** adj non-stop;
P~zeichen nt call sign; (*MUS*) rest

Pauspapier ['pauspapiːr] nt tracing paper

Pavillon ['paviljõ] (**-s, -s**) m pavilion

Pazif- [pa'tsiːf] zW: **~ik** (**-s**) m Pacific;
p~istisch adj pacifist

Pech [pɛç] (**-s, -e**) nt pitch; (*fig*) bad luck; **~
haben** to be unlucky; **p~schwarz** adj
pitch-black; **~strähne** (*umg*) m unlucky
patch; **~vogel** (*umg*) m unlucky person

Pedal [pe'daːl] (**-s, -e**) nt pedal

Pedant [pe'dant] m pedant; **~e'rie** f
pedantry; **p~isch** adj pedantic

Pediküre [pedi'kyːrə] f (*Fußpflege*) pedicure

Pegel ['peːgəl] (**-s, -**) m water gauge;
~stand m water level

peilen ['pailən] vt to get a fix on

Pein [pain] (**-**) f agony, pain; **p~igen** vt to
torture; (*plagen*) to torment; **p~lich** adj
(*unangenehm*) embarrassing, awkward,
painful; (*genau*) painstaking

Peitsche ['paitʃə] f whip; **p~n** vt to whip;
(*Regen*) to lash

Pelle ['pɛlə] f skin; **p~n** vt to skin, to peel

Pellkartoffeln pl jacket potatoes

Pelz [pɛlts] (**-es, -e**) m fur

Pendel ['pɛndəl] (**-s, -**) nt pendulum; **p~n** vi
(*Zug, Fähre etc*) to operate a shuttle service;
(*Mensch*) to commute; **~verkehr** m shuttle
traffic; (*für Pendler*) commuter traffic

Pendler ['pɛndlər] (**-s, -**) m commuter

penetrant [pene'trant] adj sharp; (*Person*)
pushing

Penis ['peːnɪs] (**-, -se**) m penis

pennen ['pɛnən] (*umg*) vi to kip

Penner (*umg: pej*) m (*Landstreicher*) tramp

Pension [pɛnzi'oːn] f (*Geld*) pension;
(*Ruhestand*) retirement; (*für Gäste*) boarding
od guesthouse; **~är(in)** [-'nɛːr(ɪn)] (**-s, -e**)
m(f) pensioner; **p~ieren** vt to pension off;
p~iert adj retired; **~ierung** f retirement;
~sgast m boarder, paying guest

Pensum ['pɛnzʊm] (**-s, Pensen**) nt quota;
(*SCH*) curriculum

per [pɛr] präp +akk by, per; (*pro*) per; (*bis*) by

Perfekt ['pɛrfɛkt] (**-(e)s, -e**) nt perfect; **p~**
adj perfect

perforieren [pɛrfo'riːrən] vt to perforate

Pergament [pɛrga'mɛnt] nt parchment;
~papier nt greaseproof paper

Periode [peri'oːdə] f period; **periodisch** adj
periodic; (*dezimal*) recurring

Perle ['pɛrlə] f (*auch fig*) pearl; **p~n** vi to
sparkle; (*Tropfen*) to trickle

Perl- ['pɛrl] zW: **~mutt** (**-s**) nt mother-of-
pearl; **~wein** m sparkling wine

perplex [pɛr'plɛks] adj dumbfounded

Person [pɛr'zoːn] (**-, -en**) f person; **ich für
meine ~ ...** personally I ...

Personal [pɛrzo'naːl] (**-s**) nt personnel;
(*Bedienung*) servants pl; **~ausweis** m
identity card; **~computer** m personal
computer; **~ien** [-iən] pl particulars;
~mangel m undermanning; **~pronomen**
nt personal pronoun

personell [pɛrzo'nɛl] adj (*Veränderungen*)
personnel

Personen- zW: **~aufzug** m lift, elevator
(*US*); **~kraftwagen** m private motorcar;
~schaden m injury to persons; **~zug** m
stopping train; passenger train

personifizieren [pɛrzonifi'tsiːrən] vt to
personify

persönlich [pɛr'zøːnlɪç] adj personal ♦ adv
in person; personally; **P~keit** f personality

Perspektive [pɛrspɛk'tiːvə] f perspective

Perücke [pe'rʏkə] f wig

pervers [pɛr'vɛrs] adj perverse

Pessimismus [pɛsi'mɪsmʊs] m pessimism

Pessimist [pɛsi'mɪst] m pessimist; **p~isch**
adj pessimistic

Pest [pɛst] (**-**) f plague

Petersilie [petar'ziːliə] f parsley

Petroleum [pe'troːleʊm] (**-s**) nt paraffin,
kerosene (*US*)

Pfad [pfaːt] (**-(e)s, -e**) m path; **~finder** (**-s,
-**) m boy scout; **~finderin** f girl guide

Pfahl [pfaːl] (**-(e)s, ⁺e**) m post, stake

Pfand [pfant] (**-(e)s, ⁺er**) nt pledge, security;
(*Flaschenpfand*) deposit; (*im Spiel*) forfeit;

~brief m bond
pfänden ['pfɛndən] vt to seize, to distrain
Pfänderspiel nt game of forfeits
Pfandflasche f returnable bottle
Pfandschein m pawn ticket
Pfändung ['pfɛndʊŋ] f seizure, distraint
Pfanne ['pfanə] f (frying) pan
Pfannkuchen m pancake; (Berliner) doughnut
Pfarr- ['pfar] zW: **~ei** f parish; **~er (-s, -)** m priest; (evangelisch) vicar; minister; **~haus** nt vicarage; manse
Pfau [pfaʊ] **(-(e)s), -en** m peacock; **~enauge** nt peacock butterfly
Pfeffer ['pfɛfər] **(-s, -)** m pepper; **~kuchen** m gingerbread; **~minz (-es, -e)** nt peppermint; **~mühle** f pepper mill; **p~n** vt to pepper; (umg: werfen) to fling; **gepfefferte Preise/Witze** steep prices/spicy jokes
Pfeife ['pfaɪfə] f whistle; (Tabakpfeife, Orgelpfeife) pipe; **p~n** (unreg) vt, vi to whistle; **~r (-s, -)** m piper
Pfeil [pfaɪl] **(-(e)s, -e)** m arrow
Pfeiler ['pfaɪlər] **(-s, -)** m pillar, prop; (Brückenpfeiler) pier
Pfennig ['pfɛnɪç] **(-(e)s, -e)** m pfennig (hundredth part of a mark)
Pferd [pfe:rt] **(-(e)s, -e)** nt horse
Pferde- ['pfe:rdə] zW: **~rennen** nt horse race; horse racing; **~schwanz** m (Frisur) ponytail; **~stall** m stable
Pfiff [pfɪf] **(-(e)s, -e)** m whistle
Pfifferling ['pfɪfərlɪŋ] m yellow chanterelle (mushroom); **keinen ~ wert** not worth a thing
pfiffig adj sly, sharp
Pfingsten ['pfɪŋstən] **(-, -)** nt Whitsun (BRIT), Pentecost
Pfirsich ['pfɪrzɪç] **(-s, -e)** m peach
Pflanz- ['pflants] zW: **~e** f plant; **p~en** vt to plant; **~enfett** nt vegetable fat; **p~lich** adj vegetable; **~ung** f plantation
Pflaster ['pflastər] **(-s, -)** nt plaster; (Straße) pavement; **p~n** vt to pave; **~stein** m paving stone
Pflaume ['pflaʊmə] f plum

Pflege ['pfle:gə] f care; (von Idee) cultivation; (Krankenpflege) nursing; **in ~ sein** (Kind) to be fostered out; **p~bedürftig** adj needing care; **~eltern** pl foster parents; **~heim** nt nursing home; **~kind** nt foster child; **p~leicht** adj easy-care; **~mutter** f foster mother; **p~n** vt to look after; (Kranke) to nurse; (Beziehungen) to foster; **~r (-s, -)** m orderly; male nurse; **~rin** f nurse, attendant; **~vater** m foster father
Pflicht [pflɪçt] **(-, -en)** f duty; (SPORT) compulsory section; **p~bewusst** ▲ adj conscientious; **~fach** nt (SCH) compulsory subject; **~gefühl** nt sense of duty; **p~gemäß** adj dutiful ♦ adv as in duty bound; **~versicherung** f compulsory insurance
pflücken ['pflʏkən] vt to pick; (Blumen) to pick, to pluck
Pflug [pflu:k] **(-(e)s, ⁻e)** m plough
pflügen ['pfly:gən] vt to plough
Pforte ['pfɔrtə] f gate; door
Pförtner ['pfœrtnər] **(-s, -)** m porter, doorkeeper, doorman
Pfosten ['pfɔstən] **(-s, -)** m post
Pfote ['pfo:tə] f paw; (umg: Schrift) scrawl
Pfropfen (-s, -) m (Flaschenpfropfen) stopper; (Blutpfropfen) clot
pfui [pfʊɪ] excl ugh!
Pfund [pfʊnt] **(-(e)s, -e)** nt pound
pfuschen ['pfʊʃən] (umg) vi to be sloppy; **jdm ins Handwerk ~** to interfere in sb's business
Pfuscher ['pfʊʃər] **(-s, -)** (umg) m sloppy worker; (Kurpfuscher) quack; **~ei** (umg) f sloppy work; quackery
Pfütze ['pfʏtsə] f puddle
Phänomen [fɛno'me:n] **(-s, -e)** nt phenomenon
phänomenal [-'na:l] adj phenomenal
Phantasie etc [fanta'zi:] f = **Fantasie** etc
phantastisch [fan'tastɪʃ] adj = **fantastisch**
Phase ['fa:zə] f phase
Philologie [filolo'gi:] f philology
Philosoph [filo'zo:f] **(-en, -en)** m philosopher; **~ie** [-'fi:] f philosophy; **p~isch** adj philosophical

Spelling Reform: ▲ *new spelling* △ *old spelling (to be phased out)*

phlegmatisch [flɛ'gmaːtɪʃ] *adj* lethargic
Phonetik [fo'neːtɪk] *f* phonetics *sg*
phonetisch *adj* phonetic
Phosphor ['fɔsfɔr] (**-s**) *m* phosphorus
Photo *etc* ['foːto] (**-s, -s**) *nt* = **Foto** *etc*
Phrase ['fraːzə] *f* phrase; (*pej*) hollow phrase
pH-Wert [peː'haːvɛrt] *m* pH-value
Physik [fy'ziːk] *f* physics *sg*; **p~alisch**
[-'kaːlɪʃ] *adj* of physics; **~er(in)** ['fyːzɪkər(ɪn)]
(**-s, -**) *m(f)* physicist
Physiologie [fyziolo'giː] *f* physiology
physisch ['fyːzɪʃ] *adj* physical
Pianist(in) [pia'nɪst(ɪn)] *m(f)* pianist
Pickel ['pɪkəl] (**-s, -**) *m* pimple; (*Werkzeug*)
pickaxe; (*Bergpickel*) ice axe; **p~ig** *adj*
pimply, spotty
picken ['pɪkən] *vi* to pick, to peck
Picknick ['pɪknɪk] (**-s, -e** *od* **-s**) *nt* picnic; **~**
machen to have a picnic
piepen ['piːpən] *vi* to chirp
piepsen ['piːpsən] *vi* to chirp
Piepser (*umg*) *m* pager, paging device
Pier [piːər] (**-s, -s** *od* **-e**) *m od f* pier
Pietät [pie'tɛːt] *f* piety, reverence; **p~los** *adj*
impious, irreverent
Pigment [pɪg'mɛnt] *nt* pigment
Pik [piːk] (**-s, -s**) *nt* (*KARTEN*) spades
pikant [pi'kant] *adj* spicy, piquant;
(*anzüglich*) suggestive
Pilger ['pɪlgər] (**-s, -**) *m* pilgrim; **~fahrt** *f*
pilgrimage
Pille ['pɪlə] *f* pill
Pilot [pi'loːt] (**-en, -en**) *m* pilot
Pilz [pɪlts] (**-es, -e**) *m* fungus; (*essbar*)
mushroom; (*giftig*) toadstool; **~krankheit** *f*
fungal disease
Pinguin ['pɪŋguiːn] (**-s, -e**) *m* penguin
Pinie ['piːniə] *f* pine
pinkeln ['pɪŋkəln] (*umg*) *vi* to pee
Pinnwand ['pɪnvant] *f* noticeboard
Pinsel ['pɪnzəl] (**-s, -**) *m* paintbrush
Pinzette [pɪn'tsɛtə] *f* tweezers *pl*
Pionier [pio'niːr] (**-s, -e**) *m* pioneer; (*MIL*)
sapper, engineer
Pirat [pi'raːt] (**-en, -en**) *m* pirate
Piste ['pɪstə] *f* (*SKI*) run, piste; (*AVIAT*) runway
Pistole [pɪs'toːlə] *f* pistol

Pizza ['pɪtsa] (**-, -s**) *f* pizza
Pkw [peːkaː'veː] (**-(s), -(s)**) *m abk* =
Personenkraftwagen
plädieren [plɛ'diːrən] *vi* to plead
Plädoyer [plɛdoa'jeː] (**-s, -s**) *nt* speech for
the defence; (*fig*) plea
Plage ['plaːgə] *f* plague; (*Mühe*) nuisance;
~geist *m* pest, nuisance; **p~n** *vt* to
torment ♦ *vr* to toil, to slave
Plakat [pla'kaːt] (**-(e)s, -e**) *nt* placard; poster
Plan [plaːn] (**-(e)s, ⁎e**) *m* plan; (*Karte*) map
Plane *f* tarpaulin
planen *vt* to plan; (*Mord etc*) to plot
Planer (**-s, -**) *m* planner
Planet [pla'neːt] (**-en, -en**) *m* planet
planieren [pla'niːrən] *vt* to plane, to level
Planke ['plaŋkə] *f* plank
plan- ['plaːn] *zW:* **~los** *adj* (*Vorgehen*)
unsystematic; (*Umherlaufen*) aimless;
~mäßig *adj* according to plan; systematic;
(*EISENB*) scheduled
Plansoll (**-s**) *nt* output target
Plantage [plan'taːʒə] *f* plantation
Plan(t)schbecken ['plan(t)ʃbɛkən] *nt*
paddling pool
plan(t)schen ['plan(t)ʃən] *vi* to splash
Planung *f* planning
Planwirtschaft *f* planned economy
plappern ['plapərn] *vi* to chatter
plärren ['plɛrən] *vi* (*Mensch*) to cry, to
whine; (*Radio*) to blare
Plasma ['plasma] (**-s, Plasmen**) *nt* plasma
Plastik¹ ['plastɪk] *f* sculpture
Plastik² ['plastɪk] (**-s**) *nt* (*Kunststoff*) plastic;
~beutel *m* plastic bag, carrier bag; **~folie**
f plastic film
plastisch ['plastɪʃ] *adj* plastic; **stell dir das**
~ vor! just picture it!
Platane [pla'taːnə] *f* plane (tree)
Platin ['plaːtiːn] (**-s**) *nt* platinum
platonisch [pla'toːnɪʃ] *adj* platonic
platsch [platʃ] *excl* splash; **~en** *vi* to splash
plätschern ['plɛtʃərn] *vi* to babble
platschnass ▲ *adj* drenched
platt [plat] *adj* flat; (*umg: überrascht*)
flabbergasted; (*fig: geistlos*) flat, boring;
~deutsch *adj* low German; **P~e** *f*

(*Speisenplatte, PHOT, TECH*) plate; (*Steinplatte*) flag; (*Kachel*) tile; (*Schallplatte*) record; **P~enspieler** *m* record player; **P~enteller** *m* turntable

Platz [plats] **(-es, ⁺e)** *m* place; (*Sitzplatz*) seat; (*Raum*) space, room; (*in Stadt*) square; (*Sportplatz*) playing field; **~ nehmen** to take a seat; **jdm ~ machen** to make room for sb; **~angst** *f* claustrophobia; **~anweiser(in) (-s, -)** *m(f)* usher(ette)

Plätzchen ['plɛtsçən] *nt* spot; (*Gebäck*) biscuit

platzen *vi* to burst; (*Bombe*) to explode; **vor Wut ~** (*umg*) to be bursting with anger

platzieren ▲ [pla'tsi:rən] *vt* to place ♦ *vr* (*SPORT*) to be placed; (*TENNIS*) to be seeded

Platz- *zW:* **~karte** *f* seat reservation; **~mangel** *m* lack of space; **~patrone** *f* blank cartridge; **~regen** *m* downpour; **~reservierung** [-rezɛrviːrʊŋ] *f* seat reservation; **~wunde** *f* cut

Plauderei [plaʊdə'raɪ] *f* chat, conversation; (*RADIO*) talk

plaudern ['plaʊdərn] *vi* to chat, to talk

plausibel [plaʊ'zi:bəl] *adj* plausible

plazieren △ [pla'tsi:rən] *vt, vr siehe* **platzieren**

Pleite ['plaɪtə] *f* bankruptcy; (*umg: Reinfall*) flop; **~ machen** to go bust; **p~** (*umg*) *adj* broke

Plenum ['ple:nʊm] **(-s)** *nt* plenum

Plombe ['plɔmbə] *f* lead seal; (*Zahnplombe*) filling

plombieren [plɔm'bi:rən] *vt* to seal; (*Zahn*) to fill

plötzlich ['plœtslɪç] *adj* sudden ♦ *adv* suddenly

plump [plʊmp] *adj* clumsy; (*Hände*) coarse; (*Körper*) shapeless; **~sen** (*umg*) *vi* to plump down, to fall

Plunder ['plʊndər] **(-s)** *m* rubbish

plündern ['plʏndərn] *vt* to plunder; (*Stadt*) to sack ♦ *vi* to plunder; **Plünderung** *f* plundering, sack, pillage

Plural ['plu:ra:l] **(-s, -e)** *m* plural; **p~istisch** *adj* pluralistic

Plus [plʊs] **(-, -)** *nt* plus; (*FIN*) profit; (*Vorteil*) advantage; **p~** *adv* plus

Plüsch [ply:ʃ] **(-(e)s, -e)** *m* plush

Plus- [plʊs] *zW:* **~pol** *m* (*ELEK*) positive pole; **~punkt** *m* point; (*fig*) point in sb's favour

Plutonium [plu'to:niʊm] **(-s)** *nt* plutonium

PLZ *abk* = **Postleitzahl**

Po [po:] **(-s, -s)** (*umg*) *m* bottom, bum

Pöbel ['pø:bəl] **(-s)** *m* mob, rabble; **~ei** *f* vulgarity; **p~haft** *adj* low, vulgar

pochen ['pɔxən] *vi* to knock; (*Herz*) to pound; **auf etw** *akk* **~** (*fig*) to insist on sth

Pocken ['pɔkən] *pl* smallpox *sg*

Podium ['po:diʊm] *nt* podium; **~sdiskussion** *f* panel discussion

Poesie [poe'zi:] *f* poetry

Poet [po'e:t] **(-en, -en)** *m* poet; **p~isch** *adj* poetic

Pointe [po'ɛ̃:tə] *f* point

Pokal [po'ka:l] **(-s, -e)** *m* goblet; (*SPORT*) cup; **~spiel** *nt* cup tie

pökeln ['pø:kəln] *vt* to pickle, to salt

Poker ['po:kər] **(-s)** *nt od m* poker

Pol [po:l] **(-s, -e)** *m* pole; **p~ar** *adj* polar; **~arkreis** *m* Arctic circle

Pole ['po:lə] **(-n, -n)** *m* Pole

polemisch [po:le:mɪʃ] *adj* polemical

Polen ['po:lən] **(-s)** *nt* Poland

Police [po'li:s(ə)] *f* insurance policy

Polier [po'li:r] **(-s, -e)** *m* foreman

polieren *vt* to polish

Poliklinik [poli'kli:nɪk] *f* outpatients (department) *sg*

Polin *f* Pole

Politik [poli'ti:k] *f* politics *sg*; (*eine bestimmte*) policy; **~er(in)** [poli'ti:kər(ɪn)] **(-s, -)** *m(f)* politician

politisch [po'li:tɪʃ] *adj* political

Politur [poli'tu:r] *f* polish

Polizei [poli'tsaɪ] *f* police; **~beamte(r)** *m* police officer; **p~lich** *adj* police; **sich p~lich melden** to register with the police; **~revier** *nt* police station; **~staat** *m* police state; **~streife** *f* police patrol; **~stunde** *f* closing time; **~wache** *f* police station

Polizist(in) [poli'tsɪst(ɪn)] **(-en, -en)** *m(f)* policeman(-woman)

Pollen ['pɔlən] **(-s, -)** *m* pollen; **~flug** *m* pollen count

polnisch ['pɔlnɪʃ] *adj* Polish

Polohemd ['po:lohɛmt] *nt* polo shirt

Polster ['pɔlstər] **(-s, -)** *nt* cushion; *(~ung)* upholstery; *(in Kleidung)* padding; *(fig: Geld)* reserves *pl*; **~er (-s, -)** *m* upholsterer; **~möbel** *pl* upholstered furniture *sg*; **p~n** *vt* to upholster; to pad

Polterabend ['pɔltəra:bənt] *m* party on eve of wedding

poltern *vi (Krach machen)* to crash; *(schimpfen)* to rant

Polyp [po'ly:p] **(-en, -en)** *m* polyp; *(umg)* cop; **~en** *pl (MED)* adenoids

Pomade [po'ma:də] *f* pomade

Pommes frites [pɔm'frɪt] *pl* chips, French fried potatoes

Pomp [pɔmp] **(-(e)s)** *m* pomp; **p~ös** [pɔm'pøːs] *adj (Auftritt, Fest, Haus)* ostentatious, showy

Pony ['pɔni] **(-s, -s)** *nt (Pferd)* pony ♦ *m (Frisur)* fringe

Popmusik ['pɔpmuzi:k] *f* pop music

Popo [po'po:] **(-s, -s)** *(umg)* *m* bottom, bum

poppig ['pɔpɪç] *adj (Farbe etc)* gaudy

populär [popu'lɛːr] *adj* popular

Popularität [populari'tɛːt] *f* popularity

Pore ['po:rə] *f* pore

Pornografie ▲ [pɔrnograˈfiː] *f* pornography; **pornografisch** ▲ [pɔrnoˈgraːfɪʃ] *adj* pornographic

porös [po'røːs] *adj* porous

Porree ['pɔre] **(-s, -s)** *m* leek

Portefeuille [pɔrt(ə)'føːj] *nt (POL, FIN)* portfolio

Portemonnaie [pɔrtmɔ'neː] **(-s, -s)** *nt* purse

Portier [pɔrti'eː] **(-s, -s)** *m* porter

Portion [pɔrtsi'oːn] *f* portion, helping; *(umg: Anteil)* amount

Portmonee ▲ [pɔrtmo'neː] **(-s, -s)** *nt* = **Portemonnaie**

Porto ['pɔrto] **(-s, -s)** *nt* postage; **p~frei** *adj* post-free, (postage) prepaid

Portrait [pɔr'trɛː] **(-s, -s)** *nt* = **Porträt**; **p~ieren** *vt* = **porträtieren**

Porträt [pɔr'trɛː] **(-s, -s)** *nt* portrait; **p~ieren** *vt* to paint, to portray

Portugal ['pɔrtugal] **(-s)** *nt* Portugal; **Portugiese** [pɔrtu'giːzə] **(-n, -n)** *m* Portuguese; **Portu'giesin** *f* Portuguese; **portu'giesisch** *adj* Portuguese

Porzellan [pɔrtse'laːn] **(-s, -e)** *nt* china, porcelain; *(Geschirr)* china

Posaune [po'zaunə] *f* trombone

Pose ['po:zə] *f* pose

Position [pozitsi'oːn] *f* position

positiv ['po:ziti:f] *adj* positive; **P~ (-s, -e)** *nt (PHOT)* positive

possessiv ['pɔsesiːf] *adj* possessive; **P~pronomen (-s, -e)** *nt* possessive pronoun

possierlich [pɔ'siːrlɪç] *adj* funny

Post [pɔst] **(-, -en)** *f* post (office); *(Briefe)* mail; **~amt** *nt* post office; **~anweisung** *f* postal order, money order; **~bote** *m* postman; **~en (-s, -)** *m* post, position; *(COMM)* item; *(auf Liste)* entry; *(MIL)* sentry; *(Streikposten)* picket; **~er (-s, -(s))** *nt* poster; **~fach** *nt* post office box; **~karte** *f* postcard; **p~lagernd** *adv* poste restante *(BRIT)*, general delivery *(US)*; **~leitzahl** *f* postal code; **~scheckkonto** *nt* postal giro account; **~sparbuch** *nt* post office savings book; **~sparkasse** *f* post office savings bank; **~stempel** *m* postmark; **p~wendend** *adv* by return of post; **~wertzeichen** *nt* postage stamp

potent [po'tɛnt] *adj* potent

Potential △ [potɛntsi'aːl] **(-s, -e)** *nt* siehe **Potenzial**

potentiell △ [potɛntsi'el] *adj* siehe **potenziell**

Potenz [po'tɛnts] *f* power; *(eines Mannes)* potency

Potenzial ▲ [potɛn'tsiaːl] **(-s, -e)** *nt* potential

potenziell ▲ [potɛn'tsiɛl] *adj* potential

Pracht [praxt] **(-)** *f* splendour, magnificence; **prächtig** ['prɛçtɪç] *adj* splendid

Prachtstück *nt* showpiece

prachtvoll *adj* splendid, magnificent

Prädikat [predi'kaːt] **(-(e)s, -e)** *nt* title;

(*GRAM*) predicate; (*Zensur*) distinction

prägen ['prɛːgən] *vt* to stamp; (*Münze*) to mint; (*Ausdruck*) to coin; (*Charakter*) to form

prägnant [prɛ'gnant] *adj* precise, terse

Prägung ['prɛːgʊŋ] *f* minting; forming; (*Eigenart*) character, stamp

prahlen ['praːlən] *vi* to boast, to brag; **Prahle'rei** *f* boasting

Praktik ['praktɪk] *f* practice; **p~abel** [-'kaːbəl] *adj* practicable; **~ant(in)** [-'kant(ɪn)] *m(f)* trainee; **~um** (**-s, Praktika** *od* **Praktiken**) *nt* practical training

praktisch ['praktɪʃ] *adj* practical, handy; **~er Arzt** general practitioner

praktizieren [praktɪ'tsiːrən] *vt, vi* to practise

Praline [pra'liːnə] *f* chocolate

prall [pral] *adj* firmly rounded; (*Segel*) taut; (*Arme*) plump; (*Sonne*) blazing; **~en** *vi* to bounce, to rebound; (*Sonne*) to blaze

Prämie ['prɛːmiə] *f* premium; (*Belohnung*) award, prize; **p~ren** *vt* to give an award to

Präparat [prɛpa'raːt] (**-(e)s, -e**) *nt* (*BIOL*) preparation; (*MED*) medicine

Präposition [prɛpozitsi'oːn] *f* preposition

Prärie [prɛ'riː] *f* prairie

Präsens ['prɛːzɛns] (**-**) *nt* present tense

präsentieren [prɛzɛn'tiːrən] *vt* to present

Präservativ [prɛzɛrva'tiːf] (**-s, -e**) *nt* contraceptive

Präsident(in) [prɛzi'dɛnt(ɪn)] *m(f)* president; **~schaft** *f* presidency

Präsidium [prɛ'ziːdiʊm] *nt* presidency, chair(manship); (*Polizeipräsidium*) police headquarters *pl*

prasseln ['prasəln] *vi* (*Feuer*) to crackle; (*Hagel*) to drum; (*Wörter*) to rain down

Praxis ['praksɪs] (**-, Praxen**) *f* practice; (*Behandlungsraum*) surgery; (*von Anwalt*) office

Präzedenzfall [prɛtse'dɛnts-] *m* precedent

präzis [prɛ'tsiːs] *adj* precise; **P~ion** [prɛtsizi'oːn] *f* precision

predigen ['preːdɪgən] *vt, vi* to preach; **Prediger** (**-s, -**) *m* preacher

Predigt ['preːdɪçt] (**-, -en**) *f* sermon

Preis [praɪs] (**-es, -e**) *m* price; (*Siegespreis*) prize; **um keinen ~** not at any price;

p~bewusst ▲ *adj* price-conscious

Preiselbeere *f* cranberry

preis- ['praɪs] *zW:* **~en** (*unreg*) *vi* to praise; **~geben** (*unreg*) *vt* to abandon; (*opfern*) to sacrifice; (*zeigen*) to expose; **~gekrönt** *adj* prizewinning; **P~gericht** *nt* jury; **~günstig** *adj* inexpensive; **P~lage** *f* price range; **~lich** *adj* (*Lage, Unterschied*) price, in price; **P~liste** *f* price list; **P~richter** *m* judge (*in a competition*); **P~schild** *nt* price tag; **P~träger(in)** *m(f)* prizewinner; **~wert** *adj* inexpensive

Prell- [prɛl] *zW:* **~bock** *m* buffers *pl*; **p~en** *vt* to bump; (*fig*) to cheat, to swindle; **~ung** *f* bruise

Premiere [prəmi'ɛːrə] *f* premiere

Premierminister [prəmi'eː-mɪnɪstər] *m* prime minister, premier

Presse ['prɛsə] *f* press; **~agentur** *f* press agency; **~freiheit** *f* freedom of the press; **p~n** *vt* to press

Pressluft ▲ ['prɛslʊft] *f* compressed air; **~bohrer** *m* pneumatic drill

Prestige [prɛs'tiːʒə] (**-s**) *nt* prestige

prickeln ['prɪkəln] *vt, vi* to tingle; to tickle

Priester ['priːstər] (**-s, -**) *m* priest

prima *adj inv* first-class, excellent

primär [pri'mɛːr] *adj* primary

Primel ['priːməl] (**-, -n**) *f* primrose

primitiv [primi'tiːf] *adj* primitive

Prinz [prɪnts] (**-en, -en**) *m* prince; **~essin** *f* princess

Prinzip [prɪn'tsiːp] (**-s, -ien**) *nt* principle; **p~iell** [-i'ɛl] *adj, adv* on principle; **p~ienlos** *adj* unprincipled

Priorität [priori'tɛːt] *f* priority

Prise ['priːzə] *f* pinch

Prisma ['prɪsma] (**-s, Prismen**) *nt* prism

privat [pri'vaːt] *adj* private; **P~besitz** *m* private property; **P~fernsehen** *nt* commercial television; **P~patient(in)** *m(f)* private patient; **P~schule** *f* public school

Privileg [privi'leːk] (**-(e)s, -ien**) *nt* privilege

Pro [proː] (**-**) *nt* pro

pro *präp +akk* per

Probe ['proːbə] *f* test; (*Teststück*) sample; (*THEAT*) rehearsal; **jdn auf die ~ stellen** to put sb to the test; **~exemplar** *nt* specimen copy; **~fahrt** *f* test drive; **p~n** *vt* to try; (*THEAT*) to rehearse; **p~weise** *adv* on approval; **~zeit** *f* probation period

probieren [proˈbiːrən] *vt* to try; (*Wein, Speise*) to taste, to sample ♦ *vi* to try; to taste

Problem [proˈbleːm] **(-s, -e)** *nt* problem; **~atik** [-ˈmaːtɪk] *f* problem; **p~atisch** [-ˈmaːtɪʃ] *adj* problematic; **p~los** *adj* problem-free

Produkt [proˈdʊkt] **(-(e)s, -e)** *nt* product; (*AGR*) produce *no pl*; **~ion** [prodʊktsiˈoːn] *f* production; output; **p~iv** [-ˈtiːf] *adj* productive; **~ivität** *f* productivity

Produzent [produˈtsɛnt] *m* manufacturer; (*Film*) producer

produzieren [produˈtsiːrən] *vt* to produce

Professor [proˈfɛsɔr] *m* professor

Profi [ˈproːfi] **(-s, -s)** *m* (*umg, SPORT*) pro

Profil [proˈfiːl] **(-s, -e)** *nt* profile; (*fig*) image

Profit [proˈfiːt] **(-(e)s, -e)** *m* profit; **p~ieren** *vi*: **p~ieren (von)** to profit (from)

Prognose [proˈgnoːzə] *f* prediction, prognosis

Programm [proˈgram] **(-s, -e)** *nt* programme; (*COMPUT*) program; **p~ieren** [-ˈmiːrən] *vt* to programme; (*COMPUT*) to program; **~ierer(in) (-s, -)** *m(f)* programmer

progressiv [progrɛˈsiːf] *adj* progressive

Projekt [proˈjɛkt] **(-(e)s, -e)** *nt* project; **~or** [proˈjɛktɔr] *m* projector

proklamieren [proklaˈmiːrən] *vt* to proclaim

Prokurist(in) [prokuˈrɪst(ɪn)] *m(f)* ≈ company secretary

Prolet [proˈleːt] **(-en, -en)** *m* prole, pleb; **~arier** [-ˈtaːriər] **(-s, -)** *m* proletarian

Prolog [proˈloːk] **(-(e)s, -e)** *m* prologue

Promenade [proməˈnaːdə] *f* promenade

Promille [proˈmɪlə] **(-(s), -)** *nt* alcohol level

prominent [promiˈnɛnt] *adj* prominent

Prominenz [promiˈnɛnts] *f* VIPs *pl*

Promotion [promotsiˈoːn] *f* doctorate, Ph.D.

promovieren [promoˈviːrən] *vi* to do a doctorate *od* Ph.D.

prompt [prɔmpt] *adj* prompt

Pronomen [proˈnoːmɛn] **(-s, -)** *nt* pronoun

Propaganda [propaˈganda] **(-)** *f* propaganda

Propeller [proˈpɛlər] **(-s, -)** *m* propeller

Prophet [proˈfeːt] **(-en, -en)** *m* prophet

prophezeien [profeˈtsaɪən] *vt* to prophesy; **Prophezeiung** *f* prophecy

Proportion [proportsiˈoːn] *f* proportion; **p~al** [-ˈnaːl] *adj* proportional

proportioniert [proportsioˈniːrt] *adj*: **gut/ schlecht ~** well-/badly-proportioned

Prosa [ˈproːza] **(-)** *f* prose; **p~isch** [proˈzaːɪʃ] *adj* prosaic

prosit [ˈproːzɪt] *excl* cheers

Prospekt [proˈspɛkt] **(-(e)s, -e)** *m* leaflet, brochure

prost [proːst] *excl* cheers

Prostituierte [prostituˈiːrtə] *f* prostitute

Prostitution [prostitutsiˈoːn] *f* prostitution

Protest [proˈtɛst] **(-(e)s, -e)** *m* protest; **~ant(in)** [protɛsˈtant(ɪn)] *m(f)* Protestant; **p~antisch** [protɛsˈtantɪʃ] *adj* Protestant; **p~ieren** [protɛsˈtiːrən] *vi* to protest

Prothese [proˈteːzə] *f* artificial limb; (*Zahnprothese*) dentures *pl*

Protokoll [protoˈkɔl] **(-s, -e)** *nt* register; (*von Sitzung*) minutes *pl*; (*diplomatisch*) protocol; (*Polizeiprotokoll*) statement; **p~ieren** [-ˈliːrən] *vt* to take down in the minutes

protzen [ˈprɔtsən] *vi* to show off

Proviant [proviˈant] **(-s, -e)** *m* provisions *pl*, supplies *pl*

Provinz [proˈvɪnts] **(-, -en)** *f* province; **p~iell** *adj* provincial

Provision [provizi̯ˈoːn] *f* (*COMM*) commission

provisorisch [proviˈzoːrɪʃ] *adj* provisional

Provokation [provokatsiˈoːn] *f* provocation

provozieren [provoˈtsiːrən] *vt* to provoke

Prozedur [protseˈduːr] *f* procedure; (*pej*) carry-on

Prozent [proˈtsɛnt] **(-(e)s, -e)** *nt* per cent, percentage; **~satz** *m* percentage; **p~ual** [-u̯ˈaːl] *adj* percentage *cpd*; as a percentage

Prozess ▲ [proˈtsɛs] **(-es, -e)** *m* trial, case

Prozession [protsɛsiˈoːn] *f* procession

prüde [ˈpryːdə] *adj* prudish; **P~rie** [-ˈriː] *f* prudery

Prüf- ['pry:f] zW: **p~en** vt to examine, to test; (nachprüfen) to check; **~er (-s, -)** m examiner; **~ling** m examinee; **~ung** f examination; checking; **~ungsaus-schuss** ▲ m examining board

Prügel ['pry:gəl] **(-s, -)** m cudgel ♦ pl (Schläge) beating; **~ei** [-'lai] f fight; **p~n** vt to beat ♦ vr to fight; **~strafe** f corporal punishment

Prunk [prʊŋk] **(-(e)s)** m pomp, show; **p~voll** adj splendid, magnificent

PS [peː'ɛs] abk (= Pferdestärke) H.P.

Psych- ['psyç] zW: **~iater** [-i'aːtər] **(-s, -)** m psychiatrist; **p~iatrisch** adj (MED) psychiatric; **p~isch** adj psychological; **~oanalyse** [-oʔanaˈlyːzə] f psychoanalysis; **~ologe (-n, -n)** m psychologist; **~olo'gie** f psychology; **p~ologisch** adj psychological; **~otherapeut(in) (-en, -en)** m(f) psychotherapist

Pubertät [pubɛr'tɛːt] f puberty

Publikum ['puːblikʊm] **(-s)** nt audience; (SPORT) crowd

publizieren [publiˈtsiːrən] vt to publish, to publicize

Pudding ['pʊdɪŋ] **(-s, -e** od **-s)** m blancmange

Pudel ['puːdəl] **(-s)** m poodle

Puder ['puːdər] **(-s, -)** m powder; **~dose** f powder compact; **p~n** vt to powder; **~zucker** m icing sugar

Puff[1] [pʊf] **(-s, -e)** m (Wäschepuff) linen basket; (Sitzpuff) pouf

Puff[2] [pʊf] **(-s, ᵘe)** (umg) m (Stoß) push

Puff[3] [pʊf] **(-s, -)** (umg) m od nt (Bordell) brothel

Puffer (-s, -) m buffer

Pullover [pʊ'loːvər] **(-s, -)** m pullover, jumper

Puls [pʊls] **(-es, -e)** m pulse; **~ader** f artery; **p~ieren** vi to throb, to pulsate

Pult [pʊlt] **(-(e)s, -e)** nt desk

Pulver ['pʊlfər] **(-s, -)** nt powder; **p~ig** adj powdery; **~schnee** m powdery snow

pummelig ['pʊmɛlɪç] adj chubby

Pumpe ['pʊmpə] f pump; **p~n** vt to pump; (umg) to lend; to borrow

Punkt [pʊŋkt] **(-(e)s, -e)** m point; (bei Muster) dot; (Satzzeichen) full stop; **p~ieren** [-'tiːrən] vt to dot; (MED) to aspirate

pünktlich ['pʏŋktlɪç] adj punctual; **P~keit** f punctuality

Punktsieg m victory on points

Punktzahl f score

Punsch [pʊnʃ] **(-(e)s, -e)** m punch

Pupille [pu'pɪlə] f pupil

Puppe ['pʊpə] f doll; (Marionette) puppet; (Insektenpuppe) pupa, chrysalis

Puppen- zW: **~spieler** m puppeteer; **~stube** f doll's house; **~theater** nt puppet theatre

pur [puːr] adj pure; (völlig) sheer; (Whisky) neat

Püree [pyˈreː] **(-s, -s)** nt mashed potatoes pl

Purzelbaum ['pʊrtsəlbaʊm] m somersault

purzeln ['pʊrtsəln] vi to tumble

Puste ['puːstə] **(-)** (umg) f puff; (fig) steam; **p~n** vi to puff, to blow

Pute ['puːtə] f turkey hen; **~r (-s, -)** m turkey cock

Putsch [pʊtʃ] **(-(e)s, -e)** m revolt, putsch

Putz [pʊts] **(-es)** m (Mörtel) plaster, roughcast

putzen vt to clean; (Nase) to wipe, to blow ♦ vr to clean o.s.; to dress o.s. up

Putz- zW: **~frau** f charwoman; **p~ig** adj quaint, funny; **~lappen** m cloth

Puzzle ['pasəl] **(-s, -s)** nt jigsaw

PVC nt abk PVC

Pyjama [pi'dʒaːma] **(-s, -s)** m pyjamas pl

Pyramide [pyraˈmiːdə] f pyramid

Pyrenäen [pyreˈnɛːən] pl Pyrenees

Q, q

Quacksalber ['kvakzalbər] **(-s, -)** m quack (doctor)

Quader ['kvaːdər] **(-s, -)** m square stone; (MATH) cuboid

Quadrat [kva'draːt] **(-(e)s, -e)** nt square; **q~isch** adj square; **~meter** m square metre

quaken ['kvaːkən] vi to croak; (Ente) to

quack
quäken ['kvɛːkən] *vi* to screech
Qual [kvaːl] (-, -en) *f* pain, agony; *(seelisch)* anguish; **q~en** *vt* to torment ♦ *vr* to struggle; *(geistig)* to torment o.s.; **~erei** *f* torture, torment
Qualifikation [kvalifikatsiˈoːn] *f* qualification
qualifizieren [kvalifiˈtsiːrən] *vt* to qualify; *(einstufen)* to label ♦ *vr* to qualify
Qualität [kvaliˈtɛːt] *f* quality; **~sware** *f* article of high quality
Qualle ['kvalə] *f* jellyfish
Qualm [kvalm] (-(e)s) *m* thick smoke; **q~en** *vt, vi* to smoke
qualvoll ['kvaːlfɔl] *adj* excruciating, painful, agonizing
Quant- ['kvant] *zW:* **~ität** [-iˈtɛːt] *f* quantity; **q~itativ** [-itaˈtiːf] *adj* quantitative; **~um** (-s) *nt* quantity, amount
Quarantäne [karanˈtɛːnə] *f* quarantine
Quark [kvark] (-s) *m* curd cheese
Quartal [kvarˈtaːl] (-s, -e) *nt* quarter (year)
Quartier [kvarˈtiːr] (-s, -e) *nt* accommodation; *(MIL)* quarters *pl*; *(Stadtquartier)* district
Quarz [kvaːrts] (-es, -e) *m* quartz
quasseln ['kvasəln] *(umg) vi* to natter
Quatsch [kvatʃ] (-es) *m* rubbish; **q~en** *vi* to chat, to natter
Quecksilber ['kvɛkzɪlbər] *nt* mercury
Quelle ['kvɛlə] *f* spring; *(eines Flusses)* source; **q~n** *(unreg) vi (hervorquellen)* to pour *od* gush forth; *(schwellen)* to swell
quer [kveːr] *adv* crossways, diagonally; *(rechtwinklig)* at right angles; **~ auf dem Bett** across the bed; **Q~balken** *m* crossbeam; **Q~flöte** *f* flute; **Q~format** *nt* *(PHOT)* oblong format; **Q~schnitt** *m* cross-section; **~schnittsgelähmt** *adj* paralysed below the waist; **Q~straße** *f* intersecting road
quetschen ['kvɛtʃən] *vt* to squash, to crush; *(MED)* to bruise
Quetschung *f* bruise, contusion
quieken ['kviːkən] *vi* to squeak
quietschen ['kviːtʃən] *vi* to squeak
Quintessenz ['kvɪntesɛnts] *f* quintessence

Quirl [kvɪrl] (-(e)s, -e) *m* whisk
quitt [kvɪt] *adj* quits, even
Quitte *f* quince
quittieren [kvɪˈtiːrən] *vt* to give a receipt for; *(Dienst)* to leave
Quittung *f* receipt
Quiz [kvɪs] (-, -) *nt* quiz
quoll *etc* [kvɔl] *vb siehe* **quellen**
Quote ['kvoːtə] *f* number, rate

R, r

Rabatt [raˈbat] (-(e)s, -e) *m* discount
Rabattmarke *f* trading stamp
Rabe ['raːbə] (-n, -n) *m* raven
rabiat [rabiˈaːt] *adj* furious
Rache ['raxə] (-) *f* revenge, vengeance
Rachen (-s, -) *m* throat
rächen ['rɛçən] *vt* to avenge, to revenge ♦ *vr* to take (one's) revenge; **das wird sich ~** you'll pay for that
Rad [raːt] (-(e)s, ¨er) *nt* wheel; *(Fahrrad)* bike; **~ fahren** to cycle
Radar ['raːdaːr] (-s) *m od nt* radar; **~falle** *f* speed trap; **~kontrolle** *f* radar-controlled speed trap
Radau [raˈdaʊ] (-s) *(umg) m* row
radeln ['raːdəln] *(umg) vi* to cycle
Radfahr- *zW:* **r~en** △ *(unreg) vi siehe* **Rad**; **~er(in)** *m(f)* cyclist; **~weg** *m* cycle track *od* path
Radier- [raˈdiːr] *zW:* **r~en** *vt* to rub out, to erase; *(KUNST)* to etch; **~gummi** *m* rubber, eraser; **~ung** *f* etching
Radieschen [raˈdiːsçən] *nt* radish
radikal [radiˈkaːl] *adj* radical
Radio ['raːdio] (-s, -s) *nt* radio, wireless; **r~ak'tiv** *adj* radioactive; **~aktivi'tät** *f* radioactivity; **~apparat** *m* radio, wireless set
Radius ['raːdiʊs] (-, **Radien**) *m* radius
Rad- *zW:* **~kappe** *f (AUT)* hub cap; **~ler(in)** *(umg) m(f)* cyclist; **~rennen** *nt* cycle race; cycle racing; **~sport** *m* cycling; **~weg** *m* cycleway
raffen ['rafən] *vt* to snatch, to pick up; *(Stoff)*

to gather (up); (*Geld*) to pile up, to rake in
raffi'niert *adj* crafty, cunning
ragen ['ra:gən] *vi* to tower, to rise
Rahm [ra:m] **(-s)** *m* cream
Rahmen (-s, -) *m* frame(work); **im ~ des Möglichen** within the bounds of possibility; **r~** *vt* to frame
räkeln ['rɛ:kln] *vr* = **rekeln**
Rakete [ra'ke:tə] *f* rocket; **~nstützpunkt** *m* missile base
rammen ['ramən] *vt* to ram
Rampe ['rampə] *f* ramp; **~nlicht** *nt* (*THEAT*) footlights *pl*
ramponieren [rampo'ni:rən] (*umg*) *vt* to damage
Ramsch [ramʃ] **(-(e)s, -e)** *m* junk
ran [ran] (*umg*) *adv* = **heran**
Rand [rant] **(-(e)s, ⁻er)** *m* edge; (*von Brille, Tasse etc*) rim; (*Hutrand*) brim; (*auf Papier*) margin; (*Schmutzrand, unter Augen*) ring; (*fig*) verge, brink; **außer ~ und Band** wild; **am ~e bemerkt** mentioned in passing
randalieren [randa'li:rən] *vi* to (go on the) rampage
Rang [raŋ] **(-(e)s, ⁻e)** *m* rank; (*Stand*) standing; (*Wert*) quality; (*THEAT*) circle
Rangier- [rãʒi:r] *zW:* **~bahnhof** *m* marshalling yard; **r~en** *vt* (*EISENB*) to shunt, to switch (*US*) ♦ *vi* to rank, to be classed; **~gleis** *nt* siding
Ranke ['raŋkə] *f* tendril, shoot
ranzig ['rantsɪç] *adj* rancid
Rappen ['rapən] *m* (*FIN*) rappen, centime
rar [ra:r] *adj* rare; **sich ~ machen** (*umg*) to keep o.s. to o.s.; **R~i'tät** *f* rarity; (*Sammelobjekt*) curio
rasant [ra'zant] *adj* quick, rapid
rasch [raʃ] *adj* quick
rascheln [ˈraʃln] *vi* to rustle
Rasen ['ra:zən] **(-s, -)** *m* lawn; grass
rasen *vi* to rave; (*schnell*) to race; **~d** *adj* furious; **~de Kopfschmerzen** a splitting headache
Rasenmäher (-s, -) *m* lawnmower
Rasier- [ra'zi:r] *zW:* **~apparat** *m* shaver; **~creme** *f* shaving cream; **r~en** *vt, vr* to shave; **~klinge** *f* razor blade; **~messer** *nt*

razor; **~pinsel** *m* shaving brush; **~schaum** *m* shaving foam; **~seife** *f* shaving soap *od* stick; **~wasser** *nt* shaving lotion
Rasse ['rasə] *f* race; (*Tierrasse*) breed; **~hund** *m* thoroughbred dog
rasseln ['rasəln] *vi* to clatter
Rassen- *zW:* **~hass ▲** *m* race *od* racial hatred; **~trennung** *f* racial segregation
Rassismus [ra'sɪsmʊs] *m* racism
Rast [rast] **(-, -en)** *f* rest; **r~en** *vi* to rest; **~hof** *m* (*AUT*) service station; **r~los** *adj* tireless; (*unruhig*) restless; **~platz** *m* (*AUT*) layby; **~stätte** *f* (*AUT*) service station
Rasur [ra'zu:r] *f* shaving
Rat [ra:t] **(-(e)s, -schläge)** *m* advice *no pl*; **ein ~** a piece of advice; **keinen ~ wissen** not to know what to do; *siehe* **zurate**
Rate *f* instalment
raten (*unreg*) *vt, vi* to guess; (*empfehlen*): **jdm ~** to advise sb
Ratenzahlung *f* hire purchase
Ratgeber (-s, -) *m* adviser
Rathaus *nt* town hall
ratifizieren [ratifi'tsi:rən] *vt* to ratify
Ration [ratsi'o:n] *f* ration; **r~al** [-'na:l] *adj* rational; **r~ali'sieren** *vt* to rationalize; **r~ell** [-'nɛl] *adj* efficient; **r~ieren** [-'ni:rən] *vt* to ration
Rat- *zW:* **r~los** *adj* at a loss, helpless; **r~sam** *adj* advisable; **~schlag** *m* (piece of) advice
Rätsel ['rɛ:tsəl] **(-s, -)** *nt* puzzle; (*Worträtsel*) riddle; **r~haft** *adj* mysterious; **es ist mir r~haft** it's a mystery to me
Ratte ['ratə] *f* rat; **~nfänger (-s, -)** *m* ratcatcher
rattern ['ratərn] *vi* to rattle, to clatter
rau ▲ [rau] *adj* rough, coarse; (*Wetter*) harsh
Raub [raup] **(-(e)s)** *m* robbery; (*Beute*) loot, booty; **~bau** *m* ruthless exploitation; **r~en** ['raubən] *vt* to rob; (*Mensch*) to kidnap, to abduct
Räuber ['rɔybər] **(-s, -)** *m* robber
Raub- *zW:* **~mord** *m* robbery with murder; **~tier** *nt* predator; **~überfall** *m* robbery with violence; **~vogel** *m* bird of prey
Rauch [raux] **(-(e)s)** *m* smoke; **r~en** *vt, vi* to

smoke; **~er(in)** **(-s, -)** *m(f)* smoker;
~erabteil *nt* (*EISENB*) smoker; **räuchern** *vt*
to smoke, to cure; **~fleisch** *nt* smoked
meat; **r~ig** *adj* smoky
rauf [rauf] (*umg*) *adv* = **herauf; hinauf**
raufen *vt* (*Haare*) to pull out ♦ *vi, vr* to fight;
Raufe'rei *f* brawl, fight
rauh △ *etc* [rau] *adj siehe* **rau** *etc*
Raum [raum] *m* **(-(e)s, Räume)** *m* space;
(*Zimmer, Platz*) room; (*Gebiet*) area
räumen ['rɔymən] *vt* to clear; (*Wohnung,
Platz*) to vacate; (*wegbringen*) to shift, to
move; (*in Schrank etc*) to put away
Raum- *zW:* **~fähre** *f* space shuttle; **~fahrt** *f*
space travel; **~inhalt** *m* cubic capacity,
volume
räumlich ['rɔymlɪç] *adj* spatial; **R~keiten** *pl*
premises
Raum- *zW:* **~pflegerin** *f* cleaner; **~schiff**
nt spaceship; **~schifffahrt** ▲ *f* space
travel
Räumung ['rɔymuŋ] *f* vacating, evacuation;
clearing (away)
Räumungs- *zW:* **~arbeiten** *pl* clearance
operations; **~verkauf** *m* clearance sale; (*bei
Geschäftsaufgabe*) closing down sale
raunen ['raunən] *vt, vi* to whisper
Raupe ['raupə] *f* caterpillar; (*~nkette*)
(caterpillar) track
Raureif ▲ ['raurаɪf] *m* hoarfrost
raus [raus] (*umg*) *adv* = **heraus; hinaus**
Rausch [rauʃ] **(-(e)s, Räusche)** *m*
intoxication
rauschen *vi* (*Wasser*) to rush; (*Baum*) to
rustle; (*Radio etc*) to hiss; (*Mensch*) to
sweep, to sail; **~d** *adj* (*Beifall*) thunderous;
(*Fest*) sumptuous
Rauschgift *nt* drug; **~süchtige(r)** *f(m)*
drug addict
räuspern ['rɔyspərn] *vr* to clear one's throat
Razzia ['ratsia] **(-, Razzien)** *f* raid
Reagenzglas [rea'gɛntsglaːs] *nt* test tube
reagieren [rea'giːrən] *vi:* **~ (auf** +*akk*) to
react (to)
Reakt- *zW:* **~ion** [reaktsi'oːn] *f* reaction;
r~io'när *adj* reactionary; **~or** [re'aktɔr] *m*
reactor

real [re'aːl] *adj* real, material
reali'sieren *vt* (*verwirklichen: Pläne*) to carry
out
Realismus [rea'lɪsmus] *m* realism
rea'listisch *adj* realistic
Realschule *f* secondary school

Realschule

ⓘ The **Realschule** is one of the secondary
schools a German schoolchild may
attend after the **Grundschule**. On the
successful completion of six years of
schooling in the **Realschule** pupils gain the
mittlere Reife *and usually go on to
vocational training or further education.*

Rebe ['reːbə] *f* vine
rebellieren [rebɛ'liːrən] *vi* to rebel;
Rebelli'on *f* rebellion; **re'bellisch** *adj*
rebellious
Rebhuhn ['rephuːn] *nt* (*KOCH, ZOOL*)
partridge
Rechen ['rɛçən] **(-s, -)** *m* rake
Rechen- *zW:* **~fehler** *m* miscalculation;
~maschine *f* calculating machine;
~schaft *f* account; **für etw ~schaft
ablegen** to account for sth; **~schieber** *m*
slide rule
Rech- ['rɛç] *zW:* **r~nen** *vt, vi* to calculate;
jdn/etw r~nen zu to count sb/sth among;
r~nen mit to reckon with; **r~nen auf** +*akk*
to count on; **~ner** *nt* arithmetic; **~ner** **(-s,
-)** *m* calculator; (*COMPUT*) computer; **~nung**
f calculation(s); (*COMM*) bill, check (*US*);
jdm/etw ~nung tragen to take sb/sth into
account; **~nungsbetrag** *m* total amount
of a bill/invoice; **~nungsjahr** *nt* financial
year; **~nungsprüfer** *m* auditor
Recht [rɛçt] **(-(e)s, -e)** *nt* right; (*JUR*) law;
mit ~ rightly, justly; **R~ haben** to be right;
jdm R~ geben to agree with sb; **von ~s
wegen** by rights
recht *adj* right ♦ *adv* (*vor Adjektiv*) really,
quite; **das ist mir ~** that suits me; **jetzt
erst ~** now more than ever
Rechte *f* right (hand); (*POL*) Right; **r~(r, s)**
adj right; (*POL*) right-wing; **ein ~r** a right-

---

winger; **~(s)** nt right thing; **etwas/nichts ~s** something/nothing proper

recht- zW: **~eckig** adj rectangular; **~fertigen** vt insep to justify ♦ vr insep to justify o.s.; **R~fertigung** f justification; **~haberisch** (pej) adj (Mensch) opinionated; **~lich** adj (gesetzlich: Gleichstellung, Anspruch) legal; **~los** adj with no rights; **~mäßig** adj legal, lawful

rechts [rɛçts] adv on/to the right; **R~anwalt** m lawyer, barrister; **R~anwältin** f lawyer, barrister

Rechtschreibung f spelling

Rechts- zW: **~fall** m (law) case; **~händer** (-s, -) m right-handed person; **r~kräftig** adj valid, legal; **~kurve** f right-hand bend; **r~verbindlich** adj legally binding; **~verkehr** m driving on the right; **r~widrig** adj illegal; **~wissenschaft** f jurisprudence

rechtwinklig adj right-angled

rechtzeitig adj timely ♦ adv in time

Reck [rɛk] **(-(e)s, -e)** nt horizontal bar; **r~en** vt, vr to stretch

recyceln [riː'saikəln] vt to recycle

Recycling [riː'saiklɪŋ] **(-s)** nt recycling

Redakteur [redak'tøːr] m editor

Redaktion [redaktsi'oːn] f editing; (Leute) editorial staff; (Büro) editorial office(s)

Rede ['reːdə] f speech; (Gespräch) talk; **jdn zur ~ stellen** to take sb to task; **~freiheit** f freedom of speech; **r~gewandt** adj eloquent; **r~n** vi to talk, to speak ♦ vt to say; (Unsinn etc) to talk; **~nsart** f set phrase

redlich ['reːtlɪç] adj honest

Redner **(-s, -)** m speaker, orator

redselig ['reːtzeːlɪç] adj talkative, loquacious

reduzieren [redu'tsiːrən] vt to reduce

Reede ['reːdə] f protected anchorage; **~r** **(-s, -)** m shipowner; **~'rei** f shipping line od firm

reell [re'ɛl] adj fair, honest; (MATH) real

Refer- zW: **~at** [refe'raːt] **(-(e)s, -e)** nt report; (Vortrag) paper; (Gebiet) section; **~ent** [refe'rɛnt] m speaker; (Berichterstatter) reporter; (Sachbearbeiter) expert; **r~ieren** [refe'riːrən] vi: **r~ieren über** +akk to speak

od talk on

reflektieren [reflɛk'tiːrən] vt (Licht) to reflect

Reflex [re'flɛks] **(-es, -e)** m reflex; **r~iv** [-'ksiːf] adj (GRAM) reflexive

Reform [re'fɔrm] f reform; **~ati'on** f reformation; **~ationstag** m Reformation Day; **~haus** nt health food shop; **r~ieren** [-'miːrən] vt to reform

Regal [re'gaːl] **(-s, -e)** nt (book)shelves pl, bookcase; stand, rack

rege ['reːgə] adj (lebhaft: Treiben) lively; (wach, lebendig: Geist) keen

Regel ['reːgəl] **(-, -n)** f rule; (MED) period; **r~mäßig** adj regular; **~mäßigkeit** f regularity; **r~n** vt to regulate, to control; (Angelegenheit) to settle ♦ vr: **sich von selbst r~n** to take care of itself; **r~recht** adj regular, proper, thorough; **~ung** f regulation; settlement; **r~widrig** adj irregular, against the rules

Regen ['reːgən] **(-s, -)** m rain; **~bogen** m rainbow; **~bogenpresse** f tabloids pl

regenerierbar [regene'riːrbaːr] adj renewable

Regen- zW: **~mantel** m raincoat, mac(kintosh); **~schauer** m shower (of rain); **~schirm** m umbrella; **~wald** m (GEOG) rainforest; **~wurm** m earthworm; **~zeit** f rainy season

Regie [re'ʒiː] f (Film etc) direction; (THEAT) production

Regier- [re'giːr] zW: **r~en** vt, vi to govern, to rule; **~ung** f government; (Monarchie) reign; **~ungssitz** m seat of government; **~ungswechsel** m change of government; **~ungszeit** f period in government; (von König) reign

Regiment [regi'mɛnt] **(-s, -er)** nt regiment

Region [regi'oːn] f region

Regisseur [reʒɪ'søːr] m director; (THEAT) (stage) producer

Register [re'gɪstər] **(-s, -)** nt register; (in Buch) table of contents, index

registrieren [regɪs'triːrən] vt to register

Regler ['reːglər] **(-s, -)** m regulator, governor

reglos ['reːkloːs] adj motionless

regnen ['reːgnən] vi unpers to rain

regnerisch *adj* rainy

regulär [regu'lɛːr] *adj* regular

regulieren [regu'liːrən] *vt* to regulate; (*COMM*) to settle

Regung ['reːgʊŋ] *f* motion; (*Gefühl*) feeling, impulse; **r~slos** *adj* motionless

Reh [reː] (**-(e)s, -e**) *nt* deer, roe; **~bock** *m* roebuck; **~kitz** *nt* fawn

Reib- ['raib] *zW:* **~e** *f* grater; **~eisen** *nt* grater; **r~en** (*unreg*) *vt* to rub; (*KOCH*) to grate; **~fläche** *f* rough surface; **~ung** *f* friction; **r~ungslos** *adj* smooth

Reich (**-(e)s, -e**) *nt* empire, kingdom; (*fig*) realm; **das Dritte R~** the Third Reich

reich [raiç] *adj* rich

reichen *vi* to reach; (*genügen*) to be enough *od* sufficient ♦ *vt* to hold out; (*geben*) to pass, to hand; (*anbieten*) to offer; **jdm ~** to be enough *od* sufficient for sb

reich- *zW:* **~haltig** *adj* ample, rich; **~lich** *adj* ample, plenty of; **R~tum** (**-s**) *m* wealth; **R~weite** *f* range

Reif (**-(e)s, -e**) *m* (*Ring*) ring, hoop

reif [raif] *adj* ripe; (*Mensch, Urteil*) mature

Reife (**-**) *f* ripeness; maturity; **r~n** *vi* to mature; to ripen

Reifen (**-s, -**) *m* ring, hoop; (*Fahrzeugreifen*) tyre; **~druck** *m* tyre pressure; **~panne** *f* puncture

Reihe ['raiə] *f* row; (*von Tagen etc, umg: Anzahl*) series *sg*; **der ~ nach** in turn; **er ist an der ~** it's his turn; **an die ~ kommen** to have one's turn

Reihen- *zW:* **~folge** *f* sequence; **alphabetische ~folge** alphabetical order; **~haus** *nt* terraced house

reihum [rai'ʊm] *adv:* **es geht/wir machen das ~** we take turns

Reim [raim] (**-(e)s, -e**) *m* rhyme; **r~en** *vt* to rhyme

rein[1] [rain] (*umg*) *adv* = **herein; hinein**

rein[2] [rain] *adj* pure; (*sauber*) clean ♦ *adv* purely; **etw ins R~e schreiben** to make a fair copy of sth; **etw ins R~e bringen** to clear up sth; **R~fall** (*umg*) *m* let-down; **R~gewinn** *m* net profit; **R~heit** *f* purity; cleanness; **~igen** *vt* to clean; (*Wasser*) to

purify; **R~igung** *f* cleaning; purification; (*Geschäft*) cleaner's; **chemische R~igung** dry cleaning; dry cleaner's; **R~igungsmittel** *nt* cleansing agent; **~rassig** *adj* pedigree; **R~schrift** *f* fair copy

Reis [rais] (**-es, -e**) *m* rice

Reise ['raizə] *f* journey; (*Schiffsreise*) voyage; **~n** *pl* (*Herumreisen*) travels; **gute ~!** have a good journey; **~apotheke** *f* first-aid kit; **~büro** *nt* travel agency; **r~fertig** *adj* ready to start; **~führer** *m* guide(book); (*Mensch*) travel guide; **~gepäck** *nt* luggage; **~gesellschaft** *f* party of travellers; **~kosten** *pl* travelling expenses; **~leiter** *m* courier; **~lektüre** *f* reading matter for the journey; **r~n** *vi* to travel; **r~n nach** to go to; **~nde(r)** *f(m)* traveller; **~pass** ▲ *m* passport; **~proviant** *m* food and drink for the journey; **~route** *f* route, itinerary; **~ruf** *m* personal message; **~scheck** *m* traveller's cheque; **~veranstalter** *m* tour operator; **~versicherung** *f* travel insurance; **~ziel** *nt* destination

Reißbrett *nt* drawing board

reißen ['raisən] (*unreg*) *vt* to tear; (*ziehen*) to pull, to drag; (*Witz*) to crack ♦ *vi* to tear; to pull, to drag; **etw an sich ~** to snatch sth up; (*fig*) to take over sth; **sich um etw ~** to scramble for sth; **~d** *adj* (*Fluss*) raging; (*WIRTS: Verkauf*) rapid

Reiß- *zW:* **~verschluss** ▲ *m* zip(per), zip fastener; **~zwecke** *m* drawing pin (*BRIT*), thumbtack (*US*)

Reit- ['rait] *zW:* **r~en** (*unreg*) *vt, vi* to ride; **~er** (**-s, -**) *m* rider; (*MIL*) cavalryman, trooper; **~erin** *f* rider; **~hose** *f* riding breeches *pl*; **~pferd** *nt* saddle horse; **~stiefel** *m* riding boot; **~weg** *n* bridle path; **~zeug** *nt* riding outfit

Reiz [raits] (**-es, -e**) *m* stimulus; (*angenehm*) charm; (*Verlockung*) attraction; **r~bar** *adj* irritable; **~barkeit** *f* irritability; **r~en** *vt* to stimulate; (*unangenehm*) to irritate; (*verlocken*) to appeal to, to attract; **r~end** *adj* charming; **r~voll** *adj* attractive

rekeln ['reːkəln] *vr* to stretch out; (*lümmeln*)

to lounge *od* loll about

Reklamation [reklamatsi'o:n] *f* complaint

Reklame [re'kla:mə] *f* advertising; advertisement; ~ **machen für etw** to advertise sth

rekonstruieren [rekɔnstru'i:rən] *vt* to reconstruct

Rekord [re'kɔrt] **(-(e)s, -e)** *m* record; ~**leistung** *f* record performance

Rektor ['rɛktɔr] *m* (*UNIV*) rector, vice-chancellor; (*SCH*) headteacher (*BRIT*), principal (*US*); ~**at** [-'ra:t] **(-(e)s, -e)** *nt* rectorate, vice-chancellorship; headship; (*Zimmer*) rector's *etc* office

Relais [rə'le:] **(-, -)** *nt* relay

relativ [rela'ti:f] *adj* relative; **R~ität** [relativi'tɛ:t] *f* relativity

relevant [rele'vant] *adj* relevant

Relief [reli'ɛf] **(-s, -s)** *nt* relief

Religion [religi'o:n] *f* religion

religiös [religi'ø:s] *adj* religious

Reling ['re:lɪŋ] **(-, -s)** *f* (*NAUT*) rail

Remoulade [remu'la:də] *f* remoulade

Rendezvous [rãde'vu:] **(-, -)** *nt* rendezvous

Renn- ['rɛn] *zW*: ~**bahn** *f* racecourse; (*AUT*) circuit, race track; **r~en** (*unreg*) *vt, vi* to run, to race; ~**en (-s, -)** *nt* running; (*Wettbewerb*) race; ~**fahrer** *m* racing driver; ~**pferd** *nt* racehorse; ~**wagen** *m* racing car

renommiert [rɛnɔ'mi:rt] *adj* renowned

renovieren [reno'vi:rən] *vt* to renovate; **Renovierung** *f* renovation

rentabel [rɛn'ta:bəl] *adj* profitable, lucrative

Rentabilität [rɛntabili'tɛ:t] *f* profitability

Rente ['rɛntə] *f* pension

Rentenversicherung *f* pension scheme

rentieren [rɛn'ti:rən] *vr* to pay, to be profitable

Rentner(in) ['rɛntnər(ɪn)] **(-s, -)** *m(f)* pensioner

Reparatur [repara'tu:r] *f* repairing; repair; ~**werkstatt** *f* repair shop; (*AUT*) garage

reparieren [repa'ri:rən] *vt* to repair

Reportage [repɔr'ta:ʒə] *f* (on-the-spot) report; (*TV, RADIO*) live commentary *od* coverage

Reporter [re'pɔrtər] **(-s, -)** *m* reporter, commentator

repräsentativ [reprɛzɛnta'ti:f] *adj* (*stellvertretend, typisch: Menge, Gruppe*) representative; (*beeindruckend: Haus, Auto etc*) impressive

repräsentieren [reprɛzɛn'ti:rən] *vt* (*Staat, Firma*) to represent; (*darstellen: Wert*) to constitute ♦ *vi* (*gesellschaftlich*) to perform official duties

Repressalie [repre'sa:liə] *f* reprisal

Reprivatisierung [reprivati'zi:rʊŋ] *f* denationalization

Reproduktion [reprodʊktsi'o:n] *f* reproduction

reproduzieren [reprodu'tsi:rən] *vt* to reproduce

Reptil [rɛp'ti:l] **(-s, -ien)** *nt* reptile

Republik [repu'bli:k] *f* republic; **r~anisch** *adj* republican

Reservat [rezɛr'va:t] **(-(e)s, -e)** *nt* reservation

Reserve [re'zɛrvə] *f* reserve; ~**rad** *nt* (*AUT*) spare wheel; ~**spieler** *m* reserve; ~**tank** *m* reserve tank

reservieren [rezɛr'vi:rən] *vt* to reserve

Reservoir [rezɛrvo'a:r] **(-s, -e)** *nt* reservoir

Residenz [rezi'dɛnts] *f* residence, seat

resignieren [rezɪ'gni:rən] *vi* to resign

resolut [rezo'lu:t] *adj* resolute

Resonanz [rezo'nants] *f* resonance; (*fig*) response

Resozialisierung [rezotsiali'zi:rʊŋ] *f* rehabilitation

Respekt [re'spɛkt] **(-(e)s)** *m* respect; **r~ieren** [-'ti:rən] *vt* to respect; **r~los** *adj* disrespectful; **r~voll** *adj* respectful

Ressort [re'so:r] **(-s, -s)** *nt* department

Rest [rɛst] **(-(e)s, -e)** *m* remainder, rest; (*Überrest*) remains *pl*

Restaurant [rɛsto'rã:] **(-s, -s)** *nt* restaurant

restaurieren [rɛstaʊ'ri:rən] *vt* to restore

Rest- *zW*: ~**betrag** *m* remainder, outstanding sum; **r~lich** *adj* remaining; **r~los** *adj* complete

Resultat [rezʊl'ta:t] **(-(e)s, -e)** *nt* result

Retorte [re'tɔrtə] *f* retort

Retouren [rɛˈtuːrən] pl (*COMM*) returns

retten [ˈrɛtən] vt to save, to rescue

Retter(in) m(f) rescuer

Rettich [ˈrɛtɪç] (-s, -e) m radish

Rettung f rescue; (*Hilfe*) help; **seine letzte ~** his last hope

Rettungs- zW: **~boot** nt lifeboat; **~dienst** m rescue service; **r~los** adj hopeless; **~ring** m lifebelt, life preserver (*US*); **~wagen** m ambulance

retuschieren [retuˈʃiːrən] vt (*PHOT*) to retouch

Reue [ˈrɔʏə] (-) f remorse; (*Bedauern*) regret; **r~n** vt: **es reut ihn** he regrets (it) od is sorry (about it)

Revanche [reˈvãːʃə] f revenge; (*SPORT*) return match

revanchieren [revãˈʃiːrən] vr (*sich rächen*) to get one's own back, to have one's revenge; (*erwidern*) to reciprocate, to return the compliment

Revier [reˈviːr] (-s, -e) nt district; (*Jagdrevier*) preserve; (*Polizeirevier*) police station; beat

Revolte [reˈvɔltə] f revolt

revol'tieren vi (*gegen jdn/etw*) to rebel

Revolution [revolutsiˈoːn] f revolution; **~är** [-ˈnɛːr] (-s, -e) m revolutionary; **r~ieren** [-ˈniːrən] vt to revolutionize

Rezept [reˈtsɛpt] (-(e)s, -e) nt recipe; (*MED*) prescription; **r~frei** adj available without prescription; **~ion** f reception; **r~pflichtig** adj available only on prescription

R-Gespräch [ˈɛrgəʃprɛːç] nt reverse charge call (*BRIT*), collect call (*US*)

Rhabarber [raˈbarbər] (-s) m rhubarb

Rhein [raɪn] (-s) m Rhine; **r~isch** adj Rhenish

Rheinland-Pfalz nt (*GEOG*) Rheinland-Pfalz, Rhineland-Palatinate

Rhesusfaktor [ˈreːzusfaktɔr] m rhesus factor

rhetorisch [reˈtoːrɪʃ] adj rhetorical

Rheuma [ˈrɔʏma] (-s) nt rheumatism; **r~tisch** [-ˈmaːtɪʃ] adj rheumatic

rhythmisch [ˈrʏtmɪʃ] adj rhythmical

Rhythmus [ˈrʏtmʊs] m rhythm

richt- [ˈrɪçt] zW: **~en** vt to direct; (*Waffe*) to aim; (*einstellen*) to adjust; (*instandsetzen*) to

repair; (*zurechtmachen*) to prepare; (*bestrafen*) to pass judgement on ♦ vr: **sich ~en nach** to go by; **~en an** +akk to direct at; (*fig*) to direct to; **~en auf** +akk to aim at; **R~er(in)** (-s, -) m(f) judge; **~erlich** adj judicial; **R~geschwindigkeit** f recommended speed

richtig adj right, correct; (*echt*) proper ♦ adv (*umg: sehr*) really; **bin ich hier ~?** am I in the right place?; **der/die R~e** the right one/person; **das R~e** the right thing; **etw ~ stellen** to correct sth; **R~keit** f correctness

Richt- zW: **~linie** f guideline; **~preis** m recommended price

Richtung f direction; tendency, orientation

rieb etc [riːp] vb siehe **reiben**

riechen [ˈriːçən] (*unreg*) vt, vi to smell; **an etw** dat **~** to smell sth; **nach etw ~** to smell of sth; **ich kann das/ihn nicht ~** (*umg*) I can't stand it/him

rief etc [riːf] vb siehe **rufen**

Riegel [ˈriːgəl] (-s, -) m bolt; (*Schokolade usw*) bar

Riemen [ˈriːmən] (-s, -) m strap; (*Gürtel*, *TECH*) belt; (*NAUT*) oar

Riese [ˈriːzə] (-n, -n) m giant

rieseln vi to trickle; (*Schnee*) to fall gently

Riesen- zW: **~erfolg** m enormous success; **r~groß** adj colossal, gigantic, huge; **~rad** nt big wheel

riesig [ˈriːzɪç] adj enormous, huge, vast

riet etc [riːt] vb siehe **raten**

Riff [rɪf] (-(e)s, -e) nt reef

Rille [ˈrɪlə] f groove

Rind [rɪnt] (-(e)s, -er) nt ox; cow; cattle pl; (*KOCH*) beef

Rinde [ˈrɪndə] f rind; (*Baumrinde*) bark; (*Brotrinde*) crust

Rind- [ˈrɪnt] zW: **~fleisch** nt beef; **~vieh** nt cattle pl; (*umg*) blockhead, stupid oaf

Ring [rɪŋ] (-(e)s, -e) m ring; **~buch** nt ring binder; **r~en** (*unreg*) vi to wrestle; **~en** (-s) nt wrestling; **~finger** m ring finger; **~kampf** m wrestling bout; **~richter** m referee; **r~s** adv: **r~s um** round; **r~sherum** adv round about; **~straße** f ring road; **r~sum** adv (rundherum) round about; (überall) all round; **r~sumher** = **ringsum**

Rinn- ['rɪn] zW: **~e** f gutter, drain; **r~en** (unreg) vi to run, to trickle; **~stein** m gutter

Rippchen ['rɪpçən] nt small rib; cutlet

Rippe ['rɪpə] f rib

Risiko [ri:ziko] (**-s, -s** od **Risiken**) nt risk

riskant [rɪs'kant] adj risky, hazardous

riskieren [rɪs'ki:rən] vt to risk

Riss ▲ [rɪs] (**-es, -e**) m tear; (in Mauer, Tasse etc) crack; (in Haut) scratch; (TECH) design

rissig ['rɪsɪç] adj torn; cracked; scratched

Ritt [rɪt] (**-(e)s, -e**) m ride

ritt etc vb siehe **reiten**

Ritter ['rɪtər] m knight, **r~lich** adj chivalrous

Ritze ['rɪtsə] f crack, chink

Rivale [ri'va:lə] (**-n, -n**) m rival

Rivalität [rivali'tɛ:t] f rivalry

Robbe ['rɔbə] f seal

Roboter ['rɔbɔtər] (**-s, -**) m robot

robust [ro'bʊst] adj (kräftig: Mensch, Gesundheit) robust

roch etc [rɔx] vb siehe **riechen**

Rock [rɔk] (**-(e)s, ⁻e**) m skirt; (Jackett) jacket; (Uniformrock) tunic

Rodel ['ro:dəl] (**-s, -**) m toboggan; **~bahn** f toboggan run; **r~n** vi to toboggan

Rogen ['ro:gən] (**-s, -**) m roe, spawn

Roggen ['rɔgən] (**-s, -**) m rye; **~brot** nt (KOCH) rye bread

roh [ro:] adj raw; (Mensch) coarse, crude; **R~bau** m shell of a building; **R~material** nt raw material; **R~öl** nt crude oil

Rohr [ro:r] (**-(e)s, -e**) nt pipe, tube; (BOT) cane; (Schilf) reed; (Gewehrrohr) barrel; **~bruch** m burst pipe

Röhre ['rø:rə] f tube, pipe; (RADIO etc) valve; (Backröhre) oven

Rohr- zW: **~leitung** f pipeline; **~zucker** m cane sugar

Rohstoff m raw material

Rokoko ['rɔkoko] (**-s**) nt rococo

Rolladen △ m siehe **Rollladen**

Rollbahn ['rɔlba:n] f (AVIAT) runway

Rolle ['rɔlə] f roll; (THEAT, soziologisch) role; (Garnrolle etc) reel, spool; (Walze) roller;

(Wäscherolle) mangle; **keine ~ spielen** not to matter; **eine (wichtige) ~ spielen bei** to play a (major) part od role in; **r~n** vt, vi to roll; (AVIAT) to taxi; **~r** (**-s, -**) m scooter; (Welle) roller

Roll- zW: **~kragen** m rollneck, polo neck; **~laden** ▲ m shutter; **~mops** m pickled herring; **~schuh** m roller skate; **~stuhl** m wheelchair; **~stuhlfahrer(in)** m(f) wheelchair user; **~treppe** f escalator

Rom [ro:m] (**-s**) nt Rome

Roman [ro'ma:n] (**-s, -e**) m novel; **~tik** f romanticism; **~tiker** [ro'mantikər] (**-s, -**) m romanticist; **r~tisch** [ro'mantɪʃ] adj romantic; **~ze** [ro'mantsə] f romance

Römer ['rø:mər] (**-s, -**) m wineglass; (Mensch) Roman

römisch ['rø:mɪʃ] adj Roman; **~-katholisch** adj (REL) Roman Catholic

röntgen ['rœntgən] vt to X-ray; **R~bild** nt X-ray; **R~strahlen** pl X-rays

rosa ['ro:za] adj inv pink, rose(-coloured)

Rose ['ro:zə] f rose

Rosen- zW: **~kohl** m Brussels sprouts pl; **~kranz** m rosary; **~montag** m Monday before Ash Wednesday

rosig ['ro:zɪç] adj rosy

Rosine [ro'zi:nə] f raisin, currant

Ross ▲ [rɔs] (**-es, -e**) nt horse, steed; **~kastanie** f horse chestnut

Rost [rɔst] (**-(e)s, -e**) m rust; (Gitter) grill, gridiron; (Bettrost) springs pl; **~braten** m roast(ed) meat, roast; **r~en** vi to rust

rösten ['rø:stən] vt to roast; to toast; to grill

Rost- zW: **r~frei** adj rust-free; rustproof; stainless; **r~ig** adj rusty; **~schutz** m rust-proofing

rot [ro:t] adj red; **in den ~en Zahlen** in the red

Röte ['rø:tə] (**-**) f redness; **~ln** pl German measles sg; **r~n** vt, vr to redden

rothaarig adj red-haired

rotieren [ro'ti:rən] vi to rotate

Rot- zW: **~kehlchen** nt robin; **~stift** m red pencil; **~wein** m red wine

Rouge [ru:ʒ] nt blusher

Roulade [ru'la:də] f (KOCH) beef olive

Route ['ru:tə] f route

Routine [ru'ti:nə] f experience; routine

Rübe ['ry:bə] f turnip; **Gelbe ~** carrot; **Rote ~** beetroot (*BRIT*), beet (*US*)

rüber ['ry:bər] (*umg*) *adv* = **herüber; hinüber**

Rubrik [ru'bri:k] f heading; (*Spalte*) column

Ruck [rʊk] (**-(e)s, -e**) *m* jerk, jolt

Rück- ['rʏk] *zW*: **~antwort** f reply, answer; **r~bezüglich** *adj* reflexive

Rücken ['rʏkən] (**-s, -**) *m* back; (*Bergrücken*) ridge

rücken *vt, vi* to move

Rücken- *zW*: **~mark** *nt* spinal cord; **~schwimmen** *nt* backstroke

Rück- *zW*: **~erstattung** f return, restitution; **~fahrkarte** f return (ticket); **~fahrt** f return journey; **~fall** *m* relapse; **r~fällig** *adj* relapsing; **r~fällig werden** to relapse; **~flug** *m* return flight; **~frage** f question; **r~fragen** *vi* to check, to inquire (further); **~gabe** f return; **~gaberecht** *nt* right of return; **~gang** *m* decline, fall; **r~gängig** *adj*: **etw r~gängig machen** to cancel sth; **~grat** (**-(e)s, -e**) *nt* spine, backbone; **~halt** *m* (*Unterstützung*) backing, support; **~kehr** (**-, -en**) f return; **~licht** *nt* back light; **r~lings** *adv* from behind; backwards; **~nahme** f taking back; **~porto** *nt* return postage; **~reise** f return journey; (*NAUT*) home voyage; **~reiseverkehr** *m* homebound traffic; **~ruf** *m* recall

Rucksack ['rʊkzak] *m* rucksack; **~tourist(in)** *m(f)* backpacker

Rück- *zW*: **~schau** f reflection; **~schlag** *m* (*plötzliche Verschlechterung*) setback; **~schluss** ▲ *m* conclusion; **~schritt** *m* retrogression; **r~schrittlich** *adj* reactionary; retrograde; **~seite** f back; (*von Münze etc*) reverse; **~sicht** f consideration; **~sicht nehmen auf** *+akk* to show consideration for; **r~sichtslos** *adj* inconsiderate; (*Fahren*) reckless; (*unbarmherzig*) ruthless; **r~sichtsvoll** *adj* considerate; **~sitz** *m* back seat; **~spiegel** *m* (*AUT*) rear-view mirror; **~spiel** *nt* return match; **~sprache** f further discussion *od* talk; **~stand** *m* arrears *pl*; **r~ständig** *adj*

backward, out-of-date; (*Zahlungen*) in arrears; **~strahler** (**-s, -**) *m* rear reflector; **~tritt** *m* resignation; **~trittbremse** f pedal brake; **~vergütung** f repayment; (*COMM*) refund; **~versicherung** f reinsurance; **r~wärtig** *adj* rear; **r~wärts** *adv* backward(s), back; **~wärtsgang** *m* (*AUT*) reverse gear; **~weg** *m* return journey, way back; **r~wirkend** *adj* retroactive; **~wirkung** f reaction; retrospective effect; **~zahlung** f repayment; **~zug** *m* retreat

Rudel ['ru:dəl] (**-s, -**) *nt* pack; herd

Ruder ['ru:dər] (**-s, -**) *nt* oar; (*Steuer*) rudder; **~boot** *nt* rowing boat; **r~n** *vt, vi* to row

Ruf [ru:f] (**-(e)s, -e**) *m* call, cry; (*Ansehen*) reputation; **r~en** (*unreg*) *vt, vi* to call; to cry; **~name** *m* usual (first) name; **~nummer** f (tele)phone number; **~säule** f (*an Autobahn*) emergency telephone; **~zeichen** *nt* (*RADIO*) call sign; (*TEL*) ringing tone

rügen ['ry:gən] *vt* to rebuke

Ruhe ['ru:ə] (**-**) f rest; (*Ungestörtheit*) peace, quiet; (*Gelassenheit, Stille*) calm; (*Schweigen*) silence; **jdn in ~ lassen** to leave sb alone; **sich zur ~ setzen** to retire; **~!** be quiet!, silence!; **r~n** *vi* to rest; **~pause** f break; **~stand** *m* retirement; **~stätte** f: **letzte ~stätte** final resting place; **~störung** f breach of the peace; **~tag** *m* (*von Geschäft*) closing day

ruhig ['ru:ɪç] *adj* quiet; (*bewegungslos*) still; (*Hand*) steady; (*gelassen, friedlich*) calm; (*Gewissen*) clear; **kommen Sie ~ herein** just come on in; **tu das ~** feel free to do that

Ruhm [ru:m] (**-(e)s**) *m* fame, glory

rühmen ['ry:mən] *vt* to praise ♦ *vr* to boast

Rühr- [ry:r] *zW*: **~ei** *nt* scrambled egg; **r~en** *vt, vr* (*auch fig*) to move, to stir ♦ *vi*: **r~en von** to come *od* stem from; **r~en an** *+akk* to touch; (*fig*) to touch on; **r~end** *adj* touching, moving; **r~selig** *adj* sentimental, emotional; **~ung** f emotion

Ruin [ru'i:n] (**-s, -e**) *m* ruin; **~e** f ruin; **r~ieren** [-'ni:rən] *vt* to ruin

rülpsen ['rʏlpsən] *vi* to burp, to belch

Rum [rʊm] (**-s, -s**) *m* rum

Rumän- *zW:* **~ien (-s)** *nt* Ro(u)mania; **r~isch** *adj* Ro(u)manian
Rummel ['rʊməl] **(-s)** (*umg*) *m* hubbub; (*Jahrmarkt*) fair; **~platz** *m* fairground, fair
Rumpf [rʊmpf] **(-(e)s, ⁻e)** *m* trunk, torso; (*AVIAT*) fuselage; (*NAUT*) hull
rümpfen ['rʏmpfən] *vt* (*Nase*) to turn up
rund [rʊnt] *adj* round ♦ *adv* (*etwa*) around; **~ um etw** round sth; **R~brief** *m* circular; **R~e** ['rʊndə] *f* round; (*in Rennen*) lap; (*Gesellschaft*) circle; **R~fahrt** *f* (round) trip
Rundfunk ['rʊntfʊŋk] **(-(e)s)** *m* broadcasting; **im ~** on the radio; **~gerät** *nt* wireless set; **~sendung** *f* broadcast, radio programme
Rund- *zW:* **r~heraus** *adv* straight out, bluntly; **r~herum** *adv* round about; all round; **r~lich** *adj* plump, rounded; **~reise** *f* round trip; **~schreiben** *nt* (*COMM*) circular; **~(wander)weg** *m* circular path *od* route
runter ['rʊntər] (*umg*) *adv* = **herunter**; **hinunter**
Runzel ['rʊntsəl] **(-, -n)** *f* wrinkle; **r~ig** *adj* wrinkled; **r~n** *vt* to wrinkle; **die Stirn r~n** to frown
rupfen ['rʊpfən] *vt* to pluck
ruppig ['rʊpɪç] *adj* rough, gruff
Rüsche ['ry:ʃə] *f* frill
Ruß [ru:s] **(-es)** *m* soot
Russe ['rʊsə] **(-n, -n)** *m* Russian
Rüssel ['rʏsəl] **(-s, -)** *m* snout; (*Elefantenrüssel*) trunk
rußig ['ru:sɪç] *adj* sooty
Russin ['rʊsɪn] *f* Russian
russisch *adj* Russian
Russland ▲ ['rʊslant] **(-s)** *nt* Russia
rüsten ['rʏstən] *vt* to prepare ♦ *vi* to prepare; (*MIL*) to arm ♦ *vr* to prepare (o.s.); to arm o.s.
rüstig ['rʏstɪç] *adj* sprightly, vigorous
Rüstung ['rʏstʊŋ] *f* preparation; arming; (*Ritterrüstung*) armour; (*Waffen etc*) armaments *pl*; **~skontrolle** *f* arms control
Rute ['ru:tə] *f* rod
Rutsch [rʊtʃ] **(-(e)s, -e)** *m* slide; (*Erdrutsch*) landslide; **~bahn** *f* slide; **r~en** *vi* to slide; (*ausrutschen*) to slip; **r~ig** *adj* slippery
rütteln ['rʏtəln] *vt, vi* to shake, to jolt

S, s

S. *abk* (= *Seite*) p.; = **Schilling**
s. *abk* (= *siehe*) see
Saal [za:l] **(-(e)s, Säle)** *m* hall; room
Saarland ['za:rlant] *nt:* **das ~** the Saar(land)
Saat [za:t] **(-, -en)** *f* seed; (*Pflanzen*) crop; (*Säen*) sowing
Säbel ['zɛ:bəl] **(-s, -)** *m* sabre, sword
Sabotage [zabo'ta:ʒə] *f* sabotage
Sach- ['zax] *zW:* **~bearbeiter** *m* specialist; **s~dienlich** *adj* relevant, helpful; **~e** *f* thing; (*Angelegenheit*) affair, business; (*Frage*) matter; (*Pflicht*) task; **zur ~e** to the point; **s~kundig** *adj* expert; **s~lich** *adj* matter-of-fact; objective; (*Irrtum, Angabe*) factual
sächlich ['zɛxlɪç] *adj* neuter
Sachschaden *m* material damage
Sachsen ['zaksən] **(-s)** *nt* Saxony
sächsisch ['zɛksɪʃ] *adj* Saxon
sacht(e) ['zaxt(ə)] *adv* softly, gently
Sachverständige(r) *f(m)* expert
Sack [zak] **(-(e)s, ⁻e)** *m* sack; **~gasse** *f* cul-de-sac, dead-end street (*US*)
Sadismus [za'dɪsmʊs] *m* sadism
Sadist [za'dɪst] *m* sadist
säen ['zɛ:ən] *vt, vi* to sow
Safersex ▲, **Safer Sex** *m* safe sex
Saft [zaft] **(-(e)s, ⁻e)** *m* juice; (*BOT*) sap; **s~ig** *adj* juicy; **s~los** *adj* dry
Sage ['za:gə] *f* saga
Säge ['zɛ:gə] *f* saw; **~mehl** *nt* sawdust
sagen ['za:gən] *vt, vi* to say; (*mitteilen*): **jdm ~** to tell sb; **~ Sie ihm, dass ...** tell him ...
sägen *vt, vi* to saw
sagenhaft *adj* legendary; (*umg*) great, smashing
sah *etc* [za:] *vb siehe* **sehen**
Sahne ['za:nə] **(-)** *f* cream
Saison [zɛ'zõ:] **(-, -s)** *f* season
Saite ['zaɪtə] *f* string

Sakko ['zako] (-s, -s) *m od nt* jacket

Sakrament [zakra'ment] *nt* sacrament

Sakristei [zakrıs'taɪ] *f* sacristy

Salat [za'la:t] (-(e)s, -e) *m* salad; (*Kopfsalat*) lettuce; **~soße** *f* salad dressing

Salbe ['zalbə] *f* ointment

Salbei ['zalbaɪ] (-s *od* -) *m od f* sage

Saldo ['zaldo] (-s, **Salden**) *m* balance

Salmiak [zalmi'ak] (-s) *m* sal ammoniac; **~geist** *m* liquid ammonia

Salmonellenvergiftung [zalmo'nɛlən-] *f* salmonella (poisoning)

salopp [za'lɔp] *adj* casual

Salpeter [zal'pe:tər] (-s) *m* saltpetre; **~säure** *f* nitric acid

Salz [zalts] (-es, -e) *nt* salt; **s~en** (*unreg*) *vt* to salt; **s~ig** *adj* salty; **~kartoffeln** *pl* boiled potatoes; **~säure** *f* hydrochloric acid; **~streuer** *m* salt cellar; **~wasser** *nt* (*Meerwasser*) salt water

Samen ['za:mən] (-s, -) *m* seed; (*ANAT*) sperm

Sammel- ['zaməl] *zW:* **~band** *m* anthology; **~fahrschein** *m* multi-journey ticket; (*für mehrere Personen*) group ticket

sammeln ['zaməln] *vt* to collect ♦ *vr* to assemble, to gather; (*konzentrieren*) to concentrate

Sammlung ['zamlʊŋ] *f* collection; assembly, gathering; concentration

Samstag ['zamsta:k] *m* Saturday; **s~s** *adv* (on) Saturdays

Samt [zamt] (-(e)s, -e) *m* velvet; **~** *präp +dat* (along) with, together with; **~ und sonders** each and every one (of them)

sämtlich ['zɛmtlıç] *adj* all (the), entire

Sand [zant] (-(e)s, -e) *m* sand

Sandale [zan'da:lə] *f* sandal

Sand- *zW:* **~bank** *f* sandbank; **s~ig** ['zandıç] *adj* sandy; **~kasten** *m* sandpit; **~kuchen** *m* Madeira cake; **~papier** *nt* sandpaper; **~stein** *m* sandstone; **s~strahlen** *vt, vi insep* to sandblast; **~strand** *m* sandy beach

sandte *etc* ['zantə] *vb siehe* **senden**

sanft [zanft] *adj* soft, gentle; **~mütig** *adj* gentle, meek

sang *etc* [zaŋ] *vb siehe* **singen**

Sänger(in) ['zɛŋər(ın)] (-s, -) *m(f)* singer

Sani- *zW:* **s~eren** [za'ni:rən] *vt* to redevelop; (*Betrieb*) to make financially sound; ♦ *vr* to line one's pockets; to become financially sound; **s~tär** [zani'tɛ:r] *adj* sanitary; **s~täre Anlagen** sanitation *sg*; **~täter** [zani'tɛ:tər] (-s, -) *m* first-aid attendant; (*MIL*) (medical) orderly

sanktionieren [zaŋktsio'ni:rən] *vt* to sanction

Sardelle [zar'dɛlə] *f* anchovy

Sardine [zar'di:nə] *f* sardine

Sarg [zark] (-(e)s, ⁻e) *m* coffin

Sarkasmus [zar'kasmʊs] *m* sarcasm

saß *etc* [za:s] *vb siehe* **sitzen**

Satan ['za:tan] (-s, -e) *m* Satan; devil

Satellit [zate'li:t] (-en, -en) *m* satellite; **~enfernsehen** *nt* satellite television

Satire [za'ti:rə] *f* satire; **satirisch** *adj* satirical

satt [zat] *adj* full; (*Farbe*) rich, deep; **jdn/etw ~ sein** *od* **haben** to be fed up with sb/sth; **sich ~ hören/sehen an** +*dat* to hear/see enough of; **sich ~ essen** to eat one's fill; **~ machen** to be filling

Sattel ['zatəl] (-s, ⁻) *m* saddle; (*Berg*) ridge; **s~n** *vt* to saddle; **~schlepper** *m* articulated lorry

sättigen ['zɛtɪgən] *vt* to satisfy; (*CHEM*) to saturate

Satz [zats] (-es, ⁻e) *m* (*GRAM*) sentence; (*Nebensatz, Adverbialsatz*) clause; (*Theorem*) theorem; (*MUS*) movement; (*TENNIS: Briefmarken etc*) set; (*Kaffee*) grounds *pl*; (*COMM*) rate; (*Sprung*) jump; **~teil** *m* part of a sentence; **~ung** *f* (*Statut*) statute, rule; **~zeichen** *nt* punctuation mark

Sau [zaʊ] (-, **Säue**) *f* sow; (*umg*) dirty pig

sauber ['zaʊbər] *adj* clean; (*ironisch*) fine; **~ halten** to keep clean; **S~keit** *f* cleanness; (*einer Person*) cleanliness

säuberlich ['zɔybərlıç] *adv* neatly

säubern *vt* to clean; (*POL etc*) to purge; **Säuberung** *f* cleaning; purge

Sauce ['zo:sə] *f* sauce, gravy

sauer ['zaʊər] *adj* sour; (*CHEM*) acid; (*umg*)

cross; **saurer Regen** acid rain; S~**braten** *m* braised beef marinated in vinegar

Sauerei [zaʊəˈraɪ] (*umg*) *f* rotten state of affairs, scandal; (*Schmutz etc*) mess; (*Unanständigkeit*) obscenity

Sauerkraut *nt* sauerkraut, pickled cabbage

säuerlich [ˈzɔʏərlɪç] *adj* (*Geschmack*) sour; (*missvergnügt: Gesicht*) dour

Sauer- *zW*: ~**milch** *f* sour milk; ~**rahm** *m* (*KOCH*) sour cream; ~**stoff** *m* oxygen; ~**teig** *m* leaven

saufen [ˈzaʊfən] (*unreg*) (*umg*) *vt, vi* to drink, to booze; **Säufer** [ˈzɔʏfər] (**-s, -**) (*umg*) *m* boozer

saugen [ˈzaʊɡən] (*unreg*) *vt, vi* to suck

säugen [ˈzɔʏɡən] *vt* to suckle

Sauger [ˈzaʊɡər] (**-s, -**) *m* dummy, comforter (*US*); (*auf Flasche*) teat

Säugetier [ˈzɔʏɡə-] *nt* mammal

Säugling *m* infant, baby

Säule [ˈzɔʏlə] *f* column, pillar

Saum [zaʊm] (**-(e)s, Säume**) *m* hem; (*Naht*) seam

säumen [ˈzɔʏmən] *vt* to hem; to seam ♦ *vi* to delay, to hesitate

Sauna [ˈzaʊna] (**-, -s**) *f* sauna

Säure [ˈzɔʏrə] *f* acid

sausen [ˈzaʊzən] *vi* to blow; (*umg: eilen*) to rush; (*Ohren*) to buzz; **etw ~ lassen** (*umg*) not to bother with sth

Saxofon, Saxophon [zakso'foːn] (**-s, -e**) *nt* saxophone

SB *abk* = **Selbstbedienung**

S-Bahn *f abk* (= *Schnellbahn*) high speed railway; (= *Stadtbahn*) suburban railway

schaben [ˈʃaːbən] *vt* to scrape

schäbig [ˈʃɛːbɪç] *adj* shabby

Schablone [ʃaˈbloːnə] *f* stencil; (*Muster*) pattern; (*fig*) convention

Schach [ʃax] (**-s, -s**) *nt* chess; (*Stellung*) check; ~**brett** *nt* chessboard; ~**figur** *f* chessman; '~'**matt** *adj* checkmate; ~**spiel** *nt* game of chess

Schacht [ʃaxt] (**-(e)s, -̈e**) *m* shaft

Schachtel (**-, -n**) *f* box

schade [ˈʃaːdə] *adj* a pity *od* shame ♦ *excl*: **(wie) ~!** (what a) pity *od* shame; **sich** *dat*

zu ~ sein für etw to consider o.s. too good for sth

Schädel [ˈʃɛːdəl] (**-s, -**) *m* skull; ~**bruch** *m* fractured skull

Schaden [ˈʃaːdən] (**-s, -̈**) *m* damage; (*Verletzung*) injury; (*Nachteil*) disadvantage; **s~** *vi* +*dat* to hurt; **einer Sache s~** to damage sth; ~**ersatz** *m* compensation, damages *pl*; ~**freude** *f* malicious glee; **s~froh** *adj* (*Mensch, Lachen*) gloating; ~**sfall** *m*: **im ~sfall** in the event of a claim

schadhaft [ˈʃaːthaft] *adj* faulty, damaged

schäd- [ˈʃɛːt] *zW*: ~**igen** [ˈʃɛːdɪɡən] *vt* to damage; (*Person*) to do harm to, to harm; ~**lich** *adj*: ~**lich (für)** harmful (to); **S~lichkeit** *f* harmfulness; **S~ling** *m* pest

Schadstoff [ˈʃaːtʃtɔf] *m* harmful substance; **s~arm** *adj*: **s~arm sein** to contain a low level of harmful substances

Schaf [ʃaːf] (**-(e)s, -e**) *nt* sheep

Schäfer [ˈʃɛːfər] (**-s, -e**) *m* shepherd; ~**hund** *m* Alsatian (dog) (*BRIT*), German shepherd (dog) (*US*)

Schaffen [ˈʃafən] (**-s**) *nt* (creative) activity

schaffen[1] [ˈʃafən] (*unreg*) *vt* to create; (*Platz*) to make

schaffen[2] [ˈʃafən] *vt* (*erreichen*) to manage, to do; (*erledigen*) to finish; (*Prüfung*) to pass; (*transportieren*) to take ♦ *vi* (*umg: arbeiten*) to work; **sich** *dat* **etw ~** to get o.s. sth; **sich an etw** *dat* **zu ~ machen** to busy o.s. with sth

Schaffner(in) [ˈʃafnər(ɪn)] (**-s, -**) *m(f)* (*Busschaffner*) conductor(-tress); (*EISENB*) guard

Schaft [ʃaft] (**-(e)s, -̈e**) *m* shaft; (*von Gewehr*) stock; (*von Stiefel*) leg; (*BOT*) stalk; tree trunk

Schal [ʃaːl] (**-s, -e** *od* **-s**) *m* scarf

schal *adj* flat; (*fig*) insipid

Schälchen [ˈʃɛːlçən] *nt* cup, bowl

Schale [ˈʃaːlə] *f* skin; (*abgeschält*) peel; (*Nussschale, Muschelschale, Eischale*) shell; (*Geschirr*) dish, bowl

schälen [ˈʃɛːlən] *vt* to peel; to shell ♦ *vr* to peel

Schall [ʃal] (**-(e)s, -e**) *m* sound; ~**dämpfer** (**-s, -**) *m* (*AUT*) silencer; **s~dicht** *adj* soundproof; **s~en** vi to (re)sound; **s~end** adj resounding, loud; **~mauer** f sound barrier; **~platte** f (gramophone) record

Schalt- ['ʃalt] zW: **~bild** nt circuit diagram; **~brett** nt switchboard; **s~en** vt to switch, to turn ♦ vi (AUT) to change (gear); (umg: begreifen) to catch on; **~er** (-s, -) m counter; (an Gerät) switch; **~erbeamte(r)** m counter clerk; **~erstunden** pl hours of business; **~hebel** m switch; (AUT) gear lever; **~jahr** nt leap year; **~ung** f switching; (ELEK) circuit; (AUT) gear change

Scham [ʃaːm] (-) f shame; (~gefühl) modesty; (Organe) private parts pl

schämen ['ʃɛːmən] vr to be ashamed

schamlos adj shameless

Schande ['ʃandə] (-) f disgrace

schändlich ['ʃɛntlɪç] adj disgraceful, shameful

Schändung ['ʃɛndʊŋ] f violation, defilement

Schanze ['ʃantsə] f (Sprungschanze) ski jump

Schar [ʃaːr] (-, -en) f band, company; (Vögel) flock; (Menge) crowd; **in ~en** in droves; **s~en** vr to assemble, to rally

scharf [ʃarf] adj sharp; (Essen) hot, spicy; (Munition) live; **~ nachdenken** to think hard; **auf etw** akk **~ sein** (umg) to be keen on sth

Schärfe ['ʃɛrfə] f sharpness; (Strenge) rigour; **s~n** vt to sharpen

Scharf- zW: **s~machen** (umg) vt to stir up; **~richter** m executioner; **~schütze** m marksman, sharpshooter; **s~sinnig** adj astute, shrewd

Scharlach ['ʃarlax] (-s, -e) m (~fieber) scarlet fever

Scharnier [ʃar'niːr] (-s, -e) nt hinge

scharren ['ʃarən] vt, vi to scrape, to scratch

Schaschlik ['ʃaʃlɪk] (-s, -s) m od nt (shish) kebab

Schatten ['ʃatən] (-s, -) m shadow; **~riss** ▲ m silhouette; **~seite** f shady side, dark side

schattieren [ʃa'tiːrən] vt, vi to shade

schattig ['ʃatɪç] adj shady

Schatulle [ʃa'tʊlə] f casket; (Geldschatulle) coffer

Schatz [ʃats] (-es, ⁻e) m treasure; (Person) darling

schätz- [ʃɛts] zW: **~bar** adj assessable; **S~chen** nt darling, love; **~en** vt (abschätzen) to estimate; (Gegenstand) to value; (würdigen) to value, to esteem; (vermuten) to reckon; **S~ung** f estimate; estimation; valuation; **nach meiner S~ung ...** I reckon that ...

Schau [ʃau] (-) f show; (Ausstellung) display, exhibition; **etw zur ~ stellen** to make a show of sth, to show sth off; **~bild** nt diagram

Schauder ['ʃaudər] (-s, -s) m shudder; (wegen Kälte) shiver; **s~haft** adj horrible; **s~n** vi to shudder; to shiver

schauen ['ʃauən] vi to look

Schauer ['ʃauər] (-s, -) m (Regenschauer) shower; (Schreck) shudder; **~geschichte** f horror story; **s~lich** adj horrific, spine-chilling

Schaufel ['ʃaufəl] (-, -n) f shovel; (NAUT) paddle; (TECH) scoop; **s~n** vt to shovel, to scoop

Schau- zW: **~fenster** nt shop window; **~fensterbummel** m window shopping (expedition); **~kasten** m showcase

Schaukel ['ʃaukəl] (-, -n) f swing; **s~n** vi to swing, to rock; **~pferd** nt rocking horse; **~stuhl** m rocking chair

Schaulustige(r) ['ʃaulʊstɪgə(r)] f(m) onlooker

Schaum [ʃaum] (-(e)s, Schäume) m foam; (Seifenschaum) lather; **~bad** nt bubble bath

schäumen ['ʃɔymən] vi to foam

Schaum- zW: **~festiger (-s, -)** m mousse; **~gummi** m foam (rubber); **s~ig** adj frothy, foamy; **~stoff** m foam material; **~wein** m sparkling wine

Schauplatz m scene

schaurig ['ʃaurɪç] adj horrific, dreadful

Schauspiel nt spectacle; (THEAT) play; **~er(in)** m(f) actor (actress); **s~ern** vi insep to act; **Schauspielhaus** nt theatre

Scheck [ʃɛk] (-s, -s) m cheque; **~gebühr** f encashment fee; **~heft** m cheque book; **~karte** f cheque card

---

Rechtschreibreform: ▲ *neue Schreibung* △ *alte Schreibung (auslaufend)*

scheffeln ['ʃefəln] vt to amass

Scheibe ['ʃaɪbə] f disc; (Brot etc) slice; (Glasscheibe) pane; (MIL) target

Scheiben- zW: **~bremse** f (AUT) disc brake; **~wischer** m (AUT) windscreen wiper

Scheide ['ʃaɪdə] f sheath; (Grenze) boundary; (ANAT) vagina; **s~n** (unreg) vt to separate; (Ehe) to dissolve ♦ vi to depart; to part; **sich s~n lassen** to get a divorce

Scheidung f (Ehescheidung) divorce

Schein [ʃaɪn] **(-(e)s, -e)** m light; (Anschein) appearance; (Geld) (bank)note; (Bescheinigung) certificate; **zum ~** in pretence; **s~bar** adj apparent; **s~en** (unreg) vi to shine; (Anschein haben) to seem; **s~heilig** adj hypocritical; **~werfer** **(-s, -)** m floodlight; spotlight; (Suchscheinwerfer) searchlight; (AUT) headlamp

Scheiß- ['ʃaɪs] (umg) in zW bloody

Scheiße ['ʃaɪsə] **(-)** (umg) f shit

Scheitel ['ʃaɪtəl] **(-s, -)** m top; (Haarscheitel) parting; **s~n** vt to part

scheitern ['ʃaɪtərn] vi to fail

Schelle ['ʃelə] f small bell; **s~n** vi to ring

Schellfisch ['ʃelfɪʃ] m haddock

Schelm [ʃelm] **(-(e)s, -e)** m rogue; **s~isch** adj mischievous, roguish

Schelte ['ʃeltə] f scolding; **s~n** (unreg) vt to scold

Schema ['ʃeːma] **(-s, -s** od **-ta)** nt scheme, plan; (Darstellung) schema; **nach ~** quite mechanically; **s~tisch** [ʃeˈmaːtɪʃ] adj schematic; (pej) mechanical

Schemel ['ʃeːməl] **(-s, -)** m (foot)stool

Schenkel ['ʃeŋkəl] **(-s, -)** m thigh

schenken ['ʃeŋkən] vt (auch fig) to give; (Getränk) to pour; **sich** dat **etw ~** (umg) to skip sth; **das ist geschenkt!** (billig) that's a giveaway!; (nichts wert) that's worthless!

Scherbe ['ʃerbə] f broken piece, fragment; (archäologisch) potsherd

Schere ['ʃeːra] f scissors pl; (groß) shears pl; **s~n** (unreg) vt to cut; (Schaf) to shear; (kümmern) to bother ♦ vr to care; **scher dich zum Teufel!** get lost!; **~'rei** (umg) f bother, trouble

Scherz [ʃerts] **(-es, -e)** m joke; fun; **~frage** f conundrum; **s~haft** adj joking, jocular

Scheu [ʃɔy] **(-)** f shyness; (Angst) fear; (Ehrfurcht) awe; **s~** adj shy; **s~en** vr: **sich s~en vor** +dat to be afraid of, to shrink from ♦ vt to shun ♦ vi (Pferd) to shy

scheuern ['ʃɔyərn] vt to scour, to scrub

Scheune ['ʃɔynə] f barn

Scheusal ['ʃɔyzaːl] **(-s, -e)** nt monster

scheußlich ['ʃɔyslɪç] adj dreadful, frightful

Schi [ʃiː] m = **Ski**

Schicht [ʃɪçt] **(-, -en)** f layer; (Klasse) class, level; (in Fabrik etc) shift; **~arbeit** f shift work; **s~en** vt to layer, to stack

schick [ʃɪk] adj stylish, chic

schicken vt to send ♦ vr: **sich ~ (in** +akk) to resign o.s. (to) ♦ vb unpers (anständig sein) to be fitting

schicklich adj proper, fitting

Schicksal **(-s, -e)** nt fate; **~sschlag** m great misfortune, blow

Schieb- ['ʃiːb] zW: **~edach** nt (AUT) sun roof; **s~en** (unreg) vt (auch Drogen) to push; (Schuld) to put ♦ vi to push; **~etür** f sliding door; **~ung** f fiddle

Schieds- ['ʃiːts] zW: **~gericht** nt court of arbitration; **~richter** m referee; umpire; (Schlichter) arbitrator

schief [ʃiːf] adj crooked; (Ebene) sloping; (Turm) leaning; (Winkel) oblique; (Blick) funny; (Vergleich) distorted ♦ adv crooked(ly); (ansehen) askance; **etw ~ stellen** to slope sth; **~ gehen** (umg) to go wrong

Schiefer ['ʃiːfər] **(-s, -)** m slate

schielen ['ʃiːlən] vi to squint; **nach etw ~** (fig) to eye sth

schien etc [ʃiːn] vb siehe **scheinen**

Schienbein nt shinbone

Schiene ['ʃiːnə] f rail; (MED) splint; **s~n** vt to put in splints

schier [ʃiːr] adj (fig) sheer ♦ adv nearly, almost

Schieß- [ʃiːs] zW: **~bude** f shooting gallery; **s~en** (unreg) vt to shoot; (Ball) to kick; (Geschoss) to fire ♦ vi to shoot; (Salat etc) to run to seed; **s~en auf** +akk to shoot

at; **~e'rei** f shooting incident, shoot-out;
~pulver nt gunpowder; **~scharte** f
embrasure

Schiff [ʃɪf] **(-(e)s, -e)** nt ship, vessel;
(*Kirchenschiff*) nave; **s~bar** adj (*Fluß*)
navigable; **~bruch** m shipwreck;
s~brüchig adj shipwrecked; **~chen** nt
small boat; (*Weben*) shuttle; (*Mütze*) forage
cap; **~er (-s, -)** m bargeman, boatman;
~fahrt ▲ f shipping; (*Reise*) voyage

Schikane [ʃi'ka:nə] f harassment; dirty trick;
mit allen ~n with all the trimmings

schikanieren [ʃika'ni:rən] vt to harass, to
torment

Schikoree ▲ ['ʃikore:] **(-s)** m od f =
Chicorée

Schild[1] [ʃɪlt] **(-(e)s, -e)** m shield; **etw im ~e**
führen to be up to sth

Schild[2] [ʃɪlt] **(-(e)s, -er)** nt sign; nameplate;
(*Etikett*) label

Schilddrüse f thyroid gland

schildern ['ʃɪldərn] vt to depict, to portray

Schildkröte f tortoise; (*Wasserschildkröte*)
turtle

Schilf [ʃɪlf] **(-(e)s, -e)** nt (*Pflanze*) reed;
(*Material*) reeds pl, rushes pl; **~rohr** nt
(*Pflanze*) reed

schillern ['ʃɪlərn] vi to shimmer; **~d** adj
iridescent

Schilling ['ʃɪlɪŋ] m schilling

Schimmel ['ʃɪməl] **(-s, -)** m mould; (*Pferd*)
white horse; **s~ig** adj mouldy; **s~n** vi to
get mouldy

Schimmer ['ʃɪmər] **(-s)** m (*Lichtsein*)
glimmer; (*Glanz*) shimmer; **s~n** vi to
glimmer, to shimmer

Schimpanse [ʃɪm'panzə] **(-n, -n)** m
chimpanzee

schimpfen ['ʃɪmpfən] vt to scold ♦ vi to
curse, to complain; to scold

Schimpfwort nt term of abuse

schinden ['ʃɪndən] (*unreg*) vt to maltreat, to
drive too hard ♦ vr: **sich ~ (mit)** to sweat
and strain (at), to toil away (at); **Eindruck**
~ (*umg*) to create an impression

Schinde'rei f grind, drudgery

Schinken ['ʃɪŋkən] **(-s, -)** m ham

Schirm [ʃɪrm] **(-(e)s, -e)** m (*Regenschirm*)
umbrella; (*Sonnenschirm*) parasol, sunshade;
(*Wandschirm, Bildschirm*) screen;
(*Lampenschirm*) (lamp)shade; (*Mützenschirm*)
peak; (*Pilzschirm*) cap; **~mütze** f peaked
cap; **~ständer** m umbrella stand

schizophren [ʃitso'fre:n] adj schizophrenic

Schlacht [ʃlaxt] **(-, -en)** f battle; **s~en** vt to
slaughter, to kill; **~er (-s, -)** m butcher;
~feld nt battlefield; **~hof** m
slaughterhouse, abattoir; **~schiff** nt
battleship; **~vieh** nt animals kept for meat;
beef cattle

Schlaf [ʃla:f] **(-(e)s)** m sleep; **~anzug** m
pyjamas pl

Schläfe f (*ANAT*) temple

schlafen ['ʃla:fən] (*unreg*) vi to sleep; **~**
gehen to go to bed; **S~szeit** f bedtime

schlaff [ʃlaf] adj slack; (*energielos*) limp;
(*erschöpft*) exhausted

Schlaf- zW: **~gelegenheit** f sleeping
accommodation; **~lied** nt lullaby; **s~los**
adj sleepless; **~losigkeit** f sleeplessness,
insomnia; **~mittel** nt sleeping pill

schläfrig ['ʃle:frɪç] adj sleepy

Schlaf- zW: **~saal** m dormitory; **~sack** m
sleeping bag; **~tablette** f sleeping pill;
~wagen m sleeping car, sleeper;
s~wandeln vi insep to sleepwalk;
~zimmer nt bedroom

Schlag [ʃla:k] **(-(e)s, ˤe)** m (*auch fig*) blow;
(*auch MED*) stroke; (*Pulsschlag, Herzschlag*)
beat; (*ELEK*) shock; (*Blitzschlag*) bolt, stroke;
(*Autotür*) car door; (*umg: Portion*) helping;
(*Art*) kind, type; **Schläge** pl (*Tracht Prügel*)
beating sg; **mit einem ~** all at once; **~ auf**
~ in rapid succession; **~ader** f artery;
~anfall m stroke; **s~artig** adj sudden,
without warning; **~baum** m barrier

Schlägel ['ʃle:gəl] **(-s, -)** m (drum)stick;
(*Hammer*) mallet, hammer

schlagen ['ʃla:gən] (*unreg*) vt, vi to strike, to
hit; (*wiederholt ~, besiegen*) to beat;
(*Glocke*) to ring; (*Stunde*) to strike; (*Sahne*)
to whip; (*Schlacht*) to fight ♦ vr to fight;
nach jdm ~ (*fig*) to take after sb; **sich gut**
~ (*fig*) to do well; **Schlager** ['ʃla:gər] **(-s, -)**

m (auch fig) hit

Schläger ['ʃlɛːɡər] *m* brawler; (*SPORT*) bat; (*TENNIS etc*) racket; (*GOLF*) club; hockey stick; (*Waffe*) rapier; **Schläge'rei** *f* fight, punch-up

Schlagersänger(in) *m(f)* pop singer

Schlag- *zW*: **s~fertig** *adj* quick-witted; **~fertigkeit** *f* ready wit, quickness of repartee; **~loch** *nt* pothole; **~obers** (*ÖSTERR*) *nt* = **Schlagsahne; ~sahne** *f* (whipped) cream; **~seite** *f* (*NAUT*) list; **~wort** *nt* slogan, catch phrase; **~zeile** *f* headline; **~zeug** *nt* percussion; drums *pl*; **~zeuger** (**-s, -**) *m* drummer

Schlamassel [ʃlaˈmasəl] (**-s, -**) (*umg*) *m* mess

Schlamm [ʃlam] (**-(e)s, -e**) *m* mud; **s~ig** *adj* muddy

Schlamp- ['ʃlamp] *zW*: **~e** (*umg*) *f* slut; **s~en** (*umg*) *vi* to be sloppy; **~e'rei** (*umg*) *f* disorder, untidiness; sloppy work; **s~ig** (*umg*) *adj* (*Mensch, Arbeit*) sloppy, messy

Schlange ['ʃlaŋə] *f* snake; (*Menschenschlange*) queue (*BRIT*), line-up (*US*); **~ stehen** to (form a) queue, to line up

schlängeln ['ʃlɛŋəln] *vr* (*Schlange*) to wind; (*Weg*) to wind, twist; (*Fluss*) to meander

Schlangen- *zW*: **~biss** ▲ *m* snake bite; **~gift** *nt* snake venom; **~linie** *f* wavy line

schlank [ʃlaŋk] *adj* slim, slender; **S~heit** *f* slimness, slenderness; **S~heitskur** *f* diet

schlapp [ʃlap] *adj* limp; (*locker*) slack; **S~e** (*umg*) *f* setback

Schlaraffenland [ʃlaˈrafənlant] *nt* land of milk and honey

schlau [ʃlaʊ] *adj* crafty, cunning

Schlauch [ʃlaʊx] (**-(e)s, Schläuche**) *m* hose; (*in Reifen*) inner tube; (*umg: Anstrengung*) grind; **~boot** *nt* rubber dinghy; **s~en** (*umg*) *vt* to tell on, to exhaust

Schläue ['ʃlɔʏə] (**-**) *f* cunning

Schlaufe ['ʃlaʊfə] *f* loop; (*Aufhänger*) hanger

Schlauheit *f* cunning

schlecht [ʃlɛçt] *adj* bad ♦ *adv* badly; **~ gelaunt** in a bad mood; **~ und recht** after

a fashion; **jdm ist ~** sb feels sick *od* bad; **jdm geht es ~** sb is in a bad way; **~ machen** to run down; **S~igkeit** *f* badness; bad deed

schlecken ['ʃlɛkən] *vt, vi* to lick

Schlegel ['ʃleːɡəl] (**-s, -**) *m* (*KOCH*) leg; *siehe* **Schlägel**

schleichen ['ʃlaɪçən] (*unreg*) *vi* to creep, to crawl; **~d** *adj* gradual; creeping

Schleichwerbung *f* (*COMM*) plug

Schleier ['ʃlaɪər] (**-s, -**) *m* veil; **s~haft** (*umg*) *adj*: **jdm s~haft sein** to be a mystery to sb

Schleif- ['ʃlaɪf] *zW*: **~e** *f* loop; (*Band*) bow; **s~en¹** *vt, vi* to drag; **s~en²** (*unreg*) *vt* to grind; (*Edelstein*) to cut; **~stein** *m* grindstone

Schleim [ʃlaɪm] (**-(e)s, -e**) *m* slime; (*MED*) mucus; (*KOCH*) gruel; **~haut** *f* (*ANAT*) mucous membrane; **s~ig** *adj* slimy

Schlemm- ['ʃlɛm] *zW*: **s~en** *vi* to feast; **~er** (**-s, -**) *m* gourmet; **~e'rei** *f* gluttony, feasting

schlendern ['ʃlɛndərn] *vi* to stroll

schlenkern ['ʃlɛŋkərn] *vt, vi* to swing, to dangle

Schlepp- ['ʃlɛp] *zW*: **~e** *f* train; **s~en** *vt* to drag; (*Auto, Schiff*) to tow; (*tragen*) to lug; **s~end** *adj* dragging, slow; **~er** (**-s, -**) *m* tractor; (*Schiff*) tug

Schlesien ['ʃleːziən] (**-s**) *nt* Silesia

Schleuder ['ʃlɔʏdər] (**-, -n**) *f* catapult; (*Wäscheschleuder*) spin-drier; (*Butterschleuder etc*) centrifuge; **~gefahr** *f* risk of skidding; **„Achtung ~gefahr"** "slippery road ahead"; **s~n** *vt* to hurl; (*Wäsche*) to spin-dry ♦ *vi* (*AUT*) to skid; **~preis** *m* give-away price; **~sitz** *m* (*AVIAT*) ejector seat; (*fig*) hot seat; **~ware** *f* cheap *od* cut-price goods *pl*

schleunigst ['ʃlɔʏnɪçst] *adv* straight away

Schleuse ['ʃlɔʏzə] *f* lock; (*~ntor*) sluice

schlicht [ʃlɪçt] *adj* simple, plain; **~en** *vt* (*glätten*) to smooth, to dress; (*Streit*) to settle; **S~er** (**-s, -**) *m* mediator, arbitrator; **S~ung** *f* settlement; arbitration

Schlick [ʃlɪk] (**-(e)s, -e**) *m* mud; (*Ölschlick*) slick

schlief *etc* [ʃliːf] *vb siehe* **schlafen**

Schließ- [ˈʃliːs] *zW:* **s~en** (*unreg*) *vt* to close, to shut; (*beenden*) to close; (*Freundschaft, Bündnis, Ehe*) to enter into; (*folgern*): **s~en (aus)** to infer (from) ♦ *vi, vr* to close, to shut; **etw in sich s~en** to include sth; **~fach** *nt* locker; **s~lich** *adv* finally; **s~lich doch** after all

Schliff [ʃlɪf] **(-(e)s, -e)** *m* cut(ting); (*fig*) polish

schlimm [ʃlɪm] *adj* bad; **~er** *adj* worse; **~ste(r, s)** *adj* worst; **~stenfalls** *adv* at (the) worst

Schlinge [ˈʃlɪŋə] *f* loop; (*bes Henkersschlinge*) noose; (*Falle*) snare; (*MED*) sling; **s~n** (*unreg*) *vt* to wind; (*essen*) to bolt, to gobble ♦ *vi* (*essen*) to bolt one's food, to gobble

schlingern *vi* to roll

Schlips [ʃlɪps] **(-es, -e)** *m* tie

Schlitten [ˈʃlɪtən] **(-s, -)** *m* sledge, sleigh; **~fahren (-s)** *nt* tobogganing

schlittern [ˈʃlɪtərn] *vi* to slide

Schlittschuh [ˈʃlɪtʃuː] *m* skate; **~ laufen** to skate; **~bahn** *f* skating rink; **~läufer(in)** *m(f)* skater

Schlitz [ʃlɪts] **(-es, -e)** *m* slit; (*für Münze*) slot; (*Hosenschlitz*) flies *pl*; **s~äugig** *adj* slant-eyed

Schloss ▲ [ʃlɔs] **(-es, ᵘer)** *nt* lock; (*an Schmuck etc*) clasp; (*Bau*) castle; chateau

schloss ▲ *etc vb siehe* **schließen**

Schlosser [ˈʃlɔsər] **(-s, -)** *m* (*Autoschlosser*) fitter; (*für Schlüssel etc*) locksmith

Schlosserei [-ˈraɪ] *f* metal (working) shop

Schlot [ʃloːt] **(-(e)s, -e)** *m* chimney; (*NAUT*) funnel

schlottern [ˈʃlɔtərn] *vi* to shake, to tremble; (*Kleidung*) to be baggy

Schlucht [ʃlʊxt] **(-, -en)** *f* gorge, ravine

schluchzen [ˈʃlʊxtsən] *vi* to sob

Schluck [ʃlʊk] **(-(e)s, -e)** *m* swallow; (*Menge*) drop; **~auf (-s, -s)** *m* hiccups *pl*; **s~en** *vt, vi* to swallow

schludern [ˈʃluːdərn] *vi* to skimp, to do sloppy work

schlug *etc* [ʃluːk] *vb siehe* **schlagen**

Schlummer [ˈʃlʊmər] **(-s)** *m* slumber; **s~n**

vi to slumber

Schlund [ʃlʊnt] **(-(e)s, ᵘe)** *m* gullet; (*fig*) jaw

schlüpfen [ˈʃlʏpfən] *vi* to slip; (*Vogel etc*) to hatch (out)

Schlüpfer [ˈʃlʏpfər] **(-s, -)** *m* panties *pl*, knickers *pl*

schlüpfrig [ˈʃlʏpfrɪç] *adj* slippery; (*fig*) lewd; **S~keit** *f* slipperiness; (*fig*) lewdness

schlurfen [ˈʃlʊrfən] *vi* to shuffle

schlürfen [ˈʃlʏrfən] *vt, vi* to slurp

Schluss ▲ [ʃlʊs] **(-es, ᵘe)** *m* end; (*~folgerung*) conclusion; **am ~** at the end; **~ machen mit** to finish with

Schlüssel [ˈʃlʏsəl] **(-s, -)** *m* (*auch fig*) key; (*Schraubenschlüssel*) spanner, wrench; (*MUS*) clef; **~bein** *nt* collarbone; **~blume** *f* cowslip, primrose; **~bund** *m* bunch of keys; **~dienst** *m* key cutting service; **~loch** *nt* keyhole; **~position** *f* key position; **~wort** *nt* keyword

schlüssig [ˈʃlʏsɪç] *adj* conclusive

Schluss- ▲ *zW:* **~licht** *nt* taillight; (*fig*) tailender; **~strich** *m* (*fig*) final stroke; **~verkauf** *m* clearance sale

schmächtig [ˈʃmɛçtɪç] *adj* slight

schmackhaft [ˈʃmakhaft] *adj* tasty

schmal [ʃmaːl] *adj* narrow; (*Person, Buch etc*) slender, slim; (*karg*) meagre

schmälern [ˈʃmɛːlərn] *vt* to diminish; (*fig*) to belittle

Schmalfilm *m* cine film

Schmalz [ʃmalts] **(-es, -e)** *nt* dripping, lard; (*fig*) sentiment, schmaltz; **s~ig** *adj* (*fig*) schmaltzy

schmarotzen [ʃmaˈrɔtsən] *vi* to sponge; (*BOT*) to be parasitic; **Schmarotzer (-s, -)** *m* parasite; sponger

Schmarren [ˈʃmarən] **(-s, -)** *m* (*ÖSTERR*) small piece of pancake; (*fig*) rubbish, tripe

schmatzen [ˈʃmatsən] *vi* to smack one's lips; to eat noisily

schmecken [ˈʃmɛkən] *vt, vi* to taste; **es schmeckt ihm** he likes it

Schmeichel- [ˈʃmaɪçəl] *zW:* **~ei** [-ˈlaɪ] *f* flattery; **s~haft** *adj* flattering; **s~n** *vi* to flatter

schmeißen [ˈʃmaɪsən] (*unreg*) (*umg*) *vt* to

throw, to chuck

Schmelz [ʃmɛlts] **(-es, -e)** m enamel; (*Glasur*) glaze; (*von Stimme*) melodiousness; **s~en** (*unreg*) vt to melt; (*Erz*) to smelt ♦ vi to melt; **~punkt** m melting point; **~wasser** nt melted snow

Schmerz [ʃmɛrts] **(-es, -en)** m pain; (*Trauer*) grief; **s~empfindlich** adj sensitive to pain; **s~en** vt, vi to hurt; **~ensgeld** nt compensation; **s~haft** adj painful; **s~lich** adj painful; **s~los** adj painless; **~mittel** nt painkiller; **~tablette** f painkiller

Schmetterling [ʃmɛtərlɪŋ] m butterfly

schmettern [ʃmɛtərn] vt (*werfen*) to hurl; (*TENNIS: Ball*) to smash; (*singen*) to belt out (*inf*)

Schmied [ʃmiːt] **(-(e)s, -e)** m blacksmith; **~e** [ʃmiːdə] f smithy, forge; **~eeisen** nt wrought iron; **s~en** vt to forge; (*Pläne*) to devise, to concoct

schmiegen [ʃmiːɡən] vt to press, to nestle ♦ vr: **sich ~ (an** +akk) to cuddle up (to), to nestle (up to)

Schmier- [ʃmiːr] zW: **~e** f grease; (*THEAT*) greasepaint, make-up; **s~en** vt to smear; (*ölen*) to lubricate, to grease; (*bestechen*) to bribe; (*schreiben*) to scrawl ♦ vi (*schreiben*) to scrawl; **~fett** nt grease; **~geld** nt bribe; **s~ig** adj greasy; **~seife** f soft soap

Schminke [ʃmɪŋkə] f make-up; **s~n** vt, vr to make up

schmirgeln [ʃmɪrɡəln] vt to sand (down)

Schmirgelpapier nt emery paper

schmollen [ʃmɔlən] vi to sulk, to pout

Schmorbraten m stewed od braised meat

schmoren [ʃmoːrən] vt to stew, to braise

Schmuck [ʃmʊk] **(-(e)s, -e)** m jewellery; (*Verzierung*) decoration

schmücken [ʃmʏkən] vt to decorate

Schmuck- zW: **s~los** adj unadorned, plain; **~sachen** pl jewels, jewellery sg

Schmuggel [ʃmʊɡəl] **(-s)** m smuggling; **s~n** vt to smuggle

Schmuggler (-s, -) m smuggler

schmunzeln [ʃmʊntsəln] vi to smile benignly

schmusen [ʃmuːzən] (*umg*) vi (*zärtlich sein*)

to cuddle, to canoodle (*inf*)

Schmutz [ʃmʊts] **(-es)** m dirt, filth; **~fink** m filthy creature; **~fleck** m stain; **s~ig** adj dirty

Schnabel [ʃnaːbəl] **(-s, ¨)** m beak, bill; (*Ausguss*) spout

Schnalle [ʃnalə] f buckle, clasp; **s~n** vt to buckle

Schnapp- [ʃnap] zW: **s~en** vt to grab, to catch ♦ vi to snap; **~schloss** ▲ nt spring lock; **~schuss** ▲ m (*PHOT*) snapshot

Schnaps [ʃnaps] **(-es, ¨e)** m spirits pl; schnapps

schnarchen [ʃnarçən] vi to snore

schnattern [ʃnatərn] vi (*Gänse*) to gabble; (*Ente*) to quack

schnauben [ʃnaʊbən] vi to snort ♦ vr to blow one's nose

schnaufen [ʃnaʊfən] vi to puff, to pant

Schnauze f snout, muzzle; (*Ausguss*) spout; (*umg*) gob

schnäuzen ▲ [ʃnɔytsən] vr to blow one's nose

Schnecke [ʃnɛkə] f snail; **~nhaus** nt snail's shell

Schnee [ʃneː] **(-s)** m snow; (*Eischnee*) beaten egg white; **~ball** m snowball; **~flocke** f snowflake; **s~frei** adj free of snow; **~gestöber** nt snowstorm; **~glöckchen** nt snowdrop; **~grenze** f snow line; **~kette** f (*AUT*) snow chain; **~mann** m snowman; **~pflug** m snowplough; **~regen** m sleet; **~schmelze** f thaw; **~wehe** f snowdrift

Schneide [ʃnaɪdə] f edge; (*Klinge*) blade; **s~n** (*unreg*) vt to cut; (*kreuzen*) to cross, to intersect with ♦ vr to cut o.s.; to cross, to intersect; **s~nd** adj cutting; **~r (-s, -)** m tailor; **~rei** f (*Geschäft*) tailor's; **~rin** f dressmaker; **s~rn** vt to make ♦ vi to be a tailor; **~zahn** m incisor

schneien [ʃnaɪən] vi unpers to snow

Schneise [ʃnaɪzə] f clearing

schnell [ʃnɛl] adj quick, fast ♦ adv quick, quickly, fast; **S~hefter (-s, -)** m loose-leaf binder; **S~igkeit** f speed; **S~imbiss** ▲ m (*Lokal*) snack bar; **S~kochtopf** m

Spelling Reform: ▲ new spelling △ old spelling (to be phased out)

(*Dampfkochtopf*) pressure cooker;
S~reinigung *f* dry cleaner's; **~stens** *adv*
as quickly as possible; **S~straße** *f*
expressway; **S~zug** *m* fast *od* express train
schneuzen △ ['ʃnɔytsən] *vr siehe*
schnäuzen
schnippeln ['ʃnɪpəln] (*umg*) *vt*: **~ (an** +*dat*)
to snip (at)
schnippisch ['ʃnɪpɪʃ] *adj* sharp-tongued
Schnitt (**-(e)s, -e**) *m* cut(ting); (~*punkt*)
intersection; (*Querschnitt*) (cross) section;
(*Durchschnitt*) average; (~*muster*) pattern;
(*an Buch*) edge; (*umg: Gewinn*) profit
schnitt *etc vb siehe* **schneiden**
Schnitt- *zW*: **~blumen** *pl* cut flowers; **~e** *f*
slice; (*belegt*) sandwich; **~fläche** *f* section;
~lauch *m* chive; **~punkt** *m* (point of)
intersection; **~stelle** *f* (*COMPUT*) interface;
~wunde *f* cut
Schnitz- ['ʃnɪtz] *zW*: **~arbeit** *f* wood
carving; **~el** (**-s, -**) *nt* chip; (*KOCH*)
escalope; **s~en** *vt* to carve; **~er** (**-s, -**) *m*
carver; (*umg*) blunder; **~e'rei** *f* carving;
carved woodwork
schnodderig ['ʃnɔdərɪç] (*umg*) *adj* snotty
Schnorchel ['ʃnɔrçəl] (**-s, -**) *m* snorkel
Schnörkel ['ʃnœrkəl] (**-s, -**) *m* flourish;
(*ARCHIT*) scroll
schnorren ['ʃnɔrən] *vt, vi* to cadge
schnüffeln ['ʃnʏfəln] *vi* to sniff
Schnüffler (**-s, -**) *m* snooper
Schnuller ['ʃnʊlər] (**-s, -**) *m* dummy,
comforter (*US*)
Schnupfen ['ʃnʊpfən] (**-s, -**) *m* cold
schnuppern ['ʃnʊpərn] *vi* to sniff
Schnur [ʃnuːr] (**-, ⁻e**) *f* string, cord; (*ELEK*)
flex
schnüren ['ʃnyːrən] *vt* to tie
schnurgerade *adj* straight (as a die)
Schnurrbart ['ʃnʊrbaːrt] *m* moustache
schnurren ['ʃnʊrən] *vi* to purr; (*Kreisel*) to
hum
Schnürschuh *m* lace-up (shoe)
Schnürsenkel *m* shoelace
schnurstracks *adv* straight (away)
Schock [ʃɔk] (**-(e)s, -e**) *m* shock; **s~ieren**
[ʃɔ'kiːrən] *vt* to shock, to outrage

Schöffe ['ʃœfə] (**-n, -n**) *m* lay magistrate;
Schöffin *f* lay magistrate
Schokolade [ʃoko'laːdə] *f* chocolate
Scholle ['ʃɔlə] *f* clod; (*Eisscholle*) ice floe;
(*Fisch*) plaice

┌─────────────────────────────┐
│ *SCHLÜSSELWORT* │
└─────────────────────────────┘

schon [ʃoːn] *adv* **1** (*bereits*) already; **er ist
schon da** he's there already, he's already
there; **ist er schon da?** is he there yet?;
warst du schon einmal da? have you ever
been there?; **ich war schon einmal da** I've
been there before; **das war schon immer
so** that has always been the case; **schon
oft** often; **hast du schon gehört?** have
you heard?
2 (*bestimmt*) all right; **du wirst schon
sehen** you'll see (all right); **das wird
schon noch gut** that'll be OK
3 (*bloß*) just; **allein schon das Gefühl ...**
just the very feeling ...; **schon der
Gedanke** the very thought; **wenn ich das
schon höre** I only have to hear that
4 (*einschränkend*): **ja schon, aber ...** yes
(well), but ...
5: schon möglich possible; **schon gut!**
OK!; **du weißt schon** you know; **komm
schon!** come on!

└─────────────────────────────┘

schön [ʃøːn] *adj* beautiful; (*nett*) nice; **~e
Grüße** best wishes; **~e Ferien** have a nice
holiday; **~en Dank** (many) thanks; **sich ~
machen** to make o.s. look nice
schonen ['ʃoːnən] *vt* to look after ♦ *vr* to
take it easy; **~d** *adj* careful, gentle
Schön- *zW*: **~heit** *f* beauty; **~heitsfehler**
m blemish, flaw; **~heitsoperation** *f*
cosmetic surgery
Schonkost (**-**) *f* light diet; (*Spezialdiät*)
special diet
Schon- *zW*: **~ung** *f* good care; (*Nachsicht*)
consideration; (*Forst*) plantation of young
trees; **s~ungslos** *adj* unsparing, harsh;
~zeit *f* close season
Schöpf- ['ʃœpf] *zW*: **s~en** *vt* to scoop, to
ladle; (*Mut*) to summon up; (*Luft*) to
breathe in; **~er** (**-s, -**) *m* creator; **s~erisch**

adj creative; **~kelle** *f* ladle; **~ung** *f* creation

Schorf [ʃɔrf] **(-(e)s, -e)** *m* scab

Schornstein ['ʃɔrnʃtaɪn] *m* chimney; (*NAUT*) funnel; **~feger (-s, -)** *m* chimney sweep

Schoß [ʃoːs] **(-es, ⁼e)** *m* lap

schoss ▲ *etc vb siehe* **schießen**

Schoßhund *m* pet dog, lapdog

Schote ['ʃoːtə] *f* pod

Schotte ['ʃɔtə] *m* Scot, Scotsman

Schotter ['ʃɔtər] **(-s)** *m* broken stone, road metal; (*EISENB*) ballast

Schott- [ʃɔt] *zW:* **~in** *f* Scot, Scotswoman; **s~isch** *adj* Scottish, Scots; **~land** *nt* Scotland

schraffieren [ʃra'fiːrən] *vt* to hatch

schräg [ʃrɛːk] *adj* slanting, not straight; **etw ~ stellen** to put sth at an angle; **~ gegenüber** diagonally opposite; **S~e** ['ʃrɛːgə] *f* slant; **S~strich** *m* oblique stroke

Schramme ['ʃramə] *f* scratch; **s~n** *vt* to scratch

Schrank [ʃraŋk] **(-(e)s, ⁼e)** *m* cupboard; (*Kleiderschrank*) wardrobe; **~e** *f* barrier; **~koffer** *m* trunk

Schraube ['ʃraubə] *f* screw; **s~n** *vt* to screw; **~nschlüssel** *m* spanner; **~nzieher (-s, -)** *m* screwdriver

Schraubstock ['ʃraupʃtɔk] *m* (*TECH*) vice

Schreck [ʃrɛk] **(-(e)s, -e)** *m* terror; fright; **~en (-s, -)** *m* terror; fright; **s~en** *vt* to frighten, to scare; **~gespenst** *nt* spectre, nightmare; **s~haft** *adj* jumpy, easily frightened; **s~lich** *adj* terrible, dreadful

Schrei [ʃraɪ] **(-(e)s, -e)** *m* scream; (*Ruf*) shout

Schreib- ['ʃraɪb] *zW:* **~block** *m* writing pad; **s~en** (*unreg*) *vt, vi* to write; (*buchstabieren*) to spell; **~en (-s, -)** *nt* letter, communication; **s~faul** *adj* bad about writing letters; **~kraft** *f* typist; **~maschine** *f* typewriter; **~papier** *nt* notepaper; **~tisch** *m* desk; **~ung** *f* spelling; **~waren** *pl* stationery *sg*; **~weise** *f* spelling; way of writing; **~zentrale** *f* typing pool; **~zeug** *nt* writing materials *pl*

schreien ['ʃraɪən] (*unreg*) *vt, vi* to scream; (*rufen*) to shout; **~d** *adj* (*fig*) glaring; (*Farbe*) loud

Schrein [ʃraɪn] **(-(e)s, -e)** *m* shrine

Schreiner ['ʃraɪnər] **(-s, -)** *m* joiner; (*Zimmermann*) carpenter; (*Möbelschreiner*) cabinetmaker; **~ei** [-'raɪ] *f* joiner's workshop

schreiten ['ʃraɪtən] (*unreg*) *vi* to stride

schrieb *etc* [ʃriːp] *vb siehe* **schreiben**

Schrift [ʃrɪft] **(-, -en)** *f* writing; handwriting; (*~art*) script; (*Gedrucktes*) pamphlet, work; **~deutsch** *nt* written German; **~führer** *m* secretary; **s~lich** *adj* written ♦ *adv* in writing; **~sprache** *f* written language; **~steller(in) (-s, -)** *m(f)* writer; **~stück** *nt* document; **~wechsel** *m* correspondence

schrill [ʃrɪl] *adj* shrill

Schritt [ʃrɪt] **(-(e)s, -e)** *m* step; (*Gangart*) walk; (*Tempo*) pace; (*von Hose*) crutch; **~ fahren** to drive at walking pace; **~macher (-s, -)** *m* pacemaker; **~tempo** ▲ *nt:* **im ~tempo** at a walking pace

schroff [ʃrɔf] *adj* steep; (*zackig*) jagged; (*fig*) brusque

schröpfen ['ʃrœpfən] *vt* (*fig*) to fleece

Schrot [ʃroːt] **(-(e)s, -e)** *m* od *nt* (*Blei*) (small) shot; (*Getreide*) coarsely ground grain, groats *pl*; **~flinte** *f* shotgun

Schrott [ʃrɔt] **(-(e)s, -e)** *m* scrap metal; **~haufen** *m* scrap heap; **s~reif** *adj* ready for the scrap heap

schrubben ['ʃrʊbən] *vt* to scrub

Schrubber (-s, -) *m* scrubbing brush

schrumpfen ['ʃrʊmpfən] *vi* to shrink; (*Apfel*) to shrivel

Schub- ['ʃuːb] *zW:* **~fach** *nt* drawer; **~karren** *m* wheelbarrow; **~lade** *f* drawer

Schubs [ʃuːps] **(-es, -e)** (*umg*) *m* shove (*inf*), push

schüchtern ['ʃʏçtərn] *adj* shy; **S~heit** *f* shyness

Schuft [ʃʊft] **(-(e)s, -e)** *m* scoundrel

schuften (*umg*) *vi* to graft, to slave away

Schuh [ʃuː] **(-(e)s, -e)** *m* shoe; **~band** *nt* shoelace; **~creme** *f* shoe polish; **~größe** *f* shoe size; **~löffel** *m* shoehorn; **~macher (-s, -)** *m* shoemaker

Schul- *zW:* **~arbeit** *f* homework (*no pl*); **~aufgaben** *pl* homework *sg*; **~besuch** *m*

school attendance; **~buch** nt school book

Schuld [ʃʊlt] (-, -en) f guilt; (FIN) debt; (Verschulden) fault; **~ haben (an** +dat) to be to blame (for); **er hat ~** it's his fault; **jdm ~ geben** to blame sb; *siehe* **zuschulden; s~** adj: **s~ sein (an** +dat) to be to blame (for); **er ist s~** it's his fault; **s~en** ['ʃʊldən] vt to owe; **s~enfrei** adj free from debt; **~gefühl** nt feeling of guilt; **s~ig** adj guilty; (gebührend) due; **s~ig an etw** dat **sein** to be guilty of sth; **jdm etw s~ig sein** to owe sb sth; **jdm etw s~ig bleiben** not to provide sb with sth; **s~los** adj innocent, without guilt; **~ner** (-s, -) m debtor; **~schein** m promissory note, IOU

Schule ['ʃuːlə] f school; **s~n** vt to train, to school

Schüler(in) ['ʃyːlər(ɪn)] (-s, -) m(f) pupil; **~austausch** m school od student exchange; **~ausweis** m (school) student card

Schul- zW: **~ferien** pl school holidays; **s~frei** adj: **s~freier Tag** holiday; **s~frei sein** to be a holiday; **~hof** m playground; **~jahr** nt school year; **~kind** nt schoolchild; **s~pflichtig** adj of school age; **~schiff** nt (NAUT) training ship; **~stunde** f period, lesson; **~tasche** f school bag

Schulter ['ʃʊltər] (-, -n) f shoulder; **~blatt** nt shoulder blade; **s~n** vt to shoulder

Schulung f education, schooling

Schulzeugnis nt school report

Schund [ʃʊnt] (-(e)s) m trash, garbage

Schuppe ['ʃʊpə] f scale; **~n** pl (Haarschuppen) dandruff sg

Schuppen (-s, -) m shed

schuppig ['ʃʊpɪç] adj scaly

Schur [ʃuːr] (-, -en) f shearing

schüren ['ʃyːrən] vt to rake; (fig) to stir up

schürfen ['ʃʏrfən] vt, vi to scrape, to scratch; (MIN) to prospect

Schurke ['ʃʊrkə] (-n, -n) m rogue

Schurwolle f: **„reine ~"** "pure new wool"

Schürze ['ʃʏrtsə] f apron

Schuss ▲ [ʃʊs] (-es, ⁼e) m shot; (WEBEN) woof; **~bereich** m effective range

Schüssel ['ʃʏsəl] (-, -n) f bowl

Schuss- ▲ zW: **~linie** f line of fire; **~verletzung** f bullet wound; **~waffe** f firearm

Schuster ['ʃuːstər] (-s, -) m cobbler, shoemaker

Schutt [ʃʊt] (-(e)s) m rubbish; (Bauschutt) rubble

Schüttelfrost m shivering

schütteln ['ʃʏtəln] vt, vr to shake

schütten ['ʃʏtən] vt to pour; (Zucker, Kies etc) to tip; (verschütten) to spill ♦ vi unpers to pour (down)

Schutthalde f dump

Schutthaufen m heap of rubble

Schutz [ʃʊts] (-es) m protection; (Unterschlupf) shelter; **jdn in ~ nehmen** to stand up for sb; **~anzug** m overalls pl; **~blech** nt mudguard

Schütze ['ʃʏtsə] (-n, -n) m gunman; (Gewehrschütze) rifleman; (Scharfschütze, Sportschütze) marksman; (ASTROL) Sagittarius

schützen ['ʃʏtsən] vt to protect; **~ vor** +dat od **gegen** to protect from

Schützenfest nt fair featuring shooting matches

Schutz- zW: **~engel** m guardian angel; **~gebiet** nt protectorate; (Naturschutzgebiet) reserve; **~hütte** f shelter, refuge; **~impfung** f immunisation

Schützling ['ʃʏtslɪŋ] m protégé(e); (bes Kind) charge

Schutz- zW: **s~los** adj defenceless; **~mann** m policeman; **~patron** m patron saint

Schwaben ['ʃvaːbən] nt Swabia; **schwäbisch** adj Swabian

schwach [ʃvax] adj weak, feeble

Schwäche ['ʃvɛçə] f weakness; **s~n** vt to weaken

Schwachheit f weakness

schwächlich adj weakly, delicate

Schwächling m weakling

Schwach- zW: **~sinn** m imbecility; **s~sinnig** adj mentally deficient; (Idee) idiotic; **~strom** m weak current

Schwächung ['ʃvɛçʊŋ] f weakening

Schwager ['ʃvaːgər] (-s, ⁼) m brother-in-law; **Schwägerin** ['ʃvɛːgərɪn] f sister-in-law

Schwalbe ['ʃvalbə] *f* swallow

Schwall [ʃval] **(-(e)s, -e)** *m* surge; (*Worte*) flood, torrent

Schwamm [ʃvam] **(-(e)s, ⸚e)** *m* sponge; (*Pilz*) fungus

schwamm *etc vb siehe* **schwimmen**

schwammig *adj* spongy; (*Gesicht*) puffy

Schwan [ʃva:n] **(-(e)s, ⸚e)** *m* swan

schwanger ['ʃvaŋər] *adj* pregnant; **S~schaft** *f* pregnancy

schwanken *vi* to sway; (*taumeln*) to stagger, to reel; (*Preise, Zahlen*) to fluctuate; (*zögern*) to hesitate, to vacillate

Schwankung *f* fluctuation

Schwanz [ʃvants] **(-es, ⸚e)** *m* tail

schwänzen ['ʃvɛntsən] (*umg*) *vt* to skip, to cut ♦ *vi* to play truant

Schwarm [ʃvarm] **(-(e)s, ⸚e)** *m* swarm; (*umg*) heart-throb, idol

schwärm- ['ʃvɛrm] [**~en** *vi* to swarm; **~en für** to be mad *od* wild about; **S~erei** [-ə'raɪ] *f* enthusiasm; **~erisch** *adj* impassioned, effusive

Schwarte ['ʃvartə] *f* hard skin; (*Speckschwarte*) rind

schwarz [ʃvarts] *adj* black; **~es Brett** notice board; **ins S~e treffen** (*auch fig*) to hit the bull's eye; **in den ~en Zahlen** in the black; **~ sehen** (*umg*) to see the gloomy side of things; **S~arbeit** *f* illicit work, moonlighting; **S~brot** *nt* black bread; **S~e(r)** *f(m)* black (man/woman)

Schwärze ['ʃvɛrtsə] *f* blackness; (*Farbe*) blacking; (*Druckerschwärze*) printer's ink; **s~n** *vt* to blacken

Schwarz- *zW:* **s~fahren** (*unreg*) *vi* to travel without paying; to drive without a licence; **~handel** *m* black market (trade); **~markt** *m* black market; **~wald** *m* Black Forest; **s~weiß, s~-weiß** *adj* black and white

schwatzen ['ʃvatsən] *vi* to chatter

schwätzen ['ʃvɛtsən] *vi* to chatter

Schwätzer ['ʃvɛtsər] **(-s, -)** *m* gasbag

schwatzhaft *adj* talkative, gossipy

Schwebe ['ʃve:bə] *f:* **in der ~** (*fig*) in abeyance; **~bahn** *f* overhead railway; **s~n** *vi* to drift, to float; (*hoch*) to soar

Schwed- ['ʃve:d] *zW:* **~e** *m* Swede; **~en** *nt* Sweden; **~in** *f* Swede; **s~isch** *adj* Swedish

Schwefel ['ʃve:fəl] **(-s)** *m* sulphur; **s~ig** *adj* sulphurous; **~säure** *f* sulphuric acid

Schweig- ['ʃvaɪg] *zW:* **~egeld** *nt* hush money; **~en (-s)** *nt* silence; **s~en** (*unreg*) *vi* to be silent; to stop talking; **~epflicht** *f* pledge of secrecy; (*von Anwalt*) requirement of confidentiality; **s~sam** ['ʃvaɪkza:m] *adj* silent, taciturn; **~samkeit** *f* taciturnity, quietness

Schwein [ʃvaɪn] **(-(e)s, -e)** *nt* pig; (*umg*) (good) luck

Schweine- *zW:* **~fleisch** *nt* pork; **~'rei** *f* mess; (*Gemeinheit*) dirty trick; **~stall** *m* pigsty

schweinisch *adj* filthy

Schweinsleder *nt* pigskin

Schweiß [ʃvaɪs] **(-es)** *m* sweat, perspiration; **s~en** *vt, vi* to weld; **~er (-s, -)** *m* welder; **~füße** *pl* sweaty feet; **~naht** *f* weld

Schweiz [ʃvaɪts] *f* Switzerland; **~er(in)** *m(f)* Swiss; **s~erisch** *adj* Swiss

schwelgen ['ʃvɛlgən] *vi* to indulge

Schwelle ['ʃvɛlə] *f* (*auch fig*) threshold; doorstep; (*EISENB*) sleeper (*BRIT*), tie (*US*)

schwellen (*unreg*) *vi* to swell

Schwellung *f* swelling

Schwemme ['ʃvɛmə] *f* (*WIRTS:* Überangebot) surplus

Schwenk- ['ʃvɛŋk] *zW:* **s~bar** *adj* swivel-mounted; **s~en** *vt* to swing; (*Fahne*) to wave; (*abspülen*) to rinse ♦ *vi* to turn, to swivel; (*MIL*) to wheel; **~ung** *f* turn; wheel

schwer [ʃve:r] *adj* heavy; (*schwierig*) difficult, hard; (*schlimm*) serious, bad ♦ *adv* (*sehr*) very (much); (*verletzt etc*) seriously, badly; **~ erziehbar** difficult (to bring up); **jdm ~ fallen** to be difficult for sb; **jdm/sich etw ~ machen** to make sth difficult for sb/o.s.; **~ nehmen** to take to heart; **sich** *dat od akk* **~ tun** to have difficulties; **~ verdaulich** indigestible, heavy; **~ wiegend** weighty, important; **S~arbeiter** *m* manual worker, labourer; **S~behinderte(r)** *f(m)* seriously handicapped person; **S~e** *f* weight, heaviness; (*PHYS*) gravity; **~elos** *adj* weightless; (*Kammer*) zero-G; **~fällig** *adj* ponderous; **S~gewicht** *nt* heavyweight; (*fig*) emphasis; **~hörig** *adj* hard of hearing; **S~industrie** *f* heavy industry; **S~kraft** *f* gravity; **S~kranke(r)** *f(m)* person who is seriously ill; **~lich** *adv* hardly; **~mütig** *adj* melancholy; **S~punkt** *m* centre of gravity; (*fig*) emphasis, crucial point

Schwert [ʃveːrt] **(-(e)s, -er)** *nt* sword; **~lilie** *f* iris

schwer- *zW*: **S~verbrecher(in)** *m(f)* criminal, serious offender; **S~verletzte(r)** *f(m)* serious casualty; (*bei Unfall usw auch*) seriously injured person

Schwester [ˈʃvɛstər] **(-, -n)** *f* sister; (*MED*) nurse; **s~lich** *adj* sisterly

Schwieger- [ˈʃviːgər] *zW*: **~eltern** *pl* parents-in-law; **~mutter** *f* mother-in-law; **~sohn** *m* son-in-law; **~tochter** *f* daughter-in-law; **~vater** *m* father-in-law

schwierig [ˈʃviːrɪç] *adj* difficult, hard; **S~keit** *f* difficulty

Schwimm- [ˈʃvɪm] *zW*: **~bad** *nt* swimming baths *pl*; **~becken** *nt* swimming pool; **s~en** (*unreg*) *vi* to swim; (*treiben, nicht sinken*) to float; (*fig: unsicher sein*) to be all at sea; **~er (-s, -)** *m* swimmer; (*Angeln*) float; **~erin** *f* (female) swimmer; **~lehrer** *m* swimming instructor; **~weste** *f* life jacket

Schwindel [ˈʃvɪndəl] **(-s)** *m* giddiness; dizzy spell; (*Betrug*) swindle, fraud; (*Zeug*) stuff; **s~frei** *adj*: **s~frei sein** to have a good head for heights; **s~n** (*umg*) *vi* (*lügen*) to fib; **jdm s~t es** sb feels dizzy

schwinden [ˈʃvɪndən] (*unreg*) *vi* to disappear; (*sich verringern*) to decrease; (*Kräfte*) to decline

Schwindler [ˈʃvɪndlər] *m* swindler; (*Lügner*) liar

schwindlig *adj* dizzy; **mir ist ~** I feel dizzy

Schwing- [ˈʃvɪŋ] *zW*: **s~en** (*unreg*) *vt* to swing; (*Waffe etc*) to brandish ♦ *vi* to swing; (*vibrieren*) to vibrate; (*klingen*) to sound; **~tür** *f* swing door(s); **~ung** *f* vibration;

(*PHYS*) oscillation

Schwips [ʃvɪps] **(-es, -e)** *m*: **einen ~ haben** to be tipsy

schwirren [ˈʃvɪrən] *vi* to buzz

schwitzen [ˈʃvɪtsən] *vi* to sweat, to perspire

schwören [ˈʃvøːrən] (*unreg*) *vt, vi* to swear

schwul [ʃvuːl] (*umg*) *adj* gay, queer

schwül [ʃvyːl] *adj* sultry, close; **S~e (-)** *f* sultriness

Schwule(r) (*umg*) *f(m)* gay (man/woman)

Schwung [ʃvʊŋ] **(-(e)s, ⁻e)** *m* swing; (*Triebkraft*) momentum; (*fig: Energie*) verve, energy; (*umg: Menge*) batch; **s~haft** *adj* brisk, lively; **s~voll** *adj* vigorous

Schwur [ʃvuːr] **(-(e)s, ⁻e)** *m* oath; **~gericht** *nt* court with a jury

sechs [zɛks] *num* six; **~hundert** *num* six hundred; **~te(r, s)** *adj* sixth; **S~tel (-s, -)** *nt* sixth

sechzehn [ˈzɛçtseːn] *num* sixteen

sechzig [ˈzɛçtsɪç] *num* sixty

See¹ [zeː] **(-, -n)** *f* sea

See² [zeː] **(-s, -n)** *m* lake

See- [zeː] *zW*: **~bad** *nt* seaside resort; **~hund** *m* seal; **~igel** [ˈzeːʔiːgəl] *m* sea urchin; **s~krank** *adj* seasick; **~krankheit** *f* seasickness; **~lachs** *m* rock salmon

Seele [ˈzeːlə] *f* soul; **s~nruhig** *adv* calmly

Seeleute [ˈzeːlɔytə] *pl* seamen

Seel- *zW*: **s~isch** *adj* mental; **~sorge** *f* pastoral duties *pl*; **~sorger (-s, -)** *m* clergyman

See- *zW*: **~macht** *f* naval power; **~mann** (*pl* **-leute**) *m* seaman, sailor; **~meile** *f* nautical mile; **~möwe** *f* (*ZOOL*) seagull; **~not** *f* distress; **~räuber** *m* pirate; **~rose** *f* water lily; **~stern** *m* starfish; **s~tüchtig** *adj* seaworthy; **~weg** *m* sea route; **auf dem ~weg** by sea; **~zunge** *f* sole

Segel [ˈzeːgəl] **(-s, -)** *nt* sail; **~boot** *nt* yacht; **~fliegen (-s)** *nt* gliding; **~flieger** *m* glider pilot; **~flugzeug** *nt* glider; **s~n** *vt, vi* to sail; **~schiff** *nt* sailing vessel; **~sport** *m* sailing; **~tuch** *nt* canvas

Segen [ˈzeːgən] **(-s, -)** *m* blessing

Segler [ˈzeːglər] **(-s, -)** *m* sailor, yachtsman

segnen [ˈzeːgnən] *vt* to bless

Rechtschreibreform: ▲ *neue Schreibung* △ *alte Schreibung (auslaufend)*

Seh- ['zeː] zW: **s~behindert** adj partially sighted; **s~en** (unreg) vt, vi to see; (in bestimmte Richtung) to look; **mal s~en(, ob ...)** let's see (if ...); **siehe Seite 5** see page 5; **s~enswert** adj worth seeing; **~enswürdigkeiten** pl sights (of a town); **~fehler** m sight defect

Sehne ['zeːnə] f sinew; (an Bogen) string

sehnen vr: **sich ~ nach** to long od yearn for

sehnig adj sinewy

Sehn- zW: **s~lich** adj ardent; **~sucht** f longing; **s~süchtig** adj longing

sehr [zeːr] adv very; (mit Verben) a lot, (very) much; **zu ~** too much; **~ geehrte(r) ...** dear ...

seicht [zaɪçt] adj (auch fig) shallow

Seide ['zaɪdə] f silk; **s~n** adj silk; **~npapier** nt tissue paper

seidig ['zaɪdɪç] adj silky

Seife ['zaɪfə] f soap

Seifen- zW: **~lauge** f soapsuds pl; **~schale** f soap dish; **~schaum** m lather

seihen ['zaɪən] vt to strain, to filter

Seil [zaɪl] **(-(e)s, -e)** nt rope; cable; **~bahn** f cable railway; **~hüpfen (-s)** nt skipping; **~springen (-s)** nt skipping; **~tänzer(in)** m(f) tightrope walker

SCHLÜSSELWORT

sein [zaɪn] (pt **war**, pp **gewesen**) vi **1** to be; **ich bin** I am; **du bist** you are; **er/sie/es ist** he/she/it is; **wir sind/ihr seid/sie sind** we/you/they are; **wir waren** we were; **wir sind gewesen** we have been

2: seien Sie nicht böse don't be angry; **sei so gut und ...** be so kind as to ...; **das wäre gut** that would od that'd be a good thing; **wenn ich Sie wäre** if I were od was you; **das wärs** that's all, that's it; **morgen bin ich in Rom** tomorrow I'll od I will od I shall be in Rome; **waren Sie mal in Rom?** have you ever been to Rome?

3: wie ist das zu verstehen? how is that to be understood?; **er ist nicht zu ersetzen** he cannot be replaced; **mit ihr ist nicht zu reden** you can't talk to her

4: mir ist kalt I'm cold; **was ist?** what's the matter, what is it?; **ist was?** is something the matter?; **es sei denn, dass ...** unless ...; **wie dem auch sei** be that as it may; **wie wäre es mit ...?** how od what about ...?; **lass das sein!** stop that!

sein(e) ['zaɪn(ə)] adj his; its; **~e(r, s)** pron his; its; **~er** (gen von **er**) pron of him; **~erseits** adv for his part; **~erzeit** adv in those days, formerly; **~esgleichen** pron people like him; **~etwegen** adv (für ihn) for his sake; (wegen ihm) on his account; (von ihm aus) as far as he is concerned; **~etwillen** adv: **um ~etwillen** = **seinetwegen**; **~ige** pron: **der/die/das ~ige** od **S~ige** his

seit [zaɪt] präp +dat since ♦ konj since; **er ist ~ einer Woche hier** he has been here for a week; **~ langem** for a long time; **~dem** [zaɪt'deːm] adv, konj since

Seite ['zaɪtə] f side; (Buchseite) page; (MIL) flank

Seiten- zW: **~ansicht** f side view; **~hieb** m (fig) passing shot, dig; **s~s** präp +gen on the part of; **~schiff** nt aisle; **~sprung** m extramarital escapade; **~stechen** nt (a) stitch; **~straße** f side road; **~streifen** m verge; (der Autobahn) hard shoulder

seither [zaɪt'heːr] adv, konj since (then)

seit- zW: **~lich** adj on one od the side; side cpd; **~wärts** adv sidewards

Sekretär [zekre'tɛːr] m secretary; (Möbel) bureau

Sekretariat [zekretari'aːt] **(-(e)s, -e)** nt secretary's office, secretariat

Sekretärin f secretary

Sekt [zɛkt] **(-(e)s, -e)** m champagne

Sekte ['zɛktə] f sect

Sekunde [ze'kʊndə] f second

selber ['zɛlbər] = **selbst**

Selbst [zɛlpst] **(-)** nt self

SCHLÜSSELWORT

selbst [zɛlpst] pron **1: ich/er/wir selbst** I myself/he himself/we ourselves; **sie ist die Tugend selbst** she's virtue itself; **er braut**

Spelling Reform: ▲ *new spelling* △ *old spelling (to be phased out)*

sein Bier selbst he brews his own beer; **wie gehts? - gut, und selbst?** how are things? - fine, and yourself? **2** (*ohne Hilfe*) alone, on my/his/one's *etc* own; **von selbst** by itself; **er kam von selbst** he came of his own accord; **selbst gemacht** home-made

♦ *adv* even; **selbst wenn** even if; **selbst Gott** even God (himself)

---

selbständig *etc* ['zɛlpʃtɛndɪç] = **selbstständig** *etc*

Selbst- *zW*: **~auslöser** *m* (*PHOT*) delayed-action shutter release; **~bedienung** *f* self-service; **~befriedigung** *f* masturbation; **~beherrschung** *f* self-control; **~bestimmung** *f* (*POL*) self-determination; **~beteiligung** *f* (*VERSICHERUNG: bei Kosten*) (voluntary) excess; **s~bewusst** ▲ *adj* (self-)confident; **~bewusstsein** ▲ *nt* self-confidence; **~erhaltung** *f* self-preservation; **~erkenntnis** *f* self-knowledge; **s~gefällig** *adj* smug, self-satisfied; **~gespräch** *nt* conversation with o.s.; **~kostenpreis** *m* cost price; **s~los** *adj* unselfish, selfless; **~mord** *m* suicide; **~mörder(in)** *m(f)* suicide; **s~mörderisch** *adj* suicidal; **s~sicher** *adj* self-assured; **s~ständig** ▲ *adj* independent; **~ständigkeit** ▲ *f* independence; **s~süchtig** *adj* (*Mensch*) selfish; **~versorger** (**-s, -**) *m* (*im Urlaub etc*) self-caterer; **s~verständlich** ['zɛlpstfɛrʃtɛntlɪç] *adj* obvious ♦ *adv* naturally; **ich halte das für s~verständlich** I take that for granted; **~verteidigung** *f* self-defence; **~vertrauen** *nt* self-confidence; **~verwaltung** *f* autonomy, self-government

selig ['ze:lɪç] *adj* happy, blissful; (*REL*) blessed; (*tot*) late; **S~keit** *f* bliss

Sellerie ['zɛləri:] (**-s, -(s)** *od* **-, -**) *m od f* celery

selten ['zɛltən] *adj* rare ♦ *adv* seldom, rarely; **S~heit** *f* rarity

Selterswasser ['zɛltərsvasər] *nt* soda water

seltsam ['zɛltza:m] *adj* strange, curious; **S~keit** *f* strangeness

Semester [ze'mɛstər] (**-s, -**) *nt* semester; **~ferien** *pl* vacation *sg*

Semi- [zemi] *in zW* semi-; **~kolon** [-'ko:lɔn] (**-s, -s**) *nt* semicolon

Seminar [zemi'na:r] (**-s, -e**) *nt* seminary; (*Kurs*) seminar; (*UNIV: Ort*) department building

Semmel ['zɛməl] (**-, -n**) *f* roll

Senat [ze'na:t] (**-(e)s, -e**) *m* senate, council

Sende- ['zɛndə] *zW*: **~bereich** *m* transmission range; **~folge** *f* (*Serie*) series; **s~n** (*unreg*) *vt* to send; (*RADIO, TV*) to transmit, to broadcast ♦ *vi* to transmit, to broadcast; **~r** (**-s, -**) *m* station; (*Anlage*) transmitter; **~reihe** *f* series (of broadcasts)

Sendung ['zɛnduŋ] *f* consignment; (*Aufgabe*) mission; (*RADIO, TV*) transmission; (*Programm*) programme

Senf [zɛnf] (**-(e)s, -e**) *m* mustard

senil [ze'ni:l] (*pej*) *adj* senile

Senior(in) ['ze:niɔr(ɪn)] (**-s, -en**) *m(f)* (*Mensch im Rentenalter*) (old age) pensioner

Seniorenheim [zeni'o:rənhaɪm] *nt* old people's home

Senk- ['zɛŋk] *zW*: **~blei** *nt* plumb; **~e** *f* depression; **s~en** *vt* to lower ♦ *vr* to sink, to drop gradually; **s~recht** *adj* vertical, perpendicular; **~rechte** *f* perpendicular; **~rechtstarter** *m* (*AVIAT*) vertical take-off plane; (*fig*) high-flyer

Sensation [zɛnzatsi'o:n] *f* sensation; **s~ell** [-'nɛl] *adj* sensational

sensibel [zɛn'zi:bəl] *adj* sensitive

sentimental [zɛntimɛn'ta:l] *adj* sentimental; **S~i'tät** *f* sentimentality

separat [zepa'ra:t] *adj* separate

September [zɛp'tɛmbər] (**-(s), -**) *m* September

Serie ['ze:riə] *f* series

serien- *zW*: **~mäßig** *adj* standard; **S~mörder(in)** *m(f)* serial killer; **~weise** *adv* in series

seriös [zeri'ø:s] *adj* serious, bona fide

Service¹ [zɛr'vi:s] (**-(s), -**) *nt* (*Geschirr*) set, service

Service² (**-, -s**) *m* service

servieren [zɛr'vi:rən] *vt, vi* to serve

Rechtschreibreform: ▲ *neue Schreibung* △ *alte Schreibung (auslaufend)*

Serviererin [zɛr'viːrərɪn] f waitress

Serviette [zɛrvi'etə] f napkin, serviette

Servo- ['zɛrvo] zW: **~bremse** f (AUT) servo(-assisted) brake; **~lenkung** f (AUT) power steering

Sessel ['zɛsəl] **(-s, -)** m armchair; **~lift** m chairlift

sesshaft ▲ ['zɛshaft] adj settled; (ansässig) resident

setzen ['zɛtsən] vt to put, to set; (Baum etc) to plant; (Segel, TYP) to set ♦ vr to settle; (Person) to sit down ♦ vi (springen) to leap; (wetten) to bet

Setz- ['zɛts] zW: **~er (-s, -)** m (TYP) compositor; **~ling** m young plant

Seuche ['zɔʏçə] f epidemic; **~ngebiet** nt infected area

seufzen ['zɔʏftsən] vt, vi to sigh

Seufzer ['zɔʏftsər] **(-s, -)** m sigh

Sex [zɛks] **(-(es))** m sex; **~ualität** [zɛksualiˈtɛt] f sex, sexuality; **~ualkunde** [zɛksuˈaːl-] f (SCH) sex education; **s~uell** [-uˈɛl] adj sexual

Shampoo [ʃamˈpuː] **(-s, -s)** nt shampoo

Sibirien [ziˈbiːriən] nt Siberia

SCHLÜSSELWORT

sich [zɪç] pron **1** (akk): **er/sie/es ... sich** he/she/it ... himself/herself/itself; **sie** pl/ **man ... sich** they/one ... themselves/ oneself; **Sie ... sich** you ... yourself/ yourselves pl; **sich wiederholen** to repeat oneself/itself

2 (dat): **er/sie/es ... sich** he/she/it ... to himself/herself/itself; **sie** pl/**man ... sich** they/one ... to themselves/oneself; **Sie ... sich** you ... to yourself/yourselves pl; **sie hat sich einen Pullover gekauft** she bought herself a jumper; **sich die Haare waschen** to wash one's hair

3 (mit Präposition): **haben Sie Ihren Ausweis bei sich?** do you have your pass on you?; **er hat nichts bei sich** he's got nothing on him; **sie bleiben gern unter sich** they keep themselves to themselves

4 (einander) each other, one another; **sie bekämpfen sich** they fight each other od one another

5: dieses Auto fährt sich gut this car drives well; **hier sitzt es sich gut** it's good to sit here

---

Sichel ['zɪçəl] **(-, -n)** f sickle; (Mondsichel) crescent

sicher ['zɪçər] adj safe; (gewiss) certain; (zuverlässig) secure, reliable; (selbstsicher) confident; **vor jdm/etw ~ sein** to be safe from sb/sth; **ich bin nicht ~** I'm not sure od certain; **~ nicht** surely not; **aber ~!** of course!; **~gehen** (unreg) vi to make sure

Sicherheit ['zɪçərhaɪt] f safety; (auch FIN) security; (Gewissheit) certainty; (Selbstsicherheit) confidence

Sicherheits- zW: **~abstand** m safe distance; **~glas** nt safety glass; **~gurt** m safety belt; **s~halber** adv for safety; to be on the safe side; **~nadel** f safety pin; **~schloss** ▲ nt safety lock; **~vorkehrung** f safety precaution

sicher- zW: **~lich** adv certainly, surely; **~n** vt to secure; (schützen) to protect; (Waffe) to put the safety catch on; **jdm etw ~n** to secure sth for sb; **sich** dat **etw ~n** to secure sth (for o.s.); **~stellen** vt to impound; (COMPUT) to save; **S~ung** f (S~n) securing; (Vorrichtung) safety device; (an Waffen) safety catch; (ELEK) fuse; **S~ungskopie** f back-up copy

Sicht [zɪçt] **(-)** f sight; (Aussicht) view; **auf** od **nach ~** (FIN) at sight; **auf lange ~** on a long-term basis; **s~bar** adj visible; **s~en** vt to sight; (auswählen) to sort out; **s~lich** adj evident, obvious; **~verhältnisse** pl visibility sg; **~vermerk** m visa; **~weite** f visibility

sickern ['zɪkərn] vi to trickle, to seep

Sie [ziː] **(nom, akk)** pron you

sie [ziː] pron (sg: nom) she, it; (: akk) her, it; (pl: nom) they; (: akk) them

Sieb [ziːp] **(-(e)s, -e)** nt sieve; (KOCH) strainer; **s~en¹** ['ziːbən] vt to sift; (Flüssigkeit) to strain

sieben² num seven; **~hundert** num seven hundred; **S~sachen** pl belongings

siebte(r, s) ['zi:ptə(r, s)] *adj* seventh; **S~l** **(-s, -)** *nt* seventh

siebzehn ['zi:ptse:n] *num* seventeen

siebzig ['zi:ptsɪç] *num* seventy

siedeln ['zi:dəln] *vi* to settle

sieden ['zi:dən] *vt, vi* to boil, to simmer

Siedepunkt *m* boiling point

Siedler (-s, -) *m* settler

Siedlung *f* settlement; (*Häusersiedlung*) housing estate

Sieg [zi:k] **(-(e)s, -e)** *m* victory

Siegel ['zi:gəl] **(-s, -)** *nt* seal; **~ring** *m* signet ring

Sieg- *zW:* **s~en** *vi* to be victorious; (*SPORT*) to win; **~er (-s, -)** *m* victor; (*SPORT etc*) winner; **s~reich** *adj* victorious

siehe *etc* ['zi:ə] *vb siehe* **sehen**

siezen ['zi:tsən] *vt* to address as "Sie"

Signal [zɪ'gna:l] **(-s, -e)** *nt* signal

Silbe ['zɪlbə] *f* syllable

Silber ['zɪlbər] **(-s)** *nt* silver; **~hochzeit** *f* silver wedding (anniversary); **s~n** *adj* silver; **~papier** *nt* silver paper

Silhouette [zilu'ɛtə] *f* silhouette

Silvester [zɪl'vɛstər] **(-s, -)** *nt* New Year's Eve, Hogmanay (*SCOTTISH*); **~abend** *m* = **Silvester**

Silvester

ⓘ **Silvester** *is the German word for New Year's Eve. Although not an official holiday most businesses close early and shops shut at midday. Most Germans celebrate in the evening, and at midnight they let off fireworks and rockets; the revelry usually lasts until the early hours of the morning.*

---

simpel ['zɪmpəl] *adj* simple

Sims [zɪms] **(-es, -e)** *nt od m* (*Kaminsims*) mantelpiece; (*Fenstersims*) (window)sill

simulieren [zimu'li:rən] *vt* to simulate; (*vortäuschen*) to feign ♦ *vi* to feign illness

simultan [zimʊl'ta:n] *adj* simultaneous

Sinfonie [zɪnfo'ni:] *f* symphony

singen ['zɪŋən] (*unreg*) *vt, vi* to sing

Singular ['zɪŋgula:r] *m* singular

Singvogel ['zɪŋfo:gəl] *m* songbird

sinken ['zɪŋkən] (*unreg*) *vi* to sink; (*Preise etc*) to fall, to go down

Sinn [zɪn] **(-(e)s, -e)** *m* mind; (*Wahrnehmungssinn*) sense; (*Bedeutung*) sense, meaning; **~ für etw** sense of sth; **von ~en sein** to be out of one's mind; **es hat keinen ~** there's no point; **~bild** *nt* symbol; **s~en** (*unreg*) *vi* to ponder; **auf etw** *akk* **s~en** to contemplate sth; **~estäuschung** *f* illusion; **s~gemäß** *adj* faithful; (*Wiedergabe*) in one's own words; **s~ig** *adj* clever; **s~lich** *adj* sensual, sensuous; (*Wahrnehmung*) sensory; **~lichkeit** *f* sensuality; **s~los** *adj* senseless; meaningless; **~losigkeit** *f* senselessness; meaninglessness; **s~voll** *adj* meaningful; (*vernünftig*) sensible

Sintflut ['zɪntflu:t] *f* Flood

Sippe ['zɪpə] *f* clan, kin

Sippschaft ['zɪpʃaft] (*pej*) *f* relations *pl*, tribe; (*Bande*) gang

Sirene [zi're:nə] *f* siren

Sirup ['zi:rʊp] **(-s, -e)** *m* syrup

Sitt- [zɪt] *zW:* **~e** *f* custom; **~en** *pl* (*~lichkeit*) morals; **~enpolizei** *f* vice squad; **s~sam** *adj* modest, demure

Situation [zituatsi'o:n] *f* situation

Sitz [zɪts] **(-es, -e)** *m* seat; **der Anzug hat einen guten ~** the suit is a good fit; **s~en** (*unreg*) *vi* to sit; (*Bemerkung, Schlag*) to strike home, to tell; (*Gelerntes*) to have sunk in; **s~en bleiben** to remain seated; (*SCH*) to have to repeat a year; **auf etw** *dat* **s~en bleiben** to be lumbered with sth; **s~en lassen** (*SCH*) to make (sb) repeat a year; (*Mädchen*) to jilt; (*Wartenden*) to stand up; **etw auf sich** *dat* **s~en lassen** to take sth lying down; **s~end** *adj* (*Tätigkeit*) sedentary; **~gelegenheit** *f* place to sit down; **~platz** *m* seat; **~streik** *m* sit-down strike; **~ung** *f* meeting

Sizilien [zi'tsi:liən] *nt* Sicily

Skala ['ska:la] **(-, Skalen)** *f* scale

Skalpell [skal'pɛl] **(-s, -e)** *nt* scalpel

Skandal [skan'da:l] **(-s, -e)** *m* scandal; **s~ös** [-'lø:s] *adj* scandalous

Skandinav- [skandi'na:v] *zW:* **~ien** *nt*
Scandinavia; **~ier(in)** *m(f)* Scandinavian;
s~isch *adj* Scandinavian

Skelett [ske'lɛt] **(-(e)s, -e)** *nt* skeleton

Skepsis ['skɛpsɪs] **(-)** *f* scepticism

skeptisch ['skɛptɪʃ] *adj* sceptical

Ski [ʃi:] **(-s, -er)** *m* ski; **~ laufen** *od* **fahren** to
ski; **~fahrer** *m* skier; **~gebiet** *nt* ski(ing)
area; **~läufer** *m* skier; **~lehrer** *m* ski
instructor; **~lift** *m* ski-lift; **~springen** *nt*
ski-jumping; **~stock** *m* ski-pole

Skizze ['skɪtsə] *f* sketch

skizzieren [skɪ'tsi:rən] *vt, vi* to sketch

Sklave ['skla:və] **(-n, -n)** *m* slave; **~'rei** *f*
slavery; **Sklavin** *f* slave

Skonto ['skɔnto] **(-s, -s)** *m od nt* discount

Skorpion [skɔrpi'o:n] **(-s, -e)** *m* scorpion;
(*ASTROL*) Scorpio

Skrupel ['skru:pəl] **(-s, -)** *m* scruple; **s~los**
adj unscrupulous

Skulptur [skʊlp'tu:r] *f* (*Gegenstand*) sculpture

S-Kurve ['ɛskʊrvə] *f* S-bend

Slip [slɪp] **(-s, -s)** *m* (under)pants; **~einlage**
f panty liner

Slowakei [slova'kaɪ] *f*: **die ~** Slovakia

Slowenien [slo've:niən] *nt* Slovenia

Smaragd [sma'rakt] **(-(e)s, -e)** *m* emerald

Smoking ['smo:kɪŋ] **(-s, -s)** *m* dinner jacket

SCHLÜSSELWORT
---

so [zo:] *adv* **1** (*so sehr*) so; **so groß/schön**
etc so big/nice *etc*; **so groß/schön wie ...**
as big/nice as ...; **so viel (wie)** as much as;
rede nicht so viel don't talk so much; **so
weit sein** to be ready; **so weit wie** *od* **als
möglich** as far as possible; **ich bin so weit
zufrieden** by and large I'm quite satisfied;
so wenig (wie) as little (as); **das hat ihn
so geärgert, dass ...** that annoyed him so
much that ...; **so einer wie ich** somebody
like me; **na so was!** well, well!
2 (*auf diese Weise*) like this; **mach es nicht
so** don't do it like that; **so oder so** in one
way or the other; **und so weiter** and so
on; **... oder so was** ... or something like
that; **das ist gut so** that's fine; **so genannt**
so-called

3 (*umg: umsonst*): **ich habe es so
bekommen** I got it for nothing
♦ *konj:* **so dass, sodass** so that; **so wie es
jetzt ist** as things are at the moment
♦ *excl:* **so?** really?; **so, das wärs** so, that's
it then

---

s. o. *abk* = **siehe oben**

Söckchen ['zœkçən] *nt* ankle socks

Socke ['zɔkə] *f* sock

Sockel ['zɔkəl] **(-s, -)** *m* pedestal, base

sodass ▲ [zo'das] *konj* so that

Sodawasser ['zo:davasər] *nt* soda water

Sodbrennen ['zo:tbrɛnən] **(-s, -)** *nt*
heartburn

soeben [zo'e:bən] *adv* just (now)

Sofa ['zo:fa] **(-s, -s)** *nt* sofa

sofern [zo'fɛrn] *konj* if, provided (that)

sofort [zo'fɔrt] *adv* immediately, at once;
~ig *adj* immediate

Sog [zo:k] **(-(e)s, -e)** *m* (*Strömung*) undertow

sogar [zo'ga:r] *adv* even

sogleich [zo'glaɪç] *adv* straight away, at
once

Sohle ['zo:lə] *f* sole; (*Talsohle etc*) bottom;
(*MIN*) level

Sohn [zo:n] **(-(e)s, ⁻e)** *m* son

Solar- [zo'la:r] *in zW* solar; **~zelle** *f* solar
cell

solch [zɔlç] *pron* such; **ein ~e(r, s) ...** such
a ...

Soldat [zɔl'da:t] **(-en, -en)** *m* soldier

Söldner ['zœldnər] **(-s, -)** *m* mercenary

solidarisch [zoli'da:rɪʃ] *adj* in *od* with
solidarity; **sich ~ erklären** to declare one's
solidarity

Solidari'tät *f* solidarity

solid(e) [zo'li:d(ə)] *adj* solid; (*Leben, Person*)
respectable

Solist(in) [zo'lɪst(ɪn)] *m(f)* soloist

Soll [zɔl] **(-(s), -(s))** *nt* (*FIN*) debit (side);
(*Arbeitsmenge*) quota, target

SCHLÜSSELWORT
---

sollen ['zɔlən] (*pt* **sollte,** *pp* **gesollt** *od (als
Hilfsverb)* **sollen**) *Hilfsverb* **1** (*Pflicht, Befehl*)
to be supposed to; **du hättest nicht gehen**

sollen you shouldn't have gone, you oughtn't to have gone; **soll ich?** shall I?; **soll ich dir helfen?** shall I help you?; **sag ihm, er soll warten** tell him he's to wait; **was soll ich machen?** what should I do? 2 (*Vermutung*): **sie soll verheiratet sein** she's said to be married; **was soll das heißen?** what's that supposed to mean?; **man sollte glauben, dass ...** you would think that ...; **sollte das passieren, ...** if that should happen ...
♦ *vt, vi*: **was soll das?** what's all this?; **das sollst du nicht** you shouldn't do that; **was solls?** what the hell!

Solo ['zo:lo] **(-s, -s** *od* **Soli)** *nt* solo
somit [zo'mɪt] *konj* and so, therefore
Sommer ['zɔmər] **(-s, -)** *m* summer; **s~lich** *adj* summery; summer; **~reifen** *m* normal tyre; **~schlussverkauf** ▲ *m* summer sale; **~sprossen** *pl* freckles
Sonde ['zɔndə] *f* probe
Sonder- ['zɔndər] *in zW* special; **~angebot** *nt* special offer; **s~bar** *adj* strange, odd; **~fahrt** *f* special trip; **~fall** *m* special case; **s~lich** *adj* particular; (*außergewöhnlich*) remarkable; (*eigenartig*) peculiar; **~marke** *f* special issue stamp; **s~n** *konj* but ♦ *vt* to separate; **nicht nur ..., s~n auch** not only ..., but also; **~preis** *m* special reduced price; **~zug** *m* special train
Sonnabend ['zɔn|a:bənt] *m* Saturday
Sonne ['zɔnə] *f* sun; **s~n** *vr* to sun o.s.
Sonnen- *zW*: **~aufgang** *m* sunrise; **s~baden** *vi* to sunbathe; **~brand** *m* sunburn; **~brille** *f* sunglasses *pl*; **~creme** *f* suntan lotion; **~energie** *f* solar energy, solar power; **~finsternis** *f* solar eclipse; **~kollektor** *m* solar panel; **~schein** *m* sunshine; **~schirm** *m* parasol, sunshade; **~schutzfaktor** *m* protection factor; **~stich** *m* sunstroke; **~uhr** *f* sundial; **~untergang** *m* sunset; **~wende** *f* solstice
sonnig ['zɔnɪç] *adj* sunny
Sonntag ['zɔnta:k] *m* Sunday
sonst [zɔnst] *adv* otherwise; (*mit pron, in Fragen*) else; (*zu anderer Zeit*) at other times,

normally ♦ *konj* otherwise; **~ noch etwas?** anything else?; **~ nichts** nothing else; **~ jemand** anybody (at all); **~ wo** somewhere else; **~ woher** from somewhere else; **~ wohin** somewhere else; **~ig** *adj* other
sooft [zo'ɔft] *konj* whenever
Sopran [zo'pra:n] **(-s, -e)** *m* soprano
Sorge ['zɔrgə] *f* care, worry
sorgen *vi*: **für jdn ~** to look after sb ♦ *vr*: **sich ~ (um)** to worry (about); **für etw ~** to take care of *od* see to sth; **~frei** *adj* carefree; **~voll** *adj* troubled, worried
Sorgerecht *nt* custody (of a child)
Sorg- [zɔrk] *zW*: **~falt (-)** *f* care(fulness); **s~fältig** *adj* careful; **s~los** *adj* careless; (*ohne ~en*) carefree; **s~sam** *adj* careful
Sorte ['zɔrtə] *f* sort; (*Warensorte*) brand; **~n** *pl* (FIN) foreign currency *sg*
sortieren [zɔr'ti:rən] *vt* to sort (out)
Sortiment [zɔrti'mɛnt] *nt* assortment
sosehr [zo'ze:r] *konj* as much as
Soße ['zo:sə] *f* sauce; (*Bratensoße*) gravy
soufflieren [zu'fli:rən] *vt, vi* to prompt
Souterrain [zutɛ'rɛ̃:] **(-s, -s)** *nt* basement
souverän [zuva'rɛ:n] *adj* sovereign; (*überlegen*) superior
so- *zW*: **~viel** [zo'fi:l] *konj*: **~viel ich weiß** as far as I know; *siehe* **so**; **~weit** [zo'vaɪt] *konj* as far as; *siehe* **so**; **~wenig** [zo'veːnɪç] *konj* little as; *siehe* **so**; **~wie** [zo'vi:] *konj* (*~bald*) as soon as; (*ebenso*) as well as; **~wieso** [zovi'zo:] *adv* anyway
sowjetisch [zɔ'vjɛtɪʃ] *adj* Soviet
Sowjetunion *f* Soviet Union
sowohl [zo'vo:l] *konj*: **~ ... als** *od* **wie auch** both ... and
sozial [zotsi'a:l] *adj* social; **S~abgaben** *pl* national insurance contributions; **S~arbeiter(in)** *m(f)* social worker; **S~demokrat** *m* social democrat; **~demokratisch** *adj* social democratic; **S~hilfe** *f* income support (BRIT), welfare (aid) (US); **~isieren** *vt* to socialize; **S~ismus** [-'lɪsmʊs] *m* socialism; **S~ist** [-'lɪst] *m* socialist; **~istisch** *adj* socialist; **S~politik** *f* social welfare policy; **S~produkt** *nt* (net) national product;

S~staat *m* welfare state;
S~versicherung *f* national insurance
(*BRIT*), social security (*US*); **S~wohnung** *f*
council flat
soziologisch [zotsio'lo:gɪʃ] *adj* sociological
sozusagen [zotsu'za:gən] *adv* so to speak
Spachtel ['ʃpaxtəl] **(-s, -)** *m* spatula
spähen ['ʃpɛ:ən] *vi* to peep, to peek
Spalier [ʃpa'li:r] **(-s, -e)** *nt* (*Gerüst*) trellis;
(*Leute*) guard of honour
Spalt [ʃpalt] **(-(e)s, -e)** *m* crack; (*Türspalt*)
chink; (*fig: Kluft*) split; **~e** *f* crack, fissure;
(*Gletscherspalte*) crevasse; (*in Text*) column;
s~en *vt, vr* (*auch fig*) to split; **~ung** *f*
splitting
Span [ʃpa:n] **(-(e)s, ᵉe)** *m* shaving
Spanferkel *nt* sucking pig
Spange ['ʃpaŋə] *f* clasp; (*Haarspange*) hair
slide; (*Schnalle*) buckle
Spanien ['ʃpa:niən] *nt* Spain; **Spanier(in)**
m(f) Spaniard; **spanisch** *adj* Spanish
Spann- ['ʃpan] *zW:* **~beton** *m* prestressed
concrete; **~betttuch** ▲ *nt* fitted sheet; **~e**
f (*Zeitspanne*) space; (*Differenz*) gap; **s~en**
vt (*straffen*) to tighten, to tauten;
(*befestigen*) to brace ♦ *vi* to be tight;
s~end *adj* exciting, gripping; **~ung** *f*
tension; (*ELEK*) voltage; (*fig*) suspense;
(*unangenehm*) tension
Spar- ['ʃpa:r] *zW:* **~buch** *nt* savings book;
~büchse *f* money box; **s~en** *vt, vi* to
save; **sich** *dat* **etw s~en** to save o.s. sth;
(*Bemerkung*) to keep sth to o.s.; **mit etw
s~en** to be sparing with sth; **an etw** *dat*
s~en to economize on sth; **~er (-s, -)** *m*
saver
Spargel ['ʃpargəl] **(-s, -)** *m* asparagus
Sparkasse *f* savings bank
Sparkonto *nt* savings account
spärlich ['ʃpɛ:rlɪç] *adj* meagre; (*Bekleidung*)
scanty
Spar- *zW:* **~preis** *m* economy price;
s~sam *adj* economical, thrifty; **~samkeit**
f thrift, economizing; **~schwein** *nt* piggy
bank
Sparte ['ʃpartə] *f* field; line of business;
(*PRESSE*) column

Spaß [ʃpa:s] **(-es, ᵉe)** *m* joke; (*Freude*) fun;
jdm ~ machen to be fun (for sb); **viel ~!**
have fun!; **s~en** *vi* to joke; **mit ihm ist
nicht zu s~en** you can't take liberties with
him; **s~haft** *adj* funny, droll; **s~ig** *adj*
funny, droll
spät [ʃpɛ:t] *adj, adv* late; **wie ~ ist es?**
what's the time?
Spaten ['ʃpa:tən] **(-s, -)** *m* spade
später *adj, adv* later
spätestens *adv* at the latest
Spätvorstellung *f* late show
Spatz [ʃpats] **(-en, -en)** *m* sparrow
spazier- [ʃpa'tsi:r] *zW:* **~en** *vi* to stroll, to
walk; **~en fahren** to go for a drive; **~en
gehen** to go for a walk; **S~gang** *m* walk;
S~stock *m* walking stick; **S~weg** *m* path,
walk
Specht [ʃpɛçt] **(-(e)s, -e)** *m* woodpecker
Speck [ʃpɛk] **(-(e)s, -e)** *m* bacon
Spediteur [ʃpedi'tø:r] *m* carrier;
(*Möbelspediteur*) furniture remover
Spedition [ʃpeditsi'o:n] *f* carriage; (*~firma*)
road haulage contractor; removal firm
Speer [ʃpe:r] **(-(e)s, -e)** *m* spear; (*SPORT*)
javelin
Speiche ['ʃpaɪçə] *f* spoke
Speichel ['ʃpaɪçəl] **(-s)** *m* saliva, spit(tle)
Speicher ['ʃpaɪçər] **(-s, -)** *m* storehouse;
(*Dachspeicher*) attic, loft; (*Kornspeicher*)
granary; (*Wasserspeicher*) tank; (*TECH*) store;
(*COMPUT*) memory; **s~n** *vt* to store;
(*COMPUT*) to save
speien ['ʃpaɪən] (*unreg*) *vt, vi* to spit;
(*erbrechen*) to vomit; (*Vulkan*) to spew
Speise ['ʃpaɪzə] *f* food; **~eis** [-aɪs] *nt* ice-
cream; **~kammer** *f* larder, pantry; **~karte**
f menu; **s~n** *vt* to feed; to eat ♦ *vi* to dine;
~röhre *f* gullet, oesophagus; **~saal** *m*
dining room; **~wagen** *m* dining car
Speku- [ʃpeku] *zW:* **~lant** *m* speculator;
~lation [-latsi'o:n] *f* speculation; **s~lieren**
[-'li:rən] *vi* (*fig*) to speculate; **auf etw** *akk*
s~lieren to have hopes of sth
Spelunke [ʃpe'luŋkə] *f* dive
Spende ['ʃpɛndə] *f* donation; **s~n** *vt* to
donate, to give; **~r (-s, -)** *m* donor,

donator

spendieren [ʃpɛnˈdiːrən] *vt* to pay for, to buy; **jdm etw ~** to treat sb to sth, to stand sb sth

Sperling [ˈʃpɛrlɪŋ] *m* sparrow

Sperma [ˈʃpɛrma] **(-s, Spermen)** *nt* sperm

Sperr- [ˈʃpɛr] *zW:* **~e** *f* barrier; (*Verbot*) ban; **s~en** *vt* to block; (*SPORT*) to suspend, to bar; (*vom Ball*) to obstruct; (*einschließen*) to lock; (*verbieten*) to ban ♦ *vr* to baulk, to jib(e); **~gebiet** *nt* prohibited area; **~holz** *nt* plywood; **s~ig** *adj* bulky; **~müll** *m* bulky refuse; **~sitz** *m* (*THEAT*) stalls *pl*; **~stunde** *f* closing time

Spesen [ˈʃpeːzən] *pl* expenses

Spezial- [ʃpetsiˈaːl] *in zW* special; **~gebiet** *nt* specialist field; **s~iˈsieren** *vr* to specialize; **~iˈsierung** *f* specialization; **~ist** [-ˈlɪst] *m* specialist; **~iˈtät** *f* speciality

speziell [ʃpetsiˈɛl] *adj* special

spezifisch [ʃpeˈtsiːfɪʃ] *adj* specific

Sphäre [ˈsfɛːrə] *f* sphere

Spiegel [ˈʃpiːgəl] **(-s, -)** *m* mirror; (*Wasserspiegel*) level; (*MIL*) tab; **~bild** *nt* reflection; **s~bildlich** *adj* reversed; **~ei** *nt* fried egg; **s~n** *vt* to mirror, to reflect ♦ *vr* to be reflected ♦ *vi* to gleam; (*widerspiegeln*) to be reflective; **~ung** *f* reflection

Spiel [ʃpiːl] **(-(e)s, -e)** *nt* game; (*Schauspiel*) play; (*Tätigkeit*) play(ing); (*KARTEN*) deck; (*TECH*) (free) play; **s~en** *vt, vi* to play; (*um Geld*) to gamble; (*THEAT*) to perform, to act; **s~end** *adv* easily; **~er (-s, -)** *m* player; (*um Geld*) gambler; **~eˈrei** *f* trifling pastime; **~feld** *nt* pitch, field; **~film** *m* feature film; **~kasino** *nt* casino; **~plan** *m* (*THEAT*) programme; **~platz** *m* playground; **~raum** *m* room to manoeuvre, scope; **~regel** *f* rule; **~sachen** *pl* toys; **~uhr** *f* musical box; **~verderber (-s, -)** *m* spoilsport; **~waren** *pl* toys; **~zeug** *nt* toy(s)

Spieß [ʃpiːs] **(-es, -e)** *m* spear; (*Bratspieß*) spit; **~bürger** *m* bourgeois; **~er (-s, -)** (*umg*) *m* bourgeois; **s~ig** (*pej*) *adj* (petit) bourgeois

Spinat [ʃpiˈnaːt] **(-(e)s, -e)** *m* spinach

Spind [ʃpɪnt] **(-(e)s, -e)** *m od nt* locker

Spinn- [ʃpɪn] *zW:* **~e** *f* spider; **s~en** (*unreg*) *vt, vi* to spin; (*umg*) to talk rubbish; (*verrückt sein*) to be crazy *od* mad; **~eˈrei** *f* spinning mill; **~rad** *nt* spinning wheel; **~webe** *f* cobweb

Spion [ʃpiˈoːn] **(-s, -e)** *m* spy; (*in Tür*) spyhole; **~age** [ʃpio'naːʒə] *f* espionage; **s~ieren** [ʃpio'niːrən] *vi* to spy; **~in** *f* (female) spy

Spirale [ʃpiˈraːlə] *f* spiral

Spirituosen [ʃpirituˈoːzən] *pl* spirits

Spiritus [ˈʃpiːritʊs] **(-, -se)** *m* (methylated) spirit

Spital [ʃpiˈtaːl] **(-s, ⁺er)** *nt* hospital

spitz [ʃpɪts] *adj* pointed; (*Winkel*) acute; (*fig: Zunge*) sharp; (: *Bemerkung*) caustic

Spitze *f* point, tip; (*Bergspitze*) peak; (*Bemerkung*) taunt, dig; (*erster Platz*) lead, top; (*meist pl: Gewebe*) lace

Spitzel (-s, -) *m* police informer

spitzen *vt* to sharpen

Spitzenmarke *f* brand leader

spitzfindig *adj* (over)subtle

Spitzname *m* nickname

Splitter [ˈʃplɪtər] **(-s, -)** *m* splinter

sponsern [ˈʃpɔnzərn] *vt* to sponsor

spontan [ʃpɔnˈtaːn] *adj* spontaneous

Sport [ʃpɔrt] **(-(e)s, -e)** *m* sport; (*fig*) hobby; **~lehrer(in)** *m(f)* games *od* P.E. teacher; **~ler(in) (-s, -)** *m(f)* sportsman(-woman); **s~lich** *adj* sporting; (*Mensch*) sporty; **~platz** *m* playing *od* sports field; **~schuh** *m* (*Turnschuh*) training shoe, trainer; **~stadion** *nt* sports stadium; **~verein** *m* sports club; **~wagen** *m* sports car

Spott [ʃpɔt] **(-(e)s)** *m* mockery, ridicule; **s~billig** *adj* dirt-cheap; **s~en** *vi* to mock; **s~en (über** +*akk*) to mock (at), to ridicule

spöttisch [ˈʃpœtɪʃ] *adj* mocking

sprach *etc* [ʃpraːx] *vb siehe* **sprechen**

Sprach- *zW:* **s~begabt** *adj* good at languages; **~e** *f* language; **~enschule** *f* language school; **~fehler** *m* speech defect; **~führer** *m* phrasebook; **~gefühl** *nt* feeling for language; **~kenntnisse** *pl* linguistic proficiency *sg*; **~kurs** *m* language course; **~labor** *nt* language laboratory; **s~lich** *adj*

linguistic; **s~los** *adj* speechless
sprang *etc* [ʃpraŋ] *vb siehe* **springen**
Spray [spreː] **(-s, -s)** *m od nt* spray
Sprech- ['ʃpreç] *zW:* **~anlage** *f* intercom;
s~en (*unreg*) *vi* to speak, to talk ♦ *vt* to say;
(*Sprache*) to speak; (*Person*) to speak to; **mit
jdm s~en** to speak to sb; **das spricht für
ihn** that's a point in his favour; **~er(in) (-s,
-)** *m(f)* speaker; (*für Gruppe*) spokesman(-
woman); (*RADIO, TV*) announcer; **~stunde** *f*
consultation (hour); (doctor's) surgery;
~stundenhilfe *f* (doctor's) receptionist;
~zimmer *nt* consulting room, surgery,
office (*US*)
spreizen ['ʃpraɪtsən] *vt* (*Beine*) to open, to
spread; (*Finger, Flügel*) to spread
Spreng- ['ʃprɛŋ] *zW:* **s~en** *vt* to sprinkle;
(*mit ~stoff*) to blow up; (*Gestein*) to blast;
(*Versammlung*) to break up; **~stoff** *m*
explosive(s)
sprichst *etc* [ʃprɪçst] *vb siehe* **sprechen**
Sprichwort *nt* proverb; **sprichwörtlich**
adj proverbial
Spring- ['ʃprɪŋ] *zW:* **~brunnen** *m* fountain;
s~en (*unreg*) *vi* to jump; (*Glas*) to crack;
(*mit Kopfsprung*) to dive; **~er (-s, -)** *m*
jumper; (*Schach*) knight
Sprit [ʃprɪt] **(-(e)s, -e)** (*umg*) *m* juice, gas
Spritz- ['ʃprɪts] *zW:* **~e** *f* syringe; injection;
(*an Schlauch*) nozzle; **s~en** *vt* to spray;
(*MED*) to inject ♦ *vi* to splash;
(*herausspritzen*) to spurt; (*MED*) to give
injections; **~pistole** *f* spray gun; **~tour** *f*
(*umg*) spin
spröde ['ʃprøːdə] *adj* brittle; (*Person*)
reserved, coy
Sprosse ['ʃprɔsə] *f* rung
Sprössling ▲ ['ʃprœslɪŋ] (*umg*) *m* (*Kind*)
offspring (*pl inv*)
Spruch [ʃprʊx] **(-(e)s, ⁼e)** *m* saying, maxim;
(*JUR*) judgement
Sprudel ['ʃpruːdəl] **(-s, -)** *m* mineral water;
lemonade; **s~n** *vi* to bubble; **~wasser** *nt*
(*KOCH*) sparkling *od* fizzy mineral water
Sprüh- ['ʃpryː] *zW:* **~dose** *f* aerosol (can);
s~en *vi* to spray; (*fig*) to sparkle ♦ *vt* to
spray; **~regen** *m* drizzle

Sprung [ʃprʊŋ] **(-(e)s, ⁼e)** *m* jump; (*Riss*)
crack; **~brett** *nt* springboard; **s~haft** *adj*
erratic; (*Aufstieg*) rapid; **~schanze** *f* ski
jump
Spucke ['ʃpʊkə] **(-)** *f* spit; **s~n** *vt, vi* to spit
Spuk [ʃpuːk] **(-(e)s, -e)** *m* haunting; (*fig*)
nightmare; **s~en** *vi* (*Geist*) to walk; **hier
s~t es** this place is haunted
Spülbecken ['ʃpyːlbɛkən] *nt* (*in Küche*) sink
Spule ['ʃpuːlə] *f* spool; (*ELEK*) coil
Spül- ['ʃpyːl] *zW:* **~e** *f* (kitchen) sink; **s~en**
vt, vi to rinse; (*Geschirr*) to wash up;
(*Toilette*) to flush; **~maschine** *f*
dishwasher; **~mittel** *nt* washing-up liquid;
~stein *m* sink; **~ung** *f* rinsing; flush; (*MED*)
irrigation
Spur [ʃpuːr] **(-, -en)** *f* trace; (*Fußspur, Radspur,
Tonbandspur*) track; (*Fährte*) trail; (*Fahrspur*)
lane
spürbar *adj* noticeable, perceptible
spüren ['ʃpyːrən] *vt* to feel
spurlos *adv* without (a) trace
Spurt [ʃpʊrt] **(-(e)s, -s** *od* **-e)** *m* spurt; **s~en**
vi to spurt
sputen ['ʃpuːtən] *vr* to make haste
St. *abk* = **Stück** St.; (= *Sankt*) St.
Staat [ʃtaːt] **(-(e)s, -en)** *m* state; (*Prunk*)
show; (*Kleidung*) finery; **s~enlos** *adj*
stateless; **s~lich** *adj* state(-); state-run
Staats- *zW:* **~angehörige(r)** *f(m)* national;
~angehörigkeit *f* nationality; **~anwalt** *m*
public prosecutor; **~bürger** *m* citizen;
~dienst *m* civil service; **~examen** *nt*
(*UNIV*) state exam(ination); **s~feindlich** *adj*
subversive; **~mann** (*pl* **-männer**) *m*
statesman; **~oberhaupt** *nt* head of state
Stab [ʃtaːp] **(-(e)s, ⁼e)** *m* rod; (*Gitterstab*) bar;
(*Menschen*) staff; **~hochsprung** *m* pole
vault
stabil [ʃtaˈbiːl] *adj* stable; (*Möbel*) sturdy;
~i'sieren *vt* to stabilize
Stachel ['ʃtaxəl] **(-s, -n)** *m* spike; (*von Tier*)
spine; (*von Insekten*) sting; **~beere** *f*
gooseberry; **~draht** *m* barbed wire; **s~ig**
adj prickly; **~schwein** *nt* porcupine
Stadion ['ʃtaːdiɔn] **(-s, Stadien)** *nt* stadium
Stadium ['ʃtaːdiʊm] *nt* stage, phase

Spelling Reform: ▲ *new spelling* △ *old spelling (to be phased out)*

Stadt [ʃtat] (-, ̈e) f town; **~autobahn** f urban motorway; **~bahn** f suburban railway; **~bücherei** f municipal library

Städt- ['ʃtɛːt] zW: **~ebau** m town planning; **~epartnerschaft** f town twinning; **~er(in)** (-s, -) m(f) town dweller; **s~isch** adj municipal; (nicht ländlich) urban

Stadt- zW: **~kern** m town centre, city centre; **~mauer** f city wall(s); **~mitte** f town centre; **~plan** m street map; **~rand** m outskirts pl; **~rat** m (Behörde) town council, city council; **~rundfahrt** f tour of a/the city; **~teil** m district, part of town; **~zentrum** nt town centre

Staffel ['ʃtafəl] (-, -n) f rung; (SPORT) relay (team); (AVIAT) squadron; **~lauf** m (SPORT) relay (race); **s~n** vt to graduate

Stahl [ʃtaːl] (-(e)s, ̈e) m steel

stahl etc vb siehe **stehlen**

stak etc [ʃtaːk] vb siehe **stecken**

Stall [ʃtal] (-(e)s, ̈e) m stable; (Kaninchenstall) hutch; (Schweinestall) sty; (Hühnerstall) henhouse

Stamm [ʃtam] (-(e)s, ̈e) m (Baumstamm) trunk; (Menschenstamm) tribe; (GRAM) stem; **~baum** m family tree; (von Tier) pedigree; **s~eln** vt, vi to stammer; **s~en** vi: **s~en von** od **aus** to come from; **~gast** m regular (customer)

stämmig ['ʃtɛmɪç] adj sturdy; (Mensch) stocky

Stammtisch ['ʃtamtɪʃ] m table for the regulars

stampfen ['ʃtampfən] vt, vi to stamp; (stapfen) to tramp; (mit Werkzeug) to pound

Stand [ʃtant] (-(e)s, ̈e) m position; (Wasserstand, Benzinstand etc) level; (Stehen) standing position; (Zustand) state; (Spielstand) score; (Messestand etc) stand; (Klasse) class; (Beruf) profession; siehe **imstande, zustande**

stand etc vb siehe **stehen**

Standard [ʃtandart] (-s, -s) m standard

Ständer ['ʃtɛndər] (-s, -) m stand

Standes- ['ʃtandəs] zW: **~amt** nt registry office; **~beamte(r)** m registrar; **s~gemäß** adj, adv according to one's social position;

~unterschied m social difference

Stand- zW: **s~haft** adj steadfast; **s~halten** (unreg) vi: **(jdm/etw) s~halten** to stand firm (against sb/sth), to resist (sb/sth)

ständig ['ʃtɛndɪç] adj permanent; (ununterbrochen) constant, continual

Stand- zW: **~licht** nt sidelights pl, parking lights pl (US); **~ort** m location; (MIL) garrison; **~punkt** m standpoint; **~spur** f hard shoulder

Stange ['ʃtaŋə] f stick; (Stab) pole, bar; rod; (Zigaretten) carton; **von der ~** (COMM) off the peg; **eine ~ Geld** (umg) quite a packet

Stängel ▲ ['ʃtɛŋəl] (-s, -) m stalk

Stapel ['ʃtaːpəl] (-s, -) m pile; (NAUT) stocks pl; **~lauf** m launch; **s~n** vt to pile (up)

Star¹ [ʃtaːr] (-(e)s, -e) m starling; (MED) cataract

Star² [ʃtaːr] (-s, -s) m (Filmstar etc) star

starb etc [ʃtarp] vb siehe **sterben**

stark [ʃtark] adj strong; (heftig, groß) heavy; (Maßangabe) thick

Stärke ['ʃtɛrkə] f strength; heaviness; thickness; (KOCH: Wäschestärke) starch; **s~n** vt to strengthen; (Wäsche) to starch

Starkstrom m heavy current

Stärkung ['ʃtɛrkʊŋ] f strengthening; (Essen) refreshment

starr [ʃtar] adj stiff; (unnachgiebig) rigid; (Blick) staring; **~en** vi to stare; **~en vor** od **von** to be covered in; (Waffen) to be bristling with; **S~heit** f rigidity; **~köpfig** adj stubborn; **S~sinn** m obstinacy

Start [ʃtart] (-(e)s, -e) m start; (AVIAT) takeoff; **~automatik** f (AUT) automatic choke; **~bahn** f runway; **s~en** vt to start ♦ vi to start; to take off; **~er** (-s, -) m starter; **~erlaubnis** f takeoff clearance; **~hilfekabel** nt jump leads pl

Station [ʃtatsiˈoːn] f station; hospital ward; **s~är** [ʃtatsioˈnɛːr] adj (MED) in-patient attr; **s~ieren** [-ˈniːrən] vt to station

Statist [ʃtaˈtɪst] m extra, supernumerary

Statistik f statistics sg; **~er** (-s, -) m statistician

statistisch adj statistical

Stativ [ʃtaˈtiːf] (-s, -e) nt tripod

statt [ʃtat] *konj* instead of ♦ *präp* (*+gen od dat*) instead of

Stätte ['ʃtɛtə] *f* place

statt- *zW:* **~finden** (*unreg*) *vi* to take place; **~haft** *adj* admissible; **~lich** *adj* imposing, handsome

Statue ['ʃtaːtuə] *f* statue

Status ['ʃtaːtʊs] **(-, -)** *m* status

Stau [ʃtaʊ] **(-(e)s, -e)** *m* blockage; (*Verkehrsstau*) (traffic) jam

Staub [ʃtaʊp] **(-(e)s)** *m* dust; **~ saugen** to vacuum, to hoover®; **s~en** ['ʃtaʊbən] *vi* to be dusty; **s~ig** *adj* dusty; **s~saugen** *vi* to vacuum, to hoover®; **~sauger** *m* vacuum cleaner; **~tuch** *nt* duster

Staudamm *m* dam

Staude ['ʃtaʊdə] *f* shrub

stauen ['ʃtaʊən] *vt* (*Wasser*) to dam up; (*Blut*) to stop the flow of ♦ *vr* (*Wasser*) to become dammed up; (*MED: Verkehr*) to become congested; (*Menschen*) to collect; (*Gefühle*) to build up

staunen ['ʃtaʊnən] *vi* to be astonished; **S~ (-s)** *nt* amazement

Stausee ['ʃtaʊzeː] **(-s, -n)** *m* reservoir, man-made lake

Stauung ['ʃtaʊʊŋ] *f* (*von Wasser*) damming-up; (*von Blut, Verkehr*) congestion

Std. *abk* (= *Stunde*) hr.

Steak [ʃteːk] *nt* steak

Stech- ['ʃtɛç] *zW:* **s~en** (*unreg*) *vt* (*mit Nadel etc*) to prick; (*mit Messer*) to stab; (*mit Finger*) to poke; (*Biene etc*) to sting; (*Mücke*) to bite; (*Sonne*) to burn; (*KARTEN*) to take; (*ART*) to engrave; (*Torf, Spargel*) to cut; **in See s~en** to put to sea; **~en (-s, -)** *nt* (*SPORT*) play-off; jump-off; **s~end** *adj* piercing, stabbing; (*Geruch*) pungent; **~palme** *f* holly; **~uhr** *f* time clock

Steck- ['ʃtɛk] *zW:* **~brief** *m* "wanted" poster; **~dose** *f* (wall) socket; **s~en** *vt* to put, to insert; (*Nadel*) to stick; (*Pflanzen*) to plant; (*beim Nähen*) to pin ♦ *vi* (*auch unreg*) to be; (*festsitzen*) to be stuck; (*Nadeln*) to stick; **s~en bleiben** to get stuck; **s~en lassen** to leave in; **~enpferd** *nt* hobby-horse; **~er (-s, -)** *m* plug; **~nadel** *f* pin

Steg [ʃteːk] **(-(e)s, -e)** *m* small bridge; (*Anlegesteg*) landing stage; **~reif** *m:* **aus dem ~reif** just like that

stehen ['ʃteːən] (*unreg*) *vi* to stand; (*sich befinden*) to be; (*in Zeitung*) to say; (*stillstehen*) to have stopped ♦ *vi unpers:* **es steht schlecht um jdn/etw** things are bad for sb/sth; **zu jdm/etw ~** to stand by sb/sth; **jdm ~** to suit sb; **wie stehts?** how are things?; (*SPORT*) what's the score?; **~ bleiben** to remain standing; (*Uhr*) to stop; (*Fehler*) to stay as it is; **~ lassen** to leave; (*Bart*) to grow

Stehlampe ['ʃteːlampə] *f* standard lamp

stehlen ['ʃteːlən] (*unreg*) *vt* to steal

Stehplatz ['ʃteːplats] *m* standing place

steif [ʃtaɪf] *adj* stiff; **S~heit** *f* stiffness

Steig- ['ʃtaɪk] *zW:* **~bügel** *m* stirrup; **s~en** ['ʃtaɪgən] (*unreg*) *vi* to rise; (*klettern*) to climb; **s~en in** *+akk*/**auf** *+akk* to get in/on; **s~ern** *vt* to raise; (*GRAM*) to compare ♦ *vi* (*Auktion*) to bid ♦ *vr* to increase; **~erung** *f* raising; (*GRAM*) comparison; **~ung** *f* incline, gradient, rise

steil [ʃtaɪl] *adj* steep; **S~küste** *f* steep coast; (*Klippen*) cliffs *pl*

Stein [ʃtaɪn] **(-(e)s, -e)** *m* stone; (*in Uhr*) jewel; **~bock** *m* (*ASTROL*) Capricorn; **~bruch** *m* quarry; **s~ern** *adj* (made of) stone; (*fig*) stony; **~gut** *nt* stoneware; **s~ig** ['ʃtaɪnɪç] *adj* stony; **s~igen** *vt* to stone; **~kohle** *f* mineral coal; **~zeit** *f* Stone Age

Stelle ['ʃtɛlə] *f* place; (*Arbeit*) post, job; (*Amt*) office; **an Ihrer/meiner ~** in your/my place; *siehe* **anstelle**

stellen *vt* to put; (*Uhr etc*) to set; (*zur Verfügung ~*) to supply; (*fassen: Dieb*) to apprehend ♦ *vr* (*sich aufstellen*) to stand; (*sich einfinden*) to present o.s.; (*bei Polizei*) to give o.s. up; (*vorgeben*) to pretend (to be); **sich zu etw ~** to have an opinion of sth

Stellen- *zW:* **~angebot** *nt* offer of a post; (*in Zeitung*) "vacancies"; **~anzeige** *f* job advertisement; **~gesuch** *nt* application for a post; **~vermittlung** *f* employment agency

Spelling Reform: ▲ *new spelling* △ *old spelling (to be phased out)*

Stell- zW: **~ung** f position; (MIL) line; **~ung nehmen zu** to comment on; **~ungnahme** f comment; **s~vertretend** adj deputy, acting; **~vertreter** m deputy

Stelze ['fteltsə] f stilt

stemmen ['fteman] vt to lift (up); (drücken) to press; **sich ~ gegen** (fig) to resist, to oppose

Stempel ['ftempəl] (-s, -) m stamp; (BOT) pistil; **~kissen** nt ink pad; **s~n** vt to stamp; (Briefmarke) to cancel; **s~n gehen** (umg) to be od go on the dole

Stengel △ ['ftengəl] (-s, -) m = **Stängel**

Steno- [fteno] zW: **~gramm** [-'gram] nt shorthand report; **~grafie** ▲ [-gra'fi:] f shorthand; **s~grafieren** ▲ [-gra'fi:rən] vt, vi to write (in) shorthand; **~typist(in)** [-ty'pist(in)] m(f) shorthand typist

Stepp- ['ftep] zW: **~decke** f quilt; **~e** f prairie; steppe; **s~en** vt to stitch ♦ vi to tap-dance

Sterb- ['fterb] zW: **~efall** m death; **~ehilfe** f euthanasia; **s~en** (unreg) vi to die; **s~lich** ['fterpliç] adj mortal; **~lichkeit** f mortality; **~lichkeitsziffer** f death rate

stereo- ['ste:reo] in zW stereo(-); **S~anlage** f stereo (system); **~typ** [ftereo'ty:p] adj stereotype

steril [fte'ri:l] adj sterile; **~i'sieren** vt to sterilize; **S~i'sierung** f sterilization

Stern [ftern] (-(e)s, -e) m star; **~bild** nt constellation; **~schnuppe** f meteor, falling star; **~stunde** f historic moment; **~zeichen** nt sign of the zodiac

stet [fte:t] adj steady; **~ig** adj constant, continual; **~s** adv continually, always

Steuer¹ ['ftɔyər] (-s, -) nt (NAUT) helm; (~ruder) rudder; (AUT) steering wheel

Steuer² ['ftɔyər] (-, -n) f tax; **~berater(in)** m(f) tax consultant

Steuerbord nt (NAUT, AVIAT) starboard

Steuer- ['ftɔyər] zW: **~erklärung** f tax return; **s~frei** adj tax-free; **~freibetrag** m tax allowance; **~klasse** f tax group; **~knüppel** m control column; (AVIAT, COMPUT) joystick; **~mann** (pl **-männer** od **-leute**) m helmsman; **s~n** vt, vi to steer;

(Flugzeug) to pilot; (Entwicklung, Tonstärke) to control; **s~pflichtig** [-pfliçtiç] adj taxable; **~rad** nt steering wheel; **~ung** f (auch AUT) steering; piloting; control; (Vorrichtung) controls pl; **~zahler** (-s, -) m taxpayer

Steward ['stju:ərt] (-s, -s) m steward; **~ess** ▲ ['stju:ərdɛs] (-, -en) f stewardess; air hostess

Stich [ftiç] (-(e)s, -e) m (Insektenstich) sting; (Messerstich) stab; (beim Nähen) stitch; (Färbung) tinge; (KARTEN) trick; (ART) engraving; **jdn im ~ lassen** to leave sb in the lurch; **s~eln** vi (fig) to jibe; **s~haltig** adj sound, tenable; **~probe** f spot check; **~straße** f cul-de-sac; **~wahl** f final ballot; **~wort** nt cue; (in Wörterbuch) headword; (für Vortrag) note

sticken ['ftikən] vt, vi to embroider

Sticke'rei f embroidery

stickig adj stuffy, close

Stickstoff m nitrogen

Stief- ['fti:f] in zW step

Stiefel ['fti:fəl] (-s, -) m boot

Stief- zW: **~kind** nt stepchild; (fig) Cinderella; **~mutter** f stepmother; **~mütterchen** nt pansy; **s~mütterlich** adj (fig): **jdn/etw s~mütterlich behandeln** to pay little attention to sb/sth; **~vater** m stepfather

stiehlst etc [fti:lst] vb siehe **stehlen**

Stiel [fti:l] (-(e)s, -e) m handle; (BOT) stalk

Stier (-(e)s, -e) m bull; (ASTROL) Taurus

stieren vi to stare

Stierkampf m bullfight

Stierkämpfer m bullfighter

Stift [ftift] (-(e)s, -e) m peg; (Nagel) tack; (Farbstift) crayon; (Bleistift) pencil ♦ nt (charitable) foundation; (ECCL) religious institution; **s~en** vt to found; (Unruhe) to cause; (spenden) to contribute; **~er(in)** (-s, -) m(f) founder; **~ung** f donation; (Organisation) foundation; **~zahn** m post crown

Stil [fti:l] (-(e)s, -e) m style

still [ftil] adj quiet; (unbewegt) still; (heimlich) secret; **S~er Ozean** Pacific; **~ halten** to keep still; **~ stehen** to stand still; **S~e** f

stillness, quietness; **in aller S~e** quietly;
~en vt to stop; (*befriedigen*) to satisfy;
(*Säugling*) to breast-feed; **~legen** ▲ vt to
close down; **~schweigen** (*unreg*) vi to be
silent; **S~schweigen** nt silence;
~schweigend adj silent; (*Einverständnis*)
tacit ♦ adv silently; tacitly; **S~stand** m
standstill

Stimm- ['ʃtɪm] zW: **~bänder** pl vocal cords;
s~berechtigt adj entitled to vote; **~e** f
voice; (*Wahlstimme*) vote; **s~en** vt (MUS) to
tune ♦ vi to be right; **das s~te ihn traurig**
that made him feel sad; **s~en für/gegen**
to vote for/against; **s~t so!** that's right;
~enmehrheit f majority (of votes);
~enthaltung f abstention; **~gabel** f
tuning fork; **~recht** nt right to vote; **~ung**
f mood; atmosphere; **s~ungsvoll** adj
enjoyable; full of atmosphere; **~zettel** m
ballot paper

stinken ['ʃtɪŋkən] (*unreg*) vi to stink
Stipendium [ʃti'pɛndiʊm] nt grant
stirbst etc ['ʃtɪrpst] vb siehe **sterben**
Stirn [ʃtɪrn] (-, -en) f forehead, brow;
(*Frechheit*) impudence; **~band** nt
headband; **~höhle** f sinus
stöbern ['ʃtøːbərn] vi to rummage
stochern ['ʃtɔxərn] vi to poke (about)
Stock¹ [ʃtɔk] (-(e)s, ⁻e) m stick; (BOT) stock
Stock² [ʃtɔk] (-(e)s, - od **Stockwerke**) m
storey
stocken vi to stop, to pause; **~d** adj halting
Stockung f stoppage
Stockwerk nt storey, floor
Stoff [ʃtɔf] (-(e)s, -e) m (*Gewebe*) material,
cloth; (*Materie*) matter; (*von Buch etc*)
subject (matter); **s~lich** adj material; **~tier**
nt soft toy; **~wechsel** m metabolism
stöhnen ['ʃtøːnən] vi to groan
Stollen ['ʃtɔlən] (-s, -) m (MIN) gallery;
(KOCH) *cake eaten at Christmas*; (*von
Schuhen*) stud
stolpern ['ʃtɔlpərn] vi to stumble, to trip
Stolz [ʃtɔlts] (-es) m pride; **s~** adj proud;
s~ieren [ʃtɔl'tsiːrən] vi to strut
stopfen ['ʃtɔpfən] vt (*hineinstopfen*) to stuff;
(*voll stopfen*) to fill (up); (*nähen*) to darn ♦ vi

(MED) to cause constipation
Stopfgarn nt darning thread
Stoppel ['ʃtɔpəl] (-, -n) f stubble
Stopp- ['ʃtɔp] zW: **s~en** vt to stop; (*mit Uhr*)
to time ♦ vi to stop; **~schild** nt stop sign;
~uhr f stopwatch
Stöpsel ['ʃtœpsəl] (-s, -) m plug; (*für
Flaschen*) stopper
Storch [ʃtɔrç] (-(e)s, ⁻e) m stork
Stör- ['ʃtøːr] zW: **s~en** vt to disturb;
(*behindern*, RADIO) to interfere with ♦ vr:
sich an etw dat **s~en** to let sth bother
one; **s~end** adj disturbing, annoying;
~enfried (-(e)s, -e) m troublemaker
stornieren [ʃtɔr'niːrən] vt (*Auftrag*) to
cancel; (*Buchung*) to reverse
Stornogebühr ['ʃtɔrno-] f cancellation fee
störrisch ['ʃtœrɪʃ] adj stubborn, perverse
Störung f disturbance; interference
Stoß [ʃtoːs] (-es, ⁻e) m (*Schub*) push; (*Schlag*)
blow; knock; (*mit Schwert*) thrust; (*mit Fuß*)
kick; (*Erdstoß*) shock; (*Haufen*) pile;
~dämpfer (-s, -) m shock absorber; **s~en**
(*unreg*) vt (*mit Druck*) to shove, to push; (*mit
Schlag*) to knock, to bump; (*mit Fuß*) to
kick; (*Schwert etc*) to thrust; (*anstoßen: Kopf
etc*) to bump ♦ vr to get a knock ♦ vi: **s~en
an** od **auf** +akk to bump into; (*finden*) to
come across; (*angrenzen*) to be next to;
sich s~en an +dat (*fig*) to take exception
to; **~stange** f (AUT) bumper
stottern ['ʃtɔtərn] vt, vi to stutter
Str. abk (= *Straße*) St.
Straf- ['ʃtraːf] zW: **~anstalt** f penal
institution; **~arbeit** f (SCH) punishment;
lines pl; **s~bar** adj punishable; **~e** f
punishment; (JUR) penalty; (*Gefängnisstrafe*)
sentence; (*Geldstrafe*) fine; **s~en** vt to
punish
straff [ʃtraf] adj tight; (*streng*) strict; (*Stil etc*)
concise; (*Haltung*) erect; **~en** vt to tighten,
to tauten
Strafgefangene(r) f(m) prisoner, convict
Strafgesetzbuch nt penal code
sträflich ['ʃtrɛːflɪç] adj criminal
Sträfling m convict
Straf- zW: **~porto** nt excess postage

Spelling Reform: ▲ *new spelling* △ *old spelling (to be phased out)*

(charge); **~predigt** f telling-off; **~raum** m
(*SPORT*) penalty area; **~recht** nt criminal
law; **~stoß** m (*SPORT*) penalty (kick); **~tat** f
punishable act; **~zettel** m ticket

Strahl [ʃtraːl] **(-s, -en)** m ray, beam;
(*Wasserstrahl*) jet; **s~en** vi to radiate; (*fig*)
to beam; **~ung** f radiation

Strähne ['ʃtrɛːnə] f strand

stramm [ʃtram] adj tight; (*Haltung*) erect;
(*Mensch*) robust

strampeln ['ʃtrampəln] vi to kick (about), to
fidget

Strand [ʃtrant] **(-(e)s, ⸚e)** m shore; (*mit
Sand*) beach; **~bad** nt open-air swimming
pool, lido; **s~en** ['ʃtrandən] vi to run
aground; (*fig: Mensch*) to fail; **~gut** nt
flotsam; **~korb** m beach chair

Strang [ʃtraŋ] **(-(e)s, ⸚e)** m cord, rope;
(*Bündel*) skein

Strapaz- zW: **~e** [ʃtraˈpaːtsə] f strain,
exertion; **s~ieren** [ʃtrapaˈtsiːrən] vt
(*Material*) to treat roughly, to punish;
(*Mensch, Kräfte*) to wear out, to exhaust;
s~ierfähig adj hard-wearing; **s~iös**
[ʃtrapatsiˈøːs] adj exhausting, tough

Straße ['ʃtraːsə] f street, road

Straßen- zW: **~bahn** f tram, streetcar (*US*);
~glätte f slippery road surface; **~karte** f
road map; **~kehrer (-s, -)** m roadsweeper;
~sperre f roadblock; **~verkehr** m (road)
traffic; **~verkehrsordnung** f highway
code

Strateg- [ʃtraˈteːg] zW: **~e** (**-n, -n**) m
strategist; **~ie** [ʃtrateˈgiː] f strategy; **s~isch**
adj strategic

sträuben ['ʃtrɔybən] vt to ruffle ♦ vr to
bristle; (*Mensch*): **sich (gegen etw) ~** to
resist (sth)

Strauch [ʃtraux] **(-(e)s, Sträucher)** m bush,
shrub

Strauß¹ [ʃtraus] **(-es, Sträuße)** m bunch;
bouquet

Strauß² [ʃtraus] **(-es, -e)** m ostrich

Streb- ['ʃtreːb] zW: **s~en** vi to strive, to
endeavour; **s~en nach** to strive for; **~er**
(**-s, -**) (*pej*) m pusher, climber; (*SCH*) swot
(*BRIT*)

Strecke ['ʃtrɛkə] f stretch; (*Entfernung*)
distance; (*EISENB, MATH*) line; **s~n** vt to
stretch; (*Waffen*) to lay down; (*KOCH*) to eke
out ♦ vr to stretch (o.s.)

Streich [ʃtraɪç] **(-(e)s, -e)** m trick, prank;
(*Hieb*) blow; **s~eln** vt to stroke; **s~en**
(*unreg*) vt (*berühren*) to stroke; (*auftragen*) to
spread; (*anmalen*) to paint; (*durchstreichen*)
to delete; (*nicht genehmigen*) to cancel ♦ vi
(*berühren*) to brush; (*schleichen*) to prowl;
~holz nt match; **~instrument** nt string
instrument

Streif- ['ʃtraɪf] zW: **~e** f patrol; **s~en** vt
(*leicht berühren*) to brush against, to graze;
(*Blick*) to skim over; (*Thema, Problem*) to
touch on; (*abstreifen*) to take off ♦ vi
(*gehen*) to roam; **~en (-s, -)** m (*Linie*) stripe;
(*Stück*) strip; (*Film*) film; **~enwagen** m
patrol car; **~schuss** ▲ m graze, grazing
shot; **~zug** m scouting trip

Streik [ʃtraɪk] **(-(e)s, -s)** m strike; **~brecher**
(**-s, -**) m blackleg, strikebreaker; **s~en** vi to
strike; **~posten** m (strike) picket

Streit [ʃtraɪt] **(-(e)s, -e)** m argument;
dispute; **s~en** (*unreg*) vi, vr to argue; to
dispute; **~frage** f point at issue; **s~ig** adj:
jdm etw s~ig machen to dispute sb's right
to sth; **~igkeiten** pl quarrel sg, dispute sg;
~kräfte pl (*MIL*) armed forces

streng [ʃtrɛŋ] adj severe; (*Lehrer, Maßnahme*)
strict; (*Geruch etc*) sharp; **~ genommen**
strictly speaking; **S~e (-)** f severity,
strictness, sharpness; **~gläubig** adj
orthodox, strict; **~stens** adv strictly

Stress ▲ [ʃtrɛs] **(-es, -e)** m stress

stressen vt to put under stress

streuen ['ʃtrɔyən] vt to strew, to scatter, to
spread

Strich [ʃtrɪç] **(-(e)s, -e)** m (*Linie*) line;
(*Federstrich, Pinselstrich*) stroke; (*von
Geweben*) nap; (*von Fell*) pile; **auf den ~
gehen** (*umg*) to walk the streets; **jdm
gegen den ~ gehen** to rub sb up the
wrong way; **einen ~ machen durch** to
cross out; (*fig*) to foil; **~kode** m (*auf Waren*)
bar code; **~mädchen** nt streetwalker;
s~weise adv here and there

Rechtschreibreform: ▲ *neue Schreibung* △ *alte Schreibung (auslaufend)*

Strick [ʃtrɪk] (-(e)s, -e) m rope; **s~en** vt, vi to knit; **~jacke** f cardigan; **~leiter** f rope ladder; **~nadel** f knitting needle; **~waren** pl knitwear sg

strikt [strɪkt] adj strict

strittig ['ʃtrɪtɪç] adj disputed, in dispute

Stroh [ʃtro:] (-(e)s) nt straw; **~blume** f everlasting flower; **~dach** nt thatched roof; **~halm** m (drinking) straw

Strom [ʃtro:m] (-(e)s, ⁀e) m river; (fig) stream; (ELEK) current; **s~abwärts** adv downstream; **s~aufwärts** adv upstream; **~ausfall** m power failure

strömen ['ʃtrø:mən] vi to stream, to pour

Strom- zW: **~kreis** m circuit; **s~linienförmig** adj streamlined; **~sperre** f power cut

Strömung ['ʃtrø:mʊŋ] f current

Strophe ['ʃtro:fə] f verse

strotzen ['ʃtrɔtsən] vi: **~ vor** od **von** to abound in, to be full of

Strudel ['ʃtru:dəl] (-s, -) m whirlpool, vortex; (KOCH) strudel

Struktur [ʃtrʊk'tu:r] f structure

Strumpf [ʃtrʊmpf] (-(e)s, ⁀e) m stocking; **~band** nt garter; **~hose** f (pair of) tights

Stube ['ʃtu:bə] f room

Stuben- zW: **~arrest** m confinement to one's room; (MIL) confinement to quarters; **~hocker** (umg) m stay-at-home; **s~rein** adj house-trained

Stuck [ʃtʊk] (-(e)s) m stucco

Stück [ʃtʏk] (-(e)s, -e) nt piece; (etwas) bit; (THEAT) play; **~chen** nt little piece; **~lohn** m piecework wages pl; **s~weise** adv bit by bit, piecemeal; (COMM) individually

Student(in) [ʃtu'dɛnt(ɪn)] m(f) student; **s~isch** adj student, academic

Studie ['ʃtu:diə] f study

Studienfahrt f study trip

studieren [ʃtu'di:rən] vt, vi to study

Studio ['ʃtu:dio] (-s, -s) nt studio

Studium ['ʃtu:diʊm] nt studies pl

Stufe ['ʃtu:fə] f step; (Entwicklungsstufe) stage; **s~nweise** adv gradually

Stuhl [ʃtu:l] (-(e)s, ⁀e) m chair; **~gang** m bowel movement

stülpen ['ʃtʏlpən] vt (umdrehen) to turn upside down; (bedecken) to put

stumm [ʃtʊm] adj silent; (MED) dumb

Stummel ['ʃtʊməl] (-s, -) m stump; (Zigarettenstummel) stub

Stummfilm m silent film

Stümper ['ʃtʏmpər] (-s, -) m incompetent, duffer; **s~haft** adj bungling, incompetent; **s~n** vi to bungle

Stumpf [ʃtʊmpf] (-(e)s, ⁀e) m stump; **s~** adj blunt; (teilnahmslos, glanzlos) dull; (Winkel) obtuse; **~sinn** m tediousness; **s~sinnig** adj dull

Stunde ['ʃtʊndə] f hour; (SCH) lesson

stunden vt: **jdm etw ~** to give sb time to pay sth; **S~geschwindigkeit** f average speed per hour; **S~kilometer** pl kilometres per hour; **~lang** adj for hours; **S~lohn** m hourly wage; **S~plan** m timetable; **~weise** adj by the hour; every hour

stündlich ['ʃtʏntlɪç] adj hourly

Stups [ʃtʊps] (-es, -e) (umg) m push; **~nase** f snub nose

stur [ʃtu:r] adj obstinate, pigheaded

Sturm [ʃtʊrm] (-(e)s, ⁀e) m storm, gale; (MIL etc) attack, assault

stürm- ['ʃtʏrm] zW: **~en** vi (Wind) to blow hard, to rage; (rennen) to storm ♦ vt (MIL, fig) to storm ♦ vb unpers: **es ~t** there's a gale blowing; **S~er** (-s, -) m (SPORT) forward, striker; **~isch** adj stormy

Sturmwarnung f gale warning

Sturz [ʃtʊrts] (-es, ⁀e) m fall; (POL) overthrow

stürzen ['ʃtʏrtsən] vt (werfen) to hurl; (POL) to overthrow; (umkehren) to overturn ♦ vr to rush; (hineinstürzen) to plunge ♦ vi to fall; (AVIAT) to dive; (rennen) to dash

Sturzflug m nose dive

Sturzhelm m crash helmet

Stute ['ʃtu:tə] f mare

Stützbalken m brace, joist

Stütze ['ʃtʏtsə] f support; help

stutzen ['ʃtʊtsən] vt to trim; (Ohr, Schwanz) to dock; (Flügel) to clip ♦ vi to hesitate; to become suspicious

stützen vt (auch fig) to support; (Ellbogen

etc) to prop up

stutzig *adj* perplexed, puzzled; (*misstrauisch*) suspicious

Stützpunkt *m* point of support; (*von Hebel*) fulcrum; (*MIL, fig*) base

Styropor [ʃtyro'poːr] (®; **-s**) *nt* polystyrene

s. u. *abk* = **siehe unten**

Subjekt [zʊp'jɛkt] (**-(e)s, -e**) *nt* subject; **s~iv** [-'tiːf] *adj* subjective; **~ivi'tät** *f* subjectivity

Subsidiarität *f* subsidiarity

Substantiv [zʊpstan'tiːf] (**-s, -e**) *nt* noun

Substanz [zʊp'stants] *f* substance

subtil [zʊp'tiːl] *adj* subtle

subtrahieren [zʊptra'hiːrən] *vt* to subtract

subtropisch ['zʊptroːpɪʃ] *adj* subtropical

Subvention [zʊpvɛntsi'oːn] *f* subsidy; **s~ieren** *vt* to subsidize

Such- ['zuːx] *zW*: **~aktion** *f* search; **~e** *f* search; **s~en** *vt* to look (for), to seek; (*versuchen*) to try ♦ *vi* to seek, to search; **~er (-s, -)** *m* seeker, searcher; (*PHOT*) viewfinder

Sucht [zʊxt] (**-, ⁓e**) *f* mania; (*MED*) addiction, craving

süchtig ['zʏçtɪç] *adj* addicted; **S~e(r)** *f(m)* addict

Süd- ['zyːt] *zW*: **~en** ['zyːdən] (**-s**) *m* south; **~früchte** *pl* Mediterranean fruit *sg*; **s~lich** *adj* southern; **s~lich von** (to the) south of; **~pol** *m* South Pole; **s~wärts** *adv* southwards

süffig ['zʏfɪç] *adj* (*Wein*) pleasant to the taste

süffisant [zʏfi'zant] *adj* smug

suggerieren [zʊɡe'riːrən] *vt* to suggest

Sühne ['zyːnə] *f* atonement, expiation; **s~n** *vt* to atone for, to expiate

Sultan ['zʊltan] (**-s, -e**) *m* sultan; **~ine** [zʊlta'niːnə] *f* sultana

Sülze ['zʏltsə] *f* brawn

Summe ['zʊmə] *f* sum, total

summen *vt, vi* to buzz; (*Lied*) to hum

Sumpf [zʊmpf] (**-(e)s, ⁓e**) *m* swamp, marsh; **s~ig** *adj* marshy

Sünde ['zʏndə] *f* sin; **~nbock** (*umg*) *m* scapegoat; **~r(in)** (**-s, -**) *m(f)* sinner; **sündigen** *vi* to sin

Super ['zuːpər] (**-s**) *nt* (*Benzin*) four star

(*petrol*) (*BRIT*), premium (*US*); **~lativ** [-latiːf] (**-s, -e**) *m* superlative; **~macht** *f* superpower; **~markt** *m* supermarket

Suppe ['zʊpə] *f* soup; **~nteller** *m* soup plate

süß [zyːs] *adj* sweet; **S~e (-)** *f* sweetness; **~en** *vt* to sweeten; **S~igkeit** *f* sweetness; (*Bonbon etc*) sweet (*BRIT*), candy (*US*); **~lich** *adj* sweetish; (*fig*) sugary; **~sauer** *adj* (*Gurke*) pickled; (*Sauce etc*) sweet-and-sour; **S~speise** *f* pudding, sweet; **S~stoff** *m* sweetener; **S~waren** *pl* confectionery (*sing*); **S~wasser** *nt* fresh water

Symbol [zʏm'boːl] (**-s, -e**) *nt* symbol; **s~isch** *adj* symbolic(al)

Symmetrie [zʏme'triː] *f* symmetry

symmetrisch [zʏ'meːtrɪʃ] *adj* symmetrical

Sympathie [zʏmpa'tiː] *f* liking, sympathy; **sympathisch** [zʏm'paːtɪʃ] *adj* likeable; **er ist mir sympathisch** I like him; **sympathi'sieren** *vi* to sympathize

Symphonie [zʏmfo'niː] *f* (*MUS*) symphony

Symptom [zʏmp'toːm] (**-s, -e**) *nt* symptom; **s~atisch** [zʏmpto'maːtɪʃ] *adj* symptomatic

Synagoge [zʏna'goːɡə] *f* synagogue

synchron [zʏn'kroːn] *adj* synchronous; **~i'sieren** *vt* to synchronize; (*Film*) to dub

Synonym [zʏno'nyːm] (**-s, -e**) *nt* synonym; **s~** *adj* synonymous

Synthese [zʏn'teːzə] *f* synthesis

synthetisch *adj* synthetic

System [zʏs'teːm] (**-s, -e**) *nt* system; **s~atisch** *adj* systematic; **s~ati'sieren** *vt* to systematize

Szene ['stseːnə] *f* scene; **~rie** [stsenə'riː] *f* scenery

T, t

t *abk* (= *Tonne*) t

Tabak ['taːbak] (**-s, -e**) *m* tobacco

Tabell- [ta'bɛl] *zW*: **t~arisch** [tabɛ'laːrɪʃ] *adj* tabular; **~e** *f* table

Tablett [ta'blɛt] *nt* tray; **~e** *f* tablet, pill

Tabu [ta'buː] *nt* taboo; **t~** *adj* taboo

Tachometer [taxo'meːtər] (**-s, -**) *m* (*AUT*) speedometer

Tadel ['ta:dəl] **(-s, -)** m censure; scolding; (*Fehler*) fault, blemish; **t~los** adj faultless, irreproachable; **t~n** vt to scold

Tafel ['ta:fəl] **(-, -n)** f (*auch* MATH) table; (*Anschlagtafel*) board; (*Wandtafel*) blackboard; (*Schiefertafel*) slate; (*Gedenktafel*) plaque; (*Illustration*) plate; (*Schalttafel*) panel; (*Schokolade etc*) bar

Tag [ta:k] **(-(e)s, -e)** m day; daylight; **unter/über ~e** (MIN) underground/on the surface; **an den ~ kommen** to come to light; **guten ~!** good morning/afternoon!; *siehe* **zutage**; **t~aus** adv: **t~aus, ~ein** day in, day out; **~dienst** m day duty

Tage- ['ta:gə] zW: **~buch** ['ta:gəbu:x] nt diary, journal; **~geld** nt daily allowance; **t~lang** adv for days; **t~n** vi to sit, to meet ♦ vb unpers: **es tagt** dawn is breaking

Tages- zW: **~ablauf** m course of the day; **~anbruch** m dawn; **~fahrt** f day trip; **~karte** f menu of the day; (*Fahrkarte*) day ticket; **~licht** nt daylight; **~ordnung** f agenda; **~zeit** f time of day; **~zeitung** f daily (paper)

täglich ['tɛ:klɪç] adj, adv daily

tagsüber ['ta:ks|y:bər] adv during the day

Tagung f conference

Taille ['taljə] f waist

Takt [takt] **(-(e)s, -e)** m tact; (MUS) time; **~gefühl** nt tact

Taktik f tactics pl; **taktisch** adj tactical

Takt- zW: **t~los** adj tactless; **~losigkeit** f tactlessness; **~stock** m (conductor's) baton; **t~voll** adj tactful

Tal [ta:l] **(-(e)s, ⁻er)** nt valley

Talent [ta'lɛnt] **(-(e)s, -e)** nt talent; **t~iert** [talɛn'ti:rt] adj talented, gifted

Talisman ['ta:lɪsman] **(-s, -e)** m talisman

Talsohle f bottom of a valley

Talsperre f dam

Tampon ['tampɔn] **(-s, -s)** m tampon

Tandem ['tandɛm] **(-s, -s)** nt tandem

Tang [taŋ] **(-(e)s, -e)** m seaweed

Tank [taŋk] **(-s, -s)** m tank; **~anzeige** f fuel gauge; **t~en** vi to fill up with petrol (BRIT) od gas (US); (AVIAT) to (re)fuel; **~er (-s, -)** m tanker; **~schiff** nt tanker; **~stelle** f petrol (BRIT) od gas (US) station; **~wart** m petrol pump (BRIT) od gas station (US) attendant

Tanne ['tanə] f fir

Tannen- zW: **~baum** m fir tree; **~zapfen** m fir cone

Tante ['tantə] f aunt

Tanz [tants] **(-es, ⁻e)** m dance; **t~en** vt, vi to dance

Tänzer(in) ['tɛntsər(ɪn)] **(-s, -)** m(f) dancer

Tanzfläche f (dance) floor

Tanzschule f dancing school

Tapete [ta'pe:tə] f wallpaper; **~nwechsel** m (fig) change of scenery

tapezieren [tape'tsi:rən] vt to (wall)paper; **Tapezierer** [tape'tsi:rər] **(-s, -)** m (interior) decorator

tapfer ['tapfər] adj brave; **T~keit** f courage, bravery

Tarif [ta'ri:f] **(-s, -e)** m tariff, (scale of) fares od charges; **~lohn** m standard wage rate; **~verhandlungen** pl wage negotiations; **~zone** f fare zone

Tarn- ['tarn] zW: **t~en** vt to camouflage; (*Person, Absicht*) to disguise; **~ung** f camouflaging; disguising

Tasche ['taʃə] f pocket; handbag

Taschen- *in* zW pocket; **~buch** nt paperback; **~dieb** m pickpocket; **~geld** nt pocket money; **~lampe** f (electric) torch, flashlight (US); **~messer** nt penknife; **~tuch** nt handkerchief

Tasse ['tasə] f cup

Tastatur [tasta'tu:r] f keyboard

Taste ['tastə] f push-button control; (*an Schreibmaschine*) key; **t~n** vt to feel, to touch ♦ vi to feel, to grope ♦ vr to feel one's way

Tat [ta:t] **(-, -en)** f act, deed, action; **in der ~** indeed, as a matter of fact; **t~** etc vb siehe **tun**; **~bestand** m facts pl of the case; **t~enlos** adj inactive

Tät- ['tɛ:t] zW: **~er(in) (-s, -)** m(f) perpetrator, culprit; **t~ig** adj active; **in einer Firma t~ig sein** to work for a firm; **~igkeit** f activity; (*Beruf*) occupation; **t~lich** adj violent; **~lichkeit** f violence; **~lichkeiten** pl (*Schläge*) blows

tätowieren [tεto'viːrən] *vt* to tattoo
Tatsache *f* fact
tatsächlich *adj* actual ♦ *adv* really
Tau¹ [taʊ] (-(e)s, -e) *nt* rope
Tau² [taʊ] (-(e)s) *m* dew
taub [taʊp] *adj* deaf; (*Nuss*) hollow
Taube ['taʊbə] *f* dove; pigeon; ~**nschlag** *m* dovecote; **hier geht es zu wie in einem** ~**nschlag** it's a hive of activity here
taub- *zW:* **T~heit** *f* deafness; ~**stumm** *adj* deaf-and-dumb
Tauch- ['taʊx] *zW:* **t~en** *vt* to dip ♦ *vi* to dive; (*NAUT*) to submerge; ~**er** (**-s, -**) *m* diver; ~**eranzug** *m* diving suit; ~**erbrille** *f* diving goggles *pl*; ~**sieder** (**-s, -**) *m* immersion coil (*for boiling water*)
tauen ['taʊən] *vt, vi* to thaw ♦ *vb unpers:* **es taut** it's thawing
Tauf- ['taʊf] *zW:* ~**becken** *nt* font; ~**e** *f* baptism; **t~en** *vt* to christen, to baptize; ~**pate** *m* godfather; ~**patin** *f* godmother; ~**schein** *m* certificate of baptism
taug- ['taʊg] *zW:* ~**en** *vi* to be of use; ~**en für** to do for, to be good for; **nicht** ~**en** to be no good *od* useless; **T~enichts** (**-es, -e**) *m* good-for-nothing; ~**lich** ['taʊkliç] *adj* suitable; (*MIL*) fit (for service)
Taumel ['taʊməl] (**-s**) *m* dizziness; (*fig*) frenzy; **t~n** *vi* to reel, to stagger
Tausch [taʊʃ] (-(e)s, -e) *m* exchange; **t~en** *vt* to exchange, to swap
täuschen ['tɔʏʃən] *vt* to deceive ♦ *vi* to be deceptive ♦ *vr* to be wrong; ~**d** *adj* deceptive
Tauschhandel *m* barter
Täuschung *f* deception; (*optisch*) illusion
tausend ['taʊzənt] *num* (a) thousand
Tauwetter *nt* thaw
Taxi ['taksi] (-(s), -(s)) *nt* taxi; ~**fahrer** *m* taxi driver; ~**stand** *m* taxi rank
Tech- [tεç] *zW:* ~**nik** *f* technology; (*Methode, Kunstfertigkeit*) technique; ~**niker** (**-s, -**) *m* technician; **t~nisch** *adj* technical; ~**nolo'gie** *f* technology; **t~no'logisch** *adj* technological
Tee [teː] (**-s, -s**) *m* tea; ~**beutel** *m* tea bag; ~**kanne** *f* teapot; ~**löffel** *m* teaspoon

Teer [teːr] (-(e)s, -e) *m* tar; **t~en** *vt* to tar
Teesieb *nt* tea strainer
Teich [taiç] (-(e)s, -e) *m* pond
Teig [taik] (-(e)s, -e) *m* dough; **t~ig** ['taigiç] *adj* doughy; ~**waren** *pl* pasta *sg*
Teil [tail] (-(e)s, -e) *m od nt* part; (*Anteil*) share; (*Bestandteil*) component; **zum** ~ partly; **t~bar** *adj* divisible; ~**betrag** *m* instalment; ~**chen** *nt* (atomic) particle; **t~en** *vt, vr* to divide; (*mit jdm*) to share; **t~haben** (*unreg*) *vi:* **t~haben an** +*dat* to share in; ~**haber** (**-s, -**) *m* partner; ~**kaskoversicherung** *f* third party, fire and theft insurance; **t~möbliert** *adj* partially furnished; ~**nahme** *f* participation; (*Mitleid*) sympathy; **t~nahmslos** *adj* disinterested, apathetic; **t~nehmen** (*unreg*) *vi:* **t~nehmen an** +*dat* to take part in; ~**nehmer** (**-s, -**) *m* participant; **t~s** *adv* partly; ~**ung** *f* division; **t~weise** *adv* partly, in part; ~**zahlung** *f* payment by instalments; ~**zeitarbeit** *f* part-time work
Teint [tɛː] (**-s, -s**) *m* complexion
Telearbeit ['teːlelarbait] *f* teleworking
Telefax ['teːlefaks] *nt* fax
Telefon [tele'foːn] (**-s, -e**) *nt* telephone; ~**anruf** *m* (tele)phone call; ~**at** [telefo'naːt] (-(e)s, -e) *nt* (tele)phone call; ~**buch** *nt* telephone directory; ~**hörer** *m* (telephone) receiver; **t~ieren** *vi* to telephone; **t~isch** [-iʃ] *adj* telephone; (*Benachrichtigung*) by telephone; ~**ist(in)** [telefo'nist(in)] *m(f)* telephonist; ~**karte** *f* phonecard; ~**nummer** *f* (tele)phone number; ~**zelle** *f* telephone kiosk, callbox; ~**zentrale** *f* telephone exchange
Telegraf [tele'graːf] (**-en, -en**) *m* telegraph; ~**enmast** *m* telegraph pole; ~**ie** [-'fiː] *f* telegraphy; **t~ieren** [-'fiːrən] *vt, vi* to telegraph, to wire
Telegramm [tele'gram] (**-s, -e**) *nt* telegram, cable; ~**adresse** *f* telegraphic address
Tele- *zW:* ~**objektiv** ['teːlelɔpjektiːf] *nt* telephoto lens; **t~pathisch** [tele'paːtiʃ] *adj* telepathic; ~**skop** [tele'skoːp] (**-s, -e**) *nt* telescope

Teller ['tɛlər] **(-s, -)** *m* plate; **~gericht** *nt* (*KOCH*) one-course meal

Tempel ['tɛmpəl] **(-s, -)** *m* temple

Temperament [tɛmpera'mɛnt] *nt* temperament; (*Schwung*) vivacity, liveliness; **t~voll** *adj* high-spirited, lively

Temperatur [tɛmpera'tu:r] *f* temperature

Tempo¹ ['tɛmpo] **(-s, Tempi)** *nt* (*MUS*) tempo

Tempo² ['tɛmpo] **(-s, -s)** *nt* speed, pace; **~!** get a move on!; **~limit** [-lɪmɪt] **(-s, -s)** *nt* speed limit; **~taschentuch** ® *nt* tissue

Tendenz [tɛn'dɛnts] *f* tendency; (*Absicht*) intention; **t~iös** [-i'ø:s] *adj* biased, tendentious

tendieren [tɛn'di:rən] *vi:* **~ zu** to show a tendency to, to incline towards

Tennis ['tɛnɪs] **(-)** *nt* tennis; **~ball** *m* tennis ball; **~platz** *m* tennis court; **~schläger** *m* tennis racket; **~schuh** *m* tennis shoe; **~spieler(in)** *m(f)* tennis player

Tenor [te'no:r] **(-s, ⁺e)** *m* tenor

Teppich ['tɛpɪç] **(-s, -e)** *m* carpet; **~boden** *m* wall-to-wall carpeting

Termin [tɛr'mi:n] **(-s, -e)** *m* (*Zeitpunkt*) date; (*Frist*) time limit, deadline; (*Arzttermin etc*) appointment; **~kalender** *m* diary, appointments book; **~planer** *m* personal organizer

Terrasse [tɛ'rasə] *f* terrace

Terrine [tɛ'ri:nə] *f* tureen

territorial [tɛritori'a:l] *adj* territorial

Territorium [tɛri'to:riʊm] *nt* territory

Terror ['tɛror] **(-s)** *m* terror; reign of terror; **t~isieren** [tɛrori'zi:rən] *vt* to terrorize; **~ismus** [-'rɪsmʊs] *m* terrorism; **~ist** [-'rɪst] *m* terrorist

Tesafilm ['te:zafɪlm] ® *m* Sellotape ® (*BRIT*), Scotch tape ® (*US*)

Tessin [tɛ'si:n] **(-s)** *nt:* **das ~** Ticino

Test [tɛst] **(-s, -s)** *m* test

Testament [tɛsta'mɛnt] *nt* will, testament; (*REL*) Testament; **t~arisch** [-'ta:rɪʃ] *adj* testamentary

Testamentsvollstrecker *m* executor (of a will)

testen *vt* to test

Tetanus ['te:tanʊs] **(-)** *m* tetanus; **~impfung** *f* (anti-)tetanus injection

teuer ['tɔyər] *adj* dear, expensive; **T~ung** *f* increase in prices; **T~ungszulage** *f* cost of living bonus

Teufel ['tɔyfəl] **(-s, -)** *m* devil; **teuflisch** ['tɔyflɪʃ] *adj* fiendish, diabolical

Text [tɛkst] **(-(e)s, -e)** *m* text; (*Liedertext*) words *pl*; **t~en** *vi* to write the words

textil [tɛks'ti:l] *adj* textile; **T~ien** *pl* textiles; **T~industrie** *f* textile industry; **T~waren** *pl* textiles

Textverarbeitung *f* word processing

Theater [te'a:tər] **(-s, -)** *nt* theatre; (*umg*) fuss; **~ spielen** (*auch fig*) to playact; **~besucher** *m* playgoer; **~kasse** *f* box office; **~stück** *nt* (stage) play

Theke ['te:kə] *f* (*Schanktisch*) bar; (*Ladentisch*) counter

Thema ['te:ma] **(-s, Themen** *od* **-ta)** *nt* theme, topic, subject

Themse ['tɛmzə] *f* Thames

Theo- [teo] *zW:* **~loge** [-'lo:gə] **(-n, -n)** *m* theologian; **~logie** [-lo'gi:] *f* theology; **t~logisch** [-'lo:gɪʃ] *adj* theological; **~retiker** [-'re:tikər] **(-s, -)** *m* theorist; **t~retisch** [-'re:tɪʃ] *adj* theoretical; **~rie** [-'ri:] *f* theory

Thera- [tera] *zW:* **~peut** [-'pɔyt] **(-en, -en)** *m* therapist; **t~peutisch** [-'pɔytɪʃ] *adj* therapeutic; **~pie** [-'pi:] *f* therapy

Therm- *zW:* **~albad** [tɛr'ma:lba:t] *nt* thermal bath; thermal spa; **~odrucker** [tɛrmo-] *m* thermal printer; **~ometer** [tɛrmo'me:tər] **(-s, -)** *nt* thermometer; **~osflasche** ['tɛrmɔsflaʃə] ® *f* Thermos ® flask

These ['te:zə] *f* thesis

Thrombose [trɔm'bo:zə] *f* thrombosis

Thron [tro:n] **(-(e)s, -e)** *m* throne; **t~en** *vi* to sit enthroned; (*fig*) to sit in state; **~folge** *f* succession (to the throne); **~folger(in)** **(-s, -)** *m(f)* heir to the throne

Thunfisch ['tu:nfɪʃ] *m* tuna

Thüringen ['ty:rɪŋən] **(-s)** *nt* Thuringia

Thymian ['ty:mia:n] **(-s, -e)** *m* thyme

Tick [tɪk] **(-(e)s, -s)** *m* tic; (*Eigenart*) quirk;

(*Fimmel*) craze

ticken *vi* to tick

tief [ti:f] *adj* deep; (~*sinnig*) profound; (*Ausschnitt, Preis, Ton*) low; ~ **greifend** far-reaching; ~ **schürfend** profound; **T~ (-s, -s)** *nt* (*MET*) depression; **T~druck** *m* low pressure; **T~e** *f* depth; **T~ebene** *f* plain; **T~enschärfe** *f* (*PHOT*) depth of focus; **T~garage** *f* underground garage; ~**gekühlt** *adj* frozen; **T~kühlfach** *nt* deepfreeze compartment; **T~kühlkost** *f* (deep) frozen food; **T~kühltruhe** *f* deepfreeze, freezer; **T~punkt** *m* low point; (*fig*) low ebb; **T~schlag** *m* (*BOXEN, fig*) blow below the belt; **T~see** *f* deep sea; ~**sinnig** *adj* profound; melancholy; **T~stand** *m* low level; **T~stwert** *m* minimum *od* lowest value

Tier [ti:r] **(-(e)s, -e)** *nt* animal; ~**arzt** *m* vet(erinary surgeon); ~**garten** *m* zoo(logical gardens *pl*); ~**heim** *nt* cat/dog home; **t~isch** *adj* animal; (*auch fig*) brutish; (*fig: Ernst etc*) deadly; ~**kreis** *m* zodiac; ~**kunde** *f* zoology; **t~liebend** *adj* fond of animals; ~**park** *m* zoo; ~**quälerei** [-kvɛːləˈraɪ] *f* cruelty to animals; ~**schutzverein** *m* society for the prevention of cruelty to animals

Tiger(in) [ˈtiːɡər(ɪn)] **(-s, -)** *m(f)* tiger(-gress)

tilgen [ˈtɪlɡən] *vt* to erase; (*Sünden*) to expiate; (*Schulden*) to pay off

Tinte [ˈtɪntə] *f* ink

Tintenfisch *m* cuttlefish

Tipp ▲ [tɪp] *m* tip; **t~en** *vt, vi* to tap, to touch; (*umg: schreiben*) to type; (*im Lotto etc*) to bet (on); **auf jdn t~en** (*umg: raten*) to tip sb, to put one's money on sb (*fig*)

Tipp- [ˈtɪp] *zW:* ~**fehler** (*umg*) *m* typing error; **t~topp** (*umg*) *adj* tip-top; ~**zettel** *m* (pools) coupon

Tirol [tiˈroːl] *nt* the Tyrol; ~**er(in)** *m(f)* Tyrolean; **t~isch** *adj* Tyrolean

Tisch [tɪʃ] **(-(e)s, -e)** *m* table; **bei ~** at table; **vor/nach ~** before/after eating; **unter den ~ fallen** (*fig*) to be dropped; ~**decke** *f* tablecloth; ~**ler (-s, -)** *m* carpenter, joiner; ~**le'rei** *f* joiner's workshop; (*Arbeit*)

carpentry, joinery; **t~lern** *vi* to do carpentry *etc*; ~**rede** *f* after-dinner speech; ~**tennis** *nt* table tennis; ~**tuch** *nt* tablecloth

Titel [ˈtiːtəl] **(-s, -)** *m* title; ~**bild** *nt* cover (picture); (*von Buch*) frontispiece; ~**rolle** *f* title role; ~**seite** *f* cover; (*Buchtitelseite*) title page; ~**verteidiger** *m* defending champion, title holder

Toast [toːst] **(-(e)s, -s** *od* **-e)** *m* toast; ~**brot** *nt* bread for toasting; ~**er (-s, -)** *m* toaster

tob- [ˈtoːb] *zW:* ~**en** *vi* to rage; (*Kinder*) to romp about; ~**süchtig** *adj* maniacal

Tochter [ˈtɔxtər] **(-, ⸚)** *f* daughter; ~**gesellschaft** *f* subsidiary (company)

Tod [toːt] **(-(e)s, -e)** *m* death; **t~ernst** *adj* deadly serious ♦ *adv* in dead earnest

Todes- [ˈtoːdəs] *zW:* ~**angst** [-aŋst] *f* mortal fear; ~**anzeige** *f* obituary (notice); ~**fall** *m* death; ~**strafe** *f* death penalty; ~**ursache** *f* cause of death; ~**urteil** *nt* death sentence; ~**verachtung** *f* utter disgust

todkrank *adj* dangerously ill

tödlich [ˈtøːtlɪç] *adj* deadly, fatal

tod- *zW:* ~**müde** *adj* dead tired; ~**schick** (*umg*) *adj* smart, classy; ~**sicher** (*umg*) *adj* absolutely *od* dead certain; **T~sünde** *f* deadly sin

Toilette [toaˈlɛtə] *f* toilet, lavatory; (*Frisiertisch*) dressing table

Toiletten- *zW:* ~**artikel** *pl* toiletries, toilet articles; ~**papier** *nt* toilet paper; ~**tisch** *m* dressing table

toi, toi, toi [ˈtɔy'tɔy'tɔy] *excl* touch wood

tolerant [toleˈrant] *adj* tolerant

Toleranz [toleˈrants] *f* tolerance

tolerieren [toleˈriːrən] *vt* to tolerate

toll [tɔl] *adj* mad; (*Treiben*) wild; (*umg*) terrific; ~**en** *vi* to romp; **T~kirsche** *f* deadly nightshade; ~**kühn** *adj* daring; **T~wut** *f* rabies

Tomate [toˈmaːtə] *f* tomato; ~**nmark** *nt* tomato purée

Ton¹ [toːn] **(-(e)s, -e)** *m* (*Erde*) clay

Ton² [toːn] **(-(e)s, ⸚e)** *m* (*Laut*) sound; (*MUS*) note; (*Redeweise*) tone; (*Farbton, Nuance*) shade; (*Betonung*) stress;

t~angebend *adj* leading; ~art *f* (musical) key; ~band *nt* tape; ~bandgerät *nt* tape recorder

tönen ['tøːnən] *vi* to sound ♦ *vt* to shade; (*Haare*) to tint

tönern ['tøːnərn] *adj* clay

Ton- *zW:* ~fall *m* intonation; ~film *m* sound film; ~leiter *f* (*MUS*) scale; t~los *adj* soundless

Tonne ['tɔnə] *f* barrel; (*Maß*) ton

Ton- *zW:* ~taube *f* clay pigeon; ~waren *pl* pottery *sg*, earthenware *sg*

Topf [tɔpf] **(-(e)s, ⁻e)** *m* pot; ~blume *f* pot plant

Töpfer ['tœpfər] **(-s, -)** *m* potter; ~ei [-'rai] *f* piece of pottery; potter's workshop; ~scheibe *f* potter's wheel

topografisch ▲ [topo'graːfɪʃ] *adj* topographic

Tor¹ [toːr] **(-en, -en)** *m* fool

Tor² [toːr] **(-(e)s, -e)** *nt* gate; (*SPORT*) goal; ~bogen *m* archway

Torf [tɔrf] **(-(e)s)** *m* peat

Torheit *f* foolishness; foolish deed

töricht ['tøːrɪçt] *adj* foolish

torkeln ['tɔrkəln] *vi* to stagger, to reel

Torte ['tɔrtə] *f* cake; (*Obsttorte*) flan, tart

Tortur [tɔr'tuːr] *f* ordeal

Torwart (-(e)s, -e) *m* goalkeeper

tosen ['toːzən] *vi* to roar

tot [toːt] *adj* dead; ~ **geboren** stillborn; **sich ~ stellen** to pretend to be dead

total [to'taːl] *adj* total; ~itär [totali'tɛːr] *adj* totalitarian; **T~schaden** *m* (*AUT*) complete write-off

Tote(r) *f(m)* dead person

töten ['tøːtən] *vt, vi* to kill

Toten- *zW:* ~bett *nt* death bed; t~-blass ▲ *adj* deathly pale, white as a sheet; ~kopf *m* skull; ~schein *m* death certificate; ~stille *f* deathly silence

tot- *zW:* ~fahren (*unreg*) *vt* to run over; ~geboren △ *adj siehe* **tot**; ~lachen (*umg*) *vr* to laugh one's head off

Toto ['toːto] **(-s, -s)** *m od nt* pools *pl*; ~schein *m* pools coupon

tot- *zW:* **T~schlag** *m* manslaughter;

~schlagen (*unreg*) *vt* (*auch fig*) to kill; ~schweigen (*unreg*) *vt* to hush up; ~stellen △ *vr siehe* **tot**

Tötung ['tøːtʊŋ] *f* killing

Toupet [tu'peː] **(-s, -s)** *nt* toupee

toupieren [tu'piːrən] *vt* to backcomb

Tour [tuːr] **(-, -en)** *f* tour, trip; (*Umdrehung*) revolution; (*Verhaltensart*) way; **in einer ~** incessantly; ~enzähler *m* rev counter; ~ismus [tu'rɪsmʊs] *m* tourism; ~ist [tu'rɪst] *m* tourist; ~istenklasse *f* tourist class; ~nee [tʊr'neː] **(-, -n)** *f* (*THEAT etc*) tour; **auf ~nee gehen** to go on tour

Trab [traːp] **(-(e)s)** *m* trot

Trabantenstadt *f* satellite town

traben ['traːbən] *vi* to trot

Tracht [traxt] **(-, -en)** *f* (*Kleidung*) costume, dress; **eine ~ Prügel** a sound thrashing; **t~en** *vi*: **t~en (nach)** to strive (for); **jdm nach dem Leben t~en** to seek to kill sb; **danach t~en, etw zu tun** to strive *od* endeavour to do sth

trächtig ['trɛçtɪç] *adj* (*Tier*) pregnant

Tradition [traditsi'oːn] *f* tradition; **t~ell** [-'nɛl] *adj* traditional

traf *etc* [traːf] *vb siehe* **treffen**

Tragbahre *f* stretcher

tragbar *adj* (*Gerät*) portable; (*Kleidung*) wearable; (*erträglich*) bearable

träge ['trɛːgə] *adj* sluggish, slow; (*PHYS*) inert

tragen ['traːgən] (*unreg*) *vt* to carry; (*Kleidung, Brille*) to wear; (*Namen, Früchte*) to bear; (*erdulden*) to endure ♦ *vi* (*schwanger sein*) to be pregnant; (*Eis*) to hold; **sich mit einem Gedanken ~** to have an idea in mind; **zum T~ kommen** to have an effect

Träger ['trɛːgər] **(-s, -)** *m* carrier; wearer; bearer; (*Ordensträger*) holder; (*an Kleidung*) (shoulder) strap; (*Körperschaft etc*) sponsor

Tragetasche *f* carrier bag

Tragfläche *f* (*AVIAT*) wing

Tragflügelboot *nt* hydrofoil

Trägheit ['trɛːkhait] *f* laziness; (*PHYS*) inertia

Tragik ['traːgɪk] *f* tragedy; **tragisch** *adj* tragic

Tragödie [tra'gøːdiə] *f* tragedy

Tragweite *f* range; (*fig*) scope

Train- ['trɛːn] zW: **~er (-s, -)** m (SPORT)
trainer, coach; (Fußball) manager; **t~ieren**
[trɛ'niːrən] vt, vi to train; (Mensch) to train,
to coach; (Übung) to practise; **~ing (-s, -s)**
nt training; **~ingsanzug** m track suit

Traktor ['traktɔr] m tractor; (von Drucker)
tractor feed

trällern ['trɛlərn] vt, vi to trill, to sing

Tram [tram] **(-, -s)** f tram

trampeln ['trampəln] vt, vi to trample, to
stamp

trampen ['trɛmpən] vi to hitch-hike

Tramper(in) [trɛmpər(ɪn)] **(-s, -)** m(f) hitch-
hiker

Tran [traːn] **(-(e)s, -e)** m train oil, blubber

tranchieren [trãˈʃiːrən] vt to carve

Träne ['trɛːnə] f tear; **t~n** vi to water;
~ngas nt teargas

trank etc [traŋk] vb siehe **trinken**

tränken ['trɛŋkən] vt (Tiere) to water

transchieren ▲ [tranˈʃiːrən] vt to carve

Trans- zW: **~formator** [transfɔrˈmaːtɔr] m
transformer; **~istor** [tranˈzɪstɔr] m transistor;
~itverkehr [tranˈziːtfɛrkeːr] m transit traffic;
~itvisum nt transit visa; **t~parent** adj
transparent; **~parent (-(e)s, -e)** nt (Bild)
transparency; (Spruchband) banner;
~plantation [transplantatsiˈoːn] f
transplantation; (Hauttransplantation)
graft(ing)

Transport [transˈpɔrt] **(-(e)s, -e)** m
transport; **t~ieren** [transpɔrˈtiːrən] vt to
transport; **~kosten** pl transport charges,
carriage sg; **~mittel** nt means sg of
transportation; **~unternehmen** nt carrier

Traube ['traubə] f grape; bunch (of grapes);
~nzucker m glucose

trauen ['trauən] vi: **jdm/etw ~** to trust sb/
sth ♦ vr to dare ♦ vt to marry

Trauer ['trauər] **(-)** f sorrow; (für
Verstorbenen) mourning; **~fall** m death,
bereavement; **~feier** f funeral service;
~kleidung f mourning; **t~n** vi to mourn;
um jdn t~n to mourn (for) sb; **~rand** m
black border; **~spiel** nt tragedy

traulich ['traulɪç] adj cosy, intimate

Traum [traum] **(-(e)s, Träume)** m dream

Trauma (-s, -men) nt trauma

träum- ['trɔym] zW: **~en** vt, vi to dream;
T~er (-s, -) m dreamer; **T~e'rei** f
dreaming; **~erisch** adj dreamy

traumhaft adj dreamlike; (fig) wonderful

traurig ['trauriç] adj sad; **T~keit** f sadness

Trau- ['trau] zW: **~ring** m wedding ring;
~schein m marriage certificate; **~ung** f
wedding ceremony; **~zeuge** m witness (to
a marriage); **~zeugin** f witness (to a
marriage)

treffen ['trɛfən] (unreg) vt to strike, to hit;
(Bemerkung) to hurt; (begegnen) to meet;
(Entscheidung etc) to make; (Maßnahmen) to
take ♦ vi to hit ♦ vr to meet; **er hat es gut
getroffen** he did well; **~ auf** +akk to come
across, to meet with; **es traf sich, dass ...**
it so happened that ...; **es trifft sich gut**
it's convenient; **wie es so trifft** as these
things happen; **T~ (-s, -)** nt meeting; **~d**
adj pertinent, apposite

Treffer (-s, -) m hit; (Tor) goal; (Los) winner

Treffpunkt m meeting place

Treib- [traib] zW: **~eis** nt drift ice; **t~en**
(unreg) vt to drive; (Studien etc) to pursue;
(Sport) to do, to go in for ♦ vi (Schiff etc) to
drift; (Pflanzen) to sprout; (KOCH: aufgehen)
to rise; (Tee, Kaffee) to be diuretic; **~haus**
nt greenhouse; **~hauseffekt** m
greenhouse effect; **~hausgas** nt
greenhouse gas; **~stoff** m fuel

trenn- ['trɛn] zW: **~bar** adj separable; **~en**
vt to separate; (teilen) to divide ♦ vr to
separate; **sich ~en von** to part with;
T~ung f separation; **T~wand** f partition
(wall)

Trepp- ['trɛp] zW: **t~ab** adv downstairs;
t~auf adv upstairs; **~e** f stair(case);
~engeländer nt banister; **~enhaus** nt
staircase

Tresor [treˈzoːr] **(-s, -e)** m safe

Tretboot nt pedalo, pedal boat

treten ['treːtən] (unreg) vi to step; (Tränen,
Schweiß) to appear ♦ vt (mit Fußtritt) to kick;
(niedertreten) to tread, to trample; **~ nach**
to kick at; **~ in** +akk to step in(to); **in
Verbindung ~** to get in contact; **in**

Erscheinung ~ to appear
treu [trɔy] *adj* faithful, true; **T~e (-)** *f* loyalty,
faithfulness; **T~händer (-s, -)** *m* trustee;
T~handanstalt *f* trustee organization;
T~handgesellschaft *f* trust company;
~herzig *adj* innocent; **~los** *adj* faithless

Treuhandanstalt

i *The* **Treuhandanstalt** *was the
organization set up in 1990 to take over
the nationally-owned companies of the
former* **DDR**, *break them down into smaller
units and privatize them. It was based in
Berlin and had nine branches. Many
companies were closed down by the*
Treuhandanstalt *because of their outdated
equipment and inability to compete with
Western firms which resulted in rising
unemployment. Having completed its initial
task, the* **Treuhandanstalt** *was closed
down in 1995.*

Tribüne [tri'byːnə] *f* grandstand;
(*Rednertribüne*) platform
Trichter ['trɪçtər] **(-s, -)** *m* funnel; (*in Boden*)
crater
Trick [trɪk] **(-s, -e** *od* **-s)** *m* trick; **~film** *m*
cartoon
Trieb [triːp] **(-(e)s, -e)** *m* urge, drive;
(*Neigung*) inclination; (*an Baum etc*) shoot;
t~ *etc vb siehe* **treiben; ~kraft** *f* (*fig*) drive;
~täter *m* sex offender; **~werk** *nt* engine
triefen ['triːfən] *vi* to drip
triffst *etc* [trɪfst] *vb siehe* **treffen**
triftig ['trɪftɪç] *adj* good, convincing
Trikot [tri'koː] **(-s, -s)** *nt* vest; (*SPORT*) shirt
Trimester [tri'mɛstər] **(-s, -)** *nt* term
trimmen ['trɪmən] *vr* to do keep fit exercises
trink- ['trɪŋk] *zW*: **~bar** *adj* drinkable; **~en**
(*unreg*) *vt, vi* to drink; **T~er (-s, -)** *m*
drinker; **T~geld** *nt* tip; **T~halle** *f*
refreshment kiosk; **T~wasser** *nt* drinking
water
Tripper ['trɪpər] **(-s, -)** *m* gonorrhoea
Tritt [trɪt] **(-(e)s, -e)** *m* step; (*Fußtritt*) kick;
~brett *nt* (*EISENB*) step; (*AUT*) running
board

Triumph [tri'ʊmf] **(-(e)s, -e)** *m* triumph;
~bogen *m* triumphal arch; **t~ieren**
[triʊm'fiːrən] *vi* to triumph; (*jubeln*) to exult
trocken ['trɔkən] *adj* dry; **T~element** *nt*
dry cell; **T~haube** *f* hair dryer; **T~heit** *f*
dryness; **~legen** *vt* (*Sumpf*) to drain; (*Kind*)
to put a clean nappy on; **T~milch** *f* dried
milk; **T~rasur** *f* dry shave, electric shave
trocknen ['trɔknən] *vt, vi* to dry
Trödel ['trøːdəl] **(-s)** (*umg*) *m* junk; **~markt**
m flea market; **t~n** (*umg*) *vi* to dawdle
Trommel ['trɔməl] **(-, -n)** *f* drum; **~fell** *nt*
eardrum; **t~n** *vt, vi* to drum
Trompete [trɔm'peːtə] *f* trumpet; **~r (-s, -)**
m trumpeter
Tropen ['troːpən] *pl* tropics; **~helm** *m* sun
helmet
tröpfeln ['trœpfəln] *vi* to drop, to trickle
Tropfen ['trɔpfən] **(-s, -)** *m* drop; **t~** *vt, vi* to
drip ♦ *vb unpers*: **es tropft** a few raindrops
are falling; **t~weise** *adv* in drops
Tropfsteinhöhle *f* stalactite cave
tropisch ['troːpɪʃ] *adj* tropical
Trost [troːst] **(-es)** *m* consolation, comfort
trösten ['trøːstən] *vt* to console, to comfort
trost- *zW*: **~los** *adj* bleak; (*Verhältnisse*)
wretched; **T~preis** *m* consolation prize;
~reich *adj* comforting
Trott [trɔt] **(-(e)s, -e)** *m* trot; (*Routine*)
routine; **~el (-s, -)** (*umg*) *m* fool, dope;
t~en *vi* to trot
Trotz [trɔts] **(-es)** *m* pigheadedness; **etw aus
~ tun** to do sth just to show them; **jdm
zum ~** in defiance of sb; **t~** *präp* (*+gen od
dat*) in spite of; **t~dem** *adv* nevertheless, all
the same ♦ *konj* although; **t~en** *vi* (*+dat*) to
defy; (*der Kälte, Klima etc*) to withstand; (*der
Gefahr*) to brave; (*t~ig sein*) to be awkward;
t~ig *adj* defiant, pig-headed; **~kopf** *m*
obstinate child
trüb [tryːp] *adj* dull; (*Flüssigkeit, Glas*) cloudy;
(*fig*) gloomy
Trubel ['truːbəl] **(-s)** *m* hurly-burly
trüb- *zW*: **~en** ['tryːbən] *vt* to cloud ♦ *vr* to
become clouded; **T~heit** *f* dullness;
cloudiness; gloom; **T~sal (-, -e)** *f* distress;
~selig *adj* sad, melancholy; **T~sinn** *m*

depression; **~sinnig** *adj* depressed, gloomy

Trüffel ['trʏfəl] (-, -n) *f* truffle

trug *etc* [truːk] *vb siehe* **tragen**

trügen ['tryːgən] (*unreg*) *vt* to deceive ♦ *vi* to be deceptive

trügerisch *adj* deceptive

Trugschluss ▲ ['truːɡʃlʊs] *m* false conclusion

Truhe ['truːə] *f* chest

Trümmer ['trʏmər] *pl* wreckage *sg*; (*Bautrümmer*) ruins; **~haufen** *m* heap of rubble

Trumpf [trʊmpf] (-(e)s, ⁻e) *m* (*auch fig*) trump; **t~en** *vt, vi* to trump

Trunk [trʊŋk] (-(e)s, ⁻e) *m* drink; **t~en** *adj* intoxicated; **~enheit** *f* intoxication; **~enheit am Steuer** drunken driving; **~sucht** *f* alcoholism

Trupp [trʊp] (-s, -s) *m* troop; **~e** *f* troop; (*Waffengattung*) force; (*Schauspieltruppe*) troupe; **~en** *pl* (*MIL*) troops; **~enübungsplatz** *m* training area

Truthahn ['truːthaːn] *m* turkey

Tschech- ['tʃɛç] *zW*: **~e** *m* Czech; **~ien** (-s) *nt* the Czech Republic; **~in** *f* Czech; **t~isch** *adj* Czech; **~oslowakei** [-oslova'kaɪ] *f*: **die ~oslowakei** Czechoslovakia; **t~oslowakisch** [-oslo'va:kɪʃ] *adj* Czechoslovak(ian)

tschüs(s) [tʃʏs] *excl* cheerio

T-Shirt ['tiːʃəːt] *nt* T-shirt

Tube ['tuːbə] *f* tube

Tuberkulose [tuberku'loːzə] *f* tuberculosis

Tuch [tuːx] (-(e)s, ⁻er) *nt* cloth; (*Halstuch*) scarf; (*Kopftuch*) headscarf; (*Handtuch*) towel

tüchtig ['tʏçtɪç] *adj* efficient, (cap)able; (*umg: kräftig*) good, sound; **T~keit** *f* efficiency, ability

Tücke ['tʏkə] *f* (*Arglist*) malice; (*Trick*) trick; (*Schwierigkeit*) difficulty, problem

tückisch ['tʏkɪʃ] *adj* treacherous; (*böswillig*) malicious

Tugend ['tuːgənt] (-, -en) *f* virtue; **t~haft** *adj* virtuous

Tülle *f* spout

Tulpe ['tʊlpə] *f* tulip

Tumor ['tuːmɔr] (-s, -e) *m* tumour

Tümpel ['tʏmpəl] (-s, -) *m* pool, pond

Tumult [tu'mʊlt] (-(e)s, -e) *m* tumult

tun [tuːn] (*unreg*) *vt* (*machen*) to do; (*legen*) to put ♦ *vi* to act ♦ *vr*: **es tut sich etwas/ viel** something/a lot is happening; **jdm etw ~** (*antun*) to do sth to sb; **etw tut es auch** sth will do; **das tut nichts** that doesn't matter; **das tut nichts zur Sache** that's neither here nor there; **so ~ als ob** to act as if

tünchen ['tʏnçən] *vt* to whitewash

Tunfisch ▲ ['tuːnfɪʃ] *m* = **Thunfisch**

Tunke ['tʊŋkə] *f* sauce; **t~n** *vt* to dip, to dunk

tunlichst ['tuːnlɪçst] *adv* if at all possible; **~ bald** as soon as possible

Tunnel ['tʊnəl] (-s, -s *od* -) *m* tunnel

Tupfen ['tʊpfən] (-s, -) *m* dot, spot; **t~** *vt, vi* to dab; (*mit Farbe*) to dot

Tür [tyːr] (-, -en) *f* door

Turbine [tʊr'biːnə] *f* turbine

Türk- [tʏrk] *zW*: **~e** *m* Turk; **~ei** [tʏr'kaɪ] *f*: **die ~ei** Turkey; **~in** *f* Turk

Türkis [tʏr'kiːs] (-es, -e) *m* turquoise; **t~** *adj* turquoise

türkisch ['tʏrkɪʃ] *adj* Turkish

Türklinke *f* doorknob, door handle

Turm [tʊrm] (-(e)s, ⁻e) *m* tower; (*Kirchturm*) steeple; (*Sprungturm*) diving platform; (*SCHACH*) castle, rook

türmen ['tʏrmən] *vr* to tower up ♦ *vt* to heap up ♦ *vi* (*umg*) to scarper, to bolt

Turn- ['tʊrn] *zW*: **t~en** *vi* to do gymnastic exercises ♦ *vt* to perform; **~en** (-s) *nt* gymnastics; (*SCH*) physical education, P.E.; **~er(in)** (-s, -) *m(f)* gymnast; **~halle** *f* gym(nasium); **~hose** *f* gym shorts *pl*

Turnier [tʊr'niːr] (-s, -e) *nt* tournament

Turn- *zW*: **~schuh** *m* gym shoe; **~verein** *m* gymnastics club; **~zeug** *nt* gym things *pl*

Tusche ['tʊʃə] *f* Indian ink

tuscheln ['tʊʃəln] *vt, vi* to whisper

Tuschkasten *m* paintbox

Tüte ['tyːtə] *f* bag

tuten ['tuːtən] *vi* (*AUT*) to hoot (*BRIT*), to honk (*US*)

TÜV [tʏf] (**-s, -s**) *m abk* (= *Technischer Überwachungs-Verein*) ≈ MOT
Typ [ty:p] (**-s, -en**) *m* type; **~e** *f* (*TYP*) type
Typhus ['ty:fʊs] (**-**) *m* typhoid (fever)
typisch ['ty:pɪʃ] *adj*: **~** (**für**) typical (of)
Tyrann [ty'ran] (**-en, -en**) *m* tyrant; **~ei** [-'naɪ] *f* tyranny; **t~isch** *adj* tyrannical; **t~i'sieren** *vt* to tyrannize

U, u

u. a. *abk* = **unter anderem**
U-Bahn ['u:ba:n] *f* underground, tube
übel ['y:bəl] *adj* bad; (*moralisch*) bad, wicked; **jdm ist ~** sb feels sick; **~ gelaunt** bad-tempered; **jdm eine Bemerkung** *etc* **~ nehmen** to be offended at sb's remark *etc*; **Ü~** (**-s, -**) *nt* evil; (*Krankheit*) disease; **Ü~keit** *f* nausea
üben ['y:bən] *vt, vi* to exercise, to practise

SCHLÜSSELWORT

über ['y:bər] *präp +dat* **1** (*räumlich*) over, above; **zwei Grad über null** two degrees above zero

2 (*zeitlich*) over; **über der Arbeit einschlafen** to fall asleep over one's work
♦ *präp +akk* **1** (*räumlich*) over; (*hoch über auch*) above; (*quer über auch*) across
2 (*zeitlich*) over; **über Weihnachten** over Christmas; **über kurz oder lang** sooner or later
3 (*mit Zahlen*): **Kinder über 12 Jahren** children over *od* above 12 years of age; **ein Scheck über 200 Mark** a cheque for 200 marks
4 (*auf dem Wege*) via; **nach Köln über Aachen** to Cologne via Aachen; **ich habe es über die Auskunft erfahren** I found out from information
5 (*betreffend*) about; **ein Buch über ...** a book about *od* on ...; **über jdn/etw lachen** to laugh about *od* at sb/sth
6: **Macht über jdn haben** to have power over sb; **sie liebt ihn über alles** she loves him more than everything

♦ *adv* over; **über und über** over and over; **den ganzen Tag über** all day long; **jdm in etw** *dat* **über sein** to be superior to sb in sth

überall [y:bər'al] *adv* everywhere; **~'hin** *adv* everywhere
überanstrengen [y:bər'anʃtrɛŋən] *vt insep* to overexert ♦ *vr insep* to overexert o.s.
überarbeiten [y:bər'arbaɪtən] *vt insep* to revise, to rework ♦ *vr insep* to overwork (o.s.)
überaus ['y:bəraʊs] *adv* exceedingly
überbelichten ['y:bərbəlɪçtən] *vt* (*PHOT*) to overexpose
über'bieten (*unreg*) *vt insep* to outbid; (*übertreffen*) to surpass; (*Rekord*) to break
Überbleibsel ['y:bərblaɪpsəl] (**-s, -**) *nt* residue, remainder
Überblick ['y:bərblɪk] *m* view; (*fig: Darstellung*) survey, overview; (*Fähigkeit*): **~** (**über** +*akk*) grasp (of), overall view (of); **ü~en** [-'blɪkən] *vt insep* to survey
überbring- [y:bər'brɪŋ] *zW*: **~en** (*unreg*) *vt insep* to deliver, to hand over; **Ü~er** (**-s, -**) *m* bearer
überbrücken [y:bər'brʏkən] *vt insep* to bridge (over)
überbuchen ['y:bərbu:xən] *vt insep* to overbook
über'dauern *vt insep* to outlast
über'denken (*unreg*) *vt insep* to think over
überdies [y:bər'di:s] *adv* besides
überdimensional ['y:bərdimenzjona:l] *adj* oversize
Überdruss ▲ ['y:bərdrʊs] (**-es**) *m* weariness; **bis zum ~** ad nauseam
überdurchschnittlich ['y:bərdʊrçʃnɪtlɪç] *adj* above-average ♦ *adv* exceptionally
übereifrig ['y:bəraɪfrɪç] *adj* over-keen
übereilt [y:bər'aɪlt] *adj* (over)hasty, premature
überein- [y:bər'aɪn] *zW*: **~ander** [y:bərʔaɪ'nandər] *adv* one upon the other; (*sprechen*) about each other; **~kommen** (*unreg*) *vi* to agree; **Ü~kunft** (**-, -künfte**) *f* agreement; **~stimmen** *vi* to agree;

Spelling Reform: ▲ *new spelling* △ *old spelling (to be phased out)*

Ü~stimmung f agreement

überempfindlich ['y:bər|ɛmpfɪntlɪç] *adj* hypersensitive

überfahren [y:bər'fa:rən] (*unreg*) *vt insep* (*AUT*) to run over; (*fig*) to walk all over

Überfahrt ['y:bərfa:rt] f crossing

Überfall ['y:bərfal] *m* (*Banküberfall, MIL*) raid; (*auf jdn*) assault; **ü~en** [-'falən] (*unreg*) *vt insep* to attack; (*Bank*) to raid; (*besuchen*) to drop in on, to descend on

überfällig ['y:bərfɛlɪç] *adj* overdue

über'fliegen (*unreg*) *vt insep* to fly over, to overfly; (*Buch*) to skim through

Überfluss ▲ ['y:bərflʊs] *m*: ~ **(an** +*dat*) (super)abundance (of), excess (of)

überflüssig ['y:bərflʏsɪç] *adj* superfluous

über'fordern *vt insep* to demand too much of; (*Kräfte etc*) to overtax

über'führen *vt insep* (*Leiche etc*) to transport; (*Täter*) to have convicted

Über'führung f transport; conviction; (*Brücke*) bridge, overpass

über'füllt *adj* (*Schulen, Straßen*) overcrowded; (*Kurs*) oversubscribed

Übergabe ['y:bərga:bə] f handing over; (*MIL*) surrender

Übergang ['y:bərgaŋ] *m* crossing; (*Wandel, Überleitung*) transition

Übergangs- *zW*: **~lösung** f provisional solution, stopgap; **~zeit** f transitional period

über'geben (*unreg*) *vt insep* to hand over; (*MIL*) to surrender ♦ *vr insep* to be sick

übergehen ['y:bərge:ən] (*unreg*) *vi* (*Besitz*) to pass; (*zum Feind etc*) to go over, to defect; **~ in** +*akk* to turn into; **über'gehen** (*unreg*) *vt insep* to pass over, to omit

Übergewicht ['y:bərgəvɪçt] *nt* excess weight; (*fig*) preponderance

überglücklich ['y:bərglʏklɪç] *adj* overjoyed

Übergröße ['y:bərgrø:sə] f oversize

überhaupt [y:bər'haʊpt] *adv* at all; (*im Allgemeinen*) in general; (*besonders*) especially; **~ nicht/keine** not/none at all

überheblich [y:bər'he:plɪç] *adj* arrogant; Ü~keit f arrogance

über'holen *vt insep* to overtake; (*TECH*) to

overhaul

über'holt *adj* out-of-date, obsolete

Überholverbot [y:bər'ho:lfɛrbo:t] *nt* restriction on overtaking

über'hören *vt insep* not to hear; (*absichtlich*) to ignore

überirdisch ['y:bər|ɪrdɪʃ] *adj* supernatural, unearthly

über'laden (*unreg*) *vt insep* to overload ♦ *adj* (*fig*) cluttered

über'lassen (*unreg*) *vt insep*: **jdm etw ~** to leave sth to sb ♦ *vr insep*: **sich einer Sache** *dat* ~ to give o.s. over to sth

über'lasten *vt insep* to overload; (*Mensch*) to overtax

überlaufen ['y:bərlaʊfən] (*unreg*) *vi* (*Flüssigkeit*) to flow over; (*zum Feind etc*) to go over, to defect; **~ sein** to be inundated *od* besieged; **über'laufen** (*unreg*) *vt insep* (*Schauer etc*) to come over

über'leben *vt insep* to survive; **Über'lebende(r)** f(m) survivor

über'legen *vt insep* to consider ♦ *adj* superior; **ich muss es mir ~** I'll have to think about it; **Über'legenheit** f superiority

Über'legung f consideration, deliberation

über'liefern *vt insep* to hand down, to transmit

Überlieferung f tradition

überlisten [y:bər'lɪstən] *vt insep* to outwit

überm ['y:bərm] = **über dem**

Übermacht ['y:bərmaxt] f superior force, superiority; **übermächtig** ['y:bərmɛçtɪç] *adj* superior (in strength); (*Gefühl etc*) overwhelming

übermäßig ['y:bərmɛ:sɪç] *adj* excessive

Übermensch ['y:bərmɛnʃ] *m* superman; ü~lich *adj* superhuman

übermitteln [y:bər'mɪtəln] *vt insep* to convey

übermorgen ['y:bərmɔrgən] *adv* the day after tomorrow

Übermüdung [y:bər'my:dʊŋ] f fatigue, overtiredness

Übermut ['y:bərmu:t] *m* exuberance

übermütig ['y:bərmy:tɪç] *adj* exuberant,

high-spirited; **~ werden** to get overconfident

übernächste(r, s) ['y:bərnɛ:çstə(r, s)] *adj* (*Jahr*) next but one

übernacht- [y:bər'naxt] *zW*: **~en** *vi insep*: **(bei jdm) ~en** to spend the night (at sb's place); **Ü~ung** *f* overnight stay; **Ü~ung mit Frühstück** bed and breakfast; **Ü~ungsmöglichkeit** *f* overnight accommodation *no pl*

Übernahme ['y:bərna:mə] *f* taking over *od* on, acceptance

über'nehmen (*unreg*) *vt insep* to take on, to accept; (*Amt, Geschäft*) to take over ♦ *vr insep* to take on too much

über'prüfen *vt insep* to examine, to check

überqueren [y:bər'kve:rən] *vt insep* to cross

überragen [y:bər'ra:gən] *vt insep* to tower above; (*fig*) to surpass

überraschen [y:bər'raʃən] *vt insep* to surprise

Überraschung *f* surprise

überreden [y:bər're:dən] *vt insep* to persuade

überreichen [y:bər'raiçən] *vt insep* to present, to hand over

'Überrest *m* remains, remnants

überrumpeln [y:bər'rompəln] *vt insep* to take by surprise

überrunden [y:bər'rondən] *vt insep* to lap

übers ['y:bərs] = **über das**

Überschall- ['y:bərʃal] *zW*: **~flugzeug** *nt* supersonic jet; **~geschwindigkeit** *f* supersonic speed

über'schätzen *vt insep* to overestimate

'überschäumen *vi* (*Bier*) to foam over, bubble over; (*Temperament*) to boil over

Überschlag ['y:bərʃla:k] *m* (*FIN*) estimate; (*SPORT*) somersault; **ü~en** [-'ʃla:gən] (*unreg*) *vt insep* (*berechnen*) to estimate; (*auslassen*: *Seite*) to omit ♦ *vr insep* to somersault; (*Stimme*) to crack; (*AVIAT*) to loop the loop; **'überschlagen** (*unreg*) *vt* (*Beine*) to cross ♦ *vi* (*Wellen*) to break; (*Funken*) to flash

überschnappen ['y:bərʃnapən] *vi* (*Stimme*) to crack; (*umg*: *Mensch*) to flip one's lid

über'schneiden (*unreg*) *vr insep* (*auch fig*) to overlap; (*Linien*) to intersect

über'schreiben (*unreg*) *vt insep* to provide with a heading; **jdm etw ~** to transfer *od* make over sth to sb

über'schreiten (*unreg*) *vt insep* to cross over; (*fig*) to exceed; (*verletzen*) to transgress

Überschrift ['y:bərʃrift] *f* heading, title

Überschuss ▲ ['y:bərʃʊs] *m*: **~ (an** +*dat*) surplus (of); **überschüssig** ['y:bərʃysɪç] *adj* surplus, excess

über'schütten *vt insep*: **jdn/etw mit etw ~** to pour sth over sb/sth; **jdn mit etw ~** (*fig*) to shower sb with sth

überschwänglich ▲ ['y:bərʃvɛŋlɪç] *adj* effusive

überschwemmen [y:bər'ʃvemən] *vt insep* to flood

Überschwemmung *f* flood

Übersee ['y:bərze:] *f*: **nach/in ~** overseas; **ü~isch** *adj* overseas

über'sehen (*unreg*) *vt insep* to look (out) over; (*fig*: *Folgen*) to see, to get an overall view of; (: *nicht beachten*) to overlook

über'senden (*unreg*) *vt insep* to send, to forward

übersetz- *zW*: **~en** [y:bər'zetsən] *vt insep* to translate; **'übersetzen** *vi* to cross; **Ü~er(in)** [-'zetsər(ɪn)] (**-s, -**) *m(f)* translator; **Ü~ung** [-'zetsʊŋ] *f* translation; (*TECH*) gear ratio

Übersicht ['y:bərzɪçt] *f* overall view; (*Darstellung*) survey; **ü~lich** *adj* clear; (*Gelände*) open; **~lichkeit** *f* clarity, lucidity

übersiedeln ['y:bərzi:dəln] *vi sep* to move; **über'siedeln** *vi* to move

über'spannt *adj* eccentric; (*Idee*) wild, crazy

überspitzt [y:bər'ʃpɪtst] *adj* exaggerated

über'springen (*unreg*) *vt insep* to jump over; (*fig*) to skip

überstehen [y:bər'ʃte:ən] (*unreg*) *vt insep* to overcome, to get over; (*Winter etc*) to survive, to get through; **'überstehen** (*unreg*) *vi* to project

über'steigen (*unreg*) *vt insep* to climb over; (*fig*) to exceed

über'stimmen vt insep to outvote

Überstunden ['y:bərʃtʊndən] pl overtime sg

über'stürzen vt insep to rush ♦ vr insep to follow (one another) in rapid succession

überstürzt adj (over)hasty

Übertrag ['y:bərtra:k] (-(e)s, -träge) m (COMM) amount brought forward; **ü~bar** [-'tra:kba:r] adj transferable; (MED) infectious; **ü~en** [-'tra:gən] (unreg) vt insep to transfer; (RADIO) to broadcast; (übersetzen) to render; (Krankheit) to transmit ♦ vr insep to spread ♦ adj figurative; **ü~en auf** +akk to transfer to; **jdm etw ü~en** to assign sth to sb; **sich ü~en auf** +akk to spread to; **~ung** [-'tra:gʊŋ] f transfer(ence); (RADIO) broadcast; rendering; transmission

über'treffen (unreg) vt insep to surpass

über'treiben (unreg) vt insep to exaggerate; **Übertreibung** f exaggeration

übertreten [y:bər'tre:tən] (unreg) vt insep to cross; (Gebot etc) to break; **'übertreten** (unreg) vi (über Linie, Gebiet) to step (over); (SPORT) to overstep; (zu anderem Glauben) to be converted; **'übertreten (in** +akk) (POL) to go over (to)

Über'tretung f violation, transgression

übertrieben [y:bər'tri:bən] adj exaggerated, excessive

übervölkert [y:bər'fœlkərt] adj overpopulated

übervoll ['y:bərfɔl] adj overfull

übervorteilen [y:bər'fɔrtailən] vt insep to dupe, to cheat

über'wachen vt insep to supervise; (Verdächtigen) to keep under surveillance; **Überwachung** f supervision; surveillance

überwältigen [y:bər'vɛltigən] vt insep to overpower; **~d** adj overwhelming

überweisen [y:bər'vaizən] (unreg) vt insep to transfer

Überweisung f transfer; **~sauftrag** m (credit) transfer order

über'wiegen (unreg) vi insep to predominate; **~d** adj predominant

über'winden (unreg) vt insep to overcome ♦ vr insep to make an effort, to bring o.s. (to do sth)

Überwindung f effort, strength of mind

Überzahl ['y:bərtsa:l] f superiority, superior numbers pl; **in der ~ sein** to be numerically superior

überzählig ['y:bərtsɛ:lɪç] adj surplus

über'zeugen vt insep to convince; **~d** adj convincing

Überzeugung f conviction

überziehen ['y:bərtsi:ən] (unreg) vt to put on; **über'ziehen** (unreg) vt insep to cover; (Konto) to overdraw

Überziehungskredit m overdraft provision

Überzug ['y:bərtsu:k] m cover; (Belag) coating

üblich ['y:plɪç] adj usual

U-Boot ['u:bo:t] nt submarine

übrig ['y:brɪç] adj remaining; **für jdn etwas ~ haben** (umg) to be fond of sb; **die Ü~en** the others; **das Ü~e** the rest; **im Ü~en** besides; **~ bleiben** to remain, to be left (over); **~ lassen** to leave (over); **~ens** ['y:brɪgəns] adv besides; (nebenbei bemerkt) by the way

Übung ['y:bʊŋ] f practice; (Turnübung, Aufgabe etc) exercise; **~ macht den Meister** practice makes perfect

Ufer ['u:fər] (-s, -) nt bank; (Meeresufer) shore

Uhr [u:r] (-, -en) f clock; (Armbanduhr) watch; **wie viel ~ ist es?** what time is it?; **1 ~** 1 o'clock; **20 ~** 8 o'clock, 20.00 (twenty hundred) hours; **~(arm)band** nt watch strap; **~band** nt watch strap; **~macher** (-s, -) m watchmaker; **~werk** nt clockwork; works of a watch; **~zeiger** m hand; **~zeigersinn** m: **im ~zeigersinn** clockwise; **entgegen dem ~zeigersinn** anticlockwise; **~zeit** f time (of day)

Uhu ['u:hu] (-s, -s) m eagle owl

UKW [u:ka:'ve:] abk (= Ultrakurzwelle) VHF

ulkig ['ʊlkɪç] adj funny

Ulme ['ʊlmə] f elm

Ultimatum [ʊlti'ma:tʊm] (-s, Ultimaten) nt ultimatum

Ultra- ['ʊltra] zW: **~schall** m (PHYS) ultrasound; **u~violett** adj ultraviolet

um [ʊm] *präp +akk* **1** (*um herum*) (a)round; **um Weihnachten** around Christmas; **er schlug um sich** he hit about him **2** (*mit Zeitangabe*) at; **um acht (Uhr)** at eight (o'clock) **3** (*mit Größenangabe*) by; **etw um 4 cm kürzen** to shorten sth by 4 cm; **um 10% teurer** 10% more expensive; **um vieles besser** better by far; **um nichts besser** not in the least bit better **4**: **der Kampf um den Titel** the battle for the title; **um Geld spielen** to play for money; **Stunde um Stunde** hour after hour; **Auge um Auge** an eye for an eye
♦ *präp +gen*: **um ... willen** for the sake of ...; **um Gottes willen** for goodness *od* (*stärker*) God's sake
♦ *konj*: **um ... zu** (in order) to ...; **zu klug, um zu ...** too clever to ...; *siehe* **umso**
♦ *adv* **1** (*ungefähr*) about; **um (die) 30 Leute** about *od* around 30 people **2** (*vorbei*): **die 2 Stunden sind um** the two hours are up

umändern ['ʊm|ɛndərn] *vt* to alter
Umänderung *f* alteration
umarbeiten ['ʊm|arbaɪtən] *vt* to remodel; (*Buch etc*) to revise, to rework
umarmen [ʊm'|armən] *vt insep* to embrace
Umbau ['ʊmbaʊ] (**-(e)s, -e** *od* **-ten**) *m* reconstruction, alteration(s); **u~en** *vt* to rebuild, to reconstruct
umbilden ['ʊmbɪldən] *vt* to reorganize; (*POL: Kabinett*) to reshuffle
umbinden ['ʊmbɪndən] (*unreg*) *vt* (*Krawatte etc*) to put on
umblättern ['ʊmblɛtərn] *vt* to turn over
umblicken ['ʊmblɪkən] *vr* to look around
umbringen ['ʊmbrɪŋən] (*unreg*) *vt* to kill
umbuchen ['ʊmbuːxən] *vi* to change one's reservation/flight *etc* ♦ *vt* to change
umdenken ['ʊmdɛŋkən] (*unreg*) *vi* to adjust one's views
umdrehen ['ʊmdreːən] *vt* to turn (round); (*Hals*) to wring ♦ *vr* to turn (round)

Um'drehung *f* revolution; rotation
umeinander [ʊm|aɪ'nandər] *adv* round one another; (*füreinander*) for one another
umfahren ['ʊmfaːrən] (*unreg*) *vt* to run over; **um'fahren** (*unreg*) *vt insep* to drive round; to sail round
umfallen ['ʊmfalən] (*unreg*) *vi* to fall down *od* over
Umfang ['ʊmfaŋ] *m* extent; (*von Buch*) size; (*Reichweite*) range; (*Fläche*) area; (*MATH*) circumference; **u~reich** *adj* extensive; (*Buch etc*) voluminous
um'fassen *vt insep* to embrace; (*umgeben*) to surround; (*enthalten*) to include; **um'fassend** *adj* comprehensive, extensive
umformen ['ʊmfɔrmən] *vt* to transform
Umfrage ['ʊmfraːgə] *f* poll
umfüllen ['ʊmfʏlən] *vt* to transfer; (*Wein*) to decant
umfunktionieren ['ʊmfʊŋktsioniːrən] *vt* to convert, to transform
Umgang ['ʊmgaŋ] *m* company; (*mit jdm*) dealings *pl*; (*Behandlung*) way of behaving
umgänglich ['ʊmgɛŋlɪç] *adj* sociable
Umgangs- *zW*: **~formen** *pl* manners; **~sprache** *f* colloquial language
umgeben [ʊm'geːbən] (*unreg*) *vt insep* to surround
Umgebung *f* surroundings *pl*; (*Milieu*) environment; (*Personen*) people in one's circle
umgehen ['ʊmgeːən] (*unreg*) *vi* to go (a)round; **im Schlosse ~** to haunt the castle; **mit jdm grob** *etc* **~** to treat sb roughly *etc*; **mit Geld sparsam ~** to be careful with one's money; **um'gehen** *vt insep* to bypass; (*MIL*) to outflank; (*Gesetz etc*) to circumvent; (*vermeiden*) to avoid; **'umgehend** *adj* immediate
Um'gehung *f* bypassing; outflanking; circumvention; avoidance; **~sstraße** *f* bypass
umgekehrt ['ʊmgəkeːrt] *adj* reverse(d); (*gegenteilig*) opposite ♦ *adv* the other way around; **und ~** and vice versa
umgraben ['ʊmgraːbən] (*unreg*) *vt* to dig up
Umhang ['ʊmhaŋ] *m* wrap, cape

umhauen ['ʊmhaʊən] vt to fell; (fig) to bowl over

umher [ʊm'he:r] adv about, around; **~gehen** (unreg) vi to walk about; **~ziehen** (unreg) vi to wander from place to place

umhinkönnen [ʊm'hɪnkœnən] (unreg) vi: **ich kann nicht umhin, das zu tun** I can't help doing it

umhören ['ʊmhø:rən] vr to ask around

Umkehr ['ʊmke:r] (-) f turning back; (Änderung) change; **u~en** vi to turn back ♦ vt to turn round, to reverse; (Tasche etc) to turn inside out; (Gefäß etc) to turn upside down

umkippen ['ʊmkɪpən] vt to tip over ♦ vi to overturn; (umg: Mensch) to keel over; (fig: Meinung ändern) to change one's mind

Umkleide- ['ʊmklaɪdə] zW: **~kabine** f (im Schwimmbad) (changing) cubicle; **~raum** m changing od dressing room

umkommen ['ʊmkɔmən] (unreg) vi to die, to perish; (Lebensmittel) to go bad

Umkreis ['ʊmkraɪs] m neighbourhood; **im ~ von** within a radius of

Umlage ['ʊmla:gə] f share of the costs

Umlauf ['ʊmlaʊf] m (Geldumlauf) circulation; (von Gestirn) revolution; **~bahn** f orbit

Umlaut ['ʊmlaʊt] m umlaut

umlegen ['ʊmle:gən] vt to put on; (verlegen) to move, to shift; (Kosten) to share out; (umkippen) to tip over; (umg: töten) to bump off

umleiten ['ʊmlaɪtən] vt to divert

Umleitung f diversion

umliegend ['ʊmli:gənt] adj surrounding

um'randen vt insep to border, to edge

umrechnen ['ʊmrɛçnən] vt to convert

Umrechnung f conversion; **~skurs** m rate of exchange

um'reißen (unreg) vt insep to outline, to sketch

Umriss ▲ ['ʊmrɪs] m outline

umrühren ['ʊmry:rən] vt, vi to stir

ums [ʊms] = **um das**

Umsatz ['ʊmzats] m turnover; **~steuer** f sales tax

umschalten ['ʊmʃaltən] vt to switch

umschauen vr to look round

Umschlag ['ʊmʃla:k] m cover; (Buchumschlag auch) jacket; (MED) compress; (Briefumschlag) envelope; (Wechsel) change; (von Hose) turn-up; **u~en** [-gən] (unreg) vi to change; (NAUT) to capsize ♦ vt to knock over; (Ärmel) to turn up; (Seite) to turn over; (Waren) to transfer; **~platz** m (COMM) distribution centre

umschreiben ['ʊmʃraɪbən] (unreg) vt (neu schreiben) to rewrite; (übertragen) to transfer; **~ auf** +akk to transfer to; **um'schreiben** (unreg) vt insep to paraphrase; (abgrenzen) to define

umschulen ['ʊmʃu:lən] vt to retrain; (Kind) to send to another school

Umschweife ['ʊmʃvaɪfə] pl: **ohne ~** without beating about the bush, straight out

Umschwung ['ʊmʃvʊŋ] m change (around), revolution

umsehen ['ʊmze:ən] (unreg) vr to look around od about; (suchen): **sich ~ (nach)** to look out (for)

umseitig ['ʊmzaɪtɪç] adv overleaf

umsichtig ['ʊmzɪçtɪç] adj cautious, prudent

umso ▲ ['ʊmzo] konj: **~ besser/schlimmer** so much the better/worse

umsonst [ʊm'zɔnst] adv in vain; (gratis) for nothing

umspringen ['ʊmʃprɪŋən] (unreg) vi to change; (Wind auch) to veer; **mit jdm ~ to** treat sb badly

Umstand ['ʊmʃtant] m circumstance; **Umstände** pl (fig: Schwierigkeiten) fuss; **in anderen Umständen sein** to be pregnant; **Umstände machen** to go to a lot of trouble; **unter Umständen** possibly

umständlich ['ʊmʃtɛntlɪç] adj (Methode) cumbersome, complicated; (Ausdrucksweise, Erklärung) long-winded; (Mensch) ponderous

Umstandskleid nt maternity dress

Umstehende(n) ['ʊmʃte:əndə(n)] pl bystanders

umsteigen ['ʊmʃtaɪgən] (unreg) vi (EISENB) to change

umstellen ['ʊmʃtɛlən] vt (an anderen Ort) to

change round, to rearrange; (*TECH*) to convert ♦ *vr* to adapt (o.s.); **sich auf etw** *akk* ~ to adapt to sth; **um'stellen** *vt insep* to surround

Umstellung ['ʊmʃtɛlʊŋ] *f* change; (*Umgewöhnung*) adjustment; (*TECH*) conversion

umstimmen ['ʊmʃtɪmən] *vt* (*MUS*) to retune; **jdn** ~ to make sb change his mind

umstoßen ['ʊmʃtoːsən] (*unreg*) *vt* to overturn; (*Plan etc*) to change, to upset

umstritten [ʊm'ʃtrɪtən] *adj* disputed

Umsturz ['ʊmʃtʊrts] *m* overthrow

umstürzen ['ʊmʃtʏrtsən] *vt* (*umwerfen*) to overturn ♦ *vi* to collapse, to fall down; (*Wagen*) to overturn

Umtausch ['ʊmtaʊʃ] *m* exchange; **u~en** *vt* to exchange

Umverpackung ['ʊmfɛrpakʊŋ] *f* packaging

umwandeln ['ʊmvandəln] *vt* to change, to convert; (*ELEK*) to transform

umwechseln ['ʊmvɛksəln] *vt* to change

Umweg ['ʊmveːk] *m* detour, roundabout way

Umwelt ['ʊmvɛlt] *f* environment; **u~freundlich** *adj* not harmful to the environment, environment-friendly; **u~schädlich** *adj* ecologically harmful; ~**schutz** *m* environmental protection; ~**schützer** *m* environmentalist; ~**verschmutzung** *f* environmental pollution

umwenden ['ʊmvɛndən] (*unreg*) *vt, vr* to turn (round)

umwerfen ['ʊmvɛrfən] (*unreg*) *vt* to upset, to overturn; (*fig: erschüttern*) to upset, to throw; ~**d** (*umg*) *adj* fantastic

umziehen ['ʊmtsiːən] (*unreg*) *vt, vr* to change ♦ *vi* to move

Umzug ['ʊmtsuːk] *m* procession; (*Wohnungsumzug*) move, removal

unab- ['ʊn|ap] *zW*: ~**änderlich** *adj* irreversible, unalterable; ~**hängig** *adj* independent; **U~hängigkeit** *f* independence; ~**kömmlich** *adj* indispensable; **zur Zeit ~kömmlich** not free at the moment; ~**lässig** *adj* incessant,

constant; ~**sehbar** *adj* immeasurable; (*Folgen*) unforeseeable; (*Kosten*) incalculable; ~**sichtlich** *adj* unintentional; ~'**wendbar** *adj* inevitable

unachtsam ['ʊn|axtzaːm] *adj* careless; **U~keit** *f* carelessness

unan- ['ʊn|an] *zW*: ~'**fechtbar** *adj* indisputable; ~**gebracht** *adj* uncalled-for; ~**gemessen** *adj* inadequate; ~**genehm** *adj* unpleasant; **U~nehmlichkeit** *f* inconvenience; **U~nehmlichkeiten** *pl* (*Ärger*) trouble *sg*; ~**sehnlich** *adj* unsightly; ~**ständig** *adj* indecent, improper

unappetitlich ['ʊn|apetiːtlɪç] *adj* unsavoury

Unart ['ʊn|aːrt] *f* bad manners *pl*; (*Angewohnheit*) bad habit; **u~ig** *adj* naughty, badly behaved

unauf- ['ʊn|aʊf] *zW*: ~**fällig** *adj* unobtrusive; (*Kleidung*) inconspicuous; ~'**findbar** *adj* not to be found; ~**gefordert** *adj* unasked ♦ *adv* spontaneously; ~**haltsam** *adj* irresistible; ~'**hörlich** *adj* incessant, continuous; ~**merksam** *adj* inattentive; ~**richtig** *adj* insincere

unaus- ['ʊn|aʊs] *zW*: ~**geglichen** *adj* unbalanced; ~'**sprechlich** *adj* inexpressible; ~'**stehlich** *adj* intolerable

unbarmherzig ['ʊnbarmhɛrtsɪç] *adj* pitiless, merciless

unbeabsichtigt ['ʊnbə|apzɪçtɪçt] *adj* unintentional

unbeachtet ['ʊnbə|axtət] *adj* unnoticed, ignored

unbedenklich ['ʊnbədɛŋklɪç] *adj* (*Plan*) unobjectionable

unbedeutend ['ʊnbədɔʏtənt] *adj* insignificant, unimportant; (*Fehler*) slight

unbedingt ['ʊnbədɪŋt] *adj* unconditional ♦ *adv* absolutely; **musst du ~ gehen?** do you really have to go?

unbefangen ['ʊnbəfaŋən] *adj* impartial, unprejudiced; (*ohne Hemmungen*) uninhibited; **U~heit** *f* impartiality; uninhibitedness

unbefriedigend ['ʊnbəfriːdɪɡənd] *adj* unsatisfactory

unbefriedigt ['ʊnbəfriːdɪçt] *adj* unsatisfied,

Spelling Reform: ▲ *new spelling* △ *old spelling (to be phased out)*

dissatisfied
unbefugt ['ʊnbəfuːkt] *adj* unauthorized
unbegreiflich [ʊnbə'graiflɪç] *adj*
inconceivable
unbegrenzt ['ʊnbəgrɛntst] *adj* unlimited
unbegründet ['ʊnbəgryndət] *adj* unfounded
Unbehagen ['ʊnbəhaːgən] *nt* discomfort;
unbehaglich ['ʊnbəhaːklɪç] *adj*
uncomfortable; (*Gefühl*) uneasy
unbeholfen ['ʊnbəhɔlfən] *adj* awkward,
clumsy
unbekannt ['ʊnbəkant] *adj* unknown
unbekümmert ['ʊnbəkymərt] *adj*
unconcerned
unbeliebt ['ʊnbəliːpt] *adj* unpopular
unbequem ['ʊnbəkveːm] *adj* (*Stuhl*)
uncomfortable; (*Mensch*) bothersome;
(*Regelung*) inconvenient
unberechenbar [ʊnbə'rɛçənbaːr] *adj*
incalculable; (*Mensch, Verhalten*)
unpredictable
unberechtigt ['ʊnbərɛçtɪçt] *adj* unjustified;
(*nicht erlaubt*) unauthorized
unberührt ['ʊnbəryːrt] *adj* untouched,
intact; **sie ist noch ~** she is still a virgin
unbescheiden ['ʊnbəʃaidən] *adj*
presumptuous
unbeschreiblich [ʊnbə'ʃraiplɪç] *adj*
indescribable
unbeständig ['ʊnbəʃtɛndɪç] *adj* (*Mensch*)
inconstant; (*Wetter*) unsettled; (*Lage*)
unstable
unbestechlich [ʊnbə'ʃtɛçlɪç] *adj*
incorruptible
unbestimmt ['ʊnbəʃtɪmt] *adj* indefinite;
(*Zukunft auch*) uncertain
unbeteiligt [ʊnbə'tailɪçt] *adj* unconcerned,
indifferent
unbeweglich ['ʊnbəveːklɪç] *adj* immovable
unbewohnt ['ʊnbəvoːnt] *adj* uninhabited;
(*Wohnung*) unoccupied
unbewusst ▲ ['ʊnbəvʊst] *adj* unconscious
unbezahlt ['ʊnbətsaːlt] *adj* (*Rechnung*)
outstanding, unsettled; (*Urlaub*) unpaid
unbrauchbar ['ʊnbrauxbaːr] *adj* (*Arbeit*)
useless; (*Gerät auch*) unusable
und [ʊnt] *konj* and; **~ so weiter** and so on

Undank ['ʊndaŋk] *m* ingratitude; **u~bar** *adj*
ungrateful
undefinierbar [ʊndefi'niːrbaːr] *adj*
indefinable
undenkbar [ʊn'dɛŋkbaːr] *adj* inconceivable
undeutlich ['ʊndɔytlɪç] *adj* indistinct
undicht ['ʊndɪçt] *adj* leaky
Unding ['ʊndɪŋ] *nt* absurdity
undurch- ['ʊndʊrç] *zW:* **~führbar** [-'fyːrbaːr]
adj impracticable; **~lässig** [-'lɛsɪç]
waterproof, impermeable; **~sichtig** [-'zɪçtɪç]
adj opaque; (*fig*) obscure
uneben ['ʊn|eːbən] *adj* uneven
unecht ['ʊn|ɛçt] *adj* (*Schmuck*) fake;
(*vorgetäuscht: Freundlichkeit*) false
unehelich ['ʊn|eːəlɪç] *adj* illegitimate
uneinig ['ʊn|ainɪç] *adj* divided; **~ sein** to
disagree; **U~keit** *f* discord, dissension
uneins ['ʊn|ains] *adj* at variance, at odds
unempfindlich ['ʊn|ɛmpfɪntlɪç] *adj*
insensitive; (*Stoff*) practical
unendlich [ʊn'|ɛntlɪç] *adj* infinite
unent- ['ʊn|ɛnt] *zW:* **~behrlich** [-'beːrlɪç] *adj*
indispensable; **~geltlich** [-gɛltlɪç] *adj* free
(of charge); **~schieden** [-ʃiːdən] *adj*
undecided; **~schieden enden** (*SPORT*) to
end in a draw; **~schlossen** [-ʃlɔsən] *adj*
undecided; irresolute; **~wegt** [-'veːkt] *adj*
unswerving; (*unaufhörlich*) incessant
uner- ['ʊn|ɛr] *zW:* **~bittlich** [-'bɪtlɪç] *adj*
unyielding, inexorable; **~fahren** [-faːrən]
adj inexperienced; **~freulich** [-frɔylɪç]
adj unpleasant; **~gründlich** *adj* unfathomable;
~hört [-høːrt] *adj* unheard-of; (*Bitte*)
outrageous; **~lässlich** ▲ [-'lɛslɪç] *adj*
indispensable; **~laubt** *adj* unauthorized;
~messlich ▲ *adj* immeasurable,
immense; **~reichbar** *adj* (*Ziel*)
unattainable; (*Ort*) inaccessible; (*telefonisch*)
unobtainable; **~schöpflich** [-'ʃœpflɪç] *adj*
inexhaustible; **~schwinglich** [-'ʃvɪŋlɪç] *adj*
(*Preis*) exorbitant; too expensive; **~träglich**
[-'trɛːklɪç] *adj* unbearable; (*Frechheit*)
insufferable; **~wartet** *adj* unexpected;
~wünscht *adj* undesirable, unwelcome
unfähig ['ʊnfɛːɪç] *adj* incapable,
incompetent; **zu etw ~ sein** to be

incapable of sth; **U~keit** *f* incapacity; incompetence

unfair ['ʊnfɛːr] *adj* unfair

Unfall ['ʊnfal] *m* accident; **~flucht** *f* hit-and-run (driving); **~schaden** *m* damages *pl*; **~station** *f* emergency ward; **~stelle** *f* scene of the accident; **~versicherung** *f* accident insurance

unfassbar ▲ [ʊn'fasbaːr] *adj* inconceivable

unfehlbar [ʊn'feːlbaːr] *adj* infallible ♦ *adv* inevitably; **U~keit** *f* infallibility

unförmig ['ʊnfœrmɪç] *adj* (*formlos*) shapeless

unfrei ['ʊnfraɪ] *adj* not free, unfree; (*Paket*) unfranked; **~willig** *adj* involuntary, against one's will

unfreundlich ['ʊnfrɔʏntlɪç] *adj* unfriendly; **U~keit** *f* unfriendliness

Unfriede(n) ['ʊnfriːdə(n)] *m* dissension, strife

unfruchtbar ['ʊnfrʊxtbaːr] *adj* infertile; (*Gespräche*) unfruitful; **U~keit** *f* infertility; unfruitfulness

Unfug ['ʊnfuːk] **(-s)** *m* (*Benehmen*) mischief; (*Unsinn*) nonsense; **grober ~** (*JUR*) gross misconduct; malicious damage

Ungar(in) ['ʊŋgar(ɪn)] *m(f)* Hungarian; **u~isch** *adj* Hungarian; **~n** *nt* Hungary

ungeachtet ['ʊngə|axtət] *präp* +*gen* notwithstanding

ungeahnt ['ʊngə|aːnt] *adj* unsuspected, undreamt-of

ungebeten ['ʊngəbeːtən] *adj* uninvited

ungebildet ['ʊngəbɪldət] *adj* uneducated; uncultured

ungedeckt ['ʊngədɛkt] *adj* (*Scheck*) uncovered

Ungeduld ['ʊngədʊlt] *f* impatience; **u~ig** [-dɪç] *adj* impatient

ungeeignet ['ʊngə|aɪgnət] *adj* unsuitable

ungefähr ['ʊngəfɛːr] *adj* rough, approximate; **das kommt nicht von ~** that's hardly surprising

ungefährlich ['ʊngəfɛːrlɪç] *adj* not dangerous, harmless

ungehalten ['ʊngəhaltən] *adj* indignant

ungeheuer ['ʊngəhɔʏər] *adj* huge ♦ *adv* (*umg*) enormously; **U~ (-s, -)** *nt* monster;

~lich [-'hɔʏərlɪç] *adj* monstrous

ungehörig ['ʊngəhøːrɪç] *adj* impertinent, improper

ungehorsam ['ʊngəhoːrzaːm] *adj* disobedient; **U~** *m* disobedience

ungeklärt ['ʊngəklɛːrt] *adj* not cleared up; (*Rätsel*) unsolved

ungeladen ['ʊngəlaːdən] *adj* not loaded; (*Gast*) uninvited

ungelegen ['ʊngəleːgən] *adj* inconvenient

ungelernt ['ʊngəlɛrnt] *adj* unskilled

ungelogen ['ʊngəloːgən] *adv* really, honestly

ungemein ['ʊngəmaɪn] *adj* uncommon

ungemütlich ['ʊngəmyːtlɪç] *adj* uncomfortable; (*Person*) disagreeable

ungenau ['ʊngənaʊ] *adj* inaccurate; **U~igkeit** *f* inaccuracy

ungenießbar ['ʊngəniːsbaːr] *adj* inedible; undrinkable; (*umg*) unbearable

ungenügend ['ʊngənyːgənt] *adj* insufficient, inadequate

ungepflegt ['ʊngəpfleːkt] *adj* (*Garten etc*) untended; (*Person*) unkempt; (*Hände*) neglected

ungerade ['ʊngəraːdə] *adj* uneven, odd

ungerecht ['ʊngəreçt] *adj* unjust; **~fertigt** *adj* unjustified; **U~igkeit** *f* injustice, unfairness

ungern ['ʊngɛrn] *adv* unwillingly, reluctantly

ungeschehen ['ʊngəʃeːən] *adj*: **~ machen** to undo

Ungeschicklichkeit ['ʊngəʃɪklɪçkaɪt] *f* clumsiness

ungeschickt *adj* awkward, clumsy

ungeschminkt ['ʊngəʃmɪŋkt] *adj* without make-up; (*fig*) unvarnished

ungesetzlich ['ʊngəzɛtslɪç] *adj* illegal

ungestört ['ʊngəʃtøːrt] *adj* undisturbed

ungestraft ['ʊngəʃtraːft] *adv* with impunity

ungestüm ['ʊngəʃtyːm] *adj* impetuous; tempestuous

ungesund ['ʊngəzʊnt] *adj* unhealthy

ungetrübt ['ʊngətryːpt] *adj* clear; (*fig*) untroubled; (*Freude*) unalloyed

Ungetüm ['ʊngətyːm] **(-(e)s, -e)** *nt* monster

ungewiss ▲ ['ʊngəvɪs] *adj* uncertain;

U~heit *f* uncertainty
ungewöhnlich ['ʊngəvøːnlɪç] *adj* unusual
ungewohnt ['ʊngəvoːnt] *adj* unaccustomed
Ungeziefer ['ʊngətsiːfər] **(-s)** *nt* vermin
ungezogen ['ʊngətsoːgən] *adj* rude,
impertinent; **U~heit** *f* rudeness,
impertinence
ungezwungen ['ʊngətsvʊŋən] *adj* natural,
unconstrained
unglaublich [ʊn'glaʊplɪç] *adj* incredible
ungleich ['ʊnglaɪç] *adj* dissimilar; unequal
♦ *adv* incomparably; **~artig** *adj* different;
U~heit *f* dissimilarity; inequality; **~mäßig**
adj irregular, uneven
Unglück ['ʊnglʏk] **(-(e)s, -e)** *nt* misfortune;
(*Pech*) bad luck; (*~sfall*) calamity, disaster;
(*Verkehrsunglück*) accident; **u~lich** *adj*
unhappy; (*erfolglos*) unlucky; (*unerfreulich*)
unfortunate; **u~licherweise** [-'vaɪzə] *adv*
unfortunately; **~sfall** *m* accident, calamity
ungültig ['ʊngʏltɪç] *adj* invalid; **U~keit** *f*
invalidity
ungünstig ['ʊngʏnstɪç] *adj* unfavourable
ungut ['ʊnguːt] *adj* (*Gefühl*) uneasy; **nichts**
für ~ no offence
unhaltbar ['ʊnhaltbaːr] *adj* untenable
Unheil ['ʊnhaɪl] *nt* evil; (*Unglück*) misfortune;
~ anrichten to cause mischief; **u~bar** *adj*
incurable
unheimlich ['ʊnhaɪmlɪç] *adj* weird, uncanny
♦ *adv* (*umg*) tremendously
unhöflich ['ʊnhøːflɪç] *adj* impolite; **U~keit** *f*
impoliteness
unhygienisch ['ʊnhygieːnɪʃ] *adj* unhygienic
Uni ['ʊni] **(-, -s)** (*umg*) *f* university
Uniform [uni'fɔrm] *f* uniform; **u~iert**
[-'miːrt] *adj* uniformed
uninteressant ['ʊn|ɪnteresant] *adj*
uninteresting
Uni- *zW:* **~versität** [univerzi'tɛːt] *f* university;
~versum [uni'verzʊm] **(-s)** *nt* universe
unkenntlich ['ʊnkentlɪç] *adj* unrecognizable
Unkenntnis ['ʊnkentnɪs] *f* ignorance
unklar ['ʊnklaːr] *adj* unclear; **im U~en sein**
über *+akk* to be in the dark about; **U~heit**
f unclarity; (*Unentschiedenheit*) uncertainty
unklug ['ʊnkluːk] *adj* unwise

Unkosten ['ʊnkɔstən] *pl* expense(s);
~beitrag *m* contribution to costs *od*
expenses
Unkraut ['ʊnkraʊt] *nt* weed; weeds *pl*
unkündbar ['ʊnkʏntbaːr] *adj* (*Stelle*)
permanent; (*Vertrag*) binding
unlauter ['ʊnlaʊtər] *adj* unfair
unleserlich ['ʊnleːzərlɪç] *adj* illegible
unlogisch ['ʊnloːgɪʃ] *adj* illogical
unlösbar [ʊn'løːsbar] *adj* insoluble
Unlust ['ʊnlʊst] *f* lack of enthusiasm
Unmenge ['ʊnmeŋə] *f* tremendous number,
hundreds *pl*
Unmensch ['ʊnmenʃ] *m* ogre, brute;
u~lich *adj* inhuman, brutal; (*ungeheuer*)
awful
unmerklich [ʊn'merklɪç] *adj* imperceptible
unmissverständlich ▲ ['ʊnmɪsferʃtentlɪç]
adj unmistakable
unmittelbar ['ʊnmɪtəlbaːr] *adj* immediate
unmodern ['ʊnmodern] *adj* old-fashioned
unmöglich ['ʊnmøːklɪç] *adj* impossible;
U~keit *f* impossibility
unmoralisch ['ʊnmoraːlɪʃ] *adj* immoral
Unmut ['ʊnmuːt] *m* ill humour
unnachgiebig ['ʊnnaːxgiːbɪç] *adj* unyielding
unnahbar [ʊn'naːbaːr] *adj* unapproachable
unnötig ['ʊnnøːtɪç] *adj* unnecessary
unnütz ['ʊnnʏts] *adj* useless
unordentlich ['ʊn|ɔrdəntlɪç] *adj* untidy
Unordnung ['ʊn|ɔrdnʊŋ] *f* disorder
unparteiisch ['ʊnpartaɪʃ] *adj* impartial;
U~e(r) *f(m)* umpire; (*FUSSBALL*) referee
unpassend ['ʊnpasənt] *adj* inappropriate;
(*Zeit*) inopportune
unpässlich ▲ ['ʊnpeslɪç] *adj* unwell
unpersönlich ['ʊnperzøːnlɪç] *adj* impersonal
unpolitisch ['ʊnpoliːtɪʃ] *adj* apolitical
unpraktisch ['ʊnpraktɪʃ] *adj* unpractical
unpünktlich ['ʊnpʏŋktlɪç] *adj* unpunctual
unrationell ['ʊnratsionel] *adj* inefficient
unrealistisch ['ʊnrealɪstɪʃ] *adj* unrealistic
unrecht ['ʊnreçt] *adj* wrong; **U~** *nt* wrong;
zu U~ wrongly; **U~ haben** to be wrong;
~mäßig *adj* unlawful, illegal
unregelmäßig ['ʊnreːgəlmɛːsɪç] *adj*
irregular; **U~keit** *f* irregularity

unreif ['ʊnraif] adj (Obst) unripe; (fig) immature

unrentabel ['ʊnrɛnta:bəl] adj unprofitable

unrichtig ['ʊnrɪçtɪç] adj incorrect, wrong

Unruhe ['ʊnru:ə] f unrest; **~stifter** m troublemaker

unruhig ['ʊnru:ɪç] adj restless

uns [ʊns] (akk, dat von **wir**) pron us; ourselves

unsachlich ['ʊnzaxlɪç] adj not to the point, irrelevant

unsagbar [ʊn'za:kba:r] adj indescribable

unsanft ['ʊnzanft] adj rough

unsauber ['ʊnzaubər] adj unclean, dirty; (fig) crooked; (MUS) fuzzy

unschädlich ['ʊnʃɛːtlɪç] adj harmless; **jdn/ etw ~ machen** to render sb/sth harmless

unscharf ['ʊnʃarf] adj indistinct; (Bild etc) out of focus, blurred

unscheinbar ['ʊnʃainba:r] adj insignificant; (Aussehen, Haus etc) unprepossessing

unschlagbar [ʊn'ʃla:kba:r] adj invincible

unschön ['ʊnʃøːn] adj (hässlich: Anblick) ugly, unattractive; (unfreundlich: Benehmen) unpleasant, ugly

Unschuld ['ʊnʃʊlt] f innocence; **u~ig** [-dɪç] adj innocent

unselbst(st)ändig ['ʊnzɛlpʃtɛndɪç] adj dependent, over-reliant on others

unser(e) ['ʊnzər(ə)] adj our; **~e(r, s)** pron ours; **~einer** pron people like us; **~eins** pron = **unsereiner; ~erseits** adv on our part; **~twegen** adv (für uns) for our sake; (wegen uns) on our account; **~twillen** adv: **um ~twillen = unsertwegen**

unsicher ['ʊnzɪçər] adj uncertain; (Mensch) insecure; **U~heit** f uncertainty; insecurity

unsichtbar ['ʊnzɪçtba:r] adj invisible

Unsinn ['ʊnzɪn] m nonsense; **u~ig** adj nonsensical

Unsitte ['ʊnzɪtə] f deplorable habit

unsozial ['ʊnzotsia:l] adj (Verhalten) antisocial

unsportlich ['ʊnʃpɔrtlɪç] adj not sporty; unfit; (Verhalten) unsporting

unsre ['ʊnzrə] = **unsere**

unsterblich ['ʊnʃtɛrplɪç] adj immortal

Unstimmigkeit ['ʊnʃtɪmɪçkait] f inconsistency; (Streit) disagreement

unsympathisch ['ʊnzympa:tɪʃ] adj unpleasant; **er ist mir ~** I don't like him

untätig ['ʊntɛːtɪç] adj idle

untauglich ['ʊntauklɪç] adj unsuitable; (MIL) unfit

unteilbar [ʊn'tailba:r] adj indivisible

unten ['ʊntən] adv below; (im Haus) downstairs; (an der Treppe etc) at the bottom; **nach ~** down; **~ am Berg** etc at the bottom of the mountain etc; **ich bin bei ihm ~ durch** (umg) he's through with me

---

SCHLÜSSELWORT

unter ['ʊntər] präp +dat 1 (räumlich, mit Zahlen) under; (drunter) underneath, below; **unter 18 Jahren** under 18 years 2 (zwischen) among(st); **sie waren unter sich** they were by themselves; **einer unter ihnen** one of them; **unter anderem** among other things

♦ präp +akk under, below

Unterarm ['ʊntərʔarm] m forearm

unter- zW: **~belichten** vt (PHOT) to underexpose; **U~bewusstsein** ▲ nt subconscious; **~bezahlt** adj underpaid

unterbieten [ʊntər'bi:tən] (unreg) vt insep (COMM) to undercut; (Rekord) to lower

unterbrechen [ʊntər'brɛçən] (unreg) vt insep to interrupt

Unterbrechung f interruption

unterbringen ['ʊntərbrɪŋən] (unreg) vt (in Koffer) to stow; (in Zeitung) to place; (Person: in Hotel etc) to accommodate, to put up

unterdessen [ʊntər'dɛsən] adv meanwhile

Unterdruck ['ʊntərdrʊk] m low pressure

unterdrücken [ʊntər'drykən] vt insep to suppress; (Leute) to oppress

untere(r, s) ['ʊntərə(r, s)] adj lower

untereinander [ʊntərʔai'nandər] adv with each other; among themselves etc

unterentwickelt ['ʊntərʔɛntvɪkəlt] adj underdeveloped

Spelling Reform: ▲ *new spelling* △ *old spelling (to be phased out)*

unterernährt ['ʊntərɛrnɛːrt] *adj*
undernourished, underfed
Unterernährung *f* malnutrition
Unter'führung *f* subway, underpass
Untergang ['ʊntərgaŋ] *m* (down)fall,
decline; (*NAUT*) sinking; (*von Gestirn*) setting
unter'geben *adj* subordinate
untergehen ['ʊntərgeːən] (*unreg*) *vi* to go
down; (*Sonne auch*) to set; (*Staat*) to fall;
(*Volk*) to perish; (*Welt*) to come to an end;
(*im Lärm*) to be drowned
Untergeschoss ▲ ['ʊntərgəʃɔs] *nt*
basement
'Untergewicht *nt* underweight
unter'gliedern *vt insep* to subdivide
Untergrund ['ʊntərgrʊnt] *m* foundation;
(*POL*) underground; **~bahn** *f* underground,
tube, subway (*US*)
unterhalb ['ʊntərhalp] *präp* +*gen* below
♦ *adv* below; **~ von** below
Unterhalt ['ʊntərhalt] *m* maintenance;
u~en (*unreg*) *vt insep* to maintain;
(*belustigen*) to entertain ♦ *vr insep* to talk;
(*sich belustigen*) to enjoy o.s.; **u~sam** *adj*
(*Abend, Person*) entertaining, amusing;
~ung *f* maintenance; (*Belustigung*)
entertainment, amusement; (*Gespräch*) talk
Unterhändler ['ʊntərhɛntlər] *m* negotiator
Unter- *zW*: **~hemd** *nt* vest, undershirt (*US*);
~hose *f* underpants *pl*; **~kiefer** *m* lower
jaw
unterkommen ['ʊntərkɔmən] (*unreg*) *vi* to
find shelter; to find work; **das ist mir noch
nie untergekommen** I've never met with
that
unterkühlt [ʊntər'kyːlt] *adj* (*Körper*) affected
by hypothermia
Unterkunft ['ʊntərkʊnft] (**-, -künfte**) *f*
accommodation
Unterlage ['ʊntərlaːgə] *f* foundation; (*Beleg*)
document; (*Schreibunterlage etc*) pad
unter'lassen (*unreg*) *vt insep* (*versäumen*) to
fail to do; (*sich enthalten*) to refrain from
unterlaufen [ʊntər'laʊfən] (*unreg*) *vi insep* to
happen ♦ *adj*: **mit Blut ~** suffused with
blood; (*Augen*) bloodshot
unterlegen ['ʊntərleːgən] *vt* to lay *od* put

under; **unter'legen** *adj* inferior; (*besiegt*)
defeated
Unterleib ['ʊntərlaɪp] *m* abdomen
unter'liegen (*unreg*) *vi insep* (+*dat*) to be
defeated *od* overcome (by); (*unterworfen
sein*) to be subject (to)
Untermiete ['ʊntərmiːtə] *f*: **zur ~ wohnen**
to be a subtenant *od* lodger; **~r(in)** *m(f)*
subtenant, lodger
unter'nehmen (*unreg*) *vt insep* to
undertake; **Unter'nehmen (-s, -)** *nt*
undertaking, enterprise (*auch COMM*)
Unternehmer [ʊntər'neːmər] (**-s, -**) *m*
entrepreneur, businessman
'unterordnen ['ʊntərɔrdnən] *vr* +*dat* to
submit o.s. (to), to give o.s. second place
to
Unterredung [ʊntər're:dʊŋ] *f* discussion,
talk
Unterricht ['ʊntərrɪçt] (**-(e)s, -e**) *m*
instruction, lessons *pl*; **u~en** [ʊntər'rɪçtən] *vt
insep* to instruct; (*SCH*) to teach ♦ *vr insep*:
sich u~en (über +*akk*) to inform o.s.
(about), to obtain information (about);
~sfach *nt* subject (on school *etc*
curriculum)
Unterrock ['ʊntərrɔk] *m* petticoat, slip
unter'sagen *vt insep* to forbid; **jdm etw ~**
to forbid sb to do sth
Untersatz ['ʊntərzats] *m* coaster, saucer
unter'schätzen *vt insep* to underestimate
unter'scheiden (*unreg*) *vt insep* to
distinguish ♦ *vr insep* to differ
Unter'scheidung *f* (*Unterschied*)
distinction; (*Unterscheiden*) differentiation
Unterschied ['ʊntərʃiːt] (**-(e)s, -e**) *m*
difference, distinction; **im ~ zu** as distinct
from; **u~lich** *adj* varying, differing;
(*diskriminierend*) discriminatory
unterschiedslos *adv* indiscriminately
unter'schlagen (*unreg*) *vt insep* to
embezzle; (*verheimlichen*) to suppress
Unter'schlagung *f* embezzlement
Unterschlupf ['ʊntərʃlʊpf] (**-(e)s,
-schlüpfe**) *m* refuge
unter'schreiben (*unreg*) *vt insep* to sign
Unterschrift ['ʊntərʃrɪft] *f* signature

Rechtschreibreform: ▲ *neue Schreibung* △ *alte Schreibung (auslaufend)*

Unterseeboot ['ʊntərze:bo:t] *nt* submarine
Untersetzer ['ʊntərzɛtsər] *m* tablemat; (*für Gläser*) coaster
untersetzt [ʊntər'zɛtst] *adj* stocky
unterste(r, s) ['ʊntərstə(r, s)] *adj* lowest, bottom
unterstehen [ʊntər'ʃte:ən] (*unreg*) *vi insep* (+*dat*) to be under ♦ *vr insep* to dare; '**unterstehen** (*unreg*) *vi* to shelter
unterstellen [ʊntər'ʃtɛlən] *vt insep* to subordinate; (*fig*) to impute ♦ *vt* (*Auto*) to garage, to park ♦ *vr* to take shelter
unter'streichen (*unreg*) *vt insep* (*auch fig*) to underline
Unterstufe ['ʊntərʃtu:fə] *f* lower grade
unter'stützen *vt insep* to support
Unter'stützung *f* support, assistance
unter'suchen *vt insep* (*MED*) to examine; (*Polizei*) to investigate
Unter'suchung *f* examination; investigation, inquiry; **~sausschuss** ▲ *m* committee of inquiry; **~shaft** *f* imprisonment on remand
Untertasse ['ʊntərtasə] *f* saucer
untertauchen ['ʊntərtaʊxən] *vi* to dive; (*fig*) to disappear, to go underground
Unterteil ['ʊntərtaɪl] *nt od m* lower part, bottom; **u~en** [ʊntər'taɪlən] *vt insep* to divide up
Untertitel ['ʊntərti:təl] *m* subtitle
Unterwäsche ['ʊntərvɛʃə] *f* underwear
unterwegs [ʊntər've:ks] *adv* on the way
unter'werfen (*unreg*) *vt insep* to subject; (*Volk*) to subjugate ♦ *vr insep* (+*dat*) to submit (to)
unter'zeichnen *vt insep* to sign
unter'ziehen (*unreg*) *vt insep* to subject ♦ *vr insep* (+*dat*) to undergo; (*einer Prüfung*) to take
untragbar [ʊn'tra:kba:r] *adj* unbearable, intolerable
untreu ['ʊntrɔy] *adj* unfaithful; **U~e** *f* unfaithfulness
untröstlich [ʊn'trø:stlɪç] *adj* inconsolable
unüberlegt ['ʊn|y:bərle:kt] *adj* ill-considered ♦ *adv* without thinking
unübersichtlich *adj* (*Gelände*) broken;

(*Kurve*) blind
unumgänglich [ʊn|ʊm'gɛŋlɪç] *adj* indispensable, vital; absolutely necessary
ununterbrochen ['ʊn|ʊntərbrɔxən] *adj* uninterrupted
unver- ['ʊnfer] *zW*: **~änderlich** [-'ɛndərlɪç] *adj* unchangeable; **~antwortlich** [-'antvɔrtlɪç] *adj* irresponsible; (*unentschuldbar*) inexcusable; **~besserlich** *adj* incorrigible; **~bindlich** *adj* not binding; (*Antwort*) curt ♦ *adv* (*COMM*) without obligation; **~bleit** *adj* (*Benzin usw*) unleaded; **ich fahre ~bleit** I use unleaded; **~blümt** [-'bly:mt] *adj* plain, blunt ♦ *adv* plainly, bluntly; **~daulich** *adj* indigestible; **~einbar** *adj* incompatible; **~fänglich** [-'fɛŋlɪç] *adj* harmless; **~froren** *adj* impudent; **~gesslich** ▲ *adj* (*Tag, Erlebnis*) unforgettable; **~hofft** [-'hɔft] *adj* unexpected; **~meidlich** [-'maɪtlɪç] *adj* unavoidable; **~mutet** *adj* unexpected; **~nünftig** [-'nynftɪç] *adj* foolish; **~schämt** *adj* impudent; **U~schämtheit** *f* impudence, insolence; **~sehrt** *adj* uninjured; **~söhnlich** [-'zø:nlɪç] *adj* irreconcilable; **~ständlich** [-'ʃtɛntlɪç] *adj* unintelligible; **~träglich** *adj* quarrelsome; (*Meinungen, MED*) incompatible; **~zeihlich** *adj* unpardonable; **~züglich** [-'tsy:klɪç] *adj* immediate
unvollkommen ['ʊnfɔlkɔmən] *adj* imperfect
unvollständig *adj* incomplete
unvor- ['ʊnfo:r] *zW*: **~bereitet** *adj* unprepared; **~eingenommen** *adj* unbiased; **~hergesehen** [-he:rgeze:ən] *adj* unforeseen; **~sichtig** [-zɪçtɪç] *adj* careless, imprudent; **~stellbar** [-'ʃtɛlba:r] *adj* inconceivable; **~teilhaft** *adj* disadvantageous
unwahr ['ʊnva:r] *adj* untrue; **~scheinlich** *adj* improbable, unlikely ♦ *adv* (*umg*) incredibly
unweigerlich [ʊn'vaɪgərlɪç] *adj* unquestioning ♦ *adv* without fail
Unwesen ['ʊnve:zən] *nt* nuisance; (*Unfug*) mischief; **sein ~ treiben** to wreak havoc
unwesentlich *adj* inessential, unimportant; **~ besser** marginally better

---

Spelling Reform: ▲ *new spelling* △ *old spelling (to be phased out)*

Unwetter ['ʊnvɛtər] nt thunderstorm
unwichtig ['ʊnvɪçtɪç] adj unimportant
unwider- ['ʊnviːdər] zW: **~legbar** adj irrefutable; **~ruflich** adj irrevocable; **~stehlich** adj irresistible
unwill- ['ʊnvɪl] zW: **U~e(n)** m indignation; **~ig** adj indignant; (widerwillig) reluctant; **~kürlich** [-kyːrlɪç] adj involuntary ♦ adv instinctively; (lachen) involuntarily
unwirklich ['ʊnvɪrklɪç] adj unreal
unwirksam ['ʊnvɪrkzaːm] adj (Mittel, Methode) ineffective
unwirtschaftlich ['ʊnvɪrtʃaftlɪç] adj uneconomical
unwissen- ['ʊnvɪsən] zW: **~d** adj ignorant; **U~heit** f ignorance; **~tlich** adv unknowingly, unwittingly
unwohl ['ʊnvoːl] adj unwell, ill; **U~sein (-s)** nt indisposition
unwürdig ['ʊnvʏrdɪç] adj unworthy
unzählig [ʊn'tsɛːlɪç] adj innumerable, countless
unzer- [ʊntsɛr] zW: **~brechlich** adj unbreakable; **~störbar** adj indestructible; **~trennlich** adj inseparable
Unzucht ['ʊntsʊxt] f sexual offence
unzüchtig ['ʊntsʏçtɪç] adj immoral; lewd
unzu- ['ʊntsu] zW: **~frieden** adj dissatisfied; **U~friedenheit** f discontent; **~länglich** adj inadequate; **~lässig** adj inadmissible; **~rechnungsfähig** adj irresponsible; **~treffend** adj incorrect; **~verlässig** adj unreliable
unzweideutig ['ʊntsvaɪdɔytɪç] adj unambiguous
üppig ['ʏpɪç] adj (Frau) curvaceous; (Busen) full, ample; (Essen) sumptuous; (Vegetation) luxuriant, lush
Ur- ['uːr] in zW original
uralt ['uːr|alt] adj ancient, very old
Uran [u'raːn] (-s) nt uranium
Ur- zW: **~aufführung** f first performance; **~einwohner** m original inhabitant; **~eltern** pl ancestors; **~enkel(in)** m(f) great-grandchild, great-grandson (-daughter); **~großeltern** pl great-grandparents; **~heber (-s, -)** m originator;

(Autor) author; **~heberrecht** nt copyright
Urin [u'riːn] (-s, -e) m urine
Urkunde ['uːrkʊndə] f document, deed
Urlaub ['uːrlaʊp] (-(e)s, -e) m holiday(s pl) (BRIT), vacation (US); (MIL etc) leave; **~er** [-'laʊbər] (-s, -) m holiday-maker (BRIT), vacationer (US); **~sort** m holiday resort; **~szeit** f holiday season
Urne ['ʊrnə] f urn
Ursache ['uːrzaxə] f cause; **keine ~** that's all right
Ursprung ['uːrʃprʊŋ] m origin, source; (von Fluss) source
ursprünglich ['uːrʃprʏŋlɪç] adj original ♦ adv originally
Ursprungsland nt country of origin
Urteil ['ʊrtaɪl] (-s, -e) nt opinion; (JUR) sentence, judgement; **u~en** vi to judge; **~sspruch** m sentence, verdict
Urwald m jungle
Urzeit f prehistoric times pl
USA [uː'ɛs|'aː] pl abk (= Vereinigte Staaten von Amerika) USA
usw. abk (= und so weiter) etc
Utensilien [uten'ziːliən] pl utensils
Utopie [uto'piː] f pipe dream
utopisch [u'toːpɪʃ] adj utopian

V, v

vag(e) [vaːk, 'vaːgə] adj vague
Vagina [va'giːna] (-, **Vaginen**) f vagina
Vakuum ['vaːkuʊm] (-s, **Vakua** od **Vakuen**) nt vacuum
Vampir [vam'piːr] (-s, -e) m vampire
Vanille [va'nɪljə] (-) f vanilla
Variation [variatsi'oːn] f variation
variieren [vari'iːrən] vt, vi to vary
Vase ['vaːzə] f vase
Vater ['faːtər] (-s, ⁰) m father; **~land** nt native country; Fatherland
väterlich ['fɛːtərlɪç] adj fatherly
Vaterschaft f paternity
Vaterunser (-s, -) nt Lord's prayer
Vati ['faːti] m daddy
v. Chr. abk (= vor Christus) B.C.

Vegetarier(in) [vegeˈtaːriər(ɪn)] **(-s, -)** *m(f)* vegetarian

vegetarisch [vegeˈtaːrɪʃ] *adj* vegetarian

Veilchen [ˈfaɪlçən] *nt* violet

Vene [ˈveːnə] *f* vein

Ventil [vɛnˈtiːl] **(-s, -e)** *nt* valve

Ventilator [vɛntiˈlaːtɔr] *m* ventilator

verab- [fɛrˈap] *zW:* **~reden** *vt* to agree, to arrange ♦ *vr:* **sich mit jdm ~reden** to arrange to meet sb; **mit jdm ~redet sein** to have arranged to meet sb; **V~redung** *f* arrangement; *(Treffen)* appointment; **~scheuen** *vt* to detest, to abhor; **~schieden** *vt (Gäste)* to say goodbye to; *(entlassen)* to discharge; *(Gesetz)* to pass ♦ *vr* to take one's leave; **V~schiedung** *f* leave-taking; discharge; passing

ver- [fɛr] *zW:* **~achten** *vt* to despise; **~ächtlich** [-ˈʔɛçtlɪç] *adj* contemptuous; *(~achtenswert)* contemptible; **jdn ~ächtlich machen** to run sb down; **V~achtung** *f* contempt

verallgemeinern [fɛrʔalgəˈmaɪnərn] *vt* to generalize; **Verallgemeinerung** *f* generalization

veralten [fɛrˈaltən] *vi* to become obsolete *od* out-of-date

Veranda [veˈranda] **(-, Veranden)** *f* veranda

veränder- [fɛrˈɛndər] *zW:* **~lich** *adj* changeable; **~n** *vt, vr* to change, to alter; **V~ung** *f* change, alteration

veran- [fɛrˈan] *zW:* **~lagt** *adj* with a ... nature; **V~lagung** *f* disposition; **~lassen** *vt* to cause; **Maßnahmen ~lassen** to take measures; **sich ~lasst sehen** to feel prompted; **~schaulichen** *vt* to illustrate; **~schlagen** *vt* to estimate; **~stalten** *vt* to organize, to arrange; **V~stalter (-s, -)** *m* organizer; **V~staltung** *f (V~stalten)* organizing; *(Konzert etc)* event, function

verantwort- [fɛrˈʔantvɔrt] *zW:* **~en** *vt* to answer for ♦ *vr* to justify o.s.; **~lich** *adj* responsible; **V~ung** *f* responsibility; **~ungsbewusst** ▲ *adj* responsible; **~ungslos** *adj* irresponsible

verarbeiten [fɛrˈarbaɪtən] *vt* to process; *(geistig)* to assimilate; **etw zu etw ~** to make sth into sth; **Verarbeitung** *f* processing; assimilation

verärgern [fɛrˈʔɛrgərn] *vt* to annoy

verausgaben [fɛrˈʔausgaːbən] *vr* to run out of money; *(fig)* to exhaust o.s.

Verb [vɛrp] **(-s, -en)** *nt* verb

Verband [fɛrˈbant] **(-(e)s, ⁻e)** *m (MED)* bandage, dressing; *(Bund)* association, society; *(MIL)* unit; **~skasten** *m* medicine chest, first-aid box; **~zeug** *nt* bandage

verbannen [fɛrˈbanən] *vt* to banish

verbergen [fɛrˈbɛrgən] *(unreg) vt, vr:* **(sich) ~ (vor** +*dat)* to hide (from)

verbessern [fɛrˈbɛsərn] *vt, vr* to improve; *(berichtigen)* to correct (o.s.)

Verbesserung *f* improvement; correction

verbeugen [fɛrˈbɔygən] *vr* to bow

Verbeugung *f* bow

ver'biegen *(unreg) vi* to bend

ver'bieten *(unreg) vt* to forbid; **jdm etw ~** to forbid sb to do sth

verbilligen [fɛrˈbɪlɪgən] *vt* to reduce the cost of; *(Preis)* to reduce

ver'binden *(unreg) vt* to connect; *(kombinieren)* to combine; *(MED)* to bandage ♦ *vr (auch CHEM)* to combine, to join; **jdm die Augen ~** to blindfold sb

verbindlich [fɛrˈbɪntlɪç] *adj* binding; *(freundlich)* friendly

Ver'bindung *f* connection; *(Zusammensetzung)* combination; *(CHEM)* compound; *(UNIV)* club

verbissen [fɛrˈbɪsən] *adj (Kampf)* bitter; *(Gesichtsausdruck)* grim

ver'bitten *(unreg) vt:* **sich** *dat* **etw ~** not to tolerate sth, not to stand for sth

Verbleib [fɛrˈblaɪp] **(-(e)s)** *m* whereabouts; **v~en** *(unreg) vi* to remain

verbleit [fɛrˈblaɪt] *adj (Benzin)* leaded

verblüffen [fɛrˈblʏfən] *vt* to stagger, to amaze; **Verblüffung** *f* stupefaction

ver'blühen *vi* to wither, to fade

ver'bluten *vi* to bleed to death

verborgen [fɛrˈbɔrgən] *adj* hidden

Verbot [fɛrˈboːt] **(-(e)s, -e)** *nt* prohibition, ban; **v~en** *adj* forbidden; **Rauchen v~en!** no smoking; **~sschild** *nt* prohibitory sign

---

Spelling Reform: ▲ *new spelling* △ *old spelling (to be phased out)*

Verbrauch [fɛrˈbraʊx] **(-(e)s)** *m* consumption; **v~en** *vt* to use up; **~er (-s, -)** *m* consumer; **v~t** *adj* used up, finished; (*Luft*) stale; (*Mensch*) worn-out

Verbrechen [fɛrˈbrɛçən] **(-s, -)** *nt* crime

Verbrecher [fɛrˈbrɛçər] **(-s, -)** *m* criminal; **v~isch** *adj* criminal

ver'breiten *vt, vr* to spread; **sich über etw** *akk* **~** to expound on sth

verbreitern [fɛrˈbraɪtərn] *vt* to broaden

Verbreitung *f* spread(ing), propagation

verbrenn- [fɛrˈbrɛn] *zW:* **~bar** *adj* combustible; **~en** (*unreg*) *vt* to burn; (*Leiche*) to cremate; **V~ung** *f* burning; (*in Motor*) combustion; (*von Leiche*) cremation; **V~ungsmotor** *m* internal combustion engine

verbringen [fɛrˈbrɪŋən] (*unreg*) *vt* to spend

verbrühen [fɛrˈbryːən] *vt* to scald

verbuchen [fɛrˈbuːxən] *vt* (*FIN*) to register; (*Erfolg*) to enjoy; (*Misserfolg*) to suffer

verbunden [fɛrˈbʊndən] *adj* connected; **jdm ~ sein** to be obliged *od* indebted to sb; **„falsch ~"** (*TEL*) "wrong number"

verbünden [fɛrˈbyndən] *vr* to ally o.s.; **Verbündete(r)** *f(m)* ally

ver'bürgen *vr:* **sich ~ für** to vouch for

ver'büßen *vt:* **eine Strafe ~** to serve a sentence

Verdacht [fɛrˈdaxt] **(-(e)s)** *m* suspicion

verdächtig [fɛrˈdɛçtɪç] *adj* suspicious, suspect; **~en** [fɛrˈdɛçtɪɡən] *vt* to suspect

verdammen [fɛrˈdamən] *vt* to damn, to condemn; **verdammt!** damn!

verdammt (*umg*) *adj, adv* damned; **~ noch mal!** damn!, dammit!

ver'dampfen *vi* to vaporize, to evaporate

ver'danken *vt:* **jdm etw ~** to owe sb sth

verdau- [fɛrˈdaʊ] *zW:* **~en** *vt* (*auch fig*) to digest; **~lich** *adj* digestible; **das ist schwer ~lich** that is hard to digest; **V~ung** *f* digestion

Verdeck [fɛrˈdɛk] **(-(e)s, -e)** *nt* (*AUT*) hood; (*NAUT*) deck; **v~en** *vt* to cover (up); (*verbergen*) to hide

Verderb- [fɛrˈdɛrp] *zW:* **~en** [-ˈdɛrbən] **(-s)** *nt* ruin; **v~en** (*unreg*) *vt* to spoil; (*schädigen*) to ruin; (*moralisch*) to corrupt ♦ *vi* (*Essen*) to spoil, to rot; (*Mensch*) to go to the bad; **es mit jdm v~en** to get into sb's bad books; **v~lich** *adj* (*Einfluss*) pernicious; (*Lebensmittel*) perishable

verdeutlichen [fɛrˈdɔʏtlɪçən] *vt* to make clear

ver'dichten *vt, vr* to condense

ver'dienen *vt* to earn; (*moralisch*) to deserve

Ver'dienst (-(e)s, -e) *m* earnings *pl* ♦ *nt* merit; (*Leistung*) **~ (um)** service (to)

verdient [fɛrˈdiːnt] *adj* well-earned; (*Person*) deserving of esteem; **sich um etw ~ machen** to do a lot for sth

verdoppeln [fɛrˈdɔpəln] *vt* to double

verdorben [fɛrˈdɔrbən] *adj* spoilt; (*geschädigt*) ruined; (*moralisch*) corrupt

verdrängen [fɛrˈdrɛŋən] *vt* to oust, to displace (*auch PHYS*); (*PSYCH*) to repress

ver'drehen *vt* (*auch fig*) to twist; (*Augen*) to roll; **jdm den Kopf ~** (*fig*) to turn sb's head

verdrießlich [fɛrˈdriːslɪç] *adj* peevish, annoyed

Verdruss ▲ [fɛrˈdrʊs] **(-es, -e)** *m* annoyance, worry

verdummen [fɛrˈdʊmən] *vt* to make stupid ♦ *vi* to grow stupid

verdunkeln [fɛrˈdʊŋkəln] *vt* to darken; (*fig*) to obscure ♦ *vr* to darken

Verdunk(e)lung *f* blackout; (*fig*) obscuring

verdünnen [fɛrˈdʏnən] *vt* to dilute

verdunsten [fɛrˈdʊnstən] *vi* to evaporate

verdursten [fɛrˈdʊrstən] *vi* to die of thirst

verdutzt [fɛrˈdʊtst] *adj* nonplussed, taken aback

verehr- [fɛrˈʔeːr] *zW:* **~en** *vt* to venerate, to worship (*auch REL*); **jdm etw ~en** to present sb with sth; **V~er(in) (-s, -)** *m(f)* admirer, worshipper (*auch REL*); **~t** *adj* esteemed; **V~ung** *f* respect; (*REL*) worship

Verein [fɛrˈʔaɪn] **(-(e)s, -e)** *m* club, association; **v~bar** *adj* compatible; **v~baren** *vt* to agree upon; **~barung** *f* agreement; **v~en** *vt* (*Menschen, Länder*) to unite; (*Prinzipien*) to reconcile; **mit v~ten**

Kräften having pooled resources, having joined forces; **~te Nationen** United Nations; **v~fachen** vt to simplify; **v~heitlichen** [-haɪtlɪçən] vt to standardize; **v~igen** vt, vr to unite; **~igung** f union; (*Verein*) association; **v~t** adj united; **v~zelt** adj isolated

ver'eitern vi to suppurate, to fester

verengen [fɛr|ɛŋən] vr to narrow

vererb- [fɛr|ɛrb] zW: **~en** vt to bequeath; (*BIOL*) to transmit ♦ vr to be hereditary; **V~ung** f bequeathing; (*BIOL*) transmission; (*Lehre*) heredity

verewigen [fɛr|eːvɪɡən] vt to immortalize ♦ vr (*umg*) to immortalize o.s.

ver'fahren (*unreg*) vi to act ♦ vr to get lost ♦ adj tangled; **~ mit** to deal with; **Ver'fahren (-s, -)** nt procedure; (*TECH*) process; (*JUR*) proceedings pl

Verfall [fɛr'fal] (**-(e)s**) m decline; (*von Haus*) dilapidation; (*FIN*) expiry; **v~en** (*unreg*) vi to decline; (*Haus*) to be falling down; (*FIN*) to lapse; **v~en in** +akk to lapse into; **v~en auf** +akk to hit upon; **einem Laster v~en sein** to be addicted to a vice; **~sdatum** nt expiry date; (*der Haltbarkeit*) sell-by date

ver'färben vr to change colour

verfassen [fɛr'fasən] vt (*Rede*) to prepare, work out

Verfasser(in) [fɛr'fasər(ɪn)] **(-s, -)** m(f) author, writer

Verfassung f (*auch POL*) constitution

Verfassungs- zW: **~gericht** nt constitutional court; **v~widrig** adj unconstitutional

ver'faulen vi to rot

ver'fehlen vt to miss; **etw für verfehlt halten** to regard sth as mistaken

verfeinern [fɛr'faɪnərn] vt to refine

ver'filmen vt to film

verflixt [fɛr'flɪkst] (*umg*) adj damned, damn

ver'fluchen vt to curse

verfolg- [fɛr'fɔlɡ] zW: **~en** vt to pursue; (*gerichtlich*) to prosecute; (*grausam, bes POL*) to persecute; **V~er (-s, -)** m pursuer; **V~ung** f pursuit; prosecution; persecution

verfrüht [fɛr'fryːt] adj premature

verfüg- [fɛr'fyːɡ] zW: **~bar** adj available; **~en** vt to direct, to order ♦ vr to proceed ♦ vi: **~en über** +akk to have at one's disposal; **V~ung** f direction, order; **zur V~ung** at one's disposal; **jdm zur V~ung stehen** to be available to sb

verführ- [fɛr'fyːr] zW: **~en** vt to tempt; (*sexuell*) to seduce; **V~er** m tempter; seducer; **~erisch** adj seductive; **V~ung** f seduction; (*Versuchung*) temptation

ver'gammeln (*umg*) vi to go to seed; (*Nahrung*) to go off

vergangen [fɛr'ɡaŋən] adj past; **V~heit** f past

vergänglich [fɛr'ɡɛŋlɪç] adj transitory

vergasen [fɛr'ɡaːzən] vt (*töten*) to gas

Vergaser (-s, -) m (*AUT*) carburettor

vergaß etc [fɛr'ɡaːs] vb siehe **vergessen**

vergeb- [fɛr'ɡeːb] zW: **~en** (*unreg*) vt (*verzeihen*) to forgive; (*weggeben*) to give away; **jdm etw ~en** to forgive sb (for) sth; **~ens** adv in vain; **~lich** [fɛr'ɡeːplɪç] adv in vain ♦ adj vain, futile; **V~ung** f forgiveness

ver'gehen (*unreg*) vi to pass by od away ♦ vr to commit an offence; **jdm vergeht etw** sb loses sth; **sich an jdm ~** to (sexually) assault sb; **Ver'gehen (-s, -)** nt offence

ver'gelten (*unreg*) vt: **jdm etw ~** to pay sb back for sth, to repay sb for sth

Ver'geltung f retaliation, reprisal

vergessen [fɛr'ɡɛsən] (*unreg*) vt to forget; **V~heit** f oblivion

vergesslich ▲ [fɛr'ɡɛslɪç] adj forgetful; **V~keit** f forgetfulness

vergeuden [fɛr'ɡɔʏdən] vt to squander, to waste

vergewaltigen [fɛrɡə'valtɪɡən] vt to rape; (*fig*) to violate

Vergewaltigung f rape

vergewissern [fɛrɡə'vɪsərn] vr to make sure

ver'gießen (*unreg*) vt to shed

vergiften [fɛr'ɡɪftən] vt to poison

Vergiftung f poisoning

Vergissmeinnicht ▲ [fɛr'ɡɪsmaɪnnɪçt] **(-(e)s, -e)** nt forget-me-not

vergisst ▲ etc [fɛr'ɡɪst] vb siehe **vergessen**

Spelling Reform: ▲ *new spelling* △ *old spelling (to be phased out)*

Vergleich [fɛrˈglaɪç] **(-(e)s, -e)** *m*
comparison; (*JUR*) settlement; **im ~ mit** *od*
zu compared with *od* to; **v~bar** *adj*
comparable; **v~en** (*unreg*) *vt* to compare
♦ *vr* to reach a settlement

vergnügen [fɛrˈgnyːgən] *vr* to enjoy *od*
amuse o.s.; **V~ (-s, -)** *nt* pleasure; **viel V~!**
enjoy yourself!

vergnügt [fɛrˈgnyːkt] *adj* cheerful

Vergnügung *f* pleasure, amusement;
~spark *m* amusement park

vergolden [fɛrˈgɔldən] *vt* to gild

ver'graben *vt* to bury

ver'greifen (*unreg*) *vr*: **sich an jdm ~** to lay
hands on sb; **sich an etw ~** to
misappropriate sth; **sich im Ton ~** to say
the wrong thing

vergriffen [fɛrˈgrɪfən] *adj* (*Buch*) out of print;
(*Ware*) out of stock

vergrößern [fɛrˈgrøːsərn] *vt* to enlarge;
(*mengenmäßig*) to increase; (*Lupe*) to
magnify

Vergrößerung *f* enlargement; increase;
magnification; **~sglas** *nt* magnifying glass

Vergünstigung [fɛrˈgʏnstɪgʊŋ] *f*
concession, privilege

Vergütung *f* compensation

verhaften [fɛrˈhaftən] *vt* to arrest

Verhaftung *f* arrest

ver'halten (*unreg*) *vr* to be, to stand; (*sich*
benehmen) to behave ♦ *vt* to hold *od* keep
back; (*Schritt*) to check; **sich ~ (zu)** (*MATH*)
to be in proportion (to); **Ver'halten (-s)** *nt*
behaviour

Verhältnis [fɛrˈhɛltnɪs] **(-ses, -se)** *nt*
relationship; (*MATH*) proportion, ratio; **~se**
pl (*Umstände*) conditions; **über seine ~se**
leben to live beyond one's means;
v~mäßig *adj* relative, comparative ♦ *adv*
relatively, comparatively

verhandeln [fɛrˈhandəln] *vi* to negotiate;
(*JUR*) to hold proceedings ♦ *vt* to discuss;
(*JUR*) to hear; **über etw** *akk* **~** to negotiate
sth *od* about sth

Verhandlung *f* negotiation; (*JUR*)
proceedings *pl*; **~sbasis** *f* (*FIN*) basis for
negotiations

ver'hängen *vt* (*fig*) to impose, to inflict

Verhängnis [fɛrˈhɛŋnɪs] **(-ses, -se)** *nt* fate,
doom; **jdm zum ~ werden** to be sb's
undoing; **v~voll** *adj* fatal, disastrous

verharmlosen [fɛrˈharmloːzən] *vt* to make
light of, to play down

verhärten [fɛrˈhɛrtən] *vr* to harden

verhasst ▲ [fɛrˈhast] *adj* odious, hateful

verhauen [fɛrˈhaʊən] (*unreg*; *umg*) *vt*
(*verprügeln*) to beat up

verheerend [fɛrˈheːrənt] *adj* disastrous,
devastating

verheimlichen [fɛrˈhaɪmlɪçən] *vt*: **jdm etw**
~ to keep sth secret from sb

verheiratet [fɛrˈhaɪraːtət] *adj* married

ver'helfen (*unreg*) *vi*: **jdm ~ zu** to help sb
to get

ver'hindern *vt* to prevent; **verhindert sein**
to be unable to make it

verhöhnen [fɛrˈhøːnən] *vt* to mock, to
sneer at

Verhör [fɛrˈhøːr] **(-(e)s, -e)** *nt* interrogation;
(*gerichtlich*) (cross-)examination; **v~en** *vt* to
interrogate; to (cross-)examine ♦ *vr* to
misunderstand, to mishear

ver'hungern *vi* to starve, to die of hunger

ver'hüten *vt* to prevent, to avert

Ver'hütung *f* prevention; **~smittel** *nt*
contraceptive

verirren [fɛrˈʔɪrən] *vr* to go astray

ver'jagen *vt* to drive away *od* out

verkalken [fɛrˈkalkən] *vi* to calcify; (*umg*) to
become senile

Verkauf [fɛrˈkaʊf] *m* sale; **v~en** *vt* to sell

Verkäufer(in) [fɛrˈkɔyfər(ɪn)] **(-s, -)** *m(f)*
seller; salesman(-woman); (*in Laden*) shop
assistant

verkaufsoffen *adj*: **~er Samstag** *Saturday*
when the shops stay open all day

Verkehr [fɛrˈkeːr] **(-s, -e)** *m* traffic; (*Umgang*,
bes sexuell) intercourse; (*Umlauf*) circulation;
v~en *vi* (*Fahrzeug*) to ply, to run ♦ *vt*, *vr* to
turn, to transform; **v~en mit** to associate
with; **bei jdm v~en** (*besuchen*) to visit sb
regularly

Verkehrs- *zW*: **~ampel** *f* traffic lights *pl*;
~aufkommen *nt* volume of traffic;

~beruhigung f traffic calming; **~delikt** nt traffic offence; **~funk** m radio traffic service; **v~günstig** adj convenient; **~mittel** nt means of transport; **~schild** nt road sign; **~stauung** f traffic jam, stoppage; **~unfall** m traffic accident; **~verein** m tourist information office; **~zeichen** nt traffic sign

verkehrt adj wrong; (umgekehrt) the wrong way round

ver'kennen (unreg) vt to misjudge, not to appreciate

ver'klagen vt to take to court

verkleiden [fɛr'klaɪdən] vt to disguise (o.s.); (sich kostümieren) to get dressed up ♦ vt (Wand) to cover

Verkleidung f disguise; (ARCHIT) wainscoting

verkleinern [fɛr'klaɪnərn] vt to make smaller, to reduce in size

ver'kneifen (umg) vt: **sich** dat **etw ~** (Lachen) to stifle sth; (Schmerz) to hide sth; (sich versagen) to do without sth

verknüpfen [fɛr'knʏpfən] vt to tie (up), to knot; (fig) to connect

ver'kommen (unreg) vi to deteriorate, to decay; (Mensch) to go downhill, to come down in the world ♦ adj (moralisch) dissolute, depraved

ver'körpern [fɛr'kœrpərn] vt to embody, to personify

verkraften [fɛr'kraftən] vt to cope with

ver'kriechen (unreg) vr to creep away, to creep into a corner

verkrüppelt [fɛr'krʏpəlt] adj crippled

ver'kühlen vr to get a chill

ver'kümmern vi to waste away

verkünden [fɛr'kʏndən] vt to proclaim; (Urteil) to pronounce

verkürzen [fɛr'kʏrtsən] vt to shorten; (Wort) to abbreviate; **sich** dat **die Zeit ~** to while away the time

Verkürzung f shortening; abbreviation

verladen [fɛr'la:dən] (unreg) vt (Waren, Vieh) to load; (Truppen: auf Schiff) to embark, (auf Zug) to entrain, (auf Flugzeug) to enplane

Verlag [fɛr'la:k] **(-(e)s, -e)** m publishing firm

verlangen [fɛr'laŋən] vt to demand; to desire ♦ vi: **~ nach** to ask for, to desire; **~ Sie Herrn X** ask for Mr X; **V~ (-s, -)** nt: **V~ (nach)** desire (for); **auf jds V~ (hin)** at sb's request

verlängern [fɛr'lɛŋərn] vt to extend; (länger machen) to lengthen

Verlängerung f extension; (SPORT) extra time; **~sschnur** f extension cable

verlangsamen [fɛr'laŋza:mən] vt, vr to decelerate, to slow down

Verlass ▲ [fɛr'las] m: **auf ihn/das ist kein ~** he/it cannot be relied upon

ver'lassen (unreg) vt to leave ♦ vr: **sich ~ auf** +akk to depend on ♦ adj desolate; (Mensch) abandoned

verlässlich ▲ [fɛr'lɛslɪç] adj reliable

Verlauf [fɛr'lauf] m course; **v~en** (unreg) vi (zeitlich) to pass; (Farben) to run ♦ vr to get lost; (Menschenmenge) to disperse

ver'lauten vi: **etw ~ lassen** to disclose sth; **wie verlautet** as reported

ver'legen vt to move; (verlieren) to mislay; (Buch) to publish ♦ vr: **sich auf etw** akk **~** to take up od to sth ♦ adj embarrassed; **nicht ~ um** never at a loss for; **Ver'legenheit** f embarrassment; (Situation) difficulty, scrape

Verleger [fɛr'le:gər] **(-s, -)** m publisher

Verleih [fɛr'lai] **(-(e)s, -e)** m hire service; **v~en** (unreg) vt to lend; (Kraft, Anschein) to confer, to bestow; (Preis, Medaille) to award; **~ung** f lending; bestowal; award

ver'leiten vt to lead astray; **~ zu** to talk into, to tempt into

ver'lernen vt to forget, to unlearn

ver'lesen (unreg) vt to read out; (aussondern) to sort out ♦ vr to make a mistake in reading

verletz- [fɛr'lɛts] zW: **~en** vt (auch fig) to injure, to hurt; (Gesetz etc) to violate; **~end** adj (fig: Worte) hurtful; **~lich** adj vulnerable, sensitive; **V~te(r)** f(m) injured person; **V~ung** f injury; (Verstoß) violation, infringement

verleugnen [fɛr'lɔʏgnən] vt (Herkunft, Glauben) to belie; (Menschen) to disown

verleumden [fɛr'lɔymdən] *vt* to slander; **Verleumdung** *f* slander, libel

ver'lieben *vr*: **sich ~ (in** +*akk*) to fall in love (with)

verliebt [fɛr'li:pt] *adj* in love

verlieren [fɛr'li:rən] (*unreg*) *vt, vi* to lose ♦ *vr* to get lost

Verlierer *m* loser

verlob- [fɛr'lo:b] *zW*: **~en** *vr*: **sich ~en (mit)** to get engaged (to); **V~te(r)** [fɛr'lo:ptə(r)] *f(m)* fiancé *m*, fiancée *f*; **V~ung** *f* engagement

ver'locken *vt* to entice, to lure

Ver'lockung *f* temptation, attraction

verlogen [fɛr'lo:gən] *adj* untruthful

verlor *etc vb siehe* **verlieren**

verloren [fɛr'lo:rən] *adj* lost; (*Eier*) poached ♦ *vb siehe* **verlieren**; **etw ~ geben** to give sth up for lost; **~ gehen** to get lost

verlosen [fɛr'lo:zən] *vt* to raffle, to draw lots for; **Verlosung** *f* raffle, lottery

Verlust [fɛr'lʊst] **(-(e)s, -e)** *m* loss; (*MIL*) casualty

ver'machen *vt* to bequeath, to leave

Vermächtnis [fɛr'mɛçtnɪs] **(-ses, -se)** *nt* legacy

Vermählung [fɛr'mɛ:lʊŋ] *f* wedding, marriage

vermarkten [fɛr'marktən] *vt* (*COMM: Artikel*) to market

vermehren [fɛr'me:rən] *vt, vr* to multiply; (*Menge*) to increase

Vermehrung *f* multiplying; increase

ver'meiden (*unreg*) *vt* to avoid

vermeintlich [fɛr'maɪntlɪç] *adj* supposed

Vermerk [fɛr'mɛrk] **(-(e)s, -e)** *m* note; (*in Ausweis*) endorsement; **v~en** *vt* to note

ver'messen (*unreg*) *vt* to survey ♦ *adj* presumptuous, bold; **Ver'messenheit** *f* presumptuousness; recklessness

Ver'messung *f* survey(ing)

vermiet- [fɛr'mi:t] *zW*: **ver'mieten** *vt* to let, to rent (out); (*Auto*) to hire out, to rent; **Ver'mieter(in)** **(-s, -)** *m(f)* landlord(-lady); **Ver'mietung** *f* letting, renting (out); (*von Autos*) hiring (out)

vermindern [fɛr'mɪndərn] *vt, vr* to lessen, to

decrease; (*Preise*) to reduce

Verminderung *f* reduction

ver'mischen *vt, vr* to mix, to blend

vermissen [fɛr'mɪsən] *vt* to miss

vermitt- [fɛr'mɪt] *zW*: **~eln** *vi* to mediate ♦ *vt* (*Gespräch*) to connect; **jdm etw ~eln** to help sb to obtain sth; **V~ler** **(-s, -)** *m* (*Schlichter*) agent, mediator; **V~lung** *f* procurement; (*Stellenvermittlung*) agency; (*TEL*) exchange; (*Schlichtung*) mediation; **V~lungsgebühr** *f* commission

ver'mögen (*unreg*) *vt* to be capable of; **~ zu** to be able to; **Ver'mögen** **(-s, -)** *nt* wealth; (*Fähigkeit*) ability; **ein V~ kosten** to cost a fortune; **ver'mögend** *adj* wealthy

vermuten [fɛr'mu:tən] *vt* to suppose, to guess; (*argwöhnen*) to suspect

vermutlich *adj* supposed, presumed ♦ *adv* probably

Vermutung *f* supposition; suspicion

vernachlässigen [fɛr'na:xlɛsɪgən] *vt* to neglect

ver'nehmen (*unreg*) *vt* to perceive, to hear; (*erfahren*) to learn; (*JUR*) to (cross-)examine; **dem V~ nach** from what I/we *etc* hear

Vernehmung *f* (cross-)examination

verneigen [fɛr'naɪgən] *vr* to bow

verneinen [fɛr'naɪnən] *vt* (*Frage*) to answer in the negative; (*ablehnen*) to deny; (*GRAM*) to negate; **~d** *adj* negative

Verneinung *f* negation

vernichten [fɛr'nɪçtən] *vt* to annihilate, to destroy; **~d** *adj* (*fig*) crushing; (*Blick*) withering; (*Kritik*) scathing

Vernunft [fɛr'nʊnft] **(-)** *f* reason, understanding

vernünftig [fɛr'nʏnftɪç] *adj* sensible, reasonable

veröffentlichen [fɛr'|œfəntlɪçən] *vt* to publish; **Veröffentlichung** *f* publication

verordnen [fɛr'|ɔrdnən] *vt* (*MED*) to prescribe

Verordnung *f* order, decree; (*MED*) prescription

ver'pachten *vt* to lease (out)

ver'packen *vt* to pack

Ver'packung *f* packing, wrapping;

~smaterial nt packing, wrapping
ver'passen vt to miss; **jdm eine Ohrfeige ~** (umg) to give sb a clip round the ear
verpfänden [fɛr'pfɛndən] vt (Besitz) to mortgage
ver'pflanzen vt to transplant
ver'pflegen vt to feed, to cater for
Ver'pflegung f feeding, catering; (Kost) food; (in Hotel) board
verpflichten [fɛr'pflɪçtən] vt to oblige, to bind; (anstellen) to engage ♦ vr to undertake; (MIL) to sign on ♦ vi to carry obligations; **jdm zu Dank verpflichtet sein** to be obliged to sb
Verpflichtung f obligation, duty
verpönt [fɛr'pøːnt] adj disapproved (of), taboo
ver'prügeln (umg) vt to beat up, to do over
Verputz [fɛr'pʊts] m plaster, roughcast; **v~en** vt to plaster; (umg: Essen) to put away
Verrat [fɛr'raːt] **(-(e)s)** m treachery; (POL) treason; **v~en** (unreg) vt to betray; (Geheimnis) to divulge ♦ vr to give o.s. away
Verräter [fɛr'rɛːtər] **(-s, -)** m traitor(-tress); **v~isch** adj treacherous
ver'rechnen vt: **~ mit** to set off against ♦ vr to miscalculate
Verrechnungsscheck [fɛr'rɛçnʊŋsʃɛk] m crossed cheque
verregnet [fɛr'reːgnət] adj spoilt by rain, rainy
ver'reisen vi to go away (on a journey)
verrenken [fɛr'rɛŋkən] vt to contort; (MED) to dislocate; **sich** dat **den Knöchel ~** to sprain one's ankle
ver'richten vt to do, to perform
verriegeln [fɛr'riːgəln] vt to bolt up, to lock
verringern [fɛr'rɪŋərn] vt to reduce ♦ vr to diminish
Verringerung f reduction; lessening
ver'rinnen (unreg) vi to run out od away; (Zeit) to elapse
ver'rosten vi to rust
verrotten [fɛr'rɔtən] vi to rot

ver'rücken vt to move, to shift
verrückt [fɛr'rʏkt] adj crazy, mad; **V~e(r)** f(m) lunatic; **V~heit** f madness, lunacy
Verruf [fɛr'ruːf] m: **in ~ geraten/bringen** to fall/bring into disrepute; **v~en** adj notorious, disreputable
Vers [fɛrs] **(-es, -e)** m verse
ver'sagen vt: **jdm/sich etw ~** to deny sb/o.s. sth ♦ vi to fail; **Ver'sagen (-s)** nt failure
ver'salzen (unreg) vt to put too much salt in; (fig) to spoil
ver'sammeln vt, vr to assemble, to gather
Ver'sammlung f meeting, gathering
Versand [fɛr'zant] **(-(e)s)** m forwarding; dispatch; (~abteilung) dispatch department; **~haus** nt mail-order firm
versäumen [fɛr'zɔʏmən] vt to miss; (unterlassen) to neglect, to fail
ver'schaffen vt: **jdm/sich etw ~** to get od procure sth for sb/o.s.
verschämt [fɛr'ʃɛːmt] adj bashful
verschandeln [fɛr'ʃandəln] (umg) vt to spoil
verschärfen [fɛr'ʃɛrfən] vt to intensify; (Lage) to aggravate ♦ vr to intensify; to become aggravated
ver'schätzen vr to be out in one's reckoning
ver'schenken vt to give away
verscheuchen [fɛr'ʃɔʏçən] vt (Tiere) to chase off od away
ver'schicken vt to send off
ver'schieben (unreg) vt to shift; (EISENB) to shunt; (Termin) to postpone
verschieden [fɛr'ʃiːdən] adj different; (pl: mehrere) various; **sie sind ~ groß** they are of different sizes; **~tlich** adv several times
verschimmeln [fɛr'ʃɪməln] vi (Nahrungsmittel) to go mouldy
verschlafen [fɛr'ʃlaːfən] (unreg) vt to sleep through; (fig: versäumen) to miss ♦ vi, vr to oversleep ♦ adj sleepy
Verschlag [fɛr'ʃlaːk] m shed; **v~en** [-gən] (unreg) vt to board up ♦ adj cunning; **jdm den Atem v~en** to take sb's breath away; **an einen Ort v~en werden** to wind up in a place

Spelling Reform: ▲ *new spelling* △ *old spelling (to be phased out)*

verschlechtern [fɛr'ʃlɛçtərn] *vt* to make worse ♦ *vr* to deteriorate, to get worse; **Verschlechterung** *f* deterioration

Verschleiß [fɛr'ʃlaɪs] **(-es, -e)** *m* wear and tear; **v~en** (*unreg*) *vt* to wear out

ver'schleppen *vt* to carry off, to abduct; (*Krankheit*) to protract; (*zeitlich*) to drag out

ver'schleudern *vt* to squander; (*COMM*) to sell dirt-cheap

verschließbar *adj* lockable

verschließen [fɛr'ʃliːsən] (*unreg*) *vt* to close; to lock ♦ *vr:* **sich einer Sache** *dat* **~** to close one's mind to sth

verschlimmern [fɛr'ʃlɪmərn] *vt* to make worse, to aggravate ♦ *vr* to get worse, to deteriorate

verschlingen [fɛr'ʃlɪŋən] (*unreg*) *vt* to devour, to swallow up; (*Fäden*) to twist

verschlossen [fɛr'ʃlɔsən] *adj* locked; (*fig*) reserved; **v~heit** *f* reserve

ver'schlucken *vt* to swallow ♦ *vr* to choke

Verschluss ▲ [fɛr'ʃlʊs] *m* lock; (*von Kleid etc*) fastener; (*PHOT*) shutter; (*Stöpsel*) plug

verschlüsseln [fɛr'ʃlʏsəln] *vt* to encode

verschmieren [fɛr'ʃmiːrən] *vt* (*verstreichen: Gips, Mörtel*) to apply, spread on; (*schmutzig machen: Wand etc*) to smear

verschmutzen [fɛr'ʃmʊtsən] *vt* to soil; (*Umwelt*) to pollute

verschneit [fɛr'ʃnaɪt] *adj* snowed up, covered in snow

verschollen [fɛr'ʃɔlən] *adj* lost, missing

ver'schonen *vt:* **jdn mit etw ~** to spare sb sth

verschönern [fɛr'ʃøːnərn] *vt* to decorate; (*verbessern*) to improve

ver'schreiben (*unreg*) *vt* (*MED*) to prescribe ♦ *vr* to make a mistake (in writing); **sich einer Sache** *dat* **~** to devote o.s. to sth

verschreibungspflichtig *adj* (*Medikament*) available on prescription only

verschrotten [fɛr'ʃrɔtən] *vt* to scrap

verschuld- [fɛr'ʃʊld] *zW:* **~en** *vt* to be guilty of; **V~en (-s)** *nt* fault, guilt; **~et** *adj* in debt; **V~ung** *f* fault; (*Geld*) debts *pl*

ver'schütten *vt* to spill; (*zuschütten*) to fill; (*unter Trümmer*) to bury

ver'schweigen (*unreg*) *vt* to keep secret; **jdm etw ~** to keep sth from sb

verschwend- [fɛr'ʃvɛnd] *zW:* **~en** *vt* to squander; **V~er (-s, -)** *m* spendthrift; **~erisch** *adj* wasteful, extravagant; **V~ung** *f* waste; extravagance

verschwiegen [fɛr'ʃviːgən] *adj* discreet; (*Ort*) secluded; **V~heit** *f* discretion; seclusion

ver'schwimmen (*unreg*) *vi* to grow hazy, to become blurred

ver'schwinden (*unreg*) *vi* to disappear, to vanish; **Ver'schwinden (-s)** *nt* disappearance

verschwitzt [fɛr'ʃvɪtst] *adj* (*Mensch*) sweaty

verschwommen [fɛr'ʃvɔmən] *adj* hazy, vague

verschwör- [fɛr'ʃvøːr] *zW:* **~en** (*unreg*) *vr* to plot, to conspire; **V~ung** *f* conspiracy, plot

ver'sehen (*unreg*) *vt* to supply, to provide; (*Pflicht*) to carry out; (*Amt*) to fill; (*Haushalt*) to keep ♦ *vr* (*fig*) to make a mistake; **ehe er (es) sich ~ hatte ...** before he knew it ...; **Ver'sehen (-s, -)** *nt* oversight; **aus V~** by mistake; **~tlich** *adv* by mistake

Versehrte(r) [fɛr'zeːrtə(r)] *f(m)* disabled person

ver'senden (*unreg*) *vt* to forward, to dispatch

ver'senken *vt* to sink ♦ *vr:* **sich ~ in** +*akk* to become engrossed in

versessen [fɛr'zɛsən] *adj:* **~ auf** +*akk* mad about

ver'setzen *vt* to transfer; (*verpfänden*) to pawn; (*umg*) to stand up ♦ *vr:* **sich in jdn** *od* **in jds Lage ~** to put o.s. in sb's place; **jdm einen Tritt/Schlag ~** to kick/hit sb; **etw mit etw ~** to mix sth with sth; **jdn in gute Laune ~** to put sb in a good mood

Ver'setzung *f* transfer

verseuchen [fɛr'zɔʏçən] *vt* to contaminate

versichern [fɛr'zɪçərn] *vt* to assure; (*mit Geld*) to insure

Versicherung *f* assurance; insurance

Versicherungs- *zW:* **~gesellschaft** *f* insurance company; **~karte** *f* insurance card; **die grüne ~karte** the green card;

~**police** f insurance policy

ver'sinken (*unreg*) *vi* to sink

versöhnen [fɛr'zø:nən] *vt* to reconcile ♦ *vr* to become reconciled

Versöhnung f reconciliation

ver'sorgen *vt* to provide, to supply; (*Familie etc*) to look after

Ver'sorgung f provision; (*Unterhalt*) maintenance; (*Altersversorgung etc*) benefit, assistance

verspäten [fɛr'ʃpɛːtən] *vr* to be late

verspätet *adj* (*Zug, Abflug, Ankunft*) late; (*Glückwünsche*) belated

Verspätung f delay; ~ **haben** to be late

ver'sperren *vt* to bar, to obstruct

verspielt [fɛr'ʃpiːlt] *adj* (*Kind, Tier*) playful

ver'spotten *vt* to ridicule, to scoff at

ver'sprechen (*unreg*) *vt* to promise; **sich** *dat* **etw von etw ~** to expect sth from sth; **Ver'sprechen** (**-s, -**) *nt* promise

verstaatlichen [fɛr'ʃtaːtlɪçən] *vt* to nationalize

Verstand [fɛr'ʃtant] *m* intelligence; mind; **den ~ verlieren** to go out of one's mind; **über jds ~ gehen** to go beyond sb

verständig [fɛr'ʃtɛndɪç] *adj* sensible; ~**en** [fɛr'ʃtɛndɪgən] *vt* to inform ♦ *vr* to communicate; (*sich einigen*) to come to an understanding; **V~ung** f communication; (*Benachrichtigung*) informing; (*Einigung*) agreement

verständ- [fɛr'ʃtɛnt] *zW*: ~**lich** *adj* understandable, comprehensible; **V~lichkeit** f clarity, intelligibility; **V~nis** (**-ses, -se**) *nt* understanding; ~**nislos** *adj* uncomprehending; ~**nisvoll** *adj* understanding, sympathetic

verstärk- [fɛr'ʃtɛrk] *zW*: ~**en** *vt* to strengthen; (*Ton*) to amplify; (*erhöhen*) to intensify ♦ *vr* to intensify; **V~er** (**-s, -**) *m* amplifier; **V~ung** f strengthening; (*Hilfe*) reinforcements *pl*; (*von Ton*) amplification

verstauchen [fɛr'ʃtauxən] *vt* to sprain

verstauen [fɛr'ʃtauən] *vt* to stow away

Versteck [fɛr'ʃtɛk] (**-(e)s, -e**) *nt* hiding (place); **v~en** *vt, vr* to hide; **v~t** *adj* hidden

ver'stehen (*unreg*) *vt* to understand ♦ *vr* to

get on; **das versteht sich (von selbst)** that goes without saying

versteigern [fɛr'ʃtaɪgərn] *vt* to auction; **Versteigerung** f auction

verstell- [fɛr'ʃtɛl] *zW*: ~**bar** *adj* adjustable, variable; ~**en** *vt* to move, to shift; (*Uhr*) to adjust; (*versperren*) to block; (*fig*) to disguise ♦ *vr* to pretend, to put on an act; **V~ung** f pretence

versteuern [fɛr'ʃtɔyərn] *vt* to pay tax on

verstimmt [fɛr'ʃtɪmt] *adj* out of tune; (*fig*) cross, put out; (*Magen*) upset

ver'stopfen *vt* to block, to stop up; (*MED*) to constipate

Ver'stopfung f obstruction; (*MED*) constipation

verstorben [fɛr'ʃtɔrbən] *adj* deceased, late

verstört [fɛr'ʃtøːrt] *adj* (*Mensch*) distraught

Verstoß [fɛr'ʃtoːs] *m*: ~ **(gegen)** infringement (of), violation (of); **v~en** (*unreg*) *vt* to disown, to reject ♦ *vi*: **v~en gegen** to offend against

ver'streichen (*unreg*) *vt* to spread ♦ *vi* to elapse

ver'streuen *vt* to scatter (about)

verstümmeln [fɛr'ʃtyməln] *vt* to maim, to mutilate (*auch fig*)

verstummen [fɛr'ʃtumən] *vi* to go silent; (*Lärm*) to die away

Versuch [fɛr'zuːx] (**-(e)s, -e**) *m* attempt; (*SCI*) experiment, ~**en** *vt* to try; (*verlocken*) to tempt ♦ *vr*: **sich an etw** *dat* **v~en** to try one's hand at sth; ~**skaninchen** *nt* (*fig*) guinea-pig; ~**ung** f temptation

vertagen [fɛr'taːgən] *vt, vi* to adjourn

ver'tauschen *vt* to exchange; (*versehentlich*) to mix up

verteidig- [fɛr'taɪdɪg] *zW*: ~**en** *vt* to defend; **V~er** (**-s, -**) *m* defender; (*JUR*) defence counsel; **V~ung** f defence

ver'teilen *vt* to distribute; (*Rollen*) to assign; (*Salbe*) to spread

Verteilung f distribution, allotment

vertiefen [fɛr'tiːfən] *vt* to deepen ♦ *vr*: **sich in etw** *akk* ~ to become engrossed *od* absorbed in sth

Vertiefung f depression

vertikal [vɛrtiˈkaːl] *adj* vertical

vertilgen [fɛrˈtɪlgən] *vt* to exterminate; (*umg*) to eat up, to consume

vertonen [fɛrˈtoːnən] *vt* to set to music

Vertrag [fɛrˈtraːk] **(-(e)s, ⁀e)** *m* contract, agreement; (*POL*) treaty; **v~en** [-gən] (*unreg*) *vt* to tolerate, to stand ♦ *vr* to get along; (*sich aussöhnen*) to become reconciled; **v~lich** *adj* contractual

verträglich [fɛrˈtrɛːklɪç] *adj* good-natured, sociable; (*Speisen*) easily digested; (*MED*) easily tolerated; **V~keit** *f* sociability; good nature; digestibility

Vertrags- *zW*: **~bruch** *m* breach of contract; **~händler** *m* appointed retailer; **~partner** *m* party to a contract; **~werkstatt** *f* appointed repair shop; **v~widrig** *adj* contrary to contract

vertrauen [fɛrˈtrauən] *vi*: **jdm ~** to trust sb; **~ auf** +*akk* to rely on; **V~ (-s)** *nt* confidence; **V~ erweckend** inspiring trust; **~svoll** *adj* trustful; **~swürdig** *adj* trustworthy

vertraulich [fɛrˈtraulɪç] *adj* familiar; (*geheim*) confidential

vertraut [fɛrˈtraut] *adj* familiar; **V~heit** *f* familiarity

ver'treiben (*unreg*) *vt* to drive away; (*aus Land*) to expel; (*COMM*) to sell; (*Zeit*) to pass

vertret- [fɛrˈtreːt] *zW*: **~en** (*unreg*) *vt* to represent; (*Ansicht*) to hold, to advocate; **sich** *dat* **die Beine ~en** to stretch one's legs; **V~er (-s, -)** *m* representative; (*Verfechter*) advocate; **V~ung** *f* representation; advocacy

Vertrieb [fɛrˈtriːp] **(-(e)s, -e)** *m* marketing (department)

ver'trocknen *vi* to dry up

ver'trösten *vt* to put off

vertun [fɛrˈtuːn] (*unreg*) *vt* to waste ♦ *vr* (*umg*) to make a mistake

vertuschen [fɛrˈtuʃən] *vt* to hush *od* cover up

verübeln [fɛrˈyːbəln] *vt*: **jdm etw ~** to be cross *od* offended with sb on account of sth

verüben [fɛrˈyːbən] *vt* to commit

verun- [fɛrˈʊn] *zW*: **~glimpfen** *vt* to disparage; **~glücken** *vi* to have an accident; **tödlich ~glücken** to be killed in an accident; **~reinigen** *vt* to soil; (*Umwelt*) to pollute; **~sichern** *vt* to rattle; **~treuen** [-trɔyən] *vt* to embezzle

verur- [fɛrˈuːr] *zW*: **~sachen** *vt* to cause; **~teilen** [-tailən] *vt* to condemn; **V~teilung** *f* condemnation; (*JUR*) sentence

verviel- [fɛrˈfiːl] *zW*: **~fachen** *vt* to multiply; **~fältigen** [-fɛltɪgən] *vt* to duplicate, to copy; **V~fältigung** *f* duplication, copying

vervollkommnen [fɛrˈfɔlkɔmnən] *vt* to perfect

vervollständigen [fɛrˈfɔlʃtɛndɪgən] *vt* to complete

ver'wackeln *vt* (*Foto*) to blur

ver'wählen *vr* (*TEL*) to dial the wrong number

verwahren [fɛrˈvaːrən] *vt* to keep, to lock away ♦ *vr* to protest

verwalt- [fɛrˈvalt] *zW*: **~en** *vt* to manage; to administer; **V~er (-s, -)** *m* manager; (*Vermögensverwalter*) trustee; **V~ung** *f* administration; management

ver'wandeln *vt* to change, to transform ♦ *vr* to change; to be transformed; **Ver'wandlung** *f* change, transformation

verwandt [fɛrˈvant] *adj*: **~ (mit)** related (to); **V~e(r)** *f(m)* relative, relation; **V~schaft** *f* relationship; (*Menschen*) relations *pl*

ver'warnen *vt* to caution

Ver'warnung *f* caution

ver'wechseln *vt*: **~ mit** to confuse with; to mistake for; **zum V~ ähnlich** as like as two peas

Ver'wechslung *f* confusion, mixing up

Verwehung [fɛrˈveːʊŋ] *f* snowdrift; sand drift

verweichlicht [fɛrˈvaiçlɪçt] *adj* effeminate, soft

ver'weigern *vt*: **jdm etw ~** to refuse sb sth; **den Gehorsam / die Aussage ~** to refuse to obey/testify

Ver'weigerung *f* refusal

Verweis [fɛrˈvais] **(-es, -e)** *m* reprimand,

rebuke; (*Hinweis*) reference; **v~en** (*unreg*) *vt* to refer; **jdn von der Schule v~en** to expel sb (from school); **jdn des Landes v~en** to deport *od* expel sb

ver'welken *vi* to fade

verwend- [fɛr'vɛnd] *zW*: **~bar** [-'vɛntbaːr] *adj* usable; **ver'wenden** (*unreg*) *vt* to use; (*Mühe, Zeit, Arbeit*) to spend ♦ *vr* to intercede; **Ver'wendung** *f* use

ver'werfen (*unreg*) *vt* to reject

verwerflich [fɛr'vɛrflɪç] *adj* reprehensible

ver'werten *vt* to utilize

Ver'wertung *f* utilization

verwesen [fɛr'veːzən] *vi* to decay

ver'wickeln *vt* to tangle (up); (*fig*) to involve ♦ *vr* to get tangled (up); **jdn in etw** *akk* **~** to involve sb in sth; **sich in etw** *akk* **~** to get involved in sth

verwickelt [fɛr'vɪkəlt] *adj* (*Situation, Fall*) difficult, complicated

verwildern [fɛr'vɪldərn] *vi* to run wild

verwirklichen [fɛr'vɪrklɪçən] *vt* to realize, to put into effect

Verwirklichung *f* realization

verwirren [fɛr'vɪrən] *vt* to tangle (up); (*fig*) to confuse

Verwirrung *f* confusion

verwittern [fɛr'vɪtərn] *vi* to weather

verwitwet [fɛr'vɪtvət] *adj* widowed

verwöhnen [fɛr'vøːnən] *vt* to spoil

verworren [fɛr'vɔrən] *adj* confused

verwundbar [fɛr'vʊntbaːr] *adj* vulnerable

verwunden [fɛr'vʊndən] *vt* to wound

verwunder- [fɛr'vʊndər] *zW*: **~lich** *adj* surprising; **V~ung** *f* astonishment

Verwundete(r) *f(m)* injured person

Verwundung *f* wound, injury

ver'wünschen *vt* to curse

verwüsten [fɛr'vyːstən] *vt* to devastate

verzagen [fɛr'tsaːgən] *vi* to despair

ver'zählen *vr* to miscount

verzehren [fɛr'tseːrən] *vt* to consume

ver'zeichnen *vt* to list; (*Niederlage, Verlust*) to register

Verzeichnis [fɛr'tsaɪçnɪs] (**-ses, -se**) *nt* list, catalogue; (*in Buch*) index

verzeih- [fɛr'tsaɪ] *zW*: **~en** (*unreg*) *vt, vi* to

forgive; **jdm etw ~en** to forgive sb for sth; **~lich** *adj* pardonable; **V~ung** *f* forgiveness, pardon; **V~ung!** sorry!, excuse me!

verzichten [fɛr'tsɪçtən] *vi*: **~ auf** +*akk* to forgo, to give up

ver'ziehen (*unreg*) *vi* to move ♦ *vt* to put out of shape; (*Kind*) to spoil; (*Pflanzen*) to thin out ♦ *vr* to go out of shape; (*Gesicht*) to contort; (*verschwinden*) to disappear; **das Gesicht ~** to pull a face

verzieren [fɛr'tsiːrən] *vt* to decorate, to ornament

Verzierung *f* decoration

verzinsen [fɛr'tsɪnzən] *vt* to pay interest on

ver'zögern *vt* to delay

Ver'zögerung *f* delay, time lag; **~staktik** *f* delaying tactics *pl*

verzollen [fɛr'tsɔlən] *vt* to pay duty on

Verzug [fɛr'tsuːk] *m* delay

verzweif- [fɛr'tsvaɪf] *zW*: **~eln** *vi* to despair; **~elt** *adj* desperate; **V~lung** *f* despair

Veto ['veːto] (**-s, -s**) *nt* veto

Vetter ['fɛtər] (**-s, -n**) *m* cousin

vgl. *abk* (= *vergleiche*) cf.

v. H. *abk* (= *vom Hundert*) p.c.

vibrieren [vi'briːrən] *vi* to vibrate

Video ['viːdeo] *nt* video; **~gerät** *nt* video recorder; **~rekorder** *m* video recorder

Vieh [fiː] (**-(e)s**) *nt* cattle *pl*; **v~isch** *adj* bestial

viel [fiːl] *adj* a lot of, much ♦ *adv* a lot, much; **~ sagend** significant; **~ versprechend** promising; **~e** *pron pl* a lot of, many; **~ zu wenig** much too little; **~erlei** *adj* a great variety of; **~es** *pron* a lot; **~fach** *adj, adv* many times; **auf ~fachen Wunsch** at the request of many people; **V~falt** (**-**) *f* variety; **~fältig** *adj* varied, many-sided

vielleicht [fi'laɪçt] *adv* perhaps

viel- *zW*: **~mal(s)** *adv* many times; **danke ~mals** many thanks; **~mehr** *adv* rather, on the contrary; **~seitig** *adj* many-sided

vier [fiːr] *num* four; **V~eck** (**-(e)s, -e**) *nt* four-sided figure; (*gleichseitig*) square; **~eckig** *adj* four-sided; square; **V~takt-motor** *m* four-stroke engine; **~te(r, s)**

Spelling Reform: ▲ *new spelling* △ *old spelling (to be phased out)*

['fiːrtə(r, s)] *adj* fourth; **V~tel** ['fɪrtəl] **(-s, -)** *nt* quarter; **V~teljahr** *nt* quarter; **~teljährlich** *adj* quarterly; **~teln** *vt* to divide into four; (*Kuchen usw*) to divide into quarters; **V~telstunde** *f* quarter of an hour; **~zehn** ['fɪrtseːn] *num* fourteen; **in ~zehn Tagen** in a fortnight; **~zehntägig** *adj* fortnightly; **~zig** ['fɪrtsɪç] *num* forty

Villa ['vɪla] **(-, Villen)** *f* villa

violett [vio'lεt] *adj* violet

Violin- [vio'liːn] *zW:* **~e** *f* violin; **~schlüssel** *m* treble clef

virtuell [vɪrtu'εl] *adj* (*COMPUT*) virtual; **~e Realität** virtual reality

Virus ['viːrʊs] **(-, Viren)** *m od nt* (*auch COMPUT*) virus

Visa ['viːza] *pl von* **Visum**

vis-a-vis ▲, **vis-à-vis** [viza'viː] *adv* opposite

Visen ['viːzən] *pl von* **Visum**

Visier [vi'ziːr] **(-s, -e)** *nt* gunsight; (*am Helm*) visor

Visite [vi'ziːtə] *f* (*MED*) visit; **~nkarte** *f* visiting card

Visum ['viːzʊm] **(-s, Visa od Visen)** *nt* visa

vital [vi'taːl] *adj* lively, full of life, vital

Vitamin [vita'miːn] **(-s, -e)** *nt* vitamin

Vogel ['foːgəl] **(-s, ⸚)** *m* bird; **einen ~ haben** (*umg*) to have bats in the belfry; **jdm den ~ zeigen** (*umg*) to tap one's forehead (*meaning that one thinks sb stupid*); **~bauer** *nt* birdcage; **~perspektive** *f* bird's-eye view; **~scheuche** *f* scarecrow

Vokabel [vo'kaːbəl] **(-, -n)** *f* word

Vokabular [vokabu'laːr] **(-s, -e)** *nt* vocabulary

Vokal [vo'kaːl] **(-s, -e)** *m* vowel

Volk [fɔlk] **(-(e)s, ⸚er)** *nt* people; nation

Völker- ['fœlkar] *zW:* **~recht** *nt* international law; **v~rechtlich** *adj* according to international law; **~verständigung** *f* international understanding

Volkshochschule

ℹ️ The **Volkshochschule** (*VHS*) is an institution which offers Adult Education classes. No set qualifications are necessary

to attend. For a small fee adults can attend both vocational and non-vocational classes in the day-time or evening.

Volks- *zW:* **~entscheid** *m* referendum; **~fest** *nt* fair; **~hochschule** *f* adult education classes *pl*; **~lied** *nt* folksong; **~republik** *f* people's republic; **~schule** *f* elementary school; **~tanz** *m* folk dance; **~vertreter(in)** *m(f)* people's representative; **~wirtschaft** *f* economics *sg*

voll [fɔl] *adj* full; **etw ~ machen** to fill sth up; **~ tanken** to fill up; **~ und ganz** completely; **jdn für ~ nehmen** (*umg*) to take sb seriously; **~auf** *adv* amply; **V~bart** *m* full beard; **V~beschäftigung** *f* full employment; **~'bringen** (*unreg*) *vt insep* to accomplish; **~'enden** *vt insep* to finish, to complete; **~endet** *adj* (*~kommen*) completed; **~ends** ['fɔlεnts] *adv* completely; **V~'endung** *f* completion

Volleyball ['vɔlibal] *m* volleyball

Vollgas *nt:* **mit ~** at full throttle; **~ geben** to step on it

völlig ['fœlɪç] *adj* complete ♦ *adv* completely

voll- *zW:* **~jährig** *adj* of age; **V~kaskoversicherung** ['fɔlkaskofεrzɪçərʊŋ] *f* fully comprehensive insurance; **~'kommen** *adj* perfect; **V~'kommenheit** *f* perfection; **V~kornbrot** *nt* wholemeal bread; **V~macht** **(-, -en)** *f* authority, full powers *pl*; **V~milch** *f* (*KOCH*) full-cream milk; **V~mond** *m* full moon; **V~pension** *f* full board; **~ständig** ['fɔlʃtεndɪç] *adj* complete; **~'strecken** *vt insep* to execute; **~tanken** △ *vt, vi siehe* **voll**; **V~waschmittel** *nt* detergent; **V~wertkost** *f* wholefood; **~zählig** ['fɔlːsεːlɪç] *adj* complete; in full number; **~'ziehen** (*unreg*) *vt insep* to carry out ♦ *vr insep* to happen; **V~'zug** *m* execution

Volumen [vo'luːmən] **(-s, - od Volumina)** *nt* volume

vom [fɔm] = **von dem**

SCHLÜSSELWORT

von [fɔn] *präp +dat* **1** (*Ausgangspunkt*) from;

von from ... to; **von morgens bis abends** from morning till night; **von ... nach ...** from ... to ...; **von ... an** from ...; **von ... aus** from ...; **von dort aus** from there; **etw von sich aus tun** to do sth of one's own accord; **von mir aus** (*umg*) if you like, I don't mind; **von wo/wann ...?** where/when ... from?

2 (*Ursache, im Passiv*) by; **ein Gedicht von Schiller** a poem by Schiller; **von etw müde** tired from sth

3 (*als Genitiv*) of; **ein Freund von mir** a friend of mine; **nett von dir** nice of you; **jeweils zwei von zehn** two out of every ten

4 (*über*) about; **er erzählte vom Urlaub** he talked about his holiday

5: von wegen! (*umg*) no way!

voneinander *adv* from each other

vor [foːr] *präp +dat* **1** (*räumlich*) in front of; **vor der Kirche links abbiegen** turn left before the church

2 (*zeitlich*) before; **ich war vor ihm da** I was before him; **vor 2 Tagen** 2 days ago; **5 (Minuten) vor 4** 5 (minutes) to 4; **vor kurzem** a little while ago

3 (*Ursache*) with; **vor Wut/Liebe** with rage/love; **vor Hunger sterben** to die of hunger; **vor lauter Arbeit** because of work

4: vor allem, vor allen Dingen most of all
♦ *präp +akk* (*räumlich*) in front of
♦ *adv*: **vor und zurück** backwards and forwards

Vorabend ['foːrʔaːbənt] *m* evening before, eve

voran [fo'ran] *adv* before, ahead; **mach ~!** get on with it!; **~gehen** (*unreg*) *vi* to go ahead; **einer Sache** *dat* **~gehen** to precede sth; **~kommen** (*unreg*) *vi* to come along, to make progress

Voranschlag ['foːrʔanʃlaːk] *m* estimate

Vorarbeiter ['foːrʔarbaɪtər] *m* foreman

voraus [fo'raʊs] *adv* ahead; (*zeitlich*) in advance; **jdm ~ sein** to be ahead of sb; **im V~** in advance; **~gehen** (*unreg*) *vi* to go (on) ahead; (*fig*) to precede; **~haben** (*unreg*) *vt*: **jdm etw ~haben** to have the edge on sb in sth; **V~sage** *f* prediction; **~sagen** *vt* to predict; **~sehen** (*unreg*) *vt* to foresee; **~setzen** *vt* to assume; **~gesetzt, dass ...** provided that ...; **V~setzung** *f* requirement, prerequisite; **V~sicht** *f* foresight; **aller V~sicht nach** in all probability; **~sichtlich** *adv* probably

Vorbehalt ['foːrbəhalt] (**-(e)s, -e**) *m* reservation, proviso; **v~en** (*unreg*) *vt*: **sich/jdm etw v~en** to reserve sth (for o.s.)/for sb; **v~los** *adj* unconditional ♦ *adv* unconditionally

vorbei [foːr'baɪ] *adv* by, past; **das ist ~** that's over; **~gehen** (*unreg*) *vi* to pass by, to go past; **~kommen** (*unreg*) *vi*: **bei jdm ~kommen** to drop in *od* call in on sb

vor- *zW*: **~belastet** ['foːrbəlastət] *adj* (*fig*) handicapped; **~bereiten** *vt* to prepare; **V~bereitung** *f* preparation; **V~bestellung** *f* advance order; (*von Platz, Tisch etc*) advance booking; **~bestraft** ['foːrbəʃtraːft] *adj* previously convicted, with a record

vorbeugen ['foːrbɔʏɡən] *vt, vr* to lean forward ♦ *vi +dat* to prevent; **~d** *adj* preventive

Vorbeugung *f* prevention; **zur ~ gegen** for the prevention of

Vorbild ['foːrbɪlt] *nt* model; **sich** *dat* **jdn zum ~ nehmen** to model o.s. on sb; **v~lich** *adj* model, ideal

vorbringen ['foːrbrɪŋən] (*unreg*) *vt* to advance, to state

Vorder- ['fɔrdər] *zW*: **~achse** *f* front axle; **v~e(r, s)** *adj* front; **~grund** *m* foreground; **~mann** (*pl* **-männer**) *m* man in front; **jdn auf ~mann bringen** (*umg*) to get sb to shape up; **~seite** *f* front (side); **v~ste(r, s)** *adj* front

vordrängen ['foːrdrɛŋən] *vr* to push to the front

voreilig ['foːrʔaɪlɪç] *adj* hasty, rash

voreinander [foːrʔaɪ'nandər] *adv* (*räumlich*)

in front of each other

voreingenommen ['fo:r|aingənɔmən] *adj* biased; **V~heit** *f* bias

vorenthalten ['fo:r|enthaltən] (*unreg*) *vt*: **jdm etw ~** to withhold sth from sb

vorerst ['fo:r|e:rst] *adv* for the moment *od* present

Vorfahr ['fo:rfa:r] (**-en, -en**) *m* ancestor

vorfahren (*unreg*) *vi* to drive (on) ahead; (*vors Haus etc*) to drive up

Vorfahrt *f* (*AUT*) right of way; **~ achten!** give way!

Vorfahrts- *zW*: **~regel** *f* right of way; **~schild** *nt* give way sign; **~straße** *f* major road

Vorfall ['fo:rfal] *m* incident; **v~en** (*unreg*) *vi* to occur

vorfinden ['fo:rfɪndən] (*unreg*) *vt* to find

Vorfreude ['fo:rfrɔydə] *f* (joyful) anticipation

vorführen ['fo:rfy:rən] *vt* to show, to display; **dem Gericht ~** to bring before the court

Vorgabe ['fo:rga:bə] *f* (*SPORT*) start, handicap ♦ *in zW* (*COMPUT*) default

Vorgang ['fo:rgaŋ] *m* course of events; (*bes SCI*) process

Vorgänger(in) ['fo:rgɛŋər(ɪn)] (**-s, -**) *m(f)* predecessor

vorgeben ['fo:rge:bən] (*unreg*) *vt* to pretend, to use as a pretext; (*SPORT*) to give an advantage *od* a start of

vorgefertigt ['fo:rgəfɛrtɪçt] *adj* prefabricated

vorgehen ['fo:rge:ən] (*unreg*) *vi* (*voraus*) to go (on) ahead; (*nach vorn*) to go up front; (*handeln*) to act, to proceed; (*Uhr*) to be fast; (*Vorrang haben*) to take precedence; (*passieren*) to go on

Vorgehen (**-s**) *nt* action

Vorgeschichte ['fo:rgəʃɪçtə] *f* past history

Vorgeschmack ['fo:rgəʃmak] *m* foretaste

Vorgesetzte(r) ['fo:rgəzɛtstə(r)] *f(m)* superior

vorgestern ['fo:rgɛstərn] *adv* the day before yesterday

vorhaben ['fo:rha:bən] (*unreg*) *vt* to intend; **hast du schon was vor?** have you got anything on?; **V~ (-s, -)** *nt* intention

vorhalten ['fo:rhaltən] (*unreg*) *vt* to hold *od* put up ♦ *vi* to last; **jdm etw ~** (*fig*) to reproach sb for sth

vorhanden [fo:r'handən] *adj* existing; (*erhältlich*) available

Vorhang ['fo:rhaŋ] *m* curtain

Vorhängeschloss ▲ ['fo:rhɛŋəʃlɔs] *nt* padlock

vorher [fo:r'he:r] *adv* before(hand); **~bestimmen** *vt* (*Schicksal*) to preordain; **~gehen** (*unreg*) *vi* to precede; **~ig** *adj* previous

Vorherrschaft ['fo:rhɛrʃaft] *f* predominance, supremacy

vorherrschen ['fo:rhɛrʃən] *vi* to predominate

vorher- [fo:r'he:r] *zW*: **V~sage** *f* forecast; **~sagen** *vt* to forecast, to predict; **~sehbar** *adj* predictable; **~sehen** (*unreg*) *vt* to foresee

vorhin [fo:r'hɪn] *adv* not long ago, just now; **V~ein** ▲ *adv*: **im V~ein** beforehand

vorig ['fo:rɪç] *adj* previous, last

Vorkämpfer(in) ['fo:rkɛmpfər(ɪn)] *m(f)* pioneer

Vorkaufsrecht ['fo:rkaufsrɛçt] *nt* option to buy

Vorkehrung ['fo:rke:ruŋ] *f* precaution

vorkommen ['fo:rkɔmən] (*unreg*) *vi* to come forward; (*geschehen, sich finden*) to occur; (*scheinen*) to seem (to be); **sich** *dat* **dumm** *etc* **~** to feel stupid *etc*; **V~ (-s, -)** *nt* occurrence

Vorkriegs- ['fo:rkri:ks] *in zW* prewar

Vorladung ['fo:rla:duŋ] *f* summons *sg*

Vorlage ['fo:rla:gə] *f* model, pattern; (*Gesetzesvorlage*) bill; (*SPORT*) pass

vorlassen ['fo:rlasən] (*unreg*) *vt* to admit; (*vorgehen lassen*) to allow to go in front

vorläufig ['fo:rlɔyfɪç] *adj* temporary, provisional

vorlaut ['fo:rlaut] *adj* impertinent, cheeky

vorlesen ['fo:rle:zən] (*unreg*) *vt* to read (out)

Vorlesung *f* (*UNIV*) lecture

vorletzte(r, s) ['fo:rlɛtstə(r, s)] *adj* last but one

vorlieb [fo:r'li:p] *adv*: **~ nehmen mit** to

make do with

Vorliebe ['foːrliːbə] f preference, partiality

vorliegen ['foːrliːɡən] (unreg) vi to be (here); **etw liegt jdm vor** sb has sth; **~d** adj present, at issue

vormachen ['foːrmaxən] vt: **jdm etw ~** to show sb how to do sth; (fig) to fool sb; to have sb on

Vormachtstellung ['foːrmaxtʃtɛlʊŋ] f supremacy, hegemony

Vormarsch ['foːrmarʃ] m advance

vormerken ['foːrmɛrkən] vt to book

Vormittag ['foːrmɪtaːk] m morning; **v~s** adv in the morning, before noon

vorn [fɔrn] adv in front; **von ~ anfangen** to start at the beginning; **nach ~** to the front

Vorname ['foːrnaːmə] m first name, Christian name

vorne ['fɔrnə] adv = **vorn**

vornehm ['foːrneːm] adj distinguished; refined; elegant

vornehmen (unreg) vt (fig) to carry out; **sich** dat **etw ~** to start on sth; (beschließen) to decide to do sth; **sich** dat **jdn ~** to tell sb off

vornherein ['fɔrnhɛraɪn] adv: **von ~** from the start

Vorort ['foːrɔrt] m suburb

Vorrang ['foːrraŋ] m precedence, priority; **v~ig** adj of prime importance, primary

Vorrat ['foːrraːt] m stock, supply

vorrätig ['foːrrɛːtɪç] adj in stock

Vorratskammer f pantry

Vorrecht ['foːrrɛçt] nt privilege

Vorrichtung ['foːrrɪçtʊŋ] f device, contrivance

vorrücken ['foːrrʏkən] vi to advance ♦ vt to move forward

Vorsaison ['foːrzɛzõː] f early season

Vorsatz ['foːrzats] m intention; (JUR) intent; **einen ~ fassen** to make a resolution

vorsätzlich ['foːrzɛtslɪç] adj intentional; (JUR) premeditated ♦ adv intentionally

Vorschau ['foːrʃaʊ] f (RADIO, TV) (programme) preview; (Film) trailer

Vorschlag ['foːrʃlaːk] m suggestion, proposal; **v~en** (unreg) vt to suggest, to propose

vorschreiben ['foːrʃraɪbən] (unreg) vt to prescribe, to specify

Vorschrift ['foːrʃrɪft] f regulation(s); rule(s); (Anweisungen) instruction(s); **Dienst nach ~** work-to-rule; **v~smäßig** adj as per regulations/instructions

Vorschuss ▲ ['foːrʃʊs] m advance

vorsehen ['foːrzeːən] (unreg) vt to provide for, to plan ♦ vr to take care, to be careful ♦ vi to be visible

Vorsehung f providence

Vorsicht ['foːrzɪçt] f caution, care; **~!** look out!, take care!; (auf Schildern) caution!, danger!; **~, Stufe!** mind the step!; **v~ig** adj cautious, careful; **v~shalber** adv just in case

Vorsilbe ['foːrzɪlbə] f prefix

vorsingen ['foːrzɪŋən] vt (vor Zuhörern) to sing (to); (in Prüfung, für Theater etc) to audition (for) ♦ vi to sing

Vorsitz ['foːrzɪts] m chair(manship); **~ende(r)** f(m) chairman(-woman)

Vorsorge ['foːrzɔrɡə] f precaution(s), provision(s); **v~n** vi: **v~n für** to make provision(s) for; **~untersuchung** f check-up

vorsorglich ['foːrzɔrklɪç] adv as a precaution

Vorspeise ['foːrʃpaɪzə] f hors d'oeuvre, appetizer

Vorspiel ['foːrʃpiːl] nt prelude

vorspielen vt: **jdm etw ~** (MUS) to play sth for od to sb ♦ vi (zur Prüfung etc) to play for od to sb

vorsprechen ['foːrʃprɛçən] (unreg) vt to say out loud, to recite ♦ vi: **bei jdm ~** to call on sb

Vorsprung ['foːrʃprʊŋ] m projection, ledge; (fig) advantage, start

Vorstadt ['foːrʃtat] f suburbs pl

Vorstand ['foːrʃtant] m executive committee; (COMM) board (of directors); (Person) director, head

vorstehen ['foːrʃteːən] (unreg) vi to project; **einer Sache** dat **~** (fig) to be the head of sth

vorstell- ['foːrʃtɛl] zW: **~bar** adj

Spelling Reform: ▲ *new spelling* △ *old spelling (to be phased out)*

conceivable; **~en** *vt* to put forward; (*bekannt machen*) to introduce; (*darstellen*) to represent; **~en vor** +*akk* to put in front of; **sich** *dat* **etw ~en** to imagine sth; **V~ung** *f* (*Bekanntmachen*) introduction; (*THEAT etc*) performance; (*Gedanke*) idea, thought

vorstoßen ['foːrʃtoːsən] (*unreg*) *vi* (*ins Unbekannte*) to venture (forth)

Vorstrafe ['foːrʃtraːfə] *f* previous conviction

Vortag ['foːrtaːk] *m*: **am ~ einer Sache** *gen* on the day before sth

vortäuschen ['foːrtɔʏʃən] *vt* to feign, to pretend

Vorteil ['foːrtaɪl] **(-s, -e)** *m*: **~ (gegenüber)** advantage (over); **im ~ sein** to have the advantage; **v~haft** *adj* advantageous

Vortrag ['foːrtraːk] **(-(e)s, Vorträge)** *m* talk, lecture; **v~en** [-gən] (*unreg*) *vt* to carry forward; (*fig*) to recite; (*Rede*) to deliver; (*Lied*) to perform; (*Meinung etc*) to express

vortreten ['foːrtreːtən] (*unreg*) *vi* to step forward; (*Augen etc*) to protrude

vorüber [fo'ryːbər] *adv* past, over; **~gehen** (*unreg*) *vi* to pass (by); **~gehen an** +*dat* (*fig*) to pass over; **~gehend** *adj* temporary, passing

Vorurteil ['foːrʔʊrtaɪl] *nt* prejudice

Vorverkauf ['foːrfɛrkaʊf] *m* advance booking

Vorwahl ['foːrvaːl] *f* preliminary election; (*TEL*) dialling code

Vorwand ['foːrvant] **(-(e)s, Vorwände)** *m* pretext

vorwärts ['foːrvɛrts] *adv* forward; **~ gehen** to progress; **V~gang** *m* (*AUT etc*) forward gear; **~ kommen** to get on, to make progress

Vorwäsche *f* prewash

vorweg [foːr'vɛk] *adv* in advance; **~nehmen** (*unreg*) *vt* to anticipate

vorweisen ['foːrvaɪzən] (*unreg*) *vt* to show, to produce

vorwerfen ['foːrvɛrfən] (*unreg*) *vt*: **jdm etw ~** to reproach sb for sth, to accuse sb of sth; **sich** *dat* **nichts vorzuwerfen haben** to have nothing to reproach o.s. with

vorwiegend ['foːrviːgənt] *adj* predominant ♦ *adv* predominantly

vorwitzig ['foːrvɪtsɪç] *adj* (*Mensch, Bemerkung*) cheeky

Vorwort ['foːrvɔrt] **(-(e)s, -e)** *nt* preface

Vorwurf ['foːrvʊrf] *m* reproach; **jdm/sich Vorwürfe machen** to reproach sb/o.s.; **v~svoll** *adj* reproachful

vorzeigen ['foːrtsaɪgən] *vt* to show, to produce

vorzeitig ['foːrtsaɪtɪç] *adj* premature

vorziehen ['foːrtsiːən] (*unreg*) *vt* to pull forward; (*Gardinen*) to draw; (*lieber haben*) to prefer

Vorzimmer ['foːrtsɪmər] *nt* (*Büro*) outer office

Vorzug ['foːrtsuːk] *m* preference; (*gute Eigenschaft*) merit, good quality; (*Vorteil*) advantage

vorzüglich [foːr'tsyːklɪç] *adj* excellent

Vorzugspreis *m* special discount price

vulgär [vʊl'gɛːr] *adj* vulgar

Vulkan [vʊl'kaːn] **(-s, -e)** *m* volcano

W, w

Waage ['vaːgə] *f* scales *pl*; (*ASTROL*) Libra; **w~recht** *adj* horizontal

Wabe ['vaːbə] *f* honeycomb

wach [vax] *adj* awake; (*fig*) alert; **W~e** *f* guard, watch; **W~e halten** to keep watch; **W~e stehen** to stand guard; **~en** *vi* to be awake; (*Wache halten*) to guard

Wachs [vaks] **(-es, -e)** *nt* wax

wachsam ['vaxzaːm] *adj* watchful, vigilant, alert

wachsen (*unreg*) *vi* to grow

Wachstuch ['vakstuːx] *nt* oilcloth

Wachstum ['vakstuːm] **(-s)** *nt* growth

Wächter ['vɛçtər] **(-s, -)** *m* guard, warden, keeper; (*Parkplatzwächter*) attendant

wackel- ['vakəl] *zW*: **~ig** *adj* shaky, wobbly; **W~kontakt** *m* loose connection; **~n** *vi* to shake; (*fig: Position*) to be shaky

wacker ['vakər] *adj* valiant, stout ♦ *adv* well, bravely

Wade ['va:də] f (ANAT) calf
Waffe ['vafə] f weapon
Waffel ['vafəl] (-, -n) f waffle; wafer
Waffen- zW: **~schein** m gun licence;
~stillstand m armistice, truce
Wagemut ['va:gəmu:t] m daring
wagen ['va:gən] vt to venture, to dare
Wagen ['va:gən] (-s, -) m vehicle; (Auto) car;
(EISENB) carriage; (Pferdewagen) cart;
~heber (-s, -) m jack
Waggon [va'gõ:] (-s, -s) m carriage;
(Güterwaggon) goods van, freight truck (US)
Wagnis ['va:knɪs] (-ses, -se) nt risk
Wagon ▲ [va'gõ:, va'gɔ:n] (-s, -s) m
= **Waggon**
Wahl [va:l] (-, -en) f choice; (POL) election;
zweite ~ (COMM) seconds pl
wähl- ['vɛ:l] zW: **~bar** adj eligible; **~en** vt, vi
to choose; (POL) to elect, to vote (for); (TEL)
to dial; **W~er(in)** (-s, -) m(f) voter;
~erisch adj fastidious, particular
Wahl- zW: **~fach** nt optional subject;
~gang m ballot; **~kabine** f polling booth;
~kampf m election campaign; **~kreis** m
constituency; **~lokal** nt polling station;
w~los adv at random; **~recht** nt franchise;
~spruch m motto; **~urne** f ballot box
Wahn [va:n] (-(e)s) m delusion; folly; **~sinn**
m madness; **w~sinnig** adj insane, mad
♦ adv (umg) incredibly
wahr [va:r] adj true
wahren vt to maintain, to keep
während ['vɛ:rənt] präp +gen during ♦ konj
while; **~dessen** adv meanwhile
wahr- zW: **~haben** (unreg) vt: **etw nicht
~haben wollen** to refuse to admit sth;
~haft adv (tatsächlich) truly; **~haftig**
[va:r'haftɪç] adj true, real ♦ adv really;
W~heit f truth; **~nehmen** (unreg) vt to
perceive, to observe; **W~nehmung** f
perception; **~sagen** vi to prophesy, to tell
fortunes; **W~sager(in)** (-s, -) m(f) fortune
teller; **~scheinlich** [va:r'ʃaɪnlɪç] adj
probable ♦ adv probably;
W~'scheinlichkeit f probability; **aller
W~scheinlichkeit nach** in all probability
Währung ['vɛ:rʊŋ] f currency

Wahrzeichen nt symbol
Waise ['vaɪzə] f orphan; **~nhaus** nt
orphanage
Wald [valt] (-(e)s, ⁻er) m wood(s); (groß)
forest; **~brand** m forest fire; **~sterben** nt
trees dying due to pollution
Wales [weɪlz] (-) nt Wales
Wal(fisch) ['va:l(fɪʃ)] (-(e)s, -e) m whale
Waliser [va'li:zər] (-s, -) m Welshman;
Waliserin [va'li:zərɪn] f Welsh woman;
walisisch [va'li:zɪʃ] adj Welsh
Walkman ['wɔ:kman] (®; -s, Walkmen) m
Walkman ®, personal stereo
Wall [val] (-(e)s, ⁻e) m embankment;
(Bollwerk) rampart
Wallfahr- zW: **~er(in)** m(f) pilgrim; **~t** f
pilgrimage
Walnuss ▲ ['valnʊs] f walnut
Walross ▲ ['valrɔs] nt walrus
Walze ['valtsə] f (Gerät) cylinder; (Fahrzeug)
roller; **w~n** vt to roll (out)
wälzen ['vɛltsən] vt to roll (over); (Bücher) to
hunt through; (Probleme) to deliberate on
♦ vr to wallow; (vor Schmerzen) to roll
about; (im Bett) to toss and turn
Walzer ['valtsər] (-s, -) m waltz
Wand [vant] (-, ⁻e) f wall; (Trennwand)
partition; (Bergwand) precipice
Wandel ['vandəl] (-s) m change; **w~bar** adj
changeable, variable; **w~n** vt, vr to change
♦ vi (gehen) to walk
Wander- ['vandər] zW: **~er** (-s, -) m hiker,
rambler; **~karte** f map of country walks;
w~n vi to hike; (Blick) to wander;
(Gedanken) to stray; **~schaft** f travelling;
~ung f walk, hike; **~weg** m trail, walk
Wandlung f change, transformation
Wange ['vaŋə] f cheek
wanken ['vaŋkən] vi to stagger; (fig) to
waver
wann [van] adv when
Wanne ['vanə] f tub
Wanze ['vantsə] f bug
Wappen ['vapən] (-s, -) nt coat of arms,
crest; **~kunde** f heraldry
war etc [va:r] vb siehe **sein**
Ware ['va:rə] f ware

Waren- *zW*: **~haus** *nt* department store; **~lager** *nt* stock, store; **~muster** *nt* trade sample; **~probe** *f* sample; **~sendung** *f* trade sample (*sent by post*); **~zeichen** *nt*: **(eingetragenes) ~zeichen** (registered) trademark

warf *etc* [varf] *vb siehe* **werfen**

warm [varm] *adj* warm; (*Essen*) hot

Wärm- ['verm] *zW*: **~e** *f* warmth; **w~en** *vt*, *vr* to warm (up), to heat (up); **~flasche** *f* hot-water bottle

Warn- ['varn] *zW*: **~blinkanlage** *f* (*AUT*) hazard warning lights *pl*; **~dreieck** *nt* warning triangle; **w~en** *vt* to warn; **~ung** *f* warning

warten ['vartən] *vi*: **~ (auf** +*akk*) to wait (for); **auf sich ~ lassen** to take a long time

Wärter(in) ['vertər(in)] (**-s, -**) *m(f)* attendant

Warte- ['vartə] *zW*: **~saal** *m* (*EISENB*) waiting room; **~zimmer** *nt* waiting room

Wartung *f* servicing; service; **~ und Instandhaltung** maintenance

warum [va'rum] *adv* why

Warze ['vartsə] *f* wart

was [vas] *pron* what; (*umg: etwas*) something; **~ für (ein) ...** what sort of ...

waschbar *adj* washable

Waschbecken *nt* washbasin

Wäsche ['veʃə] *f* wash(ing); (*Bettwäsche*) linen; (*Unterwäsche*) underclothing

waschecht *adj* colourfast; (*fig*) genuine

Wäsche- *zW*: **~klammer** *f* clothes peg (*BRIT*), clothespin (*US*); **~leine** *f* washing line (*BRIT*)

waschen ['vaʃən] (*unreg*) *vt*, *vi* to wash ♦ *vr* to (have a) wash; **sich** *dat* **die Hände ~** to wash one's hands

Wäsche'rei *f* laundry

Wasch- *zW*: **~gelegenheit** *f* washing facilities; **~küche** *f* laundry room; **~lappen** *m* face flannel, washcloth (*US*); (*umg*) sissy; **~maschine** *f* washing machine; **~mittel** *nt* detergent, washing powder; **~pulver** *nt* detergent, washing powder; **~raum** *m* washroom; **~salon** *m* Launderette ®

Wasser ['vasər] (**-s, -**) *nt* water; **~ball** *m* water polo; **w~dicht** *adj* waterproof; **~fall** *m* waterfall; **~farbe** *f* watercolour; **~hahn** *m* tap, faucet (*US*); **~kraftwerk** *nt* hydroelectric power station; **~leitung** *f* water pipe; **~mann** *m* (*ASTROL*) Aquarius

wässern ['vesərn] *vt*, *vi* to water

Wasser- *zW*: **w~scheu** *adj* afraid of (the) water; **~ski** ['vasərʃiː] *nt* water-skiing; **~stoff** *m* hydrogen; **~waage** *f* spirit level; **~zeichen** *nt* watermark

wässrig ▲ ['vesriç] *adj* watery

Watt [vat] (**-(e)s, -en**) *nt* mud flats *pl*

Watte *f* cotton wool, absorbent cotton (*US*)

WC ['veːˈtseː] (**-s, -s**) *nt abk* (= *water closet*) W.C.

Web- ['veːb] *zW*: **w~en** (*unreg*) *vt* to weave; **~er** (**-s, -**) *m* weaver; **~e'rei** *f* (*Betrieb*) weaving mill; **~stuhl** *m* loom

Wechsel ['veksəl] (**-s, -**) *m* change; (*COMM*) bill of exchange; **~geld** *nt* change; **w~haft** *adj* (*Wetter*) variable; **~jahre** *pl* change of life *sg*; **~kurs** *m* rate of exchange; **w~n** *vt* to change; (*Blicke*) to exchange ♦ *vi* to change; to vary; (*Geldwechseln*) to have change; **~strom** *m* alternating current; **~stube** *f* bureau de change; **~wirkung** *f* interaction

Weck- ['vek] *zW*: **~dienst** *m* alarm call service; **w~en** *vt* to wake (up); to call; **~er** (**-s, -**) *m* alarm clock

wedeln ['veːdəln] *vi* (*mit Schwanz*) to wag; (*mit Fächer etc*) to wave

weder ['veːdər] *konj* neither; **~ ... noch ...** neither ... nor ...

Weg [veːk] (**-(e)s, -e**) *m* way; (*Pfad*) path; (*Route*) route; **sich auf den ~ machen** to be on one's way; **jdm aus dem ~ gehen** to keep out of sb's way; *siehe* **zuwege**

weg [vek] *adv* away, off; **über etw** *akk* **~ sein** to be over sth; **er war schon ~** he had already left; **Finger ~!** hands off!

wegbleiben (*unreg*) *vi* to stay away

wegen ['veːgən] *präp* +*gen* (*umg*: +*dat*) because of

weg- ['vek] *zW*: **~fallen** (*unreg*) *vi* to be left out; (*Ferien, Bezahlung*) to be cancelled; (*aufhören*) to cease; **~gehen** (*unreg*) *vi* to go away; to leave; **~lassen** (unreg) vt to leave out; **~laufen** (unreg) vi to run away od off; **~legen** vt to put aside; **~machen** (umg) vt to get rid of; **~müssen** (unreg; umg) vi to have to go; **~nehmen** (unreg) vt to take away; **~tun** (unreg) vt to put away; **W~weiser (-s, -)** m road sign, signpost; **~werfen** (unreg) vt to throw away

weh [ve:] adj sore; **~(e)** excl: **~(e), wenn du ...** woe betide you if ...; **o ~!** oh dear!; **~e!** just you dare!

wehen vt, vi to blow; (Fahnen) to flutter

weh- zW: **~leidig** adj whiny, whining; **~mütig** adj melancholy

Wehr [ve:r] (-, -en) f: **sich zur ~ setzen** to defend o.s.; **~dienst** m military service; **~dienstverweigerer** m ≃ conscientious objector; **w~en** vr to defend o.s.; **w~los** adj defenceless; **~pflicht** f compulsory military service; **w~pflichtig** adj liable for military service

Wehrdienst

i **Wehrdienst** is military service which is still compulsory in Germany. All young men receive their call-up papers at 18 and all those pronounced physically fit are required to spend 10 months in the **Bundeswehr**. Conscientious objectors are allowed to do **Zivildienst** as an alternative, after attending a hearing and presenting their case.

wehtun ▲ ['ve:tu:n] (unreg) vt to hurt, to be sore; **jdm/sich ~** to hurt sb/o.s.

Weib [vaip] (-(e)s, -er) nt woman, female; wife; **~chen** nt female; **w~lich** adj feminine

weich [vaiç] adj soft; **W~e** f (EISENB) points pl; **~en** (unreg) vi to yield, to give way; **W~heit** f softness; **~lich** adj soft, namby-pamby

Weide ['vaidə] f (Baum) willow; (Gras) pasture; **w~n** vi to graze ♦ vr: **sich an etw** dat **w~n** to delight in sth

weigern ['vaigərn] vr to refuse

Weigerung ['vaigəruŋ] f refusal

Weihe ['vaiə] f consecration; (Priesterweihe) ordination; **w~n** vt to consecrate; to ordain

Weihnacht- zW: **~en (-)** nt Christmas; **w~lich** adj Christmas cpd

Weihnachts- zW: **~abend** m Christmas Eve; **~lied** nt Christmas carol; **~mann** m Father Christmas, Santa Claus; **~markt** m Christmas fair; **~tag** m Christmas Day; **zweiter ~tag** Boxing Day

Weihnachtsmarkt

i The **Weihnachtsmarkt** is a market held in most large towns in Germany in the weeks prior to Christmas. People visit it to buy presents, toys and Christmas decorations, and to enjoy the festive atmosphere. Traditional Christmas food and drink can also be consumed there, for example, **Lebkuchen** and **Glühwein**.

Weihwasser nt holy water

weil [vail] konj because

Weile ['vailə] (-) f while, short time

Wein [vain] (-(e)s, -e) m wine; (Pflanze) vine; **~bau** m cultivation of vines; **~berg** m vineyard; **~bergschnecke** f snail; **~brand** m brandy

weinen vt, vi to cry; **das ist zum W~** it's enough to make you cry od weep

Wein- zW: **~glas** nt wine glass; **~karte** f wine list; **~lese** f vintage; **~probe** f wine-tasting; **~rebe** f vine; **~rot** adj burgundy, claret, wine-red; **~stock** m vine; **~stube** f wine bar; **~traube** f grape

weise ['vaizə] adj wise

Weise f manner, way; (Lied) tune; **auf diese ~** in this way

weisen (unreg) vt to show

Weisheit ['vaishait] f wisdom; **~szahn** m wisdom tooth

weiß [vais] adj white ♦ vb siehe **wissen**; **W~bier** nt weissbier (light, fizzy beer made using top-fermentation yeast); **W~brot** nt white bread; **~en** vt to whitewash; **W~glut** f (TECH) incandescence; **jdn bis zur W~glut bringen** (fig) to make sb see red; **W~kohl**

m (white) cabbage; **W~wein** *m* white wine; **W~wurst** *f* veal sausage

weit [vait] *adj* wide; (*Begriff*) broad; (*Reise, Wurf*) long ♦ *adv* far; **wie ~ ist es ...?** how far is it ...?; **in ~er Ferne** in the far distance; **~ blickend** far-seeing; **~ reichend** long-range; (*fig*) far-reaching; **~ verbreitet** widespread; **das geht zu ~** that's going too far; **~aus** *adv* by far; **~blickend** *adj* far-seeing; **W~e** *f* width; (*Raum*) space; (*von Entfernung*) distance; **~en** *vt, vr* to widen

weiter ['vaitər] *adj* wider; broader; farther (away); (*zusätzlich*) further ♦ *adv* further; **ohne ~es** without further ado; just like that; **~ nichts/niemand** nothing/nobody else; **~arbeiten** *vi* to go on working; **~bilden** *vr* to continue one's education; **~empfehlen** (*unreg*) *vt* to recommend (to others); **W~fahrt** *f* continuation of the journey; **~führen** *vi* (*Straße*) to lead on (to) ♦ *vt* (*fortsetzen*) to continue, carry on; **~gehen** (*unreg*) *vi* to go on; **~hin** *adv*: **etw ~hin tun** to go on doing sth; **~kommen** (*unreg*) *vi* (*fig: mit Arbeit*) to make progress; **~leiten** *vt* to pass on; **~machen** *vt, vi* to continue

weit- *zW*: **~gehend** *adj* considerable ♦ *adv* largely; **~läufig** *adj* (*Gebäude*) spacious; (*Erklärung*) lengthy; (*Verwandter*) distant; **~reichend** *adj* long-range; (*fig*) far-reaching; **~schweifig** *adj* long-winded; **~sichtig** *adj* (*MED*) long-sighted; (*fig*) far-sighted; **W~sprung** *m* long jump; **~verbreitet** *adj* widespread

Weizen ['vaitsən] (**-s, -**) *m* wheat

welche(r, s) *interrogativ pron* which; **welcher von beiden?** which (one) of the two?; **welchen hast du genommen?** which (one) did you take?; **welche eine ...!** what a ...!; **welche Freude!** what joy! ♦ *indef pron* some; (*in Fragen*) any; **ich habe welche** I have some; **haben Sie welche?** do you have any? ♦ *relativ pron* (*bei Menschen*) who; (*bei*

Sachen) which, that; **welche(r, s) auch immer** whoever/whichever/whatever

welk [vɛlk] *adj* withered; **~en** *vi* to wither

Welle ['vɛlə] *f* wave; (*TECH*) shaft

Wellen- *zW*: **~bereich** *m* waveband; **~länge** *f* (*auch fig*) wavelength; **~linie** *f* wavy line; **~sittich** *m* budgerigar

Welt [vɛlt] (**-, -en**) *f* world; **~all** *nt* universe; **~anschauung** *f* philosophy of life; **w~berühmt** *adj* world-famous; **~krieg** *m* world war; **w~lich** *adj* worldly; (*nicht kirchlich*) secular; **~macht** *f* world power; **~meister** *m* world champion; **~raum** *m* space; **~reise** *f* trip round the world; **~stadt** *f* metropolis; **w~weit** *adj* world-wide

wem [ve:m] (*dat von* **wer**) *pron* to whom

wen [ve:n] (*akk von* **wer**) *pron* whom

Wende ['vɛndə] *f* turn; (*Veränderung*) change; **~kreis** *m* (*GEOG*) tropic; (*AUT*) turning circle; **~ltreppe** *f* spiral staircase; **w~n** (*unreg*) *vt, vi, vr* to turn; **sich an jdn w~n** to go/come to sb

wendig ['vɛndɪç] *adj* (*Auto etc*) manœuvrable; (*fig*) agile

Wendung *f* turn; (*Redewendung*) idiom

wenig ['ve:nɪç] *adj, adv* little; **~e** *pron pl* few *pl*; **~er** *adj* less; (*mit pl*) fewer ♦ *adv* less; **~ste(r, s)** *adj* least; **am ~sten** least; **~stens** *adv* at least

wenn [vɛn] *konj* **1** (*falls, bei Wünschen*) if; **wenn auch ..., selbst wenn ...** even if ...; **wenn ich doch ...** if only I ...

2 (*zeitlich*) when; **immer wenn** whenever

wennschon ['vɛnʃoːn] *adv*: **na ~** so what?; **~, dennschon!** in for a penny, in for a pound

wer [ve:r] *pron* who

Werbe- ['vɛrbə] *zW*: **~fernsehen** *nt* commercial television; **~geschenk** *nt* gift (*from company*); (*zu Gekauftem*) free gift; **w~n** (*unreg*) *vt* to win; (*Mitglied*) to recruit ♦ *vi* to advertise; **um jdn/etw w~n** to try to win sb/sth; **für jdn/etw w~n** to promote sb/sth

Werbung f advertising; (*von Mitgliedern*) recruitment; **~ um jdn/etw** promotion of sb/sth

Werdegang ['veːrdəgaŋ] m (*Laufbahn*) development; (*beruflich*) career

---
SCHLÜSSELWORT
---

werden ['veːrdən] (*pt* **wurde**, *pp* **geworden** *od* (*bei Passiv*) **worden**) *vi* to become; **was ist aus ihm/aus der Sache geworden?** what became of him/it?; **es ist nichts/gut geworden** it came to nothing/turned out well; **es wird Nacht/Tag** it's getting dark/light; **mir wird kalt** I'm getting cold, **mir wird schlecht** I feel ill; **Erster werden** to come *od* be first; **das muss anders werden** that'll have to change; **rot/zu Eis werden** to turn red/to ice; **was willst du (mal) werden?** what do you want to be?; **die Fotos sind gut geworden** the photos have come out nicely

♦ *als Hilfsverb* **1** (*bei Futur*): **er wird es tun** he will *od* he'll do it; **er wird das nicht tun** he will not *od* he won't do it; **es wird gleich regnen** it's going to rain

2 (*bei Konjunktiv*): **ich würde ...** I would ...; **er würde gern ...** he would *od* he'd like to ...; **ich würde lieber ...** I would *od* I'd rather ...

3 (*bei Vermutung*): **sie wird in der Küche sein** she will be in the kitchen

4 (*bei Passiv*): **gebraucht werden** to be used; **er ist erschossen worden** he has *od* he's been shot; **mir wurde gesagt, dass ...** I was told that ...

---

werfen ['verfən] (*unreg*) *vt* to throw

Werft [verft] (-, -en) f shipyard, dockyard

Werk [verk] (-(e)s, -e) nt work; (*Tätigkeit*) job; (*Fabrik, Mechanismus*) works pl; **ans ~ gehen** to set to work; **~statt** (-, -stätten) f workshop; (*AUT*) garage; **~tag** m working day; **w~tags** adv on working days; **w~tätig** adj working; **~zeug** nt tool

Wermut ['veːrmuːt] (-(e)s) m wormwood;

(*Wein*) vermouth

Wert [veːrt] (-(e)s, -e) m worth; (*FIN*) value; **~ legen auf** +akk to attach importance to; **es hat doch keinen ~** it's useless; **w~** adj worth; (*geschätzt*) dear; worthy; **das ist nichts/viel w~** it's not worth anything/it's worth a lot; **das ist es/er mir w~** it's/he's worth that to me; **~angabe** f declaration of value; **~brief** m registered letter (*containing sth of value*); **w~en** vt to rate; **~gegenstände** mpl valuables; **w~los** adj worthless; **~papier** nt security; **w~voll** adj valuable

Wesen ['veːzən] (-s, -) nt (*Geschöpf*) being; (*Natur, Charakter*) nature; **w~tlich** adj significant; (*beträchtlich*) considerable

weshalb [vɛsˈhalp] adv why

Wespe ['vɛspə] f wasp

wessen ['vɛsən] (*gen von* **wer**) pron whose

Weste ['vɛstə] f waistcoat, vest (*US*); (*Wollweste*) cardigan

West- zW: **~en** (-s) m west; **~europa** nt Western Europe; **w~lich** adj western ♦ adv to the west

weswegen [vɛsˈveːgən] adv why

wett [vɛt] adj even; **W~bewerb** m competition; **W~e** f bet, wager; **~en** vt, vi to bet

Wetter ['vɛtər] (-s, -) nt weather; **~bericht** m weather report; **~dienst** m meteorological service; **~lage** f (weather) situation; **~vorhersage** f weather forecast; **~warte** f weather station

Wett- zW: **~kampf** m contest; **~lauf** m race; **w~machen** vt to make good

wichtig ['vɪçtɪç] adj important; **W~keit** f importance

wickeln ['vɪkəln] vt to wind; (*Haare*) to set; (*Kind*) to change; **jdn/etw in etw** akk **~** to wrap sb/sth in sth

Wickelraum m mothers' (and babies') room

Widder ['vɪdər] (-s, -) m ram; (*ASTROL*) Aries

wider ['viːdər] präp +akk against; **~fahren** (*unreg*) vi to happen; **~legen** vt to refute

widerlich ['viːdərlıç] adj disgusting, repulsive

wider- ['vi:dər] *zW:* **~rechtlich** *adj*
unlawful; **W~rede** *f* contradiction; **~'rufen**
(*unreg*) *vt insep* to retract; (*Anordnung*) to
revoke; (*Befehl*) to countermand; **~'setzen**
vr insep: **sich jdm/etw ~setzen** to oppose
sb/sth

widerspenstig ['vi:dərʃpɛnstɪç] *adj* wilful

wider- ['vi:dər] *zW:* **~spiegeln** *vt*
(*Entwicklung, Erscheinung*) to mirror, reflect
♦ *vr* to be reflected; **~'sprechen** (*unreg*) *vi*
insep: **jdm ~sprechen** to contradict sb

Widerspruch ['vi:dərʃprʊx] *m*
contradiction; **~slos** *adv* without arguing

Widerstand ['vi:dərʃtant] *m* resistance

Widerstands- *zW:* **~bewegung** *f*
resistance (movement); **w~fähig** *adj*
resistant, tough; **w~los** *adj* unresisting

wider'stehen (*unreg*) *vi insep:* **jdm/etw ~**
to withstand sb/sth

wider- ['vi:dər] *zW:* **~wärtig** *adj* nasty,
horrid; **W~wille** *m:* **W~wille (gegen)**
aversion (to); **~willig** *adj* unwilling,
reluctant

widmen ['vɪtmən] *vt* to dedicate; to devote
♦ *vr* to devote o.s.

widrig ['vi:drɪç] *adj* (*Umstände*) adverse

SCHLÜSSELWORT

wie [vi:] *adv* how; **wie groß/schnell?** how
big/fast?; **wie wärs?** how about it?; **wie ist
er?** what's he like?; **wie gut du das
kannst!** you're very good at it; **wie bitte?**
pardon?; (*entrüstet*) I beg your pardon!;
und wie! and how!; **wie viel** how much;
wie viel Menschen how many people;
wie weit to what extent
♦ *konj* 1 (*bei Vergleichen*): **so schön wie ...**
as beautiful as ...; **wie ich schon sagte** as I
said; **wie du** like you; **singen wie ein ...** to
sing like a ...; **wie (zum Beispiel)** such as
(for example)
2 (*zeitlich*): **wie er das hörte, ging er**
when he heard that he left; **wie er hörte, wie
der Regen fiel** he heard the rain falling

wieder ['vi:dər] *adv* again; **~ da sein** to be
back (again); **~ aufbereiten** to recycle; **~**
aufnehmen to resume; **~ erkennen** to
recognize; **~ gutmachen** to make up for;
(*Fehler*) to put right; **~ herstellen** (*Ruhe,
Frieden etc*) to restore; **~ vereinigen** to
reunite; (*POL*) to reunify; **~ verwerten** to
recycle; **gehst du schon ~?** are you off
again?; **~ ein(e) ...** another ...; **W~aufbau**
m rebuilding; **~bekommen** (*unreg*) *vt* to
get back; **W~gabe** *f* reproduction;
~geben (*unreg*) *vt* (*zurückgeben*) to return;
(*Erzählung etc*) to repeat; (*Gefühle etc*) to
convey; **W~gutmachung** *f* reparation;
~'herstellen *vt* (*Gesundheit, Gebäude*) to
restore; **~'holen** *vt insep* to repeat;
W~'holung *f* repetition; **W~hören** *nt:* **auf
W~hören** (*TEL*) goodbye; **W~kehr (-)** *f*
return; (*von Vorfall*) repetition, recurrence;
~sehen (*unreg*) *vt* to see again; **auf
W~sehen** goodbye; **~um** *adv* again;
(*andererseits*) on the other hand;
W~vereinigung *f* (*POL*) reunification;
W~wahl *f* re-election

Wiege ['vi:gə] *f* cradle; **w~n¹** *vt* (*schaukeln*)
to rock

wiegen² (*unreg*) *vt, vi* (*Gewicht*) to weigh

Wien [vi:n] *nt* Vienna

Wiese ['vi:zə] *f* meadow

Wiesel ['vi:zəl] **(-s, -)** *nt* weasel

wieso [vi:'zo:] *adv* why

wieviel △ [vi:'fi:l] *adj siehe* **wie**

wievielmal [vi:'fi:lma:l] *adv* how often

wievielte(r, s) *adj:* **zum ~n Mal?** how
many times?; **den W~n haben wir?** what's
the date?; **an ~r Stelle?** in what place?;
der ~ Besucher war er? how many
visitors were there before him?

wild [vɪlt] *adj* wild; **W~ (-(e)s)** *nt* game;
W~e(r) ['vɪldə(r)] *f(m)* savage; **~ern** *vi* to
poach; **~'fremd** (*umg*) *adj* quite strange *od*
unknown; **W~heit** *f* wildness; **W~leder** *nt*
suede; **W~nis (-, -se)** *f* wilderness;
W~schwein *nt* (wild) boar

will *etc* [vɪl] *vb siehe* **wollen**

Wille ['vɪlə] **(-ns, -n)** *m* will; **w~n** *präp +gen:*
um ... w~n for the sake of ...; **w~nsstark**
adj strong-willed

will- *zW:* **~ig** *adj* willing; **W~kommen**

Rechtschreibreform: ▲ *neue Schreibung* △ *alte Schreibung (auslaufend)*

[vɪl'kɔmən] **(-s, -)** *nt* welcome; **~kommen** *adj* welcome; **jdn ~kommen heißen** to welcome sb; **~kürlich** *adj* arbitrary; (*Bewegung*) voluntary

wimmeln ['vɪməln] *vi*: **~ (von)** to swarm (with)

wimmern ['vɪmərn] *vi* to whimper

Wimper ['vɪmpər] **(-, -n)** *f* eyelash

Wimperntusche *f* mascara

Wind [vɪnt] **(-(e)s, -e)** *m* wind; **~beutel** *m* cream puff; (*fig*) rake; **~e** *f* (*TECH*) winch, windlass; (*BOT*) bindweed; **~el** ['vɪndəl] **(-, -n)** *f* nappy, diaper (*US*); **w~en** *vi unpers* to be windy ♦ *vt* (*unreg*) to wind; (*Kranz*) to weave; (*entwinden*) to twist ♦ *vr* (*unreg*) to wind; (*Person*) to writhe; **~energie** *f* wind energy; **w~ig** ['vɪndɪç] *adj* windy; (*fig*) dubious; **~jacke** *f* windcheater; **~mühle** *f* windmill; **~pocken** *pl* chickenpox *sg*; **~schutzscheibe** *f* (*AUT*) windscreen (*BRIT*), windshield (*US*); **~stärke** *f* wind force; **w~still** *adj* (*Tag*) still, windless; (*Platz*) sheltered; **~stille** *f* calm; **~stoß** *m* gust of wind

Wink [vɪŋk] **(-(e)s, -e)** *m* (*mit Hand*) wave; (*mit Kopf*) nod; (*Hinweis*) hint

Winkel ['vɪŋkəl] **(-s, -)** *m* (*MATH*) angle; (*Gerät*) square; (*in Raum*) corner

winken ['vɪŋkən] *vt, vi* to wave

winseln ['vɪnzəln] *vi* to whine

Winter ['vɪntər] **(-s, -)** *m* winter; **w~fest** *adj* (*Pflanze*) hardy; **~garten** *m* conservatory; **w~lich** *adj* wintry; **~reifen** *m* winter tyre; **~sport** *m* winter sports *pl*

Winzer ['vɪntsər] **(-s, -)** *m* vine grower

winzig ['vɪntsɪç] *adj* tiny

Wipfel ['vɪpfəl] **(-s, -)** *m* treetop

wir [viːr] *pron* we; **~ alle** all of us, we all

Wirbel ['vɪrbəl] **(-s, -)** *m* whirl, swirl; (*Trubel*) hurly-burly; (*Aufsehen*) fuss; (*ANAT*) vertebra; **w~n** *vi* to whirl, to swirl; **~säule** *f* spine

wird [vɪrt] *vb siehe* **werden**

wirfst *etc* [vɪrfst] *vb siehe* **werfen**

wirken ['vɪrkən] *vi* to have an effect; (*erfolgreich sein*) to work; (*scheinen*) to seem ♦ *vt* (*Wunder*) to work

wirklich ['vɪrklɪç] *adj* real ♦ *adv* really;

W~keit *f* reality

wirksam ['vɪrkzaːm] *adj* effective

Wirkstoff *m* (*biologisch, chemisch, pflanzlich*) active substance

Wirkung ['vɪrkʊŋ] *f* effect; **w~slos** *adj* ineffective; **w~slos bleiben** to have no effect; **w~svoll** *adj* effective

wirr [vɪr] *adj* confused, wild; **W~warr (-s)** *m* disorder, chaos

wirst [vɪrst] *vb siehe* **werden**

Wirt(in) [vɪrt(ɪn)] **(-(e)s, -e)** *m(f)* landlord(lady); **~schaft** *f* (*Gaststätte*) pub; (*Haushalt*) housekeeping; (*eines Landes*) economy; (*umg: Durcheinander*) mess; **w~schaftlich** *adj* economical; (*POL*) economic

Wirtschafts- *zW*: **~krise** *f* economic crisis; **~politik** *f* economic policy; **~prüfer** *m* chartered accountant; **~wunder** *nt* economic miracle

Wirtshaus *nt* inn

wischen ['vɪʃən] *vt* to wipe

Wischer (-s, -) *m* (*AUT*) wiper

Wissbegier(de) ▲ ['vɪsbəɡiːr(də)] *f* thirst for knowledge; **wissbegierig** ▲ *adj* inquisitive, eager for knowledge

wissen ['vɪsən] (*unreg*) *vt* to know; **was weiß ich!** I don't know!; **W~ (-s)** *nt* knowledge; **W~schaft** *f* science; **W~schaftler(in) (-s, -)** *m(f)* scientist; **~schaftlich** *adj* scientific; **~swert** *adj* worth knowing

wittern ['vɪtərn] *vt* to scent; (*fig*) to suspect

Witterung *f* weather; (*Geruch*) scent

Witwe ['vɪtvə] *f* widow; **~r (-s, -)** *m* widower

Witz [vɪts] **(-es, -e)** *m* joke; **w~bold (-(e)s, -e)** *m* joker, wit; **w~ig** *adj* funny

wo [voː] *adv* where; (*umg: irgendwo*) somewhere; **im Augenblick, ~ ...** the moment (that) ...; **die Zeit, ~ ...** the time when ...; **~anders** [voːʔandərs] *adv* elsewhere; **~bei** [-'baɪ] *adv* (*relativ*) by/with which; (*interrogativ*) what ... in/by/with

Woche ['vɔxə] *f* week

Wochen- *zW*: **~ende** *nt* weekend; **w~lang** *adj, adv* for weeks; **~markt** *m* weekly market; **~schau** *f* newsreel

Spelling Reform: ▲ *new spelling* △ *old spelling (to be phased out)*

wöchentlich ['vœçəntlɪç] *adj, adv* weekly
wodurch [vo'dʊrç] *adv* (*relativ*) through
which; (*interrogativ*) what ... through
wofür [vo'fy:r] *adv* (*relativ*) for which;
(*interrogativ*) what ... for
wog *etc* [vo:k] *vb siehe* **wiegen**
wo- [vo:] *zW:* ~'**gegen** *adv* (*relativ*) against
which; (*interrogativ*) what ... against; ~**her**
[-'he:r] *adv* where ... from; ~**hin** [-'hɪn] *adv*
where ... to

wohl [vo:l] *adv* **1**: **sich wohl fühlen**
(*zufrieden*) to feel happy; (*gesundheitlich*) to
feel well; **jdm wohl tun** to do sb good;
wohl oder übel whether one likes it or not
2 (*wahrscheinlich*) probably; (*gewiss*)
certainly; (*vielleicht*) perhaps; **sie ist wohl
zu Hause** she's probably at home; **das ist
doch wohl nicht dein Ernst!** surely you're
not serious!; **das mag wohl sein** that may
well be; **ob das wohl stimmt?** I wonder if
that's true; **er weiß das sehr wohl** he
knows that perfectly well

Wohl [vo:l] **(-(e)s)** *nt* welfare; **zum ~!**
cheers!; **w~auf** *adv* well; ~**behagen** *nt*
comfort; ~**fahrt** *f* welfare; ~**fahrtsstaat** *m*
welfare state; **w~habend** *adj* wealthy;
w~ig *adj* contented, comfortable;
w~schmeckend *adj* delicious; ~**stand** *m*
prosperity; ~**standsgesellschaft** *f*
affluent society; ~**tat** *f* relief; act of charity;
~**täter(in)** *m(f)* benefactor; **w~tätig** *adj*
charitable; ~**tätigkeits-** *zW* charity,
charitable; **w~tun** (*unreg*) *vi* △ *siehe* **wohl**;
w~verdient *adj* well-earned, well-
deserved; **w~weislich** *adv* prudently;
~**wollen (-s)** *nt* good will; **w~wollend** *adj*
benevolent
wohn- [vo:n] *zW:* ~**en** *vi* to live;
W~gemeinschaft *f* (*Menschen*) people
sharing a flat; ~**haft** *adj* resident; **W~heim**
nt (*für Studenten*) hall of residence; (*für
Senioren*) home; (*bes für Arbeiter*) hostel;
~**lich** *adj* comfortable; **W~mobil (-s, -e)**
nt camper; **W~ort** *m* domicile; **W~sitz** *m*

place of residence; **W~ung** *f* house;
(*Etagenwohnung*) flat, apartment (*US*);
W~wagen *m* caravan; **W~zimmer** *nt*
living room
wölben ['vœlbən] *vt, vr* to curve
Wolf [vɔlf] **(-(e)s, ~e)** *m* wolf
Wolke ['vɔlkə] *f* cloud; ~**nkratzer** *m*
skyscraper; **wolkig** ['vɔlkɪç] *adj* cloudy
Wolle ['vɔlə] *f* wool; **w~n¹** *adj* woollen

wollen² ['vɔlən] (*pt* **wollte**, *pp* **gewollt** *od*
(*als Hilfsverb*) **wollen**) *vt, vi* to want; **ich
will nach Hause** I want to go home; **er
will nicht** he doesn't want to; **er wollte
das nicht** he didn't want it; **wenn du
willst** if you like; **ich will, dass du mir
zuhörst** I want you to listen to me
♦ *Hilfsverb*: **er will ein Haus kaufen** he
wants to buy a house; **ich wollte, ich wäre
...** I wish I were ...; **etw gerade tun wollen**
to be going to do sth

wollüstig ['vɔlystɪç] *adj* lusty, sensual
wo- *zW:* ~**mit** *adv* (*relativ*) with which;
(*interrogativ*) what ... with; ~**möglich** *adv*
probably, I suppose; ~**nach** *adv* (*relativ*)
after/for which; (*interrogativ*) what ... for/
after; ~**ran** *adv* (*relativ*) on/at which;
(*interrogativ*) what ... on/at; ~**rauf** *adv*
(*relativ*) on which; (*interrogativ*) what ... on;
~**raus** *adv* (*relativ*) from/out of which;
(*interrogativ*) what ... from/out of; ~**rin** *adv*
(*relativ*) in which; (*interrogativ*) what ... in
Wort [vɔrt] **(-(e)s, ~er** *od* **-e)** *nt* word; **jdn
beim ~ nehmen** to take sb at his word;
mit anderen ~en in other words;
w~brüchig *adj* not true to one's word
Wörterbuch ['vœrtərbu:x] *nt* dictionary
Wort- *zW:* **w~führer** *m* spokesman; **w~karg**
adj taciturn; ~**laut** *m* wording
wörtlich ['vœrtlɪç] *adj* literal
Wort- *zW:* **w~los** *adj* mute; **w~reich** *adj*
wordy, verbose; ~**schatz** *m* vocabulary;
~**spiel** *nt* play on words, pun
wo- *zW:* ~**rüber** *adv* (*relativ*) over/about
which; (*interrogativ*) what ... over/about;

~rum adv (relativ) about/round which; (interrogativ) what ... about/round; **~runter** adv (relativ) under which; (interrogativ) what ... under; **~von** adv (relativ) from which; (interrogativ) what ... from; **~vor** adv (relativ) in front of/before which; (interrogativ) in front of/before what; of what; **~zu** adv (relativ) to/for which; (interrogativ) what ... for/to; (warum) why

Wrack [vrak] (-(e)s, -s) nt wreck

Wucher ['vu:xər] (-s) m profiteering; **~er** (-s, -) m profiteer; **w~isch** adj profiteering; **w~n** vi (Pflanzen) to grow wild; **~ung** f (MED) growth, tumour

Wuchs [vu:ks] (-es) m (Wachstum) growth; (Statur) build

Wucht [voxt] (-) f force

wühlen ['vy:lən] vi to scrabble; (Tier) to root; (Maulwurf) to burrow; (umg: arbeiten) to slave away ♦ vt to dig

Wulst [volst] (-es, ⁻e) m bulge; (an Wunde) swelling

wund [vont] adj sore, raw; **W~e** f wound

Wunder ['vondər] (-s, -) nt miracle; **es ist kein ~** it's no wonder; **w~bar** adj wonderful, marvellous; **~kerze** f sparkler; **~kind** nt infant prodigy; **w~lich** adj odd, peculiar; **w~n** vr to be surprised ♦ vt to surprise; **sich w~n über** +akk to be surprised at; **w~schön** adj beautiful; **w~voll** adj wonderful

Wundstarrkrampf ['vontʃtarrkrampf] m tetanus, lockjaw

Wunsch [vonʃ] (-(e)s, ⁻e) m wish

wünschen ['vynʃən] vt to wish; **sich** dat **etw ~** to want sth, to wish for sth; **~swert** adj desirable

wurde etc ['vordə] vb siehe **werden**

Würde ['vyrdə] f dignity; (Stellung) honour; **w~voll** adj dignified

würdig ['vyrdıç] adj worthy; (würdevoll) dignified; **~en** vt to appreciate

Wurf [vorf] (-s, ⁻e) m throw; (Junge) litter

Würfel ['vyrfəl] (-s, -) m dice; (MATH) cube; **~becher** m (dice) cup; **w~n** vi to play dice ♦ vt to dice; **~zucker** m lump sugar

würgen ['vyrgən] vt, vi to choke

Wurm [vorm] (-(e)s, ⁻er) m worm; **w~stichig** adj worm-ridden

Wurst [vorst] (-, ⁻e) f sausage; **das ist mir ~** (umg) I don't care, I don't give a damn

Würstchen ['vyrstçən] nt sausage

Würze ['vyrtsə] f seasoning, spice

Wurzel ['vortsəl] (-, -n) f root

würzen ['vyrtsən] vt to season, to spice

würzig adj spicy

wusch etc [vuʃ] vb siehe **waschen**

wusste ▲ etc ['vostə] vb siehe **wissen**

wüst [vy:st] adj untidy, messy; (ausschweifend) wild; (öde) waste; (umg: heftig) terrible; **W~e** f desert

Wut [vu:t] (-) f rage, fury; **~anfall** m fit of rage

wüten ['vy:tən] vi to rage; **~d** adj furious, mad

X, x

X-Beine ['ıksbaınə] pl knock-knees

x-beliebig [ıksbə'li:bıç] adj any (whatever)

xerokopieren [kseroko'pi:rən] vt to xerox, to photocopy

x-mal ['ıksma:l] adv any number of times, n times

Xylofon ▲, **Xylophon** [ksylo'fo:n] (-s, -e) nt xylophone

Y, y

Yacht (-, -en) f siehe **Jacht**

Ypsilon ['ypsilən] (-(s), -s) nt the letter Y

Z, z

Zacke ['tsakə] f point; (Bergzacke) jagged peak; (Gabelzacke) prong; (Kammzacke) tooth

zackig ['tsakıç] adj jagged; (umg) smart; (Tempo) brisk

zaghaft ['tsa:khaft] adj timid

zäh [tsɛ:] adj tough; (Mensch) tenacious;

(*Flüssigkeit*) thick; (*schleppend*) sluggish;
Z~igkeit *f* toughness; tenacity
Zahl [tsaːl] (-, -en) *f* number; **z~bar** *adj*
payable; **z~en** *vt, vi* to pay; **z~en bitte!** the
bill please!
zählen ['tsɛːlən] *vt, vi* to count; **~ auf** +*akk*
to count on; **~ zu** to be numbered among
Zahlenschloss ▲ *nt* combination lock
Zähler ['tsɛːlər] (-s, -) *m* (*TECH*) meter;
(*MATH*) numerator
Zahl- *zW:* **z~los** *adj* countless; **z~reich** *adj*
numerous; **~tag** *m* payday; **~ung** *f*
payment; **~ungsanweisung** *f* giro
transfer order; **z~ungsfähig** *adj* solvent;
~wort *nt* numeral
zahm [tsaːm] *adj* tame
zähmen ['tsɛːmən] *vt* to tame; (*fig*) to curb
Zahn [tsaːn] (-(e)s, ᵉe) *m* tooth; **~arzt** *m*
dentist; **~ärztin** *f* (female) dentist;
~bürste *f* toothbrush; **~fleisch** *nt* gums
pl; **~pasta** *f* toothpaste; **~rad** *nt*
cog(wheel); **~schmerzen** *pl* toothache *sg*;
~stein *m* tartar; **~stocher** (-s, -) *m*
toothpick
Zange ['tsaŋə] *f* pliers *pl*; (*Zuckerzange etc*)
tongs *pl*; (*Beißzange, ZOOL*) pincers *pl*; (*MED*)
forceps *pl*
zanken ['tsaŋkən] *vi, vr* to quarrel
zänkisch ['tsɛŋkɪʃ] *adj* quarrelsome
Zäpfchen ['tsɛpfçən] *nt* (*ANAT*) uvula; (*MED*)
suppository
Zapfen ['tsapfən] (-s, -) *m* plug; (*BOT*) cone;
(*Eiszapfen*) icicle
zappeln ['tsapəln] *vi* to wriggle; to fidget
zart [tsart] *adj* (*weich, leise*) soft; (*Fleisch*)
tender; (*fein, schwächlich*) delicate; **Z~heit** *f*
softness; tenderness; delicacy
zärtlich ['tsɛːrtlɪç] *adj* tender, affectionate
Zauber ['tsaubər] (-s, -) *m* magic; (*~bann*)
spell; **~ei** [-'rai] *f* magic; **~er** (-s, -) *m*
magician; conjuror; **z~haft** *adj* magical,
enchanting; **~künstler** *m* conjuror;
~kunststück *nt* conjuring trick; **z~n** *vi* to
conjure, to practise magic
zaudern ['tsaudərn] *vi* to hesitate
Zaum [tsaum] (-(e)s, **Zäume**) *m* bridle; **etw
im ~ halten** to keep sth in check

Zaun [tsaun] (-(e)s, **Zäune**) *m* fence
z. B. *abk* (= *zum Beispiel*) e.g.
Zebra ['tseːbra] *nt* zebra; **~streifen** *m* zebra
crossing
Zeche ['tseçə] *f* (*Rechnung*) bill; (*Bergbau*)
mine
Zeh [tse:] (-s, -en) *m* toe
Zehe [tseːə] *f* toe; (*Knoblauchzehe*) clove
zehn [tse:n] *num* ten; **~te(r, s)** *adj* tenth;
Z~tel (-s, -) *nt* tenth (part)
Zeich- ['tsaiç] *zW:* **~en** (-s, -) *nt* sign;
z~nen *vt* to draw; (*kennzeichnen*) to mark;
(*unterzeichnen*) to sign ♦ *vi* to draw; to sign;
~ner (-s, -) *m* artist; **technischer ~ner**
draughtsman; **~nung** *f* drawing;
(*Markierung*) markings *pl*
Zeige- ['tsaigə] *zW:* **~finger** *m* index finger;
z~n *vt* to show ♦ *vi* to point ♦ *vr* to show
o.s.; **z~n auf** +*akk* to point to; to point at;
es wird sich z~n time will tell; **es zeigte
sich, dass ...** it turned out that ...; **~r** (-s,
-) *m* pointer; (*Uhrzeiger*) hand
Zeile ['tsailə] *f* line; (*Häuserzeile*) row
Zeit [tsait] (-, -en) *f* time; (*GRAM*) tense; **sich**
dat **~ lassen** to take one's time; **von ~ zu ~**
from time to time; *siehe* **zurzeit**; **~alter** *nt*
age; **~ansage** *f* (*TEL*) speaking clock;
~arbeit *f* (*COMM*) temporary job;
z~gemäß *adj* in keeping with the times;
~genosse *m* contemporary; **z~ig** *adj*
early; **z~lich** *adj* temporal; **~lupe** *f* slow
motion; **z~raubend** *adj* time-consuming;
~raum *m* period; **~rechnung** *f* time, era;
nach/vor unserer ~rechnung A.D./B.C.;
~schrift *f* periodical; **~ung** *f* newspaper;
~vertreib *m* pastime, diversion; **z~weilig**
adj temporary; **z~weise** *adv* for a time;
~wort *nt* verb
Zelle ['tsɛlə] *f* cell; (*Telefonzelle*) callbox
Zellstoff *m* cellulose
Zelt [tsɛlt] (-(e)s, -e) *nt* tent; **z~en** *vi* to
camp; **~platz** *m* camp site
Zement [tse'mɛnt] (-(e)s, -e) *m* cement;
z~ieren *vt* to cement
zensieren [tsɛn'ziːrən] *vt* to censor; (*SCH*) to
mark
Zensur [tsɛn'zuːr] *f* censorship; (*SCH*) mark

Rechtschreibreform: ▲ *neue Schreibung* △ *alte Schreibung (auslaufend)*

Zentimeter [tsɛnti'me:tər] *m od nt* centimetre

Zentner ['tsɛntnər] **(-s, -)** *m* hundredweight

zentral [tsɛn'tra:l] *adj* central; **Z~e** *f* central office; (*TEL*) exchange; **Z~heizung** *f* central heating

Zentrum ['tsɛntrʊm] **(-s, Zentren)** *nt* centre

zerbrechen [tsɛr'brɛçən] (*unreg*) *vt, vi* to break

zerbrechlich *adj* fragile

zer'drücken *vt* to squash, to crush; (*Kartoffeln*) to mash

Zeremonie [tseremo'ni:] *f* ceremony

Zerfall [tsɛr'fal] *m* decay; **z~en** (*unreg*) *vi* to disintegrate, to decay; (*sich gliedern*): **z~en (in** +*akk*) to fall (into)

zer'gehen (*unreg*) *vi* to melt, to dissolve

zerkleinern [tsɛr'klainərn] *vt* to reduce to small pieces

zerlegbar [tsɛr'le:kba:r] *adj* able to be dismantled

zerlegen [tsɛr'le:gən] *vt* to take to pieces; (*Fleisch*) to carve; (*Satz*) to analyse

zermürben [tsɛr'myrbən] *vt* to wear down

zerquetschen [tsɛr'kvɛtʃən] *vt* to squash

zer'reißen (*unreg*) *vt* to tear to pieces ♦ *vi* to tear, to rip

zerren ['tsɛrən] *vt* to drag ♦ *vi*: **~ (an** +*dat*) to tug (at)

zer'rinnen (*unreg*) *vi* to melt away

zerrissen [tsɛr'rɪsən] *adj* torn, tattered; **Z~heit** *f* tattered state; (*POL*) disunion, discord; (*innere Z~heit*) disintegration

Zerrung *f* (*MED*): **eine ~** pulled muscle

zerrütten [tsɛr'rʏtən] *vt* to wreck, to destroy

zer'schlagen (*unreg*) *vt* to shatter, to smash ♦ *vr* to fall through

zer'schneiden (*unreg*) *vt* to cut up

zer'setzen *vt, vr* to decompose, to dissolve

zer'springen (*unreg*) *vi* to shatter, to burst

Zerstäuber [tsɛr'ʃtɔybər] **(-s, -)** *m* atomizer

zerstören [tsɛr'ʃtø:rən] *vt* to destroy

Zerstörung *f* destruction

zerstreu- [tsɛr'ʃtrɔy] *zW*: **~en** *vt* to disperse, to scatter; (*unterhalten*) to divert; (*Zweifel etc*) to dispel ♦ *vr* to disperse, to scatter; to be dispelled; **~t** *adj* scattered; (*Mensch*)

absent-minded; **Z~theit** *f* absent-mindedness; **Z~ung** *f* dispersion; (*Ablenkung*) diversion

zerstückeln [tsɛr'ʃtʏkəln] *vt* to cut into pieces

zer'teilen *vt* to divide into parts

Zertifikat [tsɛrtifi'ka:t] **(-(e)s, -e)** *nt* certificate

zer'treten (*unreg*) *vt* to crush underfoot

zertrümmern [tsɛr'trʏmərn] *vt* to shatter; (*Gebäude etc*) to demolish

Zettel ['tsɛtəl] **(-s, -)** *m* piece of paper, slip; (*Notizzettel*) note; (*Formular*) form

Zeug [tsɔyk] **(-(e)s, -e)** (*umg*) *nt* stuff; (*Ausrüstung*) gear; **dummes ~** (stupid) nonsense; **das ~ haben zu** to have the makings of; **sich ins ~ legen** to put one's shoulder to the wheel

Zeuge ['tsɔygə] **(-n, -n)** *m* witness; **z~n** *vi* to bear witness, to testify ♦ *vt* (*Kind*) to father; **es zeugt von ...** it testifies to ...; **~naussage** *f* evidence; **Zeugin** ['tsɔygɪn] *f* witness

Zeugnis ['tsɔyknɪs] **(-ses, -se)** *nt* certificate; (*SCH*) report; (*Referenz*) reference; (*Aussage*) evidence, testimony; **~ geben von** to be evidence of, to testify to

z. H(d). *abk* (= *zu Händen*) attn.

Zickzack ['tsɪktsak] **(-(e)s, -e)** *m* zigzag

Ziege ['tsi:gə] *f* goat

Ziegel ['tsi:gəl] **(-s, -)** *m* brick; (*Dachziegel*) tile

ziehen ['tsi:ən] (*unreg*) *vt* to draw; (*zerren*) to pull; (*SCHACH etc*) to move; (*züchten*) to rear ♦ *vi* to draw; (*umziehen, wandern*) to move; (*Rauch, Wolke etc*) to drift; (*reißen*) to pull ♦ *vb unpers*: **es zieht** there is a draught, it's draughty ♦ *vr* (*Gummi*) to stretch; (*Grenze etc*) to run; (*Gespräche*) to be drawn out; **etw nach sich ~** to lead to sth, to entail sth

Ziehung ['tsi:ʊŋ] *f* (*Losziehung*) drawing

Ziel [tsi:l] **(-(e)s, -e)** *nt* (*einer Reise*) destination; (*SPORT*) finish; (*MIL*) target; (*Absicht*) goal; **z~bewusst** ▲ *adj* decisive; **z~en** *vi*: **z~en (auf** +*akk*) to aim (at); **z~los** *adj* aimless; **~scheibe** *f* target; **z~strebig**

adj purposeful

ziemlich ['tsi:mlɪç] *adj* quite a; fair ♦ *adv* rather; quite a bit

zieren ['tsi:rən] *vr* to act coy

zierlich ['tsi:rlɪç] *adj* dainty

Ziffer ['tsɪfər] (-, -n) *f* figure, digit; ~**blatt** *nt* dial, clock-face

zig [tsɪk] (*umg*) *adj* umpteen

Zigarette [tsɪga'retə] *f* cigarette

Zigaretten- *zW:* ~**automat** *m* cigarette machine; ~**schachtel** *f* cigarette packet; ~**spitze** *f* cigarette holder

Zigarre [tsi'garə] *f* cigar

Zigeuner(in) [tsi'gɔynər(ɪn)] (-s, -) *m(f)* gipsy

Zimmer ['tsɪmər] (-s, -) *nt* room; ~**lautstärke** *f* reasonable volume; ~**mädchen** *nt* chambermaid; ~**mann** *m* carpenter; **z~n** *vt* to make (from wood); ~**nachweis** *m* accommodation office; ~**pflanze** *f* indoor plant; ~**service** *m* room service

zimperlich ['tsɪmpərlɪç] *adj* squeamish; (*pingelig*) fussy, finicky

Zimt [tsɪmt] (-(e)s, -e) *m* cinnamon

Zink [tsɪŋk] (-(e)s) *nt* zinc

Zinn [tsɪn] (-(e)s) *nt* (*Element*) tin; (*in ~waren*) pewter; ~**soldat** *m* tin soldier

Zins [tsɪns] (-es, -en) *m* interest; ~**eszins** *m* compound interest; ~**fuß** *m* rate of interest; **z~los** *adj* interest-free; ~**satz** *m* rate of interest

Zipfel ['tsɪpfəl] (-s, -) *m* corner; (*spitz*) tip; (*Hemdzipfel*) tail; (*Wurstzipfel*) end

zirka ['tsɪrka] *adv* (round) about

Zirkel ['tsɪrkəl] (-s, -) *m* circle; (*MATH*) pair of compasses

Zirkus ['tsɪrkʊs] (-, -se) *m* circus

zischen ['tsɪʃən] *vi* to hiss

Zitat [tsi'ta:t] (-(e)s, -e) *nt* quotation, quote

zitieren [tsi'ti:rən] *vt* to quote

Zitrone [tsi'tro:nə] *f* lemon; ~**nlimonade** *f* lemonade; ~**nsaft** *m* lemon juice

zittern ['tsɪtərn] *vi* to tremble

zivil [tsi'vi:l] *adj* civil; (*Preis*) moderate; **Z~** (-s) *nt* plain clothes *pl*; (*MIL*) civilian clothing; **Z~courage** *f* courage of one's convictions;

Z~dienst *m* community service; **Z~isation** [tsivilizatsi'o:n] *f* civilization; **Z~isationskrankheit** *f* disease peculiar to civilization; ~**i'sieren** *vt* to civilize

ⓘ A young German has to complete his 13 months' **Zivildienst** or service to the community if he has opted out of military service as a conscientious objector. This is usually done in a hospital or old people's home. About 18% of young Germans choose to do this as an alternative to the **Wehrdienst**.

Zivilist [tsivi'lɪst] *m* civilian

zögern ['tsø:gərn] *vi* to hesitate

Zoll [tsɔl] (-(e)s, ⁝e) *m* customs *pl*; (*Abgabe*) duty; ~**abfertigung** *f* customs clearance; ~**amt** *nt* customs office; ~**beamte(r)** *m* customs official; ~**erklärung** *f* customs declaration; **z~frei** *adj* duty-free; ~**kontrolle** *f* customs check; **z~pflichtig** *adj* liable to duty, dutiable

Zone ['tso:nə] *f* zone

Zoo [tso:] (-s, -s) *m* zoo; ~**loge** [tsoo'lo:gə] (-n, -n) *m* zoologist; ~**lo'gie** *f* zoology; **z~'logisch** *adj* zoological

Zopf [tsɔpf] (-(e)s, ⁝e) *m* plait; pigtail; **alter** ~ antiquated custom

Zorn [tsɔrn] (-(e)s) *m* anger; **z~ig** *adj* angry

zottig ['tsɔtɪç] *adj* shaggy

z. T. *abk* = **zum Teil**

zu [tsu:] *präp +dat* **1** (*örtlich*) to; **zum Bahnhof/Arzt gehen** to go to the station/doctor; **zur Schule/Kirche gehen** to go to school/church; **sollen wir zu euch gehen?** shall we go to your place?; **sie sah zu ihm hin** she looked towards him; **zum Fenster herein** through the window; **zu meiner Linken** to *od* on my left

2 (*zeitlich*) at; **zu Ostern** at Easter; **bis zum 1. Mai** until May 1st; (*nicht später als*) by May 1st; **zu meiner Zeit** in my time

3 (*Zusatz*) with; **Wein zum Essen trinken**

to drink wine with one's meal; **sich zu jdm setzen** to sit down beside sb; **setz dich doch zu uns** (come and) sit with us; **Anmerkungen zu etw** notes on sth **4** (*Zweck*) for; **Wasser zum Waschen** water for washing; **Papier zum Schreiben** paper to write on; **etw zum Geburtstag bekommen** to get sth for one's birthday **5** (*Veränderung*) into; **zu etw werden** to turn into sth; **jdn zu etw machen** to make sb (into) sth; **zu Asche verbrennen** to burn to ashes

6 (*mit Zahlen*): **3 zu 2** (*SPORT*) 3-2; **das Stück zu 2 Mark** at 2 marks each; **zum ersten Mal** for the first time

7: **zu meiner Freude** *etc* to my joy *etc*; **zum Glück** luckily; **zu Fuß** on foot; **es ist zum Weinen** it's enough to make you cry ♦ *konj* to; **etw zu essen** sth to eat; **um besser sehen zu können** in order to see better; **ohne es zu wissen** without knowing it; **noch zu bezahlende Rechnungen** bills that are still to be paid ♦ *adv* **1** (*allzu*) too; **zu sehr** too much; **zu viel** too much; **zu wenig** too little

2 (*örtlich*) toward(s); **er kam auf mich zu** he came up to me

3 (*geschlossen*) shut, closed; **die Geschäfte haben zu** the shops are closed; „**auf/zu**" (*Wasserhahn etc*) "on/off"

4 (*umg: los*): **nur zu!** just keep on!; **mach zu!** hurry up!

zualler- [tsu'ʔalər] *zW*: **~erst** [-'ʔeːrst] *adv* first of all; **~letzt** [-'lɛtst] *adv* last of all
Zubehör ['tsuːbəhøːr] (**-(e)s, -e**) *nt* accessories *pl*
zubereiten ['tsuːbəraɪtən] *vt* to prepare
zubilligen ['tsuːbɪlɪɡən] *vt* to grant
zubinden ['tsuːbɪndən] (*unreg*) *vt* to tie up
zubringen ['tsuːbrɪŋən] (*unreg*) *vt* (*Zeit*) to spend
Zubringer (**-s, -**) *m* (*Straße*) approach *od* slip road
Zucchini [tsuˈkiːniː] *pl* (*BOT, KOCH*) courgette (*BRIT*), zucchini (*US*)
Zucht [tsʊxt] (**-, -en**) *f* (*von Tieren*) breeding;

(*von Pflanzen*) cultivation; (*Rasse*) breed; (*Erziehung*) raising; (*Disziplin*) discipline
züchten ['tsʏçtən] *vt* (*Tiere*) to breed; (*Pflanzen*) to cultivate, to grow; **Züchter** (**-s, -**) *m* breeder; grower
Zuchthaus *nt* prison, penitentiary (*US*)
züchtigen ['tsʏçtɪɡən] *vt* to chastise
Züchtung *f* (*Zuchtart, Sorte: von Tier*) breed; (*: von Pflanze*) variety
zucken ['tsʊkən] *vi* to jerk, to twitch; (*Strahl etc*) to flicker ♦ *vt* (*Schultern*) to shrug
Zucker ['tsʊkər] (**-s, -**) *m* sugar; (*MED*) diabetes; **~guss** ▲ *m* icing; **z~krank** *adj* diabetic; **~krankheit** *f* (*MED*) diabetes; **z~n** *vt* to sugar; **~rohr** *nt* sugar cane; **~rübe** *f* sugar beet
Zuckung ['tsʊkʊŋ] *f* convulsion, spasm; (*leicht*) twitch
zudecken ['tsuːdɛkən] *vt* to cover (up)
zudem [tsuˈdeːm] *adv* in addition (to this)
zudringlich ['tsuːdrɪŋlɪç] *adj* forward, pushing, obtrusive
zudrücken ['tsuːdrʏkən] *vt* to close; **ein Auge ~** to turn a blind eye
zueinander [tsuʔaɪˈnandər] *adv* to one other; (*in Verbindung*) together
zuerkennen ['tsuːʔɛrkɛnən] (*unreg*) *vt* to award; **jdm etw ~** to award sth to sb, to award sb sth
zuerst [tsuˈʔeːrst] *adv* first; (*zu Anfang*) at first; **~ einmal** first of all
Zufahrt ['tsuːfaːrt] *f* approach; **~sstraße** *f* approach road; (*von Autobahn etc*) slip road
Zufall ['tsuːfal] *m* chance; (*Ereignis*) coincidence; **durch ~** by accident; **so ein ~** what a coincidence; **z~en** (*unreg*) *vi* to close, to shut; (*Anteil, Aufgabe*) to fall
zufällig ['tsuːfɛlɪç] *adj* chance ♦ *adv* by chance; (*in Frage*) by any chance
Zuflucht ['tsuːflʊxt] *f* recourse; (*Ort*) refuge
zufolge [tsuˈfɔlɡə] *präp* (+*dat od gen*) judging by; (*laut*) according to
zufrieden [tsuˈfriːdən] *adj* content(ed), satisfied; **~ geben** to be content *od* satisfied (with); **~ stellen** to satisfy
zufrieren ['tsuːfriːrən] (*unreg*) *vi* to freeze up *od* over

Spelling Reform: ▲ *new spelling* △ *old spelling (to be phased out)*

zufügen ['tsu:fy:gən] *vt* to add; (*Leid etc*): **(jdm) etw ~** to cause (sb) sth

Zufuhr ['tsu:fu:r] (-, -en) *f* (*Herbeibringen*) supplying; (*MET*) influx

Zug [tsu:k] (-(e)s, ̈e) *m* (*EISENB*) train; (*Luftzug*) draught; (*Ziehen*) pull(ing); (*Gesichtszug*) feature; (*SCHACH etc*) move; (*Schriftzug*) stroke; (*Atemzug*) breath; (*Charakterzug*) trait; (*an Zigarette*) puff, pull, drag; (*Schluck*) gulp; (*Menschengruppe*) procession; (*von Vögeln*) flight; (*MIL*) platoon; **etw in vollen Zügen genießen** to enjoy sth to the full

Zu- ['tsu:] *zW:* **~gabe** *f* extra; (*in Konzert etc*) encore; **~gang** *m* access, approach; **z~gänglich** *adj* accessible; (*Mensch*) approachable

zugeben ['tsu:ge:bən] (*unreg*) *vt* (*beifügen*) to add, to throw in; (*zugestehen*) to admit; (*erlauben*) to permit

zugehen ['tsu:ge:ən] (*unreg*) *vi* (*schließen*) to shut; **es geht dort seltsam zu** there are strange goings-on there; **auf jdn/etw ~** to walk towards sb/sth; **dem Ende ~** to be finishing

Zugehörigkeit ['tsu:gəhø:rıçkaıt] *f:* **~ (zu)** membership (of), belonging (to)

Zügel ['tsy:gəl] (-s, -) *m* rein(s); (*fig*) curb; **z~n** *vt* to curb; (*Pferd*) to rein in

zuge- ['tsu:gə] *zW:* **Z~ständnis** (-ses, -se) *nt* concession; **~stehen** (*unreg*) *vt* to admit; (*Rechte*) to concede

Zugführer *m* (*EISENB*) guard

zugig ['tsu:gıç] *adj* draughty

zügig ['tsy:gıç] *adj* speedy, swift

zugreifen ['tsu:graıfən] (*unreg*) *vi* to seize *od* grab at; (*helfen*) to help; (*beim Essen*) to help o.s.

Zugrestaurant *nt* dining car

zugrunde, zu Grunde [tsu:'grundə] *adv:* **~ gehen** to collapse; (*Mensch*) to perish; **einer Sache dat etw ~ legen** to base sth on sth; **einer Sache dat ~ liegen** to be based on sth; **~ richten** to ruin, to destroy

zugunsten, zu Gunsten [tsu:'gunstən] *präp* (+*gen od dat*) in favour of

zugute [tsu:'gu:tə] *adv:* **jdm etw ~ halten** to concede sth to sb; **jdm ~ kommen** to be of assistance to sb

Zugvogel *m* migratory bird

zuhalten ['tsu:haltən] (*unreg*) *vt* to keep closed ♦ *vi:* **auf jdn/etw ~** to make a beeline for sb/sth

Zuhälter ['tsu:heltər] (-s, -) *m* pimp

Zuhause [tsu:'hauzə] (-) *nt* home

zuhause [tsu:'hauzə] *adv* (*österreichisch, schweizerisch*) at home

zuhören ['tsu:hø:rən] *vi* to listen

Zuhörer (-s, -) *m* listener

zukleben ['tsu:kle:bən] *vt* to paste up

zukommen ['tsu:kɔmən] (*unreg*) *vi* to come up; **auf jdn ~** to come up to sb; **jdm etw ~ lassen** to give sb sth; **etw auf sich ~ lassen** to wait and see; **jdm ~** (*sich gehören*) to be fitting for sb

Zukunft ['tsu:kunft] (-, Zukünfte) *f* future; **zukünftig** ['tsu:kynftıç] *adj* future ♦ *adv* in future; **mein zukünftiger Mann** my husband to be

Zulage ['tsu:la:gə] *f* bonus

zulassen ['tsu:lasən] (*unreg*) *vt* (*hereinlassen*) to admit; (*erlauben*) to permit; (*Auto*) to license; (*umg: nicht öffnen*) to (keep) shut

zulässig ['tsu:lesıç] *adj* permissible, permitted

Zulassung *f* (*amtlich*) authorization; (*von Kfz*) licensing

zulaufen ['tsu:laufən] (*unreg*) *vi* (*subj: Mensch*): **~ auf jdn/etw** to run up to sb/sth; (*: Straße*): **~ auf** to lead towards

zuleide, zu Leide [tsu:'laıdə] *adv:* **jdm etw ~ tun** to hurt *od* harm sb

zuletzt [tsu:'letst] *adv* finally, at last

zuliebe [tsu:'li:bə] *adv:* **jdm ~** to please sb

zum [tsum] = **zu dem**; **~ dritten Mal** for the third time; **~ Scherz** as a joke; **~ Trinken** for drinking

zumachen ['tsu:maxən] *vt* to shut; (*Kleidung*) to do up, to fasten ♦ *vi* to shut; (*umg*) to hurry up

zu- *zW:* **~mal** [tsu:'ma:l] *konj* especially (as); **~meist** [tsu:'maıst] *adv* mostly; **~mindest** [tsu:'mındəst] *adv* at least

Rechtschreibreform: ▲ *neue Schreibung* △ *alte Schreibung (auslaufend)*

zumutbar ['tsu:mu:tba:r] *adj* reasonable

zumute, zu Mute [tsu'mu:tə] *adv*: **wie ist ihm ~?** how does he feel?

zumuten ['tsu:mu:tən] *vt*: **(jdm) etw ~** to expect *od* ask sb (of sb)

Zumutung ['tsu:mu:tʊŋ] *f* unreasonable expectation *od* demand, impertinence

zunächst [tsu'nɛ:çst] *adv* first of all; **~ einmal** to start with

Zunahme ['tsu:na:mə] *f* increase

Zuname ['tsu:na:mə] *m* surname

Zünd- [tsʏnd] *zW*: **z~en** *vi* (Feuer) to light, to ignite; (Motor) to fire; (begeistern): **bei jdm z~en** to fire sb (with enthusiasm); **z~end** *adj* fiery; **~er** (**-s, -**) *m* fuse; (MIL) detonator; **~holz** ['tsʏnt-] *nt* match; **~kerze** *f* (AUT) spark(ing) plug; **~schloss** ▲ *nt* ignition lock; **~schlüssel** *m* ignition key; **~schnur** *f* fuse wire; **~stoff** *m* (fig) inflammatory stuff; **~ung** *f* ignition

zunehmen ['tsu:ne:mən] (unreg) *vi* to increase, to grow; (Mensch) to put on weight

Zuneigung ['tsu:naɪgʊŋ] *f* affection

Zunft [tsʊnft] (**-, ⁺e**) *f* guild

zünftig ['tsʏnftɪç] *adj* proper, real; (Handwerk) decent

Zunge ['tsʊŋə] *f* tongue

zunichte [tsu'nɪçtə] *adv*: **~ machen** to ruin, to destroy; **~ werden** to come to nothing

zunutze, zu Nutze [tsu'nʊtsə] *adv*: **sich** *dat* **etw ~ machen** to make use of sth

zuoberst [tsu'lo:bərst] *adv* at the top

zupfen ['tsʊpfən] *vt* to pull, to pick, to pluck; (Gitarre) to pluck

zur [tsu:r] = **zu der**

zurate, zu Rate [tsu'ra:tə] *adv*: **jdn ~ ziehen** to consult sb

zurechnungsfähig ['tsu:rɛçnʊŋsfɛ:ɪç] *adj* responsible, accountable

zurecht- [tsu:'rɛçt] *zW*: **~finden** (unreg) *vr* to find one's way (about); **~kommen** (unreg) *vi* to (be able to) cope, to manage; **~legen** *vt* to get ready; (Ausrede etc) to have ready; **~machen** *vt* to prepare ♦ *vr* to get ready; **~weisen** (unreg) *vt* to reprimand

zureden ['tsu:re:dən] *vi*: **jdm ~** to persuade *od* urge sb

zurück [tsu'rʏk] *adv* back; **~behalten** (unreg) *vt* to keep back; **~bekommen** (unreg) *vt* to get back; **~bleiben** (unreg) *vi* (Mensch) to remain behind; (nicht nachkommen) to fall behind, to lag; (Schaden) to remain; **~bringen** (unreg) *vt* to bring back; **~fahren** (unreg) *vi* to travel back; (vor Schreck) to recoil, to start ♦ *vt* to drive back; **~finden** (unreg) *vi* to find one's way back; **~fordern** *vt* to demand back; **~führen** *vt* to lead back; **etw auf etw** *akk* **~führen** to trace sth back to sth; **~geben** (unreg) *vt* to give back; (antworten) to retort with; **~geblieben** *adj* retarded; **~gehen** (unreg) *vi* to go back; (fallen) to go down, to fall; (zeitlich): **~gehen (auf** +*akk*) to date back (to); **~gezogen** *adj* retired, withdrawn; **~halten** (unreg) *vt* to hold back; (Mensch) to restrain; (hindern) to prevent ♦ *vr* (reserviert sein) to be reserved; (im Essen) to hold back; **~haltend** *adj* reserved; **Z~haltung** *f* reserve; **~kehren** *vi* to return; **~kommen** (unreg) *vi* to come back; **auf etw** *akk* **~kommen** to return to sth; **~lassen** (unreg) *vt* to leave behind; **~legen** *vt* to put back; (Geld) to put by; (reservieren) to keep back; (Strecke) to cover; **~nehmen** (unreg) *vt* to take back; **~stellen** *vt* to put back, to replace; (aufschieben) to put off, to postpone; (Interessen) to defer; (Ware) to keep; **~treten** (unreg) *vi* to step back; (vom Amt) to retire; **gegenüber etw** *od* **hinter etw** *dat* **~treten** to diminish in importance in view of sth; **~weisen** (unreg) *vt* to turn down; (Mensch) to reject; **~zahlen** *vt* to repay, to pay back; **~ziehen** (unreg) *vt* to pull back; (Angebot) to withdraw ♦ *vr* to retire

Zuruf ['tsu:ru:f] *m* shout, cry

zurzeit [tsʊr'tsaɪt] *adv* at the moment

Zusage ['tsu:za:gə] *f* promise; (Annahme) consent; **z~n** *vt* to promise ♦ *vi* to accept; **jdm z~n** (gefallen) to agree with *od* please sb

zusammen [tsu'zamən] *adv* together;

Z~arbeit *f* cooperation; **~arbeiten** *vi* to cooperate; **~beißen** (*unreg*) *vt* (*Zähne*) to clench; **~brechen** (*unreg*) *vi* to collapse; (*Mensch auch*) to break down; **~bringen** (*unreg*) *vt* to bring *od* get together; (*Geld*) to get; (*Sätze*) to put together; **Z~bruch** *m* collapse; **~fassen** *vt* to summarize; (*vereinigen*) to unite; **Z~fassung** *f* summary, résumé; **~fügen** *vt* to join (together), to unite; **~halten** (*unreg*) *vi* to stick together; **Z~hang** *m* connection; **im/aus dem Z~hang** in/out of context; **~hängen** (*unreg*) *vt* to be connected *od* linked; **~kommen** (*unreg*) *vi* to meet, to assemble; (*sich ereignen*) to occur at once *od* together; **~legen** *vt* to put together; (*stapeln*) to pile up; (*falten*) to fold; (*verbinden*) to combine, to unite; (*Termine, Fest*) to amalgamate; (*Geld*) to collect; **~nehmen** (*unreg*) *vt* to summon up ♦ *vr* to pull o.s. together; **alles ~genommen** all in all; **~passen** *vi* to go well together, to match; **~schließen** (*unreg*) *vt, vr* to join (together); **Z~schluss** ▲ *m* amalgamation; **~schreiben** (*unreg*) *vt* to write as one word; (*Bericht*) to put together; **Z~sein** (**-s**) *nt* get-together; **~setzen** *vt* to put together ♦ *vr* (*Stoff*) to be composed of; (*Menschen*) to get together; **Z~setzung** *f* composition; **~stellen** *vt* to put together; to compile; **Z~stoß** *m* collision; **~stoßen** (*unreg*) *vi* to collide; **~treffen** (*unreg*) *vi* to coincide; (*Menschen*) to meet; **Z~treffen** *nt* coincidence; meeting; **~zählen** *vt* to add up; **~ziehen** (*unreg*) *vt* (*verengern*) to draw together; (*vereinigen*) to bring together; (*addieren*) to add up ♦ *vr* to shrink; (*sich bilden*) to form, to develop

zusätzlich ['tsu:zɛtslɪç] *adj* additional ♦ *adv* in addition

zuschauen ['tsu:ʃauən] *vi* to watch, to look on; **Zuschauer(in)** (**-s, -**) *m(f)* spectator ♦ *pl* (*THEAT*) audience *sg*

zuschicken ['tsu:ʃɪkən] *vt*: (**jdm etw**) **~** to send *od* to forward (sth to sb)

Zuschlag ['tsu:ʃla:k] *m* extra charge,

surcharge; **z~en** (*unreg*) *vt* (*Tür*) to slam; (*Ball*) to hit; (*bei Auktion*) to knock down; (*Steine etc*) to knock into shape ♦ *vi* (*Fenster, Tür*) to shut; (*Mensch*) to hit, to punch; **~karte** *f* (*EISENB*) surcharge ticket; **z~pflichtig** *adj* subject to surcharge

zuschneiden ['tsu:ʃnaidən] (*unreg*) *vt* to cut out; to cut to size

zuschrauben ['tsu:ʃraubən] *vt* to screw down *od* up

zuschreiben ['tsu:ʃraibən] (*unreg*) *vt* (*fig*) to ascribe, to attribute; (*COMM*) to credit

Zuschrift ['tsu:ʃrɪft] *f* letter, reply

zuschulden, zu Schulden [tsu:ʃuldən] *adv*: **sich** *dat* **etw ~ kommen lassen** to make o.s. guilty of sth

Zuschuss ▲ ['tsu:ʃus] *m* subsidy, allowance

zusehen ['tsu:ze:ən] (*unreg*) *vi* to watch; (*dafür sorgen*) to take care; **jdm/etw ~** to watch sb/sth; **~ds** *adv* visibly

zusenden ['tsu:zɛndən] (*unreg*) *vt* to forward, to send on

zusichern ['tsu:zɪçərn] *vt*: **jdm etw ~** to assure sb of sth

zuspielen ['tsu:ʃpi:lən] *vt, vi* to pass

zuspitzen ['tsu:ʃpɪtsən] *vt* to sharpen ♦ *vr* (*Lage*) to become critical

zusprechen ['tsu:ʃprɛçən] (*unreg*) *vt* (*zuerkennen*) to award ♦ *vi* to speak; **jdm etw ~** to award sb sth *od* sth to sb; **jdm Trost ~** to comfort sb; **dem Essen/ Alkohol ~** to eat/drink a lot

Zustand ['tsu:ʃtant] *m* state, condition

zustande, zu Stande [tsu:ʃtandə] *adv*: **~ bringen** to bring about; **~ kommen** to come about

zuständig ['tsu:ʃtɛndɪç] *adj* responsible; **Z~keit** *f* competence, responsibility

zustehen ['tsu:ʃte:ən] (*unreg*) *vi*: **jdm ~** to be sb's right

zustellen ['tsu:ʃtɛlən] *vt* (*verstellen*) to block; (*Post etc*) to send

Zustellung *f* delivery

zustimmen ['tsu:ʃtɪmən] *vi* to agree

Zustimmung *f* agreement, consent

zustoßen ['tsu:ʃto:sən] (*unreg*) *vi* (*fig*) to happen

zutage, zu Tage [tsu'ta:gə] *adv*: **~ bringen** to bring to light; **~ treten** to come to light

Zutaten ['tsu:ta:tən] *pl* ingredients

zuteilen ['tsu:taɪlən] *vt* (*Arbeit, Rolle*) to designate, assign; (*Aktien, Wohnung*) to allocate

zutiefst [tsu'ti:fst] *adv* deeply

zutragen ['tsu:tra:gən] (*unreg*) *vt* to bring; (*Klatsch*) to tell ♦ *vr* to happen

zutrau- ['tsu:traʊ] *zW*: **Z~en (-s)** *nt*: **Z~en (zu)** trust (in); **~en** *vt*: **jdm etw ~en** to credit sb with sth; **~lich** *adj* trusting, friendly

zutreffen ['tsu:trɛfən] (*unreg*) *vi* to be correct; to apply; **~d** *adj* (*richtig*) accurate; **Z~des bitte unterstreichen** please underline where applicable

Zutritt ['tsu:trɪt] *m* access, admittance

Zutun ['tsu:tu:n] **(-s)** *nt* assistance

zuverlässig ['tsu:fɛrlɛsɪç] *adj* reliable; **Z~keit** *f* reliability

zuversichtlich ['tsu:fɛrzɪçtlɪç] *adj* confident

zuvor [tsu'fo:r] *adv* before, previously; **~kommen** (*unreg*) *vi* +*dat* to anticipate; **jdm ~kommen** to beat sb to it; **~kommend** *adj* obliging, courteous

Zuwachs ['tsu:vaks] **(-es)** *m* increase, growth; (*umg*) addition; **z~en** (*unreg*) *vi* to become overgrown; (*Wunde*) to heal (up)

zuwege, zu Wege [tsu've:gə] *adv*: **etw ~ bringen** to accomplish sth

zuweilen [tsu'vaɪlən] *adv* at times, now and then

zuweisen ['tsu:vaɪzən] (*unreg*) *vt* to assign, to allocate

zuwenden ['tsu:vɛndən] (*unreg*) *vt* (+*dat*) to turn (towards) ♦ *vr*: **sich jdm/etw ~** to devote o.s. to sb/sth; to turn to sb/sth

zuwider [tsu'vi:dər] *adv*: **etw ist jdm ~** sb loathes sth, sb finds sth repugnant; **~handeln** *vi*: **einer Sache** *dat* **~handeln** to act contrary to sth; **einem Gesetz ~handeln** to contravene a law

zuziehen ['tsu:tsi:ən] (*unreg*) *vt* (*schließen*: *Vorhang*) to draw, to close; (*herbeirufen*: *Experten*) to call in ♦ *vi* to move in, to come; **sich** *dat* **etw ~** (*Krankheit*) to catch sth; (*Zorn*) to incur sth

zuzüglich ['tsu:tsy:klɪç] *präp* +*gen* plus, with the addition of

Zwang [tsvaŋ] **(-(e)s, ⁔e)** *m* compulsion, coercion

zwängen ['tsvɛŋən] *vt, vr* to squeeze

zwanglos *adj* informal

Zwangs- *zW*: **~arbeit** *f* forced labour; (*Strafe*) hard labour; **~lage** *f* predicament, tight corner; **z~läufig** *adj* necessary, inevitable

zwanzig ['tsvantsɪç] *num* twenty

zwar [tsva:r] *adv* to be sure, indeed; **das ist ~ ..., aber ...** that may be ... but ...; **und ~ am Sonntag** on Sunday to be precise; **und ~ so schnell, dass ...** in fact so quickly that ...

Zweck [tsvɛk] **(-(e)s, -e)** *m* purpose, aim; **es hat keinen ~** there's no point; **z~dienlich** *adj* practical; expedient

Zwecke *f* hobnail; (*Heftzwecke*) drawing pin, thumbtack (*US*)

Zweck- *zW*: **z~los** *adj* pointless; **z~mäßig** *adj* suitable, appropriate; **z~s** *präp* +*gen* for the purpose of

zwei [tsvaɪ] *num* two; **Z~bettzimmer** *nt* twin room; **~deutig** *adj* ambiguous; (*unanständig*) suggestive; **~erlei** *adj*: **~erlei Stoff** two different kinds of material; **~erlei Meinung** of differing opinions, **~fach** *adj* double

Zweifel ['tsvaɪfəl] **(-s, -)** *m* doubt; **z~haft** *adj* doubtful, dubious; **z~los** *adj* doubtless; **z~n** *vi*: **(an etw** *dat***) z~n** to doubt (sth)

Zweig [tsvaɪk] **(-(e)s, -e)** *m* branch; **~stelle** *f* branch (office)

zwei- *zW*: **~hundert** *num* two hundred; **~mal** *adv* twice; **~sprachig** *adj* bilingual; **~spurig** *adj* (*AUT*) two-lane; **~stimmig** *adj* for two voices

zweit [tsvaɪt] *adv*: **zu ~** together; (*bei mehreren Paaren*) in twos

zweitbeste(r, s) *adj* second best

zweite(r, s) *adj* second

zweiteilig ['tsvaɪtaɪlɪç] *adj* (*Gruppe*) two-piece; (*Fernsehfilm*) two-part; (*Kleidung*)

two-piece
zweit- *zW:* **~ens** *adv* secondly; **~größte(r,
s)** *adj* second largest; **~klassig** *adj*
second-class; **~letzte(r, s)** *adj* last but one,
penultimate; **~rangig** *adj* second-rate
Zwerchfell ['tsvɛrçfɛl] *nt* diaphragm
Zwerg [tsvɛrk] **(-(e)s, -e)** *m* dwarf
Zwetsch(g)e ['tsvɛtʃ(g)ə] *f* plum
Zwieback ['tsvi:bak] **(-(e)s, -e)** *m* rusk
Zwiebel ['tsvi:bəl] **(-, -n)** *f* onion;
(*Blumenzwiebel*) bulb
Zwie- ['tsvi:] *zW:* **z~lichtig** *adj* shady,
dubious; **z~spältig** *adj* (*Gefühle*)
conflicting; (*Charakter*) contradictory;
~tracht *f* discord, dissension
Zwilling ['tsvɪlɪŋ] **(-s, -e)** *m* twin; **~e** *pl*
(*ASTROL*) Gemini
zwingen ['tsvɪŋən] (*unreg*) *vt* to force; **~d**
adj (*Grund etc*) compelling
zwinkern ['tsvɪŋkərn] *vi* to blink; (*absichtlich*)
to wink
Zwirn [tsvɪrn] **(-(e)s, -e)** *m* thread
zwischen ['tsvɪʃən] *präp* (+akk od dat)
between; **Z~bemerkung** *f* (incidental)
remark; **Z~ding** *nt* cross; **~durch** *adv* in
between; (*räumlich*) here and there;
Z~ergebnis *nt* intermediate result; **Z~fall**
m incident; **Z~frage** *f* question; **Z~handel**
m middlemen *pl*; middleman's trade;
Z~landung *f* (*AVIAT*) stopover;
~menschlich *adj* interpersonal; **Z~raum**
m space; **Z~ruf** *m* interjection; **Z~stecker**
m adaptor (plug); **Z~zeit** *f* interval; **in der
Z~zeit** in the interim, meanwhile
zwitschern ['tsvɪtʃərn] *vt, vi* to twitter, to
chirp
zwo [tsvo:] *num* two
zwölf [tsvœlf] *num* twelve
Zyklus ['tsy:klʊs] **(-, Zyklen)** *m* cycle
Zylinder [tsi'lɪndər] **(-s, -)** *m* cylinder; (*Hut*)
top hat
Zyniker ['tsy:nikər] **(-s, -)** *m* cynic
zynisch ['tsy:nɪʃ] *adj* cynical
Zypern ['tsy:pərn] *nt* Cyprus
Zyste ['tsystə] *f* cyst
zz., zzt. *abk* = **zurzeit**

PUZZLES AND WORDGAMES

PUZZLES AND WORDGAMES

Introduction

We are delighted that you have decided to invest in this Collins Pocket Dictionary! Whether you intend to use it in school, at home, on holiday or at work, we are sure that you will find it very useful.

In the pages which follow you will find explanations and wordgames (not too difficult!) designed to give you practice in exploring the dictionary's contents and in retrieving information for a variety of purposes. Answers are provided at the end. If you spend a little time on these pages you should be able to use your dictionary more efficiently and effectively. Have fun!

Supplement by
Roy Simon
reproduced by kind permission of
Tayside Region Education Department

HOW INFORMATION IS PRESENTED IN YOUR DICTIONARY

A great deal of information is packed into your Collins Pocket Dictionary using colour, various typefaces, sizes of type, symbols, abbreviations and brackets. The purpose of this section is to acquaint you with the conventions used in presenting information.

Headwords

A headword is the word you look up in a dictionary. Headwords are listed in alphabetical order throughout the dictionary. They are printed in colour so that they stand out clearly from all the other words on the dictionary page.

Note that at the top of each page a headword appears. This is a guide to the alphabetical order of words on the page. It is there to help you scan through the dictionary more quickly to find the word you want.

The German alphabet consists of the same 26 letters as the English alphabet, plus the letter ß. Although certain letters in the German alphabet take umlaut (ä, ö, ü), this does not affect the order of words in the German-English section of the dictionary.

A Dictionary Entry

An entry is made up of a headword and all the information about that headword. Entries will be short or long depending on how frequently a word is used in either English or German and how many meanings it has. Inevitably, the fuller the dictionary entry the more care is needed in sifting through it to find the information you require.

Meanings

The translations of a headword are given in ordinary type. Where there is more than one meaning or usage, a semi-colon separates one from the other.

abladen ['apla:dən] (*unreg*) *vt* to unload
Ablage ['apla:gə] *f* (*für Akten*) tray; (*für Kleider*) cloakroom
ablassen ['aplasən] (*unreg*) *vt* (*Wasser, Dampf*) to let off; (*vom Preis*) to knock off
♦ *vi*: **von etw ~** to give sth up, to abandon sth

brünett [bry'nɛt] *adj* brunette, dark-haired
Brunnen ['brʊnən] (**-s, -**) *m* fountain; (*tief*)

Bude ['bu:də] *f* booth, stall; (*umg*) digs *pl* (*BRIT*)

Ohnmacht ['o:nmaxt] *f* faint; (*fig*) impotence; **in ~ fallen** to faint
ohnmächtig ['o:nmɛçtıç] *adj* in a faint, unconscious; (*fig*) weak, impotent; **sie ist ~** she has fainted
Ohr [o:r] (**-(e)s, -en**) *nt* ear
Öhr [ø:r] (**-(e)s, -e**) *nt* eye

Gurt [gʊrt] (**-(e)s, -e**) *m* belt

klar- *zW*: **~legen** *vt* to clear up, to explain; **~machen** *vt* (*Schiff*) to get ready for sea; **jdm etw ~machen** to make sth clear to sb; **~sehen** △ (*unreg*) *vi siehe* **klar**; **K~sichtfolie** *f* transparent film; **~stellen** *vt* to clarify

Zug [tsu:k] (**-(e)s, ⁻e**) *m* (*EISENB*) train; (*Luftzug*) draught; (*Ziehen*) pull(ing); (*Gesichtszug*) feature; (*SCHACH etc*) move; (*Schriftzug*) stroke; (*Atemzug*) breath; (*Charakterzug*) trait; (*an Zigarette*) puff, pull, drag; (*Schluck*) gulp; (*Menschengruppe*) procession; (*von Vögeln*) flight; (*MIL*) platoon; **etw in vollen Zügen genießen** to enjoy sth to the full

In addition, you will often find other words appearing in *italics* in brackets before the translations. These either give some notion of the contexts in which the headword might appear (as with 'scharf' opposite – 'scharfes Essen', 'scharfe Munition', etc.) or else they provide synonyms (as with 'fremd' opposite – 'unvertraut', 'ausländisch', etc.).

Phonetic Spellings

In square brackets immediately after most headwords you will find the phonetic spelling of the word – i.e. its pronunciation. The phonetic transcription of German and English vowels and consonants is given on page xii near the front of your dictionary.

Additional Information About Headwords

Information about the usage or form of certain headwords is given in brackets between the phonetics and the translation or translations. Have a look at the entries for 'KG', 'Filiale', 'löschen' and 'Bruch' opposite.

This information is usually given in abbreviated form. A helpful list of abbreviations is given on pages viii to x at the front of your dictionary.

You should be particularly careful with colloquial words or phrases. Words labelled '(*umg*)' would not normally be used in formal speech, while those labelled '(*umg!*)' would be considered offensive.

Careful consideration of such style labels will provide indications as to the degree of formality and appropriateness of a word and could help you avoid many an embarrassing situation when using German!

Expressions in which the Headword Appears

An entry will often feature certain common expressions in which the headword appears. These expressions are in **bold** type but in black as opposed to colour. A swung dash (-) is used instead of repeating a headword in an entry. 'Schikane' and 'man' opposite illustrate this point.

Related Words

In the Pocket Dictionary words related to certain headwords are sometimes given at the end of an entry, as with 'Lohn' and 'accept' opposite. These are easily picked out as they are also in colour. To help you find these words, they are placed in alphabetical order after the headword to which they belong – see 'acceptable', 'acceptance' etc. opposite.

scharf [ʃarf] *adj* sharp; (*Essen*) hot, spicy; (*Munition*) live; **~ nachdenken** to think hard; **auf etw** *akk* **~ sein** (*umg*) to be keen on sth

fremd [frɛmt] *adj* (*unvertraut*) strange; (*ausländisch*) foreign; (*nicht eigen*) someone else's; **etw ist jdm ~** sth is foreign to sb; **~artig** *adj* strange; **F~enführer** ['frɛmdən-]

KG [kaːˈɡeː] (*-, -s*) *f abk* (= *Kommanditgesellschaft*) limited partnership

Filiale [filiˈaːlə] *f* (*COMM*) branch

löschen ['lœʃən] *vt* (*Feuer, Licht*) to put out, to extinguish; (*Durst*) to quench; (*COMM*) to cancel; (*COMPUT*) to delete; (*Tonband*) to erase; (*Fracht*) to unload ♦ *vi* (*Feuerwehr*) to put out a fire; (*Tinte*) to blot

Bruch [brʊx] (*-(e)s, ⁻e*) *m* breakage; (*zerbrochene Stelle*) break; (*fig*) split, breach; (*MED: Eingeweidebruch*) rupture, hernia; (*Beinbruch etc*) fracture; (*MATH*) fraction

Schikane [ʃiˈkaːnə] *f* harassment; dirty trick; **mit allen ~n** with all the trimmings

man [man] *pron* one, you; **~ sagt, ...** they *od* people say ...; **wie schreibt ~ das?** how do you write it?, how is it written?

gänzlich ['ɡɛntslɪç] *adj* complete, entire ♦ *adv* completely, entirely

Teufel ['tɔyfəl] (*-s, -*) *m* devil; **teuflisch** ['tɔyflɪʃ] *adj* fiendish, diabolical

schenken ['ʃɛŋkən] *vt* (*auch fig*) to give; (*Getränk*) to pour; **sich** *dat* **etw ~** (*umg*) to skip sth; **das ist geschenkt!** (*billig*) that's a giveaway!; (*nichts wert*) that's worthless!

Bombenerfolg (*umg*) *m* smash hit

Arsch [arʃ] (*-es, ⁻e*) (*umg!*) *m* arse (*BRIT!*), ass (*US!*)

Lohn [loːn] (*-(e)s, ⁻e*) *m* reward; (*Arbeitslohn*) pay, wages *pl*; **~büro** *nt* wages office; **~empfänger** *m* wage earner

accept [akˈsɛpt] *vt* (*take*) annehmen; (*agree to*) akzeptieren; **~able** *adj* annehmbar; **~ance** *n* Annahme *f*

281

'Key' Words

Your Collins Pocket Dictionary gives special status to certain German and English words which can be looked on as 'key' words in each language. These are words which have many different usages. 'werden', 'alle(r, s)' and 'sich' opposite are typical examples in German. You are likely to become familiar with them in your day-to-day language studies.

There will be occasions, however, when you want to check on a particular usage. Your dictionary can be very helpful here. Note how different parts of speech and different usages are clearly indicated by a combination of lozenges (♦) and numbers. In addition, further guides to usage are given in italics in brackets in the language of the user who needs them.

werden [ˈveːrdən] (*pt* **wurde** *od* (*bei Passiv*) **worden**) *vi* to become; **was ist aus ihm/aus der Sache geworden?** what became of him/it?; **es ist nichts/gut geworden** it came to nothing/turned out well; **es wird Nacht/Tag** it's getting dark/light; **mir wird kalt** I'm getting cold; **mir wird schlecht** I feel ill; **Erster werden** to come *od* be first; **das muss anders werden** that'll have to change; **rot/zu Eis werden** to turn red/to ice; **was willst du (mal) werden?** what do you want to be?; **die Fotos sind gut geworden** the photos have come out nicely

♦ *als Hilfsverb* **1** (*bei Futur*): **er wird es tun** he will *od* he'll do it; **er wird das nicht tun** he will not *od* he won't do it; **es wird gleich regnen** it's going to rain

2 (*bei Konjunktiv*): **ich würde ...** I would ...; **er würde gern ...** he would *od* he'd like to ...; **ich würde lieber ...** I would *od* I'd rather ...

3 (*bei Vermutung*): **sie wird in der Küche sein** she will be in the kitchen

4 (*bei Passiv*): **gebraucht werden** to be used; **er ist erschossen worden** he has *od* he's been shot; **mir wurde gesagt, dass ...** I was told that ...

alle(r, s) [ˈalə(r,s)] *adj* **1** (*sämtliche*) all; **wir alle** all of us; **alle Kinder waren da** all the children were there; **alle Kinder mögen ...** all children like ...; **alle beide** both of us/them; **sie kamen alle** they all came; **alles Gute** all the best; **alles in allem** all in all **2** (*mit Zeit- oder Maßangaben*) every; **alle vier Jahre** every four years; **alle fünf Meter** every five metres

♦ *pron* everything; **alles was er sagt** everything he says, all that he says

♦ *adv* (*zu Ende, aufgebraucht*) finished; **die Milch ist alle** the milk's all gone, there's no milk left; **etw alle machen** to finish sth up

sich [zɪç] *pron* **1** (*akk*): **er/sie/es ... sich** he/she/it ... himself/herself/itself; **sie** *pl*/**man ... sich** they/one ... themselves/oneself; **Sie ... sich** you ... yourself/yourselves *pl*; **sich wiederholen** to repeat oneself/itself

2 (*dat*): **er/sie/es ... sich** he/she/it ... to himself/herself/itself; **sie** *pl*/**man ... sich** they/one ... to themselves/oneself; **Sie ... sich** you ... to yourself/yourselves *pl*; **sie hat sich einen Pullover gekauft** she bought herself a jumper; **sich die Haare waschen** to wash one's hair

3 (*mit Präposition*): **haben Sie Ihren Ausweis bei sich?** do you have your pass on you?; **er hat nichts bei sich** he's got nothing on him; **sie bleiben gern unter sich** they keep themselves to themselves

4 (*einander*) each other, one another; **sie bekämpfen sich** they fight each other *od* one another

5: **dieses Auto fährt sich gut** this car drives well; **hier sitzt es sich gut** it's good to sit here

WORDGAME 1
HEADWORDS

Study the following sentences. In each sentence a wrong word spelt very similarly to the correct word has deliberately been put in and the sentence doesn't make sense. This word is shaded each time. Write out the correct word, which you will find in your dictionary near the wrong word.

Example   Raufen verboten

['Raufen' (= 'to pull out') is the wrong word and should be replaced by 'rauchen' (= 'to smoke')]

1. Hast du das Buch schon gekonnt?

2. Ich habe ein paar VW-Akten gekauft.

3. Wir waren gestern im Kilo.

4. Sollen wir die Theaterkarten schon kauen?

5. Unser Nachbar hat einen kleinen schwarzen Puder.

6. Ich zähle heute die Rechnung.

7. Der Student muss sich für den Kurs einschreiten.

8. Das neue Restaurant ist gar nicht über.

9. Gans viele Leute standen am Unfallort.

10. Ich habe meiner Tanne einen Brief geschrieben.

WORDGAME 2
DICTIONARY ENTRIES

Complete the crossword below by looking up the English words in the list and finding the correct German translations. There is a slight catch, however! All the English words can be translated several ways into German, but only one translation will fit correctly into each part of the crossword. So look carefully through the entries in the English-German section of your dictionary.

1. FAIR

2. CATCH

3. LEARN

4. FALL

5. HIT

6. HARD

7. CALF

8. PLACE

9. HOLD

10. PLACE

11. TRACK

12. HOME

WORDGAME 3

FINDING MEANINGS

In this list there are eight pairs of words that have some sort of connection with each other. For example, 'Diplom' (= 'diploma') and 'Student' (='student') are linked. Find the other pairs by looking up the words in your dictionary.

1. Morgenrock

2. Handtasche

3. Bett

4. Kirche

5. Fisch

6. Nest

7. Diplom

8. Lederwaren

9. Hausschuhe

10. Glockengeläut

11. Student

12. Decke

13. Elster

14. Buch

15. Schuppe

16. Regal

WORDGAME 4
SYNONYMS

Complete the crossword by supplying synonyms of the words below. You will sometimes find the words you are looking for in italics in brackets in the entries for the words in the list. Sometimes you will have to turn to the English-German section for help.

1. Art
2. probieren
3. Feuer
4. sich ereignen
5. Arroganz
6. namhaft
7. Ladung
8. Plan
9. begegnen
10. Neigung

WORDGAME 5

SPELLING

You will often use your dictionary to check spellings. The person who has compiled this list of ten German words has made <u>three</u> spelling mistakes. Find the three words which have been misspelt and write them out correctly.

1. nachsehen
2. nacht
3. Nagetier
4. Name
5. Nature
6. neuriech
7. Nickerchen
8. Nimmersatt
9. nördlich
10. nötig

WORDGAME 6
ANTONYMS

Complete the crossword by supplying ANTONYMS (i.e. opposites) in German of the words below. Use your dictionary to help.

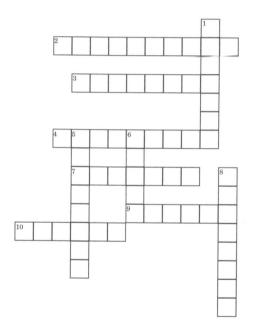

1. gestehen
2. enthüllen
3. unschuldig
4. kaufen
5. verbieten
6. Reichtum
7. ruhig
8. ankommen
9. ängstlich
10. schmutzig

WORDGAME 7
PHONETIC SPELLINGS

The phonetic transcriptions of ten German words are given below. If you study page xii near the front of your dictionary you should be able to work out what the words are.

1. frika'dɛlə

2. ʃpuːr

3. faɪn

4. 'lyːgə

5. 'ʃtaxəl

6. 'naʊtɪʃ

7. gə'vœlbə

8. 'kɔyçən

9. 'møːgən

10. 'glaʊbvʏrdɪç

WORDGAME 8

EXPRESSIONS IN WHICH THE HEADWORD APPEARS

If you look up the headword 'Satz' in the German-English section of your dictionary you will find that the word can have many meanings. Study the entry carefully and translate the following sentences into English.

1. Der Satz ist viel zu lang.

2. Unterstreicht jeden Satz, der mit einer Konjunktion beginnt.

3. Den Satz von Pythagoras kennt jeder.

4. Das Orchester hat den letzten Satz ganz ausgezeichnet gespielt.

5. Steffi Graf hat in der Meisterschaft keinen Satz verloren.

6. Der ganze Satz war in der Tasse.

7. Bei Lieferungen ins Ausland gilt ein anderer Satz.

8. Sie hat vor lauter Begeisterung einen großen Satz gemacht.

WORDGAME 9

RELATED WORDS

Fill in the blanks in the pairs of sentences below. The missing words are related to the headwords on the left. Choose the correct "relative" each time. You will find it in your dictionary near the headword provided.

HEADWORD	RELATED WORDS
Stellung	1. Ich habe die Uhr auf halb sechs _____. 2. Das Auto steht an der gleichen _____.
Hoffnung	3. _____ bleibt das Wetter so. 4. Sie _____, dass sie bald wieder gesund ist.
Betrug	5. Von ihm lassen wir uns nicht mehr _____. 6. Er ist als _____ bekannt.
sprechen	7. Hat er schon mit seiner Mutter _____? 8. Das Buch wurde in fünf _____ übersetzt.
Student	9. Er hat letztes Semester mit dem _____ begonnen. 10. Sie _____ Medizin.
kurz	11. Ich habe _____ noch mit ihm gesprochen. 12. Der Rock muss _____ werden.

WORDGAME 10

'KEY' WORDS

Study carefully the entry 'machen' in your dictionary and find translations for the following:

1. what are you doing (there)?

2. it's the cold that does that

3. that doesn't matter

4. I don't mind the cold

5. 3 and 5 are 8

6. to have the car done

7. how's the work going?

8. hurry up!

9. to set about sth

10. to turn the radio down

THE DICTIONARY AND GRAMMAR

While it is true that a dictionary can never be a substitute for a detailed grammar book, it nevertheless provides a great deal of grammatical information. If you know how to extract this information you will be able to use German more accurately both in speech and in writing.

The Collins Pocket Dictionary presents grammatical information as follows.

Parts of Speech

Parts of speech are given in italics immediately after the phonetic spellings of headwords. Abbreviated forms are used. Abbreviations can be checked on pages viii to x.

Changes in parts of speech within an entry – for example, from adjective to pronoun to adverb, or from noun to intransitive verb to transitive verb – are indicated by means of lozenges (♦), as with the German 'alle(r, s)' and the English 'fast' opposite.

German Nouns

The gender of each noun in the German-English section of the dictionary is indicated in the following way:

$$m \quad = \quad \text{Maskulinum}$$
$$f \quad = \quad \text{Femininum}$$
$$nt \quad = \quad \text{Neutrum}$$

You will occasionally see '*m od nt*' or '*m od f*' beside an entry. This indicates that the noun can be either masculine or neuter (see 'Knäuel' opposite or masculine or feminine (see 'Sellerie' opposite).

Feminine forms of nouns are shown, as with 'Schaffner(in)' opposite. This is marked *m(f)* to show that the feminine form has the ending '-in'. Nouns which have the ending '-(r)', like 'Angeklagte(r)' opposite, are formed from adjectives and are marked *f(m)* to show that they can be either masculine or feminine. Their spelling changes in the same way as adjectives, depending on their article and position in the sentence.

prosit ['pro:zɪt] *excl* cheers

leiten ['laɪtən] *vt* to lead; *(Firma)* to manage; *(in eine Richtung)* to direct; *(ELEK)* to conduct

alle(r, s) ['alə(r,s)] *adj* **1** *(sämtliche)* all; **wir alle** all of us; **alle Kinder waren da** all the children were there; **alle Kinder mögen ...** all children like ...; **alle beide** both of us/ them; **sie kamen alle** they all came, **alles Gute** all the best; **alles in allem** all in all **2** *(mit Zeit- oder Maßangaben)* every; **alle vier Jahre** every four years; **alle fünf Meter** every five metres
♦ *pron* everything; **alles was er sagt** everything he says, all that he says
♦ *adv* *(zu Ende, aufgebraucht)* finished; **die Milch ist alle** the milk's all gone, there's no milk left; **etw alle machen** to finish sth up

fast [fʊ:st] *adj* schnell; *(firm)* fest ♦ *adv* schnell; fest ♦ *n* Fasten *nt* ♦ *vi* fasten; **to be ~** *(clock)* vorgehen

Knäuel ['knɔyəl] (-s, -) *m od nt* *(Wollknäuel)* ball; *(Menschenknäuel)* knot

Sellerie ['zɛləri:] (-s, -(s) *od* -, -) *m od f* celery

Schaffner(in) ['ʃafnər(ɪn)] (-s, -) *m(f)* *(Busschaffner)* conductor(-tress); *(EISENB)* guard

Angeklagte(r) ['angəkla:ktə(r)] *f(m)* accused

So many things depend on you knowing the correct gender of a German noun – whether you use 'er', 'sie' or 'es' to translate 'it'; whether you use 'er' or 'es' to translate 'he', 'sie' or 'es' to translate 'she'; the spelling of adjectives etc. If you are in any doubt as to the gender of a noun, it is always best to check it in your dictionary.

Genitive singular and nominative plural forms of many nouns are also given (see 'Bube' and 'Scheitel' opposite). A list of regular noun endings is given on page xi and nouns which have these forms will not show genitive singular and nominative plural at the headword (see 'Rasur' and 'Forelle' opposite). Nouns formed from two or more words do not have genitive singular and nominative plural shown if the last element appears in the dictionary as a headword. For example, if you want to know how to decline 'Backenzahn', you will find the necessary information at 'Zahn'.

Adjectives

Adjectives are given in the form used when they come after a verb. If the adjective comes before a noun, the spelling changes, depending on the gender of the noun and on the article (if any), which comes before the adjective. Compare 'der Hund ist schwarz' with 'der schwarze Hund'. If you find an unfamiliar adjective in a text and want to look it up in the dictionary, you will have to decide what spelling changes have been made before you can know how it will appear in the dictionary.

Some adjectives are never used after a verb. In these cases, the dictionary shows all the possible nominative singular endings.

Adverbs

German adverbs come in three main types.

Some are just adjectives in their after-verb form, used as adverbs. Sometimes the meaning is similar to the meaning of the adjective (see 'laut'), sometimes it is rather different (see 'richtig').

Some adverbs are formed by adding '-weise', '-sweise' or '-erweise' to the adjective.

Other adverbs are not considered to be derived from particular adjectives.

In your dictionary, adjective-adverbs may be shown by a change of part of speech or by the mention 'adj, adv' at the beginning of the entry.

Fuß [fuːs] (**-es, ̈e**) *m* foot; (*von Glas, Säule etc*) base; (*von Möbel*) leg; **zu ~** on foot;

Stube ['ʃtuːbə] *f* room

Mädchen ['mɛːtçən] *nt* girl; **m~haft** *adj* girlish; **~name** *m* maiden name

Rasur [raˈzuːr] *f* shaving

Forelle [foˈrɛlə] *f* trout

schwarz [ʃvarts] *adj* black; **~es Brett** notice board; **ins S~e treffen** (*auch fig*) to hit the bull's eye; **in den ~en Zahlen** in the black; **~ sehen** (*umg*) to see the gloomy side of things; **S~arbeit** *f* illicit work, moonlighting; **S~brot** *nt* black bread; **S~e(r)** *f(m)* black (man/woman)

laut [laut] *adj* loud ♦ *adv* loudly; (*lesen*) aloud ♦ *präp* (+*gen od dat*) according to; **L~** (**-(e)s, ̈e**) *m* sound

richtig *adj* right, correct; (*echt*) proper ♦ *adv* (*umg: sehr*) really; **bin ich hier ~?** am I in the right place?; **der/die R~e** the right one/person; **das R~e** the right thing; **etw ~ stellen** to correct sth; **R~keit** *f* correctness

leider ['laɪdər] *adv* unfortunately; **ja, ~** yes, I'm afraid so; **~ nicht** I'm afraid not

oben ['oːbən] *adv* above; (*in Haus*) upstairs; **~ erwähnt, ~ genannt** above-mentioned; **nach ~** up; **von ~** down; **~ ohne** topless;

Bube ['buːbə] (**-n, -n**) *m* (*Schurke*) rogue; (*KARTEN*) jack

Scheitel ['ʃaɪtəl] (**-s, -**) *m* top; (*Haarscheitel*) parting; **s~n** *vt* to part

Backenzahn *m* molar

Zahn [tsaːn] (**-(e)s, ̈e**) *m* tooth; **~arzt** *m* dentist; **~ärztin** *f* (female) dentist; **~bürste** *f* toothbrush; **~fleisch** *nt* gums *pl*; **~pasta** *f* toothpaste; **~rad** *nt* cog(wheel); **~schmerzen** *pl* toothache *sg*; **~stein** *m* tartar; **~stocher** (**-s, -**) *m* toothpick

besondere(r, s) [bəˈzɔndərə(r, s)] *adj* special; (*eigen*) particular; (*gesondert*) separate; (*eigentümlich*) peculiar

letzte(r, s) ['lɛtstə(r, s)] *adj* last; (*neueste*) latest; **zum ~n Mal** for the last time; **~ns** *adv* lately; **~re(r, s)** *adj* latter

nett [nɛt] *adj* nice; (*freundlich*) nice, kind; **~erweise** *adv* kindly

glück- *zW*: **~lich** *adj* fortunate; (*froh*) happy; **~licherweise** *adv* fortunately; **~'selig** *adj* blissful

Adjective-plus-ending adverbs will usually appear as subentries.

Adverbs like 'oben' and 'leider' will usually appear as separate headwords.

Where a word in your text seems to be an adverb but does not appear in the dictionary, you should be able to work out a translation from the word it is related to, once you have found that in the dictionary.

Information about Verbs

A major problem facing language learners is that the form of a verb will change according to the subject and/or the tense being used. A typical German verb can take on many different forms – too many to list in a dictionary entry.

Yet, although verbs are listed in your dictionary in their infinitive forms only, this does not mean that the dictionary is of limited value when it comes to handling the verb system of the German language. On the contrary, it contains much valuable information.

First of all, your dictionary will help you with the meanings of unfamiliar verbs. If you came across the word 'füllt' in a text and looked it up in your dictionary you wouldn't find it. What you must do is assume that it is part of a verb and look for the infinitive form. Thus you will deduce that 'füllt' is a form of the verb 'füllen'. You now have the basic meaning of the word you are concerned with – something to do with English verb 'fill' – and this should be enough to help you understand the text you are reading.

It is usually an easy task to make the connection between the form of a verb and the infinitive. For example, 'füllten', 'füllst', 'füllte' and 'gefüllt' are all recognizable as parts of the infinitive 'füllen'. However, sometimes it is less obvious – for example, 'hilft', 'halfen' and 'geholfen' are all parts of 'helfen'. The only real solution to this problem is to learn the various forms of the main German irregular verbs.

And this is the second source of help offered by your dictionary as far as verbs are concerned. The irregular verb lists on pages 609 to 613 at the back of the Collins Pocket Dictionary provide the main forms of the main tenses of the basic irregular verbs. (Verbs which consist of a basic verb with prefix usually follow the rules for the basic verb.) Consider the verb 'sehen' below where the following information is given:

infinitive	present indicative (2nd, 3rd sg)	imperfect	past participle
sehen	siehst, sieht	sah	gesehen

In order to make maximum use of the information contained in these pages, a good working knowledge of the various rules affecting German verbs is required. You will acquire this in the course of your German studies and your Collins dictionary will serve as a useful 'aide-mémoire'. If you happen to forget how to form the second person singular form of the Past Tense of 'sehen' (i.e. how to translate 'You saw'), there will be no need to panic – your dictionary contains the information!

In addition, the main parts of the most common irregular verbs are listed in the body of the dictionary.

WORDGAME 11
PARTS OF SPEECH

In each sentence below a word has been shaded. Put a tick in the appropriate box to indicate the **part of speech** each time.

SENTENCE	Noun	Adj	Adv	Verb
1. Das Essen ist fertig.				
2. Er hat kein Recht dazu.				
3. Warum fahren wir nicht in die Stadt zum Essen?				
4. Ich gehe nicht mit essen.				
5. Rauchen ist strengstens verboten.				
6. Gehen Sie geradeaus und dann die erste Straße links.				
7. Das war aber ein interessanter Vortrag.				
8. Die Schauspielerin trug ein herrliches Kleid.				
9. Hast du schon von deiner Freundin gehört?				
10. Es ist immer noch recht sommerlich.				

WORDGAME 12

MEANING CHANGING WITH GENDER

Some German nouns change meaning according to their gender. Look at the pairs of sentences below and fill in the blanks with either 'ein, einen, eine' or 'der, den, die, das'.

1. Ist das _____ erste Band der Schillerausgabe?

   _____ Band ist nicht lang genug.

2. _____ Mark ist in letzter Zeit wieder gestiegen.

   Der Metzger löst _____ Mark aus den Knochen.

3. Was kostet _____ Bund Petersilie?

   _____ Bund an der Hose ist zu weit.

4. _____ Tau lag noch auf den Wiesen.

   Der Mann konnte _____ Tau nicht heben.

5. Wie steht mir _____ Hut?

   Wir müssen wirklich auf _____ Hut sein.

6. Hinter dem Haus steht _____ Kiefer.

   Er hat sich _____ Kiefer gebrochen.

WORDGAME 13
ADJECTIVES

Try to work out how the adjectives in the following phrases will appear in
the dictionary. Write your answer beside the phrase, then check in the
dictionary.

1. ein englisches Buch

2. der rote Traktor

3. letzte Nacht

4. mein kleiner Bruder

5. eine lange Reise

6. guter Käse

7. das alte Trikot

8. schwarzes Brot

9. die große Kommode

10. ein heftiger Schlag

11. der siebte Sohn

12. die neuen Nachbarn

WORDGAME 14
VERB TENSES

Use your dictionary to help you fill in the blanks in the table below.
(Remember the important pages at the back of your dictionary.)

INFINITIVE	PRESENT TENSE	IMPERFECT	PERFECT TENSE
sehen		ich	
schlafen	du		
sein			ich
schlagen		ich	
anrufen			ich
abfahren	er		
studieren			ich
haben		ich	
anfangen	du		
waschen	er		
werden		ich	
nehmen			ich

WORDGAME 15
PAST PARTICIPLES

Use your dictionary to find the past participle of these verbs.

INFINITIVE	PAST PARTICIPLE
singen	
beißen	
bringen	
frieren	
reiben	
gewinnen	
helfen	
geschehen	
liegen	
lügen	
schneiden	
kennen	
mögen	
wissen	
können	

WORDGAME 16

IDENTIFYING INFINITIVES

In the sentences below you will see various German verbs shaded. Use your dictionary to help you find the INFINITIVE form of each verb.

1. Leider habe ich Ihren Namen vergessen.

2. Bitte ruf mich doch morgen früh mal an.

3. Er ist um 16 Uhr angekommen.

4. Sie hielt an ihrem Argument fest.

5. Wir waren im Sommer in Italien.

6. Ich würde gerne kommen, wenn ich nur könnte.

7. Die Maschine flog über den Nordpol.

8. Ich würde es ja machen, aber ich habe keine Zeit.

9. Wohin fährst du diesen Winter zum Skilaufen?

10. Wen habt ihr sonst noch eingeladen?

11. Er hat deinen Brief erst gestern bekommen.

12. Liest du das Buch nicht zu Ende?

13. Meine Mutter ist letztes Jahr gestorben.

14. Er hat den Zettel aus Versehen weggeworfen.

15. Ich nahm ihn jeden Tag mit nach Hause.

MORE ABOUT MEANING

In this section we will consider some of the problems associated with using a bilingual dictionary.

Overdependence on your dictionary

That the dictionary is an invaluable tool for the language learner is beyond dispute. Nevertheless, it is possible to become overdependent on your dictionary, turning to it in an almost automatic fashion every time you come up against a new German word or phrase. Tackling an unfamiliar text in this way will turn reading in German into an extremely tedious activity. If you stop to look up every new word you may actually be *hindering* your ability to read in German – you are so concerned with the individual words that you pay no attention to the text as a whole and to the context which gives them meaning. It is therefore important to develop appropriate reading skills – using clues such as titles, headlines, illustrations, etc., understanding relations within a sentence, etc. to predict or infer what a text is about.

A detailed study of the development of reading skills is not within the scope of this supplement; we are concerned with knowing how to use a dictionary, which is only one of several important skills involved in reading. Nevertheless, it may be instructive to look at one example. You see the following text in a German newspaper and are interested in working out what it is about.

Contextual clues here include the word in large type which you would probably recognize as a German name, something that looks like a date below, and the name and address at the bottom. Some 'form' words such as 'wir', 'sind', 'und' and 'Tochter' will be familiar to you from your general studies in German. Given that we are dealing with

> *Wir sind glücklich*
> *über die Geburt*
> *unserer Tochter*
>
> ## Julia
>
> am 5. Juni 1999
>
> *Christine und Artur Landgraf*
> *Vacher Straße 50 B, Köln*

a newspaper, you will probably have worked out by now that this could be an announcement placed in the 'Personal Column'.

So you have used a series of cultural, contextual and word-formation clues to get you to the point where you have understood that Christine and Artur Landgraf have placed this notice in the 'Personal Column' of the newspaper and that something happened to Julia on 5 November 1997. And you have reached this point *without* opening your dictionary once. Common sense and your knowledge of newspaper contents in this country might suggest that this must be an announcement of someone's birth or death. Thus 'glücklich' ('happy') and 'Geburt' ('birth') become the only words that you might have to look up in order to confirm that this is indeed a birth announcement.

When learning German we are helped by the fact that some German and English words look and sound alike and have exactly the same meaning. Such words are called 'COGNATES' i.e. words derived from the same root. Many words come from a common Latin root. Other words are the same or nearly the same in both languages because the German language has borrowed a word from English or vice versa. The dictionary should not be necessary where cognates are concerned – provided you know the English word that the German word resembles!

Words With More Than One Meaning

The need to examine with care *all* the information contained in a dictionary entry must be stressed. This is particularly important with the many German words which have more than one meaning. For example, the German 'Zeit' can mean 'grammatical tense' as well as 'time'. How you translated the word would depend on the context in which you found it.

Similarly, if you were trying to translate a phrase such as 'sich vor etwas drücken', you would have to look through the whole entry for 'drücken' to get the right translation. If you restricted your search to the first couple of lines of the entry and saw that the first meaning given is 'press', you might be tempted to assume that the idiom meant 'to press o.s. in front of sth'. But if you examined the entry closely you would see that 'sich vor etwas drücken' means 'to get out of (doing) sth', as in the sentence 'Sie drückt sich immer vor dem Abwasch'.

The same need for care applies when you are using the English-German section of your dictionary to translate a word from English into German. Watch out in particular for the lozenges indicating changes in parts of speech.

If you want to translate 'You can't fool me', the capital letters at 'Narr' and 'Närrin' will remind you that these words are nouns. But watch what you are doing with the verbs or you could end up with a mistranslation like 'Sie können mich nicht herumalbern'!

Phrasal Verbs

Another potential source of difficulty is English phrasal verbs. These consist of a common verb ('go', 'make', etc.) plus an adverb and/or a preposition to give English expressions such as 'to take after', 'to make out', etc. Entries for such verbs tend to be fairly full; therefore close examination of the contents is required. Note how these verbs appear in colour within the entry.

False Friends

fool [fu:l] *n* Narr *m*, Närrin *f* ♦ *vt* (*deceive*) hereinlegen ♦ *vi* (*also:* ~ **around**) (herum)albern; ~**hardy** *adj* tollkühn; ~**ish** *adj* albern; ~**proof** *adj* idiotensicher

make [meɪk] (*pt, pp* **made**) *vt* machen; (*appoint*) ernennen (zu); (*cause to do sth*) veranlassen; (*reach*) erreichen; (*in time*) schaffen; (*earn*) verdienen ♦ *n* Marke *f*; **to ~ sth happen** etw geschehen lassen; **to ~ it** es schaffen; **what time do you ~ it?** wie spät hast du es?; **to ~ do with** auskommen mit; **~ for** *vi* gehen/fahren nach; **~ out** *vt* (*write out*) ausstellen; (*understand*) verstehen; **~ up** *vt* machen; (*face*) schminken; (*quarrel*) beilegen; (*story etc*) erfinden ♦ *vi* sich versöhnen; **~ up for** *vt* wieder gutmachen; (*COMM*) vergüten; **~-believe** *n* Fantasie *f*; **~r** *n* (*COMM*) Hersteller *m*; **~shift** *adj* behelfsmäßig, Not-; **~-up** *n* Schminke *f*, Make-up *nt*; **~-up remover** *n* Make-up-Entferner *m*; **making** *n*: **in the making** im Entstehen; **to have the makings of** das Zeug haben zu

Some German and English words have similar forms *and* meanings. There are, however, German words which *look* like English words but have a completely *different* meaning. For example, 'blank' in German means 'bright'; 'Probe' means 'rehearsal'; 'bilden' means 'to educate'. This can easily lead to serious mistranslations.

Sometimes the meaning of the German word is close to the English. For example, 'die Chips' are 'potato crisps' rather than 'chips'; 'der Hund' means a dog of any sort, not just a 'hound'. But some German words have two meanings, one the same as the English, the other completely different! 'Golf' can mean 'gulf' as well as 'golf'; 'senden' can mean 'to send' but can also mean 'to transmit/broadcast'.

Such words are often referred to as 'false friends'. You will have to look at the context in which they appear in order to arrive at the correct meaning. If they seem to fit with the sense of the passage as a whole, it will probably not be necessary to look them up. If they don't make sense, however, you may be dealing with 'false friends'.

WORDGAME 17

WORDS IN CONTEXT

Study the sentences below. Translations of the underlined words are given at the bottom. Match the number of the sentence and the letter of the translation correctly each time.

1. Sprich bitte lauter, ich kann dich nicht hören.

2. Er hört den ganzen Tag Radio.

3. Kannst du das Licht ausmachen, wenn du ins Bett gehst?

4. Können wir heute schon einen Termin ausmachen?

5. Seine Frau saß am Steuer, als der Unfall passierte.

6. Ich muss dieses Jahr viel Steuern nachzahlen.

7. Die Nachfrage nach japanischen Autos ist groß.

8. Aufgrund meiner Nachfrage konnte ich dann doch etwas erfahren.

9. Das Haus wird auf meinen Namen umgeschrieben.

10. Das Referat musst du völlig umschreiben.

11. Sind die Äpfel schon reif?

12. Für ihr Alter wirkt sie schon ziemlich reif.

a. demand
b. transferred
c. turn off
d. hear

e. ripe
f. inquiry
g. mature
h. rewrite

i. steering wheel
j. listens to
k. agree
l. tax

WORDGAME 18
FALSE FRIENDS

Look at the advertisements below. The words which have been shaded resemble English words but have different meanings here. Find a correct translation for each word in the context.

Reformhaus
Neustr. 23
Sonderangebot:
Vollkornbrot 2, 78 DM

1

2

Hotel Olympia

Alle Zimmer mit Dusche/WC
Gemütliche Atmosphäre
Bitte Prospekt anfordern

Heinrichstraße 51 –
7000 STUTTGART 25
Tel. 0711/21 56 93

3

KP-Chef Italiens fliegt
morgen nach New York

4

W. Meinzer   Lebensmittel
Heute Chips
im
Sonderangebot

5

Der Mann
im
Smoking

6

Clinton
will wieder
Präsident der
USA werden

7

Nach der
Jahrtausendwende
erst mit 65 in
Rente

8

Europaparlament

Fraktions-Flanke abdecken

9

Reise sorgenfrei
mit diesen Drei

Reisescheck
Devisen
Sparkassenbuch

BEZIRKSSPARKASSE HAUSACH
Hauptstr. 14

WORDGAME 19

WORDS WITH MORE THAN ONE MEANING

Look at the advertisements and headlines below. The words which have been shaded can have more than one meaning. Use your dictionary to help you work out the correct translation in the context.

1

Landespräsident tritt zurück

2

Vermögen:

Vom kleinen zum großen Geld

3

Ich weiß, wie ich
Schmerzen schnell los werde

Parazetamol
Aus Ihrer Apotheke

4

Heinrich Wohnmobile GmbH

Spezialisten bieten
günstige Preise

5

Hotel Restaurant Seeberger

Alle Preise inklusive
Bedienung

Marktplatz 12
Loßurg   *Telefon (07165) 33 14*

6

Müsli – Riegel

von Cadbury
– gibt Kraft und Energie!

7

Hotel - Pension Miramar

Behagliche Atmosphäre
Günstige Nachsaisonpreise

Strandstr. 6,
24340 Eckernförde
Telefon (04269) 29 51

8

Das Blatt
Finanz- und
Wirtschaftszeitung

313

HAVE FUN WITH YOUR DICTIONARY

Here are some word games for you to try. You will find your dictionary helpful as you attempt the activities.

WORDGAME 20
CODED WORDS

In the boxes below the letters of eight German words have been replaced by numbers. A number represents the same letter each time.

Try to crack the code and find the eight words. If you need help, use your dictionary.

Here is a clue: all the words you are looking for have something to do with TRANSPORT.

1 W¹ A² G³ ⁴ ⁵

2 ¹⁰ ⁸ ¹¹ ¹¹ ⁴ ¹⁰

3 ¹² ² ¹³ ¹⁴

4 ⁹ ² ⁷ ¹⁰ ¹⁰ ² ¹⁹

5 ⁹ ¹¹ ¹⁶ ³ ¹⁵ ⁴ ¹⁶ ³

6 ⁶ ² ⁷ ⁵ ⁷ ⁸ ⁹

7 ¹⁵ ¹⁶ ³

8 ¹¹ ² ¹⁸ ¹² ¹ ² ³ ⁴ ⁵

WORDGAME 21
BEHEADED WORDS

If you 'behead' certain German words, i.e. take away their first letter, you are left with another German word. For example, if you behead 'Kleider' (= 'clothes'), you get 'leider' (= 'unfortunately'), and 'dort' (= 'there') gives 'Ort' (= 'place').

The following words have their heads chopped off, i.e. the first letter has been removed. Use your dictionary to help you form a new German word by adding one letter to the start of each word below. Write down the new German word and its meaning.

1. ragen (= to tower)
2. tollen (= to romp)
3. nie (= never)
4. Rand (= edge)
5. oben (= above)
6. ich (= I)
7. Rad (= wheel)
8. innen (= inside)
9. raten (= to guess)
10. indisch (= Indian)
11. eigen (=own)
12. eben (= level)
13. Ohr (= ear)
14. pur (= pure)

WORDGAME 22

CROSSWORD

Complete this crossword by looking up the words listed below in the English-German section of your dictionary. Remember to read through the entry carefully to find the word that will fit.

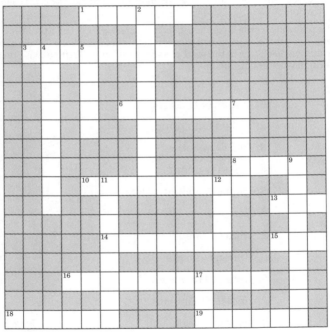

Across/Down			
1. Heavily	6. Sad	11. To start up (a car)	15. Clock
2. Tearful	7. Smooth	12. Tap	16. To dirty
3. Meal	8. Deaf	13. Place	17. Day
4. To record	9. To reassure	14. To withdraw	18. To fold
5. Mood	10. (A piece of) news		19. Profit

WORDGAME 23

There are twelve German words hidden in the grid below. Each word is made up of five letters but has been split into two parts.

Find the German words. Each group of letters can only be used once.

Use your dictionary to help you.

Re	ten	cke	er	Lad	Na
rbe	Sch	tr	Sip	eh	wei
unt	en	He	am	ank	pe
ren	be	ne	cht	se	ben

WORDGAME 24

Here is a list of German words for things you will find in the kitchen. Unfortunately, they have all been jumbled up. Try to work out what each word is and put the word in the boxes on the right. You will see that there are six shaded boxes below. With the six letters in the shaded boxes make up <u>another</u> German word for an object you can find in the kitchen.

1. CSIHT   Die Kinder decken den ____   ☐☐▨☐☐

2. DERH   Die Kasserolle steht auf dem ____   ☐▨☐☐

3. RSNAHKC   Ist die Kaffeekanne in diesem ____ ?   ☐☐☐☐☐☐▨

4. SAETS   Sie gießt den Tee in die ____   ☐☐☐▨☐

5. SRIGHCRE   Das ____ liegt im Spülbecken   ▨☐☐☐☐☐☐☐

6. HKRÜHNSKCLA   Hol die Milch aus dem ____ heraus   ☐☐☐▨☐☐☐☐☐☐☐

The word you are looking for is:

☐☐☐☐☐☐

318

WORDGAME 25

Take the four letters given each time and put them in the four empty boxes in the centre of each grid. Arrange them in such a way that you form four six-letter words. Use your dictionary to check the words.

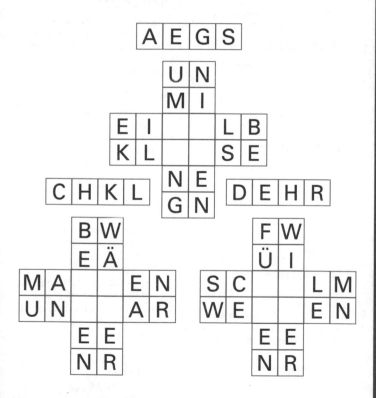

ANSWERS

WORDGAME 1

1 gekannt	6 zahle
2 Aktien	7 einschreiben
3 Kino	8 übel
4 kaufen	9 Ganz
5 Pudel	10 Tante

WORDGAME 2

1 gerecht	7 Wade
2 erreichen	8 Ort
3 erfahren	9 fassen
4 Herbst	10 Stelle
5 treffen	11 Gleis
6 schwer	12 Heim

WORDGAME 3

Morgenrock+Hausschuhe
Handtasche+Lederwaren
Bett+Decke
Kirchturm+Glockengeläut
Fisch+Schuppe
Nest+Elster
Diplom+Student
Buch+Regal

WORDGAME 4

1 Weise *or* Sorte	6 berühmt
2 versuchen	7 Last
3 Brand	8 Karte
4 passieren	9 treffen
5 Überheblichkeit	10 Tendenz

WORDGAME 5

2 Nacht   5 Natur   6 neureich

WORDGAME 6

1 leugnen	6 Armut
2 verstecken	7 lärmend
3 schuldig	8 abreisen
4 verkaufen	9 tapfer
5 erlauben	10 sauber

WORDGAME 7

1 Frikadelle	6 nautisch
2 Spur	7 Gewölbe
3 fein	8 keuchen
4 Lüge	9 mögen
5 Stachel	10 glaubwürdig

WORDGAME 8

1 The sentence is much too long.
2 Underline every clause which starts with a conjunction.
3 Everybody knows Pythagoras' theorem.
4 The orchestra performed the last movement really well.
5 Steffi Graf hasn't lost a set in the championships.
6 All the grounds were in the cup.
7 For deliveries abroad there is a different rate.
8 She jumped for joy.

WORDGAME 9

1	gestellt	7	gesprochen
2	Stelle	8	Sprachen
3	hoffentlich	9	Studium
4	hofft	10	studiert
5	betrügen	11	kürzlich
6	Betrüger	12	gekürzt

WORDGAME 11

1	adj	6	adv
2	noun	7	adj
3	noun	8	verb
4	verb	9	verb
5	adv	10	adj

WORDGAME 12

1 der/das
2 die/das
3 das (or ein)/der
4 der/das
5 der/der
6 eine/den

WORDGAME 13

1	englisch	7	alt
2	rot	8	schwarz
3	letzte(r, s)	9	groß
4	klein	10	heftig
5	lang	11	siebte(r, s)
6	gut	12	neu

WORDGAME 14

ich sah
du schläfst
ich bin gewesen
ich schlug
ich habe angerufen
er fährt ab
ich habe studiert
ich hatte
du fängst an
er wäscht
ich wurde
ich habe genommen

WORDGAME 15

gesungen	gelegen
gebissen	gelogen
gebracht	geschnitten
gefroren	gekannt
gerieben	gemocht
gewonnen	gewusst
geholfen	gekonnt
geschehen	

WORDGAME 16

1	vergessen	9	fahren
2	anrufen	10	einladen
3	ankommen	11	bekommen
4	festhalten	12	lesen
5	sein	13	sterben
6	können	14	wegwerfen
7	fliegen	15	mitnehmen
8	werden		

WORDGAME 17

1	d	5	i	9	b
2	j	6	l	10	h
3	c	7	a	11	e
4	k	8	f	12	g

WORDGAME 18

1 health food shop
2 brochure
3 boss
4 crisps
5 dinner jacket
6 wants
7 pension
8 parliamentary party
9 foreign currency

WORDGAME 19

1 resigns
2 wealth
3 know
4 offer
5 service
6 bar
7 guesthouse
8 newspaper

WORDGAME 20

1 Wagen
2 Roller
3 Taxi
4 Fahrrad
5 Flugzeug
6 Bahnhof
7 Zug
8 Lastwagen

WORDGAME 21

1 tragen (= to carry);
  fragen (= to ask)
2 Stollen (= gallery)
3 Knie (= knee)
4 Brand (= fire)
5 loben (= to praise)
6 dich (= you);
  sich (= oneself);
  mich (= me)
7 Grad (= degree)
8 sinnen (= to ponder);
  rinnen (= to trickle)
9 braten (= to roast)
10 kindisch (= childish)
11 zeigen (= to show);
  neigen (= to incline)
12 geben (= to give);
  leben (= to live);
  neben (= next to);
  beben (= to tremble);
  heben (= to raise);
  weben (= to weave)
13 Rohr (= pipe, tube)
14 Spur (= race)

WORDGAME 22

1 schwer
2 weinerlich
3 Mahlzeit
4 aufnehmen
5 Laune
6 traurig
7 glatt
8 taub
9 beruhigen
10 Nachricht
11 anlassen
12 Hahn
13 Ort
14 abheben
15 Uhr
16 beschmutzen
17 Tag
18 falten
19 Gewinn

WORDGAME 23

1	Recht	7	neben
2	Laden	8	Sippe
3	Hecke	9	unter
4	ehren	10	Scham
5	beten	11	weise
6	Narbe	12	trank

WORDGAME 24

1	Tisch	4	Tasse
2	Herd	5	Geschirr
3	Schrank	6	Kühlschrank

Hidden word – KESSEL

WORDGAME 25

ENGLISH-GERMAN DICTIONARY

WÖRTERBUCH ENGLISCH-DEUTSCH

ENGLISH – GERMAN
ENGLISCH – DEUTSCH

A, a

A [eɪ] *n* (*MUS*) A *nt*; **~ road**
Hauptverkehrsstraße *f*

KEYWORD
---

a [eɪ, ə] (*before vowel or silent h: an*) *indef art* **1**
ein; eine; **a woman** eine Frau; **a book** ein
Buch; **an eagle** ein Adler; **she's a doctor**
sie ist Ärztin

2 (*instead of the number "one"*) ein, eine; **a
year ago** vor einem Jahr; **a hundred/
thousand** *etc* **pounds** (ein) hundert/(ein)
tausend *etc* Pfund

3 (*in expressing ratios, prices etc*) pro; **3 a
day/week** 3 pro Tag/Woche, 3 am Tag/in
der Woche; **10 km an hour** 10 km pro
Stunde/in der Stunde

A.A. *n abbr* = **Alcoholics Anonymous;**
(*BRIT*) = **Automobile Association**

A.A.A. (*US*) *n abbr* = **American Automobile
Association**

aback [əˈbæk] *adv*: **to be taken ~** verblüfft
sein

abandon [əˈbændən] *vt* (*give up*) aufgeben;
(*desert*) verlassen ♦ *n* Hingabe *f*

abate [əˈbeɪt] *vi* nachlassen, sich legen

abattoir [ˈæbətwɑːr] (*BRIT*) *n* Schlachthaus *nt*

abbey [ˈæbɪ] *n* Abtei *f*

abbot [ˈæbət] *n* Abt *m*

abbreviate [əˈbriːvɪeɪt] *vt* abkürzen;
abbreviation [əbriːvɪˈeɪʃən] *n* Abkürzung *f*

abdicate [ˈæbdɪkeɪt] *vt* aufgeben ♦ *vi*
abdanken

abdomen [ˈæbdəmɛn] *n* Unterleib *m*

abduct [æbˈdʌkt] *vt* entführen

aberration [æbəˈreɪʃən] *n* (*geistige*)
Verwirrung *f*

abet [əˈbɛt] *vt see* **aid**

abeyance [əˈbeɪəns] *n*: **in ~** in der Schwebe;
(*disuse*) außer Kraft

abide [əˈbaɪd] *vt* vertragen; leiden; **~ by** *vt*
sich halten an *+acc*

ability [əˈbɪlɪtɪ] *n* (*power*) Fähigkeit *f*; (*skill*)
Geschicklichkeit *f*

abject [ˈæbdʒɛkt] *adj* (*liar*) übel; (*poverty*)
größte(r, s); (*apology*) zerknirscht

ablaze [əˈbleɪz] *adj* in Flammen

able [ˈeɪbl] *adj* geschickt, fähig; **to be ~ to
do sth** etw tun können; **~-bodied**
[ˈeɪblˈbɔdɪd] *adj* kräftig; (*seaman*) Voll-; **ably**
[ˈeɪblɪ] *adv* geschickt

abnormal [æbˈnɔːməl] *adj* regelwidrig,
abnorm

aboard [əˈbɔːd] *adv*, *prep* an Bord *+gen*

abode [əˈbəʊd] *n*: **of no fixed ~** ohne festen
Wohnsitz

abolish [əˈbɔlɪʃ] *vt* abschaffen; **abolition**
[æbəˈlɪʃən] *n* Abschaffung *f*

abominable [əˈbɔmɪnəbl] *adj* scheußlich

aborigine [æbəˈrɪdʒɪnɪ] *n* Ureinwohner *m*

abort [əˈbɔːt] *vt* abtreiben; fehlgebären; **~ion**
[əˈbɔːʃən] *n* Abtreibung *f*; (*miscarriage*)
Fehlgeburt *f*; **~ive** *adj* misslungen

abound [əˈbaʊnd] *vi* im Überfluss vorhanden
sein; **to ~ in** Überfluss haben an *+dat*

KEYWORD
---

about [əˈbaʊt] *adv* **1** (*approximately*) etwa,
ungefähr; **about a hundred/thousand** *etc*
etwa hundert/tausend *etc*; **at about 2
o'clock** etwa um 2 Uhr; **I've just about
finished** ich bin gerade fertig

2 (*referring to place*) herum, umher; **to
leave things lying about** Sachen
herumliegen lassen; **to run/walk** *etc* **about**
herumrennen/gehen *etc*

3: **to be about to do sth** im Begriff sein,
etw zu tun; **he was about to go to bed** er
wollte gerade ins Bett gehen

♦ *prep* **1** (*relating to*) über *+acc*; **a book**

about London ein Buch über London; **what is it about?** worum geht es?; (*book etc*) wovon handelt es?; **we talked about it** wir haben darüber geredet; **what** *or* **how about doing this?** wollen wir das machen? **2** (*referring to place*) um (... herum); **to walk about the town** in der Stadt herumgehen; **her clothes were scattered about the room** ihre Kleider waren über das ganze Zimmer verstreut

about-turn [ə'baut'tə:n] *n* Kehrtwendung *f*
above [ə'bʌv] *adv* oben ♦ *prep* über; **~ all** vor allem; **~ board** *adj* offen, ehrlich
abrasive [ə'breɪzɪv] *adj* Abschleif-; (*personality*) zermürbend, aufreibend
abreast [ə'brest] *adv* nebeneinander; **to keep ~ of** Schritt halten mit
abroad [ə'brɔ:d] *adv* (*be*) im Ausland; (*go*) ins Ausland
abrupt [ə'brʌpt] *adj* (*sudden*) abrupt, jäh; (*curt*) schroff; **~ly** *adv* abrupt
abscess ['æbsɪs] *n* Geschwür *nt*
abscond [əb'skɔnd] *vi* flüchten, sich davonmachen
abseil ['æbseɪl] *vi* (*also*: **~ down**) sich abseilen
absence ['æbsəns] *n* Abwesenheit *f*
absent ['æbsənt] *adj* abwesend, nicht da; (*lost in thought*) geistesabwesend; **~-minded** *adj* zerstreut
absolute ['æbsəlu:t] *adj* absolut; (*power*) unumschränkt; (*rubbish*) vollkommen, rein; **~ly** [æbsə'lu:tlɪ] *adv* absolut, vollkommen; **~ly!** ganz bestimmt!
absolve [əb'zɔlv] *vt* entbinden; freisprechen
absorb [əb'zɔ:b] *vt* aufsaugen, absorbieren; (*fig*) ganz in Anspruch nehmen, fesseln; **to be ~ed in a book** in ein Buch vertieft sein; **~ent cotton** (*US*) *n* Verbandwatte *f*; **~ing** *adj* aufsaugend; (*fig*) packend; **absorption** [əb'sɔ:pʃən] *n* Aufsaugung *f*, Absorption *f*; (*fig*) Versunkenheit *f*
abstain [əb'steɪn] *vi* (*in vote*) sich enthalten; **to ~ from** (*keep from*) sich enthalten +*gen*
abstemious [əb'sti:mɪəs] *adj* enthaltsam
abstinence ['æbstɪnəns] *n* Enthaltsamkeit *f*

abstract ['æbstrækt] *adj* abstrakt
absurd [əb'sə:d] *adj* absurd
abundance [ə'bʌndəns] *n*: **~ (of)** Überfluss *m* (an +*dat*); **abundant** [ə'bʌndənt] *adj* reichlich
abuse [*n* ə'bju:s, *vb* ə'bju:z] *n* (*rude language*) Beschimpfung *f*; (*ill usage*) Missbrauch *m*; (*bad practice*) (Amts)missbrauch *m* ♦ *vt* (*misuse*) missbrauchen; **abusive** [ə'bju:sɪv] *adj* beleidigend, Schimpf-
abysmal [ə'bɪzməl] *adj* scheußlich; (*ignorance*) bodenlos
abyss [ə'bɪs] *n* Abgrund *m*
AC *abbr* (= *alternating current*) Wechselstrom *m*
academic [ækə'demɪk] *adj* akademisch; (*theoretical*) theoretisch ♦ *n* Akademiker(in) *m(f)*
academy [ə'kædəmɪ] *n* (*school*) Hochschule *f*; (*society*) Akademie *f*
accelerate [æk'seləreɪt] *vi* schneller werden; (*AUT*) Gas geben ♦ *vt* beschleunigen; **acceleration** [ækselə'reɪʃən] *n* Beschleunigung *f*; **accelerator** [æk'seləreɪtə*] *n* Gas(pedal) *nt*
accent ['æksent] *n* Akzent *m*, Tonfall *m*; (*mark*) Akzent *m*; (*stress*) Betonung *f*
accept [ək'sept] *vt* (*take*) annehmen; (*agree to*) akzeptieren; **~able** *adj* annehmbar; **~ance** *n* Annahme *f*
access ['ækses] *n* Zugang *m*; **~ible** [æk'sesəbl] *adj* (*easy to approach*) zugänglich; (*within reach*) (leicht) erreichbar
accessory [æk'sesərɪ] *n* Zubehörteil *nt*; **toilet accessories** Toilettenartikel *pl*
accident ['æksɪdənt] *n* Unfall *m*; (*coincidence*) Zufall *m*; **by ~** zufällig; **~al** [æksɪ'dentl] *adj* unbeabsichtigt; **~ally** [æksɪ'dentəlɪ] *adv* zufällig; **~ insurance** *n* Unfallversicherung *f*; **~-prone** *adj*: **to be ~-prone** zu Unfällen neigen
acclaim [ə'kleɪm] *vt* zujubeln +*dat* ♦ *n* Beifall *m*
acclimatize [ə'klaɪmətaɪz] *vt*: **to become ~d (to)** sich gewöhnen (an +*acc*), sich akklimatisieren (in +*dat*)
accommodate [ə'kɔmədeɪt] *vt*

unterbringen; (*hold*) Platz haben für; (*oblige*) (aus)helfen +*dat*

accommodating [əˈkɔmədeɪtɪŋ] *adj* entgegenkommend

accommodation [əkɔməˈdeɪʃən] (*US* **accommodations**) *n* Unterkunft *f*

accompany [əˈkʌmpənɪ] *vt* begleiten

accomplice [əˈkʌmplɪs] *n* Helfershelfer *m*, Komplize *m*

accomplish [əˈkʌmplɪʃ] *vt* (*fulfil*) durchführen; (*finish*) vollenden; (*aim*) erreichen; **~ed** *adj* vollendet, ausgezeichnet; **~ment** *n* (*skill*) Fähigkeit *f*; (*completion*) Vollendung *f*; (*feat*) Leistung *f*

accord [əˈkɔːd] *n* Übereinstimmung *f* ♦ *vt* gewähren; **of one's own ~** freiwillig; **~ing to** nach, laut +*gen*; **~ance** *n*: **in ~ance with** in Übereinstimmung mit; **~ingly** *adv* danach, dementsprechend

accordion [əˈkɔːdɪən] *n* Akkordeon *nt*

accost [əˈkɔst] *vt* ansprechen

account [əˈkaunt] *n* (*bill*) Rechnung *f*; (*narrative*) Bericht *m*; (*report*) Rechenschaftsbericht *m*; (*in bank*) Konto *nt*; (*importance*) Geltung *f*; **~s** *npl* (*FIN*) Bücher *pl*; **on ~** auf Rechnung; **of no ~** ohne Bedeutung; **on no ~** keinesfalls; **on ~ of** wegen; **to take into ~** berücksichtigen; **~ for** *vt fus* (*expenditure*) Rechenschaft ablegen für; **how do you ~ for that?** wie erklären Sie (sich) das?; **~able** *adj* verantwortlich; **~ancy** [əˈkauntənsɪ] *n* Buchhaltung *f*; **~ant** [əˈkauntənt] *n* Wirtschaftsprüfer(in) *m(f)*; **~ number** *n* Kontonummer *f*

accumulate [əˈkjuːmjuleɪt] *vt* ansammeln ♦ *vi* sich ansammeln

accuracy [ˈækjurəsɪ] *n* Genauigkeit *f*

accurate [ˈækjurɪt] *adj* genau; **~ly** *adv* genau, richtig

accusation [ækjuˈzeɪʃən] *n* Anklage *f*, Beschuldigung *f*

accuse [əˈkjuːz] *vt* anklagen, beschuldigen; **~d** *n* Angeklagte(r) *mf*

accustom [əˈkʌstəm] *vt*: **to ~ sb (to sth)** jdn (an etw *acc*) gewöhnen; **~ed** *adj* gewohnt

ace [eɪs] *n* Ass *nt*; (*inf*) Ass *nt*, Kanone *f*

ache [eɪk] *n* Schmerz *m* ♦ *vi* (*be sore*) schmerzen, wehtun

achieve [əˈtʃiːv] *vt* zustande *or* zu Stande bringen; (*aim*) erreichen; **~ment** *n* Leistung *f*; (*act*) Erreichen *nt*

acid [ˈæsɪd] *n* Säure *f* ♦ *adj* sauer, scharf; **~ rain** *n* Saure(r) Regen *m*

acknowledge [əkˈnɔlɪdʒ] *vt* (*receipt*) bestätigen; (*admit*) zugeben; **~ment** *n* Anerkennung *f*; (*letter*) Empfangsbestätigung *f*

acne [ˈæknɪ] *n* Akne *f*

acorn [ˈeɪkɔːn] *n* Eichel *f*

acoustic [əˈkuːstɪk] *adj* akustisch; **~s** *npl* Akustik *f*

acquaint [əˈkweɪnt] *vt* vertraut machen; **to be ~ed with sb** mit jdm bekannt sein; **~ance** *n* (*person*) Bekannte(r) *f(m)*; (*knowledge*) Kenntnis *f*

acquire [əˈkwaɪəʳ] *vt* erwerben; **acquisition** [ækwɪˈzɪʃən] *n* Errungenschaft *f*; (*act*) Erwerb *m*

acquit [əˈkwɪt] *vt* (*free*) freisprechen; **to ~ o.s. well** sich bewähren; **~tal** *n* Freispruch *m*

acre [ˈeɪkəʳ] *n* Morgen *m*

acrid [ˈækrɪd] *adj* (*smell, taste*) bitter; (*smoke*) beißend

acrobat [ˈækrəbæt] *n* Akrobat *m*

across [əˈkrɔs] *prep* uber +*acc* ♦ *adv* hinüber, herüber; **he lives ~ the river** er wohnt auf der anderen Seite des Flusses; **ten metres ~** zehn Meter breit; **he lives ~ from us** er wohnt uns gegenüber; **to run/swim ~** hinüberlaufen/schwimmen

acrylic [əˈkrɪlɪk] *adj* Acryl-

act [ækt] *n* (*deed*) Tat *f*; (*JUR*) Gesetz *nt*; (*THEAT*) Akt *m*; (: *turn*) Nummer *f* ♦ *vi* (*take ~ion*) handeln; (*behave*) sich verhalten; (*pretend*) vorgeben; (*THEAT*) spielen ♦ *vt* (*in play*) spielen; **to ~ as** fungieren als; **~ing** *adj* stellvertretend ♦ *n* Schauspielkunst *f*; (*performance*) Aufführung *f*

action [ˈækʃən] *n* (*deed*) Tat *f*; Handlung *f*; (*motion*) Bewegung *f*; (*way of working*) Funktionieren *nt*; (*battle*) Einsatz *m*, Gefecht *nt*; (*lawsuit*) Klage *f*, Prozess *m*; **out of ~**

(*person*) nicht einsatzfähig; (*thing*) außer Betrieb; **to take ~** etwas unternehmen; **~ replay** n (*TV*) Wiederholung f

activate ['æktɪveɪt] vt (*mechanism*) betätigen; (*CHEM, PHYS*) aktivieren

active ['æktɪv] adj (*brisk*) rege, tatkräftig; (*working*) aktiv; (*GRAM*) aktiv, Tätigkeits-; **~ly** adv aktiv; (*dislike*) offen

activity [æk'tɪvɪtɪ] n Aktivität f; (*doings*) Unternehmungen pl; (*occupation*) Tätigkeit f; **~ holiday** n Aktivurlaub m

actor ['æktəʳ] n Schauspieler m

actress ['æktrɪs] n Schauspielerin f

actual ['æktjuəl] adj wirklich; **~ly** adv tatsächlich; **~ly no** eigentlich nicht

acumen ['ækjumən] n Scharfsinn m

acute [ə'kjuːt] adj (*severe*) heftig, akut; (*keen*) scharfsinnig

ad [æd] n abbr = **advertisement**

A.D. adv abbr (= *Anno Domini*) n. Chr.

adamant ['ædəmənt] adj eisern; hartnäckig

adapt [ə'dæpt] vt anpassen ♦ vi: **to ~ (to)** sich anpassen (an *+acc*); **~able** adj anpassungsfähig; **~ation** [ædæp'teɪʃən] n (*THEAT etc*) Bearbeitung f; (*adjustment*) Anpassung f; **~er, ~or** n (*ELEC*) Zwischenstecker m

add [æd] vt (*join*) hinzufügen; (*numbers: also:* **~ up**) addieren; **~ up** vi (*make sense*) stimmen; **~ up to** vt fus ausmachen

adder ['ædəʳ] n Kreuzotter f, Natter f

addict ['ædɪkt] n Süchtige(r) f(m); **~ed** [ə'dɪktɪd] adj: **~ed to** -süchtig; **~ion** [ə'dɪkʃən] n Sucht f; **~ive** [ə'dɪktɪv] adj: **to be ~ive** süchtig machen

addition [ə'dɪʃən] n Anhang m, Addition f; (*MATH*) Addition f, Zusammenzählen nt; **in ~** zusätzlich, außerdem; **~al** adj zusätzlich, weiter

additive ['ædɪtɪv] n Zusatz m

address [ə'drɛs] n Adresse f; (*speech*) Ansprache f ♦ vt (*letter*) adressieren; (*speak to*) ansprechen; (*make speech to*) eine Ansprache halten an *+acc*

adept ['ædɛpt] adj geschickt; **to be ~ at** gut sein in *+dat*

adequate ['ædɪkwɪt] adj angemessen

adhere [əd'hɪəʳ] vi: **to ~ to** haften an *+dat*; (*fig*) festhalten an *+dat*

adhesive [əd'hiːzɪv] adj klebend; Kleb(e)- ♦ n Klebstoff m; **~ tape** n (*BRIT*) Klebestreifen m; (*US*) Heftpflaster nt

ad hoc [æd'hɔk] adj (*decision, committee*) Ad-hoc- ♦ adv ad hoc

adjacent [ə'dʒeɪsənt] adj benachbart; **~ to** angrenzend an *+acc*

adjective ['ædʒɛktɪv] n Adjektiv nt, Eigenschaftswort nt

adjoining [ə'dʒɔɪnɪŋ] adj benachbart, Neben-

adjourn [ə'dʒəːn] vt vertagen ♦ vi abbrechen

adjudicate [ə'dʒuːdɪkeɪt] vi entscheiden, ein Urteil fällen

adjust [ə'dʒʌst] vt (*alter*) anpassen; (*put right*) regulieren, richtig stellen ♦ vi sich anpassen; **~able** adj verstellbar

ad-lib [æd'lɪb] vt, vi improvisieren ♦ adv: **ad lib** aus dem Stegreif

administer [əd'mɪnɪstəʳ] vt (*manage*) verwalten; (*dispense*) ausüben; (*justice*) sprechen; (*medicine*) geben; **administration** [ədmɪnɪs'treɪʃən] n Verwaltung f; (*POL*) Regierung f; **administrative** [əd'mɪnɪstrətɪv] adj Verwaltungs-; **administrator** [əd'mɪnɪstreɪtəʳ] n Verwaltungsbeamte(r) f(m)

Admiralty ['ædmərəltɪ] (*BRIT*) n Admiralität f

admiration [ædmə'reɪʃən] n Bewunderung f

admire [əd'maɪəʳ] vt (*respect*) bewundern; (*love*) verehren; **~r** n Bewunderer m

admission [əd'mɪʃən] n (*entrance*) Einlass m; (*fee*) Eintritt(spreis m) m; (*confession*) Geständnis nt; **~ charge** n Eintritt(spreis m

admit [əd'mɪt] vt (*let in*) einlassen; (*confess*) gestehen; (*accept*) anerkennen; **~tance** n Zulassung f; **~tedly** adv zugegebenermaßen

admonish [əd'mɔnɪʃ] vt ermahnen

ad nauseam [æd'nɔːsɪæm] adv (*repeat, talk*) endlos

ado [ə'duː] n: **without more ~** ohne weitere Umstände

adolescence [ædəu'lesns] n Jugendalter nt;
adolescent [ædəu'lesnt] adj jugendlich ♦ n
Jugendliche(r) f(m)

adopt [ə'dɔpt] vt (child) adoptieren; (idea)
übernehmen; **~ion** [ə'dɔpʃən] n Adoption f;
Übernahme f

adore [ə'dɔːʳ] vt anbeten; verehren

adorn [ə'dɔːn] vt schmücken

Adriatic [eɪdrɪ'ætɪk] n: **the ~ (Sea)** die Adria

adrift [ə'drɪft] adv Wind und Wellen
preisgegeben

adult [ædʌlt] n Erwachsene(r) f(m)

adultery [ə'dʌltərɪ] n Ehebruch m

advance [əd'vɑːns] n (progress) Vorrücken
nt; (money) Vorschuss m ♦ vt (move forward)
vorrücken; (money) vorschießen; (argument)
vorbringen ♦ vi vorwärts gehen; **in ~** im
Voraus; **~ booking** n Vorverkauf m; **~d** adj
(ahead) vorgerückt; (modern)
fortgeschritten; (study) für Fortgeschrittene

advantage [əd'vɑːntɪdʒ] n Vorteil m; **to
have an ~ over sb** jdm gegenüber im
Vorteil sein; **to take ~ of** (misuse)
ausnutzen; (profit from) Nutzen ziehen aus;
~ous [ædvən'teɪdʒəs] adj vorteilhaft

advent ['ædvənt] n Ankunft f; **A~** Advent m

adventure [əd'ventʃəʳ] n Abenteuer nt;
adventurous adj abenteuerlich, waghalsig

adverb ['ædvɜːb] n Adverb nt,
Umstandswort nt

adversary ['ædvəsərɪ] n Gegner m

adverse ['ædvɜːs] adj widrig; **adversity**
[əd'vɜːsɪtɪ] n Widrigkeit f, Missgeschick nt

advert ['ædvɜːt] n Anzeige f; **~ise** ['ædvətaɪz]
vt werben für ♦ vi annoncieren; **to ~ise for
sth** etw (per Anzeige) suchen; **~isement**
[əd'vɜːtɪsmənt] n Anzeige f, Inserat nt; **~iser**
n (in newspaper etc) Inserent m; **~ising** n
Werbung f

advice [əd'vaɪs] n Rat(schlag) m

advisable [əd'vaɪzəbl] adj ratsam

advise [əd'vaɪz] vt: **to ~ (sb)** (jdm) raten;
~dly [əd'vaɪzdlɪ] adv (deliberately) bewusst;
~r n Berater m; **advisory** [əd'vaɪzərɪ] adj
beratend, Beratungs-

advocate [vb 'ædvəkeɪt, n 'ædvəkət] vt
vertreten ♦ n Befürworter(in) m(f)

Aegean [iː'dʒiːən] n: **the ~ (Sea)** die Ägäis

aerial ['eərɪəl] n Antenne f ♦ adj Luft-

aerobics [eə'rəubɪks] n Aerobic nt

aerodynamic ['eərəudaɪ'næmɪk] adj
aerodynamisch

aeroplane ['eərəpleɪn] n Flugzeug nt

aerosol ['eərəsɔl] n Aerosol nt; Sprühdose f

aesthetic [iːs'θetɪk] adj ästhetisch

afar [ə'fɑːʳ] adv: **from ~** aus der Ferne

affable ['æfəbl] adj umgänglich

affair [ə'feəʳ] n (concern) Angelegenheit f;
(event) Ereignis nt; (love ~) Verhältnis nt; **~s**
npl (business) Geschäfte pl

affect [ə'fekt] vt (influence) (ein)wirken auf
+acc; (move deeply) bewegen; **this change
doesn't ~ us** diese Änderung betrifft uns
nicht; **~ed** adj affektiert, gekünstelt

affection [ə'fekʃən] n Zuneigung f; **~ate** adj
liebevoll

affiliated [ə'fɪleɪtɪd] adj angeschlossen

affinity [ə'fɪnɪtɪ] n (attraction) gegenseitige
Anziehung f; (relationship) Verwandtschaft f

affirmative [ə'fɜːmətɪv] adj bestätigend

afflict [ə'flɪkt] vt quälen, heimsuchen

affluence ['æfluəns] n (wealth) Wohlstand
m; **affluent** adj wohlhabend, Wohlstands-

afford [ə'fɔːd] vt sich dat leisten; (yield)
bieten, einbringen

afield [ə'fiːld] adv: **far ~** weit fort

afloat [ə'fləut] adj: **to be ~** schwimmen

afoot [ə'fut] adv im Gang

afraid [ə'freɪd] adj ängstlich; **to be ~ of**
Angst haben vor +dat; **to be ~ to do sth**
sich scheuen, etw zu tun; **I am ~ I have ...**
ich habe leider ...; **I'm ~ so/not** leider/
leider nicht; **I am ~ that ...** ich fürchte(,
dass) ...

afresh [ə'freʃ] adv von neuem

Africa ['æfrɪkə] n Afrika nt; **~n** adj afrikanisch
♦ n Afrikaner(in) m(f)

after ['ɑːftəʳ] prep nach; (following, seeking)
hinter ... dat ... her; (in imitation) nach, im
Stil von ♦ adv: **soon ~** bald danach ♦ conj
nachdem; **what are you ~?** was wollen
Sie?; **~ he left** nachdem er gegangen war;
~ you! nach Ihnen!; **~ all** letzten Endes; **~
having shaved** als er sich rasiert hatte;

~**effects** *npl* Nachwirkungen *pl*; ~**math** *n* Auswirkungen *pl*; ~**noon** *n* Nachmittag *m*; ~**s** (*inf*) *n* (*dessert*) Nachtisch *m*; ~**-sales service** (*BRIT*) *n* Kundendienst *m*; ~**shave (lotion)** *n* Rasierwasser *nt*; ~**sun** *n* Aftersunlotion *f*; ~**thought** *n* nachträgliche(r) Einfall *m*; ~**wards** *adv* danach, nachher

again [ə'gɛn] *adv* wieder, noch einmal; (*besides*) außerdem, ferner; ~ **and** ~ immer wieder

against [ə'gɛnst] *prep* gegen

age [eɪdʒ] *n* (*of person*) Alter *nt*; (*in history*) Zeitalter *nt* ♦ *vi* altern, alt werden ♦ *vt* älter machen; **to come of** ~ mündig werden; **20 years of** ~ 20 Jahre alt; **it's been** ~**s since** ... es ist ewig her, seit ...

aged¹ [eɪdʒd] *adj* ... Jahre alt, -jährig

aged² [eɪdʒɪd] *adj* (*elderly*) betagt ♦ *npl*: **the** ~ die Alten *pl*

age group *n* Altersgruppe *f*

age limit *n* Altersgrenze *f*

agency ['eɪdʒənsɪ] *n* Agentur *f*; Vermittlung *f*; (*CHEM*) Wirkung *f*; **through** *or* **by the** ~ **of** ... mithilfe *or* mit Hilfe von ...

agenda [ə'dʒɛndə] *n* Tagesordnung *f*

agent ['eɪdʒənt] *n* (*COMM*) Vertreter *m*; (*spy*) Agent *m*

aggravate ['ægrəveɪt] *vt* (*make worse*) verschlimmern; (*irritate*) reizen

aggregate ['ægrɪgɪt] *n* Summe *f*

aggression [ə'grɛʃən] *n* Aggression *f*; **aggressive** [ə'grɛsɪv] *adj* aggressiv

aghast [ə'gɑːst] *adj* entsetzt

agile ['ædʒaɪl] *adj* flink; agil; (*mind*) rege

agitate ['ædʒɪteɪt] *vt* rütteln; **to** ~ **for** sich stark machen für

AGM *n abbr* (= *annual general meeting*) JHV *f*

ago [ə'gəʊ] *adv*: **two days** ~ vor zwei Tagen; **not long** ~ vor kurzem; **it's so long** ~ es ist schon so lange her

agog [ə'gɒg] *adj* gespannt

agonizing ['ægənaɪzɪŋ] *adj* quälend

agony ['ægənɪ] *n* Qual *f*; **to be in** ~ Qualen leiden

agree [ə'griː] *vt* (*date*) vereinbaren ♦ *vi* (*have same opinion, correspond*) übereinstimmen; (*consent*) zustimmen; (*be in harmony*) sich vertragen; **to** ~ **to sth** einer Sache *dat* zustimmen; **to** ~ **that** ... (*admit*) zugeben, dass ...; **to** ~ **to do sth** sich bereit erklären, etw zu tun; **garlic doesn't** ~ **with me** Knoblauch vertrage ich nicht; **I** ~ einverstanden, ich stimme zu; **to** ~ **on sth** sich auf etw *acc* einigen; ~**able** *adj* (*pleasing*) liebenswürdig; (*willing to consent*) einverstanden; ~**d** *adj* vereinbart; ~**ment** *n* (~*ing*) Übereinstimmung *f*; (*contract*) Vereinbarung *f*, Vertrag *m*; **to be in** ~**ment** übereinstimmen

agricultural [ægrɪ'kʌltʃərəl] *adj* landwirtschaftlich, Landwirtschafts-

agriculture ['ægrɪkʌltʃər] *n* Landwirtschaft *f*

aground [ə'graʊnd] *adv*: **to run** ~ auf Grund laufen

ahead [ə'hɛd] *adv* vorwärts; **to be** ~ voraus sein; ~ **of time** der Zeit voraus; **go right** *or* **straight** ~ gehen Sie geradeaus; fahren Sie geradeaus

aid [eɪd] *n* (*assistance*) Hilfe *f*, Unterstützung *f*; (*person*) Hilfe *f*; (*thing*) Hilfsmittel *nt* ♦ *vt* unterstützen, helfen +*dat*; **in** ~ **of** zugunsten *or* zu Gunsten +*gen*; **to** ~ **and abet sb** jdm Beihilfe leisten

aide [eɪd] *n* (*person*) Gehilfe *m*; (*MIL*) Adjutant *m*

AIDS [eɪdz] *n abbr* (= *acquired immune deficiency syndrome*) Aids *nt*; **AIDS-related** aidsbedingt

ailing ['eɪlɪŋ] *adj* kränkelnd

ailment ['eɪlmənt] *n* Leiden *nt*

aim [eɪm] *vt* (*gun, camera*) richten ♦ *vi* (*with gun: also*: **take** ~) zielen; (*intend*) beabsichtigen ♦ *n* (*intention*) Absicht *f*, Ziel *nt*; (*pointing*) Zielen *nt*, Richten *nt*; **to** ~ **at sth** auf etw *dat* richten; (*fig*) etw anstreben; **to** ~ **to do sth** vorhaben, etw zu tun; ~**less** *adj* ziellos; ~**lessly** *adv* ziellos

ain't [eɪnt] (*inf*) = **am not**; **are not**; **is not**; **has not**; **have not**

air [ɛər] *n* Luft *f*; (*manner*) Miene *f*, Anschein *m*; (*MUS*) Melodie *f* ♦ *vt* lüften; (*fig*) an die Öffentlichkeit bringen ♦ *cpd* Luft-; **by** ~ (*travel*) auf dem Luftweg; **to be on the** ~

(*RADIO, TV: programme*) gesendet werden; **~bed** (*BRIT*) n Luftmatratze f; **~-conditioned** adj mit Klimaanlage; **~-conditioning** n Klimaanlage f; **~craft** n Flugzeug nt, Maschine f; **~craft carrier** n Flugzeugträger m; **~field** n Flugplatz m; **~ force** n Luftwaffe f; **~ freshener** n Raumspray nt; **~gun** n Luftgewehr nt; **~ hostess** (*BRIT*) n Stewardess f; **~ letter** (*BRIT*) n Luftpostbrief m; **~lift** n Luftbrücke f; **~line** n Luftverkehrsgesellschaft f; **~liner** n Verkehrsflugzeug nt; **~lock** n Luftblase f; **~mail** n: **by ~mail** mit Luftpost; **~ miles** npl ≃ Flugkilometer m; **~plane** (*US*) n Flugzeug nt; **~port** n Flughafen m, Flugplatz m; **~ raid** n Luftangriff m; **~sick** adj luftkrank; **~space** n Luftraum m; **~strip** n Landestreifen m; **~ terminal** n Terminal m; **~tight** adj luftdicht; **~ traffic controller** n Fluglotse m; **~y** adj luftig; (*manner*) leichtfertig

aisle [aɪl] n Gang m; **~ seat** n Sitz m am Gang

ajar [ə'dʒɑːʳ] adv angelehnt; einen Spalt offen

alarm [ə'lɑːm] n (*warning*) Alarm m; (*bell etc*) Alarmanlage f; (*anxiety*) Sorge f ♦ vt erschrecken; **~ call** n (*in hotel etc*) Weckruf m; **~ clock** n Wecker m

Albania [æl'beɪnɪə] n Albanien nt

albeit [ɔːl'biːɪt] conj obgleich

album ['ælbəm] n Album nt

alcohol ['ælkəhɒl] n Alkohol m; **~-free** adj alkoholfrei; **~ic** [ælkə'hɒlɪk] adj (*drink*) alkoholisch ♦ n Alkoholiker(in) m(f); **~ism** n Alkoholismus m

alert [ə'lɜːt] adj wachsam ♦ n Alarm m ♦ vt alarmieren; **to be on the ~** wachsam sein

Algeria [æl'dʒɪərɪə] n Algerien nt

alias ['eɪlɪəs] adv alias ♦ n Deckname m

alibi ['ælɪbaɪ] n Alibi nt

alien ['eɪlɪən] n Ausländer m ♦ adj (*foreign*) ausländisch; (*strange*) fremd; **to ~** fremd +dat; **~ate** vt entfremden

alight [ə'laɪt] adj brennend; (*of building*) in Flammen ♦ vi (*descend*) aussteigen; (*bird*) sich setzen

align [ə'laɪn] vt ausrichten

alike [ə'laɪk] adj gleich, ähnlich ♦ adv gleich, ebenso; **to look ~** sich dat ähnlich sehen

alimony ['ælɪmənɪ] n Unterhalt m, Alimente pl

alive [ə'laɪv] adj (*living*) lebend; (*lively*) lebendig, aufgeweckt; **~ (with)** (*full of*) voll (von), wimmelnd (von)

KEYWORD

all [ɔːl] adj alle(r, s); **all day/night** den ganzen Tag/die ganze Nacht; **all men are equal** alle Menschen sind gleich; **all five came** alle fünf kamen; **all the books/food** die ganzen Bücher/das ganze Essen; **all the time** die ganze Zeit (über); **all his life** sein ganzes Leben (lang)

♦ pron 1 alles; **I ate it all, I ate all of it** ich habe alles gegessen; **all of us/the boys went** wir gingen alle/alle Jungen gingen; **we all sat down** wir setzten uns alle

2 (*in phrases*): **above all** vor allem; **after all** schließlich; **at all: not at all** (*in answer to question*) überhaupt nicht; (*in answer to thanks*) gern geschehen; **I'm not at all tired** ich bin überhaupt nicht müde; **anything at all will do** es ist egal, welche(r, s); **all in all** alles in allem

♦ adv ganz; **all alone** ganz allein; **it's not as hard as all that** so schwer ist es nun auch wieder nicht; **all the more/the better** umso mehr/besser; **all but** fast; **the score is 2 all** es steht 2 zu 2

---

allay [ə'leɪ] vt (*fears*) beschwichtigen

all clear n Entwarnung f

allegation [ælɪ'geɪʃən] n Behauptung f

allege [ə'ledʒ] vt (*declare*) behaupten; (*falsely*) vorgeben; **~dly** adv angeblich

allegiance [ə'liːdʒəns] n Treue f

allergic [ə'lɜːdʒɪk] adj: **~ (to)** allergisch (gegen)

allergy ['ælədʒɪ] n Allergie f

alleviate [ə'liːvɪeɪt] vt lindern

alley ['ælɪ] n Gasse f, Durchgang m

alliance [ə'laɪəns] n Bund m, Allianz f

allied ['ælaɪd] adj vereinigt; (*powers*) alliiert; **~ (to)** verwandt (mit)

all: ~-**in** (*BRIT*) *adj, adv* (*charge*) alles inbegriffen, Gesamt-; ~-**in wrestling** *n* Freistilringen *nt*; ~-**night** *adj* (*café, cinema*) die ganze Nacht geöffnet, Nacht-

allocate ['æləkeɪt] *vt* zuteilen

allot [ə'lɒt] *vt* zuteilen; ~**ment** *n* (*share*) Anteil *m*; (*plot*) Schrebergarten *m*

all-out ['ɔ:laut] *adj* total; **all out** *adv* mit voller Kraft

allow [ə'lau] *vt* (*permit*) erlauben, gestatten; (*grant*) bewilligen; (*deduct*) abziehen; (*concede*): **to ~ that ...** annehmen, dass ...; **to ~ sb sth** jdm etw erlauben, jdm etw gestatten; **to ~ sb to do sth** jdm erlauben *or* gestatten, etw zu tun; ~ **for** *vt fus* berücksichtigen, einplanen; ~**ance** *n* Beihilfe *f*; **to make ~ances for** berücksichtigen

alloy ['ælɔɪ] *n* Metalllegierung *f*

all: ~ **right** *adv* (*well*) gut; (*correct*) richtig; (*as answer*) okay; ~-**round** *adj* (*sportsman*) allseitig, Allround-; (*view*) Rundum-; ~-**time** *adj* (*record, high*) ... aller Zeiten, Höchst-

allude [ə'lu:d] *vi*: **to ~ to** hinweisen auf +*acc*, anspielen auf +*acc*

alluring [ə'ljuərɪŋ] *adj* verlockend

ally [*n* 'ælaɪ, *vb* ə'laɪ] *n* Verbündete(r) *f(m)*; (*POL*) Alliierte(r) *f(m)* ♦ *vr*: **to ~ o.s. with** sich verbünden mit

almighty [ɔ:l'maɪtɪ] *adj* allmächtig

almond ['ɑ:mənd] *n* Mandel *f*

almost ['ɔ:lməust] *adv* fast, beinahe

alms [ɑ:mz] *npl* Almosen *nt*

alone [ə'ləun] *adj, adv* allein; **to leave sth ~** etw sein lassen; **let ~ ...** geschweige denn ...

along [ə'lɒŋ] *prep* entlang, längs ♦ *adv* (*onward*) vorwärts, weiter; ~ **with** zusammen mit; **he was limping ~** er humpelte einher; **all ~** (*all the time*) die ganze Zeit; ~**side** *adv* (*walk*) nebenher; (*come*) nebendran; (*be*) daneben ♦ *prep* (*walk, compared with*) neben +*dat*; (*come*) neben +*acc*; (*be*) entlang, neben +*dat*; (*of ship*) längsseits +*gen*

aloof [ə'lu:f] *adj* zurückhaltend ♦ *adv* fern; **to stand ~** abseits stehen

aloud [ə'laud] *adv* laut

alphabet ['ælfəbet] *n* Alphabet *nt*; ~**ical** [ælfə'betɪkl] *adj* alphabetisch

alpine ['ælpaɪn] *adj* alpin, Alpen-

Alps [ælps] *npl*: **the ~** die Alpen *pl*

already [ɔ:l'redɪ] *adv* schon, bereits

alright ['ɔ:l'raɪt] (*BRIT*) *adv* = **all right**

Alsatian [æl'seɪʃən] *n* (*dog*) Schäferhund *m*

also ['ɔ:lsəu] *adv* auch, außerdem

altar ['ɔltəʳ] *n* Altar *m*

alter ['ɔltəʳ] *vt* ändern; (*dress*) umändern; ~**ation** [ɔltə'reɪʃən] *n* Änderung *f*; Umänderung *f*; (*to building*) Umbau *m*

alternate [*adj* ɔl'tə:nɪt, *vb* 'ɔltə:neɪt] *adj* abwechselnd ♦ *vi* abwechseln; **on ~ days** jeden zweiten Tag

alternating ['ɔltə:neɪtɪŋ] *adj*: ~ **current** Wechselstrom *m*; **alternative** [ɔl'tə:nətɪv] *adj* andere(r, s) ♦ *n* Alternative *f*; **alternative medicine** Alternativmedizin *f*; **alternatively** *adv* im anderen Falle; **alternatively one could ...** oder man könnte ...; **alternator** ['ɔltə:neɪtəʳ] *n* (*AUT*) Lichtmaschine *f*

although [ɔ:l'ðəu] *conj* obwohl

altitude ['æltɪtju:d] *n* Höhe *f*

alto ['æltəu] *n* Alt *m*

altogether [ɔ:ltə'geðəʳ] *adv* (*on the whole*) im Ganzen genommen; (*entirely*) ganz und gar

aluminium [ælju'mɪnɪəm] (*BRIT*) *n* Aluminium *nt*

aluminum [ə'lu:mɪnəm] (*US*) *n* Aluminium *nt*

always ['ɔ:lweɪz] *adv* immer

Alzheimer's (disease) ['æltshaɪməz-] *n* (*MED*) Alzheimerkrankheit *f*

am [æm] *see* **be**

a.m. *adv abbr* (= *ante meridiem*) vormittags

amalgamate [ə'mælgəmeɪt] *vi* (*combine*) sich vereinigen ♦ *vt* (*mix*) amalgamieren

amass [ə'mæs] *vt* anhäufen

amateur ['æmətəʳ] *n* Amateur *m*; (*pej*) Amateur *m*, Stümper *m*; ~**ish** (*pej*) *adj* dilettantisch, stümperhaft

amaze [ə'meɪz] *vt* erstaunen; **to be ~d (at)** erstaunt sein (über); ~**ment** *n* höchste(s) Erstaunen *nt*; **amazing** *adj* höchst erstaunlich

Amazon ['æməzən] n (GEOG) Amazonas m
ambassador [æm'bæsədər] n Botschafter m
amber ['æmbər] n Bernstein m; **at ~** (BRIT: AUT) auf Gelb, gelb
ambiguous [æm'bɪgjuəs] adj zweideutig; (not clear) unklar
ambition [æm'bɪʃən] n Ehrgeiz m; **ambitious** adj ehrgeizig
amble ['æmbl] vi (usu: ~ along) schlendern
ambulance ['æmbjuləns] n Krankenwagen m; **~ man** (irreg) n Sanitäter m
ambush ['æmbuʃ] n Hinterhalt m ♦ vt (aus dem Hinterhalt) überfallen
amenable [ə'mi:nəbl] adj gefügig; **~ (to)** (reason) zugänglich (+dat); (flattery) empfänglich (für)
amend [ə'mɛnd] vt (law etc) abändern, ergänzen; **to make ~s** etw wieder gutmachen; **~ment** n Abänderung f
amenities [ə'mi:nɪtɪz] npl Einrichtungen pl
America [ə'mɛrɪkə] n Amerika nt; **~n** adj amerikanisch ♦ n Amerikaner(in) m(f)
amiable ['eɪmɪəbl] adj liebenswürdig
amicable ['æmɪkəbl] adj freundschaftlich; (settlement) gütlich
amid(st) [ə'mɪd(st)] prep mitten in or unter +dat
amiss [ə'mɪs] adv: **to take sth ~** etw übel nehmen; **there's something ~** da stimmt irgendetwas nicht
ammonia [ə'məunɪə] n Ammoniak nt
ammunition [æmju'nɪʃən] n Munition f
amnesia [æm'ni:zɪə] n Gedächtnisverlust m
amnesty ['æmnɪstɪ] n Amnestie f
amok [ə'mɔk] adv: **to run ~** Amok laufen
among(st) [ə'mʌŋ(st)] prep unter
amoral [æ'mɔrəl] adj unmoralisch
amorous ['æmərəs] adj verliebt
amount [ə'maunt] n (of money) Betrag m; (of water, sand) Menge f ♦ vi: **to ~ to** (total) sich belaufen auf +acc; **a great ~ of time / energy** ein großer Aufwand an Zeit/ Energie (dat); **this ~s to treachery** das kommt Verrat gleich; **he won't ~ to much** aus ihm wird nie was
amp(ere) [æmp(ɛər)] n Ampere nt
amphibian [æm'fɪbɪən] n Amphibie f

ample ['æmpl] adj (portion) reichlich; (dress) weit, groß; **~ time** genügend Zeit
amplifier ['æmplɪfaɪər] n Verstärker m
amuse [ə'mju:z] vt (entertain) unterhalten; (make smile) belustigen; **~ment** n (feeling) Unterhaltung f; (recreation) Zeitvertreib m; **~ment arcade** n Spielhalle f; **~ment park** n Vergnügungspark m
an [æn, ən] see **a**
anaemia [ə'ni:mɪə] n Anämie f; **anaemic** adj blutarm
anaesthetic [ænɪs'θɛtɪk] n Betäubungsmittel nt; **under ~** unter Narkose; **anaesthetist** [æ'ni:sθɪtɪst] n Anästhesist(in) m(f)
analgesic [ænæl'dʒi:sɪk] n schmerzlindernde(s) Mittel nt
analog(ue) ['ænəlɔg] adj Analog-
analogy [ə'nælədʒɪ] n Analogie f
analyse ['ænəlaɪz] (BRIT) vt analysieren
analyses [ə'næləsi:z] (BRIT) npl of **analysis**
analysis [ə'næləsɪs] (pl **analyses**) n Analyse f
analyst ['ænəlɪst] n Analytiker(in) m(f)
analytic(al) [ænə'lɪtɪk(l)] adj analytisch
analyze ['ænəlaɪz] (US) vt = **analyse**
anarchy ['ænəkɪ] n Anarchie f
anatomy [ə'nætəmɪ] n (structure) anatomische(r) Aufbau m; (study) Anatomie f
ancestor ['ænsɪstər] n Vorfahr m
anchor ['æŋkər] n Anker m ♦ vi (also: **to drop ~**) ankern, vor Anker gehen ♦ vt verankern; **to weigh ~** den Anker lichten
anchovy ['æntʃəvɪ] n Sardelle f
ancient ['eɪnʃənt] adj alt; (car etc) uralt
ancillary [æn'sɪlərɪ] adj Hilfs-
and [ænd] conj und; **~ so on** und so weiter; **try ~ come** versuche zu kommen; **better ~ better** immer besser
Andes ['ændi:z] npl: **the ~** die Anden pl
anemia etc [ə'ni:mɪə] (US) n = **anaemia** etc
anesthetic etc [ænɪs'θɛtɪk] (US) n = **anaesthetic** etc
anew [ə'nju:] adv von neuem
angel ['eɪndʒəl] n Engel m
anger ['æŋgər] n Zorn m ♦ vt ärgern

angina [æn'dʒaɪnə] *n* Angina *f*

angle ['æŋgl] *n* Winkel *m*; (*point of view*) Standpunkt *m*

angler ['æŋglə'] *n* Angler *m*

Anglican ['æŋglɪkən] *adj* anglikanisch ♦ *n* Anglikaner(in) *m(f)*

angling ['æŋglɪŋ] *n* Angeln *nt*

angrily ['æŋgrɪlɪ] *adv* ärgerlich, böse

angry ['æŋgrɪ] *adj* ärgerlich, ungehalten, böse; (*wound*) entzündet; **to be ~ with sb** auf jdn böse sein; **to be ~ at sth** über etw *acc* verärgert sein

anguish ['æŋgwɪʃ] *n* Qual *f*

angular ['æŋgjulə'] *adj* eckig, winkelförmig; (*face*) kantig

animal ['ænɪməl] *n* Tier *nt*; (*living creature*) Lebewesen *nt* ♦ *adj* tierisch

animate [*vb* 'ænɪmeɪt, *adj* 'ænɪmɪt] *vt* beleben ♦ *adj* lebhaft; **~d** *adj* lebendig; (*film*) Zeichentrick-

animosity [ænɪ'mɔsɪtɪ] *n* Feindseligkeit *f*, Abneigung *f*

aniseed ['ænɪsiːd] *n* Anis *m*

ankle ['æŋkl] *n* (Fuß)knöchel *m*; **~ sock** *n* Söckchen *nt*

annex [*n* 'æneks, *vb* ə'neks] *n* (*BRIT: also:* **~e**) Anbau *m* ♦ *vt* anfügen; (*POL*) annektieren, angliedern

annihilate [ə'naɪəleɪt] *vt* vernichten

anniversary [ænɪ'vɜːsərɪ] *n* Jahrestag *m*

announce [ə'nauns] *vt* ankündigen, anzeigen; **~ment** *n* Ankündigung *f*; (*official*) Bekanntmachung *f*; **~r** *n* Ansager(in) *m(f)*

annoy [ə'nɔɪ] *vt* ärgern; **don't get ~ed!** reg dich nicht auf!; **~ance** *n* Ärgernis *nt*, Störung *f*; **~ing** *adj* ärgerlich; (*person*) lästig

annual ['ænjuəl] *adj* jährlich; (*salary*) Jahres- ♦ *n* (*plant*) einjährige Pflanze *f*; (*book*) Jahrbuch *nt*; **~ly** *adv* jährlich

annul [ə'nʌl] *vt* aufheben, annullieren

annum ['ænəm] *n see* **per**

anonymous [ə'nɔnɪməs] *adj* anonym

anorak ['ænəræk] *n* Anorak *m*, Windjacke *f*

anorexia [ænə'reksɪə] *n* (*MED*) Magersucht *f*

another [ə'nʌðə'] *adj, pron* (*different*) ein(e) andere(r, s); (*additional*) noch eine(r, s); *see*

also **one**

answer ['ɑːnsə'] *n* Antwort *f* ♦ *vi* antworten; (*on phone*) sich melden ♦ *vt* (*person*) antworten +*dat*; (*letter, question*) beantworten; (*telephone*) gehen an +*acc*, abnehmen; (*door*) öffnen; **in ~ to your letter** in Beantwortung Ihres Schreibens; **to ~ the phone** ans Telefon gehen; **to ~ the bell** *or* **the door** aufmachen; **~ back** *vi* frech sein; **~ for** *vt fus*: **to ~ for sth** für etw verantwortlich sein; **~able** *adj*: **to be ~able to sb for sth** jdm gegenüber für etw verantwortlich sein; **~ing machine** *n* Anrufbeantworter *m*

ant [ænt] *n* Ameise *f*

antagonism [æn'tægənɪzəm] *n* Antagonismus *m*

antagonize [æn'tægənaɪz] *vt* reizen

Antarctic [ænt'ɑːktɪk] *adj* antarktisch ♦ *n*: **the ~** die Antarktis

antelope ['æntɪləup] *n* Antilope *f*

antenatal ['æntɪ'neɪtl] *adj* vor der Geburt; **~ clinic** *n* Sprechstunde *f* für werdende Mütter

antenna [æn'tenə] *n* (*BIOL*) Fühler *m*; (*RAD*) Antenne *f*

antennae [æn'teniː] *npl of* **antenna**

anthem ['ænθəm] *n* Hymne *f*; **national ~** Nationalhymne *f*

anthology [æn'θɔlədʒɪ] *n* Gedichtsammlung *f*, Anthologie *f*

anti- ['æntɪ] *prefix* Gegen-, Anti-

anti-aircraft ['æntɪ'eəkrɑːft] *adj* Flugabwehr-

antibiotic ['æntɪbaɪ'ɔtɪk] *n* Antibiotikum *nt*

antibody ['æntɪbɔdɪ] *n* Antikörper *m*

anticipate [æn'tɪsɪpeɪt] *vt* (*expect: trouble, question*) erwarten, rechnen mit; (*look forward to*) sich freuen auf +*acc*; (*do first*) vorwegnehmen; (*foresee*) ahnen, vorhersehen; **anticipation** [æntɪsɪ'peɪʃən] *n* Erwartung *f*; (*foreshadowing*) Vorwegnahme *f*

anticlimax ['æntɪ'klaɪmæks] *n* Ernüchterung *f*

anticlockwise ['æntɪ'klɔkwaɪz] *adv* entgegen dem Uhrzeigersinn

antics ['æntɪks] *npl* Possen *pl*

anti: **~cyclone** n Hoch nt, Hochdruckgebiet nt; **~dote** n Gegenmittel nt; **~freeze** n Frostschutzmittel nt; **~histamine** n Antihistamin nt

antiquated ['æntɪkweɪtɪd] adj antiquiert

antique [æn'tiːk] n Antiquität f ♦ adj antik; (old-fashioned) altmodisch; **~ shop** n Antiquitätenladen m; **antiquity** [æn'tɪkwɪtɪ] n Altertum nt

antiseptic [æntɪ'septɪk] n Antiseptikum nt ♦ adj antiseptisch

antisocial ['æntɪ'səufəl] adj (person) ungesellig; (law) unsozial

antlers ['æntləz] npl Geweih nt

anus ['eɪnəs] n After m

anvil ['ænvɪl] n Amboss m

anxiety [æŋ'zaɪətɪ] n Angst f; (worry) Sorge f; **anxious** ['æŋkʃəs] adj ängstlich; (worried) besorgt; **to be anxious to do sth** etw unbedingt tun wollen

KEYWORD

any ['enɪ] adj **1** (in questions etc): **have you any butter?** haben Sie (etwas) Butter?; **have you any children?** haben Sie Kinder?; **if there are any tickets left** falls noch Karten da sind
2 (with negative): **I haven't any money/ books** ich habe kein Geld/keine Bücher
3 (no matter which) jede(r, s) (beliebige); **any colour (at all)** jede beliebige Farbe; **choose any book you like** nehmen Sie ein beliebiges Buch
4 (in phrases): **in any case** in jedem Fall; **any day now** jeden Tag; **at any moment** jeden Moment; **at any rate** auf jeden Fall
♦ pron **1** (in questions etc): **have you got any?** haben Sie welche?; **can any of you sing?** kann (irgend)einer von euch singen?
2 (with negative): **I haven't any (of them)** ich habe keinen/keines (davon)
3 (no matter which one(s)): **take any of those books (you like)** nehmen Sie irgendeines dieser Bücher
♦ adv **1** (in questions etc): **do you want any more soup/sandwiches?** möchten Sie noch Suppe/Brote?; **are you feeling any**

better? fühlen Sie sich etwas besser?
2 (with negative): **I can't hear him any more** ich kann ihn nicht mehr hören

anybody ['enɪbɔdɪ] pron (no matter who) jede(r); (in questions etc) (irgend)jemand, (irgend)eine(r); (with negative): **I can't see ~** ich kann niemanden sehen

anyhow ['enɪhau] adv (at any rate): **I shall go ~** ich gehe sowieso; (haphazardly): **do it ~** machen Sie es, wie Sie wollen

anyone ['enɪwʌn] pron = **anybody**

KEYWORD

anything ['enɪθɪŋ] pron **1** (in questions etc) (irgend)etwas; **can you see anything?** können Sie etwas sehen?
2 (with negative): **I can't see anything** ich kann nichts sehen
3 (no matter what): **you can say anything you like** Sie können sagen, was Sie wollen; **anything will do** irgendetwas (wird genügen), irgendeine(r, s) (wird genügen); **he'll eat anything** er isst alles

anyway ['enɪweɪ] adv (at any rate) auf jeden Fall; (besides): **~, I couldn't come even if I wanted to** jedenfalls könnte ich nicht kommen, selbst wenn ich wollte; **why are you phoning, ~?** warum rufst du überhaupt an?

anywhere ['enɪweəʳ] adv (in questions etc) irgendwo; (: with direction) irgendwohin; (no matter where) überall; (: with direction) überallhin; (with negative): **I can't see him ~** ich kann ihn nirgendwo or nirgends sehen; **can you see him ~?** siehst du ihn irgendwo?; **put the books down ~** leg die Bücher irgendwohin

apart [ə'paːt] adv (parted) auseinander; (away) beiseite, abseits; **10 miles ~** 10 Meilen auseinander; **to take ~** auseinander nehmen; **~ from** prep außer

apartheid [ə'paːteɪt] n Apartheid f

apartment [ə'paːtmənt] (US) n Wohnung f; **~ building** (US) n Wohnhaus nt

apathy ['æpəθɪ] n Teilnahmslosigkeit f,

Apathie f

ape [eɪp] n (Menschen)affe m ♦ vt nachahmen

aperitif [ə'perɪti:f] n Aperitif m

aperture ['æpətfjuəʳ] n Öffnung f; (PHOT) Blende f

APEX ['eɪpeks] n abbr (AVIAT: = advance purchase excursion) APEX (im Voraus reservierte(r) Fahrkarte/Flugschein zu reduzierten Preisen)

apex ['eɪpeks] n Spitze f

apiece [ə'pi:s] adv pro Stück; (per person) pro Kopf

apologetic [əpɒlə'dʒetɪk] adj entschuldigend; **to be ~** sich sehr entschuldigen

apologize [ə'pɒlədʒaɪz] vi: **to ~ (for sth to sb)** sich (für etw bei jdm) entschuldigen; **apology** n Entschuldigung f

apostle [ə'pɒsl] n Apostel m

apostrophe [ə'pɒstrəfɪ] n Apostroph m

appal [ə'pɔ:l] vt erschrecken; **~ling** adj schrecklich

apparatus [æpə'reɪtəs] n Gerät nt

apparel [ə'pærəl] (US) n Kleidung f

apparent [ə'pærənt] adj offenbar; **~ly** adv anscheinend

apparition [æpə'rɪʃən] n (ghost) Erscheinung f, Geist m

appeal [ə'pi:l] vi dringend ersuchen; (JUR) Berufung einlegen ♦ n Aufruf m; (JUR) Berufung f; **to ~ for** dringend bitten um; **~ to** sich wenden an +acc; (to public) appellieren an +acc; **it doesn't ~ to me** es gefällt mir nicht; **~ing** adj ansprechend

appear [ə'pɪəʳ] vi (come into sight) erscheinen; (be seen) auftauchen; (seem) scheinen; **it would ~ that ...** anscheinend ...; **~ance** n (coming into sight) Erscheinen nt; (outward show) Äußere(s) nt

appease [ə'pi:z] vt beschwichtigen

appendices [ə'pendɪsi:z] npl of **appendix**

appendicitis [əpendɪ'saɪtɪs] n Blinddarmentzündung f

appendix [ə'pendɪks] (pl **appendices**) n (in book) Anhang m; (MED) Blinddarm m

appetite ['æpɪtaɪt] n Appetit m; (fig) Lust f

appetizer ['æpɪtaɪzəʳ] n Appetitanreger m; **appetizing** ['æpɪtaɪzɪŋ] adj appetitanregend

applaud [ə'plɔ:d] vi Beifall klatschen, applaudieren ♦ vt Beifall klatschen +dat; **applause** [ə'plɔ:z] n Beifall m, Applaus m

apple ['æpl] n Apfel m; **~ tree** n Apfelbaum m

appliance [ə'plaɪəns] n Gerät nt

applicable [ə'plɪkəbl] adj anwendbar; (in forms) zutreffend

applicant ['æplɪkənt] n Bewerber(in) m(f)

application [æplɪ'keɪʃən] n (request) Antrag m; (for job) Bewerbung f; (putting into practice) Anwendung f; (hard work) Fleiß m; **~ form** n Bewerbungsformular nt

applied [ə'plaɪd] adj angewandt

apply [ə'plaɪ] vi (be suitable) zutreffen; (ask): **to ~ (to)** sich wenden (an +acc); (request): **to ~ for** sich melden für +acc ♦ vt (place on) auflegen; (cream) auftragen; (put into practice) anwenden; **to ~ for sth** sich um etw bewerben; **to ~ o.s. to sth** sich bei etw anstrengen

appoint [ə'pɔɪnt] vt (to office) ernennen, berufen; (settle) festsetzen; **~ment** n (meeting) Verabredung f; (at hairdresser etc) Bestellung f; (in business) Termin m; (choice for a position) Ernennung f; (UNIV) Berufung f

appraisal [ə'preɪzl] n Beurteilung f

appreciable [ə'pri:ʃəbl] adj (perceptible) merklich; (able to be estimated) abschätzbar

appreciate [ə'pri:ʃɪeɪt] vt (value) zu schätzen wissen; (understand) einsehen ♦ vi (increase in value) im Wert steigen; **appreciation** [əpri:ʃɪ'eɪʃən] n Wertschätzung f; (COMM) Wertzuwachs m; **appreciative** [ə'pri:ʃɪətɪv] adj (showing thanks) dankbar; (showing liking) anerkennend

apprehend [æprɪ'hend] vt (arrest) festnehmen; (understand) erfassen

apprehension [æprɪ'henʃən] n Angst f

apprehensive [æprɪ'hensɪv] adj furchtsam

apprentice [ə'prentɪs] n Lehrling m; **~ship** n Lehrzeit f

approach [ə'prəʊtʃ] vi sich nähern ♦ vt herantreten an +acc; (problem) herangehen

an +*acc* ♦ *n* Annäherung *f*; (*to problem*)
Ansatz *m*; (*path*) Zugang *m*, Zufahrt *f*;
~**able** *adj* zugänglich

appropriate [*adj* ə'prəuprɪɪt, *vb* ə'prəuprɪeɪt]
adj angemessen; (*remark*) angebracht ♦ *vt*
(*take for o.s.*) sich aneignen; (*set apart*)
bereitstellen

approval [ə'pruːvəl] *n* (*show of satisfaction*)
Beifall *m*; (*permission*) Billigung *f*; **on ~**
(*COMM*) bei Gefallen

approve [ə'pruːv] *vt*, *vi* billigen; **I don't ~ of
it/him** ich halte nichts davon/von ihm; **~d
school** (*BRIT*) *n* Erziehungsheim *nt*

approximate [*adj* ə'prɔksɪmɪt, *vb*
ə'prɔksɪmeɪt] *adj* annähernd, ungefähr ♦ *vt*
nahe kommen +*dat*; **~ly** *adv* rund,
ungefähr

apricot ['eɪprɪkɔt] *n* Aprikose *f*

April ['eɪprəl] *n* April *m*; **~ Fools' Day** *n* der
erste April

apron ['eɪprən] *n* Schürze *f*

apt [æpt] *adj* (*suitable*) passend; (*able*)
begabt; (*likely*): **to be ~ to do sth** dazu
neigen, etw zu tun

aptitude ['æptɪtjuːd] *n* Begabung *f*

aqualung ['ækwəlʌŋ] *n*
Unterwasseratmungsgerät *nt*

aquarium [ə'kweərɪəm] *n* Aquarium *nt*

Aquarius [ə'kweərɪəs] *n* Wassermann *m*

aquatic [ə'kwætɪk] *adj* Wasser-

Arab ['ærəb] *n* Araber(in) *m(f)*

Arabia [ə'reɪbɪə] *n* Arabien *nt*; **~n** *adj*
arabisch

Arabic ['ærəbɪk] *adj* arabisch ♦ *n* Arabisch *nt*

arable ['ærəbl] *adj* bebaubar, Kultur-

arbitrary ['ɑːbɪtrərɪ] *adj* willkürlich

arbitration [ɑːbɪ'treɪʃən] *n* Schlichtung *f*

arc [ɑːk] *n* Bogen *m*

arcade [ɑː'keɪd] *n* Säulengang *m*; (*with video
games*) Spielhalle *f*

arch [ɑːtʃ] *n* Bogen *m* ♦ *vt* überwölben;
(*back*) krumm machen

archaeologist [ɑːkɪ'ɔlədʒɪst] *n* Archäologe
m

archaeology [ɑːkɪ'ɔlədʒɪ] *n* Archäologie *f*

archaic [ɑː'keɪɪk] *adj* altertümlich

archbishop [ɑːtʃ'bɪʃəp] *n* Erzbischof *m*

archenemy ['ɑːtʃ'enəmɪ] *n* Erzfeind *m*

archeology *etc* [ɑːkɪ'ɔlədʒɪ] (*US*) =
archaeology *etc*

archery ['ɑːtʃərɪ] *n* Bogenschießen *nt*

architect ['ɑːkɪtekt] *n* Architekt(in) *m(f)*;
~**ural** [ɑːkɪ'tektʃərəl] *adj* architektonisch;
~**ure** *n* Architektur *f*

archives ['ɑːkaɪvz] *npl* Archiv *nt*

archway ['ɑːtʃweɪ] *n* Bogen *m*

Arctic ['ɑːktɪk] *adj* arktisch ♦ *n*: **the ~** die
Arktis

ardent ['ɑːdənt] *adj* glühend

arduous ['ɑːdjuəs] *adj* mühsam

are [ɑːr] *see* **be**

area ['eərɪə] *n* Fläche *f*, (*of land*) Gebiet *nt*,
(*part of sth*) Teil *m*, Abschnitt *m*

arena [ə'riːnə] *n* Arena *f*

aren't [ɑːnt] = **are not**

Argentina [ɑːdʒən'tiːnə] *n* Argentinien *nt*;
Argentinian [ɑːdʒən'tɪnɪən] *adj*
argentinisch ♦ *n* Argentinier(in) *m(f)*

arguably ['ɑːgjuəblɪ] *adv* wohl

argue ['ɑːgjuː] *vi* diskutieren; (*angrily*)
streiten; **argument** *n* (*theory*) Argument *nt*;
(*reasoning*) Argumentation *f*; (*row*)
Auseinandersetzung *f*, Streit *m*; **to have an
argument** sich streiten; **argumentative**
[ɑːgju'mentətɪv] *adj* streitlustig

aria ['ɑːrɪə] *n* Arie *f*

Aries ['eərɪz] *n* Widder *m*

arise [ə'raɪz] (*pt* **arose**, *pp* **arisen**) *vi*
aufsteigen; (*get up*) aufstehen; (*difficulties
etc*) entstehen; (*case*) vorkommen; **to ~
from sth** herrühren von etw; ~**n** [ə'rɪzn] *pp*
of **arise**

aristocracy [ærɪs'tɔkrəsɪ] *n* Adel *m*,
Aristokratie *f*; **aristocrat** ['ærɪstəkræt] *n*
Adlige(r) *f(m)*, Aristokrat(in) *m(f)*

arithmetic [ə'rɪθmətɪk] *n* Rechnen *nt*,
Arithmetik *f*

arm [ɑːm] *n* Arm *m*; (*branch of military service*)
Zweig *m* ♦ *vt* bewaffnen; ~**s** *npl* (*weapons*)
Waffen *pl*

armaments ['ɑːməmənts] *npl* Ausrüstung *f*

armchair ['ɑːmtʃeər] *n* Lehnstuhl *m*

armed [ɑːmd] *adj* (*forces*) Streit-, bewaffnet;
~ robbery *n* bewaffnete(r) Raubüberfall *m*

armistice ['ɑːmɪstɪs] *n* Waffenstillstand *m*

armour ['ɑːməʳ] (*US* **armor**) *n* (*knight's*) Rüstung *f*; (*MIL*) Panzerplatte *f*; **~ed car** *n* Panzerwagen *m*

armpit ['ɑːmpɪt] *n* Achselhöhle *f*

armrest ['ɑːmrest] *n* Armlehne *f*

army ['ɑːmɪ] *n* Armee *f*, Heer *nt*; (*host*) Heer *nt*

aroma [ə'rəumə] *n* Duft *m*, Aroma *nt*; **~therapy** [ərəumə'θerəpɪ] *n* Aromatherapie *f*; **~tic** [ærə'mætɪk] *adj* aromatisch, würzig

arose [ə'rəuz] *pt of* **arise**

around [ə'raund] *adv* ringsherum; (*almost*) ungefähr ♦ *prep* um ... herum; **is he ~?** ist er hier?

arrange [ə'reɪndʒ] *vt* (*time, meeting*) festsetzen; (*holidays*) festlegen; (*flowers, hair, objects*) anordnen; **I ~d to meet him** ich habe mit ihm ausgemacht, ihn zu treffen; **it's all ~d** es ist alles arrangiert; **~ment** *n* (*order*) Reihenfolge *f*; (*agreement*) Vereinbarung *f*; **~ments** *npl* (*plans*) Pläne *pl*

array [ə'reɪ] *n* (*collection*) Ansammlung *f*

arrears [ə'rɪəz] *npl* (*of debts*) Rückstand *m*; (*of work*) Unerledigte(s) *nt*; **in ~** im Rückstand

arrest [ə'rest] *vt* (*person*) verhaften; (*stop*) aufhalten ♦ *n* Verhaftung *f*; **under ~** in Haft

arrival [ə'raɪvl] *n* Ankunft *f*

arrive [ə'raɪv] *vi* ankommen; **to ~ at** ankommen in +*dat*, ankommen bei

arrogance ['ærəgəns] *n* Überheblichkeit *f*, Arroganz *f*; **arrogant** ['ærəgənt] *adj* überheblich, arrogant

arrow ['ærəu] *n* Pfeil *m*

arse [ɑːs] (*infl*) *n* Arsch *m* (!)

arsenal ['ɑːsɪnl] *n* Waffenlager *nt*, Zeughaus *nt*

arsenic ['ɑːsnɪk] *n* Arsen *nt*

arson ['ɑːsn] *n* Brandstiftung *f*

art [ɑːt] *n* Kunst *f*; **A~s** *npl* (*UNIV*) Geisteswissenschaften *pl*

artery ['ɑːtərɪ] *n* Schlagader *f*, Arterie *f*

art gallery *n* Kunstgalerie *f*

arthritis [ɑː'θraɪtɪs] *n* Arthritis *f*

artichoke ['ɑːtɪtʃəuk] *n* Artischocke *f*; **Jerusalem ~** Erdartischocke *f*

article ['ɑːtɪkl] *n* (*PRESS, GRAM*) Artikel *m*; (*thing*) Gegenstand *m*, Artikel *m*; (*clause*) Abschnitt *m*, Paragraf *m*; **~ of clothing** Kleidungsstück *nt*

articulate [*adj* ɑː'tɪkjulɪt, *vb* ɑː'tɪkjuleɪt] *adj* (*able to express o.s.*) redegewandt; (*speaking clearly*) deutlich, verständlich ♦ *vt* (*connect*) zusammenfügen, gliedern; **to be ~** sich gut ausdrücken können; **~d vehicle** *n* Sattelschlepper *m*

artificial [ɑːtɪ'fɪʃəl] *adj* künstlich, Kunst-; **~ respiration** *n* künstliche Atmung *f*

artisan ['ɑːtɪzæn] *n* gelernte(r) Handwerker *m*

artist ['ɑːtɪst] *n* Künstler(in) *m(f)*; **~ic** [ɑː'tɪstɪk] *adj* künstlerisch; **~ry** *n* künstlerische(s) Können *nt*

art school *n* Kunsthochschule *f*

KEYWORD

as [æz] *conj* **1** (*referring to time*) als; **as the years went by** mit den Jahren; **he came in as I was leaving** als er hereinkam, ging ich gerade; **as from tomorrow** ab morgen

2 (*in comparisons*): **as big as** so groß wie; **twice as big as** zweimal so groß wie; **as much/many as** so viel/so viele wie; **as soon as** sobald

3 (*since, because*) da; **he left early as he had to be home by 10** er ging früher, da er um 10 zu Hause sein musste

4 (*referring to manner, way*) wie; **do as you wish** mach was du willst; **as she said** wie sie sagte

5 (*concerning*): **as for** *or* **to that** was das betrifft *or* angeht

6: as if *or* **though** als ob

♦ *prep* als; *see also* **long**; **he works as a driver** er arbeitet als Fahrer; *see also* **such**; **he gave it to me as a present** er hat es mir als Geschenk gegeben; *see also* **well**

---

a.s.a.p. *abbr* = **as soon as possible**

asbestos [æz'bestəs] *n* Asbest *m*

ascend [ə'send] *vi* aufsteigen ♦ *vt* besteigen; **ascent** *n* Aufstieg *m*; Besteigung *f*

ascertain [æsə'teɪn] vt feststellen
ascribe [ə'skraɪb] vt: **to ~ sth to sth /sth to sb** etw einer Sache/jdm etw zuschreiben
ash [æʃ] n Asche f; (tree) Esche f
ashamed [ə'ʃeɪmd] adj beschämt; **to be ~ of sth** sich für etw schämen
ashen ['æʃən] adj (pale) aschfahl
ashore [ə'ʃɔːr] adv an Land
ashtray ['æʃtreɪ] n Aschenbecher m
Ash Wednesday n Aschermittwoch m
Asia ['eɪʃə] n Asien nt; **~n** adj asiatisch ♦ n Asiat(in) m(f)
aside [ə'saɪd] adv beiseite
ask [ɑːsk] vt fragen; (permission) bitten um; **~ him his name** frage ihn nach seinem Namen; **he ~ed to see you** er wollte dich sehen; **to ~ sb to do sth** jdn bitten, etw zu tun; **to ~ sb about sth** jdn nach etw fragen; **to ~ (sb) a question** (jdn) etwas fragen; **to ~ sb out to dinner** jdn zum Essen einladen; **~ after** vt fus fragen nach; **~ for** vt fus bitten um
askance [ə'skɑːns] adv: **to look ~ at sb** jdn schief ansehen
asking price ['ɑːskɪŋ-] n Verkaufspreis m
asleep [ə'sliːp] adj: **to be ~** schlafen; **to fall ~** einschlafen
asparagus [əs'pærəgəs] n Spargel m
aspect ['æspekt] n Aspekt m
aspersions [əs'pɜːʃənz] npl: **to cast ~ on sb/sth** sich abfällig über jdn/etw äußern
asphyxiation [æsfɪksɪ'eɪʃən] n Erstickung f
aspirations [æspə'reɪʃənz] npl: **to have ~ towards sth** etw anstreben
aspire [əs'paɪər] vi: **to ~ to** streben nach
aspirin ['æsprɪn] n Aspirin nt
ass [æs] n (also fig) Esel m; (US: inf!) Arsch m (!)
assailant [ə'seɪlənt] n Angreifer m
assassin [ə'sæsɪn] n Attentäter(in) m(f); **~ate** vt ermorden; **~ation** [əsæsɪ'neɪʃən] n (geglückte(s)) Attentat nt
assault [ə'sɔːlt] n Angriff m ♦ vt überfallen; (woman) herfallen über +acc
assemble [ə'sɛmbl] vt versammeln; (parts) zusammensetzen ♦ vi sich versammeln; **assembly** n (meeting) Versammlung f; (construction) Zusammensetzung f, Montage f; **assembly line** n Fließband nt
assent [ə'sent] n Zustimmung f
assert [ə'sɜːt] vt erklären; **~ion** n Behauptung f
assess [ə'ses] vt schätzen; **~ment** n Bewertung f, Einschätzung f; **~or** n Steuerberater m
asset ['æset] n Vorteil m, Wert m; **~s** npl (FIN) Vermögen nt; (estate) Nachlass m
assign [ə'saɪn] vt zuweisen; **~ment** n Aufgabe f, Auftrag m
assimilate [ə'sɪmɪleɪt] vt sich aneignen, aufnehmen
assist [ə'sɪst] vt beistehen +dat; **~ance** n Unterstützung f, Hilfe f; **~ant** n Assistent(in) m(f), Mitarbeiter(in) m(f); (BRIT: also: **shop ~ant**) Verkäufer(in) m(f)
associate [n ə'səʊʃɪɪt, vb ə'səʊʃɪeɪt] n (partner) Kollege m, Teilhaber m; (member) außerordentliche(s) Mitglied nt ♦ vt verbinden ♦ vi (keep company) verkehren; **association** [əsəʊsɪ'eɪʃən] n Verband m, Verein m; (PSYCH) Assoziation f; (link) Verbindung f
assorted [ə'sɔːtɪd] adj gemischt
assortment [ə'sɔːtmənt] n Sammlung f; (COMM): **~ (of)** Sortiment nt (von), Auswahl f (an +dat)
assume [ə'sjuːm] vt (take for granted) annehmen; (put on) annehmen, sich geben; **~d name** n Deckname m
assumption [ə'sʌmpʃən] n Annahme f
assurance [ə'ʃʊərəns] n (firm statement) Versicherung f; (confidence) Selbstsicherheit f; (insurance) (Lebens)versicherung f
assure [ə'ʃʊər] vt (make sure) sicherstellen; (convince) versichern +dat; (life) versichern
asterisk ['æstərɪsk] n Sternchen nt
asthma ['æsmə] n Asthma nt
astonish [ə'stɒnɪʃ] vt erstaunen; **~ment** n Erstaunen nt
astound [ə'staʊnd] vt verblüffen
astray [ə'streɪ] adv in die Irre; auf Abwege; **to go ~** (go wrong) sich vertun; **to lead ~** irreführen
astride [ə'straɪd] adv rittlings ♦ prep rittlings

auf

astrologer [əsˈtrɔlədʒəʳ] n Astrologe m, Astrologin f; **astrology** n Astrologie f

astronaut [ˈæstrənɔːt] n Astronaut(in) m(f)

astronomer [əsˈtrɔnəməʳ] n Astronom m

astronomical [æstrəˈnɔmɪkl] adj astronomisch; (success) riesig

astronomy [əsˈtrɔnəmɪ] n Astronomie f

astute [əsˈtjuːt] adj scharfsinnig; schlau, gerissen

asylum [əˈsaɪləm] n (home) Heim nt; (refuge) Asyl nt

KEYWORD

at [æt] prep 1 (referring to position, direction) an +dat, bei +dat; (with place) in +dat; **at the top** an der Spitze; **at home/school** zu Hause/in der Schule; **at the baker's** beim Bäcker; **to look at sth** auf etw acc blicken; **to throw sth at sb** etw nach jdm werfen
2 (referring to time): **at 4 o'clock** um 4 Uhr; **at night** bei Nacht; **at Christmas** zu Weihnachten; **at times** manchmal
3 (referring to rates, speed etc): **at £1 a kilo** zu £1 pro Kilo; **two at a time** zwei auf einmal; **at 50 km/h** mit 50 km/h
4 (referring to manner): **at a stroke** mit einem Schlag; **at peace** in Frieden
5 (referring to activity): **to be at work** bei der Arbeit sein; **to play at cowboys** Cowboy spielen; **to be good at sth** gut in etw dat sein
6 (referring to cause): **shocked/surprised/ annoyed at sth** schockiert/überrascht/ verärgert über etw acc; **I went at his suggestion** ich ging auf seinen Vorschlag hin

---

ate [eɪt] pt of **eat**

atheist [ˈeɪθɪɪst] n Atheist(in) m(f)

Athens [ˈæθɪnz] n Athen nt

athlete [ˈæθliːt] n Athlet m, Sportler m

athletic [æθˈletɪk] adj sportlich, athletisch; **~s** n Leichtathletik f

Atlantic [ətˈlæntɪk] adj atlantisch ♦ n: **the ~ (Ocean)** der Atlantik

atlas [ˈætləs] n Atlas m

ATM abbr (= automated teller machine) Geldautomat m

atmosphere [ˈætməsfɪəʳ] n Atmosphäre f

atom [ˈætəm] n Atom nt; (fig) bisschen nt; **~ic** [əˈtɔmɪk] adj atomar, Atom-; **~(ic) bomb** n Atombombe f

atomizer [ˈætəmaɪzəʳ] n Zerstäuber m

atone [əˈtəun] vi sühnen; **to ~ for sth** etw sühnen

atrocious [əˈtrəuʃəs] adj grässlich

atrocity [əˈtrɔsɪtɪ] n Scheußlichkeit f; (deed) Gräueltat f

attach [əˈtætʃ] vt (fasten) befestigen; **to be ~ed to sb/sth** an jdm/etw hängen; **to ~ importance** etc **to sth** Wichtigkeit etc auf etw acc legen, einer Sache dat Wichtigkeit etc beimessen

attaché case [əˈtæʃeɪ] n Aktenkoffer m

attachment [əˈtætʃmənt] n (tool) Zubehörteil nt; (love): **~ (to sb)** Zuneigung f (zu jdm)

attack [əˈtæk] vt angreifen ♦ n Angriff m; (MED) Anfall m; **~er** n Angreifer(in) m(f)

attain [əˈteɪn] vt erreichen; **~ments** npl Kenntnisse pl

attempt [əˈtempt] n Versuch m ♦ vt versuchen; **~ed murder** Mordversuch m

attend [əˈtend] vt (go to) teilnehmen (an +dat); (lectures) besuchen; **to ~ to** (needs) nachkommen +dat; (person) sich kümmern um; **~ance** n (presence) Anwesenheit f; (people present) Besucherzahl f; **good ~ance** gute Teilnahme; **~ant** n (companion) Begleiter(in) m(f); Gesellschafter(in) m(f); (in car park etc) Wächter(in) m(f); (servant) Bedienstete(r) mf ♦ adj begleitend; (fig) damit verbunden

attention [əˈtenʃən] n Aufmerksamkeit f; (care) Fürsorge f; (for machine etc) Pflege f ♦ excl (MIL) Achtung!; **for the ~ of ...** zu Händen (von) ...

attentive [əˈtentɪv] adj aufmerksam

attic [ˈætɪk] n Dachstube f, Mansarde f

attitude [ˈætɪtjuːd] n (mental) Einstellung f

attorney [əˈtəːnɪ] n (solicitor) Rechtsanwalt m; **A~ General** n Justizminister m

attract [əˈtrækt] vt anziehen; (attention)

erregen; **~ion** n Anziehungskraft f; (thing) Attraktion f; **~ive** adj attraktiv

attribute [n 'ætrɪbjuːt, vb ə'trɪbjuːt] n Eigenschaft f, Attribut nt ♦ vt zuschreiben

attrition [ə'trɪʃən] n: **war of ~** Zermürbungskrieg m

aubergine ['əubəʒiːn] n Aubergine f

auburn ['ɔːbən] adj kastanienbraun

auction ['ɔːkʃən] n (also: **sale by ~**) Versteigerung f, Auktion f ♦ vt versteigern; **~eer** [ɔːkʃə'nɪəʳ] n Versteigerer m

audacity [ɔː'dæsɪtɪ] n (boldness) Wagemut m; (impudence) Unverfrorenheit f

audible ['ɔːdɪbl] adj hörbar

audience ['ɔːdɪəns] n Zuhörer pl, Zuschauer pl; (with queen) Audienz f

audiotypist ['ɔːdɪəʊ'taɪpɪst] n Phonotypistin f, Fonotypistin f

audiovisual ['ɔːdɪəʊ'vɪzjuəl] adj audiovisuell

audit ['ɔːdɪt] vt prüfen

audition [ɔː'dɪʃən] n Probe f

auditor ['ɔːdɪtəʳ] n (accountant) Rechnungsprüfer(in) m(f), Buchprüfer m

auditorium [ɔːdɪ'tɔːrɪəm] n Zuschauerraum m

augment [ɔːg'mɛnt] vt vermehren

augur ['ɔːgəʳ] vi bedeuten, voraussagen; **this ~s well** das ist ein gutes Omen

August ['ɔːgəst] n August m

aunt [ɑːnt] n Tante f; **~ie** n Tantchen nt; **~y** n = **auntie**

au pair ['əu'peəʳ] n (also: **~ girl**) Aupairmädchen nt, Au-pair-Mädchen nt

aura ['ɔːrə] n Nimbus m

auspicious [ɔːs'pɪʃəs] adj günstig; verheißungsvoll

austere [ɒs'tɪəʳ] adj streng; (room) nüchtern; **austerity** [ɒs'tɛrɪtɪ] n Strenge f; (POL) wirtschaftliche Einschränkung f

Australia [ɒs'treɪlɪə] n Australien nt; **~n** adj australisch ♦ n Australier(in) m(f)

Austria ['ɒstrɪə] n Österreich nt; **~n** adj österreichisch ♦ n Österreicher(in) m(f)

authentic [ɔː'θɛntɪk] adj echt, authentisch

author ['ɔːθəʳ] n Autor m, Schriftsteller m; (beginner) Urheber m, Schöpfer m

authoritarian [ɔːθɒrɪ'tɛərɪən] adj autoritär

authoritative [ɔː'θɒrɪtətɪv] adj (account) maßgeblich; (manner) herrisch

authority [ɔː'θɒrɪtɪ] n (power) Autorität f; (expert) Autorität f, Fachmann m; **the authorities** npl (ruling body) die Behörden pl

authorize ['ɔːθəraɪz] vt bevollmächtigen; (permit) genehmigen

auto ['ɔːtəu] (US) n Auto nt, Wagen m

autobiography [ɔːtəbaɪ'ɒgrəfɪ] n Autobiografie f

autograph ['ɔːtəgrɑːf] n (of celebrity) Autogramm nt ♦ vt mit Autogramm versehen

automatic [ɔːtə'mætɪk] adj automatisch ♦ n (gun) Selbstladepistole f; (car) Automatik m; **~ally** adv automatisch

automation [ɔːtə'meɪʃən] n Automatisierung f

automobile ['ɔːtəməbiːl] (US) n Auto(mobil) nt

autonomous [ɔː'tɒnəməs] adj autonom; **autonomy** n Autonomie f

autumn ['ɔːtəm] n Herbst m

auxiliary [ɔːg'zɪlɪərɪ] adj Hilfs-

Av. abbr = **avenue**

avail [ə'veɪl] vt: **to ~ o.s. of sth** sich einer Sache gen bedienen ♦ n: **to no ~** nutzlos

availability [əveɪlə'bɪlɪtɪ] n Erhältlichkeit f, Vorhandensein nt

available [ə'veɪləbl] adj erhältlich; zur Verfügung stehend; (person) erreichbar, abkömmlich

avalanche ['ævəlɑːnʃ] n Lawine f

Ave. abbr = **avenue**

avenge [ə'vɛndʒ] vt rächen, sühnen

avenue ['ævənjuː] n Allee f

average ['ævərɪdʒ] n Durchschnitt m ♦ adj durchschnittlich, Durchschnitts- ♦ vt (figures) den Durchschnitt nehmen von; (perform) durchschnittlich leisten; (in car etc) im Schnitt fahren; **on ~** durchschnittlich, im Durchschnitt; **~ out** vi: **to ~ out at** im Durchschnitt betragen

averse [ə'vɜːs] adj: **to be ~ to doing sth** eine Abneigung dagegen haben, etw zu tun

avert [ə'vɜːt] *vt* (*turn away*) abkehren;
(*prevent*) abwehren

aviary ['eɪvɪərɪ] *n* Vogelhaus *nt*

aviation [eɪvɪ'eɪʃən] *n* Luftfahrt *f*, Flugwesen
nt

avid ['ævɪd] *adj*: ~ **(for)** gierig (auf +*acc*)

avocado [ævə'kɑːdəʊ] *n* (*BRIT: also*: ~ **pear**)
Avocado(birne) *f*

avoid [ə'vɔɪd] *vt* vermeiden

await [ə'weɪt] *vt* erwarten, entgegensehen
+*dat*

awake [ə'weɪk] (*pt* **awoke**, *pp* **awoken** *or*
awaked) *adj* wach ♦ *vt* (auf)wecken ♦ *vi*
aufwachen; **to be ~** wach sein; **~ning** *n*
Erwachen *nt*

award [ə'wɔːd] *n* (*prize*) Preis *m* ♦ *vt*: **to ~
(sb sth)** (jdm etw) zuerkennen

aware [ə'weə³] *adj* bewusst; **to be ~**
sich bewusst sein; **~ness** *n* Bewusstsein
nt

awash [ə'wɒʃ] *adj* überflutet

away [ə'weɪ] *adv* weg, fort; **two hours ~ by
car** zwei Autostunden entfernt; **the holiday
was two weeks ~** es war noch zwei
Wochen bis zum Urlaub; **two kilometres ~**
zwei Kilometer entfernt; **~ match** *n* (*SPORT*)
Auswärtsspiel *nt*

awe [ɔː] *n* Ehrfurcht *f*; **~-inspiring** *adj*
Ehrfurcht gebietend; **~some** *adj* Ehrfurcht
gebietend

awful ['ɔːfəl] *adj* (*very bad*) furchtbar; **~ly** *adv*
furchtbar, sehr

awhile [ə'waɪl] *adv* eine Weile

awkward ['ɔːkwəd] *adj* (*clumsy*) ungeschickt,
linkisch; (*embarrassing*) peinlich

awning ['ɔːnɪŋ] *n* Markise *f*

awoke [ə'wəʊk] *pt of* **awake**; **~n** *pp of*
awake

awry [ə'raɪ] *adv* schief; (*plans*) schief gehen

axe [æks] (*US* **ax**) *n* Axt *f*, Beil *nt* ♦ *vt* (*end
suddenly*) streichen

axes¹ ['æksɪz] *npl of* **axe**

axes² ['æksiːz] *npl of* **axis**

axis ['æksɪs] (*pl* **axes**) *n* Achse *f*

axle ['æksl] *n* Achse *f*

ay(e) [aɪ] *excl* (*yes*) ja

azalea [ə'zeɪlɪə] *n* Azalee *f*

B, b

B [biː] *n* (*MUS*) H *nt*; ~ **road** (*BRIT*) Landstraße
f

B.A. *n abbr* = **Bachelor of Arts**

babble ['bæbl] *vi* schwätzen

baby ['beɪbɪ] *n* Baby *nt*; ~ **carriage** (*US*) *n*
Kinderwagen *m*; ~ **food** *n* Babynahrung *f*;
~-sit *vi* Kinder hüten, babysitten; **~-sitter**
n Babysitter *m*; **~-sitting** *n* Babysitten *nt*,
Babysitting *nt*; ~ **wipe** *n* Ölpflegetuch *nt*

bachelor ['bætʃələ³] *n* Junggeselle *m*; **B~ of
Arts** Bakkalaureus *m* der philosophischen
Fakultät; **B~ of Science** Bakkalaureus *m* der
Naturwissenschaften

back [bæk] *n* (*of person, horse*) Rücken *m*; (*of
house*) Rückseite *f*; (*of train*) Ende *nt*;
(*FOOTBALL*) Verteidiger *m* ♦ *vt* (*support*)
unterstützen; (*wager*) wetten auf +*acc*; (*car*)
rückwärts fahren ♦ *vi* (*go ~wards*) rückwärts
gehen *or* fahren ♦ *adj* hintere(r, s) ♦ *adv*
zurück; (*to the rear*) nach hinten; ~ **down**
vi zurückstecken; ~ **out** *vi* sich
zurückziehen; (*inf*) kneifen; ~ **up** *vt*
(*support*) unterstützen; (*car*) zurücksetzen;
(*COMPUT*) eine Sicherungskopie machen
von; **~ache** *n* Rückenschmerzen *pl*;
~bencher (*BRIT*) *n* Parlamentarier(in) *m(f)*;
~bone *n* Rückgrat *nt*; (*support*) Rückhalt *m*;
~cloth *n* Hintergrund *m*; **~date** *vt*
rückdatieren; **~drop** *n* (*THEAT*) = **backcloth**;
(*~ground*) Hintergrund *m*; **~fire** *vi* (*plan*)
fehlschlagen; (*TECH*) fehlzünden; **~ground**
n Hintergrund *m*; (*person's education*)
Vorbildung *f*; **family ~ground**
Familienverhältnisse *pl*; **~hand** *n* (*TENNIS*:
also: **~hand stroke**) Rückhand *f*; **~hander**
(*BRIT*) *n* (*bribe*) Schmiergeld *nt*; **~ing** *n*
(*support*) Unterstützung *f*; **~lash** *n* (*fig*)
Gegenschlag *m*; **~log** *n* (*of work*) Rückstand
m; ~ **number** *n* (*PRESS*) alte Nummer *f*;
~pack *n* Rucksack *m*; **~packer** *n*
Rucksacktourist(in) *m(f)*; ~ **pain** *n*
Rückenschmerzen *pl*; ~ **pay** *n* (Gehalts- *or*
Lohn)nachzahlung *f*; ~ **payments** *npl*

Zahlungsrückstände pl; ~ **seat** n (AUT)
Rücksitz m; **~side** (inf) n Hintern m;
~stage adv hinter den Kulissen; **~stroke** n
Rückenschwimmen nt; **~up** adj (COMPUT)
Sicherungs- ♦ n (COMPUT) Sicherungskopie
f; **~ward** adj (less developed)
zurückgeblieben; (primitive) rückständig;
~wards adv rückwärts; **~water** n (fig) Kaff
nt; **~yard** n Hinterhof m

bacon ['beikən] n Schinkenspeck m

bacteria [bæk'tɪərɪə] npl Bakterien pl

bad [bæd] adj schlecht, schlimm; **to go ~**
schlecht werden

bade [bæd] pt of **bid**

badge [bædʒ] n Abzeichen nt

badger ['bædʒə*] n Dachs m

badly ['bædlɪ] adv schlecht, schlimm; **~
wounded** schwer verwundet; **he needs it
~** er braucht es dringend; **to be ~ off (for
money)** dringend Geld nötig haben

badminton ['bædmɪntən] n Federball m,
Badminton nt

bad-tempered ['bæd'tempəd] adj schlecht
gelaunt

baffle ['bæfl] vt (puzzle) verblüffen

bag [bæg] n (sack) Beutel m; (paper) Tüte f;
(handbag) Tasche f; (suitcase) Koffer m; (inf:
old woman) alte Schachtel f ♦ vt (put in sack)
in einen Sack stecken; (hunting) erlegen; **~s
of** (inf: lots of) eine Menge +acc; **~gage**
['bægɪdʒ] n Gepäck nt; **~ allowance** n
Freigepäck nt; **~ reclaim** n
Gepäckausgabe f; **~gy** ['bægɪ] adj bauschig,
sackartig

bagpipes ['bægpaɪps] npl Dudelsack m

bail [beɪl] n (money) Kaution f ♦ vt (prisoner:
usu: grant ~ to) gegen Kaution freilassen;
(boat: also: ~ out) ausschöpfen; **on ~**
(prisoner) gegen Kaution freigelassen; **to ~
sb out** die Kaution für jdn stellen; see also
bale

bailiff ['beɪlɪf] n Gerichtsvollzieher(in) m(f)

bait [beɪt] n Köder m ♦ vt mit einem Köder
versehen; (fig) ködern

bake [beɪk] vt, vi backen; **~d beans**
gebackene Bohnen pl; **~d potatoes** npl in
der Schale gebackene Kartoffeln pl; **~r** n

Bäcker m; **~ry** n Bäckerei f; **baking** n
Backen nt; **baking powder** n Backpulver
nt

balance ['bæləns] n (scales) Waage f;
(equilibrium) Gleichgewicht nt; (FIN: state of
account) Saldo m; (difference) Bilanz f;
(amount remaining) Restbetrag m ♦ vt
(weigh) wägen; (make equal) ausgleichen; **~
of trade / payments** Handels-/
Zahlungsbilanz f; **~d** adj ausgeglichen; **~
sheet** n Bilanz f, Rechnungsabschluss m

balcony ['bælkənɪ] n Balkon m

bald [bɔːld] adj kahl; (statement) knapp

bale [beɪl] n Ballen m; **bale out** vi (from a
plane) abspringen

ball [bɔːl] n Ball m; **~ bearing** n Kugellager
nt

ballet ['bæleɪ] n Ballett nt; **~ dancer** n
Balletttänzer(in) m(f); **~ shoe** n
Balletschuh m

balloon [bə'luːn] n (Luft)ballon m

ballot ['bælət] n (geheime) Abstimmung f

ballpoint (pen) ['bɔːlpɔɪnt-] n
Kugelschreiber m

ballroom ['bɔːlrum] n Tanzsaal m

Baltic ['bɔːltɪk] n: **the ~ (Sea)** die Ostsee

bamboo [bæm'buː] n Bambus m

ban [bæn] n Verbot nt ♦ vt verbieten

banana [bə'nɑːnə] n Banane f

band [bænd] n Band nt; (group) Gruppe f; (of
criminals) Bande f; (MUS) Kapelle f, Band f;
~ together vi sich zusammentun

bandage ['bændɪdʒ] n Verband m; (elastic)
Bandage f ♦ vt (cut) verbinden; (broken
limb) bandagieren

Bandaid ['bændeɪd] (® US) n Heftpflaster nt

bandit ['bændɪt] n Bandit m, Räuber m

bandwagon ['bændwægən] n: **to jump on
the ~** (fig) auf den fahrenden Zug
aufspringen

bandy ['bændɪ] vt wechseln; **~-legged** adj
o-beinig, O-beinig

bang [bæŋ] n (explosion) Knall m; (blow) Hieb
m ♦ vt, vi knallen

Bangladesh [bæŋglə'deʃ] n Bangladesch nt

bangle ['bæŋgl] n Armspange f

bangs [bæŋz] (US) npl (fringe) Pony m

banish ['bænɪʃ] *vt* verbannen

banister(s) ['bænɪstə(z)] *n(pl)* (Treppen)geländer *nt*

bank [bæŋk] *n* (*raised ground*) Erdwall *m*; (*of lake etc*) Ufer *nt*; (*FIN*) Bank *f* ♦ *vt* (*tilt: AVIAT*) in die Kurve bringen; (*money*) einzahlen; **~ on** *vt fus*: **to ~ on sth** mit etw rechnen; **~ account** *n* Bankkonto *nt*; **~ card** *n* Scheckkarte *f*; **~er** *n* Bankier *m*; **~er's card** (*BRIT*) *n* = **bank card; B~ holiday** (*BRIT*) *n* gesetzliche(r) Feiertag *m*; **~ing** *n* Bankwesen *nt*; **~note** *n* Banknote *f*; **~ rate** *n* Banksatz *m*

---
bank holiday

ⓘ *Als* **bank holiday** *wird in Großbritannien ein gesetzlicher Feiertag bezeichnet, an dem die Banken geschlossen sind. Die meisten dieser Feiertage, abgesehen von Weihnachten und Ostern, fallen auf Montage im Mai und August. An diesen langen Wochenenden (bank holiday weekends) fahren viele Briten in Urlaub, so dass dann auf den Straßen, Flughäfen und bei der Bahn sehr viel Betrieb ist.*

---

bankrupt ['bæŋkrʌpt] *adj*: **to be ~** bankrott sein; **to go ~** Bankrott machen; **~cy** *n* Bankrott *m*

bank statement *n* Kontoauszug *m*

banned [bænd] *adj*: **he was ~ from driving** (*BRIT*) ihm wurde Fahrverbot erteilt

banner ['bænə*] *n* Banner *nt*

banns [bænz] *npl* Aufgebot *nt*

baptism ['bæptɪzəm] *n* Taufe *f*

baptize [bæp'taɪz] *vt* taufen

bar [bɑː*] *n* (*rod*) Stange *f*; (*obstacle*) Hindernis *nt*; (*of chocolate*) Tafel *f*; (*of soap*) Stück *nt*; (*for food, drink*) Buffet *nt*, Bar *f*; (*pub*) Wirtschaft *f*; (*MUS*) Takt(strich) *m* ♦ *vt* (*fasten*) verriegeln; (*hinder*) versperren; (*exclude*) ausschließen; **behind ~s** hinter Gittern; **the B~**: **to be called to the B~** als Anwalt zugelassen werden; **~ none** ohne Ausnahme

barbaric [bɑː'bærɪk] *adj* primitiv, unkultiviert

barbecue ['bɑːbɪkjuː] *n* Barbecue *nt*

barbed wire ['bɑːbd-] *n* Stacheldraht *m*

barber ['bɑːbə*] *n* Herrenfriseur *m*

bar code *n* (*COMM*) Registrierkode *f*

bare [beə*] *adj* nackt; (*trees, country*) kahl; (*mere*) bloß ♦ *vt* entblößen; **~back** *adv* ungesattelt; **~faced** *adj* unverfroren; **~foot** *adj, adv* barfuß; **~ly** *adv* kaum, knapp

bargain ['bɑːgɪn] *n* (*sth cheap*) günstiger Kauf; (*agreement: written*) Kaufvertrag *m*; (*: oral*) Geschäft *nt*; **into the ~** obendrein; **~ for** *vt*: **he got more than he ~ed for** er erlebte sein blaues Wunder

barge [bɑːdʒ] *n* Lastkahn *m*; **~ in** *vi* hereinplatzen; **~ into** *vt* rennen gegen

bark [bɑːk] *n* (*of tree*) Rinde *f*; (*of dog*) Bellen *nt* ♦ *vi* (*dog*) bellen

barley ['bɑːlɪ] *n* Gerste *f*; **~ sugar** *n* Malzbonbon *nt*

bar: **~maid** *n* Bardame *f*; **~man** (*irreg*) *n* Barkellner *m*; **~ meal** *n* einfaches Essen in einem Pub

barn [bɑːn] *n* Scheune *f*

barometer [bə'rɒmɪtə*] *n* Barometer *nt*

baron ['bærən] *n* Baron *m*; **~ess** *n* Baronin *f*

barracks ['bærəks] *npl* Kaserne *f*

barrage ['bærɑːʒ] *n* (*gunfire*) Sperrfeuer *nt*; (*dam*) Staudamm *m*; Talsperre *f*

barrel ['bærəl] *n* Fass *nt*; (*of gun*) Lauf *m*

barren ['bærən] *adj* unfruchtbar

barricade [bærɪ'keɪd] *n* Barrikade *f* ♦ *vt* verbarrikadieren

barrier ['bærɪə*] *n* (*obstruction*) Hindernis *nt*; (*fence*) Schranke *f*

barring ['bɑːrɪŋ] *prep* außer im Falle +*gen*

barrister ['bærɪstə*] (*BRIT*) *n* Rechtsanwalt *m*

barrow ['bærəu] *n* (*cart*) Schubkarren *m*

bartender ['bɑːtendə*] (*US*) *n* Barmann *or* -kellner *m*

barter ['bɑːtə*] *vt* handeln

base [beɪs] *n* (*bottom*) Boden *m*, Basis *f*; (*MIL*) Stützpunkt *m* ♦ *vt* gründen; (*opinion, theory*): **to be ~d on** basieren auf +*dat* ♦ *adj* (*low*) gemein; **I'm ~d in London** ich wohne in London; **~ball** ['beɪsbɔːl] *n* Baseball *m*; **~ment** ['beɪsmənt] *n* Kellergeschoss *nt*

bases¹ ['beɪsɪz] *npl of* **base**

bases² ['beɪsiːz] *npl of* **basis**

bash [bæʃ] (inf) vt (heftig) schlagen
bashful ['bæʃful] adj schüchtern
basic ['beɪsɪk] adj grundlegend; ~s npl: **the ~s** das Wesentliche sg; ~ally adv im Grunde
basil ['bæzl] n Basilikum nt
basin ['beɪsn] n (dish) Schüssel f; (for washing, also valley) Becken nt; (dock) (Trocken)becken nt
basis ['beɪsɪs] (pl **bases**) n Basis f, Grundlage f
bask [bɑːsk] vi: **to ~ in the sun** sich sonnen
basket ['bɑːskɪt] n Korb m; ~**ball** n Basketball m
bass [beɪs] n (MUS, also instrument) Bass m, (voice) Bassstimme f; ~ **drum** n große Trommel
bassoon [bə'suːn] n Fagott nt
bastard ['bɑːstəd] n Bastard m; (inf!) Arschloch nt (!)
bat [bæt] n (SPORT) Schlagholz nt; Schläger m; (ZOOL) Fledermaus f ♦ vt: **he didn't ~ an eyelid** er hat nicht mit der Wimper gezuckt
batch [bætʃ] n (of letters) Stoß m; (of samples) Satz m
bated ['beɪtɪd] adj: **with ~ breath** mit angehaltenem Atem
bath [bɑːθ] n Bad nt; (~ tub) Badewanne f ♦ vt baden; **to have a ~** baden; see also **baths**
bathe [beɪð] vt, vi baden; ~r n Badende(r) f(m)
bathing ['beɪðɪŋ] n Baden nt; ~ **cap** n Badekappe f; ~ **costume** n Badeanzug m; ~ **suit** (US) n Badeanzug m; ~ **trunks** (BRIT) npl Badehose f
bath: ~**robe** n Bademantel m; ~**room** n Bad(ezimmer nt) nt; ~**s** npl (Schwimm)bad nt; ~ **towel** n Badetuch nt
baton ['bætən] n (of police) Gummiknüppel m; (MUS) Taktstock m
batter ['bætə'] vt verprügeln ♦ n Schlagteig m; (for cake) Biskuitteig m; ~**ed** adj (hat, pan) verbeult
battery ['bætərɪ] n (ELEC) Batterie f; (MIL) Geschützbatterie f
battery farming n (Hühner- etc)batterien

pl
battle ['bætl] n Schlacht f; (small) Gefecht nt ♦ vi kämpfen; ~**field** n Schlachtfeld nt; ~**ship** n Schlachtschiff nt
Bavaria [bə'veərɪə] n Bayern nt; ~**n** adj bay(e)risch ♦ n (person) Bayer(in) m(f)
bawdy ['bɔːdɪ] adj unflätig
bawl [bɔːl] vi brüllen
bay [beɪ] n (of sea) Bucht f ♦ vi bellen; **to keep at ~** unter Kontrolle halten; ~ **window** n Erkerfenster nt
bazaar [bə'zɑː'] n Basar m
B. & B. abbr = **bed and breakfast**
BBC n abbr (= British Broadcasting Corporation) BBC f or m
B.C. adv abbr (= before Christ) v. Chr.

KEYWORD

be [biː] (pt **was, were**, pp **been**) aux vb
1 (with present participle: forming continuous tenses): **what are you doing?** was machst du (gerade)?; **it is raining** es regnet; **I've been waiting for you for hours** ich warte schon seit Stunden auf dich
2 (with pp: forming passives): **to be killed** getötet werden; **the thief was nowhere to be seen** der Dieb war nirgendwo zu sehen
3 (in tag questions): **it was fun, wasn't it?** es hat Spaß gemacht, nicht wahr?
4 (+to +infin): **the house is to be sold** das Haus soll verkauft werden; **he's not to open it** er darf es nicht öffnen
♦ vb +complement **1** (usu) sein; **I'm tired** ich bin müde; **I'm hot/cold** mir ist heiß/kalt; **he's a doctor** er ist Arzt; **2 and 2 are 4** 2 und 2 ist or sind 4; **she's tall/pretty** sie ist groß/hübsch; **be careful/quiet** sei vorsichtig/ruhig
2 (of health): **how are you?** wie geht es dir?; **he's very ill** er ist sehr krank; **I'm fine now** jetzt geht es mir gut
3 (of age): **how old are you?** wie alt bist du?; **I'm sixteen (years old)** ich bin sechzehn (Jahre alt)
4 (cost): **how much was the meal?** was or wie viel hat das Essen gekostet?; **that'll be £5.75, please** das macht £5.75, bitte

♦ vi **1** (exist, occur etc) sein; **is there a God?** gibt es einen Gott?; **be that as it may** wie dem auch sei; **so be it** also gut **2** (referring to place) sein; **I won't be here tomorrow** iche werde morgen nicht hier sein **3** (referring to movement): **where have you been?** wo bist du gewesen?; **I've been in the garden** ich war im Garten ♦ impers vb **1** (referring to time, distance, weather) sein; **it's 5 o'clock** es ist 5 Uhr; **it's 10 km to the village** es sind 10 km bis zum Dorf; **it's too hot/cold** es ist zu heiß/ kalt **2** (emphatic): **it's me** ich bins; **it's the postman** es ist der Briefträger

beach [biːtʃ] n Strand m ♦ vt (ship) auf den Strand setzen
beacon ['biːkən] n (signal) Leuchtfeuer nt; (traffic ~) Bake f
bead [biːd] n Perle f; (drop) Tropfen m
beak [biːk] n Schnabel m
beaker ['biːkər] n Becher m
beam [biːm] n (of wood) Balken m; (of light) Strahl m; (smile) strahlende(s) Lächeln nt ♦ vi strahlen
bean [biːn] n Bohne f; (also: baked ~s) gebackene Bohnen pl; ~ **sprouts** npl Sojasprossen pl
bear [bɛəʳ] (pt **bore**, pp **borne**) n Bär m ♦ vt (weight, crops) tragen; (tolerate) ertragen; (young) gebären ♦ vi: **to ~ right/left** sich rechts/links halten; ~ **out** vt (suspicions etc) bestätigen; ~ **up** vi sich halten
beard [bɪəd] n Bart m; ~**ed** adj bärtig
bearer ['bɛərəʳ] n Träger m
bearing ['bɛərɪŋ] n (posture) Haltung f; (relevance) Relevanz f; (relation) Bedeutung f; (TECH) Kugellager nt; ~**s** npl (direction) Orientierung f; (also: ball ~s) (Kugel)lager nt
beast [biːst] n Tier nt, Vieh nt; (person) Biest nt
beat [biːt] (pt **beat**, pp **beaten**) n (stroke) Schlag m; (pulsation) (Herz)schlag m; (police round) Runde f; Revier nt; (MUS) Takt m;

Beat m ♦ vt, vi schlagen; **to ~ it** abhauen; **off the ~en track** abgelegen; ~ **off** vt abschlagen; ~ **up** vt zusammenschlagen; ~**en** pp of **beat**; ~**ing** n Prügel pl
beautiful ['bjuːtɪful] adj schön; ~**ly** adv ausgezeichnet
beauty ['bjuːtɪ] n Schönheit f; ~ **salon** n Schönheitssalon m; ~ **spot** n Schönheitsfleck m; (BRIT: TOURISM) (besonders) schöne(r) Ort m
beaver ['biːvəʳ] n Biber m
became [bɪ'keɪm] pt of **become**
because [bɪ'kɔz] conj weil ♦ prep: ~ **of** wegen +gen, wegen +dat (inf)
beck [bɛk] n: **to be at the ~ and call of sb** nach jds Pfeife tanzen
beckon ['bɛkən] vt, vi: **to ~ to sb** jdm ein Zeichen geben
become [bɪ'kʌm] (irreg: like **come**) vi werden ♦ vt werden; (clothes) stehen +dat
becoming [bɪ'kʌmɪŋ] adj (suitable) schicklich; (clothes) kleidsam
bed [bɛd] n Bett nt; (of river) Flussbett nt; (foundation) Schicht f; (in garden) Beet nt; **to go to ~** zu Bett gehen; ~ **and breakfast** n Übernachtung f mit Frühstück; ~**clothes** npl Bettwäsche f; ~**ding** n Bettzeug nt

---

Bed and Breakfast

i Bed and Breakfast *bedeutet „Übernachtung mit Frühstück", wobei sich dies in Großbritannien nicht auf Hotels, sondern auf kleinere Pensionen, Privathäuser und Bauernhöfe bezieht, wo man wesentlich preisgünstiger übernachten kann als in Hotels. Oft wird für Bed and Breakfast, auch B & B genannt, durch ein entsprechendes Schild im Garten oder an der Einfahrt geworben.*

---

bedlam ['bɛdləm] n (uproar) tolle(s) Durcheinander nt
bed linen n Bettwäsche f
bedraggled [bɪ'dræɡld] adj ramponiert
bed: ~**ridden** adj bettlägerig; ~**room** n Schlafzimmer nt; ~**side** n: **at the ~side** am Bett; ~**sit(ter)** (BRIT) n Einzimmerwohnung

f, möblierte(s) Zimmer *nt*; **~spread** *n*
Tagesdecke *f*; **~time** *n* Schlafenszeit *f*
bee [biː] *n* Biene *f*
beech [biːtʃ] *n* Buche *f*
beef [biːf] *n* Rindfleisch *nt*; **roast ~** Roastbeef
nt; **~burger** *n* Hamburger *m*
beehive ['biːhaɪv] *n* Bienenstock *m*
beeline ['biːlaɪn] *n*: **to make a ~ for**
schnurstracks zugehen auf +*acc*
been [biːn] *pp of* **be**
beer [bɪə*r*] *n* Bier *nt*
beet [biːt] *n* (*vegetable*) Rübe *f*; (*US: also:* **red
~**) Rote Bete *f or* Rübe *f*
beetle ['biːtl] *n* Käfer *m*
beetroot ['biːtruːt] (*BRIT*) *n* Rote Bete *f*
before [bɪ'fɔː*r*] *prep* vor ♦ *conj* bevor ♦ *adv* (*of
time*) zuvor; früher; **the week ~** die Woche
zuvor *or* vorher; **I've done it ~** das hab ich
schon mal getan; **~ going** bevor er/sie *etc*
geht/ging; **~ she goes** bevor sie geht;
~hand *adv* im Voraus
beg [beg] *vt, vi* (*implore*) dringend bitten;
(*alms*) betteln
began [bɪ'gæn] *pt of* **begin**
beggar ['begə*r*] *n* Bettler(in) *m(f)*
begin [bɪ'gɪn] (*pt* **began**, *pp* **begun**) *vt, vi*
anfangen, beginnen; (*found*) gründen; **to ~
doing** *or* **to do sth** anfangen *or* beginnen,
etw zu tun; **to ~ with** zunächst (einmal);
~ner *n* Anfänger *m*; **~ning** *n* Anfang *m*
begun [bɪ'gʌn] *pp of* **begin**
behalf [bɪ'hɑːf] *n*: **on ~ of** im Namen +*gen*;
on my ~ für mich
behave [bɪ'heɪv] *vi* sich benehmen;
behaviour [bɪ'heɪvjə*r*] (*US* **behavior**) *n*
Benehmen *nt*
beheld [bɪ'held] *pt, pp of* **behold**
behind [bɪ'haɪnd] *prep* hinter ♦ *adv* (*late*) im
Rückstand; (*in the rear*) hinten ♦ *n* (*inf*)
Hinterteil *nt*; **~ the scenes** (*fig*) hinter den
Kulissen
behold [bɪ'həʊld] (*irreg: like* **hold**) *vt*
erblicken
beige [beɪʒ] *adj* beige
Beijing ['beɪ'dʒɪŋ] *n* Peking *nt*
being ['biːɪŋ] *n* (*existence*) (Da)sein *nt*;
(*person*) Wesen *nt*; **to come into ~**

entstehen
Belarus [belə'rus] *n* Weißrussland *nt*
belated [bɪ'leɪtɪd] *adj* verspätet
belch [beltʃ] *vi* rülpsen ♦ *vt* (*smoke*)
ausspeien
belfry ['belfrɪ] *n* Glockenturm *m*
Belgian ['beldʒən] *adj* belgisch ♦ *n*
Belgier(in) *m(f)*
Belgium ['beldʒəm] *n* Belgien *nt*
belie [bɪ'laɪ] *vt* Lügen strafen +*acc*
belief [bɪ'liːf] *n* Glaube *m*; (*conviction*)
Überzeugung *f*; **~ in sb/sth** Glaube an
jdn/etw
believe [bɪ'liːv] *vt* glauben +*dat*; (*think*)
glauben, meinen, denken ♦ *vi* (*have faith*)
glauben; **to ~ in sth** an etw *acc* glauben;
~r *n* Gläubige(r) *f(m)*
belittle [bɪ'lɪtl] *vt* herabsetzen
bell [bel] *n* Glocke *f*
belligerent [bɪ'lɪdʒərənt] *adj* (*person*)
streitsüchtig; (*country*) Krieg führend
bellow ['beləʊ] *vt, vi* brüllen
bellows ['beləʊz] *npl* (*TECH*) Gebläse *nt*; (*for
fire*) Blasebalg *m*
belly ['belɪ] *n* Bauch *m*
belong [bɪ'lɔŋ] *vi* gehören; **to ~ to sb** jdm
gehören; **to ~ to a club** *etc* einem Klub *etc*
angehören; **~ings** *npl* Habe *f*
beloved [bɪ'lʌvɪd] *adj* innig geliebt ♦ *n*
Geliebte(r) *f(m)*
below [bɪ'ləʊ] *prep* unter ♦ *adv* unten
belt [belt] *n* (*band*) Riemen *m*; (*round waist*)
Gürtel *m* ♦ *vt* (*fasten*) mit Riemen
befestigen; (*inf: beat*) schlagen; **~way** (*US*)
n (*AUT: ring road*) Umgehungsstraße *f*
bemused [bɪ'mjuːzd] *adj* verwirrt
bench [bentʃ] *n* (*seat*) Bank *f*; (*workshop*)
Werkbank *f*; (*judge's seat*) Richterbank *f*;
(*judges*) Richter *pl*
bend [bend] (*pt, pp* **bent**) *vt* (*curve*) biegen;
(*stoop*) beugen ♦ *vi* sich biegen; sich
beugen ♦ *n* Biegung *f*; (*BRIT: in road*) Kurve
f; **~ down** *or* **over** *vi* sich bücken
beneath [bɪ'niːθ] *prep* unter ♦ *adv* darunter
benefactor ['benɪfæktə*r*] *n* Wohltäter(in)
m(f)
beneficial [benɪ'fɪʃəl] *adj* vorteilhaft; (*to*

health) heilsam

benefit ['benɪfɪt] *n* (*advantage*) Nutzen *m*
♦ *vt* fördern ♦ *vi*: **to ~ (from)** Nutzen ziehen
(aus)

Benelux ['benɪlʌks] *n* Beneluxstaaten *pl*

benevolent [bɪ'nevələnt] *adj* wohlwollend

benign [bɪ'naɪn] *adj* (*person*) gütig; (*climate*)
mild

bent [bent] *pt, pp of* **bend** ♦ *n* (*inclination*)
Neigung *f* ♦ *adj* (*inf: dishonest*) unehrlich; **to
be ~ on** versessen sein auf +*acc*

bequest [bɪ'kwest] *n* Vermächtnis *nt*

bereaved [bɪ'riːvd] *npl*: **the ~** die
Hinterbliebenen *pl*

beret ['bereɪ] *n* Baskenmütze *f*

Berlin [bɜː'lɪn] *n* Berlin *nt*

berm [bəːm] (*US*) *n* (*AUT*) Seitenstreifen *m*

berry ['berɪ] *n* Beere *f*

berserk [bə'səːk] *adj*: **to go ~** wild werden

berth [bəːθ] *n* (*for ship*) Ankerplatz *m*; (*in
ship*) Koje *f*; (*in train*) Bett *nt* ♦ *vt* am Kai
festmachen ♦ *vi* anlegen

beseech [bɪ'siːtʃ] (*pt, pp* **besought**) *vt*
anflehen

beset [bɪ'set] (*pt, pp* **beset**) *vt* bedrängen

beside [bɪ'saɪd] *prep* neben, bei; (*except*)
außer; **to be ~ o.s. (with)** außer sich sein
(vor +*dat*); **that's ~ the point** das tut nichts
zur Sache

besides [bɪ'saɪdz] *prep* außer, neben ♦ *adv*
außerdem

besiege [bɪ'siːdʒ] *vt* (*MIL*) belagern;
(*surround*) umlagern, bedrängen

besought [bɪ'sɔːt] *pt, pp of* **beseech**

best [best] *adj* beste(r, s) ♦ *adv* am besten;
the ~ part of (*quantity*) das meiste +*gen*; **at
~** höchstens; **to make the ~ of it** das Beste
daraus machen; **to do one's ~** sein Bestes
tun; **to the ~ of my knowledge** meines
Wissens; **to the ~ of my ability** so gut ich
kann; **for the ~** zum Besten; **~-before
date** *n* Mindesthaltbarkeitsdatum *nt*; **~
man** *n* Trauzeuge *m*

bestow [bɪ'stəʊ] *vt* verleihen

bet [bet] (*pt, pp* **bet** *or* **betted**) *n* Wette *f* ♦ *vt,
vi* wetten

betray [bɪ'treɪ] *vt* verraten

better ['betər] *adj, adv* besser ♦ *vt* verbessern
♦ *n*: **to get the ~ of sb** jdn überwinden; **he
thought ~ of it** er hat sich eines Besseren
besonnen; **you had ~ leave** Sie gehen jetzt
wohl besser; **to get ~** (*MED*) gesund
werden; **~ off** *adj* (*richer*) wohlhabender

betting ['betɪŋ] *n* Wetten *nt*; **~ shop** (*BRIT*) *n*
Wettbüro *nt*

between [bɪ'twiːn] *prep* zwischen; (*among*)
unter ♦ *adv* dazwischen

beverage ['bevərɪdʒ] *n* Getränk *nt*

bevy ['bevɪ] *n* Schar *f*

beware [bɪ'weər] *vt, vi* sich hüten vor +*dat*;
"~ of the dog" „Vorsicht, bissiger Hund!"

bewildered [bɪ'wɪldəd] *adj* verwirrt

beyond [bɪ'jɒnd] *prep* (*place*) jenseits +*gen*;
(*time*) über ... hinaus; (*out of reach*)
außerhalb +*gen* ♦ *adv* darüber hinaus; **~
doubt** ohne Zweifel; **~ repair** nicht mehr
zu reparieren

bias ['baɪəs] *n* (*slant*) Neigung *f*; (*prejudice*)
Vorurteil *nt*; **~(s)ed** *adj* voreingenommen

bib [bɪb] *n* Latz *m*

Bible ['baɪbl] *n* Bibel *f*

bicarbonate of soda [baɪ'kɑːbənɪt-] *n*
Natron *nt*

bicker ['bɪkər] *vi* zanken

bicycle ['baɪsɪkl] *n* Fahrrad *nt*

bid [bɪd] (*pt* **bade** *or* **bid**, *pp* **bid(den)**) *n*
(*offer*) Gebot *nt*; (*attempt*) Versuch *m* ♦ *vt, vi*
(*offer*) bieten; **to ~ farewell** Lebewohl
sagen; **~der** *n* (*person*) Steigerer *m*; **the
highest ~der** der Meistbietende; **~ding** *n*
(*command*) Geheiß *nt*

bide [baɪd] *vt*: **to ~ one's time** abwarten

bifocals [baɪ'fəʊklz] *npl* Bifokalbrille *f*

big [bɪg] *adj* groß; **~ dipper** [-'dɪpər] *n*
Achterbahn *f*; **~headed** ['bɪg'hedɪd] *adj*
eingebildet

bigot ['bɪgət] *n* Frömmler *m*; **~ed** *adj* bigott;
~ry *n* Bigotterie *f*

big top *n* Zirkuszelt *nt*

bike [baɪk] *n* Rad *nt*

bikini [bɪ'kiːnɪ] *n* Bikini *m*

bile [baɪl] *n* (*BIOL*) Galle *f*

bilingual [baɪ'lɪŋgwəl] *adj* zweisprachig

bill [bɪl] *n* (*account*) Rechnung *f*; (*POL*)

Gesetzentwurf m; (US: FIN) Geldschein m; **to fit** or **fill the ~** (fig) der/die/das Richtige sein; **"post no ~s"** „Plakate ankleben verboten"; **~board** ['bɪlbɔːd] n Reklameschild nt

billet ['bɪlɪt] n Quartier nt

billfold ['bɪlfəuld] (US) n Geldscheintasche f

billiards ['bɪljədz] n Billard nt

billion ['bɪljən] n (BRIT) Billion f; (US) Milliarde f

bimbo ['bɪmbəu] (inf: pej) n Puppe f, Häschen nt

bin [bɪn] n Kasten m; (dustbin) (Abfall)eimer m

bind [baɪnd] (pt, pp **bound**) vt (tie) binden; (tie together) zusammenbinden; (oblige) verpflichten; **~ing** n (Buch)einband m ♦ adj verbindlich

binge [bɪndʒ] (inf) n Sauferei f

bingo ['bɪŋgəu] n Bingo nt

binoculars [bɪ'nɔkjuləz] npl Fernglas nt

bio... [baɪəu] prefix: **~chemistry** n Biochemie f; **~degradable** adj biologisch abbaubar; **~graphy** n Biografie f; **~logical** [baɪə'lɔdʒɪkl] adj biologisch; **~logy** [baɪ'ɔlədʒɪ] n Biologie f

birch [bəːtʃ] n Birke f

bird [bəːd] n Vogel m; (BRIT: inf: girl) Mädchen nt; **~'s-eye view** n Vogelschau f; **~ watcher** n Vogelbeobachter(in) m(f); **~ watching** n Vogelbeobachten nt

Biro ['baɪərəu] ® n Kugelschreiber m

birth [bəːθ] n Geburt f; **to give ~ to** zur Welt bringen; **~ certificate** n Geburtsurkunde f; **~ control** n Geburtenkontrolle f; **~day** n Geburtstag m; **~day card** n Geburtstagskarte f; **~place** n Geburtsort m; **~ rate** n Geburtenrate f

biscuit ['bɪskɪt] n Keks m

bisect [baɪ'sekt] vt halbieren

bishop ['bɪʃəp] n Bischof m

bit [bɪt] pt of **bite** ♦ n bisschen, Stückchen nt; (horse's) Gebiss nt; (COMPUT) Bit nt; **a ~ tired** etwas müde

bitch [bɪtʃ] n (dog) Hündin f; (unpleasant woman) Weibsstück nt

bite [baɪt] (pt **bit**, pp **bitten**) vt, vi beißen ♦ n

Biss m; (mouthful) Bissen m; **to ~ one's nails** Nägel kauen; **let's have a ~ to eat** lass uns etwas essen

bitten ['bɪtn] pp of **bite**

bitter ['bɪtə*] adj bitter; (memory etc) schmerzlich; (person) verbittert ♦ n (BRIT: beer) dunkle(s) Bier nt; **~ness** n Bitterkeit f

blab [blæb] vi klatschen ♦ vt (also: ~ **out**) ausplaudern

black [blæk] adj schwarz; (night) finster ♦ vt schwärzen; (shoes) wichsen; (eye) blau schlagen; (BRIT: INDUSTRY) boykottieren; **to give sb a ~ eye** jdm ein blaues Auge schlagen; **in the ~** (bank account) in den schwarzen Zahlen; **~ and blue** adj grün und blau; **~berry** n Brombeere f; **~bird** n Amsel f; **~board** n (Wand)tafel f; **~ coffee** n schwarze(r) Kaffee m; **~currant** n schwarze Johannisbeere f; **~en** vt schwärzen; (fig) verunglimpfen; **B~ Forest** n Schwarzwald m; **~ ice** n Glatteis nt; **~leg** (BRIT) n Streikbrecher(in) m(f); **~list** n schwarze Liste f; **~mail** n Erpressung f ♦ vt erpressen; **~ market** n Schwarzmarkt m; **~out** n Verdunklung f; (MED): **to have a ~out** bewusstlos werden; **~ pudding** n ≃ Blutwurst f; **B~ Sea** n: **the B~ Sea** das Schwarze Meer; **~ sheep** n schwarze(s) Schaf nt; **~smith** n Schmied m; **~ spot** n (AUT) Gefahrenstelle f; (for unemployment etc) schwer betroffene(s) Gebiet nt

bladder ['blædə*] n Blase f

blade [bleɪd] n (of weapon) Klinge f; (of grass) Halm m; (of oar) Ruderblatt nt

blame [bleɪm] n Tadel m, Schuld f ♦ vt Vorwürfe machen +dat; **to ~ sb for sth** jdm die Schuld an etw dat geben; **he is to ~** er ist daran schuld

bland [blænd] adj mild

blank [blæŋk] adj leer, unbeschrieben; (look) verdutzt; (verse) Blank- ♦ n (space) Lücke f; Zwischenraum m; (cartridge) Platzpatrone f; **~ cheque** n Blankoscheck m; (fig) Freibrief m

blanket ['blæŋkɪt] n (Woll)decke f

blare [blɛə*] vi (radio) plärren; (horn) tuten; (MUS) schmettern

blasé ['blɑːzeɪ] *adj* blasiert

blast [blɑːst] *n* Explosion *f*; (*of wind*) Windstoß *m* ♦ *vt* (*blow up*) sprengen; ~! (*inf*) verflixt!; ~**off** *n* (*SPACE*) (Raketen)abschuss *m*

blatant ['bleɪtənt] *adj* offenkundig

blaze [bleɪz] *n* (*fire*) lodernde(s) Feuer *nt* ♦ *vi* lodern ♦ *vt*: **to ~ a trail** Bahn brechen

blazer ['bleɪzə*] *n* Blazer *m*

bleach [bliːtʃ] *n* (*also*: **household ~**) Bleichmittel *nt* ♦ *vt* bleichen; ~**ed** *adj* gebleicht

bleachers ['bliːtʃəz] (*US*) *npl* (*SPORT*) unüberdachte Tribüne *f*

bleak [bliːk] *adj* kahl, rau; (*future*) trostlos

bleary-eyed ['blɪərɪ'aɪd] *adj* triefäugig; (*on waking up*) mit verschlafenen Augen

bleat [bliːt] *vi* blöken; (*fig: complain*) meckern

bled [bled] *pt, pp of* **bleed**

bleed [bliːd] (*pt, pp* **bled**) *vi* bluten ♦ *vt* (*draw blood*) zur Ader lassen; **to ~ to death** verbluten

bleeper ['bliːpə*] *n* (*of doctor etc*) Funkrufempfänger *m*

blemish ['blemɪʃ] *n* Makel *m* ♦ *vt* verunstalten

blend [blend] *n* Mischung *f* ♦ *vt* mischen ♦ *vi* sich mischen; ~**er** *n* Mixer *m*, Mixgerät *nt*

bless [bles] (*pt, pp* **blessed**) *vt* segnen; (*give thanks*) preisen; (*make happy*) glücklich machen; ~ **you!** Gesundheit!; ~**ing** *n* Segen *m*; (*at table*) Tischgebet *nt*; (*happiness*) Wohltat *f*; Segen *m*; (*good wish*) Glück *nt*

blew [bluː] *pt of* **blow**

blimey ['blaɪmɪ] (*BRIT: inf*) *excl* verflucht

blind [blaɪnd] *adj* blind; (*corner*) unübersichtlich ♦ *n* (*for window*) Rouleau *nt* ♦ *vt* blenden; ~ **alley** *n* Sackgasse *f*; ~**fold** *n* Augenbinde *f* ♦ *adj, adv* mit verbundenen Augen ♦ *vt*: **to ~fold sb** jdm die Augen verbinden; ~**ly** *adv* blind; (*fig*) blindlings; ~**ness** *n* Blindheit *f*; ~ **spot** *n* (*AUT*) tote(r) Winkel *m*; (*fig*) schwache(r) Punkt *m*

blink [blɪŋk] *vi* blinzeln; ~**ers** *npl* Scheuklappen *pl*

bliss [blɪs] *n* (Glück)seligkeit *f*

blister ['blɪstə*] *n* Blase *f* ♦ *vi* Blasen werfen

blitz [blɪts] *n* Luftkrieg *m*

blizzard ['blɪzəd] *n* Schneesturm *m*

bloated ['bləʊtɪd] *adj* aufgedunsen; (*inf: full*) nudelsatt

blob [blɒb] *n* Klümpchen *nt*

bloc [blɒk] *n* (*POL*) Block *m*

block [blɒk] *n* (*of wood*) Block *m*, Klotz *m*; (*of houses*) Häuserblock *m* ♦ *vt* hemmen; ~**ade** [blɒ'keɪd] *n* Blockade *f* ♦ *vt* blockieren; ~**age** *n* Verstopfung *f*; ~**buster** *n* Knüller *m*; ~ **letters** *npl* Blockbuchstaben *pl*; ~ **of flats** (*BRIT*) *n* Häuserblock *m*

bloke [bləʊk] (*BRIT: inf*) *n* Kerl *m*, Typ *m*

blond(e) [blɒnd] *adj* blond ♦ *n* Blondine *f*

blood [blʌd] *n* Blut *nt*; ~ **donor** *n* Blutspender *m*; ~ **group** *n* Blutgruppe *f*; ~ **poisoning** *n* Blutvergiftung *f*; ~ **pressure** *n* Blutdruck *m*; ~**shed** *n* Blutvergießen *nt*; ~**shot** *adj* blutunterlaufen; ~ **sports** *npl* Jagdsport, Hahnenkampf *etc*; ~**stained** *adj* blutbefleckt; ~**stream** *n* Blut *nt*, Blutkreislauf *m*; ~ **test** *n* Blutprobe *f*; ~**thirsty** *adj* blutrünstig; ~ **vessel** *n* Blutgefäß *nt*; ~**y** *adj* blutig; (*BRIT: inf*) verdammt; ~**y-minded** (*BRIT: inf*) *adj* stur

bloom [bluːm] *n* Blüte *f*; (*freshness*) Glanz *m* ♦ *vi* blühen

blossom ['blɒsəm] *n* Blüte *f* ♦ *vi* blühen

blot [blɒt] *n* Klecks *m* ♦ *vt* beklecksen; (*ink*) (ab)löschen; ~ **out** *vt* auslöschen

blotchy ['blɒtʃɪ] *adj* fleckig

blotting paper ['blɒtɪŋ-] *n* Löschpapier *nt*

blouse [blaʊz] *n* Bluse *f*

blow [bləʊ] (*pt* **blew**, *pp* **blown**) *n* Schlag *m* ♦ *vt* blasen ♦ *vi* (*wind*) wehen; **to ~ one's nose** sich *dat* die Nase putzen; ~ **away** *vt* wegblasen; ~ **down** *vt* umwehen; ~ **off** *vt* wegwehen ♦ *vi* wegfliegen; ~ **out** *vi* ausgehen; ~ **over** *vi* vorübergehen; ~ **up** *vi* explodieren ♦ *vt* sprengen; ~-**dry** *n*: **to have a ~-dry** sich föhnen lassen ♦ *vt* föhnen; ~**lamp** (*BRIT*) *n* Lötlampe *f*; ~**n** *pp of* **blow**; ~**out** *n* (*AUT*) geplatzte(r) Reifen *m*; ~**torch** *n* = **blowlamp**

blue [bluː] *adj* blau; (*inf: unhappy*) niedergeschlagen; (*obscene*) pornografisch;

(*joke*) anzüglich ♦ *n*: **out of the ~** (*fig*) aus heiterem Himmel; **to have the ~s** traurig sein; **~bell** *n* Glockenblume *f*; **~bottle** *n* Schmeißfliege *f*; **~ film** *n* Pornofilm *m*; **~print** *n* (*fig*) Entwurf *m*

bluff [blʌf] *vi* bluffen, täuschen ♦ *n* (*deception*) Bluff *m*; **to call sb's ~** es darauf ankommen lassen

blunder ['blʌndə^r] *n* grobe(r) Fehler *m*, Schnitzer *m* ♦ *vi* einen groben Fehler machen

blunt [blʌnt] *adj* (*knife*) stumpf; (*talk*) unverblümt ♦ *vt* abstumpfen

blur [blə:^r] *n* Fleck *m* ♦ *vt* verschwommen machen

blurb [blə:b] *n* Waschzettel *m*

blush [blʌʃ] *vi* erröten

blustery ['blʌstərɪ] *adj* stürmisch

boar [bɔ:^r] *n* Keiler *m*, Eber *m*

board [bɔ:d] *n* (*of wood*) Brett *nt*; (*of card*) Pappe *f*; (*committee*) Ausschuss *m*; (*of firm*) Aufsichtsrat *m*; (*SCH*) Direktorium *nt* ♦ *vt* (*train*) einsteigen in +*acc*; (*ship*) an Bord gehen +*gen*; **on ~** (*AVIAT, NAUT*) an Bord; **~ and lodging** Unterkunft *f* und Verpflegung; **full/half ~** (*BRIT*) Voll-/Halbpension *f*; **to go by the ~** flachfallen, über Bord gehen; **~ up** *vt* mit Brettern vernageln; **~er** *n* Kostgänger *m*; (*SCH*) Internatsschüler(in) *m(f)*; **~ game** *n* Brettspiel *nt*; **~ing card** *n* (*AVIAT, NAUT*) Bordkarte *f*; **~ing house** *n* Pension *f*; **~ing school** *n* Internat *nt*; **~room** *n* Sitzungszimmer *nt*

boast [bəust] *vi* prahlen ♦ *vt* sich rühmen +*gen* ♦ *n* Großtuerei *f*; Prahlerei *f*; **to ~ about** or **of sth** mit etw prahlen

boat [bəut] *n* Boot *nt*; (*ship*) Schiff *nt*; **~er** *n* (*hat*) Kreissäge *f*; **~swain** *n* = **bosun**; **~ train** *n* Zug *m* mit Fährenanschluss

bob [bɔb] *vi* sich auf und nieder bewegen; **~ up** *vi* auftauchen

bobbin ['bɔbɪn] *n* Spule *f*

bobby ['bɔbɪ] *n* (*BRIT: inf*) Bobby *m*

bobsleigh ['bɔbsleɪ] *n* Bob *m*

bode [bəud] *vi*: **to ~ well/ill** ein gutes/ schlechtes Zeichen sein

bodily ['bɔdɪlɪ] *adj, adv* körperlich

body ['bɔdɪ] *n* Körper *m*; (*dead*) Leiche *f*; (*group*) Mannschaft *f*; (*AUT*) Karosserie *f*; (*trunk*) Rumpf *m*; **~ building** *n* Bodybuilding *nt*; **~guard** *n* Leibwache *f*; **~work** *n* Karosserie *f*

bog [bɔg] *n* Sumpf *m* ♦ *vt*: **to get ~ged down** sich festfahren

boggle ['bɔgl] *vi* stutzen; **the mind ~s** es ist kaum auszumalen

bog-standard *adj* stinknormal (*inf*)

bogus ['bəugəs] *adj* unecht, Schein-

boil [bɔɪl] *vt, vi* kochen ♦ *n* (*MED*) Geschwür *nt*; **to come to the** (*BRIT*) or **a** (*US*) **~** zu kochen anfangen; **to ~ down to** (*fig*) hinauslaufen auf +*acc*; **~ over** *vi* überkochen; **~ed egg** *n* (*weich*) gekochte(s) Ei *nt*; **~ed potatoes** *npl* Salzkartoffeln *pl*; **~er** *n* Boiler *m*; **~er suit** (*BRIT*) *n* Arbeitsanzug *m*; **~ing point** *n* Siedepunkt *m*

boisterous ['bɔɪstərəs] *adj* ungestüm

bold [bəuld] *adj* (*fearless*) unerschrocken; (*handwriting*) fest und klar

bollard ['bɔləd] *n* (*NAUT*) Poller *m*; (*BRIT: AUT*) Pfosten *m*

bolt [bəult] *n* Bolzen *m*; (*lock*) Riegel *m* ♦ *adv*: **~ upright** kerzengerade ♦ *vt* verriegeln; (*swallow*) verschlingen ♦ *vi* (*horse*) durchgehen

bomb [bɔm] *n* Bombe *f* ♦ *vt* bombardieren; **~ard** [bɔm'bɑːd] *vt* bombardieren; **~ardment** [bɔm'bɑːdmənt] *n* Beschießung *f*; **~ disposal** *n*: **~ disposal unit** Bombenräumkommando *nt*; **~er** *n* Bomber *m*; (*terrorist*) Bombenattentäter(in) *m(f)*; **~ing** *n* Bomben *nt*; **~shell** *n* (*fig*) Bombe *f*

bona fide ['bəunə'faɪdɪ] *adj* echt

bond [bɔnd] *n* (*link*) Band *nt*; (*FIN*) Schuldverschreibung *f*

bondage ['bɔndɪdʒ] *n* Sklaverei *f*

bone [bəun] *n* Knochen *m*; (*of fish*) Gräte *f*; (*piece of ~*) Knochensplitter *m* ♦ *vt* die Knochen herausnehmen +*dat*; (*fish*) entgräten; **~ dry** *adj* (*inf*) knochentrocken; **~ idle** *adj* stinkfaul; **~ marrow** *n* (*ANAT*) Knochenmark *nt*

bonfire ['bɔnfaɪə^r] *n* Feuer *nt* im Freien

bonnet ['bɔnɪt] n Haube f; (for baby) Häubchen nt; (BRIT: AUT) Motorhaube f

bonus ['bəʊnəs] n Bonus m; (annual ~) Prämie f

bony ['bəʊnɪ] adj knochig, knochendürr

boo [bu:] vt auspfeifen

booby trap ['bu:bɪ-] n Falle f

book [bʊk] n Buch nt ♦ vt (ticket etc) vorbestellen; (person) verwarnen; **~s** npl (COMM) Bücher pl; **~case** n Bücherregal nt, Bücherschrank m; **~ing office** (BRIT) n (RAIL) Fahrkartenschalter m; (THEAT) Vorverkaufsstelle f; **~-keeping** n Buchhaltung f; **~let** n Broschüre f; **~maker** n Buchmacher m; **~seller** n Buchhändler m; **~shelf** n Bücherbord nt; **~shop** ['bʊkʃɔp], **~store** n Buchhandlung f

boom [bu:m] n (noise) Dröhnen nt; (busy period) Hochkonjunktur f ♦ vi dröhnen

boon [bu:n] n Wohltat f, Segen m

boost [bu:st] n Auftrieb m; (fig) Reklame f ♦ vt Auftrieb geben; **~er** n (MED) Wiederholungsimpfung f

boot [bu:t] n Stiefel m; (BRIT: AUT) Kofferraum m ♦ vt (kick) einen Fußtritt geben; (COMPUT) laden; **to ~** (in addition) obendrein

booth [bu:ð] n (at fair) Bude f; (telephone ~) Zelle f; (voting ~) Kabine f

booze [bu:z] (inf) n Alkohol m, Schnaps m ♦ vi saufen

border ['bɔːdəʳ] n Grenze f; (edge) Kante f; (in garden) (Blumen)rabatte f ♦ adj Grenz-; **the B~s** Grenzregion zwischen England und Schottland; **~ on** vt grenzen an +acc; **~line** n Grenze f; **~line case** n Grenzfall m

bore [bɔːʳ] pt of **bear** ♦ vt bohren; (weary) langweilen ♦ n (person) Langweiler m; (thing) langweilige Sache f; (of gun) Kaliber nt; **I am ~d** ich langweile mich; **~dom** n Langeweile f

boring ['bɔːrɪŋ] adj langweilig

born [bɔːn] adj: **to be ~** geboren werden

borne [bɔːn] pp of **bear**

borough ['bʌrə] n Stadt(gemeinde) f, Stadtbezirk m

borrow ['bɔrəʊ] vt borgen

Bosnia (and) Herzegovina ['bɔznɪə (ənd) hɜːtsəgəʊ'viːnə] n Bosnien und Herzegowina nt; **~n** n Bosnier(in) m(f) ♦ adj bosnisch

bosom ['buzəm] n Busen m

boss [bɔs] n Chef m, Boss m ♦ vt: **to ~ around** or **about** herumkommandieren; **~y** adj herrisch

bosun ['bəʊsn] n Bootsmann m

botany ['bɔtənɪ] n Botanik f

botch [bɔtʃ] vt (also: ~ up) verpfuschen

both [bəʊθ] adj beide(s) ♦ pron beide(s) ♦ adv: **~ X and Y** sowohl X wie or als auch Y; **~ (of) the books** beide Bücher; **~ of us went, we ~ went** wir gingen beide

bother ['bɔðəʳ] vt (pester) quälen ♦ vi (fuss) sich aufregen ♦ n Mühe f, Umstand m; **to ~ doing sth** sich dat die Mühe machen, etw zu tun; **what a ~!** wie ärgerlich!

bottle ['bɔtl] n Flasche f ♦ vt (in Flaschen) abfüllen; **~ up** vt aufstauen; **~ bank** n Altglascontainer m; **~d beer** n Flaschenbier nt; **~d water** n in Flaschen abgefülltes Wasser; **~neck** n (also fig) Engpass m; **~ opener** n Flaschenöffner m

bottom ['bɔtəm] n Boden m; (of person) Hintern m; (riverbed) Flussbett nt ♦ adj unterste(r, s)

bough [baʊ] n Zweig m, Ast m

bought [bɔːt] pt, pp of **buy**

boulder ['bəʊldəʳ] n Felsbrocken m

bounce [baʊns] vi (person) herumhüpfen; (ball) hochspringen; (cheque) platzen ♦ vt (auf)springen lassen ♦ n (rebound) Aufprall m; **~r** n Rausschmeißer m

bound [baʊnd] pt, pp of **bind** ♦ n Grenze f; (leap) Sprung m ♦ vi (spring, leap) (auf)springen ♦ adj (obliged) gebunden, verpflichtet; **out of ~s** Zutritt verboten; **to be ~ to do sth** verpflichtet sein, etw zu tun; **it's ~ to happen** es muss so kommen; **to be ~ for ...** nach ... fahren

boundary ['baʊndrɪ] n Grenze f

bouquet ['bʊkeɪ] n Strauß m; (of wine) Blume f

bourgeois ['bʊəʒwɑː] adj kleinbürgerlich, bourgeois ♦ n Spießbürger(in) m(f)

bout [baʊt] n (of illness) Anfall m; (of contest)

Kampf m

bow¹ [bəu] n (ribbon) Schleife f; (weapon, MUS) Bogen m

bow² [bəu] n (with head, body) Verbeugung f; (of ship) Bug m ♦ vi sich verbeugen; (submit): **to ~ to** sich beugen +dat

bowels ['bauəlz] npl (ANAT) Darm m

bowl [bəul] n (basin) Schüssel f; (of pipe) (Pfeifen)kopf m; (wooden ball) (Holz)kugel f ♦ vt, vi (die Kugel) rollen

bow-legged ['bəu'legɪd] adj o-beinig, O-beinig

bowler ['bəulər] n Werfer m; (BRIT: also: ~ **hat**) Melone f

bowling ['bəulɪŋ] n Kegeln nt; **~ alley** n Kegelbahn f; **~ green** n Rasen m zum Bowlingspiel

bowls n (game) Bowlsspiel nt

bow tie [bəu-] n Fliege f

box [bɒks] n (also: **cardboard ~**) Schachtel f; (bigger) Kasten m; (THEAT) Loge f ♦ vt einpacken ♦ vi boxen; **~er** n Boxer m; **~er shorts** (BRIT) npl Boxershorts pl; **~ing** n (SPORT) Boxen nt; **B~ing Day** (BRIT) n zweite(r) Weihnachtsfeiertag m; **~ing gloves** npl Boxhandschuhe pl; **~ing ring** n Boxring m; **~ office** n (Theater)kasse f; **~room** n Rumpelkammer f

boy [bɔɪ] n Junge m

boycott ['bɔɪkɒt] n Boykott m ♦ vt boykottieren

boyfriend ['bɔɪfrend] n Freund m

boyish ['bɔɪʃ] adj jungenhaft

B.R. n abbr = **British Rail**

bra [brɑː] n BH m

brace [breɪs] n (TECH) Stütze f; (MED)

Klammer f ♦ vt stützen; **~s** npl (BRIT) Hosenträger pl; **to ~ o.s. for sth** (fig) sich auf etw acc gefasst machen

bracelet ['breɪslɪt] n Armband nt

bracing ['breɪsɪŋ] adj kräftigend

bracken ['brækən] n Farnkraut nt

bracket ['brækɪt] n Halter m, Klammer f; (in punctuation) Klammer f; (group) Gruppe f ♦ vt einklammern; (fig) in dieselbe Gruppe einordnen

brag [bræg] vi sich rühmen

braid [breɪd] n (hair) Flechte f; (trim) Borte f

Braille [breɪl] n Blindenschrift f

brain [breɪn] n (ANAT) Gehirn nt; (intellect) Intelligenz f, Verstand m; (person) kluge(r) Kopf m; **~s** npl (intelligence) Verstand m; **~child** n Erfindung f; **~wash** vt eine Gehirnwäsche vornehmen bei; **~wave** n Geistesblitz m; **~y** adj gescheit

braise [breɪz] vt schmoren

brake [breɪk] n Bremse f ♦ vt, vi bremsen; **~ fluid** n Bremsflüssigkeit f; **~ light** n Bremslicht nt

bramble ['bræmbl] n Brombeere f

bran [bræn] n Kleie f; (food) Frühstücksflocken pl

branch [brɑːntʃ] n Ast m; (division) Zweig m ♦ vi (also: **~ out**: road) sich verzweigen

brand [brænd] n (COMM) Marke f, Sorte f; (on cattle) Brandmal nt ♦ vt brandmarken; (COMM) ein Warenzeichen geben +dat

brandish ['brændɪʃ] vt (drohend) schwingen

brand-new ['brænd'njuː] adj funkelnagelneu

brandy ['brændɪ] n Weinbrand m, Kognak m

brash [bræʃ] adj unverschämt

brass [brɑːs] n Messing nt; **the ~** (MUS) das Blech; **~ band** n Blaskapelle f

brassière ['bræsɪər] n Büstenhalter m

brat [bræt] n Gör nt

bravado [brə'vɑːdəu] n Tollkühnheit f

brave [breɪv] adj tapfer ♦ vt die Stirn bieten +dat; **~ry** n Tapferkeit f

brawl [brɔːl] n Rauferei f

brawn [brɔːn] n (ANAT) Muskeln pl; (strength) Muskelkraft f

bray [breɪ] vi schreien

brazen ['breɪzn] adj (shameless) unverschämt

♦ *vt*: **to ~ it out** sich mit Lügen und Betrügen durchsetzen

brazier ['breɪzɪər] *n* (*of workmen*) offene(r) Kohlenofen *m*

Brazil [brə'zɪl] *n* Brasilien *nt*; **~ian** *adj* brasilianisch ♦ *n* Brasilianer(in) *m(f)*

breach [briːtʃ] *n* (*gap*) Lücke *f*; (*MIL*) Durchbruch *m*; (*of discipline*) Verstoß *m* (gegen die Disziplin); (*of faith*) Vertrauensbruch *m* ♦ *vt* durchbrechen; **~ of contract** Vertragsbruch *m*; **~ of the peace** öffentliche Ruhestörung *f*

bread [bred] *n* Brot *nt*; **~ and butter** Butterbrot *nt*; **~bin** *n* Brotkasten *m*; **~ box** (*US*) *n* Brotkasten *m*; **~crumbs** *npl* Brotkrumen *pl*; (*COOK*) Paniermehl *nt*; **~line** *n*: **to be on the ~line** sich gerade so durchschlagen

breadth [bretθ] *n* Breite *f*

breadwinner ['bredwɪnər] *n* Ernährer *m*

break [breɪk] (*pt* **broke**, *pp* **broken**) *vt* (*destroy*) (ab- *or* zer)brechen; (*promise*) brechen, nicht einhalten ♦ *vi* (*fall apart*) auseinander brechen; (*collapse*) zusammenbrechen; (*dawn*) anbrechen ♦ *n* (*gap*) Lücke *f*; (*chance*) Chance *f*, Gelegenheit *f*; (*fracture*) Bruch *m*; (*rest*) Pause *f*; **~ down** *vt* (*figures, data*) aufschlüsseln; (*undermine*) überwinden ♦ *vi* (*car*) eine Panne haben; (*person*) zusammenbrechen; **~ even** *vi* die Kosten decken; **~ free** *vi* sich losreißen; **~ in** *vt* (*horse*) zureiten ♦ *vi* (*burglar*) einbrechen; **~ into** *vt fus* (*house*) einbrechen in +*acc*; **~ loose** *vi* sich losreißen; **~ off** *vi* abbrechen; **~ open** *vt* (*door etc*) aufbrechen; **~ out** *vi* ausbrechen; **to ~ out in spots** Pikkel bekommen; **~ up** *vi* zerbrechen; (*fig*) sich zerstreuen; (*BRIT: SCH*) in die Ferien gehen ♦ *vt* brechen; **~age** *n* Bruch *m*, Beschädigung *f*; **~down** *n* (*TECH*) Panne *f*; (*MED: also*: **nervous ~down**) Zusammenbruch *m*; **~down van** (*BRIT*) *n* Abschleppwagen *m*; **~er** *n* Brecher *m*

breakfast ['brekfəst] *n* Frühstück *nt*

break: **~-in** *n* Einbruch *m*; **~ing** *n*: **~ing and entering** (*JUR*) Einbruch *m*; **~through**

n Durchbruch *m*; **~water** *n* Wellenbrecher *m*

breast [brest] *n* Brust *f*; **~-feed** (*irreg: like* **feed**) *vt*, *vi* stillen; **~-stroke** *n* Brustschwimmen *nt*

breath [breθ] *n* Atem *m*; **out of ~** außer Atem; **under one's ~** flüsternd

Breathalyzer ['breθəlaɪzər] ® *n* Röhrchen *nt*

breathe [briːð] *vt*, *vi* atmen; **~ in** *vt*, *vi* einatmen; **~ out** *vt*, *vi* ausatmen; **~r** *n* Verschnaufpause *f*; **breathing** *n* Atmung *f*

breathless ['breθlɪs] *adj* atemlos

breathtaking ['breθteɪkɪŋ] *adj* atemberaubend

bred [bred] *pt*, *pp of* **breed**

breed [briːd] (*pt*, *pp* **bred**) *vi* sich vermehren ♦ *vt* züchten ♦ *n* (*race*) Rasse *f*, Zucht *f*; **~ing** *n* Züchtung *f*; (*upbringing*) Erziehung *f*

breeze [briːz] *n* Brise *f*; **breezy** *adj* windig; (*manner*) munter

brevity ['brevɪtɪ] *n* Kürze *f*

brew [bruː] *vt* (*beer*) brauen ♦ *vi* (*storm*) sich zusammenziehen; **~ery** *n* Brauerei *f*

bribe [braɪb] *n* Bestechungsgeld *nt*, Bestechungsgeschenk *nt* ♦ *vt* bestechen; **~ry** ['braɪbərɪ] *n* Bestechung *f*

bric-a-brac ['brɪkəbræk] *n* Nippes *pl*

brick [brɪk] *n* Backstein *m*; **~layer** *n* Maurer *m*; **~works** *n* Ziegelei *f*

bridal ['braɪdl] *adj* Braut-

bride [braɪd] *n* Braut *f*; **~groom** *n* Bräutigam *m*; **~smaid** *n* Brautjungfer *f*

bridge [brɪdʒ] *n* Brücke *f*; (*NAUT*) Kommandobrücke *f*; (*CARDS*) Bridge *nt*; (*ANAT*) Nasenrücken *m* ♦ *vt* eine Brücke schlagen über +*acc*; (*fig*) überbrücken

bridle ['braɪdl] *n* Zaum *m* ♦ *vt* (*fig*) zügeln; (*horse*) aufzäumen; **~ path** *n* Reitweg *m*

brief [briːf] *adj* kurz ♦ *n* (*JUR*) Akten *pl* ♦ *vt* instruieren; **~s** *npl* (*underwear*) Schlüpfer *m*, Slip *m*; **~case** *n* Aktentasche *f*; **~ing** *n* (*genaue*) Anweisung *f*; **~ly** *adv* kurz

brigadier [brɪɡə'dɪər] *n* Brigadegeneral *m*

bright [braɪt] *adj* hell; (*cheerful*) heiter; (*idea*) klug; **~en (up)** ['braɪtn-] *vt* aufhellen; (*person*) aufheitern ♦ *vi* sich aufheitern

brilliance ['brɪljəns] *n* Glanz *m*; (*of person*)

Scharfsinn *m*

brilliant ['brɪljənt] *adj* glänzend

brim [brɪm] *n* Rand *m*

brine [braɪn] *n* Salzwasser *nt*

bring [brɪŋ] (*pt, pp* **brought**) *vt* bringen; **~ about** *vt* zustande *or* zu Stande bringen; **~ back** *vt* zurückbringen; **~ down** *vt* (*price*) senken; **~ forward** *vt* (*meeting*) vorverlegen; (COMM) übertragen; **~ in** *vt* hereinbringen; (*harvest*) einbringen; **~ off** *vt* davontragen; (*success*) erzielen; **~ out** *vt* (*object*) herausbringen; **~ round** *or* **to** *vt* wieder zu sich bringen; **~ up** *vt* aufziehen; (*question*) zur Sprache bringen

brink [brɪŋk] *n* Rand *m*

brisk [brɪsk] *adj* lebhaft

bristle ['brɪsl] *n* Borste *f* ♦ *vi* sich sträuben; **bristling with** strotzend vor +*dat*

Britain ['brɪtən] *n* (*also:* **Great ~**) Großbritannien *nt*

British ['brɪtɪʃ] *adj* britisch ♦ *npl*: **the ~** die Briten *pl*; **~ Isles** *npl*: **the ~ Isles** die Britischen Inseln *pl*; **~ Rail** *n* die Britischen Eisenbahnen

Briton ['brɪtən] *n* Brite *m*, Britin *f*

Brittany ['brɪtənɪ] *n* die Bretagne

brittle ['brɪtl] *adj* spröde

broach [brəutʃ] *vt* (*subject*) anschneiden

broad [brɔːd] *adj* breit, (*hint*) deutlich; (*general*) allgemein; (*accent*) stark; **in ~ daylight** am helllichten Tag; **~cast** (*pt, pp* **broadcast**) *n* Rundfunkübertragung *f* ♦ *vt, vi* übertragen, senden; **~en** *vt* erweitern ♦ *vi* sich erweitern; **~ly** *adv* allgemein gesagt; **~-minded** *adj* tolerant

broccoli ['brɔkəlɪ] *n* Brokkoli *pl*

brochure ['brəuʃjuə*r*] *n* Broschüre *f*

broil [brɔɪl] *vt* (*grill*) grillen

broke [brəuk] *pt of* **break** ♦ *adj* (*inf*) pleite

broken ['brəukn] *pp of* **break** ♦ *adj*: **~ leg** gebrochenes Bein; **in ~ English** in gebrochenem Englisch; **~-hearted** *adj* untröstlich

broker ['brəukə*r*] *n* Makler *m*

brolly ['brɔlɪ] (BRIT: *inf*) *n* Schirm *m*

bronchitis [brɔŋ'kaɪtɪs] *n* Bronchitis *f*

bronze [brɔnz] *n* Bronze *f*

brooch [brəutʃ] *n* Brosche *f*

brood [bruːd] *n* Brut *f* ♦ *vi* brüten

brook [bruk] *n* Bach *m*

broom [brum] *n* Besen *m*

Bros. *abbr* = **Brothers**

broth [brɔθ] *n* Suppe *f*, Fleischbrühe *f*

brothel ['brɔθl] *n* Bordell *nt*

brother ['brʌðə*r*] *n* Bruder *m*; **~-in-law** *n* Schwager *m*

brought [brɔːt] *pt, pp of* **bring**

brow [brau] *n* (*eyebrow*) (Augen)braue *f*; (*forehead*) Stirn *f*; (*of hill*) Bergkuppe *f*

brown [braun] *adj* braun ♦ *n* Braun *nt* ♦ *vt* bräunen; **~ bread** *n* Mischbrot *nt*; **B~ie** *n* Wichtel *m*; **~ paper** *n* Packpapier *nt*; **~ sugar** *n* braune(r) Zucker *m*

browse [brauz] *vi* (*in books*) blättern; (*in shop*) schmökern, herumschauen

bruise [bruːz] *n* Bluterguss *m*, blaue(r) Fleck *m* ♦ *vt* einen blauen Fleck geben ♦ *vi* einen blauen Fleck bekommen

brunt [brʌnt] *n* volle Wucht *f*

brush [brʌʃ] *n* Bürste *f*; (*for sweeping*) Handbesen *m*; (*for painting*) Pinsel *m*; (*fight*) kurze(r) Kampf *m*; (MIL) Scharmützel *nt*; (*fig*) Auseinandersetzung *f* ♦ *vt* (*clean*) bürsten; (*sweep*) fegen; (*usu*: **~ past**, **~ against**) streifen; **~ aside** *vt* abtun; **~ up** *vt* (*knowledge*) auffrischen; **~wood** *n* Gestrüpp *nt*

brusque [bruːsk] *adj* schroff

Brussels ['brʌslz] *n* Brüssel *nt*; **~ sprout** *n* Rosenkohl *m*

brutal ['bruːtl] *adj* brutal

brute [bruːt] *n* (*person*) Scheusal *nt* ♦ *adj*: **by ~ force** mit roher Kraft

B.Sc. *n abbr* = **Bachelor of Science**

BSE *n abbr* (= *bovine spongiform encephalopathy*) BSE *f*

bubble ['bʌbl] *n* (Luft)blase *f* ♦ *vi* sprudeln; (*with joy*) übersprudeln; **~ bath** *n* Schaumbad *nt*; **~ gum** *n* Kaugummi *m or* *nt*

buck [bʌk] *n* Bock *m*; (US: *inf*) Dollar *m* ♦ *vi* bocken; **to pass the ~ (to sb)** die Verantwortung (auf jdn) abschieben; **~ up** (*inf*) *vi* sich zusammenreißen

bucket ['bʌkɪt] *n* Eimer *m*

Buckingham Palace

ⓘ **Buckingham Palace** *ist die offizielle Londoner Residenz der britischen Monarchen und liegt am St James Park. Der Palast wurde 1703 für den Herzog von Buckingham erbaut, 1762 von George III. gekauft, zwischen 1821 und 1836 von John Nash umgebaut, und Anfang des 20. Jahrhunderts teilweise neu gestaltet. Teile des Buckingham Palace sind heute der Öffentlichkeit zugänglich.*

---

buckle ['bʌkl] *n* Schnalle *f* ♦ *vt* (an- or zusammen)schnallen ♦ *vi* (*bend*) sich verziehen
bud [bʌd] *n* Knospe *f* ♦ *vi* knospen, keimen
Buddhism ['budɪzəm] *n* Buddhismus *m*; **Buddhist** *adj* buddhistisch ♦ *n* Buddhist(in) *m(f)*
budding ['bʌdɪŋ] *adj* angehend
buddy ['bʌdɪ] (*inf*) *n* Kumpel *m*
budge [bʌdʒ] *vt, vi* (sich) von der Stelle rühren
budgerigar ['bʌdʒərɪgɑːʳ] *n* Wellensittich *m*
budget ['bʌdʒɪt] *n* Budget *nt*; (*POL*) Haushalt *m* ♦ *vi*: **to ~ for sth** etw einplanen
budgie ['bʌdʒɪ] *n* = **budgerigar**
buff [bʌf] *adj* (*colour*) lederfarben ♦ *n* (*enthusiast*) Fan *m*
buffalo ['bʌfələu] (*pl ~ or ~es*) *n* (*BRIT*) Büffel *m*; (*US: bison*) Bison *m*
buffer ['bʌfəʳ] *n* Puffer *m*; (*COMPUT*) Pufferspeicher *m*; **~ zone** *n* Pufferzone *f*
buffet[1] ['bʌfɪt] *n* (*blow*) Schlag *m* ♦ *vt* (herum)stossen
buffet[2] ['bufeɪ] (*BRIT*) *n* (*bar*) Imbissraum *m*, Erfrischungsraum *m*; (*food*) (kaltes) Büfett *nt*; **~ car** (*BRIT*) *n* Speisewagen *m*
bug [bʌg] *n* (*also fig*) Wanze *f* ♦ *vt* verwanzen; **the room is bugged** das Zimmer ist verwanzt
bugle ['bjuːgl] *n* Jagdhorn *nt*; (*MIL: MUS*) Bügelhorn *nt*
build [bɪld] (*pt, pp* **built**) *vt* bauen ♦ *n* Körperbau *m*; **~ up** *vt* aufbauen; **~er** *n*

Bauunternehmer *m*; **~ing** *n* Gebäude *nt*; **~ing society** (*BRIT*) *n* Bausparkasse *f*
built [bɪlt] *pt, pp of* **build**; **~-in** *adj* (*cupboard*) eingebaut; **~-up area** *n* Wohngebiet *nt*
bulb [bʌlb] *n* (*BOT*) (Blumen)zwiebel *f*; (*ELEC*) Glühlampe *f*, Birne *f*
Bulgaria [bʌlˈgɛərɪə] *n* Bulgarien *nt*; **~n** *adj* bulgarisch ♦ *n* Bulgare *m*, Bulgarin *f*; (*LING*) Bulgarisch *nt*
bulge [bʌldʒ] *n* Wölbung *f* ♦ *vi* sich wölben
bulk [bʌlk] *n* Größe *f*, Masse *f*; (*greater part*) Großteil *m*; **in ~** (*COMM*) en gros; **the ~ of** der größte Teil +*gen*; **~head** *n* Schott *nt*; **~y** *adj* (sehr) umfangreich; (*goods*) sperrig
bull [bul] *n* Bulle *m*; (*cattle*) Stier *m*; **~dog** *n* Bulldogge *f*
bulldozer ['buldəuzəʳ] *n* Planierraupe *f*
bullet ['bulɪt] *n* Kugel *f*
bulletin ['bulɪtɪn] *n* Bulletin *nt*, Bekanntmachung *f*
bulletproof ['bulɪtpruːf] *adj* kugelsicher
bullfight ['bulfaɪt] *n* Stierkampf *m*; **~er** *n* Stierkämpfer *m*; **~ing** *n* Stierkamp *m*
bullion ['buljən] *n* Barren *m*
bullock ['bulək] *n* Ochse *m*
bullring ['bulrɪŋ] *n* Stierkampfarena *f*
bull's-eye ['bulzaɪ] *n* Zentrum *nt*
bully ['bulɪ] *n* Raufbold *m* ♦ *vt* einschüchtern
bum [bʌm] *n* (*inf: backside*) Hintern *m*; (*tramp*) Landstreicher *m*
bumblebee ['bʌmblbiː] *n* Hummel *f*
bump [bʌmp] *n* (*blow*) Stoß *m*; (*swelling*) Beule *f* ♦ *vt, vi* stoßen, prallen; **~ into** *vt fus* stoßen gegen ♦ *vt* (*person*) treffen; **~er** *n* (*AUT*) Stoßstange *f* ♦ *adj* (*edition*) dick; (*harvest*) Rekord-
bumpy ['bʌmpɪ] *adj* holprig
bun [bʌn] *n* Korinthenbrötchen *nt*
bunch [bʌntʃ] *n* (*of flowers*) Strauß *m*; (*of keys*) Bund *nt*; (*of people*) Haufen *m*; **~es** *npl* (*in hair*) Zöpfe *pl*
bundle ['bʌndl] *n* Bündel *nt* ♦ *vt* (*also: ~ up*) bündeln
bungalow ['bʌŋgələu] *n* einstöckige(s) Haus *nt*, Bungalow *m*
bungle ['bʌŋgl] *vt* verpfuschen
bunion ['bʌnjən] *n* entzündete(r) Fußbal-

len *m*

bunk [bʌŋk] *n* Schlafkoje *f*; ~ **beds** *npl* Etagenbett *nt*

bunker ['bʌŋkə'] *n* (*coal store*) Kohlenbunker *m*; (*GOLF*) Sandloch *nt*

bunny ['bʌnɪ] *n* (*also*: ~ **rabbit**) Häschen *nt*

bunting ['bʌntɪŋ] *n* Fahnentuch *nt*

buoy [bɔɪ] *n* Boje *f*; (*lifebuoy*) Rettungsboje *f*; ~**ant** *adj* (*floating*) schwimmend; (*fig*) heiter

burden ['bə:dn] *n* (*weight*) Ladung *f*, Last *f*; (*fig*) Bürde *f* ♦ *vt* belasten

bureau ['bjuərəu] (*pl* ~**x**) *n* (*BRIT*: *writing desk*) Sekretär *m*; (*US*: *chest of drawers*) Kommode *f*; (*for information etc*) Büro *nt*

bureaucracy [bjuə'rɔkrəsɪ] *n* Bürokratie *f*

bureaucrat ['bjuərəkræt] *n* Bürokrat(in) *m(f)*

bureaux ['bjuərəuz] *npl of* **bureau**

burglar ['bə:glə'] *n* Einbrecher *m*; ~ **alarm** *n* Einbruchssicherung *f*; ~**y** *n* Einbruch *m*

burial ['bɛrɪəl] *n* Beerdigung *f*

burly ['bə:lɪ] *adj* stämmig

Burma ['bə:mə] *n* Birma *nt*

burn [bə:n] (*pt, pp* **burned** *or* **burnt**) *vt* verbrennen ♦ *vi* brennen ♦ *n* Brandwunde *f*; ~ **down** *vt, vi* abbrennen; ~**er** *n* Brenner *m*; ~**ing** *adj* brennend; ~**t** [bə:nt] *pt, pp of* **burn**

burrow ['bʌrəu] *n* (*of fox*) Bau *m*; (*of rabbit*) Höhle *f* ♦ *vt* eingraben

bursar ['bə:sə'] *n* Kassenverwalter *m*, Quästor *m*; ~**y** (*BRIT*) *n* Stipendium *nt*

burst [bə:st] (*pt, pp* **burst**) *vt* zerbrechen ♦ *vi* platzen ♦ *n* Explosion *f*; (*outbreak*) Ausbruch *m*; (*in pipe*) Bruch(stelle *f*) *m*; **to ~ into flames** in Flammen aufgehen; **to ~ into tears** in Tränen ausbrechen; **to ~ out laughing** in Gelächter ausbrechen; ~ **into** *vt fus* (*room etc*) platzen in +*acc*; ~ **open** *vi* aufbrechen

bury ['bɛrɪ] *vt* vergraben; (*in grave*) beerdigen

bus [bʌs] *n* (Auto)bus *m*, Omnibus *m*

bush [buʃ] *n* Busch *m*; **to beat about the ~** wie die Katze um den heißen Brei herumgehen; ~**y** ['buʃɪ] *adj* buschig

busily ['bɪzɪlɪ] *adv* geschäftig

business ['bɪznɪs] *n* Geschäft *nt*; (*concern*)

Angelegenheit *f*; **it's none of your ~** es geht dich nichts an; **to mean ~** es ernst meinen; **to be away on ~** geschäftlich verreist sein; **it's my ~ to ...** es ist meine Sache, zu ...; ~**like** *adj* geschäftsmäßig; ~**man** (*irreg*) *n* Geschäftsmann *m*; ~ **trip** *n* Geschäftsreise *f*; ~**woman** (*irreg*) *n* Geschäftsfrau *f*

busker ['bʌskə'] (*BRIT*) *n* Straßenmusikant *m*

bus: ~ **shelter** *n* Wartehäuschen *nt*; ~ **station** *n* Busbahnhof *m*; ~ **stop** *n* Bushaltestelle *f*

bust [bʌst] *n* Büste *f* ♦ *adj* (*broken*) kaputt(gegangen); (*business*) pleite; **to go ~** Pleite machen

bustle ['bʌsl] *n* Getriebe *nt* ♦ *vi* hasten

bustling ['bʌslɪŋ] *adj* geschäftig

busy ['bɪzɪ] *adj* beschäftigt; (*road*) belebt ♦ *vt*: **to ~ o.s.** sich beschäftigen; ~**body** *n* Übereifrige(r) *mf*; ~ **signal** (*US*) *n* (*TEL*) Besetztzeichen *nt*

KEYWORD

but [bʌt] *conj* **1** (*yet*) aber; **not X but Y** nicht X sondern Y

2 (*however*): **I'd love to come, but I'm busy** ich würde gern kommen, bin aber beschäftigt

3 (*showing disagreement, surprise etc*): **but that's fantastic!** (aber) das ist ja fantastisch!

♦ *prep* (*apart from, except*): **nothing but trouble** nichts als Ärger; **no-one but him can do it** niemand außer ihn kann es machen; **but for your help** ohne dich/deine Hilfe; **anything but that** alles, nur das nicht

♦ *adv* (*just, only*): **she's but a child** sie ist noch ein Kind; **had I but known** wenn ich es nur gewusst hätte; **I can but try** ich kann es immerhin versuchen; **all but finished** so gut wie fertig

---

butcher ['butʃə'] *n* Metzger *m*; (*murderer*) Schlächter *m* ♦ *vt* schlachten; (*kill*) abschlachten; ~**'s (shop)** *n* Metzgerei *f*

butler ['bʌtlə'] *n* Butler *m*

butt [bʌt] n (*cask*) große(s) Fass nt; (*BRIT: fig: target*) Zielscheibe f; (*of gun*) Kolben m; (*of cigarette*) Stummel m ♦ vt (mit dem Kopf) stoßen; **~ in** vi sich einmischen

butter [ˈbʌtəʳ] n Butter f ♦ vt buttern; **~ bean** n Wachsbohne f; **~cup** n Butterblume f

butterfly [ˈbʌtəflaɪ] n Schmetterling m; (*SWIMMING: also: ~ stroke*) Butterflystil m

buttocks [ˈbʌtəks] npl Gesäß nt

button [ˈbʌtn] n Knopf m ♦ vt, vi (*also: ~ up*) zuknöpfen

buttress [ˈbʌtrɪs] n Strebepfeiler m; Stützbogen m

buxom [ˈbʌksəm] adj drall

buy [baɪ] (pt, pp **bought**) vt kaufen ♦ n Kauf m; **to ~ sb a drink** jdm einen Drink spendieren; **~er** n Käufer(in) m(f)

buzz [bʌz] n Summen nt ♦ vi summen; **~er** [ˈbʌzəʳ] n Summer m; **~ word** n Modewort nt

---

KEYWORD

by [baɪ] prep **1** (*referring to cause, agent*) of, durch; **killed by lightning** vom Blitz getötet; **a painting by Picasso** ein Gemälde von Picasso

2 (*referring to method, manner*): **by bus/car/train** mit dem Bus/Auto/Zug; **to pay by cheque** per Scheck bezahlen; **by moonlight** bei Mondschein; **by saving hard, he ...** indem er eisern sparte, ... er ...

3 (*via, through*) über +acc; **he came in by the back door** er kam durch die Hintertür herein

4 (*close to, past*) bei, an +dat; **a holiday by the sea** ein Urlaub am Meer; **she rushed by me** sie eilte an mir vorbei

5 (*not later than*): **by 4 o'clock** bis 4 Uhr; **by this time tomorrow** morgen um diese Zeit; **by the time I got here it was too late** als ich hier ankam, war es zu spät

6 (*during*): **by day** bei Tag

7 (*amount*): **by the kilo/metre** kiloweise/meterweise; **paid by the hour** stundenweise bezahlt

8 (*MATH, measure*): **to divide by 3** durch 3

teilen; **to multiply by 3** mit 3 malnehmen; **a room 3 metres by 4** ein Zimmer 3 mal 4 Meter; **it's broader by a metre** es ist (um) einem Meter breiter

9 (*according to*) nach; **it's all right by me** von mir aus gern

10: (all) by oneself etc ganz allein

11: by the way übrigens

♦ adv **1** see **go; pass** etc

2: by and by irgendwann; (*with past tenses*) nach einiger Zeit; **by and large** (*on the whole*) im Großen und Ganzen

---

bye(-bye) [ˈbaɪ(ˈbaɪ)] excl (auf) Wiedersehen

by(e)-law [ˈbaɪlɔː] n Verordnung f

by-election [ˈbaɪ.ɪlekʃən] (*BRIT*) n Nachwahl f

bygone [ˈbaɪgɒn] adj vergangen ♦ n: **let ~s be ~s** lass(t) das Vergangene vergangen sein

bypass [ˈbaɪpɑːs] n Umgehungsstraße f ♦ vt umgehen

by-product [ˈbaɪprɒdʌkt] n Nebenprodukt nt

bystander [ˈbaɪstændəʳ] n Zuschauer m

byte [baɪt] n (*COMPUT*) Byte nt

byword [ˈbaɪwɜːd] n Inbegriff m

C, c

C [siː] n (*MUS*) C nt

C. abbr (= *centigrade*) C

C.A. abbr = **chartered accountant**

cab [kæb] n Taxi nt; (*of train*) Führerstand m; (*of truck*) Führersitz m

cabaret [ˈkæbəreɪ] n Kabarett nt

cabbage [ˈkæbɪdʒ] n Kohl(kopf) m

cabin [ˈkæbɪn] n Hütte f; (*NAUT*) Kajüte f; (*AVIAT*) Kabine f; **~ crew** n (*AVIAT*) Flugbegleitpersonal nt; **~ cruiser** n Motorjacht f

cabinet [ˈkæbɪnɪt] n Schrank m; (*for china*) Vitrine f; (*POL*) Kabinett nt; **~-maker** n Kunsttischler m

cable [ˈkeɪbl] n Drahtseil nt, Tau nt; (*TEL*) (Leitungs)kabel nt; (*telegram*) Kabel nt ♦ vt kabeln, telegrafieren; **~ car** n Seilbahn f; **~ television** n Kabelfernsehen nt

cache [kæʃ] n geheime(s) (Waffen)lager nt; geheime(s) (Proviant)lager nt

cackle ['kækl] vi gackern

cacti ['kæktaɪ] npl of **cactus**

cactus ['kæktəs] (pl **cacti**) n Kaktus m, Kaktee f

caddie ['kædɪ] n (GOLF) Golfjunge m; **caddy** ['kædɪ] n = **caddie**

cadet [kə'dɛt] n Kadett m

cadge [kædʒ] vt schmarotzen

Caesarean [sɪ'zɛərɪən] adj: ~ **(section)** Kaiserschnitt m

café ['kæfeɪ] n Café nt, Restaurant nt

cafeteria [kæfɪ'tɪərɪə] n Selbstbedienungsrestaurant nt

caffein(e) ['kæfiːn] n Koffein nt

cage [keɪdʒ] n Käfig m ♦ vt einsperren

cagey ['keɪdʒɪ] adj geheimnistuerisch, zurückhaltend

cagoule [kə'guːl] n Windhemd nt

Cairo ['kaɪərəu] n Kairo nt

cajole [kə'dʒəul] vt überreden

cake [keɪk] n Kuchen m; (of soap) Stück nt; ~**d** vt verkrustet

calamity [kə'læmɪtɪ] n Unglück nt, (Schicksals)schlag m

calcium ['kælsɪəm] n Kalzium nt

calculate ['kælkjuleɪt] vt berechnen, kalkulieren; **calculating** adj berechnend; **calculation** [kælkju'leɪʃən] n Berechnung f; **calculator** n Rechner m

calendar ['kæləndər] n Kalender m; ~ **month** n Kalendermonat m

calf [kɑːf] (pl **calves**) n Kalb nt; (also: ~**skin**) Kalbsleder nt; (ANAT) Wade f

calibre ['kælɪbər] (US **caliber**) n Kaliber nt

call [kɔːl] vt rufen; (name) nennen; (meeting) einberufen; (awaken) wecken; (TEL) anrufen ♦ vi (shout) rufen; (visit: also: ~ **in**, ~ **round**) vorbeikommen ♦ n (shout) Ruf m; (TEL) Anruf m; **to be ~ed** heißen; **on** ~ in Bereitschaft; ~ **back** vi (return) wiederkommen; (TEL) zurückrufen; ~ **for** vt fus (demand) erfordern, verlangen; (fetch) abholen; ~ **off** vt (cancel) absagen; ~ **on** vt fus (visit) besuchen; (turn to) bitten; ~ **out** vi rufen; ~ **up** vt (MIL) einberufen;

~**box** (BRIT) n Telefonzelle f; ~ **centre** n Telefoncenter nt, Callcenter nt; ~**er** n Besucher(in) m(f); (TEL) Anrufer m; ~ **girl** n Callgirl nt; ~-**in** (US) n (phone-in) Phone-in nt; ~**ing** n (vocation) Berufung f; ~**ing card** (US) n Visitenkarte f

callous ['kæləs] adj herzlos

calm [kɑːm] n Ruhe f; (NAUT) Flaute f ♦ vt beruhigen ♦ adj ruhig; (person) gelassen; ~ **down** vi sich beruhigen ♦ vt beruhigen

Calor gas ['kælər-] ® n Propangas nt

calorie ['kælərɪ] n Kalorie f

calves [kɑːvz] npl of **calf**

Cambodia [kæm'bəudɪə] n Kambodscha nt

camcorder ['kæmkɔːdər] n Camcorder m

came [keɪm] pt of **come**

cameo ['kæmɪəu] n Kamee f

camera ['kæmərə] n Fotoapparat m; (CINE, TV) Kamera f; **in** ~ unter Ausschluss der Öffentlichkeit; ~**man** (irreg) n Kameramann m

camouflage ['kæməflɑːʒ] n Tarnung f ♦ vt tarnen

camp [kæmp] n Lager nt ♦ vi zelten, campen ♦ adj affektiert

campaign [kæm'peɪn] n Kampagne f; (MIL) Feldzug m ♦ vi (MIL) Krieg führen; (fig) werben, Propaganda machen; (POL) den Wahlkampf führen

camp: ~ **bed** ['kæmp'bɛd] (BRIT) n Campingbett nt; ~**er** n Camper(in) m(f); (vehicle) Campingwagen m; ~**ing** ['kæmpɪŋ] n: **to go** ~**ing** zelten, Camping machen; ~**ing gas** (US) n Campinggas nt; ~**site** ['kæmpsaɪt] n Campingplatz m

campus ['kæmpəs] n Universitätsgelände nt, Campus m

can¹ [kæn] n Büchse f, Dose f; (for water) Kanne f ♦ vt konservieren, in Büchsen einmachen

---

KEYWORD

---

can² [kæn] (negative **cannot, can't,** conditional **could**) aux vb **1** (be able to, know how to) können; **I can see you tomorrow, if you like** ich könnte Sie morgen sehen,

wenn Sie wollen; **I can swim** ich kann schwimmen; **can you speak German?** sprechen Sie Deutsch?
2 (*may*) können, dürfen; **could I have a word with you?** könnte ich Sie kurz sprechen?

Canada ['kænədə] *n* Kanada *nt*; **Canadian** [kə'neɪdɪən] *adj* kanadisch ♦ *n* Kanadier(in) *m(f)*
canal [kə'næl] *n* Kanal *m*
canapé ['kænəpeɪ] *n* Cocktail- *or* Appetithappen *m*
canary [kə'neərɪ] *n* Kanarienvogel *m*
cancel ['kænsəl] *vt* absagen; (*delete*) durchstreichen; (*train*) streichen; **~lation** [kænsə'leɪʃən] *n* Absage *f*; Streichung *f*
cancer ['kænsər] *n* (*ASTROL: C~*) Krebs *m*
candid ['kændɪd] *adj* offen, ehrlich
candidate ['kændɪdeɪt] *n* Kandidat(in) *m(f)*
candle ['kændl] *n* Kerze *f*; **~light** *n* Kerzenlicht *nt*; **~stick** *n* (*also:* **~ holder**) Kerzenhalter *m*
candour ['kændər] (*US* **candor**) *n* Offenheit *f*
candy ['kændɪ] *n* Kandis(zucker) *m*; (*US*) Bonbons *pl*; **~floss** (*BRIT*) *n* Zuckerwatte *f*
cane [keɪn] *n* (*BOT*) Rohr *nt*; (*stick*) Stock *m* ♦ *vt* (*BRIT: beat*) schlagen
canine ['keɪnaɪn] *adj* Hunde-
canister ['kænɪstər] *n* Blechdose *f*
cannabis ['kænəbɪs] *n* Hanf *m*, Haschisch *nt*
canned [kænd] *adj* Büchsen-, eingemacht
cannon ['kænən] (*pl* **~** *or* **~s**) *n* Kanone *f*
cannot ['kænɔt] = **can not**
canny ['kænɪ] *adj* schlau
canoe [kə'nuː] *n* Kanu *nt*; **~ing** *n* Kanusport *m*, Kanufahren *nt*
canon ['kænən] *n* (*clergyman*) Domherr *m*; (*standard*) Grundsatz *m*
can-opener ['kænəupnər] *n* Büchsenöffner *m*
canopy ['kænəpɪ] *n* Baldachin *m*
can't [kænt] = **can not**
cantankerous [kæn'tæŋkərəs] *adj* zänkisch, mürrisch
canteen [kæn'tiːn] *n* Kantine *f*; (*BRIT: of cutlery*) Besteckkasten *m*

canter ['kæntər] *n* Kanter *m* ♦ *vi* in kurzem Galopp reiten
canvas ['kænvəs] *n* Segeltuch *nt*; (*sail*) Segel *nt*; (*for painting*) Leinwand *f*; **under ~** (*camping*) in Zelten
canvass ['kænvəs] *vi* um Stimmen werben; **~ing** *n* Wahlwerbung *f*
canyon ['kænjən] *n* Felsenschlucht *f*
cap [kæp] *n* Mütze *f*; (*of pen*) Kappe *f*; (*of bottle*) Deckel *m* ♦ *vt* (*surpass*) übertreffen; (*SPORT*) aufstellen; (*put limit on*) einen Höchstsatz festlegen für
capability [keɪpə'bɪlɪtɪ] *n* Fähigkeit *f*
capable ['keɪpəbl] *adj* fähig
capacity [kə'pæsɪtɪ] *n* Fassungsvermögen *nt*; (*ability*) Fähigkeit *f*; (*position*) Eigenschaft *f*
cape [keɪp] *n* (*garment*) Cape *nt*, Umhang *m*; (*GEOG*) Kap *nt*
caper ['keɪpər] *n* (*COOK: usu: ~s*) Kaper *f*; (*prank*) Kapriole *f*
capital ['kæpɪtl] *n* (*~ city*) Hauptstadt *f*; (*FIN*) Kapital *nt*; (*~ letter*) Großbuchstabe *m*; **~ gains tax** *n* Kapitalertragssteuer *f*; **~ism** *n* Kapitalismus *m*; **~ist** *adj* kapitalistisch ♦ *n* Kapitalist(in) *m(f)*; **~ize** *vi*: **to ~ize on** Kapital schlagen aus; **~ punishment** *n* Todesstrafe *f*

Capitol

ⓘ **Capitol** ist das Gebäude in Washington auf dem Capitol Hill, in dem der Kongress der USA zusammentritt. Die Bezeichnung wird in vielen amerikanischen Bundesstaaten auch für das Parlamentsgebäude des jeweiligen Staates verwendet.

Capricorn ['kæprɪkɔːn] *n* Steinbock *m*
capsize [kæp'saɪz] *vt, vi* kentern
capsule ['kæpsjuːl] *n* Kapsel *f*
captain ['kæptɪn] *n* Kapitän *m*; (*MIL*) Hauptmann *m* ♦ *vt* anführen
caption ['kæpʃən] *n* (*heading*) Überschrift *f*; (*to picture*) Unterschrift *f*
captivate ['kæptɪveɪt] *vt* fesseln
captive ['kæptɪv] *n* Gefangene(r) *f(m)* ♦ *adj* gefangen (gehalten); **captivity** [kæp'tɪvɪtɪ]

n Gefangenschaft *f*

capture ['kæptʃəʳ] *vt* gefangen nehmen; (*place*) erobern; (*attention*) erregen ♦ *n* Gefangennahme *f*; (*data ~*) Erfassung *f*

car [kɑːʳ] *n* Auto *nt*, Wagen *m*; (*RAIL*) Wagen *m*

caramel ['kærəməl] *n* Karamelle *f*, Karamellbonbon *m or nt*; (*burnt sugar*) Karamell *m*

carat ['kærət] *n* Karat *nt*

caravan ['kærəvæn] *n* (*BRIT*) Wohnwagen *m*; (*in desert*) Karawane *f*; **~ning** *n* Caravaning *nt*, Urlaub *m* im Wohnwagen; **~ site** (*BRIT*) *n* Campingplatz *m* für Wohnwagen

carbohydrate [kɑːbəʊˈhaɪdreɪt] *n* Kohlenhydrat *nt*

carbon ['kɑːbən] *n* Kohlenstoff *m*; **~ copy** *n* Durchschlag *m*; **~ dioxide** *n* Kohlendioxyd *nt*; **~ monoxide** *n* Kohlenmonoxyd *nt*; **~ paper** *n* Kohlepapier *nt*

car boot sale *n* auf einem Parkplatz stattfindender Flohmarkt mit dem Kofferraum als Auslage

carburettor [kɑːbjuˈretəʳ] (*US* **carburetor**) *n* Vergaser *m*

carcass ['kɑːkəs] *n* Kadaver *m*

card [kɑːd] *n* Karte *f*; **~board** *n* Pappe *f*; **~ game** *n* Kartenspiel *nt*

cardiac ['kɑːdiæk] *adj* Herz-

cardigan ['kɑːdɪgən] *n* Strickjacke *f*

cardinal ['kɑːdɪnl] *adj*: **~ number** Kardinalzahl *f* ♦ *n* (*REL*) Kardinal *m*

card index *n* Kartei *f*; (*in library*) Katalog *m*

cardphone *n* Kartentelefon *nt*

care [kɛəʳ] *n* (*of teeth, car etc*) Pflege *f*; (*of children*) Fürsorge *f*; (*~fulness*) Sorgfalt *f*; (*worry*) Sorge *f* ♦ *vi*: **to ~ about** sich kümmern um; **~ of** bei; **in sb's ~** in jds Obhut; **I don't ~** das ist mir egal; **I couldn't ~ less** es ist mir doch völlig egal; **to take ~** aufpassen; **to take ~ of** sorgen für; **to take ~ to do sth** sich bemühen, etw zu tun; **~ for** *vt* sorgen für; (*like*) mögen

career [kəˈrɪəʳ] *n* Karriere *f*, Laufbahn *f* ♦ *vi* (*also: ~ along*) rasen; **~ woman** (*irreg*) *n* Karrierefrau *f*

care: ~free *adj* sorgenfrei; **~ful** *adj* sorgfältig; **(be) ~ful!** pass auf!; **~fully** *adv* vorsichtig; (*methodically*) sorgfältig; **~less** *adj* nachlässig; **~lessness** *n* Nachlässigkeit *f*; **~r** *n* (*MED*) Betreuer(in) *m(f)*

caress [kəˈres] *n* Liebkosung *f* ♦ *vt* liebkosen

caretaker ['kɛəteɪkəʳ] *n* Hausmeister *m*

car ferry *n* Autofähre *f*

cargo ['kɑːgəʊ] (*pl* **~es**) *n* Schiffsladung *f*

car hire *n* Autovermietung *f*

Caribbean [kærɪˈbiːən] *n*: **the ~ (Sea)** die Karibik

caricature ['kærɪkətjʊəʳ] *n* Karikatur *f*

caring ['kɛərɪŋ] *adj* (*society, organization*) sozial eingestellt; (*person*) liebevoll

carnage ['kɑːnɪdʒ] *n* Blutbad *nt*

carnation [kɑːˈneɪʃən] *n* Nelke *f*

carnival ['kɑːnɪvl] *n* Karneval *m*, Fasching *m*; (*US: fun fair*) Kirmes *f*

carnivorous [kɑːˈnɪvərəs] *adj* Fleisch fressend

carol ['kærəl] *n*: **(Christmas) ~** (Weihnachts)lied *nt*

carp [kɑːp] *n* (*fish*) Karpfen *m*

car park (*BRIT*) *n* Parkplatz *m*; (*covered*) Parkhaus *nt*

carpenter ['kɑːpɪntəʳ] *n* Zimmermann *m*; **carpentry** ['kɑːpɪntrɪ] *n* Zimmerei *f*

carpet ['kɑːpɪt] *n* Teppich *m* ♦ *vt* mit einem Teppich auslegen; **~ bombing** *n* Flächenbombardierung *f*; **~ slippers** *npl* Pantoffeln *pl*; **~ sweeper** ['kɑːpɪtswiːpəʳ] *n* Teppichkehrer *m*

car phone *n* (*TEL*) Autotelefon *nt*

car rental (*US*) *n* Autovermietung *f*

carriage ['kærɪdʒ] *n* Kutsche *f*; (*RAIL, of typewriter*) Wagen *m*; (*of goods*) Beförderung *f*; (*bearing*) Haltung *f*; **~ return** *n* (*on typewriter*) Rücklauftaste *f*; **~way** (*BRIT*) *n* (*part of road*) Fahrbahn *f*

carrier ['kærɪəʳ] *n* Träger(in) *m(f)*; (*COMM*) Spediteur *m*; **~ bag** (*BRIT*) *n* Tragetasche *f*

carrot ['kærət] *n* Möhre *f*, Karotte *f*

carry ['kærɪ] *vt*, *vi* tragen; **to get carried away** (*fig*) sich nicht mehr bremsen können; **~ on** *vi* (*continue*) weitermachen; (*inf: complain*) Theater machen; **~ out** *vt* (*orders*) ausführen; (*investigation*) durchführen; **~cot** (*BRIT*) n Babytragetasche f; **~-on** (*inf*) n (*fuss*) Theater nt

cart [kɑːt] n Wagen m, Karren m ♦ vt schleppen

cartilage [ˈkɑːtɪlɪdʒ] n Knorpel m

carton [ˈkɑːtən] n Karton m; (*of milk*) Tüte f

cartoon [kɑːˈtuːn] n (*PRESS*) Karikatur f; (*comic strip*) Comics pl; (*CINE*) (Zeichen)trickfilm m

cartridge [ˈkɑːtrɪdʒ] n Patrone f

carve [kɑːv] vt (*wood*) schnitzen; (*stone*) meißeln; (*meat*) (vor)schneiden; **~ up** vt aufschneiden; **carving** [ˈkɑːvɪŋ] n Schnitzerei f; **carving knife** n Tran(s)chiermesser nt

car wash n Autowäsche f

cascade [kæsˈkeɪd] n Wasserfall m ♦ vi kaskadenartig herabfallen

case [keɪs] n (*box*) Kasten m; (*BRIT*: also: **suitcase**) Koffer m; (*JUR, matter*) Fall m; **in ~** falls, im Falle; **in any ~** jedenfalls, auf jeden Fall

cash [kæʃ] n (Bar)geld nt ♦ vt einlösen; **~ on delivery** per Nachnahme; **~ book** n Kassenbuch nt; **~ card** n Scheckkarte f; **~ desk** (*BRIT*) n Kasse f; **~ dispenser** n Geldautomat m

cashew [kæˈʃuː] n (*also: ~ nut*) Cashewnuss f

cash flow n Cashflow m

cashier [kæˈʃɪər] n Kassierer(in) m(f)

cashmere [ˈkæʃmɪər] n Kaschmirwolle f

cash register n Registrierkasse f

casing [ˈkeɪsɪŋ] n Gehäuse nt

casino [kəˈsiːnəu] n Kasino nt

casket [ˈkɑːskɪt] n Kästchen nt; (*US: coffin*) Sarg m

casserole [ˈkæsərəul] n Kasserolle f; (*food*) Auflauf m

cassette [kæˈset] n Kassette f; **~ player** n Kassettengerät nt

cast [kɑːst] (*pt, pp* **cast**) vt werfen; (*horns*) verlieren; (*metal*) gießen; (*THEAT*) besetzen; (*vote*) abgeben ♦ n (*THEAT*) Besetzung f; (*also:* **plaster ~**) Gipsverband m; **~ off** vi (*NAUT*) losmachen

castaway [ˈkɑːstəweɪ] n Schiffbrüchige(r) f(m)

caste [kɑːst] n Kaste f

caster sugar [ˈkɑːstə-] (*BRIT*) n Raffinade f

casting vote [ˈkɑːstɪŋ-] (*BRIT*) n entscheidende Stimme f

cast iron n Gusseisen nt

castle [ˈkɑːsl] n Burg f; Schloss nt; (*CHESS*) Turm m

castor [ˈkɑːstər] n (*wheel*) Laufrolle f

castor oil n Rizinusöl nt

castrate [kæsˈtreɪt] vt kastrieren

casual [ˈkæʒjul] adj (*attitude*) nachlässig; (*dress*) leger; (*meeting*) zufällig; (*work*) Gelegenheits-; **~ly** adv (*dress*) zwanglos, leger; (*remark*) beiläufig

casualty [ˈkæʒjultɪ] n Verletzte(r) f(m); (*dead*) Tote(r) f(m); (*also: ~ department*) Unfallstation f

cat [kæt] n Katze f

catalogue [ˈkætəlɔg] (*US* **catalog**) n Katalog m ♦ vt katalogisieren

catalyst [ˈkætəlɪst] n Katalysator m

catalytic converter [kætəˈlɪtɪk kənˈvəːtər] n Katalysator m

catapult [ˈkætəpʌlt] n Schleuder f

cataract [ˈkætərækt] n (*MED*) graue(r) Star m

catarrh [kəˈtɑː] n Katarr(h) m

catastrophe [kəˈtæstrəfɪ] n Katastrophe f

catch [kætʃ] (*pt, pp* **caught**) vt fangen; (*arrest*) fassen; (*train*) erreichen; (*person: by surprise*) ertappen; (*also: ~ up*) einholen ♦ vi (*fire*) in Gang kommen; (*in branches etc*) hängen bleiben ♦ n (*fish etc*) Fang m; (*trick*) Haken m; (*of lock*) Sperrhaken m; **to ~ an illness** sich *dat* eine Krankheit holen; **to ~ fire** Feuer fangen; **~ on** vi (*understand*) begreifen; (*grow popular*) ankommen; **~ up** vi (*fig*) aufholen; **~ing** [ˈkætʃɪŋ] adj ansteckend; **~ment area** [ˈkætʃmənt-] (*BRIT*) n Einzugsgebiet nt; **~ phrase** n Slogan m; **~y** [ˈkætʃɪ] adj (*tune*) eingängig

categoric(al) [kætɪˈgɔrɪk(l)] adj kategorisch

category [ˈkætɪgərɪ] n Kategorie f

cater [ˈkeɪtər] vi versorgen; **~ for** (*BRIT*) vt fus (*party*) ausrichten; (*needs*) eingestellt sein auf +*acc*; **~er** n Lieferant(in) m(f) von Speisen und Getränken; **~ing** n

Gastronomie f

caterpillar ['kætəpɪlər] n Raupe f; **~ track** ® n Gleiskette f

cathedral [kə'θi:drəl] n Kathedrale f, Dom m

Catholic ['kæθəlɪk] adj (REL) katholisch ♦ n Katholik(in) m(f); **c~** adj (tastes etc) vielseitig

CAT scan [kæt-] n Computertomografie f

Catseye ['kæts'aɪ] (BRIT: ®) n (AUT) Katzenauge nt

cattle ['kætl] npl Vieh nt

catty ['kætɪ] adj gehässig

caucus ['kɔ:kəs] n (POL) Gremium nt; (US: meeting) Sitzung f

caught [kɔ:t] pt, pp of **catch**

cauliflower ['kɔlɪflauər] n Blumenkohl m

cause [kɔ:z] n Ursache f; (purpose) Sache f ♦ vt verursachen

causeway ['kɔ:zweɪ] n Damm m

caustic ['kɔ:stɪk] adj ätzend; (fig) bissig

caution ['kɔ:ʃən] n Vorsicht f; (warning) Verwarnung f ♦ vt verwarnen; **cautious** ['kɔ:ʃəs] adj vorsichtig

cavalry ['kævəlrɪ] n Kavallerie f

cave [keɪv] n Höhle f; **~ in** vi einstürzen; **~man** (irreg) n Höhlenmensch m

cavern ['kævən] n Höhle f

caviar(e) ['kævɪɑ:r] n Kaviar m

cavity ['kævɪtɪ] n Loch nt

cavort [kə'vɔ:t] vi umherspringen

C.B. n abbr (= Citizens' Band (Radio)) CB

C.B.I. n abbr (= Confederation of British Industry) ≃ BDI m

cc n abbr = **carbon copy**; **cubic centimetres**

CD n abbr (= compact disc) CD f

CDI n abbr (= Compact Disk Interactive) CD-I f

CD player n CD-Spieler m

CD-ROM n abbr (= compact disc read-only memory) CD-Rom f

cease [si:s] vi aufhören ♦ vt beenden; **~fire** n Feuereinstellung f; **~less** adj unaufhörlich

cedar ['si:dər] n Zeder f

ceiling ['si:lɪŋ] n Decke f; (fig) Höchstgrenze f

celebrate ['selɪbreɪt] vt, vi feiern; **~d** adj gefeiert; **celebration** [selɪ'breɪʃən] n Feier f

celebrity [sɪ'lebrɪtɪ] n gefeierte Persönlichkeit f

celery ['selərɪ] n Sellerie m or f

celibacy ['selɪbəsɪ] n Zölibat nt or m

cell [sel] n Zelle f; (ELEC) Element nt

cellar ['selər] n Keller m

cello ['tʃeləʊ] n Cello nt

Cellophane ['seləfeɪn] ® n Cellophan nt ®

cellphone ['selfəʊn] n Funktelefon nt

cellular ['seljʊlər] adj zellular

cellulose ['seljʊləʊs] n Zellulose f

Celt [kelt, selt] n Kelte m, Keltin f; **~ic** ['keltɪk, 'seltɪk] adj keltisch

cement [sə'ment] n Zement m ♦ vt zementieren; **~ mixer** n Betonmischmaschine f

cemetery ['semɪtrɪ] n Friedhof m

censor ['sensər] n Zensor m ♦ vt zensieren; **~ship** n Zensur f

censure ['senʃər] vt rügen

census ['sensəs] n Volkszählung f

cent [sent] n (US: coin) Cent m; see also **per cent**

centenary [sen'ti:nərɪ] n Jahrhundertfeier f

center ['sentər] (US) n = **centre**

centigrade ['sentɪgreɪd] adj Celsius

centimetre ['sentɪmi:tər] (US **centimeter**) n Zentimeter nt

centipede ['sentɪpi:d] n Tausendfüßler m

central ['sentrəl] adj zentral; **C~ America** n Mittelamerika nt; **~ heating** n Zentralheizung f; **~ize** vt zentralisieren; **~ reservation** (BRIT) n (AUT) Mittelstreifen m

centre ['sentər] (US **center**) n Zentrum nt ♦ vt zentrieren; **~-forward** n (SPORT) Mittelstürmer m; **~-half** n (SPORT) Stopper m

century ['sentjʊrɪ] n Jahrhundert nt

ceramic [sɪ'ræmɪk] adj keramisch; **~s** npl Keramiken pl

cereal ['si:rɪəl] n (grain) Getreide nt; (at breakfast) Getreideflocken pl

cerebral ['serɪbrəl] adj zerebral; (intellectual) geistig

ceremony ['serɪmənɪ] n Zeremonie f; **to**

stand on ~ förmlich sein

certain ['sɜːtən] *adj* sicher; (*particular*) gewiss; **for ~** ganz bestimmt; **~ly** *adv* sicher, bestimmt; **~ty** *n* Gewissheit *f*

certificate [sə'tɪfɪkɪt] *n* Bescheinigung *f*; (*SCH etc*) Zeugnis *nt*

certified mail ['sɜː:tɪfaɪd-] (*US*) *n* Einschreiben *nt*

certified public accountant ['sɜː:tɪfaɪd-] (*US*) *n* geprüfte(r) Buchhalter *m*

certify ['sɜː:tɪfaɪ] *vt* bescheinigen

cervical ['sɜː:vɪkl] *adj* (*smear, cancer*) Gebärmutterhals-

cervix ['sɜː:vɪks] *n* Gebärmutterhals *m*

cf. *abbr* (= *compare*) vgl.

CFC *n abbr* (= *chlorofluorocarbon*) FCKW *m*

ch. *abbr* (= *chapter*) Kap.

chafe [tʃeɪf] *vt* scheuern

chaffinch ['tʃæfɪntʃ] *n* Buchfink *m*

chain [tʃeɪn] *n* Kette *f* ♦ *vt* (*also*: ~ **up**) anketten; ~ **reaction** *n* Kettenreaktion *f*; **~~smoke** *vi* kettenrauchen; ~ **store** *n* Kettenladen *m*

chair [tʃeə*] *n* Stuhl *m*; (*armchair*) Sessel *m*; (*UNIV*) Lehrstuhl *m* ♦ *vt* (*meeting*) den Vorsitz führen bei; **~lift** *n* Sessellift *m*; **~man** (*irreg*) *n* Vorsitzende(r) *m*

chalet ['ʃæleɪ] *n* Chalet *nt*

chalk [tʃɔːk] *n* Kreide *f*

challenge ['tʃælɪndʒ] *n* Herausforderung *f* ♦ *vt* herausfordern; (*contest*) bestreiten; **challenging** *adj* (*tone*) herausfordernd; (*work*) anspruchsvoll

chamber ['tʃeɪmbə*] *n* Kammer *f*; ~ **of commerce** Handelskammer *f*; **~maid** *n* Zimmermädchen *nt*; ~ **music** *n* Kammermusik *f*

chamois ['ʃæmwɑː] *n* Gämse *f*

champagne [ʃæm'peɪn] *n* Champagner *m*, Sekt *m*

champion ['tʃæmpɪən] *n* (*SPORT*) Meister(in) *m(f)*; (*of cause*) Verfechter(in) *m(f)*; **~ship** *n* Meisterschaft *f*

chance [tʃɑːns] *n* (*luck*) Zufall *m*; (*possibility*) Möglichkeit *f*; (*opportunity*) Gelegenheit *f*, Chance *f*; (*risk*) Risiko *nt* ♦ *adj* zufällig ♦ *vt*: **to ~ it** es darauf ankommen lassen; **by ~**

zufällig; **to take a ~** ein Risiko eingehen

chancellor ['tʃɑːnsələ*] *n* Kanzler *m*; **C~ of the Exchequer** (*BRIT*) *n* Schatzkanzler *m*

chandelier [ʃændə'lɪə*] *n* Kronleuchter *m*

change [tʃeɪndʒ] *vt* ändern; (*replace, COMM: money*) wechseln; (*exchange*) umtauschen; (*transform*) verwandeln ♦ *vi* sich ändern; (~ *trains*) umsteigen; (~ *clothes*) sich umziehen ♦ *n* Veränderung *f*; (*money returned*) Wechselgeld *nt*; (*coins*) Kleingeld *nt*; **to ~ one's mind** es sich *dat* anders überlegen; **to ~ into sth** (*be transformed*) in etw *acc* verwandeln; **for a ~** zur Abwechslung; **~able** *adj* (*weather*) wechselhaft; ~ **machine** *n* Geldwechselautomat *m*; **~over** *n* Umstellung *f*

changing ['tʃeɪndʒɪŋ] *adj* veränderlich; ~ **room** (*BRIT*) *n* Umkleideraum *m*

channel ['tʃænl] *n* (*stream*) Bachbett *nt*; (*NAUT*) Straße *f*; (*TV*) Kanal *m*; (*fig*) Weg *m* ♦ *vt* (*efforts*) lenken; **the (English) C~** der Ärmelkanal; **~-hopping** *n* (*TV*) ständiges Umschalten; **C~ Islands** *npl*: **the C~ Islands** die Kanalinseln *pl*; **C~ Tunnel** *n*: **the C~ Tunnel** der Kanaltunnel

chant [tʃɑːnt] *n* Gesang *m*; (*of fans*) Sprechchor *m* ♦ *vt* intonieren

chaos ['keɪɔs] *n* Chaos *nt*

chap [tʃæp] (*inf*) *n* Kerl *m*

chapel ['tʃæpl] *n* Kapelle *f*

chaperon ['ʃæpərəʊn] *n* Anstandsdame *f*

chaplain ['tʃæplɪn] *n* Kaplan *m*

chapped [tʃæpt] *adj* (*skin, lips*) spröde

chapter ['tʃæptə*] *n* Kapitel *nt*

char [tʃɑː*] *vt* (*burn*) verkohlen

character ['kærɪktə*] *n* Charakter *m*, Wesen *nt*; (*in novel, film*) Figur *f*; **~istic** [kærɪktə'rɪstɪk] *adj*: **~istic (of sb/sth)** (für jdn/etw) charakteristisch *n* Kennzeichen *nt*; **~ize** *vt* charakterisieren, kennzeichnen

charade [ʃə'rɑːd] *n* Scharade *f*

charcoal ['tʃɑːkəʊl] *n* Holzkohle *f*

charge [tʃɑːdʒ] *n* (*cost*) Preis *m*; (*JUR*) Anklage *f*; (*explosive*) Ladung *f*; (*attack*) Angriff *m* ♦ *vt* (*gun, battery*) laden; (*price*) verlangen; (*JUR*) anklagen; (*MIL*) angreifen ♦ *vi* (*rush*) (an)stürmen; **bank ~s**

Bankgebühren pl; **free of ~** kostenlos; **to reverse the ~s** (TEL) ein R-Gespräch führen; **to be in ~ of** verantwortlich sein für; **to take ~** (die Verantwortung) übernehmen; **to ~ sth (up) to sb's account** jdm etw in Rechnung stellen; **~ card** n Kundenkarte f

charitable ['tʃærɪtəbl] adj wohltätig; (lenient) nachsichtig

charity ['tʃærɪtɪ] n (institution) Hilfswerk nt; (attitude) Nächstenliebe f

charm [tʃɑːm] n Charme m; (spell) Bann m; (object) Talisman m ♦ vt bezaubern; **~ing** adj reizend

chart [tʃɑːt] n Tabelle f; (NAUT) Seekarte f ♦ vt (course) abstecken

charter ['tʃɑːtəʳ] vt chartern ♦ n Schutzbrief m; **~ed accountant** n Wirtschaftsprüfer(in) m(f); **~ flight** n Charterflug m

chase [tʃeɪs] vt jagen, verfolgen ♦ n Jagd f

chasm ['kæzəm] n Kluft f

chassis ['tʃæsɪ] n Fahrgestell nt

chat [tʃæt] vi (also: **have a ~**) plaudern ♦ n Plauderei f; **~ show** (BRIT) n Talkshow f

chatter ['tʃætəʳ] vi schwatzen; (teeth) klappern ♦ n Geschwätz nt; **~box** n Quasselstrippe f

chatty ['tʃætɪ] adj geschwätzig

chauffeur ['ʃəʊfəʳ] n Chauffeur m

chauvinist ['ʃəʊvɪnɪst] n (male ~) Chauvi m (inf)

cheap [tʃiːp] adj, adv billig; **~ day return** n Tagesrückfahrkarte f (zu einem günstigeren Tarif); **~ly** adv billig

cheat [tʃiːt] vt, vi betrügen; (SCH) mogeln ♦ n Betrüger(in) m(f)

check [tʃɛk] vt (examine) prüfen; (make sure) nachsehen; (control) kontrollieren; (restrain) zügeln; (stop) anhalten ♦ n (examination, restraint) Kontrolle f; (bill) Rechnung f; (pattern) Karo(muster) nt; (US) = **cheque** ♦ adj (pattern, cloth) kariert; **~ in** vi (in hotel, airport) einchecken ♦ vt (luggage) abfertigen lassen; **~ out** vi (of hotel) abreisen; **~ up** vi nachschauen; **~ up on** vt kontrollieren; **~ered** (US) adj =

chequered; ~ers (US) n (draughts) Damespiel nt; **~-in (desk)** n Abfertigung f; **~ing account** (US) n (current account) Girokonto nt; **~mate** n Schachmatt nt; **~out** n Kasse f; **~point** n Kontrollpunkt m; **~ room** (US) n (left-luggage office) Gepäckaufbewahrung f; **~up** n (Nach)prüfung f; (MED) (ärztliche) Untersuchung f

cheek [tʃiːk] n Backe f; (fig) Frechheit f; **~bone** n Backenknochen m; **~y** adj frech

cheep [tʃiːp] vi piepsen

cheer [tʃɪəʳ] n (usu pl) Hurra- or Beifallsruf m ♦ vt zujubeln; (encourage) aufmuntern ♦ vi jauchzen; **~s!** Prost!; **~ up** vi bessere Laune bekommen ♦ vt aufmuntern; **~ up!** nun lach doch mal!; **~ful** adj fröhlich

cheerio [tʃɪərɪ'əʊ] (BRIT) excl tschüss!

cheese [tʃiːz] n Käse m; **~board** n (gemischte) Käseplatte f

cheetah ['tʃiːtə] n Gepard m

chef [ʃef] n Küchenchef m

chemical ['kemɪkl] adj chemisch ♦ n Chemikalie f

chemist ['kemɪst] n (BRIT: pharmacist) Apotheker m, Drogist m; (scientist) Chemiker m; **~ry** n Chemie f; **~'s (shop)** (BRIT) n Apotheke f; Drogerie f

cheque [tʃek] (BRIT) n Scheck m; **~book** n Scheckbuch nt; **~ card** n Scheckkarte f

chequered ['tʃekəd] adj (fig) bewegt

cherish ['tʃerɪʃ] vt (person) lieben; (hope) hegen

cherry ['tʃerɪ] n Kirsche f

chess [tʃes] n Schach nt; **~board** n Schachbrett nt; **~man** (irreg) n Schachfigur f

chest [tʃest] n (ANAT) Brust f; (box) Kiste f; **~ of drawers** Kommode f

chestnut ['tʃesnʌt] n Kastanie f

chew [tʃuː] vt, vi kauen; **~ing gum** n Kaugummi m

chic [ʃiːk] adj schick, elegant

chick [tʃɪk] n Küken nt; (US: inf: girl) Biene f

chicken ['tʃɪkɪn] n Huhn nt; (food) Hähnchen nt; **~ out** (inf) vi kneifen

chickenpox ['tʃɪkɪnpɔks] n Windpocken pl

chicory ['tʃɪkərɪ] *n* (*in coffee*) Zichorie *f*;
(*plant*) Chicorée *f*, Schikoree *f*

chief [tʃiːf] *n* (*of tribe*) Häuptling *m*; (COMM)
Chef *m* ♦ *adj* Haupt-; **~ executive** *n*
Geschäftsführer(in) *m(f)*; **~ly** *adv*
hauptsächlich

chilblain ['tʃɪlbleɪn] *n* Frostbeule *f*

child [tʃaɪld] (*pl* **~ren**) *n* Kind *nt*; **~birth** *n*
Entbindung *f*; **~hood** *n* Kindheit *f*; **~ish**
adj kindisch; **~like** *adj* kindlich; **~ minder**
(BRIT) *n* Tagesmutter *f*; **~ren** ['tʃɪldrən] *npl*
of **child**; **~ seat** *n* Kindersitz *m*

Chile ['tʃɪlɪ] *n* Chile *nt*; **~an** *adj* chilenisch

chill [tʃɪl] *n* Kühle *f*; (MED) Erkältung *f* ♦ *vt*
(CULIN) kühlen

chilli ['tʃɪlɪ] *n* Peperoni *pl*; (*meal, spice*) Chili
m

chilly ['tʃɪlɪ] *adj* kühl, frostig

chime [tʃaɪm] *n* Geläut *nt* ♦ *vi* ertönen

chimney ['tʃɪmnɪ] *n* Schornstein *m*; **~
sweep** *n* Schornsteinfeger(in) *m(f)*

chimpanzee [tʃɪmpæn'ziː] *n* Schimpanse *m*

chin [tʃɪn] *n* Kinn *nt*

China ['tʃaɪnə] *n* China *nt*

china ['tʃaɪnə] *n* Porzellan *nt*

Chinese [tʃaɪ'niːz] *adj* chinesisch ♦ *n* (*inv*)
Chinese *m*, Chinesin *f*; (LING) Chinesisch *nt*

chink [tʃɪŋk] *n* (*opening*) Ritze *f*; (*noise*)
Klirren *nt*

chip [tʃɪp] *n* (*of wood etc*) Splitter *m*; (*in poker
etc; US: crisp*) Chip *m* ♦ *vt* absplittern; **~s** *npl*
(BRIT: COOK) Pommes frites *pl*; **~ in** *vi*
Zwischenbemerkungen machen

Chip shop

ⓘ **Chip shop**, auch *fish-and-chip shop*, ist
die traditionelle britische Imbissbude, in
der vor allem fritierte Fischfilets und
Pommes frites, aber auch andere einfache
Mahlzeiten angeboten werden. Früher wurde
das Essen zum Mitnehmen in
Zeitungspapier verpackt. Manche *chip shops*
haben auch einen Essraum.

---

chiropodist [kɪ'rɔpədɪst] (BRIT) *n*
Fußpfleger(in) *m(f)*

chirp [tʃəːp] *vi* zwitschern

chisel ['tʃɪzl] *n* Meißel *m*

chit [tʃɪt] *n* Notiz *f*

chivalrous ['ʃɪvəlrəs] *adj* ritterlich; **chivalry**
['ʃɪvəlrɪ] *n* Ritterlichkeit *f*

chives [tʃaɪvz] *npl* Schnittlauch *m*

chlorine ['klɔːriːn] *n* Chlor *nt*

chock-a-block ['tʃɔkə'blɔk] *adj* voll
gepfropft

chock-full [tʃɔk'ful] *adj* voll gepfropft

chocolate ['tʃɔklɪt] *n* Schokolade *f*

choice [tʃɔɪs] *n* Wahl *f*; (*of goods*) Auswahl *f*
♦ *adj* Qualitäts-

choir ['kwaɪər] *n* Chor *m*; **~boy** *n* Chorknabe
m

choke [tʃəʊk] *vi* ersticken ♦ *vt* erdrosseln;
(*block*) (ab)drosseln ♦ *n* (AUT) Starterklappe
f

cholera ['kɔlərə] *n* Cholera *f*

cholesterol [kə'lestərɔl] *n* Cholesterin *nt*

choose [tʃuːz] (*pt* **chose**, *pp* **chosen**) *vt*
wählen; **choosy** ['tʃuːzɪ] *adj* wählerisch

chop [tʃɔp] *vt* (*wood*) spalten; (COOK: *also:* **~
up**) (zer)hacken ♦ *n* Hieb *m*; (COOK)
Kotelett *nt*; **~s** *npl* (*jaws*) Lefzen *pl*

chopper ['tʃɔpər] *n* (*helicopter*) Hubschrauber
m

choppy ['tʃɔpɪ] *adj* (*sea*) bewegt

chopsticks ['tʃɔpstɪks] *npl* (Ess)stäbchen *pl*

choral ['kɔːrəl] *adj* Chor-

chord [kɔːd] *n* Akkord *m*

chore [tʃɔːʳ] *n* Pflicht *f*; **~s** *npl* (*housework*)
Hausarbeit *f*

choreographer [kɔrɪ'ɔgrəfəʳ] *n*
Choreograf(in) *m(f)*

chorister ['kɔrɪstəʳ] *n* Chorsänger(in) *m(f)*

chortle ['tʃɔːtl] *vi* glucksen

chorus ['kɔːrəs] *n* Chor *m*; (*in song*) Refrain
m

chose [tʃəʊz] *pt of* **choose**

chosen ['tʃəʊzn] *pp of* **choose**

chowder ['tʃaʊdəʳ] (US) *n* sämige Fischsuppe
f

Christ [kraɪst] *n* Christus *m*

christen ['krɪsn] *vt* taufen; **~ing** *n* Taufe *f*

Christian ['krɪstɪən] *adj* christlich ♦ *n*
Christ(in) *m(f)*; **~ity** [krɪstɪ'ænɪtɪ] *n*
Christentum *nt*; **~ name** *n* Vorname *m*

Christmas ['krɪsməs] n Weihnachten pl;
Happy or **Merry ~!** frohe or fröhliche
Weihnachten!; **~ card** n Weihnachtskarte f;
~ Day n der erste Weihnachtstag; **~ Eve** n
Heiligabend m; **~ tree** n Weihnachtsbaum
m

chrome [krəum] n Verchromung f

chromium ['krəumɪəm] n Chrom nt

chronic ['krɔnɪk] adj chronisch

chronicle ['krɔnɪkl] n Chronik f

chronological [krɔnə'lɔdʒɪkl] adj
chronologisch

chubby ['tʃʌbɪ] adj rundlich

chuck [tʃʌk] vt werfen; (BRIT: also: ~ up)
hinwerfen; **~ out** vt (person) rauswerfen;
(old clothes etc) wegwerfen

chuckle ['tʃʌkl] vi in sich hineinlachen

chug [tʃʌg] vi tuckern

chunk [tʃʌŋk] n Klumpen m; (of food)
Brocken m

church [tʃɜ:tʃ] n Kirche f; **~yard** n Kirchhof
m

churn [tʃɜ:n] n (for butter) Butterfass nt; (for
milk) Milchkanne f; **~ out** (inf) vt
produzieren

chute [ʃu:t] n Rutsche f; (rubbish ~)
Müllschlucker m

chutney ['tʃʌtnɪ] n Chutney nt

CIA (US) n abbr (= Central Intelligence Agency)
CIA m

CID (BRIT) n abbr (= Criminal Investigation
Department) ≃ Kripo f

cider ['saɪdə'] n Apfelwein m

cigar [sɪ'gɑ:'] n Zigarre f

cigarette [sɪgə'ret] n Zigarette f; **~ case** n
Zigarettenetui nt; **~ end** n
Zigarettenstummel m

Cinderella [sɪndə'relə] n Aschenbrödel nt

cinders ['sɪndəz] npl Asche f

cine camera ['sɪnɪ-] (BRIT) n Filmkamera f

cine film (BRIT) n Schmalfilm m

cinema ['sɪnəmə] n Kino nt

cinnamon ['sɪnəmən] n Zimt m

circle ['sɜ:kl] n Kreis m; (in cinema etc) Rang
m ♦ vi kreisen ♦ vt (surround) umgeben;
(move round) kreisen um

circuit ['sɜ:kɪt] n (track) Rennbahn f; (lap)
Runde f; (ELEC) Stromkreis m

circular ['sɜ:kjulə'] adj rund ♦ n
Rundschreiben nt

circulate ['sɜ:kjuleɪt] vi zirkulieren ♦ vt in
Umlauf setzen; **circulation** [sɜ:kju'leɪʃən] n
(of blood) Kreislauf m; (of newspaper) Auflage
f; (of money) Umlauf m

circumcise ['sɜ:kəmsaɪz] vt beschneiden

circumference [sə'kʌmfərəns] n
(Kreis)umfang m

circumspect ['sɜ:kəmspekt] adj umsichtig

circumstances ['sɜ:kəmstənsɪz] npl
Umstände pl; (financial) Verhältnisse pl

circumvent [sɜ:kəm'vent] vt umgehen

circus ['sɜ:kəs] n Zirkus m

CIS n abbr (= Commonwealth of Independent
States) GUS f

cistern ['sɪstən] n Zisterne f; (of W.C.)
Spülkasten m

cite [saɪt] vt zitieren, anführen

citizen ['sɪtɪzn] n Bürger(in) m(f); **~ship** n
Staatsbürgerschaft f

citrus fruit ['sɪtrəs-] n Zitrusfrucht f

city ['sɪtɪ] n Großstadt f; **the C~** die City, das
Finanzzentrum Londons

city technology college n ≃ Technische
Fachschule f

civic ['sɪvɪk] adj (of town) städtisch; (of citizen)
Bürger-; **~ centre** (BRIT) n Stadtverwaltung
f

civil ['sɪvɪl] adj bürgerlich; (not military) zivil;
(polite) höflich; **~ engineer** n Bauingenieur
m; **~ian** [sɪ'vɪlɪən] n Zivilperson f ♦ adj zivil,
Zivil-

civilization [sɪvɪlaɪ'zeɪʃən] n Zivilisation f

civilized ['sɪvɪlaɪzd] adj zivilisiert

civil: ~ law n Zivilrecht nt; **~ servant** n
Staatsbeamte(r) m; **C~ Service** n
Staatsdienst m; **~ war** n Bürgerkrieg m

clad [klæd] adj: **~ in** gehüllt in +acc

claim [kleɪm] vt beanspruchen; (have opinion)
behaupten ♦ vi (for insurance) Ansprüche
geltend machen ♦ n (demand) Forderung f;
(right) Anspruch m; (pretension) Behauptung
f; **~ant** n Antragsteller(in) m(f)

clairvoyant [klɛə'vɔɪənt] n Hellseher(in) m(f)

clam [klæm] n Venusmuschel f

clamber ['klæmbə'] vi kraxeln

clammy ['klæmɪ] adj klamm

clamour ['klæmə'] vi: **to ~ for sth** nach etw verlangen

clamp [klæmp] n Schraubzwinge f ♦ vt einspannen; (AUT: wheel) krallen; **~ down on** vt fus Maßnahmen ergreifen gegen

clan [klæn] n Clan m

clandestine [klæn'destɪn] adj geheim

clang [klæŋ] vi scheppern

clap [klæp] vi klatschen ♦ vt Beifall klatschen +dat ♦ n (of hands) Klatschen nt; (of thunder) Donnerschlag m; **~ping** n Klatschen nt

claret ['klærət] n rote(r) Bordeaux(wein) m

clarify ['klærɪfaɪ] vt klären, erklären

clarinet [klærɪ'net] n Klarinette f

clarity ['klærɪtɪ] n Klarheit f

clash [klæʃ] n (fig) Konflikt m ♦ vi zusammenprallen; (colours) sich beißen; (argue) sich streiten

clasp [klɑːsp] n Griff m; (on jewels, bag) Verschluss m ♦ vt umklammern

class [klɑːs] n Klasse f ♦ vt einordnen; **~-conscious** adj klassenbewusst

classic ['klæsɪk] n Klassiker m ♦ adj klassisch; **~al** adj klassisch

classified ['klæsɪfaɪd] adj (information) Geheim-; **~ advertisement** n Kleinanzeige f

classify ['klæsɪfaɪ] vt klassifizieren

classmate ['klɑːsmeɪt] n Klassenkamerad(in) m(f)

classroom ['klɑːsrum] n Klassenzimmer nt

clatter ['klætə'] n klappern; (feet) trappeln

clause [klɔːz] n (JUR) Klausel f; (GRAM) Satz m

claustrophobia [klɔːstrə'fəubɪə] n Platzangst f

claw [klɔː] n Kralle f ♦ vt (zer)kratzen

clay [kleɪ] n Lehm m; (for pots) Ton m

clean [kliːn] adj sauber ♦ vt putzen; (clothes) reinigen; **~ out** vt gründlich putzen; **~ up** vt aufräumen; **~-cut** adj (person) adrett; (clear) klar; **~er** n (person) Putzfrau f; **~er's** n (also: **dry ~er's**) Reinigung f; **~ing** n Putzen nt; (clothes) Reinigung f; **~liness** ['klenlɪnɪs] n Reinlichkeit f

cleanse [klenz] vt reinigen; **~r** n (for face) Reinigungsmilch f

clean-shaven ['kliːn'ʃeɪvn] adj glatt rasiert

cleansing department ['klenzɪŋ-] (BRIT) n Stadtreinigung f

clear [klɪə'] adj klar; (road) frei ♦ vt (road etc) freimachen; (obstacle) beseitigen; (JUR: suspect) freisprechen ♦ vi klar werden; (fog) sich lichten ♦ adv: **~ of** von ... entfernt; **to ~ the table** den Tisch abräumen; **~ up** vt aufräumen; (solve) aufklären; **~ance** ['klɪərəns] n (removal) Räumung f; (free space) Lichtung f; (permission) Freigabe f; **~-cut** adj (case) eindeutig; **~ing** n Lichtung f; **~ing bank** (BRIT) n Clearingbank f; **~ly** adv klar; (obviously) eindeutig; **~way** (BRIT) n (Straße f mit) Halteverbot nt

cleaver ['kliːvə'] n Hackbeil nt

cleft [kleft] n (in rock) Spalte f

clementine ['kleməntaɪn] n (fruit) Klementine f

clench [klentʃ] vt (teeth) zusammenbeißen; (fist) ballen

clergy ['klɜːdʒɪ] n Geistliche(n) pl; **~man** (irreg) n Geistliche(r) m

clerical ['klerɪkl] adj (office) Schreib-, Büro-; (REL) geistlich

clerk [klɑːk, (US) klɜːrk] n (in office) Büroangestellte(r) mf; (US: sales person) Verkäufer(in) m(f)

clever ['klevə'] adj klug; (crafty) schlau

cliché ['kliːʃeɪ] n Klischee nt

click [klɪk] vt (tongue) schnalzen mit; (heels) zusammenklappen

client ['klaɪənt] n Klient(in) m(f); **~ele** [kliːɑ̃ː'ntel] n Kundschaft f

cliff [klɪf] n Klippe f

climate ['klaɪmɪt] n Klima nt

climax ['klaɪmæks] n Höhepunkt m

climb [klaɪm] vt besteigen ♦ vi steigen, klettern ♦ n Aufstieg m; **~-down** n Abstieg m; **~er** n Bergsteiger(in) m(f); **~ing** n Bergsteigen nt

clinch [klɪntʃ] vt (decide) entscheiden; (deal) festmachen

cling [klɪŋ] (pt, pp **clung**) vi (clothes) eng anliegen; **to ~ to** sich festklammern an +dat

clinic ['klɪnɪk] n Klinik f; **~al** adj klinisch

clink [klɪŋk] *vi* klimpern

clip [klɪp] *n* Spange *f*; (*also:* **paper ~**) Klammer *f* ♦ *vt* (*papers*) heften; (*hair, hedge*) stutzen; **~pers** *npl* (*for hedge*) Heckenschere *f*; (*for hair*) Haarschneidemaschine *f*; **~ping** *n* Ausschnitt *m*

cloak [kləuk] *n* Umhang *m* ♦ *vt* hüllen; **~room** *n* (*for coats*) Garderobe *f*; (*BRIT: W.C.*) Toilette *f*

clock [klɔk] *n* Uhr *f*; **~ in** *or* **on** *vi* stempeln; **~ off** *or* **out** *vi* stempeln; **~wise** *adv* im Uhrzeigersinn; **~work** *n* Uhrwerk *nt* ♦ *adj* zum Aufziehen

clog [klɔg] *n* Holzschuh *m* ♦ *vt* verstopfen

cloister ['klɔɪstə*r*] *n* Kreuzgang *m*

clone [kləun] *n* Klon *m*

close¹ [kləus] *adj* (*near*) in der Nähe; (*friend, connection, print*) eng; (*relative*) nahe; (*result*) knapp; (*examination*) eingehend; (*weather*) schwül; (*room*) stickig ♦ *adv* nahe, dicht; **~ by** in der Nähe; **~ at hand** in der Nähe; **to have a ~ shave** (*fig*) mit knapper Not davonkommen

close² [kləuz] *vt* (*shut*) schließen; (*end*) beenden ♦ *vi* (*shop etc*) schließen; (*door etc*) sich schließen ♦ *n* Ende *nt*; **~ down** *vi* schließen; **~d** *adj* (*shop etc*) geschlossen; **~d shop** *n* Gewerkschaftszwang *m*

close-knit ['kləus'nɪt] *adj* eng zusammengewachsen

closely ['kləuslɪ] *adv* eng; (*carefully*) genau

closet ['klɔzɪt] *n* Schrank *m*

close-up ['kləusʌp] *n* Nahaufnahme *f*

closure ['kləuʒə*r*] *n* Schließung *f*

clot [klɔt] *n* (*of blood*) Blutgerinnsel *nt*; (*fool*) Blödmann *m* ♦ *vi* gerinnen

cloth [klɔθ] *n* (*material*) Tuch *nt*; (*rag*) Lappen *m*

clothe [kləuð] *vt* kleiden

clothes [kləuðz] *npl* Kleider *pl*; **~ brush** *n* Kleiderbürste *f*; **~ line** *n* Wäscheleine *f*; **~ peg**, **~ pin** (*US*) *n* Wäscheklammer *f*

clothing ['kləuðɪŋ] *n* Kleidung *f*

clotted cream ['klɔtɪd-] (*BRIT*) *n* Sahne aus erhitzter Milch

cloud [klaud] *n* Wolke *f*; **~burst** *n* Wolkenbruch *m*; **~y** *adj* bewölkt; (*liquid*) trüb

clout [klaut] *vt* hauen

clove [kləuv] *n* Gewürznelke *f*; **~ of garlic** Knoblauchzehe *f*

clover ['kləuvə*r*] *n* Klee *m*

clown [klaun] *n* Clown *m* ♦ *vi* (*also:* **~ about**, **~ around**) kaspern

cloying ['klɔɪɪŋ] *adj* (*taste, smell*) übersüß

club [klʌb] *n* (*weapon*) Knüppel *m*; (*society*) Klub *m*; (*also:* **golf ~**) Golfschläger *m* ♦ *vt* prügeln ♦ *vi:* **to ~ together** zusammenlegen; **~s** *npl* (*CARDS*) Kreuz *nt*; **~ car** (*US*) *n* (*RAIL*) Speisewagen *m*; **~ class** *n* (*AVIAT*) Club-Klasse *f*; **~house** *n* Klubhaus *nt*

cluck [klʌk] *vi* glucken

clue [klu:] *n* Anhaltspunkt *m*; (*in crosswords*) Frage *f*; **I haven't a ~** (ich hab) keine Ahnung

clump [klʌmp] *n* Gruppe *f*

clumsy ['klʌmzɪ] *adj* (*person*) unbeholfen; (*shape*) unförmig

clung [klʌŋ] *pt, pp of* **cling**

cluster ['klʌstə*r*] *n* (*of trees etc*) Gruppe *f* ♦ *vi* sich drängen, sich scharen

clutch [klʌtʃ] *n* Griff *m*; (*AUT*) Kupplung *f* ♦ *vt* sich festklammern an +*dat*

clutter ['klʌtə*r*] *vt* voll pfropfen; (*desk*) übersäen

CND *n abbr* = **Campaign for Nuclear Disarmament**

Co. *abbr* = **county; company**

c/o *abbr* (= *care of*) c/o

coach [kəutʃ] *n* (*bus*) Reisebus *m*; (*horse-drawn*) Kutsche *f*; (*RAIL*) (Personen)wagen *m*; (*trainer*) Trainer *m* ♦ *vt* (*SCH*) Nachhilfeunterricht geben +*dat*; (*SPORT*) trainieren; **~ trip** *n* Busfahrt *f*

coal [kəul] *n* Kohle *f*; **~ face** *n* Streb *m*

coalition [kəuə'lɪʃən] *n* Koalition *f*

coalman ['kəulmən] (*irreg*) *n* Kohlenhändler *m*

coal mine *n* Kohlenbergwerk *nt*

coarse [kɔ:s] *adj* grob; (*fig*) ordinär

coast [kəust] *n* Küste *f* ♦ *vi* dahinrollen; (*AUT*) im Leerlauf fahren; **~al** *adj* Küsten-;

~guard *n* Küstenwache *f*; **~line** *n* Küste(nlinie) *f*

coat [kəut] *n* Mantel *m*; (*on animals*) Fell *nt*; (*of paint*) Schicht *f* ♦ *vt* überstreichen; **~hanger** *n* Kleiderbügel *m*; **~ing** *n* Überzug *m*; (*of paint*) Schicht *f*; **~ of arms** *n* Wappen *nt*

coax [kəuks] *vt* beschwatzen

cob [kɔb] *n see* **corn**

cobbler ['kɔblə'] *n* Schuster *m*

cobbles ['kɔblz] *npl* Pflastersteine *pl*

cobweb ['kɔbweb] *n* Spinnennetz *nt*

cocaine [kə'keɪn] *n* Kokain *nt*

cock [kɔk] *n* Hahn *m* ♦ *vt* (*gun*) entsichern; **~erel** ['kɔkərl] *n* junge(r) Hahn *m*; **~eyed** *adj* (*fig*) verrückt

cockle ['kɔkl] *n* Herzmuschel *f*

cockney ['kɔknɪ] *n* echte(r) Londoner *m*

cockpit ['kɔkpɪt] *n* (*AVIAT*) Pilotenkanzel *f*

cockroach ['kɔkrəutʃ] *n* Küchenschabe *f*

cocktail ['kɔkteɪl] *n* Cocktail *m*; **~ cabinet** *n* Hausbar *f*; **~ party** *n* Cocktailparty *f*

cocoa ['kəukəu] *n* Kakao *m*

coconut ['kəukənʌt] *n* Kokosnuss *f*

cocoon [kə'ku:n] *n* Kokon *m*

cod [kɔd] *n* Kabeljau *m*

C.O.D. *abbr* = **cash on delivery**

code [kəud] *n* Kode *m*; (*JUR*) Kodex *m*

cod-liver oil ['kɔdlɪvə-] *n* Lebertran *m*

coercion [kəu'ɜ:ʃən] *n* Zwang *m*

coffee ['kɔfɪ] *n* Kaffee *m*; **~ bar** (*BRIT*) *n* Café *nt*; **~ bean** *n* Kaffeebohne *f*; **~ break** *n* Kaffeepause *f*; **~pot** *n* Kaffeekanne *f*; **~ table** *n* Couchtisch *m*

coffin ['kɔfɪn] *n* Sarg *m*

cog [kɔg] *n* (Rad)zahn *m*

cognac ['kɔnjæk] *n* Kognak *m*

coherent [kəu'hɪərənt] *adj* zusammenhängend; (*person*) verständlich

coil [kɔɪl] *n* Rolle *f*; (*ELEC*) Spule *f*; (*contraceptive*) Spirale *f* ♦ *vt* aufwickeln

coin [kɔɪn] *n* Münze *f* ♦ *vt* prägen; **~age** ['kɔɪnɪdʒ] *n* (*word*) Prägung *f*; **~ box** (*BRIT*) *n* Münzfernsprecher *m*

coincide [kəuɪn'saɪd] *vi* (*happen together*) zusammenfallen; (*agree*) übereinstimmen; **~nce** [kəu'ɪnsɪdəns] *n* Zufall *m*

coinphone ['kɔɪnfəun] *n* Münzfernsprecher *m*

Coke [kəuk] ® *n* (*drink*) Coca-Cola ® *f*

coke [kəuk] *n* Koks *m*

colander ['kɔləndə'] *n* Durchschlag *m*

cold [kəuld] *adj* kalt ♦ *n* Kälte *f*; (*MED*) Erkältung *f*; **I'm ~** mir ist kalt; **to catch ~** sich erkälten; **in ~ blood** kaltblütig; **to give sb the ~ shoulder** jdm die kalte Schulter zeigen; **~ly** *adv* kalt; **~-shoulder** *vt* die kalte Schulter zeigen +*dat*; **~ sore** *n* Erkältungsbläschen *nt*

coleslaw ['kəulslɔ:] *n* Krautsalat *m*

colic ['kɔlɪk] *n* Kolik *f*

collaborate [kə'læbəreɪt] *vi* zusammenarbeiten

collapse [kə'læps] *vi* (*people*) zusammenbrechen; (*things*) einstürzen ♦ *n* Zusammenbruch *m*; Einsturz *m*; **collapsible** *adj* zusammenklappbar, Klapp-

collar ['kɔlə'] *n* Kragen *m*; **~bone** *n* Schlüsselbein *nt*

collateral [kə'lætərl] *n* (zusätzliche) Sicherheit *f*

colleague ['kɔli:g] *n* Kollege *m*, Kollegin *f*

collect [kə'lekt] *vt* sammeln; (*BRIT: call and pick up*) abholen ♦ *vi* sich sammeln ♦ *adv*: **to call ~** (*US: TEL*) ein R-Gespräch führen; **~ion** [kə'lekʃən] *n* Sammlung *f*; (*REL*) Kollekte *f*; (*of post*) Leerung *f*; **~ive** [kə'lektɪv] *adj* gemeinsam; (*POL*) kollektiv; **~or** [kə'lektə'] *n* Sammler *m*; (*tax ~or*) (Steuer)einnehmer *m*

college ['kɔlɪdʒ] *n* (*UNIV*) College *nt*; (*TECH*) Fach-, Berufsschule *f*

collide [kə'laɪd] *vi* zusammenstoßen

collie ['kɔlɪ] *n* Collie *m*

colliery ['kɔlɪərɪ] (*BRIT*) *n* Zeche *f*

collision [kə'lɪʒən] *n* Zusammenstoß *m*

colloquial [kə'ləukwɪəl] *adj* umgangssprachlich

colon ['kəulən] *n* Doppelpunkt *m*; (*MED*) Dickdarm *m*

colonel ['kɜ:nl] *n* Oberst *m*

colonial [kə'ləunɪəl] *adj* Kolonial-

colonize ['kɔlənaɪz] *vt* kolonisieren

colony ['kɔlənɪ] n Kolonie f

colour ['kʌləʳ] (US **color**) n Farbe f ♦ vt (also fig) färben ♦ vi sich verfärben; **~s** npl (of club) Fahne f; **~ bar** n Rassenschranke f; **~-blind** adj farbenblind; **~ed** adj farbig; **~ film** n Farbfilm m; **~ful** adj bunt; (personality) schillernd; **~ing** n (complexion) Gesichtsfarbe f; (substance) Farbstoff m; **~ scheme** n Farbgebung f; **~ television** n Farbfernsehen nt

colt [kəult] n Fohlen nt

column ['kɔləm] n Säule f; (MIL) Kolonne f; (of print) Spalte f; **~ist** ['kɔləmnɪst] n Kolumnist m

coma ['kəumə] n Koma nt

comb [kəum] n Kamm m ♦ vt kämmen; (search) durchkämmen

combat ['kɔmbæt] n Kampf m ♦ vt bekämpfen

combination [kɔmbɪ'neɪʃən] n Kombination f

combine [vb kəm'baɪn, n 'kɔmbaɪn] vt verbinden ♦ vi sich vereinigen ♦ n (COMM) Konzern m; **~ (harvester)** n Mähdrescher m

combustion [kəm'bʌstʃən] n Verbrennung f

come [kʌm] (pt **came**, pp **come**) vi kommen; **to ~ undone** aufgehen; **~ about** vi geschehen; **~ across** vt fus (find) stoßen auf +acc; **~ away** vi (person) weggehen; (handle etc) abgehen; **~ back** vi zurückkommen; **~ by** vt fus (find): **to ~ by sth** zu etw kommen; **~ down** vi (price) fallen; **~ forward** vi (volunteer) sich melden; **~ from** vt fus (result) kommen von; **where do you ~ from?** wo kommen Sie her?; **I ~ from London** ich komme aus London; **~ in** vi hereinkommen; (train) einfahren; **~ in for** vt fus abkriegen; **~ into** vt fus (inherit) erben; **~ off** vi (handle) abgehen; (succeed) klappen; **~ on** vi (progress) vorankommen; **~ on!** komm!; (hurry) beeil dich!; **~ out** vi herauskommen; **~ round** vi (MED) wieder zu sich kommen; **~ to** vi (MED) wieder zu sich kommen ♦ vt fus (bill) sich belaufen auf +acc; **~ up** vi hochkommen; (sun)

aufgehen; (problem) auftauchen; **~ up against** vt fus (resistance, difficulties) stoßen auf +acc; **~ upon** vt fus stoßen auf +acc; **~ up with** vt fus sich einfallen lassen

comedian [kə'miːdɪən] n Komiker m; **comedienne** [kəmiː'dɪ'en] n Komikerin f

comedown ['kʌmdaun] n Abstieg m

comedy ['kɔmɪdɪ] n Komödie f

comet ['kɔmɪt] n Komet m

comeuppance [kʌm'ʌpəns] n: **to get one's ~** seine Quittung bekommen

comfort ['kʌmfət] n Komfort m; (consolation) Trost m ♦ vt trösten; **~able** adj bequem; **~ably** adv (sit etc) bequem; (live) angenehm; **~ station** (US) n öffentliche Toilette f

comic ['kɔmɪk] n Comic(heft) nt; (comedian) Komiker m ♦ adj (also: **~al**) komisch; **~ strip** n Comicstrip m

coming ['kʌmɪŋ] n Kommen nt; **~(s) and going(s)** n(pl) Kommen und Gehen nt

comma ['kɔmə] n Komma nt

command [kə'mɑːnd] n Befehl m; (control) Führung f; (MIL) Kommando nt; (mastery) Beherrschung f ♦ vt befehlen +dat; (MIL) kommandieren; (be able to get) verfügen über +acc; **~eer** [kɔmən'dɪəʳ] vt requirieren; **~er** n Kommandant m; **~ment** n (REL) Gebot nt

commando [kə'mɑːndəu] n Kommandotruppe nt; (person) Mitglied nt einer Kommandotruppe

commemorate [kə'meməreɪt] vt gedenken +gen

commence [kə'mens] vt, vi beginnen

commend [kə'mend] vt (recommend) empfehlen; (praise) loben

commensurate [kə'menʃərɪt] adj: **~ with sth** einer Sache dat entsprechend

comment ['kɔment] n Bemerkung f ♦ vi: **to ~ (on)** sich äußern (zu); **~ary** n Kommentar m; **~ator** n Kommentator m; (TV) Reporter(in) m(f)

commerce ['kɔmɜːs] n Handel m

commercial [kə'mɑːʃəl] adj kommerziell, geschäftlich; (training) kaufmännisch ♦ n (TV) Fernsehwerbung f; **~ break** n

Werbespot *m*; **~ize** *vt* kommerzialisieren

commiserate [kə'mɪzəreɪt] *vi*: **to ~ with** Mitleid haben mit

commission [kə'mɪʃən] *n* (*act*) Auftrag *m*; (*fee*) Provision *f*; (*body*) Kommission *f* ♦ *vt* beauftragen; (*MIL*) zum Offizier ernennen; (*work of art*) in Auftrag geben; **out of ~** außer Betrieb; **~er** *n* (*POLICE*) Polizeipräsident *m*

commit [kə'mɪt] *vt* (*crime*) begehen; (*entrust*) anvertrauen; **to ~ o.s.** sich festlegen; **~ment** *n* Verpflichtung *f*

committee [kə'mɪtɪ] *n* Ausschuss *m*

commodity [kə'mɔdɪtɪ] *n* Ware *f*

common ['kɔmən] *adj* (*cause*) gemeinsam; (*pej*) gewöhnlich; (*widespread*) üblich, häufig ♦ *n* Gemeindeland *nt*; **C~s** *npl* (*BRIT*): **the C~s** das Unterhaus; **~er** *n* Bürgerliche(r) *mf*; **~ law** *n* Gewohnheitsrecht *nt*; **~ly** *adv* gewöhnlich; **C~ Market** *n* Gemeinsame(r) Markt *m*; **~place** *adj* alltäglich; **~ room** *n* Gemeinschaftsraum *m*; **~ sense** *n* gesunde(r) Menschenverstand *m*; **C~wealth** *n*: **the C~wealth** das Commonwealth

commotion [kə'məuʃən] *n* Aufsehen *nt*

communal ['kɔmjuːnl] *adj* Gemeinde-; Gemeinschafts-

commune [*n* 'kɔmjuːn, *vb* kə'mjuːn] *n* Kommune *f* ♦ *vi*: **to ~ with** sich mitteilen +*dat*

communicate [kə'mjuːnɪkeɪt] *vt* (*transmit*) übertragen ♦ *vi* (*be in touch*) in Verbindung stehen; (*make self understood*) sich verständigen; **communication** [kəmjuːnɪ'keɪʃən] *n* (*message*) Mitteilung *f*; (*making understood*) Kommunikation *f*; **communication cord** (*BRIT*) *n* Notbremse *f*

communion [kə'mjuːnɪən] *n* (*also*: **Holy C~**) Abendmahl *nt*, Kommunion *f*

communism ['kɔmjunɪzəm] *n* Kommunismus *m*; **communist** ['kɔmjunɪst] *n* Kommunist(in) *m(f)* ♦ *adj* kommunistisch

community [kə'mjuːnɪtɪ] *n* Gemeinschaft *f*; **~ centre** *n* Gemeinschaftszentrum *nt*; **~**

chest (*US*) *n* Wohltätigkeitsfonds *m*; **~ home** (*BRIT*) *n* Erziehungsheim *nt*

commutation ticket [kɔmju'teɪʃən-] (*US*) *n* Zeitkarte *f*

commute [kə'mjuːt] *vi* pendeln ♦ *vt* umwandeln; **~r** *n* Pendler *m*

compact [*adj* kəm'pækt, *n* 'kɔmpækt] *adj* kompakt ♦ *n* (*for make-up*) Puderdose *f*; **~ disc** *n* Compactdisc *f*, Compact Disc *f*; **~ disc player** *n* CD-Spieler *m*

companion [kəm'pænjən] *n* Begleiter(in) *m(f)*; **~ship** *n* Gesellschaft *f*

company ['kʌmpənɪ] *n* Gesellschaft *f*; (*COMM*) Firma *f*, Gesellschaft *f*; **to keep sb ~** jdm Gesellschaft leisten; **~ secretary** (*BRIT*) *n* ≈ Prokurist(in) *m(f)*

comparable ['kɔmpərəbl] *adj* vergleichbar

comparative [kəm'pærətɪv] *adj* (*relative*) relativ; **~ly** *adv* verhältnismäßig

compare [kəm'pɛə*] *vt* vergleichen ♦ *vi* sich vergleichen lassen; **comparison** [kəm'pærɪsn] *n* Vergleich *m*; **in comparison (with)** im Vergleich (mit *or* zu)

compartment [kəm'pɑːtmənt] *n* (*RAIL*) Abteil *nt*; (*in drawer*) Fach *nt*

compass ['kʌmpəs] *n* Kompass *m*; **~es** *npl* (*MATH etc*: *also*: **pair of ~es**) Zirkel *m*

compassion [kəm'pæʃən] *n* Mitleid *nt*; **~ate** *adj* mitfühlend

compatible [kəm'pætɪbl] *adj* vereinbar; (*COMPUT*) kompatibel

compel [kəm'pɛl] *vt* zwingen

compensate ['kɔmpənseɪt] *vt* entschädigen ♦ *vi*: **to ~ for** Ersatz leisten für; **compensation** [kɔmpən'seɪʃən] *n* Entschädigung *f*

compère ['kɔmpɛə*] *n* Conférencier *m*

compete [kəm'piːt] *vi* (*take part*) teilnehmen; (*vie with*) konkurrieren

competent ['kɔmpɪtənt] *adj* kompetent

competition [kɔmpɪ'tɪʃən] *n* (*contest*) Wettbewerb *m*; (*COMM, rivalry*) Konkurrenz *f*; **competitive** [kəm'petɪtɪv] *adj* Konkurrenz-; (*COMM*) konkurrenzfähig; **competitor** [kəm'petɪtə*] *n* (*COMM*) Konkurrent(in) *m(f)*; (*participant*) Teilnehmer(in) *m(f)*

compile [kəm'paɪl] vt zusammenstellen

complacency [kəm'pleɪsnsɪ] n Selbstzufriedenheit f

complacent [kəm'pleɪsnt] adj selbstzufrieden

complain [kəm'pleɪn] vi sich beklagen; (formally) sich beschweren; ~t n Klage f; (formal ~t) Beschwerde f; (MED) Leiden nt

complement [n 'kɒmplɪmənt, vb 'kɒmplɪmɛnt] n Ergänzung f; (ship's crew etc) Bemannung f ♦ vt ergänzen; ~ary [kɒmplɪ'mɛntərɪ] adj (sich) ergänzend

complete [kəm'pli:t] adj (full) vollkommen, ganz; (finished) fertig ♦ vt vervollständigen; (finish) beenden; (fill in: form) ausfüllen; ~ly adv ganz; **completion** [kəm'pli:ʃən] n Fertigstellung f; (of contract etc) Abschluss m

complex ['kɒmplɛks] adj kompliziert

complexion [kəm'plɛkʃən] n Gesichtsfarbe f; (fig) Aspekt m

complexity [kəm'plɛksɪtɪ] n Kompliziertheit f

compliance [kəm'plaɪəns] n Fügsamkeit f, Einwilligung f; **in ~ with sth** einer Sache dat gemäß

complicate ['kɒmplɪkeɪt] vt komplizieren; ~d adj kompliziert; **complication** [kɒmplɪ'keɪʃən] n Komplikation f

compliment [n 'kɒmplɪmənt, vb 'kɒmplɪmɛnt] n Kompliment nt ♦ vt ein Kompliment machen +dat; ~s npl (greetings) Grüße pl; **to pay sb a ~** jdm ein Kompliment machen; ~ary [kɒmplɪ'mɛntərɪ] adj schmeichelhaft; (free) Frei-, Gratis-

comply [kəm'plaɪ] vi: **to ~ with** erfüllen +acc; entsprechen +dat

component [kəm'pəʊnənt] adj Teil- ♦ n Bestandteil m

compose [kəm'pəʊz] vt (music) komponieren; (poetry) verfassen; **to ~ o.s.** sich sammeln; ~d adj gefasst; ~r n Komponist(in) m(f); **composition** ['kɒmpə'zɪʃən] n (MUS) Komposition f; (SCH) Aufsatz m; (structure) Zusammensetzung f, Aufbau m

composure [kəm'pəʊʒər] n Fassung f

compound ['kɒmpaʊnd] n (CHEM) Verbindung f; (enclosure) Lager nt; (LING) Kompositum nt ♦ adj zusammengesetzt; (fracture) kompliziert; ~ **interest** n Zinseszins m

comprehend [kɒmprɪ'hɛnd] vt begreifen; **comprehension** n Verständnis nt

comprehensive [kɒmprɪ'hɛnsɪv] adj umfassend ♦ n = **comprehensive school;** ~ **insurance** n Vollkasko nt; ~ **school** (BRIT) n Gesamtschule f

compress [vb kəm'prɛs, n 'kɒmprɛs] vt komprimieren ♦ n (MED) Kompresse f

comprise [kəm'praɪz] vt (also: **be ~d of**) umfassen, bestehen aus

compromise ['kɒmprəmaɪz] n Kompromiss m ♦ vt kompromittieren ♦ vi einen Kompromiss schließen

compulsion [kəm'pʌlʃən] n Zwang m; **compulsive** [kəm'pʌlsɪv] adj zwanghaft; **compulsory** [kəm'pʌlsərɪ] adj obligatorisch

computer [kəm'pju:tər] n Computer m, Rechner m; ~ **game** n Computerspiel nt; ~-**generated** adj computergeneriert; ~ize vt (information) computerisieren; (company, accounts) auf Computer umstellen; ~ **programmer** n Programmierer(in) m(f); ~ **programming** n Programmieren nt; ~ **science** n Informatik f; **computing** [kəm'pju:tɪŋ] n (science) Informatik f; (work) Computerei f

comrade ['kɒmrɪd] n Kamerad m; (POL) Genosse m

con [kɒn] vt hereinlegen ♦ n Schwindel nt

concave ['kɒnkeɪv] adj konkav

conceal [kən'si:l] vt (secret) verschweigen; (hide) verbergen

concede [kən'si:d] vt (grant) gewähren; (point) zugeben ♦ vi (admit defeat) nachgeben

conceit [kən'si:t] n Einbildung f; ~ed adj eingebildet

conceivable [kən'si:vəbl] adj vorstellbar

conceive [kən'si:v] vt (of idea) ausdenken; (imagine) sich vorstellen; (baby) empfangen ♦ vi empfangen

concentrate ['kɒnsəntreɪt] vi sich konzentrieren ♦ vt konzentrieren; **to ~ on sth** sich auf etw acc konzentrieren;

concentration [kɔnsən'treɪʃən] n Konzentration f; **concentration camp** n Konzentrationslager nt, KZ nt

concept ['kɔnsept] n Begriff m

conception [kən'sepʃən] n (*idea*) Vorstellung f; (*BIOL*) Empfängnis f

concern [kən'sɜːn] n (*affair*) Angelegenheit f; (*COMM*) Unternehmen nt; (*worry*) Sorge f ♦ vt (*interest*) angehen; (*be about*) handeln von; (*have connection with*) betreffen; **to be ~ed (about)** sich Sorgen machen (um); **~ing** prep hinsichtlich +gen

concert ['kɔnsət] n Konzert nt

concerted [kən'sɜːtɪd] adj gemeinsam

concert hall n Konzerthalle f

concertina [kɔnsə'tiːnə] n Handharmonika f

concerto [kən'tʃɛːtəu] n Konzert nt

concession [kən'seʃən] n (*yielding*) Zugeständnis nt; **tax ~** Steuerkonzession f

conciliation [kənsɪlɪ'eɪʃən] n Versöhnung f; (*official*) Schlichtung f

concise [kən'saɪs] adj präzis

conclude [kən'kluːd] vt (*end*) beenden; (*treaty*) (ab)schließen; (*decide*) schließen, folgern; **conclusion** [kən'kluːʒən] n (Ab)schluss m; (*deduction*) Schluss m; **conclusive** [kən'kluːsɪv] adj schlüssig

concoct [kən'kɔkt] vt zusammenbrauen; **~ion** [kən'kɔkʃən] n Gebräu nt

concourse ['kɔŋkɔːs] n (Bahnhofs)halle f, Vorplatz m

concrete ['kɔŋkriːt] n Beton m ♦ adj konkret

concur [kən'kɜː] vi übereinstimmen

concurrently [kən'kʌrntlɪ] adv gleichzeitig

concussion [kən'kʌʃən] n (Gehirn)erschütterung f

condemn [kən'dem] vt (*JUR*) verurteilen; (*building*) abbruchreif erklären

condensation [kɔndən'seɪʃən] n Kondensation f

condense [kən'dens] vi (*CHEM*) kondensieren ♦ vt (*fig*) zusammendrängen; **~d milk** n Kondensmilch f

condescending [kɔndɪ'sendɪŋ] adj herablassend

condition [kən'dɪʃən] n (*state*) Zustand m; (*presupposition*) Bedingung f ♦ vt (*hair etc*)

behandeln; (*accustom*) gewöhnen; **~s** npl (*circumstances*) Verhältnisse pl; **on ~ that ...** unter der Bedingung, dass ...; **~al** adj bedingt; **~er** n (*for hair*) Spülung f; (*for fabrics*) Weichspüler m

condolences [kən'dəulənsɪz] npl Beileid nt

condom ['kɔndəm] n Kondom nt or m

condominium [kɔndə'mɪnɪəm] n (*US*) Eigentumswohnung f; (*block*) Eigentumsblock m

condone [kən'dəun] vt gutheißen

conducive [kən'djuːsɪv] adj: **~ to** dienlich +dat

conduct [n 'kɔndʌkt, vb kən'dʌkt] n (*behaviour*) Verhalten nt; (*management*) Führung f ♦ vt führen; (*MUS*) dirigieren; **~ed tour** n Führung f; **~or** [kən'dʌktə] n (*of orchestra*) Dirigent m; (*in bus, US*: on train) Schaffner m; (*ELEC*) Leiter m; **~ress** [kən'dʌktrɪs] n (*in bus*) Schaffnerin f

cone [kəun] n (*MATH*) Kegel m; (*for ice cream*) (Waffel)tüte f; (*BOT*) Tannenzapfen m

confectioner's (shop) [kən'fekʃənəz-] n Konditorei f; **~y** [kən'fekʃənrɪ] n Süßigkeiten pl

confederation [kənfedə'reɪʃən] n Bund m

confer [kən'fɜː] vt (*degree*) verleihen ♦ vi (*discuss*) konferieren, verhandeln; **~ence** ['kɔnfərəns] n Konferenz f

confess [kən'fes] vt, vi gestehen; (*ECCL*) beichten; **~ion** [kən'feʃən] n Geständnis nt; (*ECCL*) Beichte f; **~ional** n Beichtstuhl m

confide [kən'faɪd] vi: **to ~ in** (sich) anvertrauen +dat

confidence ['kɔnfɪdns] n Vertrauen nt; (*assurance*) Selbstvertrauen nt; (*secret*) Geheimnis nt; **in ~** (*speak, write*) vertraulich; **~ trick** n Schwindel m

confident ['kɔnfɪdənt] adj (*sure*) überzeugt; (*self-assured*) selbstsicher

confidential [kɔnfɪ'denʃəl] adj vertraulich

confine [kən'faɪn] vt (*limit*) beschränken; (*lock up*) einsperren; **~d** adj (*space*) eng; **~ment** n (*in prison*) Haft f; (*MED*) Wochenbett nt; **~s** ['kɔnfaɪnz] npl Grenzen pl

confirm [kən'fɜːm] vt bestätigen; **~ation**

[kɔnfə'meɪʃən] n Bestätigung f; (REL) Konfirmation f; **~ed** adj unverbesserlich; (bachelor) eingefleischt

confiscate ['kɔnfɪskeɪt] vt beschlagnahmen

conflict [n 'kɔnflɪkt, vb kən'flɪkt] n Konflikt m ♦ vi im Widerspruch stehen; **~ing** [kən'flɪktɪŋ] adj widersprüchlich

conform [kən'fɔːm] vi: **to ~ (to)** (things) entsprechen +dat; (people) sich anpassen +dat; (to rules) sich richten (nach)

confound [kən'faund] vt verblüffen; (confuse) durcheinander bringen

confront [kən'frʌnt] vt (enemy) entgegentreten +dat; (problems) sich stellen +dat; **to ~ sb with sth** jdn mit etw konfrontieren; **~ation** [kɔnfrən'teɪʃən] n Konfrontation f

confuse [kən'fjuːz] vt verwirren; (sth with sth) verwechseln; **~d** adj verwirrt; **confusing** adj verwirrend; **confusion** [kən'fjuːʒən] n (perplexity) Verwirrung f; (mixing up) Verwechslung f; (tumult) Aufruhr m

congeal [kən'dʒiːl] vi (freeze) gefrieren; (clot) gerinnen

congested [kən'dʒestɪd] adj überfüllt

congestion [kən'dʒestʃən] n Stau m

conglomerate [kən'glɔmərɪt] n (COMM, GEOL) Konglomerat nt

conglomeration [kənglɔmə'reɪʃən] n Anhäufung f

congratulate [kən'grætjuleɪt] vt: **to ~ sb (on sth)** jdn (zu etw) beglückwünschen; **congratulations** [kəngrætju'leɪʃənz] npl Glückwünsche pl; **congratulations!** gratuliere!, herzlichen Glückwunsch!

congregate ['kɔŋgrɪgeɪt] vi sich versammeln; **congregation** [kɔŋgrɪ'geɪʃən] n Gemeinde f

congress ['kɔŋgres] n Kongress m; **C~man** (irreg: US) n Mitglied nt des amerikanischen Repräsentantenhauses

conifer ['kɔnɪfər] n Nadelbaum m

conjunction [kən'dʒʌŋkʃən] n Verbindung f; (GRAM) Konjunktion f

conjunctivitis [kəndʒʌŋktɪ'vaɪtɪs] n Bindehautentzündung f

conjure ['kʌndʒər] vi zaubern; **~ up** vt heraufbeschwören; **~r** n Zauberkünstler(in) m(f)

conk out [kɔŋk-] (inf) vi den Geist aufgeben

con man (irreg) n Schwindler m

connect [kə'nekt] vt verbinden; (ELEC) anschließen; **to be ~ed with** eine Beziehung haben zu; (be related to) verwandt sein mit; **~ion** [kə'nekʃən] n Verbindung f; (relation) Zusammenhang m; (ELEC, TEL, RAIL) Anschluss m

connive [kə'naɪv] vi: **to ~ at** stillschweigend dulden

connoisseur [kɔnɪ'səːr] n Kenner m

conquer ['kɔŋkər] vt (feelings) überwinden; (enemy) besiegen; (country) erobern; **~or** n Eroberer m

conquest ['kɔŋkwest] n Eroberung f

cons [kɔnz] npl see **convenience**; **pro**

conscience ['kɔnʃəns] n Gewissen nt

conscientious [kɔnʃɪ'enʃəs] adj gewissenhaft

conscious ['kɔnʃəs] adj bewusst; (MED) bei Bewusstsein; **~ness** n Bewusstsein nt

conscript ['kɔnskrɪpt] n Wehrpflichtige(r) m; **~ion** [kən'skrɪpʃən] n Wehrpflicht f

consecutive [kən'sekjutɪv] adj aufeinander folgend

consensus [kən'sensəs] n allgemeine Übereinstimmung f

consent [kən'sent] n Zustimmung f ♦ vi zustimmen

consequence ['kɔnsɪkwəns] n (importance) Bedeutung f; (effect) Folge f

consequently ['kɔnsɪkwəntlɪ] adv folglich

conservation [kɔnsə'veɪʃən] n Erhaltung f; (nature ~) Umweltschutz m

conservative [kən'səːvətɪv] adj konservativ; **C~** (BRIT) adj konservativ ♦ n Konservative(r) mf

conservatory [kən'səːvətrɪ] n (room) Wintergarten m

conserve [kən'səːv] vt erhalten

consider [kən'sɪdər] vt überlegen; (take into account) in Betracht ziehen; (regard as) halten für; **to ~ doing sth** daran denken, etw zu tun; **~able** [kən'sɪdərəbl] adj beträchtlich; **~ably** *adv* beträchtlich; **~ate** *adj* rücksichtsvoll; **~ation** [kənsɪdəˈreɪʃən] *n* Rücksicht(nahme) *f*; (*thought*) Erwägung *f*; **~ing** *prep* in Anbetracht +*gen*

consign [kənˈsaɪn] *vt* übergeben; **~ment** *n* Sendung *f*

consist [kənˈsɪst] *vi*: **to ~ of** bestehen aus

consistency [kənˈsɪstənsɪ] *n* (*of material*) Konsistenz *f*; (*of argument, person*) Konsequenz *f*

consistent [kənˈsɪstənt] *adj* (*person*) konsequent; (*argument*) folgerichtig

consolation [kɒnsəˈleɪʃən] *n* Trost *m*

console[1] [kənˈsəul] *vt* trösten

console[2] [ˈkɒnsəul] *n* Kontroll(pult) *nt*

consolidate [kənˈsɒlɪdeɪt] *vt* festigen

consommé [kɒnˈsɒmeɪ] *n* Fleischbrühe *f*

consonant [ˈkɒnsənənt] *n* Konsonant *m*, Mitlaut *m*

conspicuous [kənˈspɪkjuəs] *adj* (*prominent*) auffällig; (*visible*) deutlich sichtbar

conspiracy [kənˈspɪrəsɪ] *n* Verschwörung *f*

conspire [kənˈspaɪəʳ] *vi* sich verschwören

constable [ˈkʌnstəbl] (*BRIT*) *n* Polizist(in) *m(f)*; **chief ~** Polizeipräsident *m*; **constabulary** [kənˈstæbjulərɪ] *n* Polizei *f*

constant [ˈkɒnstənt] *adj* (*continuous*) ständig; (*unchanging*) konstant; **~ly** *adv* ständig

constellation [kɒnstəˈleɪʃən] *n* Sternbild *nt*

consternation [kɒnstəˈneɪʃən] *n* Bestürzung *f*

constipated [ˈkɒnstɪpeɪtɪd] *adj* verstopft; **constipation** [kɒnstɪˈpeɪʃən] *n* Verstopfung *f*

constituency [kənˈstɪtjuənsɪ] *n* Wahlkreis *m*

constituent [kənˈstɪtjuənt] *n* (*person*) Wähler *m*; (*part*) Bestandteil *m*

constitute [ˈkɒnstɪtjuːt] *vt* (*make up*) bilden; (*amount to*) darstellen

constitution [kɒnstɪˈtjuːʃən] *n* Verfassung *f*; **~al** *adj* Verfassungs-

constraint [kənˈstreɪnt] *n* Zwang *m*; (*shyness*) Befangenheit *f*

construct [kənˈstrʌkt] *vt* bauen; **~ion** [kənˈstrʌkʃən] *n* Konstruktion *f*; (*building*) Bau *m*; **~ive** *adj* konstruktiv

construe [kənˈstruː] *vt* deuten

consul [ˈkɒnsl] *n* Konsul *m*; **~ate** *n* Konsulat *nt*

consult [kənˈsʌlt] *vt* um Rat fragen; (*doctor*) konsultieren; (*book*) nachschlagen in +*dat*; **~ant** *n* (*MED*) Facharzt *m*; (*other specialist*) Gutachter *m*; **~ation** [kɒnsəlˈteɪʃən] *n* Beratung *f*; (*MED*) Konsultation *f*; **~ing room** *n* Sprechzimmer *nt*

consume [kənˈsjuːm] *vt* verbrauchen; (*food*) konsumieren; **~r** *n* Verbraucher *m*; **~r goods** *npl* Konsumgüter *pl*; **~rism** *n* Konsum *m*; **~r society** *n* Konsumgesellschaft *f*

consummate [ˈkɒnsʌmeɪt] *vt* (*marriage*) vollziehen

consumption [kənˈsʌmpʃən] *n* Verbrauch *m*; (*of food*) Konsum *m*

cont. *abbr* (= *continued*) Forts.

contact [ˈkɒntækt] *n* (*touch*) Berührung *f*; (*connection*) Verbindung *f*; (*person*) Kontakt *m* ♦ *vt* sich in Verbindung setzen mit; **~ lenses** *npl* Kontaktlinsen *pl*

contagious [kənˈteɪdʒəs] *adj* ansteckend

contain [kənˈteɪn] *vt* enthalten; **to ~ o.s.** sich zügeln; **~er** *n* Behälter *m*; (*transport*) Container *m*

contaminate [kənˈtæmɪneɪt] *vt* verunreinigen

cont'd *abbr* (= *continued*) Forts.

contemplate [ˈkɒntəmpleɪt] *vt* (*look at*) (nachdenklich) betrachten; (*think about*) überdenken; (*plan*) vorhaben

contemporary [kənˈtɛmpərərɪ] *adj* zeitgenössisch ♦ *n* Zeitgenosse *m*

contempt [kənˈtɛmpt] *n* Verachtung *f*; **~ of court** (*JUR*) Missachtung *f* des Gerichts; **~ible** *adj* verachtenswert; **~uous** *adj* verächtlich

contend [kənˈtɛnd] *vt* (*argue*) behaupten ♦ *vi* kämpfen; **~er** *n* (*for post*) Bewerber(in) *m(f)*; (*SPORT*) Wettkämpfer(in) *m(f)*

content [*adj, vb* kənˈtɛnt, *n* ˈkɒntɛnt] *adj* zufrieden ♦ *vt* befriedigen ♦ *n* (*also:* **~s**) Inhalt *m*; **~ed** *adj* zufrieden

contention [kənˈtɛnʃən] *n* (*dispute*) Streit *m*; (*argument*) Behauptung *f*

contentment [kənˈtɛntmənt] *n* Zufriedenheit f

contest [n 'kɔntest, vb kən'test] n
(Wett)kampf m ♦ vt (dispute) bestreiten;
(JUR) anfechten; (POL) kandidieren in +dat;
~ant [kən'testənt] n Bewerber(in) m(f)

context ['kɔntekst] n Zusammenhang m

continent ['kɔntinənt] n Kontinent m; **the
C~** (BRIT) das europäische Festland; ~al
[kɔntɪ'nentl] adj kontinental; ~al breakfast
n kleines Frühstück nt; ~al quilt (BRIT) n
Federbett nt

contingency [kən'tɪndʒənsɪ] n Möglichkeit f

contingent [kən'tɪndʒənt] n Kontingent nt

continual [kən'tɪnjuəl] adj (endless)
fortwährend; (repeated) immer
wiederkehrend; ~ly adv immer wieder

continuation [kəntɪnju'eɪʃən] n Fortsetzung
f

continue [kən'tɪnju:] vi (person)
weitermachen; (thing) weitergehen ♦ vt
fortsetzen

continuity [kɔntɪ'nju:ɪtɪ] n Kontinuität f

continuous [kən'tɪnjuəs] adj
ununterbrochen; ~ **stationery** n
Endlospapier nt

contort [kən'tɔ:t] vt verdrehen; ~ion
[kən'tɔ:ʃən] n Verzerrung f

contour ['kɔntuər] n Umriss m; (also: ~ **line**)
Höhenlinie f

contraband ['kɔntrəbænd] n
Schmuggelware f

contraception [kɔntrə'sepʃən] n
Empfängnisverhütung f

contraceptive [kɔntrə'septɪv] n
empfängnisverhütende(s) Mittel nt ♦ adj
empfängnisverhütend

contract [n 'kɔntrækt, vb kən'trækt] n Vertrag
m ♦ vi (muscle, metal) sich zusammenziehen
♦ vt zusammenziehen; **to ~ to do sth**
(COMM) sich vertraglich verpflichten, etw zu
tun; ~ion [kən'trækʃən] n (shortening)
Verkürzung f; ~or [kən'træktər] n
Unternehmer m

contradict [kɔntrə'dɪkt] vt widersprechen
+dat; ~ion [kɔntrə'dɪkʃən] n Widerspruch m

contraflow ['kɔntrəfləu] n (AUT)
Gegenverkehr m

contraption [kən'træpʃən] (inf) n Apparat m

contrary¹ ['kɔntrərɪ] adj (opposite)
entgegengesetzt ♦ n Gegenteil nt; **on the ~**
im Gegenteil

contrary² [kən'treərɪ] adj (obstinate)
widerspenstig

contrast [n 'kɔntrɑ:st, vb kən'trɑ:st] n
Kontrast m ♦ vt entgegensetzen; ~ing
[kən'trɑ:stɪŋ] adj Kontrast-

contravene [kɔntrə'vi:n] vt verstoßen
gegen

contribute [kən'trɪbju:t] vt, vi: **to ~ to**
beitragen zu; **contribution** [kɔntrɪ'bju:ʃən]
n Beitrag m; **contributor** [kən'trɪbjutər] n
Beitragende(r) f(m)

contrive [kən'traɪv] vt ersinnen ♦ vi: **to ~ to
do sth** es schaffen, etw zu tun

control [kən'trəul] vt (direct, test)
kontrollieren ♦ n Kontrolle f; ~s npl (of
vehicle) Steuerung f; (of engine) Schalttafel f;
to be in ~ of (business, office) leiten; (group
of children) beaufsichtigen; **out of ~** außer
Kontrolle; **under ~** unter Kontrolle; ~led
substance n verschreibungspflichtiges
Medikament; ~ **panel** n Schalttafel f; ~
room n Kontrollraum m; ~ **tower** n (AVIAT)
Kontrollturm m

controversial [kɔntrə'və:ʃl] adj umstritten;
controversy ['kɔntrəvə:sɪ] n Kontroverse f

conurbation [kɔnə'beɪʃən] n Ballungsgebiet
nt

convalesce [kɔnvə'les] vi genesen;
convalescence [kɔnvə'lesns] n Genesung f

convector [kən'vektər] n Heizlüfter m

convene [kən'vi:n] vt zusammenrufen ♦ vi
sich versammeln

convenience [kən'vi:nɪəns] n
Annehmlichkeit f; **all modern ~s** or (BRIT)
mod cons mit allem Komfort; **at your ~**
wann es Ihnen passt

convenient [kən'vi:nɪənt] adj günstig

convent ['kɔnvənt] n Kloster nt

convention [kən'venʃən] n Versammlung f;
(custom) Konvention f; ~al adj
konventionell

convent school n Klosterschule f

converge [kən'və:dʒ] vi zusammenlaufen

conversant [kən'vɜːsnt] *adj*: **to be ~ with** bewandert sein in +*dat*

conversation [kɔnvə'seɪʃən] *n* Gespräch *nt*; **~al** *adj* Unterhaltungs-

converse [*n* 'kɔnvɜːs, *vb* kən'vɜːs] *n* Gegenteil *nt* ♦ *vi* sich unterhalten

conversion [kən'vɜːʃən] *n* Umwandlung *f*; (REL) Bekehrung *f*

convert [*vb* kən'vɜːt, *n* 'kɔnvɜːt] *vt* (*change*) umwandeln; (REL) bekehren ♦ *n* Bekehrte(r) *mf*; Konvertit(in) *m(f)*; **~ible** *n* (AUT) Kabriolett *nt* ♦ *adj* umwandelbar; (FIN) konvertierbar

convex ['kɔnvɛks] *adj* konvex

convey [kən'veɪ] *vt* (*carry*) befördern; (*feelings*) vermitteln; **~or belt** *n* Fließband *nt*

convict [*vb* kən'vɪkt, *n* 'kɔnvɪkt] *vt* verurteilen ♦ *n* Häftling *m*; **~ion** [kən'vɪkʃən] *n* (*verdict*) Verurteilung *f*; (*belief*) Überzeugung *f*

convince [kən'vɪns] *vt* überzeugen; **~d** *adj*: **~d that** überzeugt davon, dass; **convincing** *adj* überzeugend

convoluted ['kɔnvəluːtɪd] *adj* verwickelt; (*style*) gewunden

convoy ['kɔnvɔɪ] *n* (*of vehicles*) Kolonne *f*; (*protected*) Konvoi *m*

convulse [kən'vʌls] *vt* zusammenzucken lassen; **to be ~d with laughter** sich vor Lachen krümmen; **convulsion** [kən'vʌlʃən] *n* (*esp MED*) Zuckung *f*, Krampf *m*

coo [kuː] *vi* gurren

cook [kuk] *vt*, *vi* kochen ♦ *n* Koch *m*, Köchin *f*; **~ book** *n* Kochbuch *nt*; **~er** *n* Herd *m*; **~ery** *n* Kochkunst *f*; **~ery book** (BRIT) *n* = **cook book**; **~ie** (US) *n* Plätzchen *nt*; **~ing** *n* Kochen *nt*

cool [kuːl] *adj* kühl ♦ *vt*, *vi* (ab)kühlen; **~ down** *vt*, *vi* (*fig*) (sich) beruhigen; **~ness** *n* Kühle *f*; (*of temperament*) kühle(r) Kopf *m*

coop [kuːp] *n* Hühnerstall *m* ♦ *vt*: **~ up** (*fig*) einpferchen

cooperate [kəu'ɔpəreɪt] *vi* zusammenarbeiten; **cooperation** [kəuɔpə'reɪʃən] *n* Zusammenarbeit *f*

cooperative [kəu'ɔpərətɪv] *adj* hilfsbereit; (COMM) genossenschaftlich ♦ *n* (*of farmers*) Genossenschaft *f*; (~ *store*) Konsumladen *m*

coordinate [*vb* kəu'ɔːdɪneɪt, *n* kəu'ɔːdɪnət] *vt* koordinieren ♦ *n* (MATH) Koordinate *f*; **~s** *npl* (*clothes*) Kombinationen *pl*; **coordination** [kəuɔːdɪ'neɪʃən] *n* Koordination *f*

cop [kɔp] *(inf)* *n* Polyp *m*, Bulle *m*

cope [kəup] *vi*: **to ~ with** fertig werden mit

copious ['kəupɪəs] *adj* reichhaltig

copper ['kɔpə'] *n* (*metal*) Kupfer *nt*; (*inf*: *policeman*) Polyp *m*, Bulle *m*; **~s** *npl* (*money*) Kleingeld *nt*

copse [kɔps] *n* Unterholz *nt*

copy ['kɔpɪ] *n* (*imitation*) Kopie *f*; (*of book etc*) Exemplar *nt*; (*of newspaper*) Nummer *f* ♦ *vt* kopieren, abschreiben; **~right** *n* Copyright *nt*

coral ['kɔrəl] *n* Koralle *f*; **~ reef** *n* Korallenriff *nt*

cord [kɔːd] *n* Schnur *f*; (ELEC) Kabel *nt*

cordial ['kɔːdɪəl] *adj* herzlich ♦ *n* Fruchtsaft *m*

cordon ['kɔːdn] *n* Absperrkette *f*; **~ off** *vt* abriegeln

corduroy ['kɔːdərɔɪ] *n* Kord(samt) *m*

core [kɔːʳ] *n* Kern *m* ♦ *vt* entkernen

cork [kɔːk] *n* (*bark*) Korkrinde *f*; (*stopper*) Korken *m*; **~screw** *n* Korkenzieher *m*

corn [kɔːn] *n* (BRIT: *wheat*) Getreide *nt*, Korn *nt*; (*US*: *maize*) Mais *m*; (*on foot*) Hühnerauge *nt*; **~ on the cob** Maiskolben *m*

corned beef ['kɔːnd-] *n* Cornedbeef *nt*, Corned Beef *nt*

corner ['kɔːnəʳ] *n* Ecke *f*; (*on road*) Kurve *f* ♦ *vt* in die Enge treiben; (*market*) monopolisieren ♦ *vi* (AUT) in die Kurve gehen; **~stone** *n* Eckstein *m*

cornet ['kɔːnɪt] *n* (MUS) Kornett *nt*; (BRIT: *of ice cream*) Eistüte *f*

corn: ~flakes ['kɔːnfleɪks] *npl* Cornflakes *pl* ®; **~flour** ['kɔːnflauəʳ] (BRIT) *n* Maizena *nt* ®; **~starch** ['kɔːnstɑːtʃ] (US) *n* Maizena *nt* ®

corny ['kɔːnɪ] *adj* (*joke*) blöd(e)

coronary ['kɔrənərɪ] *n* (*also*: **~ thrombosis**) Herzinfarkt *m*

coronation [kɔrə'neɪʃən] n Krönung f
coroner ['kɔrənəʳ] n Untersuchungsrichter m
corporal ['kɔːpərl] n Obergefreite(r) m ♦ adj:
~ **punishment** Prügelstrafe f
corporate ['kɔːpərɪt] adj gemeinschaftlich,
korporativ
corporation [kɔːpə'reɪʃən] n (of town)
Gemeinde f; (COMM) Körperschaft f,
Aktiengesellschaft f
corps [kɔːʳ] (pl ~) n (Armee)korps nt
corpse [kɔːps] n Leiche f
corral [kə'rɑːl] n Pferch m, Korral m
correct [kə'rekt] adj (accurate) richtig;
(proper) korrekt ♦ vt korrigieren; ~**ion**
[kə'rekʃən] n Berichtigung f
correlation [kɔrɪ'leɪʃən] n
Wechselbeziehung f
correspond [kɔrɪs'pɔnd] vi (agree)
übereinstimmen; (exchange letters)
korrespondieren; ~**ence** n (similarity)
Entsprechung f; (letters) Briefwechsel m,
Korrespondenz f; ~**ence course** n
Fernkurs m; ~**ent** n (PRESS) Berichterstatter
m
corridor ['kɔrɪdɔːʳ] n Gang m
corroborate [kə'rɔbəreɪt] vt bestätigen
corrode [kə'rəud] vt zerfressen ♦ vi rosten
corrosion [kə'rəuʒən] n Korrosion f
corrugated ['kɔrəgeɪtɪd] adj gewellt; ~ **iron**
n Wellblech nt
corrupt [kə'rʌpt] adj korrupt ♦ vt verderben;
(bribe) bestechen; ~**ion** [kə'rʌpʃən] n
Verdorbenheit f; (bribery) Bestechung f
corset ['kɔːsɪt] n Korsett nt
Corsica ['kɔːsɪkə] n Korsika nt
cosmetics [kɔz'metɪks] npl Kosmetika pl
cosmic ['kɔzmɪk] adj kosmisch
cosmonaut ['kɔzmənɔːt] n Kosmonaut(in)
m(f)
cosmopolitan [kɔzmə'pɔlɪtn] adj
international; (city) Welt-
cosmos ['kɔzmɔs] n Kosmos m
cost [kɔst] (pt, pp **cost**) n Kosten pl, Preis m
♦ vt, vi kosten; ~**s** npl (JUR) Kosten pl; **how
much does it ~?** wie viel kostet das?; **at all
~s** um jeden Preis
co-star ['kəustɑːʳ] n zweite(r) or weitere(r)

Hauptdarsteller(in) m(f)
cost: ~-effective adj rentabel; **~ly** ['kɔstlɪ]
adj kostspielig; **~-of-living** ['kɔstəv'lɪvɪŋ]
adj (index) Lebenshaltungskosten-; ~ **price**
(BRIT) n Selbstkostenpreis m
costume ['kɔstjuːm] n Kostüm nt; (fancy
dress) Maskenkostüm nt; (BRIT: also:
swimming ~) Badeanzug m; ~ **jewellery**
n Modeschmuck m
cosy ['kəuzɪ] (BRIT) adj behaglich;
(atmosphere) gemütlich
cot [kɔt] n (BRIT: child's) Kinderbett(chen) nt;
(US: camp bed) Feldbett nt
cottage ['kɔtɪdʒ] n kleine(s) Haus nt; ~
cheese n Hüttenkäse m; ~ **industry** n
Heimindustrie f; ~ **pie** n Auflauf mit
Hackfleisch und Kartoffelbrei
cotton ['kɔtn] n Baumwolle f; (thread) Garn
nt; ~ **on to** (inf) vt kapieren; ~ **candy** (US)
n Zuckerwatte f; ~ **wool** (BRIT) n Watte f
couch [kautʃ] n Couch f
couchette [kuː'ʃet] n (on train, boat)
Liegewagenplatz m
cough [kɔf] vi husten ♦ n Husten m; ~ **drop**
n Hustenbonbon nt
could [kud] pt of **can**[2]
couldn't ['kudnt] = **could not**
council ['kaunsl] n (of town) Stadtrat m; ~
estate (BRIT) n Siedlung f des sozialen
Wohnungsbaus; ~ **house** (BRIT) n Haus nt
des sozialen Wohnungsbaus, ~**lor**
['kaunsləʳ] n Stadtrat m/-rätin f
counsel ['kaunsl] n (barrister) Anwalt m;
(advice) Rat(schlag) m ♦ vt beraten; ~**lor**
['kaunsləʳ] n Berater m
count [kaunt] vt, vi zählen ♦ n (reckoning)
Abrechnung f; (nobleman) Graf m; ~ **on** vt
zählen auf +acc
countenance ['kauntɪnəns] n (old) Antlitz nt
♦ vt (tolerate) gutheißen
counter ['kauntəʳ] n (in shop) Ladentisch m;
(in café) Theke f; (in bank, post office)
Schalter m ♦ vt entgegnen
counteract ['kauntər'ækt] vt
entgegenwirken +dat
counterfeit ['kauntəfɪt] n Fälschung f ♦ vt
fälschen ♦ adj gefälscht

counterfoil ['kauntəfɔɪl] n (Kontroll)abschnitt m

counterpart ['kauntəpɑːt] n (object) Gegenstück nt; (person) Gegenüber nt

counterproductive ['kauntəprə'dʌktɪv] adj destruktiv

countersign ['kauntəsaɪn] vt gegenzeichnen

countess ['kauntɪs] n Gräfin f

countless ['kauntlɪs] adj zahllos, unzählig

country ['kʌntrɪ] n Land nt; ~ **dancing** (BRIT) n Volkstanz m; ~ **house** n Landhaus nt; ~**man** (irreg) n (national) Landsmann m; (rural) Bauer m; ~**side** n Landschaft f

county ['kauntɪ] n Landkreis m; (BRIT) Grafschaft f

coup [kuː] (pl ~s) n Coup m; (also: ~ d'état) Staatsstreich m, Putsch m

couple ['kʌpl] n Paar nt ♦ vt koppeln; **a ~ of** ein paar

coupon ['kuːpɔn] n Gutschein m

coups [kuː] npl of **coup**

courage ['kʌrɪdʒ] n Mut m; ~**ous** [kə'reɪdʒəs] adj mutig

courgette [kuə'ʒet] (BRIT) n Zucchini f or pl

courier ['kurɪə] n (for holiday) Reiseleiter m; (messenger) Kurier m

course [kɔːs] n (race) Bahn f; (of stream) Lauf m; (golf ~) Platz m; (NAUT, SCH) Kurs m; (in meal) Gang m; **of** ~ natürlich

court [kɔːt] n (royal) Hof m; (JUR) Gericht nt ♦ vt (woman) gehen mit; (danger) herausfordern; **to take to** ~ vor Gericht bringen

courteous ['kəːtɪəs] adj höflich

courtesy ['kəːtəsɪ] n Höflichkeit f

courtesy bus, courtesy coach n gebührenfreier Bus m

court: ~ **house** (US) n Gerichtsgebäude nt; ~**ier** ['kɔːtɪə] n Höfling m; ~ **martial** ['kɔːt'mɑːʃəl] (pl ~**s martial**) n Kriegsgericht nt ♦ vt vor ein Kriegsgericht stellen; ~**room** n Gerichtssaal m; ~**s martial** npl of **court martial**; ~**yard** ['kɔːtjɑːd] n Hof m

cousin ['kʌzn] n Cousin m, Vetter m; Kusine f

cove [kəuv] n kleine Bucht f

covenant ['kʌvənənt] n (ECCL) Bund m; (JUR) Verpflichtung f

cover ['kʌvə] vt (spread over) bedecken; (shield) abschirmen; (include) sich erstrecken über +acc; (protect) decken; (distance) zurücklegen; (report on) berichten über +acc ♦ n (lid) Deckel m; (for bed) Decke f; (MIL) Bedeckung f; (of book) Einband m; (of magazine) Umschlag m; (insurance) Versicherung f; **to take** ~ (from rain) sich unterstellen; (MIL) in Deckung gehen; **under** ~ (indoors) drinnen; **under** ~ **of** im Schutze +gen; **under separate** ~ (COMM) mit getrennter Post; **to** ~ **up for sb** jdn decken; ~**age** n (PRESS: reports) Berichterstattung f; (distribution) Verbreitung f; ~ **charge** n Bedienungsgeld nt; ~**ing** n Bedeckung f; ~**ing letter** (US ~ **letter**) n Begleitbrief m; ~ **note** n (INSURANCE) vorläufige(r) Versicherungsschein m

covert ['kʌvət] adj geheim

cover-up ['kʌvərʌp] n Vertuschung f

cow [kau] n Kuh f ♦ vt einschüchtern

coward ['kauəd] n Feigling m; ~**ice** ['kauədɪs] n Feigheit f; ~**ly** adj feige

cower ['kauə] vi kauern

coy [kɔɪ] adj schüchtern

coyote [kɔɪ'əutɪ] n Präriewolf m

cozy ['kəuzɪ] (US) adj = **cosy**

CPA (US) n abbr = **certified public accountant**

crab [kræb] n Krebs m

crab apple n Holzapfel m

crack [kræk] n Riss m, Sprung m; (noise) Knall m; (drug) Crack nt ♦ vt (break) springen lassen; (joke) reißen; (nut, safe) knacken; (whip) knallen lassen ♦ vi springen ♦ adj erstklassig; (troops) Elite-; ~ **down** vi: **to** ~ **down (on)** hart durchgreifen (bei); ~ **up** vi (fig) zusammenbrechen

cracked [krækt] adj (glass, plate, ice) gesprungen; (rib, bone) gebrochen, angeknackst (umg); (broken) gebrochen; (surface, walls) rissig; (inf: mad) übergeschnappt

cracker ['krækə] n (firework) Knallkörper m, Kracher m; (biscuit) Keks m; (Christmas ~)

Knallbonbon nt

crackle ['krækl] vi knistern; (fire) prasseln

cradle ['kreidl] n Wiege f

craft [krɑːft] n (skill) (Hand- or Kunst)fertigkeit f; (trade) Handwerk nt; (NAUT) Schiff nt; ~sman (irreg) n Handwerker m; ~smanship n (quality) handwerkliche Ausführung f; (ability) handwerkliche(s) Können nt

crafty ['krɑːftɪ] adj schlau

crag [kræg] n Klippe f

cram [kræm] vt voll stopfen ♦ vi (learn) pauken; **to ~ sth into sth** etw in etw acc stopfen

cramp [kræmp] n Krampf m ♦ vt (limit) einengen; (hinder) hemmen; ~ed adj (position) verkrampft; (space) eng

crampon ['kræmpən] n Steigeisen nt

cranberry ['krænbərɪ] n Preiselbeere f

crane [kreɪn] n (machine) Kran m; (bird) Kranich m

crank [kræŋk] n (lever) Kurbel f; (person) Spinner m; ~shaft n Kurbelwelle f

cranny ['krænɪ] n see **nook**

crash [kræʃ] n (noise) Krachen nt; (with cars) Zusammenstoß m; (with plane) Absturz m; (COMM) Zusammenbruch m ♦ vt (plane) abstürzen mit ♦ vi (cars) zusammenstoßen; (plane) abstürzen; (economy) zusammenbrechen; (noise) knallen; ~ **course** n Schnellkurs m; ~ **helmet** n Sturzhelm m; ~ **landing** n Bruchlandung f

crass [kræs] adj krass

crate [kreit] n (also fig) Kiste f

crater ['kreitər] n Krater m

cravat(e) [krəˈvæt] n Halstuch nt

crave [kreiv] vt verlangen nach

crawl [krɔːl] vi kriechen; (baby) krabbeln ♦ n Kriechen nt; (swim) Kraul m

crayfish ['kreɪfɪʃ] n inv (freshwater) Krebs m; (saltwater) Languste f

crayon ['kreiən] n Buntstift m

craze [kreiz] n Fimmel m

crazy ['kreizɪ] adj verrückt

creak [kriːk] vi knarren

cream [kriːm] n (from milk) Rahm m, Sahne f; (polish, cosmetic) Creme f; (fig: people)

Elite f ♦ adj cremefarbig; ~ **cake** n Sahnetorte f; ~ **cheese** n Rahmquark m; ~**y** adj sahnig

crease [kriːs] n Falte f ♦ vt falten; (wrinkle) zerknittern ♦ vi (wrinkle up) knittern; ~**d** adj zerknittert, faltig

create [kriːˈeɪt] vt erschaffen; (cause) verursachen; **creation** [kriːˈeɪʃən] n Schöpfung f; **creative** adj kreativ; **creator** n Schöpfer m

creature ['kriːtʃər] n Geschöpf nt

crèche [krɛʃ] n Krippe f

credence ['kriːdns] n: **to lend** or **give ~ to sth** etw dat Glauben schenken

credentials [krɪˈdɛnʃlz] npl Beglaubigungsschreiben nt

credibility [krɛdɪˈbɪlɪtɪ] n Glaubwürdigkeit f

credible ['krɛdɪbl] adj (person) glaubwürdig; (story) glaubhaft

credit ['krɛdɪt] n (also COMM) Kredit m ♦ vt Glauben schenken +dat; (COMM) gutschreiben; ~**s** npl (of film) Mitwirkenden pl; ~**able** adj rühmlich; ~ **card** n Kreditkarte f; ~**or** n Gläubiger m

creed [kriːd] n Glaubensbekenntnis nt

creek [kriːk] n (inlet) kleine Bucht f; (US: river) kleine(r) Wasserlauf m

creep [kriːp] (pt, pp **crept**) vi kriechen; ~**er** n Kletterpflanze f; ~**y** adj (frightening) gruselig

cremate [krɪˈmeɪt] vt einäschern; **cremation** [krɪˈmeɪʃən] n Einäscherung f; **crematorium** [krɛməˈtɔːrɪəm] n Krematorium nt

crêpe [kreɪp] n Krepp m; ~ **bandage** (BRIT) n Elastikbinde f

crept [krɛpt] pt, pp of **creep**

crescent ['krɛsnt] n (of moon) Halbmond m

cress [krɛs] n Kresse f

crest [krɛst] n (of cock) Kamm m; (of wave) Wellenkamm m; (coat of arms) Wappen nt

crestfallen ['krɛstfɔːlən] adj niedergeschlagen

Crete [kriːt] n Kreta nt

crevice ['krɛvɪs] n Riss m

crew [kruː] n Besatzung f, Mannschaft f; ~-**cut** n Bürstenschnitt m; ~ **neck** n runde(r)

Ausschnitt m

crib [krɪb] n (bed) Krippe f ♦ vt (inf) spicken

crick [krɪk] n Muskelkrampf m

cricket ['krɪkɪt] n (insect) Grille f; (game) Kricket nt

crime [kraɪm] n Verbrechen nt

criminal ['krɪmɪnl] n Verbrecher m ♦ adj kriminell; (act) strafbar

crimson ['krɪmzn] adj leuchtend rot

cringe [krɪndʒ] vi sich ducken

crinkle ['krɪŋkl] vt zerknittern

cripple ['krɪpl] n Krüppel m ♦ vt lahm legen; (MED) verkrüppeln

crisis ['kraɪsɪs] (pl crises) n Krise f

crisp [krɪsp] adj knusprig; ~s (BRIT) npl Chips pl

crisscross ['krɪskrɒs] adj gekreuzt, Kreuz-

criteria [kraɪ'tɪərɪə] npl of **criterion**

criterion [kraɪ'tɪərɪən] (pl criteria) n Kriterium n

critic ['krɪtɪk] n Kritiker(in) m(f); ~al adj kritisch; ~ally adv kritisch; (ill) gefährlich; ~ism ['krɪtɪsɪzəm] n Kritik f; ~ize ['krɪtɪsaɪz] vt kritisieren

croak [krəʊk] vi krächzen; (frog) quaken

Croatia [krəʊ'eɪʃə] n Kroatien nt

crochet ['krəʊʃeɪ] n Häkelei f

crockery ['krɒkərɪ] n Geschirr nt

crocodile ['krɒkədaɪl] n Krokodil nt

crocus ['krəʊkəs] n Krokus m

croft [krɒft] (BRIT) n kleine(s) Pachtgut nt

crony ['krəʊnɪ] (inf) n Kumpel m

crook [krʊk] n (criminal) Gauner m; (stick) Hirtenstab m

crooked ['krʊkɪd] adj krumm

crop [krɒp] n (harvest) Ernte f; (riding ~) Reitpeitsche f ♦ vt ernten; ~ up vi passieren

croquet ['krəʊkeɪ] n Krocket nt

croquette [krə'ket] n Krokette f

cross [krɒs] n Kreuz nt ♦ vt (road) überqueren; (legs) übereinander legen; kreuzen ♦ adj (annoyed) böse; ~ out vt streichen; ~ over vi hinübergehen; ~bar n Querstange f; ~-country (race) n Geländelauf m; ~-examine vt ins Kreuzverhör nehmen; ~-eyed adj: to be

~-eyed schielen; ~fire n Kreuzfeuer nt; ~ing n (~roads) (Straßen)kreuzung f; (of ship) Überfahrt f; (for pedestrians) Fußgängerüberweg m; ~ing guard (US) n Schülerlotse m; ~ purposes npl: to be at ~ purposes aneinander vorbeireden; ~-reference n Querverweis m; ~roads n Straßenkreuzung f; (fig) Scheideweg m; ~ section n Querschnitt m; ~walk (US) n Fußgängerüberweg m; ~wind n Seitenwind m; ~word (puzzle) n Kreuzworträtsel nt

crotch [krɒtʃ] n Zwickel m; (ANAT) Unterleib nt

crouch [kraʊtʃ] vi hocken

crow [krəʊ] n (bird) Krähe f; (of cock) Krähen nt ♦ vi krähen

crowbar ['krəʊbɑːʳ] n Stemmeisen nt

crowd [kraʊd] n Menge f ♦ vt (fill) überfüllen ♦ vi drängen; ~ed adj überfüllt

crown [kraʊn] n Krone f; (of head, hat) Kopf m ♦ vt krönen; ~ jewels npl Kronjuwelen pl; ~ prince n Kronprinz m

crow's-feet ['krəʊzfiːt] npl Krähenfüße pl

crucial ['kruːʃl] adj entscheidend

crucifix ['kruːsɪfɪks] n Kruzifix nt; ~ion [kruːsɪ'fɪkʃən] n Kreuzigung f

crude [kruːd] adj (raw) roh; (humour, behaviour) grob; (basic) primitiv; ~ (oil) n Rohöl nt

cruel ['kruəl] adj grausam; ~ty n Grausamkeit f

cruise [kruːz] n Kreuzfahrt f ♦ vi kreuzen; ~r n (MIL) Kreuzer m

crumb [krʌm] n Krume f

crumble ['krʌmbl] vt, vi zerbröckeln; crumbly adj krümelig

crumpet ['krʌmpɪt] n Tee(pfann)kuchen m

crumple ['krʌmpl] vt zerknittern

crunch [krʌntʃ] n: the ~ (fig) der Knackpunkt ♦ vt knirschen; ~y adj knusprig

crusade [kruː'seɪd] n Kreuzzug m

crush [krʌʃ] n Gedränge nt ♦ vt zerdrücken; (rebellion) unterdrücken

crust [krʌst] n Kruste f

crutch [krʌtʃ] n Krücke f

crux [krʌks] n springende(r) Punkt m

cry [kraɪ] vi (shout) schreien; (weep) weinen ♦ n (call) Schrei m; ~ **off** vi (plötzlich) absagen

crypt [krɪpt] n Krypta f

cryptic ['krɪptɪk] adj hintergründig

crystal ['krɪstl] n Kristall m; (glass) Kristallglas nt; (mineral) Bergkristall m; **~-clear** adj kristallklar

crystallize ['krɪstəlaɪz] vt, vi kristallisieren; (fig) klären

CSA n abbr (= Child Support Agency) Amt zur Regelung von Unterhaltszahlungen für Kinder

CTC (BRIT) n abbr = **city technology college**

cub [kʌb] n Junge(s) nt; (also: **C~ scout**) Wölfling m

Cuba ['kju:bə] n Kuba nt; **~n** adj kubanisch ♦ n Kubaner(in) m(f)

cubbyhole ['kʌbɪhəul] n Eckchen nt

cube [kju:b] n Würfel m ♦ vt (MATH) hoch drei nehmen

cubic ['kju:bɪk] adj würfelförmig; (centimetre etc) Kubik-; ~ **capacity** n Fassungsvermögen nt

cubicle ['kju:bɪkl] n Kabine f

cuckoo ['kuku:] n Kuckuck m; ~ **clock** n Kuckucksuhr f

cucumber ['kju:kʌmbər] n Gurke f

cuddle ['kʌdl] vt, vi herzen, drücken (inf)

cue [kju:] n (THEAT) Stichwort nt; (snooker ~) Billardstock m

cuff [kʌf] n (BRIT: of shirt, coat etc) Manschette f; Aufschlag m; (US) = **turn-up**; **off the ~** aus dem Handgelenk; **~link** n Manschettenknopf m

cuisine [kwɪ'zi:n] n Kochkunst f, Küche f

cul-de-sac ['kʌldəsæk] n Sackgasse f

culinary ['kʌlɪnərɪ] adj Koch-

cull [kʌl] vt (select) auswählen

culminate ['kʌlmɪneɪt] vi gipfeln; **culmination** [kʌlmɪ'neɪʃən] n Höhepunkt m

culottes [kju:'lɔts] npl Hosenrock m

culpable ['kʌlpəbl] adj schuldig

culprit ['kʌlprɪt] n Täter m

cult [kʌlt] n Kult m

cultivate ['kʌltɪveɪt] vt (AGR) bebauen; (mind) bilden; **cultivation** [kʌltɪ'veɪʃən] n

(AGR) Bebauung f; (of person) Bildung f

cultural ['kʌltʃərəl] adj kulturell, Kultur-

culture ['kʌltʃər] n Kultur f; **~d** adj gebildet

cumbersome ['kʌmbəsəm] adj (object) sperrig

cumulative ['kju:mjulətɪv] adj gehäuft

cunning ['kʌnɪŋ] n Verschlagenheit f ♦ adj schlau

cup [kʌp] n Tasse f; (prize) Pokal m

cupboard ['kʌbəd] n Schrank m

cup tie (BRIT) n Pokalspiel nt

curate ['kjuərɪt] n (Catholic) Kurat m; (Protestant) Vikar m

curator [kjuə'reɪtər] n Kustos m

curb [kə:b] vt zügeln ♦ n (on spending etc) Einschränkung f; (US) Bordstein m

curdle ['kə:dl] vi gerinnen

cure [kjuər] n Heilmittel nt; (process) Heilverfahren nt ♦ vt heilen

curfew ['kə:fju:] n Ausgangssperre f; Sperrstunde f

curio ['kjuərɪəu] n Kuriosität f

curiosity [kjuərɪ'ɔsɪtɪ] n Neugier f

curious ['kjuərɪəs] adj neugierig; (strange) seltsam

curl [kə:l] n Locke f ♦ vt locken ♦ vi sich locken; ~ **up** vi sich zusammenrollen; (person) sich ankuscheln; **~er** n Lockenwickler m; **~y** ['kə:lɪ] adj lockig

currant ['kʌrnt] n Korinthe f

currency ['kʌrnsɪ] n Währung f; **to gain ~** an Popularität gewinnen

current ['kʌrnt] n Strömung f ♦ adj (expression) gängig, üblich; (issue) neueste; ~ **account** (BRIT) n Girokonto nt; ~ **affairs** npl Zeitgeschehen nt; **~ly** adv zurzeit

curricula [kə'rɪkjulə] npl of **curriculum**

curriculum [kə'rɪkjuləm] (pl **~s** or **curricula**) n Lehrplan m; ~ **vitae** [-'vi:taɪ] n Lebenslauf m

curry ['kʌrɪ] n Currygericht nt ♦ vt: **to ~ favour with** sich einschmeicheln bei; ~ **powder** n Curry(pulver) nt

curse [kə:s] vi (swear): **to ~ (at)** fluchen (auf or über +acc) ♦ vt (insult) verwünschen ♦ n Fluch m

cursor ['kə:sər] n (COMPUT) Cursor m

cursory ['kə:sərɪ] *adj* flüchtig

curt [kə:t] *adj* schroff

curtail [kə:'teɪl] *vt* abkürzen; *(rights)* einschränken

curtain ['kə:tn] *n* Vorhang *m*

curts(e)y ['kə:tsɪ] *n* Knicks *m* ♦ *vi* knicksen

curve [kə:v] *n* Kurve *f*; *(of body, vase etc)* Rundung *f* ♦ *vi* sich biegen; *(hips, breasts)* sich runden; *(road)* einen Bogen machen

cushion ['kuʃən] *n* Kissen *nt* ♦ *vt* dämpfen

custard ['kʌstəd] *n* Vanillesoße *f*

custodian [kʌs'təudɪən] *n* Kustos *m*, Verwalter(in) *m(f)*

custody ['kʌstədɪ] *n* Aufsicht *f*; *(police ~)* Haft *f*; **to take into ~** verhaften

custom ['kʌstəm] *n* *(tradition)* Brauch *m*; *(COMM)* Kundschaft *f*; **~ary** *adj* üblich

customer ['kʌstəmər] *n* Kunde *m*, Kundin *f*

customized ['kʌstəmaɪzd] *adj* (car etc) mit Spezialausrüstung

custom-made ['kʌstəm'meɪd] *adj* speziell angefertigt

customs ['kʌstəmz] *npl* Zoll *m*; **~ duty** *n* Zollabgabe *f*; **~ officer** *n* Zollbeamte(r) *m*, Zollbeamtin *f*

cut [kʌt] *(pt, pp* **cut)** *vt* schneiden; *(wages)* kürzen; *(prices)* heruntersetzen ♦ *vi* schneiden; *(intersect)* sich schneiden ♦ *n* Schnitt *m*; *(wound)* Schnittwunde *f*; *(in income etc)* Kürzung *f*; *(share)* Anteil *m*; **to ~ a tooth** zahnen; **~ down** *vt* (tree) fällen; *(reduce)* einschränken; **~ off** *vt* (also fig) abschneiden; *(allowance)* sperren; **~ out** *vt* (shape) ausschneiden; *(delete)* streichen; **~ up** *vt* (meat) aufschneiden; **~back** *n* Kürzung *f*

cute [kju:t] *adj* niedlich

cuticle ['kju:tɪkl] *n* Nagelhaut *f*

cutlery ['kʌtlərɪ] *n* Besteck *nt*

cutlet ['kʌtlɪt] *n* (pork) Kotelett *nt*; *(veal)* Schnitzel *nt*

cut- : **~out** *n* (cardboard ~out) Ausschneidemodell *nt*; **~-price**, **~-rate** *(US) adj* verbilligt; **~throat** *n* Verbrechertyp *m* ♦ *adj* mörderisch

cutting ['kʌtɪŋ] *adj* schneidend ♦ *n* (BRIT: PRESS) Ausschnitt *m*; (: RAIL) Durchstich *m*

CV *n abbr* = **curriculum vitae**

cwt *abbr* = **hundredweight(s)**

cyanide ['saɪənaɪd] *n* Zyankali *nt*

cyberspace ['saɪbəspeɪs] *n* Cyberspace *m*

cycle ['saɪkl] *n* Fahrrad *nt*; *(series)* Reihe *f* ♦ *vi* Rad fahren; **~ hire** *n* Fahrradverleih *m*; **~ lane**, **~ path** *n* (Fahr)radweg *m*; **cycling** *n* Radfahren *nt*; **cyclist** *n* Radfahrer(in) *m(f)*

cyclone ['saɪkləun] *n* Zyklon *m*

cygnet ['sɪgnɪt] *n* junge(r) Schwan *m*

cylinder ['sɪlɪndər] *n* Zylinder *m*; *(TECH)* Walze *f*; **~ head gasket** *n* Zylinderkopfdichtung *f*

cymbals ['sɪmblz] *npl* Becken *nt*

cynic ['sɪnɪk] *n* Zyniker(in) *m(f)*; **~al** *adj* zynisch; **~ism** ['sɪnɪsɪzəm] *n* Zynismus *m*

cypress ['saɪprɪs] *n* Zypresse *f*

Cyprus ['saɪprəs] *n* Zypern *nt*

cyst [sɪst] *n* Zyste *f*

cystitis [sɪs'taɪtɪs] *n* Blasenentzündung *f*

czar [za:r] *n* Zar *m*

Czech [tʃek] *adj* tschechisch ♦ *n* Tscheche *m*, Tschechin *f*

Czechoslovakia [tʃekəslə'vækɪə] *(HIST)* *n* die Tschechoslowakei; **~n** *adj* tschechoslowakisch ♦ *n* Tschechoslowake *m*, Tchechoslowakin *f*

D, d

D [di:] *n* *(MUS)* D *nt*

dab [dæb] *vt* (wound, paint) betupfen ♦ *n* (little bit) bisschen *nt*; *(of paint)* Tupfer *m*

dabble ['dæbl] *vi*: **to ~ in sth** in etw *dat* machen

dad [dæd] *n* Papa *m*, Vati *m*; **~dy** ['dædɪ] *n* Papa *m*, Vati *m*; **~dy-long-legs** *n* Weberknecht *m*

daffodil ['dæfədɪl] *n* Osterglocke *f*

daft [dɑ:ft] *(inf) adj* blöd(e), doof

dagger ['dægər] *n* Dolch *m*

daily ['deɪlɪ] *adj* täglich ♦ *n* *(PRESS)* Tageszeitung *f*; *(BRIT: cleaner)* Haushaltshilfe *f* ♦ *adv* täglich

dainty ['deɪntɪ] *adj* zierlich

dairy ['deərɪ] *n* (shop) Milchgeschäft *nt*; *(on*

farm) Molkerei f ♦ adj Milch-; ~ **farm** n Hof m mit Milchwirtschaft; ~ **produce** n Molkereiprodukte pl; ~ **products** npl Milchprodukte pl; ~ **store** (US) n Milchgeschäft nt

dais ['deɪs] n Podium nt

daisy ['deɪzɪ] n Gänseblümchen nt

dale [deɪl] n Tal nt

dam [dæm] n (Stau)damm m ♦ vt stauen

damage ['dæmɪdʒ] n Schaden m ♦ vt beschädigen; ~**s** npl (JUR) Schaden(s)ersatz m

damn [dæm] vt verdammen ♦ n (inf): **I don't give a** ~ das ist mir total egal ♦ adj (inf: also: ~**ed**) verdammt; ~ **it!** verflucht!; ~**ing** adj vernichtend

damp [dæmp] adj feucht ♦ n Feuchtigkeit f ♦ vt (also: ~**en**) befeuchten; (discourage) dämpfen

damson ['dæmzən] n Damaszenerpflaume f

dance [dɑːns] n Tanz m ♦ vi tanzen; ~ **hall** n Tanzlokal nt; ~**r** n Tänzer(in) m(f); **dancing** n Tanzen nt

dandelion ['dændɪlaɪən] n Löwenzahn m

dandruff ['dændrəf] n (Kopf)schuppen pl

Dane [deɪn] n Däne m, Dänin f

danger ['deɪndʒə'] n Gefahr f; ~**!** (sign) Achtung!; **to be in ~ of doing sth** Gefahr laufen, etw zu tun; ~**ous** adj gefährlich

dangle ['dæŋgl] vi baumeln ♦ vt herabhängen lassen

Danish ['deɪnɪʃ] adj dänisch ♦ n Dänisch nt

dare [dɛə'] vt herausfordern ♦ vi: **to ~ (to) do sth** es wagen, etw zu tun; **I ~ say** ich würde sagen; **daring** ['dɛərɪŋ] adj (audacious) verwegen; (bold) wagemutig; (dress) gewagt ♦ n Mut m

dark [dɑːk] adj dunkel; (fig) düster, trübe; (deep colour) dunkel- ♦ n Dunkelheit f; **to be left in the ~ about** im Dunkeln sein über +acc; **after ~** nach Anbruch der Dunkelheit; ~**en** vt, vi verdunkeln; ~ **glasses** npl Sonnenbrille f; ~**ness** n Finsternis nt; ~**room** n Dunkelkammer f

darling ['dɑːlɪŋ] n Liebling m ♦ adj lieb

darn [dɑːn] vt stopfen

dart [dɑːt] n (weapon) Pfeil m; (in sewing)

Abnäher m ♦ vi sausen; ~**s** n (game) Pfeilwerfen nt; ~**board** n Zielscheibe f

dash [dæʃ] n Sprung m; (mark) (Gedanken)strich m; (small amount) bisschen nt ♦ vt (hopes) zunichte machen ♦ vi stürzen; ~ **away** vi davonstürzen; ~ **off** vi davonstürzen

dashboard ['dæʃbɔːd] n Armaturenbrett nt

dashing ['dæʃɪŋ] adj schneidig

data ['deɪtə] npl Einzelheiten pl, Daten pl; ~**base** n Datenbank f; ~ **processing** n Datenverarbeitung f

date [deɪt] n Datum nt; (for meeting etc) Termin m; (with person) Verabredung f; (fruit) Dattel f ♦ vt (letter etc) datieren; (person) gehen mit; ~ **of birth** Geburtsdatum nt; **to** ~ bis heute; **out of** ~ überholt; **up to** ~ (clothes) modisch; (report) up-to-date; (with news) auf dem Laufenden; ~**d** adj altmodisch; ~ **rape** n Vergewaltigung f nach einem Rendezvous

daub [dɔːb] vt beschmieren; (paint) schmieren

daughter ['dɔːtə'] n Tochter f; ~**-in-law** n Schwiegertochter f

daunting ['dɔːntɪŋ] adj entmutigend

dawdle ['dɔːdl] vi trödeln

dawn [dɔːn] n Morgendämmerung f ♦ vi dämmern; (fig): **it ~ed on him that ...** es dämmerte ihm, dass ...

day [deɪ] n Tag m; **the ~ before / after** am Tag zuvor/danach; **the ~ after tomorrow** übermorgen; **the ~ before yesterday** vorgestern; **by** ~ am Tage; ~**break** n Tagesanbruch m; ~**dream** vi mit offenen Augen träumen; ~**light** n Tageslicht nt; ~ **return** (BRIT) n Tagesrückfahrkarte f; ~**time** n Tageszeit f; ~**-to-~** adj alltäglich

daze [deɪz] vt betäuben ♦ n Betäubung f; **in a ~** benommen

dazzle ['dæzl] vt blenden

DC abbr (= direct current) Gleichstrom m

D-day ['diːdeɪ] n (HIST) Tag der Invasion durch die Alliierten (6.6.44); (fig) der Tag X

deacon ['diːkən] n Diakon m

dead [dɛd] adj tot; (without feeling) gefühllos ♦ adv ganz; (exactly) genau ♦ npl: **the** ~ die

Toten *pl*; **to shoot sb ~** jdn erschießen; **~ tired** todmüde; **to stop ~** abrupt stehen bleiben; **~en** *vt* (*pain*) abtöten; (*sound*) ersticken; **~ end** *n* Sackgasse *f*; **~ heat** *n* tote(s) Rennen *nt*; **~line** *n* Stichtag *m*; **~lock** *n* Stillstand *m*; **~ loss** (*inf*) *n*: **to be a ~ loss** ein hoffnungsloser Fall sein; **~ly** *adj* tödlich; **~pan** *adj* undurchdringlich; **D~ Sea** *n*: **the D~ Sea** das Tote Meer

deaf [dɛf] *adj* taub; **~en** *vt* taub machen; **~ening** *adj* (*noise*) ohrenbetäubend; (*noise*) lautstark; **~-mute** *n* Taubstumme(r) *mf*; **~ness** *n* Taubheit *f*

deal [diːl] (*pt, pp* **dealt**) *n* Geschäft *nt* ♦ *vt* austeilen; (*CARDS*) geben; **a great ~ of** sehr viel; **~ in** *vt fus* handeln mit; **~ with** *vt fus* (*person*) behandeln; (*subject*) sich befassen mit; (*problem*) in Angriff nehmen; **~er** *n* (*COMM*) Händler *m*; (*CARDS*) Kartengeber *m*; **~ings** *npl* (*FIN*) Geschäfte *pl*; (*relations*) Beziehungen *pl*; **~t** [dɛlt] *pt, pp* of **deal**

dean [diːn] *n* (*Protestant*) Superintendent *m*; (*Catholic*) Dechant *m*; (*UNIV*) Dekan *m*

dear [dɪəʳ] *adj* lieb; (*expensive*) teuer ♦ *n* Liebling *m* ♦ *excl*: **~ me!** du liebe Zeit!; **D~ Sir** Sehr geehrter Herr!; **D~ John** Lieber John!; **~ly** *adv* (*love*) herzlich; (*pay*) teuer

death [dɛθ] *n* Tod *m*; (*statistic*) Todesfall *m*; **~ certificate** *n* Totenschein *m*; **~ly** *adj* totenähnlich, Toten-; **~ penalty** *n* Todesstrafe *f*; **~ rate** *n* Sterblichkeitsziffer *f*

debar [dɪ'bɑːʳ] *vt* ausschließen

debase [dɪ'beɪs] *vt* entwerten

debatable [dɪ'beɪtəbl] *adj* anfechtbar

debate [dɪ'beɪt] *n* Debatte *f* ♦ *vt* debattieren, diskutieren; (*consider*) überlegen

debilitating [dɪ'bɪlɪteɪtɪŋ] *adj* schwächend

debit ['dɛbɪt] *n* Schuldposten *m* ♦ *vt* belasten

debris ['dɛbriː] *n* Trümmer *pl*

debt [dɛt] *n* Schuld *f*; **to be in ~** verschuldet sein; **~or** *n* Schuldner *m*

debunk [diː'bʌŋk] *vt* entlarven

decade ['dɛkeɪd] *n* Jahrzehnt *nt*

decadence ['dɛkədəns] *n* Dekadenz *f*

decaff ['diːkæf] (*inf*) *n* koffeinfreier Kaffee

decaffeinated [dɪ'kæfɪneɪtɪd] *adj* koffeinfrei

decanter [dɪ'kæntəʳ] *n* Karaffe *f*

decay [dɪ'keɪ] *n* Verfall *m*; (*tooth ~*) Karies *m* ♦ *vi* verfallen; (*teeth, meat etc*) faulen; (*leaves etc*) verrotten

deceased [dɪ'siːst] *adj* verstorben

deceit [dɪ'siːt] *n* Betrug *m*; **~ful** *adj* falsch

deceive [dɪ'siːv] *vt* täuschen

December [dɪ'sɛmbəʳ] *n* Dezember *m*

decency ['diːsənsɪ] *n* Anstand *m*

decent ['diːsənt] *adj* (*respectable*) anständig; (*pleasant*) annehmbar

deception [dɪ'sɛpʃən] *n* Betrug *m*

deceptive [dɪ'sɛptɪv] *adj* irreführend

decibel ['dɛsɪbɛl] *n* Dezibel *nt*

decide [dɪ'saɪd] *vt* entscheiden ♦ *vi* sich entscheiden; **to ~ on sth** etw beschließen; **~d** *adj* entschieden; **~dly** [dɪ'saɪdɪdlɪ] *adv* entschieden

deciduous [dɪ'sɪdjuəs] *adj* Laub-

decimal ['dɛsɪməl] *adj* dezimal ♦ *n* Dezimalzahl *f*; **~ point** *n* Komma *nt*

decipher [dɪ'saɪfəʳ] *vt* entziffern

decision [dɪ'sɪʒən] *n* Entscheidung *f*, Entschluss *m*

decisive [dɪ'saɪsɪv] *adj* entscheidend; (*person*) entschlossen

deck [dɛk] *n* (*NAUT*) Deck *nt*; (*of cards*) Pack *m*; **~chair** *n* Liegestuhl *m*

declaration [dɛklə'reɪʃən] *n* Erklärung *f*

declare [dɪ'klɛəʳ] *vt* erklären; (*CUSTOMS*) verzollen

decline [dɪ'klaɪn] *n* (*decay*) Verfall *m*; (*lessening*) Rückgang *m* ♦ *vt* (*invitation*) ablehnen ♦ *vi* (*say no*) ablehnen; (*of strength*) nachlassen

decode ['diː'kəud] *vt* entschlüsseln; **~r** *n* (*TV*) Decoder *m*

decompose [diːkəm'pəuz] *vi* (sich) zersetzen

décor ['deɪkɔːʳ] *n* Ausstattung *f*

decorate ['dɛkəreɪt] *vt* (*room: paper*) tapezieren; (: *paint*) streichen; (*adorn*) (aus)schmücken; (*cake*) verzieren; (*honour*) auszeichnen; **decoration** [dɛkə'reɪʃən] *n* (*of house*) (Wand)dekoration *f*; (*medal*) Orden *m*; **decorator** ['dɛkəreɪtəʳ] *n* Maler *m*, Anstreicher *m*

decorum [dɪ'kɔːrəm] *n* Anstand *m*

decoy ['di:kɔɪ] n Lockvogel m

decrease [n 'di:kri:s, vb di:'kri:s] n Abnahme f ♦ vt vermindern ♦ vi abnehmen

decree [dɪ'kri:] n Erlass m; ~ **nisi** n vorläufige(s) Scheidungsurteil nt

decrepit [dɪ'krepɪt] adj hinfällig

dedicate ['dedɪkeɪt] vt widmen; ~**d** adj hingebungsvoll, engagiert; (COMPUT) dediziert; **dedication** [dedɪ'keɪʃən] n (devotion) Ergebenheit f; (in book) Widmung f

deduce [dɪ'dju:s] vt: **to ~ sth (from sth)** etw (aus etw) ableiten, etw (aus etw) schließen

deduct [dɪ'dʌkt] vt abziehen; ~**ion** [dɪ'dʌkʃən] n (of money) Abzug m; (conclusion) (Schluss)folgerung f

deed [di:d] n Tat f; (document) Urkunde f

deem [di:m] vt: **to ~ sb/sth (to be) sth** jdn/etw für etw halten

deep [di:p] adj tief ♦ adv: **the spectators stood 20 ~** die Zuschauer standen in 20 Reihen hintereinander; **to be 4m ~** 4 Meter tief sein; ~**en** vt vertiefen ♦ vi (darkness) tiefer werden; ~ **end** n: **the ~ end** (of swimming pool) das Tiefe; ~**-freeze** n Tiefkühlung f; ~**-fry** vt fritttieren; ~**ly** adv tief; ~**-sea diving** n Tiefseetauchen nt; ~**-seated** adj tief sitzend

deer [dɪə*] n Reh nt; ~**skin** n Hirsch-/Rehleder nt

deface [dɪ'feɪs] vt entstellen

defamation [defə'meɪʃən] n Verleumdung f

default [dɪ'fɔ:lt] n Versäumnis nt; (COMPUT) Standardwert m ♦ vi versäumen; **by ~** durch Nichterscheinen

defeat [dɪ'fi:t] n Niederlage f ♦ vt schlagen; ~**ist** adj defätistisch ♦ n Defätist m

defect [n 'di:fekt, vb dɪ'fekt] n Fehler m ♦ vi überlaufen; ~**ive** [dɪ'fektɪv] adj fehlerhaft

defence [dɪ'fens] n Verteidigung f; ~**less** adj wehrlos

defend [dɪ'fend] vt verteidigen; ~**ant** n Angeklagte(r) m; ~**er** n Verteidiger m

defense [dɪ'fens] (US) n = **defence**

defensive [dɪ'fensɪv] adj defensiv ♦ n: **on the ~** in der Defensive

defer [dɪ'fɜ:*] vt verschieben

deference ['defərəns] n Rücksichtnahme f

defiance [dɪ'faɪəns] n Trotz m, Unnachgiebigkeit f; **in ~ of sth** einer Sache dat zum Trotz

defiant [dɪ'faɪənt] adj trotzig, unnachgiebig

deficiency [dɪ'fɪʃənsɪ] n (lack) Mangel m; (weakness) Schwäche f

deficient [dɪ'fɪʃənt] adj mangelhaft

deficit ['defɪsɪt] n Defizit nt

defile [vb dɪ'faɪl, n 'di:faɪl] vt beschmutzen ♦ n Hohlweg m

define [dɪ'faɪn] vt bestimmen; (explain) definieren

definite ['defɪnɪt] adj (fixed) definitiv; (clear) eindeutig; ~**ly** adv bestimmt

definition [defɪ'nɪʃən] n Definition f

deflate [di:'fleɪt] vt die Luft ablassen aus

deflect [dɪ'flekt] vt ablenken

deformity [dɪ'fɔ:mɪtɪ] n Missbildung f

defraud [dɪ'frɔ:d] vt betrügen

defrost [di:'frɔst] vt (fridge) abtauen; (food) auftauen; ~**er** (US) n (demister) Gebläse nt

deft [deft] adj geschickt

defunct [dɪ'fʌŋkt] adj verstorben

defuse [di:'fju:z] vt entschärfen

defy [dɪ'faɪ] vt (disobey) sich widersetzen +dat; (orders, death) trotzen +dat; (challenge) herausfordern

degenerate [v dɪ'dʒenəreɪt, adj dɪ'dʒenərɪt] vi degenerieren ♦ adj degeneriert

degrading [dɪ'greɪdɪŋ] adj erniedrigend

degree [dɪ'gri:] n Grad m; (UNIV) Universitätsabschluss m; **by ~s** allmählich; **to some ~** zu einem gewissen Grad

dehydrated [di:haɪ'dreɪtɪd] adj (person) ausgetrocknet

de-ice ['di:'aɪs] vt enteisen

deign [deɪn] vi sich herablassen

deity ['di:ɪtɪ] n Gottheit f

dejected [dɪ'dʒektɪd] adj niedergeschlagen

delay [dɪ'leɪ] vt (hold back) aufschieben ♦ vi (linger) sich aufhalten ♦ n Aufschub m, Verzögerung f; (of train etc) Verspätung f; **to be ~ed** (train) Verspätung haben; **without ~** unverzüglich

delectable [dɪ'lektəbl] adj köstlich; (fig) reizend

delegate [n 'dɛlɪgɪt, vb 'dɛlɪgeɪt] *n* Delegierte(r) *mf* ♦ *vt* delegieren

delete [dɪ'liːt] *vt* (aus)streichen

deliberate [*adj* dɪ'lɪbərɪt, vb dɪ'lɪbəreɪt] *adj* (*intentional*) absichtlich; (*slow*) bedächtig ♦ *vi* (*consider*) überlegen; (*debate*) sich beraten; **~ly** *adv* absichtlich

delicacy ['dɛlɪkəsɪ] *n* Zartheit *f*; (*weakness*) Anfälligkeit *f*; (*food*) Delikatesse *f*

delicate ['dɛlɪkɪt] *adj* (*fine*) fein; (*fragile*) zart; (*situation*) heikel; (*MED*) empfindlich

delicatessen [dɛlɪkə'tɛsn] *n* Feinkostgeschäft *nt*

delicious [dɪ'lɪʃəs] *adj* lecker

delight [dɪ'laɪt] *n* Wonne *f* ♦ *vt* entzücken; **to take ~ in sth** Freude an etw *dat* haben; **~ed** *adj*: **~ed (at** *or* **with sth)** entzückt (über +*acc* etw); **~ed to do sth** etw sehr gern tun; **~ful** *adj* entzückend, herrlich

delinquency [dɪ'lɪŋkwənsɪ] *n* Kriminalität *f*

delinquent [dɪ'lɪŋkwənt] *n* Straffällige(r) *mf* ♦ *adj* straffällig

delirious [dɪ'lɪrɪəs] *adj* im Fieberwahn

deliver [dɪ'lɪvəʳ] *vt* (*goods*) (ab)liefern; (*letter*) zustellen; (*speech*) halten; **~y** *n* (Ab)lieferung *f*; (*of letter*) Zustellung *f*; (*of speech*) Vortragsweise *f*; (*MED*) Entbindung *f*; **to take ~y of** in Empfang nehmen

delude [dɪ'luːd] *vt* täuschen

deluge ['dɛljuːdʒ] *n* Überschwemmung *f*; (*fig*) Flut *f* ♦ *vt* (*fig*) überfluten

delusion [dɪ'luːʒən] *n* (Selbst)täuschung *f*

de luxe [də'lʌks] *adj* Luxus-

delve [dɛlv] *vi*: **to ~ into** sich vertiefen in +*acc*

demand [dɪ'mɑːnd] *vt* verlangen ♦ *n* (*request*) Verlangen *nt*; (*COMM*) Nachfrage *f*; **in ~** gefragt; **on ~** auf Verlangen; **~ing** *adj* anspruchsvoll

demean [dɪ'miːn] *vt*: **to ~ o.s.** sich erniedrigen

demeanour [dɪ'miːnəʳ] (*US* **demeanor**) *n* Benehmen *nt*

demented [dɪ'mɛntɪd] *adj* wahnsinnig

demister [diː'mɪstəʳ] *n* (*AUT*) Gebläse *nt*

demo ['dɛməʊ] (*inf*) *n abbr* (= *demonstration*) Demo *f*

democracy [dɪ'mɔkrəsɪ] *n* Demokratie *f*

democrat ['dɛməkræt] *n* Demokrat *m*; **democratic** [dɛmə'krætɪk] *adj* demokratisch

demolish [dɪ'mɔlɪʃ] *vt* abreißen; (*fig*) vernichten

demolition [dɛmə'lɪʃən] *n* Abbruch *m*

demon ['diːmən] *n* Dämon *m*

demonstrate ['dɛmənstreɪt] *vt, vi* demonstrieren; **demonstration** [dɛmən'streɪʃən] *n* Demonstration *f*; **demonstrator** ['dɛmənstreɪtəʳ] *n* (*POL*) Demonstrant(in) *m(f)*

demote [dɪ'məʊt] *vt* degradieren

demure [dɪ'mjʊəʳ] *adj* ernst

den [dɛn] *n* (*of animal*) Höhle *f*; (*study*) Bude *f*

denatured alcohol [diː'neɪtʃəd-] (*US*) *n* ungenießbar gemachte(r) Alkohol *m*

denial [dɪ'naɪəl] *n* Leugnung *f*; **official ~** Dementi *nt*

denim ['dɛnɪm] *adj* Denim-; **~s** *npl* Denimjeans *pl*

Denmark ['dɛnmɑːk] *n* Dänemark *nt*

denomination [dɪnɔmɪ'neɪʃən] *n* (*ECCL*) Bekenntnis *nt*; (*type*) Klasse *f*; (*FIN*) Wert *m*

denote [dɪ'nəʊt] *vt* bedeuten

denounce [dɪ'naʊns] *vt* brandmarken

dense [dɛns] *adj* dicht; (*stupid*) schwer von Begriff; **~ly** *adv* dicht; **density** ['dɛnsɪtɪ] *n* Dichte *f*; **single/double density disk** Diskette *f* mit einfacher/doppelter Dichte

dent [dɛnt] *n* Delle *f* ♦ *vt* (*also:* **make a ~ in**) einbeulen

dental ['dɛntl] *adj* Zahn-; **~ surgeon** *n* = **dentist**

dentist ['dɛntɪst] *n* Zahnarzt(ärztin) *m(f)*

dentures ['dɛntʃəz] *npl* Gebiss *nt*

deny [dɪ'naɪ] *vt* leugnen; (*officially*) dementieren; (*help*) abschlagen

deodorant [diː'əʊdərənt] *n* Deodorant *nt*

depart [dɪ'pɑːt] *vi* abfahren; **to ~ from** (*fig: differ from*) abweichen von

department [dɪ'pɑːtmənt] *n* (*COMM*) Abteilung *f*; (*UNIV*) Seminar *nt*; (*POL*) Ministerium *nt*; **~ store** *n* Warenhaus *nt*

departure [dɪ'pɑːtʃəʳ] *n* (*of person*) Abreise *f*; (*of train*) Abfahrt *f*; (*of plane*) Abflug *m*; **new**

~ Neuerung f; ~ **lounge** n (at airport) Abflughalle f

depend [dɪ'pɛnd] vi: **to ~ on** abhängen von; (rely on) angewiesen sein auf +acc; **it ~s** es kommt darauf an; **~ing on the result ...** abhängend vom Resultat ...; **~able** adj zuverlässig; **~ant** n Angehörige(r) f(m); **~ence** n Abhängigkeit f; **~ent** adj abhängig ♦ n = **dependant**; **~ent on** abhängig von

depict [dɪ'pɪkt] vt schildern

depleted [dɪ'pliːtɪd] adj aufgebraucht

deplorable [dɪ'plɔːrəbl] adj bedauerlich

deploy [dɪ'plɔɪ] vt einsetzen

depopulation ['diːpɔpju'leɪʃən] n Entvölkerung f

deport [dɪ'pɔːt] vt deportieren; **~ation** [diːpɔː'teɪʃən] n Abschiebung f

deportment [dɪ'pɔːtmənt] n Betragen nt

deposit [dɪ'pɔzɪt] n (in bank) Guthaben nt; (down payment) Anzahlung f; (security) Kaution f; (CHEM) Niederschlag m ♦ vt (in bank) deponieren; (put down) niederlegen; **~ account** n Sparkonto nt

depot ['dɛpəu] n Depot nt

depraved [dɪ'preɪvd] adj verkommen

depreciate [dɪ'priːʃɪeɪt] vi im Wert sinken; **depreciation** [dɪpriːʃɪ'eɪʃən] n Wertminderung f

depress [dɪ'prɛs] vt (press down) niederdrücken; (in mood) deprimieren; **~ed** adj deprimiert; **~ion** [dɪ'prɛʃən] n (mood) Depression f; (in trade) Wirtschaftskrise f; (hollow) Vertiefung f; (MET) Tief(druckgebiet) nt

deprivation [dɛprɪ'veɪʃən] n Not f

deprive [dɪ'praɪv] vt: **to ~ sb of sth** jdn einer Sache gen berauben; **~d** adj (child) sozial benachteiligt; (area) unterentwickelt

depth [dɛpθ] n Tiefe f; **in the ~s of despair** in tiefster Verzweiflung

deputation [dɛpju'teɪʃən] n Abordnung f

deputize ['dɛpjutaɪz] vi: **to ~ (for sb)** (jdn) vertreten

deputy ['dɛpjuti] adj stellvertretend ♦ n (Stell)vertreter m; **~ head** (BRIT: SCOL) n Konrektor(in) m(f)

derail [dɪ'reɪl] vt: **to be ~ed** entgleisen; **~ment** n Entgleisung f

deranged [dɪ'reɪndʒd] adj verrückt

derby ['dɑːrbɪ] (US) n Melone f

derelict ['dɛrɪlɪkt] adj verlassen

deride [dɪ'raɪd] vt auslachen

derisory [dɪ'raɪsərɪ] adj spöttisch

derivative [dɪ'rɪvətɪv] n Derivat nt ♦ adj abgeleitet

derive [dɪ'raɪv] vt (get) gewinnen; (deduce) ableiten ♦ vi (come from) abstammen

dermatitis [dəːmə'taɪtɪs] n Hautentzündung f

derogatory [dɪ'rɔgətərɪ] adj geringschätzig

derrick ['dɛrɪk] n Drehkran m

descend [dɪ'sɛnd] vt, vi hinuntersteigen; **to ~ from** abstammen von; **~ant** n Nachkomme m; **descent** [dɪ'sɛnt] n (coming down) Abstieg m; (origin) Abstammung f

describe [dɪs'kraɪb] vt beschreiben

description [dɪs'krɪpʃən] n Beschreibung f; (sort) Art f

descriptive [dɪs'krɪptɪv] adj beschreibend; (word) anschaulich

desecrate ['dɛsɪkreɪt] vt schänden

desert [n 'dɛzət, vb dɪ'zəːt] n Wüste f ♦ vt verlassen; (temporarily) im Stich lassen ♦ vi (MIL) desertieren; **~s** npl (what one deserves): **to get one's just ~s** seinen gerechten Lohn bekommen; **~er** n Deserteur m; **~ion** [dɪ'zəːʃən] n (of wife) Verlassen nt; (MIL) Fahnenflucht f; **~ island** n einsame Insel f

deserve [dɪ'zəːv] vt verdienen; **deserving** adj verdienstvoll

design [dɪ'zaɪn] n (plan) Entwurf m; (planning) Design nt ♦ vt entwerfen

designate [vb 'dɛzɪgneɪt, adj 'dɛzɪgnɪt] vt bestimmen ♦ adj designiert

designer [dɪ'zaɪnər] n Designer(in) m(f); (TECH) Konstrukteur(in) m(f); (fashion ~) Modeschöpfer(in) m(f)

desirable [dɪ'zaɪərəbl] adj wünschenswert

desire [dɪ'zaɪər] n Wunsch m, Verlangen nt ♦ vt (lust) begehren; (ask for) wollen

desk [dɛsk] n Schreibtisch m; (BRIT: in shop, restaurant) Kasse f; **~top publishing** n

Desktop-Publishing *nt*

desolate ['dɛsəlɪt] *adj* öde; *(sad)* trostlos; **desolation** [dɛsə'leɪʃən] *n* Trostlosigkeit *f*

despair [dɪs'pɛəʳ] *n* Verzweiflung *f* ♦ *vi:* **to ~ (of)** verzweifeln (an +*dat*)

despatch [dɪs'pætʃ] *n, vt* = **dispatch**

desperate ['dɛspərɪt] *adj* verzweifelt; **~ly** *adv* verzweifelt; **desperation** [dɛspə'reɪʃən] *n* Verzweiflung *f*

despicable [dɪs'pɪkəbl] *adj* abscheulich

despise [dɪs'paɪz] *vt* verachten

despite [dɪs'paɪt] *prep* trotz +*gen*

despondent [dɪs'pɒndənt] *adj* mutlos

dessert [dɪ'zəːt] *n* Nachtisch *m*; **~spoon** *n* Dessertlöffel *m*

destination [dɛstɪ'neɪʃən] *n* (*of person*) (Reise)ziel *nt*; (*of goods*) Bestimmungsort *m*

destiny ['dɛstɪnɪ] *n* Schicksal *nt*

destitute ['dɛstɪtjuːt] *adj* Not leidend

destroy [dɪs'trɔɪ] *vt* zerstören; **~er** *n* (*NAUT*) Zerstörer *m*

destruction [dɪs'trʌkʃən] *n* Zerstörung *f*

destructive [dɪs'trʌktɪv] *adj* zerstörend

detach [dɪ'tætʃ] *vt* loslösen; **~able** *adj* abtrennbar; **~ed** *adj* (*attitude*) distanziert; (*house*) Einzel-; **~ment** *n* (*fig*) Abstand *m*; (*MIL*) Sonderkommando *nt*

detail ['diːteɪl] *n* Einzelheit *f*, Detail *nt* ♦ *vt* (*relate*) ausführlich berichten; (*appoint*) abkommandieren; **in ~** im Detail; **~ed** *adj* detailliert

detain [dɪ'teɪn] *vt* aufhalten; (*imprison*) in Haft halten

detect [dɪ'tɛkt] *vt* entdecken; **~ion** [dɪ'tɛkʃən] *n* Aufdeckung *f*; **~ive** *n* Detektiv *m*; **~ive story** *n* Kriminalgeschichte *f*, Krimi *m*

détente [deɪ'tɑːnt] *n* Entspannung *f*

detention [dɪ'tɛnʃən] *n* Haft *f*; (*SCH*) Nachsitzen *nt*

deter [dɪ'təːʳ] *vt* abschrecken

detergent [dɪ'təːdʒənt] *n* Waschmittel *nt*

deteriorate [dɪ'tɪərɪəreɪt] *vi* sich verschlechtern; **deterioration** [dɪtɪərɪə'reɪʃən] *n* Verschlechterung *f*

determination [dɪtəːmɪ'neɪʃən] *n* Entschlossenheit *f*

determine [dɪ'təːmɪn] *vt* bestimmen; **~d** *adj* entschlossen

deterrent [dɪ'tɛrənt] *n* Abschreckungsmittel *nt*

detest [dɪ'tɛst] *vt* verabscheuen

detonate ['dɛtəneɪt] *vt* explodieren lassen ♦ *vi* detonieren

detour ['diːtuəʳ] *n* Umweg *m*; (*US: AUT: diversion*) Umleitung *f* ♦ *vt* (*US: AUT: traffic*) umleiten

detract [dɪ'trækt] *vi:* **to ~ from** schmälern

detriment ['dɛtrɪmənt] *n:* **to the ~ of** zum Schaden +*gen*; **~al** [dɛtrɪ'mɛntl] *adj* schädlich

devaluation [diːvælju'eɪʃən] *n* Abwertung *f*

devastate ['dɛvəsteɪt] *vt* verwüsten; (*fig: shock*): **to be ~d by** niedergeschmettert sein von; **devastating** *adj* verheerend

develop [dɪ'vɛləp] *vt* entwickeln; (*resources*) erschließen ♦ *vi* sich entwickeln; **~ing country** *n* Entwicklungsland *nt*; **~ment** *n* Entwicklung *f*

deviate ['diːvɪeɪt] *vi* abweichen

device [dɪ'vaɪs] *n* Gerät *nt*

devil ['dɛvl] *n* Teufel *m*

devious ['diːvɪəs] *adj* (*means*) krumm; (*person*) verschlagen

devise [dɪ'vaɪz] *vt* entwickeln

devoid [dɪ'vɔɪd] *adj:* **~ of** ohne

devolution [diːvə'luːʃən] *n* (*POL*) Dezentralisierung *f*

devote [dɪ'vəut] *vt:* **to ~ sth (to sth)** etw (einer Sache *dat*) widmen; **~d** *adj* ergeben; **~e** [dɛvəu'tiː] *n* Anhänger(in) *m(f)*, Verehrer(in) *m(f)*; **devotion** [dɪ'vəuʃən] *n* (*piety*) Andacht *f*; (*loyalty*) Ergebenheit *f*, Hingabe *f*

devour [dɪ'vauəʳ] *vt* verschlingen

devout [dɪ'vaut] *adj* andächtig

dew [djuː] *n* Tau *m*

dexterity [dɛks'tɛrɪtɪ] *n* Geschicklichkeit *f*

DHSS (*BRIT*) *n abbr* = **Department of Health and Social Security**

diabetes [daɪə'biːtiːz] *n* Zuckerkrankheit *f*

diabetic [daɪə'bɛtɪk] *adj* zuckerkrank; (*food*) Diabetiker- ♦ *n* Diabetiker *m*

diabolical [daɪə'bɒlɪkl] (*inf*) *adj* (*weather, behaviour*) saumäßig

diagnose [daɪəg'nəuz] *vt* diagnostizieren

diagnoses [daɪəg'nəusi:z] *npl of* **diagnosis**

diagnosis [daɪəg'nəusɪs] *n* Diagnose *f*

diagonal [daɪ'ægənl] *adj* diagonal ♦ *n* Diagonale *f*

diagram ['daɪəgræm] *n* Diagramm *nt*, Schaubild *nt*

dial ['daɪəl] *n* (TEL) Wählscheibe *f*; (of clock) Zifferblatt *nt* ♦ *vt* wählen

dialect ['daɪəlɛkt] *n* Dialekt *m*

dialling code ['daɪəlɪŋ-] *n* Vorwahl *f*

dialling tone *n* Amtszeichen *nt*

dialogue ['daɪəlɒg] *n* Dialog *m*

dial tone (US) *n* = **dialling tone**

diameter [daɪ'æmɪtər] *n* Durchmesser *m*

diamond ['daɪəmənd] *n* Diamant *m*; ~s *npl* (CARDS) Karo *nt*

diaper ['daɪəpər] (US) *n* Windel *f*

diaphragm ['daɪəfræm] *n* Zwerchfell *nt*

diarrhoea [daɪə'ri:ə] (US **diarrhea**) *n* Durchfall *m*

diary ['daɪərɪ] *n* Taschenkalender *m*; (account) Tagebuch *nt*

dice [daɪs] *n* Würfel *pl* ♦ *vt* in Würfel schneiden

dictate [dɪk'teɪt] *vt* diktieren; ~s ['dɪkteɪts] *npl* Gebote *pl*; **dictation** [dɪk'teɪʃən] *n* Diktat *nt*

dictator [dɪk'teɪtər] *n* Diktator *m*; ~ship [dɪk'teɪtəʃɪp] *n* Diktatur *f*

dictionary ['dɪkʃənrɪ] *n* Wörterbuch *nt*

did [dɪd] *pt of* **do**

didn't ['dɪdnt] = **did not**

die [daɪ] *vi* sterben; **to be dying for sth** etw unbedingt haben wollen; **to be dying to do sth** darauf brennen, etw zu tun; ~ **away** *vi* schwächer werden; ~ **down** *vi* nachlassen; ~ **out** *vi* aussterben

diesel ['di:zl] *n* (car) Diesel *m*; ~ **engine** *n* Dieselmotor *m*; ~ **oil** *n* Dieselkraftstoff *m*

diet ['daɪət] *n* Nahrung *f*; (special food) Diät *f*; (slimming) Abmagerungskur *f* ♦ *vi* (also: **be on a** ~) eine Abmagerungskur machen

differ ['dɪfər] *vi* sich unterscheiden; (disagree) anderer Meinung sein; ~**ence** *n* Unterschied *m*; ~**ent** *adj* anders; (two things) verschieden; ~**entiate** [dɪfə'rɛnʃɪeɪt]

vt, vi unterscheiden; ~**ently** *adv* anders; (from one another) unterschiedlich

difficult ['dɪfɪkəlt] *adj* schwierig; ~**y** *n* Schwierigkeit *f*

diffident ['dɪfɪdənt] *adj* schüchtern

diffuse [*adj* dɪ'fju:s, *vb* dɪ'fju:z] *adj* langatmig ♦ *vt* verbreiten

dig [dɪg] (*pt, pp* **dug**) *vt* graben ♦ *n* (prod) Stoß *m*; (remark) Spitze *f*; (archaeological) Ausgrabung *f*; ~ **in** *vi* (MIL) sich eingraben; ~ **into** *vt fus* (savings) angreifen; ~ **up** *vt* ausgraben; (fig) aufgaben

digest [*vb* daɪ'dʒɛst, *n* 'daɪdʒɛst] *vt* verdauen ♦ *n* Auslese *f*; ~**ion** [dɪ'dʒɛstʃən] *n* Verdauung *f*

digit ['dɪdʒɪt] *n* Ziffer *f*; (ANAT) Finger *m*; ~**al** *adj* digital, Digital-; ~**al TV** *n* Digitalfernsehen *nt*

dignified ['dɪgnɪfaɪd] *adj* würdevoll

dignity ['dɪgnɪtɪ] *n* Würde *f*

digress [daɪ'grɛs] *vi* abschweifen

digs [dɪgz] (BRIT: inf) *npl* Bude *f*

dilapidated [dɪ'læpɪdeɪtɪd] *adj* baufällig

dilate [daɪ'leɪt] *vt* weiten ♦ *vi* sich weiten

dilemma [daɪ'lɛmə] *n* Dilemma *nt*

diligent ['dɪlɪdʒənt] *adj* fleißig

dilute [daɪ'lu:t] *vt* verdünnen

dim [dɪm] *adj* trübe; (stupid) schwer von Begriff ♦ *vt* verdunkeln; **to** ~ **one's headlights** (esp US) abblenden

dime [daɪm] (US) *n* Zehncentstück *nt*

dimension [daɪ'mɛnʃən] *n* Dimension *f*

diminish [dɪ'mɪnɪʃ] *vt, vi* verringern

diminutive [dɪ'mɪnjutɪv] *adj* winzig ♦ *n* Verkleinerungsform *f*

dimmer ['dɪmər] (US) *n* (AUT) Abblendschalter *m*; ~**s** *npl* Abblendlicht *nt*; (sidelights) Begrenzungsleuchten *pl*

dimple ['dɪmpl] *n* Grübchen *nt*

din [dɪn] *n* Getöse *nt*

dine [daɪn] *vi* speisen; ~**r** *n* Tischgast *m*; (RAIL) Speisewagen *m*

dinghy ['dɪŋgɪ] *n* Dingi *nt*; **rubber** ~ Schlauchboot *nt*

dingy ['dɪndʒɪ] *adj* armselig

dining car (BRIT) *n* Speisewagen *m*

dining room ['daɪnɪŋ-] *n* Esszimmer *nt*; (in

hotel) Speisezimmer *nt*

dinner ['dɪnəʳ] *n* (*lunch*) Mittagessen *nt*; (*evening*) Abendessen *nt*; (*public*) Festessen *nt*; ~ **jacket** *n* Smoking *m*; ~ **party** *n* Tischgesellschaft *f*; ~ **time** *n* Tischzeit *f*

dinosaur ['daɪnəsɔ:ʳ] *n* Dinosaurier *m*

dint [dɪnt] *n*: **by ~ of** durch

diocese ['daɪəsɪs] *n* Diözese *f*

dip [dɪp] *n* (*hollow*) Senkung *f*; (*bathe*) kurze(s) Baden *nt* ♦ *vt* eintauchen; (*BRIT: AUT*) abblenden ♦ *vi* (*slope*) sich senken, abfallen

diploma [dɪ'pləumə] *n* Diplom *nt*

diplomacy [dɪ'pləuməsɪ] *n* Diplomatie *f*

diplomat ['dɪpləmæt] *n* Diplomat(in) *m(f)*; **~ic** [dɪplə'mætɪk] *adj* diplomatisch

dip stick *n* Ölmessstab *m*

dipswitch ['dɪpswɪtʃ] (*BRIT*) *n* (*AUT*) Abblendschalter *m*

dire [daɪəʳ] *adj* schrecklich

direct [daɪ'rɛkt] *adj* direkt ♦ *vt* leiten; (*film*) die Regie führen +*gen*; (*aim*) richten; (*order*) anweisen; **can you ~ me to ...?** können Sie mir sagen, wo ich zu ... komme?; ~ **debit** *n* (*BRIT*) Einzugsauftrag *m*; (*transaction*) automatische Abbuchung *f*

direction [dɪ'rɛkʃən] *n* Richtung *f*; (*CINE*) Regie *f*; Leitung *f*; **~s** *npl* (*for use*) Gebrauchsanleitung *f*; (*orders*) Anweisungen *pl*; **sense of ~** Orientierungssinn *m*

directly [dɪ'rɛktlɪ] *adv* direkt; (*at once*) sofort

director [dɪ'rɛktəʳ] *n* Direktor *m*; (*of film*) Regisseur *m*

directory [dɪ'rɛktərɪ] *n* (*TEL*) Telefonbuch *nt*; ~ **enquiries**, ~ **assistance** (*US*) *n* (Fernsprech)auskunft *f*

dirt [də:t] *n* Schmutz *m*, Dreck *m*; **~-cheap** *adj* spottbillig; **~y** *adj* schmutzig ♦ *vt* beschmutzen; **~y trick** *n* gemeine(r) Trick *m*

disability [dɪsə'bɪlɪtɪ] *n* Körperbehinderung *f*

disabled [dɪs'eɪbld] *adj* körperbehindert

disadvantage [dɪsəd'vɑ:ntɪdʒ] *n* Nachteil *m*

disagree [dɪsə'gri:] *vi* nicht übereinstimmen; (*quarrel*) (sich) streiten; (*food*) **to ~ with sb** jdm nicht bekommen; **~able** *adj*

unangenehm; **~ment** *n* (*between persons*) Streit *m*; (*between things*) Widerspruch *m*

disallow ['dɪsə'lau] *vt* nicht zulassen

disappear [dɪsə'pɪəʳ] *vi* verschwinden; **~ance** *n* Verschwinden *nt*

disappoint [dɪsə'pɔɪnt] *vt* enttäuschen; **~ed** *adj* enttäuscht; **~ment** *n* Enttäuschung *f*

disapproval [dɪsə'pru:vəl] *n* Missbilligung *f*

disapprove [dɪsə'pru:v] *vi*: **to ~ of** missbilligen

disarm [dɪs'ɑ:m] *vt* entwaffnen; (*POL*) abrüsten; **~ament** *n* Abrüstung *f*

disarray [dɪsə'reɪ] *n*: **to be in ~** (*army*) in Auflösung (begriffen) sein; (*clothes*) in unordentlichen Zustand sein

disaster [dɪ'zɑ:stəʳ] *n* Katastrophe *f*; **disastrous** [dɪ'zɑ:strəs] *adj* verhängnisvoll

disband [dɪs'bænd] *vt* auflösen ♦ *vi* auseinander gehen

disbelief ['dɪsbə'li:f] *n* Ungläubigkeit *f*

disc [dɪsk] *n* Scheibe *f*; (*record*) (Schall)platte *f*; (*COMPUT*) = **disk**

discard [dɪs'kɑ:d] *vt* ablegen

discern [dɪ'sə:n] *vt* erkennen; **~ing** *adj* scharfsinnig

discharge [*vb* dɪs'tʃɑ:dʒ, *n* 'dɪstʃɑ:dʒ] *vt* (*ship*) entladen; (*duties*) nachkommen +*dat*; (*dismiss*) entlassen; (*gun*) abschießen; (*JUR*) freisprechen ♦ *n* (*of ship, ELEC*) Entladung *f*; (*dismissal*) Entlassung *f*; (*MED*) Ausfluss *m*

disciple [dɪ'saɪpl] *n* Jünger *m*

discipline ['dɪsɪplɪn] *n* Disziplin *f* ♦ *vt* (*train*) schulen; (*punish*) bestrafen

disc jockey *n* Diskjockey *m*

disclaim [dɪs'kleɪm] *vt* nicht anerkennen

disclose [dɪs'kləuz] *vt* enthüllen; **disclosure** [dɪs'kləuʒəʳ] *n* Enthüllung *f*

disco ['dɪskəu] *n abbr* = **discotheque**

discoloured [dɪs'kʌləd] (*US* **discolored**) *adj* verfärbt

discomfort [dɪs'kʌmfət] *n* Unbehagen *nt*

disconcert [dɪskən'sə:t] *vt* aus der Fassung bringen

disconnect [dɪskə'nɛkt] *vt* abtrennen

discontent [dɪskən'tɛnt] *n* Unzufriedenheit *f*; **~ed** *adj* unzufrieden

discontinue [dɪskən'tɪnju:] *vt* einstellen

discord ['dɪskɔːd] *n* Zwietracht *f*; (*noise*) Dissonanz *f*

discotheque ['dɪskəutek] *n* Diskothek *f*

discount [*n* 'dɪskaunt, *vb* dɪs'kaunt] *n* Rabatt *m* ♦ *vt* außer Acht lassen

discourage [dɪs'kʌrɪdʒ] *vt* entmutigen; (*prevent*) abraten

discourteous [dɪs'kəːtɪəs] *adj* unhöflich

discover [dɪs'kʌvəʳ] *vt* entdecken; ~y *n* Entdeckung *f*

discredit [dɪs'krɛdɪt] *vt* in Verruf bringen

discreet [dɪs'kriːt] *adj* diskret

discrepancy [dɪs'krepənsɪ] *n* Diskrepanz *f*

discriminate [dɪs'krɪmɪneɪt] *vi* unterscheiden; **to ~ against** diskriminieren; **discriminating** *adj* anspruchsvoll, **discrimination** [dɪskrɪmɪ'neɪʃən] *n* Urteilsvermögen *nt*; (*pej*) Diskriminierung *f*

discuss [dɪs'kʌs] *vt* diskutieren, besprechen; ~ion [dɪs'kʌʃən] *n* Diskussion *f*, Besprechung *f*

disdain [dɪs'deɪn] *n* Verachtung *f*

disease [dɪ'ziːz] *n* Krankheit *f*

disembark [dɪsɪm'bɑːk] *vi* von Bord gehen

disenchanted ['dɪsɪn'tʃɑːntɪd] *adj* desillusioniert

disengage [dɪsɪn'geɪdʒ] *vt* (*AUT*) auskuppeln

disentangle [dɪsɪn'tæŋgl] *vt* entwirren

disfigure [dɪs'fɪgəʳ] *vt* entstellen

disgrace [dɪs'greɪs] *n* Schande *f* ♦ *vt* Schande bringen über +*acc*; ~ful *adj* unerhört

disgruntled [dɪs'grʌntld] *adj* verärgert

disguise [dɪs'gaɪz] *vt* verkleiden; (*feelings*) verhehlen ♦ *n* Verkleidung *f*; **in ~** verkleidet, maskiert

disgust [dɪs'gʌst] *n* Abscheu *f* ♦ *vt* anwidern; ~ed *adj* angeekelt; (*at sb's behaviour*) empört; ~ing *adj* widerlich

dish [dɪʃ] *n* Schüssel *f*; (*food*) Gericht *nt*; **to do** *or* **wash the ~es** abwaschen; ~ **up** *vt* auftischen; ~ **cloth** *n* Spüllappen *m*

dishearten [dɪs'hɑːtn] *vt* entmutigen

dishevelled [dɪ'fevəld] *adj* (*hair*) zerzaust; (*clothing*) ungepflegt

dishonest [dɪs'ɔnɪst] *adj* unehrlich

dishonour [dɪs'ɔnəʳ] (*US* **dishonor**) *n* Unehre *f*; ~able *adj* unehrenhaft

dishtowel ['dɪʃtauəl] *n* Geschirrtuch *nt*

dishwasher ['dɪʃwɔʃəʳ] *n* Geschirrspülmaschine *f*

disillusion [dɪsɪ'luːʒən] *vt* enttäuschen, desillusionieren

disincentive [dɪsɪn'sentɪv] *n* Entmutigung *f*

disinfect [dɪsɪn'fɛkt] *vt* desinfizieren; ~ant *n* Desinfektionsmittel *nt*

disintegrate [dɪs'ɪntɪgreɪt] *vi* sich auflösen

disinterested [dɪs'ɪntrəstɪd] *adj* uneigennützig; (*inf*) uninteressiert

disjointed [dɪs'dʒɔɪntɪd] *adj* unzusammenhängend

disk [dɪsk] *n* (*COMPUT*) Diskette *f*; **single/ double sided ~** einseitige/beidseitige Diskette; ~ **drive** *n* Diskettenlaufwerk *nt*; ~**ette** [dɪs'ket] (*US*) *n* = **disk**

dislike [dɪs'laɪk] *n* Abneigung *f* ♦ *vt* nicht leiden können

dislocate ['dɪsləkeɪt] *vt* auskugeln

dislodge [dɪs'lɔdʒ] *vt* verschieben; (*MIL*) aus der Stellung werfen

disloyal [dɪs'lɔɪəl] *adj* treulos

dismal ['dɪzml] *adj* trostlos, trübe

dismantle [dɪs'mæntl] *vt* demontieren

dismay [dɪs'meɪ] *n* Bestürzung *f* ♦ *vt* bestürzen

dismiss [dɪs'mɪs] *vt* (*employee*) entlassen; (*idea*) von sich weisen; (*send away*) wegschicken; (*JUR*) abweisen; ~al *n* Entlassung *f*

dismount [dɪs'maunt] *vi* absteigen

disobedience [dɪsə'biːdɪəns] *n* Ungehorsam *m*; **disobedient** *adj* ungehorsam

disobey [dɪsə'beɪ] *vt* nicht gehorchen +*dat*

disorder [dɪs'ɔːdəʳ] *n* (*confusion*) Verwirrung *f*; (*commotion*) Aufruhr *m*; (*MED*) Erkrankung *f*

disorderly [dɪs'ɔːdəlɪ] *adj* (*untidy*) unordentlich; (*unruly*) ordnungswidrig

disorganized [dɪs'ɔːgənaɪzd] *adj* unordentlich

disorientated [dɪs'ɔːrɪenteɪtɪd] *adj* (*person: after journey*) verwirrt

disown [dɪs'əun] *vt* (*child*) verstoßen

disparaging [dɪs'pærɪdʒɪŋ] *adj*

geringschätzig

dispassionate [dɪs'pæʃənət] *adj* objektiv

dispatch [dɪs'pætʃ] *vt* (*goods*) abschicken, abfertigen ♦ *n* Absendung *f*; (*esp MIL*) Meldung *f*

dispel [dɪs'pel] *vt* zerstreuen

dispensary [dɪs'pensərɪ] *n* Apotheke *f*

dispense [dɪs'pens] *vt* verteilen, austeilen; ~ **with** *vt fus* verzichten auf +*acc*; ~**r** *n* (*container*) Spender *m*; **dispensing** *adj*: **dispensing chemist** (*BRIT*) Apotheker *m*

dispersal [dɪs'pə:sl] *n* Zerstreuung *f*

disperse [dɪs'pə:s] *vt* zerstreuen ♦ *vi* sich verteilen

dispirited [dɪs'pɪrɪtɪd] *adj* niedergeschlagen

displace [dɪs'pleɪs] *vt* verschieben; ~**d person** *n* Verschleppte(r) *mf*

display [dɪs'pleɪ] *n* (*of goods*) Auslage *f*; (*of feeling*) Zurschaustellung *f* ♦ *vt* zeigen; (*ostentatiously*) vorführen; (*goods*) ausstellen

displease [dɪs'pli:z] *vt* missfallen +*dat*

displeasure [dɪs'pleʒər] *n* Missfallen *nt*

disposable [dɪs'pəuzəbl] *adj* Wegwerf-; ~ **nappy** *n* Papierwindel *f*

disposal [dɪs'pəuzl] *n* (*of property*) Verkauf *m*; (*throwing away*) Beseitigung *f*; **to be at one's** ~ einem zur Verfügung stehen

dispose [dɪs'pəuz] *vi*: **to** ~ **of** loswerden; ~**d** *adj* geneigt

disposition [dɪspə'zɪʃən] *n* Wesen *nt*

disproportionate [dɪsprə'pɔ:ʃənət] *adj* unverhältnismäßig

disprove [dɪs'pru:v] *vt* widerlegen

dispute [dɪs'pju:t] *n* Streit *m*; (*also*: **industrial** ~) Arbeitskampf *m* ♦ *vt* bestreiten

disqualify [dɪs'kwɔlɪfaɪ] *vt* disqualifizieren

disquiet [dɪs'kwaɪət] *n* Unruhe *f*

disregard [dɪsrɪ'gɑːd] *vt* nicht (be)achten

disrepair ['dɪsrɪ'peər] *n*: **to fall into** ~ verfallen

disreputable [dɪs'repjutəbl] *adj* verrufen

disrespectful [dɪsrɪ'spektful] *adj* respektlos

disrupt [dɪs'rʌpt] *vt* stören; (*service*) unterbrechen; ~**ion** [dɪs'rʌpʃən] *n* Störung *f*; Unterbrechung *f*

dissatisfaction [dɪssætɪs'fækʃən] *n*

Unzufriedenheit *f*; **dissatisfied** [dɪs'sætɪsfaɪd] *adj* unzufrieden

dissect [dɪ'sekt] *vt* zerlegen, sezieren

dissent [dɪ'sent] *n* abweichende Meinung *f*

dissertation [dɪsə'teɪʃən] *n* wissenschaftliche Arbeit *f*; (*Ph.D.*) Doktorarbeit *f*

disservice [dɪs'sə:vɪs] *n*: **to do sb a** ~ jdm einen schlechten Dienst erweisen

dissident ['dɪsɪdnt] *adj* anders denkend ♦ *n* Dissident *m*

dissimilar [dɪ'sɪmɪlər] *adj*: ~ **(to sb/sth)** (jdm/etw) unähnlich

dissipate ['dɪsɪpeɪt] *vt* (*waste*) verschwenden; (*scatter*) zerstreuen

dissociate [dɪ'səuʃieɪt] *vt* trennen

dissolve [dɪ'zɔlv] *vt* auflösen ♦ *vi* sich auflösen

dissuade [dɪ'sweɪd] *vt*: **to** ~ **sb from doing sth** jdn davon abbringen, etw zu tun

distance ['dɪstns] *n* Entfernung *f*; **in the** ~ in der Ferne; **distant** *adj* entfernt, fern; (*with time*) fern

distaste [dɪs'teɪst] *n* Abneigung *f*; ~**ful** *adj* widerlich

distended [dɪs'tendɪd] *adj* (*stomach*) aufgebläht

distil [dɪs'tɪl] *vt* destillieren; ~**lery** *n* Brennerei *f*

distinct [dɪs'tɪŋkt] *adj* (*separate*) getrennt; (*clear*) klar, deutlich; **as ~ from** im Unterschied zu; ~**ion** [dɪs'tɪŋkʃən] *n* Unterscheidung *f*; (*eminence*) Auszeichnung *f*; ~**ive** *adj* bezeichnend

distinguish [dɪs'tɪŋgwɪʃ] *vt* unterscheiden; ~**ed** *adj* (*eminent*) berühmt; ~**ing** *adj* bezeichnend

distort [dɪs'tɔ:t] *vt* verdrehen; (*misrepresent*) entstellen; ~**ion** [dɪs'tɔ:ʃən] *n* Verzerrung *f*

distract [dɪs'trækt] *vt* ablenken; ~**ing** *adj* verwirrend; ~**ion** [dɪs'trækʃən] *n* (*distress*) Raserei *f*; (*diversion*) Zerstreuung *f*

distraught [dɪs'trɔ:t] *adj* bestürzt

distress [dɪs'tres] *n* Not *f*; (*suffering*) Qual *f* ♦ *vt* quälen; ~**ing** *adj* erschütternd; ~ **signal** *n* Notsignal *nt*

distribute [dɪs'trɪbju:t] *vt* verteilen; **distribution** [dɪstrɪ'bju:ʃən] *n* Verteilung *f*;

distributor n Verteiler m
district ['dɪstrɪkt] n (of country) Kreis m; (of town) Bezirk m; ~ **attorney** (US) n Oberstaatsanwalt m; ~ **nurse** n Kreiskrankenschwester f
distrust [dɪs'trʌst] n Misstrauen nt ♦ vt misstrauen +dat
disturb [dɪs'tɜːb] vt stören; (agitate) erregen; ~**ance** n Störung f; ~**ed** adj beunruhigt; **emotionally** ~**ed** emotional gestört; ~**ing** adj beunruhigend
disuse [dɪs'juːs] n: **to fall into** ~ außer Gebrauch kommen; ~**d** [dɪs'juːzd] adj außer Gebrauch; (mine, railway line) stillgelegt
ditch [dɪtʃ] n Graben m ♦ vt (person) loswerden; (plan) fallen lassen
dither ['dɪðə*] vi verdattert sein
ditto ['dɪtəu] adv dito, ebenfalls
divan [dɪ'væn] n Liegesofa nt
dive [daɪv] n (into water) Kopfsprung m; (AVIAT) Sturzflug m ♦ vi tauchen; ~**r** n Taucher m
diverge [daɪ'vɜːdʒ] vi auseinander gehen
diverse [daɪ'vɜːs] adj verschieden
diversion [daɪ'vɜːʃən] n Ablenkung f; (BRIT: AUT) Umleitung f
diversity [daɪ'vɜːsɪtɪ] n Vielfalt f
divert [daɪ'vɜːt] vt ablenken; (traffic) umleiten
divide [dɪ'vaɪd] vt teilen ♦ vi sich teilen; ~**d highway** (US) n Schnellstraße f
divine [dɪ'vaɪn] adj göttlich
diving ['daɪvɪŋ] n (SPORT) Turmspringen nt; (underwater ~) Tauchen nt; ~ **board** n Sprungbrett nt
divinity [dɪ'vɪnɪtɪ] n Gottheit f; (subject) Religion f
division [dɪ'vɪʒən] n Teilung f; (MIL) Division f; (part) Abteilung f; (in opinion) Uneinigkeit f; (BRIT: POL) (Abstimmung f durch) Hammelsprung f
divorce [dɪ'vɔːs] n (Ehe)scheidung f ♦ vt scheiden; ~**d** adj geschieden; ~**e** [dɪvɔː'siː] n Geschiedene(r) f(m)
divulge [daɪ'vʌldʒ] vt preisgeben
DIY (BRIT) n abbr = **do-it-yourself**
dizzy ['dɪzɪ] adj schwindlig
DJ n abbr = **disc jockey**

DNA fingerprinting n genetische Fingerabdrücke pl

KEYWORD

do [duː] (pt **did**, pp **done**) n (inf: party etc) Fete f
♦ aux vb 1 (in negative constructions and questions): **I don't understand** ich verstehe nicht; **didn't you know?** wusstest du das nicht?; **what do you think?** was meinen Sie?
2 (for emphasis, in polite phrases): **she does seem rather tired** sie scheint wirklich sehr müde zu sein; **do sit down/help yourself** setzen Sie sich doch hin/greifen Sie doch zu
3 (used to avoid repeating vb): **she swims better than I do** sie schwimmt besser als ich; **she lives in Glasgow - so do I** sie wohnt in Glasgow - ich auch
4 (in tag questions): **you like him, don't you?** du magst ihn doch, oder?
♦ vt 1 (carry out, perform etc) tun, machen; **what are you doing tonight?** was machst du heute Abend?; **I've got nothing to do** ich habe nichts zu tun; **to do one's hair/nails** sich die Haare/Nägel machen
2 (AUT etc) fahren
♦ vi 1 (act, behave): **do as I do** mach es wie ich
2 (get on, fare): **he's doing well/badly at school** er ist gut/schlecht in der Schule; **how do you do?** guten Tag
3 (be suitable) gehen; (be sufficient) reichen; **to make do (with)** auskommen mit
 do away with vt (kill) umbringen; (abolish: law etc) abschaffen
 do up vt (laces, dress, buttons) zumachen; (room, house) renovieren
 do with vt (need) brauchen; (be connected) zu tun haben mit
 do without vt, vi auskommen ohne

docile ['dəusaɪl] adj gefügig
dock [dɔk] n Dock nt; (JUR) Anklagebank f
♦ vi ins Dock gehen; ~**er** n Hafenarbeiter m; ~**yard** n Werft f

doctor ['dɔktəʳ] n Arzt m, Ärztin f; (UNIV) Doktor m ♦ vt (fig) fälschen; (drink etc) etw beimischen +dat; **D~ of Philosophy** n Doktor m der Philosophie

document ['dɔkjumənt] n Dokument nt; **~ary** [dɔkju'mɛntərɪ] n Dokumentarbericht m; (film) Dokumentarfilm m ♦ adj dokumentarisch; **~ation** [dɔkjumən'teɪʃən] n dokumentarische(r) Nachweis m

dodge [dɔdʒ] n Kniff m ♦ vt ausweichen +dat

dodgems ['dɔdʒəmz] (BRIT) npl Autoskooter m

doe [dəu] n (roe deer) Ricke f; (red deer) Hirschkuh f; (rabbit) Weibchen nt

does [dʌz] vb see **do**; **~n't = does not**

dog [dɔg] n Hund m; **~ collar** n Hundehalsband nt; (ECCL) Kragen m des Geistlichen; **~-eared** adj mit Eselsohren

dogged ['dɔgɪd] adj hartnäckig

dogsbody ['dɔgzbɔdɪ] n Mädchen nt für alles

doings ['duɪŋz] npl (activities) Treiben nt

do-it-yourself ['duːɪtjɔːˈsɛlf] n Do-it-yourself nt

doldrums ['dɔldrəmz] npl: **to be in the ~** (business) Flaute haben; (person) deprimiert sein

dole [dəul] (BRIT) n Stempelgeld nt; **to be on the ~** stempeln gehen; **~ out** vt ausgeben, austeilen

doleful ['dəulful] adj traurig

doll [dɔl] n Puppe f ♦ vt: **to o.s. up** sich aufdonnern

dollar ['dɔləʳ] n Dollar m

dolphin ['dɔlfɪn] n Delfin m, Delphin m

dome [dəum] n Kuppel f

domestic [də'mɛstɪk] adj häuslich; (within country) Innen-, Binnen-; (animal) Haus-; **~ated** adj (person) häuslich; (animal) zahm

dominant ['dɔmɪnənt] adj vorherrschend

dominate ['dɔmɪneɪt] vt beherrschen

domineering [dɔmɪ'nɪərɪŋ] adj herrisch

dominion [də'mɪnɪən] n (rule) Regierungsgewalt f; (land) Staatsgebiet nt mit Selbstverwaltung

domino ['dɔmɪnəu] (pl **-es**) n Dominostein m; **~es** n (game) Domino(spiel) nt

don [dɔn] (BRIT) n akademische(r) Lehrer m

donate [də'neɪt] vt (blood, money) spenden; (lot of money) stiften; **donation** [də'neɪʃən] n Spende f

done [dʌn] pp of **do**

donkey ['dɔŋkɪ] n Esel m

donor ['dəunəʳ] n Spender m; **~ card** n Organspenderausweis m

don't [dəunt] = **do not**

doodle ['duːdl] vi kritzeln

doom [duːm] n böse(s) Geschick nt; (downfall) Verderben nt ♦ vt: **to be ~ed** zum Untergang verurteilt sein; **~sday** n der Jüngste Tag

door [dɔːʳ] n Tür f; **~bell** n Türklingel f; **~handle** n Türklinke f; **~man** (irreg) n Türsteher m; **~mat** n Fußmatte f; **~step** n Türstufe f; **~way** n Türöffnung f

dope [dəup] n (drug) Aufputschmittel nt ♦ vt (horse) dopen

dopey ['dəupɪ] (inf) adj bekloppt

dormant ['dɔːmənt] adj latent

dormitory ['dɔːmɪtrɪ] n Schlafsaal m

dormouse ['dɔːmaus] (pl **-mice**) n Haselmaus f

DOS [dɔs] n abbr (= disk operating system) DOS nt

dosage ['dəusɪdʒ] n Dosierung f

dose [dəus] n Dosis f

dosh [dɔʃ] (inf) n (money) Moos nt, Knete f

doss house ['dɔs-] (BRIT) n Bleibe f

dot [dɔt] n Punkt m; **~ted with** übersät mit; **on the ~** pünktlich

dote [dəut]: **to ~ on** vt fus vernarrt sein in +acc

dotted line ['dɔtɪd-] n punktierte Linie f

double ['dʌbl] adj, adv doppelt ♦ n Doppelgänger m ♦ vt verdoppeln ♦ vi sich verdoppeln; **~s** npl (TENNIS) Doppel nt; **on or at the ~** im Laufschritt; **~ bass** n Kontrabass m; **~ bed** n Doppelbett nt; **~ bend** (BRIT) n S-Kurve f; **~-breasted** adj zweireihig; **~-cross** vt hintergehen; **~-decker** n Doppeldecker m; **~ glazing** (BRIT) n Doppelverglasung f; **~ room** n Doppelzimmer nt

doubly ['dʌblɪ] adv doppelt

doubt [daut] n Zweifel m ♦ vt bezweifeln; **~ful** adj zweifelhaft; **~less** adv ohne Zweifel

dough [dəu] n Teig m; **~nut** n Berliner m

douse [dauz] vt (drench) mit Wasser begießen, durchtränken; (extinguish) ausmachen

dove [dʌv] n Taube f

dovetail ['dʌvteɪl] vi (plans) übereinstimmen

dowdy ['daudɪ] adj unmodern

down [daun] n (fluff) Flaum m; (hill) Hügel m ♦ adv unten; (motion) herunter; hinunter ♦ prep: **to go ~ the street** die Straße hinuntergehen ♦ vt niederschlagen; **~ with X!** nieder mit X!; **~-and-out** n Tramp m; **~-at-heel** adj schäbig; **~cast** adj niedergeschlagen; **~fall** n Sturz m; **~hearted** adj niedergeschlagen; **~hill** adv bergab; **~ payment** n Anzahlung f; **~pour** n Platzregen m; **~right** adj ausgesprochen; **~size** vi (ECON: company) sich verkleinern

Downing Street

i Downing Street *ist die Straße in London, die von Whitehall zum St James Park führt und in der sich der offizielle Wohnsitz des Premierministers (Nr. 10) und des Finanzministers (Nr. 11) befindet. Im weiteren Sinne bezieht sich der Begriff Downing Street auf die britische Regierung.*

Down's syndrome [daunz-] n (MED) Down-Syndrom nt

down: **~stairs** adv unten; (motion) nach unten; **~stream** adv flussabwärts; **~-to-earth** adj praktisch; **~town** adv in der Innenstadt; (motion) in die Innenstadt; **~ under** (BRIT: inf) adv in/nach Australien/Neuseeland; **~ward** adj Abwärts-, nach unten ♦ adv abwärts, nach unten; **~wards** adv abwärts, nach unten

dowry ['daurɪ] n Mitgift f

doz. abbr (= dozen) Dtzd.

doze [dəuz] vi dösen; **~ off** vi einnicken

dozen ['dʌzn] n Dutzend nt; **a ~ books** ein Dutzend Bücher; **~s of** dutzende or Dutzende von

Dr. abbr = doctor; drive

drab [dræb] adj düster, eintönig

draft [drɑːft] n Entwurf m; (FIN) Wechsel m; (US: MIL) Einberufung f ♦ vt skizzieren; see also **draught**

draftsman ['drɑːftsmən] (US: irreg) n = **draughtsman**

drag [dræg] vt schleppen; (river) mit einem Schleppnetz absuchen ♦ vi sich (dahin)schleppen ♦ n (bore) etwas Blödes; **in ~** als Tunte; **a man in ~** eine Tunte; **~ on** vi sich in die Länge ziehen; **~ and drop** vt (COMPUT) Drag & Drop nt

dragon ['drægn] n Drache m; **~fly** ['drægənflaɪ] n Libelle f

drain [dreɪn] n Abfluss m; (fig: burden) Belastung f ♦ vt ableiten; (exhaust) erschöpfen ♦ vi (of water) abfließen; **~age** n Kanalisation f; **~ing board** (US **~board**) n Ablaufbrett nt; **~pipe** n Abflussrohr nt

dram [dræm] n Schluck m

drama ['drɑːmə] n Drama nt; **~tic** [drə'mætɪk] adj dramatisch; **~tist** ['dræmətɪst] n Dramatiker m; **~tize** ['dræmətaɪz] vt (events) dramatisieren; (for TV etc) bearbeiten

drank [dræŋk] pt of **drink**

drape [dreɪp] vt drapieren; **~s** (US) npl Vorhänge pl

drastic ['dræstɪk] adj drastisch

draught [drɑːft] (US **draft**) n Zug m; (NAUT) Tiefgang m; **~s** n Damespiel nt; **on ~** (beer) vom Fass; **~ beer** n Bier nt vom Fass; **~board** (BRIT) n Zeichenbrett n

draughtsman ['drɑːftsmən] (irreg) n technische(r) Zeichner m

draw [drɔː] (pt drew, pp drew) vt ziehen; (crowd) anlocken; (picture) zeichnen; (money) abheben; (water) schöpfen ♦ vi (SPORT) unentschieden spielen ♦ n (SPORT) Unentschieden nt; (lottery) Ziehung f; **~ near** vi näher rücken; **~ out** vi (train) ausfahren; (lengthen) sich hinziehen; **~ up** vi (stop) halten ♦ vt (document) aufsetzen

drawback ['drɔːbæk] n Nachteil m

drawbridge ['drɔːbrɪdʒ] n Zugbrücke f

drawer [drɔːʳ] *n* Schublade *f*

drawing [ˈdrɔːɪŋ] *n* Zeichnung *f*; Zeichnen *nt*; ~ **board** *n* Reißbrett *nt*; ~ **pin** (*BRIT*) *n* Reißzwecke *f*; ~ **room** *n* Salon *m*

drawl [drɔːl] *n* schleppende Sprechweise *f*

drawn [drɔːn] *pp of* **draw**

dread [dred] *n* Furcht *f* ♦ *vt* fürchten; ~**ful** *adj* furchtbar

dream [driːm] (*pt, pp* **dreamed** *or* **dreamt**) *n* Traum *m* ♦ *vt* träumen ♦ *vi*: **to ~ (about)** träumen (von); ~**er** *n* Träumer *m*; ~**t** [dremt] *pt, pp of* **dream**; ~**y** *adj* verträumt

dreary [ˈdrɪərɪ] *adj* trostlos, öde

dredge [dredʒ] *vt* ausbaggern

dregs [dregz] *npl* Bodensatz *m*; (*fig*) Abschaum *m*

drench [drentʃ] *vt* durchnässen

dress [dres] *n* Kleidung *f*; (*garment*) Kleid *nt* ♦ *vt* anziehen; (*MED*) verbinden; **to get ~ed** sich anziehen; ~ **up** *vi* sich fein machen; ~ **circle** (*BRIT*) *n* erste(r) Rang *m*; ~**er** *n* (*furniture*) Anrichte *f*; ~**ing** *n* (*MED*) Verband *m*; (*COOK*) Soße *f*; ~**ing gown** (*BRIT*) *n* Morgenrock *m*; ~**ing room** *n* (*THEAT*) Garderobe *f*; (*SPORT*) Umkleideraum *m*; ~**ing table** *n* Toilettentisch *m*; ~**maker** *n* Schneiderin *f*; ~ **rehearsal** *n* Generalprobe *f*

drew [druː] *pt of* **draw**

dribble [ˈdrɪbl] *vi* sabbern ♦ *vt* (*ball*) dribbeln

dried [draɪd] *adj* getrocknet; (*fruit*) Dörr-, gedörrte(r, s); ~ **milk** *n* Milchpulver *nt*

drier [ˈdraɪəʳ] *n* = **dryer**

drift [drɪft] *n* Strömung *f*; (*snowdrift*) Schneewehe *f*; (*fig*) Richtung *f* ♦ *vi* sich treiben lassen; ~**wood** *n* Treibholz *nt*

drill [drɪl] *n* Bohrer *m*; (*MIL*) Drill *m* ♦ *vt* bohren; (*MIL*) ausbilden ♦ *vi*: **to ~ (for)** bohren (nach)

drink [drɪŋk] (*pt* **drank**, *pp* **drunk**) *n* Getränk *nt*; (*spirits*) Drink *m* ♦ *vt, vi* trinken; **to have a ~** etwas trinken; ~**er** *n* Trinker *m*; ~**ing water** *n* Trinkwasser *nt*

drip [drɪp] *n* Tropfen *m* ♦ *vi* tropfen; ~-**dry** *adj* bügelfrei; ~**ping** *n* Bratenfett *nt*

drive [draɪv] (*pt* **drove**, *pp* **driven**) *n* Fahrt *f*; (*road*) Einfahrt *f*; (*campaign*) Aktion *f*; (*energy*) Schwung *m*; (*SPORT*) Schlag *m*; (*also*: **disk ~**) Diskettenlaufwerk *nt* ♦ *vt* (*car*) fahren; (*animals, people, objects*) treiben; (*power*) antreiben ♦ *vi* fahren; **left-/right-hand ~** Links-/Rechtssteuerung *f*; **to ~ sb mad** jdn verrückt machen; ~-**by shooting** *n* Schusswaffenangriff aus einem vorbeifahrenden Wagen

drivel [ˈdrɪvl] *n* Faselei *f*

driven [ˈdrɪvn] *pp of* **drive**

driver [ˈdraɪvəʳ] *n* Fahrer *m*; ~**'s license** (*US*) *n* Führerschein *m*

driveway [ˈdraɪvweɪ] *n* Auffahrt *f*; (*longer*) Zufahrtsstraße *f*

driving [ˈdraɪvɪŋ] *adj* (*rain*) stürmisch; ~ **instructor** *n* Fahrlehrer *m*; ~ **lesson** *n* Fahrstunde *f*; ~ **licence** (*BRIT*) *n* Führerschein *m*; ~ **school** *n* Fahrschule *f*; ~ **test** *n* Fahrprüfung *f*

drizzle [ˈdrɪzl] *n* Nieselregen *m* ♦ *vi* nieseln

droll [drəul] *adj* drollig

drone [drəun] *n* (*sound*) Brummen *nt*; (*bee*) Drohne *f*

drool [druːl] *vi* sabbern

droop [druːp] *vi* (schlaff) herabhängen

drop [drɔp] *n* (*of liquid*) Tropfen *m*; (*fall*) Fall *m* ♦ *vt* fallen lassen; (*lower*) senken; (*abandon*) fallen lassen ♦ *vi* (*fall*) herunterfallen; ~**s** *npl* (*MED*) Tropfen *pl*; ~ **off** *vi* (*sleep*) einschlafen ♦ *vt* (*passenger*) absetzen; ~ **out** *vi* (*withdraw*) ausscheiden; ~-**out** *n* Aussteiger *m*; ~**per** *n* Pipette *f*; ~**pings** *npl* Kot *m*

drought [draut] *n* Dürre *f*

drove [drəuv] *pt of* **drive**

drown [draun] *vt* ertränken; (*sound*) übertönen ♦ *vi* ertrinken

drowsy [ˈdrauzɪ] *adj* schläfrig

drudgery [ˈdrʌdʒərɪ] *n* Plackerei *f*

drug [drʌg] *n* (*MED*) Arznei *f*; (*narcotic*) Rauschgift *nt* ♦ *vt* betäuben; ~ **addict** *n* Rauschgiftsüchtige(r) *f(m)*; ~**gist** (*US*) *n* Drogist(in) *m(f)*; ~**store** (*US*) *n* Drogerie *f*

drum [drʌm] *n* Trommel *f* ♦ *vi* trommeln; ~**s** *npl* (*MUS*) Schlagzeug *nt*; ~**mer** *n* Trommler *m*

drunk [drʌŋk] *pp of* **drink** ♦ *adj* betrunken

♦ n (also: **~ard**) Trinker(in) m(f); **~en** adj betrunken

dry [draɪ] adj trocken ♦ vt (ab)trocknen ♦ vi trocknen; **~ up** vi austrocknen ♦ vt (dishes) abtrocknen; **~ cleaner's** n chemische Reinigung f; **~ cleaning** n chemische Reinigung f; **~er** n Trockner m; (US: spin-dryer) (Wäsche)schleuder f; **~ goods store** (US) n Kurzwarengeschäft nt; **~ness** n Trockenheit f; **~ rot** n Hausschwamm m

DSS (BRIT) n abbr (= Department of Social Security) ≈ Sozialministerium nt

DTP n abbr (= desktop publishing) DTP nt

dual ['djuəl] adj doppelt; **~ carriageway** (BRIT) n zweispurige Fahrbahn f; **~ nationality** n doppelte Staatsangehörigkeit f; **~-purpose** adj Mehrzweck-

dubbed [dʌbd] adj (film) synchronisiert

dubious ['djuːbɪəs] adj zweifelhaft

duchess ['dʌtʃɪs] n Herzogin f

duck [dʌk] n Ente f ♦ vi sich ducken; **~ling** n Entchen nt

duct [dʌkt] n Röhre f

dud [dʌd] n Niete f ♦ adj (cheque) ungedeckt

due [djuː] adj fällig; (fitting) angemessen ♦ n Gebühr f; (right) Recht nt ♦ adv (south etc) genau; **~s** npl (for club) Beitrag m; (NAUT) Gebühren pl; **~ to** wegen +gen

duel ['djuːəl] n Duell nt

duet [djuː'et] n Duett nt

duffel ['dʌfl] adj: **~ bag** Matchbeutel m, Matchsack m

dug [dʌg] pt, pp of **dig**

duke [djuːk] n Herzog m

dull [dʌl] adj (colour, weather) trübe; (stupid) schwer von Begriff; (boring) langweilig ♦ vt abstumpfen

duly ['djuːlɪ] adv ordnungsgemäß

dumb [dʌm] adj stumm; (inf: stupid) doof, blöde; **~founded** [dʌm'faʊndɪd] adj verblüfft

dummy ['dʌmɪ] n Schneiderpuppe f; (substitute) Attrappe f; (BRIT: for baby) Schnuller m ♦ adj Schein-

dump [dʌmp] n Abfallhaufen m; (MIL) Stapelplatz m; (inf: place) Nest nt ♦ vt abladen, auskippen; **~ing** n (COMM) Schleuderexport m; (of rubbish) Schuttabladen nt

dumpling ['dʌmplɪŋ] n Kloß m, Knödel m

dumpy ['dʌmpɪ] adj pummelig

dunce [dʌns] n Dummkopf m

dune [djuːn] n Düne f

dung [dʌŋ] n Dünger m

dungarees [dʌŋgə'riːz] npl Latzhose f

dungeon ['dʌndʒən] n Kerker m

dupe [djuːp] n Gefoppte(r) m ♦ vt hintergehen, anführen

duplex ['djuːpleks] (US) n zweistöckige Wohnung f

duplicate [n 'djuːplɪkət, vb 'djuːplɪkeɪt] n Duplikat nt ♦ vt verdoppeln; (make copies) kopieren; **in ~** in doppelter Ausführung

duplicity [djuː'plɪsɪtɪ] n Doppelspiel nt

durable ['djuərəbl] adj haltbar

duration [djuə'reɪʃən] n Dauer f

duress [djuə'res] n: **under ~** unter Zwang

during ['djuərɪŋ] prep während +gen

dusk [dʌsk] n Abenddämmerung f

dust [dʌst] n Staub m ♦ vt abstauben; (sprinkle) bestäuben; **~bin** (BRIT) n Mülleimer m; **~er** n Staubtuch nt; **~ jacket** n Schutzumschlag m; **~man** (BRIT: irreg) n Müllmann m; **~y** adj staubig

Dutch [dʌtʃ] adj holländisch, niederländisch ♦ n (LING) Holländisch nt, Niederländisch nt; **the ~** npl (people) die Holländer pl, die Niederländer pl; **to go ~** getrennte Kasse machen; **~man/woman** (irreg) n Holländer(in) m(f), Niederländer(in) m(f)

dutiful ['djuːtɪful] adj pflichtbewusst

duty ['djuːtɪ] n Pflicht f; (job) Aufgabe f; (tax) Einfuhrzoll m; **on ~** im Dienst; **~ chemist's** n Apotheke f im Bereitschaftsdienst; **~-free** adj zollfrei

duvet ['duːveɪ] (BRIT) n Daunendecke nt

dwarf [dwɔːf] (pl **dwarves**) n Zwerg m ♦ vt überragen

dwell [dwel] (pt, pp **dwelt**) vi wohnen; **~ on** vt fus verweilen bei; **~ing** n Wohnung f

dwelt [dwelt] pt, pp of **dwell**

dwindle ['dwɪndl] vi schwinden

dye [daɪ] n Farbstoff m ♦ vt färben

dying ['daɪɪŋ] adj (person) sterbend;

(*moments*) letzt

dyke [daɪk] (*BRIT*) *n* (*channel*) Kanal *m*; (*barrier*) Deich *m*, Damm *m*

dynamic [daɪˈnæmɪk] *adj* dynamisch

dynamite [ˈdaɪnəmaɪt] *n* Dynamit *nt*

dynamo [ˈdaɪnəməu] *n* Dynamo *m*

dyslexia [dɪsˈleksɪə] *n* Legasthenie *f*

E, e

E [iː] *n* (*MUS*) E *nt*

each [iːtʃ] *adj* jeder/jede/jedes ♦ *pron* (ein) jeder/(eine) jede/(ein) jedes; ~ **other** einander, sich; **they have two books** ~ sie haben je zwei Bücher

eager [ˈiːgəʳ] *adj* eifrig

eagle [ˈiːgl] *n* Adler *m*

ear [ɪəʳ] *n* Ohr *nt*; (*of corn*) Ähre *f*; ~**ache** *n* Ohrenschmerzen *pl*; ~**drum** *n* Trommelfell *nt*

earl [əːl] *n* Graf *m*

earlier [ˈəːlɪəʳ] *adj*, *adv* früher; **I can't come any** ~ ich kann nicht früher *or* eher kommen

early [ˈəːlɪ] *adj*, *adv* früh; ~ **retirement** *n* vorzeitige Pensionierung

earmark [ˈɪəmɑːk] *vt* vorsehen

earn [əːn] *vt* verdienen

earnest [ˈəːnɪst] *adj* ernst; **in** ~ im Ernst

earnings [ˈəːnɪŋz] *npl* Verdienst *m*

ear: ~**phones** [ˈɪəfəunz] *npl* Kopfhörer *pl*; ~**ring** [ˈɪərɪŋ] *n* Ohrring *m*; ~**shot** [ˈɪəʃɒt] *n* Hörweite *f*

earth [əːθ] *n* Erde *f*; (*BRIT*: *ELEC*) Erdung *f* ♦ *vt* erden; ~**enware** *n* Steingut *nt*; ~**quake** *n* Erdbeben *nt*; ~**y** *adj* roh

earwig [ˈɪəwɪg] *n* Ohrwurm *m*

ease [iːz] *n* (*simplicity*) Leichtigkeit *f*; (*social*) Ungezwungenheit *f* ♦ *vt* (*pain*) lindern; (*burden*) erleichtern; **at** ~ ungezwungen; (*MIL*) rührt euch!; ~ **off** *or* **up** *vi* nachlassen

easel [ˈiːzl] *n* Staffelei *f*

easily [ˈiːzɪlɪ] *adv* leicht

east [iːst] *n* Osten *m* ♦ *adj* östlich ♦ *adv* nach Osten

Easter [ˈiːstəʳ] *n* Ostern *nt*; ~ **egg** *n* Osterei *nt*

east: ~**erly** *adj* östlich, Ost-; ~**ern** *adj* östlich; ~**ward(s)** *adv* ostwärts

easy [ˈiːzɪ] *adj* (*task*) einfach; (*life*) bequem; (*manner*) ungezwungen, natürlich ♦ *adv* leicht; ~ **chair** *n* Sessel *m*; ~-**going** *adj* gelassen; (*lax*) lässig

eat [iːt] (*pt* **ate**, *pp* **eaten**) *vt* essen; (*animals*) fressen; (*destroy*) (zer)fressen ♦ *vi* essen; fressen; ~ **away** *vt* zerfressen; ~ **into** *vt fus* zerfressen; ~**en** *pp* of **eat**

eau de Cologne [ˈəudəkəˈləun] *n* Kölnischwasser *nt*

eaves [iːvz] *npl* Dachrand *m*

eavesdrop [ˈiːvzdrɒp] *vi* lauschen; **to** ~ **on sb** jdn belauschen

ebb [eb] *n* Ebbe *f* ♦ *vi* (*fig: also:* ~ **away**) (ab)ebben

ebony [ˈebənɪ] *n* Ebenholz *nt*

EC *n abbr* (= *European Community*) EG *f*

eccentric [ɪkˈsentrɪk] *adj* exzentrisch ♦ *n* Exzentriker(in) *m(f)*

ecclesiastical [ɪkliːzɪˈæstɪkl] *adj* kirchlich

echo [ˈekəu] (*pl* ~**es**) *n* Echo *nt* ♦ *vt* zurückwerfen; (*fig*) nachbeten ♦ *vi* widerhallen

eclipse [ɪˈklɪps] *n* Finsternis *f* ♦ *vt* verfinstern

ecology [ɪˈkɒlədʒɪ] *n* Ökologie *f*

economic [iːkəˈnɒmɪk] *adj* wirtschaftlich; ~**al** *adj* wirtschaftlich; (*person*) sparsam; ~ **refugee** *n* Wirtschaftsflüchtling *m*; ~**s** *n* Volkswirtschaft *f*

economist [ɪˈkɒnəmɪst] *n* Volkswirt(schaftler) *m*

economize [ɪˈkɒnəmaɪz] *vi* sparen

economy [ɪˈkɒnəmɪ] *n* (*thrift*) Sparsamkeit *f*; (*of country*) Wirtschaft *f*; ~ **class** *n* Touristenklasse *f*

ecstasy [ˈekstəsɪ] *n* Ekstase *f*; (*drug*) Ecstasy *nt*; **ecstatic** [eksˈtætɪk] *adj* hingerissen

ECU [ˈeɪkjuː] *n abbr* (= *European Currency Unit*) ECU *m(f)*

eczema [ˈeksɪmə] *n* Ekzem *nt*

edge [edʒ] *n* Rand *m*; (*of knife*) Schneide *f* ♦ *vt* (*SEWING*) einfassen; **on** ~ (*fig*) = **edgy**; **to** ~ **away from** langsam abrücken von;

~ways adv: he couldn't get a word in ~ways er kam überhaupt nicht zu Wort
edgy ['edʒɪ] adj nervös
edible ['edɪbl] adj essbar
edict ['iːdɪkt] n Erlass m
edit ['edɪt] vt redigieren; ~ion [ɪ'dɪʃən] n Ausgabe f; ~or n (of newspaper) Redakteur m; (of book) Lektor m
editorial [edɪ'tɔːrɪəl] adj Redaktions- ♦ n Leitartikel m
educate ['edjukeɪt] vt erziehen, (aus)bilden; ~d adj gebildet; education [edju'keɪʃən] n (teaching) Unterricht m; (system) Schulwesen nt; (schooling) Erziehung f; Bildung f; educational adj pädagogisch
eel [iːl] n Aal m
eerie ['ɪərɪ] adj unheimlich
effect [ɪ'fekt] n Wirkung f ♦ vt bewirken; ~s npl (sound, visual) Effekte pl; in ~ in der Tat; to take ~ (law) in Kraft treten; (drug) wirken; ~ive adj wirksam, effektiv; ~ively adv wirksam, effektiv
effeminate [ɪ'femɪnɪt] adj weibisch
effervescent [efə'vesnt] adj (also fig) sprudelnd
efficiency [ɪ'fɪʃənsɪ] n Leistungsfähigkeit f
efficient [ɪ'fɪʃənt] adj tüchtig; (TECH) leistungsfähig; (method) wirksam
effigy ['efɪdʒɪ] n Abbild nt
effort ['efət] n Anstrengung f; ~less adj mühelos
effusive [ɪ'fjuːsɪv] adj überschwänglich
e.g. adv abbr (= exempli gratia) z. B.
egalitarian [ɪgælɪ'teərɪən] adj Gleichheits-, egalitär
egg [eg] n Ei nt; ~ on vt anstacheln; ~cup n Eierbecher m; ~plant n (esp US) Aubergine f; ~shell n Eierschale f
ego ['iːgəu] n Ich nt, Selbst nt; ~tism ['egəutɪzəm] n Ichbezogenheit f; ~tist ['egəutɪst] n Egozentriker m
Egypt ['iːdʒɪpt] n Ägypten nt; ~ian [ɪ'dʒɪpʃən] adj ägyptisch ♦ n Ägypter(in) m(f)
eiderdown ['aɪdədaun] n Daunendecke f
eight [eɪt] num acht; ~een num achtzehn; ~h [eɪtθ] adj achte(r, s) ♦ n Achtel nt; ~y num achtzig

Eire ['eərə] n Irland nt
either ['aɪðər] conj: ~ ... or entweder ... oder ♦ pron: ~ of the two eine(r, s) von beiden ♦ adj: on ~ side auf beiden Seiten ♦ adv: I don't ~ ich auch nicht; I don't want ~ ich will keins von beiden
eject [ɪ'dʒekt] vt ausstoßen, vertreiben
eke [iːk] vt: to ~ out strecken
elaborate [adj ɪ'læbərɪt, vb ɪ'læbəreɪt] adj sorgfältig ausgearbeitet, ausführlich ♦ vt sorgfältig ausarbeiten ♦ vi ausführlich darstellen
elapse [ɪ'læps] vi vergehen
elastic [ɪ'læstɪk] n Gummiband nt ♦ adj elastisch; ~ band n (BRIT) n Gummiband nt
elated [ɪ'leɪtɪd] adj froh
elation [ɪ'leɪʃən] n gehobene Stimmung f
elbow ['elbəu] n Ellbogen m
elder ['eldər] adj älter ♦ n Ältere(r) f(m); ~ly adj ältere(r, s) ♦ npl: the ~ly die Älteren pl; eldest ['eldɪst] adj älteste(r, s) ♦ n Älteste(r) f(m)
elect [ɪ'lekt] vt wählen ♦ adj zukünftig; ~ion [ɪ'lekʃən] n Wahl f; ~ioneering [ɪlekʃə'nɪərɪŋ] n Wahlpropaganda f; ~or n Wähler m; ~oral adj Wahl-; ~orate n Wähler pl, Wählerschaft f
electric [ɪ'lektrɪk] adj elektrisch, Elektro-; ~al adj elektrisch; ~ blanket n Heizdecke f; ~ chair n elektrische(r) Stuhl m; ~ fire n elektrische(r) Heizofen m
electrician [ɪlek'trɪʃən] n Elektriker m
electricity [ɪlek'trɪsɪtɪ] n Elektrizität f
electrify [ɪ'lektrɪfaɪ] vt elektrifizieren; (fig) elektrisieren
electrocute [ɪ'lektrəkjuːt] vt durch elektrischen Strom töten
electronic [ɪlek'trɒnɪk] adj elektronisch, Elektronen-; ~ mail n elektronische(r) Briefkasten m; ~s n Elektronik f
elegance ['elɪgəns] n Eleganz f; elegant ['elɪgənt] adj elegant
element ['elɪmənt] n Element nt; ~ary [elɪ'mentərɪ] adj einfach; (primary) Grund-
elephant ['elɪfənt] n Elefant m
elevate ['elɪveɪt] vt emporheben; elevation [elɪ'veɪʃən] n (height) Erhebung f; (ARCHIT)

(Quer)schnitt *m*; **elevator** (*US*) *n* Fahrstuhl *m*, Aufzug *m*

eleven [ɪ'lɛvn] *num* elf; **~ses** (*BRIT*) *npl* ≃ zweite(s) Frühstück *nt*; **~th** *adj* elfte(r, s)

elicit [ɪ'lɪsɪt] *vt* herausbekommen

eligible ['ɛlɪdʒəbl] *adj* wählbar; **to be ~ for a pension** pensionsberechtigt sein

eliminate [ɪ'lɪmɪneɪt] *vt* ausschalten

elite [eɪ'liːt] *n* Elite *f*

elm [ɛlm] *n* Ulme *f*

elocution [ɛlə'kjuːʃən] *n* Sprecherziehung *f*

elongated ['iːlɒŋɡeɪtɪd] *adj* verlängert

elope [ɪ'ləʊp] *vi* entlaufen

eloquence ['ɛləkwəns] *n* Beredsamkeit *f*; **eloquent** *adj* redegewandt

else [ɛls] *adv* sonst; **who ~?** wer sonst?; **somebody ~** jemand anders; **or ~** sonst; **~where** *adv* anderswo, woanders

elude [ɪ'luːd] *vt* entgehen +*dat*

elusive [ɪ'luːsɪv] *adj* schwer fassbar

emaciated [ɪ'meɪsɪeɪtɪd] *adj* abgezehrt

E-mail ['iːmeɪl] *n abbr* (= *electronic mail*) E-Mail *f*

emancipation [ɪmænsɪ'peɪʃən] *n* Emanzipation *f*; Freilassung *f*

embankment [ɪm'bæŋkmənt] *n* (*of river*) Uferböschung *f*; (*of road*) Straßendamm *m*

embargo [ɪm'bɑːɡəʊ] (*pl* **~es**) *n* Embargo *nt*

embark [ɪm'bɑːk] *vi* sich einschiffen; **~ on** *vt fus* unternehmen; **~ation** [ɛmbɑː'keɪʃən] *n* Einschiffung *f*

embarrass [ɪm'bærəs] *vt* in Verlegenheit bringen; **~ed** *adj* verlegen; **~ing** *adj* peinlich; **~ment** *n* Verlegenheit *f*

embassy ['ɛmbəsɪ] *n* Botschaft *f*

embed [ɪm'bɛd] *vt* einbetten

embellish [ɪm'bɛlɪʃ] *vt* verschönern

embers ['ɛmbəz] *npl* Glut(asche) *f*

embezzle [ɪm'bɛzl] *vt* unterschlagen; **~ment** *n* Unterschlagung *f*

embitter [ɪm'bɪtəʳ] *vt* verbittern

embody [ɪm'bɒdɪ] *vt* (*ideas*) verkörpern; (*new features*) (in sich) vereinigen

embossed [ɪm'bɒst] *adj* geprägt

embrace [ɪm'breɪs] *vt* umarmen; (*include*) einschließen ♦ *vi* sich umarmen ♦ *n* Umarmung *f*

embroider [ɪm'brɔɪdəʳ] *vt* (be)sticken; (*story*) ausschmücken; **~y** *n* Stickerei *f*

emerald ['ɛmərəld] *n* Smaragd *m*

emerge [ɪ'mɜːdʒ] *vi* auftauchen; (*truth*) herauskommen; **~nce** *n* Erscheinen *nt*

emergency [ɪ'mɜːdʒənsɪ] *n* Notfall *m*; **~ cord** (*US*) *n* Notbremse *f*; **~ exit** *n* Notausgang *m*; **~ landing** *n* Notlandung *f*; **~ services** *npl* Notdienste *pl*

emery board ['ɛmərɪ-] *n* Papiernagelfeile *f*

emigrant ['ɛmɪɡrənt] *n* Auswanderer *m*

emigrate ['ɛmɪɡreɪt] *vi* auswandern; **emigration** [ɛmɪ'ɡreɪʃən] *n* Auswanderung *f*

eminence ['ɛmɪnəns] *n* hohe(r) Rang *m*

eminent ['ɛmɪnənt] *adj* bedeutend

emission [ɪ'mɪʃən] *n* Ausströmen *nt*; **~s** *npl* Emissionen *fpl*

emit [ɪ'mɪt] *vt* von sich *dat* geben

emotion [ɪ'məʊʃən] *n* Emotion *f*, Gefühl *nt*; **~al** *adj* (*person*) emotional; (*scene*) ergreifend

emotive [ɪ'məʊtɪv] *adj* gefühlsbetont

emperor ['ɛmpərəʳ] *n* Kaiser *m*

emphases ['ɛmfəsiːz] *npl* of **emphasis**

emphasis ['ɛmfəsɪs] *n* (*LING*) Betonung *f*; (*fig*) Nachdruck *m*; **emphasize** ['ɛmfəsaɪz] *vt* betonen

emphatic [ɛm'fætɪk] *adj* nachdrücklich; **~ally** *adv* nachdrücklich

empire ['ɛmpaɪəʳ] *n* Reich *nt*

empirical [ɛm'pɪrɪkl] *adj* empirisch

employ [ɪm'plɔɪ] *vt* (*hire*) anstellen; (*use*) verwenden; **~ee** [ɪmplɔɪ'iː] *n* Angestellte(r) *f(m)*; **~er** *n* Arbeitgeber(in) *m(f)*; **~ment** *n* Beschäftigung *f*; **~ment agency** *n* Stellenvermittlung *f*

empower [ɪm'paʊəʳ] *vt*: **to ~ sb to do sth** jdn ermächtigen, etw zu tun

empress ['ɛmprɪs] *n* Kaiserin *f*

emptiness ['ɛmptɪnɪs] *n* Leere *f*

empty ['ɛmptɪ] *adj* leer ♦ *n* (*bottle*) Leergut *nt* ♦ *vt* (*contents*) leeren; (*container*) ausleeren ♦ *vi* (*water*) abfließen; (*river*) münden; (*house*) sich leeren; **~-handed** *adj* mit leeren Händen

EMU ['iːmjuː] *n abbr* (= *economic and monetary union*) EWU *f*

emulate ['emjuleɪt] vt nacheifern +dat

emulsion [ɪ'mʌlʃən] n Emulsion f

enable [ɪ'neɪbl] vt: **to ~ sb to do sth** es jdm ermöglichen, etw zu tun

enact [ɪ'nækt] vt (law) erlassen; (play) aufführen; (role) spielen

enamel [ɪ'næməl] n Email nt; (of teeth) (Zahn)schmelz m

encased [ɪn'keɪst] adj: **~ in** (enclosed) eingeschlossen in +dat; (covered) verkleidet mit

enchant [ɪn'tʃɑ:nt] vt bezaubern; **~ing** adj entzückend

encircle [ɪn'sɜːkl] vt umringen

encl. abbr (= enclosed) Anl.

enclose [ɪn'kləʊz] vt einschließen; **to ~ sth (in** or **with a letter)** etw (einem Brief) beilegen; **~d** (in letter) beiliegend, anbei; **enclosure** [ɪn'kləʊʒəʳ] n Einfriedung f; (in letter) Anlage f

encompass [ɪn'kʌmpəs] vt (include) umfassen

encore [ɔŋ'kɔːʳ] n Zugabe f

encounter [ɪn'kaʊntəʳ] n Begegnung f; (MIL) Zusammenstoß m ♦ vt treffen; (resistance) stoßen auf +acc

encourage [ɪn'kʌrɪdʒ] vt ermutigen; **~ment** n Ermutigung f, Förderung f; **encouraging** adj ermutigend, viel versprechend

encroach [ɪn'krəʊtʃ] vi: **to ~ (up)on** eindringen in +acc; (time) in Anspruch nehmen

encrusted [ɪn'krʌstɪd] adj: **~ with** besetzt mit

encyclop(a)edia [ensaɪkləʊ'piːdɪə] n Konversationslexikon nt

end [end] n Ende nt, Schluss m; (purpose) Zweck m ♦ vt (also: **bring to an ~, put an ~ to**) beenden ♦ vi zu Ende gehen; **in the ~** zum Schluss; **on ~** (object) hochkant; **to stand on ~** (hair) zu Berge stehen; **for hours on ~** stundenlang; **~ up** vi landen

endanger [ɪn'deɪndʒəʳ] vt gefährden; **~ed species** n eine vom Aussterben bedrohte Art

endearing [ɪn'dɪərɪŋ] adj gewinnend

endeavour [ɪn'devəʳ] (US **endeavor**) n Bestrebung f ♦ vi sich bemühen

ending ['endɪŋ] n Ende nt

endless ['endlɪs] adj endlos

endorse [ɪn'dɔːs] vt unterzeichnen; (approve) unterstützen; **~ment** n (AUT) Eintrag m

endow [ɪn'daʊ] vt: **to ~ sb with sth** jdm etw verleihen; (with money) jdm etw stiften

endurance [ɪn'djʊərəns] n Ausdauer f

endure [ɪn'djʊəʳ] vt ertragen ♦ vi (last) (fort)dauern

enemy ['enəmɪ] n Feind m ♦ adj feindlich

energetic [enə'dʒetɪk] adj tatkräftig

energy ['enədʒɪ] n Energie f

enforce [ɪn'fɔːs] vt durchsetzen

engage [ɪn'geɪdʒ] vt (employ) einstellen; (in conversation) verwickeln; (TECH) einschalten ♦ vi (TECH) ineinander greifen; (clutch) fassen; **to ~ in** sich beteiligen an +dat; **~d** adj verlobt; (BRIT: TEL, toilet) besetzt; (: busy) beschäftigt; **to get ~d** sich verloben; **~d tone** (BRIT) n (TEL) Besetztzeichen nt; **~ment** n (appointment) Verabredung f; (to marry) Verlobung f; (MIL) Gefecht nt; **~ment ring** n Verlobungsring m; **engaging** adj gewinnend

engender [ɪn'dʒendəʳ] vt hervorrufen

engine ['endʒɪn] n (AUT) Motor m; (RAIL) Lokomotive f; **~ driver** n Lok(omotiv)führer(in) m(f)

engineer [endʒɪ'nɪəʳ] n Ingenieur m; (US: RAIL) Lok(omotiv)führer(in) m(f); **~ing** [endʒɪ'nɪərɪŋ] n Technik f

England ['ɪŋglənd] n England nt

English ['ɪŋglɪʃ] adj englisch ♦ n (LING) Englisch nt; **the ~** npl (people) die Engländer pl; **~ Channel** n: **the ~ Channel** der Ärmelkanal m; **~man/ woman** (irreg) n Engländer(in) m(f)

engraving [ɪn'greɪvɪŋ] n Stich m

engrossed [ɪn'grəʊst] adj vertieft

engulf [ɪn'gʌlf] vt verschlingen

enhance [ɪn'hɑːns] vt steigern, heben

enigma [ɪ'nɪgmə] n Rätsel nt; **~tic** [enɪg'mætɪk] adj rätselhaft

enjoy [ɪn'dʒɔɪ] vt genießen; (privilege) besitzen; **to ~ o.s.** sich amüsieren; **~able**

adj erfreulich; **~ment** *n* Genuss *m*, Freude *f*

enlarge [ɪn'lɑːdʒ] *vt* erweitern; (*PHOT*) vergrößern ♦ *vi*: **to ~ on sth** etw weiter ausführen; **~ment** *n* Vergrößerung *f*

enlighten [ɪn'laɪtn] *vt* aufklären; **~ment** *n*: **the E~ment** (*HIST*) die Aufklärung

enlist [ɪn'lɪst] *vt* gewinnen ♦ *vi* (*MIL*) sich melden

enmity ['enmɪtɪ] *n* Feindschaft *f*

enormity [ɪ'nɔːmɪtɪ] *n* Ungeheuerlichkeit *f*

enormous [ɪ'nɔːməs] *adj* ungeheuer

enough [ɪ'nʌf] *adj, adv* genug; **funnily ~** komischerweise

enquire [ɪn'kwaɪə*] *vt, vi* = **inquire**

enrage [ɪn'reɪdʒ] *vt* wütend machen

enrich [ɪn'rɪtʃ] *vt* bereichern

enrol [ɪn'rəul] *vt* einschreiben ♦ *vi* (*register*) sich anmelden; **~ment** *n* (*for course*) Anmeldung *f*

en route [ɒn'ruːt] *adv* unterwegs

ensign ['ensaɪn, 'ensən] *n* (*NAUT*) Flagge *f*; (*MIL*) Fähnrich *m*

enslave [ɪn'sleɪv] *vt* versklaven

ensue [ɪn'sjuː] *vi* folgen, sich ergeben

en suite [ɒnswiːt] *adj*: **room with ~ bathroom** Zimmer *nt* mit eigenem Bad

ensure [ɪn'ʃuə*] *vt* garantieren

entail [ɪn'teɪl] *vt* mit sich bringen

entangle [ɪn'tæŋgl] *vt* verwirren, verstricken; **~d** *adj*: **to become ~d (in)** (*in net, rope etc*) sich verfangen (in +*dat*)

enter ['entə*] *vt* eintreten in +*dat*, betreten; (*club*) beitreten +*dat*; (*in book*) eintragen ♦ *vi* hereinkommen, hineingehen; **~ for** *vt fus* sich beteiligen an +*dat*; **~ into** *vt fus* (*agreement*) eingehen; (*plans*) eine Rolle spielen bei; **~ (up)on** *vt fus* beginnen

enterprise ['entəpraɪz] *n* (*in person*) Initiative *f*; (*COMM*) Unternehmen *nt*; **enterprising** ['entəpraɪzɪŋ] *adj* unternehmungslustig

entertain [entə'teɪn] *vt* (*guest*) bewirten; (*amuse*) unterhalten; **~er** *n* Unterhaltungskünstler(in) *m(f)*; **~ing** *adj* unterhaltsam; **~ment** *n* Unterhaltung *f*

enthralled [ɪn'θrɔːld] *adj* gefesselt

enthusiasm [ɪn'θuːzɪæzəm] *n* Begeisterung *f*

enthusiast [ɪn'θuːzɪæst] *n* Enthusiast *m*; **~ic** [ɪnθuːzɪ'æstɪk] *adj* begeistert

entice [ɪn'taɪs] *vt* verleiten, locken

entire [ɪn'taɪə*] *adj* ganz; **~ly** *adv* ganz, völlig; **~ty** [ɪn'taɪərətɪ] *n*: **in its ~ty** in seiner Gesamtheit

entitle [ɪn'taɪtl] *vt* (*allow*) berechtigen; (*name*) betiteln; **~d** *adj* (*book*) mit dem Titel; **to be ~d to sth** das Recht auf etw *acc* haben; **to be ~d to do sth** das Recht haben, etw zu tun

entity ['entɪtɪ] *n* Ding *nt*, Wesen *nt*

entourage [ɒntu'rɑːʒ] *n* Gefolge *nt*

entrails ['entreɪlz] *npl* Eingeweide *pl*

entrance [*n* 'entrns, *vb* ɪn'trɑːns] *n* Eingang *m*; (*entering*) Eintritt *m* ♦ *vt* hinreißen; **~ examination** *n* Aufnahmeprüfung *f*; **~ fee** *n* Eintrittsgeld *nt*; **~ ramp** (*US*) *n* (*AUT*) Einfahrt *f*

entrant ['entrnt] *n* (*for exam*) Kandidat *m*; (*in race*) Teilnehmer *m*

entreat [en'triːt] *vt* anflehen

entrenched [en'trentʃt] *adj* (*fig*) verwurzelt

entrepreneur ['ɒntrəprə'nəː*] *n* Unternehmer(in) *m(f)*

entrust [ɪn'trʌst] *vt*: **to ~ sb with sth** *or* **sth to sb** jdm etw anvertrauen

entry ['entrɪ] *n* Eingang *m*; (*THEAT*) Auftritt *m*; (*in account*) Eintragung *f*; (*in dictionary*) Eintrag *m*; **"no ~"** „Eintritt verboten"; (*for cars*) „Einfahrt verboten"; **~ form** *n* Anmeldeformular *nt*; **~ phone** *n* Sprechanlage *f*

enumerate [ɪ'njuːməreɪt] *vt* aufzählen

enunciate [ɪ'nʌnsɪeɪt] *vt* aussprechen

envelop [ɪn'veləp] *vt* einhüllen

envelope ['envələup] *n* Umschlag *m*

enviable ['envɪəbl] *adj* beneidenswert

envious ['envɪəs] *adj* neidisch

environment [ɪn'vaɪərnmənt] *n* Umgebung *f*; (*ECOLOGY*) Umwelt *f*; **~al** [ɪnvaɪərn'mentl] *adj* Umwelt-; **~-friendly** *adj* umweltfreundlich

envisage [ɪn'vɪzɪdʒ] *vt* sich *dat* vorstellen

envoy ['envɔɪ] *n* Gesandte(r) *mf*

envy ['envɪ] *n* Neid *m* ♦ *vt*: **to ~ sb sth** jdn um etw beneiden

enzyme ['enzaɪm] *n* Enzym *nt*

epic ['epɪk] n Epos nt ♦ adj episch
epidemic [epɪ'demɪk] n Epidemie f
epilepsy ['epɪlepsɪ] n Epilepsie f; **epileptic**
[epɪ'leptɪk] adj epileptisch ♦ n Epileptiker(in)
m(f)
episode ['epɪsəud] n (incident) Vorfall m;
(story) Episode f
epitaph ['epɪtɑ:f] n Grabinschrift f
epitomize [ɪ'pɪtəmaɪz] vt verkörpern
equable ['ekwəbl] adj ausgeglichen
equal ['i:kwl] adj gleich ♦ n Gleichgestellte(r)
mf ♦ vt gleichkommen +dat; **~ to the task**
der Aufgabe gewachsen; **equality**
[i:'kwɔlɪtɪ] n Gleichheit f; (equal rights)
Gleichberechtigung f; **~ize** vt
gleichmachen ♦ vi (SPORT) ausgleichen;
~izer n (SPORT) Ausgleich(streffer) m; **~ly**
adv gleich
equanimity [ekwə'nɪmɪtɪ] n Gleichmut m
equate [ɪ'kweɪt] vt gleichsetzen
equation [ɪ'kweɪʃən] n Gleichung f
equator [ɪ'kweɪtər] n Äquator m
equestrian [ɪ'kwestrɪən] adj Reit-
equilibrium [i:kwɪ'lɪbrɪəm] n Gleichgewicht
nt
equinox ['i:kwɪnɔks] n Tagundnachtgleiche f
equip [ɪ'kwɪp] vt ausrüsten; **to be well ~ped**
gut ausgerüstet sein; **~ment** n Ausrüstung
f; (TECH) Gerät nt
equitable ['ekwɪtəbl] adj gerecht, billig
equities ['ekwɪtɪz] (BRIT) npl (FIN)
Stammaktien pl
equivalent [ɪ'kwɪvələnt] adj gleichwertig,
entsprechend ♦ n Äquivalent nt; (in money)
Gegenwert m; **~ to** gleichwertig +dat,
entsprechend +dat
equivocal [ɪ'kwɪvəkl] adj zweideutig
era ['ɪərə] n Epoche f, Ära f
eradicate [ɪ'rædɪkeɪt] vt ausrotten
erase [ɪ'reɪz] vt ausradieren; (tape) löschen;
~r n Radiergummi m
erect [ɪ'rekt] adj aufrecht ♦ vt errichten;
~ion [ɪ'rekʃən] n Errichtung f; (ANAT)
Erektion f
ERM n abbr (= Exchange Rate Mechanism)
Wechselkursmechanismus m
erode [ɪ'rəud] vt zerfressen; (land)

auswaschen
erotic [ɪ'rɔtɪk] adj erotisch
err [ə:r] vi sich irren
errand ['erənd] n Besorgung f
erratic [ɪ'rætɪk] adj unberechenbar
erroneous [ɪ'rəunɪəs] adj irrig
error ['erər] n Fehler m
erupt [ɪ'rʌpt] vi ausbrechen; **~ion** [ɪ'rʌpʃən] n
Ausbruch m

escalate ['eskəleɪt] vi sich steigern
escalator ['eskəleɪtər] n Rolltreppe f
escape [ɪs'keɪp] n Flucht f; (of gas)
Entweichen nt ♦ vi entkommen; (prisoners)
fliehen; (leak) entweichen ♦ vt entkommen
+dat; **escapism** n Flucht f (vor der
Wirklichkeit)
escort [n 'eskɔ:t, vb ɪs'kɔ:t] n (person
accompanying) Begleiter m; (guard) Eskorte f
♦ vt (lady) begleiten; (MIL) eskortieren
Eskimo ['eskɪməu] n Eskimo(frau) m(f)
especially [ɪs'peʃlɪ] adv besonders
espionage ['espɪənɑ:ʒ] n Spionage f
esplanade [esplə'neɪd] n Promenade f
Esquire [ɪs'kwaɪər] n: **J. Brown ~** Herrn J.
Brown
essay ['eseɪ] n Aufsatz m; (LITER) Essay m
essence ['esns] n (quality) Wesen nt;
(extract) Essenz f
essential [ɪ'senʃl] adj (necessary)
unentbehrlich; (basic) wesentlich ♦ n
Allernötigste(s) nt; **~ly** adv eigentlich
establish [ɪs'tæblɪʃ] vt (set up) gründen;
(prove) nachweisen; **~ed** adj anerkannt;
(belief, laws etc) herrschend; **~ment** n
(setting up) Einrichtung f
estate [ɪs'teɪt] n Gut nt; (BRIT: housing ~)
Siedlung f; (will) Nachlass m; **~ agent**
(BRIT) n Grundstücksmakler m; **~ car** (BRIT)
n Kombiwagen m
esteem [ɪs'ti:m] n Wertschätzung f
esthetic [ɪs'θetɪk] (US) adj = **aesthetic**
estimate [n 'estɪmət, vb 'estɪmeɪt] n
Schätzung f; (of price) (Kosten)voranschlag
m ♦ vt schätzen; **estimation** [estɪ'meɪʃən] n
Einschätzung f; (esteem) Achtung f
estranged [ɪs'treɪndʒd] adj entfremdet
estuary ['estjuərɪ] n Mündung f

etc *abbr* (= *et cetera*) usw
etching ['etʃɪŋ] *n* Kupferstich *m*
eternal [ɪ'tɜːnl] *adj* ewig
eternity [ɪ'tɜːnɪtɪ] *n* Ewigkeit *f*
ether ['iːθəʳ] *n* Äther *m*
ethical ['εθɪkl] *adj* ethisch
ethics ['εθɪks] *n* Ethik *f* ♦ *npl* Moral *f*
Ethiopia [iːθɪ'əʊpɪə] *n* Äthiopien *nt*
ethnic ['εθnɪk] *adj* Volks-, ethnisch; ~
  minority *n* ethnische Minderheit *f*
ethos ['iːθɒs] *n* Gesinnung *f*
etiquette ['εtɪket] *n* Etikette *f*
EU *abbr* (= *European Union*) EU *f*
euphemism ['juːfəmɪzəm] *n* Euphemismus
  m
euro ['jʊərəʊ] *n* (*FIN*) Euro *m*
Eurocheque ['jʊərəʊtʃεk] *n* Euroscheck *m*
Europe ['jʊərəp] *n* Europa *nt*; ~an
  [jʊərə'piːən] *adj* europäisch ♦ *n* Europäer(in)
  m(f); **~an Community** *n*: **the ~an**
  Community die Europäische Gemeinschaft
Euro-sceptic ['jʊərəʊskeptɪk] *n* Kritiker der
  Europäischen Gemeinschaft
evacuate [ɪ'vækjʊeɪt] *vt* (*place*) räumen;
  (*people*) evakuieren; **evacuation**
  [ɪvækjʊ'eɪʃən] *n* Räumung *f*; Evakuierung *f*
evade [ɪ'veɪd] *vt* (*escape*) entkommen +*dat*;
  (*avoid*) meiden; (*duty*) sich entziehen +*dat*
evaluate [ɪ'væljʊeɪt] *vt* bewerten;
  (*information*) auswerten
evaporate [ɪ'væpəreɪt] *vi* verdampfen ♦ *vt*
  verdampfen lassen; **~d milk** *n*
  Kondensmilch *f*
evasion [ɪ'veɪʒən] *n* Umgehung *f*
evasive [ɪ'veɪsɪv] *adj* ausweichend
eve [iːv] *n*: **on the ~ of** am Vorabend +*gen*
even ['iːvn] *adj* eben; gleichmäßig; (*score
  etc*) unentschieden; (*number*) gerade ♦ *adv*:
  ~ **you** sogar du; **to get ~ with sb** jdm
  heimzahlen; ~ **if** selbst wenn; ~ **so**
  dennoch; ~ **though** obwohl; ~ **more** sogar
  noch mehr; ~ **out** *vi* sich ausgleichen
evening ['iːvnɪŋ] *n* Abend *m*; **in the ~**
  abends, am Abend; ~ **class** *n* Abendschule
  f; ~ **dress** *n* (*man's*) Gesellschaftsanzug *m*;
  (*woman's*) Abendkleid *nt*
event [ɪ'vεnt] *n* (*happening*) Ereignis *nt*;

(*SPORT*) Disziplin *f*; **in the ~ of** im Falle +*gen*;
  ~ful *adj* ereignisreich
eventual [ɪ'vεntʃʊəl] *adj* (*final*) schließlich;
  ~ity [ɪvεntʃu'ælɪt] *n* Möglichkeit *f*; **~ly** *adv*
  am Ende; (*given time*) schließlich
ever ['εvəʳ] *adv* (*always*) immer; (*at any time*)
  je(mals) ♦ *conj* seit; ~ **since** seitdem; **have**
  you ~ seen it? haben Sie es je gesehen?;
  ~green *n* Immergrün *nt*; **~lasting** *adj*
  immer während
every ['εvrɪ] *adj* jede(r, s); ~ **other/third day**
  jeden zweiten/dritten Tag; ~ **one of them**
  alle; **I have ~ confidence in him** ich habe
  uneingeschränktes Vertrauen in ihn; **we**
  wish you ~ success wir wünschen Ihnen
  viel Erfolg; **he's ~ bit as clever as his**
  brother er ist genauso klug wie sein
  Bruder; ~ **now and then** ab und zu;
  ~body *pron* = **everyone**; **~day** *adj* (*daily*)
  täglich; (*commonplace*) alltäglich, Alltags-;
  ~one *pron* jeder, alle *pl*; **~thing** *pron* alles;
  ~where *adv* überall(hin); (*wherever*) wohin;
  ~where you go wohin du auch gehst
evict [ɪ'vɪkt] *vt* ausweisen; **~ion** [ɪ'vɪkʃən] *n*
  Ausweisung *f*
evidence ['εvɪdns] *n* (*sign*) Spur *f*; (*proof*)
  Beweis *m*; (*testimony*) Aussage *f*
evident ['εvɪdnt] *adj* augenscheinlich; **~ly**
  adv offensichtlich
evil ['iːvl] *adj* böse ♦ *n* Böse *nt*
evocative [ɪ'vɒkətɪv] *adj*: **to be ~ of sth** an
  etw *acc* erinnern
evoke [ɪ'vəʊk] *vt* hervorrufen
evolution [iːvə'luːʃən] *n* Entwicklung *f*; (*of
  life*) Evolution *f*
evolve [ɪ'vɒlv] *vt* entwickeln ♦ *vi* sich
  entwickeln
ewe [juː] *n* Mutterschaf *nt*
ex- [εks] *prefix* Ex-, Alt-, ehemalig
exacerbate [εks'æsəbeɪt] *vt* verschlimmern
exact [ɪg'zækt] *adj* genau ♦ *vt* (*demand*)
  verlangen; **~ing** *adj* anspruchsvoll; **~ly** *adv*
  genau
exaggerate [ɪg'zædʒəreɪt] *vt, vi* übertreiben;
  exaggeration [ɪgzædʒə'reɪʃən] *n*
  Übertreibung *f*
exalted [ɪg'zɔːltɪd] *adj* (*position, style*) hoch;

(*person*) exaltiert

exam [ɪgˈzæm] *n abbr* (*SCH*) = **examination**

examination [ɪgzæmɪˈneɪʃən] *n* Untersuchung *f*; (*SCH*) Prüfung *f*, Examen *nt*; (*customs*) Kontrolle *f*

examine [ɪgˈzæmɪn] *vt* untersuchen; (*SCH*) prüfen; (*consider*) erwägen; **~r** *n* Prüfer *m*

example [ɪgˈzɑːmpl] *n* Beispiel *nt*; **for ~** zum Beispiel

exasperate [ɪgˈzɑːspəreɪt] *vt* zur Verzweiflung bringen; **exasperating** *adj* ärgerlich, zum Verzweifeln bringend; **exasperation** [ɪgzɑːspəˈreɪʃən] *n* Verzweiflung *f*

excavate [ˈekskəveɪt] *vt* ausgraben; **excavation** [ekskəˈveɪʃən] *n* Ausgrabung *f*

exceed [ɪkˈsiːd] *vt* überschreiten; (*hopes*) übertreffen; **~ingly** *adv* äußerst

excel [ɪkˈsel] *vi* sich auszeichnen; **~lence** [ˈeksələns] *n* Vortrefflichkeit *f*; **E~lency** [ˈeksələnsɪ] *n*: **His E~lency** Seine Exzellenz *f*; **~lent** [ˈeksələnt] *adj* ausgezeichnet

except [ɪkˈsept] *prep* (*also:* **~ for, ~ing**) außer +*dat* ♦ *vt* ausnehmen; **~ion** [ɪkˈsepʃən] *n* Ausnahme *f*; **to take ~ion to** Anstoß nehmen an +*dat*; **~ional** [ɪkˈsepʃənl] *adj* außergewöhnlich

excerpt [ˈeksɜːpt] *n* Auszug *m*

excess [ɪkˈses] *n* Übermaß *nt*; **an ~ of** ein Übermaß an +*dat*; **~ baggage** *n* Mehrgepäck *nt*; **~ fare** *n* Nachlösegebühr *f*; **~ive** *adj* übermäßig

exchange [ɪksˈtʃeɪndʒ] *n* Austausch *m*; (*also:* **telephone ~**) Zentrale *f* ♦ *vt* (*goods*) tauschen; (*greetings*) austauschen; (*money, blows*) wechseln; **~ rate** *n* Wechselkurs *m*

Exchequer [ɪksˈtʃekəʳ] (*BRIT*) *n*: **the ~** das Schatzamt

excise [ˈeksaɪz] *n* Verbrauchssteuer *f*

excite [ɪkˈsaɪt] *vt* erregen; **to get ~d** sich aufregen; **~ment** *n* Aufregung *f*; **exciting** *adj* spannend

exclaim [ɪksˈkleɪm] *vi* ausrufen

exclamation [ekskləˈmeɪʃən] *n* Ausruf *m*; **~ mark** *n* Ausrufezeichen *nt*

exclude [ɪksˈkluːd] *vt* ausschließen

exclusion [ɪksˈkluːʒən] *n* Ausschluss *m*; **~**

zone *n* Sperrzone *f*

exclusive [ɪksˈkluːsɪv] *adj* (*select*) exklusiv; (*sole*) ausschließlich, Allein-; **~ of** exklusive +*gen*; **~ly** *adv* nur, ausschließlich

excommunicate [ekskəˈmjuːnɪkeɪt] *vt* exkommunizieren

excrement [ˈekskrəmənt] *n* Kot *m*

excruciating [ɪksˈkruːʃieɪtɪŋ] *adj* qualvoll

excursion [ɪksˈkɜːʃən] *n* Ausflug *m*

excusable [ɪksˈkjuːzəbl] *adj* entschuldbar

excuse [*n* ɪksˈkjuːs, *vb* ɪksˈkjuːz] *n* Entschuldigung *f* ♦ *vt* entschuldigen; **~ me!** entschuldigen Sie!

ex-directory [ˈeksdɪˈrektərɪ] (*BRIT*) *adj*: **to be ~** nicht im Telefonbuch stehen

execute [ˈeksɪkjuːt] *vt* (*carry out*) ausführen; (*kill*) hinrichten; **execution** [eksɪˈkjuːʃən] *n* Ausführung *f*; (*killing*) Hinrichtung *f*; **executioner** [eksɪˈkjuːʃnəʳ] *n* Scharfrichter *m*

executive [ɪgˈzekjutɪv] *n* (*COMM*) Geschäftsführer *m*; (*POL*) Exekutive *f* ♦ *adj* Exekutiv-, ausführend

executor [ɪgˈzekjutəʳ] *n* Testamentsvollstrecker *m*

exemplary [ɪgˈzemplərɪ] *adj* musterhaft

exemplify [ɪgˈzemplɪfaɪ] *vt* veranschaulichen

exempt [ɪgˈzempt] *adj* befreit ♦ *vt* befreien; **~ion** [ɪqˈzempʃən] *n* Befreiung *f*

exercise [ˈeksəsaɪz] *n* Übung *f* ♦ *vt* (*power*) ausüben; (*muscle, patience*) üben; (*dog*) ausführen ♦ *vi* Sport treiben; **~ bike** *n* Heimtrainer *m*; **~ book** *n* (Schul)heft *nt*

exert [ɪgˈzɜːt] *vt* (*influence*) ausüben; **to ~ o.s.** sich anstrengen; **~ion** [ɪgˈzɜːʃən] *n* Anstrengung *f*

exhale [eksˈheɪl] *vt, vi* ausatmen

exhaust [ɪgˈzɔːst] *n* (*fumes*) Abgase *pl*; (*pipe*) Auspuffrohr *nt* ♦ *vt* erschöpfen; **~ed** *adj* erschöpft; **~ion** [ɪgˈzɔːstʃən] *n* Erschöpfung *f*; **~ive** *adj* erschöpfend

exhibit [ɪgˈzɪbɪt] *n* (*JUR*) Beweisstück *nt*; (*ART*) Ausstellungsstück *nt* ♦ *vt* ausstellen; **~ion** [eksɪˈbɪʃən] *n* (*ART*) Ausstellung *f*; (*of temper etc*) Zurschaustellung *f*; **~ionist** [eksɪˈbɪʃnɪst] *n* Exhibitionist *m*

exhilarating [ɪgˈzɪləreɪtɪŋ] *adj* erhebend

ex-husband *n* Ehemann *m*

exile ['ɛksaɪl] *n* Exil *nt*; (*person*) Verbannte(r) *f(m)* ♦ *vt* verbannen

exist [ɪg'zɪst] *vi* existieren; **~ence** *n* Existenz *f*; **~ing** *adj* bestehend

exit ['ɛksɪt] *n* Ausgang *m*; (*THEAT*) Abgang *m* ♦ *vi* (*THEAT*) abtreten; (*COMPUT*) aus einem Programm herausgehen; **~ poll** *n bei Wahlen unmittelbar nach Verlassen der Wahllokale durchgeführte Umfrage*; **~ ramp** (*US*) *n* (*AUT*) Ausfahrt *f*

exodus ['ɛksədəs] *n* Auszug *m*

exonerate [ɪg'zɔnəreɪt] *vt* entlasten

exorbitant [ɪg'zɔ:bɪtnt] *adj* übermäßig; (*price*) Fantasie-

exotic [ɪg'zɔtɪk] *adj* exotisch

expand [ɪks'pænd] *vt* ausdehnen ♦ *vi* sich ausdehnen

expanse [ɪks'pæns] *n* Fläche *f*

expansion [ɪks'pænʃən] *n* Erweiterung *f*

expatriate [ɛks'pætrɪət] *n* Ausländer(in) *m(f)*

expect [ɪks'pɛkt] *vt* erwarten; (*suppose*) annehmen ♦ *vi*: **to be ~ing** ein Kind erwarten; **~ancy** *n* Erwartung *f*; **~ant mother** *n* werdende Mutter *f*; **~ation** [ɛkspɛk'teɪʃən] *n* Hoffnung *f*

expedient [ɪks'pi:dɪənt] *adj* zweckdienlich ♦ *n* (Hilfs)mittel *nt*

expedition [ɛkspə'dɪʃən] *n* Expedition *f*

expel [ɪks'pɛl] *vt* ausweisen; (*student*) (ver)weisen

expend [ɪks'pɛnd] *vt* (*effort*) aufwenden; **~iture** *n* Ausgaben *pl*

expense [ɪks'pɛns] *n* Kosten *pl*; **~s** *npl* (*COMM*) Spesen *pl*; **at the ~ of** auf Kosten von; **~ account** *n* Spesenkonto *nt*; **expensive** [ɪks'pɛnsɪv] *adj* teuer

experience [ɪks'pɪərɪəns] *n* (*incident*) Erlebnis *nt*; (*practice*) Erfahrung *f* ♦ *vt* erleben; **~d** *adj* erfahren

experiment [ɪks'pɛrɪmənt] *n* Versuch *m*, Experiment *nt* ♦ *vi* experimentieren; **~al** [ɪksperɪ'mɛntl] *adj* experimentell

expert ['ɛkspə:t] *n* Fachmann *m*; (*official*) Sachverständige(r) *m* ♦ *adj* erfahren; **~ise** [ɛkspə:'ti:z] *n* Sachkenntnis *f*

expire [ɪks'paɪə˚] *vi* (*end*) ablaufen; (*ticket*)

verfallen; (*die*) sterben; **expiry** *n* Ablauf *m*

explain [ɪks'pleɪn] *vt* erklären

explanation [ɛksplə'neɪʃən] *n* Erklärung *f*; **explanatory** [ɪks'plænətrɪ] *adj* erklärend

explicit [ɪks'plɪsɪt] *adj* ausdrücklich

explode [ɪks'pləʊd] *vi* explodieren ♦ *vt* (*bomb*) sprengen

exploit [*n* 'ɛksplɔɪt, *vb* ɪks'plɔɪt] *n* (Helden)tat *f* ♦ *vt* ausbeuten; **~ation** [ɛksplɔɪ'teɪʃən] *n* Ausbeutung *f*

exploration [ɛksplɔ:'reɪʃən] *n* Erforschung *f*

exploratory [ɪks'plɔrətrɪ] *adj* Probe-

explore [ɪks'plɔ:˚] *vt* (*travel*) erforschen; (*search*) untersuchen; **~r** *n* Erforscher(in) *m(f)*

explosion [ɪks'pləʊʒən] *n* Explosion *f*; (*fig*) Ausbruch *m*

explosive [ɪks'pləʊsɪv] *adj* explosiv, Spreng- ♦ *n* Sprengstoff *m*

export [*vb* ɛks'pɔ:t, *n* 'ɛkspɔ:t] *vt* exportieren ♦ *n* Export *m* ♦ *cpd* (*trade*) Export-; **~er** [ɛks'pɔ:tə˚] *n* Exporteur *m*

expose [ɪks'pəʊz] *vt* (*to danger etc*) aussetzen; (*impostor*) entlarven; **to ~ sb to sth** jdn einer Sache *dat* aussetzen; **~d** *adj* (*position*) exponiert; **exposure** [ɪks'pəʊʒə˚] *n* (*MED*) Unterkühlung *f*; (*PHOT*) Belichtung *f*; **exposure meter** *n* Belichtungsmesser *m*

express [ɪks'prɛs] *adj* ausdrücklich; (*speedy*) Express-, Eil- ♦ *n* (*RAIL*) Schnellzug *m* ♦ *adv* (*send*) per Express ♦ *vt* ausdrücken; **to ~ o.s.** sich ausdrücken; **~ion** [ɪks'prɛʃən] *n* Ausdruck *m*; **~ive** *adj* ausdrucksvoll; **~ly** *adv* ausdrücklich; **~way** (*US*) *n* (*urban motorway*) Schnellstraße *f*

expulsion [ɪks'pʌlʃən] *n* Ausweisung *f*

exquisite [ɛks'kwɪzɪt] *adj* erlesen

extend [ɪks'tɛnd] *vt* (*visit etc*) verlängern; (*building*) ausbauen; (*hand*) ausstrecken; (*welcome*) bieten ♦ *vi* (*land*) sich erstrecken

extension [ɪks'tɛnʃən] *n* Erweiterung *f*; (*of building*) Anbau *m*; (*TEL*) Apparat *m*

extensive [ɪks'tɛnsɪv] *adj* (*knowledge*) umfassend; (*use*) weitgehend, weit gehend

extent [ɪks'tɛnt] *n* Ausdehnung *f*; (*fig*) Ausmaß *nt*; **to a certain ~** bis zu einem gewissen Grade; **to such an ~ that ...** dermaßen, dass ...; **to what ~?** inwieweit?

extenuating [ɪks'tɛnjueɪtɪŋ] *adj* mildernd

exterior [eks'tɪərɪər] *adj* äußere(r, s), Außen- ♦ *n* Äußere(s) *nt*

exterminate [ɪks'tə:mɪneɪt] *vt* ausrotten

external [eks'tə:nl] *adj* äußere(r, s), Außen-

extinct [ɪks'tɪŋkt] *adj* ausgestorben; **~ion** [ɪks'tɪŋkʃən] *n* Aussterben *nt*

extinguish [ɪks'tɪŋgwɪʃ] *vt* (aus)löschen

extort [ɪks'tɔ:t] *vt* erpressen; **~ion** [ɪks'tɔ:ʃən] *n* Erpressung *f*; **~ionate** [ɪks'tɔ:ʃnɪt] *adj* überhöht, erpresserisch

extra ['ɛkstrə] *adj* zusätzlich ♦ *adv* besonders ♦ *n* (*for car etc*) Extra *nt*; (*charge*) Zuschlag *m*; (*THEAT*) Statist *m* ♦ *prefix* außer...

extract [v ɪks'trækt, n 'ɛkstrækt] *vt* (heraus)ziehen ♦ *n* (*from book etc*) Auszug *m*; (*COOK*) Extrakt *m*

extracurricular ['ɛkstrəkə'rɪkjulər] *adj* außerhalb des Stundenplans

extradite ['ɛkstrədaɪt] *vt* ausliefern

extramarital ['ɛkstrə'mærɪtl] *adj* außerehelich

extramural ['ɛkstrə'mjuərl] *adj* (*course*) Volkshochschul-

extraordinary [ɪks'trɔ:dnrɪ] *adj* außerordentlich; (*amazing*) erstaunlich

extravagance [ɪks'trævəgəns] *n* Verschwendung *f*; (*lack of restraint*) Zügellosigkeit *f*; (*an ~*) Extravaganz *f*

extravagant [ɪks'trævəgənt] *adj* extravagant

extreme [ɪks'tri:m] *adj* (*edge*) äußerste(r, s), hinterste(r, s); (*cold*) äußerste(r, s); (*behaviour*) außergewöhnlich, übertrieben ♦ *n* Extrem *nt*; **~ly** *adv* äußerst, höchst;

extremist *n* Extremist(in) *m(f)*

extremity [ɪks'trɛmɪtɪ] *n* (*end*) Spitze *f*, äußerste(s) Ende *nt*; (*hardship*) bitterste Not *f*; (*ANAT*) Hand *f*; Fuß *m*

extricate ['ɛkstrɪkeɪt] *vt* losmachen, befreien

extrovert ['ɛkstrəvə:t] *n* extrovertierte(r) Mensch *m*

exuberant [ɪg'zju:bərnt] *adj* ausgelassen

exude [ɪg'zju:d] *vt* absondern

eye [aɪ] *n* Auge *nt*; (*of needle*) Öhr *nt* ♦ *vt* betrachten; (*up and down*) mustern; **to keep an ~ on** aufpassen auf +*acc*; **~ball** *n* Augapfel *m*; **~bath** *n* Augenbad *nt*; **~brow** *n* Augenbraue *f*; **~brow pencil** *n* Augenbrauenstift *m*; **~drops** *npl* Augentropfen *pl*; **~lash** *n* Augenwimper *f*; **~lid** *n* Augenlid *nt*; **~liner** *n* Eyeliner *nt*; **~-opener** *n*: **that was an ~-opener** das hat mir/ihm *etc* die Augen geöffnet; **~shadow** *n* Lidschatten *m*; **~sight** *n* Sehkraft *f*; **~sore** *n* Schandfleck *m*; **~ witness** *n* Augenzeuge *m*

F, f

F [ɛf] *n* (*MUS*) F *nt*

F. *abbr* (= *Fahrenheit*) F

fable ['feɪbl] *n* Fabel *f*

fabric ['fæbrɪk] *n* Stoff *m*; (*fig*) Gefüge *nt*

fabrication [fæbrɪ'keɪʃən] *n* Erfindung *f*

fabulous ['fæbjuləs] *adj* sagenhaft

face [feɪs] *n* Gesicht *nt*; (*surface*) Oberfläche *f*; (*of clock*) Zifferblatt *nt* ♦ *vt* (*point towards*) liegen nach; (*situation, difficulty*) sich stellen +*dat*; **~ down** (*person*) mit dem Gesicht nach unten; (*card*) mit der Vorderseite nach unten; **to make** *or* **pull a ~** das Gesicht verziehen; **in the ~ of** angesichts +*gen*; **on the ~ of it** so, wie es aussieht; **~ to ~** Auge in Auge; **to ~ up to sth** einer Sache *dat* ins Auge sehen; **~ cloth** (*BRIT*) *n* Waschlappen *m*; **~ cream** *n* Gesichtscreme *f*; **~ lift** *n* Facelifting *nt*; **~ powder** *n* (Gesichts)puder *m*

facet ['fæsɪt] *n* Aspekt *m*; (*of gem*) Facette *f*, Fassette *f*

facetious [fə'si:ʃəs] *adj* witzig

face value *n* Nennwert *m*; **to take sth at (its) ~** (*fig*) etw für bare Münze nehmen

facial ['feɪʃl] *adj* Gesichts-

facile ['fæsaɪl] *adj* (*easy*) leicht

facilitate [fə'sɪlɪteɪt] *vt* erleichtern

facilities [fə'sɪlɪtɪz] *npl* Einrichtungen *pl*; **credit ~** Kreditmöglichkeiten *pl*

facing ['feɪsɪŋ] *adj* zugekehrt ♦ *prep* gegenüber

facsimile [fæk'sɪmɪlɪ] *n* Faksimile *nt*;

(*machine*) Telekopierer *m*

fact [fækt] *n* Tatsache *f*; **in ~** in der Tat

faction ['fækʃən] *n* Splittergruppe *f*

factor ['fæktə^r] *n* Faktor *m*

factory ['fæktəri] *n* Fabrik *f*

factual ['fæktjuəl] *adj* sachlich

faculty ['fækəlti] *n* Fähigkeit *f*; (*UNIV*) Fakultät *f*; (*US: teaching staff*) Lehrpersonal *nt*

fad [fæd] *n* Tick *m*; (*fashion*) Masche *f*

fade [feɪd] *vi* (*lose colour*) verblassen; (*dim*) nachlassen; (*sound, memory*) schwächer werden; (*wilt*) verwelken

fag [fæg] (*inf*) *n* (*cigarette*) Kippe *f*

fail [feɪl] *vt* (*exam*) nicht bestehen; (*student*) durchfallen lassen; (*courage*) verlassen; (*memory*) im Stich lassen ♦ *vi* (*supplies*) zu Ende gehen; (*student*) durchfallen; (*eyesight*) nachlassen; (*light*) schwächer werden; (*crop*) fehlschlagen; (*remedy*) nicht wirken; **to ~ to do sth** (*neglect*) es unterlassen, etw zu tun; (*be unable*) es nicht schaffen, etw zu tun; **without ~** unbedingt; **~ing** *n* Schwäche *f* ♦ *prep* mangels +*gen*; **~ure** ['feɪljə^r] *n* (*person*) Versager *m*; (*act*) Versagen *nt*; (*TECH*) Defekt *m*

faint [feɪnt] *adj* schwach ♦ *n* Ohnmacht *f* ♦ *vi* ohnmächtig werden

fair [feə^r] *adj* (*just*) gerecht, fair; (*hair*) blond; (*skin*) hell; (*weather*) schön; (*not very good*) mittelmäßig; (*sizeable*) ansehnlich ♦ *adv* (*play*) fair ♦ *n* (*COMM*) Messe *f*; (*BRIT: funfair*) Jahrmarkt *m*; **~ly** *adv* (*honestly*) gerecht, fair; (*rather*) ziemlich; **~ness** *n* Fairness *f*

fairy ['feəri] *n* Fee *f*; **~ tale** *n* Märchen *nt*

faith [feɪθ] *n* Glaube *m*; (*trust*) Vertrauen *nt*; (*sect*) Bekenntnis *nt*; **~ful** *adj* treu; **~fully** *adv* treu; **yours ~fully** (*BRIT*) hochachtungsvoll

fake [feɪk] *n* (*thing*) Fälschung *f*; (*person*) Schwindler *m* ♦ *adj* vorgetäuscht ♦ *vt* fälschen

falcon ['fɔːlkən] *n* Falke *m*

fall [fɔːl] (*pt* **fell**, *pp* **fallen**) *n* Fall *m*, Sturz *m*; (*decrease*) Fallen *nt*; (*of snow*) (Schnee)fall *m*; (*US: autumn*) Herbst *m* ♦ *vi* (*also fig*) fallen; (*night*) hereinbrechen; **~s** *npl* (*waterfall*) Fälle *pl*; **to ~ flat** platt hinfallen;

(*joke*) nicht ankommen; **~ back** *vi* zurückweichen; **~ back on** *vt fus* zurückgreifen auf +*acc*; **~ behind** *vi* zurückbleiben; **~ down** *vi* (*person*) hinfallen; (*building*) einstürzen; **~ for** *vt fus* (*trick*) hereinfallen auf +*acc*; (*person*) sich verknallen in +*acc*; **~ in** *vi* (*roof*) einstürzen; **~ off** *vi* herunterfallen; (*diminish*) sich vermindern; **~ out** *vi* sich streiten; (*MIL*) wegtreten; **~ through** *vi* (*plan*) ins Wasser fallen

fallacy ['fæləsi] *n* Trugschluss *m*

fallen ['fɔːlən] *pp* of **fail**

fallible ['fæləbl] *adj* fehlbar

fallout ['fɔːlaut] *n* radioaktive(r) Niederschlag *m*; **~ shelter** *n* Atombunker *m*

fallow ['fæləu] *adj* brach(liegend)

false [fɔːls] *adj* falsch; (*artificial*) künstlich; **under ~ pretences** unter Vorspiegelung falscher Tatsachen; **~ alarm** *n* Fehlalarm *m*; **~ teeth** (*BRIT*) *npl* Gebiss *nt*

falter ['fɔːltə^r] *vi* schwanken; (*in speech*) stocken

fame [feɪm] *n* Ruhm *m*

familiar [fə'mɪliə^r] *adj* bekannt; (*intimate*) familiär; **to be ~ with** vertraut sein mit; **~ize** *vt* vertraut machen

family ['fæmɪli] *n* Familie *f*; (*relations*) Verwandtschaft *f*; **~ business** *n* Familienunternehmen *nt*; **~ doctor** *n* Hausarzt *m*

famine ['fæmɪn] *n* Hungersnot *f*

famished ['fæmɪʃt] *adj* ausgehungert

famous ['feɪməs] *adj* berühmt

fan [fæn] *n* (*folding*) Fächer *m*; (*ELEC*) Ventilator *m*; (*admirer*) Fan *m* ♦ *vt* fächeln; **~ out** *vi* sich (fächerförmig) ausbreiten

fanatic [fə'nætɪk] *n* Fanatiker(in) *m(f)*

fan belt *n* Keilriemen *m*

fanciful ['fænsɪful] *adj* (*odd*) seltsam; (*imaginative*) fantasievoll

fancy ['fænsi] *n* (*liking*) Neigung *f*; (*imagination*) Einbildung *f* ♦ *adj* schick ♦ *vt* (*like*) gern haben; wollen; (*imagine*) sich einbilden; **he fancies her** er mag sie; **~ dress** *n* Maskenkostüm *nt*; **~-dress ball** *n* Maskenball *m*

fang [fæŋ] n Fangzahn m; (of snake) Giftzahn m

fantastic [fæn'tæstɪk] adj fantastisch

fantasy ['fæntəsɪ] n Fantasie f

far [fɑːʳ] adj weit ♦ adv weit entfernt; (very much) weitaus; **by ~** bei weitem; **so ~** so weit; bis jetzt; **go as ~ as the station** gehen Sie bis zum Bahnhof; **as ~ as I know** soweit or soviel ich weiß; **~away** adj weit entfernt

farce [fɑːs] n Farce f; **farcical** ['fɑːsɪkl] adj lächerlich

fare [feəʳ] n Fahrpreis m; Fahrgeld nt; (food) Kost f; **half/full ~** halber/voller Fahrpreis m

Far East n: **the ~** der Ferne Osten

farewell [feə'wel] n Abschied(sgruß) m ♦ excl lebe wohl!

farm [fɑːm] n Bauernhof m, Farm f ♦ vt bewirtschaften; **~er** n Bauer m, Landwirt m; **~hand** n Landarbeiter m; **~house** n Bauernhaus nt; **~ing** n Landwirtschaft f; **~land** n Ackerland nt; **~yard** n Hof m

far-reaching ['fɑː'riːtʃɪŋ] adj (reform, effect) weitreichend, weit reichend

fart [fɑːt] (inf!) n Furz m ♦ vi furzen

farther ['fɑːðəʳ] adv weiter; **farthest** ['fɑːðɪst] adj fernste(r, s) ♦ adv am weitesten

fascinate ['fæsɪneɪt] vt faszinieren; **fascinating** adj faszinierend; **fascination** [fæsɪ'neɪʃən] n Faszination f

fascism ['fæʃɪzəm] n Faschismus m

fashion ['fæʃən] n (of clothes) Mode f; (manner) Art f (und Weise f) ♦ vt machen; **in ~** in Mode; **out of ~** unmodisch; **~able** adj (clothes) modisch; (place) elegant; **~ show** n Mode(n)schau f

fast [fɑːst] adj schnell; (firm) fest ♦ adv schnell; fest ♦ n Fasten nt ♦ vi fasten; **to be ~** (clock) vorgehen

fasten ['fɑːsn] vt (attach) befestigen; (with rope) zuschnüren; (seat belt) festmachen; (coat) zumachen ♦ vi sich schließen lassen; **~er** n Verschluss m; **~ing** n Verschluss m

fast food n Fastfood nt, Fast Food nt

fastidious [fæs'tɪdɪəs] adj wählerisch

fat [fæt] adj dick ♦ n Fett nt

fatal ['feɪtl] adj tödlich; (disastrous) verhängnisvoll; **~ity** [fə'tælɪtɪ] n (road death etc) Todesopfer nt; **~ly** adv tödlich

fate [feɪt] n Schicksal nt; **~ful** adj (prophetic) schicksalsschwer; (important) schicksalhaft

father ['fɑːðəʳ] n Vater m; (REL) Pater m; **~-in-law** n Schwiegervater m; **~ly** adj väterlich

fathom ['fæðəm] n Klafter m ♦ vt ausloten; (fig) ergründen

fatigue [fə'tiːg] n Ermüdung f

fatten ['fætn] vt dick machen; (animals) mästen ♦ vi dick werden

fatty ['fætɪ] adj fettig ♦ n (inf) Dickerchen nt

fatuous ['fætjuəs] adj albern, affig

faucet ['fɔːsɪt] (US) n Wasserhahn m

fault [fɔːlt] n (defect) Defekt m; (ELEC) Störung f; (blame) Schuld f; (GEOG) Verwerfung f; **it's your ~** du bist daran schuld; **to find ~ with (sth/sb)** etwas auszusetzen haben an (etw/jdm); **at ~** im Unrecht; **~less** adj tadellos; **~y** adj fehlerhaft, defekt

fauna ['fɔːnə] n Fauna f

favour ['feɪvəʳ] (US **favor**) n (approval) Wohlwollen nt; (kindness) Gefallen m ♦ vt (prefer) vorziehen; **in ~ of** für; zugunsten or zu Gunsten +gen; **to find ~ with sb** bei jdm Anklang finden; **~able** ['feɪvrəbl] adj günstig; **~ite** ['feɪvrɪt] adj Lieblings- ♦ n (child) Liebling m; (SPORT) Favorit m

fawn [fɔːn] adj rehbraun ♦ n (animal) (Reh)kitz nt ♦ vi: **to ~ (up)on** (fig) katzbuckeln vor +dat

fax [fæks] n (document) Fax nt; (machine) Telefax nt ♦ vt: **to ~ sth to sb** jdm etw faxen

FBI (US) n abbr (= Federal Bureau of Investigation) FBI nt

fear [fɪəʳ] n Furcht f ♦ vt fürchten; **~ful** adj (timid) furchtsam; (terrible) fürchterlich; **~less** adj furchtlos

feasible ['fiːzəbl] adj durchführbar

feast [fiːst] n Festmahl nt; (REL: also: **~ day**) Feiertag m ♦ vi: **to ~ (on)** sich gütlich tun (an +dat)

feat [fiːt] n Leistung f

feather ['feðəʳ] n Feder f

feature ['fiːtʃəʳ] n (Gesichts)zug m;

(*important part*) Grundzug m; (*CINE, PRESS*) Feature nt ♦ vt darstellen; (*advertising etc*) groß herausbringen ♦ vi vorkommen; **featuring X** mit X; ~ **film** n Spielfilm m

February ['februəri] n Februar m

fed [fed] pt, pp of **feed**

federal ['fedərəl] adj Bundes-

federation [fedə'reɪʃən] n (*society*) Verband m; (*of states*) Staatenbund m

fed up adj: **to be ~ with sth** etw satt haben; **I'm ~** ich habe die Nase voll

fee [fi:] n Gebühr f

feeble ['fi:bl] adj (*person*) schwach; (*excuse*) lahm

feed [fi:d] (*pt, pp* **fed**) n (*for animals*) Futter nt ♦ vt füttern; (*support*) ernähren; (*data*) eingeben; **to ~ on** fressen; **~back** n (*information*) Feed-back nt, Feedback nt; **~ing bottle** (*BRIT*) n Flasche f

feel [fi:l] (*pt, pp* **felt**) n: **it has a soft ~** es fühlt sich weich an ♦ vt (*sense*) fühlen; (*touch*) anfassen; (*think*) meinen ♦ vi (*person*) sich fühlen; (*thing*) sich anfühlen; **to get the ~ of sth** sich an etw acc gewöhnen; **I ~ cold** mir ist kalt; **I ~ like a cup of tea** ich habe Lust auf eine Tasse Tee; **~ about** or **around** vi herumsuchen; **~er** n Fühler m; **~ing** n Gefühl nt; (*opinion*) Meinung f

feet [fi:t] npl of **foot**

feign [feɪn] vt vortäuschen

feline ['fi:laɪn] adj katzenartig

fell [fel] pt of **fall** ♦ vt (*tree*) fällen

fellow ['feləʊ] n (*man*) Kerl m; ~ **citizen** n Mitbürger(in) m(f); ~ **countryman** (*irreg*) n Landsmann m; ~ **men** npl Mitmenschen pl; **~ship** n (*group*) Körperschaft f; (*friendliness*) Kameradschaft f; (*scholarship*) Forschungsstipendium nt; ~ **student** n Kommilitone m, Kommilitonin f

felony ['feləni] n schwere(s) Verbrechen nt

felt [felt] pt, pp of **feel** ♦ n Filz m; **~-tip pen** n Filzstift m

female ['fi:meɪl] n (*of animals*) Weibchen nt ♦ adj weiblich

feminine ['femɪnɪn] adj (*LING*) weiblich; (*qualities*) fraulich

feminist ['femɪnɪst] n Feminist(in) m(f)

fence [fens] n Zaun m ♦ vt (*also:* ~ **in**) einzäunen ♦ vi fechten; **fencing** ['fensɪŋ] n Zaun m; (*SPORT*) Fechten nt

fend [fend] vi: **to ~ for o.s.** sich (allein) durchschlagen; ~ **off** vt abwehren

fender ['fendə] n Kaminvorsetzer m; (*US: AUT*) Kotflügel m

ferment [vb fə'ment, n 'fɜ:ment] vi (*CHEM*) gären ♦ n (*unrest*) Unruhe f

fern [fɜːn] n Farn m

ferocious [fə'rəʊʃəs] adj wild, grausam

ferret ['ferɪt] n Frettchen nt ♦ vt: **to ~ out** aufspüren

ferry ['feri] n Fähre f ♦ vt übersetzen

fertile ['fɜːtaɪl] adj fruchtbar

fertilize ['fɜːtɪlaɪz] vt (*AGR*) düngen; (*BIOL*) befruchten; **~r** n (Kunst)dünger m

fervent ['fɜːvənt] adj (*admirer*) glühend; (*hope*) innig

fervour ['fɜːvə] (*US* **fervor**) n Leidenschaft f

fester ['festə] vi eitern

festival ['festɪvəl] n (*REL etc*) Fest nt; (*ART, MUS*) Festspiele pl

festive ['festɪv] adj festlich; **the ~ season** (*Christmas*) die Festzeit; **festivities** [fes'tɪvɪtɪz] npl Feierlichkeiten pl

festoon [fes'tu:n] vt: **to ~ with** schmücken mit

fetch [fetʃ] vt holen; (*in sale*) einbringen

fetching ['fetʃɪŋ] adj reizend

fête [feɪt] n Fest nt

fetus ['fi:təs] (*esp US*) n = **foetus**

feud [fju:d] n Fehde f

feudal ['fju:dl] adj Feudal-

fever ['fi:və] n Fieber nt; **~ish** adj (*MED*) fiebrig; (*fig*) fieberhaft

few [fju:] adj wenig; **a ~** einige; **~er** adj weniger; **~est** adj wenigste(r,s)

fiancé [fɪ'ɑ̃:ŋseɪ] n Verlobte(r) m; **~e** n Verlobte f

fib [fɪb] n Flunkerei f ♦ vi flunkern

fibre ['faɪbə] (*US* **fiber**) n Faser f; **~glass** n Glaswolle f

fickle ['fɪkl] adj unbeständig

fiction ['fɪkʃən] n (*novels*) Romanliteratur f; (*story*) Erdichtung f; **~al** adj erfunden

fictitious [fɪk'tɪʃəs] *adj* erfunden, fingiert

fiddle ['fɪdl] *n* Geige *f*; (*trick*) Schwindelei *f*
♦ *vt* (*BRIT: accounts*) frisieren; **~ with** *vt fus*
herumfummeln an +*dat*

fidelity [fɪ'delɪtɪ] *n* Treue *f*

fidget ['fɪdʒɪt] *vi* zappeln

field [fi:ld] *n* Feld *nt*; (*range*) Gebiet *nt*; **~
marshal** *n* Feldmarschall *m*; **~work** *n*
Feldforschung *f*

fiend [fi:nd] *n* Teufel *m*

fierce [fɪəs] *adj* wild

fiery ['faɪərɪ] *adj* (*person*) hitzig

fifteen [fɪf'ti:n] *num* fünfzehn

fifth [fɪfθ] *adj* fünfte(r, s) ♦ *n* Fünftel *nt*

fifty ['fɪftɪ] *num* fünfzig; **~-fifty** *adj, adv*
halbe-halbe, fifty-fifty (*inf*)

fig [fɪg] *n* Feige *f*

fight [faɪt] (*pt, pp* **fought**) *n* Kampf *m*; (*brawl*)
Schlägerei *f*; (*argument*) Streit *m* ♦ *vt*
kämpfen gegen; sich schlagen mit; (*fig*)
bekämpfen ♦ *vi* kämpfen; sich schlagen;
streiten; **~er** *n* Kämpfer(in) *m(f)*; (*plane*)
Jagdflugzeug *nt*; **~ing** *n* Kämpfen *nt*; (*war*)
Kampfhandlungen *pl*

figment ['fɪgmənt] *n*: **~ of the imagination**
reine Einbildung *f*

figurative ['fɪgjʊrətɪv] *adj* bildlich

figure ['fɪgər] *n* (*of person*) Figur *f*; (*person*)
Gestalt *f*; (*number*) Ziffer *f* ♦ *vt* (*US: imagine*)
glauben ♦ *vi* (*appear*) erscheinen; **~ out** *vt*
herausbekommen; **~head** *n* (*NAUT, fig*)
Galionsfigur *f*; **~ of speech** *n* Redensart *f*

file [faɪl] *n* (*tool*) Feile *f*; (*dossier*) Akte *f*;
(*folder*) Aktenordner *m*; (*COMPUT*) Datei *f*;
(*row*) Reihe *f* ♦ *vt* (*metal, nails*) feilen;
(*papers*) abheften; (*claim*) einreichen ♦ *vi*: **to
~ in/out** hintereinander hereinkommen/
hinausgehen; **to ~ past** vorbeimarschieren;
filing ['faɪlɪŋ] *n* Ablage *f*; **filing cabinet** *n*
Aktenschrank *m*

fill [fɪl] *vt* füllen; (*occupy*) ausfüllen; (*satisfy*)
sättigen ♦ *n*: **to eat one's ~** sich richtig
satt essen; **~ in** *vt* (*hole*) (auf)füllen; (*form*)
ausfüllen; **~ up** *vt* (*container*) auffüllen;
(*form*) ausfüllen ♦ *vi* (*AUT*) tanken

fillet ['fɪlɪt] *n* Filet *nt*; **~ steak** *n* Filetsteak *nt*

filling ['fɪlɪŋ] *n* (*COOK*) Füllung *f*; (*for tooth*)

(Zahn)plombe *f*; **~ station** *n* Tankstelle *f*

film [fɪlm] *n* Film *m* ♦ *vt* (*scene*) filmen; **~
star** *n* Filmstar *m*

filter ['fɪltər] *n* Filter *m* ♦ *vt* filtern; **~ lane**
(*BRIT*) *n* Abbiegespur *f*; **~-tipped** *adj* Filter-

filth [fɪlθ] *n* Dreck *m*; **~y** *adj* dreckig;
(*weather*) scheußlich

fin [fɪn] *n* Flosse *f*

final ['faɪnl] *adj* letzte(r, s); End-; (*conclusive*)
endgültig ♦ *n* (*FOOTBALL etc*) Endspiel *nt*; **~s**
npl (*UNIV*) Abschlussexamen *nt*; (*SPORT*)
Schlussrunde *f*

finale [fɪ'nɑ:lɪ] *n* (*MUS*) Finale *nt*

final: ~ist *n* (*SPORT*) Schluss-
rundenteilnehmer *m*; **~ize** *vt* endgültige
Form geben +*dat*; abschließen; **~ly** *adv*
(*lastly*) zuletzt; (*eventually*) endlich;
(*irrevocably*) endgültig

finance [faɪ'næns] *n* Finanzwesen *nt* ♦ *vt*
finanzieren; **~s** *npl* (*funds*) Finanzen *pl*;
financial [faɪ'nænʃəl] *adj* Finanz-; finanziell

find [faɪnd] (*pt, pp* **found**) *vt* finden ♦ *n* Fund
m; **to ~ sb guilty** jdn für schuldig erklären;
~ out *vt* herausfinden; **~ings** *npl* (*JUR*)
Ermittlungsergebnis *nt*; (*of report*) Befund *m*

fine [faɪn] *adj* fein; (*good*) gut; (*weather*)
schön ♦ *adv* (*well*) gut; (*small*) klein ♦ *n* (*JUR*)
Geldstrafe *f* ♦ *vt* (*JUR*) mit einer Geldstrafe
belegen; **~ arts** *npl* schöne(n) Künste *pl*

finger ['fɪŋgər] *n* Finger *m* ♦ *vt* befühlen;
~nail *n* Fingernagel *m*; **~print** *n*
Fingerabdruck *m*; **~tip** *n* Fingerspitze *f*

finicky ['fɪnɪkɪ] *adj* pingelig

finish ['fɪnɪʃ] *n* Ende *nt*; (*SPORT*) Ziel *nt*; (*of
object*) Verarbeitung *f*; (*of paint*)
Oberflächenwirkung *f* ♦ *vt* beenden; (*book*)
zu Ende lesen ♦ *vi* aufhören; (*SPORT*) ans
Ziel kommen; **to be ~ed with sth** fertig
sein mit etw; **to ~ doing sth** mit etw fertig
werden; **~ off** *vt* (*complete*) fertig machen;
(*kill*) den Gnadenstoß geben +*dat*; (*knock
out*) erledigen (*umg*); **~ up** *vt* (*food*)
aufessen; (*drink*) austrinken ♦ *vi* (*end up*)
enden; **~ing line** *n* Ziellinie *f*; **~ing
school** *n* Mädchenpensionat *nt*

finite ['faɪnaɪt] *adj* endlich, begrenzt

Finland ['fɪnlənd] *n* Finnland *nt*

Finn [fɪn] *n* Finne *m*, Finnin *f*; **~ish** *adj*
finnisch ♦ *n* (*LING*) Finnisch *nt*

fir [fəːʳ] *n* Tanne *f*

fire ['faɪəʳ] *n* Feuer *nt*; (*in house etc*) Brand *m*
♦ *vt* (*gun*) abfeuern; (*imagination*)
entzünden; (*dismiss*) hinauswerfen ♦ *vi*
(*AUT*) zünden; **to be on ~** brennen; **~**
alarm *n* Feueralarm *m*; **~arm** *n*
Schusswaffe *f*; **~ brigade** (*BRIT*) *n*
Feuerwehr *f*; **~ department** (*US*) *n*
Feuerwehr *f*; **~ engine** *n* Feuerwehrauto
nt; **~ escape** *n* Feuerleiter *f*; **~**
extinguisher *n* Löschgerät *nt*; **~man**
(*irreg*) *n* Feuerwehrmann *m*; **~place** *n*
Kamin *m*; **~side** *n* Kamin *m*; **~ station** *n*
Feuerwehrwache *f*; **~wood** *n* Brennholz *nt*;
~works *npl* Feuerwerk *nt*; **~ squad** *n*
Exekutionskommando *nt*

firm [fəːm] *adj* fest ♦ *n* Firma *f*; **~ly** ['fəːmlɪ]
adv (*grasp, speak*) fest; (*push, tug*) energisch;
(*decide*) endgültig

first [fəːst] *adj* erste(r, s) ♦ *adv* zuerst; (*arrive*)
als Erste(r); (*happen*) zum ersten Mal ♦ *n*
(*person: in race*) Erste(r) *mf*; (*UNIV*) Eins *f*;
(*AUT*) erste(r) Gang *m*; **at ~** zuerst; **~ of all**
zuallererst; **~ aid** *n* erste Hilfe *f*; **~-aid kit** *n*
Verbandskasten *m*; **~-class** *adj* erstklassig;
(*travel*) erster Klasse; **~-hand** *adj* aus erster
Hand; **~ lady** (*US*) *n* First Lady *f*; **~ly** *adv*
erstens; **~ name** *n* Vorname *m*; **~-rate** *adj*
erstklassig

fiscal ['fɪskl] *adj* Finanz-

fish [fɪʃ] *n inv* Fisch *m* ♦ *vi* fischen; angeln; **to**
go ~ing angeln gehen; (*in sea*) fischen
gehen; **~erman** (*irreg*) *n* Fischer *m*; **~ farm**
n Fischzucht *f*; **~ fingers** (*BRIT*) *npl*
Fischstäbchen *pl*; **~ing boat** *n* Fischerboot
nt; **~ing line** *n* Angelschnur *f*; **~ing rod** *n*
Angel(rute) *f*; **~ing tackle** *n* (*for sport*)
Angelgeräte *pl*; **~monger's (shop)** *n*
Fischhändler *m*; **~ slice** *n*
Fischvorlegemesser *nt*; **~ sticks** (*US*) *npl* =
fish fingers

fishy ['fɪʃɪ] (*inf*) *adj* (*suspicious*) faul

fission ['fɪʃən] *n* Spaltung *f*

fissure ['fɪʃəʳ] *n* Riss *m*

fist [fɪst] *n* Faust *f*

fit [fɪt] *adj* (*MED*) gesund; (*SPORT*) in Form, fit;
(*suitable*) geeignet ♦ *vt* passen +*dat*; (*insert,
attach*) einsetzen ♦ *vi* passen; (*in space, gap*)
hineinpassen ♦ *n* (*of clothes*) Sitz *m*; (*MED, of
anger*) Anfall *m*; (*of laughter*) Krampf *m*; **by**
~s and starts (*move*) ruckweise; (*work*)
unregelmäßig; **~ in** *vi* hineinpassen; (*fig:
person*) passen; **~ out** *vt* (*also: ~ up*)
ausstatten; **~ful** *adj* (*sleep*) unruhig; **~ment**
n Einrichtungsgegenstand *m*; **~ness** *n*
(*suitability*) Eignung *f*; (*MED*) Gesundheit *f*;
(*SPORT*) Fitness *f*; **~ted carpet** *n*
Teppichboden *m*; **~ted kitchen** *n*
Einbauküche *f*; **~ter** *n* (*TECH*) Monteur *m*;
~ting *adj* passend ♦ *n* (*of dress*) Anprobe *f*;
(*piece of equipment*) (Ersatz)teil *nt*; **~tings**
npl (*equipment*) Zubehör *nt*; **~ting room** *n*
Anproberaum *m*

five [faɪv] *num* fünf; **~r** (*inf*) *n* (*BRIT*)
Fünfpfundnote *f*; (*US*) Fünfdollarnote *f*

fix [fɪks] *vt* befestigen; (*settle*) festsetzen;
(*repair*) reparieren ♦ *n*: **in a ~** in der
Klemme; **~ up** *vt* (*meeting*) arrangieren; **to**
~ sb up with sth jdm etw *acc* verschaffen;
~ation [fɪk'seɪʃən] *n* Fixierung *f*; **~ed** [fɪkst]
adj fest; **~ture** *n* ['fɪkstʃəʳ] *n* Installationsteil *m*;
(*SPORT*) Spiel *nt*

fizzy ['fɪzɪ] *adj* Sprudel-, sprudelnd

flabbergasted ['flæbəgɑːstɪd] (*inf*) *adj* platt

flabby ['flæbɪ] *adj* wabbelig

flag [flæg] *n* Fahne *f* ♦ *vi* (*strength*)
nachlassen; (*spirit*) erlahmen; **~ down** *vt*
anhalten; **~pole** ['flægpəul] *n* Fahnenstange
f

flair [flɛəʳ] *n* Talent *nt*

flak [flæk] *n* Flakfeuer *nt*

flake [fleɪk] *n* (*of snow*) Flocke *f*; (*of rust*)
Schuppe *f* ♦ *vi* (*also: ~ off*) abblättern

flamboyant [flæm'bɔɪənt] *adj* extravagant

flame [fleɪm] *n* Flamme *f*

flamingo [flə'mɪŋgəu] *n* Flamingo *m*

flammable ['flæməbl] *adj* brennbar

flan [flæn] (*BRIT*) *n* Obsttorte *f*

flank [flæŋk] *n* Flanke *f* ♦ *vt* flankieren

flannel ['flænl] *n* Flanell *m*; (*BRIT: also*: **face**
~) Waschlappen *m*; (: *inf*) Geschwafel *nt*;
~s *npl* (*trousers*) Flanellhose *f*

flap [flæp] n Klappe f; (inf: crisis) (helle) Aufregung f ♦ vt (wings) schlagen mit ♦ vi flattern

flare [flɛəʳ] n (signal) Leuchtsignal nt; (in skirt etc) Weite f; ~ **up** vi aufflammen; (fig) aufbrausen; (revolt) (plötzlich) ausbrechen

flash [flæʃ] n Blitz m; (also: **news** ~) Kurzmeldung f; (PHOT) Blitzlicht nt ♦ vt aufleuchten lassen ♦ vi aufleuchten; **in a** ~ im Nu; ~ **by** or **past** vi vorbeirasen; ~**back** n Rückblende f; ~**bulb** n Blitzlichtbirne f; ~ **cube** n Blitzwürfel m; ~**light** n Blitzlicht nt

flashy ['flæʃɪ] (pej) adj knallig

flask [flɑːsk] n (CHEM) Kolben m; (also: **vacuum** ~) Thermosflasche f ®

flat [flæt] adj flach; (dull) matt; (MUS) erniedrigt; (beer) schal; (tyre) platt ♦ n (BRIT: rooms) Wohnung f; (MUS) b nt; (AUT) Platte(r) m; **to work** ~ **out** auf Hochtouren arbeiten; ~**ly** adv glatt; ~**-screen** adj (TV, COMPUT) mit flachem Bildschirm; ~**ten** vt (also: ~**ten out**) ebnen

flatter ['flætəʳ] vt schmeicheln +dat; ~**ing** adj schmeichelhaft; ~**y** n Schmeichelei f

flatulence ['flætjuləns] n Blähungen pl

flaunt [flɔːnt] vt prunken mit

flavour ['fleɪvəʳ] (US **flavor**) n Geschmack m ♦ vt würzen; ~**ed** adj: **strawberry-~ed** mit Erdbeergeschmack; ~**ing** n Würze f

flaw [flɔː] n Fehler m; ~**less** adj einwandfrei

flax [flæks] n Flachs m; ~**en** adj flachsfarben

flea [fliː] n Floh m

fleck [flɛk] n (mark) Fleck m; (pattern) Tupfen m

fled [flɛd] pt, pp of **flee**

flee [fliː] (pt, pp **fled**) vi fliehen ♦ vt fliehen vor +dat; (country) fliehen aus

fleece [fliːs] n Vlies nt ♦ vt (inf) schröpfen

fleet [fliːt] n Flotte f

fleeting ['fliːtɪŋ] adj flüchtig

Flemish ['flemɪʃ] adj flämisch

flesh [flɛʃ] n Fleisch nt; ~ **wound** n Fleischwunde f

flew [fluː] pt of **fly**

flex [flɛks] n Kabel nt ♦ vt beugen; ~**ibility** [flɛksɪ'bɪlɪtɪ] n Biegsamkeit f; (fig) Flexibilität f; ~**ible** adj biegsam; (plans) flexibel

flick [flɪk] n leichte(r) Schlag m ♦ vt leicht schlagen; ~ **through** vt fus durchblättern

flicker ['flɪkəʳ] n Flackern nt ♦ vi flackern

flier ['flaɪəʳ] n Flieger m

flight [flaɪt] n Flug m; (fleeing) Flucht f; (also: ~ **of steps**) Treppe f; **to take** ~ die Flucht ergreifen; ~ **attendant** (US) n Steward(ess) m(f); ~ **deck** n Flugdeck nt

flimsy ['flɪmzɪ] adj (thin) hauchdünn; (excuse) fadenscheinig

flinch [flɪntʃ] vi: **to** ~ **(away from)** zurückschrecken (vor +dat)

fling [flɪŋ] (pt, pp **flung**) vt schleudern

flint [flɪnt] n Feuerstein m

flip [flɪp] vt werfen

flippant ['flɪpənt] adj schnippisch

flipper ['flɪpəʳ] n Flosse f

flirt [flɜːt] vi flirten ♦ n: **he/she is a** ~ er/sie flirtet gern

flit [flɪt] vi flitzen

float [fləʊt] n (FISHING) Schwimmer m; (esp in procession) Plattformwagen m ♦ vi schwimmen; (in air) schweben ♦ vt (COMM) gründen; (currency) floaten

flock [flɔk] n (of sheep, REL) Herde f; (of birds) Schwarm m

flog [flɔg] vt prügeln; (inf: sell) verkaufen

flood [flʌd] n Überschwemmung f; (fig) Flut f ♦ vt überschwemmen; ~**ing** n Überschwemmung f; ~**light** n Flutlicht nt

floor [flɔːʳ] n (Fuß)boden m; (storey) Stock m ♦ vt (person) zu Boden schlagen; **ground** ~ (BRIT) Erdgeschoss nt; **first** ~ (BRIT) erste(r) Stock m; (US) Erdgeschoss nt; ~**board** n Diele f; ~ **show** n Kabarettvorstellung f

flop [flɔp] n Plumps m; (failure) Reinfall m ♦ vi (fail) durchfallen

floppy ['flɔpɪ] adj hängend; ~ **(disk)** n (COMPUT) Diskette f

flora ['flɔːrə] n Flora f; ~**l** adj Blumen-

florist ['flɔrɪst] n Blumenhändler(in) m(f); ~**'s (shop)** n Blumengeschäft nt

flotation [fləʊ'teɪʃən] n (FIN) Auflegung f

flounce [flauns] n Volant m

flounder ['flaundəʳ] vi (fig) ins Schleudern kommen ♦ n (ZOOL) Flunder f

flour ['flaʊəʳ] *n* Mehl *nt*

flourish ['flʌrɪʃ] *vi* blühen; gedeihen ♦ *n* (*waving*) Schwingen *nt*; (*of trumpets*) Tusch *m*, Fanfare *f*

flout [flaʊt] *vt* missachten

flow [fləʊ] *n* Fließen *nt*; (*of sea*) Flut *f* ♦ *vi* fließen; ~ **chart** *n* Flussdiagramm *nt*

flower ['flaʊəʳ] *n* Blume *f* ♦ *vi* blühen; ~ **bed** *n* Blumenbeet *nt*; ~**pot** *n* Blumentopf *m*; ~**y** *adj* (*style*) blumenreich

flown [fləʊn] *pp of* **fly**

flu [flu:] *n* Grippe *f*

fluctuate ['flʌktjʊeɪt] *vi* schwanken; **fluctuation** [flʌktjʊ'eɪʃən] *n* Schwankung *f*

fluency ['flu:ənsɪ] *n* Flüssigkeit *f*

fluent ['flu:ənt] *adj* fließend; ~**ly** *adv* fließend

fluff [flʌf] *n* Fussel *f*; ~**y** *adj* flaumig

fluid ['flu:ɪd] *n* Flüssigkeit *f* ♦ *adj* flüssig; (*fig: plans*) veränderbar

fluke [flu:k] (*inf*) *n* Dusel *m*

flung [flʌŋ] *pt, pp of* **fling**

fluoride ['flʊəraɪd] *n* Fluorid *nt*; ~ **toothpaste** *n* Fluorzahnpasta *f*

flurry ['flʌrɪ] *n* (*of snow*) Gestöber *nt*; (*of activity*) Aufregung *f*

flush [flʌʃ] *n* Erröten *nt*; (*excited*) Glühen *nt* ♦ *vt* (*aus*)spülen ♦ *vi* erröten ♦ *adj* glatt; ~ **out** *vt* aufstöbern; ~**ed** *adj* rot

flustered ['flʌstəd] *adj* verwirrt

flute [flu:t] *n* Querflöte *f*

flutter ['flʌtəʳ] *n* Flattern *nt* ♦ *vi* flattern

flux [flʌks] *n*: **in a state of** ~ im Fluss

fly [flaɪ] (*pt* **flew**, *pp* **flown**) *n* (*insect*) Fliege *f*; (*on trousers: also:* **flies**) (Hosen)schlitz *m* ♦ *vt* fliegen ♦ *vi* fliegen; (*flee*) fliehen; (*flag*) wehen; ~ **away** *or* **off** *vi* (*bird, insect*) wegfliegen; ~~-**drive** *n*: ~~-**drive holiday** Fly & Drive-Urlaub *m*; ~**ing** *n* Fliegen *nt* ♦ *adj*: **with** ~**ing colours** mit fliegenden Fahnen; ~**ing start** gute(r) Start *m*; ~**ing visit** Stippvisite *f*; ~**ing saucer** *n* fliegende Untertasse *f*; ~**over** (*BRIT*) *n* Überführung *f*; ~**sheet** *n* (*for tent*) Regendach *nt*

foal [fəʊl] *n* Fohlen *nt*

foam [fəʊm] *n* Schaum *m* ♦ *vi* schäumen; ~ **rubber** *n* Schaumgummi *m*

fob [fɔb] *vt*: **to** ~ **sb off with sth** jdm etw andrehen; (*with promise*) jdn mit etw abspeisen

focal ['fəʊkl] *adj* Brenn-; ~ **point** *n* (*of room, activity*) Mittelpunkt *m*

focus ['fəʊkəs] (*pl* ~**es**) *n* Brennpunkt *m* ♦ *vt* (*attention*) konzentrieren; (*camera*) scharf einstellen ♦ *vi*: **to** ~ (**on**) sich konzentrieren (auf +*acc*); **in** ~ scharf eingestellt; **out of** ~ unscharf

fodder ['fɔdəʳ] *n* Futter *nt*

foe [fəʊ] *n* Feind *m*

foetus ['fi:təs] (*US* **fetus**) *n* Fötus *m*

fog [fɔg] *n* Nebel *m*; ~**gy** *adj* neblig; ~ **lamp** (*BRIT*), ~ **light** (*US*) *n* (*AUT*) Nebelscheinwerfer *m*

foil [fɔɪl] *vt* vereiteln ♦ *n* (*metal, also fig*) Folie *f*; (*FENCING*) Florett *nt*

fold [fəʊld] *n* (*bend, crease*) Falte *f*; (*AGR*) Pferch *m* ♦ *vt* falten; ~ **up** *vi* (*map etc*) zusammenfalten ♦ *vi* (*business*) eingehen; ~**er** *n* Schnellhefter *m*; ~**ing** *adj* (*chair etc*) Klapp-

foliage ['fəʊlɪɪdʒ] *n* Laubwerk *nt*

folk [fəʊk] *npl* Leute *pl* ♦ *adj* Volks-; ~**s** *npl* (*family*) Leute *pl*; ~**lore** ['fəʊklɔ:ʳ] *n* (*study*) Volkskunde *f*; (*tradition*) Folklore *f*; ~ **song** *n* Volkslied *nt*; (*modern*) Folksong *m*

follow ['fɔləʊ] *vt* folgen +*dat*; (*fashion*) mitmachen ♦ *vi* folgen; ~ **up** *vt* verfolgen; ~**er** *n* Anhänger(in) *m(f)*; ~**ing** *adj* folgend ♦ *n* (*people*) Gefolgschaft *f*; ~-**on call** *n* weiteres Gespräch in einer Telefonzelle um Guthaben zu verbrauchen

folly ['fɔlɪ] *n* Torheit *f*

fond [fɔnd] *adj*: **to be** ~ **of** gern haben

fondle ['fɔndl] *vt* streicheln

font [fɔnt] *n* Taufbecken *nt*

food [fu:d] *n* Essen *nt*; (*fodder*) Futter *nt*; ~ **mixer** *n* Küchenmixer *m*; ~ **poisoning** *n* Lebensmittelvergiftung *f*; ~ **processor** *n* Küchenmaschine *f*; ~**stuffs** *npl* Lebensmittel *pl*

fool [fu:l] *n* Narr *m*, Närrin *f* ♦ *vt* (*deceive*) hereinlegen ♦ *vi* (*also:* ~ **around**) (*herum*)albern; ~**hardy** *adj* tollkühn; ~**ish** *adj* albern; ~**proof** *adj* idiotensicher

foot [fʊt] (*pl* **feet**) *n* Fuß *m* ♦ *vt* (*bill*)

bezahlen; **on ~** zu Fuß
footage ['futɪdʒ] *n* (CINE) Filmmaterial *nt*
football ['futbɔːl] *n* Fußball *m*; (*game*: BRIT)
Fußball *m*; (: US) Football *m*; **~ player** *n*
(BRIT: *also*: **~er**) Fußballspieler *m*, Fußballer
m; (US) Footballer *m*

Football Pools
---

i Football Pools, *umgangssprachlich*
auch the pools *genannt, ist das in*
Großbritannien sehr beliebte Fußballtoto,
bei dem auf die Ergebnisse der
samstäglichen Fußballspiele gewettet wird.
Teilnehmer schicken ihren ausgefüllten
Totoschein vor den Spielen an die
Totogesellschaft und vergleichen nach den
Spielen die Ergebnisse mit ihrem Schein. Die
Gewinne können sehr hoch sein und
gelegentlich Millionen von Pfund betragen.

---

foot: **~brake** *n* Fußbremse *f*; **~bridge** *n*
Fußgängerbrücke *f*; **~hills** *npl* Ausläufer *pl*;
~hold *n* Halt *m*; **~ing** *n* Halt *m*; (*fig*)
Verhältnis *nt*; **~lights** *npl* Rampenlicht *nt*;
~man (*irreg*) *n* Bedienstete(r) *m*; **~note** *n*
Fußnote *f*; **~path** *n* Fußweg *m*; **~print** *n*
Fußabdruck *m*; **~sore** *adj* fußkrank; **~step**
n Schritt *m*; **~wear** *n* Schuhzeug *nt*

KEYWORD
---

for [fɔːʳ] *prep* **1** für; **is this for me?** ist das für
mich?; **the train for London** der Zug nach
London; **he went for the paper** er ging die
Zeitung holen; **give it to me – what for?**
gib es mir – warum?
2 (*because of*) wegen; **for this reason** aus
diesem Grunde
3 (*referring to distance*): **there are**
roadworks for 5 km die Baustelle ist 5 km
lang; **we walked for miles** wir sind
meilenweit gegangen
4 (*referring to time*) seit; (: *with future sense*)
für; **he was away for 2 years** er war zwei
Jahre lang weg
5 (*+infin clauses*): **it is not for me to decide**
das kann ich nicht entscheiden; **for this to**
be possible ... damit dies möglich wird/

wurde ...
6 (*in spite of*) trotz +*gen or* (*inf*) *dat* ; **for all**
his complaints obwohl er sich ständig
beschwert
♦ *conj* denn

---

forage ['fɔrɪdʒ] *n* (Vieh)futter *nt*
foray ['fɔreɪ] *n* Raubzug *m*
forbad(e) [fə'bæd] *pt of* **forbid**
forbid [fə'bɪd] (*pt* **forbad(e)**, *pp* **forbidden**)
vt verbieten; **~ding** *adj* einschüchternd
force [fɔːs] *n* Kraft *f*; (*compulsion*) Zwang *m*
♦ *vt* zwingen; (*lock*) aufbrechen; **the F~s**
npl (BRIT) die Streitkräfte; **in ~** (*rule*) gültig;
(*group*) in großer Stärke; **~d** *adj* (*smile*)
gezwungen; (*landing*) Not-; **~-feed** *vt*
zwangsernähren; **~ful** *adj* (*speech*) kraftvoll;
(*personality*) resolut
forceps ['fɔːseps] *npl* Zange *f*
forcibly ['fɔːsəblɪ] *adv* zwangsweise
ford [fɔːd] *n* Furt *f* ♦ *vt* durchwaten
fore [fɔːʳ] *n*: **to the ~** in den Vordergrund;
~arm ['fɔːrɑːm] *n* Unterarm *m*; **~boding**
[fɔː'bəudɪŋ] *n* Vorahnung *f*; **~cast** ['fɔːkɑːst]
(*irreg*: *like* **cast**) *n* Vorhersage *f* ♦ *vt*
voraussagen; **~court** ['fɔːkɔːt] *n* (*of garage*)
Vorplatz *m*; **~fathers** ['fɔːfɑːðəz] *npl*
Vorfahren *pl*; **~finger** ['fɔːfɪŋgəʳ] *n*
Zeigefinger *m*; **~front** ['fɔːfrʌnt] *n* Spitze *f*
forego [fɔː'gəu] (*irreg*: *like* **go**) *vt* verzichten
auf +*acc*
fore: **~gone** ['fɔːgɔn] *adj*: **it's a ~gone**
conclusion es steht von vornherein fest;
~ground ['fɔːgraund] *n* Vordergrund *m*;
~head ['fɔrɪd] *n* Stirn *f*
foreign ['fɔrɪn] *adj* Auslands-; (*accent*)
ausländisch; (*trade*) Außen-; (*body*) Fremd-;
~er *n* Ausländer(in) *m(f)*; **~ exchange** *n*
Devisen *pl*; **F~ Office** (BRIT) *n*
Außenministerium *nt*; **F~ Secretary** (BRIT)
n Außenminister *m*
fore: **~leg** *n* Vorderbein *nt*; **~man** (*irreg*) *n* Vorarbeiter *m*; **~most** *adj* erste(r,
s) ♦ *adv*: **first and ~most** vor allem
forensic [fə'rensɪk] *adj* gerichtsmedizinisch
fore ['fɔː-]: **~runner** *n* Vorläufer *m*; **~see**
[fɔː'siː] (*irreg*: *like* **see**) *vt* vorhersehen;

~**seeable** adj absehbar; ~**shadow** [ˈfɔːˈʃædəu] vt andeuten; ~**sight** [ˈfɔːsaɪt] n Voraussicht f

forest [ˈfɒrɪst] n Wald m

forestall [fɔːˈstɔːl] vt zuvorkommen +dat

forestry [ˈfɒrɪstrɪ] n Forstwirtschaft f

foretaste [ˈfɔːteɪst] n Vorgeschmack m

foretell [fɔːˈtel] (irreg: like **tell**) vt vorhersagen

forever [fəˈrevər] adv für immer

foreword [ˈfɔːwəːd] n Vorwort nt

forfeit [ˈfɔːfɪt] n Einbuße f ♦ vt verwirken

forgave [fəˈɡeɪv] pt of **forgive**

forge [fɔːdʒ] n Schmiede f ♦ vt fälschen; (iron) schmieden; ~ **ahead** vi Fortschritte machen; ~**d** adj gefälscht; ~**d banknotes** Blüten (inf) pl; ~**r** n Fälscher m; ~**ry** n Fälschung f

forget [fəˈɡet] (pt **forgot**, pp **forgotten**) vt, vi vergessen; ~**ful** adj vergesslich; ~**-me-not** n Vergissmeinnicht nt

forgive [fəˈɡɪv] (pt **forgave**, pp **forgiven**) vt verzeihen; **to ~ sb (for sth)** jdm (etw) verzeihen; ~**ness** n Verzeihung f

forgot [fəˈɡɒt] pt of **forget**; ~**ten** pp of **forget**

fork [fɔːk] n Gabel f; (in road) Gabelung f ♦ vi (road) sich gabeln; ~ **out** (inf) vt (pay) blechen; ~**-lift truck** n Gabelstapler m

forlorn [fəˈlɔːn] adj (person) verlassen; (hope) vergeblich

form [fɔːm] n Form f; (type) Art f; (figure) Gestalt f; (SCH) Klasse f; (bench) (Schul)bank f; (document) Formular nt ♦ vt formen; (be part of) bilden

formal [ˈfɔːməl] adj formell; (occasion) offiziell; ~**ly** adv (ceremoniously) formell; (officially) offiziell

format [ˈfɔːmæt] n Format nt ♦ vt (COMPUT) formatieren

formation [fɔːˈmeɪʃən] n Bildung f; (AVIAT) Formation f

formative [ˈfɔːmətɪv] adj (years) formend

former [ˈfɔːmər] adj früher; (opposite of latter) erstere(r, s); ~**ly** adv früher

formidable [ˈfɔːmɪdəbl] adj furchtbar

formula [ˈfɔːmjulə] (pl ~**e** or ~**s**) n Formel f; ~**e** [ˈfɔːmjuliː] npl of **formula**; ~**te**

[ˈfɔːmjuleɪt] vt formulieren

fort [fɔːt] n Feste f, Fort nt

forte [ˈfɔːtɪ] n Stärke f, starke Seite f

forth [fɔːθ] adv: **and so ~** und so weiter; ~**coming** adj kommend; (character) entgegenkommend; ~**right** adj offen; ~**with** adv umgehend

fortify [ˈfɔːtɪfaɪ] vt (ver)stärken; (protect) befestigen

fortitude [ˈfɔːtɪtjuːd] n Seelenstärke f

fortnight [ˈfɔːtnaɪt] (BRIT) n vierzehn Tage pl; ~**ly** (BRIT) adj zweiwöchentlich ♦ adv alle vierzehn Tage

fortress [ˈfɔːtrɪs] n Festung f

fortunate [ˈfɔːtʃənɪt] adj glücklich; ~**ly** adv glücklicherweise, zum Glück

fortune [ˈfɔːtʃən] n Glück nt; (money) Vermögen nt; ~**-teller** n Wahrsager(in) m(f)

forty [ˈfɔːtɪ] num vierzig

forum [ˈfɔːrəm] n Forum nt

forward [ˈfɔːwəd] adj vordere(r, s); (movement) Vorwärts-; (person) vorlaut; (planning) Voraus- ♦ adv vorwärts ♦ n (SPORT) Stürmer m ♦ vt (send) schicken; (help) fördern; ~**s** adv vorwärts

fossil [ˈfɒsl] n Fossil nt, Versteinerung f

foster [ˈfɒstər] vt (talent) fördern; ~ **child** n Pflegekind nt; ~ **mother** n Pflegemutter f

fought [fɔːt] pt, pp of **fight**

foul [faul] adj schmutzig; (language) gemein; (weather) schlecht ♦ n (SPORT) Foul nt ♦ vt (mechanism) blockieren; (SPORT) foulen; ~ **play** n (SPORT) Foulspiel nt; (LAW) Verbrechen nt

found [faund] pt, pp of **find** ♦ vt gründen; ~**ation** [faunˈdeɪʃən] n (act) Gründung f; (fig) Fundament nt; (also: ~**ation cream**) Grundierungscreme f; ~**ations** npl (of house) Fundament nt; ~**er** n Gründer(in) m(f) ♦ vi sinken

foundry [ˈfaundrɪ] n Gießerei f

fountain [ˈfauntɪn] n (Spring)brunnen m; ~ **pen** n Füllfederhalter m

four [fɔːr] num vier; **on all ~s** auf allen vieren; ~**-poster** n Himmelbett nt; ~**some** n Quartett nt; ~**teen** num vierzehn;

~teenth *adj* vierzehnte(r, s); **~th** *adj* vierte(r, s)

fowl [faul] *n* Huhn *nt*; *(food)* Geflügel *nt*

fox [fɔks] *n* Fuchs *m* ♦ *vt* täuschen

foyer ['fɔɪeɪ] *n* Foyer *nt*, Vorhalle *f*

fraction ['frækʃən] *n* (MATH) Bruch *m*; *(part)* Bruchteil *m*

fracture ['fræktʃəʳ] *n* (MED) Bruch *m* ♦ *vt* brechen

fragile ['frædʒaɪl] *adj* zerbrechlich

fragment ['frægmənt] *n* Bruchstück *nt*; *(small part)* Splitter *m*

fragrance ['freɪgrəns] *n* Duft *m*; **fragrant** ['freɪgrənt] *adj* duftend

frail [freɪl] *adj* schwach, gebrechlich

frame [freɪm] *n* Rahmen *m*; *(of spectacles: also:* **~s**) Gestell *nt*; *(body)* Gestalt *f* ♦ *vt* einrahmen; **to ~ sb** *(inf: incriminate)* jdm etwas anhängen; **~ of mind** Verfassung *f*; **~work** *n* Rahmen *m*; *(of society)* Gefüge *nt*

France [frɑːns] *n* Frankreich *nt*

franchise ['fræntʃaɪz] *n* (POL) (aktives) Wahlrecht *nt*; (COMM) Lizenz *f*

frank [fræŋk] *adj* offen ♦ *vt (letter)* frankieren; **~ly** *adv* offen gesagt

frantic ['fræntɪk] *adj* verzweifelt

fraternal [frə'tɜːnl] *adj* brüderlich

fraternity [frə'tɜːnɪtɪ] *n (club)* Vereinigung *f*; *(spirit)* Brüderlichkeit *f*; (US: SCH) Studentenverbindung *f*

fraternize ['frætənaɪz] *vi* fraternisieren

fraud [frɔːd] *n (trickery)* Betrug *m*; *(person)* Schwindler(in) *m(f)*; **~ulent** ['frɔːdjulənt] *adj* betrügerisch

fraught [frɔːt] *adj*: **~ with** voller +*gen*

fray [freɪ] *vt, vi* ausfransen; **tempers were ~ed** die Gemüter waren erhitzt

freak [friːk] *n* Monstrosität *f* ♦ *cpd (storm etc)* anormal

freckle ['frekl] *n* Sommersprosse *f*

free [friː] *adj* frei; *(loose)* lose; *(liberal)* freigebig ♦ *vt (set ~)* befreien; *(unblock)* freimachen; **~ (of charge)** gratis, umsonst; **for ~** gratis, umsonst; **~dom** ['friːdəm] *n* Freiheit *f*; **F~fone** ® *n*: **call F~fone 0800 ...** rufen Sie gebührenfrei 0800 ... an; **~-for-all** *n (fight)* allgemeine(s)

Handgemenge *nt*; **~ gift** *n* Geschenk *nt*; **~ kick** *n* Freistoß *m*; **~lance** *adj* frei; *(artist)* freischaffend; **~ly** *adv* frei; *(admit)* offen; **F~post** ® *n* ≈ Gebühr zahlt Empfänger; **~~range** *adj (hen)* Farmhof-; *(eggs)* Land-; **~ trade** *n* Freihandel *m*; **~way** *n (US) n* Autobahn *f*; **~wheel** *vi* im Freilauf fahren; **~ will** *n*: **of one's own ~ will** aus freien Stücken

freeze [friːz] *(pt* froze, *pp* frozen) *vi* gefrieren; *(feel cold)* frieren ♦ *vt (also fig)* einfrieren ♦ *n (fig, FIN)* Stopp *m*; **~r** *n* Tiefkühltruhe *f*; *(in fridge)* Gefrierfach *nt*; **freezing** *adj* eisig; *(freezing cold)* eiskalt; **freezing point** *n* Gefrierpunkt *m*

freight [freɪt] *n* Fracht *f*; **~ train** *n* Güterzug *m*

French [frentʃ] *adj* französisch ♦ *n* (LING) Französisch *nt*; **the ~** *npl (people)* die Franzosen *pl*; **~ bean** *n* grüne Bohne *f*; **~ fried potatoes** *(BRIT) npl* Pommes frites *pl*; **~ fries** *(US) npl* Pommes frites *pl*; **~ horn** *n* (MUS) (Wald)horn *nt*; **~ kiss** *n* Zungenkuss *m*; **~ loaf** *n* Baguette *f*; **~man/woman** *(irreg) n* Franzose *m*/Französin *f*; **~ window** *n* Verandatür *f*

frenzy ['frenzɪ] *n* Raserei *f*

frequency ['friːkwənsɪ] *n* Häufigkeit *f*; (PHYS) Frequenz *f*

frequent [*adj* 'friːkwənt, *vb* frɪ'kwent] *adj* häufig ♦ *vt (regelmäßig)* besuchen; **~ly** *adv (often)* häufig, oft

fresh [freʃ] *adj* frisch; **~en** *vi (also:* **~en up**) (sich) auffrischen; *(person)* sich frisch machen; **~er** *(inf: BRIT) n* (UNIV) Erstsemester *nt*; **~ly** *adv* gerade; **~man** *(irreg) (US) n* = **fresher**; **~ness** *n* Frische *f*; **~water** *adj (fish)* Süßwasser-

fret [fret] *vi* sich *dat* Sorgen machen

friar ['fraɪəʳ] *n* Klosterbruder *m*

friction ['frɪkʃən] *n (also fig)* Reibung *f*

Friday ['fraɪdɪ] *n* Freitag *m*

fridge [frɪdʒ] *(BRIT) n* Kühlschrank *m*

fried [fraɪd] *adj* gebraten

friend [frend] *n* Freund(in) *m(f)*; **~ly** *adj* freundlich; *(relations)* freundschaftlich; **~ly fire** *n* Beschuss *m* durch die eigene Seite;

~**ship** n Freundschaft f
frieze [fri:z] n Fries m
frigate ['frɪgɪt] n Fregatte f
fright [fraɪt] n Schrecken m; **to take ~** es mit der Angst zu tun bekommen; **~en** vt erschrecken; **to be ~ened** Angst haben; **~ening** adj schrecklich; **~ful** (inf) adj furchtbar
frigid ['frɪdʒɪd] adj frigide
frill [frɪl] n Rüsche f
fringe [frɪndʒ] n Besatz m; (BRIT: of hair) Pony m; (fig) Peripherie f; **~ benefits** npl zusätzliche Leistungen pl
Frisbee ['frɪzbɪ] ® n Frisbee ® nt
frisk [frɪsk] vt durchsuchen
frisky ['frɪskɪ] adj lebendig, ausgelassen
fritter ['frɪtəʳ] vt: **to ~ away** vergeuden
frivolous ['frɪvələs] adj frivol
frizzy ['frɪzɪ] adj kraus
fro [frəʊ] adv see **to**
frock [frɒk] n Kleid nt
frog [frɒg] n Frosch m; **~man** (irreg) n Froschmann m
frolic ['frɒlɪk] vi ausgelassen sein

from [frɒm] prep **1** (indicating starting place) of; (indicating origin etc) aus +dat; **a letter/ telephone call from my sister** ein Brief/ Anruf von meiner Schwester; **where do you come from?** woher kommen Sie?; **to drink from the bottle** aus der Flasche trinken
2 (indicating time) von ... an; (: past) seit; **from one o'clock to** or **until** or **till two** von ein Uhr bis zwei; **from January (on)** ab Januar
3 (indicating distance) von ... (entfernt)
4 (indicating price, number etc) ab +dat; **from £10** ab £10; **there were from 20 to 30 people there** es waren zwischen 20 und 30 Leute da
5 (indicating difference): **he can't tell red from green** er kann nicht zwischen Rot und Grün unterscheiden; **to be different from sb/sth** anders sein als jd/etw
6 (because of, based on): **from what he says** aus dem, was er sagt; **weak from hunger** schwach vor Hunger

front [frʌnt] n Vorderseite f; (of house) Fassade f; (promenade: also: **sea ~**) Strandpromenade f; (MIL, POL, MET) Front f; (fig: appearances) Fassade f ♦ adj (forward) vordere(r, s), Vorder-; (first) vorderste(r, s); **in ~** vorne; **in ~ of** vor; **~age** ['frʌntɪdʒ] n Vorderfront f; **~ door** n Haustür f; **~ier** ['frʌntɪəʳ] n Grenze f; **~ page** n Titelseite f; **~ room** (BRIT) n Wohnzimmer nt; **~-wheel drive** n Vorderradantrieb m
frost [frɒst] n Frost m; **~bite** n Erfrierung f; **~ed** adj (glass) Milch-; **~y** adj frostig
froth [frɒθ] n Schaum m
frown [fraʊn] n Stirnrunzeln nt ♦ vi die Stirn runzeln
froze [frəʊz] pt of **freeze**
frozen ['frəʊzn] pp of **freeze**
frugal ['fru:gl] adj sparsam, bescheiden
fruit [fru:t] n inv (as collective) Obst nt; (particular) Frucht f; **~ful** adj fruchtbar; **~ion** [fru:'ɪʃən] n: **to come to ~ion** in Erfüllung gehen; **~ juice** n Fruchtsaft m; **~ machine** n (BRIT) Spielautomat m; **~ salad** n Obstsalat m
frustrate [frʌs'treɪt] vt vereiteln; **~d** adj gehemmt; (PSYCH) frustriert
fry [fraɪ] (pt, pp **fried**) vt braten ♦ npl: **small ~** kleine Fische pl; **~ing pan** n Bratpfanne f
ft. abbr = **foot**; **feet**
fuddy-duddy ['fʌdɪdʌdɪ] n altmodische(r) Kauz m
fudge [fʌdʒ] n Fondant m
fuel ['fjuəl] n Treibstoff m; (for heating) Brennstoff m; (for lighter) Benzin nt; **~ oil** n (diesel fuel) Heizöl nt; **~ tank** n Tank m
fugitive ['fju:dʒɪtɪv] n Flüchtling m
fulfil [fʊl'fɪl] vt (duty) erfüllen; (promise) einhalten; **~ment** n Erfüllung f
full [fʊl] adj (box, bottle, price) voll; (person: satisfied) satt; (member, power, employment) Voll-; (complete) vollständig, Voll-; (speed) höchste(r, s); (skirt) weit ♦ adv: **~ well** sehr wohl; **in ~** vollständig; **a ~ two hours** volle

zwei Stunden; **~-length** adj (lifesize) lebensgroß; **a ~-length photograph** eine Ganzaufnahme; **~ moon** n Vollmond m; **~-scale** adj (attack) General-; (drawing) in Originalgröße; **~ stop** n Punkt m; **~-time** adj (job) Ganztags- ♦ adv (work) ganztags ♦ n (SPORT) Spielschluss nt; **~y** adv völlig; **~y fledged** adj (also fig) flügge; **~y licensed** adj (hotel, restaurant) mit voller Schankkonzession or -erlaubnis

fumble ['fʌmbl] vi: **to ~ (with)** herumfummeln (an +dat)

fume [fjuːm] vi qualmen; (fig) kochen (inf); **~s** npl (of fuel, car) Abgase pl

fumigate ['fjuːmɪɡeɪt] vt ausräuchern

fun [fʌn] n Spaß m; **to make ~ of** sich lustig machen über +acc

function ['fʌŋkʃən] n Funktion f; (occasion) Veranstaltung f ♦ vi funktionieren; **~al** adj funktionell

fund [fʌnd] n (money) Geldmittel pl, Fonds m; (store) Vorrat m; **~s** npl (resources) Mittel pl

fundamental [fʌndə'mɛntl] adj fundamental, grundlegend

funeral ['fjuːnərəl] n Beerdigung f; **~ parlour** n Leichenhalle f; **~ service** n Trauergottesdienst m

funfair ['fʌnfeə'] (BRIT) n Jahrmarkt m

fungi ['fʌŋɡaɪ] npl of **fungus**

fungus ['fʌŋɡəs] n Pilz m

funnel ['fʌnl] n Trichter m; (NAUT) Schornstein m

funny ['fʌnɪ] adj komisch

fur [fɜː'] n Pelz m; **~ coat** n Pelzmantel m

furious ['fjuərɪəs] adj wütend; (attempt) heftig

furlong ['fɜːlɔŋ] n = 201.17 m

furnace ['fɜːnɪs] n (Brenn)ofen m

furnish ['fɜːnɪʃ] vt einrichten; (supply) versehen; **~ings** npl Einrichtung f

furniture ['fɜːnɪtʃə'] n Möbel pl; **piece of ~** Möbelstück nt

furrow ['fʌrəu] n Furche f

furry ['fɜːrɪ] adj (tongue) pelzig; (animal) Pelz-

further ['fɜːðə'] adj weitere(r, s) ♦ adv weiter ♦ vt fördern; **~ education** n Weiterbildung

f; Erwachsenenbildung f; **~more** adv ferner

furthest ['fɜːðɪst] superl of **far**

furtive ['fɜːtɪv] adj verstohlen

fury ['fjuərɪ] n Wut f, Zorn m

fuse [fjuːz] (US **fuze**) n (ELEC) Sicherung f; (of bomb) Zünder m ♦ vt verschmelzen ♦ vi (BRIT: ELEC) durchbrennen; **~ box** n Sicherungskasten m

fuselage ['fjuːzəlɑːʒ] n Flugzeugrumpf m

fusion ['fjuːʒən] n Verschmelzung f

fuss [fʌs] n Theater nt; **~y** adj kleinlich

futile ['fjuːtaɪl] adj zwecklos, sinnlos; **futility** [fjuː'tɪlɪtɪ] n Zwecklosigkeit f

future ['fjuːtʃə'] adj zukünftig ♦ n Zukunft f; **in (the) ~** in Zukunft

fuze [fjuːz] (US) = **fuse**

fuzzy ['fʌzɪ] adj (indistinct) verschwommen; (hair) kraus

G, g

G [dʒiː] n (MUS) G nt

G7 n abbr (= Group of Seven) G7 f

gabble ['ɡæbl] vi plappern

gable ['ɡeɪbl] n Giebel m

gadget ['ɡædʒɪt] n Vorrichtung f

Gaelic ['ɡeɪlɪk] adj gälisch ♦ n (LING) Gälisch nt

gaffe [ɡæf] n Fauxpas m

gag [ɡæɡ] n Knebel m; (THEAT) Gag m ♦ vt knebeln

gaiety ['ɡeɪtɪ] n Fröhlichkeit f

gain [ɡeɪn] vt (obtain) erhalten; (win) gewinnen ♦ vi (clock) vorgehen ♦ n Gewinn m; **to ~ in sth** an etw dat gewinnen; **~ on** vt fus einholen

gait [ɡeɪt] n Gang m

gal. abbr = **gallon**

gala ['ɡɑːlə] n Fest nt

galaxy ['ɡæləksɪ] n Sternsystem nt

gale [ɡeɪl] n Sturm m

gallant ['ɡælənt] adj tapfer; (polite) galant

gallbladder [ɡɔːl-] n Gallenblase f

gallery ['ɡælərɪ] n (also: **art ~**) Galerie f

galley ['ɡælɪ] n (ship's kitchen) Kombüse f; (ship) Galeere f

gallon ['gæln] *n* Gallone *f*

gallop ['gæləp] *n* Galopp *m* ♦ *vi* galoppieren

gallows ['gæləuz] *n* Galgen *m*

gallstone ['gɔːlstəun] *n* Gallenstein *m*

galore [gə'lɔːʳ] *adv* in Hülle und Fülle

galvanize ['gælvənaɪz] *vt* (*metal*) galvanisieren; (*fig*) elektrisieren

gambit ['gæmbɪt] *n* (*fig*): **opening ~** (einleitende(r)) Schachzug *m*

gamble ['gæmbl] *vi* (um Geld) spielen ♦ *vt* (*risk*) aufs Spiel setzen ♦ *n* Risiko *nt*; **~r** *n* Spieler(in) *m(f)*; **gambling** *n* Glücksspiel *nt*

game [geɪm] *n* Spiel *nt*; (*hunting*) Wild *nt* ♦ *adj*: **~ (for)** bereit (zu); **~keeper** *n* Wildhüter *m*; **~s console** *n* (*COMPUT*) Gameboy *m* ®, Konsole *f*

gammon ['gæmən] *n* geräucherte(r) Schinken *m*

gamut ['gæmət] *n* Tonskala *f*

gang [gæŋ] *n* (*of criminals, youths*) Bande *f*; (*of workmen*) Kolonne *f* ♦ *vi*: **to ~ up on sb** sich gegen jdn verschwören

gangrene ['gæŋgriːn] *n* Brand *m*

gangster ['gæŋstəʳ] *n* Gangster *m*

gangway ['gæŋweɪ] *n* (*NAUT*) Laufplanke *f*; (*aisle*) Gang *m*

gaol [dʒeɪl] (*BRIT*) *n*, *vt* = **jail**

gap [gæp] *n* Lücke *f*

gape [geɪp] *vi* glotzen; **gaping** ['geɪpɪŋ] *adj* (*wound*) klaffend; (*hole*) gähnend

garage ['gærɑːʒ] *n* Garage *f*; (*for repair*) (Auto)reparaturwerkstatt *f*; (*for petrol*) Tankstelle *f*

garbage ['gɑːbɪdʒ] *n* Abfall *m*; **~ can** (*US*) *n* Mülltonne *f*

garbled ['gɑːbld] *adj* (*story*) verdreht

garden ['gɑːdn] *n* Garten *m*; **~s** *npl* (*public park*) Park *m*; (*private*) Gartenanlagen *pl*; **~er** *n* Gärtner(in) *m(f)*; **~ing** *n* Gärtnern *nt*

gargle ['gɑːgl] *vi* gurgeln

gargoyle ['gɑːgɔɪl] *n* Wasserspeier *m*

garish ['gɛərɪʃ] *adj* grell

garland ['gɑːlənd] *n* Girlande *f*

garlic ['gɑːlɪk] *n* Knoblauch *m*

garment ['gɑːmənt] *n* Kleidungsstück *nt*

garnish ['gɑːnɪʃ] *vt* (*food*) garnieren

garrison ['gærɪsn] *n* Garnison *f*

garter ['gɑːtəʳ] *n* Strumpfband *nt*; (*US*) Strumpfhalter *m*

gas [gæs] *n* Gas *nt*; (*esp US: petrol*) Benzin *nt* ♦ *vt* vergasen; **~ cooker** (*BRIT*) *n* Gasherd *m*; **~ cylinder** *n* Gasflasche *f*; **~ fire** *n* Gasofen *m*

gash [gæʃ] *n* klaffende Wunde *f* ♦ *vt* tief verwunden

gasket ['gæskɪt] *n* Dichtungsring *m*

gas mask *n* Gasmaske *f*

gas meter *n* Gaszähler *m*

gasoline ['gæsəliːn] (*US*) *n* Benzin *nt*

gasp [gɑːsp] *vi* keuchen; (*in surprise*) tief Luft holen ♦ *n* Keuchen *nt*

gas: **~ ring** *n* Gasring *m*; **~ station** (*US*) *n* Tankstelle *f*; **~ tap** *n* Gashahn *m*

gastric ['gæstrɪk] *adj* Magen-

gate [geɪt] *n* Tor *nt*; (*barrier*) Schranke *f*

gateau ['gætəu] (*pl* **~x**) *n* Torte *f*

gatecrash ['geɪtkræʃ] (*BRIT*) *vt* (*party*) platzen in +*acc*

gateway ['geɪtweɪ] *n* Toreingang *m*

gather ['gæðəʳ] *vt* (*people*) versammeln; (*things*) sammeln; (*understand*) annehmen ♦ *vi* (*assemble*) sich versammeln; **to ~ speed** schneller werden; **to ~ (from)** schließen (aus); **~ing** *n* Versammlung *f*

gauche [gəuʃ] *adj* linkisch

gaudy ['gɔːdɪ] *adj* schreiend

gauge [geɪdʒ] *n* (*instrument*) Messgerät *nt*; (*RAIL*) Spurweite *f*; (*dial*) Anzeiger *m*; (*measure*) Maß *nt* ♦ *vt* (ab)messen; (*fig*) abschätzen

gaunt [gɔːnt] *adj* hager

gauze [gɔːz] *n* Gaze *f*

gave [geɪv] *pt* of **give**

gay [geɪ] *adj* (*homosexual*) schwul; (*lively*) lustig

gaze [geɪz] *n* Blick *m* ♦ *vi* starren; **to ~ at sth** etw *dat* anstarren

gazelle [gə'zɛl] *n* Gazelle *f*

gazumping [gə'zʌmpɪŋ] (*BRIT*) *n* Hausverkauf an Höherbietenden trotz Zusage an anderen

GB *n abbr* = **Great Britain**

GCE (*BRIT*) *n abbr* = **General Certificate of Education**

GCSE (*BRIT*) *n abbr* = **General Certificate of Secondary Education**

gear [gɪəʳ] *n* Getriebe *nt*; (*equipment*) Ausrüstung *f*; (*AUT*) Gang *m* ♦ *vt* (*fig: adapt*): **to be ~ed to** ausgerichtet sein auf +*acc*; **top ~** höchste(r) Gang *m*; **high ~** (*US*) höchste(r) Gang *m*; **low ~** niedrige(r) Gang *m*; **in ~** eingekuppelt; **~ box** *n* Getriebe(gehäuse) *nt*; **~ lever** *n* Schalthebel *m*; **~ shift** (*US*) *n* Schalthebel *m*

geese [giːs] *npl of* **goose**

gel [dʒɛl] *n* Gel *nt*

gelatin(e) ['dʒɛləti:n] *n* Gelatine *f*

gem [dʒɛm] *n* Edelstein *m*; (*fig*) Juwel *nt*

Gemini ['dʒɛmɪnaɪ] *n* Zwillinge *pl*

gender ['dʒɛndəʳ] *n* (*GRAM*) Geschlecht *nt*

gene [dʒiːn] *n* Gen *nt*

general ['dʒɛnərəl] *n* General *m* ♦ *adj* allgemein; **~ delivery** (*US*) *n* Ausgabe(schalter *m*) *f* postlagernder Sendungen; **~ election** *n* allgemeine Wahlen *pl*; **~ize** *vi* verallgemeinern; **~ knowledge** *n* Allgemeinwissen *nt*; **~ly** *adv* allgemein, im Allgemeinen; **~ practitioner** *n* praktische(r) Arzt *m*, praktische Ärztin *f*

generate ['dʒɛnəreɪt] *vt* erzeugen

generation [dʒɛnə'reɪʃən] *n* Generation *f*; (*act*) Erzeugung *f*

generator ['dʒɛnəreɪtəʳ] *n* Generator *m*

generosity [dʒɛnə'rɔsɪtɪ] *n* Großzügigkeit *f*

generous ['dʒɛnərəs] *adj* großzügig

genetic [dʒɪ'nɛtɪk] *adj* genetisch; **~ally** *adv* genetisch; **~ally modified** genmanipuliert; **~ engineering** *n* Gentechnik *f*; **~ fingerprinting** [-'fɪŋɡəprɪntɪŋ] *n* genetische Fingerabdrücke *pl*

genetics [dʒɪ'nɛtɪks] *n* Genetik *f*

Geneva [dʒɪ'niːvə] *n* Genf *nt*

genial ['dʒiːnɪəl] *adj* freundlich, jovial

genitals ['dʒɛnɪtlz] *npl* Genitalien *pl*

genius ['dʒiːnɪəs] *n* Genie *nt*

genocide ['dʒɛnəʊsaɪd] *n* Völkermord *m*

gent [dʒɛnt] *n abbr* = **gentleman**

genteel [dʒɛn'tiːl] *adj* (*polite*) wohlanständig; (*affected*) affektiert

gentle ['dʒɛntl] *adj* sanft, zart

gentleman ['dʒɛntlmən] (*irreg*) *n* Herr *m*; (*polite*) Gentleman *m*

gentleness ['dʒɛntlnɪs] *n* Zartheit *f*, Milde *f*

gently ['dʒɛntlɪ] *adv* zart, sanft

gentry ['dʒɛntrɪ] *n* Landadel *m*

gents [dʒɛnts] *n*: **G~** (*lavatory*) Herren *pl*

genuine ['dʒɛnjuɪn] *adj* echt

geographic(al) [dʒɪə'græfɪk(l)] *adj* geografisch

geography [dʒɪ'ɔɡrəfɪ] *n* Geografie *f*

geological [dʒɪə'lɔdʒɪkl] *adj* geologisch

geology [dʒɪ'ɔlədʒɪ] *n* Geologie *f*

geometric(al) [dʒɪə'mɛtrɪk(l)] *adj* geometrisch

geometry [dʒɪ'ɔmɪtrɪ] *n* Geometrie *f*

geranium [dʒɪ'reɪnɪəm] *n* Geranie *f*

geriatric [dʒɛrɪ'ætrɪk] *adj* Alten- ♦ *n* Greis(in) *m(f)*

germ [dʒəːm] *n* Keim *m*; (*MED*) Bazillus *m*

German ['dʒəːmən] *adj* deutsch ♦ *n* Deutsche(r) *f(m)*; (*LING*) Deutsch *nt*; **~ measles** *n* Röteln *pl*; **~y** *n* Deutschland *nt*

germination [dʒəːmɪ'neɪʃən] *n* Keimen *nt*

gesticulate [dʒɛs'tɪkjuleɪt] *vi* gestikulieren

gesture ['dʒɛstjəʳ] *n* Geste *f*

KEYWORD

---

get [gɛt] (*pt, pp* **got**, *pp* **gotten** (*US*)) *vi* **1** (*become, be*) werden; **to get old/tired** alt/müde werden; **to get married** heiraten
2 (*go*) (an)kommen, gehen
3 (*begin*): **to get to know sb** jdn kennen lernen; **let's get going** *or* **started!** fangen wir an!
4 (*modal aux vb*): **you've got to do it** du musst es tun
♦ *vt* **1**: **to get sth done** (*do*) etw machen; (*have done*) etw machen lassen; **to get sth going** *or* **to go** etw in Gang bringen *or* bekommen; **to get sb to do sth** jdn dazu bringen, etw zu tun
2 (*obtain: money, permission, results*) erhalten; (*find: job, flat*) finden; (*fetch: person, object*) holen; **to get sth for sb** jdm etw besorgen; **get me Mr Jones, please** (*TEL*) verbinden Sie mich bitte mit Mr Jones
3 (*receive: present, letter*) bekommen, kriegen; (*acquire: reputation etc*) erwerben

4 (*catch*) bekommen, kriegen; (*hit: target etc*) treffen, erwischen; **get him!** (*to dog*) fass!

5 (*take, move*) bringen; **to get sth to sb** jdm etw bringen

6 (*understand*) verstehen; (*hear*) mitbekommen; **I've got it!** ich habs!

7 (*have, possess*): **to have got sth** etw haben

get about *vi* herumkommen; (*news*) sich verbreiten

get along *vi* (*people*) (gut) zurechtkommen; (*depart*) sich *acc* auf den Weg machen

get at *vt* (*facts*) herausbekommen; **to get at sb** (*nag*) an jdm herumnörgeln

get away *vi* (*leave*) sich *acc* davonmachen; (*escape*): **to get away from sth** von etw *dat* entkommen; **to get away with sth** mit etw davonkommen

get back *vi* (*return*) zurückkommen ♦ *vt* zurückbekommen

get by *vi* (*pass*) vorbeikommen; (*manage*) zurechtkommen

get down *vi* (her)untergehen ♦ *vt* (*depress*) fertig machen; **to get down to** in Angriff nehmen; (*find time to do*) kommen zu

get in *vi* (*train*) ankommen; (*arrive home*) heimkommen

get into *vt* (*enter*) hinein-/hereinkommen in +*acc*; (*: car, train etc*) einsteigen in +*acc*; (*clothes*) anziehen

get off *vi* (*from train etc*) aussteigen; (*from horse*) absteigen ♦ *vt* aussteigen aus; absteigen von

get on *vi* (*progress*) vorankommen; (*be friends*) auskommen; (*age*) alt werden; (*onto train etc*) einsteigen; (*onto horse*) aufsteigen ♦ *vt* einsteigen in +*acc*; auf etw *acc* aufsteigen

get out *vi* (*of house*) herauskommen; (*of vehicle*) aussteigen ♦ *vt* (*take out*) herausholen

get out of *vt* (*duty etc*) herumkommen um

get over *vt* (*illness*) sich *acc* erholen von;

(*surprise*) verkraften; (*news*) fassen; (*loss*) sich abfinden mit

get round *vt* herumkommen; (*fig: person*) herumkriegen

get through to *vt* (*TEL*) durchkommen zu

get together *vi* zusammenkommen

get up *vi* aufstehen ♦ *vt* hinaufbringen; (*go up*) hinaufgehen; (*organize*) auf die Beine stellen

get up to *vt* (*reach*) erreichen; (*prank etc*) anstellen

---

getaway [ˈgetəweɪ] *n* Flucht *f*

get-up [ˈgetʌp] (*inf*) *n* Aufzug *m*

geyser [ˈgiːzəʳ] *n* Geiser *m*; (*heater*) Durchlauferhitzer *m*

ghastly [ˈgɑːstlɪ] *adj* grässlich

gherkin [ˈgəːkɪn] *n* Gewürzgurke *f*

ghetto [ˈgetəu] *n* G(h)etto *nt*; **~ blaster** *n* (große(r)) Radiorekorder *m*

ghost [gəust] *n* Gespenst *nt*

giant [ˈdʒaɪənt] *n* Riese *m* ♦ *adj* riesig, Riesen-

gibberish [ˈdʒɪbərɪʃ] *n* dumme(s) Geschwätz *nt*

gibe [dʒaɪb] *n* spöttische Bemerkung *f*

giblets [ˈdʒɪblɪts] *npl* Geflügelinnereien *pl*

giddiness [ˈgɪdɪnɪs] *n* Schwindelgefühl *nt*

giddy [ˈgɪdɪ] *adj* schwindlig

gift [gɪft] *n* Geschenk *nt*; (*ability*) Begabung *f*; **~ed** *adj* begabt; **~ shop** *n* Geschenkeladen *m*; **~ token**, **~ voucher** *n* Geschenkgutschein *m*

gigantic [dʒaɪˈgæntɪk] *adj* riesenhaft

giggle [ˈgɪgl] *vi* kichern ♦ *n* Gekicher *nt*

gild [gɪld] *vt* vergolden

gill [dʒɪl] *n* (*1/4 pint*) Viertelpinte *f*

gills [gɪlz] *npl* (*of fish*) Kiemen *pl*

gilt [gɪlt] *n* Vergoldung *f* ♦ *adj* vergoldet; **~~ edged** *adj* mündelsicher

gimmick [ˈgɪmɪk] *n* Gag *m*

gin [dʒɪn] *n* Gin *m*

ginger [ˈdʒɪndʒəʳ] *n* Ingwer *m*; **~ ale** *n* Ingwerbier *nt*; **~ beer** *n* Ingwerbier *nt*; **~bread** *n* Pfefferkuchen *m*; **~~haired** *adj* rothaarig

gingerly [ˈdʒɪndʒəlɪ] *adv* behutsam

gipsy ['dʒɪpsɪ] n Zigeuner(in) m(f)

giraffe [dʒɪ'rɑːf] n Giraffe f

girder ['gɜːdər] n Eisenträger m

girdle ['gɜːdl] n Hüftgürtel m

girl [gɜːl] n Mädchen nt; **an English ~** eine (junge) Engländerin; **~friend** n Freundin f; **~ish** adj mädchenhaft

giro ['dʒaɪrəʊ] n (bank ~) Giro nt; (post office ~) Postscheckverkehr m

girth [gɜːθ] n (measure) Umfang m; (strap) Sattelgurt m

gist [dʒɪst] n Wesentliche(s) nt

give [gɪv] (pt **gave**, pp **given**) vt geben ♦ vi (break) nachgeben; **~ away** vt verschenken; (betray) verraten; **~ back** vt zurückgeben; **~ in** vi nachgeben ♦ vt (hand in) abgeben; **~ off** vt abgeben; **~ out** vt verteilen; (announce) bekannt geben; **~ up** vt, vi aufgeben; **to ~ o.s. up** sich stellen; (after siege) sich ergeben; **~ way** vi (BRIT: traffic) Vorfahrt lassen; (to feelings): **to ~ way to** nachgeben +dat

glacier ['glæsɪər] n Gletscher m

glad [glæd] adj froh; **~ly** ['glædlɪ] adv gern(e)

glamorous ['glæmərəs] adj reizvoll

glamour ['glæmər] n Glanz m

glance [glɑːns] n Blick m ♦ vi: **to ~ (at)** (hin)blicken (auf +acc); **~ off** vt fus (fly off) abprallen von; **glancing** ['glɑːnsɪŋ] adj (blow) Streif-

gland [glænd] n Drüse f

glare [gleər] n (light) grelle(s) Licht nt; (stare) wilde(r) Blick m ♦ vi grell scheinen; (angrily): **to ~ at** böse ansehen; **glaring** ['gleərɪŋ] adj (injustice) schreiend; (mistake) krass

glass [glɑːs] n Glas nt; (mirror: also: **looking ~**) Spiegel m; **~es** npl (spectacles) Brille f; **~house** n Gewächshaus nt; **~ware** n Glaswaren pl; **~y** adj glasig

glaze [gleɪz] vt verglasen; (finish with a ~) glasieren ♦ n Glasur f; **~d** adj (eye) glasig; (pot) glasiert; **glazier** ['gleɪzɪər] n Glaser m

gleam [gliːm] n Schimmer m ♦ vi schimmern

glean [gliːn] vt (fig) ausfindig machen

glen [glɛn] n Bergtal nt

glib [glɪb] adj oberflächlich

glide [glaɪd] vi gleiten; **~r** n (AVIAT) Segelflugzeug nt; **gliding** ['glaɪdɪŋ] n Segelfliegen nt

glimmer ['glɪmər] n Schimmer m

glimpse [glɪmps] n flüchtige(r) Blick m ♦ vt flüchtig erblicken

glint [glɪnt] n Glitzern nt ♦ vi glitzern

glisten ['glɪsn] vi glänzen

glitter ['glɪtər] vi funkeln ♦ n Funkeln nt

gloat [gləʊt] vi: **to ~ over** sich weiden an +dat

global ['gləʊbl] adj: **~ warming** globale(r) Temperaturanstieg m

globe [gləʊb] n Erdball m; (sphere) Globus m

gloom [gluːm] n (darkness) Dunkel nt; (depression) düstere Stimmung f; **~y** adj düster

glorify ['glɔːrɪfaɪ] vt verherrlichen

glorious ['glɔːrɪəs] adj glorreich

glory ['glɔːrɪ] n Ruhm m

gloss [glɔs] n (shine) Glanz m; **~ over** vt fus übertünchen

glossary ['glɔsərɪ] n Glossar nt

glossy ['glɔsɪ] adj (surface) glänzend

glove [glʌv] n Handschuh m; **~ compartment** n (AUT) Handschuhfach nt

glow [gləʊ] vi glühen ♦ n Glühen nt

glower ['glaʊər] vi: **to ~ at** finster anblicken

glucose ['gluːkəʊs] n Traubenzucker m

glue [gluː] n Klebstoff m ♦ vt kleben

glum [glʌm] adj bedrückt

glut [glʌt] n Überfluss m

glutton ['glʌtn] n Vielfraß m; **a ~ for work** ein Arbeitstier nt

glycerin(e) ['glɪsəriːn] n Glyzerin nt

GM abbr = **genetically modified**

gnarled [nɑːld] adj knorrig

gnat [næt] n Stechmücke f

gnaw [nɔː] vt nagen an +dat

gnome [nəʊm] n Gnom m

go [gəʊ] (pt **went**, pp **gone**, pl **~es**) vi gehen; (travel) reisen, fahren; (depart: train) (ab)fahren; (be sold) verkauft werden; (work) gehen, funktionieren; (fit, suit) passen; (become) werden; (break etc) nachgeben ♦ n (energy) Schwung m;

(*attempt*) Versuch *m*; **he's ~ing to do it** er wird es tun; **to ~ for a walk** spazieren gehen; **to ~ dancing** tanzen gehen; **how did it ~?** wie was?; **to ~ with** (*be suitable*) passen zu; **to have a ~ at sth** etw versuchen; **to be on the ~** auf Trab sein; **whose ~ is it?** wer ist dran?; ~ **about** *vi* (*rumour*) umgehen ♦ *vt fus*: **how do I ~ about this?** wie packe ich das an?; ~ **after** *vt fus* (*pursue: person*) nachgehen +*dat*; ~ **ahead** ♦ *vt fus* (*proceed*) weitergehen; ~ **along** *vi* dahingehen, dahinfahren ♦ *vt* entlanggehen, entlangfahren; **to ~ along with** (*support*) zustimmen +*dat*; ~ **away** *vi* (*depart*) weggehen; ~ **back** *vi* (*return*) zurückgehen; ~ **back on** *vt fus* (*promise*) nicht halten; ~ **by** *vi* (*years, time*) vergehen ♦ *vt fus* sich richten nach; ~ **down** *vi* (*sun*) untergehen ♦ *vt fus* hinuntergehen, hinunterfahren; ~ **for** *vt fus* (*fetch*) holen (gehen); (*like*) mögen; (*attack*) sich stürzen auf +*acc*; ~ **in** *vi* hineingehen; ~ **in for** *vt fus* (*competition*) teilnehmen an; ~ **into** *vt fus* (*enter*) hineingehen in +*acc*; (*study*) sich befassen mit; ~ **off** *vi* (*depart*) weggehen; (*lights*) ausgehen; (*milk etc*) sauer werden; (*explode*) losgehen ♦ *vt fus* (*dislike*) nicht mehr mögen; ~ **on** *vi* (*continue*) weitergehen; (*inf: complain*) meckern; (*lights*) angehen; **to ~ on with sth** mit etw weitermachen; ~ **out** *vi* (*fire, light*) ausgehen; (*of house*) hinausgehen; ~ **over** *vi* (*ship*) kentern ♦ *vt fus* (*examine, check*) durchgehen; ~ **past** *vi*: **to ~ past sth** an etw *dat* vorbeigehen; ~ **round** *vi* (*visit*): **to ~ round (to sb's)** (bei jdm) vorbeigehen; ~ **through** *vt fus* (*town etc*) durchgehen, durchfahren; ~ **up** *vi* (*price*) steigen; ~ **with** *vt fus* (*suit*) zu etw passen; ~ **without** *vt fus* sich behelfen ohne; (*food*) entbehren

goad [gəud] *vt* anstacheln

go-ahead ['gəuəhɛd] *adj* zielstrebig; (*progressive*) fortschrittlich ♦ *n* grüne(s) Licht *nt*

goal [gəul] *n* Ziel *nt*; (*SPORT*) Tor *nt*; **~keeper** *n* Torwart *m*; ~ **post** *n*

Torpfosten *m*

goat [gəut] *n* Ziege *f*

gobble ['gɔbl] *vt* (*also*: ~ **down**, ~ **up**) hinunterschlingen

go-between ['gəubɪtwiːn] *n* Mittelsmann *m*

god [gɔd] *n* Gott *m*; **G~** *n* Gott *m*; **~child** *n* Patenkind *nt*; **~daughter** *n* Patentochter *f*; **~dess** *n* Göttin *f*; **~father** *n* Pate *m*; **~forsaken** *adj* gottverlassen; **~mother** *n* Patin *f*; **~send** *n* Geschenk *nt* des Himmels; **~son** *n* Patensohn *m*

goggles ['gɔglz] *npl* Schutzbrille *f*

going ['gəuɪŋ] *n* (*HORSE-RACING*) Bahn *f* ♦ *adj* (*rate*) gängig; (*concern*) gut gehend; **it's hard ~** es ist schwierig

gold [gəuld] *n* Gold *nt* ♦ *adj* golden; **~en** *adj* golden, Gold-; **~fish** *n* Goldfisch *m*; ~ **mine** *n* Goldgrube *f*; **~-plated** *adj* vergoldet; **~smith** *n* Goldschmied(in) *m(f)*

golf [gɔlf] *n* Golf *nt*; ~ **ball** *n* Golfball *m*; (*on typewriter*) Kugelkopf *m*; ~ **club** *n* (*society*) Golfklub *m*; (*stick*) Golfschläger *m*; ~ **course** *n* Golfplatz *m*; **~er** *n* Golfspieler(in) *m(f)*

gondola ['gɔndələ] *n* Gondel *f*

gone [gɔn] *pp of* **go**

gong [gɔŋ] *n* Gong *m*

good [gud] *n* (*benefit*) Wohl *nt*; (*moral excellence*) Güte *f* ♦ *adj* gut; **~s** *npl* (*merchandise etc*) Waren *pl*, Güter *pl*; **a ~ deal (of)** ziemlich viel; **a ~ many** ziemlich viele; ~ **morning!** guten Morgen!; ~ **afternoon!** guten Tag!; ~ **evening!** guten Abend!; ~ **night!** gute Nacht!; **would you be ~ enough to ...?** könnten Sie bitte ...?

goodbye [gud'baɪ] *excl* auf Wiedersehen!

good: **G~ Friday** *n* Karfreitag *m*; **~-looking** *adj* gut aussehend; **~-natured** *adj* gutmütig; (*joke*) harmlos; **~ness** *n* Güte *f*; (*virtue*) Tugend *f*; **~s train** *n* (*BRIT*) Güterzug *m*; **~will** *n* (*favour*) Wohlwollen *nt*; (*COMM*) Firmenansehen *nt*

goose [guːs] *n* (*pl* **geese**) Gans *f*

gooseberry ['guzbərɪ] *n* Stachelbeere *f*

gooseflesh ['guːsflɛʃ] *n* Gänsehaut *f*

goose pimples *npl* Gänsehaut *f*

gore [gɔːʳ] *vt* aufspießen ♦ *n* Blut *nt*

gorge [gɔːdʒ] n Schlucht f ♦ vt: **to ~ o.s.** (sich voll) fressen

gorgeous ['gɔːdʒəs] adj prächtig

gorilla [gə'rɪlə] n Gorilla m

gorse [gɔːs] n Stechginster m

gory ['gɔːrɪ] adj blutig

go-slow ['gəu'sləu] (BRIT) n Bummelstreik m

gospel ['gɔspl] n Evangelium nt

gossip ['gɔsɪp] n Klatsch m; (person) Klatschbase f ♦ vi klatschen

got [gɔt] pt, pp of **get**

gotten ['gɔtn] (US) pp of **get**

gout [gaut] n Gicht f

govern ['gʌvən] vt regieren; verwalten

governess ['gʌvənɪs] n Gouvernante f

government ['gʌvnmənt] n Regierung f

governor ['gʌvənə*] n Gouverneur m

gown [gaun] n Gewand nt; (UNIV) Robe f

G.P. n abbr = **general practitioner**

grab [græb] vt packen

grace [greɪs] n Anmut f; (blessing) Gnade f; (prayer) Tischgebet nt ♦ vt (adorn) zieren; (honour) auszeichnen; **5 days' ~** 5 Tage Aufschub; **~ful** adj anmutig

gracious ['greɪʃəs] adj gnädig; (kind) freundlich

grade [greɪd] n Grad m; (slope) Gefälle nt ♦ vt (classify) einstufen; **~ crossing** (US) n Bahnübergang m; **~ school** (US) n Grundschule f

gradient ['greɪdɪənt] n Steigung f; Gefälle nt

gradual ['grædjuəl] adj allmählich; **~ly** adv allmählich

graduate [n 'grædjuɪt, vb 'grædjueɪt] n: **to be a ~** das Staatsexamen haben ♦ vi das Staatsexamen machen; **graduation** [grædju'eɪʃən] n Abschlussfeier f

graffiti [grə'fiːtɪ] npl Graffiti pl

graft [grɑːft] n (hard work) Schufterei f; (MED) Verpflanzung f ♦ vt pfropfen; (fig) aufpfropfen; (MED) verpflanzen

grain [greɪn] n Korn nt; (in wood) Maserung f

gram [græm] n Gramm nt

grammar ['græmə*] n Grammatik f; **~ school** (BRIT) n Gymnasium nt; **grammatical** [grə'mætɪkl] adj grammat(ikal)isch

gramme [græm] n = **gram**

granary ['grænərɪ] n Kornspeicher m

grand [grænd] adj großartig; **~child** (pl **~children**) n Enkelkind nt, Enkel(in) m(f); **~dad** n Opa m; **~daughter** n Enkelin f; **~eur** ['grændjə*] n Erhabenheit f; **~father** n Großvater m; **~iose** ['grændɪəus] adj (imposing) großartig; (pompous) schwülstig; **~ma** n Oma f; **~mother** n Großmutter f; **~pa** n = **granddad**; **~parents** npl Großeltern pl; **~ piano** n Flügel m; **~son** n Enkel m; **~stand** n Haupttribüne f

granite ['grænɪt] n Granit m

granny ['grænɪ] n Oma f

grant [grɑːnt] vt gewähren ♦ n Unterstützung f; (UNIV) Stipendium nt; **to take sth for ~ed** etw als selbstverständlich (an)nehmen

granulated sugar ['grænjuleɪtɪd-] n Zuckerraffinade f

granule ['grænjuːl] n Körnchen nt

grape [greɪp] n (Wein)traube f

grapefruit ['greɪpfruːt] n Pampelmuse f, Grapefruit f

graph [grɑːf] n Schaubild nt; **~ic** ['græfɪk] adj (descriptive) anschaulich; (drawing) grafisch; **~ics** npl Grafik f

grapple ['græpl] vi: **to ~ with** kämpfen mit

grasp [grɑːsp] vt ergreifen; (understand) begreifen ♦ n Griff m; (of subject) Beherrschung f; **~ing** adj habgierig

grass [grɑːs] n Gras nt; **~hopper** n Heuschrecke f; **~land** n Weideland nt; **~-roots** adj an der Basis; **~ snake** n Ringelnatter f

grate [greɪt] n Kamin m ♦ vi (sound) knirschen ♦ vt (cheese etc) reiben; **to ~ on the nerves** auf die Nerven gehen

grateful ['greɪtful] adj dankbar

grater ['greɪtə*] n Reibe f

gratify ['grætɪfaɪ] vt befriedigen; **~ing** adj erfreulich

grating ['greɪtɪŋ] n (iron bars) Gitter nt ♦ adj (noise) knirschend

gratitude ['grætɪtjuːd] n Dankbarkeit f

gratuity [grə'tjuːɪtɪ] n Gratifikation f

grave [greɪv] n Grab nt ♦ adj (serious) ernst

gravel ['grævl] n Kies m
gravestone ['greɪvstəʊn] n Grabstein m
graveyard ['greɪvjɑːd] n Friedhof m
gravity ['grævɪtɪ] n Schwerkraft f; (*seriousness*) Schwere f
gravy ['greɪvɪ] n (Braten)soße f
gray [greɪ] adj = **grey**
graze [greɪz] vi grasen ♦ vt (*touch*) streifen; (*MED*) abschürfen ♦ n Abschürfung f
grease [griːs] n (*fat*) Fett nt; (*lubricant*) Schmiere f ♦ vt (ab)schmieren; **~proof** (*BRIT*) adj (*paper*) Butterbrot-; **greasy** ['griːsɪ] adj fettig
great [greɪt] adj groß; (*inf: good*) prima; **G~ Britain** n Großbritannien nt; **~-grandfather** n Urgroßvater m; **~-grandmother** n Urgroßmutter f; **~ly** adv sehr
Greece [griːs] n Griechenland nt
greed [griːd] n (*also:* **~iness**) Gier f; (*meanness*) Geiz m; **~(iness) for** Gier nach; **~y** adj gierig
Greek [griːk] adj griechisch ♦ n Grieche m, Griechin f; (*LING*) Griechisch nt
green [griːn] adj grün ♦ n (*village ~*) Dorfwiese f; **~ belt** n Grüngürtel m; **~ card** n (*AUT*) grüne Versicherungskarte f; **~ery** n Grün nt; grüne(s) Laub nt; **~gage** n Reneklode f, Reineclaude f; **~grocer** (*BRIT*) n Obst- und Gemüsehändler m; **~house** n Gewächshaus nt; **~house effect** n Treibhauseffekt m; **~house gas** n Treibhausgas nt
Greenland ['griːnlənd] n Grönland nt
greet [griːt] vt grüßen; **~ing** n Gruß m; **~ing(s) card** n Glückwunschkarte f
gregarious [grə'ɡɛərɪəs] adj gesellig
grenade [grə'neɪd] n Granate f
grew [gruː] pt of **grow**
grey [greɪ] adj grau; **~-haired** adj grauhaarig; **~hound** n Windhund m
grid [grɪd] n Gitter nt; (*ELEC*) Leitungsnetz nt; (*on map*) Gitternetz nt
gridlock ['grɪdlɒk] n (*AUT: traffic jam*) totale(r) Stau m; **~ed** adj: **to be ~ed** (*roads*) total verstopft sein; (*talks etc*) festgefahren sein

grief [griːf] n Gram m, Kummer m
grievance ['ɡriːvəns] n Beschwerde f
grieve [griːv] vi sich grämen ♦ vt betrüben
grievous ['ɡriːvəs] adj: **~ bodily harm** (*JUR*) schwere Körperverletzung f
grill [grɪl] n Grill m ♦ vt (*BRIT*) grillen; (*question*) in die Mangel nehmen
grille [grɪl] n (*AUT*) (Kühler)gitter nt
grim [grɪm] adj grimmig; (*situation*) düster
grimace [grɪ'meɪs] n Grimasse f ♦ vi Grimassen schneiden
grime [graɪm] n Schmutz m; **grimy** ['graɪmɪ] adj schmutzig
grin [grɪn] n Grinsen nt ♦ vi grinsen
grind [graɪnd] (*pt, pp* **ground**) vt mahlen; (*US: meat*) durch den Fleischwolf drehen; (*sharpen*) schleifen; (*teeth*) knirschen mit ♦ n (*bore*) Plackerei f
grip [grɪp] n Griff m; (*suitcase*) Handkoffer m ♦ vt packen; **~ping** adj (*exciting*) spannend
grisly ['grɪzlɪ] adj grässlich
gristle ['grɪsl] n Knorpel m
grit [grɪt] n Splitt m; (*courage*) Mut m ♦ vt (*teeth*) zusammenbeißen; (*road*) (mit Splitt be)streuen
groan [grəʊn] n Stöhnen nt ♦ vi stöhnen
grocer ['grəʊsər] n Lebensmittelhändler m; **~ies** npl Lebensmittel pl; **~'s (shop)** n Lebensmittelgeschäft nt
groggy ['grɒɡɪ] adj benommen
groin [grɔɪn] n Leistengegend f
groom [gruːm] n (*also:* **bridegroom**) Bräutigam m; (*for horses*) Pferdeknecht m ♦ vt (*horse*) striegeln; **(well-)~ed** gepflegt
groove [gruːv] n Rille f, Furche f
grope [grəʊp] vi tasten; **~ for** vt fus suchen nach
gross [grəʊs] adj (*coarse*) dick, plump; (*bad*) grob, schwer; (*COMM*) brutto; **~ly** adv höchst
grotesque [grə'tesk] adj grotesk
grotto ['grɒtəʊ] n Grotte f
ground [graʊnd] pt, pp of **grind** ♦ n Boden m; (*land*) Grundbesitz m; (*reason*) Grund m; (*US: also:* **~ wire**) Endleitung f ♦ vi (*run ashore*) stranden, auflaufen; **~s** npl (*dregs*) Bodensatz m; (*around house*)

(Garten)anlagen pl; **on the ~** am Boden; **to the ~** zu Boden; **to gain/lose ~** Boden gewinnen/verlieren; **~ cloth** (US) n = **groundsheet; ~ing** n (instruction) Anfangsunterricht m; **~less** adj grundlos; **~sheet** (BRIT) n Zeltboden m; **~ staff** n Bodenpersonal nt; **~work** n Grundlage f

group [gru:p] n Gruppe f ♦ vt (also: **~ together**) gruppieren ♦ vi sich gruppieren

grouse [graus] n inv (bird) schottische(s) Moorhuhn nt

grove [grəuv] n Gehölz nt, Hain m

grovel ['grɔvl] vi (fig) kriechen

grow [grəu] (pt **grew**, pp **grown**) vi wachsen; (become) werden ♦ vt (raise) anbauen; **~ up** vi aufwachsen; **~er** n Züchter m; **~ing** adj zunehmend

growl [graul] vi knurren

grown [grəun] pp of **grow**; **~-up** n Erwachsene(r) mf

growth [grəuθ] n Wachstum nt; (increase) Zunahme f; (of beard etc) Wuchs m

grub [grʌb] n Made f, Larve f; (inf: food) Futter nt; **~by** ['grʌbɪ] adj schmutzig

grudge [grʌdʒ] n Groll m ♦ vt: **to ~ sb sth** jdm etw missgönnen; **to bear sb a ~** einen Groll gegen jdn hegen

gruelling ['gruəlɪŋ] adj (climb, race) mörderisch

gruesome ['gru:səm] adj grauenhaft

gruff [grʌf] adj barsch

grumble ['grʌmbl] vi murren

grumpy ['grʌmpɪ] adj verdrießlich

grunt [grʌnt] vi grunzen ♦ n Grunzen nt

G-string ['dʒi:strɪŋ] n Minislip m

guarantee [gærən'ti:] n Garantie f ♦ vt garantieren

guard [ga:d] n (sentry) Wache f; (BRIT: RAIL) Zugbegleiter m ♦ vt bewachen

guarded ['ga:dɪd] adj vorsichtig

guardian ['ga:dɪən] n Vormund m; (keeper) Hüter m

guard's van ['ga:dz-] (BRIT) n (RAIL) Dienstwagen m

guerrilla [gə'rɪlə] n Guerilla(kämpfer) m; **~ warfare** n Guerillakrieg m

guess [gɛs] vt, vi (er)raten, schätzen ♦ n Vermutung f; **~work** n Raterei f

guest [gɛst] n Gast m; **~ house** n Pension f; **~ room** n Gastzimmer nt

guffaw [gʌ'fɔ:] vi schallend lachen

guidance ['gaɪdəns] n (control) Leitung f; (advice) Beratung f

guide [gaɪd] n Führer m; (also: **girl ~**) Pfadfinderin f ♦ vt führen; **~book** n Reiseführer m; **~ dog** n Blindenhund m; **~lines** npl Richtlinien pl

guild [gɪld] n (HIST) Gilde f

guillotine ['gɪləti:n] n Guillotine f

guilt [gɪlt] n Schuld f; **~y** adj schuldig

guinea pig ['gɪnɪ-] n Meerschweinchen nt; (fig) Versuchskaninchen nt

guise [gaɪz] n: **in the ~ of** in der Form +gen

guitar [gɪ'ta:ʳ] n Gitarre f

gulf [gʌlf] n Golf m; (fig) Abgrund m

gull [gʌl] n Möwe f

gullet ['gʌlɪt] n Schlund m

gullible ['gʌlɪbl] adj leichtgläubig

gully ['gʌlɪ] n (Wasser)rinne f

gulp [gʌlp] vt (also: **~ down**) hinunterschlucken ♦ vi (gasp) schlucken

gum [gʌm] n (around teeth) Zahnfleisch nt; (glue) Klebstoff m; (also: **chewing ~**) Kaugummi m ♦ vt gummieren; **~boots** (BRIT) npl Gummistiefel pl

gun [gʌn] n Schusswaffe f; **~boat** n Kanonenboot nt; **~fire** n Geschützfeuer nt; **~man** (irreg) n bewaffnete(r) Verbrecher m; **~point** n: **at ~point** mit Waffengewalt; **~powder** n Schießpulver nt; **~shot** n Schuss m

gurgle ['gə:gl] vi gluckern

gush [gʌʃ] vi (rush out) hervorströmen; (fig) schwärmen

gust [gʌst] n Windstoß m, Bö f

gusto ['gʌstəu] n Genuss m, Lust f

gut [gʌt] n (ANAT) Gedärme pl; (string) Darm m; **~s** npl (fig) Schneid m

gutter ['gʌtəʳ] n Dachrinne f; (in street) Gosse f

guttural ['gʌtərl] adj guttural, Kehl-

guy [gaɪ] n (also: **~rope**) Halteseil nt; (man) Typ m, Kerl m

---

Guy Fawkes' Night

ⓘ **Guy Fawkes' Night**, *auch bonfire night genannt, erinnert an den Gunpowder Plot, einen Attentatsversuch auf James I. und sein Parlament am 5. November 1605. Einer der Verschwörer, Guy Fawkes, wurde auf frischer Tat ertappt, als er das Parlamentsgebäude in die Luft sprengen wollte. Vor der Guy Fawkes' Night basteln Kinder in Großbritannien eine Puppe des Guy Fawkes, mit der sie Geld für Feuerwerkskörper von Passanten erbetteln, und die dann am 5. November auf einem Lagerfeuer mit Feuerwerk verbrannt wird.*

guzzle [ˈgʌzl] *vt, vi* (*drink*) saufen; (*eat*) fressen

gym [dʒɪm] *n* (*also:* **~nasium**) Turnhalle *f*; (*also:* **~nastics**) Turnen *nt*

gymnast [ˈdʒɪmnæst] *n* Turner(in) *m(f)*

gymnastics [dʒɪmˈnæstɪks] *n* Turnen *nt*, Gymnastik *f*

gym shoes *npl* Turnschuhe *pl*

gynaecologist [gaɪnɪˈkɔlədʒɪst] (*US* **gynecologist**) *n* Frauenarzt(-ärztin) *m(f)*

gypsy [ˈdʒɪpsɪ] *n* = **gipsy**

gyrate [dʒaɪˈreɪt] *vi* kreisen

H, h

haberdashery [hæbəˈdæʃərɪ] (*BRIT*) *n* Kurzwaren *pl*

habit [ˈhæbɪt] *n* (An)gewohnheit *f*; (*monk's*) Habit *nt or m*

habitable [ˈhæbɪtəbl] *adj* bewohnbar

habitat [ˈhæbɪtæt] *n* Lebensraum *m*

habitual [həˈbɪtjuəl] *adj* gewohnheitsmäßig; **~ly** *adv* gewöhnlich

hack [hæk] *vt* hacken ♦ *n* Hieb *m*; (*writer*) Schreiberling *m*

hacker [ˈhækəʳ] *n* (*COMPUT*) Hacker *m*

hackneyed [ˈhæknɪd] *adj* abgedroschen

had [hæd] *pt, pp of* **have**

haddock [ˈhædək] (*pl* **~** *or* **~s**) *n* Schellfisch *m*

hadn't [ˈhædnt] = **had not**

haemorrhage [ˈhemərɪdʒ] (*US* **hemorrhage**) *n* Blutung *f*

haemorrhoids [ˈhemərɔɪdz] (*US* **hemorrhoids**) *npl* Hämorr(ho)iden *pl*

haggard [ˈhægəd] *adj* abgekämpft

haggle [ˈhægl] *vi* feilschen

Hague [heɪg] *n* (*GEOG*) **The ~** Den Haag *nt*

hail [heɪl] *n* Hagel *m* ♦ *vt* umjubeln ♦ *vi* hageln; **~stone** *n* Hagelkorn *nt*

hair [heəʳ] *n* Haar *nt*, Haare *pl*; (*one ~*) Haar *nt*; **~brush** *n* Haarbürste *f*; **~cut** *n* Haarschnitt *m*; **to get a ~cut** sich *dat* die Haare schneiden lassen; **~do** *n* Frisur *f*; **~dresser** *n* Friseur *m*, Friseuse *f*; **~dresser's** *n* Friseursalon *m*; **~ dryer** *n* Trockenhaube *f*; (*hand-held*) Föhn *m*, Fön *m* ⓡ; **~ gel** *n* Haargel *nt*; **~grip** *n* Klemme *f*; **~net** *n* Haarnetz *nt*; **~pin** *n* Haarnadel *f*; **~pin bend** (*US* **~pin curve**) *n* Haarnadelkurve *f*; **~raising** *adj* haarsträubend; **~ removing cream** *n* Enthaarungscreme *nt*; **~ spray** *n* Haarspray *nt*; **~style** *n* Frisur *f*

hairy [ˈheərɪ] *adj* haarig

hake [heɪk] *n* Seehecht *m*

half [hɑːf] (*pl* **halves**) *n* Hälfte *f* ♦ *adj* halb ♦ *adv* halb, zur Hälfte; **~ an hour** eine halbe Stunde; **two and a ~** zweieinhalb; **to cut sth in ~** etw halbieren; **~ a dozen** ein halbes Dutzend, sechs; **~ board** *n* Halbpension *f*; **~caste** *n* Mischling *m*; **~ fare** *n* halbe(r) Fahrpreis *m*; **~hearted** *adj* lustlos; **~hour** *n* halbe Stunde *f*; **~price** *n*: **(at) ~price** zum halben Preis; **~ term** (*BRIT*) *n* (*SCH*) Ferien *pl* in der Mitte des Trimesters; **~time** *n* Halbzeit *f*; **~way** *adv* halbwegs, auf halbem Wege

halibut [ˈhælɪbət] *n inv* Heilbutt *m*

hall [hɔːl] *n* Saal *m*; (*entrance ~*) Hausflur *m*; (*building*) Halle *f*; **~ of residence** (*BRIT*) *n* Studentenwohnheim *nt*

hallmark [ˈhɔːlmɑːk] *n* Stempel *m*

hallo [həˈləu] *excl* = **hello**

Hallowe'en [ˈhæləuˈiːn] *n* Tag *m* vor Allerheiligen

Hallowe'en

ⓘ **Hallowe'en** *ist der 31. Oktober, der Vorabend von Allerheiligen und nach altem Glauben der Abend, an dem man Geister und Hexen sehen kann. In Großbritannien und vor allem in den USA feiern die Kinder Hallowe'en, indem sie sich verkleiden und mit selbst gemachten Laternen aus Kürbissen von Tür zu Tür ziehen.*

---

hallucination [həluːsɪˈneɪʃən] *n* Halluzination *f*

hallway [ˈhɔːlweɪ] *n* Korridor *m*

halo [ˈheɪləu] *n* Heiligenschein *m*

halt [hɔːlt] *n* Halt *m* ♦ *vt, vi* anhalten

halve [hɑːv] *vt* halbieren

halves [hɑːvz] *pl of* **half**

ham [hæm] *n* Schinken *m*

hamburger [ˈhæmbɜːgəʳ] *n* Hamburger *m*

hamlet [ˈhæmlɪt] *n* Weiler *m*

hammer [ˈhæməʳ] *n* Hammer *m* ♦ *vt, vi* hämmern

hammock [ˈhæmək] *n* Hängematte *f*

hamper [ˈhæmpəʳ] *vt* (be)hindern ♦ *n* Picknickkorb *m*

hamster [ˈhæmstəʳ] *n* Hamster *m*

hand [hænd] *n* Hand *f*; (*of clock*) (Uhr)zeiger *m*; (*worker*) Arbeiter *m* ♦ *vt* (*pass*) geben; **to give sb a ~** jdm helfen; **at ~** nahe; **to ~** zur Hand; **in ~** (*under control*) unter Kontrolle; (*being done*) im Gange; (*extra*) übrig; **on ~** zur Verfügung; **on the one ~ ..., on the other ~ ...** einerseits ..., andererseits ...; **~ in** *vt* abgeben; (*forms*) einreichen; **~ out** *vt* austeilen; **~ over** *vt* (*deliver*) übergeben; (*surrender*) abgeben; **~bag** *n* Handtasche *f*; **~book** *n* Handbuch *nt*; **~brake** *n* Handbremse *f*; **~cuffs** *npl* Handschellen *pl*; **~ful** *n* Hand *f* voll; (*inf: person*) Plage *f*

handicap [ˈhændɪkæp] *n* Handikap *nt* ♦ *vt* benachteiligen; **mentally/physically ~ped** geistig/körperlich behindert

handicraft [ˈhændɪkrɑːft] *n* Kunsthandwerk *nt*

handiwork [ˈhændɪwɜːk] *n* Arbeit *f*; (*fig*) Werk *nt*

handkerchief [ˈhæŋkətʃɪf] *n* Taschentuch *nt*

handle [ˈhændl] *n* (*of door etc*) Klinke *f*; (*of cup etc*) Henkel *m*; (*for winding*) Kurbel *f* ♦ *vt* (*touch*) anfassen; (*deal with: things*) sich befassen mit; (*: people*) umgehen mit; **~bar(s)** *n(pl)* Lenkstange *f*

hand: ~ luggage *n* Handgepäck *nt*; **~made** *adj* handgefertigt; **~out** *n* (*distribution*) Verteilung *f*; (*charity*) Geldzuwendung *f*; (*leaflet*) Flugblatt *nt*; **~rail** *n* Geländer *nt*; (*on ship*) Reling *f*; **~set** *n* (*TEL*) Hörer *m*; **please replace the ~set** bitte legen Sie auf; **~shake** *n* Händedruck *f*

handsome [ˈhænsəm] *adj* gut aussehend

handwriting [ˈhændraɪtɪŋ] *n* Handschrift *f*

handy [ˈhændɪ] *adj* praktisch; (*shops*) leicht erreichbar; **~man** [ˈhændɪmæn] (*irreg*) *n* Bastler *m*

hang [hæŋ] (*pt, pp* **hung**) *vt* aufhängen; (*pt, pp* **hanged**: *criminal*) hängen ♦ *vi* hängen ♦ *n*: **to get the ~ of sth** (*inf*) den richtigen Dreh bei etw herauskriegen; **~ about, ~ around** *vi* sich herumtreiben; **~ on** *vi* (*wait*) warten; **~ up** *vi* (*TEL*) auflegen

hangar [ˈhæŋəʳ] *n* Hangar *m*

hanger [ˈhæŋəʳ] *n* Kleiderbügel *m*

hanger-on [hæŋərˈɔn] *n* Anhänger(in) *m(f)*

hang [ˈhæŋ-]: **~-gliding** *n* Drachenfliegen *nt*; **~over** *n* Kater *m*; **~-up** *n* Komplex *m*

hanker [ˈhæŋkəʳ] *vi*: **to ~ for** *or* **after** sich sehnen nach

hankie [ˈhæŋkɪ] *n abbr* = **handkerchief**

hanky [ˈhæŋkɪ] *n abbr* = **handkerchief**

haphazard [hæpˈhæzəd] *adj* zufällig

happen [ˈhæpən] *vi* sich ereignen, passieren; **as it ~s I'm going there today** zufällig(erweise) gehe ich heute (dort)hin; **~ing** *n* Ereignis *nt*

happily [ˈhæpɪlɪ] *adv* glücklich; (*fortunately*) glücklicherweise

happiness [ˈhæpɪnɪs] *n* Glück *nt*

happy [ˈhæpɪ] *adj* glücklich; **~ birthday!** alles Gute zum Geburtstag!; **~-go-lucky** *adj* sorglos; **~ hour** *n* Happy Hour *f*

harass ['hærəs] *vt* plagen; **~ment** *n*
Belästigung *f*

harbour ['hɑːbəʳ] (*US* **harbor**) *n* Hafen *m*
♦ *vt* (*hope etc*) hegen; (*criminal etc*)
Unterschlupf gewähren

hard [hɑːd] *adj* (*firm*) hart; (*difficult*) schwer;
(*harsh*) hart(herzig) ♦ *adv* (*work*) hart; (*try*)
sehr; (*push, hit*) fest; **no ~ feelings!** ich
nehme es dir nicht übel; **~ of hearing**
schwerhörig; **to be ~ done by** übel dran
sein; **~back** *n* kartonierte Ausgabe *f*; **~
cash** *n* Bargeld *nt*; **~ disk** *n* (*COMPUT*)
Festplatte *f*; **~en** *vt* erhärten; (*fig*) verhärten
♦ *vi* hart werden; (*fig*) sich verhärten; **~-
headed** *adj* nüchtern; **~ labour** *n*
Zwangsarbeit *f*

hardly ['hɑːdlɪ] *adv* kaum

hard: ~ship *n* Not *f*; **~ shoulder** (*BRIT*) *n*
(*AUT*) Seitenstreifen *m*; **~ up** *adj* knapp bei
Kasse; **~ware** *n* Eisenwaren *pl*; (*COMPUT*)
Hardware *f*; **~ware shop** *n*
Eisenwarenhandlung *f*; **~-wearing** *adj*
strapazierfähig; **~-working** *adj* fleißig

hardy ['hɑːdɪ] *adj* widerstandsfähig

hare [heəʳ] *n* Hase *m*; **~-brained** *adj*
schwachsinnig

harm [hɑːm] *n* Schaden *m* ♦ *vt* schaden
+*dat*; **out of ~'s way** in Sicherheit; **~ful** *adj*
schädlich; **~less** *adj* harmlos

harmonica [hɑːˈmɒnɪkə] *n* Mundharmonika
f

harmonious [hɑːˈməʊnɪəs] *adj* harmonisch

harmonize ['hɑːmənaɪz] *vt* abstimmen ♦ *vi*
harmonieren

harmony ['hɑːmənɪ] *n* Harmonie *f*

harness ['hɑːnɪs] *n* Geschirr *nt* ♦ *vt* (*horse*)
anschirren; (*fig*) nutzbar machen

harp [hɑːp] *n* Harfe *f* ♦ *vi*: **to ~ on about sth**
auf etw *dat* herumreiten

harpoon [hɑːˈpuːn] *n* Harpune *f*

harrowing ['hærəʊɪŋ] *adj* nervenaufreibend

harsh [hɑːʃ] *adj* (*rough*) rau; (*severe*) streng;
~ness *n* Härte *f*

harvest ['hɑːvɪst] *n* Ernte *f* ♦ *vt, vi* ernten

has [hæz] *vb see* **have**

hash [hæʃ] *vt* klein hacken ♦ *n* (*mess*)
Kuddelmuddel *m*

hashish ['hæʃɪʃ] *n* Haschisch *nt*

hasn't ['hæznt] = **has not**

hassle ['hæsl] (*inf*) *n* Theater *nt*

haste [heɪst] *n* Eile *f*; **~n** ['heɪsn] *vt*
beschleunigen ♦ *vi* eilen; **hasty** *adj* hastig;
(*rash*) vorschnell

hat [hæt] *n* Hut *m*

hatch [hætʃ] *n* (*NAUT: also:* **~way**) Luke *f*; (*in
house*) Durchreiche *f* ♦ *vi* (*young*)
ausschlüpfen ♦ *vt* (*brood*) ausbrüten; (*plot*)
aushecken; **~back** ['hætʃbæk] *n* (*AUT*) (Auto
nt mit) Heckklappe *f*

hatchet ['hætʃɪt] *n* Beil *nt*

hate [heɪt] *vt* hassen ♦ *n* Hass *m*; **~ful** *adj*
verhasst

hatred ['heɪtrɪd] *n* Hass *m*

haughty ['hɔːtɪ] *adj* hochnäsig, überheblich

haul [hɔːl] *vt* ziehen ♦ *n* (*catch*) Fang *m*;
~age *n* Spedition *f*; **~ier** (*US* **hauler**) *n*
Spediteur *m*

haunch [hɔːntʃ] *n* Lende *f*

haunt [hɔːnt] *vt* (*ghost*) spuken in +*dat*;
(*memory*) verfolgen; (*pub*) häufig besuchen
♦ *n* Lieblingsplatz *m*; **the castle is ~ed** in
dem Schloss spukt es

KEYWORD

---

have [hæv] (*pt, pp* **had**) *aux vb* **1** haben; (*esp
with vbs of motion*) sein; **to have arrived/
slept** angekommen sein/geschlafen haben;
to have been gewesen sein; **having eaten**
or **when he had eaten, he left** nachdem
er gegessen hatte, ging er
2 (*in tag questions*): **you've done it,
haven't you?** du hast es doch gemacht,
oder nicht?
3 (*in short answers and questions*): **you've
made a mistake – so I have/no I haven't**
du hast einen Fehler gemacht – ja,
stimmt/nein; **we haven't paid – yes we
have!** wir haben nicht bezahlt – doch; **I've
been there before, have you?** ich war
schon einmal da, du auch?
♦ *modal aux vb* (*be obliged*): **to have (got)
to do sth** etw tun müssen; **you haven't to
tell her** du darfst es ihr nicht erzählen
♦ *vt* **1** (*possess*) haben; **he has (got) blue**

eyes er hat blaue Augen; **I have (got) an idea** ich habe eine Idee
2 (*referring to meals etc*): **to have breakfast/a cigarette** frühstücken/eine Zigarette rauchen
3 (*receive, obtain etc*) haben; **may I have your address?** kann ich Ihre Adresse haben?; **to have a baby** ein Kind bekommen
4 (*maintain, allow*): **he will have it that he is right** er besteht darauf, dass er Recht hat; **I won't have it** das lasse ich mir nicht bieten
5: **to have sth done** etw machen lassen; **to have sb do sth** jdn etw machen lassen; **he soon had them all laughing** er brachte sie alle zum Lachen
6 (*experience, suffer*): **she had her bag stolen** man hat ihr die Tasche gestohlen; **he had his arm broken** er hat sich den Arm gebrochen
7 (*+noun: take, hold etc*): **to have a walk/rest** spazieren gehen/sich ausruhen; **to have a meeting/party** eine Besprechung/Party haben
have out *vt*: **to have it out with sb** (*settle problem*) etw mit jdm bereden

haven ['heɪvn] *n* Zufluchtsort *m*
haven't ['hævnt] = **have not**
havoc ['hævək] *n* Verwüstung *f*
hawk [hɔːk] *n* Habicht *m*
hay [heɪ] *n* Heu *nt*; **~ fever** *n* Heuschnupfen *m*; **~stack** *n* Heuschober *m*
haywire ['heɪwaɪə'] (*inf*) *adj* durcheinander
hazard ['hæzəd] *n* Risiko *nt* ♦ *vt* aufs Spiel setzen; **~ous** *adj* gefährlich; **~ (warning) lights** *npl* (*AUT*) Warnblinklicht *nt*
haze [heɪz] *n* Dunst *m*
hazelnut ['heɪzlnʌt] *n* Haselnuss *f*
hazy ['heɪzɪ] *adj* (*misty*) dunstig; (*vague*) verschwommen
he [hiː] *pron* er
head [hed] *n* Kopf *m*; (*leader*) Leiter *m* ♦ *vt* (an)führen, leiten; (*ball*) köpfen; **~s (or tails)** Kopf (oder Zahl); **~ first** mit dem Kopf nach unten; **~ over heels** kopfüber;

~ for *vt fus* zugehen auf +*acc*; **~ache** *n* Kopfschmerzen *pl*; **~dress** *n* Kopfschmuck *m*; **~ing** *n* Überschrift *f*; **~lamp** (*BRIT*) *n* Scheinwerfer *m*; **~land** *n* Landspitze *f*; **~light** *n* Scheinwerfer *m*; **~line** *n* Schlagzeile *f*; **~long** *adv* kopfüber; **~master** *n* (*of primary school*) Rektor *m*; (*of secondary school*) Direktor *m*; **~mistress** *n* Rektorin *f*; Direktorin *f*; **~ office** *n* Zentrale *f*; **~-on** *adj* Frontal-; **~phones** *npl* Kopfhörer *pl*; **~quarters** *npl* Zentrale *f*; (*MIL*) Hauptquartier *nt*; **~rest** *n* Kopfstütze *f*; **~room** *n* (*of bridges etc*) lichte Höhe *f*; **~scarf** *n* Kopftuch *nt*; **~strong** *adj* eigenwillig; **~teacher** (*BRIT*) *n* Schulleiter(in) *m(f)*; (*of secondary school also*) Direktor(in) *m*; **~ waiter** *n* Oberkellner *m*; **~way** *n* Fortschritte *pl*; **~wind** *n* Gegenwind *m*; **~y** *adj* berauschend
heal [hiːl] *vt* heilen ♦ *vi* verheilen
health [helθ] *n* Gesundheit *f*; **~ food** *n* Reformkost *f*; **H~ Service** (*BRIT*) *n*: **the H~ Service** das Gesundheitswesen; **~y** *adj* gesund
heap [hiːp] *n* Haufen *m* ♦ *vt* häufen
hear [hɪə'] (*pt, pp heard*) *vt* hören; (*listen to*) anhören ♦ *vi* hören; **~d** [hɜːd] *pt, pp of* **hear**; **~ing** *n* Gehör *nt*; (*JUR*) Verhandlung *f*; **~ing aid** *n* Hörapparat *m*; **~say** *n* Hörensagen *nt*
hearse [hɜːs] *n* Leichenwagen *m*
heart [hɑːt] *n* Herz *nt*; **~s** *npl* (*CARDS*) Herz *nt*; **by ~** auswendig; **~ attack** *n* Herzanfall *m*; **~beat** *n* Herzschlag *m*; **~breaking** *adj* herzzerbrechend; **~broken** *adj* untröstlich; **~burn** *n* Sodbrennen *nt*; **~ failure** *n* Herzschlag *m*; **~felt** *adj* aufrichtig
hearth [hɑːθ] *n* Herd *m*
heartily ['hɑːtɪlɪ] *adv* herzlich; (*eat*) herzhaft
heartless ['hɑːtlɪs] *adj* herzlos
hearty ['hɑːtɪ] *adj* kräftig; (*friendly*) freundlich
heat [hiːt] *n* Hitze *f*; (*of food, water etc*) Wärme *f*; (*SPORT: also:* **qualifying ~**) Ausscheidungsrunde *f* ♦ *vt* (*house*) heizen; (*substance*) heiß machen, erhitzen; **~ up** *vi* warm werden ♦ *vt* aufwärmen; **~ed** *adj* erhitzt; (*fig*) hitzig; **~er** *n* (Heiz)ofen *m*

heath [hi:θ] (*BRIT*) *n* Heide *f*
heathen ['hi:ðn] *n* Heide *m*/Heidin *f* ♦ *adj* heidnisch, Heiden-
heather ['hɛðəʳ] *n* Heidekraut *nt*
heat: ~**ing** *n* Heizung *f*; ~~**seeking** *adj* Wärme suchend; ~**stroke** *n* Hitzschlag *m*; ~ **wave** *n* Hitzewelle *f*
heave [hi:v] *vt* hochheben; (*sigh*) ausstoßen ♦ *vi* wogen; (*breast*) sich heben ♦ *n* Heben *nt*
heaven ['hɛvn] *n* Himmel *m*; ~**ly** *adj* himmlisch
heavily ['hɛvɪlɪ] *adv* schwer
heavy ['hɛvɪ] *adj* schwer; ~ **goods vehicle** *n* Lastkraftwagen *m*; ~**weight** *n* (*SPORT*) Schwergewicht *nt*
Hebrew ['hi:bru:] *adj* hebräisch ♦ *n* (*LING*) Hebräisch *nt*
Hebrides ['hɛbrɪdi:z] *npl* Hebriden *pl*
heckle ['hɛkl] *vt* unterbrechen
hectic ['hɛktɪk] *adj* hektisch
he'd [hi:d] = **he had; he would**
hedge [hɛdʒ] *n* Hecke *f* ♦ *vt* einzäunen ♦ *vi* (*fig*) ausweichen; **to** ~ **one's bets** sich absichern
hedgehog ['hɛdʒhɔg] *n* Igel *m*
heed [hi:d] *vt* (*also:* **take** ~ **of**) beachten ♦ *n* Beachtung *f*; ~**less** *adj* achtlos
heel [hi:l] *n* Ferse *f*; (*of shoe*) Absatz *m* ♦ *vt* mit Absätzen versehen
hefty ['hɛftɪ] *adj* (*person*) stämmig; (*portion*) reichlich
heifer ['hɛfəʳ] *n* Färse *f*
height [haɪt] *n* (*of person*) Größe *f*; (*of object*) Höhe *f*; ~**en** *vt* erhöhen
heir [ɛəʳ] *n* Erbe *m*; ~**ess** ['ɛəres] *n* Erbin *f*; ~**loom** *n* Erbstück *nt*
held [hɛld] *pt, pp of* **hold**
helicopter ['hɛlɪkɔptəʳ] *n* Hubschrauber *m*
heliport ['hɛlɪpɔ:t] *n* Hubschrauber-landeplatz *m*
hell [hɛl] *n* Hölle *f* ♦ *excl* verdammt!
he'll [hi:l] = **he will; he shall**
hellish ['hɛlɪʃ] *adj* höllisch, verteufelt
hello [hə'ləu] *excl* hallo
helm [hɛlm] *n* Ruder *nt*, Steuer *nt*
helmet ['hɛlmɪt] *n* Helm *m*

help [hɛlp] *n* Hilfe *f* ♦ *vt* helfen +*dat*; **I can't** ~ **it** ich kann nichts dafür; ~ **yourself** bedienen Sie sich; ~**er** *n* Helfer *m*; ~**ful** *adj* hilfreich; ~**ing** *n* Portion *f*; ~**less** *adj* hilflos
hem [hɛm] *n* Saum *m* ♦ *vt* säumen; ~ **in** *vt* einengen
hemorrhage ['hɛmərɪdʒ] (*US*) *n* = **haemorrhage**
hemorrhoids ['hɛmərɔɪdz] (*US*) *npl* = **haemorrhoids**
hen [hɛn] *n* Henne *f*
hence [hɛns] *adv* von jetzt an; (*therefore*) daher; ~**forth** *adv* von nun an; (*from then on*) von da an
henchman ['hɛntʃmən] (*irreg*) *n* Gefolgsmann *m*
her [hɑ:ʳ] *pron* (*acc*) sie; (*dat*) ihr ♦ *adj* ihr; *see also* **me; my**
herald ['hɛrəld] *n* (Vor)bote *m* ♦ *vt* verkünden
heraldry ['hɛrəldrɪ] *n* Wappenkunde *f*
herb [hə:b] *n* Kraut *nt*
herd [hə:d] *n* Herde *f*
here [hɪəʳ] *adv* hier; (*to this place*) hierher; ~**after** [hɪərˈɑ:ftəʳ] *adv* hernach, künftig ♦ *n* Jenseits *nt*; ~**by** [hɪəˈbaɪ] *adv* hiermit
hereditary [hɪˈrɛdɪtrɪ] *adj* erblich
heredity [hɪˈrɛdɪtɪ] *n* Vererbung *f*
heritage ['hɛrɪtɪdʒ] *n* Erbe *nt*
hermit ['hə:mɪt] *n* Einsiedler *m*
hernia ['hə:nɪə] *n* Bruch *m*
hero ['hɪərəu] (*pl* ~**es**) *n* Held *m*; ~**ic** [hɪˈrəuɪk] *adj* heroisch
heroin ['hɛrəuɪn] *n* Heroin *nt*
heroine ['hɛrəuɪn] *n* Heldin *f*
heroism ['hɛrəuɪzəm] *n* Heldentum *nt*
heron ['hɛrən] *n* Reiher *m*
herring ['hɛrɪŋ] *n* Hering *m*
hers [hə:z] *pron* ihre(r, s); *see also* **mine²**
herself [hə:ˈsɛlf] *pron* sich (selbst); (*emphatic*) selbst; *see also* **oneself**
he's [hi:z] = **he is; he has**
hesitant ['hɛzɪtənt] *adj* zögernd
hesitate ['hɛzɪteɪt] *vi* zögern; **hesitation** [hɛzɪˈteɪʃən] *n* Zögern *nt*
heterosexual ['hɛtərəuˈsɛksjuəl] *adj* heterosexuell ♦ *n* Heterosexuelle(r) *mf*

hew [hju:] (*pt* **hewed**, *pp* **hewn**) *vt* hauen, hacken

hexagonal [hɛkˈsægənl] *adj* sechseckig

heyday [ˈheɪdeɪ] *n* Blüte *f*, Höhepunkt *m*

HGV *n abbr* = **heavy goods vehicle**

hi [haɪ] *excl* he, hallo

hibernate [ˈhaɪbəneɪt] *vi* Winterschlaf *m* halten; **hibernation** [haɪbəˈneɪʃən] *n* Winterschlaf *m*

hiccough [ˈhɪkʌp] *vi* den Schluckauf haben; **~s** *npl* Schluckauf *m*

hiccup [ˈhɪkʌp] = **hiccough**

hid [hɪd] *pt of* **hide**; **~den** [ˈhɪdn] *pp of* **hide**

hide [haɪd] (*pt* **hid**, *pp* **hidden**) *n* (*skin*) Haut *f*, Fell *nt* ♦ *vt* verstecken ♦ *vi* sich verstecken; **~-and-seek** *n* Versteckspiel *nt*; **~away** *n* Versteck *nt*

hideous [ˈhɪdɪəs] *adj* abscheulich

hiding [ˈhaɪdɪŋ] *n* (*beating*) Tracht *f* Prügel; **to be in ~** (*concealed*) sich versteckt halten; **~ place** *n* Versteck *nt*

hi-fi [ˈhaɪfaɪ] *n* Hi-fi *nt* ♦ *adj* Hi-Fi-

high [haɪ] *adj* hoch; (*wind*) stark ♦ *adv* hoch; **it is 20m ~** es ist 20 Meter hoch; **~brow** *adj* (betont) intellektuell; **~chair** *n* Hochstuhl *m*; **~er education** *n* Hochschulbildung *f*; **~-handed** *adj* eigenmächtig; **~-heeled** *adj* hochhackig; **~ jump** *n* (*SPORT*) Hochsprung *m*; **H~lands** *npl*: **the H~lands** das schottische Hochland; **~light** *n* (*fig*) Höhepunkt *m* ♦ *vt* hervorheben; **~ly** *adv* höchst; **~ly strung** *adj* überempfindlich; **~ness** *n* Höhe *f*; **Her H~ness** Ihre Hoheit *f*; **~-pitched** *adj* hoch; **~-rise block** *n* Hochhaus *nt*; **~ school** (*US*) *n* Oberschule *f*; **~ season** (*BRIT*) *n* Hochsaison *f*; **~ street** (*BRIT*) *n* Hauptstraße *f*

highway [ˈhaɪweɪ] *n* Landstraße *f*; **H~ Code** (*BRIT*) *n* Straßenverkehrsordnung *f*

hijack [ˈhaɪdʒæk] *vt* entführen; **~er** *n* Entführer(in) *m(f)*

hike [haɪk] *vi* wandern ♦ *n* Wanderung *f*; **~r** *n* Wanderer *m*; **hiking** *n* Wandern *nt*

hilarious [hɪˈlɛərɪəs] *adj* lustig

hill [hɪl] *n* Berg *m*; **~side** *n* (Berg)hang *m*; **~ walking** *n* Bergwandern *nt*; **~y** *adj* hügelig

hilt [hɪlt] *n* Heft *nt*; **(up) to the ~** ganz und gar

him [hɪm] *pron* (*acc*) ihn; (*dat*) ihm; *see also* **me**; **~self** *pron* sich (selbst); (*emphatic*) selbst; *see also* **oneself**

hind [haɪnd] *adj* hinter, Hinter-

hinder [ˈhɪndəʳ] *vt* (*stop*) hindern; (*delay*) behindern; **hindrance** *n* (*delay*) Behinderung *f*; (*obstacle*) Hindernis *nt*

hindsight [ˈhaɪndsaɪt] *n*: **with ~** im nachhinein

Hindu [ˈhɪndu:] *n* Hindu *m*

hinge [hɪndʒ] *n* Scharnier *nt*; (*on door*) Türangel *f* ♦ *vi* (*fig*): **to ~ on** abhängen von

hint [hɪnt] *n* Tipp *m*; (*trace*) Anflug *m* ♦ *vt*: **to ~ that** andeuten, dass ♦ *vi*: **to ~ at** andeuten

hip [hɪp] *n* Hüfte *f*

hippie [ˈhɪpɪ] *n* Hippie *m*

hippo [ˈhɪpəʊ] (*inf*) *n* Nilpferd *nt*

hippopotami [hɪpəˈpɒtəmaɪ] *npl of* **hippopotamus**

hippopotamus [hɪpəˈpɒtəməs] (*pl* **~es** *or* **hippopotami**) *n* Nilpferd *nt*

hire [ˈhaɪəʳ] *vt* (*worker*) anstellen; (*BRIT: car*) mieten ♦ *n* Miete *f*; **for ~** (*taxi*) frei; **~(d) car** (*BRIT*) *n* Mietwagen *m*, Leihwagen *m*; **~ purchase** (*BRIT*) *n* Teilzahlungskauf *m*

his [hɪz] *adj* sein ♦ *pron* seine(r, s); *see also* **my**; **mine**[2]

hiss [hɪs] *vi* zischen ♦ *n* Zischen *nt*

historian [hɪˈstɔ:rɪən] *n* Historiker *m*

historic [hɪˈstɒrɪk] *adj* historisch; **~al** *adj* historisch, geschichtlich

history [ˈhɪstərɪ] *n* Geschichte *f*

hit [hɪt] (*pt, pp* **hit**) *vt* schlagen; (*injure*) treffen ♦ *n* (*blow*) Schlag *m*; (*success*) Erfolg *m*; (*MUS*) Hit *m*; **to ~ it off with sb** prima mit jdm auskommen; **~-and-run driver** *n* jemand, der Fahrerflucht begeht

hitch [hɪtʃ] *vt* festbinden; (*also:* **~ up**) hochziehen ♦ *n* (*difficulty*) Haken *m*; **to ~ a lift** trampen; **~hike** *vi* trampen; **~hiker** *n* Tramper *m*; **~hiking** *n* Trampen *nt*

hi-tech [ˈhaɪˈtɛk] *adj* Hightech- ♦ *n* Spitzentechnologie *f*

hitherto [hɪðəˈtu:] *adv* bislang

hit man (*inf*) (*irreg*) *n* Killer *m*

HIV *n abbr*: **HIV-negative/-positive** HIV-negativ/-positiv

hive [haɪv] *n* Bienenkorb *m*

HMS *abbr* = **His/Her Majesty's Ship**

hoard [hɔːd] *n* Schatz *m* ♦ *vt* horten, hamstern

hoarding ['hɔːdɪŋ] *n* Bretterzaun *m*; (*BRIT: for posters*) Reklamewand *f*

hoarse [hɔːs] *adj* heiser, rau

hoax [həʊks] *n* Streich *m*

hob [hɔb] *n* Kochmulde *f*

hobble ['hɔbl] *vi* humpeln

hobby ['hɔbɪ] *n* Hobby *nt*

hobby-horse ['hɔbɪhɔːs] *n* (*fig*) Steckenpferd *nt*

hobo ['həʊbəʊ] (*US*) *n* Tippelbruder *m*

hockey ['hɔkɪ] *n* Hockey *nt*

hoe [həʊ] *n* Hacke *f* ♦ *vt* hacken

hog [hɔg] *n* Schlachtschwein *m* ♦ *vt* mit Beschlag belegen; **to go the whole ~** aufs Ganze gehen

hoist [hɔɪst] *n* Winde *f* ♦ *vt* hochziehen

hold [həʊld] (*pt, pp* **held**) *vt* halten; (*contain*) enthalten; (*be able to contain*) fassen; (*breath*) anhalten; (*meeting*) abhalten ♦ *vi* (*withstand pressure*) aushalten ♦ *n* (*grasp*) Halt *m*; (*NAUT*) Schiffsraum *m*; **~ the line!** (*TEL*) bleiben Sie am Apparat!; **to ~ one's own** sich behaupten; **~ back** *vt* zurückhalten; **~ down** *vt* niederhalten; (*job*) behalten; **~ off** *vt* (*enemy*) abwehren; **~ on** *vi* sich festhalten; (*resist*) durchhalten; (*wait*) warten; **~ on to** *vt fus* festhalten an +*dat*; (*keep*) behalten; **~ out** *vt* hinhalten ♦ *vi* aushalten; **~ up** *vt* (*delay*) aufhalten; (*rob*) überfallen; **~all** (*BRIT*) *n* Reisetasche *f*; **~er** *n* Behälter *m*; **~ing** *n* (*share*) (Aktien)anteil *m*; **~up** *n* (*BRIT: in traffic*) Stockung *f*; (*robbery*) Überfall *m*; (*delay*) Verzögerung *f*

hole [həʊl] *n* Loch *nt*; **~ in the wall** (*inf*) *n* (*cash dispenser*) Geldautomat *m*

holiday ['hɔlɪdeɪ] *n* (*day*) Feiertag *m*; freie(r) Tag *m*; (*vacation*) Urlaub *m*; (*SCH*) Ferien *pl*; **~-maker** (*BRIT*) *n* Urlauber(in) *m(f)*; **~ resort** *n* Ferienort *m*

Holland ['hɔlənd] *n* Holland *nt*

hollow ['hɔləʊ] *adj* hohl; (*fig*) leer ♦ *n* Vertiefung *f*; **~ out** *vt* aushöhlen

holly ['hɔlɪ] *n* Stechpalme *f*

holocaust ['hɔləkɔːst] *n* Inferno *nt*

holster ['həʊlstər] *n* Pistolenhalfter *m*

holy ['həʊlɪ] *adj* heilig; **H~ Ghost** *or* **Spirit** *n*: **the H~ Ghost** *or* **Spirit** der Heilige Geist

homage ['hɔmɪdʒ] *n* Huldigung *f*; **to pay ~ to** huldigen +*dat*

home [həʊm] *n* Zuhause *nt*; (*institution*) Heim *nt*, Anstalt *f* ♦ *adj* einheimisch; (*POL*) inner ♦ *adv* heim, nach Hause; **at ~** zu Hause; **~ address** *n* Heimatadresse *f*; **~coming** *n* Heimkehr *f*; **~land** *n* Heimat(land) *nt*; **~less** *adj* obdachlos; **~ly** *adj* häuslich; (*US: ugly*) unscheinbar; **~made** *adj* selbst gemacht; **~ match** *adj* Heimspiel *nt*; **H~ Office** (*BRIT*) *n* Innenministerium *nt*; **~ rule** *n* Selbstverwaltung *f*; **H~ Secretary** (*BRIT*) *n* Innenminister(in) *m(f)*; **~sick** *adj*: **to be ~sick** Heimweh haben; **~ town** *n* Heimatstadt *f*; **~ward** *adj* (*journey*) Heim-; **~work** *n* Hausaufgaben *pl*

homicide ['hɔmɪsaɪd] (*US*) *n* Totschlag *m*

homoeopathic [həʊmɪə'pæθɪk] (*US* **homeopathic**) *adj* homöopathisch; **homoeopathy** [həʊmɪ'ɔpəθɪ] (*US* **homeopathy**) *n* Homöopathie *f*

homogeneous [hɔməʊ'dʒiːnɪəs] *adj* homogen

homosexual [hɔməʊ'sɛksjʊəl] *adj* homosexuell ♦ *n* Homosexuelle(r) *mf*

honest ['ɔnɪst] *adj* ehrlich; **~ly** *adv* ehrlich; **~y** *n* Ehrlichkeit *f*

honey ['hʌnɪ] *n* Honig *m*; **~comb** *n* Honigwabe *f*; **~moon** *n* Flitterwochen *pl*, Hochzeitsreise *f*; **~suckle** ['hʌnɪsʌkl] *n* Geißblatt *nt*

honk [hɔŋk] *vi* hupen

honor *etc* ['ɔnər] (*US*) *vt, n* = **honour** *etc*

honorary ['ɔnərərɪ] *adj* Ehren-

honour ['ɔnər] (*US* **honor**) *vt* ehren; (*cheque*) einlösen ♦ *n* Ehre *f*; **~able** *adj* ehrenwert; (*intention*) ehrenhaft; **~s degree** *n* (*UNIV*) *akademischer Grad mit Prüfung im*

Spezialfach

hood [hud] n Kapuze f; (BRIT: AUT) Verdeck nt; (US: AUT) Kühlerhaube f

hoof [hu:f] (pl **hooves**) n Huf m

hook [huk] n Haken m ♦ vt einhaken

hooligan ['hu:lɪgən] n Rowdy m

hoop [hu:p] n Reifen m

hooray [hu:'reɪ] excl = **hurrah**

hoot [hu:t] vi (AUT) hupen; **~er** n (NAUT) Dampfpfeife f; (BRIT: AUT) (Auto)hupe f

Hoover ['hu:vər] (®; BRIT) n Staubsauger m ♦ vt: **to h~** staubsaugen, Staub saugen

hooves [hu:vz] pl of **hoof**

hop [hɔp] vi hüpfen, hopsen ♦ n (jump) Hopser m

hope [həup] vt, vi hoffen ♦ n Hoffnung f; **I ~ so/not** hoffentlich/hoffentlich nicht; **~ful** adj hoffnungsvoll; (promising) viel versprechend; **~fully** adv hoffentlich; **~less** adj hoffnungslos

hops [hɔps] npl Hopfen m

horizon [hə'raɪzn] n Horizont m; **~tal** [hɔrɪ'zɔntl] adj horizontal

hormone ['hɔ:məun] n Hormon nt

horn [hɔ:n] n Horn nt; (AUT) Hupe f

hornet ['hɔ:nɪt] n Hornisse f

horny ['hɔ:nɪ] adj schwielig; (US: inf) scharf

horoscope ['hɔrəskəup] n Horoskop nt

horrendous [hə'rendəs] adj (crime) abscheulich; (error) schrecklich

horrible ['hɔrɪbl] adj fürchterlich

horrid ['hɔrɪd] adj scheußlich

horrify ['hɔrɪfaɪ] vt entsetzen

horror ['hɔrər] n Schrecken m; **~ film** n Horrorfilm m

hors d'oeuvre [ɔ:'də:vrə] n Vorspeise f

horse [hɔ:s] n Pferd nt; **~back** n: **on ~back** beritten; **~ chestnut** n Rosskastanie f; **~man/woman** (irreg) n Reiter(in) m(f); **~power** n Pferdestärke f; **~-racing** n Pferderennen nt; **~radish** n Meerrettich m; **~shoe** n Hufeisen nt

horticulture ['hɔ:tɪkʌltʃər] n Gartenbau m

hose [həuz] n (also: **~pipe**) Schlauch m

hosiery ['həuzɪərɪ] n Strumpfwaren pl

hospitable ['hɔspɪtəbl] adj gastfreundlich

hospital ['hɔspɪtl] n Krankenhaus nt

hospitality [hɔspɪ'tælɪtɪ] n Gastfreundschaft f

host [həust] n Gastgeber m; (innkeeper) (Gast)wirt m; (large number) Heerschar f; (ECCL) Hostie f

hostage ['hɔstɪdʒ] n Geisel f

hostel ['hɔstl] n Herberge f; (also: **youth ~**) Jugendherberge f

hostess ['həustɪs] n Gastgeberin f

hostile ['hɔstaɪl] adj feindlich; **hostility** [hɔ'stɪlɪtɪ] n Feindschaft f; **hostilities** npl (fighting) Feindseligkeiten pl

hot [hɔt] adj heiß; (food, water) warm; (spiced) scharf; **I'm ~** mir ist heiß; **~bed** n (fig) Nährboden m; **~ dog** n heiße(s) Würstchen nt

hotel [həu'tel] n Hotel nt; **~ier** [həu'telɪər] n Hotelier m

hot: ~house n Treibhaus nt; **~ line** n (POL) heiße(r) Draht m; **~ly** adv (argue) hitzig; **~plate** n Kochplatte f; **~pot** ['hɔtpɔt] (BRIT) n Fleischeintopf m; **~-water bottle** n Wärmflasche f

hound [haund] n Jagdhund m ♦ vt hetzen

hour ['auər] n Stunde f; (time of day) (Tages)zeit f; **~ly** adj, adv stündlich

house [n haus, vb hauz] n Haus nt ♦ vt unterbringen; **on the ~** auf Kosten des Hauses; **~ arrest** n (POL, MIL) Hausarrest m; **~boat** n Hausboot nt; **~breaking** n Einbruch m; **~coat** n Morgenmantel m; **~hold** n Haushalt m; **~keeper** n Haushälterin f; **~keeping** n Haushaltung f; **~-warming party** n Einweihungsparty f; **~wife** (irreg) n Hausfrau f; **~work** n Hausarbeit f

housing ['hauzɪŋ] n (act) Unterbringung f; (houses) Wohnungen pl; (POL) Wohnungsbau m; (covering) Gehäuse nt; **~ estate** (US **~ development**) n (Wohn)siedlung f

hovel ['hɔvl] n elende Hütte f

hover ['hɔvər] vi (bird) schweben; (person) herumstehen; **~craft** n Luftkissenfahrzeug nt

how [hau] adv wie; **~ are you?** wie geht es Ihnen?; **~ much milk?** wie viel Milch?; **~**

many people? wie viele Leute?

however [hauˈevə[r]] *adv* (*but*) (je)doch, aber; **~ you phrase it** wie Sie es auch ausdrücken

howl [haul] *n* Heulen *nt* ♦ *vi* heulen

H.P. *abbr* = **hire purchase**

h.p. *abbr* = **horsepower**

H.Q. *abbr* = **headquarters**

hub [hʌb] *n* Radnabe *f*

hubbub [ˈhʌbʌb] *n* Tumult *m*

hubcap [ˈhʌbkæp] *n* Radkappe *f*

huddle [ˈhʌdl] *vi*: **to ~ together** sich zusammendrängen

hue [hjuː] *n* Färbung *f*; **~ and cry** *n* Zetergeschrei *nt*

huff [hʌf] *n*: **to go into a ~** einschnappen

hug [hʌg] *vt* umarmen ♦ *n* Umarmung *f*

huge [hjuːdʒ] *adj* groß, riesig

hulk [hʌlk] *n* (*ship*) abgetakelte(s) Schiff *nt*; (*person*) Koloss *m*

hull [hʌl] *n* Schiffsrumpf *m*

hullo [həˈləu] *excl* = **hello**

hum [hʌm] *vt, vi* summen

human [ˈhjuːmən] *adj* menschlich ♦ *n* (*also:* **~ being**) Mensch *m*

humane [hjuːˈmein] *adj* human

humanitarian [hjuːmænɪˈtɛəriən] *adj* humanitär

humanity [hjuːˈmænɪtɪ] *n* Menschheit *f*; (*kindliness*) Menschlichkeit *f*

humble [ˈhʌmbl] *adj* demütig; (*modest*) bescheiden ♦ *vt* demütigen

humbug [ˈhʌmbʌg] *n* Humbug *m*; (*BRIT: sweet*) Pfefferminzbonbon *nt*

humdrum [ˈhʌmdrʌm] *adj* stumpfsinnig

humid [ˈhjuːmɪd] *adj* feucht; **~ity** [hjuːˈmɪdɪtɪ] *n* Feuchtigkeit *f*

humiliate [hjuːˈmɪlieɪt] *vt* demütigen; **humiliation** [hjuːmɪlɪˈeɪʃən] *n* Demütigung *f*

humility [hjuːˈmɪlɪtɪ] *n* Demut *f*

humor [ˈhjuːmə[r]] (*US*) *n, vt* = **humour**

humorous [ˈhjuːmərəs] *adj* humorvoll

humour [ˈhjuːmə[r]] (*US* **humor**) *n* (*fun*) Humor *m*; (*mood*) Stimmung *f* ♦ *vt* bei Stimmung halten

hump [hʌmp] *n* Buckel *m*

hunch [hʌntʃ] *n* Buckel *m*; (*premonition*) (Vor)ahnung *f*; **~back** *n* Bucklige(r) *mf*; **~ed** *adj* gekrümmt

hundred [ˈhʌndrəd] *num* hundert; **~weight** *n* Zentner *m* (*BRIT* = 50.8 kg; *US* = 45.3 kg)

hung [hʌŋ] *pt, pp of* **hang**

Hungarian [hʌŋˈgɛəriən] *adj* ungarisch ♦ *n* Ungar(in) *m(f)*; (*LING*) Ungarisch *nt*

Hungary [ˈhʌŋgəri] *n* Ungarn *nt*

hunger [ˈhʌŋgə[r]] *n* Hunger *m* ♦ *vi* hungern

hungry [ˈhʌŋgri] *adj* hungrig; **to be ~** Hunger haben

hunk [hʌŋk] *n* (*of bread*) Stück *nt*

hunt [hʌnt] *vt, vi* jagen ♦ *n* Jagd *f*; **to ~ for** suchen; **~er** *n* Jäger *m*; **~ing** *n* Jagd *f*

hurdle [ˈhəːdl] *n* (*also fig*) Hürde *f*

hurl [həːl] *vt* schleudern

hurrah [huˈrɑː] *n* Hurra *nt*

hurray [huˈrei] *n* Hurra *nt*

hurricane [ˈhʌrɪkən] *n* Orkan *m*

hurried [ˈhʌrɪd] *adj* eilig; (*hasty*) übereilt; **~ly** *adv* übereilt, hastig

hurry [ˈhʌri] *n* Eile *f* ♦ *vi* sich beeilen ♦ *vt* (an)treiben; (*job*) übereilen; **to be in a ~** es eilig haben; **~ up** *vi* sich beeilen ♦ *vt* (*person*) zur Eile antreiben; (*work*) vorantreiben

hurt [həːt] (*pt, pp* **hurt**) *vt* wehtun +*dat*; (*injure, fig*) verletzen ♦ *vi* wehtun; **~ful** *adj* schädlich; (*remark*) verletzend

hurtle [ˈhəːtl] *vi* sausen

husband [ˈhʌzbənd] *n* (Ehe)mann *m*

hush [hʌʃ] *n* Stille *f* ♦ *vt* zur Ruhe bringen ♦ *excl* pst, still

husky [ˈhʌski] *adj* (*voice*) rau ♦ *n* Eskimohund *m*

hustle [ˈhʌsl] *vt* (*push*) stoßen; (*hurry*) antreiben ♦ *n*: **~ and bustle** Geschäftigkeit *f*

hut [hʌt] *n* Hütte *f*

hutch [hʌtʃ] *n* (Kaninchen)stall *m*

hyacinth [ˈhaiəsinθ] *n* Hyazinthe *f*

hydrant [ˈhaidrənt] *n* (*also:* **fire ~**) Hydrant *m*

hydraulic [harˈdrɔːlik] *adj* hydraulisch

hydroelectric [ˈhaidrəuˈlektrik] *adj* (*energy*) durch Wasserkraft erzeugt; **~ power**

station n Wasserkraftwerk nt
hydrofoil ['haɪdrəfɔɪl] n Tragflügelboot nt
hydrogen ['haɪdrədʒən] n Wasserstoff m
hyena [haɪ'i:nə] n Hyäne f
hygiene ['haɪdʒi:n] n Hygiene f; **hygienic** [haɪ'dʒi:nɪk] adj hygienisch
hymn [hɪm] n Kirchenlied nt
hype [haɪp] (inf) n Publicity f
hypermarket ['haɪpəmɑ:kɪt] (BRIT) n Hypermarket m
hyphen ['haɪfn] n Bindestrich m
hypnosis [hɪp'nəʊsɪs] n Hypnose f
hypnotize ['hɪpnətaɪz] vt hypnotisieren
hypocrisy [hɪ'pɔkrɪsɪ] n Heuchelei f
hypocrite ['hɪpəkrɪt] n Heuchler m;
hypocritical [hɪpə'krɪtɪkl] adj scheinheilig, heuchlerisch
hypothermia [haɪpə'θə:mɪə] n Unterkühlung f
hypotheses [haɪ'pɔθɪsi:z] npl of **hypothesis**
hypothesis [haɪ'pɔθɪsɪs] (pl **hypotheses**) n Hypothese f
hypothetic(al) [haɪpəʊ'θetɪk(l)] adj hypothetisch
hysterical [hɪ'sterɪkl] adj hysterisch
hysterics [hɪ'sterɪks] npl hysterische(r) Anfall m

I, i

I [aɪ] pron ich
ice [aɪs] n Eis nt ♦ vi (also: ~ up) vereisen; ~ **axe** n Eispickel m; ~**berg** n Eisberg m; ~**box** (US) n Kühlschrank m; ~ **cream** n Eis nt; ~ **cube** n Eiswürfel m; ~**d** [aɪst] adj (cake) mit Zuckerguss überzogen, glasiert; (tea, coffee) Eis-; ~ **hockey** n Eishockey nt
Iceland ['aɪslənd] n Island nt
ice: ~ **lolly** (BRIT) n Eis nt am Stiel; ~ **rink** n (Kunst)eisbahn f; ~ **skating** n Schlittschuhlaufen nt
icicle ['aɪsɪkl] n Eiszapfen m
icing ['aɪsɪŋ] n (on cake) Zuckerguss m; (on window) Vereisung f; ~ **sugar** (BRIT) n Puderzucker m

icon ['aɪkɔn] n Ikone f
icy ['aɪsɪ] adj (slippery) vereist; (cold) eisig
I'd [aɪd] = I would; I had
idea [aɪ'dɪə] n Idee f
ideal [aɪ'dɪəl] n Ideal nt ♦ adj ideal
identical [aɪ'dentɪkl] adj identisch; (twins) eineiig
identification [aɪdentɪfɪ'keɪʃən] n Identifizierung f; **means of ~** Ausweispapiere pl
identify [aɪ'dentɪfaɪ] vt identifizieren; (regard as the same) gleichsetzen
Identikit [aɪ'dentɪkɪt] ® n: ~ **picture** Phantombild nt
identity [aɪ'dentɪtɪ] n Identität f; ~ **card** n Personalausweis m
ideology [aɪdɪ'ɔlədʒɪ] n Ideologie f
idiom ['ɪdɪəm] n (expression) Redewendung f; (dialect) Idiom nt; ~**atic** [ɪdɪə'mætɪk] adj idiomatisch
idiosyncrasy [ɪdɪəʊ'sɪŋkrəsɪ] n Eigenart f
idiot ['ɪdɪət] n Idiot(in) m(f); ~**ic** [ɪdɪ'ɔtɪk] adj idiotisch
idle ['aɪdl] adj (doing nothing) untätig; (lazy) faul; (useless) nutzlos; (machine) still(stehend); (threat, talk) leer ♦ vi (machine) leer laufen ♦ vt: **to ~ away the time** die Zeit vertrödeln; ~**ness** n Müßiggang m; Faulheit f
idol ['aɪdl] n Idol nt; ~**ize** vt vergöttern
i.e. abbr (= id est) d. h.

KEYWORD

if [ɪf] conj **1** wenn; (in case also) falls; **if I were you** wenn ich Sie wäre
2 (although): (**even**) **if** (selbst or auch) wenn
3 (whether) ob
4: if so/not wenn ja/nicht; **if only ...** wenn ... doch nur ...; **if only I could** wenn ich doch könnte; see also **as**

ignite [ɪg'naɪt] vt (an)zünden ♦ vi sich entzünden; **ignition** [ɪg'nɪʃən] n Zündung f; **to switch on/off the ignition** den Motor anlassen/abstellen; **ignition key** n (AUT) Zündschlüssel m

ignorance ['ignərəns] *n* Unwissenheit *f*

ignorant ['ignərənt] *adj* unwissend; **to be ~ of** nicht wissen

ignore [ig'nɔːʳ] *vt* ignorieren

I'll [aɪl] = **I will; I shall**

ill [ɪl] *adj* krank ♦ *n* Übel *nt* ♦ *adv* schlecht; **~-advised** *adj* unklug; **~-at-ease** *adj* unbehaglich

illegal [ɪ'liːgl] *adj* illegal

illegible [ɪ'ledʒɪbl] *adj* unleserlich

illegitimate [ɪlɪ'dʒɪtɪmət] *adj* unehelich

ill-fated [ɪl'feɪtɪd] *adj* unselig

ill feeling *n* Verstimmung *f*

illicit [ɪ'lɪsɪt] *adj* verboten

illiterate [ɪ'lɪtərət] *adj* ungebildet

ill-mannered [ɪl'mænəd] *adj* ungehobelt

illness ['ɪlnɪs] *n* Krankheit *f*

illogical [ɪ'lɒdʒɪkl] *adj* unlogisch

ill-treat [ɪl'triːt] *vt* misshandeln

illuminate [ɪ'luːmɪneɪt] *vt* beleuchten; **illumination** [ɪluːmɪ'neɪʃən] *n* Beleuchtung *f*; **illuminations** *pl* (*decorative lights*) festliche Beleuchtung *f*

illusion [ɪ'luːʒən] *n* Illusion *f*; **to be under the ~ that ...** sich *dat* einbilden, dass ...

illustrate ['ɪləstreɪt] *vt* (*book*) illustrieren; (*explain*) veranschaulichen; **illustration** [ɪlə'streɪʃən] *n* Illustration *f*; (*explanation*) Veranschaulichung *f*

illustrious [ɪ'lʌstrɪəs] *adj* berühmt

I'm [aɪm] = **I am**

image ['ɪmɪdʒ] *n* Bild *nt*; (*public ~*) Image *nt*; **~ry** *n* Symbolik *f*

imaginary [ɪ'mædʒɪnərɪ] *adj* eingebildet; (*world*) Fantasie-

imagination [ɪmædʒɪ'neɪʃən] *n* Einbildung *f*; (*creative*) Fantasie *f*

imaginative [ɪ'mædʒɪnətɪv] *adj* fantasiereich, einfallsreich

imagine [ɪ'mædʒɪn] *vt* sich vorstellen; (*wrongly*) sich einbilden

imbalance [ɪm'bæləns] *n* Unausge-glichenheit *f*

imbecile ['ɪmbəsiːl] *n* Schwachsinnige(r) *mf*

imitate ['ɪmɪteɪt] *vt* imitieren; **imitation** [ɪmɪ'teɪʃən] *n* Imitation *f*

immaculate [ɪ'mækjulət] *adj* makellos;

(*dress*) tadellos; (*ECCL*) unbefleckt

immaterial [ɪmə'tɪərɪəl] *adj* unwesentlich; **it is ~ whether ...** es ist unwichtig, ob ...

immature [ɪmə'tjuəʳ] *adj* unreif

immediate [ɪ'miːdɪət] *adj* (*instant*) sofortig; (*near*) unmittelbar; (*relatives*) nächste(r, s); (*needs*) dringlich; **~ly** *adv* sofort; **~ly next to** direkt neben

immense [ɪ'mens] *adj* unermesslich

immerse [ɪ'məːs] *vt* eintauchen; **to be ~d in** (*fig*) vertieft sein in +*acc*

immersion heater [ɪ'məːʃən-] (*BRIT*) *n* Boiler *m*

immigrant ['ɪmɪgrənt] *n* Einwanderer *m*

immigrate ['ɪmɪgreɪt] *vi* einwandern; **immigration** [ɪmɪ'greɪʃən] *n* Einwanderung *f*

imminent ['ɪmɪnənt] *adj* bevorstehend

immobile [ɪ'məubaɪl] *adj* unbeweglich; **immobilize** [ɪ'məubɪlaɪz] *vt* lähmen

immoral [ɪ'mɔrl] *adj* unmoralisch; **~ity** [ɪmə'rælɪtɪ] *n* Unsittlichkeit *f*

immortal [ɪ'mɔːtl] *adj* unsterblich

immune [ɪ'mjuːn] *adj* (*secure*) sicher; (*MED*) immun; **~ from** sicher vor +*dat*; **immunity** *n* (*MED, JUR*) Immunität *f*; (*fig*) Freiheit *f*; **immunize** ['ɪmjunaɪz] *vt* immunisieren

impact ['ɪmpækt] *n* Aufprall *m*; (*fig*) Wirkung *f*

impair [ɪm'peəʳ] *vt* beeinträchtigen

impart [ɪm'pɑːt] *vt* mitteilen; (*knowledge*) vermitteln; (*exude*) abgeben

impartial [ɪm'pɑːʃl] *adj* unparteiisch

impassable [ɪm'pɑːsəbl] *adj* unpassierbar

impassive [ɪm'pæsɪv] *adj* gelassen

impatience [ɪm'peɪʃəns] *n* Ungeduld *f*; **impatient** *adj* ungeduldig; **impatiently** *adv* ungeduldig

impeccable [ɪm'pekəbl] *adj* tadellos

impede [ɪm'piːd] *vt* (be)hindern; **impediment** [ɪm'pedɪmənt] *n* Hindernis *nt*; **speech impediment** Sprachfehler *m*

impending [ɪm'pendɪŋ] *adj* bevorstehend

impenetrable [ɪm'penɪtrəbl] *adj* (*also fig*) undurchdringlich

imperative [ɪm'perətɪv] *adj* (*necessary*) unbedingt erforderlich

imperceptible [ɪmpə'sɛptɪbl] *adj* nicht
wahrnehmbar

imperfect [ɪm'pə:fɪkt] *adj* (*faulty*) fehlerhaft;
~ion [ɪmpə:'fɛkʃən] *n* Unvollkommenheit *f*;
(*fault*) Fehler *m*

imperial [ɪm'pɪərɪəl] *adj* kaiserlich

impersonal [ɪm'pə:sənl] *adj* unpersönlich

impersonate [ɪm'pə:səneɪt] *vt* sich
ausgeben als; (*for fun*) imitieren

impertinent [ɪm'pə:tɪnənt] *adj* unverschämt,
frech

impervious [ɪm'pə:vɪəs] *adj* (*fig*): **~ (to)**
unempfänglich (für)

impetuous [ɪm'pɛtjʊəs] *adj* ungestüm

impetus [ɪmpətəs] *n* Triebkraft *f*; (*fig*)
Auftrieb *m*

impinge [ɪm'pɪndʒ]: **~ on** *vt* beeinträchtigen

implacable [ɪm'plækəbl] *adj* unerbittlich

implement [*n* 'ɪmplɪmənt, *vb* 'ɪmplɪmɛnt] *n*
Werkzeug *nt* ♦ *vt* ausführen

implicate ['ɪmplɪkeɪt] *vt* verwickeln;
implication [ɪmplɪ'keɪʃən] *n* (*effect*)
Auswirkung *f*; (*in crime*) Verwicklung *f*

implicit [ɪm'plɪsɪt] *adj* (*suggested*)
unausgesprochen; (*utter*) vorbehaltlos

implore [ɪm'plɔ:ʳ] *vt* anflehen

imply [ɪm'plaɪ] *vt* (*hint*) andeuten; (*be
evidence for*) schließen lassen auf +*acc*

impolite [ɪmpə'laɪt] *adj* unhöflich

import [*vb* ɪm'pɔ:t, *n* 'ɪmpɔ:t] *vt* einführen
♦ *n* Einfuhr *f*; (*meaning*) Bedeutung *f*

importance [ɪm'pɔ:tns] *n* Bedeutung *f*

important [ɪm'pɔ:tənt] *adj* wichtig; **it's not
~** es ist unwichtig

importer [ɪm'pɔ:təʳ] *n* Importeur *m*

impose [ɪm'pəuz] *vt, vi*: **to ~ (on)** auferlegen
(+*dat*); (*penalty, sanctions*) verhängen
(gegen); **to ~ (o.s.) on sb** sich jdm
aufdrängen

imposing [ɪm'pəuzɪŋ] *adj* eindrucksvoll

imposition [ɪmpə'zɪʃən] *n* (*of burden, fine*)
Auferlegung *f*; **to be an ~** (*on person*) eine
Zumutung sein

impossible [ɪm'pɔsɪbl] *adj* unmöglich

impostor [ɪm'pɔstəʳ] *n* Hochstapler *m*

impotent ['ɪmpətnt] *adj* machtlos; (*sexually*)
impotent

impound [ɪm'paund] *vt* beschlagnahmen

impoverished [ɪm'pɔvərɪʃt] *adj* verarmt

impracticable [ɪm'præktɪkəbl] *adj*
undurchführbar

impractical [ɪm'præktɪkl] *adj* unpraktisch

imprecise [ɪmprɪ'saɪs] *adj* ungenau

impregnable [ɪm'prɛgnəbl] *adj* (*castle*)
uneinnehmbar

impregnate ['ɪmprɛgneɪt] *vt* (*saturate*)
sättigen; (*fertilize*) befruchten

impress [ɪm'prɛs] *vt* (*influence*)
beeindrucken; (*imprint*) (auf)drücken; **to ~
sth on sb** jdm etw einschärfen; **~ed** *adj*
beeindruckt; **~ion** [ɪm'prɛʃən] *n* Eindruck *m*;
(*on wax, footprint*) Abdruck *m*; (*of book*)
Auflage *f*; (*take-off*) Nachahmung *f*; **I was
under the ~ion** ich hatte den Eindruck;
~ionable *adj* leicht zu beeindrucken; **~ive**
adj eindrucksvoll

imprint ['ɪmprɪnt] *n* Abdruck *m*

imprison [ɪm'prɪzn] *vt* ins Gefängnis
schicken; **~ment** *n* Inhaftierung *f*

improbable [ɪm'prɔbəbl] *adj*
unwahrscheinlich

impromptu [ɪm'prɔmptju:] *adj, adv* aus dem
Stegreif, improvisiert

improper [ɪm'prɔpəʳ] *adj* (*indecent*)
unanständig; (*unsuitable*) unpassend

improve [ɪm'pru:v] *vt* verbessern ♦ *vi* besser
werden; **~ment** *n* (Ver)besserung *f*

improvise ['ɪmprəvaɪz] *vt, vi* improvisieren

imprudent [ɪm'pru:dnt] *adj* unklug

impudent ['ɪmpjudnt] *adj* unverschämt

impulse ['ɪmpʌls] *n* Impuls *m*; **to act on ~**
spontan handeln; **impulsive** [ɪm'pʌlsɪv] *adj*
impulsiv

impure [ɪm'pjuəʳ] *adj* (*dirty*) verunreinigt;
(*bad*) unsauber; **impurity** [ɪm'pjuərɪtɪ] *n*
Unreinheit *f*; (*TECH*) Verunreinigung *f*

KEYWORD

in [ɪn] *prep* **1** (*indicating place, position*) in
+*dat*; (*with motion*) in +*acc*; **in here/there**
hier/dort; **in London** in London; **in the
United States** in den Vereinigten Staaten
2 (*indicating time: during*) in +*dat*; **in
summer** im Sommer; **in 1988** (im Jahre)

1988; **in the afternoon** nachmittags, am Nachmittag
3 (*indicating time*: *in the space of*) innerhalb von; **I'll see you in 2 weeks** *or* **in 2 weeks' time** ich sehe Sie in zwei Wochen
4 (*indicating manner, circumstances, state etc*) in +*dat*; **in the sun/rain** in der Sonne/im Regen; **in English/French** auf Englisch/ Französisch; **in a loud/soft voice** mit lauter/leiser Stimme
5 (*with ratios, numbers*): **1 in 10** jeder Zehnte; **20 pence in the pound** 20 Pence pro Pfund; **they lined up in twos** sie stellten sich in Zweierreihe auf
6 (*referring to people, works*): **the disease is common in children** die Krankheit ist bei Kindern häufig; **in Dickens** bei Dickens; **we have a loyal friend in him** er ist uns ein treuer Freund
7 (*indicating profession etc*): **to be in teaching/the army** Lehrer(in)/beim Militär sein; **to be in publishing** im Verlagswesen arbeiten
8 (*with present participle*): **in saying this, I ...** wenn ich das sage, ... ich; **in accepting this view, he ...** weil er diese Meinung akzeptierte, ... er
♦ *adv*: **to be in** (*person*: *at home, work*) da sein; (*train, ship, plane*) angekommen sein; (*in fashion*) in sein; **to ask sb in** jdn hereinbitten; **to run/limp** *etc* **in** hereingerannt/gehumpelt *etc* kommen
♦ *n*: **the ins and outs** (*of proposal, situation etc*) die Feinheiten

in. *abbr* = **inch**
inability [ɪnəˈbɪlɪtɪ] *n* Unfähigkeit *f*
inaccessible [ɪnəkˈsɛsɪbl] *adj* unzugänglich
inaccurate [ɪnˈækjʊrət] *adj* ungenau; (*wrong*) unrichtig
inactivity [ɪnækˈtɪvɪtɪ] *n* Untätigkeit *f*
inadequate [ɪnˈædɪkwət] *adj* unzulänglich
inadvertently [ɪnədˈvɜːtntlɪ] *adv* unabsichtlich
inadvisable [ɪnədˈvaɪzəbl] *adj* nicht ratsam
inane [ɪˈneɪn] *adj* dumm, albern
inanimate [ɪnˈænɪmət] *adj* leblos

inappropriate [ɪnəˈprəʊprɪət] *adj* (*clothing*) ungeeignet; (*remark*) unangebracht
inarticulate [ɪnɑːˈtɪkjʊlət] *adj* unklar
inasmuch as [ɪnəzˈmʌtʃ-] *adv* da; (*in so far as*) so weit
inaudible [ɪnˈɔːdɪbl] *adj* unhörbar
inauguration [ɪnɔːɡjuˈreɪʃən] *n* Eröffnung *f*; (*feierliche*) Amtseinführung *f*
inborn [ɪnˈbɔːn] *adj* angeboren
inbred [ɪnˈbred] *adj* angeboren
Inc. *abbr* = **incorporated**
incalculable [ɪnˈkælkjʊləbl] *adj* (*consequences*) unabsehbar
incapable [ɪnˈkeɪpəbl] *adj*: **~ (of doing sth)** unfähig(, etw zu tun)
incapacitate [ɪnkəˈpæsɪteɪt] *vt* untauglich machen
incapacity [ɪnkəˈpæsɪtɪ] *n* Unfähigkeit *f*
incarcerate [ɪnˈkɑːsəreɪt] *vt* einkerkern
incarnation [ɪnkɑːˈneɪʃən] *n* (*ECCL*) Menschwerdung *f*; (*fig*) Inbegriff *m*
incendiary [ɪnˈsɛndɪərɪ] *adj* Brand-
incense [*n* ˈɪnsɛns, *vb* ɪnˈsɛns] *n* Weihrauch *m* ♦ *vt* erzürnen
incentive [ɪnˈsɛntɪv] *n* Anreiz *m*
incessant [ɪnˈsɛsnt] *adj* unaufhörlich
incest [ˈɪnsɛst] *n* Inzest *m*
inch [ɪntʃ] *n* Zoll *m* ♦ *vi*: **to ~ forward** sich Stückchen für Stückchen vorwärts bewegen; **to be within an ~ of** kurz davor sein; **he didn't give an ~** er gab keinen Zentimeter nach
incidence [ˈɪnsɪdns] *n* Auftreten *nt*; (*of crime*) Quote *f*
incident [ˈɪnsɪdnt] *n* Vorfall *m*; (*disturbance*) Zwischenfall *m*
incidental [ɪnsɪˈdɛntl] *adj* (*music*) Begleit-; (*unimportant*) nebensächlich; (*remark*) beiläufig; **~ly** *adv* übrigens
incinerator [ɪnˈsɪnəreɪtə*] *n* Verbrennungsofen *m*
incision [ɪnˈsɪʒən] *n* Einschnitt *m*
incisive [ɪnˈsaɪsɪv] *adj* (*style*) treffend; (*person*) scharfsinnig
incite [ɪnˈsaɪt] *vt* anstacheln
inclination [ɪnklɪˈneɪʃən] *n* Neigung *f*
incline [*n* ˈɪnklaɪn, *vb* ɪnˈklaɪn] *n* Abhang *m*

♦ *vt* neigen; (*fig*) veranlassen ♦ *vi* sich neigen; **to be ~d to do sth** dazu neigen, etw zu tun

include [ɪnˈkluːd] *vt* einschließen; (*on list, in group*) aufnehmen; **including** *prep*: **including X** X inbegriffen; **inclusion** [ɪnˈkluːʒən] *n* Aufnahme *f*; **inclusive** [ɪnˈkluːsɪv] *adj* einschließlich; (*COMM*) inklusive; **inclusive of** einschließlich +*gen*

incoherent [ɪnkəuˈhɪərənt] *adj* zusammenhanglos

income [ˈɪnkʌm] *n* Einkommen *nt*; (*from business*) Einkünfte *pl*; **~ tax** *n* Lohnsteuer *f*; (*of self-employed*) Einkommenssteuer *f*

incoming [ˈɪnkʌmɪŋ] *adj*: **~ flight** eintreffende Maschine *f*

incomparable [ɪnˈkɒmpərəbl] *adj* unvergleichlich

incompatible [ɪnkəmˈpætɪbl] *adj* unvereinbar; (*people*) unverträglich

incompetence [ɪnˈkɒmpɪtns] *n* Unfähigkeit *f*; **incompetent** *adj* unfähig

incomplete [ɪnkəmˈpliːt] *adj* unvollständig

incomprehensible [ɪnkɒmprɪˈhensɪbl] *adj* unverständlich

inconceivable [ɪnkənˈsiːvəbl] *adj* unvorstellbar

incongruous [ɪnˈkɒŋgruəs] *adj* seltsam; (*remark*) unangebracht

inconsiderate [ɪnkənˈsɪdərət] *adj* rücksichtslos

inconsistency [ɪnkənˈsɪstənsɪ] *n* Widersprüchlichkeit *f*; (*state*) Unbeständigkeit *f*

inconsistent [ɪnkənˈsɪstnt] *adj* (*action, speech*) widersprüchlich; (*person, work*) unbeständig; **~ with** nicht übereinstimmend mit

inconspicuous [ɪnkənˈspɪkjuəs] *adj* unauffällig

incontinent [ɪnˈkɒntɪnənt] *adj* (*MED*) nicht fähig, Stuhl und Harn zurückzuhalten

inconvenience [ɪnkənˈviːnjəns] *n* Unbequemlichkeit *f*; (*trouble to others*) Unannehmlichkeiten *pl*

inconvenient [ɪnkənˈviːnjənt] *adj* ungelegen; (*journey*) unbequem

incorporate [ɪnˈkɔːpəreɪt] *vt* (*include*) aufnehmen; (*contain*) enthalten; **~d** *adj*: **~d company** (*US*) eingetragene Aktiengesellschaft *f*

incorrect [ɪnkəˈrekt] *adj* unrichtig

incorrigible [ɪnˈkɒrɪdʒɪbl] *adj* unverbesserlich

incorruptible [ɪnkəˈrʌptɪbl] *adj* unzerstörbar; (*person*) unbestechlich

increase [*n* ˈɪnkriːs, *vb* ɪnˈkriːs] *n* Zunahme *f*; (*pay ~*) Gehaltserhöhung *f*; (*in size*) Vergrößerung *f* ♦ *vt* erhöhen; (*wealth, rage*) vermehren; (*business*) erweitern ♦ *vi* zunehmen; (*prices*) steigen; (*in size*) größer werden; (*in number*) sich vermehren; **increasing** *adj* (*number*) steigend; **increasingly** [ɪnˈkriːsɪŋlɪ] *adv* zunehmend

incredible [ɪnˈkredɪbl] *adj* unglaublich

incredulous [ɪnˈkredjuləs] *adj* ungläubig

increment [ˈɪnkrɪmənt] *n* Zulage *f*

incriminate [ɪnˈkrɪmɪneɪt] *vt* belasten

incubation [ɪnkjuˈbeɪʃən] *n* Ausbrüten *nt*

incubator [ˈɪnkjubeɪtə*] *n* Brutkasten *m*

incumbent [ɪnˈkʌmbənt] *n* ♦ *adj*: **it is ~ on him to ...** es obliegt ihm, ...

incur [ɪnˈkəː*] *vt* sich zuziehen; (*debts*) machen

incurable [ɪnˈkjuərəbl] *adj* unheilbar

indebted [ɪnˈdetɪd] *adj* (*obliged*): **~ (to sb)** (jdm) verpflichtet

indecent [ɪnˈdiːsnt] *adj* unanständig; **~ assault** (*BRIT*) *n* Notzucht *f*; **~ exposure** *n* Exhibitionismus *m*

indecisive [ɪndɪˈsaɪsɪv] *adj* (*battle*) nicht entscheidend; (*person*) unentschlossen

indeed [ɪnˈdiːd] *adv* tatsächlich, in der Tat; **yes ~!** allerdings!

indefinite [ɪnˈdefɪnɪt] *adj* unbestimmt; **~ly** *adv* auf unbestimmte Zeit; (*wait*) unbegrenzt lange

indelible [ɪnˈdelɪbl] *adj* unauslöschlich

indemnity [ɪnˈdemnɪtɪ] *n* (*insurance*) Versicherung *f*; (*compensation*) Entschädigung *f*

independence [ɪndɪˈpendns] *n* Unabhängigkeit *f*; **independent** *adj* unabhängig

---

| **Independence Day** |

i **Independence Day** *(der 4. Juli) ist in den USA ein gesetzlicher Feiertag zum Gedenken an die Unabhängigkeitserklärung am 4. Juli 1776, mit der die 13 amerikanischen Kolonien ihre Freiheit und Unabhängigkeit von Großbritannien erklärten.*

---

indestructible [ɪndɪs'trʌktəbl] *adj* unzerstörbar

indeterminate [ɪndɪ'tə:mɪnɪt] *adj* unbestimmt

index ['ɪndeks] *(pl ~es or indices)* *n* Index *m*; ~ **card** *n* Karteikarte *f*; ~ **finger** *n* Zeigefinger *m*; **~-linked** *(US ~ed) adj* *(salaries)* der Inflationsrate *dat* angeglichen; *(pensions)* dynamisch

India ['ɪndɪə] *n* Indien *nt*; **~n** *adj* indisch ♦ *n* Inder(in) *m(f)*; **American ~n** Indianer(in) *m(f)*; **~n Ocean** *n*: **the ~n Ocean** der Indische Ozean

indicate ['ɪndɪkeɪt] *vt* anzeigen; *(hint)* andeuten; **indication** [ɪndɪ'keɪʃən] *n* Anzeichen *nt*; *(information)* Angabe *f*; **indicative** [ɪn'dɪkətɪv] *adj*: **indicative of** bezeichnend für; **indicator** *n* (An)zeichen *nt*; *(AUT)* Richtungsanzeiger *m*

indict [ɪn'daɪt] *vt* anklagen; **~ment** *n* Anklage *f*

indifference [ɪn'dɪfrəns] *n* Gleichgültigkeit *f*; Unwichtigkeit *f*; **indifferent** *adj* gleichgültig; *(mediocre)* mäßig

indigenous [ɪn'dɪdʒɪnəs] *adj* einheimisch

indigestion [ɪndɪ'dʒestʃən] *n* Verdauungsstörung *f*

indignant [ɪn'dɪgnənt] *adj*: **to be ~ about sth** über etw *acc* empört sein

indignation [ɪndɪg'neɪʃən] *n* Entrüstung *f*

indignity [ɪn'dɪgnɪtɪ] *n* Demütigung *f*

indirect [ɪndɪ'rekt] *adj* indirekt

indiscreet [ɪndɪs'kri:t] *adj (insensitive)* taktlos; *(telling secrets)* indiskret; **indiscretion** [ɪndɪs'kreʃən] *n* Taktlosigkeit *f*; Indiskretion *f*

indiscriminate [ɪndɪs'krɪmɪnət] *adj* wahllos; kritiklos

indispensable [ɪndɪs'pensəbl] *adj* unentbehrlich

indisposed [ɪndɪs'pəuzd] *adj* unpässlich

indisputable [ɪndɪs'pju:təbl] *adj* unbestreitbar; *(evidence)* unanfechtbar

indistinct [ɪndɪs'tɪŋkt] *adj* undeutlich

individual [ɪndɪ'vɪdjuəl] *n* Individuum *nt* ♦ *adj* individuell; *(case)* Einzel-; *(of, for one person)* eigen, individuell; *(characteristic)* eigentümlich; **~ly** *adv* einzeln, individuell

indivisible [ɪndɪ'vɪzɪbl] *adj* unteilbar

indoctrinate [ɪn'dɔktrɪneɪt] *vt* indoktrinieren

Indonesia [ɪndə'ni:zɪə] *n* Indonesien *nt*

indoor ['ɪndɔ:r] *adj* Haus-; Zimmer-; Innen-; *(SPORT)* Hallen-; **~s** [ɪn'dɔ:z] *adv* drinnen, im Haus

induce [ɪn'dju:s] *vt* dazu bewegen; *(reaction)* herbeiführen

induction course [ɪn'dʌkʃən-] *(BRIT) n* Einführungskurs *m*

indulge [ɪn'dʌldʒ] *vt (give way)* nachgeben +*dat*; *(gratify)* frönen +*dat* ♦ *vi*: **to ~ (in)** frönen (+*dat*); **~nce** *n* Nachsicht *f*; *(enjoyment)* Genuss *m*; **~nt** *adj* nachsichtig; *(pej)* nachgiebig

industrial [ɪn'dʌstrɪəl] *adj* Industrie-, industriell; *(dispute, injury)* Arbeits-; ~ **action** *n* Arbeitskampfmaßnahmen *pl*; ~ **estate** *(BRIT) n* Industriegebiet *nt*; **~ist** *n* Industrielle(r) *mf*; **~ize** *vt* industrialisieren; ~ **park** *(US) n* Industriegebiet *nt*

industrious [ɪn'dʌstrɪəs] *adj* fleißig

industry ['ɪndəstrɪ] *n* Industrie *f*; *(diligence)* Fleiß *m*

inebriated [ɪ'ni:brɪeɪtɪd] *adj* betrunken

inedible [ɪn'edɪbl] *adj* ungenießbar

ineffective [ɪnɪ'fektɪv] *adj* unwirksam; *(person)* untauglich

ineffectual [ɪnɪ'fektʃuəl] *adj* = **ineffective**

inefficiency [ɪnɪ'fɪʃənsɪ] *n* Ineffizienz *f*

inefficient [ɪnɪ'fɪʃənt] *adj* ineffizient; *(ineffective)* unwirksam

inept [ɪ'nept] *adj (remark)* unpassend; *(person)* ungeeignet

inequality [ɪnɪ'kwɔlɪtɪ] *n* Ungleichheit *f*

inert [ɪ'nə:t] *adj* träge; *(CHEM)* inaktiv;

(*motionless*) unbeweglich

inescapable [ɪnɪ'skeɪpəbl] *adj* unvermeidbar

inevitable [ɪn'evɪtəbl] *adj* unvermeidlich; **inevitably** *adv* zwangsläufig

inexcusable [ɪnɪks'kju:zəbl] *adj* unverzeihlich

inexhaustible [ɪnɪg'zɔ:stɪbl] *adj* unerschöpflich

inexpensive [ɪnɪk'spensɪv] *adj* preiswert

inexperience [ɪnɪk'spɪərɪəns] *n* Unerfahrenheit *f*; **~d** *adj* unerfahren

inexplicable [ɪnɪk'splɪkəbl] *adj* unerklärlich

inextricably [ɪnɪk'strɪkəblɪ] *adv* untrennbar

infallible [ɪn'fælɪbl] *adj* unfehlbar

infamous ['ɪnfəməs] *adj* (*deed*) schändlich; (*person*) niederträchtig

infancy ['ɪnfənsɪ] *n* frühe Kindheit *f*; (*fig*) Anfangsstadium *nt*

infant ['ɪnfənt] *n* kleine(s) Kind *nt*, Säugling *m*; **~ile** [-aɪl] *adj* kindisch, infantil; **~ school** (*BRIT*) *n* Vorschule *f*

infatuated [ɪn'fætjueɪtɪd] *adj* vernarrt; **to become ~ with** sich vernarren in +*acc*; **infatuation** [ɪnfætjʊ'eɪʃən] *n*: **infatuation (with)** Vernarrtheit *f* (in +*acc*)

infect [ɪn'fekt] *vt* anstecken (*also fig*); **~ed with** (*illness*) infiziert mit; **~ion** [ɪn'fekʃən] *n* Infektion *f*; **~ious** [ɪn'fekʃəs] *adj* ansteckend

infer [ɪn'fɜ:r] *vt* schließen

inferior [ɪn'fɪərɪər] *adj* (*rank*) untergeordnet; (*quality*) minderwertig ♦ *n* Untergebene(r) *m*; **~ity** [ɪnfɪərɪ'ɔrətɪ] *n* Minderwertigkeit *f*; (*in rank*) untergeordnete Stellung *f*; **~ity complex** *n* Minderwertigkeitskomplex *m*

infernal [ɪn'fɜ:nl] *adj* höllisch

infertile [ɪn'fɜ:taɪl] *adj* unfruchtbar; **infertility** [ɪnfə'tɪlɪtɪ] *n* Unfruchtbarkeit *f*

infested [ɪn'festɪd] *adj*: **to be ~ with** wimmeln von

infidelity [ɪnfɪ'delɪtɪ] *n* Untreue *f*

infighting ['ɪnfaɪtɪŋ] *n* Nahkampf *m*

infiltrate ['ɪnfɪltreɪt] *vt* infiltrieren; (*spies*) einschleusen ♦ *vi* (*MIL, liquid*) einsickern; (*POL*): **to ~ (into)** unterwandern (+*acc*)

infinite ['ɪnfɪnɪt] *adj* unendlich

infinitive [ɪn'fɪnɪtɪv] *n* Infinitiv *m*

infinity [ɪn'fɪnɪtɪ] *n* Unendlichkeit *f*

infirm [ɪn'fɜ:m] *adj* gebrechlich; **~ary** *n* Krankenhaus *nt*

inflamed [ɪn'fleɪmd] *adj* entzündet

inflammable [ɪn'flæməbl] (*BRIT*) *adj* feuergefährlich

inflammation [ɪnflə'meɪʃən] *n* Entzündung *f*

inflatable [ɪn'fleɪtəbl] *adj* aufblasbar

inflate [ɪn'fleɪt] *vt* aufblasen; (*tyre*) aufpumpen; (*prices*) hoch treiben; **inflation** [ɪn'fleɪʃən] *n* Inflation *f*; **inflationary** [ɪn'fleɪʃənrɪ] *adj* (*increase*) inflationistisch; (*situation*) inflationär

inflexible [ɪn'fleksɪbl] *adj* (*person*) nicht flexibel; (*opinion*) starr; (*thing*) unbiegsam

inflict [ɪn'flɪkt] *vt*: **to ~ sth on sb** jdm etw zufügen; (*wound*) jdm etw beibringen

influence ['ɪnfluəns] *n* Einfluss *m* ♦ *vt* beeinflussen

influential [ɪnflu'enʃl] *adj* einflussreich

influenza [ɪnflu'enzə] *n* Grippe *f*

influx ['ɪnflʌks] *n* (*of people*) Zustrom *m*; (*of ideas*) Eindringen *nt*

infomercial ['ɪnfəʊmə:ʃl] *n* Werbeinformationssendung *f*

inform [ɪn'fɔ:m] *vt* informieren ♦ *vi*: **to ~ on sb** jdn denunzieren; **to keep sb ~ed** jdn auf dem Laufenden halten

informal [ɪn'fɔ:ml] *adj* zwanglos; **~ity** [ɪnfɔ:'mælɪtɪ] *n* Ungezwungenheit *f*

informant [ɪn'fɔ:mənt] *n* Informant(in) *m(f)*

information [ɪnfə'meɪʃən] *n* Auskunft *f*, Information *f*; **a piece of ~** eine Auskunft, eine Information; **~ desk** *n* Auskunftsschalter *m*; **~ office** *n* Informationsbüro *nt*

informative [ɪn'fɔ:mətɪv] *adj* informativ; (*person*) mitteilsam

informer [ɪn'fɔ:məʳ] *n* Denunziant(in) *m(f)*

infra-red [ɪnfrə'red] *adj* infrarot

infrequent [ɪn'fri:kwənt] *adj* selten

infringe [ɪn'frɪndʒ] *vt* (*law*) verstoßen gegen; **~ upon** *vt* verletzen; **~ment** *n* Verstoß *m*, Verletzung *f*

infuriating [ɪn'fjʊərɪeɪtɪŋ] *adj* ärgerlich

ingenuity [ɪndʒɪ'nju:ɪtɪ] *n* Genialität *f*

ingenuous [ɪn'dʒɛnjuəs] *adj* aufrichtig; (*naive*) naiv

ingot ['ɪŋɡət] *n* Barren *m*

ingrained [ɪn'ɡreɪnd] *adj* tief sitzend

ingratiate [ɪn'ɡreɪʃɪeɪt] *vt*: **to ~ o.s. with sb** sich bei jdm einschmeicheln

ingratitude [ɪn'ɡrætɪtjuːd] *n* Undankbarkeit *f*

ingredient [ɪn'ɡriːdɪənt] *n* Bestandteil *m*; (*COOK*) Zutat *f*

inhabit [ɪn'hæbɪt] *vt* bewohnen; **~ant** *n* Bewohner(in) *m(f)*; (*of island, town*) Einwohner(in) *m(f)*

inhale [ɪn'heɪl] *vt* einatmen; (*MED, cigarettes*) inhalieren

inherent [ɪn'hɪərənt] *adj*: **~ (in)** innewohnend (+*dat*)

inherit [ɪn'herɪt] *vt* erben; **~ance** *n* Erbe *nt*, Erbschaft *f*

inhibit [ɪn'hɪbɪt] *vt* hemmen; **to ~ sb from doing sth** jdn daran hindern, etw zu tun; **~ion** [ɪnhɪ'bɪʃən] *n* Hemmung *f*

inhospitable [ɪnhɔs'pɪtəbl] *adj* (*person*) ungastlich; (*country*) unwirtlich

inhuman [ɪn'hjuːmən] *adj* unmenschlich

initial [ɪ'nɪʃl] *adj* anfänglich, Anfangs- ♦ *n* Initiale *f* ♦ *vt* abzeichnen; (*POL*) paraphieren; **~ly** *adv* anfangs

initiate [ɪ'nɪʃɪeɪt] *vt* einführen; (*negotiations*) einleiten; **to ~ proceedings against sb** (*JUR*) gerichtliche Schritte gegen jdn einleiten; **initiation** [ɪnɪʃɪ'eɪʃən] *n* Einführung *f*; Einleitung *f*

initiative [ɪ'nɪʃətɪv] *n* Initiative *f*

inject [ɪn'dʒekt] *vt* einspritzen; (*fig*) einflößen; **~ion** [ɪn'dʒekʃən] *n* Spritze *f*

injunction [ɪn'dʒʌŋkʃən] *n* Verfügung *f*

injure ['ɪndʒər] *vt* verletzen; **~d** *adj* (*person, arm*) verletzt; **injury** ['ɪndʒərɪ] *n* Verletzung *f*; **to play injury time** (*SPORT*) nachspielen

injustice [ɪn'dʒʌstɪs] *n* Ungerechtigkeit *f*

ink [ɪŋk] *n* Tinte *f*

inkling ['ɪŋklɪŋ] *n* (dunkle) Ahnung *f*

inlaid ['ɪnleɪd] *adj* eingelegt, Einlege-

inland [*adj* 'ɪnlənd, *adv* ɪn'lænd] *adj* Binnen-; (*domestic*) Inlands- ♦ *adv* landeinwärts; **~ revenue** (*BRIT*) *n* Fiskus *m*

in-laws ['ɪnlɔːz] *npl* (*parents-in-law*) Schwiegereltern *pl*; (*others*) angeheiratete Verwandte *pl*

inlet ['ɪnlet] *n* Einlass *m*; (*bay*) kleine Bucht *f*

inmate ['ɪnmeɪt] *n* Insasse *m*

inn [ɪn] *n* Gasthaus *nt*, Wirtshaus *nt*

innate [ɪ'neɪt] *adj* angeboren

inner ['ɪnər] *adj* inner, Innen-; (*fig*) verborgen; **~ city** *n* Innenstadt *f*; **~ tube** *n* (*of tyre*) Schlauch *m*

innings ['ɪnɪŋz] *n* (*CRICKET*) Innenrunde *f*

innocence ['ɪnəsns] *n* Unschuld *f*; (*ignorance*) Unkenntnis *f*

innocent ['ɪnəsnt] *adj* unschuldig

innocuous [ɪ'nɔkjuəs] *adj* harmlos

innovation [ɪnəu'veɪʃən] *n* Neuerung *f*

innuendo [ɪnjuː'endəu] *n* (versteckte) Anspielung *f*

innumerable [ɪ'njuːmrəbl] *adj* unzählig

inoculation [ɪnɔkjuː'leɪʃən] *n* Impfung *f*

inopportune [ɪn'ɔpətjuːn] *adj* (*remark*) unangebracht; (*visit*) ungelegen

inordinately [ɪ'nɔːdɪnətlɪ] *adv* unmäßig

inpatient ['ɪnpeɪʃənt] *n* stationäre(r) Patient *m*/stationäre Patientin *f*

input ['ɪnput] *n* (*COMPUT*) Eingabe *f*; (*power ~*) Energiezufuhr *f*; (*of energy, work*) Aufwand *m*

inquest ['ɪnkwest] *n* gerichtliche Untersuchung *f*

inquire [ɪn'kwaɪər] *vi* sich erkundigen ♦ *vt* (*price*) sich erkundigen nach; **~ into** *vt* untersuchen; **inquiry** [ɪn'kwaɪərɪ] *n* (*question*) Erkundigung *f*; (*investigation*) Untersuchung *f*; **inquiries** Auskunft *f*; **inquiry office** (*BRIT*) *n* Auskunft(sbüro *nt* f)

inquisitive [ɪn'kwɪzɪtɪv] *adj* neugierig

ins. *abbr* = **inches**

insane [ɪn'seɪn] *adj* wahnsinnig; (*MED*) geisteskrank; **insanity** [ɪn'sænɪtɪ] *n* Wahnsinn *m*

insatiable [ɪn'seɪʃəbl] *adj* unersättlich

inscribe [ɪn'skraɪb] *vt* eingravieren; **inscription** [ɪn'skrɪpʃən] *n* (*on stone*) Inschrift *f*; (*in book*) Widmung *f*

insect- ['ɪnsekt] *n* Insekt *nt*; **~icide** [ɪn'sektɪsaɪd] *n* Insektenvertilgungsmittel *nt*; **~ repellent** *n* Insektenbekämpfungsmittel *nt*

insecure [ɪnsɪ'kjuər] *adj* (*person*) unsicher;

(*thing*) nicht fest *or* sicher; **insecurity** [ɪnsɪ'kjʊərɪtɪ] *n* Unsicherheit *f*

insemination [ɪnsɛmɪ'neɪʃən] *n*: **artificial ~** künstliche Befruchtung *f*

insensible [ɪn'sɛnsɪbl] *adj* (*unconscious*) bewusstlos

insensitive [ɪn'sɛnsɪtɪv] *adj* (*to pain*) unempfindlich; (*unfeeling*) gefühllos

inseparable [ɪn'sɛprəbl] *adj* (*people*) unzertrennlich; (*word*) untrennbar

insert [*vb* ɪn'sɜːt, *n* 'ɪnsɜːt] *vt* einfügen; (*coin*) einwerfen; (*stick into*) hineinstecken; (*advertisement*) aufgeben ♦ *n* (*in book*) Einlage *f*; (*in magazine*) Beilage *f*; **~ion** [ɪn'sɜːʃən] *n* Einfügung *f*; (*PRESS*) Inserat *nt*

in-service ['ɪn'sɜːvɪs] *adj* (*training*) berufsbegleitend

inshore ['ɪn'ʃɔː] *adj* Küsten- ♦ *adv* an der Küste

inside ['ɪn'saɪd] *n* Innenseite *f*, Innere(s) *nt* ♦ *adj* innere(r, s), Innen- ♦ *adv* (*place*) innen; (*direction*) nach innen, hinein ♦ *prep* (*place*) in +*dat*; (*direction*) in +*acc* ... hinein; (*time*) innerhalb +*gen*; **~s** *npl* (*inf*) Eingeweide *nt*; **~ 10 minutes** unter 10 Minuten; **~ information** *n* interne Informationen *pl*; **~ lane** *n* (*AUT: in Britain*) linke Spur; **~ out** *adv* linksherum; (*know*) in- und auswendig

insider dealing, insider trading [ɪn'saɪdə-] *n* (*STOCK EXCHANGE*) Insiderhandel *m*

insidious [ɪn'sɪdɪəs] *adj* heimtückisch

insight ['ɪnsaɪt] *n* Einsicht *f*; **~ into** Einblick *m* in +*acc*

insignificant [ɪnsɪg'nɪfɪknt] *adj* unbedeutend

insincere [ɪnsɪn'sɪə] *adj* unaufrichtig

insinuate [ɪn'sɪnjueɪt] *vt* (*hint*) andeuten

insipid [ɪn'sɪpɪd] *adj* fad(e)

insist [ɪn'sɪst] *vi*: **to ~ (on)** bestehen (auf +*acc*); **~ence** *n* Bestehen *nt*; **~ent** *adj* hartnäckig; (*urgent*) dringend

insole ['ɪnsəʊl] *n* Einlegesohle *f*

insolence ['ɪnsələns] *n* Frechheit *f*

insolent ['ɪnsələnt] *adj* frech

insoluble [ɪn'sɔljʊbl] *adj* unlösbar; (*CHEM*) unlöslich

insolvent [ɪn'sɔlvənt] *adj* zahlungsunfähig

insomnia [ɪn'sɔmnɪə] *n* Schlaflosigkeit *f*

inspect [ɪn'spɛkt] *vt* prüfen; (*officially*) inspizieren; **~ion** [ɪn'spɛkʃən] *n* Inspektion *f*; **~or** *n* (*official*) Inspektor *m*; (*police*) Polizeikommissar *m*; (*BRIT: on buses, trains*) Kontrolleur *m*

inspiration [ɪnspə'reɪʃən] *n* Inspiration *f*

inspire [ɪn'spaɪə] *vt* (*person*) inspirieren; **to ~ sth in sb** (*respect*) jdm etw einflößen; (*hope*) etw in jdm wecken

instability [ɪnstə'bɪlɪtɪ] *n* Unbeständigkeit *f*, Labilität *f*

install [ɪn'stɔːl] *vt* (*put in*) installieren; (*telephone*) anschließen; (*establish*) einsetzen; **~ation** [ɪnstə'leɪʃən] *n* (*of person*) (Amts)einsetzung *f*; (*of machinery*) Installierung *f*; (*machines etc*) Anlage *f*

instalment [ɪn'stɔːlmənt] (*US* **installment**) *n* Rate *f*; (*of story*) Fortsetzung *f*; **to pay in ~s** in Raten zahlen

instance ['ɪnstəns] *n* Fall *m*; (*example*) Beispiel *nt*; **for ~** zum Beispiel; **in the first ~** zunächst

instant ['ɪnstənt] *n* Augenblick *m* ♦ *adj* augenblicklich, sofortig; **~aneous** [ɪnstən'teɪnɪəs] *adj* unmittelbar; **~ coffee** *n* Pulverkaffee *m*; **~ly** *adv* sofort

instead [ɪn'stɛd] *adv* stattdessen; **~ of** *prep* anstatt +*gen*

instep ['ɪnstɛp] *n* Spann *m*; (*of shoe*) Blatt *nt*

instil [ɪn'stɪl] *vt* (*fig*): **to ~ sth in sb** jdm etw beibringen

instinct ['ɪnstɪŋkt] *n* Instinkt *m*; **~ive** [ɪn'stɪŋktɪv] *adj* instinktiv

institute ['ɪnstɪtjuːt] *n* Institut *nt* ♦ *vt* einführen; (*search*) einleiten

institution [ɪnstɪ'tjuːʃən] *n* Institution *f*; (*home*) Anstalt *f*

instruct [ɪn'strʌkt] *vt* anweisen; (*officially*) instruieren; **~ion** [ɪn'strʌkʃən] *n* Unterricht *m*; **~ions** *npl* (*orders*) Anweisungen *pl*; (*for use*) Gebrauchsanweisung *f*; **~or** *n* Lehrer *m*

instrument ['ɪnstrumənt] *n* Instrument *nt*; **~al** [ɪnstru'mɛntl] *adj* (*MUS*) Instrumental-;

(*helpful*): **~al (in)** behilflich (bei); **~ panel** *n* Armaturenbrett *nt*

insubordinate [ɪnsə'bɔ:dənɪt] *adj* aufsässig, widersetzlich

insufferable [ɪn'sʌfrəbl] *adj* unerträglich

insufficient [ɪnsə'fɪʃənt] *adj* ungenügend

insular ['ɪnsjulə²] *adj* (*fig*) engstirnig

insulate ['ɪnsjuleɪt] *vt* (*ELEC*) isolieren; (*fig*): **to ~ (from)** abschirmen (vor +*dat*); **insulating tape** *n* Isolierband *nt*; **insulation** [ɪnsju'leɪʃən] *n* Isolierung *f*

insulin ['ɪnsjulɪn] *n* Insulin *nt*

insult [*n* 'ɪnsʌlt, *vb* ɪn'sʌlt] *n* Beleidigung *f* ♦ *vt* beleidigen

insurance [ɪn'ʃuərəns] *n* Versicherung *f*; **fire/life** ~ Feuer-/Lebensversicherung; **~ agent** *n* Versicherungsvertreter *m*; **~ policy** *n* Versicherungspolice *f*

insure [ɪn'ʃuə²] *vt* versichern

intact [ɪn'tækt] *adj* unversehrt

intake ['ɪnteɪk] *n* (*place*) Einlassöffnung *f*; (*act*) Aufnahme *f*; (*BRIT: SCH*): **an ~ of 200 a year** ein Neuzugang von 200 im Jahr

intangible [ɪn'tændʒɪbl] *adj* nicht greifbar

integral ['ɪntɪgrəl] *adj* (*essential*) wesentlich; (*complete*) vollständig; (*MATH*) Integral-

integrate ['ɪntɪgreɪt] *vt* integrieren ♦ *vi* sich integrieren

integrity [ɪn'tɛgrɪtɪ] *n* (*honesty*) Redlichkeit *f*, Integrität *f*

intellect ['ɪntəlɛkt] *n* Intellekt *m*; **~ual** [ɪntə'lɛktjuəl] *adj* geistig, intellektuell ♦ *n* Intellektuelle(r) *mf*

intelligence [ɪn'tɛlɪdʒəns] *n* (*understanding*) Intelligenz *f*; (*news*) Information *f*; (*MIL*) Geheimdienst *m*; **~ service** *n* Nachrichtendienst *m*, Geheimdienst *m*

intelligent [ɪn'tɛlɪdʒənt] *adj* intelligent; **~ly** *adv* klug; (*write, speak*) verständlich

intelligentsia [ɪntɛlɪ'dʒɛntsɪə] *n* Intelligenz *f*

intelligible [ɪn'tɛlɪdʒɪbl] *adj* verständlich

intend [ɪn'tɛnd] *vt* beabsichtigen; **that was ~ed for you** das war für dich gedacht

intense [ɪn'tɛns] *adj* stark, intensiv; (*person*) ernsthaft; **~ly** *adv* äußerst; (*study*) intensiv

intensify [ɪn'tɛnsɪfaɪ] *vt* verstärken, intensivieren

intensity [ɪn'tɛnsɪtɪ] *n* Intensität *f*

intensive [ɪn'tɛnsɪv] *adj* intensiv; **~ care unit** *n* Intensivstation *f*

intent [ɪn'tɛnt] *n* Absicht *f* ♦ *adj*: **to be ~ on doing sth** fest entschlossen sein, etw zu tun; **to all ~s and purposes** praktisch

intention [ɪn'tɛnʃən] *n* Absicht *f*; **~al** *adj* absichtlich

intently [ɪn'tɛntlɪ] *adv* konzentriert

interact [ɪntər'ækt] *vi* aufeinander einwirken; **~ion** [ɪntər'ækʃən] *n* Wechselwirkung *f*; **~ive** *adj* (*COMPUT*) interaktiv

intercept [ɪntə'sɛpt] *vt* abfangen

interchange [*n* 'ɪntətʃeɪndʒ, *vb* ɪntə'tʃeɪndʒ] *n* (*exchange*) Austausch *m*; (*on roads*) Verkehrskreuz *n* ♦ *vt* austauschen; **~able** [ɪntə'tʃeɪndʒəbl] *adj* austauschbar

intercom ['ɪntəkɔm] *n* (Gegen)sprechanlage *f*

intercourse ['ɪntəkɔ:s] *n* (*exchange*) Beziehungen *pl*; (*sexual*) Geschlechtsverkehr *m*

interest ['ɪntrɪst] *n* Interesse *nt*; (*FIN*) Zinsen *pl*; (*COMM: share*) Anteil *m*; (*group*) Interessengruppe *f* ♦ *vt* interessieren; **~ed** *adj* (*having claims*) beteiligt; (*attentive*) interessiert; **to be ~ed in** sich interessieren für; **~ing** *adj* interessant; **~ rate** *n* Zinssatz *m*

interface ['ɪntəfeɪs] *n* (*COMPUT*) Schnittstelle *f*, Interface *nt*

interfere [ɪntə'fɪə²] *vi*: **to ~ (with)** (*meddle*) sich einmischen (in +*acc*); (*disrupt*) stören +*acc*; **~nce** [ɪntə'fɪərəns] *n* Einmischung *f*; (*TV*) Störung *f*

interim ['ɪntərɪm] *n*: **in the ~** inzwischen

interior [ɪn'tɪərɪə²] *n* Innere(s) *nt* ♦ *adj* innere(r, s), Innen-; **~ designer** *n* Innenarchitekt(in) *m(f)*

interjection [ɪntə'dʒɛkʃən] *n* Ausruf *m*

interlock [ɪntə'lɔk] *vi* ineinander greifen

interlude ['ɪntəlu:d] *n* Pause *f*

intermediary [ɪntə'mi:dɪərɪ] *n* Vermittler *m*

intermediate [ɪntə'mi:dɪət] *adj* Zwischen-, Mittel-

interminable [ɪn'tə:mɪnəbl] *adj* endlos

intermission [ɪntə'mɪʃən] *n* Pause *f*

intermittent [ɪntə'mɪtnt] *adj* periodisch, stoßweise

intern [*vb* ɪn'tɜːn, *n* 'ɪntɜːn] *vt* internieren ♦ *n* (*US*) Assistenzarzt *m*/-ärztin *f*

internal [ɪn'tɜːnl] *adj* (*inside*) innere(r, s); (*domestic*) Inlands-; **~ly** *adv* innen; (*MED*) innerlich; **"not to be taken ~ly"** „nur zur äußerlichen Anwendung"; **Internal Revenue Service** (*US*) *n* Finanzamt *nt*

international [ɪntə'næʃənl] *adj* international ♦ *n* (*SPORT*) Nationalspieler(in) *m(f)*; (: *match*) internationale(s) Spiel *nt*

Internet ['ɪntənet] *n*: **the ~** das Internet; **~ café** *n* Internet-Café *nt*

interplay ['ɪntəpleɪ] *n* Wechselspiel *nt*

interpret [ɪn'tɜːprɪt] *vt* (*explain*) auslegen, interpretieren; (*translate*) dolmetschen; **~er** *n* Dolmetscher(in) *m(f)*

interrelated [ɪntərɪ'leɪtɪd] *adj* untereinander zusammenhängend

interrogate [ɪn'terəʊgeɪt] *vt* verhören; **interrogation** [ɪnterəʊ'geɪʃən] *n* Verhör *nt*

interrupt [ɪntə'rʌpt] *vt* unterbrechen; **~ion** [ɪntə'rʌpʃən] *n* Unterbrechung *f*

intersect [ɪntə'sekt] *vt* (durch)schneiden ♦ *vi* sich schneiden; **~ion** [ɪntə'sekʃən] *n* (*of roads*) Kreuzung *f*; (*of lines*) Schnittpunkt *m*

intersperse [ɪntə'spɜːs] *vt*: **to ~ sth with sth** etw mit etw durchsetzen

intertwine [ɪntə'twaɪn] *vt* verflechten ♦ *vi* sich verflechten

interval ['ɪntəvl] *n* Abstand *m*; (*BRIT: THEAT, SPORT*) Pause *f*; **at ~s** in Abständen

intervene [ɪntə'viːn] *vi* dazwischenliegen; (*act*): **to ~ (in)** einschreiten (gegen); **intervention** [ɪntə'venʃən] *n* Eingreifen *nt*, Intervention *f*

interview ['ɪntəvjuː] *n* (*PRESS etc*) Interview *nt*; (*for job*) Vorstellungsgespräch *nt* ♦ *vt* interviewen; **~er** *n* Interviewer *m*

intestine [ɪn'testɪn] *n*: **large/small ~** Dick-/Dünndarm *m*

intimacy ['ɪntɪməsɪ] *n* Intimität *f*

intimate [*adj* 'ɪntɪmət, *vb* 'ɪntɪmeɪt] *adj* (*inmost*) innerste(r, s); (*knowledge*) eingehend; (*familiar*) vertraut; (*friends*) eng ♦ *vt* andeuten

intimidate [ɪn'tɪmɪdeɪt] *vt* einschüchtern

into ['ɪntʊ] *prep* (*motion*) in +*acc* ... hinein; **5 ~ 25** 25 durch 5

intolerable [ɪn'tɔlərəbl] *adj* unerträglich

intolerant [ɪn'tɔlərnt] *adj*: **~ of** unduldsam gegen(über)

intoxicate [ɪn'tɔksɪkeɪt] *vt* berauschen; **~d** *adj* betrunken; **intoxication** [ɪntɔksɪ'keɪʃən] *n* Rausch *m*

intractable [ɪn'træktəbl] *adj* schwer zu handhaben; (*problem*) schwer lösbar

intransitive [ɪn'trænsɪtɪv] *adj* intransitiv

intravenous [ɪntrə'viːnəs] *adj* intravenös

in-tray ['ɪntreɪ] *n* Eingangskorb *m*

intrepid [ɪn'trepɪd] *adj* unerschrocken

intricate ['ɪntrɪkət] *adj* kompliziert

intrigue [ɪn'triːg] *n* Intrige *f* ♦ *vt* faszinieren ♦ *vi* intrigieren

intrinsic [ɪn'trɪnsɪk] *adj* innere(r, s); (*difference*) wesentlich

introduce [ɪntrə'djuːs] *vt* (*person*) vorstellen; (*sth new*) einführen; (*subject*) anschneiden; **to ~ sb to sb** jdm jdn vorstellen; **to ~ sb to sth** jdn in etw *acc* einführen; **introduction** [ɪntrə'dʌkʃən] *n* Einführung *f*; (*to book*) Einleitung *f*; **introductory** [ɪntrə'dʌktərɪ] *adj* Einführungs-, Vor-

introspective [ɪntrəʊ'spektɪv] *adj* nach innen gekehrt

introvert ['ɪntrəʊvɜːt] *n* Introvertierte(r) *mf* ♦ *adj* introvertiert

intrude [ɪn'truːd] *vi*: **to ~ (on sb/sth)** (jdn/etw) stören; **~r** *n* Eindringling *m*

intrusion [ɪn'truːʒən] *n* Störung *f*

intrusive [ɪn'truːsɪv] *adj* aufdringlich

intuition [ɪntjuː'ɪʃən] *n* Intuition *f*

inundate ['ɪnʌndeɪt] *vt* (*also fig*) überschwemmen

invade [ɪn'veɪd] *vt* einfallen in +*acc*; **~r** *n* Eindringling *m*

invalid¹ ['ɪnvəlɪd] *n* (*disabled*) Invalide *m* ♦ *adj* (*ill*) krank; (*disabled*) invalide

invalid² [ɪn'vælɪd] *adj* (*not valid*) ungültig

invaluable [ɪn'væljuəbl] *adj* unschätzbar

invariable [ɪn'veərɪəbl] *adj* unveränderlich; **invariably** *adv* ausnahmslos

invent [ɪn'vent] *vt* erfinden; **~ion** [ɪn'venʃən]

n Erfindung *f*; **~ive** *adj* erfinderisch; **~or** *n* Erfinder *m*

inventory ['ɪnvəntrɪ] *n* Inventar *nt*

inverse [ɪn'vɜːs] *n* Umkehrung *f* ♦ *adj* umgekehrt

invert [ɪn'vɜːt] *vt* umdrehen; **~ed commas** (*BRIT*) *npl* Anführungsstriche *pl*

invest [ɪn'vest] *vt* investieren

investigate [ɪn'vestɪgeɪt] *vt* untersuchen; **investigation** [ɪnvestɪ'geɪʃən] *n* Untersuchung *f*; **investigator** [ɪn'vestɪgeɪtər] *n* Untersuchungsbeamte(r) *m*

investiture [ɪn'vestɪtʃər] *n* Amtseinsetzung *f*

investment [ɪn'vestmənt] *n* Investition *f*

investor [ɪn'vestər] *n* (Geld)anleger *m*

invigilate [ɪn'vɪdʒɪleɪt] *vi* (*in exam*) Aufsicht führen ♦ *vt* Aufsicht führen bei; **invigilator** *n* Aufsicht *f*

invigorating [ɪn'vɪgəreɪtɪŋ] *adj* stärkend

invincible [ɪn'vɪnsɪbl] *adj* unbesiegbar

invisible [ɪn'vɪzɪbl] *adj* unsichtbar

invitation [ɪnvɪ'teɪʃən] *n* Einladung *f*

invite [ɪn'vaɪt] *vt* einladen

invoice ['ɪnvɔɪs] *n* Rechnung *f* ♦ *vt* (*goods*): **to ~ sb for sth** jdm etw *acc* in Rechnung stellen

invoke [ɪn'vəʊk] *vt* anrufen

involuntary [ɪn'vɒləntrɪ] *adj* unabsichtlich

involve [ɪn'vɒlv] *vt* (*entangle*) verwickeln; (*entail*) mit sich bringen; **~d** *adj* verwickelt; **~ment** *n* Verwicklung *f*

inward ['ɪnwəd] *adj* innere(r, s); (*curve*) Innen- ♦ *adv* nach innen; **~ly** *adv* im Innern; **~s** *adv* nach innen

I/O *abbr* (*COMPUT*) (= *input/output*) I/O

iodine ['aɪəʊdiːn] *n* Jod *nt*

ioniser ['aɪənaɪzər] *n* Ionisator *m*

iota [aɪ'əʊtə] *n* (*fig*) bisschen *nt*

IOU *n abbr* (= *I owe you*) Schuldschein *m*

IQ *n abbr* (= *intelligence quotient*) IQ *m*

IRA *n abbr* (= *Irish Republican Army*) IRA *f*

Iran [ɪ'rɑːn] *n* Iran *m*; **~ian** [ɪ'reɪnɪən] *adj* iranisch ♦ *n* Iraner(in) *m(f)*; (*LING*) Iranisch *nt*

Iraq [ɪ'rɑːk] *n* Irak *m*; **~i** *adj* irakisch ♦ *n* Iraker(in) *m(f)*

irate [aɪ'reɪt] *adj* zornig

Ireland ['aɪələnd] *n* Irland *nt*

iris ['aɪrɪs] (*pl* **~es**) *n* Iris *f*

Irish ['aɪrɪʃ] *adj* irisch ♦ *npl*: **the ~** die Iren *pl*, die Irländer *pl*; **~man** (*irreg*) *n* Ire *m*, Irländer *m*; **~ Sea** *n*: **the ~ Sea** die Irische See *f*; **~woman** (*irreg*) *n* Irin *f*, Irländerin *f*

irksome ['ɜːksəm] *adj* lästig

iron ['aɪən] *n* Eisen *nt*; (*for ~ing*) Bügeleisen *nt* ♦ *adj* eisern ♦ *vt* bügeln; **~ out** *vt* (*also fig*) ausbügeln; **Iron Curtain** *n* (*HIST*) Eiserne(r) Vorhang *m*

ironic(al) [aɪ'rɒnɪk(l)] *adj* ironisch; (*coincidence etc*) witzig

iron: **~ing** *n* Bügeln *nt*; (*laundry*) Bügelwäsche *f*; **~ing board** *n* Bügelbrett *nt*; **~monger's (shop)** *n* Eisen- und Haushaltswarenhandlung *f*

irony ['aɪrənɪ] *n* Ironie *f*

irrational [ɪ'ræʃənl] *adj* irrational

irreconcilable [ɪrekən'saɪləbl] *adj* unvereinbar

irrefutable [ɪrɪ'fjuːtəbl] *adj* unwiderlegbar

irregular [ɪ'regjələr] *adj* unregelmäßig; (*shape*) ungleich(mäßig); (*fig*) unüblich; (: *behaviour*) ungehörig

irrelevant [ɪ'reləvənt] *adj* belanglos, irrelevant

irreparable [ɪ'reprəbl] *adj* nicht wieder gutzumachen

irreplaceable [ɪrɪ'pleɪsəbl] *adj* unersetzlich

irresistible [ɪrɪ'zɪstɪbl] *adj* unwiderstehlich

irrespective [ɪrɪ'spektɪv]: **~ of** *prep* ungeachtet +*gen*

irresponsible [ɪrɪ'spɒnsɪbl] *adj* verantwortungslos

irreverent [ɪ'revərnt] *adj* respektlos

irrevocable [ɪ'revəkəbl] *adj* unwiderrufbar

irrigate ['ɪrɪgeɪt] *vt* bewässern

irritable ['ɪrɪtəbl] *adj* reizbar

irritate ['ɪrɪteɪt] *vt* irritieren, reizen (*also MED*); **irritating** *adj* ärgerlich, irritierend; **he is irritating** er kann einem auf die Nerven gehen; **irritation** [ɪrɪ'teɪʃən] *n* (*anger*) Ärger *m*; (*MED*) Reizung *f*

IRS *n abbr* = **Internal Revenue Service**

is [ɪz] *vb see* **be**

Islam ['ɪzlɑːm] *n* Islam *m*; **~ic** [ɪz'læmɪk] *adj*

islamisch

island ['aɪlənd] n Insel f; **~er** n Inselbewohner(in) m(f)

isle [aɪl] n (kleine) Insel f

isn't ['ɪznt] = **is not**

isolate ['aɪsəleɪt] vt isolieren; **~d** adj isoliert; (case) Einzel-; **isolation** [aɪsə'leɪʃən] n Isolierung f

Israel ['ɪzreɪl] n Israel nt; **~i** [ɪz'reɪlɪ] adj israelisch ♦ n Israeli mf

issue ['ɪʃjuː] n (matter) Frage f; (outcome) Ausgang m; (of newspaper, shares) Ausgabe f; (offspring) Nachkommenschaft f ♦ vt ausgeben; (warrant) erlassen; (documents) ausstellen; (orders) erteilen; (books) herausgeben; (verdict) aussprechen; **to be at ~** zur Debatte stehen; **to take ~ with sb over sth** jdm in etw dat widersprechen

---

KEYWORD

it [ɪt] pron **1** (specific: subject) er/sie/es; (: direct object) ihn/sie/es; (: indirect object) ihm/ihr/ihm; **about/from/in/of it** darüber/davon/darin/davon

2 (impers) es; **it's raining** es regnet; **it's Friday tomorrow** morgen ist Freitag; **who is it? – it's me** wer ist da? – ich (bins)

Italian [ɪ'tæljən] adj italienisch ♦ n Italiener(in) m(f); (LING) Italienisch nt

italic [ɪ'tælɪk] adj kursiv; **~s** npl Kursivschrift f

Italy ['ɪtəlɪ] n Italien nt

itch [ɪtʃ] n Juckreiz m; (fig) Lust f ♦ vi jucken; **to be ~ing to do sth** darauf brennen, etw zu tun; **~y** adj juckend

it'd ['ɪtd] = **it would**; **it had**

item ['aɪtəm] n Gegenstand m; (on list) Posten m; (in programme) Nummer f; (in agenda) (Programm)punkt m; (in newspaper) (Zeitungs)notiz f; **~ize** vt verzeichnen

itinerant [ɪ'tɪnərənt] adj (person) umherreisend

itinerary [aɪ'tɪnərərɪ] n Reiseroute f

it'll ['ɪtl] = **it will**; **it shall**

its [ɪts] adj (masculine, neuter) sein; (feminine) ihr

it's [ɪts] = **it is**; **it has**

itself [ɪt'self] pron sich (selbst); (emphatic) selbst

ITV (BRIT) n abbr = **Independent Television**

I.U.D. n abbr (= intra-uterine device) Pessar nt

I've [aɪv] = **I have**

ivory ['aɪvərɪ] n Elfenbein nt

ivy ['aɪvɪ] n Efeu nt

J, j

jab [dʒæb] vt (hinein)stechen ♦ n Stich m, Stoß m; (inf) Spritze f

jack [dʒæk] n (AUT) (Wagen)heber m; (CARDS) Bube m; **~ up** vt aufbocken

jackal ['dʒækl] n (ZOOL) Schakal m

jackdaw ['dʒækdɔː] n Dohle f

jacket ['dʒækɪt] n Jacke f; (of book) Schutzumschlag m; (TECH) Ummantelung f; **~ potatoes** npl in der Schale gebackene Kartoffeln pl

jackknife ['dʒæknaɪf] vi (truck) sich zusammenschieben

jack plug n (ELEC) Buchsenstecker m

jackpot ['dʒækpɒt] n Haupttreffer m

jaded ['dʒeɪdɪd] adj ermattet

jagged ['dʒægɪd] adj zackig

jail [dʒeɪl] n Gefängnis nt ♦ vt einsperren; **~er** n Gefängniswärter m

jam [dʒæm] n Marmelade f; (also: **traffic ~**) (Verkehrs)stau m; (inf: trouble) Klemme f ♦ vt (wedge) einklemmen; (cram) hineinzwängen; (obstruct) blockieren ♦ vi sich verklemmen; **to ~ sth into sth** etw in etw acc hineinstopfen

Jamaica [dʒə'meɪkə] n Jamaika nt

jam jar n Marmeladenglas nt

jammed [dʒæmd] adj: **it's ~** es klemmt

jam-packed [dʒæm'pækt] adj überfüllt, proppenvoll

jangle ['dʒæŋgl] vt, vi klimpern

janitor ['dʒænɪtə] n Hausmeister m

January ['dʒænjuərɪ] n Januar m

Japan [dʒə'pæn] n Japan nt; **~ese** [dʒæpə'niːz] adj japanisch ♦ n inv Japaner(in) m(f); (LING) Japanisch nt

jar [dʒɑː] n Glas nt ♦ vi kreischen; (colours

etc) nicht harmonieren

jargon ['dʒɑːgən] n Fachsprache f, Jargon m

jaundice ['dʒɔːndɪs] n Gelbsucht f; **~d** adj (fig) missgünstig

jaunt [dʒɔːnt] n Spritztour f

javelin ['dʒævlɪn] n Speer m

jaw [dʒɔː] n Kiefer m

jay [dʒeɪ] n (ZOOL) Eichelhäher m

jaywalker ['dʒeɪwɔːkəʳ] n unvorsichtige(r) Fußgänger m

jazz [dʒæz] n Jazz m; **~ up** vt (MUS) verjazzen; (enliven) aufpolieren

jealous ['dʒeləs] adj (envious) missgünstig; (husband) eifersüchtig; **~y** n Missgunst f; Eifersucht f

jeans [dʒiːnz] npl Jeans pl

Jeep [dʒiːp] ® n Jeep m ®

jeer [dʒɪəʳ] vi: **to ~ (at sb)** (über jdn) höhnisch lachen, (jdn) verspotten

Jehovah's Witness [dʒɪ'həʊvəz-] n Zeuge m/Zeugin f Jehovas

jelly ['dʒelɪ] n Gelee nt; (dessert) Grütze f; **~fish** n Qualle f

jeopardize ['dʒepədaɪz] vt gefährden

jeopardy ['dʒepədɪ] n: **to be in jeopardy** in Gefahr sein

jerk [dʒɜːk] n Ruck m; (inf: idiot) Trottel m ♦ vt ruckartig bewegen ♦ vi sich ruckartig bewegen

jerky ['dʒɜːkɪ] adj (movement) ruckartig; (ride) rüttelnd

jersey ['dʒɜːzɪ] n Pullover m

jest [dʒest] n Scherz m ♦ vi spaßen; **in ~** im Spaß

Jesus ['dʒiːzəs] n Jesus m

jet [dʒet] n (stream: of water etc) Strahl m; (spout) Düse f; (AVIAT) Düsenflugzeug nt; **~-black** adj rabenschwarz; **~ engine** n Düsenmotor m; **~ lag** n Jetlag m

jettison ['dʒetɪsn] vt über Bord werfen

jetty ['dʒetɪ] n Landesteg m, Mole f

Jew [dʒuː] n Jude m

jewel ['dʒuːəl] n (also fig) Juwel nt; **~ler** (US **jeweler**) n Juwelier m; **~ler's (shop)** n Juwelier m; **~lery** (US **jewelry**) n Schmuck m

Jewess ['dʒuːɪs] n Jüdin f

Jewish ['dʒuːɪʃ] adj jüdisch

jibe [dʒaɪb] n spöttische Bemerkung f

jiffy ['dʒɪfɪ] (inf) n: **in a ~** sofort

jigsaw ['dʒɪgsɔː] n (also: ~ **puzzle**) Puzzle(spiel) nt

jilt [dʒɪlt] vt den Laufpass geben +dat

jingle ['dʒɪŋgl] n (advertisement) Werbesong m ♦ vi klimpern; (bells) bimmeln ♦ vt klimpern mit; bimmeln lassen

jinx [dʒɪŋks] n: **there's a ~ on it** es ist verhext

jitters ['dʒɪtəz] (inf) npl: **to get the ~** einen Bammel kriegen

job [dʒɒb] n (piece of work) Arbeit f; (position) Stellung f; (duty) Aufgabe f; (difficulty) Mühe f; **it's a good ~ he ...** es ist ein Glück, dass er ...; **just the ~** genau das Richtige; **J~centre** (BRIT) n Arbeitsamt nt; **~less** adj arbeitslos

jockey ['dʒɒkɪ] n Jockei m, Jockey m ♦ vi: **to ~ for position** sich in eine gute Position drängeln

jocular ['dʒɒkjʊləʳ] adj scherzhaft

jog [dʒɒg] vt (an)stoßen ♦ vi (run) joggen; **to ~ along** vor sich acc hinwursteln; (work) seinen Gang gehen; **~ging** n Jogging nt

join [dʒɔɪn] vt (club) beitreten +dat; (person) sich anschließen +dat; (fasten): **to ~ (sth to sth)** (etw mit etw) verbinden ♦ vi (unite) sich vereinigen ♦ n Verbindungsstelle f, Naht f; **~ in** vt, vi: **to ~ in (sth)** (bei etw) mitmachen; **~ up** vi (MIL) zur Armee gehen

joiner ['dʒɔɪnəʳ] n Schreiner m; **~y** n Schreinerei f

joint [dʒɔɪnt] n (TECH) Fuge f; (of bones) Gelenk nt; (of meat) Braten m; (inf: place) Lokal nt ♦ adj gemeinsam; **~ account** n (with bank etc) gemeinsame(s) Konto nt; **~ly** adv gemeinsam

joke [dʒəʊk] n Witz m ♦ vi Witze machen; **to play a ~ on sb** jdm einen Streich spielen

joker [dʒəʊkəʳ] n Witzbold m; (CARDS) Joker m

jolly ['dʒɒlɪ] adj lustig ♦ adv (inf) ganz schön

jolt [dʒəʊlt] n (shock) Schock m; (jerk) Stoß m

♦ *vt* (*push*) stoßen; (*shake*) durchschütteln; (*fig*) aufrütteln ♦ *vi* holpern

Jordan ['dʒɔːdən] *n* Jordanien *nt*

jostle ['dʒɒsl] *vt* anrempeln

jot [dʒɒt] *n*: **not one** ~ kein Jota *nt*; ~ **down** *vt* notieren; ~**ter** (*BRIT*) *n* Notizblock *m*

journal ['dʒɜːnl] *n* (*diary*) Tagebuch *nt*; (*magazine*) Zeitschrift *f*; ~**ism** *n* Journalismus *m*; ~**ist** *n* Journalist(in) *m(f)*

journey ['dʒɜːnɪ] *n* Reise *f*

jovial ['dʒəʊvɪəl] *adj* jovial

joy [dʒɔɪ] *n* Freude *f*; ~**ful** *adj* freudig; ~**ous** *adj* freudig; ~ **ride** *n* Schwarzfahrt *f*; ~**rider** *n* Autodieb, der den Wagen nur für eine Spritztour stiehlt; ~**stick** *n* Steuerknüppel *m*; (*COMPUT*) Joystick *m*

J.P. *n abbr* = **Justice of the Peace**

Jr *abbr* = **junior**

jubilant ['dʒuːbɪlnt] *adj* triumphierend

jubilee ['dʒuːbɪliː] *n* Jubiläum *nt*

judge [dʒʌdʒ] *n* Richter *m*; (*fig*) Kenner *m* ♦ *vt* (*JUR*: *person*) die Verhandlung führen über +*acc*; (*case*) verhandeln; (*assess*) beurteilen; (*estimate*) einschätzen; ~**ment** *n* (*JUR*) Urteil *nt*; (*ECCL*) Gericht *nt*; (*ability*) Urteilsvermögen *nt*

judicial [dʒuː'dɪʃl] *adj* gerichtlich, Justiz-

judiciary [dʒuː'dɪʃɪərɪ] *n* Gerichtsbehörden *pl*; (*judges*) Richterstand *m*

judicious [dʒuː'dɪʃəs] *adj* weise

judo ['dʒuːdəʊ] *n* Judo *nt*

jug [dʒʌg] *n* Krug *m*

juggernaut ['dʒʌgənɔːt] (*BRIT*) *n* (*huge truck*) Schwertransporter *m*

juggle ['dʒʌgl] *vt*, *vi* jonglieren; ~**r** *n* Jongleur *m*

Jugoslav *etc* ['juːgəʊˈslɑːv] = **Yugoslav** *etc*

juice [dʒuːs] *n* Saft *m*; **juicy** ['dʒuːsɪ] *adj* (*also fig*) saftig

jukebox ['dʒuːkbɒks] *n* Musikautomat *m*

July [dʒuː'laɪ] *n* Juli *m*

jumble ['dʒʌmbl] *n* Durcheinander *nt* ♦ *vt* (*also*: ~ **up**) durcheinander werfen; (*facts*) durcheinander bringen

jumble sale (*BRIT*) *n* Basar *m*, Flohmarkt *m*

Jumble sale

ⓘ **Jumble sale** *ist ein Wohltätigkeitsbasar, meist in einer Aula oder einem Gemeindehaus abgehalten, bei dem alle möglichen Gebrauchtwaren (vor allem Kleidung, Spielzeug, Bücher, Geschirr und Möbel) verkauft werden. Der Erlös fließt entweder einer Wohltätigkeitsorganisation zu oder wird für örtliche Zwecke verwendet, z.B. die Pfadfinder, die Grundschule, Reparatur der Kirche usw.*

---

jumbo (jet) ['dʒʌmbəʊ-] *n* Jumbo(jet) *m*

jump [dʒʌmp] *vi* springen; (*nervously*) zusammenzucken ♦ *vt* überspringen ♦ *n* Sprung *m*; **to** ~ **the queue** (*BRIT*) sich vordrängeln

jumper ['dʒʌmpə*r*] *n* (*BRIT*: *pullover*) Pullover *m*; (*US*: *dress*) Trägerkleid *nt*

jump leads *BRIT*, **jumper cables** *US npl* Überbrückungskabel *nt*

jumpy ['dʒʌmpɪ] *adj* nervös

Jun. *abbr* = **junior**

junction ['dʒʌŋkʃən] *n* (*BRIT*: *of roads*) (Straßen)kreuzung *f*; (*RAIL*) Knotenpunkt *m*

juncture ['dʒʌŋktʃə*r*] *n*: **at this** ~ in diesem Augenblick

June [dʒuːn] *n* Juni *m*

jungle ['dʒʌŋgl] *n* Dschungel *m*

junior ['dʒuːnɪə*r*] *adj* (*younger*) jünger; (*after name*) junior; (*SPORT*) Junioren-; (*lower position*) untergeordnet; (*for young people*) Junioren- ♦ *n* Jüngere(r) *mf*; ~ **school** (*BRIT*) *n* Grundschule *f*

junk [dʒʌŋk] *n* (*rubbish*) Plunder *m*; (*ship*) Dschunke *f*; ~ **bond** *n* (*COMM*) niedrig eingestuftes Wertpapier mit hohen Ertragschancen bei erhöhtem Risiko; ~ **food** *n* Junk food *nt*; ~ **mail** *n* Reklame, die unangefordert in den Briefkasten gesteckt wird; ~ **shop** *n* Ramschladen *m*

Junr *abbr* = **junior**

jurisdiction [dʒʊərɪs'dɪkʃən] *n* Gerichtsbarkeit *f*; (*range of authority*) Zuständigkeit(sbereich *m*) *f*

juror ['dʒuərər] n Geschworene(r) mf; (in competition) Preisrichter m

jury ['dʒuərɪ] n (court) Geschworene pl; (panel) Jury f

just [dʒʌst] adj gerecht ♦ adv (recently, now) gerade, eben; (barely) gerade noch; (exactly) genau, gerade; (only) nur, bloß; (a small distance) gleich; (absolutely) einfach; ~ **as I arrived** gerade als ich ankam; ~ **as nice** genauso nett; ~ **as well** umso besser; ~ **now** soeben, gerade; ~ **try** versuch es mal; **she's ~ left** sie ist gerade or (so)eben gegangen; **he's ~ done it** er hat es gerade or (so)eben getan; ~ **before** gerade or kurz bevor; ~ **enough** gerade genug; **he ~ missed** er hat fast or beinahe getroffen

justice ['dʒʌstɪs] n (fairness) Gerechtigkeit f; **J~ of the Peace** n Friedensrichter m

justifiable [dʒʌstɪ'faɪəbl] adj berechtigt

justification [dʒʌstɪfɪ'keɪʃən] n Rechtfertigung f

justify ['dʒʌstɪfaɪ] vt rechtfertigen; (text) justieren

justly ['dʒʌstlɪ] adv (say) mit Recht; (condemn) gerecht

jut [dʒʌt] vi (also: ~ **out**) herausragen, vorstehen

juvenile ['dʒuːvənaɪl] adj (young) jugendlich; (for the young) Jugend- ♦ n Jugendliche(r) mf

juxtapose ['dʒʌkstəpəʊz] vt nebeneinander stellen

K, k

K [keɪ] abbr (= one thousand) Tsd.; (= kilobyte) K

kangaroo [kæŋɡə'ruː] n Känguru nt

karate [kə'rɑːtɪ] n Karate nt

kebab [kə'bæb] n Kebab m

keel [kiːl] n Kiel m; **on an even ~** (fig) im Lot

keen [kiːn] adj begeistert; (wind, blade, intelligence) scharf; (sight, hearing) gut; **to be ~ to do** or **on doing sth** etw unbedingt tun wollen; **to be ~ on sth/sb** scharf auf etw/jdn sein

keep [kiːp] (pt, pp **kept**) vt (retain) behalten; (have) haben; (animals, one's word) halten; (support) versorgen; (maintain in state) halten; (preserve) aufbewahren; (restrain) abhalten ♦ vi (continue in direction) sich halten; (food) sich halten; (remain: quiet etc) bleiben ♦ n Unterhalt m; (tower) Burgfried m; (inf): **for ~s** für immer; **to ~ sth to o.s.** etw für sich behalten; **it ~s happening** es passiert immer wieder; ~ **back** vt fern halten; (information) verschweigen; ~ **on** vi: ~ **on doing sth** etw immer weiter tun; ~ **out** vt nicht hereinlassen; "~ **out**" „Eintritt verboten!"; ~ **up** vi Schritt halten ♦ vt aufrechterhalten; (continue) weitermachen; **to ~ up with** Schritt halten mit; ~**er** n Wärter(in) m(f); (goalkeeper) Torhüter(in) m(f); ~**-fit** n Keep-fit nt; ~**ing** n (care) Obhut f; **in ~ing with** in Übereinstimmung mit; ~**sake** n Andenken nt

keg [kɛg] n Fass nt

kennel ['kɛnl] n Hundehütte f; ~**s** npl: **to put a dog in ~s** (for boarding) einen Hund in Pflege geben

Kenya ['kɛnjə] n Kenia nt; ~**n** adj kenianisch ♦ n Kenianer(in) m(f)

kept [kɛpt] pt, pp of **keep**

kerb [kəːb] (BRIT) n Bordstein m

kernel ['kəːnl] n Kern m

kerosene ['kɛrəsiːn] n Kerosin nt

kettle ['kɛtl] n Kessel m; ~**drum** n Pauke f

key [kiː] n Schlüssel m; (of piano, typewriter) Taste f; (MUS) Tonart f ♦ vt (also: ~ **in**) eingeben; ~**board** n Tastatur f; ~**ed up** adj (person) überdreht; ~**hole** n Schlüsselloch nt; ~**hole surgery** n minimal invasive Chirurgie f, Schlüssellochchirurgie f; ~**note** n Grundton m; ~ **ring** n Schlüsselring m

khaki ['kɑːkɪ] n K(h)aki nt ♦ adj k(h)aki(farben)

kick [kɪk] vt einen Fußtritt geben +dat, treten ♦ vi treten; (baby) strampeln; (horse) ausschlagen ♦ n (Fuß)tritt m; (thrill) Spaß m; **he does it for ~s** er macht das aus Jux;

~ off vi (SPORT) anstoßen; **~-off** n (SPORT) Anstoß m

kid [kɪd] n (inf: child) Kind nt; (goat) Zicklein nt; (leather) Glacéleder nt, Glaceeleder nt ♦ vi (inf) Witze machen

kidnap ['kɪdnæp] vt entführen; **~per** n Entführer m; **~ping** n Entführung f

kidney ['kɪdnɪ] n Niere f

kill [kɪl] vt töten, umbringen ♦ vi töten ♦ n (hunting) (Jagd)beute f; **~er** n Mörder(in) m(f); **~ing** n Mord m; **~joy** n Spaßverderber(in) m(f)

kiln [kɪln] n Brennofen m

kilo ['kiːləʊ] n Kilo nt; **~byte** n (COMPUT) Kilobyte nt; **~gram(me)** n Kilogramm nt; **~metre** ['kɪləmiːtəʳ] (US **kilometer**) n Kilometer m; **~watt** n Kilowatt nt

kilt [kɪlt] n Schottenrock m

kind [kaɪnd] adj freundlich ♦ n Art f; **a ~ of** eine Art von; **(two) of a ~** (zwei) von der gleichen Art; **in ~** auf dieselbe Art; (in goods) in Naturalien

kindergarten ['kɪndəgɑːtn] n Kindergarten m

kind-hearted [kaɪnd'hɑːtɪd] adj gutherzig

kindle ['kɪndl] vt (set on fire) anzünden; (rouse) reizen, (er)wecken

kindly ['kaɪndlɪ] adj freundlich ♦ adv liebenswürdig(erweise); **would you ~ ...?** wären Sie so freundlich und ...?

kindness ['kaɪndnɪs] n Freundlichkeit f

kindred ['kɪndrɪd] adj: **~ spirit** Gleichgesinnte(r) mf

king [kɪŋ] n König m; **~dom** n Königreich nt

kingfisher ['kɪŋfɪʃəʳ] n Eisvogel m

king-size(d) ['kɪŋsaɪz(d)] adj (cigarette) Kingsize

kinky ['kɪŋkɪ] (inf) adj (person, ideas) verrückt; (sexual) abartig

kiosk ['kiːɒsk] (BRIT) n (TEL) Telefonhäuschen nt

kipper ['kɪpəʳ] n Räucherhering m

kiss [kɪs] n Kuss m ♦ vt küssen ♦ vi: **they ~ed** sie küssten sich; **~ of life** (BRIT) n: **the ~ of life** Mund-zu-Mund-Beatmung f

kit [kɪt] n Ausrüstung f; (tools) Werkzeug nt

kitchen ['kɪtʃɪn] n Küche f; **~ sink** n Spülbecken nt

kite [kaɪt] n Drachen m

kitten ['kɪtn] n Kätzchen nt

kitty ['kɪtɪ] n (money) Kasse f

km abbr (= kilometre) km

knack [næk] n Dreh m, Trick m

knapsack ['næpsæk] n Rucksack m; (MIL) Tornister m

knead [niːd] vt kneten

knee [niː] n Knie nt; **~cap** n Kniescheibe f

kneel [niːl] (pt, pp knelt) vi (also: **~ down**) knien

knelt [nɛlt] pt, pp of **kneel**

knew [njuː] pt of **know**

knickers ['nɪkəz] (BRIT) npl Schlüpfer m

knife [naɪf] (pl **knives**) n Messer nt ♦ vt erstechen

knight [naɪt] n Ritter m; (chess) Springer m; **~hood** n (title): **to get a ~hood** zum Ritter geschlagen werden

knit [nɪt] vt stricken ♦ vi stricken; (bones) zusammenwachsen; **~ting** n (occupation) Stricken nt; (work) Strickzeug nt; **~ting needle** n Stricknadel f; **~wear** n Strickwaren pl

knives [naɪvz] pl of **knife**

knob [nɒb] n Knauf m; (on instrument) Knopf m; (BRIT: of butter etc) kleine(s) Stück nt

knock [nɒk] vt schlagen; (criticize) heruntermachen ♦ vi: **to ~ at** or **on the door** an die Tür klopfen ♦ n Schlag m; (on door) Klopfen nt; **~ down** vt umwerfen; (with car) anfahren; **~ off** vt (do quickly) hinhauen; (inf: steal) klauen ♦ vi (finish) Feierabend machen; **~ out** vt ausschlagen; (BOXING) k. o. schlagen; **~ over** vt (person, object) umwerfen; (with car) anfahren; **~er** n (on door) Türklopfer m; **~out** n K.-o.-Schlag m; (fig) Sensation f

knot [nɒt] n Knoten m ♦ vt (ver)knoten

knotty ['nɒtɪ] adj (fig) kompliziert

know [nəʊ] (pt knew, pp known) vt, vi wissen; (be able to) können; (be acquainted with) kennen; (recognize) erkennen; **to ~ how to do sth** wissen, wie man etw macht, etw tun können; **to ~ about** or **of sth/sb** etw/jdn kennen; **~-all** n Alleswisser

m; **~-how** *n* Kenntnis *f,* Know-how *nt;*
~ing *adj (look, smile)* wissend; **~ingly** *adv*
wissend; *(intentionally)* wissentlich
knowledge [ˈnɔlɪdʒ] *n* Wissen *nt,* Kenntnis
f; **~able** *adj* informiert
known [nəʊn] *pp* of **know**
knuckle [ˈnʌkl] *n* Fingerknöchel *m*
K.O. *n abbr* = **knockout**
Koran [kɔˈrɑːn] *n* Koran *m*
Korea [kəˈrɪə] *n* Korea *nt*
kosher [ˈkəʊʃər] *adj* koscher

L, l

L [ɛl] *abbr (BRIT: AUT)* (= *learner*) am Auto
angebrachtes Kennzeichen für Fahrschüler; =
lake; (= *large*) gr.; (= *left*) l.
l. *abbr* = **litre**
lab [læb] *(inf) n* Labor *nt*
label [ˈleɪbl] *n* Etikett *nt* ♦ *vt* etikettieren
labor *etc* [ˈleɪbər] *(US)* = **labour** *etc*
laboratory [ləˈbɔrətəri] *n* Laboratorium *nt*
laborious [ləˈbɔːrɪəs] *adj* mühsam
labour [ˈleɪbər] *(US* labor) *n* Arbeit *f;*
(workmen) Arbeitskräfte *pl; (MED)* Wehen *pl*
♦ *vi:* **to ~ (at)** sich abmühen (mit) ♦ *vt*
breittreten *(inf);* **in ~** *(MED)* in den Wehen;
L~ *(BRIT: also:* **the L~ party**) die Labour
Party; **~ed** *adj (movement)* gequält; *(style)*
schwerfällig; **~er** *n* Arbeiter *m;* **farm ~er**
(Land)arbeiter *m*
lace [leɪs] *n (fabric)* Spitze *f;* *(of shoe)*
Schnürsenkel *m; (braid)* Litze *f* ♦ *vt (also: ~*
up) (zu)schnüren
lack [læk] *n* Mangel *m* ♦ *vt* nicht haben; **sb**
~s sth jdm fehlt etw *nom;* **to be ~ing**
fehlen; **sb is ~ing in sth** es fehlt jdm an
etw *dat;* **for** *or* **through ~ of** aus Mangel an
+*dat*
lacquer [ˈlækər] *n* Lack *m*
lad [læd] *n* Junge *m*
ladder [ˈlædər] *n* Leiter *f; (BRIT: in tights)*
Laufmasche *f* ♦ *vt (BRIT: tights)* Laufmaschen
bekommen in +*dat*
laden [ˈleɪdn] *adj* beladen, voll
ladle [ˈleɪdl] *n* Schöpfkelle *f*

lady [ˈleɪdɪ] *n* Dame *f; (title)* Lady *f;* **young ~**
junge Dame; **the ladies' (room)** die
Damentoilette; **~bird** *(US* **~bug**) *n*
Marienkäfer *m;* **~like** *adj* damenhaft,
vornehm; **~ship** *n:* **your L~ship** Ihre
Ladyschaft
lag [læg] *vi (also: ~* **behind**) zurückbleiben
♦ *vt (pipes)* verkleiden
lager [ˈlɑːgər] *n* helle(s) Bier *nt*
lagging [ˈlægɪŋ] *n* Isolierung *f*
lagoon [ləˈguːn] *n* Lagune *f*
laid [leɪd] *pt, pp* of **lay; ~ back** *(inf) adj* cool
lain [leɪn] *pp* of **lie**
lair [lɛər] *n* Lager *nt*
lake [leɪk] *n* See *m*
lamb [læm] *n* Lamm *nt; (meat)* Lammfleisch
nt; **~ chop** *n* Lammkotelett *nt;* **~swool** *n*
Lammwolle *f*
lame [leɪm] *adj* lahm; *(excuse)* faul
lament [ləˈmɛnt] *n* Klage *f* ♦ *vt* beklagen
laminated [ˈlæmɪneɪtɪd] *adj* beschichtet
lamp [læmp] *n* Lampe *f; (in street)*
Straßenlaterne *f;* **~post** *n* Laternenpfahl *m;*
~shade *n* Lampenschirm *m*
lance [lɑːns] *n* Lanze *f;* **~ corporal** *(BRIT) n*
Obergefreite(r) *m*
land [lænd] *n* Land *nt* ♦ *vi (from ship)* an
Land gehen; *(AVIAT, end up)* landen ♦ *vt*
(obtain) kriegen; *(passengers)* absetzen;
(goods) abladen; *(troops, space probe)*
landen; **~fill site** [ˈlændfɪl-] *n* Mülldeponie
f; **~ing** *n* Landung *f; (on stairs)*
(Treppen)absatz *m;* **~ing gear** *n*
Fahrgestell *nt;* **~ing stage** *(BRIT) n*
Landesteg *m;* **~ing strip** *n* Landebahn *f;*
~lady *n* (Haus)wirtin *f;* **~locked** *adj*
landumschlossen, Binnen-; **~lord** *n (of*
house) Hauswirt *m,* Besitzer *m; (of pub)*
Gastwirt *m; (of area)* Grundbesitzer *m;*
~mark *n* Wahrzeichen *nt; (fig)* Meilenstein
m; **~owner** *n* Grundbesitzer *m;* **~scape** *n*
Landschaft *f;* **~ gardener** *n*
Landschaftsgärtner(in) *m(f);* **~slide** *n*
(GEOG) Erdrutsch *m; (POL)*
überwältigende(r) Sieg *m*
lane [leɪn] *n (in town)* Gasse *f; (in country)*
Weg *m; (of motorway)* Fahrbahn *f,* Spur *f;*

(*SPORT*) Bahn f; **"get in ~"** „bitte
einordnen"
language ['læŋgwɪdʒ] n Sprache f; **bad ~**
unanständige Ausdrücke pl; **~ laboratory**
n Sprachlabor nt
languish ['læŋgwɪʃ] vi schmachten
lank [læŋk] adj dürr
lanky ['læŋkɪ] adj schlaksig
lantern ['læntən] n Laterne f
lap [læp] n Schoß m; (*SPORT*) Runde f ♦ vt
(*also:* ~ **up**) auflecken ♦ vi (*water*)
plätschern
lapel [lə'pɛl] n Revers nt or m
Lapland ['læplænd] n Lappland nt
lapse [læps] n (*moral*) Fehltritt m ♦ vi
(*decline*) nachlassen; (*expire*) ablaufen;
(*claims*) erlöschen; **to ~ into bad habits**
sich schlechte Gewohnheiten angewöhnen
laptop (computer) ['læptɔp-] n Laptop(-
Computer) m
lard [lɑːd] n Schweineschmalz nt
larder ['lɑːdə'] n Speisekammer f
large [lɑːdʒ] adj groß; **at ~** auf freiem Fuß;
~ly adv zum größten Teil; **~-scale** adj
groß angelegt, Groß-
lark [lɑːk] n (*bird*) Lerche f; (*joke*) Jux m; **~
about** (*inf*) vi herumalbern
laryngitis [lærɪn'dʒaɪtɪs] n Kehlkopf-
entzündung f
laser ['leɪzə'] n Laser m; **~ printer** n
Laserdrucker m
lash [læʃ] n Peitschenhieb m; (*eyelash*)
Wimper f ♦ vt (*rain*) schlagen gegen; (*whip*)
peitschen; (*bind*) festbinden; **~ out** vi (*with
fists*) um sich schlagen
lass [læs] n Mädchen nt
lasso [læ'suː] n Lasso nt
last [lɑːst] adj letzte(r, s) ♦ adv zuletzt; (~
time) das letzte Mal ♦ vi (*continue*) dauern;
(*remain good*) sich halten; (*money*)
ausreichen; **at ~** endlich; **~ night** gestern
Abend; **~ week** letzte Woche; **~ but one**
vorletzte(r, s); **~-ditch** adj (*attempt*) in
letzter Minute; **~ing** adj dauerhaft; (*shame
etc*) andauernd; **~ly** adv schließlich; **~-
minute** adj in letzter Minute
latch [lætʃ] n Riegel m

late [leɪt] adj spät; (*dead*) verstorben ♦ adv
spät; (*after proper time*) zu spät; **to be ~** zu
spät kommen; **of ~** in letzter Zeit; **in ~
May** Ende Mai; **~comer** n Nachzügler(in)
m(f); **~ly** adv in letzter Zeit; **later** ['leɪtə']
adj (*date*) später; (*version*) neuer ♦ adv
später
lateral ['lætərəl] adj seitlich
latest ['leɪtɪst] adj (*fashion*) neueste(r, s) ♦ n
(*news*) Neu(e)ste(s) nt; **at the ~** spätestens
lathe [leɪð] n Drehbank f
lather ['lɑːðə'] n (*Seifen*)schaum m ♦ vt
einschäumen ♦ vi schäumen
Latin ['lætɪn] n Latein nt ♦ adj lateinisch;
(*Roman*) römisch; **~ America** n
Lateinamerika nt; **~ American** adj
lateinamerikanisch
latitude ['lætɪtjuːd] n (*GEOG*) Breite f;
(*freedom*) Spielraum m
latter ['lætə'] adj (*second of two*) letztere;
(*coming at end*) letzte(r, s), später ♦ n: **the ~**
der/die/das letztere, die letzteren; **~ly** adv
in letzter Zeit
lattice ['lætɪs] n Gitter nt
laudable ['lɔːdəbl] adj löblich
laugh [lɑːf] n Lachen nt ♦ vi lachen; **~ at** vt
lachen über +acc; **~ off** vt lachend abtun;
~able adj lachhaft; **~ing stock** n
Zielscheibe f des Spottes; **~ter** n Gelächter
nt
launch [lɔːntʃ] n (*of ship*) Stapellauf m; (*of
rocket*) Abschuss m; (*boat*) Barkasse f; (*of
product*) Einführung f ♦ vt (*set afloat*) vom
Stapel lassen; (*rocket*) (ab)schießen;
(*product*) auf den Markt bringen; **~(ing)
pad** n Abschussrampe f
launder ['lɔːndə'] vt waschen
Launderette [lɔːn'drɛt] (® *BRIT*) n
Waschsalon m
Laundromat ['lɔːndrəmæt] (® *US*) n
Waschsalon m
laundry ['lɔːndrɪ] n (*place*) Wäscherei f;
(*clothes*) Wäsche f; **to do the ~** waschen
laureate ['lɔːrɪət] adj see **poet**
laurel ['lɔrl] n Lorbeer m
lava ['lɑːvə] n Lava f
lavatory ['lævətərɪ] n Toilette f

lavender [ˈlævəndəʳ] *n* Lavendel *m*

lavish [ˈlævɪʃ] *adj* (*extravagant*)
verschwenderisch; (*generous*) großzügig
♦ *vt* (*money*): **to ~ sth on sth** etw auf etw
acc verschwenden; (*attention, gifts*): **to ~ sth
on sb** jdn mit etw überschütten

law [lɔ:] *n* Gesetz *nt*; (*system*) Recht *nt*; (*as
studies*) Jura *no art*; **~-abiding** *adj*
gesetzestreu; **~ and order** *n* Recht *nt* und
Ordnung *f*; **~ court** *n* Gerichtshof *m*; **~ful**
adj gesetzlich; **~less** *adj* gesetzlos

lawn [lɔ:n] *n* Rasen *m*; **~mower** *n*
Rasenmäher *m*; **~ tennis** *n* Rasentennis *m*

law: ~ school *n* Rechtsakademie *f*; **~suit** *n*
Prozess *m*; **~yer** *n* Rechtsanwalt *m*,
Rechtsanwältin *f*

lax [læks] *adj* (*behaviour*) nachlässig;
(*standards*) lax

laxative [ˈlæksətɪv] *n* Abführmittel *nt*

lay [leɪ] (*pt, pp* laid) *pt of* lie ♦ *adj* Laien- ♦ *vt*
(*place*) legen; (*table*) decken; (*egg*) legen;
(*trap*) stellen; (*money*) wetten; **~ aside** *vt*
zurücklegen; **~ by** *vt* (*set aside*) beiseite
legen; **~ down** *vt* hinlegen; (*rules*)
vorschreiben; (*arms*) strecken; **to ~ down
the law** Vorschriften machen; **~ off** *vt*
(*workers*) (vorübergehend) entlassen; **~ on**
vt (*water, gas*) anschließen; (*concert etc*)
veranstalten; **~ out** *vt* (her)auslegen;
(*money*) ausgeben; (*corpse*) aufbahren; **~
up** *vt* (*subj: illness*) ans Bett fesseln; **~about**
n Faulenzer *m*; **~-by** *n* (*BRIT*) Parkbucht *f*;
(*bigger*) Rastplatz *m*

layer [ˈleɪəʳ] *n* Schicht *f*

layman [ˈleɪmən] (*irreg*) *n* Laie *m*

layout [ˈleɪaut] *n* Anlage *f*; (*ART*) Lay-out *nt*,
Layout *nt*

laze [leɪz] *vi* faulenzen

laziness [ˈleɪzɪnɪs] *n* Faulheit *f*

lazy [ˈleɪzɪ] *adj* faul; (*slow-moving*) träge

lb. *abbr* = **pound** (*weight*)

lead¹ [led] *n* (*chemical*) Blei *nt*; (*of pencil*)
(Bleistift)mine *f* ♦ *adj* bleiern, Blei-

lead² [li:d] (*pt, pp* led) *n* (*front position*)
Führung *f*; (*distance, time ahead*) Vorsprung
f; (*example*) Vorbild *nt*; (*clue*) Tipp *m*; (*of
police*) Spur *f*; (*THEAT*) Hauptrolle *f*; (*dog's*)

Leine *f* ♦ *vt* (*guide*) führen; (*group etc*) leiten
♦ *vi* (*be first*) führen; **in the ~** (*SPORT, fig*) in
Führung; **~ astray** *vt* irreführen; **~ away**
vt wegführen; (*prisoner*) abführen; **~ back**
vi zurückführen; **~ on** *vt* anführen; **~ on
to** *vt* (*induce*) dazu bringen; **~ to** *vt* (*street*)
(hin)führen nach; (*result in*) führen zu; **~
up to** *vt* (*drive*) führen zu; (*speaker etc*)
hinführen auf +*acc*

leaded petrol [ˈlɛdɪd-] *n* verbleites Benzin
nt

leaden [ˈlɛdn] *adj* (*sky, sea*) bleiern; (*heavy:
footsteps*) bleischwer

leader [ˈli:dəʳ] *n* Führer *m*, Leiter *m*; (*of
party*) Vorsitzende(r) *m*; (*PRESS*) Leitartikel *m*;
~ship *n* (*office*) Leitung *f*; (*quality*)
Führerschaft *f*

lead-free [ˈlɛdfri:] *adj* (*petrol*) bleifrei

leading [ˈli:dɪŋ] *adj* führend; **~ lady** *n*
(*THEAT*) Hauptdarstellerin *f*; **~ light** *n*
(*person*) führende(r) Geist *m*

lead singer [li:d-] *n* Leadsänger(in) *m(f)*

leaf [li:f] (*pl* leaves) *n* Blatt *nt* ♦ *vi*: **to ~
through** durchblättern; **to turn over a new
~** einen neuen Anfang machen

leaflet [ˈli:flɪt] *n* (*advertisement*) Prospekt *m*;
(*pamphlet*) Flugblatt *nt*; (*for information*)
Merkblatt *nt*

league [li:g] *n* (*union*) Bund *m*; (*SPORT*) Liga
f; **to be in ~ with** unter einer Decke
stecken mit

leak [li:k] *n* undichte Stelle *f*; (*in ship*) Leck *nt*
♦ *vt* (*liquid etc*) durchlassen ♦ *vi* (*pipe etc*)
undicht sein; (*liquid etc*) auslaufen; **the
information was ~ed to the enemy** die
Information wurde dem Feind zugespielt; **~
out** *vi* (*liquid etc*) auslaufen; (*information*)
durchsickern; **~y** [ˈli:kɪ] *adj* undicht

lean [li:n] (*pt, pp* leaned *or* leant) *adj* mager
♦ *vi* sich neigen ♦ *vt* (an)lehnen; **to ~
against sth** an etw *dat* angelehnt sein; sich
an etw *acc* anlehnen; **~ back** *vi* sich
zurücklehnen; **~ forward** *vi* sich
vorbeugen; **~ on** *vt fus* sich stützen auf
+*acc*; **~ out** *vi* sich hinauslehnen; **~ over**
vi sich hinüberbeugen; **~ing** *n* Neigung *f*
♦ *adj* schief; **~t** [lɛnt] *pt, pp of* lean; **~-to** *n*

Anbau *m*

leap [li:p] (*pt, pp* **leaped** *or* **leapt**) *n* Sprung *m* ♦ *vi* springen; **~frog** *n* Bockspringen *nt*; **~t** [lɛpt] *pt, pp of* **leap**; **~ year** *n* Schaltjahr *nt*

learn [lɜːn] (*pt, pp* **learned** *or* **learnt**) *vt, vi* lernen; (*find out*) erfahren; **to ~ how to do sth** etw (er)lernen; **~ed** ['lɜːnɪd] *adj* gelehrt; **~er** *n* Anfänger(in) *m(f)*; (*AUT: BRIT: also:* **~er driver**) Fahrschüler(in) *m(f)*; **~ing** *n* Gelehrsamkeit *f*; **~t** [lɜːnt] *pt, pp of* **learn**

lease [li:s] *n* (*of property*) Mietvertrag *m* ♦ *vt* pachten

leash [li:ʃ] *n* Leine *f*

least [li:st] *adj* geringste(r, s) ♦ *adv* am wenigsten ♦ *n* Mindeste(s) *nt*; **the ~ possible effort** möglichst geringer Aufwand; **at ~** zumindest; **not in the ~!** durchaus nicht!

leather ['lɛðə*] *n* Leder *nt*

leave [li:v] (*pt, pp* **left**) *vt* verlassen; (*~ behind*) zurücklassen; (*forget*) vergessen; (*allow to remain*) lassen; (*after death*) hinterlassen; (*entrust*) **to ~ sth to sb** jdm etw überlassen ♦ *vi* weggehen, wegfahren; (*for journey*) abreisen; (*bus, train*) abfahren ♦ *n* Erlaubnis *f*; (*MIL*) Urlaub *m*; **to be left** (*remain*) übrig bleiben; **there's some milk left over** es ist noch etwas Milch übrig; **on ~** auf Urlaub; **~ behind** *vt* (*person, object*) dalassen; (*forget*) liegen lassen, stehen lassen; **~ out** *vt* auslassen; **~ of absence** *n* Urlaub *m*

leaves [li:vz] *pl of* **leaf**

Lebanon ['lɛbənən] *n* Libanon *m*

lecherous ['lɛtʃərəs] *adj* lüstern

lecture ['lɛktʃə*] *n* Vortrag *m*; (*UNIV*) Vorlesung *f* ♦ *vi* einen Vortrag halten; (*UNIV*) lesen ♦ *vt* (*scold*) abkanzeln; **to give a ~ on sth** einen Vortrag über etw halten; **~r** ['lɛktʃərə*] *n* Vortragende(r) *mf*; (*BRIT: UNIV*) Dozent(in) *m(f)*

led [lɛd] *pt, pp of* **lead**[2]

ledge [lɛdʒ] *n* Leiste *f*; (*window ~*) Sims *m or nt*; (*of mountain*) (Fels)vorsprung *m*

ledger ['lɛdʒə*] *n* Hauptbuch *nt*

leech [li:tʃ] *n* Blutegel *m*

leek [li:k] *n* Lauch *m*

leer [lɪə*] *vi*: **to ~ (at sb)** (nach jdm) schielen

leeway ['li:weɪ] *n* (*fig*): **to have some ~** etwas Spielraum haben

left [lɛft] *pt, pp of* **leave** ♦ *adj* linke(r, s) ♦ *n* (*side*) linke Seite *f* ♦ *adv* links; **on the ~** links; **to the ~** nach links; **the L~** (*POL*) die Linke *f*; **~-hand** *adj*: **~-hand drive** mit Linkssteuerung; **~-handed** *adj* linkshändig; **~-hand side** *n* linke Seite *f*; **~-luggage locker** *n* Gepäckschließfach *nt*; **~-luggage (office)** (*BRIT*) *n* Gepäckaufbewahrung *f*; **~-overs** *npl* Reste *pl*; **~-wing** *adj* linke(r, s)

leg [lɛg] *n* Bein *nt*; (*of meat*) Keule *f*; (*stage*) Etappe *f*; **1st/2nd ~** (*SPORT*) 1./2. Etappe

legacy ['lɛgəsɪ] *n* Erbe *nt*, Erbschaft *f*

legal ['li:gl] *adj* gesetzlich; (*allowed*) legal; **~ holiday** (*US*) *n* gesetzliche(r) Feiertag *m*; **~ize** *vt* legalisieren; **~ly** *adv* gesetzlich; legal; **~ tender** *n* gesetzliche(s) Zahlungsmittel *nt*

legend ['lɛdʒənd] *n* Legende *f*; **~ary** *adj* legendär

leggings ['lɛgɪŋz] *npl* Leggings *pl*

legible ['lɛdʒəbl] *adj* leserlich

legislation [lɛdʒɪs'leɪʃən] *n* Gesetzgebung *f*; **legislative** ['lɛdʒɪslətɪv] *adj* gesetzgebend; **legislature** ['lɛdʒɪslətʃə*] *n* Legislative *f*

legitimate [lɪ'dʒɪtɪmət] *adj* rechtmäßig, legitim; (*child*) ehelich

legroom ['lɛgru:m] *n* Platz *m* für die Beine

leisure ['lɛʒə*] *n* Freizeit *f*; **to be at ~** Zeit haben; **~ centre** *n* Freizeitzentrum *nt*; **~ly** *adj* gemächlich

lemon ['lɛmən] *n* Zitrone *f*; (*colour*) Zitronengelb *nt*; **~ade** [lɛmə'neɪd] *n* Limonade *f*; **~ tea** *n* Zitronentee *m*

lend [lɛnd] (*pt, pp* **lent**) *vt* leihen; **to ~ sb sth** jdm etw leihen; **~ing library** *n* Leihbibliothek *f*

length [lɛŋθ] *n* Länge *f*; (*of road, pipe etc*) Strecke *f*; (*of material*) Stück *nt*; **at ~** (*lengthily*) ausführlich; (*at last*) schließlich; **~en** *vt* verlängern ♦ *vi* länger werden; **~ways** *adv* längs; **~y** *adj* sehr lang, langatmig

lenient ['li:nɪənt] *adj* nachsichtig

lens [lɛnz] *n* Linse *f*; (*PHOT*) Objektiv *nt*

Lent [lɛnt] *n* Fastenzeit *f*

lent [lɛnt] *pt, pp of* **lend**

lentil [ˈlɛntɪl] *n* Linse *f*

Leo [ˈliːəu] *n* Löwe *m*

leotard [ˈliːətɑːd] *n* Trikot *nt*, Gymnastikanzug *m*

leper [ˈlɛpəʳ] *n* Leprakranke(r) *f(m)*

leprosy [ˈlɛprəsi] *n* Lepra *f*

lesbian [ˈlɛzbɪən] *adj* lesbisch ♦ *n* Lesbierin *f*

less [lɛs] *adj, adv* weniger ♦ *n* weniger ♦ *pron* weniger; **~ than half** weniger als die Hälfte; **~ than ever** weniger denn je; **~ and ~** immer weniger; **the ~ he works** je weniger er arbeitet; **~en** [ˈlɛsn] *vi* abnehmen ♦ *vt* verringern, verkleinern; **~er** [ˈlɛsəʳ] *adj* kleiner, geringer; **to a ~er extent** in geringerem Maße

lesson [ˈlɛsn] *n* (*SCH*) Stunde *f*; (*unit of study*) Lektion *f*; (*fig*) Lehre *f*; (*ECCL*) Lesung *f*; **a maths ~** eine Mathestunde

lest [lɛst] *conj:* **~ it happen** damit es nicht passiert

let [lɛt] (*pt, pp* **let**) *vt* lassen; (*BRIT: lease*) vermieten; **to ~ sb do sth** jdn etw tun lassen; **to ~ sb know sth** jdn etw wissen lassen; **~'s go!** gehen wir!; **~ him come** soll er doch kommen; **~ down** *vt* hinunterlassen; (*disappoint*) enttäuschen; **~ go** *vi* loslassen ♦ *vt* (*things*) loslassen; (*person*) gehen lassen; **~ in** *vt* hereinlassen; (*water*) durchlassen; **~ off** *vt* (*gun*) abfeuern; (*steam*) ablassen; (*forgive*) laufen lassen; **~ on** *vi* durchblicken lassen; (*pretend*) vorgeben; **~ out** *vt* herauslassen; (*scream*) fahren lassen; **~ up** *vi* nachlassen; (*stop*) aufhören

lethal [ˈliːθl] *adj* tödlich

lethargic [lɛˈθɑːdʒɪk] *adj* lethargisch

letter [ˈlɛtəʳ] *n* Brief *m*; (*of alphabet*) Buchstabe *m*; **~ bomb** *n* Briefbombe *f*; **~box** (*BRIT*) *n* Briefkasten *m*; **~ing** *n* Beschriftung *f*; **~ of credit** *n* Akkreditiv *m*

lettuce [ˈlɛtɪs] *n* (Kopf)salat *m*

let-up [ˈlɛtʌp] (*inf*) *n* Nachlassen *nt*

leukaemia [luːˈkiːmɪə] (*US* **leukemia**) *n* Leukämie *f*

level [ˈlɛvl] *adj* (*ground*) eben; (*at same height*) auf gleicher Höhe; (*equal*) gleich gut; (*head*) kühl ♦ *adv* auf gleicher Höhe ♦ *n* (*instrument*) Wasserwaage *f*; (*altitude*) Höhe *f*; (*flat place*) ebene Fläche *f*; (*position on scale*) Niveau *nt*; (*amount, degree*) Grad *m* ♦ *vt* (*ground*) einebnen; **to draw ~ with** gleichziehen mit; **to be ~ with** auf einer Höhe sein mit; **A ~s** (*BRIT*) ≃ Abitur *nt*; **O ~s** (*BRIT*) ≃ mittlere Reife *f*; **on the ~** (*fig: honest*) ehrlich; **to ~ sth at sb** (*blow*) jdm etw versetzen; (*remark*) etw gegen jdn richten; **~ off** *or* **out** *vi* flach *or* eben werden; (*fig*) sich ausgleichen; (*plane*) horizontal fliegen ♦ *vt* (*ground*) planieren; (*differences*) ausgleichen; **~ crossing** (*BRIT*) *n* Bahnübergang *m*; **~-headed** *adj* vernünftig

lever [ˈliːvəʳ] *n* Hebel *m*; (*fig*) Druckmittel *nt* ♦ *vt* (hoch)stemmen; **~age** *n* Hebelkraft *f*; (*fig*) Einfluss *m*

levy [ˈlɛvɪ] *n* (*of taxes*) Erhebung *f*; (*tax*) Abgaben *pl*; (*MIL*) Aushebung *f* ♦ *vt* erheben; (*MIL*) ausheben

lewd [luːd] *adj* unzüchtig, unanständig

liability [laɪəˈbɪlɪtɪ] *n* (*burden*) Belastung *f*; (*duty*) Pflicht *f*; (*debt*) Verpflichtung *f*; (*responsibility*) Haftung *f*; (*proneness*) Anfälligkeit *f*

liable [ˈlaɪəbl] *adj* (*responsible*) haftbar; (*prone*) anfällig; **to be ~ for sth** etw *dat* unterliegen; **it's ~ to happen** es kann leicht vorkommen

liaise [liːˈeɪz] *vi:* **to ~ (with sb)** (mit jdm) zusammenarbeiten; **liaison** *n* Verbindung *f*

liar [ˈlaɪəʳ] *n* Lügner *m*

libel [ˈlaɪbl] *n* Verleumdung *f* ♦ *vt* verleumden

liberal [ˈlɪbərl] *adj* (*generous*) großzügig; (*open-minded*) aufgeschlossen; (*POL*) liberal

liberate [ˈlɪbəreɪt] *vt* befreien; **liberation** [lɪbəˈreɪʃən] *n* Befreiung *f*

liberty [ˈlɪbətɪ] *n* Freiheit *f*; (*permission*) Erlaubnis *f*; **to be at ~ to do sth** etw tun dürfen; **to take the ~ of doing sth** sich *dat* erlauben, etw zu tun

Libra [ˈliːbrə] *n* Waage *f*

librarian [laɪˈbrɛərɪən] n Bibliothekar(in) m(f)
library [ˈlaɪbrərɪ] n Bibliothek f; (lending ~)
Bücherei f
Libya [ˈlɪbɪə] n Libyen nt; ~n adj libysch ♦ n
Libyer(in) m(f)
lice [laɪs] npl of **louse**
licence [ˈlaɪsns] (US **license**) n (permit)
Erlaubnis f; (also: driving ~, (US) driver's ~)
Führerschein m
license [ˈlaɪsns] n (US) = **licence** ♦ vt
genehmigen, konzessionieren; ~d adj (for
alcohol) konzessioniert (für den
Alkoholausschank); ~ **plate** (US) n (AUT)
Nummernschild nt
lichen [ˈlaɪkən] n Flechte f
lick [lɪk] vt lecken ♦ n Lecken nt; a ~ of paint
ein bisschen Farbe
licorice [ˈlɪkərɪs] (US) n = **liquorice**
lid [lɪd] n Deckel m; (eyelid) Lid nt
lie [laɪ] (pt **lay**, pp **lain**) vi (rest, be situated)
liegen; (put o.s. in position) sich legen; (pt,
pp **lied**: tell lies) lügen ♦ n Lüge f; to ~ low
(fig) untertauchen; ~ **about** vi (things)
herumliegen; (people) faulenzen; ~-**down**
(BRIT) n: to have a ~-down ein Nickerchen
machen; ~-**in** (BRIT) n: to have a ~-in sich
ausschlafen
lieu [luː] n: in ~ of anstatt +gen
lieutenant [lefˈtenənt, (US) luːˈtenənt] n
Leutnant m
life [laɪf] (pl **lives**) n Leben nt; ~ **assurance**
(BRIT) n = **life insurance**; ~-**belt** (BRIT) n
Rettungsring m; ~-**boat** n Rettungsboot nt;
~-**guard** n Rettungsschwimmer m; ~
insurance n Lebensversicherung f; ~
jacket n Schwimmweste f; ~-**less** adj
(dead) leblos; (dull) langweilig; ~-**like** adj
lebenswahr, naturgetreu; ~-**line** n
Rettungsleine f; (fig) Rettungsanker m;
~-**long** adj lebenslang; ~ **preserver** (US) n
= **lifebelt**; ~-**saver** n Lebensretter(in) m(f);
~-**saving** adj lebensrettend, Rettungs-; ~
sentence n lebenslängliche Freiheitsstrafe
f; ~ **span** n Lebensspanne f; ~-**style** n
Lebensstil m; ~ **support system** n (MED)
Lebenserhaltungssystem nt; ~-**time** n: in
his ~-time während er lebte; once in a

~-**time** einmal im Leben
lift [lɪft] vt hochheben ♦ vi sich heben ♦ n
(BRIT: elevator) Aufzug m, Lift m; to give sb
a ~ jdn mitnehmen; ~-**off** n Abheben nt
(vom Boden)
ligament [ˈlɪgəmənt] n Band nt
light [laɪt] (pt, pp **lighted** or **lit**) n Licht nt;
(for cigarette etc): have you got a ~? haben
Sie Feuer? ♦ vt beleuchten; (lamp)
anmachen; (fire, cigarette) anzünden ♦ adj
(bright) hell; (pale) hell-; (not heavy, easy)
leicht; (punishment) milde; (touch) leicht; ~**s**
npl (AUT) Beleuchtung f; ~ **up** vi (lamp)
angehen; (face) aufleuchten ♦ vt (illuminate)
beleuchten; (~s) anmachen; ~ **bulb** n
Glühbirne f; ~**en** vi (brighten) hell werden;
(~ning) blitzen ♦ vt (give ~ to) erhellen;
(hair) aufhellen; (gloom) aufheitern; (make
less heavy) leichter machen; (fig) erleichtern;
~**er** n Feuerzeug nt; ~-**headed** adj
(thoughtless) leichtsinnig; (giddy) schwindlig;
~-**hearted** adj leichtherzig, fröhlich;
~**house** n Leuchtturm m; ~**ing** n
Beleuchtung f; ~**ly** adv leicht; (irresponsibly)
leichtfertig; to get off ~**ly** mit einem blauen
Auge davonkommen; ~**ness** n (of weight)
Leichtigkeit f; (of colour) Helle f
lightning [ˈlaɪtnɪŋ] n Blitz m; ~ **conductor**
(US ~ **rod**) n Blitzableiter m
light: ~ **pen** n Lichtstift m; ~**weight** adj
(suit) leicht; ~**weight** n (BOXING)
Leichtgewichtler m; ~ **year** n Lichtjahr nt
like [laɪk] vt mögen, gern haben ♦ prep wie
♦ adj (similar) ähnlich; (equal) gleich ♦ n:
the ~ dergleichen; I would or I'd ~ ich
möchte gern; would you ~ a coffee?
möchten Sie einen Kaffee?; to be or look ~
sb/sth jdm/etw ähneln; that's just ~ him
das ist typisch für ihn; do it ~ this mach es
so; it is nothing ~ ... es ist nicht zu
vergleichen mit ...; what does it look ~?
wie sieht es aus?; what does it sound ~?
wie hört es sich an?; what does it taste ~?
wie schmeckt es?; his ~**s** and dislikes was
er mag und was er nicht mag; ~**able** adj
sympathisch
likelihood [ˈlaɪklɪhud] n Wahrscheinlichkeit f

likely ['laɪklɪ] *adj* wahrscheinlich; **he's ~ to leave** er geht möglicherweise; **not ~!** wohl kaum!

likeness ['laɪknɪs] *n* Ähnlichkeit *f*; (*portrait*) Bild *nt*

likewise ['laɪkwaɪz] *adv* ebenso

liking ['laɪkɪŋ] *n* Zuneigung *f*; (*taste*) Vorliebe *f*

lilac ['laɪlək] *n* Flieder *m* ♦ *adj* (*colour*) fliederfarben

lily ['lɪlɪ] *n* Lilie *f*; **~ of the valley** *n* Maiglöckchen *nt*

limb [lɪm] *n* Glied *nt*

limber up ['lɪmbə-] *vi* sich auflockern; (*fig*) sich vorbereiten

limbo ['lɪmbəʊ] *n*: **to be in ~** (*fig*) in der Schwebe sein

lime [laɪm] *n* (*tree*) Linde *f*; (*fruit*) Limone *f*; (*substance*) Kalk *m*

limelight ['laɪmlaɪt] *n*: **to be in the ~** (*fig*) im Rampenlicht stehen

limestone ['laɪmstəʊn] *n* Kalkstein *m*

limit ['lɪmɪt] *n* Grenze *f*; (*inf*) Höhe *f* ♦ *vt* begrenzen, einschränken; **~ation** [lɪmɪ'teɪʃən] *n* Einschränkung *f*; **~ed** *adj* beschränkt; **to be ~ed to** sich beschränken auf +*acc*; **~ed (liability) company** (*BRIT*) *n* Gesellschaft *f* mit beschränkter Haftung

limousine ['lɪməzi:n] *n* Limousine *f*

limp [lɪmp] *n* Hinken *nt* ♦ *vi* hinken ♦ *adj* schlaff

limpet ['lɪmpɪt] *n* (*fig*) Klette *f*

line [laɪn] *n* Linie *f*; (*rope*) Leine *f*; (*on face*) Falte *f*; (*row*) Reihe *f*; (*of hills*) Kette *f*; (*US: queue*) Schlange *f*; (*company*) Linie *f*, Gesellschaft *f*; (*RAIL*) Strecke *f*; (*TEL*) Leitung *f*; (*written*) Zeile *f*; (*direction*) Richtung *f*; (*fig: business*) Branche *f*; (*range of items*) Kollektion *f* ♦ *vt* (*coat*) füttern; (*border*) säumen; **~s** *npl* (*RAIL*) Gleise *pl*; **in ~ with** in Übereinstimmung mit; **~ up** *vi* sich aufstellen ♦ *vt* aufstellen; (*prepare*) sorgen für; (*support*) mobilisieren; (*surprise*) planen; **~ar** ['lɪnɪə-] *adj* gerade; (*measure*) Längen-; **~d** *adj* (*face*) faltig; (*paper*) liniert

linen ['lɪnɪn] *n* Leinen *nt*; (*sheets etc*) Wäsche *f*

liner ['laɪnə-] *n* Überseedampfer *m*

linesman ['laɪnzmən] (*irreg*) *n* (*SPORT*) Linienrichter *m*

line-up ['laɪnʌp] *n* Aufstellung *f*

linger ['lɪŋgə-] *vi* (*remain long*) verweilen; (*taste*) (zurück)bleiben; (*delay*) zögern, verharren

lingerie ['lænʒəri:] *n* Damenunterwäsche *f*

lingering ['lɪŋgərɪŋ] *adj* (*doubt*) zurückbleibend; (*disease*) langwierig; (*taste*) nachhaltend; (*look*) lang

lingo ['lɪŋgəʊ] (*pl* **~es**) (*inf*) *n* Sprache *f*

linguist ['lɪŋgwɪst] *n* Sprachkundige(r) *mf*; (*UNIV*) Sprachwissenschaftler(in) *m(f)*; **~ic** [lɪŋ'gwɪstɪk] *adj* sprachlich; sprachwissenschaftlich; **~ics** *n* Sprachwissenschaft *f*, Linguistik *f*

lining ['laɪnɪŋ] *n* Futter *nt*

link [lɪŋk] *n* Glied *nt*; (*connection*) Verbindung *f* ♦ *vt* verbinden; **~s** *npl* (*GOLF*) Golfplatz *m*; **~ up** *vt* verbinden ♦ *vi* zusammenkommen; (*companies*) sich zusammenschließen; **~-up** *n* (*TEL*) Verbindung *f*; (*of spaceships*) Kopplung *f*

lino ['laɪnəʊ] *n* = **linoleum**

linoleum [lɪ'nəʊlɪəm] *n* Linoleum *nt*

linseed oil ['lɪnsi:d-] *n* Leinöl *nt*

lion ['laɪən] *n* Löwe *m*; **~ess** *n* Löwin *f*

lip [lɪp] *n* Lippe *f*; (*of jug*) Schnabel *m*; **to pay ~ service (to)** ein Lippenbekenntnis ablegen (zu)

liposuction ['lɪpəʊsʌkʃən] *n* Fettabsaugen *nt*

lip: **~read** (*irreg*) *vi* von den Lippen ablesen; **~ salve** *n* Lippenbalsam *m*; **~stick** *n* Lippenstift *m*

liqueur [lɪ'kjʊə-] *n* Likör *m*

liquid ['lɪkwɪd] *n* Flüssigkeit *f* ♦ *adj* flüssig

liquidate ['lɪkwɪdeɪt] *vt* liquidieren

liquidize ['lɪkwɪdaɪz] *vt* (*COOK*) (im Mixer) pürieren; **~r** ['lɪkwɪdaɪzə-] *n* Mixgerät *nt*

liquor ['lɪkə-] *n* Alkohol *m*

liquorice ['lɪkərɪs] (*BRIT*) *n* Lakritze *f*

liquor store (*US*) *n* Spirituosengeschäft *nt*

Lisbon ['lɪzbən] *n* Lissabon *f*

lisp [lɪsp] *n* Lispeln *nt* ♦ *vt, vi* lispeln

list [lɪst] *n* Liste *f*, Verzeichnis *nt*; (*of ship*) Schlagseite *f* ♦ *vt* (*write down*) eine Liste

machen von; (*verbally*) aufzählen ♦ *vi* (*ship*)
Schlagseite haben
listen ['lɪsn] *vi* hören; **~ to** *vt* zuhören +*dat*;
~er *n* (Zu)hörer(in) *m(f)*
listless ['lɪstlɪs] *adj* lustlos
lit [lɪt] *pt, pp of* **light**
liter ['liːtə'] (*US*) *n* = **litre**
literacy ['lɪtərəsɪ] *n* Fähigkeit *f* zu lesen und
zu schreiben
literal ['lɪtərəl] *adj* buchstäblich; (*translation*)
wortwörtlich; **~ly** *adv* wörtlich;
buchstäblich
literary ['lɪtərərɪ] *adj* literarisch
literate ['lɪtərət] *adj* des Lesens und
Schreibens kundig
literature ['lɪtrɪtʃə'] *n* Literatur *f*
litigation [lɪtɪ'geɪʃən] *n* Prozess *m*
litre ['liːtə'] (*US* **liter**) *n* Liter *m*
litter ['lɪtə'] *n* (*rubbish*) Abfall *m*; (*of animals*)
Wurf *m* ♦ *vt* in Unordnung bringen; **~ed with** übersät sein mit; **~ bin** (*BRIT*) *n*
Abfalleimer *m*
little ['lɪtl] *adj* klein ♦ *adv, n* wenig; **a ~** ein
bisschen; **~ by ~** nach und nach
live¹ [laɪv] *adj* lebendig; (*MIL*) scharf; (*ELEC*)
geladen; (*broadcast*) live
live² [lɪv] *vi* leben; (*dwell*) wohnen ♦ *vt* (*life*)
führen; **~ down** *vt*: **I'll never ~ it down**
das wird man mir nie vergessen; **~ on** *vi*
weiterleben ♦ *vt fus*: **to ~ on sth** von etw
leben; **~ together** *vi* zusammenleben;
(*share a flat*) zusammenwohnen; **~ up to**
vt (*standards*) gerecht werden +*dat*;
(*principles*) anstreben; (*hopes*) entsprechen
+*dat*
livelihood ['laɪvlɪhud] *n* Lebensunterhalt *m*
lively ['laɪvlɪ] *adj* lebhaft, lebendig
liven up ['laɪvn-] *vt* beleben
liver ['lɪvə'] *n* (*ANAT*) Leber *f*
lives [laɪvz] *pl of* **life**
livestock ['laɪvstɔk] *n* Vieh *nt*
livid ['lɪvɪd] *adj* bläulich; (*furious*)
fuchsteufelswild
living ['lɪvɪŋ] *n* (Lebens)unterhalt *m* ♦ *adj*
lebendig; (*language etc*) lebend; **to earn** *or*
make a ~ sich *dat* seinen Lebensunterhalt
verdienen; **~ conditions** *npl*

Wohnverhältnisse *pl*; **~ room** *n*
Wohnzimmer *nt*; **~ standards** *npl*
Lebensstandard *m*; **~ wage** *n*
ausreichender Lohn *m*
lizard ['lɪzəd] *n* Eidechse *f*
load [ləud] *n* (*burden*) Last *f*; (*amount*)
Ladung *f* ♦ *vt* (*also*: **~ up**) (be)laden;
(*COMPUT*) laden; (*camera*) Film einlegen in
+*acc*; (*gun*) laden; **a ~ of, ~s of** (*fig*) jede
Menge; **~ed** *adj* beladen; (*dice*) präpariert;
(*question*) Fang-; (*inf: rich*) steinreich; **~ing
bay** *n* Ladeplatz *m*
loaf [ləuf] (*pl* **loaves**) *n* Brot *nt* ♦ *vi* (*also*: **~
about, ~ around**) herumlungern, faulenzen
loan [ləun] *n* Leihgabe *f*; (*FIN*) Darlehen *nt*
♦ *vt* leihen; **on ~** geliehen
loath [ləuθ] *adj*: **to be ~ to do sth** etw
ungern tun
loathe [ləuð] *vt* verabscheuen
loaves [ləuvz] *pl of* **loaf**
lobby ['lɔbɪ] *n* Vorhalle *f*; (*POL*) Lobby *f* ♦ *vt*
politisch beeinflussen (wollen)
lobster ['lɔbstə'] *n* Hummer *m*
local ['ləukl] *adj* ortsansässig, Orts- ♦ *n* (*pub*)
Stammwirtschaft *f*; **the ~s** *npl* (*people*) die
Ortsansässigen *pl*; **~ anaesthetic** *n* (*MED*)
örtliche Betäubung *f*; **~ authority** *n*
städtische Behörden *pl*; **~ call** *n* (*TEL*)
Ortsgespräch *nt*; **~ government** *n*
Gemeinde-/Kreisverwaltung *f*; **~ity**
[ləu'kælɪtɪ] *n* Ort *m*; **~ly** *adv* örtlich, am Ort
locate [ləu'keɪt] *vt* ausfindig machen;
(*establish*) errichten; **location** [ləu'keɪʃən] *n*
Platz *m*, Lage *f*; **on location** (*CINE*) auf
Außenaufnahme
loch [lɔx] (*SCOTTISH*) *n* See *m*
lock [lɔk] *n* Schloss *nt*; (*NAUT*) Schleuse *f*; (*of
hair*) Locke *f* ♦ *vt* (*fasten*) (ver)schließen ♦ *vi*
(*door etc*) sich schließen (lassen); (*wheels*)
blockieren; **~ up** *vt* (*criminal, mental patient*)
einsperren; (*house*) abschließen
locker ['lɔkə'] *n* Spind *m*
locket ['lɔkɪt] *n* Medaillon *nt*
lock ['lɔk-]: **~out** *n* Aussperrung *f*; **~smith** *n*
Schlosser(in) *m(f)*; **~up** *n* (*jail*) Gefängnis *nt*;
(*garage*) Garage *f*
locum ['ləukəm] *n* (*MED*) Vertreter(in) *m(f)*

lodge [lɔdʒ] n (*gatehouse*) Pförtnerhaus nt; (*freemasons'*) Loge f ♦ vi (*get stuck*) stecken (bleiben); (*in Untermiete*): **to ~ (with)** wohnen (bei) ♦ vt (*protest*) einreichen; **~r** n (Unter)mieter m; **lodgings** n (Miet)wohnung f

loft [lɔft] n (*Dach*)boden m

lofty ['lɔftɪ] adj hoch(ragend); (*proud*) hochmütig

log [lɔg] n Klotz m; (*book*) = **logbook**

logbook ['lɔgbuk] n Bordbuch nt; (*for lorry*) Fahrtenschreiber m; (*AUT*) Kraftfahrzeugbrief m

loggerheads ['lɔgəhedz] npl: **to be at ~** sich in den Haaren liegen

logic ['lɔdʒɪk] n Logik f; **~al** adj logisch

logistics [lɔ'dʒɪstɪks] npl Logistik f

logo ['laugəu] n Firmenzeichen nt

loin [lɔɪn] n Lende f

loiter ['lɔɪtə*] vi herumstehen

loll [lɔl] vi (*also:* **~ about**) sich rekeln or räkeln

lollipop ['lɔlɪpɔp] n (Dauer)lutscher m; **~ man/lady** (*irreg*; *BRIT*) n ≃ Schülerlotse m

---
Lollipop man/lady
---

i Lollipop man/lady *heißen in Großbritannien die Männer bzw. Frauen, die mit Hilfe eines runden Stoppschildes den Verkehr anhalten, damit Schulkinder die Straße gefahrlos überqueren können. Der Name bezieht sich auf die Form des Schildes, die an einen Lutscher erinnert.*

lolly ['lɔlɪ] (*inf*) n (*sweet*) Lutscher m

London ['lʌndən] n London nt; **~er** n Londoner(in) m(f)

lone [ləun] adj einsam

loneliness ['ləunlɪnɪs] n Einsamkeit f

lonely ['ləunlɪ] adj einsam

loner ['ləunə*] n Einzelgänger(in) m(f)

long [lɔŋ] adj lang; (*distance*) weit ♦ adv lange ♦ vi: **to ~ for** sich sehnen nach; **before ~** bald; **as ~ as** solange; **in the ~ run** auf die Dauer; **don't be ~!** beeil dich!; **how ~ is the street?** wie lang ist die Straße?; **how ~ is the lesson?** wie lange dauert die Stunde?; **6 metres ~** 6 Meter lang; **6 months ~** 6 Monate lang; **all night ~** die ganze Nacht; **he no ~er comes** er kommt nicht mehr; **~ ago** vor langer Zeit; **~ before** lange vorher; **at ~ last** endlich; **~-distance** adj Fern-

longevity [lɔn'dʒevɪtɪ] n Langlebigkeit f

long: **~-haired** adj langhaarig; **~hand** n Langschrift f; **~ing** n Sehnsucht f ♦ adj sehnsüchtig

longitude ['lɔŋgɪtjuːd] n Längengrad m

long: **~ jump** n Weitsprung m; **~-life** adj (*batteries etc*) mit langer Lebensdauer; **~-lost** adj längst verloren geglaubt; **~-playing record** n Langspielplatte f; **~-range** adj Langstrecken-, Fern-; **~-sighted** adj weitsichtig; **~-standing** adj alt, seit langer Zeit bestehend; **~-suffering** adj schwer geprüft; **~-term** adj langfristig; **~ wave** n Langwelle f; **~-winded** adj langatmig

loo [luː] (*BRIT*: *inf*) n Klo nt

look [luk] vi schauen; (*seem*) aussehen; (*building etc*): **to ~ on to the sea** aufs Meer gehen ♦ n Blick m; **~s** npl (*appearance*) Aussehen nt; **~ after** vt (*care for*) sorgen für; (*watch*) aufpassen auf +acc; **~ at** vt ansehen; (*consider*) sich überlegen; **~ back** vi sich umsehen; (*fig*) zurückblicken; **~ down on** vt (*fig*) herabsehen auf +acc; **~ for** vt (*seek*) suchen; **~ forward to** vt sich freuen auf +acc; (*in letters*): **we ~ forward to hearing from you** wir hoffen, bald von Ihnen zu hören; **~ into** vt untersuchen; **~ on** vi zusehen; **~ out** vi hinaussehen; (*take care*) aufpassen; **~ out for** vt Ausschau halten nach; (*be careful*) Acht geben auf +acc; **~ round** vi sich umsehen; **~ to** vt (*take care of*) Acht geben auf +acc; (*rely on*) sich verlassen auf +acc; **~ up** vi aufblicken; (*improve*) sich bessern ♦ vt (*word*) nachschlagen; (*person*) besuchen; **~ up to** vt aufsehen zu; **~out** n (*watch*) Ausschau f; (*person*) Wachposten m; (*place*) Ausguck m; (*prospect*) Aussichten pl; **to be on the ~ out for sth** nach etw Ausschau halten

loom [lu:m] *n* Webstuhl *m* ♦ *vi* sich abzeichnen

loony ['lu:ni] (*inf*) *n* Verrückte(r) *mf*

loop [lu:p] *n* Schlaufe *f*; **~hole** *n* (*fig*) Hintertürchen *nt*

loose [lu:s] *adj* lose, locker; (*free*) frei; (*inexact*) unpräzise ♦ *vt* lösen, losbinden; **~ change** *n* Kleingeld *nt*; **~ chippings** *npl* (*on road*) Rollsplit *m*; **~ end** *n*: **to be at a ~ end** (*BRIT*) *or* **at ~ ends** (*US*) nicht wissen, was man tun soll; **~ly** *adv* locker, lose; **~n** *vt* lockern, losmachen

loot [lu:t] *n* Beute *f* ♦ *vt* plündern

lop off [lɔp-] *vt* abhacken

lopsided ['lɔp'saidid] *adj* schief

lord [lɔ:d] *n* (*ruler*) Herr *m*; (*BRIT: title*) Lord *m*; **the L~** (*God*) der Herr; **the (House of) L~s** das Oberhaus; **~ship** *n*: **Your L~ship** Eure Lordschaft

lorry ['lɔri] (*BRIT*) *n* Lastwagen *m*; **~ driver** (*BRIT*) *n* Lastwagenfahrer(in) *m(f)*

lose [lu:z] (*pt, pp* **lost**) *vt* verlieren; (*chance*) verpassen ♦ *vi* verlieren; **to ~ (time)** (*clock*) nachgehen; **~r** *n* Verlierer *m*

loss [lɔs] *n* Verlust *m*; **at a ~** (*COMM*) mit Verlust; (*unable*) außerstande, außer Stande

lost [lɔst] *pt, pp of* **lose** ♦ *adj* verloren; **~ property** (*US* **- and found**) *n* Fundsachen *pl*

lot [lɔt] *n* (*quantity*) Menge *f*; (*fate, at auction*) Los *nt*; (*inf: people, things*) Haufen *m*; **the ~** alles; (*people*) alle; **a ~ of** (*with sg*) viel; (*with pl*) viele; **~s of** massenhaft, viel(e); **I read a ~** ich lese viel; **to draw ~s for sth** etw verlosen

lotion ['ləuʃən] *n* Lotion *f*

lottery ['lɔtəri] *n* Lotterie *f*

loud [laud] *adj* laut; (*showy*) schreiend ♦ *adv* laut; **~ly** *adv* laut; **~speaker** *n* Lautsprecher *m*

lounge [laundʒ] *n* (*in hotel*) Gesellschaftsraum *m*; (*in house*) Wohnzimmer *nt* ♦ *vi* sich herumlümmeln

louse [laus] (*pl* **lice**) *n* Laus *f*

lousy ['lauzi] *adj* (*fig*) miserabel

lout [laut] *n* Lümmel *m*

louvre ['lu:vər] (*US* **louver**) *adj* (*door, window*)

Jalousie-

lovable ['lʌvəbl] *adj* liebenswert

love [lʌv] *n* Liebe *f*; (*person*) Liebling *m*; (*SPORT*) null ♦ *vt* (*person*) lieben; (*activity*) gerne mögen; **to be in ~ with sb** in jdn verliebt sein; **to make ~** sich lieben; **for the ~ of** aus Liebe zu; **"15 ~"** (*TENNIS*) „15 null"; **to ~ to do sth** etw (sehr) gerne tun; **~ affair** *n* (Liebes)verhältnis *nt*; **~ letter** *n* Liebesbrief *m*; **~ life** *n* Liebesleben *nt*

lovely ['lʌvli] *adj* schön

lover ['lʌvər] *n* Liebhaber(in) *m(f)*

loving ['lʌviŋ] *adj* liebend, liebevoll

low [ləu] *adj* niedrig; (*rank*) niedere(r, s); (*level, note, neckline*) tief; (*intelligence, density*) gering; (*vulgar*) ordinär; (*not loud*) leise; (*depressed*) gedrückt ♦ *adv* (*not high*) niedrig; (*not loudly*) leise ♦ *n* (*~ point*) Tiefstand *m*; (*MET*) Tief *nt*; **to feel ~** sich mies fühlen; **to turn (down)** ~ leiser stellen; **~ alcohol** *adj* alkoholarm; **~-calorie** *adj* kalorienarm; **~-cut** *adj* (*dress*) tief ausgeschnitten; **~er** *vt* herunterlassen; (*eyes, gun*) senken; (*reduce*) herabsetzen, senken ♦ *vr*: **to ~er o.s.** (*fig*) sich herablassen zu; **~er sixth** (*BRIT*) *n* (*SCOL*) ≈ zwölfte Klasse; **~-fat** *adj* fettarm, Mager-; **~lands** *npl* (*GEOG*) Flachland *nt*; **~ly** *adj* bescheiden; **~-lying** *adj* tief gelegen

loyal ['lɔiəl] *adj* treu; **~ty** *n* Treue *f*

lozenge ['lɔzindʒ] *n* Pastille *f*

L-plates ['elpleits] (*BRIT*) *npl* L-Schild *nt* (*für Fahrschüler*)

L-Plates

i Als **L-Plates** werden in Großbritannien die weißen Schilder mit einem roten „L" bezeichnet, die vorne und hinten an jedem von einem Fahrschüler geführten Fahrzeug befestigt werden müssen. Fahrschüler müssen einen vorläufigen Führerschein beantragen und dürfen damit unter der Aufsicht eines erfahrenen Autofahrers auf allen Straßen außer Autobahnen fahren.

Ltd *abbr* (= *limited company*) GmbH

lubricant ['lu:brikənt] *n* Schmiermittel *nt*

lubricate ['lu:brɪkeɪt] vt schmieren
lucid ['lu:sɪd] adj klar; (sane) bei klarem Verstand; (moment) licht
luck [lʌk] n Glück nt; **bad** or **hard** or **tough** **~!** (so ein) Pech!; **good ~!** viel Glück!; **~ily** adv glücklicherweise, zum Glück; **~y** adj Glücks-; **to be ~y** Glück haben
lucrative ['lu:krətɪv] adj einträglich
ludicrous ['lu:dɪkrəs] adj grotesk
lug [lʌg] vt schleppen
luggage ['lʌgɪdʒ] n Gepäck nt; **~ rack** n Gepäcknetz nt
lukewarm ['lu:kwɔ:m] adj lauwarm; (indifferent) lau
lull [lʌl] n Flaute f ♦ vt einlullen; (calm) beruhigen
lullaby ['lʌləbaɪ] n Schlaflied nt
lumbago [lʌm'beɪgəu] n Hexenschuss m
lumber ['lʌmbər] n Plunder m; (wood) Holz nt; **~jack** n Holzfäller m
luminous ['lu:mɪnəs] adj Leucht-
lump [lʌmp] n Klumpen m; (MED) Schwellung f; (in breast) Knoten m; (of sugar) Stück nt ♦ vt (also: **~ together**) zusammentun; (judge together) in einen Topf werfen; **~ sum** n Pauschalsumme f; **~y** adj klumpig
lunacy ['lu:nəsɪ] n Irrsinn m
lunar ['lu:nər] adj Mond-
lunatic ['lu:nətɪk] n Wahnsinnige(r) mf ♦ adj wahnsinnig, irr
lunch [lʌntʃ] n Mittagessen nt; **~eon** ['lʌntʃən] n Mittagessen nt; **~eon meat** n Frühstücksfleisch nt; **~eon voucher** (BRIT) n Essenmarke f; **~time** n Mittagszeit f
lung [lʌŋ] n Lunge f
lunge [lʌndʒ] vi (also: **~ forward**) (los)stürzen; **to ~ at** sich stürzen auf +acc
lurch [lə:tʃ] vi taumeln; (NAUT) schlingern ♦ n Ruck m; (NAUT) Schlingern nt; **to leave sb in the ~** jdn im Stich lassen
lure [luər] n Köder m; (fig) Lockung f ♦ vt (ver)locken
lurid ['luərɪd] adj (shocking) grausig, widerlich; (colour) grell
lurk [lə:k] vi lauern
luscious ['lʌʃəs] adj köstlich

lush [lʌʃ] adj satt; (vegetation) üppig
lust [lʌst] n Wollust f; (greed) Gier f ♦ vi: **to ~ after** gieren nach
lustre ['lʌstər] (US **luster**) n Glanz m
Luxembourg ['lʌksəmbə:g] n Luxemburg nt
luxuriant [lʌg'zjuərɪənt] adj üppig
luxurious [lʌg'zjuərɪəs] adj luxuriös, Luxus-
luxury ['lʌkʃərɪ] n Luxus m ♦ cpd Luxus-
lying ['laɪŋ] n Lügen nt ♦ adj verlogen
lynx [lɪŋks] n Luchs m
lyric ['lɪrɪk] n Lyrik f ♦ adj lyrisch; **~s** pl (words for song) (Lied)text m; **~al** adj lyrisch, gefühlvoll

M, m

m abbr = **metre**; **mile**; **million**
M.A. n abbr = **Master of Arts**
mac [mæk] (BRIT: inf) n Regenmantel m
macaroni [mækə'rəunɪ] n Makkaroni pl
machine [mə'ʃi:n] n Maschine f ♦ vt (dress etc) mit der Maschine nähen; **~ gun** n Maschinengewehr nt; **~ language** n (COMPUT) Maschinensprache f; **~ry** n Maschinerie f
macho ['mætʃəu] adj macho
mackerel ['mækrl] n Makrele f
mackintosh ['mækɪntɒʃ] (BRIT) n Regenmantel m
mad [mæd] adj verrückt; (dog) tollwütig; (angry) wütend; **~ about** (fond of) verrückt nach, versessen auf +acc
madam ['mædəm] n gnädige Frau f
madden ['mædn] vt verrückt machen; (make angry) ärgern
made [meɪd] pt, pp of **make**
made-to-measure ['meɪdtə'mɛʒər] (BRIT) adj Maß-
mad ['mæd-]: **~ly** adv wahnsinnig; **~man** (irreg) n Verrückte(r) m, Irre(r) m; **~ness** n Wahnsinn m
magazine [mægə'zi:n] n Zeitschrift f; (in gun) Magazin nt
maggot ['mægət] n Made f
magic ['mædʒɪk] n Zauberei f, Magie f; (fig) Zauber m ♦ adj magisch, Zauber-; **~al** adj

magisch; **~ian** [mə'dʒɪʃən] n Zauberer m

magistrate ['mædʒɪstreɪt] n (Friedens)richter m

magnanimous [mæg'nænɪməs] adj großmütig

magnet ['mægnɪt] n Magnet m; **~ic** [mæg'netɪk] adj magnetisch; **~ic tape** n Magnetband nt; **~ism** n Magnetismus m; (fig) Ausstrahlungskraft f

magnificent [mæg'nɪfɪsnt] adj großartig

magnify ['mægnɪfaɪ] vt vergrößern; **~ing glass** n Lupe f

magnitude ['mægnɪtjuːd] n (size) Größe f; (importance) Ausmaß nt

magpie ['mægpaɪ] n Elster f

mahogany [mə'hɒgənɪ] n Mahagoni nt ♦ cpd Mahagoni-

maid [meɪd] n Dienstmädchen nt; **old ~** alte Jungfer f

maiden ['meɪdn] n Maid f ♦ adj (flight, speech) Jungfern-; **~ name** n Mädchenname m

mail [meɪl] n Post f ♦ vt aufgeben; **~ box** (US) n Briefkasten m; **~ing list** n Anschreibeliste f; **~ order** n Bestellung f durch die Post; **~ order firm** n Versandhaus nt

maim [meɪm] vt verstümmeln

main [meɪn] adj hauptsächlich, Haupt- ♦ n (pipe) Hauptleitung f; **the ~s** npl (ELEC) das Stromnetz; **in the ~** im Großen und Ganzen; **~frame** n (COMPUT) Großrechner m; **~land** n Festland nt; **~ly** adv hauptsächlich; **~ road** n Hauptstraße f; **~stay** n (fig) Hauptstütze f; **~stream** n Hauptrichtung f

maintain [meɪn'teɪn] vt (machine, roads) instand or in Stand halten; (support) unterhalten; (keep up) aufrechterhalten; (claim) behaupten; (innocence) beteuern

maintenance ['meɪntənəns] n (TECH) Wartung f; (of family) Unterhalt m

maize [meɪz] n Mais m

majestic [mə'dʒestɪk] adj majestätisch

majesty ['mædʒɪstɪ] n Majestät f

major ['meɪdʒəʳ] n Major m ♦ adj (MUS) Dur; (more important) Haupt-; (bigger) größer

Majorca [mə'jɔːkə] n Mallorca nt

majority [mə'dʒɒrɪtɪ] n Mehrheit f; (JUR) Volljährigkeit f

make [meɪk] (pt, pp **made**) vt machen; (appoint) ernennen (zu); (cause to do sth) veranlassen; (reach) erreichen; (in time) schaffen; (earn) verdienen ♦ n Marke f; **to ~ sth happen** etw geschehen lassen; **to ~ it** es schaffen; **what time do you ~ it?** wie spät hast du es?; **to ~ do with** auskommen mit; **~ for** vi gehen/fahren nach; **~ out** vt (write out) ausstellen; (understand) verstehen; **~ up** vt machen; (face) schminken; (quarrel) beilegen; (story etc) erfinden ♦ vi sich versöhnen; **~ up for** vt wieder gutmachen; (COMM) vergüten; **~believe** n Fantasie f; **~r** n (COMM) Hersteller m; **~shift** adj behelfsmäßig, Not-; **~up** n Schminke f, Make-up nt; **~up remover** n Make-up-Entferner m; **making** n: **in the making** im Entstehen; **to have the makings of** das Zeug haben zu

malaria [mə'leərɪə] n Malaria f

Malaysia [mə'leɪzɪə] n Malaysia nt

male [meɪl] n Mann m; (animal) Männchen nt ♦ adj männlich

malevolent [mə'levələnt] adj übel wollend

malfunction [mæl'fʌŋkʃən] n (MED) Funktionsstörung f; (of machine) Defekt m

malice ['mælɪs] n Bosheit f; **malicious** [mə'lɪʃəs] adj böswillig, gehässig

malign [mə'laɪn] vt verleumden ♦ adj böse

malignant [mə'lɪgnənt] adj bösartig

mall [mɔːl] n (also: **shopping ~**) Einkaufszentrum nt

malleable ['mælɪəbl] adj formbar

mallet ['mælɪt] n Holzhammer m

malnutrition [mælnjuː'trɪʃən] n Unterernährung f

malpractice [mæl'præktɪs] n Amtsvergehen nt

malt [mɔːlt] n Malz nt

Malta ['mɔːltə] n Malta nt; **Maltese** [mɔːl'tiːz] adj inv maltesisch ♦ n inv Malteser(in) m(f)

maltreat [mæl'triːt] vt misshandeln

mammal ['mæml] n Säugetier nt

mammoth ['mæməθ] *n* Mammut *nt* ♦ *adj* Mammut-

man [mæn] (*pl* **men**) *n* Mann *m*; (*human race*) der Mensch, die Menschen *pl* ♦ *vt* bemannen; **an old ~** ein alter Mann, ein Greis *m*; **~ and wife** Mann und Frau

manage ['mænɪdʒ] *vi* zurechtkommen ♦ *vt* (*control*) führen, leiten; (*cope with*) fertig werden mit; **~able** *adj* (*person, animal*) fügsam; (*object*) handlich; **~ment** *n* (*control*) Führung *f*, Leitung *f*; (*directors*) Management *nt*; **~r** *n* Geschäftsführer *m*; **~ress** [mænɪdʒə'res] *n* Geschäftsführerin *f*; **~rial** [mænɪ'dʒɪərɪəl] *adj* (*post*) leitend; (*problem etc*) Management-; **managing** [mænɪdʒɪŋ] *adj*: **managing director** Betriebsleiter *m*

mandarin ['mændərɪn] *n* (*fruit*) Mandarine *f*

mandatory ['mændətərɪ] *adj* obligatorisch

mane [meɪn] *n* Mähne *f*

maneuver [mə'nu:vər] (*US*) = **manoeuvre**

manfully ['mænfəlɪ] *adv* mannhaft

mangle ['mæŋgl] *vt* verstümmeln ♦ *n* Mangel *f*

mango ['mæŋgəʊ] (*pl* **~es**) *n* Mango(pflaume) *f*

mangy ['meɪndʒɪ] *adj* (*dog*) räudig

man ['mæn-]: **~handle** *vt* grob behandeln; **~hole** *n* (Straßen)schacht *m*; **~hood** *n* Mannesalter *nt*; (*~liness*) Männlichkeit *f*; **~-hour** *n* Arbeitsstunde *f*; **~hunt** *n* Fahndung *f*

mania ['meɪnɪə] *n* Manie *f*; **~c** ['meɪnɪæk] *n* Wahnsinnige(r) *mf*

manic ['mænɪk] *adj* (*behaviour, activity*) hektisch

manicure ['mænɪkjʊər] *n* Maniküre *f*; **~ set** *n* Necessaire *nt*, Nessessär *f*

manifest ['mænɪfest] *vt* offenbaren ♦ *adj* offenkundig; **~ation** [mænɪfes'teɪʃən] *n* (*sign*) Anzeichen *nt*

manifesto [mænɪ'festəʊ] *n* Manifest *nt*

manipulate [mə'nɪpjuleɪt] *vt* handhaben; (*fig*) manipulieren

man [mæn-]: **~kind** *n* Menschheit *f*; **~ly** ['mænlɪ] *adj* männlich; mannhaft; **~-made** *adj* (*fibre*) künstlich

manner ['mænər] *n* Art *f*, Weise *f*; **~s** *npl* (*behaviour*) Manieren *pl*; **in a ~ of speaking** sozusagen; **~ism** *n* (*of person*) Angewohnheit *f*; (*of style*) Manieriertheit *f*

manoeuvre [mə'nu:vər] (*US* **maneuver**) *vt, vi* manövrieren ♦ *n* (*MIL*) Feldzug *m*; (*general*) Manöver *nt*, Schachzug *m*

manor ['mænər] *n* Landgut *nt*

manpower ['mænpaʊər] *n* Arbeitskräfte *pl*

mansion ['mænʃən] *n* Villa *f*

manslaughter ['mænslɔ:tər] *n* Totschlag *m*

mantelpiece ['mæntlpi:s] *n* Kaminsims *m*

manual ['mænjuəl] *adj* manuell, Hand- ♦ *n* Handbuch *nt*

manufacture [mænju'fæktʃər] *vt* herstellen ♦ *n* Herstellung *f*; **~r** *n* Hersteller *m*

manure [mə'njʊər] *n* Dünger *m*

manuscript ['mænjuskrɪpt] *n* Manuskript *nt*

Manx [mæŋks] *adj* der Insel Man

many ['menɪ] *adj, pron* viele; **a great ~** sehr viele; **~ a time** oft

map [mæp] *n* (Land)karte *f*; (*of town*) Stadtplan *m* ♦ *vt* eine Karte machen von; **~ out** *vt* (*fig*) ausarbeiten

maple ['meɪpl] *n* Ahorn *m*

mar [mɑ:r] *vt* verderben

marathon ['mærəθən] *n* (*SPORT*) Marathonlauf *m*; (*fig*) Marathon *m*

marble ['mɑ:bl] *n* Marmor *m*; (*for game*) Murmel *f*

March [mɑ:tʃ] *n* März *m*

march [mɑ:tʃ] *vi* marschieren ♦ *n* Marsch *m*

mare [meər] *n* Stute *f*

margarine [mɑ:dʒə'ri:n] *n* Margarine *f*

margin ['mɑ:dʒɪn] *n* Rand *m*; (*extra amount*) Spielraum *m*; (*COMM*) Spanne *f*; **~al** *adj* (*note*) Rand-; (*difference etc*) geringfügig; **~al (seat)** *n* (*POL*) Wahlkreis, der nur mit knapper Mehrheit gehalten wird

marigold ['mærɪgəʊld] *n* Ringelblume *f*

marijuana [mærɪ'wɑ:nə] *n* Marihuana *nt*

marina [mə'ri:nə] *n* Jachthafen *m*

marinate ['mærɪneɪt] *vt* marinieren

marine [mə'ri:n] *adj* Meeres-, See- ♦ *n* (*MIL*) Marineinfanterist *m*

marital ['mærɪtl] *adj* ehelich, Ehe-; **~ status** *n* Familienstand *m*

maritime ['mærɪtaɪm] *adj* See-

mark [mɑːk] *n* (*coin*) Mark *f*; (*spot*) Fleck *m*; (*scar*) Kratzer *m*; (*sign*) Zeichen *nt*; (*target*) Ziel *nt*; (*SCH*) Note *f* ♦ *vt* (*make ~ on*) Flecken/Kratzer machen auf +*acc*; (*indicate*) markieren; (*exam*) korrigieren; **to ~ time** (*also fig*) auf der Stelle treten; **~ out** *vt* bestimmen; (*area*) abstecken; **~ed** *adj* deutlich; **~er** *n* (*in book*) (Lese)zeichen *nt*; (*on road*) Schild *nt*

market ['mɑːkɪt] *n* Markt *m*; (*stock ~*) Börse *f* ♦ *vt* (*COMM: new product*) auf den Markt bringen; (*sell*) vertreiben; **~ garden** (*BRIT*) *n* Handelsgärtnerei *f*; **~ing** *n* Marketing *nt*; **~ research** *n* Marktforschung *f*; **~ value** *n* Marktwert *m*

marksman ['mɑːksmən] (*irreg*) *n* Scharfschütze *m*

marmalade ['mɑːməleɪd] *n* Orangenmarmelade *f*

maroon [mə'ruːn] *vt* aussetzen ♦ *adj* (*colour*) kastanienbraun

marquee [mɑː'kiː] *n* große(s) Zelt *nt*

marriage ['mærɪdʒ] *n* Ehe *f*; (*wedding*) Heirat *f*; **~ bureau** *n* Heiratsinstitut *nt*; **~ certificate** *n* Heiratsurkunde *f*

married ['mærɪd] *adj* (*person*) verheiratet; (*couple, life*) Ehe-

marrow ['mærəʊ] *n* (Knochen)mark *nt*; (*BOT*) Kürbis *m*

marry ['mærɪ] *vt* (*join*) trauen; (*take as husband, wife*) heiraten ♦ *vi* (*also:* **get married**) heiraten

marsh [mɑːʃ] *n* Sumpf *m*

marshal ['mɑːʃl] *n* (*US*) Bezirkspolizeichef *m* ♦ *vt* (an)ordnen, arrangieren

marshy ['mɑːʃɪ] *adj* sumpfig

martial law ['mɑːʃl] *n* Kriegsrecht *nt*

martyr ['mɑːtə*] *n* (*also fig*) Märtyrer(in) *m(f)* ♦ *vt* zum Märtyrer machen; **~dom** *n* Martyrium *nt*

marvel ['mɑːvl] *n* Wunder *nt* ♦ *vi*: **to ~ (at)** sich wundern (über +*acc*); **~lous** (*US* **marvelous**) *adj* wunderbar

Marxist ['mɑːksɪst] *n* Marxist(in) *m(f)*

marzipan ['mɑːzɪpæn] *n* Marzipan *nt*

mascara [mæs'kɑːrə] *n* Wimperntusche *f*

mascot ['mæskət] *n* Maskottchen *nt*

masculine ['mæskjulɪn] *adj* männlich

mash [mæʃ] *n* Brei *m*; **~ed potatoes** *npl* Kartoffelbrei *m or* -püree *nt*

mask [mɑːsk] *n* (*also fig*) Maske *f* ♦ *vt* maskieren, verdecken

mason ['meɪsn] *n* (*stonemason*) Steinmetz *m*; (*freemason*) Freimaurer *m*; **~ry** *n* Mauerwerk *nt*

masquerade [mæskə'reɪd] *n* Maskerade *f* ♦ *vi*: **to ~ as** sich ausgeben als

mass [mæs] *n* Masse *f*; (*greater part*) Mehrheit *f*; (*REL*) Messe *f* ♦ *vi* sich sammeln; **the ~es** *npl* (*people*) die Masse(n) *f(pl)*

massacre ['mæsəkə*] *n* Blutbad *nt* ♦ *vt* niedermetzeln, massakrieren

massage ['mæsɑːʒ] *n* Massage *f* ♦ *vt* massieren

massive ['mæsɪv] *adj* gewaltig, massiv

mass media *npl* Massenmedien *pl*

mass production *n* Massenproduktion *f*

mast [mɑːst] *n* Mast *m*

master ['mɑːstə*] *n* Herr *m*; (*NAUT*) Kapitän *m*; (*teacher*) Lehrer *m*; (*artist*) Meister *m* ♦ *vt* meistern; (*language etc*) beherrschen; **~ly** *adj* meisterhaft; **~mind** *n* Kapazität *f* ♦ *vt* geschickt lenken; **M~ of Arts** *n* Magister *m* der philosophischen Fakultät; **M~ of Science** *n* Magister *m* der naturwissenschaftlichen Fakultät; **~piece** *n* Meisterwerk *nt*; **~ plan** *n* kluge(r) Plan *m*; **~y** *n* Können *nt*

masturbate ['mæstəbeɪt] *vi* masturbieren, onanieren

mat [mæt] *n* Matte *f*; (*for table*) Untersetzer *m* ♦ *adj* = **matt**

match [mætʃ] *n* Streichholz *nt*; (*sth corresponding*) Pendant *nt*; (*SPORT*) Wettkampf *m*; (*ball games*) Spiel *nt* ♦ *vt* (*be like, suit*) passen zu; (*equal*) gleichkommen +*dat* ♦ *vi* zusammenpassen; **it's a good ~ (for)** es passt gut (zu); **~box** *n* Streichholzschachtel *f*; **~ing** *adj* passend

mate [meɪt] *n* (*companion*) Kamerad *m*; (*spouse*) Lebensgefährte *m*; (*of animal*) Weibchen *nt*/Männchen *nt*; (*NAUT*) Schiffsoffizier *m* ♦ *vi* (*animals*) sich paaren

♦ vt (animals) paaren

material [məˈtɪərɪəl] n Material nt; (for book, cloth) Stoff m ♦ adj (important) wesentlich; (damage) Sach-; (comforts etc) materiell; ~**s** npl (for building etc) Materialien pl; ~**istic** [mətɪərɪəˈlɪstɪk] adj materialistisch; ~**ize** vi sich verwirklichen, zustande or zu Stande kommen

maternal [məˈtɜːnl] adj mütterlich, Mutter-

maternity [məˈtɜːnɪtɪ] adj (dress) Umstands-; (benefit) Wochen-; ~ **hospital** n Entbindungsheim nt

math [mæθ] (US) n = **maths**

mathematical [mæθəˈmætɪkl] adj mathematisch; **mathematics** n Mathematik f; **maths** (US **math**) n Mathe f

matinée [ˈmætɪneɪ] n Matinee f

matrices [ˈmeɪtrɪsiːz] npl of **matrix**

matriculation [mətrɪkjuˈleɪʃən] n Immatrikulation f

matrimonial [mætrɪˈməʊnɪəl] adj ehelich, Ehe-

matrimony [ˈmætrɪmənɪ] n Ehestand m

matrix [ˈmeɪtrɪks] (pl **matrices**) n Matrize f; (GEOL etc) Matrix f

matron [ˈmeɪtrən] n (MED) Oberin f; (SCH) Hausmutter f

matt [mæt] adj (paint) matt

matted [ˈmætɪd] adj verfilzt

matter [ˈmætər] n (substance) Materie f; (affair) Angelegenheit f ♦ vi darauf ankommen; **no ~ how/what** egal wie/was; **what is the ~?** was ist los?; **as a ~ of course** selbstverständlich; **as a ~ of fact** eigentlich; **it doesn't ~** es macht nichts; ~**-of-fact** adj sachlich, nüchtern

mattress [ˈmætrɪs] n Matratze f

mature [məˈtjuər] adj reif ♦ vi reif werden; **maturity** [məˈtjuərɪtɪ] n Reife f

maul [mɔːl] vt übel zurichten

maxima [ˈmæksɪmə] npl of **maximum**

maximum [ˈmæksɪməm] (pl **maxima**) adj Höchst-, Maximal- ♦ n Maximum nt

May [meɪ] n Mai m

may [meɪ] (conditional **might**) vi (be possible) können; (have permission) dürfen; **he ~ come** er kommt vielleicht; ~**be** [ˈmeɪbiː] adv vielleicht

May Day n der 1. Mai

mayhem [ˈmeɪhem] n Chaos nt; (US) Körperverletzung f

mayonnaise [meɪəˈneɪz] n Majonäse f, Mayonnaise f

mayor [mɛər] n Bürgermeister m; ~**ess** n Bürgermeisterin f; (wife) (die) Frau f Bürgermeister

maypole [ˈmeɪpəʊl] n Maibaum m

maze [meɪz] n Irrgarten m; (fig) Wirrwarr nt

M.D. abbr = **Doctor of Medicine**

KEYWORD

me [miː] pron **1** (direct) mich; **it's me** ich bins

2 (indirect) mir; **give them to me** gib sie mir

3 (after prep: +acc) mich; (: +dat) mir; **with/without me** mit mir/ohne mich

---

meadow [ˈmedəʊ] n Wiese f

meagre [ˈmiːɡər] (US **meager**) adj dürftig, spärlich

meal [miːl] n Essen nt, Mahlzeit f; (grain) Schrotmehl nt; **to have a ~** essen (gehen); ~**time** n Essenszeit f

mean [miːn] (pt, pp **meant**) adj (stingy) geizig; (spiteful) gemein; (average) durchschnittlich, Durchschnitts- ♦ vt (signify) bedeuten; (intend) vorhaben, beabsichtigen ♦ n (average) Durchschnitt m; ~**s** npl (wherewithal) Mittel pl; (wealth) Vermögen nt; **do you ~ me?** meinst du mich?; **do you ~ it?** meinst du das ernst?; **what do you ~?** was willst du damit sagen?; **to be ~t for sb/sth** für jdn/etw bestimmt sein; **by ~s of** durch; **by all ~s** selbstverständlich; **by no ~s** keineswegs

meander [mɪˈændər] vi sich schlängeln

meaning [ˈmiːnɪŋ] n Bedeutung f; (of life) Sinn m; ~**ful** adj bedeutungsvoll; (life) sinnvoll; ~**less** adj sinnlos

meanness [ˈmiːnnɪs] n (stinginess) Geiz m; (spitefulness) Gemeinheit f

meant [ment] pt, pp of **mean**

meantime [ˈmiːntaɪm] adv inzwischen

meanwhile ['mi:nwaɪl] *adv* inzwischen
measles ['mi:zlz] *n* Masern *pl*
measly ['mi:zlɪ] (*inf*) *adj* poplig
measure ['meʒəʳ] *vt, vi* messen ♦ *n* Maß *nt*; (*step*) Maßnahme *f*; **~ments** *npl* Maße *pl*
meat [mi:t] *n* Fleisch *nt*; **cold ~** Aufschnitt *m*; **~ ball** *n* Fleischkloß *m*; **~ pie** *n* Fleischpastete *f*; **~y** *adj* fleischig; (*fig*) gehaltvoll
Mecca ['mekə] *n* Mekka *nt* (*also fig*)
mechanic [mɪ'kænɪk] *n* Mechaniker *m*; **~al** *adj* mechanisch; **~s** *n* Mechanik *f* ♦ *npl* Technik *f*
mechanism ['mekənɪzəm] *n* Mechanismus *m*
mechanize ['mekənaɪz] *vt* mechanisieren
medal ['medl] *n* Medaille *f*; (*decoration*) Orden *m*; **~list** (*US* **medalist**) *n* Medaillengewinner(in) *m(f)*
meddle ['medl] *vi*: **to ~ (in)** sich einmischen (in +*acc*); **to ~ with sth** sich an etw *dat* zu schaffen machen
media ['mi:dɪə] *npl* Medien *pl*
mediaeval [medi'i:vl] *adj* = **medieval**
median ['mi:dɪən] (*US*) *n* (*also:* **~ strip**) Mittelstreifen *m*
mediate ['mi:dɪeɪt] *vi* vermitteln; **mediator** *n* Vermittler *m*
Medicaid ['medɪkeɪd] (® *US*) *n* medizinisches Versorgungsprogramm für sozial Schwache
medical ['medɪkl] *adj* medizinisch; Medizin-; ärztlich ♦ *n* (ärztliche) Untersuchung *f*
Medicare ['medɪkeəʳ] (*US*) *n* staatliche Krankenversicherung besonders für Ältere
medicated ['medɪkeɪtɪd] *adj* medizinisch
medication [medɪ'keɪʃən] *n* (*drugs etc*) Medikamente *pl*
medicinal [me'dɪsɪnl] *adj* medizinisch, Heil-
medicine ['medsɪn] *n* Medizin *f*; (*drugs*) Arznei *f*
medieval [medi'i:vl] *adj* mittelalterlich
mediocre [mi:dɪ'əukəʳ] *adj* mittelmäßig
meditate ['medɪteɪt] *vi* meditieren; **to ~ (on sth)** (über etw *acc*) nachdenken; **meditation** [medɪ'teɪʃən] *n* Nachsinnen *nt*; Meditation *f*

Mediterranean [medɪtə'reɪnɪən] *adj* Mittelmeer-; (*person*) südländisch; **the ~ (Sea)** das Mittelmeer
medium ['mi:dɪəm] *adj* mittlere(r, s), Mittel-, mittel- ♦ *n* Mitte *f*; (*means*) Mittel *nt*; (*person*) Medium *nt*; **happy ~** goldener Mittelweg *m*; **~-sized** *adj* mittelgroß; **~ wave** *n* Mittelwelle *f*
medley ['medlɪ] *n* Gemisch *nt*
meek [mi:k] *adj* sanft(mütig); (*pej*) duckmäuserisch
meet [mi:t] (*pt, pp* **met**) *vt* (*encounter*) treffen, begegnen +*dat*; (*by arrangement*) sich treffen mit; (*difficulties*) stoßen auf +*acc*; (*get to know*) kennen lernen; (*fetch*) abholen; (*join*) zusammentreffen mit; (*satisfy*) entsprechen +*dat* ♦ *vi* sich treffen; (*become acquainted*) sich kennen lernen; **~ with** *vt* (*problems*) stoßen auf +*acc*; (*US: people*) zusammentreffen mit; **~ing** *n* Treffen *nt*; (*business ~ing*) Besprechung *f*; (*of committee*) Sitzung *f*; (*assembly*) Versammlung *f*
mega- ['megə-] (*inf*) *prefix* Mega-; **~byte** *n* (*COMPUT*) Megabyte *nt*; **~phone** *n* Megafon *nt*, Megaphon *nt*
melancholy ['melənkəlɪ] *adj* (*person*) melancholisch; (*sight, event*) traurig
mellow ['meləu] *adj* mild, weich; (*fruit*) reif; (*fig*) gesetzt ♦ *vi* reif werden
melodious [mɪ'ləudɪəs] *adj* wohlklingend
melody ['melədɪ] *n* Melodie *f*
melon ['melən] *n* Melone *f*
melt [melt] *vi* schmelzen; (*anger*) verfliegen ♦ *vt* schmelzen; **~ away** *vi* dahinschmelzen; **~ down** *vt* einschmelzen; **~down** *n* (*in nuclear reactor*) Kernschmelze *f*; **~ing point** *n* Schmelzpunkt *m*; **~ing pot** *n* (*fig*) Schmelztiegel *m*
member ['membəʳ] *n* Mitglied *nt*; (*of tribe, species*) Angehörige(r) (*f)m*; (*ANAT*) Glied *nt*; **M~ of Parliament** (*BRIT*) *n* Parlamentsmitglied *nt*; **M~ of the European Parliament** (*BRIT*) *n* Mitglied *nt* des Europäischen Parlaments; **~ship** *n* Mitgliedschaft *f*; **to seek ~ship of** einen Antrag auf Mitgliedschaft stellen; **~ship**

card *n* Mitgliedskarte *f*

memento [məˈmentəu] *n* Andenken *nt*

memo [ˈmeməu] *n* Mitteilung *f*

memoirs [ˈmemwɑːz] *npl* Memoiren *pl*

memorable [ˈmemərəbl] *adj* denkwürdig

memoranda [meməˈrændə] *npl of* **memorandum**

memorandum [meməˈrændəm] (*pl* **memoranda**) *n* Mitteilung *f*

memorial [mɪˈmɔːrɪəl] *n* Denkmal *nt* ♦ *adj* Gedenk-

memorize [ˈmeməraɪz] *vt* sich einprägen

memory [ˈmeməri] *n* Gedächtnis *nt*; (*of computer*) Speicher *m*; (*sth recalled*) Erinnerung *f*

men [men] *pl of* **man** ♦ *n* (*human race*) die Menschen *pl*

menace [ˈmenɪs] *n* Drohung *f*; Gefahr *f* ♦ *vt* bedrohen; **menacing** *adj* drohend

menagerie [mɪˈnædʒərɪ] *n* Tierschau *f*

mend [mend] *vt* reparieren, flicken ♦ *vi* (ver)heilen ♦ *n* ausgebesserte Stelle *f*; **on the ~** auf dem Wege der Besserung; **~ing** *n* (*articles*) Flickarbeit *f*

menial [ˈmiːnɪəl] *adj* niedrig

meningitis [menɪnˈdʒaɪtɪs] *n* Hirnhautentzündung *f*, Meningitis *f*

menopause [ˈmenəupɔːz] *n* Wechseljahre *pl*, Menopause *f*

menstruation [menstruˈeɪʃən] *n* Menstruation *f*

mental [ˈmentl] *adj* geistig, Geistes-; (*arithmetic*) Kopf-; (*hospital*) Nerven-; (*cruelty*) seelisch; (*inf: abnormal*) verrückt; **~ity** [menˈtælɪtɪ] *n* Mentalität *f*

menthol [ˈmenθɒl] *n* Menthol *nt*

mention [ˈmenʃən] *n* Erwähnung *f* ♦ *vt* erwähnen; **don't ~ it!** bitte (sehr), gern geschehen

mentor [ˈmentɔːr] *n* Mentor *m*

menu [ˈmenjuː] *n* Speisekarte *f*

MEP *n abbr* = **Member of the European Parliament**

mercenary [ˈmɜːsɪnərɪ] *adj* (*person*) geldgierig ♦ *n* Söldner *m*

merchandise [ˈmɜːtʃəndaɪz] *n* (Handels)ware *f*

merchant [ˈmɜːtʃənt] *n* Kaufmann *m*; **~ bank** (*BRIT*) *n* Handelsbank *f*; **~ navy** (*US* **~ marine**) *n* Handelsmarine *f*

merciful [ˈmɜːsɪful] *adj* gnädig

merciless [ˈmɜːsɪlɪs] *adj* erbarmungslos

mercury [ˈmɜːkjurɪ] *n* Quecksilber *nt*

mercy [ˈmɜːsɪ] *n* Erbarmen *nt*; Gnade *f*; **at the ~ of** ausgeliefert +*dat*

mere [mɪər] *adj* bloß; **~ly** *adv* bloß

merge [mɜːdʒ] *vt* verbinden; (*COMM*) fusionieren ♦ *vi* verschmelzen; (*roads*) zusammenlaufen; (*COMM*) fusionieren; **~r** *n* (*COMM*) Fusion *f*

meringue [məˈræŋ] *n* Baiser *nt*

merit [ˈmerɪt] *n* Verdienst *nt*; (*advantage*) Vorzug *m* ♦ *vt* verdienen

mermaid [ˈmɜːmeɪd] *n* Wassernixe *f*

merry [ˈmerɪ] *adj* fröhlich; **~-go-round** *n* Karussell *nt*

mesh [meʃ] *n* Masche *f*

mesmerize [ˈmezməraɪz] *vt* hypnotisieren; (*fig*) faszinieren

mess [mes] *n* (*untidiness*) Unordnung *f*; (*dirt*) Schmutz *m*; (*trouble*) Schwierigkeiten *pl*; (*MIL*) Messe *f*; **~ about** *or* **around** *vi* (*play the fool*) herumalbern; (*do nothing in particular*) herumgammeln; **~ about** *or* **around with** *vt fus* (*tinker with*) herummurksen an +*dat*; **~ up** *vt* verpfuschen; (*make untidy*) in Unordnung bringen

message [ˈmesɪdʒ] *n* Mitteilung *f*; **to get the ~** kapieren

messenger [ˈmesɪndʒər] *n* Bote *m*

Messrs [ˈmesəz] *abbr* (*on letters*) die Herren

messy [ˈmesɪ] *adj* schmutzig; (*untidy*) unordentlich

met [met] *pt, pp of* **meet**

metabolism [meˈtæbəlɪzəm] *n* Stoffwechsel *m*

metal [ˈmetl] *n* Metall *nt*; **~lic** *adj* metallisch; (*made of ~*) aus Metall

metaphor [ˈmetəfər] *n* Metapher *f*

meteorology [miːtɪəˈrɒlədʒɪ] *n* Meteorologie *f*

meter [ˈmiːtər] *n* Zähler *m*; (*US*) = **metre**

method [ˈmeθəd] *n* Methode *f*; **~ical** [mɪˈθɒdɪkl] *adj* methodisch; **M~ist**

['mɛθədɪst] *adj* methodistisch ♦ *n*
Methodist(in) *m(f)*; **~ology** [mɛθə'dɔlədʒɪ] *n*
Methodik *f*

meths [mɛθs] *(BRIT) n(pl)* = **methylated spirit(s)**

methylated spirit(s) ['mɛθɪleɪtɪd-] *(BRIT) n*
(Brenn)spiritus *m*

meticulous [mɪ'tɪkjʊləs] *adj* (über)genau

metre ['mi:tər] *(US* **meter**) *n* Meter *m or nt*

metric ['mɛtrɪk] *adj (also:* **~al**) metrisch

metropolitan [mɛtrə'pɔlɪtn] *adj* der
Großstadt; **M~ Police** *(BRIT) n:* **the M~
Police** die Londoner Polizei

mettle ['mɛtl] *n* Mut *m*

mew [mju:] *vi (cat)* miauen

mews [mju:z] *n:* **~ cottage** ehemaliges
Kutscherhäuschen

Mexican ['mɛksɪkən] *adj* mexikanisch ♦ *n*
Mexikaner(in) *m(f)*

Mexico ['mɛksɪkəu] *n* Mexiko *nt*

miaow [miː'au] *vi* miauen

mice [maɪs] *pl of* **mouse**

micro ['maɪkrəu] *n (also:* **~computer**)
Mikrocomputer *m;* **~chip** *n* Mikrochip *m;*
~cosm ['maɪkrəukɔzəm] *n* Mikrokosmos *m;*
~phone *n* Mikrofon *nt*, Mikrophon *nt;*
~scope *n* Mikroskop *nt;* **~wave** *n (also:*
~wave oven) Mikrowelle(nherd *nt*) *f*

mid [mɪd] *adj:* **in ~ afternoon** am
Nachmittag; **in ~ air** in der Luft; **in ~ May**
Mitte Mai

midday [mɪd'deɪ] *n* Mittag *m*

middle ['mɪdl] *n* Mitte *f; (waist)* Taille *f* ♦ *adj*
mittlere(r, s), Mittel-; **in the ~ of** mitten in
+dat; **~-aged** *adj* mittleren Alters; **M~
Ages** *npl* die **M~ Ages** das Mittelalter;
~-class *adj* Mittelstands-; **M~ East** *n:* **the
M~ East** der Nahe Osten; **~man** *(irreg) n*
(COMM) Zwischenhändler *m;* **~ name** *n*
zweiter Vorname *m;* **~ weight** *n (BOXING)*
Mittelgewicht *nt*

middling ['mɪdlɪŋ] *adj* mittelmäßig

midge [mɪdʒ] *n* Mücke *f*

midget ['mɪdʒɪt] *n* Liliputaner(in) *m(f)*

midnight ['mɪdnaɪt] *n* Mitternacht *f*

midriff ['mɪdrɪf] *n* Taille *f*

midst [mɪdst] *n:* **in the ~ of** *(persons)* mitten

unter *+dat; (things)* mitten in *+dat*

mid [mɪd'-]: **~summer** *n* Hochsommer *m;*
~way *adv* auf halbem Wege ♦ *adj* Mittel-;
~week *adv* in der Mitte der Woche

midwife ['mɪdwaɪf] *(irreg) n* Hebamme *f;* **~ry**
['mɪdwɪfərɪ] *n* Geburtshilfe *f*

midwinter [mɪd'wɪntər] *n* tiefste(r) Winter *m*

might [maɪt] *vi see* **may** ♦ *n* Macht *f*, Kraft *f;*
I ~ come ich komme vielleicht; **~y** *adj, adv*
mächtig

migraine ['miːgreɪn] *n* Migräne *f*

migrant ['maɪgrənt] *adj* Wander-; *(bird)* Zug-

migrate [maɪ'greɪt] *vi* (ab)wandern; *(birds)*
(fort)ziehen; **migration** [maɪ'greɪʃən] *n*
Wanderung *f*, Zug *m*

mike [maɪk] *n* = **microphone**

Milan [mɪ'læn] *n* Mailand *nt*

mild [maɪld] *adj* mild; *(medicine, interest)*
leicht; *(person)* sanft ♦ *n (beer)* leichtes
dunkles Bier

mildew ['mɪldju:] *n (on plants)* Mehltau *m;*
(on food) Schimmel *m*

mildly ['maɪldlɪ] *adv* leicht; **to put it ~**
gelinde gesagt

mile [maɪl] *n* Meile *f;* **~age** *n* Meilenzahl *f;*
~ometer *n* = **milometer;** **~stone** *n (also*
fig) Meilenstein *m*

militant ['mɪlɪtnt] *adj* militant ♦ *n*
Militante(r) *mf*

military ['mɪlɪtərɪ] *adj* militärisch, Militär-,
Wehr-

militate ['mɪlɪteɪt] *vi:* **to ~ against**
entgegenwirken *+dat*

militia [mɪ'lɪʃə] *n* Miliz *f*

milk [mɪlk] *n* Milch *f* ♦ *vt (also fig)* melken; **~
chocolate** *n* Milchschokolade *f;* **~man**
(irreg) n Milchmann *m;* **~ shake** *n*
Milchmixgetränk *nt;* **~y** *adj* milchig; **M~y
Way** *n* Milchstraße *f*

mill [mɪl] *n* Mühle *f; (factory)* Fabrik *f* ♦ *vt*
mahlen ♦ *vi* umherlaufen

millennia [mɪ'lɛnɪə] *npl of* **millennium**

millennium [mɪ'lɛnɪəm] *(pl* **~s** *or* **millennia**)
n Jahrtausend *nt;* **~ bug** *n (COMPUT)*
Jahrtausendfehler *m*

miller ['mɪlər] *n* Müller *m*

milligram(me) ['mɪlɪgræm] *n* Milligramm *nt*

millimetre ['mɪlɪmiːtəʳ] (*US* **millimeter**) *n* Millimeter *m*

million ['mɪljən] *n* Million *f*; **a ~ times** tausendmal; **~aire** [mɪljə'nɛəʳ] *n* Millionär(in) *m(f)*

millstone ['mɪlstəun] *n* Mühlstein *m*

milometer [maɪ'lɔmɪtəʳ] *n* ≈ Kilometerzähler *m*

mime [maɪm] *n* Pantomime *f* ♦ *vt, vi* mimen

mimic ['mɪmɪk] *n* Mimiker *m* ♦ *vt, vi* nachahmen; **~ry** *n* Nachahmung *f*; (*BIOL*) Mimikry *f*

min. *abbr* = **minutes**; **minimum**

mince [mɪns] *vt* (zer)hacken ♦ *n* (*meat*) Hackfleisch *nt*; **~meat** *n* süße Pastetenfüllung *f*; **~ pie** *n* gefüllte (süße) Pastete *f*; **~r** *n* Fleischwolf *m*

mind [maɪnd] *n* Verstand *m*, Geist *m*; (*opinion*) Meinung *f* ♦ *vt* aufpassen auf +*acc*; (*object to*) etwas haben gegen; **on my ~** auf dem Herzen; **to my ~** meiner Meinung nach; **to be out of one's ~** wahnsinnig sein; **to bear** *or* **keep in ~** bedenken; **to change one's ~** es sich *dat* anders überlegen; **to make up one's ~** sich entschließen; **I don't ~** das macht mir nichts aus; **~ you**, ... allerdings ...; **never ~!** macht nichts!; **"~ the step"** „Vorsicht Stufe"; **~ your own business** kümmern Sie sich um Ihre eigenen Angelegenheiten; **~er** *n* Aufpasser(in) *m(f)*; **~ful** *adj*: **~ful of** achtsam auf +*acc*; **~less** *adj* sinnlos

mine[1] [maɪn] *n* (*coalmine*) Bergwerk *nt*; (*MIL*) Mine *f* ♦ *vt* abbauen; (*MIL*) verminen

mine[2] [maɪn] *pron* meine(r, s); **that book is ~** das Buch gehört mir; **a friend of ~** ein Freund von mir

minefield ['maɪnfiːld] *n* Minenfeld *nt*

miner ['maɪnəʳ] *n* Bergarbeiter *m*

mineral ['mɪnərəl] *adj* mineralisch, Mineral- ♦ *n* Mineral *nt*; **~s** *npl* (*BRIT: soft drinks*) alkoholfreie Getränke *pl*; **~ water** *n* Mineralwasser *nt*

minesweeper ['maɪnswiːpəʳ] *n* Minensuchboot *nt*

mingle ['mɪŋgl] *vi*: **to ~ (with)** sich mischen (unter +*acc*)

miniature ['mɪnətʃəʳ] *adj* Miniatur- ♦ *n* Miniatur *f*

minibus ['mɪnɪbʌs] *n* Kleinbus *m*

minimal ['mɪnɪml] *adj* minimal

minimize ['mɪnɪmaɪz] *vt* auf das Mindestmaß beschränken

minimum ['mɪnɪməm] (*pl* **minima**) *n* Minimum *nt* ♦ *adj* Mindest-

mining ['maɪnɪŋ] *n* Bergbau *m* ♦ *adj* Bergbau-, Berg-

miniskirt ['mɪnɪskəːt] *n* Minirock *m*

minister ['mɪnɪstəʳ] *n* (*BRIT: POL*) Minister *m*; (*ECCL*) Pfarrer *m* ♦ *vi*: **to ~ to sb/sb's needs** sich um jdn kümmern; **~ial** [mɪnɪs'tɪərəl] *adj* ministeriell, Minister-

ministry ['mɪnɪstrɪ] *n* (*BRIT: POL*) Ministerium *nt*; (*ECCL: office*) geistliche(s) Amt *nt*

mink [mɪŋk] *n* Nerz *m*

minnow ['mɪnəu] *n* Elritze *f*

minor ['maɪnəʳ] *adj* kleiner; (*operation*) leicht; (*problem, poet*) unbedeutend; (*MUS*) Moll ♦ *n* (*BRIT: under 18*) Minderjährige(r) *mf*

minority [maɪ'nɔrɪtɪ, maɪ'nɔrɪtɪ] *n* Minderheit *f*

mint [mɪnt] *n* Minze *f*; (*sweet*) Pfefferminzbonbon *nt* ♦ *vt* (*coins*) prägen; **the (Royal** (*BRIT*) *or* **US** (*US*)) **M~** die Münzanstalt; **in ~ condition** in tadellosem Zustand

minus ['maɪnəs] *n* Minuszeichen *nt*; (*amount*) Minusbetrag *m* ♦ *prep* minus, weniger

minuscule ['mɪnəskjuːl] *adj* winzig

minute[1] [maɪ'njuːt] *adj* winzig; (*detailed*) minutiös, minuziös

minute[2] ['mɪnɪt] *n* Minute *f*; (*moment*) Augenblick *m*; **~s** *npl* (*of meeting etc*) Protokoll *nt*

miracle ['mɪrəkl] *n* Wunder *nt*

miraculous [mɪ'rækjuləs] *adj* wunderbar

mirage ['mɪrɑːʒ] *n* Fata Morgana *f*

mire ['maɪəʳ] *n* Morast *m*

mirror ['mɪrəʳ] *n* Spiegel *m* ♦ *vt* (wider)spiegeln

mirth [məːθ] *n* Heiterkeit *f*

misadventure [mɪsəd'vɛntʃəʳ] *n* Missgeschick *nt*, Unfall *m*

misanthropist [mɪ'zænθrəpɪst] *n*

Menschenfeind *m*

misapprehension ['mɪsæprɪ'henʃən] *n* Missverständnis *nt*

misbehave [mɪsbɪ'heɪv] *vi* sich schlecht benehmen

miscalculate [mɪs'kælkjuleɪt] *vt* falsch berechnen

miscarriage ['mɪskærɪdʒ] *n* (*MED*) Fehlgeburt *f*; ~ **of justice** Fehlurteil *nt*

miscellaneous [mɪsɪ'leɪnɪəs] *adj* verschieden

mischief ['mɪstʃɪf] *n* Unfug *m*; **mischievous** ['mɪstʃɪvəs] *adj* (*person*) durchtrieben; (*glance*) verschmitzt; (*rumour*) bösartig

misconception ['mɪskən'sepʃən] *n* fälschliche Annahme *f*

misconduct [mɪs'kɔndʌkt] *n* Vergehen *nt*; **professional** ~ Berufsvergehen *nt*

misconstrue [mɪskən'stru:] *vt* missverstehen

misdemeanour [mɪsdɪ'mi:nər] (*US* **misdemeanor**) *n* Vergehen *nt*

miser ['maɪzər] *n* Geizhals *m*

miserable ['mɪzərəbl] *adj* (*unhappy*) unglücklich; (*headache, weather*) fürchterlich; (*poor*) elend; (*contemptible*) erbärmlich

miserly ['maɪzəlɪ] *adj* geizig

misery ['mɪzərɪ] *n* Elend *nt*, Qual *f*

misfire [mɪs'faɪər] *vi* (*gun*) versagen; (*engine*) fehlzünden; (*plan*) fehlgehen

misfit ['mɪsfɪt] *n* Außenseiter *m*

misfortune [mɪs'fɔ:tʃən] *n* Unglück *nt*

misgiving(s) [mɪs'gɪvɪŋ(z)] *n(pl)* Bedenken *pl*

misguided [mɪs'gaɪdɪd] *adj* fehlgeleitet; (*opinions*) irrig

mishandle [mɪs'hændl] *vt* falsch handhaben

mishap ['mɪshæp] *n* Missgeschick *nt*

misinform [mɪsɪn'fɔ:m] *vt* falsch unterrichten

misinterpret [mɪsɪn'tə:prɪt] *vt* falsch auffassen

misjudge [mɪs'dʒʌdʒ] *vt* falsch beurteilen

mislay [mɪs'leɪ] (*irreg: like* **lay**) *vt* verlegen

mislead [mɪs'li:d] (*irreg: like* **lead**[2]) *vt*

(*deceive*) irreführen; ~**ing** *adj* irreführend

mismanage [mɪs'mænɪdʒ] *vt* schlecht verwalten

misnomer [mɪs'nəumər] *n* falsche Bezeichnung *f*

misplace [mɪs'pleɪs] *vt* verlegen

misprint ['mɪsprɪnt] *n* Druckfehler *m*

Miss [mɪs] *n* Fräulein *nt*

miss [mɪs] *vt* (*fail to hit, catch*) verfehlen; (*not notice*) verpassen; (*be too late*) versäumen, verpassen; (*omit*) auslassen; (*regret the absence of*) vermissen ♦ *vi* fehlen ♦ *n* (*shot*) Fehlschuss *m*; (*failure*) Fehlschlag *m*; **I ~ you** du fehlst mir; ~ **out** *vt* auslassen

misshapen [mɪs'ʃeɪpən] *adj* missgestaltet

missile ['mɪsaɪl] *n* Rakete *f*

missing ['mɪsɪŋ] *adj* (*person*) vermisst; (*thing*) fehlend; **to be** ~ fehlen

mission ['mɪʃən] *n* (*work*) Auftrag *m*; (*people*) Delegation *f*; (*REL*) Mission *f*; ~**ary** *n* Missionar(in) *m(f)*; ~ **statement** *n* Kurzdarstellung *f* der Firmenphilosophie

misspell ['mɪs'spel] (*irreg: like* **spell**) *vt* falsch schreiben

misspent ['mɪs'spent] *adj* (*youth*) vergeudet

mist [mɪst] *n* Dunst *m*, Nebel *m* ♦ *vi* (*also:* ~ **over**, ~ **up**) sich trüben; (*BRIT: windows*) sich beschlagen

mistake [mɪs'teɪk] (*irreg: like* **take**) *n* Fehler *m* ♦ *vt* (*misunderstand*) missverstehen; (*mix up*): **to ~ (sth for sth)** (etw mit etw) verwechseln; **to make a ~** einen Fehler machen; **by ~** aus Versehen; **to ~ A for B** A mit B verwechseln; ~**n** *pp of* **mistake** ♦ *adj* (*idea*) falsch; **to be ~n** sich irren

mister ['mɪstər] *n* (*inf*) Herr *m*; *see* **Mr**

mistletoe ['mɪsltəu] *n* Mistel *f*

mistook [mɪs'tuk] *pt of* **mistake**

mistress ['mɪstrɪs] *n* (*teacher*) Lehrerin *f*; (*in house*) Herrin *f*; (*lover*) Geliebte *f*; *see* **Mrs**

mistrust [mɪs'trʌst] *vt* misstrauen +*dat*

misty ['mɪstɪ] *adj* neblig

misunderstand [mɪsʌndə'stænd] (*irreg: like* **understand**) *vt, vi* missverstehen, falsch verstehen; ~**ing** *n* Missverständnis *nt*; (*disagreement*) Meinungsverschiedenheit *f*

misuse [*n* mɪs'ju:s, *vb* mɪs'ju:z] *n* falsche(r)

Gebrauch *m* ♦ *vt* falsch gebrauchen

mitigate ['mɪtɪgeɪt] *vt* mildern

mitt(en) ['mɪt(n)] *n* Fausthandschuh *m*

mix [mɪks] *vt* (*blend*) (ver)mischen ♦ *vi* (*liquids*) sich (ver)mischen lassen; (*people: get on*) sich vertragen; (: *associate*) Kontakt haben ♦ *n* (*~ture*) Mischung *f*; **~ up** *vt* zusammenmischen; (*confuse*) verwechseln; **~ed** *adj* gemischt; **~ed-up** *adj* durcheinander; **~er** *n* (*for food*) Mixer *m*; **~ture** *n* Mischung *f*; **~-up** *n* Durcheinander *nt*

mm *abbr* (= *millimetre(s)*) mm

moan [məun] *n* Stöhnen *nt*; (*complaint*) Klage *f* ♦ *vi* stöhnen; (*complain*) maulen

moat [məut] *n* (Burg)graben *m*

mob [mɔb] *n* Mob *m*; (*the masses*) Pöbel *m* ♦ *vt* herfallen über +*acc*

mobile ['məubaɪl] *adj* beweglich; (*library etc*) fahrbar ♦ *n* (*decoration*) Mobile *nt*; **~ home** *n* Wohnwagen *m*; **~ phone** *n* (*TEL*) Mobiltelefon *nt*; **mobility** [məu'bɪlɪtɪ] *n* Beweglichkeit *f*; **mobilize** ['məubɪlaɪz] *vt* mobilisieren

mock [mɔk] *vt* verspotten; (*defy*) trotzen +*dat* ♦ *adj* Schein-; **~ery** *n* Spott *m*; (*person*) Gespött *nt*

mod [mɔd] *adj see* **convenience**

mode [məud] *n* (Art *f* und) Weise *f*

model ['mɔdl] *n* Modell *nt*; (*example*) Vorbild *nt*; (*in fashion*) Mannequin *nt* ♦ *adj* (*railway*) Modell-; (*perfect*) Muster-; vorbildlich ♦ *vt* (*make*) bilden; (*clothes*) vorführen ♦ *vi* als Mannequin arbeiten

modem ['məudɛm] *n* (*COMPUT*) Modem *nt*

moderate [*adj, n* 'mɔdərət, *vb* 'mɔdəreɪt] *adj* gemäßigt ♦ *n* (*POL*) Gemäßigte(r) *mf* ♦ *vi* sich mäßigen ♦ *vt* mäßigen; **moderation** [mɔdə'reɪʃən] *n* Mäßigung *f*; **in moderation** mit Maßen

modern ['mɔdən] *adj* modern; (*history, languages*) neuere(r, s); **~ize** *vt* modernisieren

modest ['mɔdɪst] *adj* bescheiden; **~y** *n* Bescheidenheit *f*

modicum ['mɔdɪkəm] *n* bisschen *nt*

modification [mɔdɪfɪ'keɪʃən] *n*

(Ab)änderung *f*

modify ['mɔdɪfaɪ] *vt* abändern

module ['mɔdjuːl] *n* (*component*) (Bau)element *nt*; (*SPACE*) (Raum)kapsel *f*

mogul ['məugl] *n* (*fig*) Mogul *m*

mohair ['məuheəʳ] *n* Mohär *m*, Mohair *m*

moist [mɔɪst] *adj* feucht; **~en** ['mɔɪsn] *vt* befeuchten; **~ure** ['mɔɪstʃəʳ] *n* Feuchtigkeit *f*; **~urizer** ['mɔɪstʃəraɪzəʳ] *n* Feuchtigkeitscreme *f*

molar ['məuləʳ] *n* Backenzahn *m*

molasses [mə'læsɪz] *n* Melasse *f*

mold [məuld] *n* (*US*) = **mould**

mole [məul] *n* (*spot*) Leberfleck *m*; (*animal*) Maulwurf *m*; (*pier*) Mole *f*

molest [mə'lɛst] *vt* belästigen

mollycoddle ['mɔlɪkɔdl] *vt* verhätscheln

molt [məult] *n* (*US*) *vi* = **moult**

molten ['məultən] *adj* geschmolzen

mom [mɔm] *n* (*US*) = **mum**

moment ['məumənt] *n* Moment *m*, Augenblick *m*; (*importance*) Tragweite *f*; **at the ~** im Augenblick; **~ary** *adj* kurz; **~ous** [məu'mɛntəs] *adj* folgenschwer

momentum [məu'mɛntəm] *n* Schwung *m*; **to gather ~** in Fahrt kommen

mommy ['mɔmɪ] *n* (*US*) = **mummy**

Monaco ['mɔnəkəu] *n* Monaco *nt*

monarch ['mɔnək] *n* Herrscher(in) *m(f)*; **~y** *n* Monarchie *f*

monastery ['mɔnəstərɪ] *n* Kloster *nt*

monastic [mə'næstɪk] *adj* klösterlich, Kloster-

Monday ['mʌndɪ] *n* Montag *m*

monetary ['mʌnɪtərɪ] *adj* Geld-; (*of currency*) Währungs-

money ['mʌnɪ] *n* Geld *nt*; **to make ~** Geld verdienen; **~ belt** *n* Geldgürtel *nt*; **~lender** *n* Geldverleiher *m*; **~ order** *n* Postanweisung *f*; **~-spinner** (*inf*) *n* Verkaufsschlager *m*

mongol ['mɔngəl] *n* (*MED*) mongoloide(s) Kind *nt* ♦ *adj* mongolisch; (*MED*) mongoloid

mongrel ['mʌngrəl] *n* Promenadenmischung *f*

monitor ['mɔnɪtəʳ] *n* (*SCH*) Klassenordner *m*; (*television ~*) Monitor *m* ♦ *vt* (*broadcasts*) abhören; (*control*) überwachen

monk [mʌŋk] n Mönch m

monkey ['mʌŋkɪ] n Affe m; ~ **nut** (*BRIT*) n
Erdnuss f; ~ **wrench** n (*TECH*) Engländer m,
Franzose m

monochrome ['mɒnəkrəum] adj schwarzweiß, schwarzweiß

monopolize [mə'nɒpəlaɪz] vt beherrschen

monopoly [mə'nɒpəlɪ] n Monopol nt

monosyllable ['mɒnəsɪləbl] n einsilbige(s)
Wort nt

monotone ['mɒnətəun] n gleich
bleibende(r) Ton(fall) m; **to speak in a ~**
monoton sprechen; **monotonous**
[mə'nɒtənəs] adj eintönig; **monotony**
[mə'nɒtənɪ] n Eintönigkeit f, Monotonie f

monsoon [mɒn'suːn] n Monsun m

monster ['mɒnstər] n Ungeheuer nt; (*person*)
Scheusal nt

monstrosity [mɒn'strɒsɪtɪ] n
Ungeheuerlichkeit f; (*thing*) Monstrosität f

monstrous ['mɒnstrəs] adj (*shocking*)
grässlich, ungeheuerlich; (*huge*) riesig

month [mʌnθ] n Monat m; **~ly** adj
monatlich, Monats- ♦ adv einmal im Monat
♦ n (*magazine*) Monatsschrift f

monument ['mɒnjumənt] n Denkmal nt;
~al [mɒnju'mentl] adj (*huge*) gewaltig;
(*ignorance*) ungeheuer

moo [muː] vi muhen

mood [muːd] n Stimmung f, Laune f; **to be
in a good/bad ~** gute/schlechte Laune
haben; **~y** adj launisch

moon [muːn] n Mond m; **~light** n
Mondlicht nt; **~lighting** n Schwarzarbeit f;
~lit adj mondhell

moor [muər] n Heide f, Hochmoor nt ♦ vt
(*ship*) festmachen, verankern ♦ vi anlegen;
~ings npl Liegeplatz m; **~land** ['muələnd] n
Heidemoor nt

moose [muːs] n Elch m

mop [mɒp] n Mopp m ♦ vt (auf)wischen; **~
up** vt aufwischen

mope [məup] vi Trübsal blasen

moped ['məuped] n Moped nt

moral ['mɒrl] adj moralisch; (*values*) sittlich;
(*virtuous*) tugendhaft ♦ n Moral f; **~s** npl

(*ethics*) Moral f

morale [mɒ'rɑːl] n Moral f

morality [mə'rælɪtɪ] n Sittlichkeit f

morass [mə'ræs] n Sumpf m

morbid ['mɔːbɪd] adj krankhaft; (*jokes*)
makaber

KEYWORD

more [mɔːr] adj (*greater in number etc*) mehr;
(*additional*) noch mehr; **do you want
(some) more tea?** möchten Sie noch
etwas Tee?; **I have no** or **I don't have any
more money** ich habe kein Geld mehr
♦ pron (*greater amount*) mehr; (*further or
additional amount*) noch mehr; **Is there any
more?** gibt es noch mehr?; (*left over*) ist
noch etwas da?; **there's no more** es ist
nichts mehr da
♦ adv mehr; **more dangerous/easily** etc
(**than**) gefährlicher/einfacher etc (als); **more
and more** immer mehr; **more and more
excited** immer aufgeregter; **more or less**
mehr oder weniger; **more than ever** mehr
denn je; **more beautiful than ever** schöner
denn je

---

moreover [mɔː'rəuvər] adv überdies

morgue [mɔːg] n Leichenschauhaus nt

Mormon ['mɔːmən] n Mormone m,
Mormonin f

morning ['mɔːnɪŋ] n Morgen m; **in the ~**
am Morgen; **7 o'clock in the ~** 7 Uhr
morgens; **~ sickness** n
(Schwangerschafts)übelkeit f

Morocco [mə'rɒkəu] n Marokko nt

moron ['mɔːrɒn] n Schwachsinnige(r) mf

morose [mə'rəus] adj mürrisch

morphine ['mɔːfiːn] n Morphium nt

Morse [mɔːs] n (*also:* ~ **code**)
Morsealphabet nt

morsel ['mɔːsl] n Bissen m

mortal ['mɔːtl] adj sterblich; (*deadly*) tödlich;
(*very great*) Todes- ♦ n (*human being*)
Sterbliche(r) mf; **~ity** [mɔː'tælɪtɪ] n
Sterblichkeit f; (*death rate*)
Sterblichkeitsziffer f

mortar ['mɔːtər] n (*for building*) Mörtel m;

(*MIL*) Granatwerfer m

mortgage ['mɔːgɪdʒ] n Hypothek f ♦ vt hypothekarisch belasten; ~ **company** (*US*) n ≃ Bausparkasse f

mortify ['mɔːtɪfaɪ] vt beschämen

mortuary ['mɔːtjʊərɪ] n Leichenhalle f

mosaic [məʊ'zeɪɪk] n Mosaik nt

Moscow ['mɒskəʊ] n Moskau nt

Moslem ['mɒzləm] = **Muslim**

mosque [mɒsk] n Moschee f

mosquito [mɒs'kiːtəʊ] n (pl ~**es**) n Moskito m

moss [mɒs] n Moos nt

most [məʊst] adj meiste(r, s) ♦ adv am meisten; (*very*) höchst ♦ n das meiste, der größte Teil; (*people*) die meisten; ~ **men** die meisten Männer; **at the (very)** ~ allerhöchstens; **to make the** ~ **of** das Beste machen aus; **a** ~ **interesting book** ein höchstinteressantes Buch; ~**ly** adv größtenteils

MOT (*BRIT*) n abbr (= Ministry of Transport): **the MOT (test)** ≃ der TÜV

motel [məʊ'tel] n Motel nt

moth [mɒθ] n Nachtfalter m; (*wool-eating*) Motte f; ~**ball** n Mottenkugel f

mother ['mʌðər] n Mutter f ♦ vt bemuttern; ~**hood** n Mutterschaft f; ~**in-law** n Schwiegermutter f; ~**ly** adj mütterlich; ~**of-pearl** n Perlmut nt; **M~'s Day** (*BRIT*) n Muttertag m; ~**to-be** n werdende Mutter f; ~ **tongue** n Muttersprache f

motif [məʊ'tiːf] n Motiv nt

motion ['məʊʃən] n Bewegung f; (*in meeting*) Antrag m ♦ vt, vi: **to** ~ **(to) sb** jdm winken, jdm zu verstehen geben; ~**less** adj regungslos; ~ **picture** n Film m

motivated ['məʊtɪveɪtɪd] adj motiviert

motivation [məʊtɪ'veɪʃən] n Motivierung f

motive ['məʊtɪv] n Motiv nt, Beweggrund m ♦ adj treibend

motley ['mɒtlɪ] adj bunt

motor ['məʊtər] n Motor m; (*BRIT: inf: vehicle*) Auto nt ♦ adj Motor-; ~**bike** n Motorrad nt; ~**boat** n Motorboot nt; ~**car** (*BRIT*) n Auto nt; ~**cycle** n Motorrad nt; ~**cyclist** n Motorradfahrer(in) m(f); ~**ing** (*BRIT*) n Autofahren nt ♦ adj Auto-; ~**ist** n

Autofahrer(in) m(f); ~ **mechanic** n Kraftfahrzeugmechaniker(in) m(f), Kfz-Mechaniker(in) m(f); ~ **racing** (*BRIT*) n Autorennen nt; ~ **vehicle** n Kraftfahrzeug nt; ~**way** (*BRIT*) n Autobahn f

mottled ['mɒtld] adj gesprenkelt

mould [məʊld] (*US* **mold**) n Form f; (*mildew*) Schimmel m ♦ vt (*also fig*) formen; ~**y** adj schimmelig

moult [məʊlt] (*US* **molt**) vi sich mausern

mound [maʊnd] n (Erd)hügel m

mount [maʊnt] n (*liter: hill*) Berg m; (*horse*) Pferd nt; (*for jewel etc*) Fassung f ♦ vt (*horse*) steigen auf +acc; (*put in setting*) fassen; (*exhibition*) veranstalten; (*attack*) unternehmen ♦ vi (*also:* ~ **up**) sich häufen; (*on horse*) aufsitzen

mountain ['maʊntɪn] n Berg m ♦ cpd Berg-; ~ **bike** n Mountainbike nt; ~**eer** n Bergsteiger(in) m(f); ~**eering** [maʊntɪ'nɪərɪŋ] n Bergsteigen nt; ~**ous** adj bergig; ~ **rescue team** n Bergwacht f; ~**side** n Berg(ab)hang m

mourn [mɔːn] vt betrauern, beklagen ♦ vi: **to** ~ **(for sb)** (um jdn) trauern; ~**er** n Trauernde(r) mf; ~**ful** adj traurig; ~**ing** n (*grief*) Trauer f ♦ cpd (*dress*) Trauer-; **in** ~**ing** (*period etc*) in Trauer; (*dress*) in Trauerkleidung f

mouse [maʊs] (pl **mice**) n Maus f; ~**trap** n Mausefalle f

mousse [muːs] n (*COOK*) Creme f; (*cosmetic*) Schaumfestiger m

moustache [məs'tɑːʃ] n Schnurrbart m

mousy ['maʊsɪ] adj (*colour*) mausgrau; (*person*) schüchtern

mouth [maʊθ] n Mund m; (*opening*) Öffnung f; (*of river*) Mündung f; ~**ful** n Mund m voll; ~ **organ** n Mundharmonika f; ~**piece** n Mundstück nt; (*fig*) Sprachrohr nt; ~**wash** n Mundwasser nt; ~**watering** adj lecker, appetitlich

movable ['muːvəbl] adj beweglich

move [muːv] n (~**ment**) Bewegung f; (*in game*) Zug m; (*step*) Schritt m; (*of house*) Umzug m ♦ vt bewegen; (*people*) transportieren; (*in job*) versetzen;

(*emotionally*) bewegen ♦ *vi* sich bewegen; (*vehicle, ship*) fahren; (*~ house*) umziehen; **to get a ~ on** sich beeilen; **to ~ sb to do sth** jdn veranlassen, etw zu tun; **~ about** *or* **around** *vi* sich hin und her bewegen; (*travel*) unterwegs sein; **~ along** *vi* weitergehen; (*cars*) weiterfahren; **~ away** *vi* weggehen; (*to the rear*) zurückweichen; (*to the rear*) zurückweichen; **~ forward** *vi* vorwärts gehen, sich vorwärts bewegen ♦ *vt* vorschieben; (*time*) vorverlegen; **~ in** *vi* (*to house*) einziehen; (*troops*) einrücken; **~ on** *vi* weitergehen ♦ *vt* weitergehen lassen; **~ out** *vi* (*of house*) ausziehen; (*troops*) abziehen; **~ over** *vi* zur Seite rücken; **~ up** *vi* aufsteigen; (*in job*) befördert werden ♦ *vt* nach oben bewegen; (*in job*) befördern; **~ment** ['muːvmənt] *n* Bewegung *f*

movie ['muːvɪ] *n* Film *m*; **to go to the ~s** ins Kino gehen; **~ camera** *n* Filmkamera *f*

moving ['muːvɪŋ] *adj* beweglich; (*touching*) ergreifend

mow [məu] (*pt* **mowed**, *pp* **mowed** *or* **mown**) *vt* mähen; **~ down** *vt* (*fig*) niedermähen; **~er** *n* (*lawnmower*) Rasenmäher *m*; **~n** *pp of* **mow**

MP *n abbr* = **Member of Parliament**

m.p.h. *abbr* = **miles per hour**

Mr ['mɪstəʳ] (*US* **Mr.**) *n* Herr *m*

Mrs ['mɪsɪz] (*US* **Mrs.**) *n* Frau *f*

Ms [mɪz] (*US* **Ms.**) *n* (= *Miss or Mrs*) Frau *f*

M.Sc. *n abbr* = **Master of Science**

much [mʌtʃ] *adj* viel ♦ *adv* sehr; viel ♦ *n* viel, eine Menge; **how ~ is it?** wie viel kostet das?; **too ~** zu viel; **it's not ~** es ist nicht viel; **as ~ as** so sehr, so viel; **however ~ he tries** sosehr er es auch versucht

muck [mʌk] *n* Mist *m*; (*fig*) Schmutz *m*; **~ about** *or* **around** (*inf*) *vi*: **to ~ about** *or* **around (with sth)** (an etw *dat*) herumalbern; **~ up** *vt* (*inf*: *ruin*) vermasseln; (*dirty*) dreckig machen; **~y** *adj* (*dirty*) dreckig

mud [mʌd] *n* Schlamm *m*

muddle ['mʌdl] *n* Durcheinander *nt* ♦ *vt* (*also:* **~ up**) durcheinander bringen; **~**

through *vi* sich durchwursteln

mud ['mʌd-]: **~dy** *adj* schlammig; **~guard** *n* Schutzblech *nt*; **~-slinging** (*inf*) *n* Verleumdung *f*

muesli ['mjuːzlɪ] *n* Müsli *nt*

muffin ['mʌfɪn] *n* süße(s) Teilchen *nt*

muffle ['mʌfl] *vt* (*sound*) dämpfen; (*wrap up*) einhüllen; **~d** *adj* gedämpft; **~r** (*US*) *n* (*AUT*) Schalldämpfer *m*

mug [mʌg] *n* (*cup*) Becher *m*; (*inf*: *face*) Visage *f*; (: *fool*) Trottel *m* ♦ *vt* überfallen und ausrauben; **~ger** *n* Straßenräuber *m*; **~ging** *n* Überfall *m*

muggy ['mʌgɪ] *adj* (*weather*) schwül

mule [mjuːl] *n* Maulesel *m*

mull [mʌl]: **~ over** *vt* nachdenken über +*acc*

multicoloured ['mʌltɪkʌləd] (*US* **multicolored**) *adj* mehrfarbig

multi-level ['mʌltɪlevl] (*US*) *adj* = **multistorey**

multiple ['mʌltɪpl] *n* Vielfache(s) *nt* ♦ *adj* mehrfach; (*many*) mehrere; **~ sclerosis** *n* multiple Sklerose *f*

multiplex cinema ['mʌltɪpleks-] *n* Kinocenter *nt*

multiplication [mʌltɪplɪˈkeɪʃən] *n* Multiplikation *f*; (*increase*) Vervielfachung *f*

multiply ['mʌltɪplaɪ] *vt*: **to ~ (by)** multiplizieren (mit) ♦ *vi* (*BIOL*) sich vermehren

multistorey ['mʌltɪˈstɔːrɪ] (*BRIT*) *adj* (*building, car park*) mehrstöckig

multitude ['mʌltɪtjuːd] *n* Menge *f*

mum [mʌm] *n* (*BRIT*: *inf*) Mutti *f* ♦ *adj*: **to keep ~ (about)** den Mund halten (über +*acc*)

mumble ['mʌmbl] *vt, vi* murmeln ♦ *n* Gemurmel *nt*

mummy ['mʌmɪ] *n* (*dead body*) Mumie *f*; (*BRIT*: *inf*) Mami *f*

mumps [mʌmps] *n* Mumps *m*

munch [mʌntʃ] *vt, vi* mampfen

mundane [mʌnˈdeɪn] *adj* banal

municipal [mjuːˈnɪsɪpl] *adj* städtisch, Stadt-

mural ['mjuərl] *n* Wandgemälde *nt*

murder ['mɜːdəʳ] *n* Mord *m* ♦ *vt* ermorden; **~er** *n* Mörder *m*; **~ous** *adj* Mord-; (*fig*) mörderisch

murky ['mɜ:kɪ] *adj* finster

murmur ['mɜ:mər] *n* Murmeln *nt*; (*of water, wind*) Rauschen *nt* ♦ *vt, vi* murmeln

muscle ['mʌsl] *n* Muskel *m*; **~ in** *vi* mitmischen; **muscular** ['mʌskjʊlər] *adj* Muskel-; (*strong*) muskulös

museum [mju:'zɪəm] *n* Museum *nt*

mushroom ['mʌʃrʊm] *n* Champignon *m*; Pilz *m* ♦ *vi* (*fig*) emporschießen

music ['mju:zɪk] *n* Musik *f*; (*printed*) Noten *pl*; **~al** *adj* (*sound*) melodisch; (*person*) musikalisch ♦ *n* (*show*) Musical *nt*; **~al instrument** *n* Musikinstrument *nt*; **~ centre** *n* Stereoanlage *f*; **~ hall** (*BRIT*) *n* Varietee *nt*, Varieté *nt*; **~ian** [mju:'zɪʃən] *n* Musiker(in) *m(f)*

Muslim ['mʌzlɪm] *adj* moslemisch ♦ *n* Moslem *m*

muslin ['mʌzlɪn] *n* Musselin *m*

mussel ['mʌsl] *n* Miesmuschel *f*

must [mʌst] *vb aux* müssen; (*in negation*) dürfen ♦ *n* Muss *nt*; **the film is a ~** den Film muss man einfach gesehen haben

mustard ['mʌstəd] *n* Senf *m*

muster ['mʌstər] *vt* (*MIL*) antreten lassen; (*courage*) zusammennehmen

mustn't ['mʌsnt] = **must not**

musty ['mʌstɪ] *adj* muffig

mute [mju:t] *adj* stumm ♦ *n* (*person*) Stumme(r) *mf*; (*MUS*) Dämpfer *m*; **~d** *adj* gedämpft

mutilate ['mju:tɪleɪt] *vt* verstümmeln

mutiny ['mju:tɪnɪ] *n* Meuterei *f* ♦ *vi* meutern

mutter ['mʌtər] *vt, vi* murmeln

mutton ['mʌtn] *n* Hammelfleisch *nt*

mutual ['mju:tʃʊəl] *adj* gegenseitig; beiderseitig; **~ly** *adv* gegenseitig; für beide Seiten

muzzle ['mʌzl] *n* (*of animal*) Schnauze *f*; (*for animal*) Maulkorb *m*; (*of gun*) Mündung *f* ♦ *vt* einen Maulkorb anlegen +*dat*

my [maɪ] *adj* mein; **this is ~ car** das ist mein Auto; **I've washed ~ hair** ich habe mir die Haare gewaschen

myself [maɪ'self] *pron* mich *acc*; mir *dat*; (*emphatic*) selbst; *see also* **oneself**

mysterious [mɪs'tɪərɪəs] *adj* geheimnisvoll

mystery ['mɪstərɪ] *n* (*secret*) Geheimnis *nt*; (*sth difficult*) Rätsel *nt*

mystify ['mɪstɪfaɪ] *vt* ein Rätsel *nt* sein +*dat*; verblüffen

mystique [mɪs'ti:k] *n* geheimnisvolle Natur *f*

myth [mɪθ] *n* Mythos *m*; (*fig*) Erfindung *f*; **~ology** [mɪ'θɒlədʒɪ] *n* Mythologie *f*

N, n

n/a *abbr* (= *not applicable*) nicht zutreffend

nab [næb] (*inf*) *vt* schnappen

naff [næf] (*BRIT: inf*) *adj* blöd

nag [næg] *n* (*horse*) Gaul *m*; (*person*) Nörgler(in) *m(f)* ♦ *vt, vi*: **to ~ (at) sb** an jdm herumnörgeln; **~ging** *adj* (*doubt*) nagend ♦ *n* Nörgelei *f*

nail [neɪl] *n* Nagel *m* ♦ *vt* nageln; **to ~ sb down to doing sth** jdn darauf festnageln, etw zu tun; **~brush** *n* Nagelbürste *f*; **~file** *n* Nagelfeile *f*; **~ polish** *n* Nagellack *m*; **~ polish remover** *n* Nagellackentferner *m*; **~ scissors** *npl* Nagelschere *f*; **~ varnish** (*BRIT*) *n* = **nail polish**

naïve [naɪ'i:v] *adj* naiv

naked ['neɪkɪd] *adj* nackt

name [neɪm] *n* Name *m*; (*reputation*) Ruf *m* ♦ *vt* nennen; (*sth new*) benennen; (*appoint*) ernennen; **by ~** mit Namen; **I know him only by ~** ich kenne ihn nur dem Namen nach; **what's your ~?** wie heißen Sie?; **in the ~ of** im Namen +*gen*; (*for the sake of*) um +*gen* ... willen; **~less** *adj* namenlos; **~ly** *adv* nämlich; **~sake** *n* Namensvetter *m*

nanny ['nænɪ] *n* Kindermädchen *nt*

nap [næp] *n* (*sleep*) Nickerchen *nt*; (*on cloth*) Strich *m* ♦ *vi*: **to be caught ~ping** (*fig*) überrumpelt werden

nape [neɪp] *n* Nacken *m*

napkin ['næpkɪn] *n* (*at table*) Serviette *f*; (*BRIT: for baby*) Windel *f*

nappy ['næpɪ] (*BRIT*) *n* (*for baby*) Windel *f*; **~ rash** *n* wunde Stellen *pl*

narcotic [nɑ:'kɒtɪk] *adj* betäubend ♦ *n* Betäubungsmittel *nt*

narrative ['nærətɪv] n Erzählung f ♦ adj erzählend

narrator [nə'reɪtəʳ] n Erzähler(in) m(f)

narrow ['nærəʊ] adj eng, schmal; (limited) beschränkt ♦ vi sich verengen; **to have a ~ escape** mit knapper Not davonkommen; **to ~ sth down to sth** etw auf etw acc einschränken; **~ly** adv (miss) knapp; (escape) mit knapper Not; **~-minded** adj engstirnig

nasty ['nɑːstɪ] adj ekelhaft, fies; (business, wound) schlimm

nation ['neɪʃən] n Nation f, Volk nt; **~al** ['næʃənl] adj national, National-, Landes- ♦ n Staatsangehörige(r) mf; **~al anthem** (BRIT) n Nationalhymne f; **~al dress** n Tracht f; **N~al Health Service** (BRIT) n staatliche(r) Gesundheitsdienst m; **N~al Insurance** (BRIT) n Sozialversicherung f; **~alism** ['næʃnəlɪzəm] n Nationalismus m; **~alist** ['næʃnəlɪst] n Nationalist(in) m(f) ♦ adj nationalistisch; **~ality** [næʃə'nælɪtɪ] n Staatsangehörigkeit f; **~alize** ['næʃnəlaɪz] vt verstaatlichen; **~ally** ['næʃnəlɪ] adv national, auf Staatsebene; **~al park** (BRIT) n Nationalpark m; **~wide** ['neɪʃənwaɪd] adj, adv allgemein, landesweit

National Trust

i Der **National Trust** ist ein 1895 gegründeter Natur- und Denkmalschutzverband in Großbritannien, der Gebäude und Gelände von besonderem historischen oder ästhetischen Interesse erhält und der Öffentlichkeit zugänglich macht. Viele Gebäude im Besitz des National Trust sind (z.T. gegen ein Eintrittsgeld) zu besichtigen.

native ['neɪtɪv] n (born in) Einheimische(r) mf; (original inhabitant) Eingeborene(r) mf ♦ adj einheimisch; Eingeborenen-; (belonging by birth) heimatlich, Heimat-; (inborn) angeboren, natürlich; **a ~ of Germany** ein gebürtiger Deutscher; **a ~ speaker of French** ein französischer Muttersprachler; **N~ American** n

Indianer(in) m(f), Ureinwohner(in) m(f) Amerikas; **~ language** n Muttersprache f

Nativity [nə'tɪvɪtɪ] n: **the ~** Christi Geburt no art

NATO ['neɪtəʊ] n abbr (= North Atlantic Treaty Organization) NATO f

natural ['nætʃrəl] adj natürlich; Natur-; (inborn) (an)geboren; **~ gas** n Erdgas nt; **~ist** n Naturkundler(in) m(f); **~ly** adv natürlich

nature ['neɪtʃəʳ] n Natur f; **by ~** von Natur (aus)

naught [nɔːt] n = **nought**

naughty ['nɔːtɪ] adj (child) unartig, ungezogen; (action) ungehörig

nausea ['nɔːsɪə] n (sickness) Übelkeit f; (disgust) Ekel m; **~te** ['nɔːsɪeɪt] vt anekeln

nautical ['nɔːtɪkl] adj nautisch; See-; (expression) seemännisch

naval ['neɪvl] adj Marine-, Flotten-; **~ officer** n Marineoffizier m

nave [neɪv] n Kirchen(haupt)schiff nt

navel ['neɪvl] n Nabel m

navigate ['nævɪgeɪt] vi navigieren; **navigation** [nævɪ'geɪʃən] n Navigation f; **navigator** ['nævɪgeɪtəʳ] n Steuermann m; (AVIAT) Navigator m; (AUT) Beifahrer(in) m(f)

navvy ['nævɪ] (BRIT) n Straßenarbeiter m

navy ['neɪvɪ] n (Kriegs)marine f ♦ adj (also: ~ blue) marineblau

Nazi ['nɑːtsɪ] n Nazi m

NB abbr (= nota bene) NB

near [nɪəʳ] adj nah ♦ adv in der Nähe ♦ prep (also: ~ **to**: space) in der Nähe +gen; (: time) um +acc ... herum ♦ vt sich nähern +dat; **a ~ miss** knapp daneben; **~by** adj nahe (gelegen) ♦ adv in der Nähe; **~ly** adv fast; **I ~ly fell** ich wäre fast gefallen; **~side** n (AUT) Beifahrerseite f ♦ adj auf der Beifahrerseite; **~-sighted** adj kurzsichtig

neat [niːt] adj (tidy) ordentlich; (solution) sauber; (pure) pur; **~ly** adv (tidily) ordentlich

necessarily ['nesɪsrɪlɪ] adv unbedingt

necessary ['nesɪsrɪ] adj notwendig, nötig; **he did all that was ~** er erledigte alles, was nötig war; **it is ~ to/that ...** man muss ...

necessitate [nɪ'sesɪteɪt] *vt* erforderlich machen

necessity [nɪ'sesɪtɪ] *n* (*need*) Not *f*; (*compulsion*) Notwendigkeit *f*; **necessities** *npl* (*things needed*) das Notwendigste

neck [nɛk] *n* Hals *m* ♦ *vi* (*inf*) knutschen; **~ and ~** Kopf an Kopf; **~lace** ['nɛklɪs] *n* Halskette *f*; **~line** ['nɛklaɪn] *n* Ausschnitt *m*; **~tie** ['nɛktaɪ] (*US*) *n* Krawatte *f*

née [neɪ] *adj* geborene

need [niːd] *n* Bedürfnis *nt*; (*lack*) Mangel *m*; (*necessity*) Notwendigkeit *f*; (*poverty*) Not *f* ♦ *vt* brauchen; **I ~ to do it** ich muss es tun; **you don't ~ to go** du brauchst nicht zu gehen

needle ['niːdl] *n* Nadel *f* ♦ *vt* (*fig*: *inf*) ärgern

needless ['niːdlɪs] *adj* unnötig; **~ to say** natürlich

needlework ['niːdlwəːk] *n* Handarbeit *f*

needn't ['niːdnt] = **need not**

needy ['niːdɪ] *adj* bedürftig

negative ['nɛɡətɪv] *n* (*PHOT*) Negativ *nt* ♦ *adj* negativ; (*answer*) abschlägig; **~ equity** *n* Differenz zwischen gefallenem Wert und hypothekarischer Belastung eines Wohneigentums

neglect [nɪ'ɡlɛkt] *vt* vernachlässigen ♦ *n* Vernachlässigung *f*; **~ed** *adj* vernachlässigt

negligee ['nɛɡlɪʒeɪ] *n* Negligee *nt*, Negligé *nt*

negligence ['nɛɡlɪdʒəns] *n* Nachlässigkeit *f*

negligible ['nɛɡlɪdʒɪbl] *adj* unbedeutend, geringfügig

negotiable [nɪ'ɡəʊʃɪəbl] *adj* (*cheque*) übertragbar, einlösbar

negotiate [nɪ'ɡəʊʃɪeɪt] *vi* verhandeln ♦ *vt* (*treaty*) abschließen; (*difficulty*) überwinden; (*corner*) nehmen; **negotiation** [nɪɡəʊʃɪ'eɪʃən] *n* Verhandlung *f*; **negotiator** *n* Unterhändler *m*

neigh [neɪ] *vi* wiehern

neighbour ['neɪbəʳ] (*US* **neighbor**) *n* Nachbar(in) *m(f)*; **~hood** *n* Nachbarschaft *f*; Umgebung *f*; **~ing** *adj* benachbart, angrenzend; **~ly** *adj* (*person, attitude*) nachbarlich

neither ['naɪðəʳ] *adj, pron* keine(r, s) (von beiden) ♦ *conj*: **he can't do it, and ~ can I** er kann es nicht und ich auch nicht ♦ *adv*: **~ good nor bad** weder gut noch schlecht; **~ story is true** keine der beiden Geschichten stimmt

neon ['niːɔn] *n* Neon *nt*; **~ light** *n* Neonlampe *f*

nephew ['nɛvjuː] *n* Neffe *m*

nerve [nəːv] *n* Nerv *m*; (*courage*) Mut *m*; (*impudence*) Frechheit *f*; **to have a fit of ~s** in Panik geraten; **~-racking** *adj* nervenaufreibend

nervous ['nəːvəs] *adj* (*of the nerves*) Nerven-; (*timid*) nervös, ängstlich; **~ breakdown** *n* Nervenzusammenbruch *m*; **~ness** *n* Nervosität *f*

nest [nɛst] *n* Nest *nt* ♦ *vi* nisten; **~ egg** *n* (*fig*) Notgroschen *m*

nestle ['nɛsl] *vi* sich kuscheln

net [nɛt] *n* Netz *nt* ♦ *adj* netto, Netto- ♦ *vt* netto einnehmen; **~ball** *n* Netzball *m*

Netherlands ['nɛðələndz] *npl*: **the ~** die Niederlande *pl*

nett [nɛt] *adj* = **net**

netting ['nɛtɪŋ] *n* Netz(werk) *nt*

nettle ['nɛtl] *n* Nessel *f*

network ['nɛtwəːk] *n* Netz *nt*

neurotic [njuə'rɔtɪk] *adj* neurotisch

neuter ['njuːtəʳ] *adj* (*BIOL*) geschlechtslos; (*GRAM*) sächlich ♦ *vt* kastrieren

neutral ['njuːtrəl] *adj* neutral ♦ *n* (*AUT*) Leerlauf *m*; **~ity** [njuː'trælɪtɪ] *n* Neutralität *f*; **~ize** *vt* (*fig*) ausgleichen

never ['nɛvəʳ] *adv* nie(mals); **I ~ went** ich bin gar nicht gegangen; **~ in my life** nie im Leben; **~-ending** *adj* endlos; **~theless** [nɛvəðə'lɛs] *adv* trotzdem, dennoch

new [njuː] *adj* neu; **N~ Age** *adj* Newage-, New-Age-; **~born** *adj* neugeboren; **~comer** ['njuːkʌməʳ] *n* Neuankömmling *m*; **~fangled** (*pej*) *adj* neumodisch; **~found** *adj* neu entdeckt; **~ly** *adv* frisch, neu; **~lyweds** *npl* Frischvermählte *pl*; **~ moon** *n* Neumond *m*

news [njuːz] *n* Nachricht *f*; (*RAD, TV*) Nachrichten *pl*; **a piece of ~** eine

Nachricht; **~ agency** n Nachrichtenagentur f; **~agent** (BRIT) n Zeitungshändler m; **~caster** n Nachrichtensprecher(in) m(f); **~ flash** n Kurzmeldung f; **~letter** n Rundschreiben nt; **~paper** n Zeitung f; **~print** n Zeitungspapier nt; **~reader** n = newscaster; **~reel** n Wochenschau f; **~ stand** n Zeitungsstand m

newt [njuːt] n Wassermolch m

New Year n Neujahr nt; **~'s Day** n Neujahrstag m; **~'s Eve** n Silvester(abend m) nt

New Zealand [-'ziːlənd] n Neuseeland nt; **~er** n Neuseeländer(in) m(f)

next [nɛkst] adj nächste(r, s) ♦ adv (after) dann, darauf; (~ time) das nächste Mal; **the ~ day** am nächsten or folgenden Tag; **~ time** das nächste Mal; **~ year** nächstes Jahr; **~ door** adv nebenan ♦ adj (neighbour, flat) von nebenan; **~ of kin** n nächste(r) Verwandte(r) mf; **~ to** prep neben; **~ to nothing** so gut wie nichts

NHS n abbr = **National Health Service**

nib [nɪb] n Spitze f

nibble ['nɪbl] vt knabbern an +dat

nice [naɪs] adj (person) nett; (thing) schön; (subtle) fein; **~-looking** adj gut aussehend; **~ly** adv gut, nett; **~ties** ['naɪsɪtɪz] npl Feinheiten pl

nick [nɪk] n Einkerbung f ♦ vt (inf: steal) klauen; **in the ~ of time** gerade rechtzeitig

nickel ['nɪkl] n Nickel nt; (US) Nickel m (5 cents)

nickname ['nɪkneɪm] n Spitzname m ♦ vt taufen

nicotine patch ['nɪkətiːn-] n Nikotinpflaster nt

niece [niːs] n Nichte f

Nigeria [naɪ'dʒɪərɪə] n Nigeria nt

niggling ['nɪglɪŋ] adj pedantisch; (doubt, worry) quälend

night [naɪt] n Nacht f; (evening) Abend m; **the ~ before last** vorletzte Nacht; **at** or **by ~** (before midnight) abends; (after midnight) nachts; **~cap** n (drink) Schlummertrunk m; **~club** n Nachtlokal nt; **~dress** n

Nachthemd nt; **~fall** n Einbruch m der Nacht; **~ gown** n = **nightdress**; **~ie** (inf) n Nachthemd nt

nightingale ['naɪtɪŋgeɪl] n Nachtigall f

night: ~life ['naɪtlaɪf] n Nachtleben nt; **~ly** ['naɪtlɪ] adj, adv jeden Abend; jede Nacht; **~mare** ['naɪtmɛəʳ] n Albtraum m; **~ porter** n Nachtportier m; **~ school** n Abendschule f; **~ shift** n Nachtschicht f; **~time** n Nacht f

nil [nɪl] n Null f

Nile [naɪl] n: **the ~** der Nil

nimble ['nɪmbl] adj beweglich

nine [naɪn] num neun; **~teen** num neunzehn; **~ty** num neunzig

ninth [naɪnθ] adj neunte(r, s)

nip [nɪp] vt kneifen ♦ n Kneifen nt

nipple ['nɪpl] n Brustwarze f

nippy ['nɪpɪ] (inf) adj (person) flink; (BRIT: car) flott; (: cold) frisch

nitrogen ['naɪtrədʒən] n Stickstoff m

KEYWORD

no [nəʊ] (pl noes) adv (opposite of yes) nein; **to answer no** (to question) mit Nein antworten; (to request) Nein or nein sagen; **no thank you** nein, danke
♦ adj (not any) kein(e); **I have no money/time** ich habe kein Geld/keine Zeit; **"no smoking"** „Rauchen verboten"
♦ n Nein nt; (no vote) Neinstimme f

---

nobility [nəʊ'bɪlɪtɪ] n Adel m

noble ['nəʊbl] adj (rank) adlig; (splendid) nobel, edel

nobody ['nəʊbədɪ] pron niemand, keiner

nocturnal [nɔk'tɜːnl] adj (tour, visit) nächtlich; (animal) Nacht-

nod [nɔd] vi nicken ♦ vt nicken mit ♦ n Nicken nt; **~ off** vi einnicken

noise [nɔɪz] n (sound) Geräusch nt; (unpleasant, loud) Lärm m; **noisy** ['nɔɪzɪ] adj laut; (crowd) lärmend

nominal ['nɔmɪnl] adj nominell

nominate ['nɔmɪneɪt] vt (suggest) vorschlagen; (in election) aufstellen; (appoint) ernennen; **nomination**

[nɔmɪ'neɪʃən] *n* (*election*) Nominierung *f*; (*appointment*) Ernennung *f*; **nominee** [nɔmɪ'ni:] *n* Kandidat(in) *m(f)*
non... [nɔn] *prefix* Nicht-, un-; **~-alcoholic** *adj* alkoholfrei
nonchalant ['nɔnʃələnt] *adj* lässig
non-committal [nɔnkə'mɪtl] *adj* (*reserved*) zurückhaltend; (*uncommitted*) unverbindlich
nondescript ['nɔndɪskrɪpt] *adj* mittelmäßig
none [nʌn] *adj, pron* kein(e, er, es) ♦ *adv*: **he's ~ the worse for it** es hat ihm nicht geschadet; **~ of you** keiner von euch; **I've ~ left** ich habe keinen mehr
nonentity [nɔ'nentɪtɪ] *n* Null *f* (*inf*)
nonetheless ['nʌnðə'les] *adv* nichtsdestoweniger
non-existent [nɔnɪg'zɪstənt] *adj* nicht vorhanden
non-fiction [nɔn'fɪkʃən] *n* Sachbücher *pl*
nonplussed [nɔn'plʌst] *adj* verdutzt
nonsense ['nɔnsəns] *n* Unsinn *m*
non: ~-smoker *n* Nichtraucher(in) *m(f)*; **~-smoking** *adj* Nichtraucher-; **~-stick** *adj* (*pan, surface*) Teflon- ®; **~-stop** *adj* Nonstop-, Non-Stop-
noodles ['nu:dlz] *npl* Nudeln *pl*
nook [nuk] *n* Winkel *m*; **~s and crannies** Ecken und Winkel
noon [nu:n] *n* (12 Uhr) Mittag *m*
no one ['nəuwʌn] *pron* = **nobody**
noose [nu:s] *n* Schlinge *f*
nor [nɔ:r] *conj* = **neither** ♦ *adv see* **neither**
norm [nɔ:m] *n* (*convention*) Norm *f*; (*rule, requirement*) Vorschrift *f*
normal ['nɔ:məl] *adj* normal; **~ly** *adv* normal; (*usually*) normalerweise
Normandy ['nɔ:məndɪ] *n* Normandie *f*
north [nɔ:θ] *n* Norden *m* ♦ *adj* nördlich, Nord- ♦ *adv* nördlich, nach *or* im Norden; **N~ Africa** *n* Nordafrika *nt*; **N~ America** *n* Nordamerika *nt*; **~-east** *n* Nordosten *m*; **~erly** ['nɔ:ðəlɪ] *adj* nördlich; **~ern** ['nɔ:ðən] *adj* nördlich; **N~ern Ireland** *n* Nordirland *nt*; **N~ Pole** *n* Nordpol *m*; **N~ Sea** *n* Nordsee *f*; **~ward(s)** ['nɔ:θwəd(z)] *adv* nach Norden; **~-west** *n* Nordwesten *m*
Norway ['nɔ:weɪ] *n* Norwegen *nt*

Norwegian [nɔ:'wi:dʒən] *adj* norwegisch ♦ *n* Norweger(in) *m(f)*; (*LING*) Norwegisch *nt*
nose [nəuz] *n* Nase *f* ♦ *vi*: **to ~ about** herumschnüffeln; **~bleed** *n* Nasenbluten *nt*; **~ dive** *n* Sturzflug *m*; **~y** *adj* = **nosy**
nostalgia [nɔs'tældʒɪə] *n* Nostalgie *f*; **nostalgic** *adj* nostalgisch
nostril ['nɔstrɪl] *n* Nasenloch *nt*
nosy ['nəuzɪ] (*inf*) *adj* neugierig
not [nɔt] *adv* nicht; **he is ~** *or* **isn't here** er ist nicht hier; **it's too late, isn't it?** es ist zu spät, oder *or* nicht wahr?; **~ yet/now** noch nicht/nicht jetzt; *see also* **all**; **only**
notably ['nəutəblɪ] *adv* (*especially*) besonders; (*noticeably*) bemerkenswert
notary ['nəutərɪ] *n* Notar(in) *m(f)*
notch [nɔtʃ] *n* Kerbe *f*, Einschnitt *m*
note [nəut] *n* (*MUS*) Note *f*, Ton *m*; (*short letter*) Nachricht *f*; (*POL*) Note *f*; (*comment, attention*) Notiz *f*; (*of lecture etc*) Aufzeichnung *f*; (*banknote*) Schein *m*; (*fame*) Ruf *m* ♦ *vt* (*observe*) bemerken; (*also: ~ down*) notieren; **~book** *n* Notizbuch *nt*; **~d** *adj* bekannt; **~pad** *n* Notizblock *m*; **~paper** *n* Briefpapier *nt*
nothing ['nʌθɪŋ] *n* nichts; **~ new/much** nichts Neues/nicht viel; **for ~** umsonst
notice ['nəutɪs] *n* (*announcement*) Bekanntmachung *f*; (*warning*) Ankündigung *f*; (*dismissal*) Kündigung *f* ♦ *vt* bemerken; **to take ~ of** beachten; **at short ~** kurzfristig; **until further ~** bis auf weiteres; **to hand in one's ~** kündigen; **~able** *adj* merklich; **~ board** *n* Anschlagtafel *f*
notify ['nəutɪfaɪ] *vt* benachrichtigen
notion ['nəuʃən] *n* Idee *f*
notorious [nəu'tɔ:rɪəs] *adj* berüchtigt
notwithstanding [nɔtwɪθ'stændɪŋ] *adv* trotzdem; **~ this** ungeachtet dessen
nought [nɔ:t] *n* Null *f*
noun [naun] *n* Substantiv *nt*
nourish ['nʌrɪʃ] *vt* nähren; **~ing** *adj* nahrhaft; **~ment** *n* Nahrung *f*
novel ['nɔvl] *n* Roman *m* ♦ *adj* neu(artig); **~ist** *n* Schriftsteller(in) *m(f)*; **~ty** *n* Neuheit *f*

November [nəuˈvɛmbəʳ] n November m

novice [ˈnɔvɪs] n Neuling m

now [nau] adv jetzt; **right ~** jetzt, gerade; **by ~** inzwischen; **just ~** gerade; **~ and then**, **~ and again** ab und zu, manchmal; **from ~ on** von jetzt an; **~adays** adv heutzutage

nowhere [ˈnəuwɛəʳ] adv nirgends

nozzle [ˈnɔzl] n Düse f

nuclear [ˈnjuːklɪəʳ] adj (energy etc) Atom-, Kern-

nuclei [ˈnjuːklɪaɪ] npl of nucleus

nucleus [ˈnjuːklɪəs] n Kern m

nude [njuːd] adj nackt ♦ n (ART) Akt m; **in the ~** nackt

nudge [nʌdʒ] vt leicht anstoßen

nudist [ˈnjuːdɪst] n Nudist(in) m(f)

nudity [ˈnjuːdɪtɪ] n Nacktheit f

nuisance [ˈnjuːsns] n Ärgernis nt; **what a ~!** wie ärgerlich!

nuke [njuːk] (inf) n Kernkraftwerk nt ♦ vt atomar vernichten

null [nʌl] adj: **~ and void** null und nichtig

numb [nʌm] adj taub, gefühllos ♦ vt betäuben

number [ˈnʌmbəʳ] n Nummer f; (numeral also) Zahl f; (quantity) (An)zahl f ♦ vt nummerieren; (amount to) sein; **to be ~ed among** gezählt werden zu; **a ~ of** (several) einige; **they were ten in ~** sie waren zehn an der Zahl; **~ plate** (BRIT) n (AUT) Nummernschild nt

numeral [ˈnjuːmərəl] n Ziffer f

numerate [ˈnjuːmərɪt] adj rechenkundig

numerical [njuːˈmɛrɪkl] adj (order) zahlenmäßig

numerous [ˈnjuːmərəs] adj zahlreich

nun [nʌn] n Nonne f

nurse [nɜːs] n Krankenschwester f; (for children) Kindermädchen nt ♦ vt (patient) pflegen; (doubt etc) hegen

nursery [ˈnɜːsərɪ] n (for children) Kinderzimmer nt; (for plants) Gärtnerei f; (for trees) Baumschule f; **~ rhyme** n Kinderreim m; **~ school** n Kindergarten m; **~ slope** (BRIT) n (SKI) Idiotenhügel m (inf), Anfängerhügel m

nursing [ˈnɜːsɪŋ] n (profession) Krankenpflege f; **~ home** n Privatklinik f

nurture [ˈnɜːtʃəʳ] vt aufziehen

nut [nʌt] n Nuss f; (TECH) Schraubenmutter f; (inf) Verrückte(r) mf; **he's ~s** er ist verrückt; **~crackers** [ˈnʌtkrækəz] npl Nussknacker m

nutmeg [ˈnʌtmɛg] n Muskat(nuss f) m

nutrient [ˈnjuːtrɪənt] n Nährstoff m

nutrition [njuːˈtrɪʃən] n Nahrung f; **nutritious** [njuːˈtrɪʃəs] adj nahrhaft

nutshell [ˈnʌtʃɛl] n Nussschale f; **in a ~** (fig) kurz gesagt

nutter [ˈnʌtəʳ] (BRIT: inf) n Spinner(in) m(f)

nylon [ˈnaɪlɔn] n Nylon nt ♦ adj Nylon-

O, o

oak [əuk] n Eiche f ♦ adj Eichen(holz)-

O.A.P. abbr = **old-age pensioner**

oar [ɔːʳ] n Ruder nt

oases [əuˈeɪsiːz] npl of oasis

oasis [əuˈeɪsɪs] n Oase f

oath [əuθ] n (statement) Eid m, Schwur m; (swearword) Fluch m

oatmeal [ˈəutmiːl] n Haferschrot m

oats [əuts] npl Hafer m

obedience [əˈbiːdɪəns] n Gehorsam m

obedient [əˈbiːdɪənt] adj gehorsam

obesity [əuˈbiːsɪtɪ] n Fettleibigkeit f

obey [əˈbeɪ] vt, vi: **to ~ (sb)** (jdm) gehorchen

obituary [əˈbɪtjuərɪ] n Nachruf m

object [n ˈɔbdʒɪkt, vb əbˈdʒɛkt] n (thing) Gegenstand m, Objekt nt; (purpose) Ziel nt ♦ vi dagegen sein; **expense is no ~** Ausgaben spielen keine Rolle; **I ~!** ich protestiere!; **to ~ to sth** Einwände gegen etw haben; (morally) Anstoß an etw acc nehmen; **to ~ that** einwenden, dass; **~ion** [əbˈdʒɛkʃən] n (reason against) Einwand m, Einspruch m; (dislike) Abneigung f; **I have no ~ion to ...** ich habe nichts gegen ... einzuwenden; **~ionable** [əbˈdʒɛkʃənəbl] adj nicht einwandfrei; (language) anstößig

objective [əbˈdʒɛktɪv] n Ziel nt ♦ adj objektiv

obligation [ɔblɪˈgeɪʃən] n Verpflichtung f; **without ~** unverbindlich; **obligatory**

[ə'blɪɡətərɪ] *adj* obligatorisch

oblige [ə'blaɪdʒ] *vt (compel)* zwingen; *(do a favour)* einen Gefallen tun *+dat*; **to be ~d to sb for sth** jdm für etw verbunden sein

obliging [ə'blaɪdʒɪŋ] *adj* entgegenkommend

oblique [ə'bliːk] *adj* schräg, schief ♦ *n* Schrägstrich *m*

obliterate [ə'blɪtəreɪt] *vt* auslöschen

oblivion [ə'blɪvɪən] *n* Vergessenheit *f*

oblivious [ə'blɪvɪəs] *adj* nicht bewusst

oblong ['ɒblɒŋ] *n* Rechteck *nt* ♦ *adj* länglich

obnoxious [əb'nɒkʃəs] *adj* widerlich

oboe ['əʊbəʊ] *n* Oboe *f*

obscene [əb'siːn] *adj* obszön; **obscenity** [əb'senɪtɪ] *n* Obszönität *f*; **obscenities** *npl (oaths)* Zoten *pl*

obscure [əb'skjʊəʳ] *adj* unklar; *(indistinct)* undeutlich; *(unknown)* unbekannt, obskur; *(dark)* düster ♦ *vt* verdunkeln; *(view)* verbergen; *(confuse)* verwirren; **obscurity** [əb'skjʊərɪtɪ] *n* Unklarheit *f*; *(darkness)* Dunkelheit *f*

observance [əb'zɜːvəns] *n* Befolgung *f*

observant [əb'zɜːvənt] *adj* aufmerksam

observation [ɒbzə'veɪʃən] *n (noticing)* Beobachtung *f*; *(surveillance)* Überwachung *f*; *(remark)* Bemerkung *f*

observatory [əb'zɜːvətrɪ] *n* Sternwarte *f*, Observatorium *nt*

observe [əb'zɜːv] *vt (notice)* bemerken; *(watch)* beobachten; *(customs)* einhalten; **~r** *n* Beobachter(in) *m(f)*

obsess [əb'ses] *vt* verfolgen, quälen; **~ion** [əb'seʃən] *n* Besessenheit *f*, Wahn *m*; **~ive** *adj* krankhaft

obsolete ['ɒbsəliːt] *adj* überholt, veraltet

obstacle ['ɒbstəkl] *n* Hindernis *nt*; **~ race** *n* Hindernisrennen *nt*

obstetrics [ɒb'stetrɪks] *n* Geburtshilfe *f*

obstinate ['ɒbstɪnɪt] *adj* hartnäckig, stur

obstruct [əb'strʌkt] *vt* versperren; *(pipe)* verstopfen; *(hinder)* hemmen; **~ion** [əb'strʌkʃən] *n* Versperrung *f*; Verstopfung *f*; *(obstacle)* Hindernis *nt*

obtain [əb'teɪn] *vt* erhalten, bekommen; *(result)* erzielen

obtrusive [əb'truːsɪv] *adj* aufdringlich

obvious ['ɒbvɪəs] *adj* offenbar, offensichtlich; **~ly** *adv* offensichtlich

occasion [ə'keɪʒən] *n* Gelegenheit *f*; *(special event)* Ereignis *nt*; *(reason)* Anlass *m* ♦ *vt* veranlassen; **~al** *adj* gelegentlich; **~ally** *adv* gelegentlich

occupant ['ɒkjʊpənt] *n* Inhaber(in) *m(f)*; *(of house)* Bewohner(in) *m(f)*

occupation [ɒkjʊ'peɪʃən] *n (employment)* Tätigkeit *f*, Beruf *m*; *(pastime)* Beschäftigung *f*; *(of country)* Besetzung *f*, Okkupation *f*; **~al hazard** *n* Berufsrisiko *nt*

occupier ['ɒkjʊpaɪəʳ] *n* Bewohner(in) *m(f)*

occupy ['ɒkjʊpaɪ] *vt (take possession of)* besetzen; *(seat)* belegen; *(live in)* bewohnen; *(position, office)* bekleiden; *(position in sb's life)* einnehmen; *(time)* beanspruchen; **to ~ o.s. with sth** sich mit etw beschäftigen; **to ~ o.s. by doing sth** sich damit beschäftigen, etw zu tun

occur [ə'kɜːʳ] *vi* vorkommen; **to ~ to sb** jdm einfallen; **~rence** *n (event)* Ereignis *nt*; *(appearing)* Auftreten *nt*

ocean ['əʊʃən] *n* Ozean *m*, Meer *nt*; **~-going** *adj* Hochsee-

o'clock [ə'klɒk] *adv*: **it is 5 ~** es ist 5 Uhr

OCR *n abbr* = **optical character reader**

octagonal [ɒk'tægənl] *adj* achteckig

October [ɒk'təʊbəʳ] *n* Oktober *m*

octopus ['ɒktəpəs] *n* Krake *f*; *(small)* Tintenfisch *m*

odd [ɒd] *adj (strange)* sonderbar; *(not even)* ungerade; *(sock etc)* einzeln; *(surplus)* übrig; **60-~** so um die 60; **at ~ times** ab und zu; **to be the ~ one out** *(person)* das fünfte Rad am Wagen sein; *(thing)* nicht dazugehören; **~ity** *n (strangeness)* Merkwürdigkeit *f*; *(queer person)* seltsame(r) Kauz *m*; *(thing)* Kuriosität *f*; **~-job man** *(irreg)* *n* Mädchen *nt* für alles; **~ jobs** *npl* gelegentlich anfallende Arbeiten; **~ly** *adv* seltsam; **~ments** *npl* Reste *pl*; **~s** *npl* Chancen *pl*; *(betting)* Gewinnchancen *pl*; **it makes no ~s** es spielt keine Rolle; **at ~s** uneinig; **~s and ends** *npl* Krimskrams *m*

odometer [ɒ'dɒmɪtəʳ] *(esp US)* *n* Tacho(meter) *m*

odour ['əudəʳ] (*US* **odor**) *n* Geruch *m*

⎡KEYWORD⎤

of [ɒv, əv] *prep* **1** von +*dat*; *use of gen*; **the history of Germany** die Geschichte Deutschlands; **a friend of ours** ein Freund von uns; **a boy of 10** ein 10-jähriger Junge; **that was kind of you** das war sehr freundlich von Ihnen

2 (*expressing quantity, amount, dates etc*): **a kilo of flour** ein Kilo Mehl; **how much of this do you need?** wie viel brauchen Sie (davon)?; **there were 3 of them** (*people*) sie waren zu dritt; (*objects*) es gab 3 (davon); **a cup of tea/vase of flowers** eine Tasse Tee/Vase mit Blumen; **the 5th of July** der 5. Juli

3 (*from, out of*) aus; **a bridge made of wood** eine Holzbrücke, eine Brücke aus Holz

off [ɔf] *adj, adv* (*absent*) weg, fort; (*switch*) aus(geschaltet), ab(geschaltet); (*BRIT: food: bad*) schlecht; (*cancelled*) abgesagt ♦ *prep* von +*dat*; **to be ~** (*to leave*) gehen; **to be ~ sick** krank sein; **a day ~** ein freier Tag; **to have an ~ day** einen schlechten Tag haben; **he had his coat ~** er hatte seinen Mantel aus; **10% ~** (*COMM*) 10% Rabatt; **5 km ~ (the road)** 5 km (von der Straße) entfernt; **~ the coast** vor der Küste; **I'm ~ meat** (*no longer eat it*) ich esse kein Fleisch mehr; (*no longer like it*) ich mag kein Fleisch mehr; **on the ~ chance** auf gut Glück

offal ['ɔfl] *n* Innereien *pl*

off-colour ['ɔf'kʌləʳ] *adj* nicht wohl

offence [ə'fens] (*US* **offense**) *n* (*crime*) Vergehen *nt*, Straftat *f*; (*insult*) Beleidigung *f*; **to take ~ at** gekränkt sein wegen

offend [ə'fend] *vt* beleidigen; **~er** *n* Gesetzesübertreter *m*

offense [ə'fens] (*US*) *n* = **offence**

offensive [ə'fensɪv] *adj* (*unpleasant*) übel, abstoßend; (*weapon*) Kampf-; (*remark*) verletzend ♦ *n* Angriff *m*

offer ['ɔfəʳ] *n* Angebot *nt* ♦ *vt* anbieten; (*opinion*) äußern; (*resistance*) leisten; **on ~**

zum Verkauf angeboten; **~ing** *n* Gabe *f*

offhand [ɔf'hænd] *adj* lässig ♦ *adv* ohne weiteres

office ['ɔfɪs] *n* Büro *nt*; (*position*) Amt *nt*; **doctor's ~** (*US*) Praxis *f*; **to take ~** sein Amt antreten; (*POL*) die Regierung übernehmen; **~ automation** *n* Büroautomatisierung *f*; **~ block** (*US* **~ building**) *n* Büro(hoch)haus *nt*; **~ hours** *npl* Dienstzeit *f*; (*US: MED*) Sprechstunde *f*

officer ['ɔfɪsəʳ] *n* (*MIL*) Offizier *m*; (*public ~*) Beamte(r) *m*

official [ə'fɪʃl] *adj* offiziell, amtlich ♦ *n* Beamte(r) *m*; **~dom** *n* Beamtentum *nt*

officiate [ə'fɪʃɪeɪt] *vi* amtieren

officious [ə'fɪʃəs] *adj* aufdringlich

offing ['ɔfɪŋ] *n*: **in the ~** in (Aus)sicht

⎡Off-licence⎤

ⓘ Off-licence *ist ein Geschäft (oder eine Theke in einer Gaststätte), wo man alkoholische Getränke kaufen kann, die aber anderswo konsumiert werden müssen. In solchen Geschäften, die oft von landesweiten Ketten betrieben werden, kann man auch andere Getränke, Süßigkeiten, Zigaretten und Knabbereien kaufen.*

off: **~-licence** (*BRIT*) *n* (*shop*) Wein- und Spirituosenhandlung *f*; **~-line** *adj* (*COMPUT*) Offline- ♦ *adv* (*COMPUT*) offline; **~-peak** *adj* (*charges*) verbilligt; **~-putting** (*BRIT*) *adj* (*person, remark etc*) abstoßend; **~-road vehicle** *n* Geländefahrzeug *nt*; **~-season** *adj* außer Saison; **~-set** (*irreg: like* **set**) *vt* ausgleichen ♦ *n* (*also:* **~-set printing**) Offset(druck) *m*; **~-shoot** *n* (*fig: of organization*) Zweig *m*; (*: of discussion etc*) Randergebnis *nt*; **~-shore** *adv* in einiger Entfernung von der Küste ♦ *adj* küstennah, Küsten-; **~-side** *adj* (*SPORT*) im Abseits ♦ *adv* abseits ♦ *n* (*AUT*) Fahrerseite *f*; **~-spring** *n* Nachkommenschaft *f*; (*one*) Sprössling *m*; **~-stage** *adv* hinter den Kulissen; **~-the-cuff** *adj* unvorbereitet, aus dem Stegreif; **~-the-peg** (*US* **~-the-rack**) *adv* von der Stange; **~-white** *adj* naturweiß

Oftel ['ɔftel] *n* Überwachungsgremium zum Verbraucherschutz nach Privatisierung der Telekommunikationsindustrie

often ['ɔfn] *adv* oft

Ofwat ['ɔfwɔt] *n* Überwachungsgremium zum Verbraucherschutz nach Privatisierung der Wasserindustrie

ogle ['əugl] *vt* liebäugeln mit

oil [ɔɪl] *n* Öl *nt* ♦ *vt* ölen; **~can** *n* Ölkännchen *nt*; **~field** *n* Ölfeld *nt*; **~ filter** *n* (AUT) Ölfilter *m*; **~-fired** *adj* Öl-; **~ painting** *n* Ölgemälde *nt*; **~ rig** *n* Ölplattform *f*; **~skins** *npl* Ölzeug *nt*; **~ slick** *n* Ölteppich *m*; **~ tanker** *n* (Öl)tanker *m*; **~ well** *n* Ölquelle *f*; **~y** *adj* ölig; (*dirty*) ölbeschmiert

ointment ['ɔɪntmənt] *n* Salbe *f*

O.K. ['əu'keɪ] *excl* in Ordnung, O. K., o. k. ♦ *adj* in Ordnung ♦ *vt* genehmigen

okay ['əu'keɪ] = **O.K.**

old [əuld] *adj* alt; **how ~ are you?** wie alt bist du?; **he's 10 years ~** er ist 10 Jahre alt; **~er brother** ältere(r) Bruder *m*; **~ age** *n* Alter *nt*; **~-age pensioner** (BRIT) *n* Rentner(in) *m(f)*; **~-fashioned** *adj* altmodisch

olive ['ɔlɪv] *n* (*fruit*) Olive *f*; (*colour*) Olive *nt* ♦ *adj* Oliven-; (*coloured*) olivenfarbig; **~ oil** *n* Olivenöl *nt*

Olympic [əu'lɪmpɪk] *adj* olympisch; **the ~ Games, the ~s** die Olympischen Spiele

omelet(te) ['ɔmlɪt] *n* Omelett *nt*

omen ['əumən] *n* Omen *nt*

ominous ['ɔmɪnəs] *adj* bedrohlich

omission [əu'mɪʃən] *n* Auslassung *f*; (*neglect*) Versäumnis *nt*

omit [əu'mɪt] *vt* auslassen; (*fail to do*) versäumen

KEYWORD
---

on [ɔn] *prep* **1** (*indicating position*) auf +*dat*; (*with vb of motion*) auf +*acc*; (*on vertical surface, part of body*) an +*dat/acc*; **it's on the table** es ist auf dem Tisch; **she put the book on the table** sie legte das Buch auf den Tisch; **on the left** links

2 (*indicating means, method, condition etc*): **on foot** (*go, be*) zu Fuß; **on the train/**

plane (*go*) mit dem Zug/Flugzeug; (*be*) im Zug/Flugzeug; **on the telephone/ television** am Telefon/im Fernsehen; **to be on drugs** Drogen nehmen; **to be on holiday/business** im Urlaub/auf Geschäftsreise sein

3 (*referring to time*): **on Friday** (am) Freitag; **on Fridays** freitags; **on June 20th** am 20. Juni; **a week on Friday** Freitag in einer Woche; **on arrival he ...** als er ankam, ... er ...

4 (*about, concerning*) über +*acc*

♦ *adv* **1** (*referring to dress*) an; **she put her boots/hat on** sie zog ihre Stiefel an/setzte ihren Hut auf

2 (*further, continuously*) weiter; **to walk on** weitergehen

♦ *adj* **1** (*functioning, in operation: machine, TV, light*) an; (: *tap*) aufgedreht; (: *brakes*) angezogen; **is the meeting still on?** findet die Versammlung noch statt?; **there's a good film on** es läuft ein guter Film

2: that's not on! (*inf: of behaviour*) das liegt nicht drin!

once [wʌns] *adv* einmal ♦ *conj* wenn ... einmal; **~ he had left/it was done** nachdem er gegangen war/es fertig war; **at ~** sofort; (*at the same time*) gleichzeitig; **~ a week** einmal in der Woche; **~ more** noch einmal; **~ and for all** ein für alle Mal; **~ upon a time** es war einmal

oncoming ['ɔnkʌmɪŋ] *adj* (*traffic*) Gegen-, entgegenkommend

---
KEYWORD
---

one [wʌn] *num* eins; (*with noun, referring back to noun*) ein/eine/ein; **it is one (o'clock)** es ist eins, es ist ein Uhr; **one hundred and fifty** einhundertfünfzig

♦ *adj* **1** (*sole*) einzige(r, s); **the one book which** das einzige Buch, welches

2 (*same*) derselbe/dieselbe/dasselbe; **they came in the one car** sie kamen alle in dem einen Auto

3 (*indef*): **one day I discovered ...** eines Tages bemerkte ich ...

♦ pron 1 eine(r, s); **do you have a red one?** haben Sie einen roten/eine rote/ein rotes?; **this one** diese(r, s); **that one** der/die/das; **which one?** welche(r, s)?; **one by one** einzeln

2: **one another** einander; **do you two ever see one another?** seht ihr beide euch manchmal?

3 (impers) man; **one never knows** man kann nie wissen; **to cut one's finger** sich in den Finger schneiden

one: **~-armed bandit** n einarmiger Bandit m; **~-day excursion** (US) n (day return) Tagesrückfahrkarte f; **~-man** adj Einmann-; **~-man band** n Einmannkapelle f; (fig) Einmannbetrieb m; **~-off** (BRIT: inf) n Einzelfall m

oneself [wʌn'sɛlf] pron (reflexive: after prep) sich; (~ personally) sich selbst or selber; (emphatic) (sich) selbst; **to hurt ~** sich verletzen

one: **~-sided** adj (argument) einseitig; **~-to-~** adj (relationship) eins-zu-eins; **~-upmanship** n die Kunst, anderen um eine Nasenlänge voraus zu sein; **~-way** adj (street) Einbahn-

ongoing ['ɔngəuɪŋ] adj momentan; (progressing) sich entwickelnd

onion ['ʌnjən] n Zwiebel f

on-line ['ɔnlaɪn] adj (COMPUT) Online-

onlooker ['ɔnlukə'] n Zuschauer(in) m(f)

only ['əunlɪ] adv nur, bloß ♦ adj einzige(r, s) ♦ conj nur, bloß; **an ~ child** ein Einzelkind; **not ~ ... but also ...** nicht nur ..., sondern auch ...

onset ['ɔnset] n (start) Beginn m

onshore ['ɔnʃɔː'] adj (wind) See-

onslaught ['ɔnslɔːt] n Angriff m

onto ['ɔntu] prep = **on to**

onus ['əunəs] n Last f, Pflicht f

onward(s) ['ɔnwəd(z)] adv (place) voran, vorwärts; **from that day ~** von dem Tag an; **from today ~** ab heute

ooze [uːz] vi sickern

opaque [əu'peɪk] adj undurchsichtig

OPEC ['əupek] n abbr (= Organization of Petroleum-Exporting Countries) OPEC f

open ['əupn] adj offen; (public) öffentlich; (mind) aufgeschlossen ♦ vt öffnen, aufmachen; (trial, motorway, account) eröffnen ♦ vi (begin) anfangen; (shop) aufmachen; (door, flower) aufgehen; (play) Premiere haben; **in the ~ (air)** im Freien; **~ on to** vt fus sich öffnen auf +acc; **~ up** vt (route) erschließen; (shop, prospects) eröffnen ♦ vi öffnen; **~ing** n (hole) Öffnung f; (beginning) Anfang m; (good chance) Gelegenheit f; **~ing hours** npl Öffnungszeiten pl; **~ learning centre** n Weiterbildungseinrichtung auf Teilzeitbasis; **~ly** adv offen, (publicly) öffentlich; **~-minded** adj aufgeschlossen; **~-necked** adj offen; **~-plan** adj (office) Großraum-; (flat etc) offen angelegt

┌─────────────────────┐
│ **Open University** │
└─────────────────────┘

i **Open University** *ist eine 1969 in Großbritannien gegründete Fernuniversität für Spätstudierende. Der Unterricht findet durch Fernseh- und Radiosendungen statt, schriftliche Arbeiten werden mit der Post verschickt, und der Besuch von Sommerkursen ist Pflicht. Die Studenten müssen eine bestimmte Anzahl von Unterrichtseinheiten in einem bestimmten Zeitraum absolvieren und für die Verleihung eines akademischen Grades eine Mindestzahl von Scheinen machen.*

opera ['ɔpərə] n Oper f; **~ house** n Opernhaus nt

operate ['ɔpəreɪt] vt (machine) bedienen; (brakes, light) betätigen ♦ vi (machine) laufen, in Betrieb sein; (person) arbeiten; (MED): **to ~ on** operieren

operatic [ɔpə'rætɪk] adj Opern-

operating ['ɔpəreɪtɪŋ] adj: **~ table/theatre** Operationstisch m/-saal m

operation [ɔpə'reɪʃən] n (working) Betrieb m; (MED) Operation f; (undertaking) Unternehmen nt; (MIL) Einsatz m; **to be in ~** (JUR) in Kraft sein; (machine) in Betrieb sein; **to have an ~** (MED) operiert werden;

~al adj einsatzbereit

operative ['ɔpərətɪv] adj wirksam

operator ['ɔpəreɪtəʳ] n (of machine) Arbeiter m; (TEL) Telefonist(in) m(f)

opinion [ə'pɪnjən] n Meinung f; **in my ~** meiner Meinung nach; **~ated** adj starrsinnig; **~ poll** n Meinungsumfrage f

opponent [ə'pəunənt] n Gegner m

opportunity [ɔpə'tjuːnɪtɪ] n Gelegenheit f, Möglichkeit f; **to take the ~ of doing sth** die Gelegenheit ergreifen, etw zu tun

oppose [ə'pəuz] vt entgegentreten +dat; (argument, idea) ablehnen; (plan) bekämpfen; **to be ~d to sth** gegen etw sein; **as ~d to** im Gegensatz zu; **opposing** adj gegnerisch; (points of view) entgegengesetzt

opposite ['ɔpəzɪt] adj (house) gegenüberliegend; (direction) entgegengesetzt ♦ adv gegenüber ♦ prep gegenüber ♦ n Gegenteil nt

opposition [ɔpə'zɪʃən] n (resistance) Widerstand m; (POL) Opposition f; (contrast) Gegensatz m

oppress [ə'prɛs] vt unterdrücken; (heat etc) bedrücken; **~ion** [ə'prɛʃən] n Unterdrückung f; **~ive** adj (authority, law) repressiv; (burden, thought) bedrückend; (heat) drückend

opt [ɔpt] vi: **to ~ for** sich entscheiden für; **to ~ to do sth** sich entscheiden, etw zu tun; **to ~ out of** sich drücken vor +dat

optical ['ɔptɪkl] adj optisch; **~ character reader** n optische(s) Lesegerät nt

optician [ɔp'tɪʃən] n Optiker m

optimist ['ɔptɪmɪst] n Optimist m; **~ic** [ɔptɪ'mɪstɪk] adj optimistisch

optimum ['ɔptɪməm] adj optimal

option ['ɔpʃən] n Wahl f; (COMM) Option f; **to keep one's ~s open** sich alle Möglichkeiten offen halten; **~al** adj freiwillig; (subject) wahlfrei; **~al extras** npl Extras auf Wunsch

or [ɔːʳ] conj oder; **he could not read ~ write** er konnte weder lesen noch schreiben; **~ else** sonst

oral ['ɔːrəl] adj mündlich ♦ n (exam) mündliche Prüfung f

orange ['ɔrɪndʒ] n (fruit) Apfelsine f, Orange f; (colour) Orange nt ♦ adj orange

orator ['ɔrətəʳ] n Redner(in) m(f)

orbit ['ɔːbɪt] n Umlaufbahn f

orbital (motorway) ['ɔːbɪtəl-] n Ringautobahn f

orchard ['ɔːtʃəd] n Obstgarten m

orchestra ['ɔːkɪstrə] n Orchester nt; (US: seating) Parkett nt; **~l** [ɔː'kɛstrəl] adj Orchester-, orchestral

orchid ['ɔːkɪd] n Orchidee f

ordain [ɔː'deɪn] vt (ECCL) weihen

ordeal [ɔː'diːl] n Qual f

order ['ɔːdəʳ] n (sequence) Reihenfolge f; (good arrangement) Ordnung f; (command) Befehl m; (JUR) Anordnung f; (peace) Ordnung f; (condition) Zustand m; (rank) Klasse f; (COMM) Bestellung f; (ECCL, honour) Orden m ♦ vt (also: **put in ~**) ordnen; (command) befehlen; (COMM) bestellen; **in ~** in der Reihenfolge; **in (working) ~** in gutem Zustand; **in ~ to do sth** um etw zu tun; **on ~** (COMM) auf Bestellung; **to ~ sb to do sth** jdm befehlen, etw zu tun; **to ~ sth** (command) etw acc befehlen; **~ form** n Bestellschein m; **~ly** n (MIL) Sanitäter m; (MED) Pfleger m ♦ adj (tidy) ordentlich; (well-behaved) ruhig

ordinary ['ɔːdnrɪ] adj gewöhnlich ♦ n: **out of the ~** außergewöhnlich

Ordnance Survey ['ɔːdnəns] (BRIT) n amtliche(r) Kartografiedienst m

ore [ɔːʳ] n Erz nt

organ ['ɔːgən] n (MUS) Orgel f; (BIOL, fig) Organ nt

organic [ɔː'gænɪk] adj (food, farming etc) biodynamisch

organization [ɔːgənaɪ'zeɪʃən] n Organisation f; (make-up) Struktur f

organize ['ɔːgənaɪz] vt organisieren; **~r** n Organisator m, Veranstalter m

orgasm ['ɔːgæzəm] n Orgasmus m

orgy ['ɔːdʒɪ] n Orgie f

Orient ['ɔːrɪənt] n Orient m; **o~al** [ɔːrɪ'ɛntl] adj orientalisch

origin ['ɔrɪdʒɪn] n Ursprung m; (of the world)

Anfang *m*, Entstehung *f*; ~al [ə'rɪdʒɪnl] *adj* (*first*) ursprünglich; (*painting*) original; (*idea*) originell ♦ *n* Original *nt*; ~ally *adv* ursprünglich; originell; ~ate [ə'rɪdʒɪneɪt] *vi* entstehen ♦ *vt* ins Leben rufen; **to ~ate from** stammen aus

Orkney ['ɔːknɪ] *npl* (*also*: **the ~ Islands**) die Orkneyinseln *pl*

ornament ['ɔːnəmənt] *n* Schmuck *m*; (*on mantelpiece*) Nippesfigur *f*; ~al [ɔːnə'mentl] *adj* Zier-

ornate [ɔː'neɪt] *adj* reich verziert

orphan ['ɔːfn] *n* Waise *f*, Waisenkind *nt* ♦ *vt*: **to be ~ed** Waise werden; ~age *n* Waisenhaus *nt*

orthodox ['ɔːθədɔks] *adj* orthodox; ~y *n* Orthodoxie *f*; (*fig*) Konventionalität *f*

orthopaedic [ɔːθə'piːdɪk] (*US* **orthopedic**) *adj* orthopädisch

ostentatious [ɔsten'teɪʃəs] *adj* großtuerisch, protzig

ostracize ['ɔstrəsaɪz] *vt* ausstoßen

ostrich ['ɔstrɪtʃ] *n* Strauß *m*

other ['ʌðə*r*] *adj* andere(r, s) ♦ *pron* andere(r, s) ♦ *adv*: **~ than** anders als; **the ~ (one)** der/die/das andere; **the ~ day** neulich; **~s** (*~ people*) andere; ~wise *adv* (*in a different way*) anders; (*or else*) sonst

otter ['ɔtə*r*] *n* Otter *m*

ouch [autʃ] *excl* aua

ought [ɔːt] *vb aux* sollen; **I ~ to do it** ich sollte es tun; **this ~ to have been corrected** das hätte korrigiert werden sollen

ounce [auns] *n* Unze *f*

our ['auə*r*] *adj* unser; *see also* **my**; **~s** *pron* unsere(r, s); *see also* **mine²**; **~selves** *pron* uns (selbst); (*emphatic*) (wir) selbst; *see also* **oneself**

oust [aust] *vt* verdrängen

out [aut] *adv* hinaus/heraus; (*not indoors*) draußen; (*not alight*) aus; (*unconscious*) bewusstlos; (*results*) bekannt gegeben; **to eat/go ~** auswärts essen/ausgehen; **~ there** da draußen; **he is ~** (*absent*) er ist nicht da; **he was ~ in his calculations** seine Berechnungen waren nicht richtig; **~**

loud laut; **~ of** aus; (*away from*) außerhalb +*gen*; **to be ~ of milk** *etc* keine Milch *etc* mehr haben; **~ of order** außer Betrieb; ~**-and-~** *adj* (*liar, thief etc*) ausgemacht; ~**back** *n* Hinterland *nt*; ~**board (motor)** *n* Außenbordmotor *m*; ~**break** *n* Ausbruch *m*; ~**burst** *n* Ausbruch *m*; ~**cast** *n* Ausgestoßene(r) *mf*; ~**come** *n* Ergebnis *nt*; ~**crop** *n* (*of rock*) Felsnase *f*; ~**cry** *n* Protest *m*; ~**dated** *adj* überholt; ~**do** (*irreg: like* **do**) *vt* übertrumpfen; ~**door** *adj* Außen-; (*SPORT*) im Freien; ~**doors** *adv* im Freien

outer ['autə*r*] *adj* äußere(r, s); **~ space** *n* Weltraum *m*

outfit ['autfɪt] *n* Kleidung *f*

out: ~**going** *adj* (*character*) aufgeschlossen; ~**goings** (*BRIT*) *npl* Ausgaben *pl*; ~**grow** (*irreg: like* **grow**) *vt* (*clothes*) herauswachsen aus; (*habit*) ablegen; ~**house** *n* Nebengebäude *nt*

outing ['autɪŋ] *n* Ausflug *m*

outlandish [aut'lændɪʃ] *adj* eigenartig

out: ~**law** *n* Geächtete(r) *f(m)* ♦ *vt* ächten; (*thing*) verbieten; ~**lay** *n* Auslage *f*; ~**let** *n* Auslass *m*, Abfluss *m*; (*also:* **retail ~let**) Absatzmarkt *m*; (*US: ELEC*) Steckdose *f*; (*for emotions*) Ventil *nt*

outline ['autlaɪn] *n* Umriss *m*

out: ~**live** *vt* überleben; ~**look** *n* (*also fig*) Aussicht *f*; (*attitude*) Einstellung *f*; ~**lying** *adj* entlegen; (*district*) Außen-; ~**moded** *adj* veraltet; ~**number** *vt* zahlenmäßig überlegen sein +*dat*; ~**-of-date** *adj* (*passport*) abgelaufen; (*clothes etc*) altmodisch; (*ideas etc*) überholt; ~**-of-the-way** *adj* abgelegen; ~**patient** *n* ambulante(r) Patient *m*/ambulante Patientin *f*; ~**post** *n* (*MIL, fig*) Vorposten *m*; ~**put** *n* Leistung *f*, Produktion *f*; (*COMPUT*) Ausgabe *f*

outrage ['autreɪdʒ] *n* (*cruel deed*) Ausschreitung *f*; (*indecency*) Skandal *m* ♦ *vt* (*morals*) verstoßen gegen; (*person*) empören; ~**ous** [aut'reɪdʒəs] *adj* unerhört

outreach worker [aut'riːtʃ-] *n* Streetworker(in) *m(f)*

outright [*adv* aut'raɪt, *adj* 'autraɪt] *adv* (*at*

once) sofort; (*openly*) ohne Umschweife
♦ *adj* (*denial*) völlig; (*sale*) Total-; (*winner*)
unbestritten

outset ['autset] *n* Beginn *m*

outside [aut'said] *n* Außenseite *f* ♦ *adj*
äußere(r, s), Außen-; (*chance*) gering ♦ *adv*
außen ♦ *prep* außerhalb +*gen*; **at the ~** (*fig*)
maximal; (*time*) spätestens; **to go ~** nach
draußen gehen; **~ lane** *n* (*AUT*) äußere
Spur *f*; **~ line** *n* (*TEL*) Amtsanschluss *m*; **~r**
n Außenseiter(in) *m(f)*

out: **~size** *adj* übergroß; **~skirts** *npl*
Stadtrand *m*; **~spoken** *adj* freimütig;
~standing *adj* hervorragend; (*debts etc*)
ausstehend; **~stay** *vt*: **to ~stay one's
welcome** länger bleiben als erwünscht;
~stretched *adj* ausgestreckt; **~strip** *vt*
übertreffen; **~ tray** *n* Ausgangskorb *m*

outward ['autwəd] *adj* äußere(r, s); (*journey*)
Hin-; (*freight*) ausgehend ♦ *adv* nach außen;
~ly *adv* äußerlich

outweigh [aut'wei] *vt* (*fig*) überwiegen

outwit [aut'wit] *vt* überlisten

oval ['əuvl] *adj* oval ♦ *n* Oval *nt*

Oval Office

ⓘ **Oval Office**, *ein großer ovaler Raum im
Weißen Haus, ist das private Büro des
amerikanischen Präsidenten. Im weiteren
Sinne bezieht sich dieser Begriff oft auf die
Präsidentschaft selbst.*

ovary ['əuvəri] *n* Eierstock *m*

ovation [əu'veiʃən] *n* Beifallssturm *m*

oven ['ʌvn] *n* Backofen *m*; **~proof** *adj*
feuerfest

over ['əuvər] *adv* (*across*) hinüber/herüber;
(*finished*) vorbei; (*left*) übrig; (*again*) wieder,
noch einmal ♦ *prep* über ♦ *prefix* (*excessively*)
übermäßig; **~ here** hier(hin); **~ there**
dort(hin); **all ~** (*everywhere*) überall;
(*finished*) vorbei; **~ and ~** immer wieder; **~
and above** darüber hinaus; **to ask sb ~**
jdn einladen; **to bend ~** sich bücken

overall [*adj, n* 'əuvərɔːl, *adv* əuvər'ɔːl] *adj*
(*situation*) allgemein; (*length*) Gesamt- ♦ *n*
(*BRIT*) Kittel *m* ♦ *adv* insgesamt; **~s** *npl* (for

man) Overall *m*

over: **~awe** *vt* (*frighten*) einschüchtern;
(*make impression*) überwältigen; **~balance**
vi Übergewicht bekommen; **~bearing** *adj*
aufdringlich; **~board** *adv* über Bord;
~book *vi* überbuchen

overcast ['əuvəkɑːst] *adj* bedeckt

overcharge [əuvə'tʃɑːdʒ] *vt*: **to ~ sb** von
jdm zu viel verlangen

overcoat ['əuvəkəut] *n* Mantel *m*

overcome [əuvə'kʌm] (*irreg: like* **come**) *vt*
überwinden

over: **~crowded** *adj* überfüllt; **~crowding**
n Überfüllung *f*; **~do** (*irreg: like* **do**) *vt* (*cook
too much*) verkochen; (*exaggerate*)
übertreiben; **~done** *adj* übertrieben;
(*COOK*) verbraten, verkocht; **~dose** *n*
Überdosis *f*; **~draft** *n* (*Konto)überziehung
f; **~drawn** *adj* (*account*) überzogen; **~due**
adj überfällig; **~estimate** *vt* überschätzen;
~excited *adj* überreizt; (*children*) aufgeregt

overflow [əuvə'fləu] *vi* überfließen ♦ *n*
(*excess*) Überschuss *m*; (*also:* **~ pipe**)
Überlaufrohr *nt*

overgrown [əuvə'grəun] *adj* (*garden*)
verwildert

overhaul [*vb* əuvə'hɔːl, *n* 'əuvəhɔːl] *vt* (*car*)
überholen; (*plans*) überprüfen ♦ *n*
Überholung *f*

overhead [*adv* əuvə'hed, *adj, n* 'əuvəhed] *adv*
oben ♦ *adj* Hoch-; (*wire*) oberirdisch;
(*lighting*) Decken- ♦ *n* (*US*) = **overheads**; **~s**
npl (*costs*) allgemeine Unkosten *pl*; **~
projector** *n* Overheadprojektor *m*

over: **~hear** (*irreg: like* **hear**) *vt* (mit
an)hören; **~heat** *vi* (*engine*) heiß laufen;
~joyed *adj* überglücklich; **~kill** *n* (*fig*)
Rundumschlag *m*

overland ['əuvəlænd] *adj* Überland- ♦ *adv*
(*travel*) über Land

overlap [*vb* əuvə'læp, *n* 'əuvəlæp] *vi* sich
überschneiden; (*objects*) sich teilweise
decken ♦ *n* Überschneidung *f*

over: **~leaf** *adv* umseitig; **~load** *vt*
überladen; **~look** *vt* (*view from above*)
überblicken; (*not notice*) übersehen;
(*pardon*) hinwegsehen über +*acc*

overnight [adv əuvə'naɪt, adj 'əuvənaɪt] adv über Nacht ♦ adj (journey) Nacht-; **~ stay** Übernachtung f; **to stay ~** übernachten

overpass ['əuvəpɑːs] n Überführung f

overpower [əuvə'pauə'] vt überwältigen

over: ~rate vt überschätzen; **~ride** (irreg: like ride) vt (order, decision) aufheben; (objection) übergehen; **~riding** adj vorherrschend; **~rule** vt verwerfen; **~run** (irreg: like run) vt (country) einfallen in; (time limit) überziehen

overseas [əuvə'siːz] adv nach/in Übersee ♦ adj überseeisch, Übersee-

overseer ['əuvəsiə'] n Aufseher m

overshadow [əuvə'ʃædəu] vt überschatten

overshoot [əuvə'ʃuːt] (irreg: like shoot) vt (runway) hinausschießen über +acc

oversight ['əuvəsaɪt] n (mistake) Versehen nt

over: ~sleep (irreg: like sleep) vi verschlafen; **~spill** n (Bevölkerungs)überschuss m; **~state** vt übertreiben; **~step** vt: **to ~step the mark** zu weit gehen

overt [əu'vəːt] adj offen(kundig)

overtake [əuvə'teɪk] (irreg: like take) vt, vi überholen

over: ~throw (irreg: like throw) vt (POL) stürzen; **~time** n Überstunden pl; **~tone** n (fig) Note f

overture ['əuvətʃuə'] n Ouvertüre f

over: ~turn vt, vi umkippen; **~weight** adj zu dick; **~whelm** vt überwältigen; **~work** n Überarbeitung f ♦ vt überlasten ♦ vi sich überarbeiten; **~wrought** adj überreizt

owe [əu] vt schulden; **to ~ sth to sb** (money) jdm etw schulden; (favour etc) jdm etw verdanken; **owing to** prep wegen +gen

owl [aul] n Eule f

own [əun] vt besitzen ♦ adj eigen; **a room of my ~** mein eigenes Zimmer; **to get one's ~ back** sich rächen; **on one's ~** allein; **~ up** vi: **to ~ up (to sth)** (etw) zugeben; **~er** n Besitzer(in) m(f); **~ership** n Besitz m

ox [ɔks] (pl **~en**) n Ochse m

oxtail ['ɔksteɪl] n: **~ soup** Ochsenschwanzsuppe f

oxygen ['ɔksɪdʒən] n Sauerstoff m; **~ mask** n Sauerstoffmaske f; **~ tent** n Sauerstoffzelt nt

oyster ['ɔɪstə'] n Auster f

oz. abbr = **ounce(s)**

ozone ['əuzəun] n Ozon nt; **~-friendly** adj (aerosol) ohne Treibgas; (fridge) FCKW-frei; **~ hole** n Ozonloch nt; **~ layer** n Ozonschicht f

P, p

p abbr = **penny; pence**

pa [pɑː] (inf) n Papa m

P.A. n abbr = **personal assistant; public address system**

p.a. abbr = **per annum**

pace [peɪs] n Schritt m; (speed) Tempo nt ♦ vi schreiten; **to keep ~ with** Schritt halten mit; **~maker** n Schrittmacher m

pacific [pə'sɪfɪk] adj pazifisch ♦ n: **the P~ (Ocean)** der Pazifik

pacifist ['pæsɪfɪst] n Pazifist m

pacify ['pæsɪfaɪ] vt befrieden; (calm) beruhigen

pack [pæk] n (of goods) Packung f; (of hounds) Meute f; (of cards) Spiel nt; (gang) Bande f ♦ vt (case) packen; (clothes) einpacken ♦ vi packen; **to ~ sb off to ...** jdn nach ... schicken; **~ it in!** lass es gut sein!

package ['pækɪdʒ] n Paket nt; **~ tour** n Pauschalreise f

packed [pækt] adj abgepackt; **~ lunch** n Lunchpaket nt

packet ['pækɪt] n Päckchen nt

packing ['pækɪŋ] n (action) Packen nt; (material) Verpackung f; **~ case** n (Pack)kiste f

pact [pækt] n Pakt m, Vertrag m

pad [pæd] n (of paper) (Schreib)block m; (stuffing) Polster nt ♦ vt polstern; **~ding** n Polsterung f

paddle ['pædl] n Paddel nt; (US: SPORT) Schläger m ♦ vt (boat) paddeln ♦ vi (in sea) plan(t)schen; **~ steamer** n Raddampfer m

paddling pool ['pædlɪŋ-] (BRIT) n

Plan(t)schbecken nt

paddock ['pædɔk] n Koppel f

paddy field ['pædɪ-] n Reisfeld nt

padlock ['pædlɔk] n Vorhängeschloss nt ♦ vt verschließen

paediatrics [piːdɪ'ætrɪks] (*US* **pediatrics**) n Kinderheilkunde f

pagan ['peɪɡən] adj heidnisch ♦ n Heide m, Heidin f

page [peɪdʒ] n Seite f; (*person*) Page m ♦ vt (*in hotel*) ausrufen lassen

pageant ['pædʒənt] n Festzug m; **~ry** n Gepränge nt

pager ['peɪdʒəʳ] n (*TEL*) Funkrufempfänger m, Piepser m (*inf*)

paging device ['peɪdʒɪŋ-] n (*TEL*) = **pager**

paid [peɪd] pt, pp of **pay** ♦ adj bezahlt; **to put ~ to** (*BRIT*) zunichte machen

pail [peɪl] n Eimer m

pain [peɪn] n Schmerz m; **to be in ~** Schmerzen haben; **on ~ of death** bei Todesstrafe; **to take ~s to do sth** sich *dat* Mühe geben, etw zu tun; **~ed** adj (*expression*) gequält; **~ful** adj (*physically*) schmerzhaft; (*embarrassing*) peinlich; (*difficult*) mühsam; **~fully** adv (*fig: very*) schrecklich; **~killer** n Schmerzmittel nt; **~less** adj schmerzlos; **~staking** ['zteɪkɪŋ] adj gewissenhaft

paint [peɪnt] n Farbe f ♦ vt anstreichen; (*picture*) malen; **to ~ the door blue** die Tür blau streichen; **~brush** n Pinsel m; **~er** n Maler m; **~ing** n Malerei f; (*picture*) Gemälde nt; **~work** n Anstrich m; (*of car*) Lack m

pair [peəʳ] n Paar nt; **~ of scissors** Schere f; **~ of trousers** Hose f

pajamas [pə'dʒɑːməz] (*US*) npl Schlafanzug m

Pakistan [pɑːkɪ'stɑːn] n Pakistan nt; **~i** adj pakistanisch ♦ n Pakistani mf

pal [pæl] (*inf*) n Kumpel m

palace ['pæləs] n Palast m, Schloss nt

palatable ['pælɪtəbl] adj schmackhaft

palate ['pælɪt] n Gaumen m

palatial [pə'leɪʃəl] adj palastartig

pale [peɪl] adj blass, bleich ♦ n: **to be**

beyond the ~ die Grenzen überschreiten

Palestine ['pælɪstaɪn] n Palästina nt; **Palestinian** [pælɪs'tɪnɪən] adj palästinensisch ♦ n Palästinenser(in) m(f)

palette ['pælɪt] n Palette f

paling ['peɪlɪŋ] n (*stake*) Zaunpfahl m; (*fence*) Lattenzaun m

pall [pɔːl] vi jeden Reiz verlieren, verblassen

pallet ['pælɪt] n (*for goods*) Palette f

pallid ['pælɪd] adj blass, bleich

pallor ['pæləʳ] n Blässe f

palm [pɑːm] n (*of hand*) Handfläche f; (*also:* **~ tree**) Palme f ♦ vt: **to ~ sth off on sb** jdm etw andrehen; **P~ Sunday** n Palmsonntag m

palpable ['pælpəbl] adj (*also fig*) greifbar

palpitation [pælpɪ'teɪʃən] n Herzklopfen nt

paltry ['pɔːltrɪ] adj armselig

pamper ['pæmpəʳ] vt verhätscheln

pamphlet ['pæmflət] n Broschüre f

pan [pæn] n Pfanne f ♦ vi (*CINE*) schwenken

panache [pə'næʃ] n Schwung m

pancake ['pænkeɪk] n Pfannkuchen m

pancreas ['pæŋkrɪəs] n Bauchspeicheldrüse f

panda ['pændə] n Panda m; **~ car** (*BRIT*) n (Funk)streifenwagen m

pandemonium [pændɪ'məunɪəm] n Hölle f; (*noise*) Höllenlärm m

pander ['pændəʳ] vi: **to ~ to** sich richten nach

pane [peɪn] n (*Fenster*)scheibe f

panel ['pænl] n (*of wood*) Tafel f; (*TV*) Diskussionsrunde f; **~ling** (*US* **paneling**) n Täfelung f

pang [pæŋ] n: **~s of hunger** quälende(r) Hunger m; **~s of conscience** Gewissensbisse pl

panic ['pænɪk] n Panik f ♦ vi in Panik geraten; **don't ~** (nur) keine Panik; **~ky** adj (*person*) überängstlich; **~-stricken** adj von panischem Schrecken erfasst; (*look*) panisch

pansy ['pænzɪ] n Stiefmütterchen nt; (*inf*) Schwule(r) m

pant [pænt] vi keuchen; (*dog*) hecheln

panther ['pænθəʳ] n Pant(h)er m

panties ['pæntɪz] *npl* (Damen)slip *m*

pantihose ['pæntɪhəʊz] (*US*) *n* Strumpfhose *f*

pantomime ['pæntəmaɪm] (*BRIT*) *n* Märchenkomödie *f* um Weihnachten

---
Pantomime

ⓘ **Pantomime** *oder umgangssprachlich* **panto** *ist in Großbritannien ein zur Weihnachtszeit aufgeführtes Märchenspiel mit possenhaften Elementen, Musik, Standardrollen (ein als Frau verkleideter Mann, ein Junge, ein Bösewicht) und aktuellen Witzen. Publikumsbeteiligung wird gern gesehen (z.B. warnen die Kinder den Helden mit dem Ruf „He's behind you" vor einer drohenden Gefahr), und viele der Witze sprechen vor allem Erwachsene an, so dass pantomimes Unterhaltung für die ganze Familie bieten.*

---

pantry ['pæntrɪ] *n* Vorratskammer *f*

pants [pænts] *npl* (*BRIT*: woman's) Schlüpfer *m*; (: man's) Unterhose *f*; (*US*: trousers) Hose *f*

papal ['peɪpəl] *adj* päpstlich

paper ['peɪpə'] *n* Papier *nt*; (newspaper) Zeitung *f*; (essay) Referat *nt* ♦ *adj* Papier-, aus Papier ♦ *vt* (wall) tapezieren; **~s** *npl* (identity ~s) Ausweis(papiere *pl*) *m*; **~back** *n* Taschenbuch *nt*; **~ bag** *n* Tüte *f*; **~ clip** *n* Büroklammer *f*; **~ hankie** *n* Tempotaschentuch *nt* ®; **~weight** *n* Briefbeschwerer *m*; **~work** *n* Schreibarbeit *f*

par [pɑː'] *n* (*COMM*) Nennwert *m*; (*GOLF*) Par *nt*; **on a ~ with** ebenbürtig +*dat*

parable ['pærəbl] *n* (*REL*) Gleichnis *nt*

parachute ['pærəʃuːt] *n* Fallschirm *m* ♦ *vi* (mit dem Fallschirm) abspringen

parade [pə'reɪd] *n* Parade *f* ♦ *vt* aufmarschieren lassen; (fig) zur Schau stellen ♦ *vi* paradieren, vorbeimarschieren

paradise ['pærədaɪs] *n* Paradies *nt*

paradox ['pærədɒks] *n* Paradox *nt*; **~ically** [pærə'dɒksɪklɪ] *adv* paradoxerweise

paraffin ['pærəfɪn] (*BRIT*) *n* Paraffin *nt*

paragraph ['pærəgrɑːf] *n* Absatz *m*

parallel ['pærəlel] *adj* parallel ♦ *n* Parallele *f*

paralyse ['pærəlaɪz] (*US* **paralyze**) *vt* (*MED*) lähmen, paralysieren; (fig: organization, production etc) lahm legen; **~d** *adj* gelähmt; **paralysis** [pə'rælɪsɪs] *n* Lähmung *f*

paralyze ['pærəlaɪz] (*US*) = **paralyse** *vt*

parameter [pə'ræmɪtə'] *n* Parameter *m*; **~s** *npl* (framework, limits) Rahmen *m*

paramount ['pærəmaʊnt] *adj* höchste(r, s), oberste(r, s)

paranoid ['pærənɔɪd] *adj* (person) an Verfolgungswahn leidend, paranoid; (feeling) krankhaft

parapet ['pærəpɪt] *n* Brüstung *f*

paraphernalia [pærəfə'neɪlɪə] *n* Zubehör *nt*, Utensilien *pl*

paraphrase ['pærəfreɪz] *vt* umschreiben

paraplegic [pærə'pliːdʒɪk] *n* Querschnittsgelähmte(r) *f(m)*

parasite ['pærəsaɪt] *n* (also fig) Schmarotzer *m*, Parasit *m*

parasol ['pærəsɒl] *n* Sonnenschirm *m*

paratrooper ['pærətruːpə'] *n* Fallschirmjäger *m*

parcel ['pɑːsl] *n* Paket *n* ♦ *vt* (also: ~ **up**) einpacken

parch [pɑːtʃ] *vt* (aus)dörren; **~ed** *adj* ausgetrocknet; (person) am Verdursten

parchment ['pɑːtʃmənt] *n* Pergament *nt*

pardon ['pɑːdn] *n* Verzeihung *f* ♦ *vt* (*JUR*) begnadigen; **~ me!, I beg your ~!** verzeihen Sie bitte!; **~ me?** (*US*) wie bitte?; **(I beg your) ~?** wie bitte?

parent ['pɛərənt] *n* Elternteil *m*; **~s** *npl* (mother and father) Eltern *pl*; **~al** [pə'rentl] *adj* elterlich, Eltern-

parentheses [pə'renθɪsiːz] *npl* of **parenthesis**

parenthesis [pə'renθɪsɪs] *n* Klammer *f*; (sentence) Parenthese *f*

Paris ['pærɪs] *n* Paris *nt*

parish ['pærɪʃ] *n* Gemeinde *f*

park [pɑːk] *n* Park *m* ♦ *vt*, *vi* parken

parking ['pɑːkɪŋ] *n* Parken *nt*; **"no ~"** „Parken verboten"; **~ lot** (*US*) *n* Parkplatz *m*; **~ meter** *n* Parkuhr *f*; **~ ticket** *n*

Strafzettel *m*

parlance ['pɑːləns] *n* Sprachgebrauch *m*

parliament ['pɑːləmənt] *n* Parlament *nt*; **~ary** [pɑːlə'mɛntəri] *adj* parlamentarisch, Parlaments-

parlour ['pɑːləʳ] (*US* **parlor**) *n* Salon *m*

parochial [pə'rəukiəl] *adj* (*narrow-minded*) eng(stirnig)

parole [pə'rəul] *n*: **on ~** (*prisoner*) auf Bewährung

parrot ['pærət] *n* Papagei *m*

parry ['pæri] *vt* parieren, abwehren

parsley ['pɑːsli] *n* Petersilie *m*

parsnip ['pɑːsnip] *n* Pastinake *f*

parson ['pɑːsn] *n* Pfarrer *m*

part [pɑːt] *n* (*piece*) Teil *m*; (*THEAT*) Rolle *f*; (*of machine*) Teil *nt* ♦ *adv* = **partly**; ♦ *vt* trennen; (*hair*) scheiteln ♦ *vi* (*people*) sich trennen; **to take ~ in** teilnehmen an *+dat*; **to take sth in good ~** etw nicht übel nehmen; **to take sb's ~** sich auf jds Seite *acc* stellen; **for my ~** ich für meinen Teil; **for the most ~** meistens, größtenteils; **in ~ exchange** (*BRIT*) in Zahlung; **~ with** *vt fus* hergeben; (*renounce*) aufgeben; **~ial** ['pɑːʃl] *adj* (*incomplete*) teilweise; (*biased*) parteiisch; **to be ~ial to** eine (besondere) Vorliebe haben für

participant [pɑː'tisipənt] *n* Teilnehmer(in) *m(f)*

participate [pɑː'tisipeit] *vi*: **to ~ (in)** teilnehmen (an *+dat*); **participation** [pɑːtisi'peiʃən] *n* Teilnahme *f*; (*sharing*) Beteiligung *f*

participle ['pɑːtisipl] *n* Partizip *nt*

particle ['pɑːtikl] *n* Teilchen *nt*

particular [pə'tikjuləʳ] *adj* bestimmt; (*exact*) genau; (*fussy*) eigen; **in ~** besonders; **~ly** *adv* besonders

particulars *npl* (*details*) Einzelheiten *pl*; (*of person*) Personalien *pl*

parting ['pɑːtiŋ] *n* (*separation*) Abschied *m*; (*BRIT: of hair*) Scheitel *m* ♦ *adj* Abschieds-

partition [pɑː'tiʃən] *n* (*wall*) Trennwand *f*; (*division*) Teilung *f* ♦ *vt* aufteilen

partly ['pɑːtli] *adv* zum Teil, teilweise

partner ['pɑːtnəʳ] *n* Partner *m* ♦ *vt* der

Partner sein von; **~ship** *n* Partnerschaft *f*; (*COMM*) Teilhaberschaft *f*

partridge ['pɑːtridʒ] *n* Rebhuhn *nt*

part-time ['pɑːt'taim] *adj* Teilzeit- ♦ *adv* stundenweise

party ['pɑːti] *n* (*POL, JUR*) Partei *f*; (*group*) Gesellschaft *f*; (*celebration*) Party *f* ♦ *adj* (*dress*) Party-; (*politics*) Partei-; **~ line** *n* (*TEL*) Gemeinschaftsanschluss *m*

pass [pɑːs] *vt* (*on foot*) vorbeigehen an *+dat*; (*driving*) vorbeifahren an *+dat*; (*surpass*) übersteigen; (*hand on*) weitergeben; (*approve*) genehmigen; (*time*) verbringen; (*exam*) bestehen ♦ *vi* (*go by*) vorbeigehen; vorbeifahren; (*years*) vergehen; (*be successful*) bestehen ♦ *n* (*in mountains, SPORT*) Pass *m*; (*permission*) Passierschein *m*; (*in exam*): **to get a ~** bestehen; **to ~ sth through sth** etw durch etw führen; **to make a ~ at sb** (*inf*) bei jdm Annäherungsversuche machen; **~ away** *vi* (*euph*) verscheiden; **~ by** *vi* vorbeigehen; vorbeifahren; (*years*) vergehen; **~ on** *vt* weitergeben; **~ out** *vi* (*faint*) ohnmächtig werden; **~ up** *vt* vorbeigehen lassen; **~able** *adj* (*road*) passierbar; (*fairly good*) passabel

passage ['pæsidʒ] *n* (*corridor*) Gang *m*; (*in book*) (Text)stelle *f*; (*voyage*) Überfahrt *f*; **~way** *n* Durchgang *m*

passbook ['pɑːsbuk] *n* Sparbuch *nt*

passenger ['pæsindʒəʳ] *n* Passagier *m*; (*on bus*) Fahrgast *m*

passer-by [pɑːsə'bai] *n* Passant(in) *m(f)*

passing ['pɑːsiŋ] *adj* (*car*) vorbeifahrend; (*thought, affair*) momentan ♦ *n*: **in ~** beiläufig; **~ place** *n* (*AUT*) Ausweichstelle *f*

passion ['pæʃən] *n* Leidenschaft *f*; **~ate** *adj* leidenschaftlich

passive ['pæsiv] *adj* passiv; (*LING*) passivisch; **~ smoking** *n* Passivrauchen *nt*

Passover ['pɑːsəuvəʳ] *n* Passahfest *nt*

passport ['pɑːspɔːt] *n* (Reise)pass *m*; **~ control** *n* Passkontrolle *f*; **~ office** *n* Passamt *nt*

password ['pɑːswɜːd] *n* Parole *f*, Kennwort *nt*, Losung *f*

past [pɑːst] prep (motion) an +dat ... vorbei; (position) hinter +dat; (later than) nach ♦ adj (years) vergangen; (president etc) ehemalig ♦ n Vergangenheit f; **he's ~ forty** er ist über vierzig; **for the ~ few/3 days** in den letzten paar/3 Tagen; **to run ~** vorbeilaufen; **ten/quarter ~ eight** zehn/Viertel nach acht

pasta ['pæstə] n Teigwaren pl

paste [peɪst] n (fish ~ etc) Paste f; (glue) Kleister m ♦ vt kleben

pasteurized ['pæstʃəraɪzd] adj pasteurisiert

pastime ['pɑːstaɪm] n Zeitvertreib m

pastor ['pɑːstə*] n Pfarrer m

pastry ['peɪstrɪ] n Blätterteig m; **pastries** npl (tarts etc) Stückchen pl

pasture ['pɑːstʃə*] n Weide f

pasty [n 'pæstɪ, adj 'peɪstɪ] n (Fleisch)pastete f ♦ adj blässlich, käsig

pat [pæt] n leichte(r) Schlag m, Klaps m ♦ vt tätscheln

patch [pætʃ] n Fleck m ♦ vt flicken; **(to go through) a bad ~** eine Pechsträhne (haben); **~ up** vt flicken; (quarrel) beilegen; **~ed** adj geflickt; **~y** adj (irregular) ungleichmäßig

pâté ['pæteɪ] n Pastete f

patent ['peɪtɪt] n Patent nt ♦ vt patentieren lassen; (by authorities) patentieren ♦ adj offenkundig; **~ leather** n Lackleder nt

paternal [pə'tɜːnl] adj väterlich

paternity [pə'tɜːnɪtɪ] n Vaterschaft f

path [pɑːθ] n Pfad m; Weg m

pathetic [pə'θetɪk] adj (very bad) kläglich

pathological [pæθə'lɔdʒɪk] adj pathologisch

pathology [pə'θɔlədʒɪ] n Pathologie f

pathos ['peɪθɒs] n Rührseligkeit f

pathway ['pɑːθweɪ] n Weg m

patience ['peɪʃns] n Geduld f; (BRIT: CARDS) Patience f

patient ['peɪʃnt] n Patient(in) m(f), Kranke(r) mf ♦ adj geduldig

patio ['pætɪəʊ] n Terrasse f

patriotic [pætrɪ'ɔtɪk] adj patriotisch

patrol [pə'trəʊl] n Patrouille f; (police) Streife f ♦ vt patrouillieren in +dat ♦ vi (police) die

Runde machen; (MIL) patrouillieren; **~ car** n Streifenwagen m; **~man** (US) (irreg) n (Streifen)polizist m

patron ['peɪtrən] n (in shop) (Stamm)kunde m; (in hotel) (Stamm)gast m; (supporter) Förderer m; **~ of the arts** Mäzen m; **~age** ['pætrənɪdʒ] n Schirmherrschaft f; **~ize** ['pætrənaɪz] vt (support) unterstützen; (shop) besuchen; (treat condescendingly) von oben herab behandeln; **~ saint** n Schutzpatron(in) m(f)

patter ['pætə*] n (sound: of feet) Trappeln nt; (: of rain) Prasseln nt; (sales talk) Gerede nt ♦ vi (feet) trappeln; (rain) prasseln

pattern ['pætən] n Muster nt; (SEWING) Schnittmuster nt; (KNITTING) Strickanleitung f

pauper ['pɔːpə*] n Arme(r) mf

pause [pɔːz] n Pause f ♦ vi innehalten

pave [peɪv] vt pflastern; **to ~ the way for** den Weg bahnen für

pavement ['peɪvmənt] (BRIT) n Bürgersteig m

pavilion [pə'vɪlɪən] n Pavillon m; (SPORT) Klubhaus nt

paving ['peɪvɪŋ] n Straßenpflaster nt; **~ stone** n Pflasterstein m

paw [pɔː] n Pfote f; (of big cats) Tatze f, Pranke f ♦ vt (scrape) scharren; (handle) betatschen

pawn [pɔːn] n Pfand nt; (chess) Bauer m ♦ vt verpfänden; **~broker** n Pfandleiher m; **~shop** n Pfandhaus nt

pay [peɪ] (pt, pp **paid**) n Bezahlung f, Lohn m ♦ vt bezahlen ♦ vi zahlen; (be profitable) sich bezahlt machen; **to ~ attention (to)** Acht geben (auf +acc); **to ~ sb a visit** jdn besuchen; **~ back** vt zurückzahlen; **~ for** vt fus bezahlen; **~ in** vt einzahlen; **~ off** vt abzahlen ♦ vi (scheme, decision) sich bezahlt machen; **~ up** vi bezahlen; **~able** adj zahlbar, fällig; **~ee** n Zahlungsempfänger m; **~ envelope** (US) n Lohntüte f; **~ment** n Bezahlung f; **advance ~ment** Vorauszahlung f; **monthly ~ment** monatliche Rate f; **~ packet** (BRIT) n Lohntüte f; **~phone** n Münzfernsprecher

m; ~**roll** n Lohnliste f; ~ **slip** n Lohn-/
Gehaltsstreifen m; ~ **television** n
Abonnenten-Fernsehen nt

PC n abbr = **personal computer**

p.c. abbr = **per cent**

pea [piː] n Erbse f

peace [piːs] n Friede(n) m; ~**able** adj
friedlich; ~**ful** adj friedlich, ruhig;
~**keeping** adj Friedens-

peach [piːtʃ] n Pfirsich m

peacock ['piːkɔk] n Pfau m

peak [piːk] n Spitze f; (of mountain) Gipfel m;
(fig) Höhepunkt m; ~ **hours** npl (traffic)
Hauptverkehrszeit f; (telephone, electricity)
Hauptbelastungszeit f; ~ **period** n Stoßzeit
f, Hauptzeit f

peal [piːl] n (Glocken)läuten nt; ~**s of
laughter** schallende(s) Gelächter nt

peanut ['piːnʌt] n Erdnuss f; ~ **butter** n
Erdnussbutter f

pear [pɛəʳ] n Birne f

pearl [pɜːl] n Perle f

peasant ['pɛznt] n Bauer m

peat [piːt] n Torf m

pebble ['pɛbl] n Kiesel m

peck [pɛk] vt, vi picken ♦ n (with beak)
Schnabelhieb m; (kiss) flüchtige(r) Kuss m;
~**ing order** n Hackordnung f; ~**ish** (BRIT:
inf) adj ein bisschen hungrig

peculiar [pɪˈkjuːlɪəʳ] adj (odd) seltsam; ~ **to**
charakteristisch für; ~**ity** [pɪkjuːlɪˈærɪtɪ] n
(singular quality) Besonderheit f;
(strangeness) Eigenartigkeit f

pedal ['pɛdl] n Pedal nt ♦ vt, vi (cycle) fahren,
Rad fahren

pedantic [pɪˈdæntɪk] adj pedantisch

peddler ['pɛdləʳ] n Hausierer(in) m(f); (of
drugs) Drogenhändler(in) m(f)

pedestal ['pɛdəstl] n Sockel m

pedestrian [pɪˈdɛstrɪən] n Fußgänger m
♦ adj Fußgänger-; (humdrum) langweilig; ~
crossing (BRIT) n Fußgängerüberweg m;
~**ized** n in eine Fußgängerzone
umgewandelt; ~ **precinct** (BRIT), ~ **zone**
(US) n Fußgängerzone f

pediatrics [piːdɪˈætrɪks] (US) n = **paediatrics**

pedigree ['pɛdɪgriː] n Stammbaum m ♦ cpd

(animal) reinrassig, Zucht-

pee [piː] (inf) vi pissen, pinkeln

peek [piːk] vi gucken

peel [piːl] n Schale f ♦ vt schälen ♦ vi (paint
etc) abblättern; (skin) sich schälen

peep [piːp] n (BRIT: look) kurze(r) Blick m;
(sound) Piepsen nt ♦ vi (BRIT: look) gucken;
~ **out** vi herausgucken; ~**hole** n Guckloch
nt

peer [pɪəʳ] vi starren; (peep) gucken ♦ n
(nobleman) Peer m; (equal) Ebenbürtige(r)
m; ~**age** n Peerswürde f

peeved [piːvd] adj (person) sauer

peg [pɛg] n (stake) Pflock m; (BRIT: also:
clothes ~) Wäscheklammer f

Pekinese [piːkɪˈniːz] n (dog) Pekinese m

pelican ['pɛlɪkən] n Pelikan m; ~ **crossing**
(BRIT) n (AUT) Ampelüberweg m

pellet ['pɛlɪt] n Kügelchen nt

pelmet ['pɛlmɪt] n Blende f

pelt [pɛlt] vt bewerfen ♦ vi (rain) schütten
♦ n Pelz m, Fell nt

pelvis ['pɛlvɪs] n Becken nt

pen [pɛn] n (fountain ~) Federhalter m; (ballpoint ~) Kuli m; (for sheep) Pferch m

penal ['piːnl] adj Straf-; ~**ize** vt (punish)
bestrafen; (disadvantage) benachteiligen

penalty ['pɛnltɪ] n Strafe f; (FOOTBALL)
Elfmeter m; ~ **(kick)** n Elfmeter m

penance ['pɛnəns] n Buße f

pence [pɛns] (BRIT) npl of **penny**

pencil ['pɛnsl] n Bleistift m; ~ **case** n
Federmäppchen nt; ~ **sharpener** n
Bleistiftspitzer m

pendant ['pɛndnt] n Anhänger m

pending ['pɛndɪŋ] prep bis (zu) ♦ adj
unentschieden, noch offen

pendulum ['pɛndjuləm] n Pendel nt

penetrate ['pɛnɪtreɪt] vt durchdringen;
(enter into) eindringen in +acc;
penetration [pɛnɪˈtreɪʃən] n Durchdringen
nt; Eindringen nt

penfriend ['pɛnfrɛnd] (BRIT) n Brieffreund(in)
m(f)

penguin ['pɛŋgwɪn] n Pinguin m

penicillin [pɛnɪˈsɪlɪn] n Penizillin nt

peninsula [pəˈnɪnsjulə] n Halbinsel f

penis ['pi:nɪs] n Penis m
penitentiary [penɪ'tenʃərɪ] (US) n Zuchthaus nt
penknife ['pennaɪf] n Federmesser nt
pen name n Pseudonym nt
penniless ['penɪlɪs] adj mittellos
penny ['penɪ] (pl **pennies** or (BRIT) **pence**) n Penny m; (US) Centstück nt
penpal ['penpæl] n Brieffreund(in) m(f)
pension ['penʃən] n Rente f; **~er** (BRIT) n Rentner(in) m(f); **~ fund** n Rentenfonds m; **~ plan** n Rentenversicherung f
pensive ['pensɪv] adj nachdenklich

Pentagon

i Pentagon heißt das fünfeckige Gebäude in Arlington, Virginia, in dem das amerikanische Verteidigungsministerium untergebracht ist. Im weiteren Sinne bezieht sich dieses Wort auf die amerikanische Militärführung.

pentathlon [pen'tæθlən] n Fünfkampf m
Pentecost ['pentɪkɒst] n Pfingsten pl or nt
penthouse ['penthaus] n Dach-terrassenwohnung f
pent-up ['pentʌp] adj (feelings) angestaut
penultimate [pe'nʌltɪmət] adj vorletzte(r, s)
people ['pi:pl] n (nation) Volk nt ♦ npl (persons) Leute pl; (inhabitants) Bevölkerung f ♦ vt besiedeln; **several ~ came** mehrere Leute kamen; **~ say that ...** man sagt, dass ...
pepper ['pepə*] n Pfeffer m; (vegetable) Paprika m ♦ vt (pelt) bombardieren; **~ mill** n Pfeffermühle f; **~mint** n (plant) Pfefferminze f; (sweet) Pfefferminz nt
pep talk [pep] (inf) n Anstachelung f
per [pə:*] prep pro; **~ day/person** pro Tag/Person; **~ annum** adv pro Jahr; **~ capita** adj (income) Pro-Kopf- ♦ adv pro Kopf
perceive [pə'si:v] vt (realize) wahrnehmen; (understand) verstehen
per cent n Prozent nt; **percentage** [pə'sentɪdʒ] n Prozentsatz m
perception [pə'sepʃən] n Wahrnehmung f; (insight) Einsicht f

perceptive [pə'septɪv] adj (person) aufmerksam; (analysis) tief gehend
perch [pə:tʃ] n Stange f; (fish) Flussbarsch m ♦ vi sitzen, hocken
percolator ['pə:kəleɪtə*] n Kaffeemaschine f
percussion [pə'kʌʃən] n (MUS) Schlagzeug nt
perennial [pə'renɪəl] adj wiederkehrend; (everlasting) unvergänglich
perfect [adj, n 'pə:fɪkt, vb pə'fekt] adj vollkommen; (crime, solution) perfekt ♦ n (GRAM) Perfekt nt ♦ vt vervollkommnen; **~ion** n Vollkommenheit f; **~ly** adv vollkommen, perfekt; (quite) ganz, einfach
perforate ['pə:fəreɪt] vt durchlöchern; **perforation** [pə:fə'reɪʃən] n Perforieren nt; (line of holes) Perforation f
perform [pə'fɔ:m] vt (carry out) durch- or ausführen; (task) verrichten; (THEAT) spielen, geben ♦ vi (THEAT) auftreten; **~ance** n Durchführung f; (efficiency) Leistung f; (show) Vorstellung f; **~er** n Künstler(in) m(f)
perfume ['pə:fju:m] n Duft m; (lady's) Parfüm nt
perhaps [pə'hæps] adv vielleicht
peril ['perɪl] n Gefahr f
perimeter [pə'rɪmɪtə*] n Peripherie f; (of circle etc) Umfang m
period ['pɪərɪəd] n Periode f; (GRAM) Punkt m; (MED) Periode f ♦ adj (costume) historisch; **~ic** [pɪərɪ'ɒdɪk] adj periodisch; **~ical** [pɪərɪ'ɒdɪkl] n Zeitschrift f; **~ically** [pɪərɪ'ɒdɪklɪ] adv periodisch
peripheral [pə'rɪfərəl] adj Rand-, peripher ♦ n (COMPUT) Peripheriegerät nt
perish ['perɪʃ] vi umkommen; (fruit) verderben; **~able** adj leicht verderblich
perjury ['pə:dʒərɪ] n Meineid m
perk [pə:k] (inf) n (fringe benefit) Vergünstigung f; **~ up** vi munter werden; **~y** adj keck
perm [pə:m] n Dauerwelle f
permanent ['pə:mənənt] adj dauernd, ständig
permeate ['pə:mɪeɪt] vt, vi durchdringen
permissible [pə'mɪsɪbl] adj zulässig
permission [pə'mɪʃən] n Erlaubnis f

permissive [pəˈmɪsɪv] adj nachgiebig; **the ~ society** die permissive Gesellschaft

permit [n ˈpəːmɪt, vb pəˈmɪt] n Zulassung f ♦ vt erlauben, zulassen

perpendicular [pəːpənˈdɪkjuləʳ] adj senkrecht

perpetrate [ˈpəːpɪtreɪt] vt begehen

perpetual [pəˈpetjuəl] adj dauernd, ständig

perpetuate [pəˈpetjueɪt] vt verewigen, bewahren

perplex [pəˈpleks] vt verblüffen

persecute [ˈpəːsɪkjuːt] vt verfolgen; **persecution** [pəːsɪˈkjuːʃən] n Verfolgung f

perseverance [pəːsɪˈvɪərns] n Ausdauer f

persevere [pəːsɪˈvɪəʳ] vi durchhalten

Persian [ˈpəːʃən] adj persisch ♦ n Perser(in) m(f); **the (Persian) Gulf** der Persische Golf

persist [pəˈsɪst] vi (in belief etc) bleiben; (rain, smell) andauern; (continue) nicht aufhören; **to ~ in** bleiben bei; **~ence** n Beharrlichkeit f; **~ent** adj beharrlich; (unending) ständig

person [ˈpəːsn] n Person f; **in ~** persönlich; **~able** adj gut aussehen; **~al** adj persönlich; (private) privat; (of body) körperlich, Körper-; **~al assistant** n Assistent(in) m(f); **~al column** n private Kleinanzeigen pl; **~al computer** n Personalcomputer m; **~ality** [pəːsəˈnælɪtɪ] n Persönlichkeit f; **~ally** adv persönlich; **~al organizer** n Terminplaner m, Zeitplaner m; (electronic) elektronisches Notizbuch nt; **~al stereo** n Walkman m ®; **~ify** [pəˈsɒnɪfaɪ] vt verkörpern

personnel [pəːsəˈnel] n Personal nt

perspective [pəˈspektɪv] n Perspektive f

Perspex [ˈpəːspeks] ® n Acrylglas nt, Akrylglas nt

perspiration [pəːspɪˈreɪʃən] n Transpiration f

perspire [pəˈspaɪəʳ] vi transpirieren

persuade [pəˈsweɪd] vt überreden; (convince) überzeugen

persuasion [pəˈsweɪʒən] n Überredung f; Überzeugung f

persuasive [pəˈsweɪsɪv] adj überzeugend

pert [pəːt] adj keck

pertaining [pəːˈteɪnɪŋ]: **~ to** prep betreffend +acc

pertinent [ˈpəːtɪnənt] adj relevant

perturb [pəˈtəːb] vt beunruhigen

pervade [pəˈveɪd] vt erfüllen

perverse [pəˈvəːs] adj pervers; (obstinate) eigensinnig

pervert [n ˈpəːvəːt, vb pəˈvəːt] n perverse(r) Mensch m ♦ vt verdrehen; (morally) verderben

pessimist [ˈpesɪmɪst] n Pessimist m; **~ic** adj pessimistisch

pest [pest] n (insect) Schädling m; (fig: person) Nervensäge f; (: thing) Plage f; **~er** [ˈpestəʳ] vt plagen; **~icide** [ˈpestɪsaɪd] n Insektenvertilgungsmittel nt

pet [pet] n (animal) Haustier nt ♦ vt liebkosen, streicheln

petal [ˈpetl] n Blütenblatt nt

peter out [ˈpiːtə-] vi allmählich zu Ende gehen

petite [pəˈtiːt] adj zierlich

petition [pəˈtɪʃən] n Bittschrift f

petrified [ˈpetrɪfaɪd] adj versteinert; (person) starr (vor Schreck)

petrify [ˈpetrɪfaɪ] vt versteinern; (person) erstarren lassen

petrol [ˈpetrəl] (BRIT) n Benzin nt, Kraftstoff m; **two-/four-star ~** ≈ Normal-/ Superbenzin nt; **~ can** n Benzinkanister m

petroleum [pəˈtrəʊlɪəm] n Petroleum nt

petrol: ~ pump (BRIT) n (in car) Benzinpumpe f; (at garage) Zapfsäule f; **~ station** (BRIT) n Tankstelle f; **~ tank** (BRIT) n Benzintank m

petticoat [ˈpetɪkəʊt] n Unterrock m

petty [ˈpetɪ] adj (unimportant) unbedeutend; (mean) kleinlich; **~ cash** n Portokasse f; **~ officer** n Maat m

pew [pjuː] n Kirchenbank f

pewter [ˈpjuːtəʳ] n Zinn nt

phantom [ˈfæntəm] n Phantom nt

pharmacist [ˈfɑːməsɪst] n Pharmazeut m; (druggist) Apotheker m

pharmacy [ˈfɑːməsɪ] n Pharmazie f; (shop) Apotheke f

phase [feɪz] n Phase f ♦ vt: **to ~ sth in** etw allmählich einführen; **to ~ sth out** etw auslaufen lassen

Ph.D. *n abbr* = **Doctor of Philosophy**

pheasant ['fez

nt] *n* Fasan *m*

phenomena [fə'nɔmınə] *npl of* **phenomenon**

phenomenon [fə'nɔmınən] *n* Phänomen *nt*

philanthropist [fɪ'lænθrəpɪst] *n* Philanthrop *m*, Menschenfreund *m*

Philippines ['fɪlɪpi:nz] *npl:* **the ~** die Philippinen *pl*

philosopher [fɪ'lɔsəfər] *n* Philosoph *m*; **philosophical** [fɪlə'sɔfɪkl] *adj* philosophisch; **philosophy** [fɪ'lɔsəfɪ] *n* Philosophie *f*

phlegm [flɛm] *n* (MED) Schleim *m*

phobia ['fəubjə] *n* (*irrational fear: of insects, flying, water etc*) Phobie *f*

phone [fəun] *n* Telefon *nt* ♦ *vt, vi* telefonieren, anrufen; **to be on the ~** telefonieren; **~ back** *vt, vi* zurückrufen; **~ up** *vt, vi* anrufen; **~ bill** *n* Telefonrechnung *f*; **~ book** *n* Telefonbuch *nt*; **~ booth** *n* Telefonzelle *f*; **~ box** *n* Telefonzelle *f*; **~ call** *n* Telefonanruf *m* (TEL) Telefonkarte *f*; **~-in** *n* (RAD, TV) Phone-in *nt*; **~ number** *n* Telefonnummer *f*

phonetics [fə'nɛtɪks] *n* Phonetik *f*

phoney ['fəunɪ] (*inf*) *adj* unecht ♦ *n* (*person*) Schwindler *m*; (*thing*) Fälschung *f*; (*banknote*) Blüte *f*

phony ['fəunɪ] *adj, n* = **phoney**

photo ['fəutəu] *n* Foto *nt* ♦; **~copier** ['fəutəukɔpɪər] *n* Kopiergerät *nt*; **~copy** ['fəutəukɔpɪ] *n* Fotokopie *f* ♦ *vt* fotokopieren; **~genic** [fəutəu'dʒɛnɪk] *adj* fotogen; **~graph** *n* Fotografie *f*, Aufnahme *f* ♦ *vt* fotografieren; **~grapher** [fə'tɔgrəfər] *n* Fotograf *m*; **~graphic** [fəutə'græfɪk] *adj* fotografisch; **~graphy** [fə'tɔgrəfɪ] *n* Fotografie *f*

phrase [freɪz] *n* Satz *m*; (*expression*) Ausdruck *m* ♦ *vt* ausdrücken, formulieren; **~ book** *n* Sprachführer *m*

physical ['fɪzɪkl] *adj* physikalisch; (*bodily*) körperlich, physisch; **~ education** *n* Turnen *nt*; **~ly** *adv* physikalisch

physician [fɪ'zɪʃən] *n* Arzt *m*

physicist ['fɪzɪsɪst] *n* Physiker(in) *m(f)*

physics ['fɪzɪks] *n* Physik *f*

physiotherapist [fɪzɪəu'θɛrəpɪst] *n* Physiotherapeut(in) *m(f)*

physiotherapy [fɪzɪəu'θɛrəpɪ] *n* Heilgymnastik *f*, Physiotherapie *f*

physique [fɪ'zi:k] *n* Körperbau *m*

pianist ['pi:ənɪst] *n* Pianist(in) *m(f)*

piano [pɪ'ænəu] *n* Klavier *nt*

pick [pɪk] *n* (*tool*) Pickel *m*; (*choice*) Auswahl *f* ♦ *vt* (*fruit*) pflücken; (*choose*) aussuchen; **take your ~** such dir etwas aus; **to ~ sb's pocket** jdn bestehlen; **~ on** *vt fus* (*person*) herumhacken auf +*dat*; **~ out** *vt* auswählen; **~ up** *vi* (*improve*) sich erholen ♦ *vt* (*lift up*) aufheben; (*learn*) (schnell) mitbekommen; (*collect*) abholen; (*girl*) (sich *dat*) anlachen; (AUT: *passenger*) mitnehmen; (*speed*) gewinnen an +*dat*; **to ~ o.s. up** aufstehen

picket ['pɪkɪt] *n* (*striker*) Streikposten *m* ♦ *vt* (*factory*) (Streik)posten aufstellen vor +*dat* ♦ *vi* (Streik)posten stehen

pickle ['pɪkl] *n* (*salty mixture*) Pökel *m*; (*inf*) Klemme *f* ♦ *vt* (in Essig) einlegen; einpökeln

pickpocket ['pɪkpɔkɪt] *n* Taschendieb *m*

pick-up ['pɪkʌp] *n* (BRIT: *on record player*) Tonabnehmer *m*; (*small truck*) Lieferwagen *m*

picnic ['pɪknɪk] *n* Picknick *nt* ♦ *vi* picknicken; **~ area** *n* Rastplatz *m*

pictorial [pɪk'tɔ:rɪəl] *adj* in Bildern

picture ['pɪktʃər] *n* Bild *nt* ♦ *vt* (*visualize*) sich *dat* vorstellen; **the ~s** *npl* (BRIT) das Kino; **~ book** *n* Bilderbuch *nt*

picturesque [pɪktʃə'rɛsk] *adj* malerisch

pie [paɪ] *n* (*meat*) Pastete *f*; (*fruit*) Torte *f*

piece [pi:s] *n* Stück *nt* ♦ *vt*: **to ~ together** zusammenstückeln; (*fig*) sich *dat* zusammenreimen; **to take to ~s** in Einzelteile zerlegen; **~meal** *adv* stückweise, Stück für Stück; **~work** *n* Akkordarbeit *f*

pie chart *n* Kreisdiagramm *nt*

pier [pɪər] *n* Pier *m*, Mole *f*

pierce [pɪəs] *vt* durchstechen, durchbohren (*also look*); **~d** *adj* durchgestochen; **piercing** ['pɪəsɪŋ] *adj* (*cry*) durchdringend

pig [pɪg] *n* Schwein *nt*

pigeon ['pɪdʒən] *n* Taube *f*; **~hole** *n* (*compartment*) Ablegefach *nt*

piggy bank ['pɪgɪ-] *n* Sparschwein *nt*

pig: **~headed** ['pɪg'hɛdɪd] *adj* dickköpfig; **~let** ['pɪglɪt] *n* Ferkel *nt*; **~skin** ['pɪgskɪn] *n* Schweinsleder *nt*; **~sty** ['pɪgstaɪ] *n* Schweinestall *m*; **~tail** ['pɪgteɪl] *n* Zopf *m*

pike [paɪk] *n* Pike *f*; (*fish*) Hecht *m*

pilchard ['pɪltʃəd] *n* Sardine *f*

pile [paɪl] *n* Haufen *m*; (*of books, wood*) Stapel *m*; (*in ground*) Pfahl *m*; (*on carpet*) Flausch *m* ♦ *vt* (*also:* **~ up**) anhäufen ♦ *vi* (*also:* **~ up**) sich anhäufen

piles [paɪlz] *npl* Hämorr(ho)iden *pl*

pile-up ['paɪlʌp] *n* (*AUT*) Massenzusammenstoß *m*

pilfering ['pɪlfərɪŋ] *n* Diebstahl *m*

pilgrim ['pɪlgrɪm] *n* Pilger(in) *m(f)*; **~age** *n* Wallfahrt *f*

pill [pɪl] *n* Tablette *f*, Pille *f*; **the ~** die (Antibaby)pille

pillage ['pɪlɪdʒ] *vt* plündern

pillar ['pɪlə'] *n* Pfeiler *m*, Säule *f* (*also fig*); **~ box** (*BRIT*) *n* Briefkasten *m*

pillion ['pɪljən] *n* Soziussitz *m*

pillow ['pɪləu] *n* Kissen *nt*; **~case** *n* Kissenbezug *m*

pilot ['paɪlət] *n* Pilot *m*; (*NAUT*) Lotse *m* ♦ *adj* (*scheme etc*) Versuchs- ♦ *vt* führen; (*ship*) lotsen; **~ light** *n* Zündflamme *f*

pimp [pɪmp] *n* Zuhälter *m*

pimple ['pɪmpl] *n* Pickel *m*

PIN *n abbr* (= *personal identification number*) PIN *f*

pin [pɪn] *n* Nadel *f*; (*for sewing*) Stecknadel *f*; (*TECH*) Stift *m*, Bolzen *m* ♦ *vt* stecken; (*keep in one position*) pressen, drücken; **to ~ sth to sth** etw an etw *acc* heften; **to ~ sth on sb** (*fig*) jdm etw anhängen; **~s and needles** Kribbeln *nt*; **~ down** *vt* (*fig: person*): **to ~ sb down (to sth)** jdn (auf etw *acc*) festnageln

pinafore ['pɪnəfɔː'] *n* Schürze *f*; **~ dress** *n* Kleiderrock *m*

pinball ['pɪnbɔːl] *n* Flipper *m*

pincers ['pɪnsəz] *npl* Kneif- or Beißzange *f*; (*MED*) Pinzette *f*

pinch [pɪntʃ] *n* Zwicken *nt*, Kneifen *nt*; (*of salt*) Prise *f* ♦ *vt* zwicken, kneifen; (*inf: steal*) klauen ♦ *vi* (*shoe*) drücken; **at a ~** notfalls, zur Not

pincushion ['pɪnkuʃən] *n* Nadelkissen *nt*

pine [paɪn] *n* (*also:* **~ tree**) Kiefer *f* ♦ *vi*: **to ~ for** sich sehnen nach; **~ away** *vi* sich zu Tode sehnen

pineapple ['paɪnæpl] *n* Ananas *f*

ping [pɪŋ] *n* Klingeln *nt*; **~-pong** ® *n* Pingpong *nt*

pink [pɪŋk] *adj* rosa *inv* ♦ *n* Rosa *nt*; (*BOT*) Nelke *f*

pinnacle ['pɪnəkl] *n* Spitze *f*

PIN (number) *n* Geheimnummer *f*

pinpoint ['pɪnpɔɪnt] *vt* festlegen

pinstripe ['pɪnstraɪp] *n* Nadelstreifen *m*

pint [paɪnt] *n* Pint *nt*; (*BRIT: inf: of beer*) große(s) Bier *nt*

pioneer [paɪə'nɪə'] *n* Pionier *m*; (*fig also*) Bahnbrecher *m*

pious ['paɪəs] *adj* fromm

pip [pɪp] *n* Kern *m*; **the ~s** *npl* (*BRIT: RAD*) das Zeitzeichen

pipe [paɪp] *n* (*smoking*) Pfeife *f*; (*tube*) Rohr *nt*; (*in house*) (Rohr)leitung *f* ♦ *vt* (durch Rohre) leiten; (*MUS*) blasen; **~s** *npl* (*also:* **bagpipes**) Dudelsack *m*; **~ down** *vi* (*be quiet*) die Luft anhalten; **~ cleaner** *n* Pfeifenreiniger *m*; **~ dream** *n* Luftschloss *nt*; **~line** *n* (*for oil*) Pipeline *f*; **~r** *n* Pfeifer *m*; (*bagpipes*) Dudelsackbläser *m*

piping ['paɪpɪŋ] *adv*: **~ hot** siedend heiß

pique ['piːk] *n* gekränkte(r) Stolz *m*

pirate ['paɪərət] *n* Pirat *m*, Seeräuber *m*; **~d** *adj*: **~d version** Raubkopie *f*; **~ radio** (*BRIT*) *n* Piratensender *m*

Pisces ['paɪsiːz] *n* Fische *pl*

piss [pɪs] (*inf*) *vi* pissen; **~ed** (*inf*) *adj* (*drunk*) voll

pistol ['pɪstl] *n* Pistole *f*

piston ['pɪstən] *n* Kolben *m*

pit [pɪt] *n* Grube *f*; (*THEAT*) Parterre *nt*; (*orchestra ~*) Orchestergraben *m* ♦ *vt* (*mark with scars*) zerfressen; (*compare*): **to ~ sb against sb** jdn an jdm messen; **the ~s** *npl* (*MOTOR RACING*) die Boxen *pl*

pitch [pɪtʃ] n Wurf m; (of trader) Stand m; (SPORT) (Spiel)feld nt; (MUS) Tonlage f; (substance) Pech nt ♦ vt werfen; (set up) aufschlagen ♦ vi (NAUT) rollen; **to ~ a tent** ein Zelt aufbauen; **~-black** adj pechschwarz; **~ed battle** n offene Schlacht f

piteous ['pɪtɪəs] adj kläglich, erbärmlich

pitfall ['pɪtfɔːl] n (fig) Falle f

pith [pɪθ] n Mark nt

pithy ['pɪθɪ] adj prägnant

pitiful ['pɪtɪful] adj (deserving pity) bedauernswert; (contemptible) jämmerlich

pitiless ['pɪtɪlɪs] adj erbarmungslos

pittance ['pɪtns] n Hungerlohn m

pity ['pɪtɪ] n (sympathy) Mitleid nt ♦ vt Mitleid haben mit; **what a ~!** wie schade!

pivot ['pɪvət] n Drehpunkt m ♦ vi: **to ~ (on)** sich drehen (um)

pizza ['piːtsə] n Pizza f

placard ['plækɑːd] n Plakat nt, Anschlag m

placate [pləˈkeɪt] vt beschwichtigen

place [pleɪs] n Platz m; (spot) Stelle f; (town etc) Ort m ♦ vt setzen, stellen, legen; (order) aufgeben; (SPORT) platzieren; (identify) unterbringen; **to take ~** stattfinden; **out of ~** nicht am rechten Platz; (fig: remark) unangebracht; **in the first ~** erstens; **to change ~s with sb** mit jdm den Platz tauschen; **to be ~d third** (in race, exam) auf dem dritten Platz liegen

placid ['plæsɪd] adj gelassen, ruhig

plagiarism ['pleɪdʒjərɪzəm] n Plagiat nt

plague [pleɪg] n Pest f; (fig) Plage f ♦ vt plagen

plaice [pleɪs] n Scholle f

plaid [plæd] n Plaid nt

plain [pleɪn] adj (clear) klar, deutlich; (simple) einfach, schlicht; (not beautiful) alltäglich ♦ n Ebene f; **in ~ clothes** (police) in Zivil(kleidung); **~ chocolate** n Bitterschokolade f

plaintiff ['pleɪntɪf] n Kläger m

plaintive ['pleɪntɪv] adj wehleidig

plait [plæt] n Zopf m ♦ vt flechten

plan [plæn] n Plan m ♦ vt, vi planen; **according to ~** planmäßig; **to ~ to do sth** vorhaben, etw zu tun

plane [pleɪn] n Ebene f; (AVIAT) Flugzeug nt; (tool) Hobel m; (tree) Platane f

planet ['plænɪt] n Planet m

plank [plæŋk] n Brett nt

planning ['plænɪŋ] n Planung f; **family ~** Familienplanung f; **~ permission** n Baugenehmigung f

plant [plɑːnt] n Pflanze f; (TECH) (Maschinen)anlage f; (factory) Fabrik f, Werk nt ♦ vt pflanzen; (set firmly) stellen; **~ation** [plænˈteɪʃən] n Plantage f

plaque [plæk] n Gedenktafel f; (on teeth) (Zahn)belag m

plaster ['plɑːstər] n Gips m; (in house) Verputz m; (BRIT: also: **sticking ~**) Pflaster nt; (for fracture: **~ of Paris**) Gipsverband m ♦ vt gipsen; (hole) zugipsen; (ceiling) verputzen; (fig: with pictures etc) bekleben, verkleben; **~ed** (inf) adj besoffen; **~er** n Gipser m

plastic ['plæstɪk] n Plastik nt or f ♦ adj (made of ~) Plastik-; (ART) plastisch, bildend; **~ bag** n Plastiktüte f

plasticine ['plæstɪsiːn] ® n Plastilin nt

plastic surgery n plastische Chirurgie f

plate [pleɪt] n Teller m; (gold/silver ~) vergoldete(s)/versilberte(s) Tafelgeschirr nt; (in book) (Bild)tafel f

plateau ['plætəʊ] (pl **~s** or **~x**) n (GEOG) Plateau nt, Hochebene f

plateaux ['plætəʊz] npl of **plateau**

plate glass n Tafelglas nt

platform ['plætfɔːm] n (at meeting) Plattform f, Podium nt; (RAIL) Bahnsteig m; (POL) Parteiprogramm nt; **~ ticket** n Bahnsteigkarte f

platinum ['plætɪnəm] n Platin nt

platoon [pləˈtuːn] n (MIL) Zug m

platter ['plætər] n Platte f

plausible ['plɔːzɪbl] adj (theory, excuse, statement) plausibel; (person) überzeugend

play [pleɪ] n (also THEAT) Spiel nt; (THEAT) (Theater)stück nt ♦ vt spielen; (another team) spielen gegen ♦ vi spielen; **to ~ safe** auf Nummer sicher or Sicher gehen; **~ down** vt herunterspielen; **~ up** vi (cause *trouble*) frech werden; (*bad leg etc*) wehtun ♦ *vt* (*person*) plagen; **to ~ up to sb** jdm flattieren; **~-acting** *n* Schauspielerei *f*; **~er** *n* Spieler(in) *m(f)*; **~ful** *adj* spielerisch; **~ground** *n* Spielplatz *m*; **~group** *n* Kindergarten *m*; **~ing card** *n* Spielkarte *f*; **~ing field** *n* Sportplatz *m*; **~mate** *n* Spielkamerad *m*; **~-off** *n* (*SPORT*) Entscheidungsspiel *nt*; **~pen** *n* Laufstall *m*; **~school** *n* = **playgroup**; **~thing** *n* Spielzeug *nt*; **~time** *n* (kleine) Pause *f*; **~wright** ['pleɪraɪt] *n* Theaterschriftsteller *m*

plc *abbr* (= *public limited company*) AG

plea [pliː] *n* Bitte *f*; (*general appeal*) Appell *m*; (*JUR*) Plädoyer *nt*; **~ bargaining** *n* (*LAW*) *Aushandeln der Strafe zwischen Staatsanwaltschaft und Verteidigung*

plead [pliːd] *vt* (*poverty*) zur Entschuldigung anführen; (*JUR: sb's case*) vertreten ♦ *vi* (*beg*) dringend bitten; (*JUR*) plädieren; **to ~ with sb** jdn dringend bitten

pleasant ['plɛznt] *adj* angenehm; **~ries** *npl* (*polite remarks*) Nettigkeiten *pl*

please [pliːz] *vt, vi* (*be agreeable to*) gefallen +*dat*; **~!** bitte!; **~ yourself!** wie du willst!; **~d** *adj* zufrieden; (*glad*): **~d (about sth)** erfreut (über etw *acc*); **~d to meet you** angenehm; **pleasing** ['pliːzɪŋ] *adj* erfreulich

pleasure ['plɛʒəʳ] *n* Freude *f* ♦ *cpd* Vergnügungs-; **"it's a ~"** „gern geschehen"

pleat [pliːt] *n* Falte *f*

plectrum ['plɛktrəm] *n* Plektron *nt*

pledge [plɛdʒ] *n* Pfand *nt*; (*promise*) Versprechen *nt* ♦ *vt* verpfänden; (*promise*) geloben, versprechen

plentiful ['plɛntɪful] *adj* reichlich

plenty ['plɛntɪ] *n* Fülle *f*, Überfluss *m*; **~ of** eine Menge, viel

pleurisy ['plʊərɪsɪ] *n* Rippenfellentzündung *f*

pliable ['plaɪəbl] *adj* biegsam; (*person*) beeinflussbar

pliers ['plaɪəz] *npl* (Kneif)zange *f*

plight [plaɪt] *n* (Not)lage *f*

plimsolls ['plɪmsəlz] (*BRIT*) *npl* Turnschuhe *pl*

plinth [plɪnθ] *n* Sockel *m*

P.L.O. *n abbr* (= *Palestine Liberation*

Organization) PLO *f*

plod [plɒd] *vi* (*work*) sich abplagen; (*walk*) trotten

plonk [plɒŋk] *n* (*BRIT: inf: wine*) billige(r) Wein *m* ♦ *vt*: **to ~ sth down** etw hinknallen

plot [plɒt] *n* Komplott *nt*; (*story*) Handlung *f*; (*of land*) Grundstück *nt* ♦ *vt* markieren; (*curve*) zeichnen; (*movements*) nachzeichnen ♦ *vi* (*plan secretly*) sich verschwören

plough [plaʊ] (*US* **plow**) *n* Pflug *m* ♦ *vt* pflügen; **~ back** *vt* (*COMM*) wieder in das Geschäft stecken; **~ through** *vt fus* (*water*) durchpflügen; (*book*) sich kämpfen durch

plow [plaʊ] (*US*) = **plough**

ploy [plɔɪ] *n* Masche *f*

pluck [plʌk] *vt* (*fruit*) pflücken; (*guitar*) zupfen; (*goose etc*) rupfen ♦ *n* Mut *m*; **to ~ up courage** all seinen Mut zusammennehmen

plug [plʌg] *n* Stöpsel *m*; (*ELEC*) Stecker *m*; (*inf: publicity*) Schleichwerbung *f*; (*AUT*) Zündkerze *f* ♦ *vt* (zu)stopfen; (*inf: advertise*) Reklame machen für; **~ in** *vt* (*ELEC*) anschließen

plum [plʌm] *n* Pflaume *f*, Zwetsch(g)e *f*

plumage ['pluːmɪdʒ] *n* Gefieder *nt*

plumber ['plʌməʳ] *n* Klempner *m*, Installateur *m*; **plumbing** ['plʌmɪŋ] *n* (*craft*) Installieren *nt*; (*fittings*) Leitungen *pl*

plummet ['plʌmɪt] *vi* (ab)stürzen

plump [plʌmp] *adj* rundlich, füllig ♦ *vt* plumpsen lassen; **to ~ for** (*inf: choose*) sich entscheiden für

plunder ['plʌndəʳ] *n* Plünderung *f*; (*loot*) Beute *f* ♦ *vt* plündern

plunge [plʌndʒ] *n* Sturz *m* ♦ *vt* stoßen ♦ *vi* (sich) stürzen; **to take the ~** den Sprung wagen; **plunging** ['plʌndʒɪŋ] *adj* (*neckline*) hochherzig

plural ['plʊərl] *n* Plural *m*, Mehrzahl *f*

plus [plʌs] *n* (*also: ~ sign*) Plus(zeichen) *nt* ♦ *prep* plus, und; **ten/twenty ~** mehr als zehn/zwanzig

plush [plʌʃ] *adj* (*also: ~y: inf*) feudal

ply [plaɪ] *vt* (*trade*) (be)treiben; (*with questions*) zusetzen +*dat*; (*ship, taxi*) befahren ♦ *vi* (*ship, taxi*) verkehren ♦ *n*:

three-~ (*wool*) Dreifach-; **to ~ sb with drink** jdn zum Trinken animieren; **~wood** *n* Sperrholz *nt*

P.M. *n abbr* = **prime minister**

p.m. *adv abbr* (= *post meridiem*) nachmittags

pneumatic drill *n* Presslufthammer *m*

pneumonia [nju:ˈməʊnɪə] *n* Lungenentzündung *f*

poach [pəʊtʃ] *vt* (COOK) pochieren; (*game*) stehlen ♦ *vi* (*steal*) wildern; **~ed** *adj* (*egg*) verloren; **~er** *n* Wilddieb *m*

P.O. Box *n abbr* = **Post Office Box**

pocket [ˈpɒkɪt] *n* Tasche *f*; (*of resistance*) (Widerstands)nest *nt* ♦ *vt* einstecken; **to be out of ~** (BRIT) draufzahlen; **~book** *n* Taschenbuch *nt*; **~ calculator** *n* Taschenrechner *m*; **~ knife** *n* Taschenmesser *nt*; **~ money** *n* Taschengeld *nt*

pod [pɒd] *n* Hülse *f*; (*of peas also*) Schote *f*

podgy [ˈpɒdʒɪ] *adj* pummelig

podiatrist [pɔˈdiːətrɪst] (US) *n* Fußpfleger(in) *m(f)*

poem [ˈpəʊɪm] *n* Gedicht *nt*

poet [ˈpəʊɪt] *n* Dichter *m*, Poet *m*; **~ic** [pəʊˈetɪk] *adj* poetisch, dichterisch; **~ laureate** *n* Hofdichter *m*; **~ry** *n* Poesie *f*; (*poems*) Gedichte *pl*

poignant [ˈpɔɪnjənt] *adj* (*touching*) ergreifend

point [pɔɪnt] *n* (*also in discussion, scoring*) Punkt *m*; (*spot*) Punkt *m*, Stelle *f*; (*sharpened tip*) Spitze *f*; (*moment*) (Zeit)punkt *m*; (*purpose*) Zweck *m*; (*idea*) Argument *nt*; (*decimal*) Dezimalstelle *f*; (*personal characteristic*) Seite *f* ♦ *vt* zeigen mit; (*gun*) richten ♦ *vi* zeigen; **~s** *npl* (RAIL) Weichen *pl*; **to be on the ~ of doing sth** drauf und dran sein, etw zu tun; **to make a ~ of** Wert darauf legen; **to get the ~** verstehen, worum es geht; **to come to the ~** zur Sache kommen; **there's no ~ (in doing sth)** es hat keinen Sinn(, etw zu tun); **~ out** *vt* hinweisen auf +*acc*; **~ to** *vt fus* zeigen auf +*acc*; **~-blank** *adv* (*at close range*) aus nächster Entfernung; (*bluntly*) unverblümt; **~ed** *adj* (*also fig*) spitz, scharf;

~edly *adv* (*fig*) spitz; **~er** *n* Zeigestock *m*; (*on dial*) Zeiger *m*; **~less** *adj* sinnlos; **~ of view** *n* Stand- or Gesichtspunkt *m*

poise [pɔɪz] *n* Haltung *f*; (*fig*) Gelassenheit *f*

poison [ˈpɔɪzn] *n* (*also fig*) Gift *nt* ♦ *vt* vergiften; **~ing** *n* Vergiftung *f*; **~ous** *adj* giftig, Gift-

poke [pəʊk] *vt* stoßen; (*put*) stecken; (*fire*) schüren; (*hole*) bohren; **~ about** *vi* herumstochern; (*nose around*) herumwühlen

poker [ˈpəʊkər] *n* Schürhaken *m*; (CARDS) Poker *nt*

poky [ˈpəʊkɪ] *adj* eng

Poland [ˈpəʊlənd] *n* Polen *nt*

polar [ˈpəʊlər] *adj* Polar-, polar; **~ bear** *n* Eisbär *m*

Pole [pəʊl] *n* Pole *m*, Polin *f*

pole [pəʊl] *n* Stange *f*, Pfosten *m*; (*flagpole, telegraph ~*) Stange *f*, Mast *m*; (ELEC, GEOG) Pol *m*; (SPORT: *vaulting ~*) Stab *m*; (*ski ~*) Stock *m*; **~ bean** (US) *n* (*runner bean*) Stangenbohne *f*; **~ vault** *n* Stabhochsprung *m*

police [pəˈliːs] *n* Polizei *f* ♦ *vt* kontrollieren; **~ car** *n* Polizeiwagen *m*; **~man** (*irreg*) *n* Polizist *m*; **~ state** *n* Polizeistaat *m*; **~ station** *n* (Polizei)revier *nt*, Wache *f*; **~woman** (*irreg*) *n* Polizistin *f*

policy [ˈpɒlɪsɪ] *n* Politik *f*; (*insurance*) (Versicherungs)police *f*

polio [ˈpəʊlɪəʊ] *n* (*spinale*) Kinderlähmung *f*, Polio *f*

Polish [ˈpəʊlɪʃ] *adj* polnisch ♦ *n* (LING) Polnisch *nt*

polish [ˈpɒlɪʃ] *n* Politur *f*; (*for floor*) Wachs *nt*; (*for shoes*) Creme *f*; (*for nails*) Lack *m*; (*shine*) Glanz *m*; (*of furniture*) Politur *f*; (*fig*) Schliff *m* ♦ *vt* polieren; (*shoes*) putzen; (*fig*) den letzten Schliff geben +*dat*; **~ off** *vt* (*inf: food*) wegputzen; (: *drink*) hinunterschütten; **~ed** *adj* glänzend; (*manners*) verfeinert

polite [pəˈlaɪt] *adj* höflich; **~ly** *adv* höflich; **~ness** *n* Höflichkeit *f*

politic-: ~al [pəˈlɪtɪkl] *adj* politisch; **~ally** [pəˈlɪtɪklɪ] *adv* politisch; **~ally correct**

politisch korrekt; **~ian** [pɔlɪ'tɪʃən] *n* Politiker *m*; **~s** *npl* Politik *f*

polka dot ['pɔlkə-] *n* Tupfen *m*

poll [pəul] *n* Abstimmung *f*; (*in election*) Wahl *f*; (*votes cast*) Wahlbeteiligung *f*; (*opinion ~*) Umfrage *f* ♦ *vt* (*votes*) erhalten

pollen ['pɔlən] *n* (*BOT*) Blütenstaub *m*, Pollen *m*

polling ['pəulɪŋ-]: **~ booth** (*BRIT*) *n* Wahlkabine *f*; **~ day** (*BRIT*) *n* Wahltag *m*; **~ station** (*BRIT*) *n* Wahllokal *nt*

pollute [pə'luːt] *vt* verschmutzen, verunreinigen; **~d** *adj* verschmutzt; **pollution** [pə'luːʃən] *n* Verschmutzung *f*

polo ['pəuləu] *n* Polo *nt*; **~ neck** *n* (*also: ~-necked sweater*) Rollkragen *m*; Rollkragenpullover *m*; **~ shirt** *n* Polohemd *nt*

polystyrene [pɔlɪ'staɪriːn] *n* Styropor *nt*

polytechnic [pɔlɪ'teknɪk] *n* technische Hochschule *f*

polythene ['pɔlɪθiːn] *n* Plastik *nt*; **~ bag** *n* Plastiktüte *f*

pomegranate ['pɔmɪgrænɪt] *n* Granatapfel *m*

pompom ['pɔmpɔm] *n* Troddel *f*, Pompon *m*

pompous ['pɔmpəs] *adj* aufgeblasen; (*language*) geschwollen

pond [pɔnd] *n* Teich *m*, Weiher *m*

ponder ['pɔndəʳ] *vt* nachdenken über +*acc*; **~ous** *adj* schwerfällig

pong [pɔŋ] (*BRIT: inf*) *n* Mief *m*

pontiff ['pɔntɪf] *n* Pontifex *m*

pontoon [pɔn'tuːn] *n* Ponton *m*; (*CARDS*) 17-und-4 *nt*

pony ['pəunɪ] *n* Pony *nt*; **~tail** *n* Pferdeschwanz *m*; **~ trekking** (*BRIT*) *n* Ponyreiten *nt*

poodle ['puːdl] *n* Pudel *m*

pool [puːl] *n* (*swimming ~*) Schwimmbad *nt*; (: *private*) Swimmingpool *m*; (*of liquid, blood*) Lache *f*; (*fund*) gemeinsame Kasse *f*; (*billiards*) Poolspiel *nt* ♦ *vt* (*money etc*) zusammenlegen; (**football**) **~s** Toto *nt*

poor [puəʳ] *adj* arm; (*not good*) schlecht ♦ *npl*: **the ~** die Armen *pl*; **~ in** (*resources*)

arm an +*dat*; **~ly** *adv* schlecht; (*dressed*) ärmlich ♦ *adj* schlecht

pop [pɔp] *n* Knall *m*; (*music*) Popmusik *f*; (*drink*) Limo(nade) *f*; (*US: inf*) Pa *m* ♦ *vt* (*put*) stecken; (*balloon*) platzen lassen ♦ *vi* knallen; **~ in** *vi* kurz vorbeigehen *or* vorbeikommen; **~ out** *vi* (*person*) kurz rausgehen; (*thing*) herausspringen; **~ up** *vi* auftauchen; **~corn** *n* Puffmais *m*

pope [pəup] *n* Papst *m*

poplar ['pɔpləʳ] *n* Pappel *f*

poppy ['pɔpɪ] *n* Mohn *m*

Popsicle ['pɔpsɪkl] (® *US*) *n* (*ice lolly*) Eis *nt* am Stiel

populace ['pɔpjuləs] *n* Volk *nt*

popular ['pɔpjuləʳ] *adj* beliebt, populär; (*of the people*) volkstümlich; (*widespread*) allgemein; **~ity** [pɔpju'lærɪtɪ] *n* Beliebtheit *f*, Popularität *f*; **~ly** *adv* allgemein, überall

population [pɔpju'leɪʃən] *n* Bevölkerung *f*; (*of town*) Einwohner *pl*

populous ['pɔpjuləs] *adj* dicht besiedelt

porcelain ['pɔːslɪn] *n* Porzellan *nt*

porch [pɔːtʃ] *n* Vorbau *m*, Veranda *f*

porcupine ['pɔːkjupaɪn] *n* Stachelschwein *nt*

pore [pɔːʳ] *n* Pore *f* ♦ *vi*: **to ~ over** brüten über +*dat*

pork [pɔːk] *n* Schweinefleisch *nt*

porn [pɔːn] *n* Porno *m*; **~ographic** [pɔːnə'græfɪk] *adj* pornografisch; **~ography** [pɔː'nɔgrəfɪ] *n* Pornografie *f*

porous ['pɔːrəs] *adj* porös; (*skin*) porig

porpoise ['pɔːpəs] *n* Tümmler *m*

porridge ['pɔrɪdʒ] *n* Haferbrei *m*

port [pɔːt] *n* Hafen *m*; (*town*) Hafenstadt *f*; (*NAUT: left side*) Backbord *nt*; (*wine*) Portwein *m*; **~ of call** Anlaufhafen *m*

portable ['pɔːtəbl] *adj* tragbar

porter ['pɔːtəʳ] *n* Pförtner(in) *m(f)*; (*for luggage*) (Gepäck)träger *m*

portfolio [pɔːt'fəulɪəu] *n* (*case*) Mappe *f*; (*POL*) Geschäftsbereich *m*; (*FIN*) Portefeuille *nt*; (*of artist*) Kollektion *f*

porthole ['pɔːthəul] *n* Bullauge *nt*

portion ['pɔːʃən] *n* Teil *m*, Stück *nt*; (*of food*) Portion *f*

portrait ['pɔːtreɪt] *n* Porträt *nt*

portray [pɔː'treɪ] vt darstellen; **~al** n Darstellung f

Portugal ['pɔːtjʊgl] n Portugal nt

Portuguese [pɔːtjuː'giːz] adj portugiesisch ♦ n inv Portugiese m, Portugiesin f; (LING) Portugiesisch nt

pose [pəʊz] n Stellung f, Pose f; (affectation) Pose f ♦ vi posieren ♦ vt stellen

posh [pɔʃ] (inf) adj (piek)fein

position [pə'zɪʃən] n Stellung f; (place) Lage f; (job) Stelle f; (attitude) Standpunkt m ♦ vt aufstellen

positive ['pɔzɪtɪv] adj positiv; (convinced) sicher; (definite) eindeutig

posse ['pɔsɪ] (US) n Aufgebot nt

possess [pə'zɛs] vt besitzen; **~ion** [pə'zɛʃən] n Besitz m; **~ive** adj besitzergreifend, eigensüchtig

possibility [pɔsɪ'bɪlɪtɪ] n Möglichkeit f

possible ['pɔsɪbl] adj möglich; **as big as ~** so groß wie möglich, möglichst groß; **possibly** adv möglicherweise, vielleicht; **I cannot possibly come** ich kann unmöglich kommen

post [pəʊst] n (BRIT: letters, delivery) Post f; (pole) Pfosten m, Pfahl m; (place of duty) Posten m; (job) Stelle f ♦ vt (notice) anschlagen; (BRIT: letters) aufgeben; (: appoint) versetzen; (soldiers) aufstellen; **~age** n Postgebühr f, Porto nt; **~al** adj Post-; **~al order** n Postanweisung f; **~box** (BRIT) n Briefkasten m; **~card** n Postkarte f; **~code** (BRIT) n Postleitzahl f

postdate ['pəʊst'deɪt] vt (cheque) nachdatieren

poster ['pəʊstər] n Plakat nt, Poster nt

poste restante [pəʊst'rɛstɑ̃:nt] n Aufbewahrungsstelle f für postlagernde Sendungen

posterior [pɔs'tɪərɪər] (inf) n Hintern m

posterity [pɔs'tɛrɪtɪ] n Nachwelt f

postgraduate ['pəʊst'grædjuət] n Weiterstudierende(r) f

posthumous ['pɔstjuməs] adj post(h)um

postman ['pəʊstmən] (irreg) n Briefträger m

postmark ['pəʊstmɑːk] n Poststempel m

post-mortem [pəʊst'mɔːtəm] n Autopsie f

post office n Postamt nt, Post f; (organization) Post f; **Post Office Box** n Postfach nt

postpone [pəʊs'pəʊn] vt verschieben

postscript ['pəʊstskrɪpt] n Postskript nt; (to affair) Nachspiel nt

posture ['pɔstʃər] n Haltung f ♦ vi posieren

postwar [pəʊst'wɔːr] adj Nachkriegs-

postwoman ['pəʊstwʊmən] (irreg) n Briefträgerin f

posy ['pəʊzɪ] n Blumenstrauß m

pot [pɔt] n Topf m; (teapot) Kanne f; (inf: marijuana) Hasch m ♦ vt (plant) eintopfen; **to go to ~** (inf: work) auf den Hund kommen

potato [pə'teɪtəʊ] (pl **~es**) n Kartoffel f; **~ peeler** n Kartoffelschäler m

potent ['pəʊtnt] adj stark; (argument) zwingend

potential [pə'tɛnʃl] adj potenziell, potentiell ♦ n Potenzial nt, Potential nt; **~ly** adv potenziell, potentiell

pothole ['pɔthəʊl] n (in road) Schlagloch nt; (BRIT: underground) Höhle f; **potholing** (BRIT) n: **to go potholing** Höhlen erforschen

potion ['pəʊʃən] n Trank m

potluck [pɔt'lʌk] n: **to take ~ with sth** etw auf gut Glück nehmen

pot plant n Topfpflanze f

potter ['pɔtər] n Töpfer m ♦ vi herumhantieren; **~y** n Töpferwaren pl; (place) Töpferei f

potty ['pɔtɪ] adj (inf: mad) verrückt ♦ n Töpfchen nt

pouch [paʊtʃ] n Beutel m

pouf(fe) [puːf] n Sitzkissen nt

poultry ['pəʊltrɪ] n Geflügel nt

pounce [paʊns] vi sich stürzen ♦ n Sprung m, Satz m; **to ~ on** sich stürzen auf +acc

pound [paʊnd] n (FIN, weight) Pfund nt; (for cars, animals) Auslösestelle f ♦ vt (zer)stampfen ♦ vi klopfen, hämmern; **~ sterling** n Pfund Sterling nt

pour [pɔːr] vt gießen, schütten ♦ vi gießen; (crowds etc) strömen; **~ away** vt abgießen; **~ in** vi (people) hereinströmen; **~ off** vt abgießen; **~ out** vi (people) herausströmen

♦ *vt* (*drink*) einschenken; **~ing** *adj*: **~ing rain** strömende(r) Regen *m*

pout [paut] *vi* schmollen

poverty ['pɔvətɪ] *n* Armut *f*; **~-stricken** *adj* verarmt, sehr arm

powder ['paudəʳ] *n* Pulver *nt*; (*cosmetic*) Puder *m* ♦ *vt* pulverisieren; **to ~ one's nose** sich *dat* die Nase pudern; **~ compact** *n* Puderdose *f*; **~ed milk** *n* Milchpulver *nt*; **~ room** *n* Damentoilette *f*; **~y** *adj* pulverig

power ['pauəʳ] *n* (*also POL*) Macht *f*; (*ability*) Fähigkeit *f*; (*strength*) Stärke *f*; (*MATH*) Potenz *f*; (*ELEC*) Strom *m* ♦ *vt* betreiben, antreiben; **to be in ~** (*POL etc*) an der Macht sein; **~ cut** *n* Stromausfall *m*; **~ed** *adj*: **~ed by** betrieben mit; **~ failure** (*US*) *n* Stromausfall *m*; **~ful** *adj* (*person*) mächtig; (*engine, government*) stark; **~less** *adj* machtlos; **~ point** (*BRIT*) *n* elektrische(r) Anschluss *m*; **~ station** *n* Elektrizitätswerk *nt*; **~ struggle** *n* Machtkampf *m*

p.p. *abbr* (= *per procurationem*): **p.p. J. Smith** i. A. J. Smith

PR *n abbr* = **public relations**

practicable ['præktɪkəbl] *adj* durchführbar

practical ['præktɪkl] *adj* praktisch; **~ity** [præktɪ'kælɪtɪ] *n* (*of person*) praktische Veranlagung *f*; (*of situation etc*) Durchführbarkeit *f*; **~ joke** *n* Streich *m*; **~ly** *adv* praktisch

practice ['præktɪs] *n* Übung *f*; (*reality, also of doctor, lawyer*) Praxis *f*; (*custom*) Brauch *m*; (*in business*) Usus *m* ♦ *vt, vi* (*US*) = **practise**; **in ~** (*in reality*) in der Praxis; **out of ~** außer Übung; **practicing** (*US*) *adj* = **practising**

practise ['præktɪs] (*US* **practice**) *vt* üben; (*profession*) ausüben ♦ *vi* (sich) üben; (*doctor, lawyer*) praktizieren; **practising** (*US* **practicing**) *adj* praktizierend; (*Christian etc*) aktiv

practitioner [præk'tɪʃənəʳ] *n* praktische(r) Arzt *m*, praktische Ärztin *f*

pragmatic [præg'mætɪk] *adj* pragmatisch

prairie ['prɛərɪ] *n* Prärie *f*, Steppe *f*

praise [preɪz] *n* Lob *nt* ♦ *vt* loben; **~worthy** *adj* lobenswert

pram [præm] (*BRIT*) *n* Kinderwagen *m*

prance [prɑːns] *vi* (*horse*) tänzeln; (*person*) stolzieren

prank [præŋk] *n* Streich *m*

prawn [prɔːn] *n* Garnele *f*; Krabbe *f*; **~ cocktail** *n* Krabbencocktail *m*

pray [preɪ] *vi* beten; **~er** [prɛəʳ] *n* Gebet *nt*

preach [priːtʃ] *vi* predigen; **~er** *n* Prediger *m*

preamble [prɪ'æmbl] *n* Einleitung *f*

precarious [prɪ'kɛərɪəs] *adj* prekär, unsicher

precaution [prɪ'kɔːʃən] *n* (Vorsichts)maßnahme *f*

precede [prɪ'siːd] *vi* vorausgehen ♦ *vt* vorausgehen +*dat*; **~nce** ['prɛsɪdəns] *n* Vorrang *m*; **~nt** ['prɛsɪdənt] *n* Präzedenzfall *m*; **preceding** [prɪ'siːdɪŋ] *adj* vorhergehend

precinct ['priːsɪŋkt] *n* (*US: district*) Bezirk *m*; **~s** *npl* (*round building*) Gelände *nt*; (*area, environs*) Umgebung *f*; **pedestrian ~** Fußgängerzone *f*; **shopping ~** Geschäftsviertel *nt*

precious ['prɛʃəs] *adj* kostbar, wertvoll; (*affected*) pretiös, preziös, geziert

precipice ['prɛsɪpɪs] *n* Abgrund *m*

precipitate [*adj* prɪ'sɪpɪtɪt, *vb* prɪ'sɪpɪteɪt] *adj* überstürzt, übereilt ♦ *vt* hinunterstürzen; (*events*) heraufbeschwören

precise [prɪ'saɪs] *adj* genau, präzis; **~ly** *adv* genau, präzis

precision [prɪ'sɪʒən] *n* Präzision *f*

preclude [prɪ'kluːd] *vt* ausschließen

precocious [prɪ'kəuʃəs] *adj* frühreif

preconceived [priːkən'siːvd] *adj* (*idea*) vorgefasst

precondition ['priːkən'dɪʃən] *n* Vorbedingung *f*, Voraussetzung *f*

precursor [priː'kɜːsəʳ] *n* Vorläufer *m*

predator ['prɛdətəʳ] *n* Raubtier *nt*

predecessor ['priːdɪsɛsəʳ] *n* Vorgänger *m*

predicament [prɪ'dɪkəmənt] *n* missliche Lage *f*

predict [prɪ'dɪkt] *vt* voraussagen; **~able** *adj* vorhersagbar; **~ion** [prɪ'dɪkʃən] *n* Voraussage *f*

predominantly [prɪ'dɔmɪnəntlɪ] *adv*

überwiegend, hauptsächlich

predominate [prɪˈdɔmɪneɪt] *vi* vorherrschen; (*fig*) vorherrschen, überwiegen

pre-eminent [priːˈemɪnənt] *adj* hervorragend, herausragend

pre-empt [priːˈemt] *vt* (*action, decision*) vorwegnehmen

preen [priːn] *vt* putzen; **to ~ o.s.** (*person*) sich brüsten

prefab [ˈpriːfæb] *n* Fertighaus *nt*

preface [ˈprefəs] *n* Vorwort *nt*

prefect [ˈpriːfekt] *n* Präfekt *m*; (*SCH*) Aufsichtsschüler(in) *m(f)*

prefer [prɪˈfəːr] *vt* vorziehen, lieber mögen; **to ~ to do sth** etw lieber tun; **~ably** [ˈprefrəblɪ] *adv* vorzugsweise, am liebsten; **~ence** [ˈprefrəns] *n* Präferenz *f*, Vorzug *m*; **~ential** [prefəˈrenʃəl] *adj* bevorzugt, Vorzugs-

prefix [ˈpriːfɪks] *n* Vorsilbe *f*, Präfix *nt*

pregnancy [ˈpregnənsɪ] *n* Schwangerschaft *f*

pregnant [ˈpregnənt] *adj* schwanger

prehistoric [ˈpriːhɪsˈtɔrɪk] *adj* prähistorisch, vorgeschichtlich

prejudice [ˈpredʒudɪs] *n* (*bias*) Voreingenommenheit *f*; (*opinion*) Vorurteil *nt*; (*harm*) Schaden *m* ♦ *vt* beeinträchtigen; **~d** *adj* (*person*) voreingenommen

preliminary [prɪˈlɪmɪnərɪ] *adj* einleitend, Vor-

prelude [ˈpreljuːd] *n* Vorspiel *nt*; (*fig*) Auftakt *m*

premarital [ˈpriːˈmærɪtl] *adj* vorehelich

premature [ˈpremətjuər] *adj* vorzeitig, verfrüht; (*birth*) Früh-

premeditated [priːˈmedɪteɪtɪd] *adj* geplant; (*murder*) vorsätzlich

premenstrual syndrome [priːˈmenstruəl-] *n* prämenstruelles Syndrom *nt*

premier [ˈpremɪər] *adj* erste(r, s) ♦ *n* Premier *m*

première [ˈpremɪeər] *n* Premiere *f*; Uraufführung *f*

Premier League [-liːg] *n* ≈ 1. Bundesliga (*höchste Spielklasse im Fußball*)

premise [ˈpremɪs] *n* Voraussetzung *f*;

Prämisse *f*; **~s** *npl* (*shop*) Räumlichkeiten *pl*; (*grounds*) Gelände *nt*; **on the ~s** im Hause

premium [ˈpriːmɪəm] *n* Prämie *f*; **to be at a ~** über pari stehen; **~ bond** (*BRIT*) *n* Prämienanleihe *f*

premonition [preməˈnɪʃən] *n* Vorahnung *f*

preoccupation [priːɔkjuˈpeɪʃən] *n* Sorge *f*

preoccupied [priːˈɔkjupaɪd] *adj* (*look*) geistesabwesend

prep [prep] *n* (*SCH*) Hausaufgabe *f*

prepaid [priːˈpeɪd] *adj* vorausbezahlt; (*letter*) frankiert

preparation [prepəˈreɪʃən] *n* Vorbereitung *f*

preparatory [prɪˈpærətərɪ] *adj* Vor(bereitungs)-; **~ school** *n* (*BRIT*) *private Vorbereitungsschule für die Public School*; (*US*) *private Vorbereitungsschule für die Hochschule*

prepare [prɪˈpeər] *vt* vorbereiten ♦ *vi* sich vorbereiten; **to ~ for / prepare sth for** sich/etw vorbereiten auf +*acc*; **to be ~d to ...** bereit sein zu ...

preponderance [prɪˈpɔndərns] *n* Übergewicht *nt*

preposition [prepəˈzɪʃən] *n* Präposition *f*, Verhältniswort *nt*

preposterous [prɪˈpɔstərəs] *adj* absurd

prep school *n* = **preparatory school**

prerequisite [priːˈrekwɪzɪt] *n* (unerlässliche) Voraussetzung *f*

prerogative [prɪˈrɔgətɪv] *n* Vorrecht *nt*

Presbyterian [prezbɪˈtɪərɪən] *adj* presbyterianisch ♦ *n* Presbyterier(in) *m(f)*

preschool [ˈpriːˈskuːl] *adj* Vorschul-

prescribe [prɪˈskraɪb] *vt* vorschreiben; (*MED*) verschreiben

prescription [prɪˈskrɪpʃən] *n* (*MED*) Rezept *nt*

presence [ˈprezns] *n* Gegenwart *f*; **~ of mind** Geistesgegenwart *f*

present [*adj, n* ˈpreznt, *vb* prɪˈzent] *adj* (*here*) anwesend; (*current*) gegenwärtig ♦ *n* Gegenwart *f*; (*gift*) Geschenk *nt* ♦ *vt* vorlegen; (*introduce*) vorstellen; (*show*) zeigen; (*give*): **to ~ sb with sth** jdm etw überreichen; **at ~** im Augenblick; **to give sb a ~** jdm ein Geschenk machen; **~able** [prɪˈzentəbl] *adj* präsentabel; **~ation**

[prezn'teɪʃən] n Überreichung f; **~-day** adj
heutig; **~er** [prɪ'zentə^r] n (RAD, TV)
Moderator(in) m(f); **~ly** adv bald; (at ~) im
Augenblick

preservation [prezə'veɪʃən] n Erhaltung f

preservative [prɪ'zə:vətɪv] n
Konservierungsmittel nt

preserve [prɪ'zə:v] vt erhalten; (food)
einmachen ♦ n (jam) Eingemachte(s) nt;
(reserve) Schutzgebiet nt

preside [prɪ'zaɪd] vi den Vorsitz haben

president ['prezɪdənt] n Präsident m; **~ial**
[prezɪ'denʃl] adj Präsidenten-; (election)
Präsidentschafts-; (system) Präsidial-

press [pres] n Presse f; (printing house)
Druckerei f ♦ vt drücken; (iron) bügeln;
(urge) (be)drängen ♦ vi (push) drücken; **to
be ~ed for time** unter Zeitdruck stehen; **to
~ for sth** drängen auf etw acc; **~ on** vi
vorwärts drängen; **~ agency** n
Presseagentur f; **~ conference** n
Pressekonferenz f; **~ed** adj (clothes)
gebügelt; **~ing** adj dringend; **~ stud** (BRIT)
n Druckknopf m; **~-up** (BRIT) n Liegestütz m

pressure ['preʃə^r] n Druck m; **~ cooker** n
Schnellkochtopf m; **~ gauge** n
Druckmesser m

pressurized ['preʃəraɪzd] adj Druck-

prestige [pres'ti:ʒ] n Prestige nt;
prestigious [pres'tɪdʒəs] adj Prestige-

presumably [prɪ'zju:məblɪ] adv vermutlich

presume [prɪ'zju:m] vt, vi annehmen; **to ~
to do sth** sich erlauben, etw zu tun;
presumption [prɪ'zʌmpʃən] n Annahme f;
presumptuous [prɪ'zʌmpʃəs] adj
anmaßend

pretence [prɪ'tens] (US **pretense**) n Vorgabe
f, Vortäuschung f; (false claim) Vorwand m

pretend [prɪ'tend] vt vorgeben, so tun als
ob ... ♦ vi so tun; **to ~ to sth** Anspruch
erheben auf etw acc

pretense [prɪ'tens] (US) n = **pretence**

pretension [prɪ'tenʃən] n Anspruch m;
(impudent claim) Anmaßung f

pretentious [prɪ'tenʃəs] adj angeberisch

pretext ['pri:tekst] n Vorwand m

pretty ['prɪtɪ] adj hübsch ♦ adv (inf) ganz

schön

prevail [prɪ'veɪl] vi siegen; (custom)
vorherrschen; **to ~ against** or **over** siegen
über +acc; **to ~ (up)on sb to do sth** jdn
dazu bewegen, etw zu tun; **~ing** adj
vorherrschend

prevalent ['prevələnt] adj vorherrschend

prevent [prɪ'vent] vt (stop) verhindern,
verhüten; **to ~ sb from doing sth** jdn
(daran) hindern, etw zu tun; **~ative** n
Vorbeugungsmittel nt; **~ion** [prɪ'venʃən] n
Verhütung f; **~ive** adj vorbeugend, Schutz-

preview ['pri:vju:] n private Voraufführung
f; (trailer) Vorschau f

previous ['pri:vɪəs] adj früher, vorherig; **~ly**
adv früher

prewar [pri:'wɔ:^r] adj Vorkriegs-

prey [preɪ] n Beute f; **~ on** vt fus Jagd
machen auf +acc; **it was ~ing on his mind**
es quälte sein Gewissen

price [praɪs] n Preis m; (value) Wert m ♦ vt
(label) auszeichnen; **~less** adj (also fig)
unbezahlbar; **~ list** n Preisliste f

prick [prɪk] n Stich m ♦ vt, vi stechen; **to ~
up one's ears** die Ohren spitzen

prickle ['prɪkl] n Stachel m, Dorn m

prickly ['prɪklɪ] adj stachelig; (fig: person)
reizbar; **~ heat** n Hitzebläschen pl

pride [praɪd] n Stolz m; (arrogance) Hochmut
m ♦ vt: **to ~ o.s. on sth** auf etw acc stolz
sein

priest [pri:st] n Priester m; **~hood** n
Priesteramt nt

prim [prɪm] adj prüde

primarily ['praɪmərɪlɪ] adv vorwiegend

primary ['praɪmərɪ] adj (main) Haupt-; (SCH)
Grund-; **~ school** (BRIT) n Grundschule f

prime [praɪm] adj erste(r, s); (excellent)
erstklassig ♦ vt vorbereiten; (gun) laden; **in
the ~ of life** in der Blüte der Jahre; **~
minister** n Premierminister m,
Ministerpräsident m; **~r** ['praɪmə^r] n Fibel f

primeval [praɪ'mi:vl] adj vorzeitlich; (forests)
Ur-

primitive ['prɪmɪtɪv] adj primitiv

primrose ['prɪmrəuz] n (gelbe) Primel f

primus (stove) ['praɪməs-] (® BRIT) n

Primuskocher *m*

prince [prɪns] *n* Prinz *m*; (*ruler*) Fürst *m*; **princess** [prɪn'ses] *n* Prinzessin *f*; Fürstin *f*

principal ['prɪnsɪpl] *adj* Haupt- ♦ *n* (*SCH*) (Schul)direktor *m*, Rektor *m*; (*money*) (Grund)kapital *nt*

principle ['prɪnsɪpl] *n* Grundsatz *m*, Prinzip *nt*; **in ~** im Prinzip; **on ~** aus Prinzip, prinzipiell

print [prɪnt] *n* Druck *m*; (*made by feet, fingers*) Abdruck *m*; (*PHOT*) Abzug *m* ♦ *vt* drucken; (*name*) in Druckbuchstaben schreiben; (*PHOT*) abziehen; **out of ~** vergriffen; **~ed matter** *n* Drucksache *f*; **~er** *n* Drucker *m*; **~ing** *n* Drucken *nt*; (*of photos*) Abziehen *nt*; **~out** *n* (*COMPUT*) Ausdruck *m*

prior ['praɪə*] *adj* früher ♦ *n* Prior *m*; **~ to sth** vor etw *dat*; **~ to going abroad, she had ...** bevor sie ins Ausland ging, hatte sie ...

priority [praɪ'ɔrɪtɪ] *n* Vorrang *m*; Priorität *f*

prise [praɪz] *vt*: **to ~ open** aufbrechen

prison ['prɪzn] *n* Gefängnis *nt* ♦ *adj* Gefängnis-; (*system etc*) Strafvollzugs-; **~er** *n* Gefangene(r) *mf*

pristine ['prɪstiːn] *adj* makellos

privacy ['prɪvəsɪ] *n* Ungestörtheit *f*, Ruhe *f*; Privatleben *nt*

private ['praɪvɪt] *adj* privat, Privat-; (*secret*) vertraulich, geheim ♦ *n* einfache(r) Soldat *m*; **"~"** (*on envelope*) „persönlich"; (*on door*) „Privat"; **in ~** privat, unter vier Augen; **~ enterprise** *n* Privatunternehmen *nt*; **~ eye** *n* Privatdetektiv *m*; **~ property** *n* Privatbesitz *m*; **~ school** *n* Privatschule *f*; **privatize** *vt* privatisieren

privet ['prɪvɪt] *n* Liguster *m*

privilege ['prɪvɪlɪdʒ] *n* Privileg *nt*; **~d** *adj* bevorzugt, privilegiert

privy ['prɪvɪ] *adj* geheim, privat; **P~ Council** *n* Geheime(r) Staatsrat *m*

prize [praɪz] *n* Preis *m* ♦ *adj* (*example*) erstklassig; (*idiot*) Voll- ♦ *vt* (hoch) schätzen; **~-giving** *n* Preisverteilung *f*; **~winner** *n* Preisträger(in) *m(f)*

pro [prəʊ] *n* (*professional*) Profi *m*; **the ~s and cons** das Für und Wider

probability [prɒbə'bɪlɪtɪ] *n* Wahrscheinlichkeit *f*

probable ['prɒbəbl] *adj* wahrscheinlich; **probably** *adv* wahrscheinlich

probation [prə'beɪʃən] *n* Probe(zeit) *f*; (*JUR*) Bewährung *f*; **on ~** auf Probe; auf Bewährung

probe [prəʊb] *n* Sonde *f*; (*enquiry*) Untersuchung *f* ♦ *vt*, *vi* erforschen

problem ['prɒbləm] *n* Problem *nt*; **~atic** [prɒblə'mætɪk] *adj* problematisch

procedure [prə'siːdʒə*] *n* Verfahren *nt*

proceed [prə'siːd] *vi* (*advance*) vorrücken; (*start*) anfangen; (*carry on*) fortfahren; (*set about*) vorgehen; **~ings** *npl* Verfahren *nt*

proceeds ['prəʊsiːdz] *npl* Erlös *m*

process ['prəʊses] *n* Prozess *m*; (*method*) Verfahren *nt* ♦ *vt* bearbeiten; (*food*) verarbeiten; (*film*) entwickeln; **~ing** *n* (*PHOT*) Entwickeln *nt*

procession [prə'seʃən] *n* Prozession *f*, Umzug *m*; **funeral ~** Trauerprozession *f*

pro-choice [prəʊ'tʃɔɪs] *adj* (*movement*) Pro-Abtreibungs-; **~ campaigner** Abtreibungsbefürworter(in) *m(f)*

proclaim [prə'kleɪm] *vt* verkünden

procrastinate [prəʊ'kræstɪneɪt] *vi* zaudern

procure [prə'kjʊə*] *vt* beschaffen

prod [prɒd] *vt* stoßen ♦ *n* Stoß *m*

prodigal ['prɒdɪgl] *adj*: **~ (with** *or* **of)** verschwenderisch (mit)

prodigy ['prɒdɪdʒɪ] *n* Wunder *nt*

produce [*n* 'prɒdjuːs, *vb* prə'djuːs] *n* (*AGR*) (Boden)produkte *pl*, (Natur)erzeugnis *nt* ♦ *vt* herstellen, produzieren; (*cause*) hervorrufen; (*farmer*) erzeugen; (*yield*) liefern, bringen; (*play*) inszenieren; **~r** *n* Hersteller *m*, Produzent *m* (*also CINE*); Erzeuger *m*

product ['prɒdʌkt] *n* Produkt *nt*, Erzeugnis *nt*; **~ion** [prə'dʌkʃən] *n* Produktion *f*, Herstellung *f*; (*thing*) Erzeugnis *nt*, Produkt *nt*; (*THEAT*) Inszenierung *f*; **~ion line** *n* Fließband *nt*; **~ive** [prə'dʌktɪv] *adj* produktiv; (*fertile*) ertragreich, fruchtbar

productivity [prɒdʌk'tɪvɪtɪ] *n* Produktivität *f*

profane [prə'feɪn] *adj* weltlich, profan; (*language etc*) gotteslästerlich

profess [prəˈfes] vt bekennen; (*show*) zeigen; (*claim to be*) vorgeben

profession [prəˈfeʃən] n Beruf m; (*declaration*) Bekenntnis nt; **~al** n Fachmann m; (*SPORT*) Berufsspieler(in) m(f) ♦ adj Berufs-; (*expert*) fachlich; (*player*) professionell; **~ally** adv beruflich, fachmännisch

professor [prəˈfesər] n Professor m

proficiency [prəˈfiʃənsi] n Können nt

proficient [prəˈfiʃənt] adj fähig

profile [ˈprəufaɪl] n Profil nt; (*fig: report*) Kurzbiografie f

profit [ˈprɒfɪt] n Gewinn m ♦ vi: **to ~ (by** or **from)** profitieren (von); **~ability** [prɒfɪtəˈbɪlɪtɪ] n Rentabilität f; **~able** adj einträglich, rentabel; **~eering** [prɒfɪˈtɪərɪŋ] n Profitmacherei f

profound [prəˈfaund] adj tief

profuse [prəˈfjuːs] adj überreich; **~ly** [prəˈfjuːslɪ] adv überschwänglich; (*sweat*) reichlich; **profusion** [prəˈfjuːʒən] n: **profusion (of)** Überfülle f (von), Überfluss m (an +dat)

program [ˈprəugræm] n (*COMPUT*) Programm nt ♦ vt (*machine*) programmieren; **~me** (*US* **program**) n Programm nt ♦ vt planen; (*computer*) programmieren; **~mer** (*US* **programer**) n Programmierer(in) m(f)

progress [n ˈprəugres, vb prəˈgres] n Fortschritt m ♦ vi fortschreiten, weitergehen; **in ~** im Gang; **~ion** [prəˈgreʃən] n Folge f; **~ive** [prəˈgresɪv] adj fortschrittlich, progressiv

prohibit [prəˈhɪbɪt] vt verbieten; **to ~ sb from doing sth** jdm untersagen, etw zu tun; **~ion** [prəuɪˈbɪʃən] n Verbot nt; (*US*) Alkoholverbot nt, Prohibition f; **~ive** adj unerschwinglich

project [n ˈprɒdʒekt, vb prəˈdʒekt] n Projekt nt ♦ vt vorausplanen; (*film etc*) projizieren; (*personality, voice*) zum Tragen bringen ♦ vi (*stick out*) hervorragen, (her)vorstehen

projectile [prəˈdʒektaɪl] n Geschoss nt

projection [prəˈdʒekʃən] n Projektion f; (*sth prominent*) Vorsprung m

projector [prəˈdʒektər] n Projektor m

proletariat [prəulɪˈtɛərɪət] n Proletariat nt

pro-life [prəuˈlaɪf] adj (*movement*) Anti-Abtreibungs-; **~ campaigner** Abtreibungsgegner(in) m(f)

prolific [prəˈlɪfɪk] adj fruchtbar; (*author etc*) produktiv

prologue [ˈprəulɒg] n Prolog m; (*event*) Vorspiel nt

prolong [prəˈlɒŋ] vt verlängern

prom [prɒm] n abbr = **promenade**; **promenade concert**

Prom

ⓘ **Prom** (*promenade concert*) ist in Großbritannien ein Konzert, bei dem ein Teil der Zuhörer steht (ursprünglich spazieren ging). Die seit 1895 alljährlich stattfindenden Proms (seit 1941 immer in der Londoner Royal Albert Hall) zählen zu den bedeutendsten Musikereignissen in England. Der letzte Abend der Proms steht ganz im Zeichen des Patriotismus und gipfelt im Singen des Lieds „Land of Hope and Glory". In den USA und Kanada steht das Wort für **promenade**, ein Ball an einer High School oder einem College.

---

promenade [prɒməˈnɑːd] n Promenade f; **~ concert** n Promenadenkonzert nt

prominence [ˈprɒmɪnəns] n (große) Bedeutung f

prominent [ˈprɒmɪnənt] adj bedeutend; (*politician*) prominent; (*easily seen*) herausragend, auffallend

promiscuous [prəˈmɪskjuəs] adj lose

promise [ˈprɒmɪs] n Versprechen nt; (*hope*: **~ of sth**) Aussicht f auf etw acc ♦ vt, vi versprechen; **promising** adj viel versprechend

promontory [ˈprɒməntrɪ] n Vorsprung m

promote [prəˈməut] vt befördern; (*help on*) fördern, unterstützen; **~r** n (*in entertainment, sport*) Veranstalter m; (*for charity etc*) Organisator m; **promotion** [prəˈməuʃən] n (*in rank*) Beförderung f; (*furtherance*) Förderung f; (*COMM*): **promotion (of)** Werbung f (für)

prompt [prɔmpt] *adj* prompt, schnell ♦ *adv* (*punctually*) genau ♦ *n* (*COMPUT*) Meldung *f* ♦ *vt* veranlassen; (*THEAT*) soufflieren +*dat*; **to ~ sb to do sth** jdn dazu veranlassen, etw zu tun; **~ly** *adv* sofort

prone [prəun] *adj* hingestreckt; **to be ~ to sth** zu etw neigen

prong [prɔŋ] *n* Zinke *f*

pronoun ['prəunaun] *n* Fürwort *nt*

pronounce [prə'nauns] *vt* aussprechen; (*JUR*) verkünden ♦ *vi*: **to ~ (on)** sich äußern (zu)

pronunciation [prənʌnsɪ'eɪʃən] *n* Aussprache *f*

proof [pruːf] *n* Beweis *m*; (*PRINT*) Korrekturfahne *f*; (*of alcohol*) Alkoholgehalt *m* ♦ *adj* sicher

prop [prɔp] *n* (*also fig*) Stütze *f*; (*THEAT*) Requisit *nt* ♦ *vt* (*also*: ~ **up**) (ab)stützen

propaganda [prɔpə'gændə] *n* Propaganda *f*

propel [prə'pel] *vt* (an)treiben; **~ler** *n* Propeller *m*; **~ling pencil** (*BRIT*) *n* Drehbleistift *m*

propensity [prə'pensɪtɪ] *n* Tendenz *f*

proper ['prɔpə*] *adj* richtig; (*seemly*) schicklich; **~ly** *adv* richtig; ~ **noun** *n* Eigenname *m*

property ['prɔpətɪ] *n* Eigentum *nt*; (*quality*) Eigenschaft *f*; (*land*) Grundbesitz *m*; ~ **owner** *n* Grundbesitzer *m*

prophecy ['prɔfɪsɪ] *n* Prophezeiung *f*

prophesy ['prɔfɪsaɪ] *vt* prophezeien

prophet ['prɔfɪt] *n* Prophet *m*

proportion [prə'pɔːʃən] *n* Verhältnis *nt*; (*share*) Teil *m* ♦ *vt*: **to ~ (to)** abstimmen (auf +*acc*); **~al** *adj* proportional; **~ate** *adj* verhältnismäßig

proposal [prə'pəuzl] *n* Vorschlag *m*; (*of marriage*) Heiratsantrag *m*

propose [prə'pəuz] *vt* vorschlagen; (*toast*) ausbringen ♦ *vi* (*offer marriage*) einen Heiratsantrag machen; **to ~ to do sth** beabsichtigen, etw zu tun

proposition [prɔpə'zɪʃən] *n* Angebot *nt*; (*statement*) Satz *m*

proprietor [prə'praɪətə*] *n* Besitzer *m*, Eigentümer *m*

propriety [prə'praɪətɪ] *n* Anstand *m*

pro rata [prəu'rɑːtə] *adv* anteilmäßig

prose [prəuz] *n* Prosa *f*

prosecute ['prɔsɪkjuːt] *vt* (strafrechtlich) verfolgen; **prosecution** [prɔsɪ'kjuːʃən] *n* (*JUR*) strafrechtliche Verfolgung *f*; (*party*) Anklage *f*; **prosecutor** *n* Vertreter *m* der Anklage; **Public Prosecutor** Staatsanwalt *m*

prospect [*n* 'prɔspekt, *vb* prə'spekt] *n* Aussicht *f* ♦ *vt* auf Bodenschätze hin untersuchen ♦ *vi*: **to ~ (for)** suchen (nach); **~ing** ['prɔspektɪŋ] *n* (*for minerals*) Suche *f*; **~ive** [prə'spektɪv] *adj* (*son-in-law etc*) zukünftig; (*customer, candidate*) voraussichtlich

prospectus [prə'spektəs] *n* (Werbe)prospekt *m*

prosper ['prɔspə*] *vi* blühen, gedeihen; (*person*) erfolgreich sein; **~ous** *adj* wohlhabend, reich

prostitute ['prɔstɪtjuːt] *n* Prostituierte *f*

prostrate ['prɔstreɪt] *adj* ausgestreckt (liegend)

protagonist [prə'tægənɪst] *n* Hauptperson *f*, Held *m*

protect [prə'tekt] *vt* (be)schützen; **~ed species** *n* geschützte Art; **~ion** [prə'tekʃən] *n* Schutz *m*; **~ive** *adj* Schutz-, (be)schützend

protégé ['prəuteʒeɪ] *n* Schützling *m*

protein ['prəutiːn] *n* Protein *nt*, Eiweiß *nt*

protest [*n* 'prəutest, *vb* prə'test] *n* Protest *m* ♦ *vi* protestieren ♦ *vt* (*affirm*) beteuern

Protestant ['prɔtɪstənt] *adj* protestantisch ♦ *n* Protestant(in) *m(f)*

protester [prə'testə*] *n* (*demonstrator*) Demonstrant(in) *m(f)*

protracted [prə'træktɪd] *adj* sich hinziehend

protrude [prə'truːd] *vi* (her)vorstehen

proud [praud] *adj*: ~ **(of)** stolz (auf +*acc*)

prove [pruːv] *vt* beweisen ♦ *vi*: **to ~ (to be) correct** sich als richtig erweisen; **to ~ o.s.** sich bewähren

proverb ['prɔvəːb] *n* Sprichwort *nt*; **~ial** [prə'vəːbɪəl] *adj* sprichwörtlich

provide [prə'vaɪd] *vt* versehen; (*supply*) besorgen; **to ~ sb with sth** jdn mit etw

versorgen; **~ for** *vt fus* sorgen für; (*emergency*) Vorkehrungen treffen für; **~d (that)** *conj* vorausgesetzt(, dass)
providing [prə'vaɪdɪŋ] *conj* vorausgesetzt(, dass)
province ['prɒvɪns] *n* Provinz *f*; (*division of work*) Bereich *m*; **provincial** [prə'vɪnʃəl] *adj* provinziell, Provinz-
provision [prə'vɪʒən] *n* Vorkehrung *f*; (*condition*) Bestimmung *f*; **~s** *npl* (*food*) Vorräte *pl*, Proviant *m*; **~al** *adj* provisorisch
proviso [prə'vaɪzəʊ] *n* Bedingung *f*
provocative [prə'vɒkətɪv] *adj* provozierend
provoke [prə'vəʊk] *vt* provozieren; (*cause*) hervorrufen
prowess ['praʊɪs] *n* überragende(s) Können *nt*
prowl [praʊl] *vi* herumstreichen; (*animal*) schleichen ♦ *n*: **on the ~** umherstreifend; **~er** *n* Herumtreiber(in) *m(f)*
proximity [prɒk'sɪmɪtɪ] *n* Nähe *f*
proxy ['prɒksɪ] *n* (Stell)vertreter *m*; (*authority, document*) Vollmacht *f*; **by ~** durch einen Stellvertreter
prudent ['pru:dnt] *adj* klug, umsichtig
prudish ['pru:dɪʃ] *adj* prüde
prune [pru:n] *n* Backpflaume *f* ♦ *vt* ausputzen; (*fig*) zurechtstutzen
pry [praɪ] *vi*: **to ~ (into)** seine Nase stecken (in +*acc*)
PS *n abbr* (= *postscript*) PS
pseudonym ['sju:dənɪm] *n* Pseudonym *nt*, Deckname *m*
psychiatric [saɪkɪ'ætrɪk] *adj* psychiatrisch
psychiatrist [saɪ'kaɪətrɪst] *n* Psychiater *m*
psychic ['saɪkɪk] *adj* (*also*: **~al**) übersinnlich; (*person*) paranormal begabt
psychoanalyse [saɪkəʊ'ænəlaɪz] (*US* **psychoanalyze**) *vt* psychoanalytisch behandeln; **psychoanalyst** [saɪkəʊ'ænəlɪst] *n* Psychoanalytiker(in) *m(f)*
psychological [saɪkə'lɒdʒɪkl] *adj* psychologisch; **psychologist** [saɪ'kɒlədʒɪst] *n* Psychologe *m*, Psychologin *f*; **psychology** [saɪ'kɒlədʒɪ] *n* Psychologie *f*
PTO *abbr* = **please turn over**
pub [pʌb] *n abbr* (= *public house*) Kneipe *f*

Pub

i **Pub** *ist ein Gasthaus mit einer Lizenz zum Ausschank von alkoholischen Getränken. Ein Pub besteht meist aus verschiedenen gemütlichen (**lounge, snug**) oder einfacheren Räumen (**public bar**), in der oft auch Spiele wie Darts, Domino und Poolbillard zur Verfügung stehen. In Pubs werden vor allem mittags oft auch Mahlzeiten angeboten. Pubs sind normalerweise von 11 bis 23 Uhr geöffnet, aber manchmal nachmittags geschlossen.*

---

pubic ['pju:bɪk] *adj* Scham-
public ['pʌblɪk] *adj* öffentlich ♦ *n* (*also*: **general ~**) Öffentlichkeit *f*; **in ~** in der Öffentlichkeit; **~ address system** *n* Lautsprecheranlage *f*
publican ['pʌblɪkən] *n* Wirt *m*
publication [pʌblɪ'keɪʃən] *n* Veröffentlichung *f*
public: ~ company *n* Aktiengesellschaft *f*; **~ convenience** (*BRIT*) *n* öffentliche Toiletten *pl*; **~ holiday** *n* gesetzliche(r) Feiertag *m*; **~ house** (*BRIT*) *n* Lokal *nt*, Kneipe *f*
publicity [pʌb'lɪsɪtɪ] *n* Publicity *f*, Werbung *f*
publicize ['pʌblɪsaɪz] *vt* bekannt machen; (*advertise*) Publicity machen für
publicly ['pʌblɪklɪ] *adv* öffentlich
public: ~ opinion *n* öffentliche Meinung *f*; **~ relations** *npl* Publicrelations *pl*, Public Relations *pl*; **~ school** *n* (*BRIT*) Privatschule *f*; (*US*) staatliche Schule *f*; **~-spirited** *adj* mit Gemeinschaftssinn; **~ transport** *n* öffentliche Verkehrsmittel *pl*
publish ['pʌblɪʃ] *vt* veröffentlichen; (*event*) bekannt geben; **~er** *n* Verleger *m*; **~ing** *n* (*business*) Verlagswesen *nt*
pub lunch *n* in Pubs servierter Imbiss
pucker ['pʌkər] *vt* (*face*) verziehen; (*lips*) kräuseln
pudding ['pʊdɪŋ] *n* (*BRIT*: *course*) Nachtisch *m*; Pudding *m*; **black ~** ≈ Blutwurst *f*
puddle ['pʌdl] *n* Pfütze *f*
puff [pʌf] *n* (*of wind etc*) Stoß *m*; (*cosmetic*)

Puderquaste f ♦ vt blasen, pusten; (pipe) paffen ♦ vi keuchen, schnaufen; (smoke) paffen; **to ~ out smoke** Rauch ausstoßen; **~ pastry** (US **~ paste**) n Blätterteig m; **~y** adj aufgedunsen

pull [pʊl] n Ruck m; (influence) Beziehung f ♦ vt ziehen; (trigger) abdrücken ♦ vi ziehen; **to ~ sb's leg** jdn auf den Arm nehmen; **to ~ to pieces** in Stücke reißen; (fig) verreißen; **to ~ one's punches** sich zurückhalten; **to ~ one's weight** sich in die Riemen legen; **to ~ o.s. together** sich zusammenreißen; **~ apart** vt (break) zerreißen; (dismantle) auseinander nehmen; (separate) trennen; **~ down** vt (house) abreißen; **~ in** vi hineinfahren; (stop) anhalten; (RAIL) einfahren; **~ off** vt (deal etc) abschließen; **~ out** vi (car) herausfahren; (fig: partner) aussteigen ♦ vt herausziehen; **~ over** vi (AUT) an die Seite fahren; **~ through** vi durchkommen; **~ up** vi anhalten ♦ vt (uproot) herausreißen; (stop) anhalten

pulley ['pʊlɪ] n Rolle f, Flaschenzug m
pullover ['pʊləʊvəʳ] n Pullover m
pulp [pʌlp] n Brei m; (of fruit) Fruchtfleisch nt
pulpit ['pʊlpɪt] n Kanzel f
pulsate [pʌl'seɪt] vi pulsieren
pulse [pʌls] n Puls m; **~s** npl (BOT) Hülsenfrüchte pl
pummel ['pʌml] vt mit den Fäusten bearbeiten
pump [pʌmp] n Pumpe f; (shoe) leichter (Tanz)schuh m ♦ vt pumpen; **~ up** vt (tyre) aufpumpen
pumpkin ['pʌmpkɪn] n Kürbis m
pun [pʌn] n Wortspiel nt
punch [pʌntʃ] n (tool) Locher m; (blow) (Faust)schlag m; (drink) Punsch m, Bowle f ♦ vt lochen; (strike) schlagen, boxen; **~ line** n Pointe f; **~-up** n (BRIT: inf) Keilerei f
punctual ['pʌŋktjʊəl] adj pünktlich
punctuate ['pʌŋktjueɪt] vt mit Satzzeichen versehen; (fig) unterbrechen; **punctuation** [pʌŋktju'eɪʃən] n Zeichensetzung f, Interpunktion f
puncture ['pʌŋktʃəʳ] n Loch nt; (AUT)

Reifenpanne f ♦ vt durchbohren
pundit ['pʌndɪt] n Gelehrte(r) m
pungent ['pʌndʒənt] adj scharf
punish ['pʌnɪʃ] vt bestrafen; (in boxing etc) übel zurichten; **~ment** n Strafe f; (action) Bestrafung f
punk [pʌŋk] n (also: ~ rocker) Punker(in) m(f); (also: ~ rock) Punk m; (US: inf: hoodlum) Ganove m
punt [pʌnt] n Stechkahn m
punter ['pʌntəʳ] (BRIT) n (better) Wetter m
puny ['pju:nɪ] adj kümmerlich
pup [pʌp] n = **puppy**
pupil ['pju:pl] n Schüler(in) m(f); (in eye) Pupille f
puppet ['pʌpɪt] n Puppe f; Marionette f
puppy ['pʌpɪ] n junge(r) Hund m
purchase ['pə:tʃɪs] n Kauf m; (grip) Halt m ♦ vt kaufen, erwerben; **~r** n Käufer(in) m(f)
pure [pjʊəʳ] adj (also fig) rein; **~ly** ['pjʊəlɪ] adv rein
purgatory ['pə:gətərɪ] n Fegefeuer nt
purge [pə:dʒ] n (also POL) Säuberung f ♦ vt reinigen; (body) entschlacken
purify ['pjʊərɪfaɪ] vt reinigen
purity ['pjʊərɪtɪ] n Reinheit f
purple ['pə:pl] adj violett; (face) dunkelrot
purport [pə:'pɔ:t] vi vorgeben
purpose ['pə:pəs] n Zweck m, Ziel nt; (of person) Absicht f; **on ~** absichtlich; **~ful** adj zielbewusst, entschlossen
purr [pə:ʳ] n Schnurren nt ♦ vi schnurren
purse [pə:s] n Portemonnaie nt, Portmonee nt, Geldbeutel m ♦ vt (lips) zusammenpressen, schürzen
purser ['pə:səʳ] n Zahlmeister m
pursue [pə'sju:] vt verfolgen; (study) nachgehen +dat; **~r** n Verfolger m; **pursuit** [pə'sju:t] n Verfolgung f; (occupation) Beschäftigung f
pus [pʌs] n Eiter m
push [pʊʃ] n Stoß m, Schub m; (MIL) Vorstoß m ♦ vt stoßen, schieben; (button) drücken; (idea) durchsetzen ♦ vi stoßen, schieben; **~ aside** vt beiseite schieben; **~ off** (inf) vi abschieben; **~ on** vi weitermachen; **~ through** vt durchdrücken; (policy)

durchsetzen; **~ up** *vt* (*total*) erhöhen;
(*prices*) hoch treiben; **~chair** (*BRIT*) *n*
(Kinder)sportwagen *m*; **~er** *n* (*drug dealer*)
Pusher *m*; **~over** (*inf*) *n* Kinderspiel *nt*; **~-
up** (*US*) *n* (*press-up*) Liegestütz *m*; **~y** (*inf*)
adj aufdringlich

puss [pus] *n* Mieze(katze) *f*; **~y(cat)** *n*
Mieze(katze) *f*

put [put] (*pt, pp* put) *vt* setzen, stellen, legen;
(*express*) ausdrücken, sagen; (*write*)
schreiben; **~ about** *vi* (*turn back*) wenden
♦ *vt* (*spread*) verbreiten; **~ across** *vt*
(*explain*) erklären; **~ away** *vt* weglegen;
(*store*) beiseite legen; **~ back** *vt*
zurückstellen *or* -legen; **~ by** *vt*
zurücklegen, sparen; **~ down** *vt* hinstellen
or -legen; (*rebellion*) niederschlagen;
(*animal*) einschläfern; (*in writing*)
niederschreiben; **~ forward** *vt* (*idea*)
vorbringen; (*clock*) vorstellen; **~ in** *vt*
(*application, complaint*) einreichen; **~ off** *vt*
verschieben; (*discourage*): **to ~ sb off sth**
jdn von etw abbringen; **~ on** *vt* (*clothes
etc*) anziehen; (*light etc*) anschalten,
anmachen; (*play etc*) aufführen; (*brake*)
anziehen; **~ out** *vt* (*hand etc*)
(her)ausstrecken; (*news, rumour*) verbreiten;
(*light etc*) ausschalten, ausmachen; **~
through** *vt* (*TEL: person*) verbinden; (: *call*)
durchstellen; **~ up** *vt* (*tent*) aufstellen;
(*building*) errichten; (*price*) erhöhen; (*person*)
unterbringen; **~ up with** *vt fus* sich
abfinden mit

putrid ['pjuːtrɪd] *adj* faul

putt [pʌt] *vt* (*golf*) putten ♦ *n* (*golf*) Putten *nt*;
~ing green *n* kleine(r) Golfplatz *m* nur
zum Putten

putty ['pʌtɪ] *n* Kitt *m*; (*fig*) Wachs *nt*

put-up ['putʌp] *adj*: **~ job** abgekartete(s)
Spiel *nt*

puzzle ['pʌzl] *n* Rätsel *nt*; (*toy*) Geduldspiel
nt ♦ *vt* verwirren ♦ *vi* sich den Kopf
zerbrechen; **~d** *adj* verdutzt, verblüfft;
puzzling *adj* rätselhaft, verwirrend

pyjamas [pə'dʒɑːməz] (*BRIT*) *npl* Schlafanzug
m, Pyjama *m*

pylon ['paɪlən] *n* Mast *m*

pyramid ['pɪrəmɪd] *n* Pyramide *f*

Q, q

quack [kwæk] *n* Quaken *nt*; (*doctor*)
Quacksalber *m* ♦ *vi* quaken

quad [kwɒd] *n abbr* = **quadrangle**;
quadruplet

quadrangle ['kwɒdræŋgl] *n* (*court*) Hof *m*;
(*MATH*) Viereck *nt*

quadruple [kwɒ'druːpl] *adj* ♦ *vi* sich
vervierfachen ♦ *vt* vervierfachen

quadruplets [kwɒ'druːplɪts] *npl* Vierlinge *pl*

quagmire ['kwægmaɪə'] *n* Morast *m*

quail [kweɪl] *n* (*bird*) Wachtel *f* ♦ *vi* (*vor
Angst*) zittern

quaint [kweɪnt] *adj* kurios; malerisch

quake [kweɪk] *vi* beben, zittern ♦ *n abbr* =
earthquake

qualification [kwɒlɪfɪ'keɪʃən] *n* Qualifikation
f; (*sth which limits*) Einschränkung *f*

qualified ['kwɒlɪfaɪd] *adj* (*competent*)
qualifiziert; (*limited*) bedingt

qualify ['kwɒlɪfaɪ] *vt* (*prepare*) befähigen;
(*limit*) einschränken ♦ *vi* sich qualifizieren;
to ~ as a doctor/lawyer sein
medizinisches/juristisches Staatsexamen
machen

quality ['kwɒlɪtɪ] *n* Qualität *f*; (*characteristic*)
Eigenschaft *f*

      Quality press

ⓘ **Quality press** *bezeichnet die seriösen
Tages- und Wochenzeitungen, im
Gegensatz zu den Massenblättern. Diese
Zeitungen sind fast alle großformatig und
wenden sich an den anspruchsvolleren Leser,
der voll informiert sein möchte und bereit
ist, für die Zeitungslektüre viel Zeit
aufzuwenden. Siehe auch* **tabloid press.**

quality time *n* intensiv genutzte Zeit

qualm [kwɑːm] *n* Bedenken *nt*

quandary ['kwɒndrɪ] *n*: **to be in a ~** in
Verlegenheit sein

quantity ['kwɒntɪtɪ] *n* Menge *f*; **~ surveyor**

n Baukostenkalkulator m

quarantine ['kwɔrnti:n] n Quarantäne f

quarrel ['kwɔrl] n Streit m ♦ vi sich streiten; **~some** adj streitsüchtig

quarry ['kwɔrɪ] n Steinbruch m; (animal) Wild nt; (fig) Opfer nt

quarter ['kwɔːtəʳ] n Viertel nt; (of year) Quartal nt ♦ vt (divide) vierteln; (MIL) einquartieren; **~s** npl (esp MIL) Quartier nt; **~ of an hour** Viertelstunde f; **~ final** n Viertelfinale nt; **~ly** adj vierteljährlich

quartet(te) [kwɔː'tet] n Quartett nt

quartz [kwɔːts] n Quarz m

quash [kwɔʃ] vt (verdict) aufheben

quaver ['kweɪvəʳ] vi (tremble) zittern

quay [kiː] n Kai m

queasy ['kwiːzɪ] adj übel

queen [kwiːn] n Königin f; **~ mother** n Königinmutter f

queer [kwɪəʳ] adj seltsam ♦ n (inf: homosexual) Schwule(r) m

quell [kwel] vt unterdrücken

quench [kwentʃ] vt (thirst) löschen

querulous ['kweruləs] adj nörglerisch

query ['kwɪərɪ] n (question) (An)frage f; (question mark) Fragezeichen nt ♦ vt in Zweifel ziehen, infrage or in Frage stellen

quest [kwest] n Suche f

question ['kwestʃən] n Frage f ♦ vt (ask) (be)fragen; (suspect) verhören; (doubt) infrage or in Frage stellen, bezweifeln; **beyond ~** ohne Frage; **out of the ~** ausgeschlossen; **~able** adj zweifelhaft; **~ mark** n Fragezeichen nt

questionnaire [kwestʃə'neəʳ] n Fragebogen m

queue [kjuː] (BRIT) n Schlange f ♦ vi (also: ~ up) Schlange stehen

quibble ['kwɪbl] vi kleinlich sein

quick [kwɪk] adj schnell ♦ n (of nail) Nagelhaut f; **be ~!** mach schnell!; **cut to the ~** (fig) tief getroffen; **~en** vt (hasten) beschleunigen ♦ vi sich beschleunigen; **~ly** adv schnell; **~sand** n Treibsand m; **~-witted** adj schlagfertig

quid [kwɪd] (BRIT: inf) n Pfund nt

quiet ['kwaɪət] adj (without noise) leise;

(peaceful, calm) still, ruhig ♦ n Stille f, Ruhe f ♦ vt, vi (US) = **quieten**; **keep ~!** sei still!; **~en** vi (also: **~en down**) ruhig werden ♦ vt beruhigen; **~ly** adv leise, ruhig; **~ness** n Ruhe f, Stille f

quilt [kwɪlt] n (continental ~) Steppdecke f

quin [kwɪn] n abbr = **quintuplet**

quintuplets [kwɪn'tjuːplɪts] npl Fünflinge pl

quip [kwɪp] n witzige Bemerkung f

quirk [kwɔːk] n (oddity) Eigenart f

quit [kwɪt] (pt, pp **quit** or **quitted**) vt verlassen ♦ vi aufhören

quite [kwaɪt] adv (completely) ganz, völlig; (fairly) ziemlich; **~ a few of them** ziemlich viele von ihnen; **~ (so)!** richtig!

quits [kwɪts] adj quitt; **let's call it ~** lassen wirs gut sein

quiver ['kwɪvəʳ] vi zittern ♦ n (for arrows) Köcher m

quiz [kwɪz] n (competition) Quiz nt ♦ vt prüfen; **~zical** adj fragend

quota ['kwəʊtə] n Anteil m; (COMM) Quote f

quotation [kwəʊ'teɪʃən] n Zitat nt; (price) Kostenvoranschlag m; **~ marks** npl Anführungszeichen pl

quote [kwəʊt] n = **quotation** ♦ vi (from book) zitieren ♦ vt zitieren; (price) angeben

R, r

rabbi ['ræbaɪ] n Rabbiner m; (title) Rabbi m

rabbit ['ræbɪt] n Kaninchen nt; **~ hole** n Kaninchenbau m; **~ hutch** n Kaninchenstall m

rabble ['ræbl] n Pöbel m

rabies ['reɪbiːz] n Tollwut f

RAC (BRIT) n abbr = **Royal Automobile Club**

raccoon [rə'kuːn] n Waschbär m

race [reɪs] n (species) Rasse f; (competition) Rennen nt; (on foot) Rennen nt, Wettlauf m; (rush) Hetze f ♦ vt um die Wette laufen mit; (horses) laufen lassen ♦ vi (run) rennen; (in contest) am Rennen teilnehmen; **~ car** (US) n = **racing car**; **~ car driver** (US) n = **racing driver**; **~course** n (for horses) Rennbahn f; **~horse** n Rennpferd nt; **~r** n

(*person*) Rennfahrer(in) *m(f)*; (*car*)
Rennwagen *m*; **~track** *n* (*for cars etc*)
Rennstrecke *f*

racial ['reɪʃl] *adj* Rassen-

racing ['reɪsɪŋ] *n* Rennen *nt*; **~ car** (*BRIT*) *n*
Rennwagen *m*; **~ driver** (*BRIT*) *n*
Rennfahrer *m*

racism ['reɪsɪzəm] *n* Rassismus *m*; **racist**
['reɪsɪst] *n* Rassist *m ♦ adj* rassistisch

rack [ræk] *n* Ständer *m*, Gestell *nt ♦ vt*
plagen; **to go to ~ and ruin** verfallen; **to ~
one's brains** sich *dat* den Kopf zerbrechen

racket ['rækɪt] *n* (*din*) Krach *m*; (*scheme*)
(Schwindel)geschäft *nt*; (*TENNIS*)
(Tennis)schläger *m*

racquet ['rækɪt] *n* (Tennis)schläger *m*

racy ['reɪsɪ] *adj* gewagt; (*style*) spritzig

radar ['reɪdɑːʳ] *n* Radar *nt or m*

radial ['reɪdɪəl] *adj* (*also: US*: **~-ply**) radial

radiant ['reɪdɪənt] *adj* strahlend; (*giving out
rays*) Strahlungs-

radiate ['reɪdɪeɪt] *vi* ausstrahlen; (*roads, lines*)
strahlenförmig wegführen *♦ vt* ausstrahlen;
radiation [reɪdɪ'eɪʃən] *n* (Aus)strahlung *f*

radiator ['reɪdɪeɪtəʳ] *n* (*for heating*)
Heizkörper *m*; (*AUT*) Kühler *m*

radical ['rædɪkl] *adj* radikal

radii ['reɪdɪaɪ] *npl of* **radius**

radio ['reɪdɪəu] *n* Rundfunk *m*, Radio *nt*; (*set*)
Radio *nt*, Radioapparat *m*; **on the ~** im
Radio; **~active** ['reɪdɪəu'æktɪv] *adj*
radioaktiv; **~ cassette** *n* Radiorekorder *m*;
~-controlled *adj* ferngesteuert; **~logy**
[reɪdɪ'ɔlədʒɪ] *n* Strahlenkunde *f*; **~ station** *n*
Rundfunkstation *f*; **~therapy**
['reɪdɪəu'θerəpɪ] *n* Röntgentherapie *f*

radish ['rædɪʃ] *n* (*big*) Rettich *m*; (*small*)
Radieschen *nt*

radius ['reɪdɪəs] (*pl* **radii**) *n* Radius *m*; (*area*)
Umkreis *m*

RAF *n abbr* = **Royal Air Force**

raffle ['ræfl] *n* Verlosung *f*, Tombola *f ♦ vt*
verlosen

raft [rɑːft] *n* Floß *nt*

rafter ['rɑːftəʳ] *n* Dachsparren *m*

rag [ræg] *n* (*cloth*) Lumpen *m*, Lappen *m*;
(*inf: newspaper*) Käseblatt *nt*; (*UNIV: for*

charity) studentische Sammelaktion *f ♦ vt*
(*BRIT*) auf den Arm nehmen; **~s** *npl* (*cloth*)
Lumpen *pl*; **~ doll** *n* Flickenpuppe *f*

rage [reɪdʒ] *n* Wut *f*; (*fashion*) große Mode *f
♦ vi* wüten, toben

ragged ['rægɪd] *adj* (*edge*) gezackt; (*clothes*)
zerlumpt

raid [reɪd] *n* Überfall *m*; (*MIL*) Angriff *m*; (*by
police*) Razzia *f ♦ vt* überfallen

rail [reɪl] *n* (*also RAIL*) Schiene *f*; (*on stair*)
Geländer *nt*; (*of ship*) Reling *f*; **~s** *npl* (*RAIL*)
Geleise *pl*; **by ~** per Bahn; **~ing(s)** *n(pl)*
Geländer *nt*; **~road** (*US*) *n* Eisenbahn *f*;
~way (*BRIT*) *n* Eisenbahn *f*; **~way line**
(*BRIT*) *n* (Eisen)bahnlinie *f*; (*track*) Gleis *nt*;
~wayman (*irreg; BRIT*) *n* Eisenbahner *m*;
~way station (*BRIT*) *n* Bahnhof *m*

rain [reɪn] *n* Regen *m ♦ vt, vi* regnen; **in the
~** im Regen; **it's ~ing** es regnet; **~bow** *n*
Regenbogen *m*; **~coat** *n* Regenmantel *m*;
~drop *n* Regentropfen *m*; **~fall** *n*
Niederschlag *m*; **~forest** *n* Regenwald *m*;
~y *adj* (*region, season*) Regen-; (*day*)
regnerisch, verregnet

raise [reɪz] *n* (*esp US: increase*)
(Gehalts)erhöhung *f ♦ vt* (*lift*) (hoch)heben;
(*increase*) erhöhen; (*question*) aufwerfen;
(*doubts*) äußern; (*funds*) beschaffen; (*family*)
großziehen; (*livestock*) züchten; **to ~ one's
voice** die Stimme erheben

raisin ['reɪzn] *n* Rosine *f*

rake [reɪk] *n* Rechen *m*, Harke *f*; (*person*)
Wüstling *m ♦ vt* rechen, harken; (*search*)
(durch)suchen

rally ['rælɪ] *n* (*POL etc*) Kundgebung *f*; (*AUT*)
Rallye *f ♦ vt* (*MIL*) sammeln *♦ vi* Kräfte
sammeln; **~ round** *vt fus* (sich) scharen
um; (*help*) zu Hilfe kommen *+dat ♦ vi* zu
Hilfe kommen

RAM [ræm] *n abbr* (= *random access memory*)
RAM *m*

ram [ræm] *n* Widder *m ♦ vt* (*hit*) rammen;
(*stuff*) (hinein)stopfen

ramble ['ræmbl] *n* Wanderung *f ♦ vi* (*talk*)
schwafeln; **~r** *n* Wanderer *m*; **rambling** *adj*
(*speech*) weitschweifig; (*town*) ausgedehnt

ramp [ræmp] *n* Rampe *f*; **on/off ~** (*US: AUT*)

Ein-/Ausfahrt f

rampage [ræm'peɪdʒ] n: **to be on the ~** randalieren ♦ vi randalieren

rampant ['ræmpənt] adj wild wuchernd

rampart ['ræmpɑːt] n (Schutz)wall m

ram raid n Raubüberfall, bei dem eine Geschäftsfront mit einem Fahrzeug gerammt wird

ramshackle ['ræmʃækl] adj baufällig

ran [ræn] pt of **run**

ranch [rɑːntʃ] n Ranch f

rancid ['rænsɪd] adj ranzig

rancour ['ræŋkəʳ] (US **rancor**) n Verbitterung f, Groll m

random ['rændəm] adj ziellos, wahllos ♦ n: **at ~** aufs Geratewohl; **~ access** n (COMPUT) wahlfreie(r) Zugriff m

randy ['rændɪ] (BRIT: inf) adj geil, scharf

rang [ræŋ] pt of **ring**

range [reɪndʒ] n Reihe f; (of mountains) Kette f; (COMM) Sortiment nt; (reach) (Reich)weite f; (of gun) Schussweite f; (for shooting practice) Schießplatz m; (stove) (großer) Herd m ♦ vt (set in row) anordnen, aufstellen; (roam) durchstreifen ♦ vi: **to ~ over** (wander) umherstreifen in +dat; (extend) sich erstrecken auf +acc; **a ~ of** (selection) eine (große) Auswahl an +dat; **prices ranging from £5 to £10** Preise, die sich zwischen £5 und £10 bewegen; **~r** ['reɪndʒəʳ] n Förster m

rank [ræŋk] n (row) Reihe f; (BRIT: also: **taxi ~**) (Taxi)stand m; (MIL) Rang m; (social position) Stand m ♦ vi (have ~): **to ~ among** gehören zu ♦ adj (strong-smelling) stinkend; (extreme) kraß; **the ~ and file** (fig) die breite Masse

rankle ['ræŋkl] vi nagen

ransack ['rænsæk] vt (plunder) plündern; (search) durchwühlen

ransom ['rænsəm] n Lösegeld nt; **to hold sb to ~** jdn gegen Lösegeld festhalten

rant [rænt] vi hochtrabend reden

rap [ræp] n Schlag m; (music) Rap m ♦ vt klopfen

rape [reɪp] n Vergewaltigung f; (BOT) Raps m ♦ vt vergewaltigen; **~(seed) oil** n Rapsöl nt

rapid ['ræpɪd] adj rasch, schnell; **~ity** [rə'pɪdɪtɪ] n Schnelligkeit f; **~s** npl Stromschnellen pl

rapist ['reɪpɪst] n Vergewaltiger m

rapport [ræ'pɔːʳ] n gute(s) Verhältnis nt

rapture ['ræptʃəʳ] n Entzücken nt; **rapturous** ['ræptʃərəs] adj (applause) stürmisch; (expression) verzückt

rare [rɛəʳ] adj selten, rar; (underdone) nicht durchgebraten; **~ly** ['rɛəlɪ] adv selten

raring ['rɛərɪŋ] adj: **to be ~ to go** (inf) es kaum erwarten können, bis es losgeht

rarity ['rɛərɪtɪ] n Seltenheit f

rascal ['rɑːskl] n Schuft m

rash [ræʃ] adj übereilt; (reckless) unbesonnen ♦ n (Haut)ausschlag m

rasher ['ræʃəʳ] n Speckscheibe f

raspberry ['rɑːzbərɪ] n Himbeere f

rasping ['rɑːspɪŋ] adj (noise) kratzend; (voice) krächzend

rat [ræt] n (animal) Ratte f; (person) Halunke m

rate [reɪt] n (proportion) Rate f; (price) Tarif m; (speed) Tempo nt ♦ vt (ein)schätzen; **~s** npl (BRIT: tax) Grundsteuer f; **to ~ as** für etw halten; **~able value** (BRIT) n Einheitswert m (als Bemessungsgrundlage); **~payer** (BRIT) n Steuerzahler(in) m(f)

rather ['rɑːðəʳ] adv (in preference) lieber, eher; (to some extent) ziemlich; **I would** or **I'd ~ go** ich würde lieber gehen; **it's ~ expensive** (quite) es ist ziemlich teuer; (too) es ist etwas zu teuer; **there's ~ a lot** es ist ziemlich viel

ratify ['rætɪfaɪ] vt (POL) ratifizieren

rating ['reɪtɪŋ] n Klasse f

ratio ['reɪʃɪəu] n Verhältnis nt; **in the ~ of 100 to 1** im Verhältnis 100 zu 1

ration ['ræʃən] n (usu pl) Ration f ♦ vt rationieren

rational ['ræʃənl] adj rational

rationale [ræʃə'nɑːl] n Grundprinzip nt

rationalize ['ræʃnəlaɪz] vt rationalisieren

rat race n Konkurrenzkampf m

rattle ['rætl] n (sound) Rasseln nt; (toy) Rassel f ♦ vi ratteln, klappern ♦ vt rasseln mit; **~snake** n Klapperschlange f

raucous ['rɔːkəs] *adj* heiser, rau

rave [reɪv] *vi* (*talk wildly*) fantasieren; (*rage*) toben ♦ *n* (*BRIT: inf: party*) Rave *m*, Fete *f*

raven ['reɪvən] *n* Rabe *m*

ravenous ['rævənəs] *adj* heißhungrig

ravine [rə'viːn] *n* Schlucht *f*

raving ['reɪvɪŋ] *adj*: **~ lunatic** völlig Wahnsinnige(r) *mf*

ravishing ['rævɪʃɪŋ] *adj* atemberaubend

raw [rɔː] *adj* roh; (*tender*) wund (gerieben); (*inexperienced*) unerfahren; **to get a ~ deal** (*inf*) schlecht wegkommen; **~ material** *n* Rohmaterial *nt*

ray [reɪ] *n* (*of light*) Strahl *m*; **~ of hope** Hoffnungsschimmer *m*

raze [reɪz] *vt* (*also*: **~ to the ground**) dem Erdboden gleichmachen

razor ['reɪzə*] *n* Rasierapparat *m*; **~ blade** *n* Rasierklinge *f*

Rd *abbr* = **road**

RE (*BRIT: SCH*) *abbr* (= *religious education*) Religionsunterricht *m*

re [riː] *prep* (*COMM*) betreffs +*gen*

reach [riːtʃ] *n* Reichweite *f*; (*of river*) Strecke *f* ♦ *vt* (*arrive at*) erreichen; (*give*) reichen ♦ *vi* (*stretch*) sich erstrecken; **within ~** (*shops etc*) in erreichbarer Weite *or* Entfernung; **out of ~** außer Reichweite; **to ~ for** (*try to get*) langen nach; **~ out** *vi* die Hand ausstrecken; **to ~ out for sth** nach etw greifen

react [riː'ækt] *vi* reagieren; **~ion** [riː'ækʃən] *n* Reaktion *f*; **~or** [riː'æktə*] *n* Reaktor *m*

read¹ [rɛd] *pt, pp of* **read²**

read² [riːd] (*pt, pp* **read**) *vt, vi* lesen; (*aloud*) vorlesen; **~ out** *vt* vorlesen; **~able** *adj* leserlich; (*worth ~ing*) lesenswert; **~er** *n* (*person*) Leser(in) *m(f)*; **~ership** *n* Leserschaft *f*

readily ['rɛdɪlɪ] *adv* (*willingly*) bereitwillig; (*easily*) prompt

readiness ['rɛdɪnɪs] *n* (*willingness*) Bereitwilligkeit *f*; (*being ready*) Bereitschaft *f*; **in ~** (*prepared*) bereit

reading ['riːdɪŋ] *n* Lesen *nt*

readjust [riːə'dʒʌst] *vt* neu einstellen ♦ *vi* (*person*): **to ~ to** sich wieder anpassen an

+*acc*

ready ['rɛdɪ] *adj* (*prepared, willing*) bereit ♦ *adv*: **~-cooked** vorgekocht ♦ *n*: **at the ~** bereit; **~-made** *adj* gebrauchsfertig, Fertig-; (*clothes*) Konfektions-; **~ money** *n* Bargeld *nt*; **~ reckoner** *n* Rechentabelle *f*; **~-to-wear** *adj* Konfektions-

real [rɪəl] *adj* wirklich; (*actual*) eigentlich; (*not fake*) echt; **in ~ terms** effektiv; **~ estate** *n* Grundbesitz *m*; **~istic** [rɪə'lɪstɪk] *adj* realistisch

reality [riː'ælɪtɪ] *n* Wirklichkeit *f*, Realität *f*; **in ~** in Wirklichkeit

realization [rɪəlaɪ'zeɪʃən] *n* (*understanding*) Erkenntnis *f*; (*fulfilment*) Verwirklichung *f*

realize ['rɪəlaɪz] *vt* (*understand*) begreifen; (*make real*) verwirklichen; **I didn't ~ ...** ich wusste nicht, ...

really ['rɪəlɪ] *adv* wirklich; **~?** (*indicating interest*) tatsächlich?; (*expressing surprise*) wirklich?

realm [rɛlm] *n* Reich *nt*

realtor ['rɪəltɔː*] (*US*) *n* Grundstücks-makler(in) *m(f)*

reap [riːp] *vt* ernten

reappear [riːə'pɪə*] *vi* wieder erscheinen

rear [rɪə*] *adj* hintere(r, s), Rück- ♦ *n* Rückseite *f*; (*last part*) Schluss *m* ♦ *vt* (*bring up*) aufziehen ♦ *vi* (*horse*) sich aufbäumen; **~guard** *n* Nachhut *f*

rearmament [riː'ɑːməmənt] *n* Wiederaufrüstung *f*

rearrange [riːə'reɪndʒ] *vt* umordnen

rear-view mirror ['rɪəvjuː-] *n* Rückspiegel *m*

reason ['riːzn] *n* (*cause*) Grund *m*; (*ability to think*) Verstand *m*; (*sensible thoughts*) Vernunft *f* ♦ *vi* (*think*) denken; (*use arguments*) argumentieren; **it stands to ~ that** es ist logisch, dass; **to ~ with sb** mit jdm diskutieren; **~able** *adj* vernünftig; **~ably** *adv* vernünftig; (*fairly*) ziemlich; **~ed** *adj* (*argument*) durchdacht; **~ing** *n* Urteilen *nt*; (*argumentation*) Beweisführung *f*

reassurance [riːə'ʃʊərəns] *n* Beruhigung *f*; (*confirmation*) Bestätigung *f*; **reassure** [riːə'ʃʊə*] *vt* beruhigen; **to reassure sb of**

sth jdm etw versichern
rebate ['ri:beit] n Rückzahlung f
rebel [n 'rebl, vb rɪ'bel] n Rebell m ♦ vi rebellieren; **~lion** [rɪ'beljən] n Rebellion f, Aufstand m; **~lious** [rɪ'beljəs] adj rebellisch
rebirth [ri:'bə:θ] n Wiedergeburt f
rebound [vb rɪ'baund, n 'ri:baund] vi zurückprallen ♦ n Rückprall m
rebuff [rɪ'bʌf] n Abfuhr f ♦ vt abblitzen lassen
rebuild [ri:'bɪld] (irreg) vt wieder aufbauen; (fig) wieder herstellen
rebuke [rɪ'bju:k] n Tadel m ♦ vt tadeln, rügen
rebut [rɪ'bʌt] vt widerlegen
recall [vb rɪ'kɔ:l, n 'ri:kɔ:l] vt (call back) zurückrufen; (remember) sich erinnern an +acc ♦ n Rückruf m
recap ['ri:kæp] vt, vi wiederholen
rec'd abbr (= received) Eing.
recede [rɪ'si:d] vi zurückweichen; **receding** adj: **receding hairline** Stirnglatze f
receipt [rɪ'si:t] n (document) Quittung f; (receiving) Empfang m; **~s** npl (ECON) Einnahmen pl
receive [rɪ'si:v] vt erhalten; (visitors etc) empfangen; **~r** n (TEL) Hörer m
recent ['ri:snt] adj vor kurzem (geschehen), neuerlich; (modern) neu; **~ly** adv kürzlich, neulich
receptacle [rɪ'septɪkl] n Behälter m
reception [rɪ'sepʃən] n Empfang m; **~ desk** n Empfang m; (in hotel) Rezeption f; **~ist** n (in hotel) Empfangschef m, Empfangsdame f; (MED) Sprechstundenhilfe f
receptive [rɪ'septɪv] adj aufnahmebereit
recess [rɪ'ses] n (break) Ferien pl; (hollow) Nische f
recession [rɪ'seʃən] n Rezession f
recharge [ri:'tʃɑ:dʒ] vt (battery) aufladen
recipe ['resɪpɪ] n Rezept nt
recipient [rɪ'sɪpɪənt] n Empfänger m
reciprocal [rɪ'sɪprəkl] adj gegenseitig; (mutual) wechselseitig
recital [rɪ'saɪtl] n Vortrag m
recite [rɪ'saɪt] vt vortragen, aufsagen
reckless ['rekləs] adj leichtsinnig; (driving)

fahrlässig
reckon ['rekən] vt (count) rechnen, berechnen, errechnen; (estimate) schätzen; (think): **I ~ that ...** ich nehme an, dass ...; **~ on** vt fus rechnen mit; **~ing** n (calculation) Rechnen nt
reclaim [rɪ'kleɪm] vt (expenses) zurückverlangen; (land): **to ~ (from sth)** (etw dat) gewinnen; **reclamation** [reklə'meɪʃən] n (of land) Gewinnung f
recline [rɪ'klaɪn] vi sich zurücklehnen; **reclining** adj Liege-
recluse [rɪ'klu:s] n Einsiedler m
recognition [rekəg'nɪʃən] n (recognizing) Erkennen nt; (acknowledgement) Anerkennung f; **transformed beyond ~** völlig verändert
recognizable ['rekəgnaɪzəbl] adj erkennbar
recognize ['rekəgnaɪz] vt erkennen; (POL, approve) anerkennen; **to ~ as** anerkennen als; **to ~ by** erkennen an +dat
recoil [rɪ'kɔɪl] vi (in horror) zurückschrecken; (rebound) zurückprallen; (person): **to ~ from doing sth** davor zurückschrecken, etw zu tun
recollect [rekə'lekt] vt sich erinnern an +acc; **~ion** [rekə'lekʃən] n Erinnerung f
recommend [rekə'mend] vt empfehlen; **~ation** [rekəmen'deɪʃən] n Empfehlung f
recompense ['rekəmpens] n (compensation) Entschädigung f; (reward) Belohnung f ♦ vt entschädigen; belohnen
reconcile ['rekənsaɪl] vt (facts) vereinbaren; (people) versöhnen; **to ~ o.s. to sth** sich mit etw abfinden; **reconciliation** [rekənsɪlɪ'eɪʃən] n Versöhnung f
recondition [ri:kən'dɪʃən] vt (machine) generalüberholen
reconnoitre [rekə'nɔɪtər] (US **reconnoiter**) vt erkunden ♦ vi aufklären
reconsider [ri:kən'sɪdər] vt von neuem erwägen, noch einmal überdenken ♦ vi es noch einmal überdenken
reconstruct [ri:kən'strʌkt] vt wieder aufbauen; (crime) rekonstruieren
record [n 'rekɔ:d, vb rɪ'kɔ:d] n Aufzeichnung f; (MUS) Schallplatte f; (best performance)

Rekord *m* ♦ *vt* aufzeichnen; (*music etc*) aufnehmen; **off the ~** vertraulich, im Vertrauen; **in ~ time** in Rekordzeit; **~ card** *n* (*in file*) Karteikarte *f*; **~ed delivery** (*BRIT*) *n* (*POST*) Einschreiben *nt*; **~er** *n* (*TECH*) Registriergerät *nt*; (*MUS*) Blockflöte *f*; **~ holder** *n* (*SPORT*) Rekordinhaber *m*; **~ing** *n* (*MUS*) Aufnahme *f*; **~ player** *n* Plattenspieler *m*

recount [rɪˈkaunt] *vt* (*tell*) berichten

re-count [ˈriːkaunt] *n* Nachzählung *f*

recoup [rɪˈkuːp] *vt*: **to ~ one's losses** seinen Verlust wieder gutmachen

recourse [rɪˈkɔːs] *n*: **to have ~ to** Zuflucht nehmen zu *or* bei

recover [rɪˈkʌvəʳ] *vt* (*get back*) zurückerhalten ♦ *vi* sich erholen

re-cover [riːˈkʌvəʳ] *vt* (*quilt etc*) neu überziehen

recovery [rɪˈkʌvərɪ] *n* Wiedererlangung *f*; (*of health*) Erholung *f*

recreate [riːkrɪˈeɪt] *vt* wieder herstellen

recreation [rekrɪˈeɪʃən] *n* Erholung *f*; **~al** *adj* Erholungs-; **~al drug** *n* Freizeitdroge *f*

recrimination [rɪkrɪmɪˈneɪʃən] *n* Gegenbeschuldigung *f*

recruit [rɪˈkruːt] *n* Rekrut *m* ♦ *vt* rekrutieren; **~ment** *n* Rekrutierung *f*

rectangle [ˈrektæŋgl] *n* Rechteck *nt*; **rectangular** [rekˈtæŋgjuləʳ] *adj* rechteckig, rechtwinklig

rectify [ˈrektɪfaɪ] *vt* berichtigen

rector [ˈrektəʳ] *n* (*REL*) Pfarrer *m*; (*SCH*) Direktor(in) *m(f)*; **~y** [ˈrektərɪ] *n* Pfarrhaus *nt*

recuperate [rɪˈkjuːpəreɪt] *vi* sich erholen

recur [rɪˈkəːʳ] *vi* sich wiederholen; **~rence** *n* Wiederholung *f*; **~rent** *adj* wiederkehrend

recycle [riːˈsaɪkl] *vt* wieder verwerten, wieder aufbereiten; **recycling** *n* Recycling *nt*

red [red] *n* Rot *nt*; (*POL*) Rote(r) *m* ♦ *adj* rot; **in the ~** in den roten Zahlen; **~ carpet treatment** *n* Sonderbehandlung *f*, große(r) Bahnhof *m*; **R~ Cross** *n* Rote(s) Kreuz *nt*; **~currant** *n* rote Johannisbeere *f*; **~den** *vi* sich röten; (*blush*) erröten ♦ *vt* röten; **~dish** *adj* rötlich

redecorate [riːˈdekəreɪt] *vt* neu tapezieren, neu streichen

redeem [rɪˈdiːm] *vt* (*COMM*) einlösen; (*save*) retten; **~ing** *adj*: **~ing feature** versöhnende(s) Moment *nt*

redeploy [riːdɪˈplɔɪ] *vt* (*resources*) umverteilen

red: ~-haired [redˈheəd] *adj* rothaarig; **~-handed** [redˈhændɪd] *adv*: **to be caught ~-handed** auf frischer Tat ertappt werden; **~head** [ˈredhed] *n* Rothaarige(r) *mf*; **~ herring** *n* Ablenkungsmanöver *nt*; **~-hot** [redˈhɒt] *adj* rot glühend

redirect [riːdaɪˈrekt] *vt* umleiten

red light *n*: **to go through a ~** (*AUT*) bei Rot über die Ampel fahren; **red-light district** *n* Strichviertel *nt*

redo [riːˈduː] (*irreg: like* **do**) *vt* nochmals machen

redolent [ˈredələnt] *adj*: **~ of** (*fig*) erinnernd an +*acc*

redouble [riːˈdʌbl] *vt*: **to ~ one's efforts** seine Anstrengungen verdoppeln

redress [rɪˈdres] *vt* wieder gutmachen

red: R~ Sea *n*: **the R~ Sea** das Rote Meer; **~skin** [ˈredskɪn] *n* Rothaut *f*; **~ tape** *n* Bürokratismus *m*

reduce [rɪˈdjuːs] *vt* (*speed, temperature*) vermindern; (*photo*) verkleinern; **"~ speed now"** (*AUT*) ≃ "langsam"; **to ~ the price (to)** den Preis herabsetzen (auf +*acc*); **at a ~d price** zum ermäßigten Preis

reduction [rɪˈdʌkʃən] *n* Verminderung *f*; Verkleinerung *f*; Herabsetzung *f*; (*amount of money*) Nachlass *m*

redundancy [rɪˈdʌndənsɪ] *n* Überflüssigkeit *f*; (*of workers*) Entlassung *f*

redundant [rɪˈdʌndnt] *adj* überflüssig; (*workers*) ohne Arbeitsplatz; **to be made ~** arbeitslos werden

reed [riːd] *n* Schilf *nt*; (*MUS*) Rohrblatt *nt*

reef [riːf] *n* Riff *nt*

reek [riːk] *vi*: **to ~ (of)** stinken (nach)

reel [riːl] *n* Spule *f*, Rolle *f* ♦ *vt* (*also*: **~ in**) wickeln, spulen ♦ *vi* (*stagger*) taumeln

ref [ref] (*inf*) *n abbr* (= *referee*) Schiri *m*

refectory [rɪˈfektərɪ] *n* (*UNIV*) Mensa *f*; (*SCH*)

Speisesaal *m*; (*ECCL*) Refektorium *nt*

refer [rɪˈfəːʳ] *vt*: **to ~ sb to sb/sth** jdn an jdn/etw verweisen ♦ *vi*: **to ~ to** (*to book*) nachschlagen in +*dat*; (*mention*) sich beziehen auf +*acc*

referee [refəˈriː] *n* Schiedsrichter *m*; (*BRIT: for job*) Referenz *f* ♦ *vt* schiedsrichtern

reference [ˈrefrəns] *n* (*for job*) Referenz *f*; (*in book*) Verweis *m*; (*number, code*) Aktenzeichen *nt*; (*allusion*): **~ (to)** Anspielung (auf +*acc*); **with ~ to** in Bezug auf +*acc*; **~ book** *n* Nachschlagewerk *nt*; **~ number** *n* Aktenzeichen *nt*

referenda [refəˈrenda] *npl of* **referendum**

referendum [refəˈrendəm] (*pl* **-da**) *n* Volksabstimmung *f*

refill [*vb* riːˈfɪl, *n* ˈriːfɪl] *vt* nachfüllen ♦ *n* (*for pen*) Ersatzmine *f*

refine [rɪˈfaɪn] *vt* (*purify*) raffinieren; **~d** *adj* kultiviert; **~ment** *n* Kultiviertheit *f*; **~ry** *n* Raffinerie *f*

reflect [rɪˈflekt] *vt* (*light*) reflektieren; (*fig*) (wider)spiegeln ♦ *vi* (*meditate*): **to ~ (on)** nachdenken (über +*acc*); **it ~s badly/well on him** das stellt ihn in ein schlechtes/ gutes Licht; **~ion** [rɪˈflekʃən] *n* Reflexion *f*; (*image*) Spiegelbild *nt*; (*thought*) Überlegung *f*; **on ~ion** wenn man sich *dat* das recht überlegt

reflex [ˈriːfleks] *adj* Reflex- ♦ *n* Reflex *m*; **~ive** [rɪˈfleksɪv] *adj* reflexiv

reform [rɪˈfɔːm] *n* Reform *f* ♦ *vt* (*person*) bessern; **~atory** (*US*) *n* Besserungsanstalt *f*

refrain [rɪˈfreɪn] *vi*: **to ~ from** unterlassen ♦ *n* Refrain *m*

refresh [rɪˈfreʃ] *vt* erfrischen; **~er course** (*BRIT*) *n* Wiederholungskurs *m*; **~ing** *adj* erfrischend; **~ments** *npl* Erfrischungen *pl*

refrigeration [rɪfrɪdʒəˈreɪʃən] *n* Kühlung *f*

refrigerator [rɪˈfrɪdʒəreɪtəʳ] *n* Kühlschrank *m*

refuel [riːˈfjuəl] *vt*, *vi* auftanken

refuge [ˈrefjuːdʒ] *n* Zuflucht *f*; **to take ~ in** sich flüchten in +*acc*; **~e** [refjuˈdʒiː] *n* Flüchtling *m*

refund [*n* ˈriːfʌnd, *vb* rɪˈfʌnd] *n* Rückvergütung *f* ♦ *vt* zurückerstatten

refurbish [riːˈfəːbɪʃ] *vt* aufpolieren

refusal [rɪˈfjuːzəl] *n* (Ver)weigerung *f*; **first ~** Vorkaufsrecht *nt*

refuse¹ [rɪˈfjuːz] *vt* abschlagen ♦ *vi* sich weigern

refuse² [ˈrefjuːs] *n* Abfall *m*, Müll *m*; **~ collection** *n* Müllabfuhr *f*

refute [rɪˈfjuːt] *vt* widerlegen

regain [rɪˈɡeɪn] *vt* wiedergewinnen; (*consciousness*) wiedererlangen

regal [ˈriːɡl] *adj* königlich

regalia [rɪˈɡeɪlɪə] *npl* Insignien *pl*

regard [rɪˈɡaːd] *n* Achtung *f* ♦ *vt* ansehen; **to send one's ~s to sb** jdn grüßen lassen; **"with kindest ~s"** „mit freundlichen Grüßen"; **~ing** *or* **as ~s** *or* **with ~ to** bezüglich +*gen*, in Bezug auf +*acc*; **~less** *adj*: **~less of** ohne Rücksicht auf +*acc* ♦ *adv* trotzdem

regenerate [rɪˈdʒenəreɪt] *vt* erneuern

régime [reɪˈʒiːm] *n* Regime *nt*

regiment [*n* ˈredʒɪmənt, *vb* ˈredʒɪment] *n* Regiment *nt* ♦ *vt* (*fig*) reglementieren; **~al** [redʒɪˈmentl] *adj* Regiments-

region [ˈriːdʒən] *n* Region *f*; **in the ~ of** (*fig*) so um; **~al** *adj* örtlich, regional

register [ˈredʒɪstəʳ] *n* Register *nt* ♦ *vt* (*list*) registrieren; (*emotion*) zeigen; (*write down*) eintragen ♦ *vi* (*at hotel*) sich eintragen; (*with police*) sich melden; (*make impression*) wirken, ankommen; **~ed** (*BRIT*) *adj* (*letter*) Einschreibe-, eingeschrieben; **~ed trademark** *n* eingetragene(s) Warenzeichen *nt*

registrar [ˈredʒɪstraːʳ] *n* Standesbeamte(r) *m*

registration [redʒɪsˈtreɪʃən] *n* (*act*) Registrierung *f*; (*AUT: also:* **~ number**) polizeiliche(s) Kennzeichen *nt*

registry [ˈredʒɪstrɪ] *n* Sekretariat *nt*; **~ office** (*BRIT*) *n* Standesamt *nt*; **to get married in a ~ office** standesamtlich heiraten

regret [rɪˈɡret] *n* Bedauern *nt* ♦ *vt* bedauern; **~fully** *adv* mit Bedauern, ungern; **~table** *adj* bedauerlich

regroup [riːˈɡruːp] *vt* umgruppieren ♦ *vi* sich umgruppieren

regular [ˈreɡjuləʳ] *adj* regelmäßig; (*usual*) üblich; (*inf*) regelrecht ♦ *n* (*client etc*)

Stammkunde *m*; **~ity** [regju'lærɪtɪ] *n* Regelmäßigkeit *f*; **~ly** *adv* regelmäßig

regulate ['regjuleɪt] *vt* regeln, regulieren; **regulation** [regju'leɪʃən] *n* (*rule*) Vorschrift *f*; (*control*) Regulierung *f*

rehabilitation ['ri:əbɪlɪ'teɪʃən] *n* (*of criminal*) Resozialisierung *f*

rehearsal [rɪ'hə:səl] *n* Probe *f*

rehearse [rɪ'hə:s] *vt* proben

reign [reɪn] *n* Herrschaft *f* ♦ *vi* herrschen

reimburse [ri:ɪm'bə:s] *vt*: **to ~ sb for sth** jdn für etw entschädigen; jdm etw zurückzahlen

rein [reɪn] *n* Zügel *m*

reincarnation [ri:ɪnkɑ:'neɪʃən] *n* Wiedergeburt *f*

reindeer ['reɪndɪər] *n* Ren *nt*

reinforce [ri:ɪn'fɔ:s] *vt* verstärken; **~d concrete** *n* Stahlbeton *m*; **~ment** *n* Verstärkung *f*; **~ments** *npl* (*MIL*) Verstärkungstruppen *pl*

reinstate [ri:ɪn'steɪt] *vt* wieder einsetzen

reissue [ri:'ɪʃju:] *vt* neu herausgeben

reiterate [ri:'ɪtəreɪt] *vt* wiederholen

reject [*n* 'ri:dʒekt, *vb* rɪ'dʒekt] *n* (*COMM*) Ausschuss(artikel) *m* ♦ *vt* ablehnen; **~ion** [rɪ'dʒekʃən] *n* Zurückweisung *f*

rejoice [rɪ'dʒɔɪs] *vi*: **to ~ at** *or* **over** sich freuen über +*acc*

rejuvenate [rɪ'dʒu:vəneɪt] *vt* verjüngen

rekindle [ri:'kɪndl] *vt* wieder anfachen

relapse [rɪ'læps] *n* Rückfall *m*

relate [rɪ'leɪt] *vt* (*tell*) erzählen; (*connect*) verbinden ♦ *vi*: **to ~ to** zusammenhängen mit; (*form relationship*) eine Beziehung aufbauen zu; **~d** *adj*: **~d (to)** verwandt (mit); **relating** *prep*: **relating to** bezüglich +*gen*; **relation** [rɪ'leɪʃən] *n* Verwandte(r) *mf*; (*connection*) Beziehung *f*; **relationship** *n* Verhältnis *nt*, Beziehung *f*

relative ['relətɪv] *n* Verwandte(r) *mf* ♦ *adj* relativ; **~ly** *adv* verhältnismäßig

relax [rɪ'læks] *vi* (*slacken*) sich lockern; (*muscles, person*) sich entspannen ♦ *vt* (*ease*) lockern, entspannen; **~ation** [ri:læk'seɪʃən] *n* Entspannung *f*; **~ed** *adj* entspannt, locker; **~ing** *adj* entspannend

relay [*n* 'ri:leɪ, *vb* rɪ'leɪ] *n* (*SPORT*) Staffel *f* ♦ *vt* (*message*) weiterleiten; (*RAD, TV*) übertragen

release [rɪ'li:s] *n* (*freedom*) Entlassung *f*; (*TECH*) Auslöser *m* ♦ *vt* befreien; (*prisoner*) entlassen; (*report, news*) verlautbaren, bekannt geben

relegate ['relɪgeɪt] *vt* (*SPORT*): **to be ~d** absteigen

relent [rɪ'lent] *vi* nachgeben; **~less** *adj* unnachgiebig

relevant ['relɪvənt] *adj* wichtig, relevant; **~ to** relevant für

reliability [rɪlaɪə'bɪlɪtɪ] *n* Zuverlässigkeit *f*

reliable [rɪ'laɪəbl] *adj* zuverlässig; **reliably** *adv* zuverlässig; **to be reliably informed that ...** aus zuverlässiger Quelle wissen, dass ...

reliance [rɪ'laɪəns] *n*: **~ (on)** Abhängigkeit *f* (von)

relic ['relɪk] *n* (*from past*) Überbleibsel *nt*; (*REL*) Reliquie *f*

relief [rɪ'li:f] *n* Erleichterung *f*; (*help*) Hilfe *f*; (*person*) Ablösung *f*

relieve [rɪ'li:v] *vt* (*ease*) erleichtern; (*help*) entlasten; (*person*) ablösen; **to ~ sb of sth** jdm etw abnehmen; **to ~ o.s.** (*euph*) sich erleichtern (*euph*); **~d** *adj* erleichtert

religion [rɪ'lɪdʒən] *n* Religion *f*; **religious** [rɪ'lɪdʒəs] *adj* religiös

relinquish [rɪ'lɪŋkwɪʃ] *vt* aufgeben

relish ['relɪʃ] *n* Würze *f* ♦ *vt* genießen; **to ~ doing** gern tun

relocate [ri:ləu'keɪt] *vt* verlegen ♦ *vi* umziehen

reluctance [rɪ'lʌktəns] *n* Widerstreben *nt*, Abneigung *f*

reluctant [rɪ'lʌktənt] *adj* widerwillig; **~ly** *adv* ungern

rely [rɪ'laɪ] *vt fus*: **to ~ on** sich verlassen auf +*acc*

remain [rɪ'meɪn] *vi* (*be left*) übrig bleiben; (*stay*) bleiben; **~der** *n* Rest *m*; **~ing** *adj* übrig (geblieben); **~s** *npl* Überreste *pl*

remake ['ri:meɪk] *n* (*CINE*) Neuverfilmung *f*

remand [rɪ'mɑ:nd] *n*: **on ~** in Untersuchungshaft ♦ *vt*: **to ~ in custody** in Untersuchungshaft schicken; **~ home**

(BRIT) n Untersuchungsgefängnis nt für Jugendliche

remark [rɪˈmɑːk] n Bemerkung f ♦ vt bemerken; **~able** adj bemerkenswert; **remarkably** adv außergewöhnlich

remarry [riːˈmærɪ] vi sich wieder verheiraten

remedial [rɪˈmiːdɪəl] adj Heil-; (teaching) Hilfsschul-

remedy [ˈremədɪ] n Mittel nt ♦ vt (pain) abhelfen +dat; (trouble) in Ordnung bringen

remember [rɪˈmembəʳ] vt sich erinnern an +acc; **remembrance** [rɪˈmembrəns] n Erinnerung f; (official) Gedenken nt; **R~ Day** n ≈ Volkstrauertag m

---

Remembrance Day

i **Remembrance Day** oder **Remembrance Sunday** ist der britische Gedenktag für die Gefallenen der beiden Weltkriege und anderer Konflikte. Er fällt auf einen Sonntag vor oder nach dem 11. November (am 11. November 1918 endete der erste Weltkrieg) und wird mit einer Schweigeminute, Kranzniederlegungen an Kriegerdenkmälern und dem Tragen von Anstecknadeln in Form einer Mohnblume begangen.

---

remind [rɪˈmaɪnd] vt: **to ~ sb to do sth** jdn daran erinnern, etw zu tun; **to ~ sb of sth** jdn an etw acc erinnern; **she ~s me of her mother** sie erinnert mich an ihre Mutter; **~er** n Mahnung f

reminisce [remɪˈnɪs] vi in Erinnerungen schwelgen; **~nt** [remɪˈnɪsnt] adj: **to be ~nt of sth** an etw acc erinnern

remiss [rɪˈmɪs] adj nachlässig

remission [rɪˈmɪʃən] n Nachlass m; (of debt, sentence) Erlass m

remit [rɪˈmɪt] vt (money): **to ~ (to)** überweisen (an +acc); **~tance** n Geldanweisung f

remnant [ˈremnənt] n Rest m; **~s** npl (COMM) Einzelstücke pl

remorse [rɪˈmɔːs] n Gewissensbisse pl; **~ful** adj reumütig; **~less** adj unbarmherzig

remote [rɪˈməut] adj abgelegen; (slight) gering; **~ control** n Fernsteuerung f; **~ly** adv entfernt

remould [ˈriːməuld] (BRIT) n runderneuerte(r) Reifen m

removable [rɪˈmuːvəbl] adj entfernbar

removal [rɪˈmuːvəl] n Beseitigung f; (of furniture) Umzug m; (from office) Entlassung f; **~ van** (BRIT) n Möbelwagen m

remove [rɪˈmuːv] vt beseitigen, entfernen; **~rs** npl Möbelspedition f

remuneration [rɪmjuːnəˈreɪʃən] n Vergütung f, Honorar nt

render [ˈrendəʳ] vt machen; (translate) übersetzen; **~ing** n (MUS) Wiedergabe f

rendezvous [ˈrɒndɪvuː] n (meeting) Rendezvous nt; (place) Treffpunkt m ♦ vi sich treffen

renew [rɪˈnjuː] vt erneuern; (contract, licence) verlängern; (replace) ersetzen; **~able** adj regenerierbar; **~al** n Erneuerung f; Verlängerung f

renounce [rɪˈnauns] vt (give up) verzichten auf +acc; (disown) verstoßen

renovate [ˈrenəveɪt] vt renovieren; (building) restaurieren

renown [rɪˈnaun] n Ruf m; **~ed** adj namhaft

rent [rent] n Miete f; (for land) Pacht f ♦ vt (hold as tenant) mieten; pachten; (let) vermieten; verpachten; (car etc) mieten; (firm) vermieten; **~al** n Miete f

renunciation [rɪnʌnsɪˈeɪʃən] n: **~ (of)** Verzicht m (auf +acc)

reorganize [riːˈɔːɡənaɪz] vt umgestalten, reorganisieren

rep [rep] n abbr (COMM) = **representative**; (THEAT) = **repertory**

repair [rɪˈpeəʳ] n Reparatur f ♦ vt reparieren; (damage) wieder gutmachen; **in good/bad ~** in gutem/schlechtem Zustand; **~ kit** n Werkzeugkasten m

repartee [repɑːˈtiː] n Witzeleien pl

repatriate [riːˈpætrɪeɪt] vt in die Heimat zurückschicken

repay [riːˈpeɪ] (irreg) vt zurückzahlen; (reward) vergelten; **~ment** n Rückzahlung f; (fig) Vergeltung f

repeal [rɪˈpiːl] vt aufheben

repeat [rɪ'piːt] n (*RAD, TV*) Wiederholung(ssendung) f ♦ vt wiederholen; **~edly** adv wiederholt

repel [rɪ'pɛl] vt (*drive back*) zurückschlagen; (*disgust*) abstoßen; **~lent** adj abstoßend ♦ n: **insect ~lent** Insektenmittel nt

repent [rɪ'pɛnt] vt, vi: **to ~ (of)** bereuen; **~ance** n Reue f

repercussion [riːpə'kʌʃən] n Auswirkung f; **to have ~s** ein Nachspiel haben

repertory ['rɛpətərɪ] n Repertoire nt

repetition [rɛpɪ'tɪʃən] n Wiederholung f

repetitive [rɪ'pɛtɪtɪv] adj sich wiederholend

replace [rɪ'pleɪs] vt ersetzen; (*put back*) zurückstellen; **~ment** n Ersatz m

replay ['riːpleɪ] n (*of match*) Wiederholungsspiel nt; (*of tape, film*) Wiederholung f

replenish [rɪ'plɛnɪʃ] vt ergänzen

replica ['rɛplɪkə] n Kopie f

reply [rɪ'plaɪ] n Antwort f ♦ vi antworten; **~ coupon** n Antwortschein m

report [rɪ'pɔːt] n Bericht m; (*BRIT: SCH*) Zeugnis nt ♦ vt (*tell*) berichten; (*give information against*) melden; (*to police*) anzeigen ♦ vi (*make ~*) Bericht erstatten; (*present o.s.*): **to ~ (to sb)** sich (bei jdm) melden; **~ card** n (*US, SCOTTISH*) n Zeugnis nt; **~edly** adv wie verlautet; **~er** n Reporter m

reprehensible [rɛprɪ'hɛnsɪbl] adj tadelnswert

represent [rɛprɪ'zɛnt] vt darstellen; (*speak for*) vertreten; **~ation** [rɛprɪzɛn'teɪʃən] n Darstellung f; (*being ~ed*) Vertretung f; **~ations** npl (*protest*) Vorhaltungen pl; **~ative** n (*person*) Vertreter m; (*US: POL*) Abgeordnete(r) mf ♦ adj repräsentativ

repress [rɪ'prɛs] vt unterdrücken; **~ion** [rɪ'prɛʃən] n Unterdrückung f

reprieve [rɪ'priːv] n (*JUR*) Begnadigung f; (*fig*) Gnadenfrist f ♦ vt (*JUR*) begnadigen

reprimand ['rɛprɪmɑːnd] n Verweis m ♦ vt einen Verweis erteilen +dat

reprint [n 'riːprɪnt, vb riː'prɪnt] n Neudruck m ♦ vt wieder abdrucken

reprisal [rɪ'praɪzl] n Vergeltung f

reproach [rɪ'prəʊtʃ] n Vorwurf m ♦ vt Vorwürfe machen +dat; **to ~ sb with sth** jdm etw vorwerfen; **~ful** adj vorwurfsvoll

reproduce [riːprə'djuːs] vt reproduzieren ♦ vi (*have offspring*) sich vermehren; **reproduction** [riːprə'dʌkʃən] n (*ART, PHOT*) Reproduktion f; (*breeding*) Fortpflanzung f; **reproductive** [riːprə'dʌktɪv] adj reproduktiv; (*breeding*) Fortpflanzungs-

reprove [rɪ'pruːv] vt tadeln

reptile ['rɛptaɪl] n Reptil nt

republic [rɪ'pʌblɪk] n Republik f

repudiate [rɪ'pjuːdɪeɪt] vt zurückweisen

repugnant [rɪ'pʌgnənt] adj widerlich

repulse [rɪ'pʌls] vt (*drive back*) zurückschlagen; (*reject*) abweisen

repulsive [rɪ'pʌlsɪv] adj abstoßend

reputable ['rɛpjutəbl] adj angesehen

reputation [rɛpju'teɪʃən] n Ruf m

reputed [rɪ'pjuːtɪd] adj angeblich; **~ly** [rɪ'pjuːtɪdlɪ] adv angeblich

request [rɪ'kwɛst] n Bitte f ♦ vt (*thing*) erbitten; **to ~ sth of or from sb** jdn um etw bitten; (*formally*) jdn um etw ersuchen; **~ stop** (*BRIT*) n Bedarfshaltestelle f

require [rɪ'kwaɪə] vt (*need*) brauchen; (*demand*) erfordern; **~ment** n (*condition*) Anforderung f; (*need*) Bedarf m

requisite ['rɛkwɪzɪt] adj erforderlich

requisition [rɛkwɪ'zɪʃən] n Anforderung f ♦ vt beschlagnahmen

rescue ['rɛskjuː] n Rettung f ♦ vt retten; **~ party** n Rettungsmannschaft f; **~r** n Retter m

research [rɪ'səːtʃ] n Forschung f ♦ vi forschen ♦ vt erforschen; **~er** n Forscher m

resemblance [rɪ'zɛmbləns] n Ähnlichkeit f

resemble [rɪ'zɛmbl] vt ähneln +dat

resent [rɪ'zɛnt] vt übel nehmen; **~ful** adj nachtragend, empfindlich; **~ment** n Verstimmung f, Unwille m

reservation [rɛzə'veɪʃən] n (*booking*) Reservierung f; (*THEAT*) Vorbestellung f; (*doubt*) Vorbehalt m; (*land*) Reservat nt

reserve [rɪ'zəːv] n (*store*) Vorrat m, Reserve f; (*manner*) Zurückhaltung f; (*game ~*) Naturschutzgebiet nt; (*SPORT*)

Ersatzspieler(in) *m(f)* ♦ *vt* reservieren; (*judgement*) sich *dat* vorbehalten; **~s** *npl* (*MIL*) Reserve *f*; **in ~** in Reserve; **~d** *adj* reserviert

reshuffle [riːˈʃʌfl] *n* (*POL*): **cabinet ~** Kabinettsumbildung *f* ♦ *vt* (*POL*) umbilden

reside [rɪˈzaɪd] *vi* wohnen, ansässig sein

residence [ˈrezɪdəns] *n* (*house*) Wohnsitz *m*; (*living*) Aufenthalt *m*; **~ permit** (*BRIT*) *n* Aufenthaltserlaubnis *f*

resident [ˈrezɪdənt] *n* (*in house*) Bewohner *m*; (*in area*) Einwohner *m* ♦ *adj* wohnhaft, ansässig; **~ial** [rezɪˈdenʃəl] *adj* Wohn-

residue [ˈrezɪdjuː] *n* Rest *m*; (*CHEM*) Rückstand *m*; (*fig*) Bodensatz *m*

resign [rɪˈzaɪn] *vt* (*office*) aufgeben, zurücktreten von ♦ *vi* (*from office*) zurücktreten; (*employee*) kündigen; **to be ~ed to sth, to ~ o.s. to sth** sich mit etw abfinden; **~ation** [rezɪɡˈneɪʃən] *n* (*from job*) Kündigung *f*; (*POL*) Rücktritt *m*; (*submission*) Resignation *f*; **~ed** *adj* resigniert

resilience [rɪˈzɪlɪəns] *n* Spannkraft *f*; (*of person*) Unverwüstlichkeit *f*; **resilient** [rɪˈzɪlɪənt] *adj* unverwüstlich

resin [ˈrezɪn] *n* Harz *nt*

resist [rɪˈzɪst] *vt* widerstehen +*dat*; **~ance** *n* Widerstand *m*

resit [*vb* riːˈsɪt, *n* ˈriːsɪt] *vt* (*exam*) wiederholen ♦ *n* Wiederholung(sprüfung) *f*

resolute [ˈrezəluːt] *adj* entschlossen, resolut; **resolution** [rezəˈluːʃən] *n* (*firmness*) Entschlossenheit *f*; (*intention*) Vorsatz *m*; (*decision*) Beschluss *m*

resolve [rɪˈzɒlv] *n* Entschlossenheit *f* ♦ *vt* (*decide*) beschließen ♦ *vi* sich lösen; **~d** *adj* (*fest*) entschlossen

resonant [ˈrezənənt] *adj* voll

resort [rɪˈzɔːt] *n* (*holiday place*) Erholungsort *m*; (*help*) Zuflucht *f* ♦ *vi*: **to ~ to** Zuflucht nehmen zu; **as a last ~** als letzter Ausweg

resound [rɪˈzaund] *vi*: **to ~ (with)** widerhallen (von); **~ing** *adj* nachhallend; (*success*) groß

resource [rɪˈsɔːs] *n* Findigkeit *f*; **~s** *npl* (*financial*) Geldmittel *pl*; (*natural*) Bodenschätze *pl*; **~ful** *adj* findig

respect [rɪsˈpekt] *n* Respekt *m* ♦ *vt* achten, respektieren; **~s** *npl* (*regards*) Grüße *pl*; **with ~ to** in Bezug auf +*acc*, hinsichtlich +*gen*; **in this ~** in dieser Hinsicht; **~able** *adj* anständig; (*not bad*) leidlich; **~ful** *adj* höflich

respective [rɪsˈpektɪv] *adj* jeweilig; **~ly** *adv* beziehungsweise

respiration [respɪˈreɪʃən] *n* Atmung *f*

respite [ˈrespaɪt] *n* Ruhepause *f*

resplendent [rɪsˈplendənt] *adj* strahlend

respond [rɪsˈpɒnd] *vi* antworten; (*react*): **to ~ (to)** reagieren (auf +*acc*); **response** [rɪsˈpɒns] *n* Antwort *f*; Reaktion *f*; (*to advert*) Resonanz *f*

responsibility [rɪspɒnsɪˈbɪlɪtɪ] *n* Verantwortung *f*

responsible [rɪsˈpɒnsɪbl] *adj* verantwortlich; (*reliable*) verantwortungsvoll

responsive [rɪsˈpɒnsɪv] *adj* empfänglich

rest [rest] *n* Ruhe *f*; (*break*) Pause *f*; (*remainder*) Rest *m* ♦ *vi* sich ausruhen; (*be supported*) (auf)liegen ♦ *vt* (*lean*): **to ~ sth on/against sth** etw gegen etw *acc* lehnen; **the ~ of them** die Übrigen; **it ~s with him to ...** es liegt bei ihm, zu ...

restaurant [ˈrestərɒn] *n* Restaurant *nt*; **~ car** (*BRIT*) *n* Speisewagen *m*

restful [ˈrestful] *adj* erholsam, ruhig

rest home *n* Erholungsheim *nt*

restive [ˈrestɪv] *adj* unruhig

restless [ˈrestlɪs] *adj* unruhig

restoration [restəˈreɪʃən] *n* Rückgabe *f*; (*of building etc*) Rückerstattung *f*

restore [rɪsˈtɔːr] *vt* (*order*) wieder herstellen; (*customs*) wieder einführen; (*person to position*) wieder einsetzen; (*give back*) zurückgeben; (*renovate*) restaurieren

restrain [rɪsˈtreɪn] *vt* zurückhalten; (*curiosity etc*) beherrschen; (*person*): **to ~ sb from doing sth** jdn davon abhalten, etw zu tun; **~ed** *adj* (*style etc*) gedämpft, verhalten; **~t** *n* (*self-control*) Zurückhaltung *f*

restrict [rɪsˈtrɪkt] *vt* einschränken; **~ion** [rɪsˈtrɪkʃən] *n* Einschränkung *f*; **~ive** *adj* einschränkend

rest room (*US*) *n* Toilette *f*

restructure [riː'strʌktʃəʳ] vt umstrukturieren

result [rɪ'zʌlt] n Resultat nt, Folge f; (of exam, game) Ergebnis nt ♦ vi: **to ~ in sth** etw zur Folge haben; **as a ~ of** als Folge +gen

resume [rɪ'zjuːm] vt fortsetzen; (occupy again) wieder einnehmen ♦ vi (work etc) wieder beginnen

résumé ['reɪzjuːmeɪ] n Zusammenfassung f

resumption [rɪ'zʌmpʃən] n Wiederaufnahme f

resurgence [rɪ'səːdʒəns] n Wiedererwachen nt

resurrection [rezə'rekʃən] n Auferstehung f

resuscitate [rɪ'sʌsɪteɪt] vt wieder beleben; **resuscitation** [rɪsʌsɪ'teɪʃən] n Wiederbelebung f

retail [n, adj 'riːteɪl, vb 'riː'teɪl] n Einzelhandel m ♦ adj Einzelhandels- ♦ vt im Kleinen verkaufen ♦ vi im Einzelhandel kosten; **~er** ['riːteɪləʳ] n Einzelhändler m, Kleinhändler m; **~ price** n Ladenpreis m

retain [rɪ'teɪn] vt (keep) (zurück)behalten; **~er** n (fee) (Honorar)vorschuss m

retaliate [rɪ'tælɪeɪt] vi zum Vergeltungsschlag ausholen; **retaliation** [rɪtælɪ'eɪʃən] n Vergeltung f

retarded [rɪ'tɑːdɪd] adj zurückgeblieben

retch [retʃ] vi würgen

retentive [rɪ'tentɪv] adj (memory) gut

reticent ['retɪsnt] adj schweigsam

retina ['retɪnə] n Netzhaut f

retire [rɪ'taɪəʳ] vi (from work) in den Ruhestand treten; (withdraw) sich zurückziehen; (go to bed) schlafen gehen; **~d** adj (person) pensioniert, im Ruhestand; **~ment** n Ruhestand m

retiring [rɪ'taɪərɪŋ] adj zurückhaltend

retort [rɪ'tɔːt] n (reply) Erwiderung f ♦ vi (scharf) erwidern

retrace [rɪ'treɪs] vt zurückverfolgen; **to ~ one's steps** denselben Weg zurückgehen

retract [rɪ'trækt] vt (statement) zurücknehmen; (claws) einziehen ♦ vi einen Rückzieher machen; **~able** adj (aerial) ausziehbar

retrain [riː'treɪn] vt umschulen

retread ['riːtred] n (tyre) Reifen m mit erneuerter Lauffläche

retreat [rɪ'triːt] n Rückzug m; (place) Zufluchtsort m ♦ vi sich zurückziehen

retribution [retrɪ'bjuːʃən] n Strafe f

retrieval [rɪ'triːvəl] n Wiedergewinnung f

retrieve [rɪ'triːv] vt wiederbekommen; (rescue) retten; **~r** n Apportierhund m

retrograde ['retrəgreɪd] adj (step) Rück-; (policy) rückschrittlich

retrospect ['retrəspekt] n: **in ~** im Rückblick, rückblickend; **~ive** [retrə'spektɪv] adj (action) rückwirkend; (look) rückblickend

return [rɪ'təːn] n Rückkehr f; (profits) Ertrag m; (BRIT: rail ticket etc) Rückfahrkarte f; (: plane ticket) Rückflugkarte f ♦ adj (journey, match) Rück- ♦ vi zurückkehren, zurückkommen ♦ vt zurückgeben, zurücksenden; (pay back) zurückzahlen; (elect) wählen; (verdict) aussprechen; **~s** npl (COMM) Gewinn m; (receipts) Einkünfte pl; **in ~** dafür; **by ~ of post** postwendend; **many happy ~s!** herzlichen Glückwunsch zum Geburtstag!

reunion [riː'juːnɪən] n Wiedervereinigung f; (SCH etc) Treffen nt

reunite [riːjuː'naɪt] vt wieder vereinigen

reuse [riː'juːz] vt wieder verwenden, wieder verwerten

rev [rev] n abbr (AUT: = revolution) Drehzahl f

revamp [riː'væmp] vt aufpolieren

reveal [rɪ'viːl] vt enthüllen; **~ing** adj aufschlussreich

revel ['revl] vi: **to ~ in sth/in doing sth** seine Freude an etw dat haben/daran haben, etw zu tun

revelation [revə'leɪʃən] n Offenbarung f

revelry ['revlrɪ] n Rummel m

revenge [rɪ'vendʒ] n Rache f; **to take ~ on** sich rächen an +dat

revenue ['revənjuː] n Einnahmen pl

reverberate [rɪ'vəːbəreɪt] vi widerhallen

revere [rɪ'vɪəʳ] vt (ver)ehren; **~nce** ['revərəns] n Ehrfurcht f

Reverend ['revərənd] adj: **the ~ Robert Martin** ≃ Pfarrer Robert Martin

reversal [rɪ'vəːsl] n Umkehrung f

reverse [rɪ'vəːs] n Rückseite f; (AUT: gear)

Rückwärtsgang m ♦ adj (order, direction) entgegengesetzt ♦ vt umkehren ♦ vi (BRIT: AUT) rückwärts fahren; **~-charge call** (BRIT) n R-Gespräch nt; **reversing lights** npl (AUT) Rückfahrscheinwerfer pl

revert [rɪ'vəːt] vi: **to ~ to** zurückkehren zu; (to bad state) zurückfallen in +acc

review [rɪ'vjuː] n (of book) Rezension f; (magazine) Zeitschrift f ♦ vt Rückschau halten auf +acc; (MIL) mustern; (book) rezensieren; (reexamine) von neuem untersuchen; **~er** n (critic) Rezensent m

revise [rɪ'vaɪz] vt (book) überarbeiten; (reconsider) ändern, revidieren; **revision** [rɪ'vɪʒən] n Prüfung f; (COMM) Revision f; (SCH) Wiederholung f

revitalize [riː'vaɪtəlaɪz] vt neu beleben

revival [rɪ'vaɪvəl] n Wiederbelebung f; (REL) Erweckung f; (THEAT) Wiederaufnahme f

revive [rɪ'vaɪv] vt wieder beleben; (fig) wieder auffrischen ♦ vi wieder erwachen; (fig) wieder aufleben

revoke [rɪ'vəuk] vt aufheben

revolt [rɪ'vəult] n Aufstand m, Revolte f ♦ vi sich auflehnen ♦ vt entsetzen; **~ing** adj widerlich

revolution [revə'luːʃən] n (turn) Umdrehung f; (POL) Revolution f; **~ary** adj revolutionär ♦ n Revolutionär m; **~ize** vt revolutionieren

revolve [rɪ'vɔlv] vi kreisen; (on own axis) sich drehen

revolver [rɪ'vɔlvər] n Revolver m

revolving door [rɪ'vɔlvɪŋ-] n Drehtür f

revulsion [rɪ'vʌlʃən] n Ekel m

reward [rɪ'wɔːd] n Belohnung f ♦ vt belohnen; **~ing** adj lohnend

rewind [riː'waɪnd] (irreg: like **wind**) vt (tape etc) zurückspulen

rewire [riː'waɪər] vt (house) neu verkabeln

reword [riː'wəːd] vt anders formulieren

rewrite [riː'raɪt] (irreg: like **write**) vt umarbeiten, neu schreiben

rheumatism ['ruːmətɪzəm] n Rheumatismus m, Rheuma nt

Rhine [raɪn] n: **the ~** der Rhein

rhinoceros [raɪ'nɔsərəs] n Nashorn nt

Rhone [rəun] n: **the ~** die Rhone

rhubarb ['ruːbɑːb] n Rhabarber m

rhyme [raɪm] n Reim m

rhythm ['rɪðm] n Rhythmus m

rib [rɪb] n Rippe f ♦ vt (mock) hänseln, aufziehen

ribbon ['rɪbən] n Band nt; **in ~s** (torn) in Fetzen

rice [raɪs] n Reis m; **~ pudding** n Milchreis m

rich [rɪtʃ] adj reich; (food) reichhaltig ♦ npl: **the ~** die Reichen pl; **~es** npl Reichtum m; **~ly** adv reich; (deserve) völlig

rickets ['rɪkɪts] n Rachitis f

rickety ['rɪkɪtɪ] adj wack(e)lig

rickshaw ['rɪkʃɔː] n Riksha f

ricochet ['rɪkəʃeɪ] n Abprallen nt; (shot) Querschläger m ♦ vi abprallen

rid [rɪd] (pt, pp rid) vt befreien; **to get ~ of** loswerden

riddle ['rɪdl] n Rätsel nt ♦ vt: **to be ~d with** völlig durchlöchert sein von

ride [raɪd] (pt rode, pp ridden) n (in vehicle) Fahrt f; (on horse) Ritt m ♦ vt (horse) reiten; (bicycle) fahren ♦ vi fahren, reiten; **to take sb for a ~** mit jdm eine Fahrt etc machen; (fig) jdn aufs Glatteis führen; **~r** n Reiter m

ridge [rɪdʒ] n Kamm m; (of roof) First m

ridicule ['rɪdɪkjuːl] n Spott m ♦ vt lächerlich machen

ridiculous [rɪ'dɪkjuləs] adj lächerlich

riding ['raɪdɪŋ] n Reiten nt; **~ school** n Reitschule f

rife [raɪf] adj weit verbreitet; **to be ~** grassieren; **to be ~ with** voll sein von

riffraff ['rɪfræf] n Pöbel m

rifle ['raɪfl] n Gewehr nt ♦ vt berauben; **~ range** n Schießstand m

rift [rɪft] n Spalte f; (fig) Bruch m

rig [rɪg] n (oil ~) Bohrinsel f ♦ vt (election etc) manipulieren; **~ out** (BRIT) vt ausstatten; **~ up** vt zusammenbasteln; **~ging** n Takelage f

right [raɪt] adj (correct, just) richtig, recht; (~ side) rechte(r, s) ♦ n Recht nt; (not left, POL) Rechte f ♦ adv (on the ~) rechts; (to the ~) nach rechts; (look, work) richtig, recht; (directly) gerade; (exactly) genau ♦ vt in

Ordnung bringen, korrigieren ♦ *excl* gut; **on the ~** rechts; **to be in the ~** im Recht sein; **by ~s** von Rechts wegen; **to be ~** Recht haben; **~ away** sofort; **~ now** in diesem Augenblick, eben; **~ in the middle** genau in der Mitte; **~ angle** *n* rechte(r) Winkel *m*; **~eous** ['raɪtʃəs] *adj* rechtschaffen; **~ful** *adj* rechtmäßig; **~-hand** *adj*: **~-hand drive** mit Rechtssteuerung; **~-handed** *adj* rechtshändig; **~-hand man** (*irreg*) *n* rechte Hand *f*; **~-hand side** *n* rechte Seite *f*; **~ly** *adv* mit Recht; **~ of way** *n* Vorfahrt *f*; **~-wing** *adj* rechtsorientiert

rigid ['rɪdʒɪd] *adj* (*stiff*) starr, steif; (*strict*) streng; **~ity** [rɪ'dʒɪdɪtɪ] *n* Starrheit *f*; Strenge *f*

rigmarole ['rɪgmərəul] *n* Gewäsch *nt*

rigor ['rɪgəʳ] (*US*) *n* = **rigour**

rigorous ['rɪgərəs] *adj* streng

rigour ['rɪgəʳ] (*US* **rigor**) *n* Strenge *f*, Härte *f*

rile [raɪl] *vt* ärgern

rim [rɪm] *n* (*edge*) Rand *m*; (*of wheel*) Felge *f*

rind [raɪnd] *n* Rinde *f*

ring [rɪŋ] (*pt* **rang**, *pp* **rung**) *n* Ring *m*; (*of people*) Kreis *m*; (*arena*) Manege *f*; (*of telephone*) Klingeln *nt* ♦ *vt*, *vi* (*bell*) läuten; (*BRIT*) anrufen; **~ back** (*BRIT*) *vt*, *vi* zurückrufen; **~ off** (*BRIT*) *vi* aufhängen; **~ up** (*BRIT*) *vt* anrufen; **~ binder** *n* Ringbuch *nt*; **~ing** *n* Klingeln *nt*; (*of large bell*) Läuten *nt*; (*in ears*) Klingen *nt*; **~ing tone** *n* (*TEL*) Rufzeichen *nt*

ringleader ['rɪŋliːdəʳ] *n* Anführer *m*, Rädelsführer *m*

ringlets ['rɪŋlɪts] *npl* Ringellocken *pl*

ring road (*BRIT*) *n* Umgehungsstraße *f*

rink [rɪŋk] *n* (*ice ~*) Eisbahn *f*

rinse [rɪns] *n* Spülen *nt* ♦ *vt* spülen

riot ['raɪət] *n* Aufruhr *m* ♦ *vi* randalieren; **to run ~** (*people*) randalieren; (*vegetation*) wuchern; **~er** *n* Aufrührer *m*; **~ous** *adj* aufrührerisch; (*noisy*) lärmend

rip [rɪp] *n* Schlitz *m*, Riss *m* ♦ *vt*, *vi* (zer)reißen; **~cord** *n* Reißleine *f*

ripe [raɪp] *adj* reif; **~n** *vi* reifen ♦ *vt* reifen lassen

rip-off ['rɪpɔf] (*inf*) *n*: **it's a ~~!** das ist Wucher!

ripple ['rɪpl] *n* kleine Welle *f* ♦ *vt* kräuseln ♦ *vi* sich kräuseln

rise [raɪz] (*pt* **rose**, *pp* **risen**) *n* (*slope*) Steigung *f*; (*esp in wages: BRIT*) Erhöhung *f*; (*growth*) Aufstieg *m* ♦ *vi* (*sun*) aufgehen; (*smoke*) aufsteigen; (*mountain*) sich erheben; (*ground*) ansteigen; (*prices*) steigen; (*in revolt*) sich erheben; **to give ~ to** Anlass geben zu; **to ~ to the occasion** sich der Lage gewachsen zeigen; **~n** [rɪzn] *pp of* **rise**; **~r** ['raɪzəʳ] *n*: **to be an early ~r** ein(e) Frühaufsteher(in) *m(f)* sein; **rising** ['raɪzɪŋ] *adj* (*tide, prices*) steigend; (*sun, moon*) aufgehend ♦ *n* (*uprising*) Aufstand *m*

risk [rɪsk] *n* Gefahr *f*, Risiko *nt* ♦ *vt* (*venture*) wagen; (*chance loss of*) riskieren, aufs Spiel setzen; **to take** *or* **run the ~ of doing sth** das Risiko eingehen, etw zu tun; **at ~** in Gefahr; **at one's own ~** auf eigene Gefahr; **~y** *adj* riskant

risqué ['riːskeɪ] *adj* gewagt

rissole ['rɪsəul] *n* Fleischklößchen *nt*

rite [raɪt] *n* Ritus *m*; **last ~s** Letzte Ölung *f*

ritual ['rɪtjuəl] *n* Ritual *nt* ♦ *adj* ritual, Ritual-; (*fig*) rituell

rival ['raɪvl] *n* Rivale *m*, Konkurrent *m* ♦ *adj* rivalisierend ♦ *vt* rivalisieren mit; (*COMM*) konkurrieren mit; **~ry** *n* Rivalität *f*; Konkurrenz *f*

river ['rɪvəʳ] *n* Fluss *m*, Strom *m* ♦ *cpd* (*port, traffic*) Fluss-; **up/down ~** flussaufwärts/-abwärts; **~bank** *n* Flussufer *nt*; **~bed** *n* Flussbett *nt*

rivet ['rɪvɪt] *n* Niete *f* ♦ *vt* (*fasten*) (ver)nieten

Riviera [rɪvɪ'ɛərə] *n*: **the ~** die Riviera

road [rəud] *n* Straße *f* ♦ *cpd* Straßen-; **major/minor ~** Haupt-/Nebenstraße *f*; **~ accident** *n* Verkehrsunfall *m*; **~block** *n* Straßensperre *f*; **~hog** *n* Verkehrsrowdy *m*; **~ map** *n* Straßenkarte *f*; **~ rage** *n* Aggressivität *f* im Straßenverkehr; **~ safety** *n* Verkehrssicherheit *f*; **~side** *n* Straßenrand *m* ♦ *adj* an der Landstraße (gelegen); **~ sign** *n* Straßenschild *nt*; **~ user** *n* Verkehrsteilnehmer *m*; **~way** *n* Fahrbahn *f*;

~ works npl Straßenbauarbeiten pl;
~worthy adj verkehrssicher

roam [rəum] vi (umher)streifen ♦ vt
durchstreifen

roar [rɔːʳ] n Brüllen nt, Gebrüll nt ♦ vi
brüllen; **to ~ with laughter** vor Lachen
brüllen; **to do a ~ing trade** ein
Riesengeschäft machen

roast [rəust] n Braten m ♦ vt braten,
schmoren; **~ beef** n Roastbeef nt

rob [rɔb] vt bestehlen, berauben; (bank)
ausrauben; **to ~ sb of sth** jdm etw rauben;
~ber n Räuber m; **~bery** n Raub m

robe [rəub] n (dress) Gewand nt; (US)
Hauskleid nt; (judge's) Robe f

robin ['rɔbɪn] n Rotkehlchen nt

robot ['rəubɔt] n Roboter m

robust [rəu'bʌst] adj (person) robust;
(appetite, economy) gesund

rock [rɔk] n Felsen m; (BRIT: sweet)
Zuckerstange f ♦ vt, vi wiegen, schaukeln;
on the ~s (drink) mit Eis(würfeln);
(marriage) gescheitert; (ship) aufgelaufen; **~
and roll** n Rock and Roll m; **~-bottom** n
(fig) Tiefpunkt m; **~ery** n Steingarten m

rocket ['rɔkɪt] n Rakete f

rocking chair ['rɔkɪŋ-] n Schaukelstuhl m

rocking horse n Schaukelpferd nt

rocky ['rɔkɪ] adj felsig

rod [rɔd] n (bar) Stange f; (stick) Rute f

rode [rəud] pt of **ride**

rodent ['rəudnt] n Nagetier nt

roe [rəu] n (also: ~ **deer**) Reh nt; (of fish:
also: **hard ~**) Rogen m; **soft ~** Milch f

rogue [rəug] n Schurke m

role [rəul] n Rolle f; **~ play** n Rollenspiel nt

roll [rəul] n Rolle f; (bread) Brötchen nt; (list)
(Namens)liste f; (of drum) Wirbel m ♦ vt
(turn) rollen, (herum)wälzen; (grass etc)
walzen ♦ vi (swing) schlingern; (sound)
rollen, grollen; **~ about** or **around** vi
herumkugeln; (ship) schlingern; (dog etc)
sich wälzen; **~ by** vi (time) verfließen; **~
over** vi sich (herum)drehen; **~ up** vi
(arrive) kommen, auftauchen ♦ vt (carpet)
aufrollen; **~ call** n Namensaufruf m; **~er** n
Rolle f, Walze f; (road ~er) Straßenwalze f;

R~erblade ® n Rollerblade m; **~er
coaster** n Achterbahn f; **~er skates** npl
Rollschuhe pl; **~-skating** n Rollschuhlaufen
nt

rolling ['rəulɪŋ] adj (landscape) wellig; **~ pin**
n Nudel- or Wellholz nt; **~ stock** n
Wagenmaterial nt

ROM [rɔm] n abbr (= read only memory) ROM
m

Roman ['rəumən] adj römisch ♦ n Römer(in)
m(f); **~ Catholic** adj römisch-katholisch ♦ n
Katholik(in) m(f)

romance [rə'mæns] n Romanze f; (story)
(Liebes)roman m

Romania [rəu'meɪnɪə] n = **Rumania**; **~n** n =
Rumanian

Roman numeral n römische Ziffer

romantic [rə'mæntɪk] adj romantisch; **~ism**
[rə'mæntɪsɪzəm] n Romantik f

Rome [rəum] n Rom nt

romp [rɔmp] n Tollen nt ♦ vi (also: ~ **about**)
herumtollen

rompers ['rɔmpəz] npl Spielanzug m

roof [ruːf] (pl **~s**) n Dach nt; (of mouth)
Gaumen m ♦ vt überdachen, überdecken;
~ing n Deckmaterial nt; **~ rack** n (AUT)
Dachgepäckträger m

rook [ruk] n (bird) Saatkrähe f; (chess) Turm m

room [ruːm] n Zimmer nt, Raum m; (space)
Platz m; (fig) Spielraum m; **~s** npl
(accommodation) Wohnung f; **"~s to let**
(BRIT) or **for rent** (US)" „Zimmer zu
vermieten"; **single/double ~** Einzel-/
Doppelzimmer nt; **~ing house** (US) n
Mietshaus nt (mit möblierten Wohnungen);
~mate n Mitbewohner(in) m(f); **~ service**
n Zimmerbedienung f; **~y** adj geräumig

roost [ruːst] n Hühnerstange f ♦ vi auf der
Stange hocken

rooster ['ruːstər] n Hahn m

root [ruːt] n (also fig) Wurzel f ♦ vi wurzeln;
~ about vi (fig) herumwühlen; **~ for** vt
fus Stimmung machen für; **~ out** vt
ausjäten; (fig) ausrotten

rope [rəup] n Seil nt ♦ vt (tie) festschnüren;
to know the ~s sich auskennen; **to ~ sb
in** jdn gewinnen; **~ off** vt absperren;

~ **ladder** n Strickleiter f
rosary ['rəʊzərɪ] n Rosenkranz m
rose [rəʊz] pt of **rise** ♦ n Rose f ♦ adj Rosen-, rosenrot
rosé ['rəʊzeɪ] n Rosé m
rosebud ['rəʊzbʌd] n Rosenknospe f
rosebush ['rəʊzbʊʃ] n Rosenstock m
rosemary ['rəʊzmərɪ] n Rosmarin m
rosette [rəʊ'zet] n Rosette f
roster ['rɒstə'] n Dienstplan m
rostrum ['rɒstrəm] n Rednerbühne f
rosy ['rəʊzɪ] adj rosig
rot [rɒt] n Fäulnis f; (nonsense) Quatsch m
♦ vi verfaulen ♦ vt verfaulen lassen
rota ['rəʊtə] n Dienstliste f
rotary ['rəʊtərɪ] adj rotierend
rotate [rəʊ'teɪt] vt rotieren lassen; (take turns) turnusmäßig wechseln ♦ vi rotieren; **rotating** adj rotierend; **rotation** [rəʊ'teɪʃən] n Umdrehung f
rote [rəʊt] n: **by** ~ auswendig
rotten ['rɒtn] adj faul; (fig) schlecht, gemein; **to feel** ~ (ill) sich elend fühlen
rotund [rəʊ'tʌnd] adj rundlich
rouble ['ruːbl] (US **ruble**) n Rubel m
rough [rʌf] adj (not smooth) rau; (path) uneben; (violent) roh, grob; (crossing) stürmisch; (without comforts) hart, unbequem; (unfinished, makeshift) grob; (approximate) ungefähr ♦ n (BRIT: person) Rowdy m, Rohling m; (GOLF): **in the** ~ im Rau ♦ vt: **to ~ it** primitiv leben; **to sleep** ~ im Freien schlafen; **~age** n Ballaststoffe pl; **~-and-ready** adj provisorisch; (work) zusammengehauen; ~ **copy** n Entwurf m; ~ **draft** n Entwurf m; **~ly** adv grob; (about) ungefähr; **~ness** n Rauheit f; (of manner) Ungeschliffenheit f
roulette [ruː'let] n Roulett(e) nt
Roumania [ruː'meɪnɪə] n = **Rumania**
round [raʊnd] adj rund; (figures) aufgerundet ♦ adv (in a circle) rundherum ♦ prep um ... herum ♦ n Runde f; (of ammunition) Magazin nt ♦ vt (corner) biegen um; **all** ~ überall; **the long way** ~ der Umweg; **all the year** ~ das ganze Jahr über; **it's just** ~ **the corner** (fig) es ist gerade um die Ecke;

~ **the clock** rund um die Uhr; **to go** ~ **to sb's (house)** jdn besuchen; **to go** ~ **the back** hintenherum gehen; **enough to go** ~ genug für alle; **to go the ~s** (story) die Runde machen; **a** ~ **of applause** ein Beifall m; **a** ~ **of drinks** eine Runde Drinks; **a** ~ **of sandwiches** ein Sandwich nt or m, ein belegtes Brot; ~ **off** vt abrunden; ~ **up** vt (end) abschließen; (figures) aufrunden; (criminals) hochnehmen; **~about** n (BRIT: traffic) Kreisverkehr m; (: merry-go-~) Karussell nt ♦ adj auf Umwegen; **~ers** npl (game) ≈ Schlagball m; **~ly** adv (fig) gründlich; **~-shouldered** adj mit abfallenden Schultern; ~ **trip** n Rundreise f; **~up** n Zusammentreiben nt, Sammeln nt
rouse [raʊz] vt (waken) (auf)wecken; (stir up) erregen; **rousing** adj (welcome) stürmisch; (speech) zündend
route [ruːt] n Weg m, Route f; ~ **map** (BRIT) n (for journey) Streckenkarte f
routine [ruː'tiːn] n Routine f ♦ adj Routine-
row¹ [rəʊ] n (noise) Lärm m; (dispute) Streit m ♦ vi sich streiten
row² [rəʊ] n (line) Reihe f ♦ vt, vi (boat) rudern; **in a** ~ (fig) hintereinander; **~boat** ['rəʊbəʊt] (US) n Ruderboot nt
rowdy ['raʊdɪ] adj rüpelhaft ♦ n (person) Rowdy m
rowing ['rəʊɪŋ] n Rudern nt; (SPORT) Rudersport m; ~ **boat** (BRIT) n Ruderboot nt
royal ['rɔɪəl] adj königlich, Königs-; **R~ Air Force** n Königliche Luftwaffe f; **~ty** ['rɔɪəltɪ] n (family) königliche Familie f; (for novel etc) Tantieme f
rpm abbr (= revs per minute) U/min
R.S.V.P. abbr (= répondez s'il vous plaît) u. A. w. g.
Rt. Hon. (BRIT) abbr (= Right Honourable) Abgeordnete(r) mf
rub [rʌb] n (with cloth) Polieren nt; (on person) Reiben nt ♦ vt reiben; **to ~ sb up** (BRIT) or **to ~ sb** (US) **the wrong way** jdn aufreizen; ~ **off** vi (also fig): **to ~ off (on)** abfärben (auf +acc); ~ **out** vt herausreiben; (with eraser) ausradieren
rubber ['rʌbə'] n Gummi m; (BRIT)

Radiergummi *m*; ~ **band** *n* Gummiband *nt*; ~ **plant** *n* Gummibaum *m*

rubbish ['rʌbɪʃ] *n* (*waste*) Abfall *m*; (*nonsense*) Blödsinn *m*, Quatsch *m*; ~ **bin** (*BRIT*) *n* Mülleimer *m*; ~ **dump** *n* Müllabladeplatz *m*

rubble ['rʌbl] *n* (*Stein*)schutt *m*

ruby ['ruːbɪ] *n* Rubin *m* ♦ *adj* rubinrot

rucksack ['rʌksæk] *n* Rucksack *m*

rudder ['rʌdəʳ] *n* Steuerruder *nt*

ruddy ['rʌdɪ] *adj* (*colour*) rötlich; (*inf: bloody*) verdammt

rude [ruːd] *adj* unverschämt; (*shock*) hart; (*awakening*) unsanft; (*unrefined, rough*) grob; **~ness** *n* Unverschämtheit *f*; Grobheit *f*

rudiment ['ruːdɪmənt] *n* Grundlage *f*

rueful ['ruːful] *adj* reuevoll

ruffian ['rʌfɪən] *n* Rohling *m*

ruffle ['rʌfl] *vt* kräuseln

rug [rʌg] *n* Brücke *f*; (*in bedroom*) Bettvorleger *m*; (*BRIT: for knees*) (Reise)decke *f*

rugby ['rʌgbɪ] *n* (*also*: ~ **football**) Rugby *nt*

rugged ['rʌgɪd] *adj* (*coastline*) zerklüftet; (*features*) markig

rugger ['rʌgəʳ] (*BRIT: inf*) *n* = **rugby**

ruin ['ruːɪn] *n* Ruine *f*; (*downfall*) Ruin *m* ♦ *vt* ruinieren; **~s** *npl* (*fig*) Trümmer *pl*; **~ous** *adj* ruinierend

rule [ruːl] *n* Regel *f*; (*government*) Regierung *f*; (*for measuring*) Lineal *nt* ♦ *vt* (*govern*) herrschen über +*acc*, regieren; (*decide*) anordnen, entscheiden; (*make lines on*) linieren ♦ *vi* herrschen, regieren; entscheiden; **as a** ~ in der Regel; ~ **out** *vt* ausschließen; **~d** *adj* (*paper*) liniert; **~r** *n* Lineal *nt*; Herrscher *m*; **ruling** ['ruːlɪŋ] *adj* (*party*) Regierungs-; (*class*) herrschend ♦ *n* (*JUR*) Entscheid *m*

rum [rʌm] *n* Rum *m*

Rumania [ruːˈmeɪnɪə] *n* Rumänien *nt*; **~n** *adj* rumänisch ♦ *n* Rumäne *m*, Rumänin *f*; (*LING*) Rumänisch *nt*

rumble ['rʌmbl] *n* Rumpeln *nt*; (*of thunder*) Grollen *nt* ♦ *vi* rumpeln; grollen

rummage ['rʌmɪdʒ] *vi* durchstöbern

rumour ['ruːməʳ] (*US* **rumor**) *n* Gerücht *nt*

♦ *vt*: **it is ~ed that** man sagt *or* man munkelt, dass

rump [rʌmp] *n* Hinterteil *nt*; ~ **steak** *n* Rumpsteak *nt*

rumpus ['rʌmpəs] *n* Spektakel *m*

run [rʌn] (*pt* **ran**, *pp* **run**) *n* Lauf *m*; (*in car*) (Spazier)fahrt *f*; (*series*) Serie *f*, Reihe *f*; (*ski* ~) (Ski)abfahrt *f*; (*in stocking*) Laufmasche *f* ♦ *vt* (*cause to* ~) laufen lassen; (*car, train, bus*) fahren; (*race, distance*) laufen, rennen; (*manage*) leiten; (*COMPUT*) laufen lassen; (*pass: hand, eye*) gleiten lassen ♦ *vi* laufen; (*move quickly*) laufen, rennen; (*bus, train*) fahren; (*flow*) fließen, laufen; (*colours*) (ab)färben; **there was a** ~ **on** (*meat, tickets*) es gab einen Ansturm auf +*acc*; **on the** ~ auf der Flucht; **in the long** ~ auf die Dauer; **I'll** ~ **you to the station** ich fahre dich zum Bahnhof; **to** ~ **a risk** ein Risiko eingehen; ~ **about** *or* **around** *vi* (*children*) umherspringen; ~ **across** *vt fus* (*find*) stoßen auf +*acc*; ~ **away** *vi* weglaufen; ~ **down** *vi* (*clock*) ablaufen ♦ *vt* (*production, factory*) allmählich auflösen; (*with car*) überfahren; (*talk against*) heruntermachen; **to be** ~ **down** erschöpft *or* abgespannt sein; ~ **in** (*BRIT*) *vt* (*car*) einfahren; ~ **into** *vt fus* (*meet: person*) zufällig treffen; (*trouble*) bekommen; (*collide with*) rennen gegen; fahren gegen; ~ **off** *vi* fortlaufen; ~ **out** *vi* (*person*) hinausrennen; (*liquid*) auslaufen; (*lease*) ablaufen; (*money*) ausgeben; **he ran out of money/petrol** ihm ging das Geld/ Benzin aus; ~ **over** *vt* (*in accident*) überfahren; ~ **through** *vt* (*instructions*) durchgehen; ~ **up** *vt* (*debt, bill*) machen; ~ **up against** *vt fus* (*difficulties*) stoßen auf +*acc*; **~away** *adj* (*horse*) ausgebrochen; (*person*) flüchtig

rung [rʌŋ] *pp of* **ring** ♦ *n* Sprosse *f*

runner ['rʌnəʳ] *n* Läufer(in) *m(f)*; (*for sleigh*) Kufe *f*; ~ **bean** (*BRIT*) *n* Stangenbohne *f*; **~-up** *n* Zweite(r) *mf*

running ['rʌnɪŋ] *n* (*of business*) Leitung *f*; (*of machine*) Betrieb *m* ♦ *adj* (*water*) fließend; (*commentary*) laufend; **to be in/out of the** ~ **for sth** im/aus dem Rennen für etw sein;

3 days ~ 3 Tage lang *or* hintereinander; **~ costs** npl (*of car, machine*) Unterhaltungskosten *pl*

runny ['rʌnɪ] *adj* dünn; (*nose*) laufend

run-of-the-mill ['rʌnəvðə'mɪl] *adj* gewöhnlich, alltäglich

runt [rʌnt] *n* (*animal*) Kümmerer *m*

run-up ['rʌnʌp] *n*: **the ~~~ to** (*election etc*) die Endphase vor *+dat*

runway ['rʌnweɪ] *n* Startbahn *f*

rupture ['rʌptʃə*] *n* (*MED*) Bruch *m*

rural ['ruərl] *adj* ländlich, Land-

ruse [ru:z] *n* Kniff *m*, List *f*

rush [rʌʃ] *n* Eile *f*, Hetze *f*; (*FIN*) starke Nachfrage *f ♦ vt* (*carry along*) auf dem schnellsten Wege schaffen *or* transportieren; (*attack*) losstürmen auf *+acc ♦ vi* (*hurry*) eilen, stürzen; **don't ~ me** dräng mich nicht; **~ hour** *n* Hauptverkehrszeit *f*

rusk [rʌsk] *n* Zwieback *m*

Russia ['rʌʃə] *n* Russland *nt*; **~n** *adj* russisch *♦ n* Russe *m*, Russin *f*; (*LING*) Russisch *nt*

rust [rʌst] *n* Rost *m ♦ vi* rosten

rustic ['rʌstɪk] *adj* bäuerlich, ländlich

rustle ['rʌsl] *vi* rauschen, rascheln *♦ vt* rascheln lassen

rustproof ['rʌstpru:f] *adj* rostfrei

rusty ['rʌstɪ] *adj* rostig

rut [rʌt] *n* (*in track*) Radspur *f*; **to be in a ~** im Trott stecken

ruthless ['ru:θlɪs] *adj* rücksichtslos

rye [raɪ] *n* Roggen *m*; **~ bread** *n* Roggenbrot *nt*

S, s

sabbath ['sæbəθ] *n* Sabbat *m*

sabotage ['sæbəta:ʒ] *n* Sabotage *f ♦ vt* sabotieren

saccharin ['sækərɪn] *n* Sa(c)charin *nt*

sachet ['sæʃeɪ] *n* (*of shampoo etc*) Briefchen *nt*, Kissen *nt*

sack [sæk] *n* Sack *m ♦ vt* (*inf*) hinauswerfen; (*pillage*) plündern; **to get the ~** rausfliegen; **~ing** *n* (*material*) Sackleinen *nt*; (*inf*)

Rausschmiss *m*

sacrament ['sækrəmənt] *n* Sakrament *nt*

sacred ['seɪkrɪd] *adj* heilig

sacrifice ['sækrɪfaɪs] *n* Opfer *nt ♦ vt* (*also fig*) opfern

sacrilege ['sækrɪlɪdʒ] *n* Schändung *f*

sad [sæd] *adj* traurig; **~den** *vt* traurig machen, betrüben

saddle ['sædl] *n* Sattel *m ♦ vt* (*burden*): **to ~ sb with sth** jdm etw aufhalsen; **~bag** *n* Satteltasche *f*

sadistic [sə'dɪstɪk] *adj* sadistisch

sadly ['sædlɪ] *adv* traurig; (*unfortunately*) leider

sadness ['sædnɪs] *n* Traurigkeit *f*

s.a.e. *abbr* (= *stamped addressed envelope*) adressierte(r) Rückumschlag *m*

safe [seɪf] *adj* (*careful*) vorsichtig *♦ n* Safe *m*; **~ and sound** gesund und wohl; **(just) to be on the ~ side** um ganz sicherzugehen; **~ from** (*attack*) sicher vor *+dat*; **~~conduct** *n* freie(s) Geleit *nt*; **~~deposit** *n* (*vault*) Tresorraum *m*; (*box*) Banksafe *m*; **~guard** *n* Sicherung *f ♦ vt* sichern, schützen; **~keeping** *n* sichere Verwahrung *f*; **~ly** *adv* sicher; (*arrive*) wohlbehalten; **~ sex** *n* geschützter Sex *m*

safety ['seɪftɪ] *n* Sicherheit *f*; **~ belt** *n* Sicherheitsgurt *m*; **~ pin** *n* Sicherheitsnadel *f*; **~ valve** *n* Sicherheitsventil *nt*

sag [sæg] *vi* (durch)sacken

sage [seɪdʒ] *n* (*herb*) Salbei *m*; (*person*) Weise(r) *mf*

Sagittarius [sædʒɪ'tɛərɪəs] *n* Schütze *m*

Sahara [sə'ha:rə] *n*: **the ~ (Desert)** die (Wüste) Sahara

said [sed] *pt*, *pp of* **say**

sail [seɪl] *n* Segel *nt*; (*trip*) Fahrt *f ♦ vt* segeln *♦ vi* segeln; (*begin voyage: person*) abfahren; (*: ship*) auslaufen; (*fig: cloud etc*) dahinsegeln; **to go for a ~** segeln gehen; **they ~ed into Copenhagen** sie liefen in Kopenhagen ein; **~ through** *vt fus*, *vi* (*fig*) (es) spielend schaffen; **~boat** (*US*) *n* Segelboot *nt*; **~ing** *n* Segeln *nt*; **~ing ship** *n* Segelschiff *nt*; **~or** *n* Matrose *m*, Seemann *m*

saint [seint] *n* Heilige(r) *mf*; **~ly** *adj* heilig, fromm

sake [seik] *n*: **for the ~ of** um +*gen* willen

salad ['sæləd] *n* Salat *m*; **~ bowl** *n* Salatschüssel *f*; **~ cream** (*BRIT*) *n* Salatmayonnaise *f*, Salatmajonäse *f*; **~ dressing** *n* Salatsoße *f*

salary ['sæləri] *n* Gehalt *nt*

sale [seil] *n* Verkauf *m*; (*reduced prices*) Schlussverkauf *m*; **"for ~"** „zu verkaufen"; **on ~** zu verkaufen; **~room** *n* Verkaufsraum *m*; **~s assistant** *n* Verkäufer(in) *m(f)*; **~s clerk** (*US*) *n* Verkäufer(in) *m(f)*; **~sman** (*irreg*) *n* Verkäufer *m*; (*representative*) Vertreter *m*; **~s rep** *n* (*COMM*) Vertreter(in) *m(f)*; **~swoman** (*irreg*) *n* Verkäuferin *f*

salient ['seiliənt] *adj* bemerkenswert

saliva [sə'laivə] *n* Speichel *m*

sallow ['sæləu] *adj* fahl; (*face*) bleich

salmon ['sæmən] *n* Lachs *m*

salon ['sælɔn] *n* Salon *m*

saloon [sə'lu:n] *n* (*BRIT: AUT*) Limousine *f*; (*ship's lounge*) Salon *m*; **~ car** (*BRIT*) *n* Limousine *f*

salt [sɔ:lt] *n* Salz *nt* ♦ *vt* (*cure*) einsalzen; (*flavour*) salzen; **~cellar** *n* Salzfass *nt*; **~water** *adj* Salzwasser-; **~y** *adj* salzig

salute [sə'lu:t] *n* (*MIL*) Gruß *m*; (*with guns*) Salutschüsse *pl* ♦ *vt* (*MIL*) salutieren

salvage ['sælvidʒ] *n* (*from ship*) Bergung *f*; (*property*) Rettung *f* ♦ *vt* bergen; retten

salvation [sæl'veiʃən] *n* Rettung *f*; **S~ Army** *n* Heilsarmee *f*

same [seim] *adj, pron* (*similar*) gleiche(r, s); (*identical*) derselbe/dieselbe/dasselbe; **the ~ book as** das gleiche Buch wie; **at the ~ time** zur gleichen Zeit, gleichzeitig; (*however*) zugleich, andererseits; **all or just the ~** trotzdem; **the ~ to you!** gleichfalls!; **to do the ~ (as sb)** das Gleiche tun (wie jd)

sample ['sɑ:mpl] *n* Probe *f* ♦ *vt* probieren

sanctify ['sæŋktifai] *vt* weihen

sanctimonious [sæŋkti'məuniəs] *adj* scheinheilig

sanction ['sæŋkʃən] *n* Sanktion *f*

sanctity ['sæŋktiti] *n* Heiligkeit *f*; (*fig*) Unverletzlichkeit *f*

sanctuary ['sæŋktjuəri] *n* (*for fugitive*) Asyl *nt*; (*refuge*) Zufluchtsort *m*; (*for animals*) Schutzgebiet *nt*

sand [sænd] *n* Sand *m* ♦ *vt* (*furniture*) schmirgeln

sandal ['sændl] *n* Sandale *f*

sand: **~box** (*US*) *n* = **sandpit;** **~castle** *n* Sandburg *f*; **~ dune** *n* (Sand)düne *f*; **~paper** *n* Sandpapier *nt*; **~pit** *n* Sandkasten *m*; **~stone** *n* Sandstein *m*

sandwich ['sændwitʃ] *n* Sandwich *m or nt* ♦ *vt* (*also:* **~ in**) einklemmen; **cheese/ham ~** Käse-/Schinkenbrot; **~ed between** eingeklemmt zwischen; **~ board** *n* Reklametafel *f*; **~ course** (*BRIT*) *n* Theorie und Praxis abwechselnde(r) Ausbildungsgang *m*

sandy ['sændi] *adj* sandig; (*hair*) rotblond

sane [sein] *adj* geistig gesund *or* normal; (*sensible*) vernünftig, gescheit

sang [sæŋ] *pt of* **sing**

sanitary ['sænitəri] *adj* hygienisch; **~ towel** *n* (Monats)binde *f*

sanitation [sæni'teiʃən] *n* sanitäre Einrichtungen *pl*; **~ department** (*US*) *n* Stadtreinigung *f*

sanity ['sæniti] *n* geistige Gesundheit *f*; (*sense*) Vernunft *f*

sank [sæŋk] *pt of* **sink**

Santa Claus [sæntə'klɔːz] *n* Nikolaus *m*, Weihnachtsmann *m*

sap [sæp] *n* (*of plants*) Saft *m* ♦ *vt* (*strength*) schwächen

sapling ['sæpliŋ] *n* junge(r) Baum *m*

sapphire ['sæfaiə*] *n* Saphir *m*

sarcasm ['sɑ:kæzm] *n* Sarkasmus *m*

sarcastic [sɑː'kæstik] *adj* sarkastisch

sardine [sɑː'di:n] *n* Sardine *f*

Sardinia [sɑː'diniə] *n* Sardinien *nt*

sardonic [sɑː'dɔnik] *adj* zynisch

sash [sæʃ] *n* Schärpe *f*

sat [sæt] *pt, pp of* **sit**

Satan ['seitn] *n* Satan *m*

satchel ['sætʃl] *n* (*for school*) Schulmappe *f*

satellite ['sætəlait] *n* Satellit *m*; **~ dish** *n* (*TECH*) Parabolantenne *f*, Satellitenantenne *f;* **~ television** *n* Satellitenfernsehen *nt*

satisfaction [sætɪsˈfækʃən] *n* Befriedigung *f*, Genugtuung *f*; **satisfactory** [sætɪsˈfæktərɪ] *adj* zufrieden stellend, befriedigend; **satisfied** *adj* befriedigt

satisfy [ˈsætɪsfaɪ] *vt* befriedigen, zufrieden stellen; (*convince*) überzeugen; (*conditions*) erfüllen; **~ing** *adj* befriedigend; (*meal*) sättigend

saturate [ˈsætʃəreɪt] *vt* (durch)tränken

Saturday [ˈsætədɪ] *n* Samstag *m*, Sonnabend *m*

sauce [sɔːs] *n* Soße *f*, Sauce *f*; **~pan** *n* Kasserolle *f*

saucer [ˈsɔːsəʳ] *n* Untertasse *f*

saucy [ˈsɔːsɪ] *adj* frech, keck

Saudi [ˈsaʊdɪ]: **~ Arabia** *n* Saudi-Arabien *nt*; **~ (Arabian)** *adj* saudi-arabisch ♦ *n* Saudi-Araber(in) *m(f)*

sauna [ˈsɔːnə] *n* Sauna *f*

saunter [ˈsɔːntəʳ] *vi* schlendern

sausage [ˈsɔsɪdʒ] *n* Wurst *f*; **~ roll** *n* Wurst *f* im Schlafrock, Wurstpastete *f*

sauté [ˈsəʊteɪ] *adj* Röst-

savage [ˈsævɪdʒ] *adj* wild ♦ *n* Wilde(r) *mf* ♦ *vt* (*animals*) zerfleischen

save [seɪv] *vt* retten; (*money, electricity etc*) sparen; (*strength etc*) aufsparen; (*COMPUT*) speichern ♦ *vi* (*also:* **~ up**) sparen ♦ *n* (*SPORT*) (Ball)abwehr *f* ♦ *prep, conj* außer, ausgenommen

saving [ˈseɪvɪŋ] *adj*: **the ~ grace of** das Versöhnende an +*dat* ♦ *n* Sparen *nt*, Ersparnis *f*; **~s** *npl* (*money*) Ersparnisse *pl*; **~s account** *n* Sparkonto *nt*; **~s bank** *n* Sparkasse *f*

saviour [ˈseɪvjəʳ] (*US* **savior**) *n* (*REL*) Erlöser *m*

savour [ˈseɪvəʳ] (*US* **savor**) *vt* (*taste*) schmecken; (*fig*) genießen; **~y** *adj* pikant, würzig

saw [sɔː] (*pt* **sawed**, *pp* **sawed** *or* **sawn**) *pt of* **see** ♦ *n* (*tool*) Säge *f* ♦ *vt, vi* sägen; **~dust** *n* Sägemehl *nt*; **~mill** *n* Sägewerk *nt*; **~n** *pp of* **saw**; **~n-off shotgun** *n* Gewehr *nt* mit abgesägtem Lauf

sax [sæks] (*inf*) *n* Saxofon *nt*, Saxophon *nt*

saxophone [ˈsæksəfəʊn] *n* Saxofon *nt*, Saxophon *nt*

say [seɪ] (*pt, pp* **said**) *n*: **to have a/no ~ in sth** Mitspracherecht/kein Mitspracherecht bei etw haben ♦ *vt, vi* sagen; **let him have his ~** lass ihn doch reden; **to ~ yes/no** Ja/Nein *or* ja/nein sagen; **that goes without ~ing** das versteht sich von selbst; **that is to ~** das heißt; **~ing** *n* Sprichwort *nt*

scab [skæb] *n* Schorf *m*; (*pej*) Streikbrecher *m*

scaffold [ˈskæfəld] *n* (*for execution*) Schafott *nt*; **~ing** *n* (Bau)gerüst *nt*

scald [skɔːld] *n* Verbrühung *f* ♦ *vt* (*burn*) verbrühen

scale [skeɪl] *n* (*of fish*) Schuppe *f*; (*MUS*) Tonleiter *f*; (*on map, size*) Maßstab *m*; (*gradation*) Skala *f* ♦ *vt* (*climb*) erklimmen; **~s** *npl* (*balance*) Waage *f*; **on a large ~** (*fig*) im Großen, in großem Umfang; **~ of charges** Gebührenordnung *f*; **~ down** *vt* verkleinern; **~ model** *n* maßstabgetreue(s) Modell *nt*

scallop [ˈskɔləp] *n* Kammmuschel *f*

scalp [skælp] *n* Kopfhaut *f*

scamper [ˈskæmpəʳ] *vi*: **to ~ away** *or* **off** sich davonmachen

scampi [ˈskæmpɪ] *npl* Scampi *pl*

scan [skæn] *vt* (*examine*) genau prüfen; (*quickly*) überfliegen; (*horizon*) absuchen

scandal [ˈskændl] *n* Skandal *m*; (*piece of gossip*) Skandalgeschichte *f*

Scandinavia [skændɪˈneɪvɪə] *n* Skandinavien *nt*; **~n** *adj* skandinavisch ♦ *n* Skandinavier(in) *m(f)*

scant [skænt] *adj* knapp; **~ily** *adv* knapp, dürftig; **~y** *adj* knapp, unzureichend

scapegoat [ˈskeɪpgəʊt] *n* Sündenbock *m*

scar [skɑːʳ] *n* Narbe *f* ♦ *vt* durch Narben entstellen

scarce [skɛəs] *adj* selten, rar; (*goods*) knapp; **~ly** *adv* kaum; **scarcity** *n* Mangel *m*

scare [skɛəʳ] *n* Schrecken *m* ♦ *vt* erschrecken; **bomb ~** Bombendrohung *f*; **to ~ sb stiff** jdn zu Tode erschrecken; **to be ~d** Angst haben; **~ away** *vt* (*animal*) verscheuchen; **~ off** *vt* = **scare away**;

~crow n Vogelscheuche f
scarf [skɑːf] (pl **scarves**) n Schal m;
(*headscarf*) Kopftuch nt
scarlet ['skɑːlɪt] adj scharlachrot ♦ n
Scharlachrot nt; **~ fever** n Scharlach m
scarves [skɑːvz] npl of **scarf**
scary ['skɛərɪ] (inf) adj schaurig
scathing ['skeɪðɪŋ] adj scharf, vernichtend
scatter ['skætəʳ] vt (*sprinkle*) (ver)streuen;
(*disperse*) zerstreuen ♦ vi sich zerstreuen;
~brained adj flatterhaft, schusselig
scavenger ['skævəndʒəʳ] n (*animal*)
Aasfresser m
scenario [sɪ'nɑːrɪəʊ] n (THEAT, CINE)
Szenarium nt; (fig) Szenario nt
scene [siːn] n (*of happening*) Ort m; (*of play,
incident*) Szene f; (*view*) Anblick m;
(*argument*) Szene f, Auftritt m; **~ry** ['siːnərɪ]
n (THEAT) Bühnenbild nt; (*landscape*)
Landschaft f
scenic ['siːnɪk] adj landschaftlich
scent [sɛnt] n Parfüm nt; (*smell*) Duft m ♦ vt
parfümieren
sceptical ['skɛptɪkl] (US **skeptical**) adj
skeptisch
schedule ['ʃɛdjuːl, (US) 'skɛdjuːl] n (*list*) Liste
f; (*plan*) Programm nt; (*of work*) Zeitplan m
♦ vt planen; **on ~** pünktlich; **to be ahead
of/behind ~** dem Zeitplan voraus/im
Rückstand sein; **~d flight** n (*not charter*)
Linienflug m
scheme [skiːm] n Schema nt; (*dishonest*)
Intrige f; (*plan of action*) Plan m ♦ vi
intrigieren ♦ vt planen; **scheming**
['skiːmɪŋ] adj intrigierend
scholar ['skɔləʳ] n Gelehrte(r) m; (*holding
~ship*) Stipendiat m; **~ly** adj gelehrt; **~ship**
n Gelehrsamkeit f; (*grant*) Stipendium nt
school [skuːl] n Schule f; (UNIV) Fakultät f
♦ vt schulen; **~ age** n schulpflichtige(s)
Alter nt; **~book** n Schulbuch nt; **~boy** n
Schüler m; **~children** npl Schüler pl,
Schulkinder pl; **~days** npl (alte) Schulzeit f;
~girl n Schülerin f; **~ing** n Schulung f,
Ausbildung f; **~master** n Lehrer m;
~mistress n Lehrerin f; **~teacher** n
Lehrer(in) m(f)

sciatica [saɪ'ætɪkə] n Ischias m or nt
science ['saɪəns] n Wissenschaft f; (*natural
~*) Naturwissenschaft f; **~ fiction** n
Sciencefiction f; **scientific** [saɪən'tɪfɪk] adj
wissenschaftlich; (*natural ~s*)
naturwissenschaftlich; **scientist** ['saɪəntɪst]
n Wissenschaftler(in) m(f)
scintillating ['sɪntɪleɪtɪŋ] adj sprühend
scissors ['sɪzəz] npl Schere f; **a pair of ~**
eine Schere
scoff [skɔf] vt (BRIT: inf: eat) fressen ♦ vi
(*mock*): **to ~ (at)** spotten (über +acc)
scold [skəʊld] vt schimpfen
scone [skɔn] n weiche(s) Teegebäck nt
scoop [skuːp] n Schaufel f; (*news*)
sensationelle Erstmeldung f; **~ out** vt
herausschaufeln; **~ up** vt aufschaufeln;
(*liquid*) aufschöpfen
scooter ['skuːtəʳ] n Motorroller m; (*child's*)
Roller m
scope [skəʊp] n Ausmaß nt; (*opportunity*)
(Spiel)raum m
scorch [skɔːtʃ] n Brandstelle f ♦ vt
versengen; **~ing** adj brennend
score [skɔːʳ] n (*in game*) Punktzahl f; (*final ~*)
(Spiel)ergebnis nt; (MUS) Partitur f; (*line*)
Kratzer m; (*twenty*) zwanzig, zwanzig Stück
♦ vt (*goal*) schießen; (*points*) machen;
(*mark*) einritzen ♦ vi (*keep record*) Punkte
zählen; **on that ~** in dieser Hinsicht;
what's the ~? wie stehts?; **to ~ 6 out of
10** 6 von 10 Punkten erzielen; **~ out** vt
ausstreichen; **~board** n Anschreibetafel f;
~r n Torschütze m; (*recorder*) (Auf)schreiber
m
scorn [skɔːn] n Verachtung f ♦ vt verhöhnen;
~ful adj verächtlich
Scorpio ['skɔːpɪəʊ] n Skorpion m
Scot [skɔt] n Schotte m, Schottin f
Scotch [skɔtʃ] n Scotch m
scotch [skɔtʃ] vt (*end*) unterbinden
scot-free ['skɔt'friː] adv: **to get off ~~**
(*unpunished*) ungeschoren davonkommen
Scotland ['skɔtlənd] n Schottland nt
Scots [skɔts] adj schottisch; **~man/woman**
(*irreg*) n Schotte m/Schottin f
Scottish ['skɔtɪʃ] adj schottisch

scoundrel ['skaʊndrl] n Schuft m

scour ['skaʊəʳ] vt (search) absuchen; (clean) schrubben

scourge [skɔːdʒ] n (whip) Geißel f; (plague) Qual f

scout [skaʊt] n (MIL) Späher m; (also: **boy ~**) Pfadfinder m; **~ around** vi: **to ~ around (for)** sich umsehen (nach)

scowl [skaʊl] n finstere(r) Blick m ♦ vi finster blicken

scrabble ['skræbl] vi (also: **~ around**: search) (herum)tasten; (claw): **to ~ (at)** kratzen (an +dat) ♦ n: **S~** ® Scrabble nt ®

scraggy ['skrægɪ] adj dürr, hager

scram [skræm] (inf) vi abhauen

scramble ['skræmbl] n (climb) Kletterei f; (struggle) Kampf m ♦ vi klettern; (fight) sich schlagen; **to ~ out/through** krabbeln aus/durch; **to ~ for sth** sich um etw raufen; **~d eggs** npl Rührei nt

scrap [skræp] n (bit) Stückchen nt; (fight) Keilerei f; (also: **~ iron**) Schrott m ♦ vt verwerfen ♦ vi (fight) streiten, sich prügeln; **~s** npl (leftovers) Reste pl; (waste) Abfall m; **~book** n Einklebealbum nt; **~ dealer** n Schrotthändler(in) m(f)

scrape [skreɪp] n Kratzen nt; (trouble) Klemme f ♦ vt kratzen; (car) zerkratzen; (clean) abkratzen ♦ vi (make harsh noise) kratzen; **to ~ through** gerade noch durchkommen; **~r** n Kratzer m

scrap: **~ heap** n Schrotthaufen m; **on the ~ heap** (fig) beim alten Eisen; **~ iron** n Schrott m; **~ merchant** (BRIT) n Altwarenhändler(in) m(f); **~ paper** n Schmierpapier nt

scrappy ['skræpɪ] adj zusammengestoppelt

scratch [skrætʃ] n (wound) Kratzer m, Schramme f ♦ adj: **~ team** zusammengewürfelte Mannschaft ♦ vt kratzen; (car) zerkratzen ♦ vi (sich) kratzen; **to start from ~** ganz von vorne anfangen; **to be up to ~** den Anforderungen entsprechen

scrawl [skrɔːl] n Gekritzel nt ♦ vt, vi kritzeln

scrawny ['skrɔːnɪ] adj (person, neck) dürr

scream [skriːm] n Schrei m ♦ vi schreien

scree [skriː] n Geröll(halde f) nt

screech [skriːtʃ] n Schrei m ♦ vi kreischen

screen [skriːn] n (protective) Schutzschirm m; (CINE) Leinwand f; (TV) Bildschirm m ♦ vt (shelter) (be)schirmen; (film) zeigen, vorführen; **~ing** n (MED) Untersuchung f; **~play** n Drehbuch nt; **~ saver** n (COMPUT) Bildschirmschoner m

screw [skruː] n Schraube f ♦ vt (fasten) schrauben; (vulgar) bumsen; **~ up** vt (paper etc) zerknüllen; (inf: ruin) vermasseln (inf); **~driver** n Schraubenzieher m

scribble ['skrɪbl] n Gekritzel nt ♦ vt kritzeln

script [skrɪpt] n (handwriting) Handschrift f; (for film) Drehbuch nt; (THEAT) Manuskript nt, Text m

Scripture ['skrɪptʃəʳ] n Heilige Schrift f

scroll [skrəʊl] n Schriftrolle f

scrounge [skraʊndʒ] (inf) vt: **to ~ sth off** or **from sb** etw bei jdm abstauben ♦ n: **on the ~** beim Schnorren

scrub [skrʌb] n (clean) Schrubben nt; (in countryside) Gestrüpp nt ♦ vt (clean) schrubben

scruff [skrʌf] n: **by the ~ of the neck** am Genick

scruffy ['skrʌfɪ] adj unordentlich, vergammelt

scrum(mage) ['skrʌm(ɪdʒ)] n Getümmel nt

scruple ['skruːpl] n Skrupel m, Bedenken pl

scrupulous ['skruːpjʊləs] adj peinlich genau, gewissenhaft

scrutinize ['skruːtɪnaɪz] vt genau prüfen; **scrutiny** ['skruːtɪnɪ] n genaue Untersuchung f

scuff [skʌf] vt (shoes) abstoßen

scuffle ['skʌfl] n Handgemenge nt

sculptor ['skʌlptəʳ] n Bildhauer(in) m(f)

sculpture ['skʌlptʃəʳ] n (ART) Bildhauerei f; (statue) Skulptur f

scum [skʌm] n (also fig) Abschaum m

scurry ['skʌrɪ] vi huschen

scuttle ['skʌtl] n (also: **coal ~**) Kohleneimer m ♦ vt (ship) versenken ♦ vi (scamper): **to ~ away** or **off** sich davonmachen

scythe [saɪð] n Sense f

SDP (BRIT) n abbr = **Social Democratic**

Party

sea [si:] n Meer nt, See f; (fig) Meer nt ♦ adj Meeres-, See-; **by ~** (travel) auf dem Seeweg; **on the ~** (boat) auf dem Meer; (town) am Meer; **out to ~** aufs Meer hinaus; **out at ~** aufs Meer; **~board** n Küste f; **~food** n Meeresfrüchte pl; **~ front** n Strandpromenade f; **~going** adj seetüchtig, Hochsee-; **~gull** n Möwe f

seal [si:l] n (animal) Robbe f, Seehund m; (stamp, impression) Siegel nt ♦ vt versiegeln; **~ off** vt (place) abriegeln

sea level n Meeresspiegel m

sea lion n Seelöwe m

seam [si:m] n Saum m; (edges joining) Naht f; (of coal) Flöz nt

seaman ['si:mən] (irreg) n Seemann m

seaplane ['si:plein] n Wasserflugzeug nt

seaport ['si:pɔ:t] n Seehafen m

search [sə:tʃ] n (for person, thing) Suche f; (of drawer, pockets, house) Durchsuchung f ♦ vi suchen ♦ vt durchsuchen; **in ~ of** auf der Suche nach; **to ~ for** suchen nach; **~ through** vt durchsuchen; **~ing** adj (look) forschend; **~light** n Scheinwerfer m; **~ party** n Suchmannschaft f; **~ warrant** n Durchsuchungsbefehl m

sea: **~shore** ['si:ʃɔ:r] n Meeresküste f; **~sick** ['si:sik] adj seekrank; **~side** ['si:said] n Küste f; **~side resort** n Badeort m

season ['si:zn] n Jahreszeit f; (Christmas etc) Zeit f, Saison f ♦ vt (flavour) würzen; **~al** adj Saison-; **~ed** adj (fig) erfahren; **~ing** n Gewürz nt, Würze f; **~ ticket** n (RAIL) Zeitkarte f; (THEAT) Abonnement nt

seat [si:t] n Sitz m, Platz m; (in Parliament) Sitz m; (part of body) Gesäß nt; (of trousers) Hosenboden m ♦ vt (place) setzen; (have space for) Sitzplätze bieten für; **to be ~ed** sitzen; **~ belt** n Sicherheitsgurt m

sea: **~ water** n Meerwasser nt; **~weed** ['si:wi:d] n (See)tang m; **~worthy** ['si:wə:ði] adj seetüchtig

sec. abbr (= second(s)) Sek.

secluded [si'klu:did] adj abgelegen

seclusion [si'klu:ʒən] n Zurückgezogenheit f

second ['sekənd] adj zweite(r,s) ♦ adv (in ~ position) an zweiter Stelle ♦ n Sekunde f; (person) Zweite(r) mf; (COMM: imperfect) zweite Wahl f; (SPORT) Sekundant m; (AUT: also: **~ gear**) zweite(r) Gang m; (BRIT: UNIV: degree) mittlere Note bei Abschlussprüfungen ♦ vt (support) unterstützen; **~ary** adj zweitrangig; **~ary school** n höhere Schule f, Mittelschule f; **~-class** adj zweiter Klasse; **~hand** adj aus zweiter Hand; (car etc) gebraucht; **~ hand** n (on clock) Sekundenzeiger m; **~ly** adv zweitens

secondment [si'kɔndmənt] (BRIT) n Abordnung f

second-rate ['sekənd'reit] adj mittelmäßig

second thoughts npl: **to have ~** es sich dat anders überlegen; **on ~** (BRIT) or **thought** (US) oder lieber (nicht)

secrecy ['si:krəsi] n Geheimhaltung f

secret ['si:krit] n Geheimnis nt ♦ adj geheim, Geheim-; **in ~** geheim

secretarial [sekri'teəriəl] adj Sekretärinnen-

secretary ['sekrətəri] n Sekretär(in) m(f); **S~ of State** (BRIT) n (POL): **S~ of State (for)** Minister(in) m(f) (für)

secretion [si'kri:ʃən] n Absonderung f

secretive ['si:krətiv] adj geheimtuerisch

secretly ['si:kritli] adv geheim

sectarian [sek'teəriən] adj (riots etc) Konfessions-, zwischen den Konfessionen

section ['sekʃən] n Teil m; (department) Abteilung f; (of document) Abschnitt m

sector ['sektər] n Sektor m

secular ['sekjulər] adj weltlich, profan

secure [si'kjuər] adj (safe) sicher; (firmly fixed) fest ♦ vt (make firm) befestigen, sichern; (obtain) sichern; **security** [si'kjuəriti] n Sicherheit f; (pledge) Pfand nt; (document) Wertpapier nt; (national security) Staatssicherheit f; **security guard** n Sicherheitsbeamte(r) m, Wächter m, Wache f

sedan [sə'dæn] (US) n (AUT) Limousine f

sedate [si'deit] adj gesetzt ♦ vt (MED) ein Beruhigungsmittel geben +dat; **sedation** [si'deiʃən] n (MED) Einfluss m von Beruhigungsmitteln; **sedative** ['sedətiv] n

Beruhigungsmittel *nt* ♦ *adj* beruhigend, einschläfernd

sediment ['sɛdɪmənt] *n* (Boden)satz *m*

seduce [sɪ'dju:s] *vt* verführen; **seductive** [sɪ'dʌktɪv] *adj* verführerisch

see [si:] (*pt* **saw**, *pp* **seen**) *vt* sehen; (*understand*) (ein)sehen, erkennen; (*visit*) besuchen ♦ *vi* (*be aware*) sehen; (*find out*) nachsehen ♦ *n* (*ECCL: R.C.*) Bistum *nt*; (: *Protestant*) Kirchenkreis *m*; **to ~ sb to the door** jdn hinausbegleiten; **to ~ that** (*ensure*) dafür sorgen, dass; **~ you soon!** bis bald!; **~ about** *vt fus* sich kümmern um; **~ off** *vt*: **to ~ sb off** jdn zum Zug *etc* begleiten; **~ through** *vt*: **to ~ sth through** etw durchfechten; **to ~ through sb/sth** jdn/ etw durchschauen; **~ to** *vt fus*: **to ~ to it** dafür sorgen

seed [si:d] *n* Samen *m* ♦ *vt* (*TENNIS*) platzieren; **to go to ~** (*plant*) schießen; (*fig*) herunterkommen; **~ling** *n* Setzling *m*; **~y** *adj* (*café*) übel; (*person*) zweifelhaft

seeing ['si:ɪŋ] *conj*: **~ (that)** da

seek [si:k] (*pt*, *pp* **sought**) *vt* suchen

seem [si:m] *vi* scheinen; **it ~s that ...** es scheint, dass ...; **~ingly** *adv* anscheinend

seen [si:n] *pp of* **see**

seep [si:p] *vi* sickern

seesaw ['si:sɔ:] *n* Wippe *f*

seethe [si:ð] *vi*: **to ~ with anger** vor Wut kochen

see-through ['si:θru:] *adj* (*dress etc*) durchsichtig

segment ['sɛgmənt] *n* Teil *m*; (*of circle*) Ausschnitt *m*

segregate ['sɛgrɪgeɪt] *vt* trennen

seize [si:z] *vt* (*grasp*) (er)greifen, packen; (*power*) ergreifen; (*take legally*) beschlagnahmen; **~ (up)on** *vt fus* sich stürzen auf +*acc*; **~ up** *vi* (*TECH*) sich festfressen; **seizure** ['si:ʒəʳ] *n* (*illness*) Anfall *m*

seldom ['sɛldəm] *adv* selten

select [sɪ'lɛkt] *adj* ausgewählt ♦ *vt* auswählen; **~ion** [sɪ'lɛkʃən] *n* Auswahl *f*; **~ive** *adj* (*person*) wählerisch

self [sɛlf] (*pl* **selves**) *pron* selbst ♦ *n* Selbst

nt, Ich *nt*; **the ~** das Ich; **~-assured** *adj* selbstbewusst; **~-catering** (*BRIT*) *adj* für Selbstversorger; **~-centred** (*US* **self-centered**) *adj* egozentrisch; **~-coloured** (*US* **self-colored**) *adj* (*of one colour*) einfarbig, uni; **~-confidence** *n* Selbstvertrauen *nt*, Selbstbewusstsein *nt*; **~-conscious** *adj* gehemmt, befangen; **~-contained** *adj* (*complete*) (in sich) geschlossen; (*person*) verschlossen; (*BRIT: flat*) separat; **~-control** *n* Selbstbeherrschung *f*; **~-defence** (*US* **self-defense**) *n* Selbstverteidigung *f*; (*JUR*) Notwehr *f*; **~-discipline** *n* Selbstdisziplin *f*; **~-employed** *adj* frei(schaffend); **~-evident** *adj* offensichtlich; **~-governing** *adj* selbst verwaltet; **~-indulgent** *adj* zügellos; **~-interest** *n* Eigennutz *m*

selfish ['sɛlfɪʃ] *adj* egoistisch, selbstsüchtig; **~ness** *n* Egoismus *m*, Selbstsucht *f*

self: ~lessly *adv* selbstlos; **~-made** *adj*: **~-made man** Selfmademan *m*; **~-pity** *n* Selbstmitleid *nt*; **~-portrait** *n* Selbstbildnis *nt*; **~-possessed** *adj* selbstbeherrscht; **~-preservation** *n* Selbsterhaltung *f*; **~-reliant** *adj* unabhängig; **~-respect** *n* Selbstachtung *f*; **~-righteous** *adj* selbstgerecht; **~-sacrifice** *n* Selbstaufopferung *f*; **~-satisfied** *adj* selbstzufrieden; **~-service** *adj* Selbstbedienungs-; **~-sufficient** *adj* selbstgenügsam; **~-taught** *adj* selbst erlernt; **~-taught person** Autodidakt *m*

sell [sɛl] (*pt*, *pp* **sold**) *vt* verkaufen ♦ *vi* verkaufen; (*goods*) sich verkaufen; **to ~ at** *or* **for £10** für £10 verkaufen; **~ off** *vt* verkaufen; **~ out** *vi* alles verkaufen; **~-by date** *n* Verfalldatum *nt*; **~er** *n* Verkäufer *m*; **~ing price** *n* Verkaufspreis *m*

Sellotape ['sɛləʊteɪp] (® *BRIT*) *n* Tesafilm *m* ®

sellout ['sɛlaʊt] *n* (*of tickets*): **it was a ~** es war ausverkauft

selves [sɛlvz] *npl of* **self**

semaphore ['sɛməfɔ:ʳ] *n* Winkzeichen *pl*

semblance ['sɛmblns] *n* Anschein *m*

semen ['si:mən] *n* Sperma *nt*

semester [sɪˈmɛstəʳ] (US) n Semester nt
semi [ˈsɛmɪ] n = **semidetached house**;
  ~circle n Halbkreis m; **~colon** n
  Semikolon nt; **~conductor** n Halbleiter m;
  ~detached house (BRIT) n halbe(s)
  Doppelhaus nt; **~final** n Halbfinale nt
seminary [ˈsɛmɪnərɪ] n (REL) Priesterseminar
  nt
semiskilled [sɛmɪˈskɪld] adj angelernt
semi-skimmed [sɛmɪˈskɪmd] adj (milk)
  teilentrahmt, Halbfett-
senate [ˈsɛnɪt] n Senat m; **senator** n
  Senator m
send [sɛnd] (pt, pp **sent**) vt senden,
  schicken; (inf: inspire) hinreißen; **~ away**
  vt wegschicken; **~ away for** vt fus
  anfordern; **~ back** vt zurückschicken; **~**
  for vt fus holen lassen; **~ off** vt (goods)
  abschicken; (BRIT: SPORT: player) vom Feld
  schicken; **~ out** vt (invitation) aussenden; **~**
  up vt hinaufsenden; (BRIT: parody) verulken;
  ~er n Absender m; **~-off** n: **to give sb a**
  good ~-off jdn (ganz) groß verabschieden
senior [ˈsiːnɪəʳ] adj (older) älter; (higher rank)
  Ober- ♦ n (older person) Ältere(r) mf; (higher
  ranking) Rangälteste(r) mf; **~ citizen** n
  ältere(r) Mitbürger(in) m(f); **~ity** [siːnɪˈɔrɪtɪ]
  n (of age) höhere(s) Alter nt; (in rank)
  höhere(r) Dienstgrad m
sensation [sɛnˈseɪʃən] n Gefühl nt;
  (excitement) Sensation f, Aufsehen nt; **~al**
  adj (wonderful) wunderbar; (result)
  sensationell; (headlines etc) reißerisch
sense [sɛns] n Sinn m; (understanding)
  Verstand m, Vernunft f; (feeling) Gefühl nt
  ♦ vt fühlen, spüren; **~ of humour** Humor
  m; **to make ~** Sinn ergeben; **~less** adj
  sinnlos; (unconscious) besinnungslos
sensibility [sɛnsɪˈbɪlɪtɪ] n Empfindsamkeit f;
  (feeling hurt) Empfindlichkeit f; **sensibilities**
  npl (feelings) Zartgefühl nt
sensible [ˈsɛnsɪbl] adj vernünftig
sensitive [ˈsɛnsɪtɪv] adj: **~ (to)** empfindlich
  (gegen); **sensitivity** [sɛnsɪˈtɪvɪtɪ] n
  Empfindlichkeit f; (artistic) Feingefühl nt;
  (tact) Feinfühligkeit f
sensual [ˈsɛnsjuəl] adj sinnlich

sensuous [ˈsɛnsjuəs] adj sinnlich
sent [sɛnt] pt, pp of **send**
sentence [ˈsɛntns] n Satz m; (JUR) Strafe f;
  Urteil nt ♦ vt: **to ~ sb to death/to 5 years**
  jdn zum Tode/zu 5 Jahren verurteilen
sentiment [ˈsɛntɪmənt] n Gefühl nt;
  (thought) Gedanke m; **~al** [sɛntɪˈmɛntl] adj
  sentimental; (of feelings rather than reason)
  gefühlsmäßig
sentry [ˈsɛntrɪ] n (Schild)wache f
separate [adj ˈsɛprɪt, vb ˈsɛpəreɪt] adj
  getrennt, separat ♦ vt trennen ♦ vi sich
  trennen; **~ly** adv getrennt; **~s** npl (clothes)
  Röcke, Pullover etc; **separation** [sɛpəˈreɪʃən]
  n Trennung f
September [sɛpˈtɛmbəʳ] n September m
septic [ˈsɛptɪk] adj vereitert, septisch; **~ tank**
  n Klärbehälter m
sequel [ˈsiːkwl] n Folge f
sequence [ˈsiːkwəns] n (Reihen)folge f
sequin [ˈsiːkwɪn] n Paillette f
Serbia [ˈsəːbɪə] n Serbien nt
serene [sɪˈriːn] adj heiter
sergeant [ˈsɑːdʒənt] n Feldwebel m; (POLICE)
  (Polizei)wachtmeister m
serial [ˈsɪərɪəl] n Fortsetzungsroman m; (TV)
  Fernsehserie f ♦ adj (number) (fort)laufend;
  ~ize vt in Fortsetzungen veröffentlichen; in
  Fortsetzungen senden
series [ˈsɪərɪz] n inv Serie f, Reihe f
serious [ˈsɪərɪəs] adj ernst; (injury) schwer;
  ~ly adv ernst(haft); (hurt) schwer; **~ness** n
  Ernst m, Ernsthaftigkeit f
sermon [ˈsəːmən] n Predigt f
serrated [sɪˈreɪtɪd] adj gezackt
servant [ˈsəːvənt] n Diener(in) m(f)
serve [səːv] vt dienen +dat; (guest, customer)
  bedienen; (food) servieren ♦ vi dienen,
  nützen; (at table) servieren; (TENNIS) geben,
  aufschlagen; **it ~s him right** das geschieht
  ihm recht; **that'll ~ as a table** das geht als
  Tisch; **to ~ a summons (on sb)** (jdn) vor
  Gericht laden; **~ out** or **up** vt (food)
  auftragen, servieren
service [ˈsəːvɪs] n (help) Dienst m; (trains etc)
  Verbindung f; (hotel) Service m, Bedienung
  f; (set of dishes) Service nt; (REL)

Gottesdienst *m*; *(car)* Inspektion *f*; *(for TVs etc)* Kundendienst *m*; *(TENNIS)* Aufschlag *m* ♦ *vt (AUT, TECH)* warten, überholen; **the S~s** *npl (armed forces)* die Streitkräfte *pl*; **to be of ~ to sb** jdm einen großen Dienst erweisen; **~ included/not included** Bedienung inbegriffen/nicht inbegriffen; **~able** *adj* brauchbar; **~ area** *n (on motorway)* Raststätte *f*; **~ charge** *(BRIT) n* Bedienung *f*; **~man** *(irreg) n (soldier etc)* Soldat *m*; **~ station** *n* (Groß)tankstelle *f*

serviette [sɜːvɪˈet] *n* Serviette *f*

servile [ˈsɜːvaɪl] *adj* unterwürfig

session [ˈseʃən] *n* Sitzung *f*; *(POL)* Sitzungsperiode *f*; **to be in ~** tagen

set [set] *(pt, pp* set*) n (collection of things)* Satz *m*, Set *nt*; *(RAD, TV)* Apparat *m*; *(TENNIS)* Satz *m*; *(group of people)* Kreis *m*; *(CINE)* Szene *f*; *(THEAT)* Bühnenbild *nt* ♦ *adj* festgelegt; *(ready)* bereit ♦ *vt (place)* setzen, stellen, legen; *(arrange)* (an)ordnen; *(table)* decken; *(time, price)* festsetzen; *(alarm, watch, task)* stellen; *(jewels)* (ein)fassen; *(exam)* ausarbeiten ♦ *vi (sun)* untergehen; *(become hard)* fest werden; *(bone)* zusammenwachsen; **to be ~ on doing sth** etw unbedingt tun wollen; **to ~ to music** vertonen; **to ~ on fire** anstecken; **to ~ free** freilassen; **to ~ sth going** etw in Gang bringen; **to ~ sail** losfahren; **~ about** *vt fus (task)* anpacken; **~ aside** *vt* beiseite legen; **~ back** *vt*: **to ~ back (by)** zurückwerfen (um); **~ off** *vi* aufbrechen ♦ *vt (explode)* sprengen; *(alarm)* losgehen lassen; *(show up well)* hervorheben; **~ out** *vi*: **to ~ out to do sth** vorhaben, etw zu tun ♦ *vt (arrange)* anlegen, arrangieren; *(state)* darlegen; **~ up** *vt (organization)* aufziehen; *(record)* aufstellen; *(monument)* erstellen; **~back** *n* Rückschlag *m*; **~ meal** *n* Menü *nt*; **~ menu** *n* Tageskarte *f*

settee [seˈtiː] *n* Sofa *nt*

setting [ˈsetɪŋ] *n* Hintergrund *m*

settle [ˈsetl] *vt* beruhigen; *(pay)* begleichen, bezahlen; *(agree)* regeln ♦ *vi* sich einleben; *(come to rest)* sich niederlassen; *(sink)* sich setzen; *(calm down)* sich beruhigen; **to ~ for**

sth sich mit etw zufrieden geben; **to ~ on** sth sich für etw entscheiden; **to ~ up with sb** mit jdm abrechnen; **~ down** *vi (feel at home)* sich einleben; *(calm down)* sich beruhigen; **~ in** *vi* sich eingewöhnen; **~ment** *n* Regelung *f*; *(payment)* Begleichung *f*; *(colony)* Siedlung *f*; **~r** *n* Siedler *m*

setup [ˈsetʌp] *n (situation)* Lage *f*

seven [ˈsevn] *num* sieben; **~teen** *num* siebzehn; **~th** *adj* siebte(r, s) ♦ *n* Siebtel *nt*; **~ty** *num* siebzig

sever [ˈsevər] *vt* abtrennen

several [ˈsevrəl] *adj* mehrere, verschiedene ♦ *pron* mehrere; **~ of us** einige von uns

severance [ˈsevərəns] *n*: **~ pay** Abfindung *f*

severe [sɪˈvɪər] *adj (strict)* streng; *(serious)* schwer; *(climate)* rau; **severity** [sɪˈverɪtɪ] *n* Strenge *f*; Schwere *f*; Rauheit *f*

sew [səʊ] *(pt* sewed, *pp* sewn*) vt, vi* nähen; **~ up** *vt* zunähen

sewage [ˈsuːɪdʒ] *n* Abwässer *pl*

sewer [ˈsuːər] *n* (Abwasser)kanal *m*

sewing [ˈsəʊɪŋ] *n* Näharbeit *f*; **~ machine** *n* Nähmaschine *f*

sewn [səʊn] *pp of* sew

sex [seks] *n* Sex *m*; *(gender)* Geschlecht *nt*; **to have ~ with sb** mit jdm Geschlechtsverkehr haben; **~ism** *n* Sexismus *m*; **~ist** *adj* sexistisch ♦ *n* Sexist(in) *m(f)*; **~ual** [ˈseksjuəl] *adj* sexuell, geschlechtlich, Geschlechts-; **~uality** [seksjuˈælɪtɪ] *n* Sexualität *f*; **~y** *adj* sexy

shabby [ˈʃæbɪ] *adj (also fig)* schäbig

shack [ʃæk] *n* Hütte *f*

shackles [ˈʃæklz] *npl (also fig)* Fesseln *pl*, Ketten *pl*

shade [ʃeɪd] *n* Schatten *m*; *(for lamp)* Lampenschirm *m*; *(colour)* Farbton *m* ♦ *vt* abschirmen; **in the ~** im Schatten; **a ~ smaller** ein bisschen kleiner

shadow [ˈʃædəʊ] *n* Schatten *m* ♦ *vt (follow)* beschatten ♦ *adj*: **~ cabinet** *(BRIT: POL)* Schattenkabinett *nt*; **~y** *adj* schattig

shady [ˈʃeɪdɪ] *adj* schattig; *(fig)* zwielichtig

shaft [ʃɑːft] *n (of spear etc)* Schaft *m*; *(in mine)* Schacht *m*; *(TECH)* Welle *f*; *(of light)*

Strahl *m*

shaggy ['ʃægɪ] *adj* struppig

shake [ʃeɪk] (*pt* **shook**, *pp* **shaken**) *vt* schütteln, rütteln; (*shock*) erschüttern ♦ *vi* (*move*) schwanken; (*tremble*) zittern, beben ♦ *n* (*jerk*) Schütteln *nt*, Rütteln *nt*; **to ~ hands with** die Hand geben +*dat*; **to ~ one's head** den Kopf schütteln; **~ off** *vt* abschütteln; **~ up** *vt* aufschütteln; (*fig*) aufrütteln; **~n** ['ʃeɪkn] *pp of* **shake**; **shaky** ['ʃeɪkɪ] *adj* zittrig; (*weak*) unsicher

shall [ʃæl] *vb aux*: **I ~ go** ich werde gehen; **~ I open the door?** soll ich die Tür öffnen?; **I'll buy some cake, ~ I?** soll ich Kuchen kaufen?, ich kaufe Kuchen, oder?

shallow ['ʃæləʊ] *adj* seicht

sham [ʃæm] *n* Schein *m* ♦ *adj* unecht, falsch

shambles ['ʃæmblz] *n* Durcheinander *nt*

shame [ʃeɪm] *n* Scham *f*; (*disgrace, pity*) Schande *f* ♦ *vt* beschämen; **it is a ~ that** es ist schade, dass; **it is a ~ to do ...** es ist eine Schande, ... zu tun; **what a ~!** wie schade!; **~faced** *adj* beschämt; **~ful** *adj* schändlich; **~less** *adj* schamlos

shampoo [ʃæm'puː] *n* Shampoo(n) *nt* ♦ *vt* (*hair*) waschen; **~ and set** *n* Waschen *nt* und Legen

shamrock ['ʃæmrɔk] *n* Kleeblatt *nt*

shandy ['ʃændɪ] *n* Bier *nt* mit Limonade

shan't [ʃɑːnt] = **shall not**

shantytown ['ʃæntɪtaʊn] *n* Bidonville *f*

shape [ʃeɪp] *n* Form *f* ♦ *vt* formen, gestalten ♦ *vi* (*also:* **~ up**) sich entwickeln; **to take ~** Gestalt annehmen; **~d** *suffix*: **heart-~d** herzförmig; **~less** *adj* formlos; **~ly** *adj* wohlproportioniert

share [ʃɛəʳ] *n* (An)teil *m*; (*FIN*) Aktie *f* ♦ *vt* teilen; **to ~ out (among/between)** verteilen (unter/zwischen); **~holder** *n* Aktionär(in) *m(f)*

shark [ʃɑːk] *n* Hai(fisch) *m*; (*swindler*) Gauner *m*

sharp [ʃɑːp] *adj* scharf; (*pin*) spitz; (*person*) clever; (*MUS*) erhöht ♦ *n* Kreuz *nt* ♦ *adv* zu hoch; **nine o'clock ~** Punkt neun; **~en** *vt* schärfen; (*pencil*) spitzen; **~ener** *n* (*also:* **pencil ~ener**) Anspitzer *m*; **~-eyed** *adj*

scharfsichtig; **~ly** *adv* (*turn, stop*) plötzlich; (*stand out, contrast*) deutlich; (*criticize, retort*) scharf

shatter ['ʃætəʳ] *vt* zerschmettern; (*fig*) zerstören ♦ *vi* zerspringen

shave [ʃeɪv] *n* Rasur *f* ♦ *vt* rasieren ♦ *vi* sich rasieren; **to have a ~** sich rasieren (lassen); **~r** *n* (*also:* **electric ~r**) Rasierapparat *m*

shaving ['ʃeɪvɪŋ] *n* (*action*) Rasieren *nt*; **~s** *npl* (*of wood etc*) Späne *pl*; **~ brush** *n* Rasierpinsel *m*; **~ cream** *n* Rasiercreme *f*; **~ foam** *n* Rasierschaum *m*

shawl [ʃɔːl] *n* Schal *m*, Umhang *m*

she [ʃiː] *pron* sie ♦ *adj* weiblich

sheaf [ʃiːf] (*pl* **sheaves**) *n* Garbe *f*

shear [ʃɪəʳ] (*pt* **sheared**, *pp* **sheared** *or* **shorn**) *vt* scheren; **~ off** *vi* abbrechen; **~s** *npl* Heckenschere *f*

sheath [ʃiːθ] *n* Scheide *f*; (*condom*) Kondom *m or nt*

sheaves [ʃiːvz] *npl of* **sheaf**

shed [ʃed] (*pt, pp* **shed**) *n* Schuppen *m*; (*for animals*) Stall *m* ♦ *vt* (*leaves etc*) verlieren; (*tears*) vergießen

she'd [ʃiːd] = **she had**; **she would**

sheen [ʃiːn] *n* Glanz *m*

sheep [ʃiːp] *n inv* Schaf *nt*; **~dog** *n* Schäferhund *m*; **~ish** *adj* verlegen; **~skin** *n* Schaffell *nt*

sheer [ʃɪəʳ] *adj* bloß, rein; (*steep*) steil; (*transparent*) (hauch)dünn ♦ *adv* (*directly*) direkt

sheet [ʃiːt] *n* Betttuch *nt*, Bettlaken *nt*; (*of paper*) Blatt *nt*; (*of metal etc*) Platte *f*; (*of ice*) Fläche *f*

sheik(h) [ʃeɪk] *n* Scheich *m*

shelf [ʃelf] (*pl* **shelves**) *n* Bord *nt*, Regal *nt*

shell [ʃel] *n* Schale *f*; (*seashell*) Muschel *f*; (*explosive*) Granate *f* ♦ *vt* (*peas*) schälen; (*fire on*) beschießen

she'll [ʃiːl] = **she will**; **she shall**

shellfish ['ʃelfɪʃ] *n* Schalentier *nt*; (*as food*) Meeresfrüchte *pl*

shell suit *n* Ballonseidenanzug *m*

shelter ['ʃeltəʳ] *n* Schutz *m*; (*air-raid ~*) Bunker *m* ♦ *vt* schützen, bedecken; (*refugees*) aufnehmen ♦ *vi* sich unterstellen;

~ed adj (life) behütet; (spot) geschützt; ~ **housing** n (for old people) Altenwohnungen pl; (for handicapped people) Behindertenwohnungen pl

shelve [ʃelv] vt aufschieben ♦ vi abfallen

shelves [ʃelvz] npl of **shelf**

shepherd [ˈʃepəd] n Schäfer m ♦ vt treiben, führen; **~'s pie** n Auflauf aus Hackfleisch und Kartoffelbrei

sheriff [ˈʃerɪf] n Sheriff m; (SCOTTISH) Friedensrichter m

she's [ʃiːz] = **she is; she has**

Shetland [ˈʃetlənd] n (also: **the ~s, the ~ Isles**) die Shetlandinseln pl

shield [ʃiːld] n Schild m; (fig) Schirm m ♦ vt (be)schirmen; (TECH) abschirmen

shift [ʃɪft] n Verschiebung f; (work) Schicht f ♦ vt (ver)rücken, verschieben; (arm) wegnehmen ♦ vi sich verschieben; **~less** adj (person) träge; ~ **work** n Schichtarbeit f; **~y** adj verschlagen

shilly-shally [ˈʃɪlɪʃælɪ] vi zögern

shin [ʃɪn] n Schienbein nt

shine [ʃaɪn] (pt, pp **shone**) n Glanz m, Schein m ♦ vt polieren ♦ vi scheinen; (fig) glänzen; **to ~ a torch on sb** jdn (mit einer Lampe) anleuchten

shingle [ˈʃɪŋgl] n Strandkies m; **~s** npl (MED) Gürtelrose f

shiny [ˈʃaɪnɪ] adj glänzend

ship [ʃɪp] n Schiff nt ♦ vt verschiffen; **~building** n Schiffbau m; **~ment** n Schiffsladung f; **~per** n Verschiffer m; **~ping** n (act) Verschiffung f; (~s) Schifffahrt f; **~wreck** n Schiffbruch m; (destroyed ~) Wrack nt ♦ vt: **to be ~wrecked** Schiffbruch erleiden; **~yard** n Werft f

shire [ˈʃaɪəʳ] (BRIT) n Grafschaft f

shirk [ʃəːk] vt ausweichen +dat

shirt [ʃəːt] n (Ober)hemd nt; **in ~ sleeves** in Hemdsärmeln

shit [ʃɪt] (infl) excl Scheiße (!)

shiver [ˈʃɪvəʳ] n Schauer m ♦ vi frösteln, zittern

shoal [ʃəul] n (Fisch)schwarm m

shock [ʃɔk] n Erschütterung f; (mental)

Schock m; (ELEC) Schlag m ♦ vt erschüttern; (offend) schockieren; ~ **absorber** n Stoßdämpfer m; **~ed** adj geschockt, schockiert, erschüttert; **~ing** adj unerhört

shod [ʃɔd] pt, pp of **shoe**

shoddy [ˈʃɔdɪ] adj schäbig

shoe [ʃuː] (pt, pp **shod**) n Schuh m; (of horse) Hufeisen nt ♦ vt (horse) beschlagen; **~brush** n Schuhbürste f; **~horn** n Schuhlöffel m; **~lace** n Schnürsenkel m; ~ **polish** n Schuhcreme f; ~ **shop** n Schuhgeschäft nt; **~string** n (fig): **on a ~string** mit sehr wenig Geld

shone [ʃɔn] pt, pp of **shine**

shoo [ʃuː] excl sch; (to dog etc) pfui

shook [ʃuk] pt of **shake**

shoot [ʃuːt] (pt, pp **shot**) n (branch) Schössling m ♦ vt (gun) abfeuern; (goal, arrow) schießen; (person) anschießen; (kill) erschießen; (film) drehen ♦ vi (move quickly) schießen; **to ~ (at)** schießen (auf +acc); ~ **down** vt abschießen; ~ **in** vi hineinschießen; ~ **out** vi hinausschießen; ~ **up** vi (fig) aus dem Boden schießen; **~ing** n Schießerei f; **~ing star** n Sternschnuppe f

shop [ʃɔp] n (esp BRIT) Geschäft nt, Laden m; (workshop) Werkstatt f ♦ vi (also: **go ~ping**) einkaufen gehen; ~ **assistant** (BRIT) n Verkäufer(in) m(f); ~ **floor** (BRIT) n Werkstatt f; **~keeper** n Geschäftsinhaber m; **~lifting** n Ladendiebstahl m; **~per** n Käufer(in) m(f); **~ping** n Einkaufen nt, Einkauf m; **~ping bag** n Einkaufstasche f; **~ping centre** (US **shopping center**) n Einkaufszentrum nt; **~-soiled** adj angeschmutzt; ~ **steward** (BRIT) n (INDUSTRY) Betriebsrat m; ~ **window** n Schaufenster nt

shore [ʃɔːʳ] n Ufer nt; (of sea) Strand m ♦ vt: **to ~ up** abstützen

shorn [ʃɔːn] pp of **shear**

short [ʃɔːt] adj kurz; (person) klein; (curt) kurz angebunden; (measure) zu knapp ♦ n (also: ~ **film**) Kurzfilm m ♦ adv (suddenly) plötzlich ♦ vi (ELEC) einen Kurzschluss haben; **~s** npl (clothes) Shorts pl; **to be ~ of sth** nicht genug von etw haben; **in ~** kurz gesagt; **~ of doing sth** ohne so weit zu gehen, etw zu tun; **everything ~ of ...** alles außer ...; **it is ~ for** das ist die Kurzform von; **to cut ~** abkürzen; **to fall ~ of sth** etw nicht erreichen; **to stop ~** plötzlich anhalten; **to stop ~ of** Halt machen vor; **~age** n Knappheit f, Mangel m; **~bread** n Mürbegebäck nt; **~change** vt: **to ~change sb** jdm zu wenig herausgeben; **~circuit** n Kurzschluss m ♦ vi einen Kurzschluss haben ♦ vt kurzschließen; **~coming** n Mangel m; **~(crust) pastry** (BRIT) n Mürbeteig m; **~ cut** n Abkürzung f; **~en** vt (ab)kürzen; (clothes) kürzer machen; **~fall** n Defizit nt; **~hand** (BRIT) n Stenografie f; **~hand typist** (BRIT) n Stenotypistin f; **~ list** (BRIT) n (for job) engere Wahl f; **~lived** adj kurzlebig; **~ly** adv bald; **~ notice** n: **at ~ notice** kurzfristig; **~sighted** (BRIT) adj (also fig) kurzsichtig; **~staffed** adj: **to be ~staffed** zu wenig Personal haben; **~stay** n (car park) Kurzparken nt; **~ story** n Kurzgeschichte f; **~tempered** adj leicht aufbrausend; **~term** adj (effect) kurzfristig; **~ wave** n (RAD) Kurzwelle f

shot [ʃɔt] pt, pp of **shoot** ♦ n (from gun) Schuss m; (person) Schütze m; (try) Versuch m; (injection) Spritze f; (PHOT) Aufnahme f; **like a ~** wie der Blitz; **~gun** n Schrotflinte f

should [ʃud] vb aux: **I ~ go now** ich sollte jetzt gehen; **he ~ be there now** er sollte eigentlich schon da sein; **I ~ go if I were you** ich würde gehen, wenn ich du wäre; **I ~ like to** ich möchte gerne

shoulder ['ʃəuldər] n Schulter f; (BRIT: of road): **hard ~** Seitenstreifen m (rifle) schultern; (fig) auf sich nehmen; **~ bag** n Umhängetasche f; **~ blade** n Schulterblatt nt; **~ strap** n (of dress etc) Träger m

shouldn't ['ʃudnt] = **should not**

shout [ʃaut] n Schrei m; (call) Ruf m ♦ vt rufen ♦ vi schreien; **~ down** vt niederbrüllen; **~ing** n Geschrei nt

shove [ʃʌv] n Schubs m, Stoß m ♦ vt

schieben, stoßen, schubsen; (inf: put): **to ~ sth in(to) sth** etw in etw acc hineinschieben; **~ off** vi (NAUT) abstoßen; (fig: inf) abhauen

shovel ['ʃʌvl] n Schaufel f ♦ vt schaufeln

show [ʃəu] (pt **showed**, pp **shown**) n (display) Schau f; (exhibition) Ausstellung f; (CINE, THEAT) Vorstellung f, Show f ♦ vt zeigen; (kindness) erweisen ♦ vi zu sehen sein; **to be on ~** (exhibits etc) ausgestellt sein; **to ~ sb in** jdn hereinführen; **to ~ sb out** jdn hinausbegleiten; **~ off** vi (pej) angeben ♦ vt (display) ausstellen; **~ up** vi (stand out) sich abheben, (arrive) erscheinen ♦ vt aufzeigen; (unmask) bloßstellen; **~ business** n Showbusiness nt; **~down** n Kraftprobe f

shower ['ʃauər] n Schauer m; (of stones) (Stein)hagel m; (~ bath) Dusche f ♦ vi duschen ♦ vt: **to ~ sb with sth** jdn mit etw überschütten; **~proof** adj Wasser abstoßend

showing ['ʃəuɪŋ] n Vorführung f

show jumping n Turnierreiten nt

shown [ʃəun] pp of **show**

show: **~off** ['ʃəuɔf] n Angeber(in) m(f); **~piece** ['ʃəupiːs] n Paradestück nt; **~room** ['ʃəurum] n Ausstellungsraum m

shrank [ʃræŋk] pt of **shrink**

shred [ʃred] n Fetzen m ♦ vt zerfetzen; (COOK) raspeln; **~der** n (COOK) Gemüseschneider m; (for documents) Reißwolf m

shrewd [ʃruːd] adj clever

shriek [ʃriːk] n Schrei m ♦ vt, vi kreischen, schreien

shrill [ʃrɪl] adj schrill

shrimp [ʃrɪmp] n Krabbe f, Garnele f

shrine [ʃraɪn] n Schrein m; (fig) Gedenkstätte f

shrink [ʃrɪŋk] (pt **shrank**, pp **shrunk**) vi schrumpfen, eingehen ♦ vt einschrumpfen lassen; **to ~ from doing sth** davor zurückschrecken, etw zu tun; **~age** n Schrumpfung f; **~wrap** vt einschweißen

shrivel ['ʃrɪvl] vt, vi (also: ~ **up**) schrumpfen, schrumpeln

shroud [ʃraud] *n* Leichentuch *nt* ♦ *vt*: **~ed in mystery** mit einem Geheimnis umgeben

Shrove Tuesday ['ʃrəuv-] *n* Fastnachtsdienstag *m*

shrub [ʃrʌb] *n* Busch *m*, Strauch *m*; **~bery** *n* Gebüsch *nt*

shrug [ʃrʌg] *n* Achselzucken *nt* ♦ *vt, vi*: **to ~ (one's shoulders)** die Achseln zucken; **~ off** *vt* auf die leichte Schulter nehmen

shrunk [ʃrʌŋk] *pp of* **shrink**

shudder ['ʃʌdə'] *n* Schauder *m* ♦ *vi* schaudern

shuffle ['ʃʌfl] *vt* (*cards*) mischen; **to ~ (one's feet)** schlurfen

shun [ʃʌn] *vt* scheuen, (ver)meiden

shunt [ʃʌnt] *vt* rangieren

shut [ʃʌt] (*pt, pp* **shut**) *vt* schließen, zumachen ♦ *vi* sich schließen (lassen); **~ down** *vt, vi* schließen; **~ off** *vt* (*supply*) abdrehen; **~ up** *vi* (*keep quiet*) den Mund halten ♦ *vt* (*close*) zuschließen; **~ter** *n* Fensterladen *m*; (*PHOT*) Verschluss *m*

shuttle ['ʃʌtl] *n* (*plane, train etc*) Pendelflugzeug *nt*/-zug *m etc*; (*space ~*) Raumtransporter *m*; (*also*: **~ service**) Pendelverkehr *m*; **~cock** ['ʃʌtlkɔk] *n* Federball *m*; **~ diplomacy** *n* Pendeldiplomatie *f*

shy [ʃaɪ] *adj* schüchtern; **~ness** *n* Schüchternheit *f*

Siamese [saɪə'miːz] *adj*: **~ cat** Siamkatze *f*

Siberia [saɪ'bɪərɪə] *n* Sibirien *nt*

sibling ['sɪblɪŋ] *n* Geschwister *nt*

Sicily ['sɪsɪlɪ] *n* Sizilien *nt*

sick [sɪk] *adj* krank; (*joke*) makaber; **I feel ~** mir ist schlecht; **I was ~** ich habe gebrochen; **to be ~ of sb/sth** jdn/etw satt haben; **~ bay** *n* (Schiffs)lazarett *nt*; **~en** *vt* (*disgust*) krank machen ♦ *vi* krank werden; **~ening** *adj* (*annoying*) zum Weinen

sickle ['sɪkl] *n* Sichel *f*

sick: **~ leave** *n*: **to be on ~ leave** krankgeschrieben sein; **~ly** *adj* kränklich, blass; (*causing nausea*) widerlich; **~ness** *n* Krankheit *f*; (*vomiting*) Übelkeit *f*, Erbrechen *nt*; **~ note** *n* Arbeitsunfähigkeits- bescheinigung *f*; **~ pay** *n* Krankengeld

nt

side [saɪd] *n* Seite *f* ♦ *adj* (*door, entrance*) Seiten-, Neben- ♦ *vi*: **to ~ with sb** jds Partei ergreifen; **by the ~ of** neben; **~ by ~** nebeneinander; **on all ~s** von allen Seiten; **to take ~s (with)** Partei nehmen (für); **from all ~s** von allen Seiten; **~board** *n* Sideboard *nt*; **~boards** (*BRIT*) *npl* Koteletten *pl*; **~burns** *npl* Koteletten *pl*; **~car** *n* Beiwagen *m*; **~ drum** *n* (*MUS*) kleine Trommel; **~ effect** *n* Nebenwirkung *f*; **~light** *n* (*AUT*) Parkleuchte *f*; **~line** *n* (*SPORT*) Seitenlinie *f*; (*fig: hobby*) Nebenbeschäftigung *f*; **~long** *adj* Seiten-; **~ order** *n* Beilage *f*; **~saddle** *adv* im Damensattel; **~ show** *n* Nebenausstellung *f*; **~step** *vt* (*fig*) ausweichen; **~ street** *n* Seitenstraße *f*; **~track** *vt* (*fig*) ablenken; **~walk** (*US*) *n* Bürgersteig *m*; **~ways** *adv* seitwärts

siding ['saɪdɪŋ] *n* Nebengleis *nt*

sidle ['saɪdl] *vi*: **to ~ up (to)** sich heranmachen (an +*acc*)

siege [siːdʒ] *n* Belagerung *f*

sieve [sɪv] *n* Sieb *nt* ♦ *vt* sieben

sift [sɪft] *vt* sieben; (*fig*) sichten

sigh [saɪ] *n* Seufzer *m* ♦ *vi* seufzen

sight [saɪt] *n* (*power of seeing*) Sehvermögen *nt*; (*look*) Blick *m*; (*fact of seeing*) Anblick *m*; (*of gun*) Visier *nt* ♦ *vt* sichten; **in ~** in Sicht; **out of ~** außer Sicht; **~seeing** *n* Besuch *m* von Sehenswürdigkeiten; **to go ~seeing** Sehenswürdigkeiten besichtigen

sign [saɪn] *n* Zeichen *nt*; (*notice, road ~ etc*) Schild *nt* ♦ *vt* unterschreiben; **to ~ sth over to sb** jdm etw überschreiben; **~ on** *vi* (*as unemployed*) sich (arbeitslos) melden ♦ *vt* (*employee*) anstellen; **~ up** *vi* (*MIL*) sich verpflichten ♦ *vt* verpflichten

signal ['sɪgnl] *n* Signal *nt* ♦ *vt* ein Zeichen geben +*dat*; **~man** (*irreg*) *n* (*RAIL*) Stellwerkswärter *m*

signature ['sɪgnətʃə'] *n* Unterschrift *f*; **~ tune** *n* Erkennungsmelodie *f*

signet ring ['sɪgnət-] *n* Siegelring *m*

significance [sɪg'nɪfɪkəns] *n* Bedeutung *f*

significant [sɪg'nɪfɪkənt] *adj* (*meaning sth*)

bedeutsam; (*important*) bedeutend
signify ['sɪgnɪfaɪ] *vt* bedeuten; (*show*) andeuten, zu verstehen geben
sign language *n* Zeichensprache *f*, Fingersprache *f*
signpost ['saɪnpəʊst] *n* Wegweiser *m*
silence ['saɪləns] *n* Stille *f*; (*of person*) Schweigen *nt* ♦ *vt* zum Schweigen bringen; **~r** *n* (*on gun*) Schalldämpfer *m*; (*BRIT: AUT*) Auspufftopf *m*
silent ['saɪlənt] *adj* still; (*person*) schweigsam; **to remain ~** schweigen; **~ partner** *n* (*COMM*) stille(r) Teilhaber *m*
silicon chip ['sɪlɪkən-] *n* Siliciumchip *m*, Siliziumchip *m*
silk [sɪlk] *n* Seide *f* ♦ *adj* seiden, Seiden-; **~y** *adj* seidig
silly ['sɪlɪ] *adj* dumm, albern
silt [sɪlt] *n* Schlamm *m*, Schlick *m*
silver ['sɪlvə*r*] *n* Silber *nt* ♦ *adj* silbern, Silber-; **~ paper** (*BRIT*) *n* Silberpapier *nt*; **~-plated** *adj* versilbert; **~smith** *n* Silberschmied *m*; **~ware** *n* Silber *nt*; **~y** *adj* silbern
similar ['sɪmɪlə*r*] *adj*: **~ (to)** ähnlich (+*dat*); **~ity** [sɪmɪ'lærɪtɪ] *n* Ähnlichkeit *f*; **~ly** *adv* in ähnlicher Weise
simmer ['sɪmə*r*] *vi* sieden ♦ *vt* sieden lassen
simple ['sɪmpl] *adj* einfach; **~(-minded)** *adj* einfältig
simplicity [sɪm'plɪsɪtɪ] *n* Einfachheit *f*; (*of person*) Einfältigkeit *f*
simplify ['sɪmplɪfaɪ] *vt* vereinfachen
simply ['sɪmplɪ] *adv* einfach
simulate ['sɪmjʊleɪt] *vt* simulieren
simultaneous [sɪməl'teɪnɪəs] *adj* gleichzeitig
sin [sɪn] *n* Sünde *f* ♦ *vi* sündigen
since [sɪns] *adv* seither ♦ *prep* seit, seitdem ♦ *conj* (*time*) seit; (*because*) da, weil; **~ then** seitdem
sincere [sɪn'sɪə*r*] *adj* aufrichtig; **~ly** *adv*: **yours ~ly** mit freundlichen Grüßen; **sincerity** [sɪn'serɪtɪ] *n* Aufrichtigkeit *f*
sinew ['sɪnju:] *n* Sehne *f*
sinful ['sɪnfʊl] *adj* sündig, sündhaft
sing [sɪŋ] (*pt* **sang**, *pp* **sung**) *vt*, *vi* singen
Singapore [sɪŋgə'pɔ:*r*] *n* Singapur *nt*

singe [sɪndʒ] *vt* versengen
singer ['sɪŋə*r*] *n* Sänger(in) *m(f)*
singing ['sɪŋɪŋ] *n* Singen *nt*, Gesang *m*
single ['sɪŋgl] *adj* (*one only*) einzig; (*bed, room*) Einzel-, einzeln; (*unmarried*) ledig; (*BRIT: ticket*) einfach; (*having one part only*) einzeln ♦ *n* (*BRIT: also:* **~ ticket**) einfache Fahrkarte *f*; **in ~ file** hintereinander; **~ out** *vt* aussuchen, auswählen; **~ bed** *n* Einzelbett *nt*; **~-breasted** *adj* einreihig; **~-handed** *adj* allein; **~-minded** *adj* zielstrebig; **~ parent** *n* Alleinerziehende(r) *f(m)*; **~ room** *n* Einzelzimmer *nt*; **~s** *n* (*TENNIS*) Einzel *nt*; **~-track road** *n* einspurige Straße (mit Ausweichstellen)
singly *adv* einzeln, allein
singular ['sɪŋgjʊlə*r*] *adj* (*odd*) merkwürdig, seltsam ♦ *n* (*GRAM*) Einzahl *f*, Singular *m*
sinister ['sɪnɪstə*r*] *adj* (*evil*) böse; (*ghostly*) unheimlich
sink [sɪŋk] (*pt* **sank**, *pp* **sunk**) *n* Spülbecken *nt* ♦ *vt* (*ship*) versenken ♦ *vi* sinken; **to ~ sth into** (*teeth, claws*) etw schlagen in +*acc*; **~ in** *vi* (*news etc*) eingehen
sinner ['sɪnə*r*] *n* Sünder(in) *m(f)*
sinus ['saɪnəs] *n* (*ANAT*) Sinus *m*
sip [sɪp] *n* Schlückchen *nt* ♦ *vt* nippen an +*dat*
siphon ['saɪfən] *n* Siphon(flasche *f*) *m*; **~ off** *vt* absaugen; (*fig*) abschöpfen
sir [sə*r*] *n* (*respect*) Herr *m*; (*knight*) Sir *m*; **S~ John Smith** Sir John Smith; **yes ~** ja(wohl, mein Herr)
siren ['saɪərn] *n* Sirene *f*
sirloin ['sə:lɔɪn] *n* Lendenstück *nt*
sissy ['sɪsɪ] (*inf*) *n* Waschlappen *m*
sister ['sɪstə*r*] *n* Schwester *f*; (*BRIT: nurse*) Oberschwester *f*; (*nun*) Ordensschwester *f*; **~-in-law** *n* Schwägerin *f*
sit [sɪt] (*pt, pp* **sat**) *vi* sitzen; (*hold session*) tagen ♦ *vt* (*exam*) machen; **~ down** *vi* sich hinsetzen; **~ in on** *vt fus* dabei sein bei; **~ up** *vi* (*after lying*) sich aufsetzen; (*straight*) sich gerade setzen; (*at night*) aufbleiben
sitcom ['sɪtkɔm] *n abbr* (= *situation comedy*) Situationskomödie *f*
site [saɪt] *n* Platz *m*; (*also*: **building ~**)

Baustelle f ♦ vt legen

sitting ['sɪtɪŋ] n (meeting) Sitzung f; ~ **room** n Wohnzimmer nt

situated ['sɪtjueɪtɪd] adj: **to be** ~ liegen

situation [sɪtju'eɪʃən] n Situation f, Lage f; (place) Lage f; (employment) Stelle f; **"~s vacant"** (BRIT) „Stellenangebote" pl

six [sɪks] num sechs; **~teen** num sechzehn; **~th** adj sechste(r, s) ♦ n Sechstel nt; **~ty** num sechzig

size [saɪz] n Größe f; (of project) Umfang m; ~ **up** vt (assess) abschätzen, einschätzen; **~able** adj ziemlich groß, ansehnlich

sizzle ['sɪzl] vi zischen; (COOK) brutzeln

skate [skeɪt] n Schlittschuh m; (fish: pl inv) Rochen m ♦ vi Schlittschuh laufen; **~board** n Skateboard nt; **~boarding** n Skateboardfahren nt; **~r** n Schlittschuhläufer(in) m(f); **skating** ['skeɪtɪŋ] n Eislauf m; **to go skating** Eis laufen gehen; **skating rink** n Eisbahn f

skeleton ['skelɪtn] n Skelett nt; (fig) Gerüst nt; ~ **key** n Dietrich m; ~ **staff** n Notbesetzung f

skeptical ['skeptɪkl] (US) adj = **sceptical**

sketch [sketʃ] n Skizze f; (THEAT) Sketch m ♦ vt skizzieren; **~book** n Skizzenbuch nt; **~y** adj skizzenhaft

skewer ['skjuːəʳ] n Fleischspieß m

ski [skiː] n Ski m, Schi m ♦ vi Ski or Schi laufen; ~ **boot** n Skistiefel m

skid [skɪd] n (AUT) Schleudern nt ♦ vi rutschen; (AUT) schleudern

ski: **~er** ['skiːəʳ] n Skiläufer(in) m(f); **~ing** ['skiːɪŋ] n: **to go ~ing** Ski laufen gehen; **~-jump** n Sprungschanze f ♦ vi Ski springen

skilful ['skɪlful] adj geschickt

ski-lift n Skilift m

skill [skɪl] n Können nt; **~ed** adj geschickt; (worker) Fach-, gelernt

skim [skɪm] vt (liquid) abschöpfen; (glide over) gleiten über +acc ♦ vi: ~ **through** (book) überfliegen; **~med milk** n Magermilch f

skimp [skɪmp] vt (do carelessly) oberflächlich tun; **~y** adj (dress) knapp

skin [skɪn] n Haut f; (peel) Schale f ♦ vt abhäuten; schälen; ~ **cancer** n Hautkrebs m; **~-deep** adj oberflächlich; ~ **diving** n Schwimmtauchen nt; **~head** n Skinhead m; **~ny** adj dünn; **~tight** adj (dress etc) hauteng

skip [skɪp] n Sprung m ♦ vi hüpfen; (with rope) Seil springen ♦ vt (pass over) übergehen

ski: ~ **pants** npl Skihosen pl; ~ **pass** n Skipass nt; ~ **pole** n Skistock m

skipper ['skɪpəʳ] n Kapitän m ♦ vt führen

skipping rope ['skɪpɪŋ-] (BRIT) n Hüpfseil nt

skirmish ['skəːmɪʃ] n Scharmützel nt

skirt [skəːt] n Rock m ♦ vt herumgehen um; (fig) umgehen; **~ing board** (BRIT) n Fußleiste f

ski suit n Skianzug m

skit [skɪt] n Parodie f

ski tow n Schlepplift m

skittle ['skɪtl] n Kegel m; **~s** n (game) Kegeln nt

skive [skaɪv] (BRIT: inf) vi schwänzen

skulk [skʌlk] vi sich herumdrücken

skull [skʌl] n Schädel m

skunk [skʌŋk] n Stinktier nt

sky [skaɪ] n Himmel m; **~light** n Oberlicht nt; **~scraper** n Wolkenkratzer m

slab [slæb] n (of stone) Platte f

slack [slæk] adj (loose) locker; (business) flau; (careless) nachlässig, lasch ♦ vi nachlässig sein ♦ n: **to take up the** ~ straff ziehen; **~s** npl (trousers) Hose(n pl) f; **~en** vi (also: **~en off**) locker werden; (: slow down) stocken, nachlassen ♦ vt (: loosen) lockern

slag [slæg] (BRIT) vt: ~ **off** (criticize) (he)runtermachen

slag heap [slæg-] n Halde f

slain [sleɪn] pp of **slay**

slam [slæm] n Knall m ♦ vt (door) zuschlagen; (throw down) knallen ♦ vi zuschlagen

slander ['slɑːndəʳ] n Verleumdung f ♦ vt verleumden

slang [slæŋ] n Slang m; (jargon) Jargon m

slant [slɑːnt] n Schräge f; (fig) Tendenz f ♦ vt schräg legen ♦ vi schräg liegen; **~ed** adj schräg; **~ing** adj schräg

slap [slæp] n Klaps m ♦ vt einen Klaps geben +dat ♦ adv (directly) geradewegs; **~dash** adj salopp; **~stick** n (comedy) Klamauk m; **~-up** (BRIT) adj (meal) erstklassig, prima

slash [slæʃ] n Schnittwunde f ♦ vt (auf)schlitzen

slat [slæt] n Leiste f

slate [sleɪt] n (stone) Schiefer m; (roofing) Dachziegel m ♦ vt (criticize) verreißen

slaughter ['slɔːtəʳ] n (of animals) Schlachten nt; (of people) Gemetzel nt ♦ vt schlachten; (people) niedermetzeln; **~house** n Schlachthof m

Slav [slɑːv] adj slawisch

slave [sleɪv] n Sklave m, Sklavin f ♦ vi schuften, sich schinden; **~ry** n Sklaverei f

slay [sleɪ] (pt slew, pp slain) vt ermorden

sleazy ['sliːzɪ] adj (place) schmierig

sledge [slɛdʒ] n Schlitten m

sledgehammer ['slɛdʒhæməʳ] n Schmiedehammer m

sledging n Schlittenfahren nt

sleek [sliːk] adj glatt; (shape) rassig

sleep [sliːp] (pt, pp slept) n Schlaf m ♦ vi schlafen; **to go to ~** einschlafen; **~ in** vi ausschlafen; (oversleep) verschlafen; **~er** n (person) Schläfer m; (BRIT: RAIL) Schlafwagen m; (: beam) Schwelle f; **~ing bag** n Schlafsack m; **~ing car** n Schlafwagen m; **~ing partner** n = **silent partner**; **~ing pill** n Schlaftablette f; **~less** adj (night) schlaflos; **~walker** n Schlafwandler(in) m(f); **~y** adj schläfrig

sleet [sliːt] n Schneeregen m

sleeve [sliːv] n Ärmel m; (of record) Umschlag m; **~less** adj ärmellos

sleigh [sleɪ] n Pferdeschlitten m

sleight [slaɪt] n: **~ of hand** Fingerfertigkeit f

slender ['slɛndəʳ] adj schlank; (fig) gering

slept [slɛpt] pt, pp of **sleep**

slew [sluː] vi (veer) (herum)schwenken ♦ pt of **slay**

slice [slaɪs] n Scheibe f ♦ vt in Scheiben schneiden

slick [slɪk] adj (clever) raffiniert, aalglatt ♦ n Ölteppich m

slid [slɪd] pt, pp of **slide**

slide [slaɪd] (pt, pp slid) n Rutschbahn f; (PHOT) Dia(positiv) nt; (BRIT: for hair) (Haar)spange f ♦ vt schieben ♦ vi (slip) gleiten, rutschen; **sliding** ['slaɪdɪŋ] adj (door) Schiebe-; **sliding scale** n gleitende Skala f

slight [slaɪt] adj zierlich; (trivial) geringfügig; (small) gering ♦ n Kränkung f ♦ vt (offend) kränken; **not in the ~est** nicht im Geringsten; **~ly** adv etwas, ein bisschen

slim [slɪm] adj schlank; (book) dünn; (chance) gering ♦ vi eine Schlankheitskur machen

slime [slaɪm] n Schleim m

slimming ['slɪmɪŋ] n Schlankheitskur f

slimy ['slaɪmɪ] adj glitschig; (dirty) schlammig; (person) schmierig

sling [slɪŋ] (pt, pp slung) n Schlinge f; (weapon) Schleuder f ♦ vt schleudern

slip [slɪp] n (mistake) Flüchtigkeitsfehler m; (petticoat) Unterrock m; (of paper) Zettel m ♦ vt (put) stecken, schieben ♦ vi (lose balance) ausrutschen; (move) gleiten, rutschen; (decline) nachlassen; (move smoothly): **to ~ in/out** (person) hinein-/hinausschlüpfen; **to give sb the ~** jdm entwischen; **~ of the tongue** Versprecher m; **it ~ped my mind** das ist mir entfallen; **to ~ sth on/off** etw über-/abstreifen; **~ away** vi sich wegstehlen; **~ in** vt hineingleiten lassen ♦ vi (errors) sich einschleichen; **~ped disc** n Bandscheibenschaden m

slipper ['slɪpəʳ] n Hausschuh m

slippery ['slɪpərɪ] adj glatt

slip: **~ road** (BRIT) n Auffahrt f/Ausfahrt f; **~shod** adj schlampig; **~-up** n Panne f; **~way** n Auslaufbahn f

slit [slɪt] (pt, pp slit) n Schlitz m ♦ vt aufschlitzen

slither ['slɪðəʳ] vi schlittern; (snake) sich schlängeln

sliver ['slɪvəʳ] n (of glass, wood) Splitter m; (of cheese) Scheibchen nt

slob [slɔb] (inf) n Klotz m

slog [slɔg] vi (work hard) schuften ♦ n: **it was a ~** es war eine Plackerei

slogan ['sləʊgən] n Schlagwort nt; (COMM)

Werbespruch *m*

slop [slɔp] *vi* (*also:* ~ **over**) überschwappen ♦ *vt* verschütten

slope [sləup] *n* Neigung *f*; (*of mountains*) (Ab)hang *m* ♦ *vi:* **to** ~ **down** sich senken; **to** ~ **up** ansteigen; **sloping** ['sləupɪŋ] *adj* schräg

sloppy ['slɔpɪ] *adj* schlampig

slot [slɔt] *n* Schlitz *m* ♦ *vt:* **to** ~ **sth in** in etw einlegen

sloth [sləuθ] *n* (*laziness*) Faulheit *f*

slot machine *n* (*BRIT*) Automat *m*; (*for gambling*) Spielautomat *m*

slouch [slautʃ] *vi:* **to** ~ **about** (*laze*) herumhängen (*inf*)

slovenly ['slʌvənlɪ] *adj* schlampig; (*speech*) salopp

slow [sləu] *adj* langsam ♦ *adv* langsam; **to be** ~ (*clock*) nachgehen; (*stupid*) begriffsstutzig sein; **"~"** (*road sign*) „Langsam"; **in** ~ **motion** in Zeitlupe; ~ **down** *vi* langsamer werden ♦ *vt* verlangsamen; ~ **up** *vi* sich verlangsamen, sich verzögern ♦ *vt* aufhalten, langsamer machen; ~**ly** *adv* langsam

sludge [slʌdʒ] *n* Schlamm *m*

slug [slʌg] *n* Nacktschnecke *f*; (*inf: bullet*) Kugel *f*

sluggish ['slʌgɪʃ] *adj* träge; (*COMM*) schleppend

sluice [slu:s] *n* Schleuse *f*

slum [slʌm] *n* (*house*) Elendsquartier *nt*

slump [slʌmp] *n* Rückgang *m* ♦ *vi* fallen, stürzen

slung [slʌŋ] *pt, pp of* **sling**

slur [slɜːʳ] *n* Undeutlichkeit *f*; (*insult*) Verleumdung *f*; ~**red** [slɜːd] *adj* (*pronunciation*) undeutlich

slush [slʌʃ] *n* (*snow*) Schneematsch *m*; ~ **fund** *n* Schmiergeldfonds *m*

slut [slʌt] *n* Schlampe *f*

sly [slaɪ] *adj* schlau

smack [smæk] *n* Klaps *m* ♦ *vt* einen Klaps geben +*dat* ♦ *vi:* **to** ~ **of** riechen nach; **to** ~ **one's lips** schmatzen, sich *dat* die Lippen lecken

small [smɔːl] *adj* klein; **in the** ~ **hours** in den frühen Morgenstunden; ~ **ads** (*BRIT*) *npl* Kleinanzeigen *pl*; ~ **change** *n* Kleingeld *nt*; ~**holder** (*BRIT*) *n* Kleinbauer *m*; ~**pox** *n* Pocken *pl*; ~ **talk** *n* Geplauder *nt*

smart [smɑːt] *adj* (*fashionable*) elegant, schick; (*neat*) adrett; (*clever*) clever; (*quick*) scharf ♦ *vi* brennen, schmerzen; ~ **card** *n* Chipkarte *f*; ~**en up** *vi* sich in Schale werfen ♦ *vt* herausputzen

smash [smæʃ] *n* Zusammenstoß *m*; (*TENNIS*) Schmetterball *m* ♦ *vt* (*break*) zerschmettern; (*destroy*) vernichten ♦ *vi* (*break*) zersplittern, zerspringen; ~**ing** (*inf*) *adj* toll

smattering ['smætərɪŋ] *n* oberflächliche Kenntnis *f*

smear [smɪəʳ] *n* Fleck *m* ♦ *vt* beschmieren

smell [smɛl] (*pt, pp* **smelt** *or* **smelled**) *n* Geruch *m*; (*sense*) Geruchsinn *m* ♦ *vt* riechen ♦ *vi:* **to** ~ (**of**) riechen (nach); (*fragrantly*) duften (nach); ~**y** *adj* übel riechend

smile [smaɪl] *n* Lächeln *nt* ♦ *vi* lächeln

smiling ['smaɪlɪŋ] *adj* lächelnd

smirk [smɜːk] *n* blöde(s) Grinsen *nt*

smock [smɔk] *n* Kittel *m*

smoke [sməuk] *n* Rauch *m* ♦ *vt* rauchen; (*food*) räuchern ♦ *vi* rauchen; ~**d** *adj* (*bacon*) geräuchert; (*glass*) Rauch-; ~**r** *n* Raucher(in) *m(f)*; (*RAIL*) Raucherabteil *nt*; ~ **screen** *n* Rauchwand *f*

smoking ['sməukɪŋ] *n:* **"no** ~**"** „Rauchen verboten"; ~ **compartment** (*BRIT*), ~ **car** (*US*) *n* Raucherabteil *nt*

smoky ['sməukɪ] *adj* rauchig; (*room*) verraucht; (*taste*) geräuchert

smolder ['sməuldəʳ] (*US*) *vi* = **smoulder**

smooth [smu:ð] *adj* glatt ♦ *vt* (*also:* ~ **out**) glätten, glatt streichen

smother ['smʌðəʳ] *vt* ersticken

smoulder ['sməuldəʳ] (*US* **smolder**) *vi* schwelen

smudge [smʌdʒ] *n* Schmutzfleck *m* ♦ *vt* beschmieren

smug [smʌg] *adj* selbstgefällig

smuggle ['smʌgl] *vt* schmuggeln; ~**r** *n* Schmuggler *m*

smuggling ['smʌglɪŋ] *n* Schmuggel *m*

smutty ['smʌtɪ] *adj* schmutzig
snack [snæk] *n* Imbiss *m*; ~ **bar** *n* Imbissstube *f*
snag [snæg] *n* Haken *m*
snail [sneɪl] *n* Schnecke *f*
snake [sneɪk] *n* Schlange *f*
snap [snæp] *n* Schnappen *nt*; (*photograph*) Schnappschuss *m* ♦ *adj* (*decision*) schnell ♦ *vt* (*break*) zerbrechen; (*PHOT*) knipsen ♦ *vi* (*break*) brechen; (*speak*) anfauchen; **to ~ shut** zuschnappen; ~ **at** *vt fus* schnappen nach; ~ **off** *vt* (*break*) abbrechen ~ **up** *vt* aufschnappen; **~shot** *n* Schnappschuss *m*
snare [snɛəʳ] *n* Schlinge *f* ♦ *vt* mit einer Schlinge fangen
snarl [snɑːl] *n* Zähnefletschen *nt* ♦ *vi* (*dog*) knurren
snatch [snætʃ] *n* (*small amount*) Bruchteil *m* ♦ *vt* schnappen, packen
sneak [sniːk] *vi* schleichen ♦ *n* (*inf*) Petze(r) *mf*; **~ers** ['sniːkəz] (*US*) *npl* Freizeitschuhe *pl*; **~y** ['sniːkɪ] *adj* raffiniert
sneer [snɪəʳ] *n* Hohnlächeln *nt* ♦ *vi* spötteln
sneeze [sniːz] *n* Niesen *nt* ♦ *vi* niesen
sniff [snɪf] *n* Schnüffeln *nt* ♦ *vi* schnieben; (*smell*) schnüffeln ♦ *vt* schnuppern
snigger ['snɪgəʳ] *n* Kichern *nt* ♦ *vi* hämisch kichern
snip [snɪp] *n* Schnippel *m*, Schnipsel *m* ♦ *vt* schnippeln
sniper ['snaɪpəʳ] *n* Heckenschütze *m*
snippet ['snɪpɪt] *n* Schnipsel *m*; (*of conversation*) Fetzen *m*
snivelling ['snɪvlɪŋ] *adj* weinerlich
snob [snɔb] *n* Snob *m*
snooker ['snuːkəʳ] *n* Snooker *nt*
snoop [snuːp] *vi*: **to ~ about** herumschnüffeln
snooze [snuːz] *n* Nickerchen *nt* ♦ *vi* ein Nickerchen machen, dösen
snore [snɔːʳ] *vi* schnarchen ♦ *n* Schnarchen *nt*
snorkel ['snɔːkl] *n* Schnorchel *m*
snort [snɔːt] *n* Schnauben *nt* ♦ *vi* schnauben
snout [snaut] *n* Schnauze *f*
snow [snəu] *n* Schnee *m* ♦ *vi* schneien; **~ball** *n* Schneeball *m* ♦ *vi* eskalieren;

~bound *adj* eingeschneit; **~drift** *n* Schneewehe *f*; **~drop** *n* Schneeglöckchen *nt*; **~fall** *n* Schneefall *m*; **~flake** *n* Schneeflocke *f*; **~man** (*irreg*) *n* Schneemann *m*; **~plough** (*US* **snowplow**) *n* Schneepflug *m*; ~ **shoe** *n* Schneeschuh *m*; **~storm** *n* Schneesturm *m*
snub [snʌb] *vt* schroff abfertigen ♦ *n* Verweis *m*; **~-nosed** *adj* stupsnasig
snuff [snʌf] *n* Schnupftabak *m*
snug [snʌg] *adj* gemütlich, behaglich
snuggle ['snʌgl] *vi*: **to ~ up to sb** sich an jdn kuscheln

---

KEYWORD

so [səu] *adv* **1** (*thus*) so; (*likewise*) auch; **so saying he walked away** indem er das sagte, ging er; **if so** wenn ja; **I didn't do it – you did so!** ich hab das nicht gemacht – hast du wohl!; **so do I, so am I** *etc* ich auch; **so it is!** tatsächlich!; **I hope/think so** hoffentlich/ich glaube schon; **so far** bis jetzt
2 (*in comparisons etc: to such a degree*) so; **so quickly/big (that)** so schnell/groß, dass; **I'm so glad to see you** ich freue mich so, dich zu sehen
3: **so many** so viele; **so much work** so viel Arbeit; **I love you so much** ich liebe dich so sehr
4 (*phrases*): **10 or so** etwa 10; **so long!** (*inf: goodbye*) tschüss!
♦ *conj* **1** (*expressing purpose*): **so as to** um ... zu; **so (that)** damit
2 (*expressing result*) also; **so I was right after all** ich hatte also doch Recht; **so you see ...** wie du siehst ...

---

soak [səuk] *vt* durchnässen; (*leave in liquid*) einweichen ♦ *vi* (ein)weichen; ~ **in** *vi* einsickern; ~ **up** *vt* aufsaugen; **~ed** *adj* völlig durchnässt; **~ing** *adj* klitschnass, patschnass
so-and-so ['səuənsəu] *n* (*somebody*) Soundso *m*
soap [səup] *n* Seife *f*; **~flakes** *npl* Seifenflocken *pl*; ~ **opera** *n* Familienserie *f*

(im Fernsehen, Radio); ~ **powder** n Waschpulver nt; ~**y** adj seifig, Seifen-

soar [sɔ:ʳ] vi aufsteigen; *(prices)* in die Höhe schnellen

sob [sɒb] n Schluchzen nt ♦ vi schluchzen

sober ['səʊbəʳ] adj *(also fig)* nüchtern; ~ **up** vi nüchtern werden

so-called ['səʊ'kɔ:ld] adj so genannt

soccer ['sɒkəʳ] n Fußball m

sociable ['səʊʃəbl] adj gesellig

social ['səʊʃl] adj sozial; *(friendly, living with others)* gesellig ♦ n gesellige(r) Abend m; ~ **club** n Verein m *(für Freizeitgestaltung)*; ~**ism** n Sozialismus m; ~**ist** n Sozialist(in) m(f) ♦ adj sozialistisch; ~**ize** vi: **to ~ize (with)** gesellschaftlich verkehren (mit); ~**ly** adv gesellschaftlich, privat; ~ **security** n Sozialversicherung f; ~ **work** n Sozialarbeit f; ~ **worker** n Sozialarbeiter(in) m(f)

society [sə'saɪətɪ] n Gesellschaft f; *(fashionable world)* die große Welt

sociology [səʊsɪ'ɒlədʒɪ] n Soziologie f

sock [sɒk] n Socke f

socket ['sɒkɪt] n *(ELEC)* Steckdose f; *(of eye)* Augenhöhle f

sod [sɒd] n Rasenstück nt; *(inf!)* Saukerl m (!)

soda ['səʊdə] n Soda f; *(also:* ~ **water)** Soda(wasser) nt; *(US: also:* ~ **pop)** Limonade f

sodden ['sɒdn] adj durchweicht

sodium ['səʊdɪəm] n Natrium nt

sofa ['səʊfə] n Sofa nt

soft [sɒft] adj weich; *(not loud)* leise; *(weak)* nachgiebig; ~ **drink** n alkoholfreie(s) Getränk nt; ~**en** ['sɒfn] vt weich machen; *(blow)* abschwächen, mildern ♦ vi weich werden; ~**ly** adv sanft; leise; ~**ness** n Weichheit f; *(fig)* Sanftheit f

software ['sɒftwɛəʳ] n *(COMPUT)* Software f

soggy ['sɒgɪ] adj *(ground)* sumpfig; *(bread)* aufgeweicht

soil [sɔɪl] n Erde f ♦ vt beschmutzen

solace ['sɒlɪs] n Trost m

solar ['səʊləʳ] adj Sonnen-; ~ **cell** n Solarzelle f; ~ **energy** n Sonnenenergie f; ~ **panel** n Sonnenkollektor m; ~ **power** n Sonnenenergie f

sold [səʊld] pt, pp of **sell**; ~ **out** *(COMM)* ausverkauft

solder ['səʊldəʳ] vt löten

soldier ['səʊldʒəʳ] n Soldat m

sole [səʊl] n Sohle f; *(fish)* Seezunge f ♦ adj alleinig, Allein-; ~**ly** adv ausschließlich

solemn ['sɒləm] adj feierlich

sole trader n *(COMM)* Einzelunternehmen nt

solicit [sə'lɪsɪt] vt *(request)* bitten um ♦ vi *(prostitute)* Kunden anwerben

solicitor [sə'lɪsɪtəʳ] n Rechtsanwalt m/-anwältin f

solid ['sɒlɪd] adj *(hard)* fest; *(of same material, not hollow)* massiv; *(without break)* voll, ganz; *(reliable, sensible)* solide ♦ n Festkörper m; ~**arity** [sɒlɪ'dærɪtɪ] n Solidarität f; ~**ify** [sə'lɪdɪfaɪ] vi fest werden

solitary ['sɒlɪtərɪ] adj einsam, einzeln; ~ **confinement** n Einzelhaft f

solitude ['sɒlɪtju:d] n Einsamkeit f

solo ['səʊləʊ] n Solo nt; ~**ist** ['səʊləʊɪst] n Solist(in) m(f)

soluble ['sɒljʊbl] adj *(substance)* löslich; *(problem)* (auf)lösbar

solution [sə'lu:ʃən] n *(also fig)* Lösung f; *(of mystery)* Erklärung f

solve [sɒlv] vt (auf)lösen

solvent ['sɒlvənt] adj *(FIN)* zahlungsfähig ♦ n *(CHEM)* Lösungsmittel nt

sombre ['sɒmbəʳ] *(US* **somber)** adj düster

KEYWORD
---

some [sʌm] adj **1** *(a certain amount or number of)* ein paar; *(a few)* einige; *(with singular nouns)* etwas; **some tea/biscuits** etwas Tee/ein paar Plätzchen; **I've got some money, but not much** ich habe ein bisschen Geld, aber nicht viel

2 *(certain: in contrasts)* manche(r, s); **some people say that ...** manche Leute sagen, dass ...

3 *(unspecified)* irgendein(e); **some woman was asking for you** da hat eine Frau nach Ihnen gefragt; **some day** eines Tages; **some day next week** irgendwann nächste Woche

♦ *pron* **1** (*a certain number*) einige; **have you got some?** haben Sie welche?
2 (*a certain amount*) etwas; **I've read some of the book** ich habe das Buch teilweise gelesen
♦ *adv*: **some 10 people** etwa 10 Leute

somebody ['sʌmbədɪ] *pron* = **someone**
somehow ['sʌmhau] *adv* (*in some way, for some reason*) irgendwie
someone ['sʌmwʌn] *pron* jemand; (*direct obj*) jemand(en); (*indirect obj*) jemandem
someplace ['sʌmpleɪs] (*US*) *adv* = **somewhere**
somersault ['sʌməsɔːlt] *n* Salto *m* ♦ *vi* einen Salto machen
something ['sʌmθɪŋ] *pron* etwas
sometime ['sʌmtaɪm] *adv* (irgend)einmal
sometimes ['sʌmtaɪmz] *adv* manchmal
somewhat ['sʌmwɔt] *adv* etwas
somewhere ['sʌmwɛəʳ] *adv* irgendwo; (*to a place*) irgendwohin; **~ else** irgendwo anders
son [sʌn] *n* Sohn *m*
sonar ['səunɑːʳ] *n* Echolot *nt*
song [sɔŋ] *n* Lied *nt*
sonic boom ['sɔnɪk-] *n* Überschallknall *m*
son-in-law ['sʌnɪnlɔː] *n* Schwiegersohn *m*
soon [suːn] *adv* bald; **~ afterwards** kurz danach; **~er** *adv* (*time*) früher; (*for preference*) lieber; **~er or later** früher oder später
soot [sut] *n* Ruß *m*
soothe [suːð] *vt* (*person*) beruhigen; (*pain*) lindern
sophisticated [sə'fɪstɪkeɪtɪd] *adj* (*person*) kultiviert; (*machinery*) hoch entwickelt
sophomore ['sɔfəmɔːʳ] (*US*) *n* College-student *m* im 2. Jahr
soporific [sɔpə'rɪfɪk] *adj* einschläfernd
sopping ['sɔpɪŋ] *adj* patschnass
soppy ['sɔpɪ] (*inf*) *adj* schmalzig
soprano [sə'prɑːnəu] *n* Sopran *m*
sorcerer ['sɔːsərəʳ] *n* Hexenmeister *m*
sordid ['sɔːdɪd] *adj* erbärmlich
sore [sɔːʳ] *adj* schmerzend; (*point*) wund ♦ *n* Wunde *f*; **~ly** *adv* (*tempted*) stark, sehr

sorrow ['sɔrəu] *n* Kummer *m*, Leid *nt*; **~ful** *adj* sorgenvoll
sorry ['sɔrɪ] *adj* traurig, erbärmlich; **~!** Entschuldigung!; **to feel ~ for sb** jdn bemitleiden; **I feel ~ for him** er tut mir Leid; **~?** (*pardon*) wie bitte?
sort [sɔːt] *n* Art *f*, Sorte *f* ♦ *vt* (*also:* **~ out**: *papers*) sortieren; (: *problems*) sichten, in Ordnung bringen; **~ing office** *n* Sortierstelle *f*
SOS *n* SOS *nt*
so-so ['səusəu] *adv* so(so) lala
sought [sɔːt] *pt, pp* of **seek**
soul [səul] *n* Seele *f*; (*music*) Soul *m*; **~-destroying** *adj* trostlos; **~ful** *adj* seelenvoll
sound [saund] *adj* (*healthy*) gesund; (*safe*) sicher; (*sensible*) vernünftig; (*theory*) stichhaltig; (*thorough*) tüchtig, gehörig ♦ *adv*: **to be ~ asleep** fest schlafen ♦ *n* (*noise*) Geräusch *nt*, Laut *m*; (*GEOG*) Sund *m* ♦ *vt* erschallen lassen; (*alarm*) (Alarm) schlagen ♦ *vi* (*make a ~*) schallen, tönen; (*seem*) klingen; **to ~ like** sich anhören wie; **~ out** *vt* erforschen; (*person*) auf den Zahn fühlen +*dat*; **~ barrier** *n* Schallmauer *f*; **~ bite** *n* (*RAD, TV*) prägnante(s) Zitat *nt*; **~ effects** *npl* Toneffekte *pl*; **~ly** *adv* (*sleep*) fest; (*beat*) tüchtig; **~proof** *adj* (*room*) schalldicht; **~ track** *n* Tonstreifen *m*; (*music*) Filmmusik *f*
soup [suːp] *n* Suppe *f*; **~ plate** *n* Suppenteller *m*; **~spoon** *n* Suppenlöffel *m*
sour ['sauəʳ] *adj* (*also fig*) sauer; **it's ~ grapes** (*fig*) die Trauben hängen zu hoch
source [sɔːs] *n* (*also fig*) Quelle *f*
south [sauθ] *n* Süden *m* ♦ *adj* Süd-, südlich ♦ *adv* nach Süden, südwärts; **S~ Africa** *n* Südafrika *nt*; **S~ African** *adj* südafrikanisch ♦ *n* Südafrikaner(in) *m(f)*; **S~ America** *n* Südamerika *nt*; **S~ American** *adj* südamerikanisch ♦ *n* Südamerikaner(in) *m(f)*; **~-east** *n* Südosten *m*; **~erly** ['sʌðəlɪ] *adj* südlich; **~ern** ['sʌðən] *adj* südlich, Süd-; **S~ Pole** *n* Südpol *m*; **S~ Wales** *n* Südwales *nt*; **~ward(s)** *adv* südwärts, nach Süden; **~-west** *n* Südwesten *m*
souvenir [suːvə'nɪəʳ] *n* Souvenir *nt*

sovereign ['sɔvrɪn] n (*ruler*) Herrscher(in) m(f) ♦ adj (*independent*) souverän

soviet ['səʊvɪət] adj sowjetisch; **the S~ Union** die Sowjetunion

sow¹ [saʊ] n Sau f

sow² [səʊ] (*pt* **sowed**, *pp* **sown**) vt (*also fig*) säen

soya ['sɔɪə] (*US* **soy**) n: ~ **bean** Sojabohne f; ~ **sauce** Sojasauce f

spa [spɑː] n (*place*) Kurort m

space [speɪs] n Platz m, Raum m; (*universe*) Weltraum m, All nt; (*length of time*) Abstand m ♦ vt (*also:* ~ **out**) verteilen; **~craft** n Raumschiff nt; **~man** (*irreg*) n Raumfahrer m; ~ **ship** n Raumschiff nt

spacing ['speɪsɪŋ] n Abstand m; (*also:* ~ **out**) Verteilung f

spacious ['speɪʃəs] adj geräumig, weit

spade [speɪd] n Spaten m; **~s** npl (*CARDS*) Pik nt

Spain [speɪn] n Spanien nt

span [spæn] n Spanne f; (*of bridge etc*) Spannweite f ♦ vt überspannen

Spaniard ['spænjəd] n Spanier(in) m(f)

spaniel ['spænjəl] n Spaniel m

Spanish ['spænɪʃ] adj spanisch ♦ n (*LING*) Spanisch nt; **the** ~ npl (*people*) die Spanier pl

spank [spæŋk] vt verhauen, versohlen

spanner ['spænə'] (*BRIT*) n Schraubenschlüssel m

spar [spɑː'] n (*NAUT*) Sparren m ♦ vi (*BOXING*) einen Sparring machen

spare [speə'] adj Ersatz- ♦ n = **spare part** ♦ vt (*lives, feelings*) verschonen; (*trouble*) ersparen; **to** ~ (*surplus*) übrig; ~ **part** n Ersatzteil nt; ~ **time** n Freizeit f; ~ **wheel** n (*AUT*) Reservereifen m

sparing ['speərɪŋ] adj: **to be** ~ **with** geizen mit; **~ly** adv sparsam; (*eat, spend etc*) in Maßen

spark [spɑːk] n Funken m; **~(ing) plug** n Zündkerze f

sparkle ['spɑːkl] n Funkeln nt; (*gaiety*) Schwung m ♦ vi funkeln; **sparkling** adj funkelnd; (*wine*) Schaum-; (*mineral water*) mit Kohlensäure; (*conversation*) spritzig, geistreich

sparrow ['spærəʊ] n Spatz m

sparse [spɑːs] adj spärlich

spasm ['spæzəm] n (*MED*) Krampf m; (*fig*) Anfall m; **~odic** [spæz'mɔdɪk] adj (*fig*) sprunghaft

spastic ['spæstɪk] (*old*) n Spastiker(in) m(f) ♦ adj spastisch

spat [spæt] *pt, pp* of **spit**

spate [speɪt] n (*fig*) Flut f, Schwall m; **in** ~ (*river*) angeschwollen

spatter ['spætə'] vt bespritzen, verspritzen

spatula ['spætjʊlə] n Spatel m

spawn [spɔːn] vi laichen ♦ n Laich m

speak [spiːk] (*pt* **spoke**, *pp* **spoken**) vt sprechen, reden; (*truth*) sagen; (*language*) sprechen ♦ vi: **to** ~ (**to**) sprechen (mit or zu); **to** ~ **to sb** of or **about sth** mit jdm über etw acc sprechen; ~ **up!** sprich lauter!; **~er** n Sprecher(in) m(f), Redner(in) m(f); (*loudspeaker*) Lautsprecher m; (*POL*): **the S~er** der Vorsitzende des Parlaments (*BRIT*) or des Kongresses (*US*)

spear [spɪə'] n Speer m ♦ vt aufspießen; **~head** vt (*attack etc*) anführen

spec [spek] (*inf*) n: **on** ~ auf gut Glück

special ['speʃl] adj besondere(r, s); **~ist** n (*TECH*) Fachmann m; (*MED*) Facharzt m/ Fachärztin f; **~ity** [speʃɪ'ælɪtɪ] n Spezialität f; (*study*) Spezialgebiet nt; **~ize** vi: **to** ~**ize (in)** sich spezialisieren (auf +acc); **~ly** adv besonders; (*explicitly*) extra; ~ **needs** adj: ~ **needs children** behinderte Kinder pl; **~ty** (*esp US*) n = **speciality**

species ['spiːʃiːz] n Art f

specific [spə'sɪfɪk] adj spezifisch; **~ally** adv spezifisch

specification [spesɪfɪ'keɪʃən] n Angabe f; (*stipulation*) Bedingung f; **~s** npl (*TECH*) technische Daten pl

specify ['spesɪfaɪ] vt genau angeben

specimen ['spesɪmən] n Probe f

speck [spek] n Fleckchen nt

speckled ['spekld] adj gesprenkelt

specs [speks] (*inf*) npl Brille f

spectacle ['spektəkl] n Schauspiel nt; **~s** npl (*glasses*) Brille f

spectacular [spɛk'tækjʊləʳ] *adj* sensationell; (*success etc*) spektakulär

spectator [spɛk'teɪtəʳ] *n* Zuschauer(in) *m(f)*

spectre ['spɛktəʳ] (*US* **specter**) *n* Geist *m*, Gespenst *nt*

speculate ['spɛkjʊleɪt] *vi* spekulieren

speech [spi:tʃ] *n* Sprache *f*; (*address*) Rede *f*; (*way one speaks*) Sprechweise *f*; **~less** *adj* sprachlos

speed [spi:d] *n* Geschwindigkeit *f*; (*gear*) Gang *m* ♦ *vi* (*JUR*) (zu) schnell fahren; **at full** *or* **top ~** mit Höchstgeschwindigkeit; **~ up** *vt* beschleunigen ♦ *vi* schneller werden; schneller fahren; **~boat** *n* Schnellboot *nt*; **~ily** *adv* schleunigst; **~ing** *n* Geschwindigkeitsüberschreitung *f*; **~ limit** *n* Geschwindigkeitsbegrenzung *f*; **~ometer** [spɪ'dɒmɪtəʳ] *n* Tachometer *m*; **~way** *n* (*bike racing*) Motorradrennstrecke *f*; **~y** *adj* schnell

spell [spɛl] (*pt*, *pp* **spelt** (*BRIT*) *or* **spelled**) *n* (*magic*) Bann *m*; (*period of time*) (eine) Zeit lang ♦ *vt* buchstabieren; (*imply*) bedeuten; **to cast a ~ on sb** jdn verzaubern; **~bound** *adj* (wie) gebannt; **~ing** *n* Rechtschreibung *f*

spelt [spɛlt] (*BRIT*) *pt*, *pp* of **spell**

spend [spɛnd] (*pt*, *pp* **spend**) *vt* (*money*) ausgeben; (*time*) verbringen; **~thrift** *n* Verschwender(in) *m(f)*

spent [spɛnt] *pt*, *pp* of **spend**

sperm [spə:m] *n* (*BIOL*) Samenflüssigkeit *f*

spew [spju:] *vt* (er)brechen

sphere [sfɪəʳ] *n* (*globe*) Kugel *f*; (*fig*) Sphäre *f*, Gebiet *nt*; **spherical** ['sfɛrɪkl] *adj* kugelförmig

spice [spaɪs] *n* Gewürz *nt* ♦ *vt* würzen

spick-and-span ['spɪkən'spæn] *adj* blitzblank

spicy ['spaɪsɪ] *adj* (*food*) stark gewürzt; (*fig*) pikant

spider ['spaɪdəʳ] *n* Spinne *f*

spike [spaɪk] *n* Dorn *m*, Spitze *f*

spill [spɪl] (*pt*, *pp* **spilt** *or* **spilled**) *vt* verschütten ♦ *vi* sich ergießen; **~ over** *vi* überlaufen; (*fig*) sich ausbreiten

spilt [spɪlt] *pt*, *pp* of **spill**

spin [spɪn] (*pt*, *pp* **spun**) *n* (*trip in car*) Spazierfahrt *f*; (*AVIAT*) (Ab)trudeln *nt*; (*on ball*) Drall *m* ♦ *vt* (*thread*) spinnen; (*like top*) (herum)wirbeln ♦ *vi* sich drehen; **~ out** *vt* in die Länge ziehen

spinach ['spɪnɪtʃ] *n* Spinat *m*

spinal ['spaɪnl] *adj* Rückgrat-; **~ cord** *n* Rückenmark *nt*

spindly ['spɪndlɪ] *adj* spindeldürr

spin doctor *n* PR-Fachmann *m*, PR-Fachfrau *f*

spin-dryer [spɪn'draɪəʳ] (*BRIT*) *n* Wäscheschleuder *f*

spine [spaɪn] *n* Rückgrat *nt*; (*thorn*) Stachel *m*; **~less** *adj* (*also fig*) rückgratlos

spinning ['spɪnɪŋ] *n* Spinnen *nt*; **~ top** *n* Kreisel *m*; **~ wheel** *n* Spinnrad *nt*

spin-off ['spɪnɒf] *n* Nebenprodukt *nt*

spinster ['spɪnstəʳ] *n* unverheiratete Frau *f*; (*pej*) alte Jungfer *f*

spiral ['spaɪərl] *n* Spirale *f* ♦ *adj* spiralförmig; (*movement etc*) in Spiralen ♦ *vi* sich (hoch)winden; **~ staircase** *n* Wendeltreppe *f*

spire ['spaɪəʳ] *n* Turm *m*

spirit ['spɪrɪt] *n* Geist *m*; (*humour, mood*) Stimmung *f*; (*courage*) Mut *m*; (*verve*) Elan *m*; (*alcohol*) Alkohol *m*; **~s** *npl* (*drink*) Spirituosen *pl*; **in good ~s** gut aufgelegt; **~ed** *adj* beherzt; **~ level** *n* Wasserwaage *f*

spiritual ['spɪrɪtjʊəl] *adj* geistig, seelisch; (*REL*) geistlich ♦ *n* Spiritual *nt*

spit [spɪt] (*pt*, *pp* **spat**) *n* (*for roasting*) (Brat)spieß *m*; (*saliva*) Spucke *f* ♦ *vi* spucken; (*rain*) sprühen; (*make a sound*) zischen; (*cat*) fauchen

spite [spaɪt] *n* Gehässigkeit *f* ♦ *vt* kränken; **in ~ of** trotz; **~ful** *adj* gehässig

spittle ['spɪtl] *n* Speichel *m*, Spucke *f*

splash [splæʃ] *n* Spritzer *m*; (*of colour*) (Farb)fleck *m* ♦ *vt* bespritzen ♦ *vi* spritzen

spleen [spli:n] *n* (*ANAT*) Milz *f*

splendid ['splendɪd] *adj* glänzend

splendour ['splendəʳ] (*US* **splendor**) *n* Pracht *f*

splint [splɪnt] *n* Schiene *f*

splinter ['splɪntəʳ] *n* Splitter *m* ♦ *vi* (zer)splittern

split [splɪt] (*pt, pp* **split**) *n* Spalte *f*; (*fig*) Spaltung *f*; (*division*) Trennung *f* ♦ *vt* spalten *vi* ♦ *vi* (*divide*) reißen *vi*; ~ **up** *vi* sich trennen

splutter ['splʌtər] *vi* stottern

spoil [spɔɪl] (*pt, pp* **spoilt** *or* **spoiled**) *vt* (*ruin*) verderben; (*child*) verwöhnen; ~**s** *npl* Beute *f*; ~**sport** *n* Spielverderber *m*; ~**t** *pt, pp of* **spoil**

spoke [spəuk] *pt of* **speak** ♦ *n* Speiche *f*; ~**n** *pp of* **speak**

spokesman ['spəuksmən] (*irreg*) *n* Sprecher *m*; **spokeswoman** ['spəukswumən] (*irreg*) *n* Sprecherin *f*

sponge [spʌndʒ] *n* Schwamm *m* ♦ *vt* abwaschen ♦ *vi*: **to ~ on** auf Kosten +*gen* leben; ~ **bag** (*BRIT*) *n* Kulturbeutel *m*; ~ **cake** *n* Rührkuchen *m*

sponsor ['spɒnsər] *n* Sponsor *m* ♦ *vt* fördern; ~**ship** *n* Finanzierung *f*; (*public*) Schirmherrschaft *f*

spontaneous [spɒn'teɪnɪəs] *adj* spontan

spooky ['spu:kɪ] (*inf*) *adj* gespenstisch

spool [spu:l] *n* Spule *f*, Rolle *f*

spoon [spu:n] *n* Löffel *m*; ~**-feed** (*irreg*) *vt* mit dem Löffel füttern; (*fig*) hochpäppeln; ~**ful** *n* Löffel *m* (voll)

sport [spɔ:t] *n* Sport *m*; (*person*) feine(r) Kerl *m*; ~**ing** *adj* (*fair*) sportlich, fair; **to give sb a ~ing chance** jdm eine faire Chance geben; ~ **jacket** (*US*) *n* = **sports jacket**; ~**s car** *n* Sportwagen *m*; ~**s jacket** *n* Sportjackett *nt*; ~**sman** (*irreg*) *n* Sportler *m*; ~**smanship** *n* Sportlichkeit *f*; ~**swear** *n* Sportkleidung *f*; ~**swoman** (*irreg*) *n* Sportlerin *f*; ~**y** *adj* sportlich

spot [spɒt] *n* Punkt *m*; (*dirty*) Fleck(en) *m*; (*place*) Stelle *f*; (*MED*) Pickel *m* ♦ *vt* erspähen; (*mistake*) bemerken; **on the ~** an Ort und Stelle; (*at once*) auf der Stelle; ~ **check** *n* Stichprobe *f*; ~**less** *adj* fleckenlos; ~**light** *n* Scheinwerferlicht *nt*; (*lamp*) Scheinwerfer *m*; ~**ted** *adj* gefleckt; ~**ty** *adj* (*face*) pickelig

spouse [spaus] *n* Gatte *m*/Gattin *f*

spout [spaut] *n* (*of pot*) Tülle *f*; (*jet*) Wasserstrahl *m* ♦ *vi* speien

sprain [spreɪn] *n* Verrenkung *f* ♦ *vt* verrenken

sprang [spræŋ] *pt of* **spring**

sprawl [sprɔ:l] *vi* sich strecken

spray [spreɪ] *n* Spray *nt*; (*off sea*) Gischt *f*; (*of flowers*) Zweig *m* ♦ *vt* besprühen, sprayen

spread [spred] (*pt, pp* **spread**) *n* (*extent*) Verbreitung *f*; (*inf: meal*) Schmaus *m*; (*for bread*) Aufstrich *m* ♦ *vt* ausbreiten; (*scatter*) verbreiten; (*butter*) streichen ♦ *vi* sich ausbreiten; ~ **out** *vi* (*move apart*) sich verteilen; ~**-eagled** [spredɪ:gld] *adj*: **to be ~-eagled** alle viere von sich strecken; ~**sheet** *n* Tabellenkalkulation *f*

spree [spri:] *n* (*shopping*) Einkaufsbummel *m*; **to go on a ~** einen draufmachen

sprightly ['spraɪtlɪ] *adj* munter, lebhaft

spring [sprɪŋ] (*pt* **sprang**, *pp* **sprung**) *n* (*leap*) Sprung *m*; (*TECH*) Feder *f*; (*season*) Frühling *m*; (*water*) Quelle *f* ♦ *vi* (*leap*) springen; ~ **up** *vi* (*problem*) auftauchen; ~**board** *n* Sprungbrett *nt*; ~**-clean** *n* (*also*: ~**-cleaning**) Frühjahrsputz *m*; ~**time** *n* Frühling *m*; ~**y** *adj* federnd, elastisch

sprinkle ['sprɪŋkl] *vt* (*salt*) streuen; (*liquid*) sprenkeln; **to ~ water on, to ~ with water** mit Wasser besprengen; ~**r** ['sprɪŋklər] *n* (*for lawn*) Sprenger *m*; (*for fire fighting*) Sprinkler *m*

sprint [sprɪnt] *n* (*race*) Sprint *m* ♦ *vi* (*run fast*) rennen; (*SPORT*) sprinten; ~**er** *n* Sprinter(in) *m(f)*

sprout [spraut] *vi* sprießen

sprouts [sprauts] *npl* (*also*: **Brussels ~**) Rosenkohl *m*

spruce [spru:s] *n* Fichte *f* ♦ *adj* schmuck, adrett

sprung [sprʌŋ] *pp of* **spring**

spry [spraɪ] *adj* flink, rege

spun [spʌn] *pt, pp of* **spin**

spur [spə:r] *n* Sporn *m*; (*fig*) Ansporn *m* ♦ *vt* (*also*: ~ **on**: *fig*) anspornen; **on the ~ of the moment** spontan

spurious ['spjuərɪəs] *adj* falsch

spurn [spə:n] *vt* verschmähen

spurt [spə:t] *n* (*jet*) Strahl *m*; (*acceleration*) Spurt *m* ♦ *vi* (*liquid*) schießen

spy [spaɪ] n Spion(in) m(f) ♦ vi spionieren ♦ vt erspähen; **~ing** n Spionage f

sq. abbr = **square**

squabble ['skwɔbl] n Zank m ♦ vi sich zanken

squad [skwɔd] n (MIL) Abteilung f; (POLICE) Kommando nt

squadron ['skwɔdrn] n (cavalry) Schwadron f; (NAUT) Geschwader nt; (air force) Staffel f

squalid ['skwɔlɪd] adj verkommen

squall [skwɔːl] n Bö(e) f, Windstoß m

squalor ['skwɔləʳ] n Verwahrlosung f

squander ['skwɔndəʳ] vt verschwenden

square [skwɛəʳ] n Quadrat nt; (open space) Platz m; (instrument) Winkel m; (inf: person) Spießer m ♦ adj viereckig; (inf: ideas, tastes) spießig ♦ vt (arrange) ausmachen; (MATH) ins Quadrat erheben ♦ vi (agree) übereinstimmen; **all ~** quitt; **a ~ meal** eine ordentliche Mahlzeit; **2 metres ~** 2 Meter im Quadrat; **1 ~ metre** 1 Quadratmeter; **~ly** adv fest, gerade

squash [skwɔʃ] n (BRIT: drink) Saft m; (game) Squash nt ♦ vt zerquetschen

squat [skwɔt] adj untersetzt ♦ vi hocken; **~ter** n Hausbesetzer m

squawk [skwɔːk] vi kreischen

squeak [skwiːk] vi quiek(s)en; (spring, door etc) quietschen

squeal [skwiːl] vi schrill schreien

squeamish ['skwiːmɪʃ] adj empfindlich

squeeze [skwiːz] vt pressen, drücken; (orange) auspressen; **~ out** vt ausquetschen

squelch [skwɛltʃ] vi platschen

squib [skwɪb] n Knallfrosch m

squid [skwɪd] n Tintenfisch m

squiggle ['skwɪgl] n Schnörkel m

squint [skwɪnt] vi schielen ♦ n: **to have a ~** schielen; **to ~ at sb/sth** nach jdm/etw schielen

squirm [skwəːm] vi sich winden

squirrel ['skwɪrəl] n Eichhörnchen nt

squirt [skwəːt] vt, vi spritzen

Sr abbr (= senior) sen.

St abbr (= saint) hl., St.; (= street) Str.

stab [stæb] n (blow) Stich m; (inf: try) Versuch m ♦ vt erstechen

stabilize ['steɪbəlaɪz] vt stabilisieren ♦ vi sich stabilisieren

stable ['steɪbl] adj stabil ♦ n Stall m

stack [stæk] n Stapel m ♦ vt stapeln

stadium ['steɪdɪəm] n Stadion nt

staff [stɑːf] n (stick, MIL) Stab m; (personnel) Personal nt; (BRIT: SCH) Lehrkräfte pl ♦ vt besetzen

stag [stæg] n Hirsch m

stage [steɪdʒ] n Bühne f; (of journey) Etappe f; (degree) Stufe f; (point) Stadium nt ♦ vt (put on) aufführen; (simulate) inszenieren; (demonstration) veranstalten; **in ~s** etappenweise; **~coach** n Postkutsche f; **~ door** n Bühneneingang m; **~ manager** n Intendant m

stagger ['stægəʳ] vi wanken, taumeln ♦ vt (amaze) verblüffen; (hours) staffeln; **~ing** adj unglaublich

stagnant ['stægnənt] adj stagnierend; (water) stehend; **stagnate** [stæg'neɪt] vi stagnieren

stag party n Männerabend m (vom Bräutigam vor der Hochzeit gegeben)

staid [steɪd] adj gesetzt

stain [steɪn] n Fleck m ♦ vt beflecken; **~ed glass window** buntes Glasfenster nt; **~less** adj (steel) rostfrei; **~ remover** n Fleckentferner m

stair [stɛəʳ] n (Treppen)stufe f; **~s** npl (flight of steps) Treppe f; **~case** n Treppenhaus nt, Treppe f; **~way** n Treppenaufgang m

stake [steɪk] n (post) Pfahl m; (money) Einsatz m ♦ vt (bet: money) setzen; **to be at ~** auf dem Spiel stehen

stale [steɪl] adj alt; (bread) altbacken

stalemate ['steɪlmeɪt] n (CHESS) Patt nt; (fig) Stillstand m

stalk [stɔːk] n Stängel m, Stiel m ♦ vt (game) jagen; **~ off** vi abstolzieren

stall [stɔːl] n (in stable) Stand m, Box f; (in market) (Verkaufs)stand m ♦ vt (AUT) abwürgen ♦ vi (AUT) stehen bleiben; (fig) Ausflüchte machen; **~s** npl (BRIT: THEAT) Parkett nt

stallion ['stæljən] n Zuchthengst m

stalwart ['stɔːlwət] *n* treue(r) Anhänger *m*

stamina ['stæmɪnə] *n* Durchhaltevermögen *nt*, Zähigkeit *f*

stammer ['stæmə'] *n* Stottern *nt* ♦ *vt, vi* stottern, stammeln

stamp [stæmp] *n* Briefmarke *f*; (*for document*) Stempel *m* ♦ *vi* stampfen ♦ *vt* (*mark*) stempeln; (*mail*) frankieren, (*foot*) stampfen mit; **~ album** *n* Briefmarkenalbum *nt*; **~ collecting** *n* Briefmarkensammeln *nt*

stampede [stæm'piːd] *n* panische Flucht *f*

stance [stæns] *n* Haltung *f*

stand [stænd] (*pt, pp* **stood**) *n* (*for objects*) Gestell *nt*; (*seats*) Tribüne *f* ♦ *vi* stehen; (*rise*) aufstehen; (*decision*) feststehen ♦ *vt* setzen, stellen; (*endure*) aushalten; (*person*) ausstehen; (*nonsense*) dulden; **to make a ~** Widerstand leisten; **to ~ for parliament** (*BRIT*) für das Parlament kandidieren; **~ by** *vi* (*be ready*) bereitstehen ♦ *vt fus* (*opinion*) treu bleiben +*dat*; **~ down** *vi* (*withdraw*) zurücktreten; **~ for** *vt fus* (*signify*) stehen für; (*permit, tolerate*) hinnehmen; **~ in for** *vt fus* einspringen für; **~ out** *vi* (*be prominent*) hervorstechen; **~ up** *vi* (*rise*) aufstehen; **~ up for** *vt fus* sich einsetzen für; **~ up to** *vt fus*: **to ~ up to sth** einer Sache *dat* gewachsen sein; **to ~ up to sb** sich jdm gegenüber behaupten

standard ['stændəd] *n* (*measure*) Norm *f*; (*flag*) Fahne *f* ♦ *adj* (*size etc*) Normal-; **~s** *npl* (*morals*) Maßstäbe *pl*; **~ize** *vt* vereinheitlichen; **~ lamp** (*BRIT*) *n* Stehlampe *f*; **~ of living** *n* Lebensstandard *m*

stand: **~-by** *n* Reserve *f*; **to be on ~-by** in Bereitschaft sein; **~-by ticket** *n* (*AVIAT*) Standbyticket *nt*; **~-in** ['stændɪn] *n* Ersatz *m*

standing ['stændɪŋ] *adj* (*erect*) stehend; (*permanent*) ständig; (*invitation*) offen ♦ *n* (*duration*) Dauer *f*; (*reputation*) Ansehen *nt*; **of many years' ~** langjährig; **~ order** (*BRIT*) *n* (*at bank*) Dauerauftrag *m*; **~ room** *n* Stehplatz *m*

stand: **~-offish** [stænd'ɔfɪʃ] *adj* zurückhaltend, sehr reserviert; **~point** ['stændpɔɪnt] *n* Standpunkt *m*; **~still**

~still *n*: **to be at a ~still** stillstehen; **to come to a ~still** zum Stillstand kommen

stank [stæŋk] *pt of* **stink**

staple ['steɪpl] *n* (*in paper*) Heftklammer *f*; (*article*) Haupterzeugnis *nt* ♦ *adj* Grund-, Haupt- ♦ *vt* (*fest*)klammern; **~r** *n* Heftmaschine *f*

star [stɑː'] *n* Stern *m*; (*person*) Star *m* ♦ *vi* die Hauptrolle spielen ♦ *vt*: **~ring ...** in der Hauptrolle/den Hauptrollen ...

starboard ['stɑːbɔːd] *n* Steuerbord *nt*

starch [stɑːtʃ] *n* Stärke *f*

stardom ['stɑːdəm] *n* Berühmtheit *f*

stare [steə'] *n* starre(r) Blick *m* ♦ *vi*: **to ~ at** starren auf +*acc*, anstarren

starfish ['stɑːfɪʃ] *n* Seestern *m*

stark [stɑːk] *adj* öde ♦ *adv*: **~ naked** splitternackt

starling ['stɑːlɪŋ] *n* Star *m*

starry ['stɑːrɪ] *adj* Sternen-; **~-eyed** *adj* (*innocent*) blauäugig

start [stɑːt] *n* Anfang *m*; (*SPORT*) Start *m*; (*lead*) Vorsprung *m* ♦ *vt* in Gang setzen; (*car*) anlassen ♦ *vi* anfangen; (*car*) anspringen; (*on journey*) aufbrechen; (*SPORT*) starten; (*with fright*) zusammenfahren; **to ~ doing** *or* **to do sth** anfangen, etw zu tun; **~ off** *vi* anfangen; (*begin moving*) losgehen; losfahren; **~ up** *vi* anfangen ♦ *vt* beginnen; (*car*) anlassen; (*engine*) starten; **~er** *n* (*AUT*) Anlasser *m*; (*for race*) Starter *m*; (*BRIT*: *COOK*) Vorspeise *f*; **~ing point** *n* Ausgangspunkt *m*

startle ['stɑːtl] *vt* erschrecken; **startling** *adj* erschreckend

starvation [stɑː'veɪʃən] *n* Verhungern *nt*

starve [stɑːv] *vi* verhungern ♦ *vt* verhungern lassen; **I'm starving** ich sterbe vor Hunger

state [steɪt] *n* (*condition*) Zustand *m*; (*POL*) Staat *m* ♦ *vt* erklären; (*facts*) angeben; **the S~s** (*USA*) die Staaten; **to be in a ~** durchdrehen; **~ly** *adj* würdevoll; **~ly home** *n* herrschaftliches Anwesen *nt*, Schloss *nt*; **~ment** *n* Aussage *f*; (*POL*) Erklärung *f*; **~sman** (*irreg*) *n* Staatsmann *m*

static ['stætɪk] *n* (*also*: **~ electricity**) Reibungselektrizität *f*

station ['steɪʃən] n (RAIL etc) Bahnhof m; (police etc) Wache f; (in society) Stand m ♦ vt stationieren

stationary ['steɪʃnərɪ] adj stillstehend; (car) parkend

stationer's n (shop) Schreibwarengeschäft nt; **~y** n Schreibwaren pl

station master n Bahnhofsvorsteher m

station wagon n Kombiwagen m

statistics [stə'tɪstɪks] n Statistik f

statue ['stætjuː] n Statue f

stature ['stætʃəʳ] n Größe f

status ['steɪtəs] n Status m

statute ['stætjuːt] n Gesetz nt; **statutory** ['stætjutrɪ] adj gesetzlich

staunch [stɔːntʃ] adj standhaft

stay [steɪ] n Aufenthalt m ♦ vi bleiben; (reside) wohnen; **to ~ put** an Ort und Stelle bleiben; **to ~ the night** übernachten; **~ behind** vi zurückbleiben; **~ in** vi (at home) zu Hause bleiben; **~ on** vi (continue) länger bleiben; **~ out** vi (of house) wegbleiben; **~ up** vi (at night) aufbleiben; **~ing power** n Durchhaltevermögen nt

stead [stɛd] n: **in sb's ~** an jds Stelle dat; **to stand sb in good ~** jdm zugute kommen

steadfast ['stɛdfɑːst] adj standhaft, treu

steadily ['stɛdɪlɪ] adv stetig, regelmäßig

steady ['stɛdɪ] adj (firm) fest, stabil; (regular) gleichmäßig; (reliable) beständig; (hand) ruhig; (job, boyfriend) fest ♦ vt festigen; **to ~ o.s. on/against sth** sich stützen auf/ gegen etw acc

steak [steɪk] n Steak nt; (fish) Filet nt

steal [stiːl] (pt **stole**, pp **stolen**) vt stehlen ♦ vi stehlen; (go quietly) sich stehlen

stealth [stɛlθ] n Heimlichkeit f; **~y** adj verstohlen, heimlich

steam [stiːm] n Dampf m ♦ vt (COOK) im Dampfbad erhitzen ♦ vi dampfen; **~ engine** n Dampfmaschine f; **~er** n Dampfer m; **~roller** n Dampfwalze f; **~ship** n = **steamer**; **~y** adj dampfig

steel [stiːl] n Stahl m ♦ adj Stahl-; (fig) stählern; **~works** n Stahlwerke pl

steep [stiːp] adj steil; (price) gepfeffert ♦ vt einweichen

steeple ['stiːpl] n Kirchturm m; **~chase** n Hindernisrennen nt

steer [stɪəʳ] vt, vi steuern; (car etc) lenken; **~ing** n (AUT) Steuerung f; **~ing wheel** n Steuer- or Lenkrad nt

stem [stɛm] n Stiel m ♦ vt aufhalten; **~ from** vt fus abstammen von

stench [stɛntʃ] n Gestank m

stencil ['stɛnsl] n Schablone f ♦ vt (auf)drucken

stenographer [stɛ'nɔgrəfəʳ] (US) n Stenograf(in) m(f)

step [stɛp] n Schritt m; (stair) Stufe f ♦ vi treten, schreiten; **~s** npl (BRIT) = **stepladder**; **to take ~s** Schritte unternehmen; **in/out of ~ (with)** im/nicht im Gleichklang (mit); **~ down** vi (fig) abtreten; **~ off** vt fus aussteigen aus; **~ up** vt steigern

stepbrother ['stɛpbrʌðəʳ] n Stiefbruder m

stepdaughter ['stɛpdɔːtəʳ] n Stieftochter f

stepfather ['stɛpfɑːðəʳ] n Stiefvater m

stepladder ['stɛplædəʳ] n Trittleiter f

stepmother ['stɛpmʌðəʳ] n Stiefmutter f

stepping stone ['stɛpɪŋ-] n Stein m; (fig) Sprungbrett nt

stepsister ['stɛpsɪstəʳ] n Stiefschwester f

stepson ['stɛpsʌn] n Stiefsohn m

stereo ['stɛrɪəu] n Stereoanlage f ♦ adj (also: **~phonic**) stereofonisch, stereophonisch

stereotype ['stɪərɪətaɪp] n (fig) Klischee nt ♦ vt stereotypieren; (fig) stereotyp machen

sterile ['stɛraɪl] adj steril; (person) unfruchtbar; **sterilize** vt sterilisieren

sterling ['stəːlɪŋ] adj (FIN) Sterling-; (character) gediegen ♦ n (ECON) das Pfund Sterling; **a pound ~** ein Pfund Sterling

stern [stəːn] adj streng ♦ n Heck nt, Achterschiff nt

stew [stjuː] n Eintopf m ♦ vt, vi schmoren

steward ['stjuəd] n Steward m; **~ess** n Stewardess f

stick [stɪk] (pt, pp **stuck**) n Stock m; (of chalk etc) Stück nt ♦ vt (stab) stechen; (fix) stecken; (put) stellen; (gum) (an)kleben; (inf: tolerate) vertragen ♦ vi (stop) stecken bleiben; (get stuck) klemmen; (hold fast) kleben, haften; **~ out** vi (*project*) hervorstehen; **~ up** vi (*project*) in die Höhe stehen; **~ up for** vt fus (*defend*) eintreten für; **~er** n Aufkleber m; **~ing plaster** n Heftpflaster nt

stickler ['stɪkləʳ] n: **~ (for)** Pedant m (in +acc)

stick-up ['stɪkʌp] (*inf*) n (Raub)überfall m

sticky ['stɪkɪ] adj klebrig; (*atmosphere*) stickig

stiff [stɪf] adj steif; (*difficult*) hart; (*paste*) dick; (*drink*) stark; **to have a ~ neck** einen steifen Hals haben; **~en** vt versteifen, (ver)stärken ♦ vi sich versteifen

stifle ['staɪfl] vt unterdrücken; **stifling** adj drückend

stigma ['stɪgmə] (*pl BOT, MED, REL* **~ta**; *fig* **~s**) n Stigma nt

stigmata [stɪg'mɑːtə] npl of **stigma**

stile [staɪl] n Steige f

stiletto [stɪ'lɛtəu] (*BRIT*) n (*also:* **~ heel**) Pfennigabsatz m

still [stɪl] adj still ♦ adv (*immer*) noch; (*anyhow*) immerhin; **~born** adj tot geboren; **~ life** n Stillleben nt

stilt [stɪlt] n Stelze f

stilted ['stɪltɪd] adj gestelzt

stimulate ['stɪmjuleɪt] vt anregen, stimulieren

stimuli ['stɪmjulaɪ] npl of **stimulus**

stimulus ['stɪmjuləs] (*pl* **-li**) n Anregung f, Reiz m

sting [stɪŋ] (*pt, pp* **stung**) n Stich m; (*organ*) Stachel m ♦ vi stechen; (*on skin*) brennen ♦ vt stechen

stingy ['stɪndʒɪ] adj geizig, knauserig

stink [stɪŋk] (*pt* **stank**, *pp* **stunk**) n Gestank m ♦ vi stinken; **~ing** adj (*fig*) widerlich

stint [stɪnt] n (*period*) Betätigung f; **to do one's ~** seine Arbeit tun; (*share*) seinen Teil beitragen

stipulate ['stɪpjuleɪt] vt festsetzen

stir [stəːʳ] n Bewegung f; (*COOK*) Rühren nt; (*sensation*) Aufsehen nt ♦ vt (um)rühren ♦ vi sich rühren; **~ up** vt (*mob*) aufhetzen; (*mixture*) umrühren; (*dust*) aufwirbeln

stirrup ['stɪrəp] n Steigbügel m

stitch [stɪtʃ] n (*with needle*) Stich m; (*MED*)

Faden m; (*of knitting*) Masche f; (*pain*) Stich m ♦ vt nähen

stoat [stəut] n Wiesel nt

stock [stɔk] n Vorrat m; (*COMM*) (Waren)lager nt; (*livestock*) Vieh nt; (*COOK*) Brühe f; (*FIN*) Grundkapital nt ♦ adj stets vorrätig; (*standard*) Normal- ♦ vt (*in shop*) führen; **~s** npl (*FIN*) Aktien pl; **in/out of ~** vorrätig/nicht vorrätig; **to take ~ of** Inventur machen von; (*fig*) Bilanz ziehen aus; **~s and shares** Effekten pl; **~ up** vi: **to ~ up (with)** Reserven anlegen (von); **~broker** ['stɔkbrəukəʳ] n Börsenmakler m; **~ cube** n Brühwürfel m; **~ exchange** n Börse f

stocking ['stɔkɪŋ] n Strumpf m

stock: ~ market n Börse f; **~ phrase** n Standardsatz m; **~pile** n Vorrat m ♦ vt aufstapeln; **~taking** (*BRIT*) n (*COMM*) Inventur f, Bestandsaufnahme f

stocky ['stɔkɪ] adj untersetzt

stodgy ['stɔdʒɪ] adj pampig

stoke [stəuk] vt schüren

stole [stəul] pt of **steal** ♦ n Stola f

stolen ['stəuln] pp of **steal**

stomach ['stʌmək] n Bauch m, Magen m ♦ vt vertragen; **~-ache** n Magen- or Bauchschmerzen pl

stone [stəun] n Stein m; (*BRIT: weight*) *Gewichtseinheit = 6.35 kg* ♦ vt (*olive*) entkernen; (*kill*) steinigen; **~-cold** adj eiskalt; **~-deaf** adj stocktaub; **~work** n Mauerwerk nt; **stony** ['stəunɪ] adj steinig

stood [stud] pt, pp of **stand**

stool [stuːl] n Hocker m

stoop [stuːp] vi sich bücken

stop [stɔp] n Halt m; (*bus ~*) Haltestelle f; (*punctuation*) Punkt m ♦ vt anhalten; (*bring to an end*) aufhören (mit), sein lassen ♦ vi aufhören; (*clock*) stehen bleiben; (*remain*) bleiben; **to ~ doing sth** aufhören, etw zu tun; **to ~ dead** innehalten; **~ off** vi kurz Halt machen; **~ up** vt (*hole*) zustopfen, verstopfen; **~gap** n Notlösung f; **~lights** npl (*AUT*) Bremslichter pl; **~over** n (*on journey*) Zwischenaufenthalt m; **~page** ['stɔpɪdʒ] n (An)halten nt; (*traffic*)

Verkehrsstockung f; (strike) Arbeitseinstellung f; ~per ['stɔpər] n Propfen m, Stöpsel m; ~ press n letzte Meldung f; ~watch ['stɔpwɔtʃ] n Stoppuhr f

storage ['stɔːrɪdʒ] n Lagerung f; ~ heater n (Nachtstrom)speicherofen m

store [stɔːʳ] n Vorrat m; (place) Lager nt, Warenhaus nt; (BRIT: large shop) Kaufhaus nt; (US) Laden m ♦ vt lagern; ~s npl (supplies) Vorräte pl; ~ up vt sich eindecken mit; ~room n Lagerraum m, Vorratsraum m

storey ['stɔːrɪ] (US story) n Stock m

stork [stɔːk] n Storch m

storm [stɔːm] n (also fig) Sturm m ♦ vt, vi stürmen; ~y adj stürmisch

story ['stɔːrɪ] n Geschichte f; (lie) Märchen nt; (US) = storey; ~book n Geschichtenbuch nt; ~teller n Geschichtenerzähler m

stout [staut] adj (bold) tapfer; (fat) beleibt ♦ n Starkbier nt; (also: sweet ~) ≈ Malzbier nt

stove [stəuv] n (Koch)herd m; (for heating) Ofen m

stow [stəu] vt verstauen; ~away n blinde(r) Passagier m

straddle ['strædl] vt (horse, fence) rittlings sitzen auf +dat; (fig) überbrücken

straggle ['strægl] vi (people) nachhinken; ~r n Nachzügler m; **straggly** adj (hair) zottig

straight [streɪt] adj gerade; (honest) offen, ehrlich; (drink) pur ♦ adv (direct) direkt, geradewegs; **to put** or **get sth** ~ etw in Ordnung bringen; ~ **away** sofort; ~ **off** sofort; ~en vt (also: ~en out) gerade machen; (fig) klarstellen; ~-faced adv ohne die Miene zu verziehen ♦ adj: **to be** ~-faced keine Miene verziehen; ~forward adj einfach, unkompliziert

strain [streɪn] n Belastung f; (streak, trace) Zug m; (of music) Fetzen m ♦ vt überanstrengen; (stretch) anspannen; (muscle) zerren; (filter) (durch)seihen ♦ vi sich anstrengen; ~ed adj (laugh) gezwungen; (relations) gespannt; ~er n Sieb nt

strait [streɪt] n Straße f, Meerenge f; ~jacket n Zwangsjacke f; ~-laced adj engherzig, streng

strand [strænd] n (of hair) Strähne f; (also fig) Faden m

stranded ['strændɪd] adj (also fig) gestrandet

strange [streɪndʒ] adj fremd; (unusual) seltsam; ~r n Fremde(r) mf

strangle ['stræŋgl] vt erwürgen; ~hold n (fig) Umklammerung f

strap [stræp] n Riemen m; (on clothes) Träger m ♦ vt (fasten) festschnallen

strapping ['stræpɪŋ] adj stramm

strata ['strɑːtə] npl of **stratum**

strategic [strə'tiːdʒɪk] adj strategisch

strategy ['strætɪdʒɪ] n (fig) Strategie f

stratum ['strɑːtəm] (pl -ta) n Schicht f

straw [strɔː] n Stroh nt; (single stalk, drinking ~) Strohhalm m; **that's the last** ~! das ist der Gipfel!

strawberry ['strɔːbərɪ] n Erdbeere f

stray [streɪ] adj (animal) verirrt ♦ vi herumstreunen

streak [striːk] n Streifen m; (in character) Einschlag m; (in hair) Strähne f ♦ vt streifen ♦ vi zucken; (move quickly) flitzen; ~ **of bad luck** Pechsträhne f; ~y adj gestreift; (bacon) durchwachsen

stream [striːm] n (brook) Bach m; (fig) Strom m ♦ vt (SCH) in (Leistungs)gruppen einteilen ♦ vi strömen; **to** ~ **in/out** (people) hinein-/ hinausströmen

streamer ['striːmər] n (flag) Wimpel m; (of paper) Luftschlange f

streamlined ['striːmlaɪnd] adj stromlinienförmig; (effective) rationell

street [striːt] n Straße f ♦ adj Straßen-; ~car (US) n Straßenbahn f; ~ **lamp** n Straßenlaterne f; ~ **plan** n Stadtplan m; ~wise (inf) adj: **to be** ~wise wissen, wo es langgeht

strength [streŋθ] n (also fig) Stärke f; Kraft f; ~en vt (ver)stärken

strenuous ['strenjuəs] adj anstrengend

stress [stres] n Druck m; (mental) Stress m; (GRAM) Betonung f ♦ vt betonen

stretch [stretʃ] n Strecke f ♦ vt ausdehnen,

strecken ♦ *vi* sich erstrecken; *(person)* sich strecken; ~ **out** *vi* sich ausstrecken ♦ *vt* ausstrecken

stretcher ['stretʃəʳ] *n* Tragbahre *f*

stretchy ['stretʃi] *adj* elastisch, dehnbar

strewn [struːn] *adj*: ~ **with** übersät mit

stricken ['strikən] *adj (person)* ergriffen; *(city, country)* heimgesucht; ~ **with** *(disease)* leidend unter +*dat*

strict [strikt] *adj (exact)* genau; *(severe)* streng; ~**ly** *adv* streng, genau

stridden ['stridn] *pp of* **stride**

stride [straid] *(pt* **strode***, pp* **stridden***) n* lange(r) Schritt *m* ♦ *vi* schreiten

strident ['straidnt] *adj* schneidend, durchdringend

strife [straif] *n* Streit *m*

strike [straik] *(pt, pp* **struck***) n* Streik *m*; *(attack)* Schlag *m* ♦ *vt (hit)* schlagen; *(collide)* stoßen gegen; *(come to mind)* einfallen +*dat*; *(stand out)* auffallen +*dat*; *(find)* finden ♦ *vi (stop work)* streiken; *(attack)* zuschlagen; *(clock)* schlagen; **on** ~ *(workers)* im Streik; **to** ~ **a match** ein Streichholz anzünden; ~ **down** *vt (lay low)* niederschlagen; ~ **out** *vt (cross out)* ausstreichen; ~ **up** *vt (music)* anstimmen; *(friendship)* schließen; ~**r** *n* Streikende(r) *mf*; **striking** ['straikiŋ] *adj* auffallend

string [striŋ] *(pt, pp* **strung***) n* Schnur *f*; *(row)* Reihe *f*; *(MUS)* Saite *f* ♦ *vt*: **to** ~ **together** aneinander reihen ♦ *vi*: **to** ~ **out** *(sich)* verteilen; **the** ~**s** *npl (MUS)* die Streichinstrumente *pl*; **to pull** ~**s** *(fig)* Fäden ziehen; ~ **bean** *n* grüne Bohne *f*; ~**(ed) instrument** *n (MUS)* Saiteninstrument *nt*

stringent ['strindʒənt] *adj* streng

strip [strip] *n* Streifen *m* ♦ *vt (uncover)* abstreifen, abziehen; *(clothes)* ausziehen; *(TECH)* auseinander nehmen ♦ *vi (undress)* sich ausziehen; ~ **cartoon** *n* Bildserie *f*

stripe [straip] *n* Streifen *m*; ~**d** *adj* gestreift

strip lighting *n* Neonlicht *nt*

stripper ['stripəʳ] *n* Stripteasetänzerin *f*

strip-search ['stripsəːtʃ] *n* Leibesvisitation *f (bei der man sich ausziehen muss)* ♦ *vt*: **to be** ~~~**ed** sich ausziehen müssen und

durchsucht werden

stripy ['straipi] *adj* gestreift

strive [straiv] *(pt* **strove***, pp* **striven***) vi*: **to** ~ **(for)** streben (nach)

strode [strəud] *pt of* **stride**

stroke [strəuk] *n* Schlag *m*; *(SWIMMING, ROWING)* Stoß *m*; *(MED)* Schlaganfall *m*; *(caress)* Streicheln *nt* ♦ *vt* streicheln; **at a** ~ mit einem Schlag

stroll [strəul] *n* Spaziergang *m* ♦ *vi* schlendern; ~**er** *(US) n (pushchair)* Sportwagen *m*

strong [strɔŋ] *adj* stark; *(firm)* fest; **they are 50** ~ sie sind 50 Mann stark; ~**box** *n* Kassette *f*; ~**hold** *n* Hochburg *f*; ~**ly** *adv* stark; ~**room** *n* Tresor *m*

strove [strəuv] *pt of* **strive**

struck [strʌk] *pt, pp of* **strike**

structure ['strʌktʃəʳ] *n* Struktur *f*, Aufbau *m*; *(building)* Bau *m*

struggle ['strʌgl] *n* Kampf *m* ♦ *vi (fight)* kämpfen

strum [strʌm] *vt (guitar)* klimpern auf +*dat*

strung [strʌŋ] *pt, pp of* **string**

strut [strʌt] *n* Strebe *f*, Stütze *f* ♦ *vi* stolzieren

stub [stʌb] *n* Stummel *m*; *(of cigarette)* Kippe *f* ♦ *vt*: **to** ~ **one's toe** sich *dat* den Zeh anstoßen; ~ **out** *vt* ausdrücken

stubble ['stʌbl] *n* Stoppel *f*

stubborn ['stʌbən] *adj* hartnäckig

stuck [stʌk] *pt, pp of* **stick** ♦ *adj (jammed)* klemmend; ~~**up** *adj* hochnäsig

stud [stʌd] *n (button)* Kragenknopf *m*; *(place)* Gestüt *nt* ♦ *vt (fig)*: ~**ded with** übersät mit

student ['stjuːdənt] *n* Student(in) *m(f)*; *(US)* Student(in) *m(f)*, Schüler(in) *m(f)* ♦ *adj* Studenten-; ~ **driver** *(US) n* Fahrschüler(in) *m(f)*

studio ['stjuːdiəu] *n* Studio *nt*; *(for artist)* Atelier *nt*; ~ **apartment** *(US) n* Appartement *nt*; ~ **flat** *n* Appartement *nt*

studious ['stjuːdiəs] *adj* lernbegierig

study ['stʌdi] *n* Studium *nt*; *(investigation)* Studium *nt*, Untersuchung *f*; *(room)* Arbeitszimmer *nt*; *(essay etc)* Studie *f* ♦ *vt* studieren; *(face)* erforschen; *(evidence)* prüfen ♦ *vi* studieren

stuff [stʌf] n Stoff m; (inf) Zeug nt ♦ vt stopfen, füllen; (animal) ausstopfen; **~ing** n Füllung f; **~y** adj (room) schwül; (person) spießig

stumble ['stʌmbl] vi stolpern; **to ~ across** (fig) zufällig stoßen auf +acc

stumbling block ['stʌmblɪŋ-] n Hindernis nt

stump [stʌmp] n Stumpf m

stun [stʌn] vt betäuben; (shock) niederschmettern

stung [stʌŋ] pt, pp of **sting**

stunk [stʌŋk] pp of **stink**

stunned adj benommen, fassungslos

stunning ['stʌnɪŋ] adj betäubend; (news) überwältigend, umwerfend

stunt [stʌnt] n Kunststück nt, Trick m

stunted ['stʌntɪd] adj verkümmert

stuntman ['stʌntmæn] (irreg) n Stuntman m

stupefy ['stjuːpɪfaɪ] vt betäuben; (by news) bestürzen

stupendous [stjuːˈpɛndəs] adj erstaunlich, enorm

stupid ['stjuːpɪd] adj dumm; **~ity** [stjuːˈpɪdɪtɪ] n Dummheit f

stupor ['stjuːpəʳ] n Betäubung f

sturdy ['stɜːdɪ] adj kräftig, robust

stutter ['stʌtəʳ] n Stottern nt ♦ vi stottern

sty [staɪ] n Schweinestall m

stye [staɪ] n Gerstenkorn nt

style [staɪl] n Stil m; (fashion) Mode f; **stylish** ['staɪlɪʃ] adj modisch; **stylist** ['staɪlɪst] n (hair stylist) Friseur m, Friseuse f

stylus ['staɪləs] n (Grammofon)nadel f

suave [swɑːv] adj zuvorkommend

sub... [sʌb] prefix Unter...; **~conscious** adj unterbewusst ♦ n: **the ~conscious** das Unterbewusste; **~contract** vt (vertraglich) untervermitteln; **~divide** vt unterteilen; **~dued** adj (lighting) gedämpft; (person) still

subject [n, adj 'sʌbdʒɪkt, vb səbˈdʒɛkt] n (of kingdom) Untertan m; (citizen) Staatsangehörige(r) mf; (topic) Thema nt; (SCH) Fach nt; (GRAM) Subjekt nt ♦ adj: **to be ~ to** unterworfen sein +dat; (exposed) ausgesetzt sein +dat ♦ vt (subdue) unterwerfen; (expose) aussetzen; **~ive**

[səbˈdʒɛktɪv] adj subjektiv; **~ matter** n Thema nt

sublet [sʌbˈlɛt] (irreg: like **let**) vt untervermieten

sublime [səˈblaɪm] adj erhaben

submachine gun ['sʌbməˈʃiːn-] n Maschinenpistole f

submarine [sʌbməˈriːn] n Unterseeboot nt, U-Boot nt

submerge [səbˈmɜːdʒ] vt untertauchen; (flood) überschwemmen ♦ vi untertauchen

submission [səbˈmɪʃən] n (obedience) Gehorsam m; (claim) Behauptung f; (of plan) Unterbreitung f; **submissive** [səbˈmɪsɪv] adj demütig, unterwürfig (pej)

submit [səbˈmɪt] vt behaupten; (plan) unterbreiten ♦ vi sich ergeben

subnormal [sʌbˈnɔːml] adj minderbegabt

subordinate [səˈbɔːdɪnət] adj untergeordnet ♦ n Untergebene(r) mf

subpoena [səˈpiːnə] n Vorladung f ♦ vt vorladen

subscribe [səbˈskraɪb] vi: **to ~ to** (view etc) unterstützen; (newspaper) abonnieren; **~r** n (to periodical) Abonnent m; (TEL) Telefonteilnehmer m

subscription [səbˈskrɪpʃən] n Abonnement nt; (money subscribed) (Mitglieds)beitrag m

subsequent ['sʌbsɪkwənt] adj folgend, später; **~ly** adv später

subside [səbˈsaɪd] vi sich senken; **~nce** [səbˈsaɪdns] n Senkung f

subsidiarity [səbsɪdɪˈærɪtɪ] n (POL) Subsidiarität f

subsidiary [səbˈsɪdɪərɪ] adj Neben- ♦ n Tochtergesellschaft f

subsidize ['sʌbsɪdaɪz] vt subventionieren

subsidy ['sʌbsɪdɪ] n Subvention f

subsistence [səbˈsɪstəns] n Unterhalt m

substance ['sʌbstəns] n Substanz f

substantial [səbˈstænʃl] adj (strong) fest, kräftig; (important) wesentlich; **~ly** adv erheblich

substantiate [səbˈstænʃɪeɪt] vt begründen, belegen

substitute ['sʌbstɪtjuːt] n Ersatz m ♦ vt ersetzen; **substitution** [sʌbstɪˈtjuːʃən] n

Ersetzung *f*

subterfuge ['sʌbtəfju:dʒ] *n* Vorwand *m*; (*trick*) Trick *m*

subterranean [sʌbtə'reɪnɪən] *adj* unterirdisch

subtitle ['sʌbtaɪtl] *n* Untertitel *m*; **~d** *adj* untertitelt, mit Untertiteln versehen

subtle ['sʌtl] *adj* fein; **~ty** *n* Feinheit *f*

subtotal [sʌb'təʊtl] *n* Zwischensumme *f*

subtract [səb'trækt] *vt* abziehen; **~ion** [səb'trækʃən] *n* Abziehen *nt*, Subtraktion *f*

suburb ['sʌbə:b] *n* Vorort *m*; **the ~s** die Außenbezirke *pl*; **~an** [sə'bə:bən] *adj* Vorort(s)-; **~ia** [sə'bə:bɪə] *n* Vorstadt *f*

subversive [səb'vɜ:sɪv] *adj* subversiv

subway ['sʌbweɪ] *n* (*US*) U-Bahn *f*; (*BRIT*) Unterführung *f*

succeed [sək'si:d] *vi* (*person*) erfolgreich sein, Erfolg haben; (*plan etc also*) gelingen ♦ *vt* (nach)folgen +*dat*; **he ~ed in doing it** es gelang ihm, es zu tun; **~ing** *adj* (nach)folgend

success [sək'ses] *n* Erfolg *m*; **~ful** *adj* erfolgreich; **to be ~ful (in doing sth)** Erfolg haben (bei etw); **~fully** *adv* erfolgreich

succession [sək'seʃən] *n* (Aufeinander)folge *f*; (*to throne*) Nachfolge *f*

successive [sək'sesɪv] *adj* aufeinander folgend

successor [sək'sesər] *n* Nachfolger(in) *m(f)*

succinct [sək'sɪŋkt] *adj* knapp

succulent ['sʌkjulənt] *adj* saftig

succumb [sə'kʌm] *vi*: **to ~ (to)** erliegen (+*dat*); (*yield*) nachgeben (+*dat*)

such [sʌtʃ] *adj* solche(r, s); **~ a book** so ein Buch; **~ books** solche Bücher; **~ courage** so ein Mut; **~ a long trip** so eine lange Reise; **~ a lot of** so viel(e); **~ as** wie; **a noise ~ as to** ein derartiger Lärm, dass; **as ~** an sich; **~~and~~ a time** die und die Zeit

suck [sʌk] *vt* saugen; (*lollipop etc*) lutschen

sucker ['sʌkər] (*inf*) *n* Idiot *m*

suction ['sʌkʃən] *n* Saugkraft *f*

sudden ['sʌdn] *adj* plötzlich; **all of a ~** auf einmal; **~ly** *adv* plötzlich

suds [sʌdz] *npl* Seifenlauge *f*; (*lather*) Seifenschaum *m*

sue [su:] *vt* verklagen

suede [sweɪd] *n* Wildleder *nt*

suet ['su:ɪt] *n* Nierenfett *nt*

Suez ['su:ɪz] *n*: **the ~ Canal** der Suezkanal

suffer ['sʌfər] *vt* (er)leiden ♦ *vi* leiden; **~er** *n* Leidende(r) *mf*; **~ing** *n* Leiden *nt*

suffice [sə'faɪs] *vi* genügen

sufficient [sə'fɪʃənt] *adj* ausreichend; **~ly** *adv* ausreichend

suffix ['sʌfɪks] *n* Nachsilbe *f*

suffocate ['sʌfəkeɪt] *vt*, *vi* ersticken

suffrage ['sʌfrɪdʒ] *n* Wahlrecht *nt*

sugar ['ʃugər] *n* Zucker *m* ♦ *vt* zuckern; **~ beet** *n* Zuckerrübe *f*; **~ cane** *n* Zuckerrohr *nt*; **~y** *adj* süß

suggest [sə'dʒest] *vt* vorschlagen; (*show*) schließen lassen auf +*acc*; **~ion** [sə'dʒestʃən] *n* Vorschlag *m*; **~ive** *adj* anregend; (*indecent*) zweideutig

suicide ['suɪsaɪd] *n* Selbstmord *m*; **to commit ~** Selbstmord begehen

suit [su:t] *n* Anzug *m*; (*CARDS*) Farbe *f* ♦ *vt* passen +*dat*; (*clothes*) stehen +*dat*; **well ~ed** (*well matched*) gut zusammenpassend; **~able** *adj* geeignet, passend; **~ably** *adv* passend, angemessen

suitcase ['su:tkeɪs] *n* (Hand)koffer *m*

suite [swi:t] *n* (*of rooms*) Zimmerflucht *f*; (*of furniture*) Einrichtung *f*; (*MUS*) Suite *f*

suitor ['su:tər] *n* (*JUR*) Kläger(in) *m(f)*

sulfur ['sʌlfər] (*US*) *n* = **sulphur**

sulk [sʌlk] *vi* schmollen; **~y** *adj* schmollend

sullen ['sʌlən] *adj* mürrisch

sulphur ['sʌlfər] (*US* **sulfur**) *n* Schwefel *m*

sultana [sʌl'tɑ:nə] *n* (*fruit*) Sultanine *f*

sultry ['sʌltrɪ] *adj* schwül

sum [sʌm] *n* Summe *f*; (*money*) Betrag *m*, Summe *f*; (*arithmetic*) Rechenaufgabe *f*; **~ up** *vt*, *vi* zusammenfassen

summarize ['sʌməraɪz] *vt* kurz zusammenfassen

summary ['sʌmərɪ] *n* Zusammenfassung *f* ♦ *adj* (*justice*) kurzerhand erteilt

summer ['sʌmər] *n* Sommer *m* ♦ *adj* Sommer-; **~house** *n* (*in garden*) Gartenhaus *nt*; **~time** *n* Sommerzeit *f*

summit ['sʌmɪt] *n* Gipfel *m*; **~**

(conference) n Gipfelkonferenz f
summon ['sʌmən] vt herbeirufen; (JUR)
vorladen; (gather up) aufbringen; **~s** (JUR) n
Vorladung f ♦ vt vorladen
sump [sʌmp] (BRIT) n (AUT) Ölwanne f
sumptuous ['sʌmptjuəs] adj prächtig
sun [sʌn] n Sonne f; **~bathe** vi sich sonnen;
~block n Sonnenschutzcreme f; **~burn** n
Sonnenbrand m; **~burnt** adj
sonnenverbrannt, sonnengebräunt; **to be**
~burnt (painfully) einen Sonnenbrand
haben
Sunday ['sʌndɪ] n Sonntag m; **~ school** n
Sonntagsschule f
sundial ['sʌndaɪəl] n Sonnenuhr f
sundown ['sʌndaun] n Sonnenuntergang m
sundries ['sʌndrɪz] npl (miscellaneous items)
Verschiedene(s) nt
sundry ['sʌndrɪ] adj verschieden; **all and ~**
alle
sunflower ['sʌnflauəʳ] n Sonnenblume f
sung [sʌŋ] pp of **sing**
sunglasses ['sʌnglɑːsɪz] npl Sonnenbrille f
sunk [sʌŋk] pp of **sink**
sun: **~light** ['sʌnlaɪt] n Sonnenlicht nt; **~lit**
['sʌnlɪt] adj sonnenbeschienen; **~ny** ['sʌnɪ]
adj sonnig; **~rise** n Sonnenaufgang m; **~**
roof n (AUT) Schiebedach nt; **~screen**
['sʌnskriːn] n Sonnenschutzcreme f; **~set**
['sʌnset] n Sonnenuntergang m; **~shade**
['sʌnʃeɪd] n Sonnenschirm m; **~shine**
['sʌnʃaɪn] n Sonnenschein m; **~stroke**
['sʌnstrəuk] n Hitzschlag m; **~tan** ['sʌntæn] n
(Sonnen)Bräune f; **~tan oil** n Sonnenöl nt
super ['suːpəʳ] (inf) adj prima, klasse
superannuation [suːpərænjuˈeɪʃən] n
Pension f
superb [suːˈpəːb] adj ausgezeichnet,
hervorragend
supercilious [suːpəˈsɪlɪəs] adj herablassend
superficial [suːpəˈfɪʃəl] adj oberflächlich
superfluous [suˈpəːfluəs] adj überflüssig
superhuman [suːpəˈhjuːmən] adj (effort)
übermenschlich
superimpose ['suːpərɪmˈpəuz] vt
übereinander legen
superintendent [suːpərɪnˈtendənt] n
Polizeichef m
superior [suˈpɪərɪəʳ] adj überlegen; (better)
besser ♦ n Vorgesetzte(r) mf; **~ity**
[supɪərɪˈɔrɪtɪ] n Überlegenheit f
superlative [suˈpəːlətɪv] adj überragend
super: **~man** ['suːpəmæn] (irreg) n
Übermensch m; **~market** ['suːpəmɑːkɪt] n
Supermarkt m; **~natural** ['suːpəˈnætʃərəl] adj
übernatürlich; **~power** ['suːpəpauəʳ] n
Weltmacht f
supersede [suːpəˈsiːd] vt ersetzen
supersonic ['suːpəˈsɔnɪk] adj Überschall-
superstition [suːpəˈstɪʃən] n Aberglaube m;
superstitious [suːpəˈstɪʃəs] adj
abergläubisch
supervise ['suːpəvaɪz] vt beaufsichtigen,
kontrollieren; **supervision** [suːpəˈvɪʒən] n
Aufsicht f; **supervisor** ['suːpəvaɪzəʳ] n
Aufsichtsperson f; **supervisory**
['suːpəvaɪzərɪ] adj Aufsichts-
supper ['sʌpəʳ] n Abendessen nt
supplant [səˈplɑːnt] vt (person, thing)
ersetzen
supple ['sʌpl] adj geschmeidig
supplement [n 'sʌplɪmənt, vb sʌplɪˈment] n
Ergänzung f; (in book) Nachtrag m ♦ vt
ergänzen; **~ary** [sʌplɪˈmentərɪ] adj
ergänzend; **~ary benefit** (BRIT: old) n ≈
Sozialhilfe f
supplier [səˈplaɪəʳ] n Lieferant m
supplies [səˈplaɪz] npl (food) Vorräte pl; (MIL)
Nachschub m
supply [səˈplaɪ] vt liefern ♦ n Vorrat m; (~ing)
Lieferung f; see also **supplies**; **~ teacher**
(BRIT) n Vertretung f
support [səˈpɔːt] n Unterstützung f; (TECH)
Stütze f ♦ vt (hold up) stützen, tragen;
(provide for) ernähren; (be in favour of)
unterstützen; **~er** n Anhänger(in) m(f)
suppose [səˈpəuz] vt, vi annehmen; **to be**
~d to do sth etw tun sollen; **~dly**
[səˈpəuzɪdlɪ] adv angeblich; **supposing** conj
angenommen; **supposition** [sʌpəˈzɪʃən] n
Voraussetzung f
suppress [səˈpres] vt unterdrücken
supremacy [suˈpreməsɪ] n Vorherrschaft f,
Oberhoheit f

supreme [suˈpriːm] *adj* oberste(r, s), höchste(r, s)

surcharge [ˈsəːtʃɑːdʒ] *n* Zuschlag *m*

sure [ʃuəʳ] *adj* sicher, gewiss; ~! (*of course*) klar!; **to make ~ of sth/that** sich einer Sache *gen* vergewissern/vergewissern, dass; **~ enough** (*with past*) tatsächlich; (*with future*) ganz bestimmt; **~-footed** *adj* sicher (auf den Füßen); **~ly** *adv* (*certainly*) sicherlich, gewiss; **~ly it's wrong** das ist doch wohl falsch

surety [ˈʃuərətɪ] *n* Sicherheit *f*

surf [səːf] *n* Brandung *f*

surface [ˈsəːfɪs] *n* Oberfläche *f* ♦ *vt* (*roadway*) teeren ♦ *vi* auftauchen; ~ **mail** *n* gewöhnliche Post *f*

surfboard [ˈsəːfbɔːd] *n* Surfbrett *nt*

surfeit [ˈsəːfɪt] *n* Übermaß *nt*

surfing [ˈsəːfɪŋ] *n* Surfen *nt*

surge [səːdʒ] *n* Woge *f* ♦ *vi* wogen

surgeon [ˈsəːdʒən] *n* Chirurg(in) *m(f)*

surgery [ˈsəːdʒərɪ] *n* (*BRIT: place*) Praxis *f*; (: *time*) Sprechstunde *f*; (*treatment*) Operation *f*; **to undergo ~** operiert werden; ~ **hours** (*BRIT*) *npl* Sprechstunden *pl*

surgical [ˈsəːdʒɪkl] *adj* chirurgisch; ~ **spirit** (*BRIT*) *n* Wundbenzin *nt*

surly [ˈsəːlɪ] *adj* verdrießlich, grob

surmount [səːˈmaunt] *vt* überwinden

surname [ˈsəːneɪm] *n* Zuname *m*

surpass [səːˈpɑːs] *vt* übertreffen

surplus [ˈsəːpləs] *n* Überschuss *m* ♦ *adj* überschüssig, Über(schuss)-

surprise [səˈpraɪz] *n* Überraschung *f* ♦ *vt* überraschen; **~d** *adj* überrascht; **surprising** *adj* überraschend; **surprisingly** *adv* überraschend(erweise)

surrender [səˈrɛndəʳ] *n* Kapitulation *f* ♦ *vi* sich ergeben

surreptitious [sʌrəpˈtɪʃəs] *adj* heimlich; (*look also*) verstohlen

surrogate [ˈsʌrəgɪt] *n* Ersatz *m*; ~ **mother** *n* Leihmutter *f*

surround [səˈraund] *vt* umgeben; **~ing** *adj* (*countryside*) umliegend; **~ings** *npl* Umgebung *f*; (*environment*) Umwelt *f*

surveillance [səːˈveɪləns] *n* Überwachung *f*

survey [*n* ˈsəːveɪ, *vb* səːˈveɪ] *n* Übersicht *f* ♦ *vt* überblicken; (*land*) vermessen; **~or** [səˈveɪəʳ] *n* Land(ver)messer(in) *m(f)*

survival [səˈvaɪvl] *n* Überleben *nt*

survive [səˈvaɪv] *vt*, *vi* überleben; **survivor** [səˈvaɪvəʳ] *n* Überlebende(r) *mf*

susceptible [səˈsɛptəbl] *adj*: ~ (**to**) empfindlich (gegen); (*charms etc*) empfänglich (für)

suspect [*n* ˈsʌspɛkt, *vb* səsˈpɛkt] *n* Verdächtige(r) *mf* ♦ *adj* verdächtig ♦ *vt* verdächtigen; (*think*) vermuten

suspend [səsˈpɛnd] *vt* verschieben; (*from work*) suspendieren; (*hang up*) aufhängen; (*SPORT*) sperren; **~ed sentence** *n* (*JUR*) zur Bewährung ausgesetzte Strafe; **~er belt** *n* Strumpf(halter)gürtel *m*; **~ers** *npl* (*BRIT*) Strumpfhalter *pl*; (*US*) Hosenträger *m*

suspense [səsˈpɛns] *n* Spannung *f*

suspension [səsˈpɛnʃən] *n* (*from work*) Suspendierung *f*; (*SPORT*) Sperrung *f*; (*AUT*) Federung *f*; ~ **bridge** *n* Hängebrücke *f*

suspicion [səsˈpɪʃən] *n* Misstrauen *nt*; Verdacht *m*; **suspicious** [səsˈpɪʃəs] *adj* misstrauisch; (*causing ~*) verdächtig

sustain [səsˈteɪn] *vt* (*maintain*) aufrechterhalten; (*confirm*) bestätigen; (*injury*) davontragen; **~able** *adj* (*development, growth etc*) aufrechtzuerhalten; **~ed** *adj* (*effort*) anhaltend

sustenance [ˈsʌstɪnəns] *n* Nahrung *f*

swab [swɔb] *n* (*MED*) Tupfer *m*

swagger [ˈswægəʳ] *vi* stolzieren

swallow [ˈswɔləu] *n* (*bird*) Schwalbe *f*; (*of food etc*) Schluck *m* ♦ *vt* (ver)schlucken; ~ **up** *vt* verschlingen

swam [swæm] *pt of* swim

swamp [swɔmp] *n* Sumpf *m* ♦ *vt* überschwemmen

swan [swɔn] *n* Schwan *m*

swap [swɔp] *n* Tausch *m* ♦ *vt*: **to ~ sth (for sth)** etw (gegen etw) tauschen *or* eintauschen

swarm [swɔːm] *n* Schwarm *m* ♦ *vi*: **to ~** *or* **be ~ing with** wimmeln von

swarthy ['swɔːðɪ] adj dunkel, braun

swastika ['swɒstɪkə] n Hakenkreuz nt

swat [swɒt] vt totschlagen

sway [sweɪ] vi schwanken; (branches) schaukeln, sich wiegen ♦ vt schwenken; (influence) beeinflussen

swear [sweəʳ] (pt swore, pp sworn) vi (promise) schwören; (curse) fluchen; **to ~ to sth** schwören auf etw acc; **~word** n Fluch m

sweat [swɛt] n Schweiß m ♦ vi schwitzen

sweater ['swɛtəʳ] n Pullover m

sweatshirt ['swɛtʃəːt] n Sweatshirt nt

sweaty ['swɛtɪ] adj verschwitzt

Swede [swiːd] n Schwede m, Schwedin f

swede [swiːd] (BRIT) n Steckrübe f

Sweden ['swiːdn] n Schweden nt

Swedish ['swiːdɪʃ] adj schwedisch ♦ n (LING) Schwedisch nt

sweep [swiːp] (pt, pp swept) n (chimney ~) Schornsteinfeger m ♦ vt fegen, kehren; **~ away** vt wegfegen; **~ past** vi vorbeisausen; **~ up** vt zusammenkehren; **~ing** adj (gesture) schwungvoll; (statement) verallgemeinernd

sweet [swiːt] n (course) Nachtisch m; (candy) Bonbon ♦ adj süß; **~corn** n Zuckermais m; **~en** vt süßen; (fig) versüßen; **~heart** n Liebste(r) mf; **~ness** n Süße f; **~ pea** n Gartenwicke f

swell [swɛl] (pt swelled, pp swollen or swelled) n Seegang m ♦ adj (inf) todschick ♦ vt (numbers) vermehren ♦ vi (also: ~ up) (an)schwellen; **~ing** n Schwellung f

sweltering ['swɛltərɪŋ] adj drückend

swept [swɛpt] pt, pp of sweep

swerve [swɜːv] vt, vi ausscheren

swift [swɪft] n Mauersegler m ♦ adj geschwind, schnell, rasch; **~ly** adv geschwind, schnell, rasch

swig [swɪg] n Zug m

swill [swɪl] n (for pigs) Schweinefutter nt ♦ vt spülen

swim [swɪm] (pt swam, pp swum) n: **to go for a ~** schwimmen gehen ♦ vi schwimmen ♦ vt (cross) (durch)schwimmen; **~mer** n Schwimmer(in) m(f); **~ming** n

Schwimmen nt; **~ming cap** n Badehaube f, Badekappe f; **~ming costume** (BRIT) n Badeanzug m; **~ming pool** n Schwimmbecken nt; (private) Swimmingpool m; **~ming trunks** npl Badehose f; **~suit** n Badeanzug m

swindle ['swɪndl] n Schwindel m, Betrug m ♦ vt betrügen

swine [swaɪn] n (also fig) Schwein nt

swing [swɪŋ] (pt, pp swung) n (child's) Schaukel f; (movement) Schwung m ♦ vt schwingen ♦ vi schwingen, schaukeln; (turn quickly) schwenken; **in full ~** in vollem Gange; **~ bridge** n Drehbrücke f; **~ door** (BRIT) n Schwingtür f

swingeing ['swɪndʒɪŋ] (BRIT) adj hart; (taxation, cuts) extrem

swinging door ['swɪŋɪŋ-] (US) n Schwingtür f

swipe [swaɪp] n Hieb m ♦ vt (inf: hit) hart schlagen; (: steal) klauen

swirl [swɜːl] vi wirbeln

swish [swɪʃ] adj (inf: smart) schick ♦ vi zischen; (grass, skirts) rascheln

Swiss [swɪs] adj Schweizer, schweizerisch ♦ n Schweizer(in) m(f); **the ~** npl (people) die Schweizer pl

switch [swɪtʃ] n (ELEC) Schalter m; (change) Wechsel m ♦ vt (ELEC) schalten; (change) wechseln ♦ vi wechseln; **~ off** vt ab- or ausschalten; **~ on** vt an- or einschalten; **~board** n Zentrale f; (board) Schaltbrett nt

Switzerland ['swɪtsələnd] n die Schweiz

swivel ['swɪvl] vt (also: ~ round) drehen ♦ vi (also: ~ round) sich drehen

swollen ['swəulən] pp of swell

swoon [swuːn] vi (old) in Ohnmacht fallen

swoop [swuːp] n Sturzflug m; (esp by police) Razzia f ♦ vi (also: ~ down) stürzen

swop [swɒp] = swap

sword [sɔːd] n Schwert nt; **~fish** n Schwertfisch m

swore [swɔːʳ] pt of swear

sworn [swɔːn] pp of swear

swot [swɒt] vt, vi pauken

swum [swʌm] pp of swim

swung [swʌŋ] pt, pp of swing

sycamore ['sɪkəmɔːʳ] n (US) Platane f; (BRIT) Bergahorn m
syllable ['sɪləbl] n Silbe f
syllabus ['sɪləbəs] n Lehrplan m
symbol ['sɪmbl] n Symbol nt; **~ic(al)** [sɪm'bɒlɪk(l)] adj symbolisch
symmetry ['sɪmɪtrɪ] n Symmetrie f
sympathetic [sɪmpə'θetɪk] adj mitfühlend
sympathize ['sɪmpəθaɪz] vi mitfühlen; **~r** n (POL) Sympathisant(in) m(f)
sympathy ['sɪmpəθɪ] n Mitleid nt, Mitgefühl nt; (condolence) Beileid nt; **with our deepest ~** mit tief empfundenem Beileid
symphony ['sɪmfənɪ] n Sinfonie f
symptom ['sɪmptəm] n Symptom nt; **~atic** [sɪmptə'mætɪk] adj (fig): **~atic of** bezeichnend für
synagogue ['sɪnəgɒg] n Synagoge f
synchronize ['sɪŋkrənaɪz] vt synchronisieren
syndicate ['sɪndɪkɪt] n Konsortium nt
synonym ['sɪnənɪm] n Synonym nt; **~ous** [sɪ'nɒnɪməs] adj gleichbedeutend
synopsis [sɪ'nɒpsɪs] n Zusammenfassung f
synthetic [sɪn'θetɪk] adj synthetisch; **~s** npl (man-made fabrics) Synthetik f
syphon ['saɪfən] = **siphon**
Syria ['sɪrɪə] n Syrien nt
syringe [sɪ'rɪndʒ] n Spritze f
syrup ['sɪrəp] n Sirup m; (of sugar) Melasse f
system ['sɪstəm] n System nt; **~atic** [sɪstə'mætɪk] adj systematisch; **~ disk** n (COMPUT) Systemdiskette f; **~s analyst** n Systemanalytiker(in) m(f)

T, t

ta [tɑː] (BRIT: inf) excl danke!
tab [tæb] n Aufhänger m; (name ~) Schild nt; **to keep ~s on** (fig) genau im Auge behalten
tabby ['tæbɪ] n (also: ~ cat) getigerte Katze f
table ['teɪbl] n Tisch m; (list) Tabelle f ♦ vt (PARL: propose) vorlegen, einbringen; **to lay** or **set the ~** den Tisch decken; **~cloth** n Tischtuch nt; **~ d'hôte** [tɑːbl'dəut] n Tagesmenü nt; **~ lamp** n Tischlampe f;

~mat n Untersatz m; **~ of contents** n Inhaltsverzeichnis nt; **~spoon** n Esslöffel m; **~spoonful** n Esslöffel m (voll)
tablet ['tæblɪt] n (MED) Tablette f
table tennis n Tischtennis nt
table wine n Tafelwein m
tabloid ['tæblɔɪd] n Zeitung f in kleinem Format; (pej) Boulevardzeitung f

tabloid press

i Der Ausdruck **tabloid press** bezieht sich auf kleinformatige Zeitungen (ca 30 x 40cm); sie sind in Großbritannien fast ausschließlich Massenblätter. Im Gegensatz zur **quality press** verwenden diese Massenblätter viele Fotos und einen knappen, oft reißerischen Stil. Sie kommen den Lesern entgegen, die mehr Wert auf Unterhaltung legen.

tabulate ['tæbjuleɪt] vt tabellarisch ordnen
tacit ['tæsɪt] adj stillschweigend
taciturn ['tæsɪtɜːn] adj wortkarg
tack [tæk] n (small nail) Stift m; (US: thumbtack) Reißzwecke f; (stitch) Heftstich m; (NAUT) Lavieren nt; (course) Kurs m ♦ vt (nail) nageln; (stitch) heften ♦ vi aufkreuzen
tackle ['tækl] n (for lifting) Flaschenzug m; (NAUT) Takelage f; (SPORT) Tackling nt ♦ vt (deal with) anpacken, in Angriff nehmen; (person) festhalten; (player) angehen
tacky ['tækɪ] adj klebrig
tact [tækt] n Takt m; **~ful** adj taktvoll
tactical ['tæktɪkl] adj taktisch
tactics ['tæktɪks] npl Taktik f
tactless ['tæktlɪs] adj taktlos
tadpole ['tædpəul] n Kaulquappe f
taffy ['tæfɪ] (US) n Sahnebonbon nt
tag [tæg] n (label) Schild nt, Anhänger m; (maker's name) Etikett nt; **~ along** vi mitkommen
tail [teɪl] n Schwanz m; (of list) Schluss m ♦ vt folgen +dat; **~ away** or **off** vi abfallen, schwinden; **~back** (BRIT) n (AUT) (Rück)stau m; **~ coat** n Frack m; **~ end** n Schluss m, Ende nt; **~gate** n (AUT) Heckklappe f
tailor ['teɪləʳ] n Schneider m; **~ing** n

Schneidern nt; **~-made** adj
maßgeschneidert; (fig): **~-made for sb** jdm
wie auf den Leib geschnitten
tailwind ['teɪlwɪnd] n Rückenwind m
tainted ['teɪntɪd] adj verdorben
take [teɪk] (pt **took**, pp **taken**) vt nehmen;
(trip, exam, PHOT) machen; (capture: person)
fassen; (: town; also COMM, FIN) einnehmen;
(carry to a place) bringen; (get for o.s.) sich
dat nehmen; (gain, obtain) bekommen; (put
up with) hinnehmen; (respond to)
aufnehmen; (interpret) auffassen; (assume)
annehmen; (contain) Platz haben für;
(GRAM) stehen mit; **to ~ sth from sb** jdm
etw wegnehmen; **to ~ sth from sth** (MATH:
subtract) etw von etw abziehen; (extract,
quotation) etw einer Sache dat entnehmen;
~ after vt fus ähnlich sein +dat; **~ apart**
vt auseinander nehmen; **~ away** vt
(remove) wegnehmen; (carry off)
wegbringen; **~ back** vt (return)
zurückbringen; (retract) zurücknehmen; **~
down** vt (pull down) abreißen; (write down)
aufschreiben; **~ in** vt (deceive) hereinlegen;
(understand) begreifen; (include)
einschließen; **~ off** vi (plane) starten ♦ vt
(remove) wegnehmen; (clothing) ausziehen;
(imitate) nachmachen; **~ on** vt (undertake)
übernehmen; (engage) einstellen;
(opponent) antreten gegen; **~ out** vt (girl,
dog) ausführen; (extract) herausnehmen;
(insurance) abschließen; (licence) sich dat
geben lassen; (book) ausleihen; (remove)
entfernen; **to ~ sth out of sth** (drawer,
pocket etc) etw aus etw herausnehmen; **~
over** vt übernehmen ♦ vi: **to ~ over from
sb** jdn ablösen; **~ to** vt fus (like) mögen;
(adopt as practice) sich dat angewöhnen; **~
up** vt (raise) aufnehmen; (dress etc) kürzer
machen; (occupy) in Anspruch nehmen;
(engage in) sich befassen mit; **~away** adj
zum Mitnehmen; **~-home pay** n
Nettolohn m; **~n** pp of **take**; **~off** n (AVIAT)
Start m; (imitation) Nachahmung f; **~out**
(US) adj = **takeaway**; **~over** n (COMM)
Übernahme f; **takings** ['teɪkɪŋz] npl (COMM)
Einnahmen pl

talc [tælk] n (also: **~um powder**)
Talkumpuder m
tale [teɪl] n Geschichte f, Erzählung f; **to tell
~s** (fig: lie) Geschichten erfinden
talent ['tælnt] n Talent nt; **~ed** adj begabt
talk [tɔːk] n (conversation) Gespräch nt;
(rumour) Gerede nt; (speech) Vortrag m ♦ vi
sprechen, reden; **~s** npl (POL etc) Gespräche
pl; **to ~ about** sprechen von +dat or über
+acc; **to ~ sb into doing sth** jdn
überreden, etw zu tun; **to ~ sb out of
doing sth** jdm ausreden, etw zu tun; **to ~
shop** fachsimpeln; **~ over** vt besprechen;
~ative adj gesprächig
tall [tɔːl] adj groß; (building) hoch; **to be 1 m
80 ~** 1,80 m groß sein; **~boy** (BRIT) n
Kommode f; **~ story** n übertriebene
Geschichte f
tally ['tælɪ] n Abrechnung f ♦ vi
übereinstimmen
talon ['tælən] n Kralle f
tame [teɪm] adj zahm; (fig) fade
tamper ['tæmpə*] vi: **to ~ with**
herumpfuschen an +dat
tampon ['tæmpɔn] n Tampon m
tan [tæn] n (Sonnen)bräune f; (colour)
Gelbbraun nt ♦ adj (colour) (gelb)braun ♦ vt
bräunen ♦ vi braun werden
tang [tæŋ] n Schärfe f
tangent ['tændʒənt] n Tangente f; **to go off
at a ~** (fig) vom Thema abkommen
tangerine [tændʒə'riːn] n Mandarine f
tangible ['tændʒəbl] adj greifbar
tangle ['tæŋgl] n Durcheinander nt; (trouble)
Schwierigkeiten pl; **to get in(to) a ~** sich
verheddern
tank [tæŋk] n (container) Tank m, Behälter m;
(MIL) Panzer m; **~er** ['tæŋkə*] n (ship) Tanker
m; (vehicle) Tankwagen m
tanned [tænd] adj gebräunt
tantalizing ['tæntəlaɪzɪŋ] adj verlockend;
(annoying) quälend
tantamount ['tæntəmaunt] adj: **~ to**
gleichbedeutend mit
tantrum ['tæntrəm] n Wutanfall m
tap [tæp] n Hahn m; (gentle blow) Klopfen nt
♦ vt (strike) klopfen; (supply) anzapfen;

(*telephone*) abhören; **on ~** (*fig: resources*) zur Hand; **~-dancing** n Steppen nt

tape [teɪp] n Band nt; (*magnetic*) (Ton)band nt; (*adhesive*) Klebstreifen m ♦ vt (*record*) aufnehmen; **~ deck** n Tapedeck nt; **~ measure** n Maßband nt

taper ['teɪpəʳ] vi spitz zulaufen

tape recorder n Tonbandgerät nt

tapestry ['tæpɪstrɪ] n Wandteppich m

tar [tɑ:] n Teer m

target ['tɑ:gɪt] n Ziel nt; (*board*) Zielscheibe f

tariff ['tærɪf] n (*duty paid*) Zoll m; (*list*) Tarif m

tarmac ['tɑ:mæk] n (*AVIAT*) Rollfeld nt

tarnish ['tɑ:nɪʃ] vt matt machen; (*fig*) beflecken

tarpaulin [tɑ:'pɔ:lɪn] n Plane f

tarragon ['tærəgən] n Estragon m

tart [tɑ:t] n (Obst)torte f; (*inf*) Nutte f ♦ adj scharf; **~ up** (*inf*) vt aufmachen; (*person*) auftakeln

tartan ['tɑ:tn] n Schottenkaro nt ♦ adj mit Schottenkaro

tartar ['tɑ:təʳ] n Zahnstein m

tartar(e) sauce ['tɑ:tə-] n Remouladensoße f

task [tɑ:sk] n Aufgabe f; **to take sb to ~** sich dat jdn vornehmen; **~ force** n Sondertrupp m

tassel ['tæsl] n Quaste f

taste [teɪst] n Geschmack m; (*sense*) Geschmackssinn m; (*small quantity*) Kostprobe f; (*liking*) Vorliebe f ♦ vt schmecken; (*try*) probieren ♦ vi schmecken; **can I have a ~ of this wine?** kann ich diesen Wein probieren?; **to have a ~ for sth** etw mögen; **in good/bad ~** geschmackvoll/geschmacklos; **you can ~ the garlic (in it)** man kann den Knoblauch herausschmecken; **to ~ of sth** nach einer Sache schmecken; **~ful** adj geschmackvoll; **~less** adj (*insipid*) fade; (*in bad ~*) geschmacklos; **tasty** ['teɪstɪ] adj schmackhaft

tattered ['tætəd] adj = **in tatters**

tatters ['tætəz] npl: **in ~** in Fetzen

tattoo [tə'tu:] n (*MIL*) Zapfenstreich m; (*on skin*) Tätowierung f ♦ vt tätowieren

tatty ['tætɪ] (*BRIT: inf*) adj schäbig

taught [tɔ:t] pt, pp of **teach**

taunt [tɔ:nt] n höhnische Bemerkung f ♦ vt verhöhnen

Taurus ['tɔ:rəs] n Stier m

taut [tɔ:t] adj straff

tawdry ['tɔ:drɪ] adj (bunt und) billig

tax [tæks] n Steuer f ♦ vt besteuern; (*strain*) strapazieren; (*strength*) angreifen; **~able** adj (*income*) steuerpflichtig; **~ation** [tæk'seɪʃən] n Besteuerung f; **~ avoidance** n Steuerumgehung f; **~ disc** (*BRIT*) n (*AUT*) Kraftfahrzeugsteuerplakette f; **~ evasion** n Steuerhinterziehung f; **~-free** adj steuerfrei

taxi ['tæksɪ] n Taxi nt ♦ vi (*plane*) rollen; **~ driver** n Taxifahrer m; **~ rank** (*BRIT*) n Taxistand m; **~ stand** n Taxistand m

tax: ~payer n Steuerzahler m; **~ relief** n Steuerermäßigung f; **~ return** n Steuererklärung f

TB n abbr (= *tuberculosis*) Tb f, Tbc f

tea [ti:] n Tee m; (*meal*) (frühes) Abendessen nt; **high ~** (*BRIT*) Abendessen nt; **~ bag** n Teebeutel m; **~ break** (*BRIT*) n Teepause f

teach [ti:tʃ] (pt, pp **taught**) vt lehren; (*SCH*) lehren, unterrichten; (*show*): **to ~ sb sth** jdm etw beibringen ♦ vi lehren, unterrichten; **~er** n Lehrer(in) m(f); **~er's pet** n Lehrers Liebling m; **~ing** n (*~er's work*) Unterricht m; (*doctrine*) Lehre f

tea: ~ cloth n Geschirrtuch nt; **~ cosy** n Teewärmer m; **~cup** n Teetasse f; **~ leaves** npl Teeblätter pl

team [ti:m] n (*workers*) Team nt; (*SPORT*) Mannschaft f; (*animals*) Gespann nt; **~work** n Gemeinschaftsarbeit f, Teamarbeit f

teapot ['ti:pɔt] n Teekanne f

tear¹ [tɛəʳ] (pt **tore**, pp **torn**) n Riss m ♦ vt zerreißen; (*muscle*) zerren ♦ vi (zer)reißen; (*rush*) rasen; **~ along** vi (*rush*) entlangrasen; **~ up** vt (*sheet of paper etc*) zerreißen

tear² [tɪəʳ] n Träne f; **~ful** ['tɪəful] adj weinend; (*voice*) weinerlich; **~ gas** ['tɪəgæs] n Tränengas nt

tearoom ['ti:ru:m] n Teestube f

tease [ti:z] n Hänsler m ♦ vt necken

tea set *n* Teeservice *nt*
teaspoon ['tiːspuːn] *n* Teelöffel *m*
teat [tiːt] *n* Brustwarze *f*; (*of animal*) Zitze *f*; (*of bottle*) Sauger *m*
tea time *n* (*in the afternoon*) Teestunde *f*; (*mealtime*) Abendessen *nt*
tea towel *n* Geschirrtuch *nt*
technical ['teknɪkl] *adj* technisch; (*knowledge, terms*) Fach-; **~ity** [teknɪ'kælɪtɪ] *n* technische Einzelheit *f*; (*JUR*) Formsache *f*; **~ly** *adv* technisch; (*speak*) spezialisiert; (*fig*) genau genommen
technician [tek'nɪʃən] *n* Techniker *m*
technique [tek'niːk] *n* Technik *f*
techno ['teknəʊ] *n* Techno *m*
technological [teknə'lɒdʒɪkl] *adj* technologisch
technology [tek'nɒlədʒɪ] *n* Technologie *f*
teddy (bear) ['tedɪ-] *n* Teddybär *m*
tedious ['tiːdɪəs] *adj* langweilig, ermüdend
tee [tiː] *n* (*GOLF: object*) Tee *nt*
teem [tiːm] *vi* (*swarm*): **to ~ (with)** wimmeln (von); **it is ~ing (with rain)** es gießt in Strömen
teenage ['tiːneɪdʒ] *adj* (*fashions etc*) Teenager-, jugendlich; **~r** *n* Teenager *m*, Jugendliche(r) *mf*
teens [tiːnz] *npl* Teenageralter *nt*
tee-shirt ['tiːʃəːt] *n* T-Shirt *nt*
teeter ['tiːtə*] *vi* schwanken
teeth [tiːθ] *npl* of **tooth**
teethe [tiːð] *vi* zahnen; **teething ring** *n* Beißring *m*; **teething troubles** *npl* (*fig*) Kinderkrankheiten *pl*
teetotal ['tiː'təʊtl] *adj* abstinent
tele-: **~communications** *npl* Fernmeldewesen *nt*; **~conferencing** *n* Telefon- *or* Videokonferenz *f*; **~gram** *n* Telegramm *nt*; **~graph** *n* Telegraf *m*; **~graph pole** *n* Telegrafenmast *m*
telephone ['telɪfəʊn] *n* Telefon *nt*, Fernsprecher *m* ♦ *vt* anrufen; (*message*) telefonisch mitteilen; **to be on the ~** (*talking*) telefonieren; (*possessing phone*) Telefon haben; **~ booth** *n* Telefonzelle *f*; **~ box** (*BRIT*) *n* Telefonzelle *f*; **~ call** *n* Telefongespräch *nt*, Anruf *m*; **~ directory**

n Telefonbuch *nt*; **~ number** *n* Telefonnummer *f*; **telephonist** [tə'lefənɪst] (*BRIT*) *n* Telefonist(in) *m(f)*
telephoto lens ['telɪ'fəʊtəʊ-] *n* Teleobjektiv *nt*
telescope ['telɪskəʊp] *n* Teleskop *nt*, Fernrohr *nt* ♦ *vt* ineinander schieben
televise ['telɪvaɪz] *vt* durch das Fernsehen übertragen
television ['telɪvɪʒən] *n* Fernsehen *nt*; **on ~** im Fernsehen; **~ (set)** *n* Fernsehapparat *m*, Fernseher *m*
teleworking ['telɪwəːkɪŋ] *n* Telearbeit *f*
telex ['teleks] *n* Telex *nt* ♦ *vt* per Telex schicken
tell [tel] (*pt, pp* **told**) *vt* (*story*) erzählen; (*secret*) ausplaudern; (*say, make known*) sagen; (*distinguish*) erkennen; (*be sure*) wissen ♦ *vi* (*talk*) sprechen; (*be sure*) wissen; (*divulge*) es verraten; (*have effect*) sich auswirken; **to ~ sb to do sth** jdm sagen, dass er etw tun soll; **to ~ sb sth** *or* **sth to sb** jdm etw sagen; **to ~ sb by sth** jdn an etw *dat* erkennen; **to ~ sth from** etw unterscheiden von; **to ~ of sth** von etw sprechen; **~ off** *vt*: **to ~ sb off** jdn ausschimpfen
teller ['telə*] *n* Kassenbeamte(r) *mf*
telling ['telɪŋ] *adj* verräterisch; (*blow*) hart
telltale ['telteɪl] *adj* verräterisch
telly ['telɪ] (*BRIT: inf*) *n abbr* (= *television*) TV *nt*
temp [temp] *n abbr* (= *temporary*) Aushilfssekretärin *f*
temper ['tempə*] *n* (*disposition*) Temperament *nt*; (*anger*) Zorn *m* ♦ *vt* (*tone down*) mildern; (*metal*) härten; **to be in a (bad) ~** wütend sein; **to lose one's ~** die Beherrschung verlieren
temperament ['temprəmənt] *n* Temperament *nt*; **~al** [temprə'mentl] *adj* (*moody*) launisch
temperate ['tempərət] *adj* gemäßigt
temperature ['temprətʃə*] *n* Temperatur *f*; (*MED: high ~*) Fieber *nt*; **to have** *or* **run a ~** Fieber haben
template ['templɪt] *n* Schablone *f*
temple ['templ] *n* Tempel *m*; (*ANAT*) Schlä-

fe *f*

temporal ['tɛmpərl] *adj* (*of time*) zeitlich; (*worldly*) irdisch, weltlich

temporarily ['tɛmpərərɪlɪ] *adv* zeitweilig, vorübergehend

temporary ['tɛmpərərɪ] *adj* vorläufig; (*road, building*) provisorisch

tempt [tɛmpt] *vt* (*persuade*) verleiten; (*attract*) reizen, (ver)locken; **to ~ sb into doing sth** jdn dazu verleiten, etw zu tun; **~ation** [tɛmp'teɪʃən] *n* Versuchung *f*; **~ing** *adj* (*person*) verführerisch; (*object, situation*) verlockend

ten [tɛn] *num* zehn

tenable ['tɛnəbl] *adj* haltbar

tenacious [tə'neɪʃəs] *adj* zäh, hartnäckig

tenacity [tə'næsɪtɪ] *n* Zähigkeit *f*, Hartnäckigkeit *f*

tenancy ['tɛnənsɪ] *n* Mietverhältnis *nt*

tenant ['tɛnənt] *n* Mieter *m*; (*of larger property*) Pächter *m*

tend [tɛnd] *vt* (*look after*) sich kümmern um ♦ *vi*: **to ~ to do sth** etw gewöhnlich tun

tendency ['tɛndənsɪ] *n* Tendenz *f*; (*of person*) Tendenz *f*, Neigung *f*

tender ['tɛndəʳ] *adj* zart; (*loving*) zärtlich ♦ *n* (*COMM: offer*) Kostenanschlag *m* ♦ *vt* (an)bieten; (*resignation*) einreichen; **~ness** *n* Zartheit *f*; (*being loving*) Zärtlichkeit *f*

tendon ['tɛndən] *n* Sehne *f*

tenement ['tɛnəmənt] *n* Mietshaus *nt*

tennis ['tɛnɪs] *n* Tennis *nt*; **~ ball** *n* Tennisball *m*; **~ court** *n* Tennisplatz *m*; **~ player** *n* Tennisspieler(in) *m(f)*; **~ racket** *n* Tennisschläger *m*; **~ shoes** *npl* Tennisschuhe *pl*

tenor ['tɛnəʳ] *n* Tenor *m*

tenpin bowling ['tɛnpɪn-] *n* Bowling *nt*

tense [tɛns] *adj* angespannt ♦ *n* Zeitform *f*

tension ['tɛnʃən] *n* Spannung *f*

tent [tɛnt] *n* Zelt *nt*

tentacle ['tɛntəkl] *n* Fühler *m*; (*of sea animals*) Fangarm *m*

tentative ['tɛntətɪv] *adj* (*movement*) unsicher; (*offer*) Probe-; (*arrangement*) vorläufig; (*suggestion*) unverbindlich; **~ly** *adv* versuchsweise; (*try, move*) vorsichtig

tenterhooks ['tɛntəhʊks] *npl*: **to be on ~** auf die Folter gespannt sein

tenth [tɛnθ] *adj* zehnte(r, s)

tent peg *n* Hering *m*

tent pole *n* Zeltstange *f*

tenuous ['tɛnjuəs] *adj* schwach

tenure ['tɛnjuəʳ] *n* (*of land*) Besitz *m*; (*of office*) Amtszeit *f*

tepid ['tɛpɪd] *adj* lauwarm

term [tɑ:m] *n* (*period of time*) Zeit(raum *m*) *f*; (*limit*) Frist *f*; (*SCH*) Quartal *nt*; (*UNIV*) Trimester *nt*; (*expression*) Ausdruck *m* ♦ *vt* (be)nennen; **~s** *npl* (*conditions*) Bedingungen *pl*; **in the short/long ~** auf kurze/lange Sicht; **to be on good ~s with sb** gut mit jdm auskommen; **to come to ~s with** (*person*) sich einigen mit; (*problem*) sich abfinden mit

terminal ['tɑ:mɪnl] *n* (*BRIT: also:* **coach ~**) Endstation *f*; (*AVIAT*) Terminal *m*; (*COMPUT*) Terminal *nt* or *m* ♦ *adj* Schluss-; (*MED*) unheilbar; **~ly** *adj* (*MED*): **~ly ill** unheilbar krank

terminate ['tɑ:mɪneɪt] *vt* beenden ♦ *vi* enden, aufhören

termini ['tɑ:mɪnaɪ] *npl of* **terminus**

terminus ['tɑ:mɪnəs] (*pl* **termini**) *n* Endstation *f*

terrace ['tɛrəs] *n* (*BRIT: row of houses*) Häuserreihe *f*; (*in garden etc*) Terrasse *f*; **the ~s** *npl* (*BRIT: SPORT*) die Ränge; **~d** *adj* (*garden*) terrassenförmig angelegt; (*house*) Reihen-

terrain [tɛ'reɪn] *n* Gelände *nt*

terrible ['tɛrɪbl] *adj* schrecklich, entsetzlich, fürchterlich; **terribly** *adv* fürchterlich

terrier ['tɛrɪəʳ] *n* Terrier *m*

terrific [tə'rɪfɪk] *adj* unwahrscheinlich; **~!** klasse!

terrified *adj*: **to be ~ of sth** vor etw schreckliche Angst haben

terrify ['tɛrɪfaɪ] *vt* erschrecken

territorial [tɛrɪ'tɔ:rɪəl] *adj* Gebiets-, territorial

territory ['tɛrɪtərɪ] *n* Gebiet *nt*

terror ['tɛrəʳ] *n* Schrecken *m*

terrorism ['tɛrərɪzəm] *n* Terrorismus *m*; **~ist** *n* Terrorist(in) *m(f)*; **~ize** *vt* terrorisieren

terse [tɜːs] *adj* knapp, kurz, bündig

test [tɛst] *n* Probe *f*; (*examination*) Prüfung *f*; (*PSYCH, TECH*) Test *m* ♦ *vt* prüfen; (*PSYCH*) testen

testicle ['tɛstɪkl] *n* (*ANAT*) Hoden *m*

testify ['tɛstɪfaɪ] *vi* aussagen; **to ~ to sth** etw bezeugen

testimony ['tɛstɪmənɪ] *n* (*JUR*) Zeugenaussage *f*; (*fig*) Zeugnis *nt*

test match *n* (*SPORT*) Länderkampf *m*

test tube *n* Reagenzglas *nt*

tetanus ['tɛtənəs] *n* Wundstarrkrampf *m*, Tetanus *m*

tether ['tɛðə*] *vt* anbinden ♦ *n*: **at the end of one's ~** völlig am Ende

text [tɛkst] *n* Text *m*; (*of document*) Wortlaut *m*; **~book** *n* Lehrbuch *nt*

textiles ['tɛkstaɪlz] *npl* Textilien *pl*

texture ['tɛkstʃə*] *n* Beschaffenheit *f*

Thai [taɪ] *adj* thailändisch ♦ *n* Thailänder(in) *m(f)*; **~land** *n* Thailand *nt*

Thames [tɛmz] *n*: **the ~** die Themse

than [ðæn, ðən] *prep* (*in comparisons*) als

thank [θæŋk] *vt* danken +*dat*; **you've him to ~ for your success** Sie haben Ihren Erfolg ihm zu verdanken; **~ you (very much)** danke (vielmals), danke schön; **~ful** *adj* dankbar; **~less** *adj* undankbar; **~s** *npl* Dank *m* ♦ *excl* danke!; **~s to** dank +*gen*; **T~sgiving (Day)** (*US*) *n* Thanksgiving Day *m*

Thanksgiving (Day)

i **Thanksgiving (Day)** *ist ein Feiertag in den USA, der auf den vierten Donnerstag im November fällt. Er soll daran erinnern, wie die Pilgerväter die gute Ernte im Jahre 1621 feierten. In Kanada gibt es einen ähnlichen Erntedanktag (der aber nichts mit dem Pilgervätern zu tun hat) am zweiten Montag im Oktober.*

KEYWORD

that [ðæt, ðət] *adj* (*demonstrative: pl those*) der/die/das; jene(r, s); **that one** das da
♦ *pron* **1** (*demonstrative: pl those*) das;

who's/what's that? wer ist da/was ist das?; **is that you?** bist du das?; **that's what he said** genau das hat er gesagt; **what happened after that?** was passierte danach?; **that is** das heißt

2 (*relative: subj*) der/die/das, die; (: *direct obj*) den/die/das, die; (: *indirect obj*) dem/der/dem, denen; **all (that) I have** alles, was ich habe

3 (*relative: of time*): **the day (that)** an dem Tag, als; **the winter (that) he came** in dem Winter, in dem er kam
♦ *conj* dass; **he thought that I was ill** er dachte, dass ich krank sei, er dachte, ich sei krank
♦ *adv* (*demonstrative*) so; **I can't work that much** ich kann nicht so viel arbeiten

thatched [θætʃt] *adj* strohgedeckt; (*cottage*) mit Strohdach

thaw [θɔː] *n* Tauwetter *nt* ♦ *vi* tauen; (*frozen foods, fig: people*) auftauen ♦ *vt* (auf)tauen lassen

KEYWORD

the [ðiː, ðə] *def art* **1** der/die/das; **to play the piano/violin** Klavier/Geige spielen; **I'm going to the butcher's/the cinema** ich gehe zum Fleischer/ins Kino; **Elizabeth the First** Elisabeth die Erste

2 (+*adj to form noun*) das, die; **the rich and the poor** die Reichen und die Armen

3 (*in comparisons*): **the more he works the more he earns** je mehr er arbeitet, desto mehr verdient er

theatre ['θɪətə*] (*US* **theater**) *n* Theater *nt*; (*for lectures etc*) Saal *m*; (*MED*) Operationssaal *m*; **~goer** *n* Theaterbesucher(in) *m(f)*; **theatrical** [θɪ'ætrɪkl] *adj* Theater-; (*career*) Schauspieler-; (*showy*) theatralisch

theft [θɛft] *n* Diebstahl *m*

their [ðɛə*] *adj* ihr; *see also* **my**; **~s** *pron* ihre(r, s); *see also* **mine²**

them [ðɛm, ðəm] *pron* (*acc*) sie; (*dat*) ihnen; *see also* **me**

theme [θiːm] n Thema nt; (MUS) Motiv nt; **~ park** n (thematisch gestalteter) Freizeitpark m; **~ song** n Titelmusik f

themselves [ðəmˈselvz] pl pron (reflexive) sich (selbst); (emphatic) selbst; see also **oneself**

then [ðen] adv (at that time) damals; (next) dann ♦ conj also, folglich; (furthermore) ferner ♦ adj damalig; **from ~ on** von da an; **by ~** bis dahin; **the ~ president** der damalige Präsident

theology [θɪˈɒlədʒɪ] n Theologie f

theoretical [θɪəˈretɪkl] adj theoretisch; **~ly** adv theoretisch

theory [ˈθɪərɪ] n Theorie f

therapist [ˈθerəpɪst] n Therapeut(in) m(f)

therapy [ˈθerəpɪ] n Therapie f

KEYWORD
---

there [ðeəʳ] adv 1: **there is, there are** es or da ist/sind; (there exists/exist also) es gibt; **there are 3 of them** (people, things) es gibt 3 davon; **there has been an accident** da war ein Unfall
2 (place) da, dort; (direction) dahin, dorthin; **put it in/on there** leg es dahinein/dorthinauf
3: **there, there** (esp to child) na, na

---

there: **~abouts** [ˈðeərəˈbauts] adv (place) dort in der Nähe, dort irgendwo; (amount): **20 or ~abouts** ungefähr 20; **~after** [ðeərˈɑːftəʳ] adv danach; **~by** [ˈðeəbaɪ] adv dadurch, damit

therefore [ˈðeəfɔːʳ] adv deshalb, daher

there's [ˈðeəz] = **there is; there has**

thermometer [θəˈmɒmɪtəʳ] n Thermometer nt

Thermos [ˈθəːməs] ® n Thermosflasche f

thesaurus [θɪˈsɔːrəs] n Synonymwörterbuch nt

these [ðiːz] pron, adj (pl) diese

theses [ˈθiːsiːz] npl of **thesis**

thesis [ˈθiːsɪs] (pl **theses**) n (for discussion) These f; (UNIV) Dissertation f, Doktorarbeit f

they [ðeɪ] pl pron sie; (people in general) man; **~ say that ...** (it is said that) es wird gesagt, dass; **~'d** = **they had**; **they would**; **~=** **they shall**; **they will**; **~=** **they are**; **~=** **they have**

thick [θɪk] adj dick; (forest) dicht; (liquid) dickflüssig; (slow, stupid) dumm, schwer von Begriff ♦ n: **in the ~ of** mitten in +dat; **it's 20 cm ~** es ist 20 cm dick or stark; **~en** vi (fog) dichter werden ♦ vt (sauce etc) verdicken; **~ness** n Dicke f; Dichte f; Dickflüssigkeit f; **~set** adj untersetzt; **~-skinned** adj dickhäutig

thief [θiːf] (pl **thieves**) n Dieb(in) m(f)

thieves [θiːvz] npl of **thief**

thieving [ˈθiːvɪŋ] n Stehlen nt ♦ adj diebisch

thigh [θaɪ] n Oberschenkel m

thimble [ˈθɪmbl] n Fingerhut m

thin [θɪn] adj dünn; (person) dünn, mager; (excuse) schwach ♦ vt: **to ~ (down)** (sauce, paint) verdünnen

thing [θɪŋ] n Ding nt; (affair) Sache f; **my ~s** meine Sachen pl; **the best ~ would be to ...** das Beste wäre, ...; **how are ~s?** wie gehts?

think [θɪŋk] (pt, pp **thought**) vt, vi denken; **what did you ~ of them?** was halten Sie von ihnen?; **to ~ about sth/sb** nachdenken über etw/jdn; **I'll ~ about it** ich überlege es mir; **to ~ of doing sth** vorhaben or beabsichtigen, etw zu tun; **I ~ so/not** ich glaube (schon)/glaube nicht; **to ~ well of sb** viel von jdm halten; **~ over** vt überdenken; **~ up** vt sich dat ausdenken

think tank n Expertengruppe f

thinly [ˈθɪnlɪ] adv dünn; (disguised) kaum

third [θəːd] adj dritte(r, s) ♦ n (person) Dritte(r) mf; (part) Drittel nt; **~ly** adv drittens; **~ party insurance** (BRIT) n Haftpflichtversicherung f; **~-rate** adj minderwertig; **T~ World** n: **the T~ World** die Dritte Welt f

thirst [θəːst] n (also fig) Durst m; **~y** adj (person) durstig; (work) durstig machend; **to be ~y** Durst haben

thirteen [θəːˈtiːn] num dreizehn

thirty [ˈθəːtɪ] num dreißig

this [ðɪs] *adj* (*demonstrative: pl* these) diese(r, s); **this evening** heute Abend; **this one** diese(r, s) (da)

♦ *pron* (*demonstrative: pl* these) dies, das; **who/what is this?** wer/was ist das?; **this is where I live** hier wohne ich; **this is what he said** das hat er gesagt; **this is Mr Brown** dies ist Mr Brown; (*on telephone*) hier ist Mr Brown

♦ *adv* (*demonstrative*): **this high/long** *etc* so groß/lang *etc*

thistle ['θɪsl] *n* Distel *f*

thorn [θɔ:n] *n* Dorn *m*; **~y** *adj* dornig; (*problem*) schwierig

thorough ['θʌrə] *adj* gründlich; **~bred** *n* Vollblut *nt* ♦ *adj* reinrassig, Vollblut-; **~fare** *n* Straße *f*; **"no ~fare"** „Durchfahrt verboten"; **~ly** *adv* gründlich; (*extremely*) äußerst

those [ðəuz] *pl pron* die (da), jene ♦ *adj* die, jene

though [ðəu] *conj* obwohl ♦ *adv* trotzdem

thought [θɔ:t] *pt, pp of* think ♦ *n* (*idea*) Gedanke *m*; (*thinking*) Denken *nt*, Denkvermögen *nt*; **~ful** *adj* (*thinking*) gedankenvoll, nachdenklich; (*kind*) rücksichtsvoll, aufmerksam; **~less** *adj* gedankenlos, unbesonnen; (*unkind*) rücksichtslos

thousand ['θauzənd] *num* tausend; **two ~** zweitausend; **~s of** tausende *or* Tausende (von); **~th** *adj* tausendste(r, s)

thrash [θræʃ] *vt* verdreschen; (*fig*) (vernichtend) schlagen; **~ about** *vi* um sich schlagen; **~ out** *vt* ausdiskutieren

thread [θred] *n* Faden *m*, Garn *nt*; (*TECH*) Gewinde *nt*; (*in story*) Faden *m* ♦ *vt* (*needle*) einfädeln; **~bare** *adj* fadenscheinig

threat [θret] *n* Drohung *f*; (*danger*) Gefahr *f*; **~en** *vt* bedrohen ♦ *vi* drohen; **to ~en sb with sth** jdm etw androhen

three [θri:] *num* drei; **~-dimensional** *adj* dreidimensional; **~-piece suite** *n* dreiteilige Polstergarnitur *f*; **~-wheeler** *n* Dreiradwagen *m*

thresh [θreʃ] *vt, vi* dreschen

threshold ['θreʃhəuld] *n* Schwelle *f*

threw [θru:] *pt of* throw

thrift [θrɪft] *n* Sparsamkeit *f*; **~y** *adj* sparsam

thrill [θrɪl] *n* Reiz *m*, Erregung *f* ♦ *vt* begeistern, packen; **to be ~ed with** (*gift etc*) sich unheimlich freuen über +*acc*; **~er** *n* Krimi *m*; **~ing** *adj* spannend; (*news*) aufregend

thrive [θraɪv] (*pt* thrived, *pp* thrived) *vi*: **to ~ (on)** gedeihen (bei); **thriving** ['θraɪvɪŋ] *adj* blühend

throat [θrəut] *n* Hals *m*, Kehle *f*; **to have a sore ~** Halsschmerzen haben

throb [θrɔb] *vi* klopfen, pochen

throes [θrəuz] *npl*: **in the ~ of** mitten in +*dat*

throne [θrəun] *n* Thron *m*; **on the ~** auf dem Thron

throng ['θrɔŋ] *n* (Menschen)schar *f* ♦ *vt* sich drängen in +*dat*

throttle ['θrɔtl] *n* Gashebel *m* ♦ *vt* erdrosseln

through [θru:] *prep* durch; (*time*) während +*gen*; (*because of*) aus, durch ♦ *adv* durch ♦ *adj* (*ticket, train*) durchgehend; (*finished*) fertig; **to put sb ~ (to)** jdn verbinden (mit); **to be ~** (*TEL*) eine Verbindung haben; (*have finished*) fertig sein; **no ~ way** (*BRIT*) Sackgasse *f*; **~out** [θru:'aut] *prep* (*place*) überall in +*dat*; (*time*) während +*gen* ♦ *adv* überall; die ganze Zeit

throw [θrəu] (*pt* threw, *pp* thrown) *n* Wurf *m* ♦ *vt* werfen; **to ~ a party** eine Party geben; **~ away** *vt* wegwerfen; (*waste*) verschenken; (*money*) verschwenden; **~ off** *vt* abwerfen; (*pursuer*) abschütteln; **~ out** *vt* hinauswerfen; (*rubbish*) wegwerfen; (*plan*) verwerfen; **~ up** *vt, vi* (*vomit*) speien; **~away** *adj* Wegwerf-; **~-in** *n* Einwurf *m*; **~n** *pp of* throw

thru [θru:] (*US*) = through

thrush [θrʌʃ] *n* Drossel *f*

thrust [θrʌst] (*pt, pp* thrust) *vt, vi* (*push*) stoßen

thud [θʌd] *n* dumpfe(r) (Auf)schlag *m*

thug [θʌg] *n* Schlägertyp *m*

thumb [θʌm] *n* Daumen *m* ♦ *vt (book)* durchblättern; **to ~ a lift** per Anhalter fahren (wollen); **~tack** *(US) n* Reißzwecke *f*

thump [θʌmp] *n (blow)* Schlag *m; (noise)* Bums *m* ♦ *vi* hämmern, pochen ♦ *vt* schlagen auf +*acc*

thunder ['θʌndər] *n* Donner *m* ♦ *vi* donnern; *(train etc):* **to ~ past** vorbeidonnern ♦ *vt* brüllen; **~bolt** *n* Blitz *nt;* **~clap** *n* Donnerschlag *m;* **~storm** *n* Gewitter *nt,* Unwetter *nt;* **~y** *adj* gewitterschwül

Thursday ['θɜːzdɪ] *n* Donnerstag *m*

thus [ðʌs] *adv (in this way)* so; *(therefore)* somit, also, folglich

thwart [θwɔːt] *vt* vereiteln, durchkreuzen; *(person)* hindern

thyme [taɪm] *n* Thymian *m*

thyroid ['θaɪrɔɪd] *n* Schilddrüse *f*

tiara [tɪ'ɑːrə] *n* Diadem *nt*

tic [tɪk] *n* Tick *m*

tick [tɪk] *n (sound)* Ticken *nt; (mark)* Häkchen *nt* ♦ *vi* ticken ♦ *vt* abhaken; **in a ~** *(BRIT: inf)* sofort; **~ off** *vt* abhaken; *(person)* ausschimpfen; **~ over** *vi (engine)* im Leerlauf laufen; *(fig)* auf Sparflamme laufen

ticket ['tɪkɪt] *n (for travel)* Fahrkarte *f; (for entrance)* (Eintritts)karte *f; (price ~)* Preisschild *nt; (luggage ~)* (Gepäck)schein *m; (raffle ~)* Los *nt; (parking ~)* Strafzettel *m; (in car park)* Parkschein *m;* **~ collector** *n* Fahrkartenkontrolleur *m;* **~ inspector** *n* Fahrkartenkontrolleur *m;* **~ office** *n (THEAT etc)* Kasse *f; (RAIL etc)* Fahrkartenschalter *m*

tickle ['tɪkl] *n* Kitzeln *nt* ♦ *vt* kitzeln; *(amuse)* amüsieren; **ticklish** ['tɪklɪʃ] *adj (also fig)* kitzlig

tidal ['taɪdl] *adj* Flut-, Tide-; **~ wave** *n* Flutwelle *f*

tidbit ['tɪdbɪt] *(US) n* Leckerbissen *m*

tiddlywinks ['tɪdlɪwɪŋks] *n* Floh(hüpf)spiel *nt*

tide [taɪd] *n* Gezeiten *pl;* **high/low ~** Flut *f*/ Ebbe *f*

tidy ['taɪdɪ] *adj* ordentlich ♦ *vt* aufräumen, in Ordnung bringen

tie [taɪ] *n (BRIT: neck)* Krawatte *f,* Schlips *m; (sth connecting)* Band *nt; (SPORT)* Unentschieden *nt* ♦ *vt (fasten, restrict)* binden ♦ *vi (SPORT)* unentschieden spielen; *(in competition)* punktgleich sein; **to ~ in a bow** zur Schleife binden; **to ~ a knot in sth** einen Knoten in etw *acc* machen; **~ down** *vt* festbinden; **to ~ sb down to** jdn binden an +*acc;* **~ up** *vt (dog)* anbinden; *(parcel)* verschnüren; *(boat)* festmachen; *(person)* fesseln; **to be ~d up** *(busy)* beschäftigt sein

tier [tɪər] *n* Rang *m; (of cake)* Etage *f*

tiff [tɪf] *n* Krach *m*

tiger ['taɪgər] *n* Tiger *m*

tight [taɪt] *adj (close)* eng, knapp; *(schedule)* gedrängt; *(firm)* fest; *(control)* streng; *(stretched)* stramm, (an)gespannt; *(inf: drunk)* blau, stramm ♦ *adv (squeeze)* fest; **~en** *vt* anziehen, anspannen; *(restrictions)* verschärfen ♦ *vi* sich spannen; **~-fisted** *adj* knauserig; **~ly** *adv* eng; fest; *(stretched)* straff; **~-rope** *n* Seil *nt;* **~s** *npl (esp BRIT)* Strumpfhose *f*

tile [taɪl] *n (on roof)* Dachziegel *m; (on wall or floor)* Fliese *f;* **~d** *adj (roof)* gedeckt, Ziegel-; *(floor, wall)* mit Fliesen belegt

till [tɪl] *n* Kasse *f* ♦ *vt* bestellen ♦ *prep, conj =* **until**

tiller ['tɪlər] *n* Ruderpinne *f*

tilt [tɪlt] *vt* kippen, neigen ♦ *vi* sich neigen

timber ['tɪmbər] *n (wood)* Holz *nt*

time [taɪm] *n* Zeit *f; (occasion)* Mal *nt; (rhythm)* Takt *m* ♦ *vt* zur rechten Zeit tun, zeitlich einrichten; *(SPORT)* stoppen; **in 2 weeks' ~** in 2 Wochen; **a long ~** lange; **for the ~ being** vorläufig; **4 at a ~** zu jeweils 4; **from ~ to ~** gelegentlich; **to have a good ~** sich amüsieren; **in ~** *(soon enough)* rechtzeitig; *(after some ~)* mit der Zeit; *(MUS)* im Takt; **in no ~** im Handumdrehen; **any ~** jederzeit; **on ~** pünktlich, rechtzeitig; **five ~s 5** fünfmal 5; **what ~ is it?** wie viel Uhr ist es?, wie spät ist es?; **at ~s** manchmal; **~ bomb** *n* Zeitbombe *f;* **~less** *adj (beauty)* zeitlos; **~ limit** *n* Frist *f;* **~ly** *adj* rechtzeitig; günstig; **~ off** *n* freie Zeit *f;* **~r** *n (timer switch: in kitchen)* Schaltuhr *f;* **~ scale** *n* Zeitspanne *f;* **~-share** *adj* Timesharing-; **~ switch**

(*BRIT*) *n* Zeitschalter *m*; **~table** *n* Fahrplan *m*; (*SCH*) Stundenplan *m*; **~ zone** *n* Zeitzone *f*

timid ['tɪmɪd] *adj* ängstlich, schüchtern

timing ['taɪmɪŋ] *n* Wahl *f* des richtigen Zeitpunkts, Timing *nt*

timpani ['tɪmpænɪ] *npl* Kesselpauken *pl*

tin [tɪn] *n* (*metal*) Blech *nt*; (*BRIT: can*) Büchse *f*, Dose *f*; **~foil** *n* Stanniolpapier *nt*

tinge [tɪndʒ] *n* (*colour*) Färbung *f*; (*fig*) Anflug *m* ♦ *vt* färben; **~d with** mit einer Spur von

tingle ['tɪŋgl] *n* Prickeln *nt* ♦ *vi* prickeln

tinker ['tɪŋkə'] *n* Kesselflicker *m*; **~ with** *vt fus* herumfuschen an +*dat*

tinkle ['tɪŋkl] *vi* klingeln

tinned [tɪnd] (*BRIT*) *adj* (*food*) Dosen-, Büchsen-

tin opener [-əupnə'] (*BRIT*) *n* Dosen- *or* Büchsenöffner *m*

tinsel ['tɪnsl] *n* Rauschgold *nt*

tint [tɪnt] *n* Farbton *m*; (*slight colour*) Anflug *m*; (*hair*) Tönung *f*; **~ed** *adj* getönt

tiny ['taɪnɪ] *adj* winzig

tip [tɪp] *n* (*pointed end*) Spitze *f*; (*money*) Trinkgeld *nt*; (*hint*) Wink *m*, Tipp *m* ♦ *vt* (*slant*) kippen; (*hat*) antippen; (**~** *over*) umkippen; (*waiter*) ein Trinkgeld geben +*dat*; **~-off** *n* Hinweis *m*, Tipp *m*; **~ped** (*BRIT*) *adj* (*cigarette*) Filter-

tipsy ['tɪpsɪ] *adj* beschwipst

tiptoe ['tɪptəu] *n*: **on ~** auf Zehenspitzen

tiptop [tɪp'tɔp] *adj*: **in ~ condition** tipptopp, erstklassig

tire ['taɪə'] *n* (*US*) = **tyre** ♦ *vt, vi* ermüden, müde machen/werden; **~d** *adj* müde; **to be ~d of sth** etw satt haben; **~less** *adj* unermüdlich; **~some** *adj* lästig

tiring ['taɪərɪŋ] *adj* ermüdend

tissue ['tɪʃuː] *n* Gewebe *nt*; (*paper handkerchief*) Papiertaschentuch *nt*; **~ paper** *n* Seidenpapier *nt*

tit [tɪt] *n* (*bird*) Meise *f*; **~ for tat** wie du mir, so ich dir

titbit ['tɪtbɪt] (*US* **tidbit**) *n* Leckerbissen *m*

titillate ['tɪtɪleɪt] *vt* kitzeln

title ['taɪtl] *n* Titel *m*; **~ deed** *n* Eigentumsurkunde *f*; **~ role** *n* Hauptrolle *f*

titter ['tɪtə'] *vi* kichern

titular ['tɪtjulə'] *adj* (*in name only*) nominell

TM *abbr* (= *trademark*) Wz

KEYWORD
---

to [tuː, tə] *prep* **1** (*direction*) zu, nach; **I go to France/school** ich gehe nach Frankreich/zur Schule; **to the left** nach links

2 (*as far as*) bis

3 (*with expressions of time*) vor; **a quarter to 5** Viertel vor 5

4 (*for, of*) für; **secretary to the director** Sekretärin des Direktors

5 (*expressing indirect object*): **to give sth to sb** jdm etw geben; **to talk to sb** mit jdm sprechen; **I sold it to a friend** ich habe es einem Freund verkauft

6 (*in relation to*) zu; **30 miles to the gallon** 30 Meilen pro Gallone

7 (*purpose, result*) zu; **to my surprise** zu meiner Überraschung

♦ *with vb* **1** (*infin*): **to go/eat** gehen/essen; **to want to do sth** etw tun wollen; **to try/start to do sth** versuchen/anfangen, etw zu tun; **he has a lot to lose** er hat viel zu verlieren

2 (*with vb omitted*): **I don't want to** ich will (es) nicht

3 (*purpose, result*) um; **I did it to help you** ich tat es, um dir zu helfen

4 (*after adj etc*): **ready to use** gebrauchsfertig; **too old/young to ...** zu alt/jung, um ... zu ...

♦ *adv*: **push/pull the door to** die Tür zuschieben/zuziehen

---

toad [təud] *n* Kröte *f*; **~stool** *n* Giftpilz *m*

toast [təust] *n* (*bread*) Toast *m*; (*drinking*) Trinkspruch *m* ♦ *vt* trinken auf +*acc*; (*bread*) toasten; (*warm*) wärmen; **~er** *n* Toaster *m*

tobacco [tə'bækəu] *n* Tabak *m*; **~nist** [tə'bækənɪst] *n* Tabakhändler *m*; **~nist's (shop)** *n* Tabakladen *m*

toboggan [tə'bɔgən] *n* (*Rodel*)schlitten *m*; **~ing** *n* Rodeln *nt*

today [tə'deɪ] *adv* heute; (*at the present time*) heutzutage

toddler ['tɔdlə'] n Kleinkind nt

toddy ['tɔdɪ] n (Whisky)grog m

to-do [tə'du:] n Theater nt

toe [təu] n Zehe f; (of sock, shoe) Spitze f
♦ vt: **to ~ the line** (fig) sich einfügen; **~nail**
n Zehennagel m

toffee ['tɔfɪ] n Sahnebonbon nt; **~ apple**
(BRIT) n kandierte(r) Apfel m

together [tə'geðə'] adv zusammen; (at the
same time) gleichzeitig; **~ with** zusammen
mit; gleichzeitig mit

toil [tɔɪl] n harte Arbeit f, Plackerei f ♦ vi sich
abmühen, sich plagen

toilet ['tɔɪlət] n Toilette f ♦ cpd Toiletten-; **~
bag** n Waschbeutel m; **~ paper** n
Toilettenpapier nt; **~ries** ['tɔɪlətrɪz] npl
Toilettenartikel pl; **~ roll** n Rolle f
Toilettenpapier; **~ water** n Toilettenwasser
nt

token ['təukən] n Zeichen nt; (gift ~)
Gutschein m; **book/record ~** (BRIT)
Bücher-/Plattengutschein m

Tokyo ['təukjəu] n Tokio nt

told [təuld] pt, pp of **tell**

tolerable ['tɔlərəbl] adj (bearable) erträglich;
(fairly good) leidlich

tolerant ['tɔlərnt] adj: **be ~ (of)** vertragen
+acc

tolerate ['tɔləreɪt] vt dulden; (noise) ertragen

toll [təul] n Gebühr f ♦ vi (bell) läuten

tomato [tə'mɑ:təu] (pl **~es**) n Tomate f

tomb [tu:m] n Grab(mal) nt

tomboy ['tɔmbɔɪ] n Wildfang m

tombstone ['tu:mstəun] n Grabstein m

tomcat ['tɔmkæt] n Kater m

tomorrow [tə'mɔrəu] n Morgen nt ♦ adv
morgen; **the day after ~** übermorgen; **~
morning** morgen früh; **a week ~** morgen
in einer Woche

ton [tʌn] n Tonne f (BRIT = 1016kg; US
= 907kg); **~s of** (inf) eine Unmenge von

tone [təun] n Ton m; **~ down** vt (criticism,
demands) mäßigen; (colours) abtönen; **~ up**
vt in Form bringen; **~-deaf** adj ohne
musikalisches Gehör

tongs [tɔŋz] npl Zange f; (curling ~)
Lockenstab m

tongue [tʌŋ] n Zunge f; (language) Sprache
f; **with ~ in cheek** scherzhaft; **~-tied** adj
stumm, sprachlos; **~ twister** n
Zungenbrecher m

tonic ['tɔnɪk] n (drink) Tonic nt; (MED)
Stärkungsmittel nt

tonight [tə'naɪt] adv heute Abend

tonsil ['tɔnsl] n Mandel f; **~litis** [tɔnsɪ'laɪtɪs] n
Mandelentzündung f

too [tu:] adv zu; (also) auch; **~ bad!** Pech!; **~
many** zu viele

took [tuk] pt of **take**

tool [tu:l] n (also fig) Werkzeug nt; **~box** n
Werkzeugkasten m

toot [tu:t] n Hupen nt ♦ vi tuten; (AUT)
hupen

tooth [tu:θ] (pl **teeth**) n Zahn m; **~ache** n
Zahnschmerzen pl, Zahnweh nt; **~brush** n
Zahnbürste f; **~paste** n Zahnpasta f;
~pick n Zahnstocher m

top [tɔp] n Spitze f; (of mountain) Gipfel m;
(of tree) Wipfel m; (toy) Kreisel m; (~ gear)
vierte(r)/fünfte(r) Gang m ♦ adj oberste(r, s)
♦ vt (list) an erster Stelle stehen auf +dat;
on ~ of oben auf +dat; **from ~ to bottom**
von oben bis unten; **~ off** (US) vt auffüllen;
~ up vt auffüllen; **~ floor** n oberste(s)
Stockwerk nt; **~ hat** n Zylinder m; **~-
heavy** adj kopflastig

topic ['tɔpɪk] n Thema nt,
Gesprächsgegenstand m; **~al** adj aktuell

top: ~less ['tɔplɪs] adj (bather etc) oben
ohne; **~-level** ['tɔplevl] adj auf höchster
Ebene; **~most** ['tɔpməust] adj oberste(r, s)

topple ['tɔpl] vt, vi stürzen, kippen

top-secret ['tɔp'si:krɪt] adj streng geheim

topsy-turvy ['tɔpsɪ'tə:vɪ] adv durcheinander
♦ adj auf den Kopf gestellt

torch [tɔ:tʃ] n (BRIT: ELEC) Taschenlampe f;
(with flame) Fackel f

tore [tɔ:'] pt of **tear**[1]

torment [n 'tɔ:ment, vb tɔ:'ment] n Qual f
♦ vt (distress) quälen

torn [tɔ:n] pp of **tear**[1] ♦ adj hin- und
hergerissen

torrent ['tɔrnt] n Sturzbach m; **~ial** [tɔ'renʃl]
adj wolkenbruchartig

torrid ['tɒrɪd] adj heiß

tortoise ['tɔːtəs] n Schildkröte f; **~shell** ['tɔːtəʃəl] n Schildpatt m

torture ['tɔːtʃəʳ] n Folter f ♦ vt foltern

Tory ['tɔːrɪ] (BRIT) n (POL) Tory m ♦ adj Tory-, konservativ

toss [tɒs] vt schleudern; **to ~ a coin** or **to ~ up for sth** etw mit einer Münze entscheiden; **to ~ and turn** (in bed) sich hin und her werfen

tot [tɒt] n (small quantity) bisschen nt; (small child) Knirps m

total ['təutl] n Gesamtheit f; (money) Endsumme f ♦ adj Gesamt-, total ♦ vt (add up) zusammenzählen; (amount to) sich belaufen auf

totalitarian [təutælɪ'tɛərɪən] adj totalitär

totally ['təutəlɪ] adv total

totter ['tɒtəʳ] vi wanken, schwanken

touch [tʌtʃ] n Berührung f; (sense of feeling) Tastsinn m ♦ vt (feel) berühren; (come against) leicht anstoßen; (emotionally) rühren; **a ~ of** (fig) eine Spur von; **to get in ~ with sb** sich mit jdm in Verbindung setzen; **to lose ~** (friends) Kontakt verlieren; **~ on** vt fus (topic) berühren, erwähnen; **~ up** vt (paint) auffrischen; **~-and-go** adj riskant, knapp; **~down** n Landen nt, Niedergehen nt; **~ed** adj (moved) gerührt; **~ing** adj rührend; **~line** n Seitenlinie f; **~-sensitive screen** n (COMPUT) berührungsempfindlicher Bildschirm m; **~y** adj empfindlich, reizbar

tough [tʌf] adj zäh; (difficult) schwierig ♦ n Schläger(typ) m; **~en** vt zäh machen; (make strong) abhärten

toupee ['tuːpeɪ] n Toupet nt

tour ['tuəʳ] n Tour f ♦ vi umherreisen; (THEAT) auf Tour sein; auf Tour gehen; **~ guide** n Reiseleiter(in) m(f)

tourism ['tuərɪzm] n Fremdenverkehr m, Tourismus m

tourist ['tuərɪst] n Tourist(in) m(f) ♦ cpd (class) Touristen-; **~ office** n Verkehrsamt nt

tournament ['tuənəmənt] n Turnier nt

tousled ['tauzld] adj zerzaust

tout [taut] vi: **to ~ for** auf Kundenfang gehen für ♦ n: **ticket ~** Kundenschlepper(in) m(f)

tow [təu] vt (ab)schleppen; **on** (BRIT) or **in** (US) ~ (AUT) im Schlepp

toward(s) [tə'wɔːd(z)] prep (with time) gegen; (in direction of) nach

towel ['tauəl] n Handtuch nt; **~ling** n (fabric) Frottee nt or m; **~ rack** (US) n Handtuchstange f; **~ rail** n Handtuchstange f

tower ['tauəʳ] n Turm m; **~ block** (BRIT) n Hochhaus nt; **~ing** adj hochragend

town [taun] n Stadt f; **to go to ~** (fig) sich ins Zeug legen; **~ centre** n Stadtzentrum nt; **~ clerk** n Stadtdirektor m; **~ council** n Stadtrat m; **~ hall** n Rathaus nt; **~ plan** n Stadtplan m; **~ planning** n Stadtplanung f

towrope ['təurəup] n Abschlepptau nt

tow truck (US) n Abschleppwagen m

toxic ['tɒksɪk] adj giftig, Gift-

toy [tɔɪ] n Spielzeug nt; **~ with** vt fus spielen mit; **~shop** n Spielwarengeschäft nt

trace [treɪs] n Spur f ♦ vt (follow a course) nachspüren +dat; (find out) aufspüren; (copy) durchpausen; **tracing paper** n Pauspapier nt

track [træk] n (mark) Spur f; (path) Weg m; (racetrack) Rennbahn f; (RAIL) Gleis nt ♦ vt verfolgen; **to keep ~ of sb** jdn im Auge behalten; **~ down** vt aufspüren; **~suit** n Trainingsanzug m

tract [trækt] n (of land) Gebiet nt

traction ['trækʃən] n (power) Zugkraft f; (AUT: grip) Bodenhaftung f; (MED): **in ~** im Streckverband

tractor ['træktəʳ] n Traktor m

trade [treɪd] n (commerce) Handel m; (business) Geschäft nt, Gewerbe nt; (people) Geschäftsleute pl; (skilled manual work) Handwerk nt ♦ vi: **to ~ (in)** handeln (mit) ♦ vt tauschen; **~ in** vt in Zahlung geben; **~ fair** n Messe nt; **~-in price** n Preis, zu dem etw in Zahlung genommen wird; **~mark** n Warenzeichen nt; **~ name** n Handelsbezeichnung f; **~r** n Händler m; **~sman** (irreg) n (shopkeeper) Geschäftsmann m; (workman) Handwerker *m; (delivery man)* Lieferant *m;* ~ **union** *n* Gewerkschaft *f;* ~ **unionist** *n* Gewerkschaftler(in) *m(f)*

trading ['treɪdɪŋ] *n* Handel *m;* ~ **estate** *(BRIT) n* Industriegelände *nt*

tradition [trə'dɪʃən] *n* Tradition *f;* ~**al** *adj* traditionell, herkömmlich

traffic ['træfɪk] *n* Verkehr *m; (esp in drugs):* ~ **(in)** Handel *m* (mit) ♦ *vi:* **to** ~ **in** *(esp drugs)* handeln mit; ~ **calming** *n* Verkehrsberuhigung *f;* ~ **circle** *(US) n* Kreisverkehr *m;* ~ **jam** *n* Verkehrsstauung *f;* ~ **lights** *npl* Verkehrsampel *f;* ~ **warden** *n* ≃ Verkehrspolizist *m (ohne amtliche Befugnisse)*, Politesse *f (ohne amtliche Befugnisse)*

tragedy ['trædʒədɪ] *n* Tragödie *f*

tragic ['trædʒɪk] *adj* tragisch

trail [treɪl] *n (track)* Spur *f; (of smoke)* Rauchfahne *f; (of dust)* Staubwolke *f; (road)* Pfad *m*, Weg *m* ♦ *vt (animal)* verfolgen; *(person)* folgen +*dat; (drag)* schleppen ♦ *vi (hang loosely)* schleifen; *(plants)* sich ranken; *(be behind)* hinterherhinken; *(SPORT)* weit zurückliegen; *(walk)* zuckeln; ~ **behind** *vi* zurückbleiben; ~**er** *n* Anhänger *m; (US: caravan)* Wohnwagen *m; (for film)* Vorschau *f;* ~**er truck** *(US) n* Sattelschlepper *m*

train [treɪn] *n* Zug *m; (of dress)* Schleppe *f; (series)* Folge *f* ♦ *vt (teach: person)* ausbilden; *(: animal)* abrichten; *(: mind)* schulen; *(SPORT)* trainieren; *(aim)* richten ♦ *vi (exercise)* trainieren; *(study)* ausgebildet werden; ~ **of thought** Gedankengang *m;* **to** ~ **sth on** *(aim)* etw richten auf +*acc;* ~**ed** *adj (eye)* geschult; *(person, voice)* ausgebildet; ~**ee** *n* Lehrling *m;* Praktikant(in) *m(f);* ~**er** *n (SPORT)* Trainer *m;* Ausbilder *m;* ~**ers** *npl* Turnschuhe *pl;* ~**ing** *n (for occupation)* Ausbildung *f; (SPORT)* Training *nt;* **in** ~**ing** im Training; ~**ing college** *n* pädagogische Hochschule *f*, Lehrerseminar *nt;* ~**ing shoes** *npl* Turnschuhe *pl*

traipse [treɪps] *vi* latschen

trait [treɪt] *n* Zug *m*, Merkmal *nt*

traitor ['treɪtə'] *n* Verräter *m*

trajectory [trə'dʒɛktərɪ] *n* Flugbahn *f*

tram [træm] *(BRIT) n (also:* ~**car)** Straßenbahn *f*

tramp [træmp] *n* Landstreicher *m* ♦ *vi (trudge)* stampfen, stapfen

trample ['træmpl] *vt* (nieder)trampeln ♦ *vi* (herum)trampeln; **to** ~ **(underfoot)** herumtrampeln auf +*dat*

trampoline ['træmpəliːn] *n* Trampolin *m*

tranquil ['træŋkwɪl] *adj* ruhig, friedlich; ~**lity** [træŋ'kwɪlɪtɪ] *(US* **tranquility**) *n* Ruhe *f;* ~**lizer** *(US* **tranquilizer**) *n* Beruhigungsmittel *nt*

transact [træn'zækt] *vt* abwickeln; ~**ion** [træn'zækʃən] *n* Abwicklung *f; (piece of business)* Geschäft *nt*, Transaktion *f*

transcend [træn'sɛnd] *vt* übersteigen

transcription [træn'skrɪpʃən] *n* Transkription *f; (product)* Abschrift *f*

transfer *[n* 'trænsfə', *vb* træns'fəː'] *n (~ring)* Übertragung *f; (of business)* Umzug *m; (being ~red)* Versetzung *f; (design)* Abziehbild *nt; (SPORT)* Transfer *m* ♦ *vt (business)* verlegen; *(person)* versetzen; *(prisoner)* überführen; *(drawing)* übertragen; *(money)* überweisen; **to** ~ **the charges** *(BRIT: TEL)* ein R-Gespräch führen; ~ **desk** *n (AVIAT)* Transitschalter *m*

transform [træns'fɔːm] *vt* umwandeln; ~**ation** [trænsfə'meɪʃən] *n* Umwandlung *f*, Verwandlung *f*

transfusion [træns'fjuːʒən] *n* Blutübertragung *f*, Transfusion *f*

transient ['trænzɪənt] *adj* kurz(lebig)

transistor [træn'zɪstə'] *n (ELEC)* Transistor *m; (RAD)* Transistorradio *nt*

transit ['trænzɪt] *n:* **in** ~ unterwegs

transition [træn'zɪʃən] *n* Übergang *m;* ~**al** *adj* Übergangs-

transit lounge *n* Warteraum *m*

translate [trænz'leɪt] *vt, vi* übersetzen;

translation [trænz'leɪʃən] *n* Übersetzung *f;*

translator [trænz'leɪtə'] *n* Übersetzer(in) *m(f)*

transmission [trænz'mɪʃən] *n (of information)* Übermittlung *f; (ELEC, MED, TV)* Übertragung *f; (AUT)* Getriebe *nt*

transmit [trænz'mɪt] vt (message) übermitteln; (ELEC, MED, TV) übertragen; **~ter** n Sender m

transparency [træns'peərnsɪ] n Durchsichtigkeit f; (BRIT: PHOT) Dia(positiv) nt

transparent [træns'pærnt] adj durchsichtig; (fig) offenkundig

transpire [træns'paɪəʳ] vi (turn out) sich herausstellen; (happen) passieren

transplant [vb træns'plɑːnt, n 'trænsplɑːnt] vt umpflanzen; (MED, also fig: person) verpflanzen ♦ n (MED) Transplantation f; (organ) Transplantat nt

transport [n 'trænspɔːt, vb træns'pɔːt] n Transport m, Beförderung f ♦ vt befördern; transportieren; **means of ~** Transportmittel nt; **~ation** ['trænspɔː'teɪʃən] n Transport m, Beförderung f; (means) Beförderungsmittel nt; (cost) Transportkosten pl; **~ café** (BRIT) n Fernfahrerlokal nt

trap [træp] n Falle f; (carriage) zweirädrige(r) Einspänner m; (inf: mouth) Klappe f ♦ vt fangen; (person) in eine Falle locken; **~door** n Falltür f

trappings ['træpɪŋz] npl Aufmachung f

trash [træʃ] n (rubbish) Plunder m; (nonsense) Mist m; **~ can** (US) n Mülleimer m; **~y** (inf) adj minderwertig, wertlos; (novel) Schund-

traumatic [trɔː'mætɪk] adj traumatisch

travel ['trævl] n Reisen nt ♦ vi reisen ♦ vt (distance) zurücklegen; (country) bereisen; **~s** npl (journeys) Reisen pl; **~ agency** n Reisebüro nt; **~ agent** n Reisebürokaufmann(-frau) m(f); **~ler** (US **traveler**) n Reisende(r) mf; (salesman) Handlungsreisende(r) m; **~ler's cheque** (US **traveler's check**) n Reisescheck m; **~ling** (US **traveling**) n Reisen nt; **~sick** adj reisekrank; **~ sickness** n Reisekrankheit f

trawler ['trɔːləʳ] n (NAUT, FISHING) Fischdampfer m, Trawler m

tray [treɪ] n (tea ~) Tablett nt; (for mail) Ablage f

treacherous ['tretʃərəs] adj verräterisch; (road) tückisch

treachery ['tretʃərɪ] n Verrat m

treacle ['triːkl] n Sirup m, Melasse f

tread [tred] (pt trod, pp trodden) n Schritt m, Tritt m; (of stair) Stufe f; (on tyre) Profil nt ♦ vi treten; **~ on** vt fus treten auf +acc

treason ['triːzn] n Verrat m

treasure ['treʒəʳ] n Schatz m ♦ vt schätzen

treasurer ['treʒərəʳ] n Kassenverwalter m, Schatzmeister m

treasury ['treʒərɪ] n (POL) Finanzministerium nt

treat [triːt] n besondere Freude f ♦ vt (deal with) behandeln; **to ~ sb to sth** jdm etw spendieren

treatise ['triːtɪz] n Abhandlung f

treatment ['triːtmənt] n Behandlung f

treaty ['triːtɪ] n Vertrag m

treble ['trebl] adj dreifach ♦ vt verdreifachen; **~ clef** n Violinschlüssel m

tree [triː] n Baum m; **~ trunk** n Baumstamm m

trek [trek] n Treck m, Zug m; (inf) anstrengende(r) Weg m ♦ vi trecken

trellis ['trelɪs] n Gitter nt; (for gardening) Spalier nt

tremble ['trembl] vi zittern; (ground) beben

tremendous [trɪ'mendəs] adj gewaltig, kolossal; (inf: good) prima

tremor ['treməʳ] n Zittern nt; (of earth) Beben nt

trench [trentʃ] n Graben m; (MIL) Schützengraben m

trend [trend] n Tendenz f; **~y** (inf) adj modisch

trepidation [trepɪ'deɪʃən] n Beklommenheit f

trespass ['trespəs] vi: **to ~ on** widerrechtlich betreten; **"no ~ing"** „Betreten verboten"

trestle ['tresl] n Bock m; **~ table** n Klapptisch m

trial ['traɪəl] n (JUR) Prozess m; (test) Versuch m, Probe f; (hardship) Prüfung f; **by ~ and error** durch Ausprobieren; **~ period** n Probezeit f

triangle ['traɪæŋgl] n Dreieck nt; (MUS) Triangel f; **triangular** [traɪ'æŋgjuləʳ] adj dreieckig

tribal ['traɪbl] adj Stammes-

tribe [traɪb] n Stamm m; **~sman** (irreg) n

Stammesangehörige(r) *m*

tribulation [trɪbju'leɪʃən] *n* Not *f*, Mühsal *f*

tribunal [traɪ'bju:nl] *n* Gericht *nt*; (*inquiry*) Untersuchungsausschuss *m*

tributary ['trɪbjutərɪ] *n* Nebenfluss *m*

tribute ['trɪbju:t] *n* (*admiration*) Zeichen *nt* der Hochachtung; **to pay ~ to sb/sth** jdm/einer Sache Tribut zollen

trick [trɪk] *n* Trick *m*; (*CARDS*) Stich *m* ♦ *vt* überlisten, beschwindeln; **to play a ~ on sb** jdm einen Streich spielen; **that should do the ~** daß müsste eigentlich klappen; **~ery** *n* Tricks *pl*

trickle ['trɪkl] *n* Tröpfeln *nt*; (*small river*) Rinnsal *nt* ♦ *vi* tröpfeln; (*seep*) sickern

tricky ['trɪkɪ] *adj* (*problem*) schwierig; (*situation*) kitzlig

tricycle ['traɪsɪkl] *n* Dreirad *nt*

trifle ['traɪfl] *n* Kleinigkeit *f*; (*COOK*) Trifle *m* ♦ *adv*: **a ~ ...** ein bisschen ...; **trifling** *adj* geringfügig

trigger ['trɪgəʳ] *n* Drücker *m*; **~ off** *vt* auslösen

trim [trɪm] *adj* gepflegt; (*figure*) schlank ♦ *n* (*gute*) Verfassung *f*; (*embellishment, on car*) Verzierung *f* ♦ *vt* (*clip*) schneiden; (*trees*) stutzen; (*decorate*) besetzen; (*sails*) trimmen; **~mings** *npl* (*decorations*) Verzierung *f*, Verzierungen *pl*; (*extras*) Zubehör *nt*

Trinity ['trɪnɪtɪ] *n*: **the ~** die Dreieinigkeit *f*

trinket ['trɪŋkɪt] *n* kleine(s) Schmuckstück *nt*

trip [trɪp] *n* (*kurze*) Reise *f*; (*outing*) Ausflug *m*; (*stumble*) Stolpern *nt* ♦ *vi* (*stumble*) stolpern; **on a ~** auf Reisen; **~ up** *vi* stolpern; (*fig*) stolpern, einen Fehler machen ♦ *vt* zu Fall bringen; (*fig*) hereinlegen

tripe [traɪp] *n* (*food*) Kutteln *pl*; (*rubbish*) Mist *m*

triple ['trɪpl] *adj* dreifach

triplets ['trɪplɪts] *npl* Drillinge *pl*

triplicate ['trɪplɪkət] *n*: **in ~** in dreifacher Ausfertigung

tripod ['traɪpɒd] *n* (*PHOT*) Stativ *nt*

trite [traɪt] *adj* banal

triumph ['traɪʌmf] *n* Triumph *m* ♦ *vi*: **to ~**

(over) triumphieren (über +*acc*); **~ant** [traɪ'ʌmfənt] *adj* triumphierend

trivia ['trɪvɪə] *npl* Trivialitäten *pl*

trivial ['trɪvɪəl] *adj* gering(fügig), trivial

trod [trɒd] *pt of* **tread**; **~den** *pp of* **tread**

trolley ['trɒlɪ] *n* Handwagen *m*; (*in shop*) Einkaufswagen *m*; (*for luggage*) Kofferkuli *m*; (*table*) Teewagen *m*; **~ bus** *n* Oberleitungsbus *m*, Obus *m*

trombone [trɒm'bəʊn] *n* Posaune *f*

troop [tru:p] *n* Schar *f*; (*MIL*) Trupp *m*; **~s** *npl* (*MIL*) Truppen *pl*; **~ in/out** *vi* hinein-/ hinausströmen; **~ing the colour** *n* (*ceremony*) Fahnenparade *f*

trophy ['trəʊfɪ] *n* Trophäe *f*

tropic ['trɒpɪk] *n* Wendekreis *m*; **~al** *adj* tropisch

trot [trɒt] *n* Trott *m* ♦ *vi* trotten; **on the ~** (*BRIT: fig: inf*) in einer Tour

trouble ['trʌbl] *n* (*problems*) Ärger *m*; (*worry*) Sorge *f*; (*in country, industry*) Unruhen *pl*; (*effort*) Mühe *f*; (*MED*): **stomach ~** Magenbeschwerden *pl* ♦ *vt* (*disturb*) stören; **~s** *npl* (*POL etc*) Unruhen *pl*; **to ~ to do sth** sich bemühen, etw zu tun; **to be in ~** Probleme *or* Ärger haben; **to go to the ~ of doing sth** sich die Mühe machen, etw zu tun; **what's the ~?** was ist los?; (*to sick person*) wo fehlts?; **~d** *adj* (*person*) beunruhigt; (*country*) geplagt; **~free** *adj* sorglos; **~maker** *n* Unruhestifter *m*; **~shooter** *n* Vermittler *m*; **~some** *adj* lästig, unangenehm; (*child*) schwierig

trough [trɒf] *n* Trog *m*; (*channel*) Rinne *f*, Kanal *m*; (*MET*) Tief *nt*

trousers ['traʊzəz] *npl* Hose *f*

trout [traʊt] *n* Forelle *f*

trowel ['traʊəl] *n* Kelle *f*

truant ['truənt] *n*: **to play ~** (*BRIT*) (die Schule) schwänzen

truce [tru:s] *n* Waffenstillstand *m*

truck [trʌk] *n* Lastwagen *m*; (*RAIL*) offene(r) Güterwagen *m*; **~ driver** *n* Lastwagenfahrer *m*; **~ farm** (*US*) *n* Gemüsegärtnerei *f*

trudge [trʌdʒ] *vi* sich (mühselig) dahinschleppen

true [truː] adj (exact) wahr; (genuine) echt; (friend) treu

truffle ['trʌfl] n Trüffel f or m

truly ['truːlɪ] adv wirklich; **yours ~** Ihr sehr ergebener

trump [trʌmp] n (CARDS) Trumpf m

trumpet ['trʌmpɪt] n Trompete f

truncheon ['trʌntʃən] n Gummiknüppel m

trundle ['trʌndl] vt schieben ♦ vi: **to ~ along** entlangrollen

trunk [trʌŋk] n (of tree) (Baum)stamm m; (ANAT) Rumpf m; (box) Truhe f, Überseekoffer m; (of elephant) Rüssel m; (US: AUT) Kofferraum m; **~s** npl (also: **swimming ~s**) Badehose f

truss [trʌs] vt (also: **~ up**) fesseln

trust [trʌst] n (confidence) Vertrauen nt; (for land etc) Treuhandvermögen nt ♦ vt (rely on) vertrauen +dat, sich verlassen auf +acc; (hope) hoffen; (entrust): **to ~ sth to sb** jdm etw anvertrauen; **~ed** adj treu; **~ee** [trʌs'tiː] n Vermögensverwalter m; **~ful** adj vertrauensvoll; **~ing** adj vertrauensvoll; **~worthy** adj vertrauenswürdig; (account) glaubwürdig

truth [truːθ] n Wahrheit f; **~ful** adj ehrlich

try [traɪ] n Versuch m ♦ vt (attempt) versuchen; (test) (aus)probieren; (JUR: person) unter Anklage stellen; (: case) verhandeln; (courage, patience) auf die Probe stellen ♦ vi (make effort) versuchen, sich bemühen; **to have a ~** es versuchen; **to ~ to do sth** versuchen, etw zu tun; **~ on** vt (dress) anprobieren; (hat) aufprobieren; **~ out** vt ausprobieren; **~ing** adj schwierig

T-shirt ['tiːʃəːt] n T-Shirt nt

T-square ['tiːskwɛəʳ] n Reißschiene f

tub [tʌb] n Wanne f, Kübel m; (for margarine etc) Becher m

tubby ['tʌbɪ] adj rundlich

tube [tjuːb] n Röhre f, Rohr nt; (for toothpaste etc) Tube f; (underground) U-Bahn f; (AUT) Schlauch m

tuberculosis [tjubəːkjuːˈləʊsɪs] n Tuberkulose f

tube station n (in London) U-Bahnstation f;

tubing ['tjuːbɪŋ] n Schlauch m; **tubular** ['tjuːbjʊləʳ] adj röhrenförmig

TUC (BRIT) n abbr = **Trades Union Congress**

tuck [tʌk] n (fold) Falte f, Einschlag m ♦ vt (put) stecken; (gather) fälteln, einschlagen; **~ away** vt wegstecken; **~ in** vt hineinstecken; (blanket etc) feststecken; (person) zudecken ♦ vi (eat) hineinhauen, zulangen; **~ up** vt (child) warm zudecken; **~ shop** n Süßwarenladen m

Tuesday ['tjuːzdɪ] n Dienstag m

tuft [tʌft] n Büschel m

tug [tʌg] n (jerk) Zerren nt, Ruck m; (NAUT) Schleppdampfer m ♦ vt, vi zerren, ziehen; (boat) schleppen; **~ of war** n Tauziehen nt

tuition [tjuːˈɪʃən] n (BRIT) Unterricht m; (: private ~) Privatunterricht m; (US: school fees) Schulgeld nt

tulip ['tjuːlɪp] n Tulpe f

tumble ['tʌmbl] n (fall) Sturz m ♦ vi fallen, stürzen; **~ to** vt fus kapieren; **~down** adj baufällig; **~ dryer** (BRIT) n Trockner m; **~r** ['tʌmbləʳ] n (glass) Trinkglas nt

tummy ['tʌmɪ] (inf) n Bauch m; **~ upset** n Magenverstimmung f

tumour ['tjuːməʳ] (US **tumor**) n Geschwulst f, Tumor m

tumultuous [tjuːˈmʌltjuəs] adj (welcome, applause etc) stürmisch

tuna ['tjuːnə] n T(h)unfisch m

tune [tjuːn] n Melodie f ♦ vt (MUS) stimmen; (AUT) richtig einstellen; **to sing in ~/out of ~** richtig/falsch singen; **to be out of ~ with** nicht harmonieren mit; **~ in** vi einschalten; **~ up** vi (MUS) stimmen; **~ful** adj melodisch; **~r** n (RAD) Tuner m; (person) (Instrumenten)stimmer m; **piano ~r** Klavierstimmer(in) m(f)

tunic ['tjuːnɪk] n Waffenrock m; (loose garment) lange Bluse f

tuning ['tjuːnɪŋ] n (RAD, AUT) Einstellen nt; (MUS) Stimmen nt; **~ fork** n Stimmgabel f

Tunisia [tjuːˈnɪzɪə] n Tunesien nt

tunnel ['tʌnl] n Tunnel m, Unterführung f ♦ vi einen Tunnel anlegen

turbulent ['təːbjulənt] adj stürmisch

tureen [təˈriːn] *n* Terrine *f*
turf [təːf] *n* Rasen *m*; *(piece)* Sode *f* ♦ *vt* mit Grassoden belegen; **~ out** *(inf) vt* rauswerfen
turgid [ˈtəːdʒɪd] *adj* geschwollen
Turk [təːk] *n* Türke *m*, Türkin *f*
Turkey [ˈtəːkɪ] *n* Türkei *f*
turkey [ˈtəːkɪ] *n* Puter *m*, Truthahn *m*
Turkish [ˈtəːkɪʃ] *adj* türkisch ♦ *n* (LING) Türkisch *nt*
turmoil [ˈtəːmɔɪl] *n* Aufruhr *m*, Tumult *m*
turn [təːn] *n* (rotation) (Um)drehung *f*; (performance) (Programm)nummer *f*; (MED) Schock *m* ♦ *vt* (rotate) drehen; (change position of) umdrehen, wenden; (page) umblättern; (transform): **to ~ sth into sth** etw in etw *acc* verwandeln; (direct) zuwenden ♦ *vi* (rotate) sich drehen; (change direction: in car) abbiegen; (: wind) drehen; (~ round) umdrehen, wenden; (become) werden; (leaves) sich verfärben; (milk) sauer werden; (weather) umschlagen; **to do sb a good ~** jdm etwas Gutes tun; **it's your ~** du bist dran *or* an der Reihe; **in ~, by ~s** abwechselnd; **to take ~s** sich abwechseln; **it gave me quite a ~** das hat mich schön erschreckt; **"no left ~"** (AUT) „Linksabbiegen verboten"; **~ away** *vi* sich abwenden; **~ back** *vt* umdrehen; (person) zurückschicken; (clock) zurückstellen ♦ *vi* umkehren; **~ down** *vt* (refuse) ablehnen; (fold down) umschlagen; **~ in** *vi* (go to bed) ins Bett gehen ♦ *vt* (fold inwards) einwärts biegen; **~ off** *vi* abbiegen ♦ *vt* ausschalten; (tap) zudrehen; (machine, electricity) abstellen; **~ on** *vt* (light) anschalten, einschalten; (tap) aufdrehen; (machine) anstellen; **~ out** *vi* (prove to be) sich erweisen; (people) sich entwickeln ♦ *vt* (light) ausschalten; (gas) abstellen; (produce) produzieren; **how did the cake ~ out?** wie ist der Kuchen geworden?; **~ over** *vi* (person) sich umdrehen ♦ *vt* (object) umdrehen, wenden; (page) umblättern; **~ round** *vi* (person, vehicle) sich herumdrehen; (rotate) sich drehen; **~ up** *vi* auftauchen ♦ *vt* (collar) hochklappen,

hochstellen; (nose) rümpfen; (increase: radio) lauter stellen; (: heat) höher drehen; **~ing** *n* (in road) Abzweigung *f*; **~ing point** *n* Wendepunkt *m*
turnip [ˈtəːnɪp] *n* Steckrübe *f*
turnout [ˈtəːnaut] *n* (Besucher)zahl *f*
turnover [ˈtəːnəuvər] *n* Umsatz *m*; (of staff) Wechsel *m*
turnpike [ˈtəːnpaɪk] (US) *n* gebührenpflichtige Straße *f*
turn-: ~stile [ˈtəːnstaɪl] *n* Drehkreuz *nt*; **~table** [ˈtəːnteɪbl] *n* (of record player) Plattenteller *m*; (RAIL) Drehscheibe *f*; **~-up** [ˈtəːnʌp] (BRIT) *n* (on trousers) Aufschlag *m*
turpentine [ˈtəːpəntaɪn] *n* Terpentin *nt*
turquoise [ˈtəːkwɔɪz] *n* (gem) Türkis *m*; (colour) Türkis *nt* ♦ *adj* türkisfarben
turret [ˈtʌrɪt] *n* Turm *m*
turtle [ˈtəːtl] *n* Schildkröte *f*; **~ neck (sweater)** *n* Pullover *m* mit Schildkrötkragen
tusk [tʌsk] *n* Stoßzahn *m*
tussle [ˈtʌsl] *n* Balgerei *f*
tutor [ˈtjuːtər] *n* (teacher) Privatlehrer *m*; (college instructor) Tutor *m*; **~ial** [tjuːˈtɔːrɪəl] *n* (UNIV) Kolloquium *nt*, Seminarübung *f*
tuxedo [tʌkˈsiːdəu] (US) *n* Smoking *m*
TV [tiːˈviː] *n abbr* (= television) TV *nt*
twang [twæŋ] *n* scharfe(r) Ton *m*; (of voice) Näseln *nt*
tweezers [ˈtwiːzəz] *npl* Pinzette *f*
twelfth [twelfθ] *adj* zwölfte(r, s)
twelve [twelv] *num* zwölf; **at ~ o'clock** (midday) um 12 Uhr; (midnight) um null Uhr
twentieth [ˈtwentɪɪθ] *adj* zwanzigste(r, s)
twenty [ˈtwentɪ] *num* zwanzig
twice [twaɪs] *adv* zweimal; **~ as much** doppelt so viel
twiddle [ˈtwɪdl] *vt, vi*: **to ~ (with) sth** an etw *dat* herumdrehen; **to ~ one's thumbs** (fig) Däumchen drehen
twig [twɪg] *n* dünne(r) Zweig *m* ♦ *vt* (inf) kapieren, merken
twilight [ˈtwaɪlaɪt] *n* Zwielicht *nt*
twin [twɪn] *n* Zwilling *m* ♦ *adj* Zwillings-; (very similar) Doppel- ♦ *vt* (towns) zu

Partnerstädten machen; **~-bedded room**
n Zimmer nt mit zwei Einzelbetten; **~ beds**
npl zwei (gleiche) Einzelbetten pl

twine [twaɪn] n Bindfaden m ♦ vi (plants)
sich ranken

twinge [twɪndʒ] n stechende(r) Schmerz m,
Stechen nt

twinkle ['twɪŋkl] n Funkeln nt, Blitzen nt ♦ vi
funkeln

twinned adj: **to be ~ with** die Partnerstadt
von ... sein

twirl [twə:l] n Wirbel m ♦ vt, vi
(herum)wirbeln

twist [twɪst] n (~ing) Drehung f; (bend) Kurve
f ♦ vt (turn) drehen; (make crooked)
verbiegen; (distort) verdrehen ♦ vi (wind)
sich drehen; (curve) sich winden

twit [twɪt] (inf) n Idiot m

twitch [twɪtʃ] n Zucken nt ♦ vi zucken

two [tu:] num zwei; **to put ~ and ~ together**
seine Schlüsse ziehen; **~-door** adj
zweitürig; **~-faced** adj falsch; **~-fold** adj,
adv zweifach, doppelt; **to increase ~-fold**
verdoppeln; **~-piece** adj zweiteilig; **~-
piece (suit)** n Zweiteiler m; **~-piece
(swimsuit)** n zweiteilige(r) Badeanzug m;
~-seater n (plane, car) Zweisitzer m;
~some n Paar nt; **~-way** adj (traffic)
Gegen-

tycoon [taɪ'ku:n] n: **(business) ~**
(Industrie)magnat m

type [taɪp] n Typ m, Art f; (PRINT) Type f ♦ vt,
vi Maschine schreiben, tippen; **~-cast** adj
(THEAT, TV) auf eine Rolle festgelegt; **~face**
n Schrift f; **~-script** n
maschinegeschriebene(r) Text m; **~writer**
n Schreibmaschine f; **~-written** adj
maschinegeschrieben

typhoid ['taɪfɔɪd] n Typhus m

typical ['tɪpɪkl] adj: **~ (of)** typisch (für)

typify ['tɪpɪfaɪ] vt typisch sein für

typing ['taɪpɪŋ] n Maschineschreiben nt

typist ['taɪpɪst] n Maschinenschreiber(in)
m(f), Tippse f (inf)

tyrant ['taɪərnt] n Tyrann m

tyre ['taɪə'] (US **tire**) n Reifen m; **~ pressure**
n Reifendruck m

U, u

U-bend ['ju:bɛnd] n (in pipe) U-Bogen m

udder ['ʌdə'] n Euter nt

UFO ['ju:fəu] n abbr (= unidentified flying
object) UFO nt

ugh [ə:h] excl hu

ugliness ['ʌglɪnɪs] n Hässlichkeit f

ugly ['ʌglɪ] adj hässlich; (bad) böse, schlimm

UHT abbr (= ultra heat treated): **UHT milk**
H-Milch f

UK n abbr = **United Kingdom**

ulcer ['ʌlsə'] n Geschwür nt

Ulster ['ʌlstə'] n Ulster nt

ulterior [ʌl'tɪərɪə'] adj: **~ motive**
Hintergedanke m

ultimate ['ʌltɪmət] adj äußerste(r, s),
allerletzte(r, s); **~ly** adv schließlich, letzten
Endes

ultrasound ['ʌltrəsaund] n (MED) Ultraschall
m

umbilical cord [ʌm'bɪlɪkl-] n Nabelschnur f

umbrella [ʌm'brɛlə] n Schirm m

umpire ['ʌmpaɪə'] n Schiedsrichter m ♦ vt, vi
schiedsrichtern

umpteenth [ʌmp'ti:nθ] (inf) adj zig; **for the
~ time** zum x-ten Mal

UN n abbr = **United Nations**

unable [ʌn'eɪbl] adj: **to be ~ to do sth** etw
nicht tun können

unacceptable [ʌnək'sɛptəbl] adj
unannehmbar, nicht akzeptabel

unaccompanied [ʌnə'kʌmpənɪd] adj ohne
Begleitung

unaccountably [ʌnə'kauntəblɪ] adv
unerklärlich

unaccustomed [ʌnə'kʌstəmd] adj nicht
gewöhnt; (unusual) ungewohnt; **~ to** nicht
gewöhnt an +acc

unanimous [ju:'nænɪməs] adj einmütig;
(vote) einstimmig; **~ly** adv einmütig;
einstimmig

unarmed [ʌn'ɑ:md] adj unbewaffnet

unashamed [ʌnə'ʃeɪmd] adj schamlos

unassuming [ʌnə'sju:mɪŋ] adj bescheiden

unattached [ʌnəˈtætʃt] *adj* ungebunden
unattended [ʌnəˈtendɪd] *adj* (*person*)
unbeaufsichtigt; (*thing*) unbewacht
unauthorized [ʌnˈɔːθəraɪzd] *adj* unbefugt
unavoidable [ʌnəˈvɔɪdəbl] *adj*
unvermeidlich
unaware [ʌnəˈwɛəʳ] *adj*: **to be ~ of sth** sich
dat einer Sache *gen* nicht bewusst sein; **~s**
adv unversehens
unbalanced [ʌnˈbælənst] *adj*
unausgeglichen; (*mentally*) gestört
unbearable [ʌnˈbɛərəbl] *adj* unerträglich
unbeatable [ʌnˈbiːtəbl] *adj* unschlagbar
unbeknown(st) [ʌnbɪˈnəʊn(st)] *adv*: **~ to**
me ohne mein Wissen
unbelievable [ʌnbɪˈliːvəbl] *adj* unglaublich
unbend [ʌnˈbend] (*irreg: like* **bend**) *vt*
gerade biegen ♦ *vi* aus sich herausgehen
unbias(s)ed [ʌnˈbaɪəst] *adj* unparteiisch
unborn [ʌnˈbɔːn] *adj* ungeboren
unbreakable [ʌnˈbreɪkəbl] *adj*
unzerbrechlich
unbridled [ʌnˈbraɪdld] *adj* ungezügelt
unbroken [ʌnˈbrəʊkən] *adj* (*period*)
ununterbrochen; (*spirit*) ungebrochen;
(*record*) unübertroffen
unburden [ʌnˈbəːdn] *vt*: **to ~ o.s.** (jdm) sein
Herz ausschütten
unbutton [ʌnˈbʌtn] *vt* aufknöpfen
uncalled-for [ʌnˈkɔːldfɔːʳ] *adj* unnötig
uncanny [ʌnˈkænɪ] *adj* unheimlich
unceasing [ʌnˈsiːsɪŋ] *adj* unaufhörlich
unceremonious [ʌnsɛrɪˈməʊnɪəs] *adj*
(*abrupt, rude*) brüsk; (*exit, departure*)
überstürzt
uncertain [ʌnˈsəːtn] *adj* unsicher; (*doubtful*)
ungewiss; (*unreliable*) unbeständig; (*vague*)
undeutlich, vag(e); **~ty** *n* Ungewissheit *f*
unchanged [ʌnˈtʃeɪndʒd] *adj* unverändert
unchecked [ʌnˈtʃekt] *adj* ungeprüft; (*not
stopped: advance*) ungehindert
uncivilized [ʌnˈsɪvɪlaɪzd] *adj* unzivilisiert
uncle [ˈʌŋkl] *n* Onkel *m*
uncomfortable [ʌnˈkʌmfətəbl] *adj*
unbequem, ungemütlich
uncommon [ʌnˈkɒmən] *adj* ungewöhnlich;
(*outstanding*) außergewöhnlich

uncompromising [ʌnˈkɒmprəmaɪzɪŋ] *adj*
kompromisslos, unnachgiebig
unconcerned [ʌnkənˈsəːnd] *adj*
unbekümmert; (*indifferent*) gleichgültig
unconditional [ʌnkənˈdɪʃənl] *adj*
bedingungslos
unconscious [ʌnˈkɒnʃəs] *adj* (*MED*)
bewusstlos; (*not meant*) unbeabsichtigt ♦ *n*:
the ~ das Unbewusste; **~ly** *adv* unbewusst
uncontrollable [ʌnkənˈtrəʊləbl] *adj*
unkontrollierbar, unbändig
unconventional [ʌnkənˈvenʃənl] *adj*
unkonventionell
uncouth [ʌnˈkuːθ] *adj* grob
uncover [ʌnˈkʌvəʳ] *vt* aufdecken
undecided [ʌndɪˈsaɪdɪd] *adj* unschlüssig
undeniable [ʌndɪˈnaɪəbl] *adj* unleugbar
under [ˈʌndəʳ] *prep* unter ♦ *adv* darunter; **~**
there da drunter; **~ repair** in Reparatur
underage [ʌndərˈeɪdʒ] *adj* minderjährig
undercarriage [ˈʌndəkærɪdʒ] (*BRIT*) *n* (*AVIAT*)
Fahrgestell *nt*
undercharge [ʌndəˈtʃɑːdʒ] *vt*: **to ~ sb** jdm
zu wenig berechnen
undercoat [ˈʌndəkəʊt] *n* (*paint*)
Grundierung *f*
undercover [ʌndəˈkʌvəʳ] *adj* Geheim-
undercurrent [ˈʌndəkʌrnt] *n*
Unterströmung *f*
undercut [ʌndəˈkʌt] (*irreg: like* **cut**) *vt*
unterbieten
underdeveloped [ˈʌndədɪˈveləpt] *adj*
Entwicklungs-, unterentwickelt
underdog [ˈʌndədɒg] *n* Unterlegene(r) *mf*
underdone [ʌndəˈdʌn] *adj* (*COOK*) nicht gar,
nicht durchgebraten
underestimate [ˈʌndərˈestɪmeɪt] *vt*
unterschätzen
underexposed [ˈʌndərɪksˈpəʊzd] *adj*
unterbelichtet
underfoot [ʌndəˈfut] *adv* am Boden
undergo [ʌndəˈgəʊ] (*irreg: like* **go**) *vt*
(*experience*) durchmachen; (*test, operation*)
sich unterziehen +*dat*
undergraduate [ʌndəˈgrædjuɪt] *n*
Student(in) *m(f)*
underground [ˈʌndəgraʊnd] *n* U-Bahn *f*

♦ *adj* Untergrund-

undergrowth [ˈʌndəgrəʊθ] *n* Gestrüpp *nt*, Unterholz *nt*

underhand(ed) [ʌndəˈhænd(ɪd)] *adj* hinterhältig

underlie [ʌndəˈlaɪ] (*irreg: like* **lie**) *vt* zugrunde *or* zu Grunde liegen +*dat*

underline [ʌndəˈlaɪn] *vt* unterstreichen; (*emphasize*) betonen

underling [ˈʌndəlɪŋ] *n* Handlanger *m*

undermine [ʌndəˈmaɪn] *vt* untergraben

underneath [ʌndəˈniːθ] *adv* darunter ♦ *prep* unter

underpaid [ʌndəˈpeɪd] *adj* unterbezahlt

underpants [ˈʌndəpænts] *npl* Unterhose *f*

underpass [ˈʌndəpɑːs] (*BRIT*) *n* Unterführung *f*

underprivileged [ʌndəˈprɪvɪlɪdʒd] *adj* benachteiligt, unterprivilegiert

underrate [ʌndəˈreɪt] *vt* unterschätzen

undershirt [ˈʌndəʃəːt] (*US*) *n* Unterhemd *nt*

undershorts [ˈʌndəʃɔːts] (*US*) *npl* Unterhose *f*

underside [ˈʌndəsaɪd] *n* Unterseite *f*

underskirt [ˈʌndəskəːt] (*BRIT*) *n* Unterrock *m*

understand [ʌndəˈstænd] (*irreg: like* **stand**) *vt, vi* verstehen; **I ~ that ...** ich habe gehört, dass ...; **am I to ~ that ...?** soll das (etwa) heißen, dass ...?; **what do you ~ by that?** was verstehen Sie darunter?; **it is understood that ...** es wurde vereinbart, dass ...; **to make o.s. understood** sich verständlich machen; **is that understood?** ist das klar?; **~able** *adj* verständlich; **~ing** *n* Verständnis *nt* ♦ *adj* verständnisvoll

understatement [ˈʌndəsteɪtmənt] *n* (*quality*) Untertreibung *f*; **that's an ~!** das ist untertrieben!

understood [ʌndəˈstʊd] *pt, pp of* **understand** ♦ *adj* klar; (*implied*) angenommen

understudy [ˈʌndəstʌdɪ] *n* Ersatz(schau)spieler(in) *m(f)*

undertake [ʌndəˈteɪk] (*irreg: like* **take**) *vt* unternehmen ♦ *vi*: **to ~ to do sth** sich verpflichten, etw zu tun

undertaker [ˈʌndəteɪkəʳ] *n* Leichenbestat-

ter *m*

undertaking [ˈʌndəteɪkɪŋ] *n* (*enterprise*) Unternehmen *nt*; (*promise*) Verpflichtung *f*

undertone [ˈʌndətəʊn] *n*: **in an ~** mit gedämpfter Stimme

underwater [ˈʌndəˈwɔːtəʳ] *adv* unter Wasser ♦ *adj* Unterwasser-

underwear [ˈʌndəwɛəʳ] *n* Unterwäsche *f*

underworld [ˈʌndəwəːld] *n* (*of crime*) Unterwelt *f*

underwriter [ˈʌndəraɪtəʳ] *n* Assekurant *m*

undesirable [ʌndɪˈzaɪərəbl] *adj* unerwünscht

undies [ˈʌndɪz] (*inf*) *npl* (Damen)unterwäsche *f*

undisputed [ʌndɪsˈpjuːtɪd] *adj* unbestritten

undo [ʌnˈduː] (*irreg: like* **do**) *vt* (*unfasten*) öffnen, aufmachen; (*work*) zunichte machen; **~ing** *n* Verderben *nt*

undoubted [ʌnˈdaʊtɪd] *adj* unbezweifelt; **~ly** *adv* zweifellos, ohne Zweifel

undress [ʌnˈdrɛs] *vt* ausziehen ♦ *vi* sich ausziehen

undue [ʌnˈdjuː] *adj* übermäßig

undulating [ˈʌndjuleɪtɪŋ] *adj* wellenförmig; (*country*) wellig

unduly [ʌnˈdjuːlɪ] *adv* übermäßig

unearth [ʌnˈəːθ] *vt* (*dig up*) ausgraben; (*discover*) ans Licht bringen

unearthly [ʌnˈəːθlɪ] *adj* (*hour*) nachtschlafen

uneasy [ʌnˈiːzɪ] *adj* (*worried*) unruhig; (*feeling*) ungut

uneconomic(al) [ˈʌniːkəˈnɔmɪk(l)] *adj* unwirtschaftlich

uneducated [ʌnˈɛdjukeɪtɪd] *adj* ungebildet

unemployed [ʌnɪmˈplɔɪd] *adj* arbeitslos ♦ *npl*: **the ~** die Arbeitslosen *pl*

unemployment [ʌnɪmˈplɔɪmənt] *n* Arbeitslosigkeit *f*

unending [ʌnˈɛndɪŋ] *adj* endlos

unerring [ʌnˈəːrɪŋ] *adj* unfehlbar

uneven [ʌnˈiːvn] *adj* (*surface*) uneben; (*quality*) ungleichmäßig

unexpected [ʌnɪksˈpɛktɪd] *adj* unerwartet; **~ly** *adv* unerwartet

unfailing [ʌnˈfeɪlɪŋ] *adj* nie versagend

unfair [ʌnˈfɛəʳ] *adj* ungerecht, unfair

unfaithful [ʌnˈfeɪθful] *adj* untreu

unfamiliar [ʌnfə'mɪliər] *adj* ungewohnt; *(person, subject)* unbekannt; **to be ~ with** nicht kennen +*acc*, nicht vertraut sein mit

unfashionable [ʌn'fæʃnəbl] *adj* unmodern; *(area etc)* nicht in Mode

unfasten [ʌn'fɑːsn] *vt* öffnen, aufmachen

unfavourable [ʌn'feɪvrəbl] (*US* **unfavorable**) *adj* ungünstig

unfeeling [ʌn'fiːlɪŋ] *adj* gefühllos, kalt

unfinished [ʌn'fɪnɪʃt] *adj* unvollendet

unfit [ʌn'fɪt] *adj* ungeeignet; *(in bad health)* nicht fit; **~ for sth** zu *or* für etw ungeeignet

unfold [ʌn'fəuld] *vt* entfalten; *(paper)* auseinander falten ♦ *vi (develop)* sich entfalten

unforeseen ['ʌnfɔː'siːn] *adj* unvorhergesehen

unforgettable [ʌnfə'getəbl] *adj* unvergesslich

unforgivable [ʌnfə'gɪvəbl] *adj* unverzeihlich

unfortunate [ʌn'fɔːtʃənət] *adj* unglücklich, bedauerlich; **~ly** *adv* leider

unfounded [ʌn'faundɪd] *adj* unbegründet

unfriendly [ʌn'frendlɪ] *adj* unfreundlich

ungainly [ʌn'geɪnlɪ] *adj* linkisch

ungodly [ʌn'gɒdlɪ] *adj (hour)* nachtschlafend; *(row)* heillos

ungrateful [ʌn'greɪtful] *adj* undankbar

unhappiness [ʌn'hæpɪnɪs] *n* Unglück *nt*, Unglückseligkeit *f*

unhappy [ʌn'hæpɪ] *adj* unglücklich; **~ with** *(arrangements etc)* unzufrieden mit

unharmed [ʌn'hɑːmd] *adj* wohlbehalten, unversehrt

UNHCR *n abbr* (= *United Nations High Commission for Refugees*) Flüchtlingshochkommissariat der Vereinten Nationen

unhealthy [ʌn'helθɪ] *adj* ungesund

unheard-of [ʌn'hɜːdɒv] *adj* unerhört

unhurt [ʌn'hɜːt] *adj* unverletzt

unidentified [ʌnaɪ'dentɪfaɪd] *adj* unbekannt, nicht identifiziert

uniform ['juːnɪfɔːm] *n* Uniform *f* ♦ *adj* einheitlich; **~ity** [juːnɪ'fɔːmɪtɪ] *n* Einheitlichkeit *f*

unify ['juːnɪfaɪ] *vt* vereinigen

unilateral [juːnɪ'lætərəl] *adj* einseitig

uninhabited [ʌnɪn'hæbɪtɪd] *adj* unbewohnt

unintentional [ʌnɪn'tenʃənəl] *adj* unabsichtlich

union ['juːnjən] *n (uniting)* Vereinigung *f*; *(alliance)* Bund *m*, Union *f*; *(trade ~)* Gewerkschaft *f*; **U~ Jack** *n* Union Jack *m*

unique [juː'niːk] *adj* einzig(artig)

UNISON ['juːnɪsn] *n* Gewerkschaft der Angestellten im öffentlichen Dienst

unison ['juːnɪsn] *n* Einstimmigkeit *f*; **in ~** einstimmig

unit ['juːnɪt] *n* Einheit *f*; **kitchen ~** Küchenelement *nt*

unite [juː'naɪt] *vt* vereinigen ♦ *vi* sich vereinigen; **~d** *adj* vereinigt; *(together)* vereint; **U~d Kingdom** *n* Vereinigte(s) Königreich *nt*; **U~d Nations (Organization)** *n* Vereinte Nationen *pl*; **U~d States (of America)** *n* Vereinigte Staaten *pl* (von Amerika)

unit trust (*BRIT*) *n* Treuhandgesellschaft *f*

unity ['juːnɪtɪ] *n* Einheit *f*; *(agreement)* Einigkeit *f*

universal [juːnɪ'vɜːsl] *adj* allgemein

universe ['juːnɪvɜːs] *n* (Welt)all *nt*

university [juːnɪ'vɜːsɪtɪ] *n* Universität *f*

unjust [ʌn'dʒʌst] *adj* ungerecht

unkempt [ʌn'kempt] *adj* ungepflegt

unkind [ʌn'kaɪnd] *adj* unfreundlich

unknown [ʌn'nəun] *adj*: **~ (to sb)** (jdm) unbekannt

unlawful [ʌn'lɔːful] *adj* illegal

unleaded [ʌn'ledɪd] *adj* bleifrei, unverbleit; **I use ~** ich fahre bleifrei

unleash [ʌn'liːʃ] *vt* entfesseln

unless [ʌn'les] *conj* wenn nicht, es sei denn; **~ he comes** es sei denn, er kommt; **~ otherwise stated** sofern nicht anders angegeben

unlike [ʌn'laɪk] *adj* unähnlich ♦ *prep* im Gegensatz zu

unlikely [ʌn'laɪklɪ] *adj (not likely)* unwahrscheinlich; *(unexpected: combination etc)* merkwürdig

unlimited [ʌn'lɪmɪtɪd] *adj* unbegrenzt

unlisted ['ʌn'lɪstɪd] (*US*) *adj* nicht im

Telefonbuch stehend

unload [ʌn'ləʊd] vt entladen

unlock [ʌn'lɒk] vt aufschließen

unlucky [ʌn'lʌkɪ] adj unglücklich; (person) unglückselig; **to be ~** Pech haben

unmarried [ʌn'mærɪd] adj unverheiratet, ledig

unmask [ʌn'mɑːsk] vt entlarven

unmistakable [ʌnmɪs'teɪkəbl] adj unverkennbar

unmitigated [ʌn'mɪtɪgeɪtɪd] adj ungemildert, ganz

unnatural [ʌn'nætʃrəl] adj unnatürlich

unnecessary [ʌn'nesəsərɪ] adj unnötig

unnoticed [ʌn'nəʊtɪst] adj: **to go ~** unbemerkt bleiben

UNO ['juːnəʊ] n abbr = **United Nations Organization**

unobtainable [ʌnəb'teɪnəbl] adj: **this number is ~** kein Anschluss unter dieser Nummer

unobtrusive [ʌnəb'truːsɪv] adj unauffällig

unofficial [ʌnə'fɪʃl] adj inoffiziell

unpack [ʌn'pæk] vt, vi auspacken

unparalleled [ʌn'pærəleld] adj beispiellos

unpleasant [ʌn'pleznt] adj unangenehm

unplug [ʌn'plʌg] vt den Stecker herausziehen von

unpopular [ʌn'pɒpjʊləʳ] adj (person) unbeliebt; (decision etc) unpopulär

unprecedented [ʌn'presɪdentɪd] adj beispiellos

unpredictable [ʌnprɪ'dɪktəbl] adj unvorhersehbar; (weather, person) unberechenbar

unprofessional [ʌnprə'feʃənl] adj unprofessionell

UNPROFOR n abbr (= United Nations Protection Force) UNPROFOR f

unqualified [ʌn'kwɒlɪfaɪd] adj (success) uneingeschränkt, voll; (person) unqualifiziert

unquestionably [ʌn'kwestʃənəblɪ] adv fraglos

unravel [ʌn'rævl] vt (disentangle) ausfasern, entwirren; (solve) lösen

unreal [ʌn'rɪəl] adj unwirklich

unrealistic ['ʌnrɪə'lɪstɪk] adj unrealistisch

unreasonable [ʌn'riːznəbl] adj unvernünftig; (demand) übertrieben

unrelated [ʌnrɪ'leɪtɪd] adj ohne Beziehung; (family) nicht verwandt

unrelenting [ʌnrɪ'lentɪŋ] adj unerbittlich

unreliable [ʌnrɪ'laɪəbl] adj unzuverlässig

unremitting [ʌnrɪ'mɪtɪŋ] adj (efforts, attempts) unermüdlich

unreservedly [ʌnrɪ'zɜːvɪdlɪ] adv offen; (believe, trust) uneingeschränkt; (cry) rückhaltlos

unrest [ʌn'rest] n (discontent) Unruhe f; (fighting) Unruhen pl

unroll [ʌn'rəʊl] vt aufrollen

unruly [ʌn'ruːlɪ] adj (child) undiszipliniert; schwer lenkbar

unsafe [ʌn'seɪf] adj nicht sicher

unsaid [ʌn'sed] adj: **to leave sth ~** etw ungesagt lassen

unsatisfactory ['ʌnsætɪs'fæktərɪ] adj unbefriedigend; unzulänglich

unsavoury [ʌn'seɪvərɪ] (US **unsavory**) adj (fig) widerwärtig

unscathed [ʌn'skeɪðd] adj unversehrt

unscrew [ʌn'skruː] vt aufschrauben

unscrupulous [ʌn'skruːpjʊləs] adj skrupellos

unsettled [ʌn'setld] adj (person) rastlos; (weather) wechselhaft

unshaven [ʌn'ʃeɪvn] adj unrasiert

unsightly [ʌn'saɪtlɪ] adj unansehnlich

unskilled [ʌn'skɪld] adj ungelernt

unspeakable [ʌn'spiːkəbl] adj (joy) unsagbar; (crime) scheußlich

unstable [ʌn'steɪbl] adj instabil; (mentally) labil

unsteady [ʌn'stedɪ] adj unsicher

unstuck [ʌn'stʌk] adj: **to come ~** sich lösen; (fig) ins Wasser fallen

unsuccessful [ʌnsək'sesful] adj erfolglos

unsuitable [ʌn'suːtəbl] adj unpassend

unsure [ʌn'ʃʊəʳ] adj unsicher; **to be ~ of o.s.** unsicher sein

unsuspecting [ʌnsəs'pektɪŋ] adj nichts ahnend

unsympathetic ['ʌnsɪmpə'θetɪk] adj gefühllos; (response) abweisend; (unlikeable) unsympathisch

untapped [ʌnˈtæpt] *adj* (*resources*) ungenützt

unthinkable [ʌnˈθɪŋkəbl] *adj* unvorstellbar

untidy [ʌnˈtaɪdɪ] *adj* unordentlich

untie [ʌnˈtaɪ] *vt* aufschnüren

until [ənˈtɪl] *prep, conj* bis; **~ he comes** bis er kommt; **~ then** bis dann; **~ now** bis jetzt

untimely [ʌnˈtaɪmlɪ] *adj* (*death*) vorzeitig

untold [ʌnˈtəʊld] *adj* unermesslich

untoward [ʌntəˈwɔːd] *adj* widrig

untranslatable [ʌntrænzˈleɪtəbl] *adj* unübersetzbar

unused [ʌnˈjuːzd] *adj* unbenutzt

unusual [ʌnˈjuːʒʊəl] *adj* ungewöhnlich

unveil [ʌnˈveɪl] *vt* enthüllen

unwanted [ʌnˈwɒntɪd] *adj* unerwünscht

unwavering [ʌnˈweɪvərɪŋ] *adj* standhaft, unerschütterlich

unwelcome [ʌnˈwelkəm] *adj* (*at a bad time*) unwillkommen; (*unpleasant*) unerfreulich

unwell [ʌnˈwel] *adj*: **to feel** or **be ~** sich nicht wohl fühlen

unwieldy [ʌnˈwiːldɪ] *adj* sperrig

unwilling [ʌnˈwɪlɪŋ] *adj*: **to be ~ to do sth** nicht bereit sein, etw zu tun; **~ly** *adv* widerwillig

unwind [ʌnˈwaɪnd] (*irreg: like* **wind**[2]) *vt* abwickeln ♦ *vi* (*relax*) sich entspannen

unwise [ʌnˈwaɪz] *adj* unklug

unwitting [ʌnˈwɪtɪŋ] *adj* unwissentlich

unworkable [ʌnˈwəːkəbl] *adj* (*plan*) undurchführbar

unworthy [ʌnˈwəːðɪ] *adj* (*person*): **~ (of sth)** (einer Sache *gen*) nicht wert

unwrap [ʌnˈræp] *vt* auspacken

unwritten [ʌnˈrɪtn] *adj* ungeschrieben

KEYWORD
---

up [ʌp] *prep*: **to be up sth** oben auf etw *dat* sein; **to go up sth** (auf) etw *acc* hinaufgehen; **go up that road** gehen Sie die Straße hinauf
♦ *adv* **1** (*upwards, higher*) oben; **put it up a bit higher** stell es etwas weiter nach oben; **up there** da oben, dort oben; **up above** hoch oben

2: **to be up** (*out of bed*) auf sein; (*prices, level*) gestiegen sein; (*building, tent*) stehen

3: **up to** (*as far as*) bis; **up to now** bis jetzt

4: **to be up** (*depending on*): **it's up to you** das hängt von dir ab; (*equal to*): **he's not up to it** (*job, task etc*) er ist dem nicht gewachsen; (*inf: be doing: showing disapproval, suspicion*): **what is he up to?** was führt er im Schilde?; **it's not up to me to decide** die Entscheidung liegt nicht bei mir; **his work is not up to the required standard** seine Arbeit entspricht nicht dem geforderten Niveau
♦ *n*: **ups and downs** (*in life, career*) Höhen und Tiefen *pl*

up-and-coming [ʌpəndˈkʌmɪŋ] *adj* aufstrebend

upbringing [ˈʌpbrɪŋɪŋ] *n* Erziehung *f*

update [ʌpˈdeɪt] *vt* auf den neuesten Stand bringen

upgrade [ʌpˈɡreɪd] *vt* höher einstufen

upheaval [ʌpˈhiːvl] *n* Umbruch *m*

uphill [ˈʌpˈhɪl] *adj* ansteigend; (*fig*) mühsam
♦ *adv*: **to go ~** bergauf gehen/fahren

uphold [ʌpˈhəʊld] (*irreg: like* **hold**) *vt* unterstützen

upholstery [ʌpˈhəʊlstərɪ] *n* Polster *nt*; Polsterung *f*

upkeep [ˈʌpkiːp] *n* Instandhaltung *f*

upon [əˈpɒn] *prep* auf

upper [ˈʌpəʳ] *n* (*on shoe*) Oberleder *nt* ♦ *adj* obere(r, s), höhere(r, s); **to have the ~ hand** die Oberhand haben; **~-class** *adj* vornehm; **~most** *adj* oberste(r, s), höchste(r, s); **what was ~most in my mind** was mich in erster Linie beschäftigte; **~ sixth** (*BRIT: SCOL*) *n* Abschlussklasse *f*

upright [ˈʌpraɪt] *adj* aufrecht

uprising [ˈʌpraɪzɪŋ] *n* Aufstand *m*

uproar [ˈʌprɔːʳ] *n* Aufruhr *m*

uproot [ʌpˈruːt] *vt* ausreißen

upset [n ˈʌpset, *vb, adj* ʌpˈset] (*irreg: like* **set**) *n* Aufregung *f* ♦ *vt* (*overturn*) umwerfen; (*disturb*) aufregen, bestürzen; (*plans*) durcheinander bringen ♦ *adj* (*person*) aufgeregt; (*stomach*) verdorben

upshot [ˈʌpʃɔt] n (End)ergebnis nt
upside-down [ˈʌpsaɪd-] adv verkehrt herum
upstairs [ʌpˈsteəz] adv oben; (go) nach oben
♦ adj (room) obere(r, s), Ober- ♦ n obere(s)
Stockwerk nt
upstart [ˈʌpstɑːt] n Emporkömmling m
upstream [ʌpˈstriːm] adv stromaufwärts
uptake [ˈʌpteɪk] n: **to be quick on the ~**
schnell begreifen; **to be slow on the ~**
schwer von Begriff sein
uptight [ʌpˈtaɪt] (inf) adj (nervous) nervös;
(inhibited) verklemmt
up-to-date [ˈʌptəˈdeɪt] adj (clothes) modisch,
modern; (information) neueste(r, s)
upturn [ˈʌptɜːn] n Aufschwung m
upward [ˈʌpwəd] adj nach oben gerichtet;
~(s) adv aufwärts
uranium [juəˈreɪnɪəm] n Uran nt
urban [ˈɜːbən] adj städtisch, Stadt-; **~**
clearway n Stadtautobahn f
urchin [ˈɜːtʃɪn] n (boy) Schlingel m; (sea ~)
Seeigel m
urge [ɜːdʒ] n Drang m ♦ vt: **to ~ sb to do**
sth jdn (dazu) drängen, etw zu tun
urgency [ˈɜːdʒənsɪ] n Dringlichkeit f
urgent [ˈɜːdʒənt] adj dringend
urinal [ˈjuərɪnl] n (public) Pissoir nt
urinate [ˈjuərɪneɪt] vi urinieren
urine [ˈjuərɪn] n Urin m, Harn m
urn [ɜːn] n Urne f; (tea ~) Teemaschine f
US n abbr = **United States**
us [ʌs] pron uns; see also **me**
USA n abbr = **United States of America**
usage [ˈjuːzɪdʒ] n Gebrauch m; (esp LING)
Sprachgebrauch m
use [n juːs, vb juːz] n (employment) Gebrauch
m; (point) Zweck m ♦ vt gebrauchen; **in ~**
in Gebrauch; **out of ~** außer Gebrauch; **to**
be of ~ nützlich sein; **it's no ~** es hat
keinen Zweck; **what's the ~?** was solls?;
~d to (accustomed to) gewöhnt an +acc;
she ~d to live here (formerly) sie hat früher
mal hier gewohnt; **~ up** vt aufbrauchen,
verbrauchen; **~d** adj (car) Gebraucht-; **~ful**
adj nützlich; **~fulness** n Nützlichkeit f;
~less adj nutzlos, unnütz; **~r** n Benutzer
m; **~r-friendly** adj (computer)

benutzerfreundlich
usher [ˈʌʃəʳ] n Platzanweiser m; **~ette**
[ʌʃəˈret] n Platzanweiserin f
usual [ˈjuːʒuəl] adj gewöhnlich, üblich; **as ~**
wie üblich; **~ly** adv gewöhnlich
usurp [juːˈzɜːp] vt an sich reißen
utensil [juːˈtensl] n Gerät nt; **kitchen ~s**
Küchengeräte pl
uterus [ˈjuːtərəs] n Gebärmutter f
utilitarian [juːtɪlɪˈteərɪən] adj Nützlichkeits-
utility [juːˈtɪlɪtɪ] n (usefulness) Nützlichkeit f;
(also: **public ~**) öffentliche(r)
Versorgungsbetrieb m; **~ room** n
Hauswirtschaftsraum m
utilize [ˈjuːtɪlaɪz] vt benützen
utmost [ˈʌtməust] adj äußerste(r, s) ♦ n: **to**
do one's ~ sein Möglichstes tun
utter [ˈʌtəʳ] adj äußerste(r, s), höchste(r, s),
völlig ♦ vt äußern, aussprechen; **~ance** n
Äußerung f; **~ly** adv äußerst, absolut, völlig
U-turn [ˈjuːtɜːn] n (AUT) Kehrtwendung f

V, v

v. abbr = **verse**; **versus**; **volt**; (= vide) see
vacancy [ˈveɪkənsɪ] n (BRIT: job) offene Stelle
f; (room) freie(s) Zimmer nt; **"no**
vacancies" „belegt"
vacant [ˈveɪkənt] adj leer; (unoccupied) frei;
(house) leer stehend, unbewohnt; (stupid)
(gedanken)leer; **~ lot** (US) n unbebaute(s)
Grundstück nt
vacate [vəˈkeɪt] vt (seat) frei machen; (room)
räumen
vacation [vəˈkeɪʃən] n Ferien pl, Urlaub m;
~ist (US) n Ferienreisende(r) f(m)
vaccinate [ˈvæksɪneɪt] vt impfen
vaccine [ˈvæksiːn] n Impfstoff m
vacuum [ˈvækjum] n Vakuum nt; **~ bottle**
(US) n Thermosflasche f; **~ cleaner** n
Staubsauger m; **~ flask** (BRIT) n
Thermosflasche f; **~-packed** adj
vakuumversiegelt
vagina [vəˈdʒaɪnə] n Scheide f
vague [veɪg] adj vag(e); (absent-minded)
geistesabwesend; **~ly** adv unbestimmt,

vag(e)

vain [veɪn] *adj* eitel; *(attempt)* vergeblich; **in ~** vergebens, umsonst

valentine ['væləntaɪn] *n (also: ~* **card)** Valentinsgruß *m;* **V~'s Day** *n* Valentinstag *m*

valet ['vælɪt] *n* Kammerdiener *m*

valiant ['væliənt] *adj* tapfer

valid ['vælɪd] *adj* gültig; *(argument)* stichhaltig; *(objection)* berechtigt; **~ity** [və'lɪdɪtɪ] *n* Gültigkeit *f*

valley ['vælɪ] *n* Tal *nt*

valour ['vælə'] *(US* **valor)** *n* Tapferkeit *f*

valuable ['væljuəbl] *adj* wertvoll; *(time)* kostbar; **~s** *npl* Wertsachen *pl*

valuation [vælju'eɪʃən] *n (FIN)* Schätzung *f;* Beurteilung *f*

value ['vælju:] *n* Wert *m; (usefulness)* Nutzen *m* ♦ *vt (prize)* (hoch) schätzen, werthalten; *(estimate)* schätzen; **~ added tax** *(BRIT) n* Mehrwertsteuer *f;* **~d** *adj* (hoch) geschätzt

valve [vælv] *n* Ventil *nt; (BIOL)* Klappe *f; (RAD)* Röhre *f*

van [væn] *n* Lieferwagen *m; (BRIT: RAIL)* Waggon *m*

vandal ['vændl] *n* Rowdy *m;* **~ism** *n* mutwillige Beschädigung *f;* **~ize** *vt* mutwillig beschädigen

vanguard ['vænɡɑ:d] *n (fig)* Spitze *f*

vanilla [və'nɪlə] *n* Vanille *f;* **~ ice cream** *n* Vanilleeis *nt*

vanish ['vænɪʃ] *vi* verschwinden

vanity ['vænɪtɪ] *n* Eitelkeit *f;* **~ case** *n* Schminkkoffer *m*

vantage ['vɑ:ntɪdʒ] *n:* **~ point** gute(r) Aussichtspunkt *m*

vapour ['veɪpə'] *(US* **vapor)** *n (mist)* Dunst *m; (gas)* Dampf *m*

variable ['veəriəbl] *adj* wechselhaft, veränderlich; *(speed, height)* regulierbar

variance ['veəriəns] *n:* **to be at ~ (with)** nicht übereinstimmen (mit)

variation [veəri'eɪʃən] *n* Variation *f; (in prices etc)* Schwankung *f*

varicose ['værɪkəus] *adj:* **~ veins** Krampfadern *pl*

varied ['veərɪd] *adj* unterschiedlich; *(life)* abwechslungsreich

variety [və'raɪətɪ] *n (difference)* Abwechslung *f; (varied collection)* Vielfalt *f; (COMM)* Auswahl *f; (sort)* Sorte *f,* Art *f;* **~ show** *n* Varietee *nt,* Varieté *f*

various ['veəriəs] *adj* verschieden; *(several)* mehrere

varnish ['vɑ:nɪʃ] *n* Lack *m; (on pottery)* Glasur *f* ♦ *vt* lackieren

vary ['veəri] *vt (alter)* verändern; *(give variety to)* abwechslungsreicher gestalten ♦ *vi* sich (ver)ändern; *(prices)* schwanken; *(weather)* unterschiedlich sein

vase [vɑ:z] *n* Vase *f*

Vaseline ['væsɪli:n] ® *n* Vaseline *f*

vast [vɑ:st] *adj* weit, groß, riesig

VAT [væt] *n abbr (= value added tax)* MwSt *f*

vat [væt] *n* große(s) Fass *nt*

vault [vɔ:lt] *n (of roof)* Gewölbe *nt; (tomb)* Gruft *f; (in bank)* Tresorraum *m; (leap)* Sprung *m* ♦ *vt (also: ~* **over)** überspringen

vaunted ['vɔ:ntɪd] *adj:* **much-~** viel gerühmt

VCR *n abbr =* **video cassette recorder**

VD *n abbr =* **venereal disease**

VDU *n abbr =* **visual display unit**

veal [vi:l] *n* Kalbfleisch *nt*

veer [vɪə'] *vi* sich drehen; *(of car)* ausscheren

vegan ['vi:ɡən] *n* Vegan *m,* radikale(r) Vegetarier(in) *m(f)*

vegeburger ['vedʒɪbə:ɡə'] *n* vegetarische Frikadelle *f*

vegetable ['vedʒtəbl] *n* Gemüse *nt* ♦ *adj* Gemüse-; **~s** *npl (CULIN)* Gemüse *nt*

vegetarian [vedʒɪ'teəriən] *n* Vegetarier(in) *m(f)* ♦ *adj* vegetarisch

vegetate ['vedʒɪteɪt] *vi* (dahin)vegetieren

veggieburger ['vedʒɪbə:ɡə'] *n =* **vegeburger**

vehement ['vi:ɪmənt] *adj* heftig

vehicle ['vi:ɪkl] *n* Fahrzeug *nt; (fig)* Mittel *nt*

veil [veɪl] *n (also fig)* Schleier *m* ♦ *vt* verschleiern

vein [veɪn] *n* Ader *f; (mood)* Stimmung *f*

velocity [vɪ'lɔsɪtɪ] *n* Geschwindigkeit *f*

velvet ['velvɪt] *n* Samt *m* ♦ *adj* Samt-

vendetta [ven'detə] *n* Fehde *f; (in family)*

Blutrache f

vending machine ['vendɪŋ-] n Automat m

vendor ['vendə'] n Verkäufer m

veneer [vəˈnɪə'] n Furnier(holz) nt; (fig) äußere(r) Anstrich m

venereal disease [vɪˈnɪərɪəl-] n Geschlechtskrankheit f

Venetian blind [vɪˈniːʃən-] n Jalousie f

vengeance ['vendʒəns] n Rache f; **with a ~** gewaltig

venison ['venɪsn] n Reh(fleisch) nt

venom ['venəm] n Gift nt

vent [vent] n Öffnung f; (in coat) Schlitz m; (fig) Ventil nt ♦ vt (emotion) abreagieren

ventilate ['ventɪleɪt] vt belüften; **ventilator** ['ventɪleɪtə'] n Ventilator m

ventriloquist [venˈtrɪləkwɪst] n Bauchredner m

venture ['ventʃə'] n Unternehmung f, Projekt nt ♦ vt wagen; (life) aufs Spiel setzen ♦ vi sich wagen

venue ['venjuː] n Schauplatz m

verb [vəːb] n Zeitwort nt, Verb nt; **~al** adj (spoken) mündlich; (translation) wörtlich; **~ally** adv mündlich

verbatim [vəːˈbeɪtɪm] adv Wort für Wort ♦ adj wortwörtlich

verbose [vəːˈbəus] adj wortreich

verdict ['vəːdɪkt] n Urteil nt

verge [vəːdʒ] n (BRIT) Rand m ♦ vi: **to ~ on** grenzen an +acc; **"soft ~s"** (BRIT: AUT) „Seitenstreifen nicht befahrbar"; **on the ~ of doing sth** im Begriff, etw zu tun

verify ['verɪfaɪ] vt (über)prüfen; (confirm) bestätigen; (theory) beweisen

veritable ['verɪtəbl] adj wirklich, echt

vermin ['vəːmɪn] npl Ungeziefer nt

vermouth ['vəːməθ] n Wermut m

versatile ['vəːsətaɪl] adj vielseitig

verse [vəːs] n (poetry) Poesie f; (stanza) Strophe f; (of Bible) Vers m; **in ~** in Versform

version ['vəːʃən] n Version f; (of car) Modell nt

versus ['vəːsəs] prep gegen

vertebrate ['vəːtɪbrɪt] adj Wirbel-

vertical ['vəːtɪkl] adj senkrecht

vertigo ['vəːtɪgəu] n Schwindel m

very ['verɪ] adv sehr ♦ adj (extreme) äußerste(r, s); **the ~ book which** genau das Buch, welches; **the ~ last ...** der/die/das allerletzte ...; **at the ~ least** allerwenigstens; **~ much** sehr

vessel ['vesl] n (ship) Schiff nt; (container) Gefäß nt

vest [vest] n (BRIT) Unterhemd nt; (US: waistcoat) Weste f

vested interests ['vestɪd-] npl finanzielle Beteiligung f; (people) finanziell Beteiligte pl; (fig) persönliche(s) Interesse nt

vestige ['vestɪdʒ] n Spur f

vestry ['vestrɪ] n Sakristei f

vet [vet] n abbr (= veterinary surgeon) Tierarzt(-ärztin) m(f)

veteran ['vetərn] n Veteran(in) m(f)

veterinarian [vetrɪˈnɛərɪən] (US) n Tierarzt m/-ärztin f

veterinary ['vetrɪnərɪ] adj Veterinär-; **~ surgeon** (BRIT) n Tierarzt m/-ärztin f

veto ['viːtəu] (pl **~es**) n Veto nt ♦ vt sein Veto einlegen gegen

vex [veks] vt ärgern; **~ed** adj verärgert; **~ed question** umstrittene Frage f

VHF abbr (= very high frequency) UKW f

via ['vaɪə] prep über +acc

viable ['vaɪəbl] adj (plan) durchführbar; (company) rentabel

vibrant ['vaɪbrnt] adj (lively) lebhaft; (bright) leuchtend; (full of emotion: voice) bebend

vibrate [vaɪˈbreɪt] vi zittern, beben; (machine, string) vibrieren; **vibration** [vaɪˈbreɪʃən] n Schwingung f; (of machine) Vibrieren nt

vicar ['vɪkə'] n Pfarrer m; **~age** n Pfarrhaus nt

vice [vaɪs] n (evil) Laster nt; (TECH) Schraubstock m

vice-chairman [vaɪsˈtʃɛəmən] n stellvertretende(r) Vorsitzende(r) m

vice-president [vaɪsˈprezɪdənt] n Vizepräsident m

vice squad n ≈ Sittenpolizei f

vice versa ['vaɪsɪ'vəːsə] adv umgekehrt

vicinity [vɪˈsɪnɪtɪ] n Umgebung f; (closeness) Nähe f

vicious ['vɪʃəs] *adj* gemein, böse; ~ **circle** *n* Teufelskreis *m*

victim ['vɪktɪm] *n* Opfer *nt*

victor ['vɪktə'] *n* Sieger *m*

Victorian [vɪk'tɔːrɪən] *adj* viktorianisch; *(fig)* (sitten)streng

victorious [vɪk'tɔːrɪəs] *adj* siegreich

victory ['vɪktərɪ] *n* Sieg *m*

video ['vɪdɪəʊ] *adj* Fernseh-, Bild- ♦ *n* (~ *film*) Video *nt*; *(also:* ~ **cassette***)* Videokassette *f*; *(also:* ~ **cassette recorder***)* Videorekorder *m*; ~ **tape** *n* Videoband *nt*; ~ **wall** *n* Videowand *m*

vie [vaɪ] *vi* wetteifern

Vienna [vɪ'enə] *n* Wien *nt*

Vietnam ['vjet'næm] *n* Vietnam *nt*; **~ese** *adj* vietnamesisch ♦ *n inv (person)* Vietnamese *m*, Vietnamesin *f*

view [vjuː] *n (sight)* Sicht *f*, Blick *m*; *(scene)* Aussicht *f*; *(opinion)* Ansicht *f*; *(intention)* Absicht *f* ♦ *vt (situation)* betrachten; *(house)* besichtigen; **to have sth in ~** etw beabsichtigen; **on ~** ausgestellt; **in ~ of** wegen +*gen*, angesichts +*gen*; **~er** *n (PHOT: small projector)* Gucki *m*; *(TV)* Fernsehzuschauer(in) *m(f)*; **~finder** *n* Sucher *m*; **~point** *n* Standpunkt *m*

vigil ['vɪdʒɪl] *n* (Nacht)wache *f*; **~ant** *adj* wachsam

vigorous ['vɪgərəs] *adj* kräftig; *(protest)* energisch, heftig

vile [vaɪl] *adj (mean)* gemein; *(foul)* abscheulich

villa ['vɪlə] *n* Villa *f*

village ['vɪlɪdʒ] *n* Dorf *nt*; **~r** *n* Dorfbewohner(in) *m(f)*

villain ['vɪlən] *n* Schurke *m*

vindicate ['vɪndɪkeɪt] *vt* rechtfertigen

vindictive [vɪn'dɪktɪv] *adj* nachtragend, rachsüchtig

vine [vaɪn] *n* Rebstock *m*, Rebe *f*

vinegar ['vɪnɪgə'] *n* Essig *m*

vineyard ['vɪnjɑːd] *n* Weinberg *m*

vintage ['vɪntɪdʒ] *n (of wine)* Jahrgang *m*; ~ **car** *n* Oldtimer *m* (zwischen 1919 und 1930 gebaut); ~ **wine** *n* edle(r) Wein *m*

viola [vɪ'əʊlə] *n* Bratsche *f*

violate ['vaɪəleɪt] *vt (law)* übertreten; *(rights, rule, neutrality)* verletzen; *(sanctity, woman)* schänden; **violation** [vaɪə'leɪʃən] *n* Übertretung *f*; Verletzung *f*

violence ['vaɪələns] *n (force)* Heftigkeit *f*; *(brutality)* Gewalttätigkeit *f*

violent ['vaɪələnt] *adj (strong)* heftig; *(brutal)* gewalttätig, brutal; *(contrast)* krass; *(death)* gewaltsam

violet ['vaɪələt] *n* Veilchen *n* ♦ *adj* veilchenblau, violett

violin [vaɪə'lɪn] *n* Geige *f*, Violine *f*; **~ist** *n* Geiger(in) *m(f)*

VIP *n abbr* (= *very important person*) VIP *m*

virgin ['vɜːdʒɪn] *n* Jungfrau *f* ♦ *adj* jungfräulich, unberührt; **~ity** [vɜː'dʒɪnɪtɪ] *n* Unschuld *f*

Virgo ['vɜːgəʊ] *n* Jungfrau *f*

virile ['vɪraɪl] *adj* männlich; **virility** [vɪ'rɪlɪtɪ] *n* Männlichkeit *f*

virtually ['vɜːtjʊəlɪ] *adv* praktisch, fast

virtual reality ['vɜːtjʊəl-] *n (COMPUT)* virtuelle Realität *f*

virtue ['vɜːtjuː] *n (moral goodness)* Tugend *f*; *(good quality)* Vorteil *m*, Vorzug *m*; **by ~ of** aufgrund *or* auf Grund +*gen*

virtuous ['vɜːtjʊəs] *adj* tugendhaft

virulent ['vɪrʊlənt] *adj (poisonous)* bösartig; *(bitter)* scharf, geharnischt

virus ['vaɪərəs] *n (also COMPUT)* Virus *m*

visa ['viːzə] *n* Visum *nt*

vis-à-vis [viːzɑː'viː] *prep* gegenüber

viscous ['vɪskəs] *adj* zähflüssig

visibility [vɪzɪ'bɪlɪtɪ] *n (MET)* Sicht(weite) *f*

visible ['vɪzəbl] *adj* sichtbar; **visibly** *adv* sichtlich

vision ['vɪʒən] *n (ability)* Sehvermögen *nt*; *(foresight)* Weitblick *m*; *(in dream, image)* Vision *f*

visit ['vɪzɪt] *n* Besuch *m* ♦ *vt* besuchen; *(town, country)* fahren nach; **~ing hours** *npl (in hospital etc)* Besuchszeiten *pl*; **~or** *n (in house)* Besucher(in) *m(f)*; *(in hotel)* Gast *m*; **~or centre** *n* Touristeninformation *f*

visor ['vaɪzə'] *n* Visier *nt*; *(on cap)* Schirm *m*; *(AUT)* Blende *f*

vista ['vɪstə] *n* Aussicht *f*

visual ['vɪzjuəl] adj Seh-, visuell; ~ **aid** n Anschauungsmaterial nt; ~ **display unit** n Bildschirm(gerät nt) m; ~**ize** vt sich +dat vorstellen; ~**ly-impaired** adj sehbehindert

vital ['vaɪtl] adj (important) unerlässlich; (necessary for life) Lebens-, lebenswichtig; (lively) vital; ~**ity** [vaɪˈtælɪtɪ] n Vitalität f; ~**ly** adv: ~**ly important** äußerst wichtig; ~ **statistics** npl (fig) Maße pl

vitamin ['vɪtəmɪn] n Vitamin nt

vivacious [vɪˈveɪʃəs] adj lebhaft

vivid ['vɪvɪd] adj (graphic) lebendig; (memory) lebhaft; (bright) leuchtend; ~**ly** adv lebendig; lebhaft; leuchtend

V-neck ['viːnɛk] n V-Ausschnitt m

vocabulary [vəuˈkæbjulərɪ] n Wortschatz m, Vokabular nt

vocal ['vəukl] adj Vokal-, Gesang-; (fig) lautstark; ~ **cords** npl Stimmbänder pl

vocation [vəuˈkeɪʃən] n (calling) Berufung f; ~**al** adj Berufs-

vociferous [vəˈsɪfərəs] adj lautstark

vodka ['vɒdkə] n Wodka m

vogue [vəug] n Mode f

voice [vɔɪs] n Stimme f; (fig) Mitspracherecht nt ♦ vt äußern

void [vɔɪd] n Leere f ♦ adj (invalid) nichtig, ungültig; (empty): ~ **of** ohne, bar +gen; see **null**

volatile ['vɒlətaɪl] adj (gas) flüchtig; (person) impulsiv; (situation) brisant

volcano [vɒlˈkeɪnəu] n Vulkan m

volition [vəˈlɪʃən] n Wille m; **of one's own** ~ aus freiem Willen

volley ['vɒlɪ] n (of guns) Salve f; (of stones) Hagel m; (tennis) Flugball m; ~**ball** n Volleyball m

volt [vəult] n Volt nt; ~**age** n (Volt)spannung f

volume ['vɒljuːm] n (book) Band m; (size) Umfang m; (space) Rauminhalt m; (of sound) Lautstärke f

voluntarily ['vɒləntrɪlɪ] adv freiwillig

voluntary ['vɒləntərɪ] adj freiwillig

volunteer [vɒlənˈtɪər] n Freiwillige(r) mf ♦ vi sich freiwillig melden; **to ~ to do sth** sich anbieten, etw zu tun

vomit ['vɒmɪt] n Erbrochene(s) nt ♦ vt spucken ♦ vi sich übergeben

vote [vəut] n Stimme f; (ballot) Abstimmung f; (result) Abstimmungsergebnis nt; (franchise) Wahlrecht nt ♦ vt, vi wählen; ~ **of thanks** n Dankesworte pl; ~**r** n Wähler(in) m(f); **voting** ['vəutɪŋ] n Wahl f

voucher ['vautʃər] n Gutschein m

vouch for [vautʃ-] vt bürgen für

vow [vau] n Versprechen nt; (REL) Gelübde nt ♦ vt geloben

vowel ['vauəl] n Vokal m

voyage ['vɔɪɪdʒ] n Reise f

vulgar ['vʌlgər] adj (rude) vulgär; ~**ity** [vʌlˈgærɪtɪ] n Vulgarität f

vulnerable ['vʌlnərəbl] adj (easily injured) verwundbar; (sensitive) verletzlich

vulture ['vʌltʃər] n Geier m

W, w

wad [wɒd] n (bundle) Bündel nt; (of paper) Stoß m; (of money) Packen m

waddle ['wɒdl] vi watscheln

wade [weɪd] vi: **to ~ through** waten durch

wafer ['weɪfər] n Waffel f; (REL) Hostie f; (COMPUT) Wafer f

waffle ['wɒfl] n Waffel f; (inf: empty talk) Geschwafel nt ♦ vi schwafeln

waft [wɒft] vt, vi wehen

wag [wæg] vt (tail) wedeln mit ♦ vi wedeln

wage [weɪdʒ] n (also: ~**s**) (Arbeits)lohn m ♦ vt: **to ~ war** Krieg führen; ~ **earner** n Lohnempfänger(in) m(f); ~ **packet** n Lohntüte f

wager ['weɪdʒər] n Wette f ♦ vt, vi wetten

waggle ['wægl] vt, vi wackeln

wag(g)on ['wægən] n (horse-drawn) Fuhrwerk nt; (US: AUT) Wagen m; (BRIT: RAIL) Wag(g)on m

wail [weɪl] n Wehgeschrei nt ♦ vi wehklagen, jammern

waist [weɪst] n Taille f; ~**coat** (BRIT) n Weste f; ~**line** n Taille f

wait [weɪt] n Wartezeit f ♦ vi warten; **to lie in ~ for sb** jdm auflauern; **I can't ~ to see**

him ich kanns kaum erwarten ihn zu
sehen; **"no ~ing"** (*BRIT: AUT*) „Halteverbot";
~ behind *vi* zurückbleiben; **~ for** *vt fus*
warten auf +*acc*; **~ on** *vt fus* bedienen; **~er**
n Kellner *m*; **~ing list** *n* Warteliste *f*; **~ing
room** *n* (*MED*) Wartezimmer *nt*; (*RAIL*)
Wartesaal *m*; **~ress** *n* Kellnerin *f*

waive [weɪv] *vt* verzichten auf +*acc*

wake [weɪk] (*pt* **woke, waked**, *pp* **woken**) *vt*
wecken ♦ *vi* (*also: ~ up*) aufwachen ♦ *n*
(*NAUT*) Kielwasser *nt*; (*for dead*) Totenwache
f; **to ~ up to** (*fig*) sich bewusst werden +*gen*

waken ['weɪkn] *vt* aufwecken

Wales [weɪlz] *n* Wales *nt*

walk [wɔːk] *n* Spaziergang *m*; (*gait*) Gang *m*;
(*route*) Weg *m* ♦ *vi* gehen; (*stroll*) spazieren
gehen; (*longer*) wandern; **~s of life** Sphären
pl; **a 10-minute ~** 10 Minuten zu Fuß; **to ~
out on sb** (*inf*) jdn sitzen lassen; **~er** *n*
Spaziergänger *m*; (*hiker*) Wanderer *m*; **~ie-
talkie** ['wɔːkɪ'tɔːkɪ] *n* tragbare(s)
Sprechfunkgerät *nt*; **~ing** *n* Gehen *nt*;
(*hiking*) Wandern *nt* ♦ *adj* Wander-; **~ing
shoes** *npl* Wanderschuhe *pl*; **~ing stick** *n*
Spazierstock *m*; **W~man** ['wɔːkmən] ® *n*
Walkman *m* ®; **~out** *n* Streik *m*; **~over**
(*inf*) *n* leichte(r) Sieg *m*; **~way** *n* Fußweg *m*

wall [wɔːl] *n* (*inside*) Wand *f*; (*outside*) Mauer
f; **~ed** *adj* von Mauern umgeben

wallet ['wɔlɪt] *n* Brieftasche *f*

wallflower ['wɔːlflauəʳ] *n* Goldlack *m*; **to be
a ~** (*fig*) ein Mauerblümchen sein

wallop ['wɔləp] (*inf*) *vt* schlagen, verprügeln

wallow ['wɔləu] *vi* sich wälzen

wallpaper ['wɔːlpeɪpəʳ] *n* Tapete *f*

walnut ['wɔːlnʌt] *n* Walnuss *f*

walrus ['wɔːlrəs] *n* Walross *nt*

waltz [wɔːlts] *n* Walzer *m* ♦ *vi* Walzer tanzen

wan [wɔn] *adj* bleich

wand [wɔnd] *n* (*also: **magic ~**) Zauberstab
m

wander ['wɔndəʳ] *vi* (*roam*)
(herum)wandern; (*fig*) abschweifen

wane [weɪn] *vi* abnehmen; (*fig*) schwinden

wangle ['wæŋgl] (*BRIT: inf*) *vt*: **to ~ sth** etw
richtig hindrehen

want [wɔnt] *n* (*lack*) Mangel *m* ♦ *vt* (*need*)

brauchen; (*desire*) wollen; (*lack*) nicht
haben; **~s** *npl* (*needs*) Bedürfnisse *pl*; **for ~
of** aus Mangel an +*dat*; mangels +*gen*; **to ~
to do sth** etw tun wollen; **to ~ sb to do
sth** wollen, dass jd etw tut; **~ed** *adj*
(*criminal etc*) gesucht; **"cook ~ed"** (*in
adverts*) „Koch/Köchin gesucht"; **~ing** *adj*:
to be found ~ing sich als unzulänglich
erweisen

wanton ['wɔntn] *adj* mutwillig, zügellos

war [wɔːʳ] *n* Krieg *m*; **to make ~** Krieg
führen

ward [wɔːd] *n* (*in hospital*) Station *f*; (*of city*)
Bezirk *m*; (*child*) Mündel *nt*; **~ off** *vt*
abwenden, abwehren

warden ['wɔːdn] *n* (*guard*) Wächter *m*,
Aufseher *m*; (*BRIT: in youth hostel*)
Herbergsvater *m*; (*UNIV*) Heimleiter *m*; (*BRIT:
also: **traffic ~**) ≃ Verkehrspolizist *m*, ≃
Politesse *f*

warder ['wɔːdəʳ] (*BRIT*) *n* Gefängniswärter *m*

wardrobe ['wɔːdrəub] *n* Kleiderschrank *m*;
(*clothes*) Garderobe *f*

warehouse ['weəhaus] *n* Lagerhaus *nt*

wares [weəz] *npl* Ware *f*

warfare ['wɔːfeəʳ] *n* Krieg *m*; Kriegsführung *f*

warhead ['wɔːhed] *n* Sprengkopf *m*

warily ['weərɪlɪ] *adv* vorsichtig

warlike ['wɔːlaɪk] *adj* kriegerisch

warm [wɔːm] *adj* warm; (*welcome*) herzlich
♦ *vt, vi* wärmen; **I'm ~** mir ist warm; **it's ~**
es ist warm; **~ up** *vt* aufwärmen ♦ *vi* warm
werden; **~-hearted** *adj* warmherzig; **~ly**
adv warm; herzlich; **~th** *n* Wärme *f*;
Herzlichkeit *f*

warn [wɔːn] *vt*: **to ~ (of** *or* **against)** warnen
(vor +*dat*); **~ing** *n* Warnung *f*; **without
~ing** unerwartet; **~ing light** *n* Warnlicht *nt*;
~ing triangle *n* (*AUT*) Warndreieck *nt*

warp [wɔːp] *vt* verziehen; **~ed** *adj* wellig;
(*fig*) pervers

warrant ['wɔrnt] *n* (*for arrest*) Haftbefehl *m*

warranty ['wɔrəntɪ] *n* Garantie *f*

warren ['wɔrən] *n* Labyrinth *nt*

Warsaw ['wɔːsɔː] *n* Warschau *nt*

warship ['wɔːʃɪp] *n* Kriegsschiff *nt*

wart [wɔːt] *n* Warze *f*

wartime ['wɔːtaɪm] n Krieg m
wary ['weərɪ] adj misstrauisch
was [wɒz] pt of **be**
wash [wɒʃ] n Wäsche f ♦ vt waschen; (dishes) abwaschen ♦ vi sich waschen; (do ~ing) waschen; **to have a ~** sich waschen; **~ away** vt abwaschen, wegspülen; **~ off** vt abwaschen; **~ up** vi (BRIT) spülen; (US) sich waschen; **~able** adj waschbar; **~basin** n Waschbecken nt; **~ bowl** (US) n Waschbecken nt; **~ cloth** (US) n (face cloth) Waschlappen m; **~er** n (TECH) Dichtungsring m; (machine) Waschmaschine f; **~ing** n Wäsche f; **~ing machine** n Waschmaschine f; **~ing powder** (BRIT) n Waschpulver nt; **~ing-up** n Abwasch m; **~ing-up liquid** n Spülmittel nt; **~-out** (inf) n (event) Reinfall m; (person) Niete f; **~room** n Waschraum m
wasn't ['wɒznt] = **was not**
wasp [wɒsp] n Wespe f
wastage ['weɪstɪdʒ] n Verlust m; **natural ~** Verschleiß m
waste [weɪst] n (wasting) Verschwendung f; (what is ~d) Abfall m ♦ adj (useless) überschüssig, Abfall- ♦ vt (object) verschwenden; (time, life) vergeuden ♦ vi: **to ~ away** verfallen, verkümmern; **~s** npl (land) Einöde f; **~ disposal unit** (BRIT) n Müllschlucker m; **~ful** adj verschwenderisch; (process) aufwändig, aufwendig; **~ ground** (BRIT) n unbebaute(s) Grundstück nt; **~land** n Ödland nt; **~paper basket** n Papierkorb m; **~ pipe** n Abflussrohr nt
watch [wɒtʃ] n Wache f; (for time) Uhr f ♦ vt ansehen; (observe) beobachten; (be careful of) aufpassen auf +acc; (guard) bewachen ♦ vi zusehen; **to be on the ~ (for sth)** (auf etw acc) aufpassen; **to ~ TV** fernsehen; **to ~ sb doing sth** jdm bei etw zuschauen; **~ out** vi Ausschau halten; (be careful) aufpassen; **~ out!** pass auf!; **~dog** n Wachhund m; (fig) Wächter m; **~ful** adj wachsam; **~maker** n Uhrmacher m; **~man** (irreg) n (also: **night ~man**) (Nacht)wächter m; **~ strap** n Uhrarmband nt

water ['wɔːtər] n Wasser nt ♦ vt (be)gießen; (river) bewässern; (horses) tränken ♦ vi (eye) tränen; **~s** npl (of sea, river etc) Gewässer nt; **~ down** vt verwässern; **~ closet** (BRIT) n (Wasser)klosett nt; **~colour** (US) **watercolor**) n (painting) Aquarell nt; (paint) Wasserfarbe f; **~cress** n (Brunnen)kresse f; **~fall** n Wasserfall m; **~ heater** n Heißwassergerät nt; **~ing can** n Gießkanne f; **~ level** n Wasserstand m; **~lily** n Seerose f; **~line** n Wasserlinie f; **~logged** adj (ground) voll Wasser; **~ main** n Haupt(wasser)leitung f; **~mark** n Wasserzeichen nt; (on wall) Wasserstandsmarke f; **~melon** n Wassermelone f; **~ polo** n Wasserball(spiel) nt; **~proof** adj wasserdicht; **~shed** n Wasserscheide f; **~-skiing** n Wasserskilaufen nt; **~ tank** n Wassertank m; **~tight** adj wasserdicht; **~way** n Wasserweg m; **~works** npl Wasserwerk nt; **~y** adj wäss(e)rig
watt [wɒt] n Watt nt
wave [weɪv] n Welle f; (with hand) Winken nt ♦ vt (move to and fro) schwenken; (hand, flag) winken mit ♦ vi (person) winken; (flag) wehen; **~length** n (also fig) Wellenlänge f
waver ['weɪvər] vi schwanken
wavy ['weɪvɪ] adj wellig
wax [wæks] n Wachs nt; (sealing ~) Siegellack m; (in ear) Ohrenschmalz nt ♦ vt (floor) (ein)wachsen ♦ vi (moon) zunehmen; **~works** npl Wachsfigurenkabinett nt
way [weɪ] n Weg m; (method) Art und Weise f; (direction) Richtung f; (habit) Gewohnheit f; (distance) Entfernung f; (condition) Zustand m; **which ~? - this ~** welche Richtung? - hier entlang; **on the ~** (en route) unterwegs; **to be in the ~** im Weg sein; **to go out of one's ~ to do sth** sich besonders anstrengen, um etw zu tun; **to lose one's ~** sich verirren; **"give ~"** (BRIT: AUT) „Vorfahrt achten!"; **in a ~** in gewisser Weise; **by the ~** übrigens; **in some ~s** in gewisser Hinsicht; **"~ in"** (BRIT) „Eingang"; **"~ out"** (BRIT) „Ausgang"
waylay [weɪˈleɪ] (irreg: like **lay**) vt auflauern

+*dat*

wayward ['weiwəd] *adj* eigensinnig

W.C. (*BRIT*) *n* WC *nt*

we [wiː] *pl pron* wir

weak [wiːk] *adj* schwach; **~en** *vt* schwächen ♦ *vi* schwächer werden; **~ling** *n* Schwächling *m*; **~ness** *n* Schwäche *f*

wealth [welθ] *n* Reichtum *m*; (*abundance*) Fülle *f*; **~y** *adj* reich

wean [wiːn] *vt* entwöhnen

weapon ['wepən] *n* Waffe *f*

wear [weəʳ] (*pt* **wore**, *pp* **worn**) *n* (*clothing*): **sports/baby ~** Sport-/Babykleidung *f*; (*use*) Verschleiß *m* ♦ *vt* (*have on*) tragen; (*smile etc*) haben; (*use*) abnutzen ♦ *vi* (*last*) halten; (*become old*) (sich) verschleißen; **evening ~** Abendkleidung *f*; **~ and tear** Verschleiß *m*; **~ away** *vt* verbrauchen ♦ *vi* schwinden; **~ down** *vt* (*people*) zermürben; **~ off** *vi* sich verlieren; **~ out** *vt* verschleißen; (*person*) erschöpfen

weary ['wɪərɪ] *adj* müde ♦ *vt* ermüden ♦ *vi* überdrüssig werden

weasel ['wiːzl] *n* Wiesel *nt*

weather ['weðəʳ] *n* Wetter *nt* ♦ *vt* verwittern lassen; (*resist*) überstehen; **under the ~** (*fig: ill*) angeschlagen (*inf*); **~-beaten** *adj* verwittert; **~cock** *n* Wetterhahn *m*; **~ forecast** *n* Wettervorhersage *f*; **~ vane** *n* Wetterfahne *f*

weave [wiːv] (*pt* **wove**, *pp* **woven**) *vt* weben; **~r** *n* Weber(in) *m(f)*; **weaving** *n* (*craft*) Webkunst *f*

web [web] *n* Netz *nt*; (*membrane*) Schwimmhaut *f*; **~ site** *n* (*COMPUT*) Website *f*, Webseite *f*

wed [wed] (*pt*, *pp* **wedded**) *vt* heiraten ♦ *n*: **the newly-~s** *npl* die Frischvermählten *pl*

we'd [wiːd] = **we had**; **we would**

wedding ['wedɪŋ] *n* Hochzeit *f*; **silver/golden ~ anniversary** Silberhochzeit *f*/goldene Hochzeit *f*; **~ day** *n* Hochzeitstag *m*; **~ dress** *n* Hochzeitskleid *nt*; **~ present** *n* Hochzeitsgeschenk *nt*; **~ ring** *n* Trauring *m*, Ehering *m*

wedge [wedʒ] *n* Keil *m*; (*of cheese etc*) Stück *nt* ♦ *vt* (*fasten*) festklemmen; (*pack tightly*)

einkeilen

Wednesday ['wednzdɪ] *n* Mittwoch *m*

wee [wiː] (*SCOTTISH*) *adj* klein, winzig

weed [wiːd] *n* Unkraut *nt* ♦ *vt* jäten; **~killer** *n* Unkrautvertilgungsmittel *nt*

weedy ['wiːdɪ] *adj* (*person*) schmächtig

week [wiːk] *n* Woche *f*; **a ~ today/on Friday** heute/Freitag in einer Woche; **~day** *n* Wochentag *m*; **~end** *n* Wochenende *nt*; **~ly** *adj* wöchentlich; (*wages, magazine*) Wochen- ♦ *adv* wöchentlich

weep [wiːp] (*pt*, *pp* **wept**) *vi* weinen; **~ing willow** *n* Trauerweide *f*

weigh [weɪ] *vt*, *vi* wiegen; **to ~ anchor** den Anker lichten; **~ down** *vt* niederdrücken; **~ up** *vt* abschätzen

weight [weɪt] *n* Gewicht *nt*; **to lose/put on ~** abnehmen/zunehmen; **~ing** *n* (*allowance*) Zulage *f*; **~lifter** *n* Gewichtheber *m*; **~lifting** *n* Gewichtheben *nt*; **~y** *adj* (*heavy*) gewichtig; (*important*) schwerwiegend, schwer wiegend

weir [wɪəʳ] *n* (Stau)wehr *nt*

weird [wɪəd] *adj* seltsam

welcome ['welkəm] *n* Willkommen *nt*, Empfang *m* ♦ *vt* begrüßen; **thank you - you're ~!** danke - nichts zu danken

welder ['weldəʳ] *n* (*person*) Schweißer(in) *m(f)*

welding ['weldɪŋ] *n* Schweißen *nt*

welfare ['welfeəʳ] *n* Wohl *nt*; (*social*) Fürsorge *f*; **~ state** *n* Wohlfahrtsstaat *m*; **~ work** *n* Fürsorge *f*

well [wel] *n* Brunnen *m*; (*oil* ~) Quelle *f* ♦ *adj* (*in good health*) gesund ♦ *adv* gut ♦ *excl* nun!, na schön!; **I'm ~** es geht mir gut; **get ~ soon!** gute Besserung!; **as ~** auch; **as ~ as** sowohl als auch; **~ done!** gut gemacht!; **to do ~** (*person*) gut zurechtkommen; (*business*) gut gehen; **~ up** *vi* emporsteigen; (*fig*) aufsteigen

we'll [wiːl] = **we will**; **we shall**

well: ~-behaved ['welbɪ'heɪvd] *adj* wohlerzogen; **~-being** ['wel'biːɪŋ] *n* Wohl *nt*; **~-built** ['wel'bɪlt] *adj* kräftig gebaut; **~-deserved** ['weldɪ'zɜːvd] *adj* wohlverdient; **~-dressed** ['wel'dres] *adj* gut gekleidet;

~-heeled ['wɛl'hi:ld] (inf) adj (wealthy) gut gepolstert
wellingtons ['welɪŋtənz] npl (also: **wellington boots**) Gummistiefel pl
well: **~-known** ['wɛl'nəun] adj bekannt; **~-mannered** ['wɛl'mænəd] adj wohlerzogen; **~-meaning** ['wɛl'mi:nɪŋ] adj (person) wohlmeinend; (action) gut gemeint; **~-off** ['wɛl'ɔf] adj gut situiert; **~-read** ['wɛl'rɛd] adj (sehr) belesen; **~-to-do** ['wɛltə'du:] adj wohlhabend; **~-wisher** ['welwɪʃər] n Gönner m
Welsh [wɛlʃ] adj walisisch ♦ n (LING) Walisisch nt; **the ~** npl (people) die Waliser pl; **~man/woman** (irreg) n Waliser(in) m(f)
went [wɛnt] pt of **go**
wept [wɛpt] pt, pp of **weep**
were [wɜ:r] pt pl of **be**
we're [wɪər] = **we are**
weren't [wɜ:nt] = **were not**
west [wɛst] n Westen m ♦ adj West-, westlich ♦ adv westwärts, nach Westen; **the W~** der Westen; **W~ Country** (BRIT) n: **the W~ Country** der Südwesten Englands; **~erly** adj westlich; **~ern** adj westlich, West- ♦ n (CINE) Western m; **W~ Indian** adj westindisch ♦ n Westindier(in) m(f); **W~ Indies** npl Westindische Inseln pl; **~ward(s)** adv westwärts
wet [wɛt] adj nass; **to get ~** nass werden; **"~ paint"** „frisch gestrichen"; **~ blanket** n (fig) Triefel m; **~ suit** n Taucheranzug m
we've [wi:v] = **we have**
whack [wæk] n Schlag m ♦ vt schlagen
whale [weɪl] n Wal m
wharf [wɔ:f] n Kai m
wharves [wɔ:vz] npl of **wharf**

KEYWORD

what [wɔt] adj 1 (in questions) welche(r, s), was für ein(e); **what size is it?** welche Größe ist das?
2 (in exclamations) was für ein(e); **what a mess!** was für ein Durcheinander!
♦ pron (interrogative/relative) was; **what are you doing?** was machst du gerade?; **what are you talking about?** wovon reden Sie?;

what is it called? wie heißt das?; **what about ...?** wie wärs mit ...?; **I saw what you did** ich habe gesehen, was du gemacht hast
♦ excl (disbelieving) wie, was; **what, no coffee!** wie, kein Kaffee?; **I've crashed the car - what!** ich hatte einen Autounfall - was!

whatever [wɔt'ɛvər] adj: **~ book** welches Buch auch immer ♦ pron: **do ~ is necessary** tu, was (immer auch) nötig ist; **~ happens** egal, was passiert; **nothing ~** überhaupt or absolut gar nichts; **do ~ you want** tu, was (immer) du (auch) möchtest; **no reason ~** or **whatsoever** überhaupt or absolut kein Grund
whatsoever [wɔtsəu'ɛvər] adj see **whatever**
wheat [wi:t] n Weizen m
wheedle ['wi:dl] vt: **to ~ sb into doing sth** jdn dazu überreden, etw zu tun; **to ~ sth out of sb** jdm etw abluchsen
wheel [wi:l] n Rad nt; (steering ~) Lenkrad nt; (disc) Scheibe f ♦ vt schieben; **~barrow** n Schubkarren m; **~chair** n Rollstuhl m; **~ clamp** n (AUT) Parkkralle f
wheeze [wi:z] vi keuchen

KEYWORD

when [wɛn] adv wann
♦ conj 1 (at, during, after the time that) wenn; (in past) als; **she was reading when I came in** sie las, als ich hereinkam; **be careful when you cross the road** seien Sie vorsichtig, wenn Sie über die Straße gehen
2 (on, at which) als; **on the day when I met him** an dem Tag, an dem ich ihn traf
3 (whereas) wo ... doch

whenever [wɛn'ɛvər] adv wann (auch) immer; (every time that) jedes Mal wenn ♦ conj (any time when)
where [wɛər] adv (place) wo; (direction) wohin; **~ from** woher; **this is ~ ...** hier ...; **~abouts** ['wɛərəbauts] adv wo ♦ n Aufenthaltsort m; **nobody knows his ~abouts** niemand weiß, wo er ist; **~as**

[wεər'æz] *conj* während, wo ... doch; **~by** *pron* woran, wodurch, womit, wovon; **~upon** *conj* worauf, wonach; (*at beginning of sentence*) daraufhin; **~ver** [wεər'εvər] *adv* wo (immer)

wherewithal ['wεəwiðɔːl] *n* nötige (Geld)mittel *pl*

whet [wεt] *vt* (*appetite*) anregen

whether ['wεðər] *conj* ob; **I don't know ~ to accept or not** ich weiß nicht, ob ich es annehmen soll oder nicht; **~ you go or not** ob du gehst oder nicht; **it's doubtful/ unclear ~ ...** es ist zweifelhaft/nicht klar, ob ...

KEYWORD
---

which [witʃ] *adj* **1** (*interrogative: direct, indirect*) welche(r, s); **which one?** welche(r, s)?

2: in which case in diesem Fall; **by which time** zu dieser Zeit

♦ *pron* **1** (*interrogative*) welche(r, s); (*of people also*) wer

2 (*relative*) der/die/das; (*referring to people*) was; **the apple which you ate/which is on the table** der Apfel, den du gegessen hast/der auf dem Tisch liegt; **he said he saw her, which is true** er sagte, er habe sie gesehen, was auch stimmt

---

whichever [witʃ'εvər] *adj* welche(r, s) auch immer; (*no matter which*) ganz gleich welche(r, s); **~ book you take** welches Buch du auch nimmst; **~ car you prefer** egal welches Auto du vorziehst

whiff [wif] *n* Hauch *m*

while [wail] *n* Weile *f* ♦ *conj* während; **for a ~** eine Zeit lang; **~ away** *vt* (*time*) sich *dat* vertreiben

whim [wim] *n* Laune *f*

whimper ['wimpər] *n* Wimmern *nt* ♦ *vi* wimmern

whimsical ['wimzikəl] *adj* launisch

whine [wain] *n* Gewinsel *nt*, Gejammer *nt* ♦ *vi* heulen, winseln

whip [wip] *n* Peitsche *f*; (POL) Fraktionsführer *m* ♦ *vt* (*beat*) peitschen; (*snatch*) reißen;

~ped cream *n* Schlagsahne *f*

whip-round ['wipraund] (BRIT: inf) *n* Geldsammlung *f*

whirl [wəːl] *n* Wirbel *m* ♦ *vt, vi* (herum)wirbeln; **~pool** *n* Wirbel *m*; **~wind** *n* Wirbelwind *m*

whirr [wəːr] *vi* schwirren, surren

whisk [wisk] *n* Schneebesen *m* ♦ *vt* (*cream etc*) schlagen; **to ~ sb away** *or* **off** mit jdm davon sausen

whisker ['wiskər] *n:* **~s** (*of animal*) Barthaare *pl*; (*of man*) Backenbart *m*

whisky ['wiski] (*US, IRISH* **whiskey**) *n* Whisky *m*

whisper ['wispər] *n* Flüstern *nt* ♦ *vt, vi* flüstern

whistle ['wisl] *n* Pfiff *m*; (*instrument*) Pfeife *f* ♦ *vt, vi* pfeifen

white [wait] *n* Weiß *nt*; (*of egg*) Eiweiß *nt* ♦ *adj* weiß; **~ coffee** (BRIT) *n* Kaffee *m* mit Milch; **~-collar worker** *n* Angestellte(r) *m*; **~ elephant** *n* (fig) Fehlinvestition *f*; **~ lie** *n* Notlüge *f*; **~ paper** *n* (POL) Weißbuch *nt*; **~wash** *n* (*paint*) Tünche *f*; (fig) Ehrenrettung *f* ♦ *vt* weißen, tünchen; (fig) rein waschen

whiting ['waitiŋ] *n* Weißfisch *m*

Whitsun ['witsn] *n* Pfingsten *nt*

whittle ['witl] *vt:* **to ~ away** *or* **down** stutzen, verringern

whizz [wiz] *vi:* **to ~ past** *or* **by** vorbeizischen, vorbeischwirren; **~ kid** (inf) *n* Kanone *f*

KEYWORD
---

who [huː] *pron* **1** (*interrogative*) wer; (*acc*) wen; (*dat*) wem; **who is it?, who's there?** wer ist da?

2 (*relative*) der/die/das; **the woman/man who spoke to me** die Frau/der Mann, die/ der mit mir sprach

---

whodu(n)nit [huː'dʌnit] (inf) *n* Krimi *m*

whoever [huː'εvər] *pron* wer/wen/wem auch immer; (*no matter who*) ganz gleich wer/ wen/wem

whole [həul] *adj* ganz ♦ *n* Ganze(s) *nt*; **the ~ of the town** die ganze Stadt; **on the ~** im

Großen und Ganzen; **as a ~** im Großen
und Ganzen; **~food(s)** ['hɔːlfuːd(z)] *n(pl)*
Vollwertkost *f*; **~hearted** [hɔːl'hɑːtɪd] *adj*
rückhaltlos; **~heartedly** *adv* von ganzem
Herzen; **~meal** *adj* (*bread, flour*) Vollkorn-;
~sale *n* Großhandel *m* ♦ *adj* (*trade*)
Großhandels-; (*destruction*) Massen-; **~saler**
n Großhändler *m*; **~some** *adj* bekömmlich,
gesund; **~wheat** *adj* = **wholemeal**
wholly ['hɔːlɪ] *adv* ganz, völlig

whom [huːm] *pron* **1** (*interrogative: acc*) wen;
(: *dat*) wem; **whom did you see?** wen
haben Sie gesehen?; **to whom did you
give it?** wem haben Sie es gegeben?
2 (*relative: acc*) den/die/das; (: *dat*) dem/
der/dem; **the man whom I saw/to whom
I spoke** der Mann, den ich sah/mit dem
ich sprach

whooping cough ['huːpɪŋ-] *n* Keuchhusten
m
whore [hɔːʳ] *n* Hure *f*
whose [huːz] *adj* (*possessive: interrogative*)
wessen; (: *relative*) dessen; (*after f and pl*)
deren ♦ *pron* wessen; **~ book is this?**, **~ is
this book?** wessen Buch ist dies?; **~ is
this?** wem gehört das?

why [waɪ] *adv* warum, weshalb
♦ *conj* warum, weshalb; **that's not why I'm
here** ich bin nicht deswegen hier; **that's
the reason why** deshalb
♦ *excl* (*expressing surprise, shock*) na so was;
(*explaining*) also dann; **why, it's you!** na so
was, du bist es!

wick [wɪk] *n* Docht *m*
wicked ['wɪkɪd] *adj* böse
wicker ['wɪkəʳ] *n* (*also:* **~work**) Korbgeflecht
nt
wicket ['wɪkɪt] *n* Tor *nt*, Dreistab *m*
wide [waɪd] *adj* breit; (*plain*) weit; (*in firing*)
daneben ♦ *adv*: **to open ~** weit öffnen; **to
shoot ~** danebenschießen; **~-angle lens** *n*

Weitwinkelobjektiv *nt*; **~-awake** *adj*
hellwach; **~ly** *adv* weit; (*known*) allgemein;
~n *vt* erweitern; **~ open** *adj* weit geöffnet;
~spread *adj* weitverbreitet, weit verbreitet
widow ['wɪdəu] *n* Witwe *f*; **~ed** *adj*
verwitwet; **~er** *n* Witwer *m*
width [wɪdθ] *n* Breite *f*, Weite *f*
wield [wiːld] *vt* schwingen, handhaben
wife [waɪf] (*pl* **wives**) *n* (Ehe)frau *f*, Gattin *f*
wig [wɪg] *n* Perücke *f*
wiggle ['wɪgl] *n* Wackeln *nt* ♦ *vt* wackeln mit
♦ *vi* wackeln
wild [waɪld] *adj* wild; (*violent*) heftig; (*plan,
idea*) verrückt; **~erness** ['wɪldənɪs] *n*
Wildnis *f*, Wüste *f*; **~-goose chase** *n* (*fig*)
fruchtlose(s) Unternehmen *nt*; **~life** *n*
Tierwelt *f*; **~ly** *adv* wild, ungestüm;
(*exaggerated*) irrsinnig; **~s** *npl*: **the ~s** die
Wildnis *f*
wilful ['wɪlful] (*US* **willful**) *adj* (*intended*)
vorsätzlich; (*obstinate*) eigensinnig

will [wɪl] *aux vb* **1** (*forms future tense*) werden;
I will finish it tomorrow ich mache es
morgen zu Ende
2 (*in conjectures, predictions*): **he will** *or* **he'll
be there by now** er dürfte jetzt da sein;
that will be the postman das wird der
Postbote sein
3 (*in commands, requests, offers*): **will you be
quiet!** sei endlich still!; **will you help me?**
hilfst du mir?; **will you have a cup of tea?**
trinken Sie eine Tasse Tee?; **I won't put up
with it!** das lasse ich mir nicht gefallen!
♦ *vt* wollen
♦ *n* Wille *m*; (*JUR*) Testament *nt*

willing ['wɪlɪŋ] *adj* gewillt, bereit; **~ly** *adv*
bereitwillig, gern; **~ness** *n* (Bereit)willigkeit
f
willow ['wɪləu] *n* Weide *f*
willpower ['wɪlpauəʳ] *n* Willenskraft *f*
willy-nilly ['wɪlɪ'nɪlɪ] *adv* einfach so
wilt [wɪlt] *vi* (ver)welken
wily ['waɪlɪ] *adj* gerissen
win [wɪn] (*pt, pp* **won**) *n* Sieg *m* ♦ *vt, vi*

gewinnen; **to ~ sb over** *or* **round** jdn gewinnen, jdn dazu bringen

wince [wɪns] *vi* zusammenzucken

winch [wɪntʃ] *n* Winde *f*

wind[1] [wɪnd] *n* Wind *m*; (*MED*) Blähungen *pl*

wind[2] [waɪnd] (*pt, pp* **wound**) *vt* (*rope*) winden; (*bandage*) wickeln ♦ *vi* (*turn*) sich winden; **~ up** *vt* (*clock*) aufziehen; (*debate*) (ab)schließen

windfall ['wɪndfɔːl] *n* unverhoffte(r) Glücksfall *m*

winding ['waɪndɪŋ] *adj* (*road*) gewunden

wind instrument ['wɪnd-] *n* Blasinstrument *nt*

windmill ['wɪndmɪl] *n* Windmühle *f*

window ['wɪndəu] *n* Fenster *nt*; **~ box** *n* Blumenkasten *m*; **~ cleaner** *n* Fensterputzer *m*; **~ envelope** *n* Fensterbriefumschlag *m*; **~ ledge** *n* Fenstersims *m*; **~ pane** *n* Fensterscheibe *f*; **~-shopping** *n* Schaufensterbummel *m*; **to go ~-shopping** einen Schaufensterbummel machen; **~sill** *n* Fensterbank *f*

wind: **~pipe** *n* Luftröhre *f*; **~ power** *n* Windenergie *f*; **~screen** (*BRIT*) *n* Windschutzscheibe *f*; **~screen washer** *n* Scheibenwaschanlage *f*; **~screen wiper** *n* Scheibenwischer *m*; **~shield** (*US*) *n* = **windscreen;** **~swept** *adj* vom Wind gepeitscht; (*person*) zerzaust; **~y** *adj* windig

wine [waɪn] *n* Wein *m*; **~ bar** *n* Weinlokal *nt*; **~ cellar** *n* Weinkeller *m*; **~glass** *n* Weinglas *nt*; **~ list** *n* Weinkarte *f*; **~ merchant** *n* Weinhändler *m*; **~ tasting** *n* Weinprobe *f*; **~ waiter** *n* Weinkellner *m*

wing [wɪŋ] *n* Flügel *m*; (*MIL*) Gruppe *f*; **~s** *npl* (*THEAT*) Seitenkulisse *f*; **~er** *n* (*SPORT*) Flügelstürmer *m*

wink [wɪŋk] *n* Zwinkern *nt* ♦ *vi* zwinkern, blinzeln

winner ['wɪnər] *n* Gewinner *m*; (*SPORT*) Sieger *m*

winning ['wɪnɪŋ] *adj* (*team*) siegreich, Sieger-; (*goal*) entscheidend; **~ post** *n* Ziel *nt*; **~s** *npl* Gewinn *m*

winter ['wɪntər] *n* Winter *m* ♦ *adj* (*clothes*) Winter- ♦ *vi* überwintern; **~ sports** *npl*

Wintersport *m*; **wintry** ['wɪntrɪ] *adj* Winter-, winterlich

wipe [waɪp] *n*: **to give sth a ~** etw (ab)wischen ♦ *vt* wischen; **~ off** *vt* abwischen; **~ out** *vt* (*debt*) löschen; (*destroy*) auslöschen; **~ up** *vt* aufwischen

wire ['waɪər] *n* Draht *m*; (*telegram*) Telegramm *nt* ♦ *vt* telegrafieren; **to ~ sb** jdm telegrafieren; **~less** ['waɪəlɪs] (*BRIT*) *n* Radio(apparat *m*) *nt*

wiring ['waɪərɪŋ] *n* elektrische Leitungen *pl*

wiry ['waɪərɪ] *adj* drahtig

wisdom ['wɪzdəm] *n* Weisheit *f*; (*of decision*) Klugheit *f*; **~ tooth** *n* Weisheitszahn *m*

wise [waɪz] *adj* klug, weise ♦ *suffix*: **timewise** zeitlich gesehen

wisecrack ['waɪzkræk] *n* Witzelei *f*

wish [wɪʃ] *n* Wunsch *m* ♦ *vt* wünschen; **best ~es** (*on birthday etc*) alles Gute; **with best ~es** herzliche Grüße; **to ~ sb goodbye** jdn verabschieden; **he ~ed me well** er wünschte mir Glück; **to ~ to do sth** etw tun wollen; **~ for** *vt fus* sich *dat* wünschen; **~ful thinking** *n* Wunschdenken *nt*

wishy-washy ['wɪʃɪ'wɒʃɪ] (*inf*) *adj* (*ideas, argument*) verschwommen

wisp [wɪsp] *n* (*Haar*)strähne *f*; (*of smoke*) Wölkchen *nt*

wistful ['wɪstful] *adj* sehnsüchtig

wit [wɪt] *n* (*also:* **~s**) Verstand *m no pl*; (*amusing ideas*) Witz *m*; (*person*) Witzbold *m*

witch [wɪtʃ] *n* Hexe *f*; **~craft** *n* Hexerei *f*

KEYWORD

with [wɪð, wɪθ] *prep* **1** (*accompanying, in the company of*) mit; **we stayed with friends** wir übernachteten bei Freunden; **I'll be with you in a minute** ich bin sofort da; **I'm not with you** (*I don't understand*) das verstehe ich nicht; **to be with it** (*inf: up-to-date*) auf dem Laufenden sein; (: *alert*) (voll) da sein (*inf*)
2 (*descriptive, indicating manner etc*) mit; **the man with the grey hat** der Mann mit dem grauen Hut; **red with anger** rot vor Wut

---

withdraw [wɪθ'drɔː] (*irreg: like* **draw**) *vt*

zurückziehen; (*money*) abheben; (*remark*) zurücknehmen ♦ *vi* sich zurückziehen; **~al** *n* Zurückziehung *f*; Abheben *nt*; Zurücknahme *f*; **~n** *adj* (*person*) verschlossen

wither ['wɪðə'] *vi* (ver)welken

withhold [wɪθ'həuld] (*irreg: like* hold) *vt*: **to ~ sth (from sb)** (jdm) etw vorenthalten

within [wɪð'ɪn] *prep* innerhalb +gen ♦ *adv* innen; **~ sight of** in Sichtweite von; **~ the week** innerhalb dieser Woche; **~ a mile of** weniger als eine Meile von

without [wɪð'aut] *prep* ohne; **~ sleeping** *etc* ohne zu schlafen *etc*

withstand [wɪθ'stænd] (*irreg: like* stand) *vt* widerstehen +dat

witness ['wɪtnɪs] *n* Zeuge *m*, Zeugin *f* ♦ *vt* (*see*) sehen, miterleben; (*document*) beglaubigen; **~ box** *n* Zeugenstand *m*; **~ stand** (*US*) *n* Zeugenstand *m*

witticism ['wɪtɪsɪzəm] *n* witzige Bemerkung *f*

witty ['wɪtɪ] *adj* witzig, geistreich

wives [waɪvz] *pl of* **wife**

wk *abbr* = **week**

wobble ['wɔbl] *vi* wackeln

woe [wəu] *n* Kummer *m*

woke [wəuk] *pt of* **wake**

woken ['wəukn] *pp of* **wake**

wolf [wulf] (*pl* **wolves**) *n* Wolf *m*

woman ['wumən] (*pl* **women**) *n* Frau *f*; **~ doctor** *n* Ärztin *f*; **~ly** *adj* weiblich

womb [wu:m] *n* Gebärmutter *f*

women ['wɪmɪn] *npl of* **woman**; **~'s lib** (*inf*) *n* Frauenrechtsbewegung *f*

won [wʌn] *pt, pp of* **win**

wonder ['wʌndə'] *n* (*marvel*) Wunder *nt*; (*surprise*) Staunen *nt*, Verwunderung *f* ♦ *vi* sich wundern ♦ *vt*: **I ~ whether ...** ich frage mich, ob ...; **it's no ~ that** es ist kein Wunder, dass; **to ~ at** sich wundern über +acc; **to ~ about** sich Gedanken machen über +acc; **~ful** *adj* wunderbar, herrlich

won't [wəunt] = **will not**

woo [wu:] *vt* (*audience etc*) umwerben

wood [wud] *n* Holz *nt*; (*forest*) Wald *m*; **~ carving** *n* Holzschnitzerei *f*; **~ed** *adj* bewaldet; **~en** *adj* (*also fig*) hölzern;

~pecker *n* Specht *m*; **~wind** *n* Blasinstrumente *pl*; **~work** *n* Holzwerk *nt*; (*craft*) Holzarbeiten *pl*; **~worm** *n* Holzwurm *m*

wool [wul] *n* Wolle *f*; **to pull the ~ over sb's eyes** (*fig*) jdm Sand in die Augen streuen; **~len** (*US* **woolen**) *adj* Woll-; **~lens** *npl* Wollsachen *pl*; **~ly** (*US* **wooly**) *adj* wollig; (*fig*) schwammig

word [wə:d] *n* Wort *nt*; (*news*) Bescheid *m* ♦ *vt* formulieren; **in other ~s** anders gesagt; **to break/keep one's ~** sein Wort brechen/halten; **~ing** *n* Wortlaut *m*; **~ processing** *n* Textverarbeitung *f*; **~ processor** *n* Textverarbeitung *f*

wore [wɔ:'] *pt of* **wear**

work [wə:k] *n* Arbeit *f*; (*ART, LITER*) Werk *nt* ♦ *vi* arbeiten; (*machine*) funktionieren; (*medicine*) wirken; (*succeed*) klappen; **~s** *n sg* (*BRIT: factory*) Fabrik *f*, Werk *nt* ♦ *npl* (*of watch*) Werk *nt*; **to be out of ~** arbeitslos sein; **in ~ing order** in betriebsfähigem Zustand; **~ loose** *vi* sich lockern; **~ on** *vi* weiterarbeiten ♦ *vt fus* arbeiten an +dat; (*influence*) bearbeiten; **~ out** *vi* (*sum*) aufgehen; (*plan*) klappen ♦ *vt* (*problem*) lösen; (*plan*) ausarbeiten; **it ~s out at £100** das gibt *or* macht £100; **~ up** *vt*: **to get ~ed up** sich aufregen; **~able** *adj* (*soil*) bearbeitbar; (*plan*) ausführbar; **~aholic** [wə:kə'hɔlɪk] *n* Arbeitssüchtige(r) *f(m)*; **~er** *n* Arbeiter(in) *m(f)*; **~ experience** *n* Praktikum *nt*; **~force** *n* Arbeiterschaft *f*; **~ing class** *n* Arbeiterklasse *f*; **~ing-class** *adj* Arbeiter-; **~man** (*irreg*) *n* Arbeiter *m*; **~manship** *n* Arbeit *f*, Ausführung *f*; **~sheet** *n* Arbeitsblatt *nt*; **~shop** *n* Werkstatt *f*; **~ station** *n* Arbeitsplatz *m*; **~-to-rule** (*BRIT*) *n* Dienst *m* nach Vorschrift

world [wə:ld] *n* Welt *f*; **to think the ~ of sb** große Stücke auf jdn halten; **~ly** *adj* weltlich, irdisch; **~-wide** *adj* weltweit

World-Wide Web ['wə:ld'waɪd-] *n* World Wide Web *nt*

worm [wə:m] *n* Wurm *m*

worn [wɔ:n] *pp of* **wear** ♦ *adj* (*clothes*) abgetragen; **~-out** *adj* (*object*) abgenutzt;

(*person*) völlig erschöpft

worried ['wʌrɪd] *adj* besorgt, beunruhigt

worry ['wʌrɪ] *n* Sorge *f* ♦ *vt* beunruhigen ♦ *vi* (*feel uneasy*) sich sorgen, sich *dat* Gedanken machen; **~ing** *adj* beunruhigend

worse [wəːs] *adj* schlechter, schlimmer ♦ *adv* schlimmer, ärger ♦ *n* Schlimmere(s) *nt*, Schlechtere(s) *nt*; **a change for the ~** eine Verschlechterung; **~n** *vt* verschlimmern ♦ *vi* sich verschlechtern; **~ off** *adj* (*fig*) schlechter dran

worship ['wəːʃɪp] *n* Verehrung *f* ♦ *vt* anbeten; **Your W~** (*BRIT: to mayor*) Herr/ Frau Bürgermeister; (: *to judge*) Euer Ehren

worst [wəːst] *adj* schlimmste(r, s), schlechteste(r, s) ♦ *adv* am schlimmsten, am ärgsten ♦ *n* Schlimmste(s) *nt*, Ärgste(s) *nt*; **at ~** schlimmstenfalls

worth [wəːθ] *n* Wert *m* ♦ *adj* wert; **it's ~ it** es lohnt sich; **to be ~ one's while (to do sth)** die Mühe wert sein(, etw zu tun); **~less** *adj* wertlos; (*person*) nichtsnutzig; **~while** *adj* lohnend, der Mühe wert; **~y** *adj* wert, würdig

―――――――――――――――――
| KEYWORD |
―――――――――――――――――

would [wʊd] *aux vb* **1** (*conditional tense*): **if you asked him he would do it** wenn du ihn fragtest, würde er es tun; **if you had asked him he would have done it** wenn du ihn gefragt hättest, hätte er es getan

2 (*in offers, invitations, requests*): **would you like a biscuit?** möchten Sie ein Plätzchen?; **would you ask him to come in?** würden Sie ihn bitte hineinbitten?

3 (*in indirect speech*): **I said I would do it** ich sagte, ich würde es tun

4 (*emphatic*): **it WOULD have to snow today!** es musste ja ausgerechnet heute schneien!

5 (*insistence*): **she wouldn't behave** sie wollte sich partout nicht anständig benehmen

6 (*conjecture*): **it would have been midnight** es mag ungefähr Mitternacht gewesen sein; **it would seem so** es sieht wohl so aus

7 (*indicating habit*): **he would go there on Mondays** er ging jeden Montag dorthin

―――――――――――――――――

would-be ['wʊdbiː] (*pej*) *adj* Möchtegern-

wouldn't ['wʊdnt] = **would not**

wound[1] [wuːnd] *n* (*also fig*) Wunde *f* ♦ *vt* verwunden, verletzen (*also fig*)

wound[2] [waʊnd] *pt, pp of* **wind**[2]

wove [wəʊv] *pt of* **weave**; **~n** *pp of* **weave**

wrangle ['ræŋgl] *n* Streit *m* ♦ *vi* sich zanken

wrap [ræp] *vt* einwickeln; **~ up** *vt* einwickeln; (*deal*) abschließen; **~per** *n* Umschlag *m*, Schutzhülle *f*; **~ping paper** *n* Einwickelpapier *nt*

wrath [rɔθ] *n* Zorn *m*

wreak [riːk] *vt* (*havoc*) anrichten; (*vengeance*) üben

wreath [riːθ] *n* Kranz *m*

wreck [rɛk] *n* (*ship*) Wrack *nt*; (*sth ruined*) Ruine *f* ♦ *vt* zerstören; **~age** *n* Trümmer *pl*

wren [rɛn] *n* Zaunkönig *m*

wrench [rɛntʃ] *n* (*spanner*) Schraubenschlüssel *m*; (*twist*) Ruck *m* ♦ *vt* reißen, zerren; **to ~ sth from sb** jdm etw entreißen *or* entwinden

wrestle ['rɛsl] *vi*: **to ~ (with sb)** (mit jdm) ringen; **~r** *n* Ringer(in) *m(f)*; **wrestling** *n* Ringen *nt*

wretched ['rɛtʃɪd] *adj* (*inf*) verflixt

wriggle ['rɪgl] *n* Schlängeln *nt* ♦ *vi* sich winden

wring [rɪŋ] (*pt, pp* **wrung**) *vt* wringen

wrinkle ['rɪŋkl] *n* Falte *f*, Runzel *f* ♦ *vt* runzeln ♦ *vi* sich runzeln; (*material*) knittern; **~d** *adj* faltig, schrumpelig

wrist [rɪst] *n* Handgelenk *nt*; **~watch** *n* Armbanduhr *f*

writ [rɪt] *n* gerichtliche(r) Befehl *m*

write [raɪt] (*pt* **wrote**, *pp* **written**) *vt, vi* schreiben; **~ down** *vt* aufschreiben; **~ off** *vt* (*dismiss*) abschreiben; **~ out** *vt* (*essay*) abschreiben; (*cheque*) ausstellen; **~ up** *vt* schreiben; **~-off** *n*: **it is a ~-off** das kann man abschreiben; **~r** *n* Schriftsteller *m*

writhe [raɪð] *vi* sich winden

writing ['raɪtɪŋ] *n* (*act*) Schreiben *nt*; (*handwriting*) (Hand)schrift *f*; **in ~** schriftlich;

~ **paper** n Schreibpapier nt

written ['rɪtn] pp of **write**

wrong [rɒŋ] adj (incorrect) falsch; (morally) unrecht ♦ n Unrecht nt ♦ vt Unrecht tun +dat; **he was ~ in doing that** es war nicht recht von ihm, das zu tun; **you are ~ about that, you've got it ~** da hast du Unrecht; **to be in the ~** im Unrecht sein; **what's ~ with your leg?** was ist mit deinem Bein los?; **to go ~** (plan) schief gehen; (person) einen Fehler machen; ~**ful** adj unrechtmäßig; ~**ly** adv falsch; (accuse) zu Unrecht

wrong number n (TEL): **you've got the ~** Sie sind falsch verbunden

wrote [rəʊt] pt of **write**

wrought [rɔːt] adj: ~ **iron** Schmiedeeisen nt

wrung [rʌŋ] pt, pp of **wring**

wry [raɪ] adj ironisch

wt. abbr = **weight**

X, x

Xmas ['ɛksməs] n abbr = **Christmas**

X-ray ['ɛksreɪ] n Röntgenaufnahme f ♦ vt röntgen; ~~~**s** npl Röntgenstrahlen pl

xylophone ['zaɪləfəʊn] n Xylofon nt, Xylophon nt

Y, y

yacht [jɒt] n Jacht f; ~**ing** n (Sport)segeln nt; ~**sman** (irreg) n Sportsegler m

Yank [jæŋk] (inf) n Ami m

yap [jæp] vi (dog) kläffen

yard [jɑːd] n Hof m; (measure) (englische) Elle f, Yard nt (0,91 m); ~**stick** n (fig) Maßstab m

yarn [jɑːn] n (thread) Garn nt; (story) (Seemanns)garn nt

yawn [jɔːn] n Gähnen nt ♦ vi gähnen; ~**ing** adj (gap) gähnend

yd. abbr = **yard(s)**

yeah [jɛə] (inf) adv ja

year [jɪəʳ] n Jahr nt; **to be 8 ~s old** acht Jahre alt sein; **an eight-year-old child** ein achtjähriges Kind; ~**ly** adj, adv jährlich

yearn [jɜːn] vi: **to ~ (for)** sich sehnen (nach); ~**ing** n Verlangen nt, Sehnsucht f

yeast [jiːst] n Hefe f

yell [jɛl] n gellende(r) Schrei m ♦ vi laut schreien

yellow ['jɛləʊ] adj gelb ♦ n Gelb nt

yelp [jɛlp] n Gekläff nt ♦ vi kläffen

yes [jɛs] adv ja ♦ n Ja nt, Jawort nt; **to say ~** Ja or ja sagen; **to answer ~** mit Ja antworten

yesterday ['jɛstədɪ] adv gestern ♦ n Gestern nt; ~ **morning/evening** gestern Morgen/Abend; **all day ~** gestern den ganzen Tag; **the day before ~** vorgestern

yet [jɛt] adv noch; (in question) schon; (up to now) bis jetzt ♦ conj doch, dennoch; **it is not finished ~** es ist noch nicht fertig; **the best ~** das bisher Beste; **as ~** bis jetzt; (in past) bis dahin

yew [juː] n Eibe f

yield [jiːld] n Ertrag m ♦ vt (result, crop) hervorbringen; (interest, profit) abwerfen; (concede) abtreten ♦ vi nachgeben; (MIL) sich ergeben; "~" (US: AUT) „Vorfahrt gewähren"

YMCA n abbr (= Young Men's Christian Association) CVJM m

yob [jɒb] (BRIT: inf) n Halbstarke(r) f(m), Rowdy m

yoga ['jəʊgə] n Joga m

yoghourt ['jəʊgət] n Jog(h)urt m

yog(h)urt ['jəʊgət] n = **yoghourt**

yoke [jəʊk] n (also fig) Joch nt

yolk [jəʊk] n Eidotter m, Eigelb nt

KEYWORD

you [juː] pron 1 (subj, in comparisons: familiar form: sg) du; (: pl) ihr; (in letters also) du, ihr; (: polite form) Sie; **you Germans** ihr Deutschen; **she's younger than you** sie ist jünger als du/Sie

2 (direct object, after prep +acc: familiar form: sg) dich; (: pl) euch; (in letters also) dich, euch; (: polite form) Sie; **I know you** ich kenne dich/euch/Sie

3 (*indirect object, after prep +dat: familiar form: sg*) dir; (: *pl*) euch; (*in letters also*) dir, euch; (: *polite form*) Ihnen; **I gave it to you** ich gab es dir/euch/Ihnen
4 (*impers: one: subj*) man; (: *direct object*) einen; (: *indirect object*) einem; **fresh air does you good** frische Luft tut gut

you'd [juːd] = **you had; you would**
you'll [juːl] = **you will; you shall**
young [jʌŋ] *adj* jung ♦ *npl*: **the ~** die Jungen *pl*; **~ster** *n* Junge *m*, junge(r) Bursche *m*, junge(s) Mädchen *nt*
your [jɔːʳ] *adj* (*familiar: sg*) dein; (: *pl*) euer, eure *pl*; (*polite*) Ihr; *see also* **my**
you're [juəʳ] = **you are**
yours [jɔːz] *pron* (*familiar: sg*) deine(r, s); (: *pl*) eure(r, s); (*polite*) Ihre(r, s); *see also* **mine**[2]
yourself [jɔːˈsɛlf] *pron* (*emphatic*) selbst; (*familiar: sg: acc*) dich (selbst); (: *dat*) dir (selbst); (: *pl*) euch (selbst); (*polite*) sich (selbst); *see also* **oneself**; **yourselves** *pl pron* (*reflexive: familiar*) euch; (: *polite*) sich; (*emphatic*) selbst; *see also* **oneself**
youth [juːθ] *n* Jugend *f*; (*young man*) junge(r) Mann *m*; **~s** *npl* (*young people*) Jugendliche *pl*; **~ club** *n* Jugendzentrum *nt*; **~ful** *adj* jugendlich; **~ hostel** *n* Jugendherberge *f*
you've [juːv] = **you have**
YTS (*BRIT*) *n abbr* (= *Youth Training Scheme*) staatliches Förderprogramm für arbeitslose Jugendliche
Yugoslav [ˈjuːɡəʊslɑːv] *adj* jugoslawisch ♦ *n* Jugoslawe *m*, Jugoslawin *f*; **~ia**

[juːɡəʊˈslɑːvɪə] *n* Jugoslawien *nt*
yuppie [ˈjʌpɪ] (*inf*) *n* Yuppie *m* ♦ *adj* yuppiehaft, Yuppie-
YWCA *n abbr* (= *Young Women's Christian Association*) CVJF *m*

Z, z

zany [ˈzeɪnɪ] *adj* (*ideas, sense of humour*) verrückt
zap [zæp] *vt* (*COMPUT*) löschen
zeal [ziːl] *n* Eifer *m*; **~ous** [ˈzɛləs] *adj* eifrig
zebra [ˈziːbrə] *n* Zebra *nt*; **~ crossing** (*BRIT*) *n* Zebrastreifen *m*
zero [ˈzɪərəʊ] *n* Null *f*; (*on scale*) Nullpunkt *m*
zest [zɛst] *n* Begeisterung *f*
zigzag [ˈzɪɡzæɡ] *n* Zickzack *m*
Zimbabwe [zɪmˈbɑːbwɪ] *n* Zimbabwe *nt*
Zimmer frame [ˈzɪmə-] *n* Laufgestell *nt*
zip [zɪp] *n* Reißverschluss *m* ♦ *vt* (*also*: **~ up**) den Reißverschluss zumachen +*gen*
zip code (*US*) *n* Postleitzahl *f*
zipper [ˈzɪpəʳ] (*US*) *n* Reißverschluss *m*
zit [zɪt] (*inf*) *n* Pickel *m*
zodiac [ˈzəʊdɪæk] *n* Tierkreis *m*
zombie [ˈzɒmbɪ] *n*: **like a ~** (*fig*) wie im Tran
zone [zəʊn] *n* (*also MIL*) Zone *f*, Gebiet *nt*; (*in town*) Bezirk *m*
zoo [zuː] *n* Zoo *m*
zoology [zuːˈɒlədʒɪ] *n* Zoologie *f*
zoom [zuːm] *vi*: **to ~ past** vorbeisausen; **~ lens** *n* Zoomobjektiv *nt*
zucchini [zuːˈkiːnɪ] (*US*) *npl* Zucchini *pl*

GERMAN IRREGULAR VERBS

*with 'sein'

infinitive	present indicative (2nd, 3rd sg)	imperfect	past participle
aufschrecken*	schrickst auf, schrickt auf	schrak *or* schreckte auf	aufgeschreckt
ausbedingen	bedingst aus, bedingt aus	bedang *or* bedingte aus	ausbedungen
backen	bäckst, bäckt	backte *or* buk	gebacken
befehlen	befiehlst, befiehlt	befahl	befohlen
beginnen	beginnst, beginnt	begann	begonnen
beißen	beißt, beißt	biss	gebissen
bergen	birgst, birgt	barg	geborgen
bersten*	birst, birst	barst	geborsten
bescheißen*	bescheißt, bescheißt	beschiss	beschissen
bewegen	bewegst, bewegt	bewog	bewogen
biegen	biegst, biegt	bog	gebogen
bieten	bietest, bietet	bot	geboten
binden	bindest, bindet	band	gebunden
bitten	bittest, bittet	bat	gebeten
blasen	bläst, bläst	blies	geblasen
bleiben*	bleibst, bleibt	blieb	geblieben
braten	brätst, brät	briet	gebraten
brechen*	brichst, bricht	brach	gebrochen
brennen	brennst, brennt	brannte	gebrannt
bringen	bringst, bringt	brachte	gebracht
denken	denkst, denkt	dachte	gedacht
dreschen	drisch(e)st, drischt	drosch	gedroschen
dringen*	dringst, dringt	drang	gedrungen
dürfen	darfst, darf	durfte	gedurft
empfehlen	empfiehlst, empfiehlt	empfahl	empfohlen
erbleichen*	erbleichst, erbleicht	erbleichte	erblichen
erlöschen*	erlischt, erlischt	erlosch	erloschen
erschrecken*	erschrickst, erschrickt	erschrak	erschrocken
essen	isst, isst	aß	gegessen
fahren*	fährst, fährt	fuhr	gefahren
fallen*	fällst, fällt	fiel	gefallen

infinitive	present indicative (2nd, 3rd sg)	imperfect	past participle
fangen	fängst, fängt	fing	gefangen
fechten	fichtst, ficht	focht	gefochten
finden	findest, findet	fand	gefunden
flechten	flichtst, flicht	flocht	geflochten
fliegen*	fliegst, fliegt	flog	geflogen
fliehen*	fliehst, flieht	floh	geflohen
fließen*	fließt, fließt	floss	geflossen
fressen	frisst, frisst	fraß	gefressen
frieren	frierst, friert	fror	gefroren
gären*	gärst, gärt	gor	gegoren
gebären	gebierst, gebiert	gebar	geboren
geben	gibst, gibt	gab	gegeben
gedeihen*	gedeihst, gedeiht	gedieh	gediehen
gehen*	gehst, geht	ging	gegangen
gelingen*	——, gelingt	gelang	gelungen
gelten	giltst, gilt	galt	gegolten
genesen*	gene(se)st, genest	genas	genesen
genießen	genießt, genießt	genoss	genossen
geraten*	gerätst, gerät	geriet	geraten
geschehen*	——, geschieht	geschah	geschehen
gewinnen	gewinnst, gewinnt	gewann	gewonnen
gießen	gießt, gießt	goss	gegossen
gleichen	gleichst, gleicht	glich	geglichen
gleiten*	gleitest, gleitet	glitt	geglitten
glimmen	glimmst, glimmt	glomm	geglommen
graben	gräbst, gräbt	grub	gegraben
greifen	greifst, greift	griff	gegriffen
haben	hast, hat	hatte	gehabt
halten	hältst, hält	hielt	gehalten
hängen	hängst, hängt	hing	gehangen
hauen	haust, haut	haute	gehauen
heben	hebst, hebt	hob	gehoben
heißen	heißt, heißt	hieß	geheißen
helfen	hilfst, hilft	half	geholfen
kennen	kennst, kennt	kannte	gekannt
klimmen*	klimmst, klimmt	klomm	geklommen
klingen	klingst, klingt	klang	geklungen
kneifen	kneifst, kneift	kniff	gekniffen
kommen*	kommst, kommt	kam	gekommen
können	kannst, kann	konnte	gekonnt
kriechen*	kriechst, kriecht	kroch	gekrochen
laden	lädst, lädt	lud	geladen
lassen	lässt, lässt	ließ	gelassen
laufen*	läufst, läuft	lief	gelaufen
leiden	leidest, leidet	litt	gelitten

infinitive	present indicative (2nd, 3rd sg)	imperfect	past participle
leihen	leihst, leiht	lieh	geliehen
lesen	liest, liest	las	gelesen
liegen*	liegst, liegt	lag	gelegen
lügen	lügst, lügt	log	gelogen
mahlen	mahlst, mahlt	mahlte	gemahlen
meiden	meidest, meidet	mied	gemieden
melken	melkst, melkt	melkte	gemolken
messen	misst, misst	maß	gemessen
misslingen*	——, misslingt	misslang	misslungen
mögen	magst, mag	mochte	gemocht
müssen	musst, muss	musste	gemusst
nehmen	nimmst, nimmt	nahm	genommen
nennen	nennst, nennt	nannte	genannt
pfeifen	pfeifst, pfeift	pfiff	gepfiffen
preisen	preist, preist	pries	gepriesen
quellen*	quillst, quillt	quoll	gequollen
raten	rätst, rät	riet	geraten
reiben	reibst, reibt	rieb	gerieben
reißen*	reißt, reißt	riss	gerissen
reiten*	reitest, reitet	ritt	geritten
rennen*	rennst, rennt	rannte	gerannt
riechen	riechst, riecht	roch	gerochen
ringen	ringst, ringt	rang	gerungen
rinnen*	rinnst, rinnt	rann	geronnen
rufen	rufst, ruft	rief	gerufen
salzen	salzt, salzt	salzte	gesalzen
saufen	säufst, säuft	soff	gesoffen
saugen	saugst, saugt	sog	gesogen
schaffen	schaffst, schafft	schuf	geschaffen
scheiden	scheidest, scheidet	schied	geschieden
scheinen	scheinst, scheint	schien	geschienen
schelten	schiltst, schilt	schalt	gescholten
scheren	scherst, schert	schor	geschoren
schieben	schiebst, schiebt	schob	geschoben
schießen	schießt, schießt	schoss	geschossen
schinden	schindest, schindet	schindete	geschunden
schlafen	schläfst, schläft	schlief	geschlafen
schlagen	schlägst, schlägt	schlug	geschlagen
schleichen*	schleichst, schleicht	schlich	geschlichen
schleifen	schleifst, schleift	schliff	geschliffen
schließen	schließt, schließt	schloss	geschlossen
schlingen	schlingst, schlingt	schlang	geschlungen

infinitive	present indicative (2nd, 3rd sg)	imperfect	past participle
schmeißen	schmeißt, schmeißt	schmiss	geschmissen
schmelzen*	schmilzt, schmilzt	schmolz	geschmolzen
schneiden	schneidest, schneidet	schnitt	geschnitten
schreiben	schreibst, schreibt	schrieb	geschrieben
schreien	schreist, schreit	schrie	geschrie(e)n
schreiten	schreitest, schreitet	schritt	geschritten
schweigen	schweigst, schweigt	schwieg	geschwiegen
schwellen*	schwillst, schwillt	schwoll	geschwollen
schwimmen*	schwimmst, schwimmt	schwamm	geschwommen
schwinden*	schwindest, schwindet	schwand	geschwunden
schwingen	schwingst, schwingt	schwang	geschwungen
schwören	schwörst, schwört	schwor	geschworen
sehen	siehst, sieht	sah	gesehen
sein*	bist, ist	war	gewesen
senden	sendest, sendet	sandte	gesandt
singen	singst, singt	sang	gesungen
sinken*	sinkst, sinkt	sank	gesunken
sinnen	sinnst, sinnt	sann	gesonnen
sitzen*	sitzt, sitzt	saß	gesessen
sollen	sollst, soll	sollte	gesollt
speien	speist, speit	spie	gespie(e)n
spinnen	spinnst, spinnt	spann	gesponnen
sprechen	sprichst, spricht	sprach	gesprochen
sprießen*	sprießt, sprießt	spross	gesprossen
springen*	springst, springt	sprang	gesprungen
stechen	stichst, sticht	stach	gestochen
stecken	steckst, steckt	steckte or stak	gesteckt
stehen	stehst, steht	stand	gestanden
stehlen	stiehlst, stiehlt	stahl	gestohlen
steigen*	steigst, steigt	stieg	gestiegen
sterben*	stirbst, stirbt	starb	gestorben
stinken	stinkst, stinkt	stank	gestunken
stoßen	stößt, stößt	stieß	gestoßen
streichen	streichst, streicht	strich	gestrichen
streiten*	streitest, streitet	stritt	gestritten
tragen	trägst, trägt	trug	getragen
treffen	triffst, trifft	traf	getroffen
treiben*	treibst, treibt	trieb	getrieben

infinitive	present indicative (2nd, 3rd sg)	imperfect	past participle
treten*	trittst, tritt	trat	getreten
trinken	trinkst, trinkt	trank	getrunken
trügen	trügst, trügt	trog	getrogen
tun	tust, tut	tat	getan
verderben	verdirbst, verdirbt	verdarb	verdorben
verdrießen	verdrießt, verdrießt	verdross	verdrossen
vergessen	vergisst, vergisst	vergaß	vergessen
verlieren	verlierst, verliert	verlor	verloren
verschleißen	verschleißt, verschleißt	verschliss	verschlissen
wachsen*	wächst, wächst	wuchs	gewachsen
weben	webst, webt	webte *or* wob	gewoben
wägen	wägst, wägt	wog	gewogen
waschen	wäschst, wäscht	wusch	gewaschen
weichen*	weichst, weicht	wich	gewichen
weisen	weist, weist	wies	gewiesen
wenden	wendest, wendet	wandte	gewandt
werben	wirbst, wirbt	warb	geworben
werden*	wirst, wird	wurde	geworden
werfen	wirfst, wirft	warf	geworfen
wiegen	wiegst, wiegt	wog	gewogen
winden	windest, windet	wand	gewunden
wissen	weißt, weiß	wusste	gewusst
wollen	willst, will	wollte	gewollt
wringen	wringst, wringt	wrang	gewrungen
zeihen	zeihst, zeiht	zieh	geziehen
ziehen*	ziehst, zieht	zog	gezogen
zwingen	zwingst, zwingt	zwang	gezwungen

GERMAN SPELLING CHANGES

In July 1996, all German–speaking countries signed a declaration concerning the reform of German spelling, with the result that the new spelling rules are now taught in all schools. To ensure that you have the most up–to–date information at your fingertips, the following list contains the old and new spellings of all German headwords and translations in this dictionary which are affected by the reform.

ALT/OLD	NEU/NEW	ALT/OLD	NEU/NEW
abend	Abend	aufsein	auf sein
Abfluß	Abfluss	aufwendig	aufwendig
Abflußrohr	Abflussrohr		or aufwändig
Abschluß	Abschluss	auseinanderbrechen	auseinander brechen
Abschlußexamen	Abschlussexamen	auseinanderbringen	auseinander bringen
Abschlußfeier	Abschlussfeier	auseinanderfallen	auseinander fallen
Abschlußklasse	Abschlussklasse	auseinanderfalten	auseinander falten
Abschlußprüfung	Abschlussprüfung	auseinandergehen	auseinander gehen
Abschuß	Abschuss	auseinanderhalten	auseinander halten
Abschußrampe	Abschussrampe	auseinandernehmen	auseinander nehmen
Abszeß	Abszess	auseinandersetzen	auseinander setzen
achtgeben	Acht geben	Ausfluß	Ausfluss
Adreßbuch	Adressbuch	Außuß	Ausguss
Alleinerziehende(r)	Alleinerziehende(r)	Auslaß	Auslass
	or allein Erziehende(r)	Ausschluß	Ausschluss
alleinstehend	allein stehend	Ausschuß	Ausschuss
allgemeingültig	allgemein gültig	Ausschuß(artikel)	Ausschuss(artikel)
allzuoft	allzu oft	aussein	aus sein
allzuviel	allzu viel	außerstande	außer Stande
Alptraum	Alptraum	Autobiographie	Autobiographie
	or Albtraum		or Autobiografie
Amboß	Amboss	Baß	Bass
Amtsanschluß	Amtsanschluss	Baßstimme	Bassstimme
(Amts)mißbrauch	(Amts)missbrauch		or Bass–Stimme
andersdenkend	anders denkend	Ballettänzer(in)	Balletttänzer(in)
aneinandergeraten	aneinander geraten		or Ballett–Tänzer(in)
aneinanderreihen	aneinander reihen	beeinflußbar	beeinflussbar
Anlaß	Anlass	beiseitelegen	beiseite legen
anläßlich	anlässlich	bekanntgeben	bekannt geben
Anschluß	Anschluss	bekanntmachen	bekannt machen
Anschlußflug	Anschlussflug	Beschluß	Beschluss
As	Ass	Beschuß	Beschuss
aufeinanderfolgen	aufeinander folgen	bessergehen	besser gehen
aufeinanderfolgend	aufeinander folgend	Bettuch	Betttuch
aufeinanderlegen	aufeinander legen		or Bett–Tuch
aufeinanderprallen	aufeinander prallen	(Bevölkerungs)überschuß	
Aufschluß	Aufschluss		(Bevölkerungs)überschuss
aufschlußreich	aufschlussreich	bewußt	bewusst
aufsehenerregend	Aufsehen erregend	bewußtlos	bewusstlos

ALT/OLD	NEU/NEW	ALT/OLD	NEU/NEW
Bewußtlosigkeit	Bewusstlosigkeit	durchnumerieren	durchnummerieren
Bewußtsein	Bewusstsein	ehrfurchtgebietend	Ehrfurcht gebietend
bezug	Bezug	Einfluß	Einfluss
Bibliographie	Bibliographie	Einflußbereich	Einflussbereich
	or Bibliografie	einflußreich	einflussreich
Biographie	Biographie	einigemal	einige Mal
	or Biografie	einiggehen	einig gehen
Biß	Biss	Einlaß	Einlass
biß	biss	ekelerregend	Ekel erregend
bißchen	bisschen	Elsaß	Elsass
blaß	blass	Engpaß	Engpass
bläßlich	blässlich	Entschluß	Entschluss
bleibenlassen	bleiben lassen	entschlußfreudig	entschlussfreudig
Bluterguß	Bluterguss	Entschlußkraft	Entschlusskraft
Boß	Boss	epochemachend	Epoche machend
braungebrannt	braun gebrannt	Erdgeschoß	Erdgeschoss
breitmachen	breit machen	Erdnuß	Erdnuss
Brennessel	Brennnessel	Erdnußbutter	Erdnussbutter
	or Brenn-Nessel	erfolgversprechend	Erfolg versprechend
Büroschluß	Büroschluss	Erguß	Erguss
Butterfaß	Butterfass	Erlaß	Erlass
Cashewnuß	Cashewnuss	ernstgemeint	ernst gemeint
Chicorée	Chicorée	erstemal	erste Mal
	or Schikoree	Eß-	Ess-
Choreograph(in)	Choreograph(in)	erstenmal	ersten Mal
	or Choreograf(in)	eßbar	essbar
Computertomographie	Computertomographie	Eßbesteck	Essbesteck
	or Computertomografie	Eßecke	Essecke
dabeisein	dabei sein	Eßgeschirr	Essgeschirr
dafürkönnen	dafür können	Eßkastanie	Esskastanie
dahinterkommen	dahinter kommen	Eßlöffel	Esslöffel
darauffolgend	darauf folgend	Eßlöffel(voll)	Esslöffel (voll)
dasein	da sein	(Eß)stäbchen	(Ess)stäbchen
daß	dass		or (Ess-)Stäbchen
Dekolleté	Dekolleté	Eßtisch	Esstisch
	or Dekolletee	Eßwaren	Esswaren
Delphin	Delphin	Eßzimmer	Esszimmer
	or Delfin	Expreß	Express
dessenungeachtet	dessen ungeachtet	Expreß-	Express-
dichtbevölkert	dicht bevölkert	Expreßgut	Expressgut
diensthabend	Dienst habend	Expreßzug	Expresszug
differential	differential	Exzeß	Exzess
	or differenzial	Facette	Facette
Differentialrechnung	Differentialrechnung		or Fassette
	or Differenzialrechnung	Fährenanschluß	Fährenanschluss
Diktaphon	Diktaphon	Fairneß	Fairness
	or Diktafon	fallenlassen	fallen lassen
dreiviertel	drei Viertel	Faß	Fass
durcheinanderbringen	durcheinander bringen	faßbar	fassbar
durcheinanderreden	durcheinander reden	Fehlschuß	Fehlschuss
durcheinanderwerfen	durcheinander werfen	fernhalten	fern halten

ALT/OLD	NEU/NEW	ALT/OLD	NEU/NEW
fertigbringen	**fertig bringen**	gewiß	**gewiss**
fertigmachen	**fertig machen**	Gewißheit	**Gewissheit**
fertigstellen	**fertig stellen**	gewußt	**gewusst**
fertigwerden	**fertig werden**	glattrasiert	**glatt rasiert**
festangestellt	**fest angestellt**	glattstreichen	**glatt streichen**
Fitneß	**Fitness**	gleichbleibend	**gleich bleibend**
fleischfressend	**Fleisch fressend**	gleichgesinnt	**gleich gesinnt**
floß	**floss**	Glimmstengel	**Glimmstängel**
Fluß	**Fluss**	Grammophon	**Grammophon**
Fluß–	**Fluss–**		or **Grammofon**
flußabwärts	**flussabwärts**	(Grammophon)nadel	**(Grammophon)nadel**
Flußbarsch	**Flussbarsch**		or **(Grammofon)nadel**
Flußbett	**Flussbett**	Graphiker(in)	**Graphiker(in)**
Flußdiagramm	**Flussdiagramm**		or **Grafiker(in)**
flüssigmachen	**flüssig machen**	graphisch	**graphisch**
Flußufer	**Flussufer**		or **grafisch**
Fön ®	**Fön**	gräßlich	**grässlich**
	or **Föhn ®**	Greuel	**Gräuel**
fönen	**föhnen**	Greueltat	**Gräueltat**
Fönfrisur	**Föhnfrisur**	greulich	**gräulich**
Friedensschluß	**Friedensschluss**	Grundriß	**Grundriss**
Frischvermählte	**frisch Vermählte**	Guß	**Guss**
Frischvermählten	**frisch Vermählten**	Gußeisen	**Gusseisen**
frißt	**frisst**	gutaussehend	**gut aussehend**
fritieren	**frittieren**	gutgehen	**gut gehen**
Gebiß	**Gebiss**	gutgehend	**gut gehend**
Gebührenerlaß	**Gebührenerlass**	gutgemeint	**gut gemeint**
gefangen(gehalten)	**gefangen (gehalten)**	guttun	**gut tun**
gefangenhalten	**gefangen halten**	haftenbleiben	**haften bleiben**
gefangennehmen	**gefangen nehmen**	halboffen	**halb offen**
gefaßt	**gefasst**	haltmachen	**Halt machen**
geheimhalten	**geheim halten**	Hämorrhoiden	**Hämorrhoiden**
gehenlassen	**gehen lassen**		or **Hämorriden**
Gemeinschaftsanschluß		Handvoll	**Hand voll**
	Gemeinschaftsanschluss	hängenbleiben	**hängen bleiben**
Gemse	**Gämse**	hängenlassen	**hängen lassen**
gemußt	**gemusst**	hartgekocht	**hart gekocht**
genaugenommen	**genau genommen**	Haselnuß	**Haselnuss**
Genuß	**Genuss**	Haß	**Hass**
genüßlich	**genüsslich**	häßlich	**hässlich**
Genußmittel	**Genussmittel**	Häßlichkeit	**Hässlichkeit**
Geograph	**Geograph**	haushalten	**haushalten**
	or **Geograf**		or **Haus halten**
Geographie	**Geographie**	heiligsprechen	**heilig sprechen**
	or **Geografie**	Hexenschuß	**Hexenschuss**
geographisch	**geographisch**	hierbehalten	**hier behalten**
	or **geografisch**	hierbleiben	**hier bleiben**
geringachten	**gering achten**	hierlassen	**hier lassen**
Geschäftsschluß	**Geschäftsschluss**	hierzulande	**hierzulande**
Geschoß	**Geschoss**		or **hier zu Lande**
gewinnbringend	**Gewinn bringend**	hochachten	**hoch achten**

ALT/OLD	NEU/NEW	ALT/OLD	NEU/NEW
hochbegabt	**hoch begabt**	kompromißlos	**kompromisslos**
hochdotiert	**hoch dotiert**	Kompromißlösung	**Kompromisslösung**
hochentwickelt	**hoch entwickelt**	Kongreß	**Kongress**
(hoch)geschätzt	**(hoch) geschätzt**	Kongreßzentrum	**Kongresszentrum**
(hoch)schätzen	**(hoch) schätzen**	Kontrabaß	**Kontrabass**
(Honorar)vorschuß	**(Honorar)vorschuss**	kraß	**krass**
Imbiß	**Imbiss**	Kreppapier	**Krepppapier**
Imbißhalle	**Imbisshalle**		or **Krepp-Papier**
Imbißraum	**Imbissraum**	kriegführend	**Krieg führend**
Imbißstube	**Imbissstube**	krummnehmen	**krumm nehmen**
	or **Imbiss-Stube**	Kurzbiographie	**Kurzbiographie**
immerwährend	**immer während**		or **Kurzbiografie**
imstande	**imstande**	kurzhalten	**kurz halten**
	or **im Stande**	Kurzschluß	**Kurzschluss**
ineinandergreifen	**ineinander greifen**	Kuß	**Kuss**
ineinanderschieben	**ineinander schieben**	Ladenschluß	**Ladenschluss**
Intercity-Expreßzug	**Intercity-Expresszug**	Laufpaß	**Laufpass**
ißt	**isst**	leerlaufen	**leer laufen**
Jahresabschluß	**Jahresabschluss**	leerstehend	**leer stehend**
jedesmal	**jedes Mal**	leichtfallen	**leicht fallen**
Joghurt	**Joghurt**	leichtmachen	**leicht machen**
	or **Jogurt**	Lenkradschloß	**Lenkradschloss**
kahlgeschoren	**kahl geschoren**	letztemal	**letzte Mal**
kaltbleiben	**kalt bleiben**	liebgewinnen	**lieb gewinnen**
Kammuschel	**Kammmuschel**	liebhaben	**lieb haben**
	or **Kamm-Muschel**	liegenbleiben	**liegen bleiben**
Känguruh	**Känguru**	liegenlassen	**liegen lassen**
Karamel	**Karamell**	Litfaßsäule	**Litfasssäule**
Karamelbonbon	**Karamellbonbon**		or **Litfass-Säule**
Katarrh	**Katarrh**	Lithographie	**Lithographie**
	or **Katarr**		or **Lithografie**
Kellergeschoß	**Kellergeschoss**	Luftschloß	**Luftschloss**
kennenlernen	**kennen lernen**	maschineschreiben	**Maschine schreiben**
keß	**kess**	maßhalten	**Maß halten**
klarsehen	**klar sehen**	Megaphon	**Megaphon**
klarwerden	**klar werden**		or **Megafon**
klassenbewußt	**klassenbewusst**	Meldeschluß	**Meldeschluss**
Klassenbewußtsein	**Klassenbewusstsein**	meßbar	**messbar**
klatschnaß	**klatschnass**	Meßbecher	**Messbecher**
kleinhacken	**klein hacken**	Meßgerät	**Messgerät**
kleinschneiden	**klein schneiden**	Mikrophon	**Mikrophon**
klitschnaß	**klitschnass**		or **Mikrofon**
knapphalten	**knapp halten**	Miß–	**Miss–**
Kokosnuß	**Kokosnuss**	mißachten	**missachten**
Koloß	**Koloss**	Mißachtung	**Missachtung**
Kombinationsschloß	**Kombinationsschloss**	Mißbehagen	**Missbehagen**
Kommuniqué	**Kommuniqué**	Mißbildung	**Missbildung**
	or **Kommunikee**	mißbilligen	**missbilligen**
Kompaß	**Kompass**	Mißbilligung	**Missbilligung**
Kompromiß	**Kompromiss**	Mißbrauch	**Missbrauch**
kompromißbereit	**kompromissbereit**	mißbrauchen	**missbrauchen**

ALT/OLD	NEU/NEW	ALT/OLD	NEU/NEW
Mißerfolg	**Misserfolg**	Nebenanschluß	**Nebenanschluss**
Mißfallen	**Missfallen**	nebeneinanderlegen	**nebeneinander legen**
mißfallen	**missfallen**	nebeneinanderstellen	**nebeneinander stellen**
Mißgeburt	**Missgeburt**	Nebenfluß	**Nebenfluss**
Mißgeschick	**Missgeschick**	Necessaire	**Necessaire**
mißgestaltet	**missgestaltet**		or **Nessessär**
mißglücken	**missglücken**	Negligé	**Negligé**
mißgönnen	**missgönnen**		or **Negligee**
Mißgriff	**Missgriff**	Netzanschluß	**Netzanschluss**
Mißgunst	**Missgunst**	neuentdeckt	**neu entdeckt**
mißgünstig	**missgünstig**	nichtsahnend	**nichts ahnend**
mißhandeln	**misshandeln**	nichtssagend	**nichts sagend**
Mißhandlung	**Misshandlung**	Nonstop–	**Nonstop–**
Mißklang	**Missklang**		or **Non-Stop–**
Mißkredit	**Misskredit**	notleidend	**Not leidend**
mißlich	**misslich**	numerieren	**nummerieren**
mißlingen	**misslingen**	Nuß	**Nuss**
mißlungen	**misslungen**	Nußbaum	**Nussbaum**
Mißmut	**Missmut**	Nußknacker	**Nussknacker**
mißmutig	**missmutig**	Nußschale	**Nussschale**
mißraten	**missraten**		or **Nuss-Schale**
Mißstand	**Missstand**	obenerwähnt	**oben erwähnt**
	or **Miss-Stand**	obengenannt	**oben genannt**
Mißtrauen	**Misstrauen**	Obergeschoß	**Obergeschoss**
mißtrauen	**misstrauen**	offenbleiben	**offen bleiben**
Mißtrauensantrag	**Misstrauensantrag**	offenhalten	**offen halten**
Mißtrauensvotum	**Misstrauensvotum**	offenlassen	**offen lassen**
mißtrauisch	**misstrauisch**	offenstehen	**offen stehen**
Mißverhältnis	**Missverhältnis**	Ölmeßstab	**Ölmessstab**
Mißverständnis	**Missverständnis**		or **Ölmess-Stab**
mißverstehen	**missverstehen**	Orthographie	**Orthographie**
Mißwirtschaft	**Misswirtschaft**		or **Orthografie**
mittag	**Mittag**	orthographisch	**orthographisch**
Mop	**Mopp**		or **orthografisch**
Muß	**Muss**	paarmal	**paar Mal**
mußte	**musste**	Panther	**Panther**
nachhinein	**Nachhinein**		or **Panter**
Nachlaß	**Nachlass**	Paragraph	**Paragraph**
nahegehen	**nahe gehen**		or **Paragraf**
nahekommen	**nahe kommen**	Paranuß	**Paranuss**
nahelegen	**nahe legen**	Parlamentsbeschluß	**Parlamentsbeschluss**
naheliegen	**nahe liegen**	Paß	**Pass**
naheliegend	**nahe liegend**	Paß–	**Pass–**
näherkommen	**näher kommen**	Paßamt	**Passamt**
näherrücken	**näher rücken**	Paßbild	**Passbild**
nahestehen	**nahe stehen**	Paßkontrolle	**Passkontrolle**
nahestehend	**nahe stehend**	Paßstelle	**Passstelle**
nahetreten	**nahe treten**		or **Pass-Stelle**
naß	**nass**	Paßstraße	**Passstraße**
naßkalt	**nasskalt**		or **Pass-Straße**
Naßrasur	**Nassrasur**	patschnaß	**patschnass**

ALT/OLD	NEU/NEW	ALT/OLD	NEU/NEW
pflichtbewußt	**pflichtbewusst**	rotglühend	**rot glühend**
Phantasie	**Phantasie**	Rückschluß	**Rückschluss**
	or **Fantasie**	Rußland	**Russland**
Phantasie–	**Phantasie–**	Safe(r) Sex	**Safe(r) Sex**
	or **Fantasie–**		or **Safe(r)-sex**
phantasielos	**phantasielos**	Salzfaß	**Salzfass**
	or **fantasielos**	sauberhalten	**sauber halten**
phantasiereich	**phantasiereich**	Saxophon	**Saxophon**
	or **fantasiereich**		or **Saxofon**
phantasieren	**phantasieren**	Schattenriß	**Schattenriss**
	or **fantasieren**	schiefgehen	**schief gehen**
phantasievoll	**phantasievoll**	Schiffahrt	**Schifffahrt**
	or **fantasievoll**		or **Schiff–Fahrt**
phantastisch	**phantastisch**	Schiffahrtslinie	**Schifffahrtslinie**
	or **fantastisch**	Schlangenbiß	**Schlangenbiss**
platschnaß	**platschnass**	schlechtgehen	**schlecht gehen**
plazieren	**platzieren**	schlechtmachen	**schlecht machen**
Pornographie	**Pornographie**	Schlegel	**Schlägel**
	or **Pornografie**	Schloß	**Schloss**
pornographisch	**pornographisch**	schloß	**schloss**
	or **pornografisch**	Schluß	**Schluss**
Portemonnaie	**Portemonnaie**	Schluß–	**Schluss–**
	or **Portmonee**	(Schluß)folgerung	**(Schluss)folgerung**
Potential	**Potential**	Schlußlicht	**Schlusslicht**
	or **Potenzial**	Schlußrunde	**Schlussrunde**
potentiell	**potentiell**	Schlußrundenteilnehmer	
	or **potenziell**		**Schlussrundenteilnehmer**
preisbewußt	**preisbewusst**	Schlußstrich	**Schlussstrich**
Preßluft	**Pressluft**		or **Schluss–Strich**
Preßluftbohrer	**Pressluftbohrer**	Schlußverkauf	**Schlussverkauf**
Preßlufthammer	**Presslufthammer**	Schmiß	**Schmiss**
Prozeß	**Prozess**	Schnappschloß	**Schnappschloss**
Prüfungsausschuß	**Prüfungsausschuss**	Schnappschuß	**Schnappschuss**
radfahren	**Rad fahren**	Schnellimbiß	**Schnellimbiss**
(Raketen)abschuß	**(Raketen)abschuss**	schneuzen	**schnäuzen**
Rassenhaß	**Rassenhass**	schoß	**schoss**
rauh	**rau**	Schößling	**Schössling**
Rauhreif	**Raureif**	Schrittempo	**Schritttempo**
Raumschiffahrt	**Raumschifffahrt**		or **Schritt–Tempo**
	or **Raumschiff–Fahrt**	Schuß	**Schuss**
Rausschmiß	**Rausschmiss**	Schußbereich	**Schussbereich**
Rechnungsabschluß	**Rechnungsabschluss**	Schußlinie	**Schusslinie**
reinwaschen	**rein waschen**	Schußverletzung	**Schussverletzung**
Reisepaß	**Reisepass**	Schußwaffe	**Schusswaffe**
Reißverschluß	**Reißverschluss**	Schußweite	**Schussweite**
richtigstellen	**richtig stellen**	schwererziehbar	**schwer erziehbar**
Riß	**Riss**	schwerfallen	**schwer fallen**
Rolladen	**Rollladen**	schwermachen	**schwer machen**
	or **Roll–Laden**	schwernehmen	**schwer nehmen**
Roß	**Ross**	schwertun	**schwer tun**
Roßkastanie	**Rosskastanie**	schwerverdaulich	**schwer verdaulich**

ALT/OLD	NEU/NEW	ALT/OLD	NEU/NEW
schwerverletzt	schwer verletzt		or telegrafieren
Seismograph	Seismograph	Thunfisch	Thunfisch
	or Seismograf		or Tunfisch
selbständig	selbständig	tiefausgeschnitten	tief ausgeschnitten
	or selbstständig	tiefgehend	tief gehend
Selbständigkeit	Selbständigkeit	tiefgekühlt	tief gekühlt
	or Selbstständigkeit	tiefgreifend	tief greifend
selbstbewußt	selbstbewusst	tiefschürfend	tief schürfend
Selbstbewußtsein	Selbstbewusstsein	Tip	Tipp
selbstgemacht	selbst gemacht	topographisch	topographisch
selbstverständlich	selbst verständlich		or topografisch
selbstverwaltet	selbst verwaltet	totenblaß	totenblass
seßhaft	sesshaft	totgeboren	tot geboren
Showbuneß	Showbusiness	Trugschluß	Trugschluss
Sicherheitsschloß	Sicherheitsschloss	tschüs	tschüs
sitzenbleiben	sitzen bleiben		or tschüss
sitzenlassen	sitzen lassen	übelgelaunt	übel gelaunt
Skipaß	Skipass	übelnehmen	übel nehmen
sogenannt	so genannt	übelriechend	übel riechend
Sommerschlußverkauf		übelwollend	übel wollend
	Sommerschlussverkauf	Überdruß	Überdruss
sonstjemand	sonst jemand	übereinanderlegen	übereinander legen
sonstwo	sonst wo	Überfluß	Überfluss
sonstwoher	sonst woher	Überschuß	Überschuss
sonstwohin	sonst wohin	überschwenglich	überschwänglich
Spannbettuch	Spannbetttuch	übrigbleiben	übrig bleiben
	or Spannbett-Tuch	übriggeblieben	übrig geblieben
spazierenfahren	spazieren fahren	übriglassen	übrig lassen
spazierengehen	spazieren gehen	Umriß	Umriss
Sprößling	Sprössling	unbewußt	unbewusst
steckenbleiben	stecken bleiben	Unbewußte	Unbewusste
steckenlassen	stecken lassen	unerläßlich	unerlässlich
stehenbleiben	stehen bleiben	unermeßlich	unermesslich
stehenlassen	stehen lassen	unfaßbar	unfassbar
Stengel	Stängel	ungewiß	ungewiss
Stenographie	Stenographie	Ungewißheit	Ungewissheit
	or Stenografie	unmißverständlich	unmissverständlich
stenographieren	stenographieren	unpäßlich	unpässlich
	or stenografieren	unselbständig	unselbständig
Stenograph(in)	Stenograph(in)		or unselbstständig
	or Stenograf(in)	unterbewußt	unterbewusst
stereophonisch	stereophonisch	Unterbewußte	Unterbewusste
	or stereofonisch	Unterbewußtsein	Unterbewusstsein
Stewardeß	Stewardess	Untergeschoß	Untergeschoss
Stilleben	Stillleben	Untersuchungsausschuß	
	or Still-Leben		Untersuchungsausschuss
stillegen	stilllegen	unvergeßlich	unvergesslich
Streifschuß	Streifschuss	Varieté	Varieté
strenggenommen	streng genommen		or Varietee
Streß	Stress	verantwortungsbewußt	
telegraphieren	telegraphieren		verantwortungsbewusst

2300912

GENUINENESS CERTIFICATE

This is to certify that this book is an authentic and genuine publication of Tata McGraw-Hill Publishing Company Limited

Tata McGraw-Hill Publishing Company Ltd.

7, West Patel Nagar, New Delhi - 110 008, India

A Division of *The McGraw-Hill Companies*